BRITISH BOXING YEARBOOK 1985

BRITISH BOXING YEARBOOK 1985

in association with the
British Boxing Board of Control

compiled by
BARRY J. HUGMAN

NEWNES BOOKS

Published by Newnes Books,
a Division of The Hamlyn Publishing Group Limited
84–88, The Centre, Feltham, Middlesex, England
and distributed for them by
The Hamlyn Publishing Group Limited
Rushden, Northants, England

This edition first published 1984

ISBN 0 600 35765 1 (softback)
0 600 35853 4 (cased)

Printed in Great Britain

Acknowledgements

A very special thank you is in order for Ray Clarke OBE, the General Secretary of the BBBC, for giving me the opportunity to produce this work, and to Bill Sheeran for his able support.

The book itself was made possible by excellent back up and professional expertise given by the following:

Sub-Editor: Ron Olver

A former assistant editor of *Boxing News*; former assistant editor of *Boxing World*; British correspondent for *The Ring*; Author of *The Professionals*; Author of the Boxing Section within *Encyclopaedia Britannica*; Author of *Boxing*, Foyles Library service; former co-editor of the *Boxing News Annual*; Member of the Nominating Committee of the International Hall of Fame; Member of the Commonwealth Championships Committee; Member of the BBBC Benevolent Fund Grants Committee; Member of the British Boxing Writer's Club; Vice-President of several Ex-Boxers Associations; writer of the Old-Timers feature in *Boxing News* for the past 15 years.

Records Compiler: Vic Hardwicke

Boxed as an amateur and was formerly licensed by the BBBC as a trainer, manager and matchmaker. Reported on boxing tournaments for *Boxing News*, but earlier than that, at the age of 12, began to compile records of British boxers. Has since compiled thousands which are now generally recognised as the most authentic in the country.

Official Photographer: Derek Rowe

Before starting up his own successful business, ably backed by his wife Maria in 1968, had worked for agencies including Sport and General. Now has work commissioned by Pears, ICI, Securicor, Woolworths, etc. Apart from supplying many of the portraits within the Yearbook, several of the current title fight shots were taken by Derek, who professes to being a 'boxing nut'.

Thanks must also go to David Roake who has been a friend of long standing and is an avid collector of fighter's photos, having an outstanding collection from 1880 to the present. David kindly allowed the use of his collection, which is seen to good effect in the 'Former British Champions' section. If any collectors feel they would like to contact David, he can be reached through the publisher.

Gilbert Odd, boxing historian extraordinaire and author of the *Encyclopaedia of Boxing* (Hamlyn) gave expert advice and the use of his photograph collection, which takes in the first 30 years of action title fights. Carl Gunns, the former manager of Tony Sibson, Dai Corp, the Welsh Area Secretary and Tommy Gilmour, the foremost manager in Scotland, all contributed generously with photographs, as did Roy Chaplin a leading photographer.

Harry Mullan, the editor of *Boxing News* was exceedingly helpful in this, the 75th year of the only trade paper, which still prospers. Simon Block, of the BBBC, for his great help and work on the Commonwealth Champions section, is thanked as is Dr. Adrian Whiteson, Chairman of the BBBC Medical Committee, for his article on the medical aspects of Boxing, which proves that a positive attitude to medical care is the answer to the current criticisms of the sport. Michael Featherstone must not be forgotten for his statistical help, mainly with birthdates, his speciality. I must also thank my wife Jennifer for many patient hours spent typing and sorting the mass of documentation that was needed to produce the finished product.

Tributes are in order for John Percival and his team at Sports Broker Services who have worked in a highly efficient manner behind the scenes in an effort to project the image of the sport.

Finally, thanks to John Morris, the Chairman of the Boxing Writers Club, who with Rudi and Angela of the BBBC offices helped to make the interface run smoothly.

BARRY J. HUGMAN

'NEWNES BOOKS' ANNUAL BRITISH BOXING AWARDS, 1984

THE PUBLISHERS in association with the BBBC have great pleasure in announcing the following special inaugural Awards scheme for which a panel of five acknowledged authorities have been formed to determine the recipient, chaired by Frank Butler, OBE, Honorary Secretary of the Boxing Writers Club. The other panelists are: Ray Clarke, OBE, General Secretary of the BBBC; Bill Martin, of the Press Association; Jim Watt, Former World Lightweight Champion and Barry Hugman, Editor of the *British Boxing Yearbook*.

THE AWARDS

British Boxer of the Year: For the outstanding British Boxer at any weight.

Contest of the Year: For both participants in the best all action contest seen in Great Britain during 1984.

Best Overseas Boxer of the Year: For an outstanding World Champion.

A Special Award: For contribution to the Sport.

A Special Award: For a former great British Boxer.

These Awards have been commissioned in the form of plaques designed by Morton T. Colver, the manufacturer of the Lonsdale Belt.

The Awards will be presented at the launch of the *British Boxing Yearbook*, and the winners announced in the press.

CONTENTS

Foreword

By Ray Clarke, OBE General Secretary,
British Boxing Board of Control

This yearbook could be described as an encyclopedia of current British boxing. It is the first in a series, and is unique – not only because such a comprehensive yearbook has not been published before, but because it is the first to be recognised and given authority by the British Boxing Board of Control.

Even in the days of bare-knuckle fisticuffs and long, colourful descriptions of fights, there was not a publication like this. You might be lucky enough to come across old volumes of *Pugilistica* and *Boxiana*, which contained descriptions of boxing matches amazing in their attention to detail. But these were, after all, collections of fight reports and the histories of pugilists put together as volumes in the way *Boxing News* might be bound from year to year by the enthusiasts of today.

This yearbook is more like the record books covering other sports, and might be regarded as a sort of 'boxing Wisden'. It contains up-to-date information on all aspects of professional boxing in the United Kingdom as well as facts, figures and records from a bygone age. It provides nostalgia for the keen boxing fan and essential data for all interested in, and connected with, the sport today. It also contains special articles of interest, and future editions will contain similar features as well as updating all the records.

The compiler, Barry Hugman, is to be congratulated on bringing his dedication to boxing with this outstanding work, resulting in a worthy yearbook for a great sport.

British Boxing Board of Control (1929): Structure

(Members of the World Boxing Council, the World Boxing Association and the European Boxing Union)

PRESIDENT	Alexander H. Elliot
VICE PRESIDENT	Jack Petersen TD, OBE
CHAIRMAN	David Hopkin
VICE CHAIRMAN	Norman N. Jacobs
GENERAL SECRETARY	Ray L. Clarke, OBE
ADMINISTRATIVE STEWARDS	Michael Hurt Dr. Adrian Whiteson Leslie M. Keegan William Sheeran Charles J. Hue-Williams Dr. James Shea Hon. Colin Moynihan, MP Dr. David Barnett Richard Gardner Leonard F. Read, QPM Deryck Monteith Robert Graham John Morris
STEWARDS OF APPEAL	Robin Simpson, QC John Mathew, QC Nicholas Valios Robert Harman, QC William Tudor John Geoffrey Finn Brian Capstick, QC Judge Peter Goldstone
HEAD OFFICE	70, Vauxhall Bridge Road, London SW1V 2RP Telephone: 01-828-2133 Telegrams: BRITBOX, LONDON

AREA COUNCILS	AREA SECRETARIES
AREA NO 1 (SCOTLAND)	G. Paxton Woolard 3 Woodside Terrace, Glasgow C3 Telephone 041-332-0392
AREA NO 2 (NORTHERN IRELAND)	Dr. P. MacHugh 32 Ballinderry Road, Lisburn, Co. Antrim, Northern Ireland Telephone Lisburn 2170
AREA NO 3 (WALES)	Dai Corp 113 Hill Crest, Brynna, Llanharan, Mid Glamorgan Telephone 0443 226465
AREA NO 4 (NORTHERN) (Northumberland, Cumbria, Durham, Cleveland, Tyne and Wear, North Yorkshire [north of a line drawn from Whitby to Northallerton to Richmond, including these towns].)	John Jarrett 5 Beechwood Avenue, Gosforth, Newcastle Telephone 0632 21989
AREA NO 5 (CENTRAL) (North Yorkshire [with the exception of the part included in the Northern Area – see above], Lancashire, West and South Yorkshire, Greater Manchester, Merseyside and Cheshire, Isle of Man, North Humberside.)	Edward Tully 20 Westmorland Road, Urmston, Manchester M31 1HJ Telephone 061 748 0014
AREA NO 6 (SOUTHERN) (Bedfordshire, Berkshire, Buckinghamshire, Cambridgeshire, Channel Islands, Isle of Wight, Essex, Hampshire, Kent, Hertfordshire, Greater London, Norfolk, Suffolk, Oxfordshire, East and West Sussex.)	Simon J. Block British Boxing Board of Control, 70 Vauxhall Bridge Road, London SW1V 2RP Telephone 01 828 2133
AREA NO 7 (WESTERN) (Cornwall, Devon, Somerset, Dorset, Wiltshire, Avon, Gloucestershire.)	Frank Parker 22 Ellenborough Park South, Weston-Super-Mare, Somerset BS23 1XN Telephone 0934 29910
AREA NO 8 (MIDLANDS) (Derbyshire, Nottinghamshire, Lincolnshire, Salop, Staffordshire, Hereford and Worcester, Warwickshire, West Midlands, Leicestershire, South Humberside, Northamptonshire.)	Arthur Musson 77 Ladywood Road, Kirk Hallam, Derbyshire Telephone Ilkeston 321264

Preface

My last work on boxing resulted in the *George Wimpey Amateur Boxing Yearbook* and it seems a natural progression to follow up with a book on the professional side of the sport.

In this new publication I have recorded as many of the facts as possible from the past as well as from the current boxing scene. It is produced in association with the British Boxing Board of Control, and I hope that the co-operation of the Board and Newnes, the publishers, will allow the ruling body more means of communication with the public, who too often see only the leading boxers and promoters and are unaware of the administrative work which makes professional boxing in Great Britain the envy of the boxing world.

This publication intends to provide facts and figures which not only revive memories of old events but act as a guide on the more recent ones. The Editor welcomes constructive suggestions for future contents.

The book concentrates mainly on British boxing since 1929, when the BBBC was formed, but also includes the complete list of British and Commonwealth title bouts and all European and World Champions from the beginning of the gloved era.

All post-1929 British Champions' records (some never before published) are set out in a new format which, though unfamiliar to boxing readers, summarise the facts clearly. The records of current boxers are shown in the usual manner.

The Championship Diary gives a brief description of all the Championship contests involving British boxers since 1929, a section which will evoke much nostalgia, and which brings to life fights which the bare results leave as mere statistics.

Ron Olver's splendid article on the ex-boxer's associations shows that interest among the old-timers (dare I say it) is extremely high. An inside view of the Board's attitude to health in boxing is provided by Dr Adrian Whiteson, who is more than qualified to discuss the subject – it would be beneficial if some other members of the medical profession would view boxing and its continuing popularity as constructively.

There will never be the space to display all the facts one would like, but each year new records and new articles will be inluded so that no aspect of the fight game will be forgotten.

I have closed the records at the end of June 1984, as the BBBC recognise that boxing is seasonal and that the season tends to run from early September to the end of June. There are contests in the interim of course, and these will not be overlooked in the next edition of the Yearbook.

I hope that the *British Boxing Yearbook* will become a 'must' for the fans, media personnel, including those directly connected with this great sport, and that you all enjoy this first edition.

Barry J. Hugman

Abbreviations and Definitions

The following abbreviations are used to indicate the results of contests:

PTS *Points*
CO *Count Out*
RSC *Referee Stopped Contest*
RTD *Retired*
DIS *Disqualified*
NC *No Contest*
ND *No Decision*
DREW
UNDEFEATED: an undefeated champion is one who did not lost his title in a contest, but who retired, was stripped of it, or otherwise relinquished it.

The British Boxing Board of Control (1929)

A Short History of Events Leading to the Formation of the Present Constitution

To trace the history of the British Boxing Board of Control, one has to start with the formation of the National Sporting Club, in March 1891. The National Sporting Club brought order, responsibility and respect to British professional boxing, and in adopting the Marquess of Queensberry Rules of 1865 (revised 1890), improved upon the original Broughton Rules of 1743. Incidentally, the author of the Marquess of Queensberry Rules was not Queensberry at all, but a person named John Chambers, a fellow-student of Queensberry at Oxford.

The Club revised their Rules in 1923, but before then, there had been several brushes with the law, with the legality of boxing being frequently called in question. Sir Charles Hall, Q.C., Recorder, on 21 November, 1898, stated 'There is absolutely nothing illegal in boxing itself. It is a noble and manly art, which I hope will never die out in this country'. Sir Forrest Fulton, Common Sergeant, on 12 March 1900, when charging the Jury in a case, stated 'Boxing has received the sanction of high legal authority and no less an authority than the late Lord Bramwell, who said that in a case tried before him a great many years ago (The Queen v. Young and Others), a sparring match with gloves fairly conducted was not unlawful; but a sparring match might become unlawful if the men fought on until they were so weak that a dangerous fall or blow was likely to be the result.' In 1900, the manager of the National Sporting Club and others were charged with manslaughter following the death of Mike Riley following a match with Matthew Precious. Despite the foregoing declarations, and evidence that the contest was carried out fairly in accordance with the Rules of the Club, the Magistrate sent the Officers of the Club for trial at the Old Bailey. At this trial, the Common Sergeant recited Lord Bramwell's legal sanction concerning a contest properly conducted under the National Sporting Club Rules and several witnesses had given evidence that this had been the case. He proceeded to compliment the late Sir Charles Hall, who had dismissed a similar case, and quoted his words about boxing, but to the amazement of all present, he advised the Jury to return a verdict of 'Guilty'. Fortunately, the Grand Jury returned no such verdict, and the defendants were released. Later at the Central Criminal Court, on 29 June 1901, the manager of the National Sporting Club, the referee, timekeeper, boxer Jack Roberts and others, were charged with feloniously killing and slaying Murray Livingstone, a boxer otherwise known as 'Billy Smith'. Upon the termination of the case and following the summing up of the Judge, Mr. Justice Grantham, the Jury, after two minutes, brought in a verdict of 'Not Guilty', finding that the death of Smith was an accident caused during a boxing contest, and not a fight. It seemed the legality of boxing was established, but in 1911, Jim Driscoll and Owen Moren were summoned before a Birmingham Magistrate on the evening before their proposed contest, to show cause why they should not be bound over to keep the peace. They were bound over, and the contest did not take place until two years later, at the National Sporting Club.

In February 1914, ten members of the Club, together with representatives from the Army and Navy Boxing Association, the Amateur Boxing Association and various boxing promoters, held a meeting with a view to forming a Boxing Board of Control. A further meeting was held in May 1914, but owing to the First World War, there was no further progress made until February 1918, when the first draft of a new Constitution and Regulations was drawn up. The New Board included two representatives from the Amateur Boxing Association, and although the Imperial Services Association resigned as a body they substituted individual Officers, with the Earl of Lonsdale presiding. By 1919 the Board had appointed a press agent at three guineas a week and also instituted a Boxer's Benevolent Fund.

The International Boxing Union was founded in Paris on 4 February 1920, consisting of Great Britain, United States of America, France, Australia, Canada, Denmark, Holland, Italy, Norway, Sweden, Switzerland, Brazil and the Argentine. Among its objectives were the administration of World championships, the formulation of International Rules and a mutual recognition of penalties. Sadly, although other similar bodies have since been set up, these original aims have yet to come to fruition. The President of France accepted the Presidency of the original International Boxing Union, but the Prince of Wales, who was also asked, declined, but did in fact subsequently grace with his presence various tournaments promoted at the National Sporting Club. By February 1922, Britain had resigned from the International Boxing Union, having originally joined on the understanding that the USA would be a member, which never came about.

The Board had originally started life with an Honorary Secretary, who carried out all the necessary duties and it was now decided that he should have a paid assistant, who would receive the princely sum of £2.00 per week. The first Honorary Secretary who officiated as such for any length of time was L. Bettinson, whose family were for many years connected with the running of the National Sporting Club. In 1921 Norman Clark was appointed Secretary of the Board.

In March 1922, it was regulated that the managers of boxers should not be referees, and it was also observed that: 'One or two referees were constantly betting on boxing matches, which was not considered a good tendency.' The Board then advised that certified referees should not bet on contests.

At a meeting in July 1925, a Commander Kenworthy proposed a Boxing Bill be submitted to the Home Office, but after many discussions, this was considered superfluous, in view of Judges' decisions in various cases concerning the National Sporting Club, that provided boxing was properly conducted under Rules, it would only be questioned if the Rules were disregarded, and the mens' sole concern was to damage each other maliciously. This is the reason why boxing contests, whatever the manner of their termination, are still decided on points, so far as the referee's actual card is concerned. Even if a boxer is counted out in a contest, the Rules state that the boxer counted out shall receive no points for that round whilst his opponent shall receive ten, and the contest shall be terminated.

In 1927, the decision was made to register all professional boxers, but this took some considerable time, and it was not really until after the Second World War that this was properly carried out.

On 14 May, 1928, a special meeting authorised the reconstitution of the Boxing Board of Control, it being considered that the Board and the National Sporting Club were really one and the same Body. Thus on 1 January 1929, the present British Boxing Board of Control was formed, and issued its first 'Constitution and Regulations' in March of that year.

The complete jurisdiction over professional boxing in Great Britain and Northern Ireland was now firmly established and by 1933 the National Sporting Club ceased to exist as a controlling body. The NSC Lonsdale Belt continued to be contested until 1935, with the British Boxing Board of Control taking over the administration of the belt a year later. The Board is now recognised throughout the World and by all Government deparments in the United Kingdom, even though it has received no charter, and is not a registered company, but is, in fact, a self-appointed body.

The principal objectives of today's British Boxing Board are to control and regulate professional boxing in the United Kingdom and Northern Ireland, to act as a 'Board of Appeal', to encourage boxing, to further licence holders' interests, to arrange International agreements, and to promote and safeguard the interests of British professional boxers throughout the World. Also to raise and administer a fund to be known as the British Boxing Board of Control (1929) Benevolent Fund. None of the members of the Board have any financial interest in boxing with each Area being managed and controlled by a Council consisting of promoters, referees, boxers, managers, matchmaker and representative of the trainers, seconds, timekeepers, etc. The Stewards may alternatively appoint persons not financially interested in boxing to control an Area and their championships come under the same conditions as British championships. There are two bodies of Stewards. (a) the 'Administrative Stewards', known as the 'Board' and (b) 'The Stewards of Appeal', of which the latter is composed chiefly of persons engaged in the legal profession. Members, i.e., boxers, promoters, etc., have the right to appeal to the 'Stewards of Appeal' against most decisions of the Board or an Area Council. Anyone wishing to act under the jurisdiction of the BBB of C, in this country must be in possession of a licence, which remains valid from the date of issue for one year and then renewed annually until suspended, withdrawn or surrendered. Licences other than those issued to promoters, must be carried by the holder and produced when required at any tournament at which the holder is engaged. All boxers must be registered and also be over 17 years of age. Official British, European and World championships are controlled by the 'Administrative Stewards' to be contested under National Sporting Club Rules of Boxing. Championship contests are not to exceed 12 (3 min.) rounds, eliminating bouts to be not less than 10 (3 min.) rounds, with a champion not called upon to defend his title until the expiration of six months since winning or successfully defending. A championship can be lost by default, forfeit or inability to pass the scales, but can only be won in a contest. No promoter is permitted to bill a contest or publish in the press that a contest is for a championship or an eliminator before obtaining the sanction of the Board. The British Boxing Board of Control also provides the referee, timekeeper, inspectors, gloves and bandages for all championship contests and last but not least, the Boards medical system is recognised the World over as a really high standard of attainment.

The British Boxing Board of Control have received praise and high regard from Boxing Federations and Commissions in many countries, and it is most pleasing to know that the British press often put forward our Board as an example of how a sport can be controlled and administered.

Alexander H. Elliot
(President BBBC)

Lord Lonsdale Challenge Belts: Outright Winners

The original belts were donated to the National Sporting Club by Lord Lonsdale and did not bear his name, the inscription reading 'The National Sporting Club's Challenge Belt'. It was not until the British Boxing Board of Control was formed that the emblems were reintroduced and the belts became known as the Lord Lonsdale Challenge Belts, with the first contest for which a belt was awarded being Benny Lynch versus Pat Palmer for the flyweight title 16.09.36. To win a belt outright a Champion must score three title match victories at the same weight, not necessarily consecutively.

Outright Winners of the National Sporting Club's Challenge Belt, 1909 – 1935 (19)

FLYWEIGHT	Jimmy Wilde; Jackie Brown
BANTAMWEIGHT	Digger Stanley; Joe Fox; Jim Higgins; Johnny Brown
FEATHERWEIGHT	Jim Driscoll; Tancy Lee; Johnny Cuthbert; Nel Tarleton
LIGHTWEIGHT	Freddie Welsh
WELTERWEIGHT	Johnny Basham; Jack Hood
MIDDLEWEIGHT	Pat O'Keefe; Len Harvey; Jock McAvoy
L. HEAVYWEIGHT	Dick Smith
HEAVYWEIGHT	Bombardier Billy Wells; Jack Petersen

Outright Winners of the BBBC Lord Lonsdale Challenge Belts, 1936 – 1984 (54)

FLYWEIGHT	Jackie Paterson; Terry Allen; Walter McGowan; John McCluskey
BANTAMWEIGHT	Peter Keenan (2); Freddie Gilroy; Alan Rudkin; Johnny Owen
FEATHERWEIGHT	Nel Tarleton; Ronnie Clayton (2); Charlie Hill; Howard Winstone (2); Evan Armstrong; Pat Cowdell
J. LIGHTWEIGHT	Jimmy Anderson
LIGHTWEIGHT	Eric Boon; Billy Thompson; Joe Lucy; Dave Charnley; Maurice Cullen; Ken Buchanan; Jim Watt; George Feeney
L. WELTERWEIGHT	Joey Singleton; Colin Power; Clinton McKenzie (2)
WELTERWEIGHT	Ernie Roderick; Wally Thom; Brian Curvis (2); Ralph Charles; Colin Jones
L. MIDDLEWEIGHT	Maurice Hope; Jimmy Batten; Pat Thomas
MIDDLEWEIGHT	Pat McAteer; Terry Downes; Johnny Pritchett; Bunny Sterling; Alan Minter; Kevin Finnegan; Roy Gumbs
L. HEAVYWEIGHT	Randy Turpin; Chic Calderwood; Chris Finnegan; Bunny Johnson; Tom Collins
HEAVYWEIGHT	Henry Cooper (3)

NOTES: Walter McGowan is the only champion to have been awarded a belt on the grounds that there were no challengers available.
Nel Tarleton is the only champion to have won both an NSC and a BBBC belt.
Henry Cooper holds the record number of belts won by a single fighter, three in all.
Chris and Kevin Finnegan are the only brothers to have won belts.
Jim Higgins holds the record for winning an NSC belt outright in the shortest time, 11 months and 8 days, whilst Pat Cowdell won a BBBC belt in 6 months and 23 days.

A review of the past season and future prospects

Barry J. Hugman (Editor and Compiler)

Professional boxing appears to be riding high! Forget the prophets of doom, because the sport, certainly in Britain is in good hands. The British Boxing Board of Control is second to none throughout the World and is used as an example by other countries where the sport needs to come to terms with modern developments.

There are always going to be ups and downs in boxing, metaphorically speaking that is. Although 1983/4 brought a few shocks, there was plenty to savour for the future. Looking back over last season, seven new British champions were crowned – heavyweight **David Pearce** beat an ageing Neville Meade; light-heavyweight **Dennis Andries** was twice too forceful for Tom Collins; middleweight **Mark Kaylor** was young and ambitious enough to depose of Roy Gumbs; light-middleweight **Jimmy Cable** claimed the vacant crown when beating Nick Wilshire, after **Prince Rodney** was beset by an eye condition following his great win over Jimmy Batten in October; bantamweight **John Feeney** beat the Irishman Davy Larmour, and at flyweight Kelvin Smart lost his title to the ginger headed Irishman, **Hugh Russell**. Of the new champions, Pearce had a crack at the European title, but was soundly outboxed by the Frenchman Lucien Rodriguez, albeit after having him on the deck twice and again John Feeney failed in Europe, being well beaten by Walter Giorgetti in Italy. Mark Kaylor has to overcome the effects of the recent disaster at the hands of the 'Yank', Buster Drayton, who gave away weight and administered a fearful shellacking at Wembley. Jimmy Cable also got himself taken apart by Buster, who I am informed quite reliably will not be coming back unless handcuffed. Cable then redeemed himself with a wonderful win against all the odds in France to take the vacant European light-middleweight title when he smashed Said Skouma to defeat.

Four British champions ruled throughout the season, namely, Lloyd Honeyghan, Clinton McKenzie, George Feeney and Barry McGuigan. Of the four, McGuigan made the most strides when, in beating Valerio Nati by a count out in round six, he collected the Italian's European featherweight crown and later defended it successfully with more explosive hitting against a brave, but outgunned Spaniard, Esteban Eguia. In between these fights he beat the Zambian Charm Chiteule in a Commonwealth eliminator and then destroyed Jose Caba of the Dominican Republic in another eliminator, this time for the WBC title. George Feeney defended his British lightweight title in great fashion with a shock quick victory over the then unbeaten Tony Willis and then made the Lonsdale Belt his own by successfully defending against Paul Chance. Lloyd Honeyghan put his welterweight title on the line for the first time, outpointing Cliff Gilpin, the man he had beaten for the vacant crown.

Tony Sibson came right back after the Hagler episode with a terrific disposal job on the Irish American John Collins in Atlantic City, but then, after stopping Manuel Jiminez at Wembley, he went back to the States to get himself beaten by the unheralded Don Lee in eight rounds. In his very next fight, Tony took the European middleweight title from the Frenchman Louis Acaries in a contest which saw the Englishman appear not as sharp as he would have liked, but carrying too much power for the defence-minded champion. Let us also not forget Stewart Lithgo of Hartlepool, who went to Australia and turned over the once excellent Steve Aczel to win the very first Commonwealth cruiserweight crown. Keith Wallace, the Commonwealth flyweight champion, unfortunately began to suffer with weight problems and was totally exposed by body punches when challenging for the European title against Antoine Montero back in December. The Commonwealth champion from Wales, Colin Jones, once again tried to nail the slippery Milton McCrory in Las Vegas, but was unable to deliver the *coup de grace* on the American, who won the vacant WBC welterweight title. Prior to relinquishing his European and Commonwealth light-middleweight honours, Herol Graham successfully defended the European crown in France by stopping the negative Frenchman, Germain Lemaitre, in his home town.

Outside of the titlists, Frank Bruno, the 'Bomber' from Wandsworth and unbeaten at the time, was counted out in the very last round against the American, 'Bonecrusher' Smith. Bruno appeared to be winning handily, but relaxed on the ropes and paid a heavy price. Earlier on in the season at the Albert Hall, Frank had a close call when he got caught by a tremendous sweeping right delivered by Jumbo Cummings from the States, but the bell came to his aid and he showed great resilience by coming back to stop his opponent.

Another major upset was the loss by Charlie Magri to the Filipino Frank Cedeno, which resulted in Britain losing her only World title. Charlie's only consolation was that he had at least surmounted the pinnacle of his profession.

Looking to the future, who are going to be the bright boys of British boxing? I shall list my selections in two categories: (a) champions who go on to win world titles – Colin Jones and Barry McGuigan; (b) Fighters who will come through the ranks to win British titles and possibly go on to greater glory – Frank Bruno, Herol Graham, Errol Christie, Jimmy Price, Chris Pyatt, Tony Willis and Duke McKenzie.

Colin Jones: He should be only one fight away from the World title despite a difficult contest with Billy Parks, when he suffered eye damage. His best bet would come in a fight at home against the WBA champion, Don Curry, as it is difficult to see McCrory wanting another contest with the hardest puncher around.

Barry McGuigan: He looks to be Britain's gilt-edged chance to win the World featherweight crown, especially now that both Gomez and Pedroza are thinking about moving up a weight. The Irishman could prove to be one of our greatest ever. He can box with the best of them, has ideal balance, can throw the left hook upstairs or downstairs and has a great finishing right hand punch, which can knock you dead. No one really knows whether Barry can take a punch, because he is so rarely caught, and is a natural who believes that attack is the best form of defence.

Frank Bruno: The 'bomber' is still big news, even following his defeat to 'Bonecrusher' Smith, but now has to come back. He can do it! Extra mobility is needed, but Frank can punch with the best of them and is still only a baby amongst the heavyweights.

Herol Graham: The fans tend to overlook the fact that this 'bomber' is unbeaten. Herol can do very well at the middleweight limit with his ability to avoid taking punishment and to outbox his man. He also hits hard enough to hurt.

Errol Christie: He could be our best middleweight since Randy Turpin and Terry Downes. A brilliant amateur he won more titles than anyone, putting himself into the Guinness Book of Records and was last beaten as a 14-year-old. Hopes must be high among his handlers that he will one day carry off the big prize. He looks set for a great season with more trips to the States on the line.

Jimmy Price: He was unfortunate when getting whacked by the former World champion, Ugandan Ayub Kalule. Jimmy was caught cold against a very experienced opponent, who never let him off the hook. The Liverpudlian places his punches well and will come again.

Chris Pyatt: Another great ex-amateur champion, Chris is being touted in knowledgeable quarters as one who will go the whole way. After only a handful of contests he is already rated in the Britsh top two at light-middleweight. He has handled, amongst others, both Darwin Brewster and Pat Thomas with consummate ease.

Tony Willis: He is bright enough to come again after being demolished by George Feeney in his British lightweight title challenge last December. As an amateur Tony was good enough to win an Olympic bronze medal with his classy, cultured moves. There is no reason to suspect that he will not scale the heights ultimately.

Duke McKenzie: The hard hitting flyweight brother of the British light-welterweight champion Clinton McKenzie, the young Duke has already had several fights in the States, where his explosive punching has been seen to good effect.

In 1983 there were 233 promotions throughout the United Kingdom, which incidentally compares extremely favourably with 148 promotions 20 years earlier, in 1964. Following the 1954 Entertainments Tax Bill, professional boxing, which had enjoyed a post-war boom with contests held virtually in every local bath, suddenly nose-dived. This was because no longer could the small-time promoter afford to produce a tournament cheaply and by 1964, promotions had dwindled, along with the number of professional boxers. So what is different 20 years later, with professional boxing on the upturn and in a healthy state? Three factors come readily to mind: (a) the advent of club boxing, which is supported by the membership; (b) televised boxing; (c) the flattening out of the economy which is making life more competitive again.

Since 1 January 1984, 88 newcomers from the amateur ranks have turned over and discarded their singlets for pay, including A.B.A. champions Bob McKenley and Tyrone Forbes; English Internationals Allan Coveley and Mickey Hull; Scottish champions Tommy Campbell, Alastair Laurie, John McAllister, Bobby McDermott and Dave Summers; Welsh champions Glen McLaggan, Mark Pearson, Chris Jacobs and Billy Barton; Irish champions Steve Hanna, David Irving, and Roy Webb.

The boy who turns professional does so by his own volition. He is the one who decides to leave the amateur ranks to make a living, but many purists feel that the boys should be persuaded to stay amongst the 'true blues', where they have learned their basic skills. However, amateur boxing provides the majority of the professional champions, and of the post-war A.B.A. champions who later punched for pay, Ken Buchanan, John Conteh, Charlie Magri, Alan Minter, John H. Stracey, Randy Turpin, Jim Watt, and Howard Winstone all went on to win the World title. The future will remain bright while excellent young amateurs like these continue to move up into the professional ranks.

As a spectator sport, boxing has always had great appeal, for it portrays man's inner drive, his will to win, individuality, flair, discipline, strength, controlled aggression and not least of all his sportsmanship. These are the very qualities which many of us admire and would wish to emulate.

Let us look forward with relish to the 1984/5 season and wish all of those involved well, while supporting one of the grandest sports of them all.

Barry J. Hugman

Current British Champions (including Ex-Champions still active) : Career Records

Includes the complete records of all British Champions or British boxers to win International Championships who have been active since 01.01.83. Names in brackets are real names where they differ from ring names. The first place-name given is the boxer's domicile. National and Divisional honours won as an amateur are shown. Boxers are either shown as self managed or with a named manager at the time of their last contest. Retirements will be recorded in future yearbooks.

Dennis Andries
Hackney. *Born* Guyana 05.11.53
British L. Heavyweight Champion and Former Undefeated Southern Area L. Heavyweight Champion
Manager G. Steene
Previous Amateur Club Colvestone
Divisional Honours NE London L. Heavyweight Champion 1978

16.05.78 Ray Pearce W CO 2 Newport
01.06.78 Mark Cumber W RSC 1 Heathrow
20.06.78 Bonny McKenzie L PTS 8 Southend
18.09.78 Ken Jones W PTS 6 Mayfair
31.10.78 Neville Estaban W PTS 6 Barnsley
14.11.78 Les McAteer DREW 8 Birkenhead
22.11.78 Young McEwan W RSC 7 Stoke
04.12.78 Tom Collins W PTS 8 Southend
22.01.79 Bunny Johnson L PTS 10 Wolverhampton
30.01.79 Tom Collins W CO 6 Southend
05.04.79 Francis Hand W RSC 8 Liverpool
06.06.79 Bonny McKenzie W PTS 8 Burslem
17.09.79 Johnny Waldron W RTD 10 Mayfair (*Southern Area L. Heavyweight Title Challenge*)
27.02.80 Bunny Johnson L PTS 15 Burslem (*British L. Heavyweight Title Challenge*)

Dennis Andries
Derek Rowe (Photos) Ltd

17.04.80 Mustafa Wasajja L PTS 8 Copenhagen
18.06.80 Chris Lawson W RSC 8 Burslem
23.03.81 Shaun Chalcraft W PTS 10 Mayfair (*Southern Area L. Heavyweight Title Challenge*)
16.09.81 Liam Coleman W RSC 6 Burslem
12.10.81 David Pearce L RSC 7 Bloomsbury
23.11.81 Alek Penarski W PTS 10 Chesterfield
15.03.82 Tom Collins L PTS 15 Bloomsbury (*Vacant British L. Heavyweight Title*)
13.08.82 Keith Bristol W PTS 10 Strand (*Southern Area L. Heavyweight Title Defence*)
28.02.83 Karl Canwell W CO 4 Strand (*Southern Area L. Heavyweight Title Defence & Elim. British L. Heavyweight Title*)
19.05.83 Chris Lawson W CO 4 Queensway
22.09.83 Keith Bristol W CO 4 Strand (*Southern Area L. Heavyweight Title Defence & Final Elim. British L. Heavyweight Title*)
26.01.84 Tom Collins W PTS 12 Strand (*British L. Heavyweight Title Challenge*)
06.04.84 Tom Collins W PTS 12 Watford (*British L. Heavyweight Title Defence*)
Summary: 27 contests, won 20, drew 1, lost 6

Jimmy Batten
Millwall. *Born* London 07.11.55
Former British L. Middleweight Champion
Manager G. Davidson
Previous Amateur Club West Ham
National Honours Schools Titles 1969 – 1971; Junior ABA Titles 1971 – 1972; NABC Title 1972; Young England Rep.
Divisional Honours London L. Middleweight Champion 1974

04.06.74 George Salmon W PTS 6 Kensington
01.10.74 Brian Gregory W PTS 6 Wembley

CONTINUED OVERLEAF

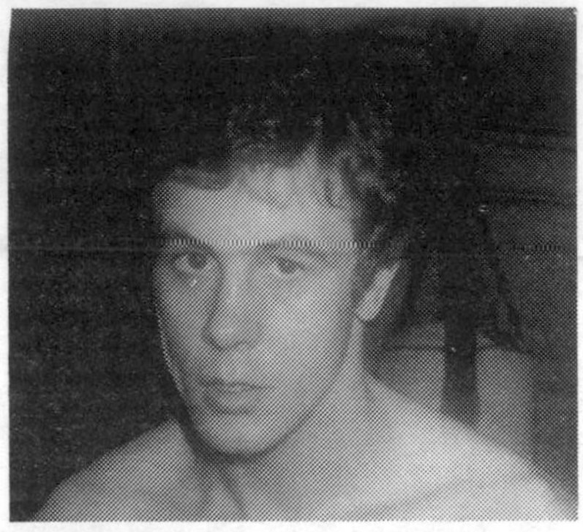

Jimmy Batten

15.10.74 Rod Griffiths **W** RSC 2 Shoreditch
21.10.74 Yotham Kunda **W** PTS 6 Bethnal Green
12.11.74 Bob Langley **W** RTD 1 Wembley
16.12.74 Brian Gregory **W** PTS 6 Bethnal Green
18.02.75 Joe Hannaford **W** RSC 2 Bethnal Green
25.03.75 Dave Davies **W** PTS 8 Kensington
29.04.75 Victor Perez **W** PTS 8 Kensington
02.12.75 Peter Cain **L** PTS 8 Bethnal Green
20.01.76 John Smith **W** PTS 8 Kensington
02.03.76 Peter Cain **L** RSC 6 Kensington
20.04.76 Roy Commosioung **W** PTS 8 Bethnal Green
01.06.76 Jim Moore **W** CO 5 Kensington
14.09.76 Jeff Burns **W** RSC 3 Kensington
26.10.76 Steve Angell **W** RSC 6 Kensington
15.11.76 Liam White **W** RSC 3 Bethnal Green
07.12.76 Kevin White **W** PTS 8 Kensington
01.02.77 Albert Hillman **W** RTD 7 Kensington
(*Vacant British L. Middleweight Title*)
22.02.77 Jimmy Savage **W** RSC 2 Kensington
29.03.77 Trevor Francis **W** PTS 10 Wembley
12.04.77 Michel Chapier **W** RSC 9 Kensington
14.06.77 Julio Garcia **W** RSC 6 Wembley
25.10.77 Larry Paul **W** RSC 4 Kensington
(*British L. Middleweight Title Defence*)
24.01.78 Clarence Howard **W** RSC 4 Kensington
25.04.78 Georges Warusfel **W** PTS 10 Kensington
12.09.78 Tony Poole **W** RTD 13 Wembley
(*British L. Middleweight Title Defence*)
21.11.78 Gilbert Cohen **L** CO 3 Wembley
(*Vacant European L. Middleweight Title*)
23.01.79 Aundra Love **W** PTS 8 Kensington
10.04.79 Dave Proud **W** RTD 6 Kensington
15.05.79 Colin Ward **W** PTS 10 Wembley
11.09.79 Pat Thomas **L** RSC 9 Wembley
(*British L. Middleweight Title Defence*)
04.12.79 George Walker **W** PTS 8 Wembley
03.06.80 Wayne Barker **W** RSC 4 Kensington
16.09.80 Charlie Malarkey **W** RSC 4 Wembley
18.11.80 George Walker **W** PTS 8 Bethnal Green
17.03.81 Billy Waith **W** PTS 8 Wembley
26.06.81 Chris Christian **L** PTS 8 Bethnal Green
21.10.81 Jesse Abrams **W** CO 5 Chicago
19.02.82 Billy Page **W** RSC 5 Chicago
03.05.82 Mario Maldonado **L** RSC 1 Atlanta City
06.09.82 Jeff Maddison **W** PTS 10 Chicago
12.11.82 Roberto Duran **L** PTS 10 Miami
25.01.83 Tony Britton **W** PTS 8 Bethnal Green
08.02.83 Jimmy Cable **W** PTS 8 Kensington
22.02.83 Dennis Sheehan **W** RSC 4 Bethnal Green
02.05.83 Greg Clark **L** PTS 10 Durban
15.08.83 Billy Page **W** RSC 5 Chicago
11.10.83 Prince Rodney **L** RSC 6 Kensington
(*Vacant British L. Middleweight Title*)

Summary: 49 contests, won 40, lost 9

Cornelius Boza-Edwards

Harrow. *Born* Uganda 27.05.56
Former Undefeated European J. Lightweight Champion. Former WBC J. Lightweight Champion
Manager M. Duff
Previous Amateur Club Fitzroy Lodge
National Honours England Int.; GB Rep.
Divisional Honours London Bantamweight Champion 1975; London Featherweight Champion 1976

13.12.76 Barry Price **W** CO 6 Mayfair
20.12.76 Paul Clemit **W** RSC 3 Walworth
25.01.77 Tommy Wright **W** RSC 1 Bethnal Green
01.02.77 Danny Connolly **W** RSC 2 Kensington
14.02.77 George McGurk **W** RSC 1 Mayfair
16.03.77 Godfrey Butler **W** CO 2 Solihull
18.04.77 Billy Vivian **W** CO 1 Mayfair
31.05.77 Tommy Glencross **W** RSC 2 Kensington
14.06.77 Mario Oliveira **W** RSC 2 Wembley
27.09.77 Des Gwilliam **L** RSC 6 Wembley
08.11.77 Bingo Crooks **W** PTS 8 Wembley
06.12.77 Dil Collins **W** CO 5 Kensington
21.02.78 Carlos Foldes **W** DIS 5 Kensington
19.07.78 Ethem Ozekalin **W** RSC 3 Bellaria

26.09.78 George Feeney **W** PTS 8 Wembley
04.11.78 Godfrey Mwamba **W** CO 3 Lusaka
18.12.78 Georges Cotin **W** RSC 1 Mayfair
13.01.79 Frank Moultry **W** PTS 8 Miami
04.03.79 Nino Jiminez **W** PTS 8 San Remo
31.03.79 Godfrey Mwamba **W** RSC 2 Lusaka
24.06.79 Fernando Jiminez **W** RTD 5 Monte Carlo
03.11.79 Jose Gonzales **W** CO 3 Glasgow
16.03.80 Fili Ramirez **W** RSC 7 Las Vegas
01.04.80 Jimmy Washington **W** RSC 2 Wembley
22.04.80 Benny Marques **W** RSC 4 Kensington
07.06.80 Jerome Artis **W** RSC 3 Glasgow
28.06.80 Ron Green **W** RSC 6 Wembley
12.07.80 Manuel Velasquez **W** RSC 3 Wembley
09.08.80 Alexis Arguello **L** RTD 8 Atlanta City
14.10.80 Roberto Torres **W** RSC 2 Kensington
28.11.80 Roman Contreras **W** PTS 10 San Diego
08.03.81 Rafael Limon **W** PTS 15 Stockton
(*WBC J. Lightweight Title Challenge*)
30.05.81 Bobby Chacon **W** RTD 13 Las Vegas
(*WBC J. Lightweight Title Defence*)
29.08.81 Rolando Navarette **L** CO 5 Via Reggio
(*WBC J. Lightweight Title Challenge*)
24.11.81 Santiago Alvarez **W** RSC 3 Wembley
09.02.82 Arturo Leon **W** RTD 4 Kensington
17.03.82 Carlos Hernandez **W** RTD 4 Kensington
(*European J. Lightweight Title Challenge*)
24.04.82 Johnny Verderosa **W** RSC 3 Atlanta City

Cornelius Boza-Edwards
Robin Nunn

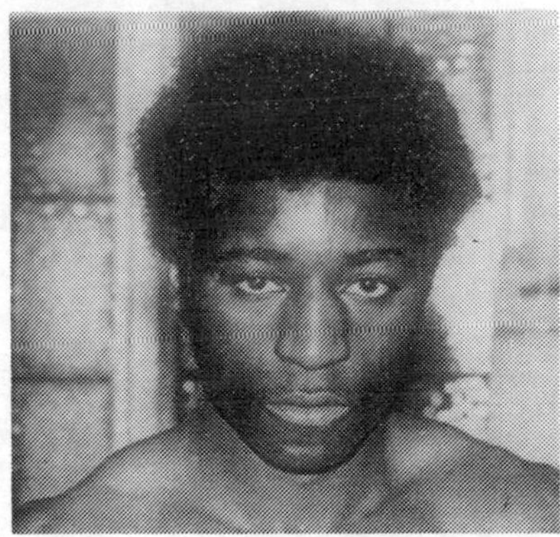

26.06.82 Roberto Elizondo **W** PTS 10 Las Vegas
09.10.82 Blaine Dickson **W** PTS 10 Las Vegas
27.02.83 Pedro Laza **W** RSC 9 Las Vegas
15.05.83 Bobby Chacon **L** PTS 12 Las Vegas
09.09.83 Rocky Lockridge **L** PTS 10 Las Vegas
17.06.84 Guy Villegas **W** RSC 7 Tampa
Summary: 44 contests, won 39, lost 5

Joe Bugner

Joe Bugner

London. *Born* Hungary 13.03.50
Former Undefeated British, Commonwealth & European Heavyweight Champion
Manager (Self)
Previous Amateur Club Bedford Lads
National Honours Young England Rep.

20.12.67 Paul Brown **L** CO 3 Mayfair
20.01.68 Paul Cassidy **W** CO 2 Bethnal Green
27.02.68 Jim McIlvaney **W** RSC 2 Bethnal Green
26.03.68 Egbert Johnson **W** CO 1 Bethnal Green
06.05.68 Mick Oliver **W** RTD 3 Mayfair
21.05.68 Billy Wynter **W** PTS 6 Bethnal Green

CONTINUED OVERLEAF

28.05.68 Paul Brown **W** RSC 4 Kensington
18.09.68 Obe Hepburn **W** RSC 1 Wembley
08.10.68 Vic Moore **W** RSC 1 Kensington
04.11.68 Paul Brown **W** RSC 3 Holborn
12.11.68 Gene Innocent **W** RSC 3 Wembley
19.12.68 George Dulaire **W** RSC 4 Bethnal Green
21.01.69 Rudolph Vaughan **W** RSC 2 Kensington
25.02.69 Terry Feeley **W** RSC 1 Kensington
11.03.69 Ulric Regis **W** PTS 8 Shoreditch
25.03.69 Lion Ven **W** RSC 5 Wembley
15.04.69 Jack O'Halloran **W** PTS 8 Kensington
20.05.69 Tony Ventura **W** PTS 8 Kensington
09.06.69 Mose Harrell **W** PTS 8 Manchester
04.08.69 Dick Hall **L** PTS 8 Manchester
14.10.69 Phil Smith **W** RSC 2 Kensington
11.11.69 Eddie Talhami **W** RSC 4 Kensington
09.12.69 Charlie Polite **W** CO 3 Kensington
20.01.70 Johnny Prescott **W** PTS 8 Kensington
10.02.70 Roberto Davila **W** RSC 3 Kensington
24.03.70 Manuel Ramos **W** PTS 8 Wembley
21.04.70 Ray Patterson **W** PTS 8 Kensington
12.05.70 Brian London **W** RSC 5 Wembley
08.09.70 Chuck Wepner **W** RSC 3 Wembley
06.10.70 Eduardo Corletti **W** PTS 10 Kensington
03.11.70 Scrap Iron Johnson **W** PTS 10 Kensington
08.12.70 Miguel Angel Paez **W** RSC 3 Kensington
19.01.71 Carl Gizzi **W** PTS 10 Kensington
10.02.71 Bill Drover DREW 10 Bethnal Green
16.03.71 Henry Cooper **W** PTS 15 Wembley
(*British, Commonwealth & European Heavyweight Title Challenge*)
11.05.71 Jurgen Blin **W** PTS 15 Wembley
(*European Heavyweight Title Defence*)
27.09.71 Jack Bodell **L** PTS 15 Wembley
(*British, Commonwealth & European Heavyweight Title Defence*)
17.11.71 Mike Boswell **W** PTS 10 Houston
24.11.71 Larry Middleton **L** PTS 10 Nottingham
28.03.72 Brian O'Melia **W** RSC 3 Wembley
25.04.72 Leroy Caldwell **W** DIS 5 Kensington
09.05.72 Mark Hans **W** RSC 3 Wembley
06.06.72 Doug Kirk **W** RSC 5 Kensington
19.07.72 Paul Neilson **W** RSC 6 Dublin
10.10.72 Jurgen Blin **W** CO 8 Kensington
(*European Heavyweight Title Challenge*)
14.11.72 Tony Doyle **W** RTD 8 Wembley
28.11.72 Dante Cane **W** RTD 6 Nottingham
16.01.73 Rudi Lubbers **W** PTS 15 Kensington
(*European Heavyweight Title Defence*)
14.02.73 Muhammad Ali **L** PTS 12 Las Vegas
02.07.73 Joe Frazier **L** PTS 12 Earls Court
02.10.73 Bepi Ros **W** PTS 15 Kensington
(*European Heavyweight Title Defence*)
13.11.73 Mac Foster **W** PTS 10 Wembley
12.03.74 Pat Duncan **W** PTS 10 Wembley
29.05.74 Mario Baruzzi **W** RTD 9 Copenhagen
(*European Heavyweight Title Defence*)
01.10.74 Jose Luis Garcia **W** CO 2 Wembley
12.11.74 Jimmy Ellis **W** PTS 10 Wembley
03.12.74 Alberto Lovell **W** RSC 2 Kensington
01.03.75 Dante Cane **W** RSC 4 Bologna
(*European Heavyweight Title Defence*)
01.07.75 Muhammad Ali **L** PTS 15 Kuala Lumpur
(*World Heavyweight Title Challenge*)
12.10.76 Richard Dunn **W** CO 1 Wembley
(*British, Commonwealth & European Heavyweight Title Challenge*)
20.03.77 Ron Lyle **L** PTS 12 Las Vegas
23.08.80 Gilberto Acuna **W** RTD 6 Los Angeles
08.05.82 Earnie Shavers **L** RSC 2 Dallas
28.10.82 Winston Allen **W** CO 3 Bloomsbury
09.12.82 Eddie Neilson **W** RSC 5 Bloomsbury
16.02.83 John Dino Dennis **W** RSC 3 Muswell Hill
20.04.83 Danny Sutton **W** RSC 9 Muswell Hill
04.06.83 Marvis Frazier **L** PTS 10 Atlantic City
13.01.84 Anders Eklund **W** PTS 10 Randers
18.02.84 Steffen Tangstad **L** PTS 10 Copenhagen

Summary: 70 contests, won 58, drew 1, lost 11

Jimmy Cable

Orpington. *Born* Penge 07.09.57
British & European L. Middleweight Champion. Former Undefeated Southern Area L. Middleweight Champion
Manager D. Bidwell
Previous Amateur Club Fitzroy Lodge

18.11.80 Mick Miller **W** PTS 6 Bethnal Green
09.12.80 Roger Ryder **W** RTD 4 Southend
06.01.81 Neville Wilson **W** PTS 6 Bethnal Green
03.02.81 Paul Goodwin **W** PTS 6 Southend
09.03.81 Steve Henty **W** PTS 6 Copthorne
13.04.81 Tony Britton **W** PTS 6 Southwark
11.05.81 Mickey Mapp **W** PTS 8 Copthorne
15.06.81 Neil Fannan **W** CO 5 Mayfair
15.09.81 Steve Buttle **W** PTS 6 Wembley

Jimmy Cable
Derek Rowe (Photos) Ltd

12.10.81 Vince Stewart W PTS 6 Copthorne
15.12.81 Tony Britton W PTS 8 Lewisham
12.01.82 George Walker W PTS 8 Bethnal Green
01.02.82 Steve Davies W PTS 8 Copthorne
16.02.82 Gary Cooper W RSC 7 Bethnal Green
17.03.82 Horace McKenzie L CO 2 Kensington
10.05.82 Joe Jackson W PTS 8 Copthorne
21.06.82 Chris Christian W PTS 10 Copthorne
(*Southern Area L. Middleweight Title Challenge*)
29.09.82 Tony Martey W PTS 8 Effingham Park
20.10.82 Arthur Davis W PTS 8 Strand
08.02.83 Jimmy Batten L PTS 8 Kensington
06.04.83 Arthur Davis W RSC 5 Mayfair
03.05.83 Nick Wilshire W PTS 10 Wembley
05.09.83 Ferdinand Pachler W RTD 5 Mayfair
11.10.83 Jake Torrance W PTS 10 Kensington
22.11.83 John Langol W RSC 1 Wembley
31.01.84 Danny Chapman W RSC 8 Kensington
22.02.84 Nick Wilshire W PTS 12 Kensington
(*Vacant British L. Middleweight Title*)
11.04.84 Buster Drayton L CO 1 Kensington
25.05.84 Said Skouma W RSC 11 Toulouse
(*Vacant European L. Middleweight Title*)

Summary: 29 contests, won 26, lost 3

Ray Cattouse

Balham. *Born* London 24.07.52
Former British Lightweight Champion & Undefeated Southern Area Lightweight Champion
Manager T. Lawless
Previous Amateur Club Fitzroy Lodge
National Honours England Int.
Divisional Honours SE London L. Welterweight R/U 1973; London Lightweight Champion 1974 – 1975

29.09.75 Barton McAllister L PTS 6 Northampton
28.10.75 Winston McKenzie W DIS 5 Southend
04.11.75 Winston McKenzie W PTS 6 Wembley
27.01.76 Willie Owen W RSC 5 Bethnal Green
23.02.76 Paddy Moore W CO 1 Nottingham
02.03.76 Keith Bundy W PTS 6 Southend
15.03.76 Lawrence Devanney W PTS 8 Mayfair
06.04.76 Von Reid W CO 4 Kensington
18.05.76 Kevin Evans W PTS 8 Walworth
20.10.76 Godfrey Butler W PTS 8 Bethnal Green
07.02.77 Dil Collins W PTS 8 Piccadilly
04.04.77 Billy Vivian W PTS 8 Piccadilly
21.06.77 Barry Price DREW 8 Piccadilly
05.08.77 Jackie McGill W RSC 3 Glasgow
18.11.77 Jeff Pritchard W PTS 8 Mayfair
31.01.78 Tommy Dunn W DIS 3 Marylebone
24.04.78 Cookie Roomes W CO 1 Walworth
20.06.78 Sylvester Gordon W PTS 8 Piccadilly
27.11.78 Tommy Davitt W DIS 7 Mayfair

CONTINUED OVERLEAF

Ray Cattouse
Universal Pictorial Press

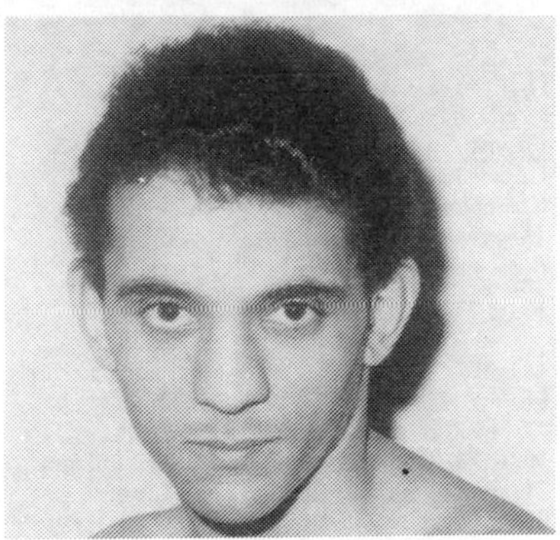

13.02.79 Johnny Claydon W RSC 10 Marylebone
(Southern Area Lightweight Title Challenge & Final Elim. British Lightweight Title)
23.10.79 George Cotin W RSC 1 Wembley
24.03.80 Dave McCabe W RSC 8 Glasgow
(Vacant British Lightweight Title)
27.09.80 Eddie Murray W PTS 8 Wembley
26.11.80 Jofre II W RTD 3 Wembley
16.02.81 Ceri Collins W PTS 8 Piccadilly
23.03.81 Dave McCabe W RSC 15 Glasgow
(British Lightweight Title Defence)
03.11.81 Teddy Hadfield W PTS 10 Kensington
24.02.82 Joey Gibilisco DREW 12 Campobasso
(European Lightweight Title Challenge)
12.10.82 George Feeney L RSC 14 Kensington
(British Lightweight Title Defence)
25.04.83 Willie Booth W RSC 7 Southwark
01.11.83 Paul Chance DREW 8 Dudley
Summary: 31 contests, won 26, drew 3, lost 2

Tom Collins
Derek Rowe (Photos) Ltd

(Elton) Tom Collins

Leeds. *Born* Curacao 01.07.55
Former British L. Heavyweight Champion & Undefeated Central Area L. Heavyweight Champion
Manager T. Callighan
Previous Amateur Club Market District

17.01.77 Ginger McIntyre W RSC 2 Birmingham
16.05.77 Mick Dolan W PTS 6 Manchester
01.06.77 Johnny Cox W CO 3 Dudley
23.11.77 George Gray W RSC 3 Stoke
19.01.78 Clint Jones W RSC 3 Wimbledon
21.03.78 Joe Jackson W PTS 8 Luton
09.05.78 Harald Skog L PTS 8 Oslo
17.07.78 Karl Canwell L RSC 6 Mayfair
28.11.78 Carlton Benoit W CO 1 Sheffield
04.12.78 Dennis Andries L PTS 8 Southend
30.01.79 Dennis Andries L CO 6 Southend
22.10.79 Danny Lawford W RSC 7 Nottingham
28.11.79 Eddie Smith W PTS 8 Solihull
25.02.80 Greg Evans W RSC 1 Bradford
(Vacant Central Area L. Heavyweight Title)
15.04.80 Chris Lawson W RSC 4 Blackpool
04.12.80 Mustafa Wasajja L PTS 8 Randers
09.03.81 Karl Canwell W PTS 10 Bradford
(Elim. British L. Heavyweight Title)
15.03.82 Dennis Andries W PTS 15 Bloomsbury
(Vacant British L. Heavyweight Title)
26.05.82 Trevor Cattouse W CO 4 Leeds
(British L. Heavyweight Title Defence)
07.10.82 John Odhiambo L RSC 5 Copenhagen
09.03.83 Antonio Harris W RSC 6 Solihull
(British L. Heavyweight Title Defence)
09.04.83 Alex Sua W PTS 12 Auckland
(Elim. Commonwealth L. Heavyweight Title)
16.12.83 Lesley Stewart L PTS 10 Trinidad
26.01.84 Dennis Andries L PTS 12 Strand
(British L. Heavyweight Title Defence)
06.04.84 Dennis Andries L PTS 12 Watford
(British L. Heavyweight Title Challenge)
Summary: 25 contests, won 16, lost 9

Pat Cowdell

Warley. *Born* Smethwick 18.08.53
Former Undefeated British & European Featherweight Champion
Manager P. Lynch
Previous Amateur Club Warley
National Honours Junior ABA Title 1970; NABC Title 1970; ABA Bantamweight Champion 1973; ABA Featherweight Champion 1976–1977; ABA Lightweight Champion 1975; Commonwealth Gold 1974; Euro. Bronze 1975; Olympic Bronze 1976; England Int.; Young England Rep.
Divisional Honours M Counties Flyweight Champion 1971–1972

05.07.77 Albert Coley W PTS 6 Wolverhampton
20.09.77 Paul Varden W RTD 5 Wolverhampton
18.10.77 Henri Koni W RSC 6 Wolverhampton
31.10.77 Lee Graham W PTS 8 Birmingham
14.12.77 Kevin Doherty W PTS 8 Kingston
23.01.78 Alan Robertson L RTD 2 Wolverhampton

Pat Cowdell

29.06.78 Alan Buchanan **W** PTS 8 Wolverhampton
18.09.78 Jackie McGill **W** PTS 8 Wolverhampton
15.11.78 Paddy Graham **W** PTS 8 Solihull
05.03.79 Les Pickett **W** PTS 12 Wolverhampton
(*Final Elim. British Featherweight Title*)
16.05.79 Jean-Jacques Souris **W** RSC 6 Wolverhampton
18.09.79 Dave Needham **L** PTS 15 Wolverhampton
(*British Featherweight Title Challenge*)
06.11.79 Dave Needham **W** PTS 15 Kensington
(*British Featherweight Title Challenge*)
21.01.80 Alain Lefol **W** PTS 10 Wolverhampton
19.02.80 Jimmy Flint **W** RTD 11 Kensington
(*British Featherweight Title Defence*)
29.05.80 Dave Needham **W** RTD 12 Wolverhampton
(*British Featherweight Title Defence*)
30.10.80 Earl Wilson **W** PTS 10 Wolverhampton
09.03.81 Modesto Gomez **W** RSC 5 Wolverhampton
01.06.81 Laurent Grimbert **W** RSC 8 Wolverhampton
05.08.81 Sammy Meck **W** PTS 10 Norwich
27.10.81 Eddie Richardson **W** PTS 10 Wolverhampton
12.12.81 Salvador Sanchez **L** PTS 15 Houston
(*WBC Featherweight Title Challenge*)
30.03.82 Salvatore Melluzzo **W** RSC 10 Wembley
(*European Featherweight Title Challenge*)
04.05.82 Thomas Diaz **W** CO 2 Wembley
20.09.82 Robert Mullins **W** PTS 10 Wolverhampton
30.10.82 Sepp Iten **W** RSC 12 Zurich
(*European Featherweight Title Defence*)
10.05.84 Kevin Pritchard **W** RSC 5 Digbeth
Summary: 27 contests, won 24, lost 3

George Feeney

Hartlepool. *Born* Hartlepool 09.02.57
British Lightweight Champion
Manager D. Mancini
Previous Amateur Club Hartlepool BW
National Honours NABC Title 1973; Young England Rep.
Divisional Honours NE Counties Featherweight S/F 1974; NE Counties Featherweight R/U 1975; NE Counties Lightweight Champion 1977

22.08.77 Eric Wood **W** RSC 4 Stockton
29.09.77 Billy Vivian **W** PTS 8 Newcastle
02.11.77 Mick Bell **W** PTS 8 Newcastle
07.02.78 Barry Price **W** RSC 3 Islington
27.02.78 Hector Molina **W** PTS 8 Middlesbrough
17.04.78 Tommy Davitt **L** PTS 8 Mayfair
26.09.78 Cornelius Boza-Edwards **L** PTS 8 Wembley
04.12.78 Eric Wood **W** PTS 8 Middlesbrough
28.02.79 Bingo Crooks **L** PTS 8 Harrogate
26.09.79 Bingo Crooks **W** PTS 8 Solihull
03.11.79 George Peacock **W** PTS 8 Glasgow
19.11.79 Chris Walker **W** CO 8 Glasgow
04.02.80 Bingo Crooks **W** PTS 8 Hammersmith
01.04.80 Clinton McKenzie **L** PTS 10 Wembley
19.07.80 Juan Jose Giminez **L** PTS 10 Grosetto
02.10.80 Ricky Beaumont **L** PTS 10 Hull
(*Elim. British Lightweight Title*)
22.01.81 Robbie Robinson **W** CO 4 Liverpool
24.02.81 Eddie Copeland **W** RTD 4 Kensington
31.03.81 Winston Spencer **W** RSC 9 Wembley
(*Elim. British Lightweight Title*)
24.09.81 Carlos Foldes **W** PTS 8 Hartlepool
23.10.81 Davidson Andeh **L** RTD 6 Lagos
25.01.82 Ken Buchanan **W** PTS 8 Piccadilly
12.10.82 Ray Cattouse **W** RSC 14 Kensington
(*British Lightweight Title Challenge*)
06.02.83 Ray Mancini **L** PTS 10 St Vincent
10.04.83 Howard Davis **L** PTS 10 San Remo
03.12.83 Tony Willis **W** RSC 1 Marylebone
10.02.84 Paul Chance **W** PTS 12 Dudley
(*British Lightweight Title Defence*)
27.04.84 Mickey Baker **W** PTS 10 Wolverhampton
Summary: 28 contests, won 19, lost 9

George Feeney

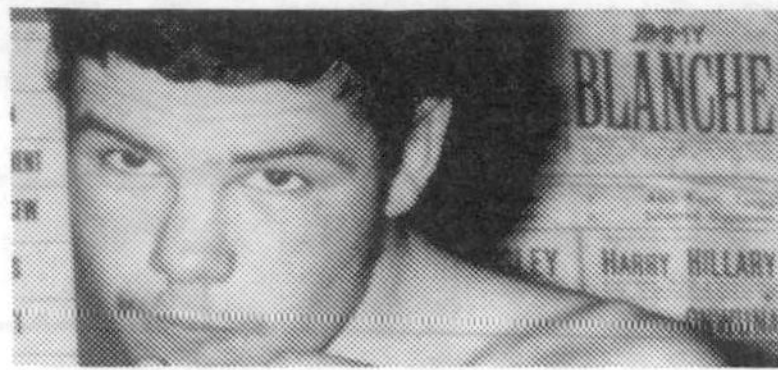

John Feeney
Arturo Fotos

John Feeney

Hartlepool. *Born* Hartlepool 15.05.58
British Bantamweight Champion
Manager D. Mancini
Previous Amateur Club Hartlepool BW
National Honours Junior ABA Title 1974; Young England Rep.; England Int.
Divisional Honours ABA Bantamweight R/U 1976; N Counties Flyweight Champion 1977

10.07.77 Larry Richards **W** RSC 2 Birmingham
22.08.77 Paul Varden **W** PTS 8 Stockton
10.10.77 Jimmy Bott **W** CO 6 Marton
18.10.77 Mohammed Younis **W** PTS 8 Wolverhampton
05.12.77 Charlie Parvin **W** PTS 8 Marton
24.01.78 George Sutton **W** RTD 6 Kensington
13.02.78 Davy Larmour **W** RSC 5 Walworth
09.10.78 Mark Bliss **W** PTS 8 Marylebone
30.10.78 Alex McIntosh **W** RTD 5 Hammersmith
11.11.78 Neil McLaughlin **W** PTS 8 Marylebone
17.01.79 Mohammed Younis **W** PTS 10 Solihull
05.02.79 Alan Robertson **W** PTS 8 Nottingham
20.02.79 Tony Kerr **W** RSC 6 Kensington
02.05.79 George Sutton **W** RSC 8 Solihull
24.09.79 Paddy Graham **W** PTS 8 Hammersmith
03.12.79 Lee Graham **W** PTS 8 Marylebone
24.01.80 Steve Enright **W** PTS 8 Hartlepool
04.03.80 Neil McLaughlin **W** RSC 3 Wembley
28.06.80 Johnny Owen **L** PTS 15 Wembley (*British & Commonwealth Bantamweight Title Challenge*)
01.11.80 Terry McKeown **W** PTS 8 Glasgow
17.11.80 Steve Sammy Sims **W** PTS 8 Gosforth
13.04.81 Mohammed Younis **W** RTD 4 Southwark
17.06.81 Valerio Nati **L** PTS 12 Cervia (*European Bantamweight Title Challenge*)
22.09.81 Dave Smith **W** RSC 8 Bethnal Green (*Vacant British Bantamweight Title*)
29.11.81 Dave Brown **W** PTS 8 Middlesbrough
02.03.82 Adrian Arreola **L** PTS 10 Kensington
02.04.82 Paul Ferreri **L** RSC 13 Sydney (*Commonwealth Bantamweight Title Challenge*)
30.06.82 Guiseppe Fossati **L** PTS 12 Sicily (*European Bantamweight Title Challenge*)
20.09.82 Kid Sumali **W** PTS 8 Mayfair
23.11.82 Vernon Penprase **W** PTS 8 Wembley
25.01.83 Hugh Russell **L** DIS 13 Belfast (*British Bantamweight Title Defence*)
09.03.83 Gerry Beard **W** PTS 8 Solihull
15.03.83 Aramado Ugalde **W** DIS 6 Wembley
16.11.83 Davy Larmour **W** RSC 3 Belfast (*British Bantamweight Title Challenge*)
28.12.83 Walter Giorgetti **L** PTS 12 Campobasso (*European Bantamweight Title Challenge*)
31.01.84 Hector Clottey **W** PTS 8 Kensington
27.04.84 Steve Topliss **W** PTS 10 Wolverhampton
15.06.84 Sepp Iten **W** PTS 8 Zurich
Summary: 38 contests, won 31, lost 7

John L. Gardner
Derek Rowe (Photos) Ltd

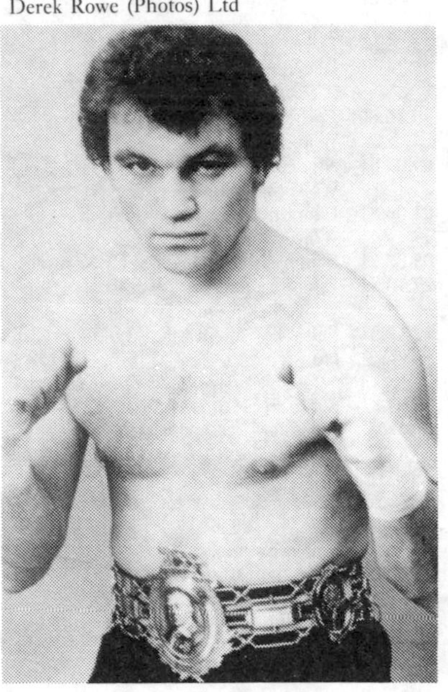

John L. Gardner

Hackney. *Born* Hackney 19.03.53
Former Undefeated Southern Area, British, Commonwealth and European Heavyweight Champion
Manager G. Steene
Previous Amateur Club Polytechnic
Divisional Honours NW London Heavyweight Champion 1973

02.10.73 Brian Hall **W** RTD 2 Kensington
30.10.73 Sid Paddock **W** RSC 3 Kensington
13.11.73 Gerald Gooding **W** PTS 6 Wembley
11.12.73 Ken Burrell **W** RSC 5 Kensington
18.12.73 Lloyd Stewart **W** CO 2 Shoreditch
15.01.74 Barry Clough **W** CO 2 Kensington
26.03.74 Les MacGowan **W** RSC 5 Kensington
07.05.74 John Celebanski **W** RSC 7 Shoreditch
21.05.74 Sid Paddock **W** RSC 4 Wembley
04.06.74 John Celebanski **W** RSC 3 Kensington
29.10.74 Tony Mikulski **W** PTS 6 Kensington
03.12.74 Tony Blackburn **W** PTS 8 Kensington
11.03.75 Peter Freeman **W** RSC 6 Wembley
29.04.75 Tony Mikulski **W** RSC 3 Kensington
14.10.75 Jerry Huston **W** RSC 5 Kensington
20.01.76 Lloyd Walford **W** CO 2 Kensington
02.03.76 Bjorn Rudi **W** RSC 3 Kensington
06.04.76 Bobby Walker **W** RSC 4 Kensington
27.04.76 Tony Moore **W** RSC 8 Kensington
01.06.76 Fred Askew **W** DIS 6 Kensington
12.10.76 Joe Gholston **W** PTS 8 Wembley
26.10.76 Neville Meade **W** RSC 6 Kensington
29.03.77 Brian O'Melia **W** RSC 2 Wembley
31.05.77 Ngozika Ekwelum **W** RSC 6 Kensington
27.09.77 Ibar Arrington L CO 1 Wembley
06.12.77 Denton Ruddock **W** RSC 8 Kensington
(*Southern Area Heavyweight Title Challenge & Final Elim. British Heavyweight Title*)
04.04.78 Dennis Jordan **W** RSC 3 Kensington
24.10.78 Billy Aird **W** RTD 5 Kensington
(*Vacant British & Commonwealth Heavyweight Titles*)
05.12.78 Greg Sorrentino **W** RSC 7 Kensington
20.02.79 Mike Koranicki **W** RSC 9 Kensington
26.06.79 Paul Sykes **W** RSC 6 Wembley
(*British & Commonwealth Heavyweight Title Defence*)
04.12.79 Jimmy Young L PTS 10 Wembley
22.04.80 Rudi Gauwe **W** RTD 9 Kensington
(*Vacant European Heavyweight Title*)
28.11.80 Lorenzo Zanon **W** CO 5 Campione
(*European Heavyweight Title Defence*)
17.03.81 Ossie Ocasio **W** CO 6 Wembley
12.06.81 Mike Dokes L CO 4 Detroit
22.09.83 Ricky James **W** RTD 6 Strand
13.10.83 Lou Benson **W** DIS 8 Bloomsbury
02.11.83 Noel Quarless L RSC 2 Bloomsbury
Summary: 39 contests, won 35, lost 4

Herol Graham
Sheffield Newspapers Ltd

Herol Graham

Sheffield. *Born* Nottingham 13.09.59
Former Undefeated British, Commonwealth, & European L. Middleweight Champion
Manager B. Ingle
Previous Amateur Club Radford
National Honours Schools Titles 1973, 1975 – 1976; Junior ABA Title 1976; NABC Title 1976; Young England Rep.; England Int.; ABA Middleweight Champion 1978
Divisional Honours M Counties Middleweight Champion 1977

28.11.78 Vivian Waite **W** PTS 6 Sheffield
04.12.78 Curtis Marsh **W** RTD 1 Sothend
22.01.79 Jimmy Roberts **W** RSC 2 Bradford
12.02.79 Dave Southwell **W** PTS 8 Reading
28.02.79 Dave Southwell **W** PTS 8 Burslem
27.03.79 George Walker **W** PTS 8 Southend
27.04.79 Mac Nicholson **W** PTS 8 Newcastle
16.05.79 Gordon George **W** PTS 8 Sheffield
26.09.79 Lloyd James **W** PTS 8 Sheffield

CONTINUED OVERLEAF

27.10.79 Billy Ahearne **W** RSC 3 Barnsley
27.11.79 Errol McKenzie **W** PTS 8 Sheffield
12.02.80 Glen McEwan **W** PTS 8 Sheffield
22.04.80 George Danahar **W** PTS 8 Sheffield
09.09.80 Joey Mack **W** PTS 8 Sheffield
30.10.80 Larry Mayes **W** RSC 4 Liverpool
22.01.81 Lancelot Innes **W** PTS 10 Liverpool
24.03.81 Pat Thomas **W** PTS 15 Sheffield
(*British L. Middleweight Title Challenge*)
17.06.81 Prince Rodney **W** RSC 1 Sheffield
25.11.81 Kenny Bristol **W** PTS 15 Sheffield
(*Commonwealth L. Middleweight Title Challenge*)
24.02.82 Chris Christian **W** RSC 9 Sheffield
(*British & Commonwealth L. Middleweight Title Defence*)
22.04.82 Fred Coranson **W** PTS 10 Liverpool
30.09.82 Hunter Clay **W** PTS 15 Lagos
(*Commonwealth L. Middleweight Title Defence*)
15.03.83 Tony Nelson **W** RTD 5 Wembley
23.05.83 Clemente Tshinza **W** CO 2 Sheffield
(*Vacant European L. Middleweight Title*)
11.10.83 Carlos Betancourt **W** CO 1 Kensington
09.12.83 Germain Le Maitre **W** RSC 8 St. Nazaire
(*European L. Middleweight Title Defence*)
Summary: 26 contests, won 26

Lloyd Honeyghan
Derek Rowe (Photos) Ltd

Roy Gumbs
Universal Pictorial Press

Roy Gumbs

Tottenham. *Born* St Kitts 05.09.54
Former British & Commonwealth Middleweight Champion. Former Undefeated Southern Area Middleweight Champion
Manager F. Warren
Previous Amateur Club Seven Feathers

18.05.76 Vernon Shaw **W** CO 6 Southend
07.06.76 Eddie Vierling L PTS 6 Piccadilly
29.06.76 Eddie Vierling L PTS 6 Southampton
21.09.76 Carlton Benoit L PTS 6 Southend
13.10.76 Len Brittain **W** RSC 3 Stoke
22.11.76 Henry Johnson **W** PTS 6 Walworth
06.12.76 Johnny Cox **W** RSC 1 Luton
19.01.77 Tony Sibson L PTS 8 Solihull
25.01.77 Peter Mullins **W** RSC 4 Piccadilly
14.02.77 Malcolm Heath **W** RSC 4 Bedford
21.02.77 Bonny McKenzie **W** PTS 8 Piccadilly
24.04.77 Wayne Bennett L DIS 7 Birmingham
14.06.77 Greg Evans L PTS 8 Wembley
18.01.78 Eddie Smith L CO 8 Solihull
28.02.78 Oscar Angus DREW 8 Aylesbury
16.03.78 Per Mullertz **W** RSC 4 Copenhagen
03.04.78 Oscar Angus **W** RSC 3 Piccadilly
28.04.78 Alfredo Naveiras L CO 3 Emines
27.09.78 Bonny McKenzie **W** PTS 8 Stoke
06.11.78 Keith Bussey DREW 8 Piccadilly
21.12.78 Greg Evans **W** RSC 6 Liverpool

19.02.79 Jan Magdziarz **W** RSC 7 Piccadilly (*Southern Area Middleweight Title Challenge*)
03.04.79 Errol McKenzie **W** RSC 4 Hammersmith
24.04.79 Bonny McKenzie **W** PTS 8 Piccadilly
15.10.79 Bonny McKenzie **W** RSC 3 Mayfair
26.11.79 Victor Attivor **W** RSC 5 Hammersmith
18.02.80 Frankie Lucas **W** PTS 10 Mayfair (*Southern Area Middleweight Title Defence*)
20.11.80 Al Styles **W** RSC 2 Piccadilly
02.02.81 Howard Mills **W** RSC 3 Piccadilly (*Vacant British Middleweight Title*)
01.10.81 Joe Henry **W** RSC 8 Toronto
29.10.81 Eddie Burke **W** RSC 6 Glasgow (*British Middleweight Title Defence*)
18.02.82 Glen McEwan **W** RSC 13 Liverpool (*British Middleweight Title Defence*)
16.04.82 Manning Galloway DREW 10 Toronto
27.09.82 Nat King **W** RSC 1 Bloomsbury
08.02.83 Ralph Hollett **W** RSC 5 Nova Scotia, (*Vacant Commonwealth Middleweight Title*)
29.03.83 Ralph Hollett **W** RSC 4 Nova Scotia, (*Commonwealth Middleweight Title Defence*)
18.05.83 Jerry Holly **W** CO 2 Bloomsbury
14.09.83 Mark Kaylor **L** CO 5 Muswell Hill (*British & Commonwealth Middleweight Title Defence*)
21.03.84 Lindell Holmes **L** CO 7 Bloomsbury
Summary: 39 contests, won 26, drew 3, lost 10

Lloyd Honeyghan

Bermondsey. *Born* Jamaica 22.04.60
British Welterweight Champion & Former Undefeated Southern Area Welterweight Champion
Manager T. Lawless
Previous Amateur Club Fisher
National Honours NABC Title 1977; Young England Rep.; England Int.
Divisional Honours SE London Welterweight R/U 1978/1980; London Welterweight Champion 1979

08.12.80 Mike Sullivan **W** PTS 6 Kensington
20.01.81 Dai Davies **W** RSC 5 Bethnal Green
10.02.81 Dave Sullivan **W** PTS 6 Bethnal Green
16.11.81 Dave Finigan **W** RSC 1 Mayfair
24.11.81 Alan Cooper **W** RSC 4 Wembley
25.01.82 Dave Finigan **W** CO 2 Mayfair
09.02.82 Granville Allen **W** RSC 5 Kensington
02.03.82 Tommy McCallum **W** PTS 6 Kensington
15.03.82 Derek McKenzie **W** RSC 6 Mayfair
23.03.82 Dave Sullivan **W** RSC 3 Bethnal Green
18.05.82 Kostas Petrou **W** PTS 8 Bethnal Green
22.09.82 Kid Murray **W** RSC 3 Mayfair
22.11.82 Frank McCord **W** CO 1 Mayfair
18.01.83 Lloyd Hibbert **W** PTS 10 Kensington (*Elim. British Welterweight Title*)
01.03.83 Sid Smith **W** CO 8 Kensington (*Southern Area Welterweight Title Challenge & Elim. British Welterweight Title*)
05.04.83 Cliff Gilpin **W** PTS 12 Kensington (*Vacant British Welterweight Title*)
09.07.83 Kevin Austin **W** RSC 10 Chicago
24.10.83 Harold Brazier **W** PTS 10 Mayfair
06.12.83 Cliff Gilpin **W** PTS 12 Kensington (*British Welterweight Title Defence*)
05.06.84 Roberto Mendez **W** PTS 8 Kensington
Summary: 20 contests, won 20

Colin Jones
Lawrence Lustig (Global Sports Photos)

Colin Jones

Gorseinon. *Born* Gorseinon 21.03.59
Commonwealth Welterweight Champion. Former Undefeated British & European Welterweight Champion
Manager E. Thomas
Previous Amateur Club Penyrhsol
National Honours School Titles 1973 – 1975; GB Rep.; Welsh Welterweight Champion 1976 – 1977; Welsh Int.

03.10.77 Mike Copp **W** RSC 5 Aberavon
01.12.77 Martin Bridge **W** RSC 4 Heathrow

CONTINUED OVERLEAF

23.01.78 Alan Reid **W** CO 1 Aberavon
07.02.78 Willie Turkington **W** RSC 1 Islington
20.03.78 Tony Martey **W** PTS 8 Aberavon
10.07.78 Frankie Decaesteker **W** PTS 6 Aberavon
03.10.78 Horace McKenzie **W** PTS 8 Aberavon
11.12.78 Johnny Pincham **W** RSC 4 Plymouth
03.04.79 Sam Hailston **W** CO 4 Caerphilly
13.05.79 Salvo Nuciforo **W** CO 4 Plymouth
05.07.79 Alain Salmon **W** RSC 1 Aberavon
30.10.79 Joey Mack **W** RSC 10 Caerphilly
(Final Elim. British Welterweight Title)
21.01.80 Billy Waith **W** CO 6 Mayfair
01.04.80 Kirkland Laing **W** RSC 9 Wembley
(British Welterweight Title Challenge)
03.06.80 Richard House **W** CO 1 Kensington
12.08.80 Peter Neal **W** RSC 5 Swansea
(British Welterweight Title Defence)
15.12.80 Clemente Tshinza **W** RSC 3 Merthyr
16.02.81 Horace McKenzie **W** RSC 7 Mayfair
03.03.81 Mark Harris **W** RSC 9 Wembley
(Vacant Commonwealth Welterweight Title)

Mark Kaylor
Derek Rowe (Photos) Ltd

28.04.81 Kirkland Laing **W** RSC 9 Kensington
(British & Commonwealth Welterweight Title Defences)
03.09.81 Curtis Ramsey L DIS 3 Cardiff
15.09.81 Pete Seward **W** RSC 3 Wembley
24.11.81 Gary Giron **W** RSC 3 Wembley
14.09.82 Sakaria Ve **W** CO 2 Wembley
(Commonwealth Welterweight Title Defence)
05.11.82 Hans Henrik Palm **W** RSC 2 Copenhagen
(European Welterweight Title Challenge)
19.03.83 Milton McCrory DREW 12 Reno Nevada
(Vacant WBC Welterweight Title)
13.08.83 Milton McCrory L PTS 12 Las Vegas
(Vacant WBC Welterweight Title)
28.03.84 Allan Braswell **W** CO 2 Aberavon
13.06.84 Billy Parks **W** RSC 10 Aberavon
Summary: 29 contests, won 26, drew 1, lost 2

Mark Kaylor

West Ham. *Born* London 11.05.61
British & Commonwealth Middleweight Champion
Manager T. Lawless
Previous Amateur Club West Ham
National Honours Schools Title 1977; NABC Title 1979; Young England Rep.; GB Rep.; ABA Middleweight Champion 1980
Divisional Honours London L. Middleweight Champion 1979

14.10.80 Peter Morris **W** RSC 5 Kensington
08.12.80 Clifton Wallace **W** RSC 3 Kensington
27.01.81 Winston Burnett **W** PTS 8 Kensington
24.02.81 Martin McEwan **W** RSC 6 Kensington
17.03.81 Peter Bassey **W** PTS 8 Wembley
26.05.81 Joe Gregory **W** RTD 6 Bethnal Green
15.09.81 Jimmy Ellis **W** RSC 5 Wembley
20.10.81 George Danahar **W** RSC 3 Bethnal Green
03.11.81 Winston Burnett **W** RSC 6 Kensington
24.11.81 Billy Savage **W** RSC 2 Wembley
09.02.82 Romal Ambrose **W** CO 1 Kensington
02.03.82 Dario D'Asa **W** RSC 3 Kensington
27.03.82 Alfonso Redondo **W** RSC 5 Kensington
20.04.82 Joel Bonnetaz **W** RSC 3 Kensington
01.06.82 Steve Williams **W** RSC 2 Kensington
22.09.82 Maurice Bufi **W** RSC 3 Mayfair

26.10.82 Doug James W RSC 2 Bethnal Green
09.11.82 Eddie Smith W RSC 3 Kensington
07.12.82 Juan Munoz-Holgado W CO 2 Kensington
18.01.83 Henry Walker W PTS 10 Kensington
01.03.83 Glen McEwan W RSC 2 Kensington
(Final Elim. British Middleweight Title)
03.05.83 Bobby Watts W RSC 4 Wembley
31.05.83 Bob West W RSC 5 Kensington
14.09.83 Roy Gumbs W CO 5 Muswell Hill
(British & Commonwealth Middleweight Title Challenge)
22.11.83 Tony Cerda L DIS 9 Wembley
31.01.84 Ralph Moncrief W RSC 5 Kensington
13.03.84 Randy Smith W PTS 10 Wembley
13.05.84 Buster Drayton L RSC 7 Wembley
Summary: 28 contests, won 26, lost 2

Kirkland Laing

Nottingham. *Born* Jamaica 20.06.54
Former British Welterweight Champion
Manager M. Duff
Previous Amateur Club Clifton
National Honours Schools Title 1970; Junior ABA Title 1971; Young England Rep., ABA Featherweight Champion 1972; Euro. Junior Bronze 1974
Divisional Honours M Counties L. Welterweight R/U 1973; M Counties Welterweight Champion 1974; M Counties L. Middleweight R/U 1975

14.04.75 Joe Hannaford W CO 2 Nottingham
12.05.75 Liam White W PTS 8 Nottingham
29.09.75 Derek Simpson W PTS 8 Nottingham
25.11.75 Oscar Angus W PTS 6 Kensington
19.01.76 Terry Schofield W PTS 8 Nottingham
12.03.76 Charlie Cooper W PTS 8 Southend
13.04.76 Mike Manley W PTS 8 Southend
17.05.76 John Laine W RSC 3 Nottingham
22.09.76 Harry Watson W RSC 5 Mayfair
11.10.76 Jim Moore W RSC 2 Nottingham
22.11.76 Jim Montague W DIS 7 Birmingham
11.01.77 John Smith W PTS 10 Wolverhampton
08.03.77 Peter Morris DREW 10 Wolverhampton
16.11.77 Peter Morris W RSC 5 Solihull
27.09.78 Achille Mitchell W PTS 12 Solihull
(Final Elim. British Welterweight Title)
04.04.79 Henry Rhiney W RSC 10 Birmingham
(British Welterweight Title Challenge)
06.11.79 Des Morrison W PTS 8 Kensington

Kirkland Laing
Lawrence Lustig (Global Sports Photos)

22.01.80 Salvo Nuciforo W RSC 6 Kensington
19.02.80 Colin Ward W RSC 5 Kensington
01.04.80 Colin Jones L RSC 9 Wembley
(British Welterweight Title Defence)
08.05.80 George Walker W PTS 8 Solihull
03.06.80 Curtis Taylor W RSC 7 Kensington
26.11.80 Joey Singleton W PTS 12 Solihull
(Final Elim. British Welterweight Title)
28.04.81 Colin Jones L RSC 9 Kensington
(British Welterweight Title Challenge)
18.11.81 Cliff Gilpin W PTS 12 Solihull
(Final Elim. British Welterweight Title)
09.02.82 Reg Ford L PTS 10 Kensington
05.05.82 Joey Mack W CO 7 Solihull
04.09.82 Roberto Duran W PTS 10 Detroit
10.09.83 Fred Hutchings L CO 10 Atlantic City
Summary: 29 contests, won 24, drew 1, lost 4

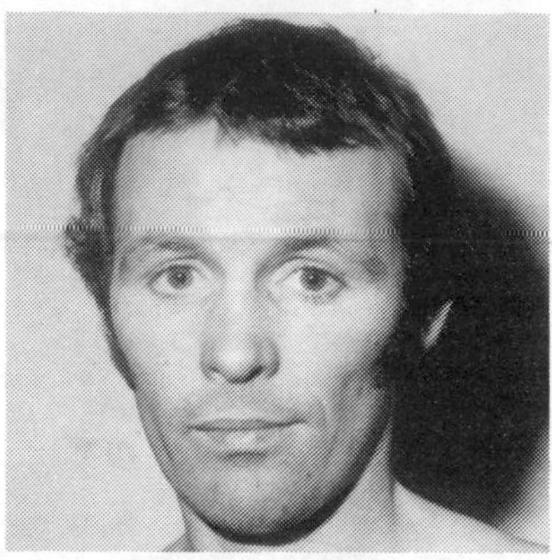

Davy Larmour
Universal Pictorial Press

Davy Larmour

Belfast. *Born* Belfast 02.04.52
N. Ireland Bantamweight Champion & Former British Bantamweight Champion
Manager (Self)
Previous Amateur Club Albert Foundry
National Honours Irish Flyweight Champion 1973/1975/1976; Irish Int.; Commonwealth Gold 1974

26.07.77 Jimmy Bott **W** CO 1 Derry
13.02.78 John Feeney **L** RSC 4 Walworth
14.03.78 George Sutton **L** RSC 6 Belfast
11.05.78 Alan Oag **W** DIS 2 Belfast
28.06.78 Johnny Owen **L** RSC 7 Caerphilly
27.10.78 Neil McLaughlin **W** PTS 10 Belfast (*N. Ireland Bantamweight Title Challenge*)
19.02.79 George Sutton **W** PTS 8 Belfast
05.04.79 Larry Richards **W** RTD 5 Belfast
26.11.79 Dave Smith **W** PTS 10 Belfast
25.02.80 Gilbert Garza **W** PTS 8 Belfast
27.05.80 Isaac Vega **W** PTS 10 Belfast
22.09.80 Steve Sammy Sims **L** PTS 8 Belfast
23.03.81 Dave Smith **L** PTS 12 Southwark (*Final Elim. British Bantamweight Title*)
20.04.82 Ivor Jones **W** PTS 8 Kensington
05.10.82 Hugh Russell **L** PTS 12 Belfast (*N. Ireland Bantamweight Title Defence & Final Elim. British Bantamweight Title*)
25.01.83 Dave George **W** RSC 6 Belfast
02.03.83 Hugh Russell **W** PTS 12 Belfast (*N. Ireland & British Bantamweight Title Challenge*)
16.11.83 John Feeney **L** RSC 3 Belfast (*British Bantamweight Title Defence*)
Summary: 18 contests, won 11, lost 7

Stewart Lithgo

Stewart Lithgo

Hartlepool. *Born* Hartlepool 02.06.57
Commonwealth Cruiserweight Champion & Northern Area Heavyweight Champion
Manager D. Mancini
Previous Amateur Club Hartlepool BW
Divisional Honours NE Counties Heavyweight Champion 1978 – 1979

26.09.79 Colin Flute **W** RSC 4 Solihull
29.10.79 Les Dunn **W** RTD 4 Birmingham
12.11.79 Mal Tetley **W** PTS 6 Middlesbrough
26.11.79 Kenny March **W** PTS 6 Hammersmith
24.01.80 Mal Tetley **W** PTS 6 Hartlepool
07.07.80 Reg Long **W** RSC 3 Middlesbrough
11.09.80 Bob Hennessey **W** PTS 6 Hartlepool

20.10.80 Manny Gabriel W RSC 4 Birmingham
21.11.80 Rudi Gauwe W PTS 8 Zele
31.01.81 Robert Amory W PTS 8 Campignon
15.06.81 Larry McDonald DREW 8 Mayfair
13.10.81 Stan McDermott W CO 8 Kensington
26.11.81 George Scott W PTS 10 Hartlepool
(*Northern Area Heavyweight Title Challenge*)
21.02.82 Gordon Ferris L RSC 2 Birmingham
(*Elim. British Heavyweight Title*)
02.05.82 Neil Malpass W DIS 6 Middlesbrough
06.07.82 Neil Malpass W RSC 3 Leeds
14.08.82 Bennie Knoetze L PTS 8 Johannesburg
07.10.82 Sylvain Watbled L PTS 8 Paris
18.11.82 Maurice Gomis DREW 8 Paris
18.01.83 Frank Bruno L RTD 4 Kensington
08.11.83 Funso Banjo L PTS 8 Bethnal Green
14.05.84 Steve Aczel W CO 11 Brisbane
(*Vacant Commonwealth Cruiserweight Title*)
Summary: 22 contests, won 15, drew 2, lost 5

Barry McGuigan
Derek Rowe (Photos) Ltd

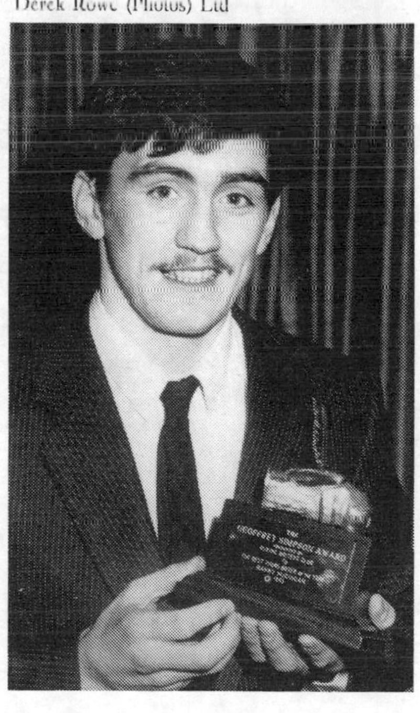

(Finbar) Barry McGuigan

Clones. *Born* Monaghan 28.02.61
British and European Featherweight Champion
Manager B. Eastwood
Previous Amateur Club Smithboro
National Honours Irish Bantamweight Champion 1978; Irish Int.; Euro. Junior Bronze 1980; Commonwealth Gold 1978

10.05.81 Selvin Bell W RSC 2 Dublin
20.06.81 Gary Lucas W RSC 4 Wembley
03.08.81 Peter Eubanks L PTS 8 Brighton
22.09.81 Jean Marc Renard W PTS 8 Belfast
26.10.81 Terry Pizzaro W RSC 4 Belfast
08.12.81 Peter Eubanks W RSC 8 Belfast
27.01.82 Luis De La Sagra W PTS 8 Belfast
08.02.82 Ian Murray W RSC 3 Mayfair
23.02.82 Angel Oliver W RSC 3 Belfast
23.03.82 Angelo Licata W RTD 2 Belfast
22.04.82 Gary Lucas W CO 1 Enniskillen
14.06.82 Young Ali W CO 6 Mayfair
05.10.82 Jimmy Duncan W RTD 4 Belfast
09.11.82 Paul Huggins W RSC 5 Belfast
(*Final Elim. British Featherweight Title*)
12.04.83 Vernon Penprase W RSC 2 Belfast
(*Vacant British Featherweight Title*)
22.05.83 Sammy Meck W RSC 6 Navan
09.07.83 Lavon McGowan W CO 1 Chicago
05.10.83 Ruben Herasme W CO 2 Belfast
16.11.83 Valerio Nati W CO 6 Belfast
(*Vacant European Featherweight Title*)
25.01.84 Charm Chiteule W RSC 10 Belfast
(*Final Elim. Commonwealth Featherweight Title*)
04.04.84 Jose Caba W RSC 7 Belfast
(*Elim. WBC Featherweight Title*)
05.06.84 Esteban Eguia W CO 3 Kensington
(*European Featherweight Title Defence*)
30.06.84 Paul De Vorce W RSC 5 Belfast
Summary: 23 contests, won 22, lost 1

Clinton McKenzie

Croydon. *Born* Croydon 15.09.55
British L. Welterweight Champion & Former European L. Welterweight Champion
Manager M. Duff
Previous Amateur Club Sir Philip Game
National Honours Junior ABA Title 1972; NABC Titles 1972 – 1973; Young England Rep.; England Int.; GB Rep.; ABA L. Welterweight Champion 1976

20.10.76 Jimmy King W PTS 8 Bethnal Green
15.11.76 Barton McAllister W PTS 8 Kensington
01.02.77 George McGurk W PTS 8 Kensington

CONTINUED OVERLEAF

Clinton McKenzie
Derek Rowe (Photos) Ltd

14.02.77 Harry Watson **W** RTD 4 Mayfair
21.03.77 Colin Power L CO 2 Mayfair
18.04.77 Al Stewart **W** RTD 3 Mayfair
07.05.77 Fernand Roelandts **W** PTS 8 Antwerp
10.06.77 Messaoud Bouachibi **W** PTS 8 Ghent
05.09.77 Johnny Pincham L PTS 8 Mayfair
10.10.77 Kevin Davies **W** PTS 8 Piccadilly
03.11.77 Erkki Meronen **W** RTD 4 Randers
16.01.78 Chris Davies **W** PTS 12 Nottingham (*Final Elim. British Welterweight Title*)
02.03.78 Mike Everett **W** PTS 10 Oslo
23.05.78 Chris Walker **W** PTS 8 Islington
11.10.78 Jim Montague **W** RSC 10 Belfast (*Vacant British L. Welterweight Title*)
15.12.78 Tony Martey **W** PTS 8 Kensington
06.02.79 Colin Power L PTS 15 Wembley (*British L. Welterweight Title Defence*)
25.02.79 Bruce Curry L PTS 10 Las Vegas
30.04.79 Des Morrison **W** PTS 12 Mayfair (*Final Elim. British L. Welterweight Title*)
11.09.79 Colin Power **W** PTS 15 Wembley (*British L. Welterweight Title Challenge*)
10.12.79 Roger Guest **W** PTS 8 Mayfair
19.02.80 Roger Guest **W** PTS 8 Kensington
01.04.80 George Feeney **W** PTS 10 Wembley
17.04.80 George Peacock **W** RSC 3 Piccadilly
12.06.80 Hans Henrik Palm L PTS 8 Randers
04.07.80 Obisia Nwankpa L PTS 15 Lagos (*Vacant Commonwealth L. Welterweight Title*)
27.08.80 Giuseppe Martinese L RTD 10 Senegalia (*Vacant European L. Welterweight Title*)
06.01.81 Des Morrison **W** RSC 14 Bethnal Green (*British L. Welterweight Title Defence*)
31.03.81 Sylvester Mittee **W** PTS 15 Wembley (*British L. Welterweight Title Defence*)
13.10.81 Antonio Guinaldo **W** PTS 12 Kensington (*European L. Welterweight Title Challenge*)
16.02.82 Steve Early **W** RSC 4 Bloomsbury (*British L. Welterweight Title Defence*)
01.06.82 Ernie Bing L DIS 1 Kensington
12.10.82 Robert Gambini L DIS 2 Kensington (*European L. Welterweight Title Defence*)
09.11.82 Luciano Navarra **W** RSC 5 Kensington
23.11.82 Memo Arreola **W** RSC 3 Wembley
08.04.83 Alan Lamb **W** PTS 12 Liverpool (*British L. Welterweight Title Defence*)
20.09.83 Tommy McCallum **W** CO 4 Mayfair
15.01.84 Sammy Young **W** RSC 7 Atlantic City
30.04.84 Irish Brett Lally **W** PTS 10 Mayfair
Summary: 39 contests, won 30, lost 9

Charlie Magri

Stepney. *Born* Tunisia 20.07.56
Former Undefeated British & European Flyweight Champion. Former WBC Flyweight Champion
Manager T. Lawless
Previous Amateur Club Arbour Youth
National Honours Junior ABA Titles 1972 – 1973; NABC Titles 1972 – 1973; Young England Rep.; England Int.; GB Rep.; ABA L. Flyweight Champion 1974 & Flyweight Champion 1975, 1976 & 1977; Euro. Junior Silver 1974; Euro. Bronze 1975

25.10.77 Neil McLaughlin **W** CO 2 Kensington
15.11.77 Bryn Griffiths **W** RSC 2 Bethnal Green
06.12.77 Dave Smith **W** RSC 7 Kensington (*Vacant British Flyweight Title*)
21.02.78 Nessim Zebilini **W** RSC 3 Kensington

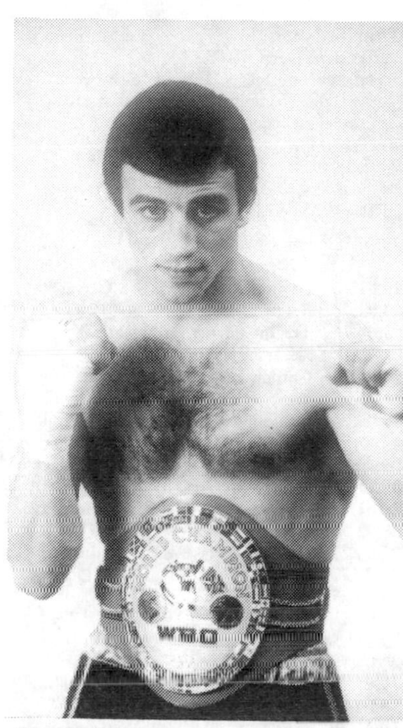

Charlie Magri
Derek Rowe (Photos) Ltd

04.04.78 Dominique Cesari W RTD 4 Kensington
25.04.78 Manuel Carrasco W PTS 8 Kensington
12.09.78 Sabatino De Filippo W RSC 7 Wembley
24.10.78 Claudio Tanda W RSC 1 Kensington
05.12.78 Mariano Garcia W CO 3 Kensington
26.01.79 Filipo Belvedere W RSC 1 Kensington
20.02.79 Mike Stuart W CO 3 Kensington
01.05.79 Franco Udella W PTS 12 Wembley
(*European Flyweight Title Challenge*)
29.05.79 Freddie Gonzales W CO 3 Kensington
25.09.79 Raul Pacheo W RSC 6 Wembley
23.10.79 Candy Iglesias W RSC 3 Wembley
04.12.79 Manuel Carrasco W PTS 12 Wembley
(*European Flyweight Title Defence*)
22.01.80 Aniceto Vargas W CO 3 Kensington
28.06.80 Giovanni Camputaro W RSC 3 Wembley
(*European Flyweight Title Defence*)
16.09.80 Alberto Lopez W PTS 10 Wembley
14.10.80 Enrique Castro W RSC 1 Kensington
08.12.80 Santos Laciar W PTS 10 Kensington
24.02.81 Enrique Rodriguez Cal W RSC 2 Kensington
(*European Flyweight Title Defence*)
20.06.81 Jose Herrera W CO 1 Wembley
13.10.81 Juan Diaz L CO 6 Kensington
02.03.82 Cipriano Arreola W PTS 10 Kensington
20.04.82 Ron Cisneros W RSC 3 Kensington
04.05.82 Jose Torres L RSC 9 Wembley
18.09.82 Enrique Rodriguez Cal W CO 2 Aviles
(*European Flyweight Title Defence*)
23.11.82 Jose Torres W PTS 10 Wembley
15.03.83 Eleoncio Mercedes W RSC 7 Wembley
(*WBC Flyweight Title Challenge*)
27.09.83 Frank Cedeno L RSC 6 Wembley
(*WBC Flyweight Title Defence*)
Summary 31 contests, won 28, lost 3

Neville Meade
Swansea. *Born* Jamaica 12.09.48
Former British & Welsh Heavyweight Champion
Manager T. Lawless
Previous Amateur Club RAF
National Honours England Int.; ABA Heavyweight Champion 1974; Commonwealth Gold 1974
Divisional Honours Combined Services Heavyweight R/U 1971; Combined Services Heavyweight Champion 1972; ABA Heavyweight R/U 1973

09.09.74 Toni Mikulski L PTS 6 Mayfair
14.10.74 Roger Barlow W RSC 3 Swansea
21.10.74 Geoff Hepplestone W CO 1 Mayfair
21.10.74 Les MacGowan W CO 1 Mayfair
21.10.74 Harold James W PTS 4 Mayfair
18.11.74 Eddie Fenton W RSC 5 Piccadilly
17.02.75 Richard Dunn L RTD 4 Mayfair
29.04.75 Tony Moore L RTD 5 Kensington
05.06.75 Tony Moore DREW 8 Hammersmith
02.07.75 Lloyd Walford W RSC 6 Swansea
06.08.75 Derek Simpkin W RSC 3 Cardiff
17.09.75 John Depledge W RSC 5 Cardiff
24.09.75 Tony Moore W PTS 8 Solihull
04.11.75 Lucien Rodriguez W RSC 3 Paris
12.03.76 Alfredo Evangelista L PTS 8 Madrid
29.03.76 Tony Blackburn W RSC 4 Swansea
(*Vacant Welsh Heavyweight Title*)
26.05.76 Garfield McEwan W RSC 9 Wolverhampton

CONTINUED OVERLEAF

Neville Meade

11.08.76 Denton Ruddock **L** RSC 7 Cardiff *(Elim. British Heavyweight Title)*
26.10.76 John L. Gardner **L** RSC 6 Kensington
02.12.76 Bjorn Rudi **W** RSC 7 Oslo
25.12.76 Jean-Pierre Coopman **L** PTS 10 Izegem
04.06.77 Kallie Knoetze **L** CO 4 Johannesburg
08.12.77 Bruce Grandham **W** RSC 3 Liverpool
31.03.78 Bruce Grandham **L** CO 3 Liverpool
15.05.78 Paul Sykes **L** RSC 5 Bradford
19.01.79 Al Syben **L** RSC 4 Brussels
22.01.80 David Pearce **W** RSC 2 Caerphilly *(Welsh Heavyweight Title Defence)*
01.10.80 Winston Allen **W** RSC 2 Swansea *(Welsh Heavyweight Title Defence)*
08.12.80 Stan McDermott **W** RSC 5 Kensington *(Elim. British Heavyweight Title)*
26.03.81 Terry Mintus **W** RSC 3 Ebbw Vale *(Final Elim. British Heavyweight Title)*
12.10.81 Gordon Ferris **W** CO 1 Birmingham *(British Heavyweight Title Challenge)*
03.11.81 Leroy Boone **L** PTS 10 Kensington
21.02.82 Rick Keller **W** CO 6 Birmingham
22.09.83 David Pearce **L** RSC 9 Cardiff *(Welsh & British Heavyweight Title Defence)*

Summary: 34 contests, won 20, drew 1, lost 13

Charlie Nash

Derry. *Born* Derry 10.05.51
Former Undefeated N. Ireland & British Lightweight Champion. Former European Lightweight Champion
Manager (Self)
Previous Amateur Club St Marys
National Honours Irish Lightweight Champion 1970 – 1973/1975; Irish Int.

02.10.75 Ray Ross **W** PTS 10 Derry *(Vacant N. Ireland Lightweight Title)*
26.01.76 Gordon Kirk **W** PTS 8 Glasgow
04.03.76 Bingo Crooks **W** PTS 8 Belfast
05.04.76 Tommy Glencross **W** PTS 8 Piccadilly
26.04.76 Gordon Kirk **W** PTS 8 Piccadilly
24.05.76 Jimmy Revie **W** RSC 3 Mayfair
22.09.76 Joey Singleton **W** RSC 9 Solihull *(Final Elim. British Lightweight Title)*
25.10.76 Guiseppe Agate **W** PTS 10 Mayfair
09.11.76 George McGurk **W** PTS 8 Derry
24.01.77 Donny Sennett **W** RSC 5 Mayfair
28.02.77 Tom Tarantino **W** RSC 1 Mayfair
22.03.77 Benny Huertas **W** PTS 10 Derry
26.07.77 Larry Stanton **W** PTS 10 Derry
04.10.77 Adolpho Osses **L** RSC 5 Belfast
28.02.78 Johnny Claydon **W** RSC 12 Derry *(Vacant British Lightweight Title)*
27.06.78 Adolpho Osses **W** CO 3 Derry
17.07.78 Rene Martin **W** RSC 7 Mayfair
18.09.78 Willie Rodriguez **W** PTS 10 Mayfair
19.02.79 Luis Vega **W** PTS 8 Mayfair
20.03.79 Jerome Artis **W** PTS 8 Mayfair

Charlie Nash
Universal Pictorial Press

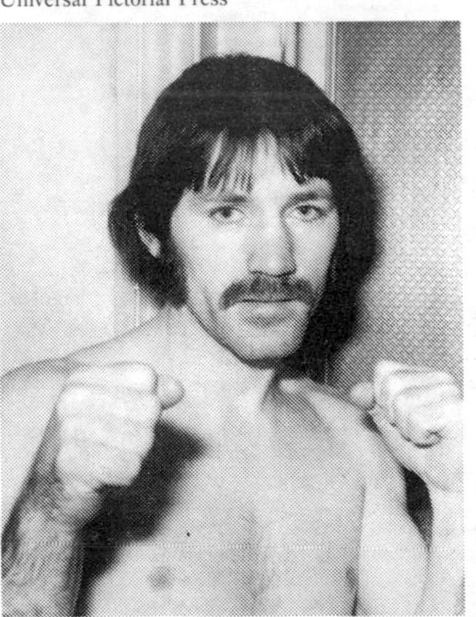

27.06.79 Andre Holyk **W** PTS 12 Derry
(*Vacant European Lightweight Title*)
06.12.79 Ken Buchanan **W** PTS 12 Copenhagen
(*European Lightweight Title Defence*)
14.03.80 Jim Watt **L** RSC 4 Glasgow
(*WBC Lightweight Title Challenge*)
27.05.80 Pedro Acosta **W** RSC 7 Belfast
14.12.80 Fransisco Leon **W** PTS 12 Dublin
(*European Lightweight Title Challenge*)
10.05.81 Joey Gibilisco **L** CO 6 Dublin
(*European Lightweight Title Defence*)
09.03.82 George Metcalf **W** RSC 2 Derry
28.09.82 Frank McCord **W** PTS 8 Derry
06.12.82 Tony Willis **L** RSC 3 Edgbaston
04.03.83 Rene Weller **L** RSC 4 Cologne
Summary: 30 contests, won 25, lost 5

David Pearce
Newport. *Born* Newport 08.05.59
British Heavyweight Champion & Former Undefeated Welsh Heavyweight Champion
Manager B. McCarthy
Previous Amateur Club Newport SC

15.11.78 Osbourne Taylor **W** RSC 1 Merthyr
01.12.78 Bob Bleau **W** CO 2 Minster
11.12.78 Theo Josephs **W** PTS 8 Plymouth
22.01.79 Mal Tetley **W** CO 1 Mayfair
22.01.79 Bob Hennessey **W** RSC 2 Mayfair
19.02.79 Bonny McKenzie **W** PTS 8 Mayfair
03.04.79 Winston Allen **W** PTS 6 Caerphilly
05.07.79 Theo Josephs **W** RSC 2 Aberavon
30.10.79 Denton Ruddock **W** RSC 7 Caerphilly
22.01.80 Neville Meade **L** RSC 2 Caerphilly
(*Welsh Heavyweight Title Challenge*)
26.01.81 John Rafferty **L** DIS 3 Glasgow
02.03.81 Bonny McKenzie **W** PTS 8 Piccadilly
16.03.81 Larry McDonald **W** CO 3 Piccadilly
08.06.81 Ishaq Hussien **W** RSC 1 Moorgate
12.10.81 Dennis Andries **W** RSC 7 Bloomsbury
01.06.82 Gordon Ferris **W** CO 5 Kensington
(*Final Elim. British Heavyweight Title*)
07.12.82 Felipe Rodriguez DREW 10 Kensington
07.04.83 Al Syben **W** CO 1 Strand
22.09.83 Neville Meade **W** RSC 9 Cardiff
(*Welsh & British Heavyweight Title Challenge*)
28.01.84 Jack Johnson **W** RSC 4 Hanley
30.03.84 Lucien Rodriguez **L** PTS 12 Limoges
(*European Heavyweight Title Challenge*)
Summary: 21 contests, won 17, drew 1, lost 3

David Pearce
Glenn Edwards

Colin Power
Paddington. *Born* London 02.02.56
Former British & European L. Welterweight Champion
Manager (Self)
Previous Amateur Club Seven Feathers
Divisional Honours NW London L. Welterweight Champion 1975

11.06.75 Kevin Quinn **W** RTD 3 Bradford
01.07.75 Hughie Clark **W** RTD 4 Southend
18.11.75 Barton McAllister **W** PTS 8 Hornsey
02.12.75 Winston McKenzie **W** RSC 4 Southend
13.01.76 Willie Owen **W** PTS 6 Hornsey
23.02.76 Danny Fearon **W** PTS 8 Nottingham
13.04.76 Tommy Dunn **W** RSC 8 Hornsey
27.04.76 George McGurk **W** PTS 8 Kensington
22.09.76 Des Morrison **L** RSC 5 Mayfair
(*Vacant Southern Area L. Welterweight Title*)
02.11.76 Terry Petersen **W** RSC 4 Southend
06.12.76 Joey Singleton **W** PTS 8 Hammersmith
17.01.77 Barton McAllister **W** RSC 5 Mayfair
25.01.77 Billy Vivian **W** RSC 4 Bethnal Green
05.02.77 Claude Lormeau **W** RSC 5 Chartres
01.03.77 Tommy Glencross **W** RSC 4 Marylebone
21.05.77 Clinton McKenzie **W** CO 2 Mayfair

CONTINUED OVERLEAF

28.05.77 Fernando Sanchez DREW 8 Miranda De Ebro
21.09.77 Efisio Pinna **W** RSC 7 Milan
19.10.77 Des Morrison **W** RSC 10 Bethnal Green
(*Vacant British L. Welterweight Title*)
06.12.77 Rudy Barro **W** PTS 10 Kensington
27.02.78 Chris Walker **W** RSC 7 Sheffield
(*British L. Welterweight Title Defence*)
05.06.78 Jean-Baptiste Piedvache **W** RTD 11 Paris
(*European L. Welterweight Title Challenge*)
09.09.78 Fernando Sanchez **L** RSC 12 Miranda De Ebro
(*European L. Welterweight Title Defence*)
06.02.79 Clinton McKenzie **W** PTS 15 Wembley
(*British L. Welterweight Title Challenge*)
29.05.79 Johnny Elliott **W** RTD 5 Southend
26.06.79 Jose Luis Ribero **W** RSC 6 Wembley
11.09.79 Clinton McKenzie **L** PTS 15 Wembley
(*British L. Welterweight Title Defence*)
22.01.80 Sylvester Mittee **L** RSC 7 Kensington
(*Elim. British L. Welterweight Title*)
15.03.82 Mike Clemow **W** RSC 6 Bloomsbury
14.04.82 Gary Pearce **W** CO 6 Strand
27.04.82 Gerry McGrath **W** RTD 3 Hornsey
07.06.82 Arthur Davis **W** CO 3 Bloomsbury
28.10.82 Chris Christian **W** PTS 8 Bloomsbury
16.02.83 Lloyd Christie **L** RSC 6 Muswell Hill

Summary: 34 contests, won 28, drew 1, lost 5

Colin Power
Universal Pictorial Press

Prince Rodney
Derek Rowe (Photos) Ltd

(Noel) Prince Rodney

Huddersfield. *Born* London 31.10.58
Former Undefeated British and Central Area L. Middleweight Champion
Manager M. Hope
Previous Amateur Club Market District

24.10.77 Russ Shaw **W** RSC 3 Manchester
08.11.77 Jackie Gilling **W** PTS 6 Darlington
01.12.77 Paddy McAleese **W** PTS 8 Caister
08.12.77 Steve Goodwin **L** PTS 6 Liverpool
19.12.77 Steve Goodwin DREW 6 Bradford
18.01.78 Billy Ahearne **W** PTS 8 Solihull
30.01.78 Dave Moore **W** RSC 6 Cleethorpes
13.02.78 Roger Guest **W** PTS 8 Manchester
02.03.78 Carl Bailey **W** PTS 8 Caister
03.04.78 Carl Bailey **W** RSC 7 Manchester
18.07.78 Horace McKenzie **W** PTS 8 Wakefield
11.09.78 Johnny Pincham **W** RSC 6 Bradford
16.10.78 Roy Commosioung **W** PTS 8 Bradford
24.10.78 Joe Lally **W** DIS 5 Blackpool
(*Vacant Central Area L. Middleweight Title*)
18.12.78 Carl Bailey **L** PTS 8 Bradford
22.01.79 Joe Oke **W** PTS 8 Bradford
13.02.79 Dave Davies **W** RTD 3 Wakefield
26.02.79 John Smith **W** PTS 8 Middlesbrough
19.03.79 Mike Copp **W** RTD 3 Bradford

28.04.79 Robert Langewuyters **W** PTS 8 Tiems
16.05.79 Mick Mills **W** RSC 4 Sheffield (*Central Area L. Middleweight Title Defence*)
25.06.79 Glen McEwan **W** PTS 8 Edgbaston
25.09.79 Danny Snyder **W** RSC 3 Wembley
19.11.79 Horace McKenzie **W** PTS 8 Stockport
04.12.79 Steve Hopkin **L** PTS 8 Wembley
14.03.80 Charlie Malarkey **L** PTS 10 Glasgow (*Elim. British L. Middleweight Title*)
25.11.80 Romal Ambrose **W** PTS 8 Wolverhampton
17.06.81 Herol Graham **L** RSC 1 Sheffield
23.11.81 Romal Ambrose **W** CO 8 Nottingham
06.04.82 Mick Mills **W** RSC 4 Leeds (*Central Area L. Middleweight Title Defence*)
26.09.82 Graeme Ahmed **W** RTD 3 Middlesbrough (*Elim. British L. Middleweight Title*)
14.03.83 Brian Anderson **W** RSC 5 Sheffield (*Central Area L. Middleweight Title Defence & Final Elim. British L. Middleweight Title*)
11.10.83 Jimmy Batten **W** RSC 6 Kensington (*Vacant British L. Middleweight Title*)
Summary: 33 contests, won 27, drew 1, lost 5

Hugh Russell
A. McCullough

Hugh Russell

Belfast. *Born* Belfast 15.12.59
British Flyweight Champion. Former British & N. Ireland Bantamweight Champion
Manager B. Eastwood
Previous Amateur Club Holy Family
National Honours Irish Flyweight Champion 1979/1981; Irish Int.; Olympic Bronze 1980; Commonwealth Bronze 1978

08.12.81 Jim Harvey **W** RSC 5 Belfast
18.01.82 Mike Wilkes **W** PTS 6 Mayfair
27.01.82 Eugene Maloney **W** DIS 4 Belfast
08.02.82 Stuart Nicol **W** RSC 3 Mayfair
23.02.82 Jimmy Bott **W** PTS 6 Belfast
23.03.82 Keith Foreman **W** RSC 1 Belfast
22.04.82 Jim Harvey **W** CO 1 Enniskillen
14.06.82 Stuart Shaw **W** PTS 8 Mayfair
05.10.82 Davy Larmour **W** PTS 12 Belfast (*N. Ireland Bantamweight Title Challenge & Final Elim. British Bantamweight Title*)
09.11.82 George Bailey **W** RSC 2 Belfast
14.12.82 Juan Fransisco Rodriguez **W** PTS 10 Belfast
25.01.83 John Feeney **W** DIS 13 Belfast (*British Bantamweight Title Challenge*)
02.03.83 Davy Larmour **L** PTS 12 Belfast (*N. Ireland & British Bantamweight Title Defence*)
05.10.83 Julio Guerrero **W** PTS 8 Belfast
16.11.83 Gabriel Kuphey **W** PTS 6 Belfast
25.01.84 Kelvin Smart **W** RTD 7 Belfast (*British Flyweight Title Challenge*)
04.04.84 Jose Torres **L** RSC 5 Belfast
Summary: 17 contests, won 15, lost 2

Tony Sibson

Leicester. *Born* Leicester 09.04.58
European Middleweight Champion.
Former Undefeated British and Commonwealth Champion.
Manager S. Burns
Previous Amateur Club Belgrave
National Honours Young England Rep.

09.04.76 Charlie Richardson **W** RSC 2 Birmingham
06.05.76 John Breen **W** PTS 6 Birmingham
26.05.76 Liam White **W** PTS 6 Wolverhampton
14.07.76 Jimmy Pickard **W** PTS 6 Wolverhampton
10.09.76 Bonny McKenzie **W** RSC 7 Digbeth
22.10.76 Clive Davidson **W** PTS 8 Digbeth
03.11.76 Neville Estaban **W** PTS 8 Caister
30.11.76 John Breen **W** RSC 5 Dudley
14.12.76 Tim McHugh **W** RSC 4 West Bromwich

CONTINUED OVERLEAF

Tony Sibson
Derek Rowe (Photos) Ltd

11.01.77 Tony Burnett **W** PTS 8 Wolverhampton
19.01.77 Roy Gumbs **W** PTS 8 Solihull
10.02.77 Arthur Winfield **W** RSC 2 Coventry
25.02.77 Tashy Jones **W** CO 1 Digbeth
24.03.77 Bonny McKenzie **W** RSC 7 Leicester
07.04.77 Steve Walker **W** PTS 8 Dudley
21.04.77 Tony Burnett **W** PTS 8 Liverpool
27.04.77 Sonny Kamunga **W** PTS 8 Leicester
18.10.77 Pat Thomas DREW 8 Wolverhampton
08.11.77 Wayne Bennett **W** PTS 8 West Bromwich
30.11.77 Oscar Angus **W** RTD 6 Wolverhampton
23.01.78 John Smith **W** CO 5 Wolverhampton
06.03.78 Errol McKenzie **W** CO 2 Wolverhampton
31.03.78 Mac Nicholson **W** RSC 7 Liverpool
04.04.78 Steve Walker **W** RSC 5 Wolverhampton
25.04.78 Mac Nicholson **W** RSC 1 Kensington
23.05.78 Lottie Mwale L CO 1 Leicester
29.06.78 Danny McLoughlin **W** CO 3 Wolverhampton
18.07.78 Bonny McKenzie **W** PTS 8 Wakefield
12.09.78 Keith Bussey **W** RSC 8 Wembley
24.10.78 Eddie Smith L PTS 8 Kensington
07.11.78 Gerard Nosley **W** RSC 7 Wembley
05.03.79 Eddie Smith **W** PTS 10 Wolverhampton
10.04.79 Frankie Lucas **W** RSC 5 Kensington (*Vacant British Middleweight Title*)
15.05.79 Al Clay **W** CO 7 Wembley
26.06.79 Jacques Chinon **W** RSC 8 Leicester
09.10.79 Willie Classen **W** CO 2 Kensington
06.11.79 Kevin Finnegan L PTS 15 Kensington (*British Middleweight Title Defence*)
29.11.79 Robert Powell **W** RSC 1 Liverpool
22.01.80 James Waire **W** PTS 10 Kensington
04.03.80 Chisanda Mutti **W** PTS 15 Wembley (*Vacant Commonwealth Middleweight Title*)
03.06.80 Marciano Bernardi **W** PTS 10 Kensington
27.09.80 Bob Coolidge **W** CO 7 Wembley
08.12.80 Matteo Salvemini **W** CO 7 Kensington (*European Middleweight Title Challenge*)
27.01.81 Norberto Cabrera **W** PTS 10 Kensington
17.03.81 Andre Mongelema **W** PTS 10 Wembley
14.05.81 Andoni Amana **W** PTS 12 Bilbao (*European Middleweight Title Defence*)
15.09.81 Alan Minter **W** CO 3 Wembley (*European Middleweight Title Defence*)
24.11.81 Nicola Cirelli **W** CO 10 Wembley (*European Middleweight Title Defence*)
21.02.82 Dwight Davidson **W** PTS 12 Birmingham (*Final Elim. WBC Middleweight Title*)
04.05.82 Jacques Chinon **W** RSC 10 Wembley (*European Middleweight Title Defence*)
14.09.82 Antonio Garrido **W** RTD 8 Wembley
11.02.83 Marvin Hagler L RSC 6 Worcester Mass. (*World Middleweight Title Challenge*)
08.10.83 John Collins **W** RSC 2 Atlantic City
22.11.83 Manuel Jiminez **W** RSC 8 Wembley
15.01.84 Don Lee L RSC 8 Atlantic City
25.02.84 Louis Acaries **W** PTS 12 Paris (*European Middleweight Title Challenge*)

Summary: 56 contests, won 50, drew 1, lost 5

Steve Sammy Sims

Newport. *Born* Newport 10.10.58
Former Undefeated British Featherweight Champion
Manager W. May
Previous Amateur Club Newport SC

18.06.79 Selvin Bell **W** PTS 6 Manchester
30.07.79 Eric Ragonesi **L** RSC 5 Mayfair
12.09.79 Joey Gilbert **W** RTD 4 Liverpool
17.10.79 Jarvis Greenidge **L** PTS 6 Evesham
17.12.79 John Henry **W** RSC 1 Wolverhampton
09.01.80 Glyn Rhodes **L** RSC 6 Burslem
19.03.80 Jarvis Greenidge **L** PTS 8 Stoke
21.04.80 Barry Winter **W** PTS 6 Nottingham
27.05.80 Philip Morris **W** PTS 6 Newport
18.06.80 Clyde Ruan **L** PTS 6 Burslem
22.09.80 Davy Lamour **W** PTS 8 Belfast
14.10.80 Don George **L** PTS 8 Nantwich
22.10.80 Peter Gabbitus **W** PTS 4 Doncaster
17.11.80 John Feeney **L** PTS 8 Gosforth
15.12.80 Vernon Penprase DREW 8 Merthyr
09.06.81 Vernon Penprase **W** PTS 10 Newport
(*Elim. British Featherweight Title*)
13.10.81 Jimmy Flint **W** CO 4 Kensington
(*Final Elim. British Featherweight Title*)
10.12.81 Jean-Marc Renard **W** PTS 8 Newport
20.09.82 Terry McKeown **W** CO 12 Glasgow
(*Vacant British Featherweight Title*)

Steve Sammy Sims

07.04.83 Loris Stecca **L** RSC 5 Sassari
(*Vacant European Featherweight Title*)
22.09.83 Chito Adigue **W** PTS 10 Cardiff
30.11.83 Nedrie Simmons **L** PTS 10 Cardiff
Summary: 22 contests, won 12, drew 1, lost 9

Kelvin Smart

Kelvin Smart

Caerphilly. *Born* Caerphilly 18.12.60
Former British Flyweight Champion
Manager M. Duff
Previous Amateur Club Wingfield
National Honours Schools Title 1976; Welsh Flyweight Champion 1979; Welsh Int.
Divisional Honours Welsh Flyweight R/U 1978

10.09.79 George Bailey **W** RSC 4 Birmingham
26.09.79 Billy Straub **W** PTS 6 Solihull
30.10.79 Bryn Jones **W** PTS 6 Caerphilly
19.11.79 Carl Gaynor **W** RSC 3 Edgbaston
28.11.79 Chris Moorcroft **W** PTS 6 Solihull
22.01.80 Ian Murray **W** PTS 6 Caerphilly
12.02.80 Iggy Jano **W** PTS 6 Wembley
19.03.80 Iggy Jano **W** PTS 8 Solihull
01.04.80 Mohammed Younis **W** PTS 8 Wembley
08.05.80 Mohammed Younis DREW 8 Solihull
26.11.80 Steve Enright **W** RSC 4 Solihull
11.03.81 Neil McLaughlin **W** PTS 8 Solihull
20.06.81 Eddie Glencross **W** CO 3 Wembley
15.09.81 Jimmy Bott **W** CO 1 Wembley
06.03.82 Enrique Rodriguez Cal **L** PTS 12 Oviedo
(*Final Elim. European Flyweight Title*)
14.09.82 Dave George **W** CO 6 Wembley
(*Vacant British Flyweight Title*)
27.09.83 Tito Abella **W** CO 1 Wembley
29.11.83 Ian Clyde **W** PTS 10 Cardiff
25.01.84 Hugh Russell **L** RTD 7 Belfast
(*British Flyweight Title Defence*)
Summary: 19 contests, won 16, drew 1, lost 2

Pat Thomas

Pat Thomas

Cardiff. *Born* St. Kitts 05.05.50
Former British Welterweight & L. Middleweight Champion. Former Undefeated Welsh L. Middleweight Champion
Manager (Self)
Previous Amateur Club Llandaff

14.12.70 Ray Farrell **W** CO 2 Manchester
12.01.71 Keith White **W** PTS 6 Shoreditch
09.02.71 Mohammed Ellah **W** PTS 6 Newport
22.02.71 Tony Bagshaw NC 6 Manchester
23.03.71 Tony Burnett **W** DIS 4 Newport
29.03.71 Alan Reid **W** PTS 6 Manchester
20.04.71 Mohammed Ellah DREW 6 Newport
03.05.71 Tony Bagshaw **W** PTS 6 Cleethorpes
17.05.71 Johnny Shields **W** PTS 6 Manchester
11.10.71 Alan Reid **L** PTS 6 Manchester
20.04.72 Jimmy Fairweather **W** PTS 8 Walworth
15.05.72 Mickey Flynn **W** PTS 8 Mayfair
19.09.72 Phil Dykes **W** RTD 3 Manchester
22.11.72 Charlie Cooper **L** DIS 7 Southend
15.01.73 Des Rea **W** PTS 8 Caerphilly
12.03.73 Amos Talbot **W** PTS 8 Caerphilly
26.09.73 Les Pearson **W** PTS 8 Solihull
05.10.73 Des Rea **W** RSC 4 Cardiff
21.11.73 Trevor Francis **L** PTS 8 Cardiff
21.01.74 Les Pearson **W** CO 1 Piccadilly
27.02.74 Des Rea **W** RTD 4 Cardiff
18.03.74 John Smith **W** PTS 8 Piccadilly
22.04.74 Mickey Flynn **W** PTS 8 Piccadilly
25.04.74 Henry Rhiney **W** PTS 8 Piccadilly
25.09.74 Kenny Webber DREW 8 Solihull
04.12.74 Henry Rhiney **W** PTS 8 Piccadilly
28.04.75 Jim Montague **W** CO 5 Glasgow
02.06.75 Jeff Gale **W** RSC 11 Piccadilly (*Final Elim. British Welterweight Title*)
08.07.75 Peter Scheibner **W** PTS 8 Caerphilly
15.12.75 Pat McCormack **W** CO 13 Walworth (*Vacant British Welterweight Title*)
16.02.76 Jim Devanney **W** RSC 8 Birmingham
09.04.76 Marco Scano **L** CO 2 Cagliari (*Vacant European Welterweight Title*)
03.06.76 Jorgen Hansen **L** RSC 3 Copenhagen
22.09.76 Trevor Francis **W** PTS 15 Mayfair (*British Welterweight Title Defence*)
07.12.76 Henry Rhiney **L** RSC 8 Luton (*British Welterweight Title Defence*)
05.03.77 Dave Davies **W** RSC 8 Liverpool (*Welsh L. Middleweight Title Challenge*)
27.05.77 Larry Paul **L** DIS 5 Digbeth (*Final Elim. British L. Middleweight Title*)
14.06.77 Henry Rhiney **W** PTS 8 Wembley
18.10.77 Tony Sibson DREW 8 Wolverhampton
11.01.78 Marijan Benes **L** PTS 8 Rotherham
20.05.78 Armat Yilderin **W** PTS 8 Rotherham
01.08.78 Chris Clarke **L** PTS 8 Nova Scotia
23.09.78 Claude Martin **L** PTS 10 St.Malo
05.10.78 Andoni Amana **L** PTS 8 Bilbao
27.11.78 Salvo Nuciforo **W** RSC 1 Kettering
05.04.79 Robbie Davies **W** PTS 12 Liverpool (*Final Elim. British L. Middleweight Title*)
29.07.79 Kenny Bristol **L** PTS 15 Georgetown (*Vacant Commonwealth L. Middleweight Title*)
11.09.79 Jimmy Batten **W** RSC 9 Wembley (*British L. Middleweight Title Challenge*)
11.12.79 Dave Proud **W** CO 7 Milton Keynes (*British L. Middleweight Title Defence*)
03.06.80 Jimmy Richards **W** PTS 8 Kensington
16.09.80 Steve Hopkin **W** RSC 15 Wembley (*British L. Middleweight Title Defence*)
24.03.81 Herol Graham **L** PTS 15 Sheffield (*British L. Middleweight Title Defence*)
13.11.81 Nino La Rocca **L** RSC 4 Rome
26.04.82 Darwin Brewster **L** PTS 10 Cardiff
21.05.82 Brian Anderson **L** PTS 10 Sheffield
31.08.82 Graham Ahmed **L** PTS 10 South Shields
15.03.84 Chris Pyatt **L** PTS 10 Leicester
Summary: 57 contests, won 35, drew 3, lost 18, NC 1

Keith Wallace

Liverpool. *Born* Prescot 29.03.61
Commonwealth Flyweight Champion
Manager F. Warren
Previous Amateur Club St. Helens Star
National Honours School Titles 1974 – 1977; NABC Title 1979; Young England Rep.; England Int.; GB Rep.; ABA Flyweight Champion 1980 & 1981
Divisional Honours W Lancs L. Flyweight Champion 1979

16.02.82 Robert Hepburn **W** RSC 2 Bloomsbury
09.03.82 Steve King **W** RSC 3 Hornsey
15.03.82 Steve Reilly **W** RSC 2 Bloomsbury
05.04.82 Jimmy Carson **W** RSC 3 Bloomsbury
07.06.82 Ray Somer **W** RSC 2 Bloomsbury
22.06.82 Alan Tombs **W** RSC 4 Hornsey
23.09.82 Jimmy Bott **W** RSC 6 Liverpool
28.10.82 Steve Whetstone **W** RSC 8 Bloomsbury
03.02.83 Steve Muchoki **W** RSC 9 Bloomsbury
(*Commonwealth Flyweight Title Challenge*)
02.03.83 Pat Doherty **W** PTS 8 Belfast
25.03.83 Henry Brent **W** PTS 10 Bloomsbury
01.09.83 Juan Diaz **W** PTS 10 Bloomsbury

Keith Wallace

07.10.83 Antoine Montero **L** CO 8 Bloomsbury
(*European Flyweight Title Challenge*)
01.02.84 Esteban Eguia **W** PTS 10 Bloomsbury
13.06.84 Peter Harris **L** PTS 10 Aberavon
Summary: 15 contests, won 13, lost 2

Active British-based Boxers: Career Records

Includes the complete records of all boxers active since 01.01.83. Does not include boxers who made their debuts outside the U.K. (unless British born). Names in brackets are real names where they differ from ring names. The first place-name given is the boxer's domicile. National and Divisional honours won as an amateur are shown. Boxers are either shown as self managed or with a named manager at the time of their last contest. Retirements will be recorded in future Yearbooks.

Steve Abadom

Newcastle. *Born* Durham 27.05.56
Heavyweight
Manager F. Deans
Previous Amateur Club Perth Green

20.04.83 Dave Garside L RSC 4 South Shields
12.06.83 Eddie Cooper **W** PTS 6 Middlesbrough
16.09.83 Tony Blackstock L PTS 4 Swindon
05.03.84 Dave Summers L PTS 4 Glasgow
21.03.84 Glenn McCrory L PTS 6 Mayfair
12.05.84 Carl Gaffney L RSC 3 Hanley
Summary: 6 contests, won 1, lost 5

Dave Adam

Kirkcaldy. *Born* Kirkcaldy 20.03.64
Featherweight
Manager T. Gilmour
Previous Amateur Club Cardenden

16.04.84 Tony Rahman **W** RSC 4 Glasgow
18.06.84 Les Walsh **W** PTS 6 Manchester
Summary: 2 contests, won 2

Tony Adams

Brixton. *Born* Wandsworth 10.10.62
L. Welterweight
Manager T. Lawless
Previous Amateur Club Fitzroy Lodge
National Honours NABC Title 1980; Young England Rep.; ABA L. Welterweight Champion 1982

12.10.82 Dennis Sullivan **W** RSC 1 Kensington
09.11.82 Ray Price **W** RSC 1 Kensington
18.01.83 Mike Essett **W** PTS 6 Kensington
08.02.83 Kid Murray **W** PTS 6 Kensington
01.03.83 Tony Laing L PTS 6 Kensington
03.05.83 Derek McKenzie **W** RTD 2 Wembley
11.10.83 Granville Allen **W** CO 2 Kensington
30.11.83 Frankie Lake **W** RSC 2 Piccadilly
31.01.84 Davey Cox **W** CO 1 Kensington
22.02.84 Frank McCord **W** RSC 8 Kensington
11.04.84 Joe Lynch **W** RSC 3 Kensington
04.06.84 Tony Brown **W** RSC 2 Mayfair
Summary: 12 contests, won 11, lost 1

Tony Adams
Derek Rowe (Photos) Ltd

Billy Ahearne

Manchester. *Born* Cardiff 21.05.57
Welterweight
Manager N. Basso
Previous Amateur Club B.D.S. Salford

17.11.75 Jimmy Pickard **W** PTS 6 Manchester
02.12.75 Joe Ward DREW 6 Leeds

09.02.76 Yotham Kunda L RSC 5 Piccadilly
08.06.76 Terry Schofield DREW 8 Bradford
13.09.76 Terry Schofield L PTS 8 Manchester
20.09.76 Russ Shaw W PTS 6 Manchester
14.09.77 Bert Green W PTS 6 Sheffield
22.09.77 Russ Shaw W PTS 6 Birkenhead
24.10.77 Carl Bailey L PTS 8 Manchester
18.01.78 Prince Rodney L PTS 8 Solihull
30.01.78 Tommy Joyce W CO 2 Cleethorpes
12.09.79 Johnny Elliott DREW 6 Liverpool
17.09.79 Phil Lewis W PTS 6 Manchester
15.10.79 Adey Allen L PTS 8 Manchester
27.10.79 Herrol Graham L RSC 3 Barnsley
09.04.80 Phil Lewis W PTS 6 Liverpool
29.04.80 Robert Armstrong W CO 1 Stockport
07.05.80 Chris Glover L RTD 3 Liverpool
16.06.80 Jeff Aspell W PTS 8 Manchester
07.07.80 Neil Fannan L RTD 3 Middlesbrough
18.05.81 Ronnie Rathbone L PTS 6 Manchester
15.06.81 Ronnie Rathbone W PTS 8 Manchester
07.09.81 Gary Petty W PTS 6 Liverpool
08.03.82 Kevin Durkin L RSC 5 Manchester
28.09.82 Alf Edwardes W PTS 6 Manchester
07.10.82 Phil Gibson W PTS 8 Morley
18.10.82 Ian Chantler L RSC 3 Blackpool
14.02.83 Ian Chantler L RSC 6 Liverpool
09.11.83 Paul Smith W PTS 6 Sheffield
22.11.83 Paul Salih W PTS 6 Manchester
05.12.83 Paul Smith DREW 8 Manchester
30.01.84 Paul Smith L RSC 5 Manchester
Summary: 32 contests, won 15, drew 4, lost 13

Barry Ahmed

South Shields. *Born* South Shields 19.06.58
Middleweight
Manager T. Cumiskey
Previous Amateur Club Perth Green
National Honours NABC Title 1977

15.09.81 Deano Wallace L PTS 6 Sunderland
02.11.81 Steve Coleman W RSC 2 South Shields
29.11.81 Joe Dean W RSC 6 Middlesbrough
24.01.82 Steve Goodwin W PTS 6 Sunderland
08.03.82 John Donnelly W RSC 2 Hamilton
18.03.82 Paul Heatley W RSC 2 South Shields
31.08.82 Winston Burnett W PTS 8 South Shields
26.09.82 Mick Morris L PTS 8 Middlesbrough
17.01.83 Blaine Longsden L PTS 6 Manchester
15.03.83 Cameron Lithgow L RTD 3 Wembley
20.04.83 Sammy Brennan DREW 8 South Shields
12.06.83 Dave Scott L PTS 8 Middlesbrough
Summary: 12 contests, won 6, drew 1, lost 5

Graeme Ahmed

South Shields. *Born* South Shields 21.11.59
L. Middleweight
Manager T. Conroy
Previous Amateur Club Perth Green
Divisional Honours NE Counties L. Middleweight R/U 1978/1980

11.09.80 Paul Murray W PTS 6 Hartlepool
13.10.80 Kevin Walsh W PTS 6 Newcastle
17.11.80 Eric Hirschmann W RSC 2 Gosforth
01.12.80 Kevin Walsh W RSC 6 Middlesbrough
12.02.81 Carl Bailey W PTS 6 South Shields
02.04.81 Jeff Lee W RSC 6 Middlesbrough
15.09.81 Dennis Pryce W PTS 8 Sunderland
02.11.81 Ronnie Rathbone W PTS 8 South Shields
29.11.81 Dave Douglas W PTS 8 Middlesbrough
24.01.82 Carl Bailey W RSC 6 Sunderland
18.03.82 Charlie Malarkey W PTS 8 South Shields
31.08.82 Pat Thomas W PTS 10 South Shields
26.09.82 Prince Rodney L RTD 3 Middlesbrough
(*Elim. British L. Middleweight Title*)
25.11.82 Darwin Brewster L PTS 10 Sunderland
10.02.83 Sammy Brennan L PTS 8 Sunderland
20.04.83 Brian Anderson L RTD 5 South Shields
Summary: 16 contests, won 12, lost 4

Peter Ahmed

Cardiff. *Born* Cardiff 28.04.58
Welterweight
Manager M. Williams
Previous Amateur Club Prince of Wales
National Honours Welsh L. Welterweight Champion 1977–1981; Welsh Int.

24.02.82 Kostas Petrou L PTS 6 Evesham
19.04.82 Sam Omidi L CO 1 Bristol
09.06.82 Derek McKenzie W PTS 6 Bristol
06.10.82 Steve Tempro W PTS 6 Solihull
19.10.82 Steve Tempro W PTS 6 Wolverhampton
17.11.82 Derek McKenzie W PTS 6 Solihull
06.12.82 Colin Neagle W RSC 2 Bristol
13.04.83 Dave Sullivan W PTS 8 Evesham
26.04.83 John Bibby L PTS 8 Bethnal Green
Summary: 9 contests, won 6, lost 3

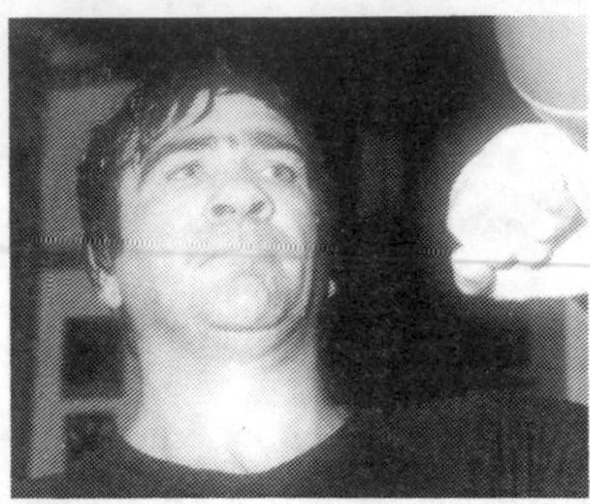

Billy Aird
Derek Rowe (Photos) Ltd

Billy Aird

Bermondsey. *Born* Liverpool 15.03.46
Former Undefeated Central Area Heavyweight Champion
Manager (Self)
Previous Amateur Club Golden Gloves
Divisional Honours W Lancs Heavyweight Champion 1967; NWC Heavyweight Champion 1968–1969

01.06.69 Paul Cassidy **W** RSC 4 Mayfair
23.06.69 George Dulaire **W** PTS 6 Mayfair
08.09.69 John Cullen **W** PTS 6 Mayfair
29.09.69 Dennis Avoth **W** PTS 6 Piccadilly
03.11.69 Richard Dunn L PTS 3 Bedford
23.02.70 Richard Dunn **W** PTS 8 Mayfair
21.04.70 Del Phillips **W** PTS 6 Kensington
07.09.70 Richard Dunn **W** RSC 6 Manchester
(*Vacant Central Area Heavyweight Title*)
11.11.70 Bunny Johnson L PTS 8 Solihull
07.12.70 Foster Bibron L PTS 10 Melbourne
11.01.71 Cliff Field **W** RSC 2 Bloomsbury
01.05.71 Arno Prick **W** PTS 10 Johannesburg
05.07.71 Cliff Field **W** RSC 7 Mayfair
28.10.71 Rocky Campbell **W** PTS 8 Bristol
07.12.71 Ted Gullick DREW 10 Kensington
09.05.72 Roger Tighe **W** PTS 8 Wembley
06.06.72 John Conteh L RSC 8 Kensington
23.10.72 Bunny Johnson L PTS 8 Mayfair
05.04.73 Brian Jewitt **W** PTS 8 Walworth
16.04.73 Rocky Campbell DREW 8 Piccadilly
14.05.73 Richard Dunn L PTS 10 Mayfair
(*Elim. British Heavyweight Title*)
09.07.73 Rocky Campbell **W** RSC 7 Mayfair
21.09.73 Greg Peralta L RSC 4 Hamburg
22.10.73 Jimmy Young DREW 8 Mayfair
12.11.73 Obie English L PTS 10 Mayfair
28.04.74 Lloyd Walford **W** PTS 8 Southend
21.06.74 Bernd August DREW 8 Berlin
04.02.75 Ngozika Ekwelum **W** PTS 8 Southend
11.03.75 Kevin Isaacs **W** PTS 8 Wembley
05.06.75 Randy Neumann L RSC 8 Hammersmith
21.03.76 Bunny Johnson DREW 10 Frimley Green
(*Elim. British Heavyweight Title*)
18.10.76 Denton Ruddock **W** RSC 10 Marylebone
(*Final Elim. British Heavyweight Title*)
28.02.77 Avenmar Peralta L DIS 5 Luton
11.10.77 Gilbert Acuna **W** RSC 6 Marylebone
03.03.78 Alfredo Evangelista L PTS 15 Leon
(*European Heavyweight Title Challenge*)
24.10.78 John L. Gardner L RTD 5 Kensington
(*Vacant British & Commonwealth Heavyweight Titles*)
21.05.79 Tommy Kiely **W** PTS 8 Walworth
01.10.79 Neil Malpass **W** PTS 10 Marylebone
21.04.80 Gordon Ferris L PTS 10 Edgbaston
(*Final Elim. British Heavyweight Title*)
18.10.80 Tony Moore **W** PTS 10 Birmingham
30.05.81 Gordon Ferris L PTS 15 Birmingham
(*Vacant British Heavyweight Title*)
23.11.81 Winston Allen **W** PTS 10 Bloomsbury
16.02.82 Larry McDonald **W** PTS 10 Bloomsbury
22.11.82 Steve Gee **W** PTS 8 Lewisham
14.02.83 Maurice Gomis **W** PTS 8 Lewisham
07.04.83 Guido Trane L RSC 5 Strand
Summary: 46 contests, won 26, drew 5, lost 15

Gilbert Alexander (Gonzaaque)

Notting Hill *Born* Holloway 16.02.61
L. Heavyweight
Manager G. Steene
Previous Amateur Club Stowe
Divisional Honours NW London Heavyweight R/U, 1982

17.04.84 Gordon Stacey **W** PTS 6 Merton
Summary: 1 contest, won 1

Adey Allen

Leicester. *Born* Leicester 12.12.58
Former Midlands Area L. Welterweight Champion
Manager R. Gray
Previous Amateur Club Belgrave
Divisional Honours M Counties Lightweight R/U 1977

06.03.78 George Metcalf **W** RSC 3 Manchester

15.03.78 Gary Collins W PTS 6 Solihull
31.03.78 Brian Snagg W RSC 4 Liverpool
12.04.78 George Metcalf W PTS 4 Evesham
17.04.78 Steve Ward W PTS 6 Mayfair
08.05.78 Kevin Quinn L PTS 6 Manchester
07.09.78 Brian Snagg L PTS 6 Liverpool
18.09.78 George O'Neill L DIS 3 Wolverhampton
02.10.78 Granville Allen L PTS 8 Nantwich
27.11.78 Hugh Smith L PTS 8 Govan
11.09.79 Chris Sanigar L PTS 6 Wembley
15.10.79 Billy Ahearne W PTS 8 Manchester
15.11.79 Kevin Quinn W PTS 8 Caister
07.01.80 John Mount W PTS 8 Manchester
10.03.80 Jarvis Greenidge L PTS 6 Wolverhampton
21.04.80 Barry Price W PTS 8 Nottingham
08.05.80 Granville Allen L PTS 8 Solihull
08.07.80 Roger Guest W PTS 8 Wolverhampton
19.10.80 Roger Guest W PTS 10 Birmingham
(Midlands Area L. Welterweight Title Challenge)
13.11.80 Kevin Walsh W PTS 8 Caister
26.01.81 Kid Murray L PTS 8 Edgbaston
09.02.81 George Peacock L PTS 8 Glasgow
09.07.81 Mickey Baker W RSC 7 Dudley
(Midlands Area L. Welterweight Title Defence)
19.11.81 Alan Lamb W RSC 3 Morecambe
21.02.82 Chris Sanigar L RSC 7 Birmingham
05.10.83 Steve Early L PTS 10 Solihull
(Midlands Area L. Welterweight Title Defence)
14.02.84 Gerry Beard DREW 8 Wolverhampton
26.03.84 Lee McKenzie L PTS 8 Glasgow
Summary: 28 contests, won 14, drew 1, lost 13

Adey Allen

Granville Allen

Wednesbury. *Born* Jamaica 15.03.56
Welterweight
Manager G. Riley
Previous Amateur Club W. Bromwich College
National Honours Young England Rep.
Divisional Honours M Counties L. Welterweight R/U 1975–1977

05.07.77 Ray Thomas W RSC 4 Wolverhampton
20.09.77 Mickey Durkin L PTS 6 Wolverhampton
11.10.77 Mick Bell W PTS 8 Coventry
31.10.77 Ian Pickersgill W RSC 2 Birmingham
30.11.77 Tommy Glencross W DIS 6 Wolverhampton
14.12.77 Tommy Glencross W PTS 8 Kingston
23.01.78 Mick Bell L CO 8 Wolverhampton
06.03.78 Dil Collins W PTS 8 Wolverhampton
04.04.78 Marty Jacobs W CO 3 Wolverhampton
21.04.78 Davy Campbell W PTS 8 Enniskillen
02.10.78 Adey Allen W PTS 8 Nantwich
23.10.78 Eric Purkis DREW 8 Piccadilly
31.10.78 Tommy Dunn W PTS 8 Birmingham
22.01.79 Dave McCabe L DIS 6 Wolverhampton
29.01.79 Chris Sanigar L CO 3 Glasgow
20.02.79 Tommy Dunn W RSC 7 Wolverhampton
21.03.79 Jimmy Roberts W PTS 8 Stoke
09.10.79 Jeff Pritchard W PTS 8 Wolverhampton
20.02.80 Dennis Sullivan W PTS 8 Evesham
18.03.80 Roy Varden W PTS 8 Wolverhampton
08.05.80 Adey Allen W PTS 8 Solihull
14.07.80 Alan Lamb L RSC 5 Mayfair
21.09.81 Eric Wood W PTS 8 Nottingham
12.10.81 Martin McGough L CO 1 Birmingham
09.02.82 Lloyd Honeyghan L RSC 5 Kensington
10.03.82 Terry Welch W PTS 8 Nottingham
23.03.82 Steve Tempro W PTS 8 Wolverhampton
07.04.82 Lee Halford L PTS 8 Evesham
19.04.82 Willie Booth L RSC 7 Glasgow
16.03.83 Steve Tempro L PTS 6 Stoke
21.03.83 Mickey Bird W CO 2 Nottingham
05.10.83 George Kerr L PTS 8 Stoke
11.10.83 Tony Adams L CO 2 Kensington
09.11.83 Roy Varden L PTS 8 Evesham
01.12.83 Lenny Gloster W PTS 6 Dudley
27.02.84 Patsy Quinn W RSC 3 Birmingham
04.06.84 Steve Craggs W PTS 8 Nottingham
Summary: 37 contests, won 23, drew 1, lost 13

Winston Allen
Cardiff. *Born* Cardiff 12.11.57
Heavyweight
Manager T. Mason
Previous Amateur Club Cardiff Y.M.C.A.
National Honours Welsh Int.

24.04.78 Terry Chard **L** PTS 6 Piccadilly
16.05.78 Terry Chard **W** RSC 3 Newport
11.09.78 Allan Bagley **W** PTS 6 Birmingham
02.11.78 John Depledge **W** PTS 8 Ebbw Vale
15.11.78 David Collins **W** CO 1 Merthyr
15.11.78 John Depledge **W** PTS 3 Merthyr
17.01.79 Terry O'Connor **L** PTS 8 Solihull
22.01.79 Danny Lawford **W** PTS 3 Mayfair
22.01.79 Bobby Hennessey **L** RSC 2 Mayfair
19.03.79 Derek Simpkin **W** PTS 8 Bradford
03.04.79 David Pearce **L** PTS 6 Caerphilly
18.06.79 Manny Gabriel **L** CO 1 Windsor
04.10.79 Bob Young **L** PTS 6 Ebbw Vale
23.10.79 Andy Palmer **W** RSC 2 Wembley
29.11.79 Glenn Adair **L** PTS 8 Ebbw Vale
07.02.80 Pete Holm **W** RSC 3 Randers
04.03.80 Stan McDermott **W** CO 1 Wembley
01.05.80 Jean Pierre Coopmans **W** CO 1 Izegem
21.06.80 Alfredo Evangelista **L** PTS 8 Barcelona
01.10.80 Neville Meade **L** RSC 2 Swansea (*Welsh Heavyweight Title Challenge*)
23.11.81 Billy Aird **L** PTS 10 Bloomsbury
28.10.82 Joe Bugner **L** CO 3 Bloomsbury
01.03.83 Frank Bruno **L** RSC 2 Kensington
14.04.83 Steve Gee **L** PTS 8 Basildon
22.09.83 Rudi Pika **L** PTS 8 Cardiff
14.04.84 Anaclet Wamba **L** PTS 8 Yffiniac
Summary: 26 contests, won 10, lost 16

Romal Ambrose
Leicester Mercury

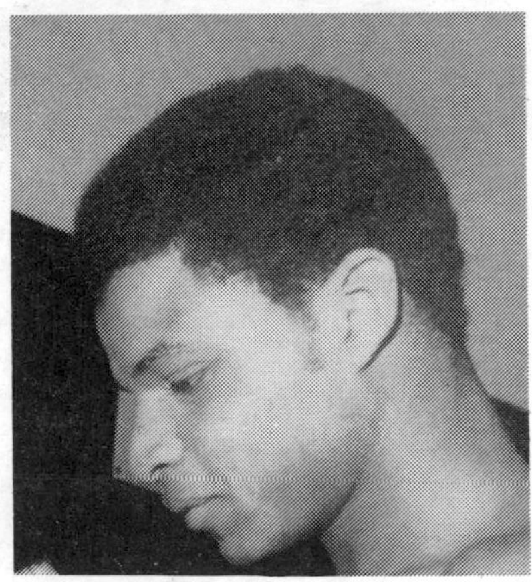

Romal Ambrose
Leicester. *Born* Leicester 22.05.57
Former Midlands Area Middleweight Champion
Manager (Self)
Previous Amateur Club Highfields

24.03.77 Cyril Bishton **W** PTS 4 Leicester
02.05.77 Dave Cammis **L** PTS 4 Walworth
27.05.77 Dennis Pryce **L** PTS 4 Digbeth
16.11.77 Roger Guest **L** PTS 4 Solihull
06.12.77 Mohammed Akram **W** PTS 4 Leeds
07.02.78 Tony Hill **L** PTS 4 Coventry
10.04.78 Clifton Wallace **W** RSC 2 Nottingham
17.04.78 Dennis Powell **W** RSC 1 Reading
07.09.78 Joey Saunders **W** RSC 5 Liverpool
18.09.78 Richard Kenyon **W** RSC 5 Manchester
09.10.78 Mick Morris **L** RTD 2 Wolverhampton
30.11.78 Richard Kenyon **W** RSC 8 Caister
21.02.79 Paul Shutt **W** CO 7 Evesham (*Vacant Midlands Area Middleweight Title*)
12.03.79 Dave Owens **W** PTS 8 Manchester
29.11.79 Dave Davies **W** RTD 5 Liverpool
05.02.80 Martin McEwan **W** PTS 10 Wolverhampton (*Midlands Area Middleweight Title Defence*)
19.03.80 Glen McEwan **L** CO 10 Solihull (*Midlands Area Middleweight Title Defence*)
20.10.80 Glen McEwan **L** CO 6 Birmingham (*Midlands Area Middleweight Title Challenge*)
25.11.80 Prince Rodney **L** PTS 8 Wolverhampton
16.03.81 Billy Savage **W** CO 3 Birmingham
30.04.81 Eddie Burke **L** CO 3 Liverpool
22.09.81 Dave Armstrong **L** CO 8 Bethnal Green
23.11.81 Prince Rodney **L** CO 8 Nottingham
09.02.82 Mark Kaylor **L** CO 1 Kensington
20.09.83 Harry Cowap **L** PTS 8 Piccadilly
18.10.83 John Humphreys **W** PTS 8 Wolverhampton
01.12.83 Roy Skeldon **W** RSC 4 Dudley
25.01.84 Cordwell Hylton **L** RSC 3 Solihull
02.05.84 Winston Burnett **W** PTS 8 Solihull
Summary: 29 contests, won 15, lost 14

Brian Anderson
Sheffield. *Born* Sheffield 09.07.61
Central Area Middleweight Champion
Manager B. Ingle
Previous Amateur Club Ridgeway
National Honours NABC Title 1980

14.04.80 Jeff Standley **W** PTS 6 Manchester
07.05.80 Jeff Aspell **W** PTS 6 Liverpool

Brian Anderson

28.05.80 Dave Ward L DIS 4 Cramlington
08.07.80 Cliff Gilpin L PTS 8 Wolverhampton
16.09.80 Dominic Bergonzi DREW 6 Wembley
29.09.80 Kevin Walsh DREW 8 Chesterfield
16.10.80 Dennis Sullivan **W** PTS 8 Bolton
29.10.80 Robbie Smith **W** PTS 6 Burslem
13.11.80 Dave Douglas **W** RTD 5 Newcastle
11.12.80 Peter Sullivan **W** PTS 6 Bolton
23.02.81 Billy Lauder **W** RTD 3 Glasgow
23.03.81 Darwin Brewster DREW 6 Mayfair
06.05.81 Harry Watson **W** RSC 2 Chesterfield
15.06.81 Carl Bailey **W** PTS 8 Manchester
21.09.81 Chris Coady **W** RTD 3 Manchester
06.11.81 Eckhard Dagge **W** RSC 2 Kiel
23.01.82 Frank Wissenbach **L** PTS 8 Berlin
18.02.82 Mick Morris **W** PTS 8 Liverpool
15.03.82 Doug James **W** PTS 8 Piccadilly
21.05.82 Pat Thomas **W** PTS 10 Sheffield
13.09.82 Darwin Brewster **W** PTS 10 Sheffield
(*Elim. British L. Middleweight Title*)
14.03.83 Prince Rodney **L** RSC 5 Sheffield
(*Central Area L. Middleweight Title Challenge & Final Elim. British L. Middleweight Title*)
20.04.83 Graeme Ahmed **W** RTD 5 South Shields
23.05.83 Jimmy Ellis **W** RSC 9 Sheffield
(*Vacant Central Area Middleweight Title*)
05.09.83 Doug James **W** RSC 1 Mayfair
09.12.83 Andre Mongelema **L** PTS 8 St Nazaire
21.05.84 Sammy Brennan **W** RTD 1 Bradford
(*Central Area Middleweight Title Defence*)
Summary: 27 contests, won 19, drew 3, lost 5

Colin Andersen

Leicester. *Born* Leicester 07.06.62
Lightweight
Manager B. Ridge
Previous Amateur Club Braunstone

30.09.83 Wayne Trigg **W** PTS 4 Leicester
14.02.84 Peter Bowen **W** PTS 6 Wolverhampton
20.02.84 Nicky Day DREW 6 Mayfair
15.03.84 Wayne Trigg **L** RSC 2 Leicester
Summary: 4 contests, won 2, drew 1, lost 1

Teddy Anderson

Wickford. *Born* Billericay 21.01.62
Lightweight
Manager A. Kasler
Previous Amateur Club Rayleigh Mill

06.10.83 Paul Boswell **W** PTS 6 Basildon
17.11.83 Mike Durvan **L** PTS 6 Basildon
16.02.84 Kenny Watson **W** PTS 6 Basildon
27.03.84 T. Roy Smith DREW 6 Bethnal Green
19.04.84 Angelo D'Amore **W** PTS 6 Basildon
31.05.84 Kenny Watson **L** PTS 6 Basildon
Summary: 6 contests, won 3, drew 1, lost 2

John Andrews

Stepney. *Born* London 18.10.62
Welterweight
Manager F. Warren
Previous Amateur Club Arbour Youth
National Honours Junior ABA Title 1979; Young England Rep.; England Int.
Divisional Honours NE London L. Welterweight R/U 1980; London Welterweight Champion 1981

23.03.82 Bert Myrie **W** CO 5 Nantwich
05.04.82 Mickey Harrison **W** RSC 3 Bloomsbury

CONTINUED OVERLEAF

14.04.82 Bert Myrie **W** RSC 5 Strand
28.04.82 Dalton Jordan **W** PTS 4 Burslem
13.09.82 Deano Wallace L RSC 4 Sheffield
28.10.82 Robert Armstrong **W** RSC 5 Bloomsbury
06.11.82 Steve Henty **W** PTS 8 Marylebone
09.12.82 Judas Clottey DREW 6 Bloomsbury
09.11.83 Johnny Wall **W** RSC 2 Southend
24.11.83 Rocky Feliciello **W** RSC 5 Kirkby
05.12.83 Phil O'Hare **W** CO 2 Manchester
14.12.83 Paul Murray **W** PTS 6 Stoke
23.02.84 Gordon Pratt **W** PTS 8 Digbeth
21.03.84 Steve Friel **W** RSC 2 Bloomsbury
Summary: 14 contests, won 12, drew 1, lost 1

Ricky Andrews

Crystal Palace. *Born* London 25.03.63
Lightweight
Manager C. Shorey
Previous Amateur Club Crystal Palace

05.09.83 Ron Shinkwin L PTS 6 Mayfair
28.11.83 Johnny Grant **W** PTS 6 Southwark
Summary: 2 contests, won 1, lost 1

(Guy) Steve Apollo (Harrison)

Leicester. *Born* Nottingham 09.04.62
L. Welterweight
Manager J. Rossi
Previous Amateur Club Highfield

07.12.83 Phil Sheridan L RSC 1 Stoke
Summary: 1 contest, lost 1

Jaswant Singh Ark

Jaswant Singh Ark

Derby. *Born* India 04.01.57
Welterweight
Manager T. Sharp
Previous Amateur Club Hogarth
Divisional Honours NW London L. Welterweight R/U 1980 & SW London L. Welterweight Champion 1981

13.08.83 Curtis Greco **W** CO 2 Kelowna BC
13.10.83 Anthony Kim **W** PTS 6 Vancouver
31.03.84 Peter Phillips **W** PTS 6 Derby
16.04.84 Tony Smith **W** RSC 2 Bradford
Summary: 4 contests, won 4

Davey Armstrong

Hackney. *Born* London 30.11.58
Former Southern Area Middleweight Champion
Manager (Self)
Previous Amateur Club Fitzroy Lodge
National Honours Junior ABA Title 1974; Schools Title 1975
Divisional Honours SE London L. Middleweight Champion 1976–1977

17.10.77 Willie Turkington **W** RSC 1 Mayfair
01.12.77 H. H. Thompson L RTD 2 Heathrow
27.11.78 Stan Thompson **W** PTS 6 Mayfair
18.12.78 Owen Slue **W** PTS 6 Mayfair
26.02.79 Lloyd Gardner **W** RSC 2 Mayfair
21.05.79 John Breen **W** RSC 2 Walworth
26.06.79 Chris Coady **W** PTS 6 Wembley
04.12.79 Gordon George **W** RSC 2 Wembley
01.04.80 Mick Morris **W** KO 1 Wembley
14.10.80 Joe Jackson L PTS 6 Kensington
18.11.80 George Danahar **W** RSC 2 Bethnal Green
20.01.81 Mike Burton **W** CO 1 Bethnal Green
10.02.81 Peter Simon **W** CO 2 Bethnal Green
03.03.81 Earl Edwards L RSC 2 Wembley (*Vacant Southern Area Middleweight Title*)
22.09.81 Romal Ambrose **W** CO 8 Bethnal Green
23.03.82 Earl Edwards **W** RSC 6 Bethnal Green (*Southern Area Middleweight Title Challenge*)
28.09.82 Glen McEwan L RSC 3 Bethnal Green (*Elim. British Middleweight Title*)
20.04.83 Devon Bailey L RSC 2 Muswell Hill
18.05.83 Gary Hobbs L RSC 1 Bloomsbury (*Southern Area Middleweight Title Defence*)
Summary: 19 contests, won 13, lost 6

Michael Armstrong
Shildon. *Born* Bishop Auckland 03.06.59
Heavyweight
Manager T. Conroy
Previous Amateur Club Shildon
Divisional Honours NE Counties L. Heavyweight Champion 1979; NE Counties L. Heavyweight S/F 1980–1981

20.04.83 Eddie Cooper W PTS 6 South Shields
19.05.83 Red Long W CO 1 Sunderland
16.09.83 Denroy Bryan L RSC 1 Swindon
14.11.83 Denroy Bryan L RSC 4 Nantwich
01.03.84 Barry Ellis L PTS 6 Queensway
Summary: 5 contests, won 2, lost 3

Robert Armstrong
Doncaster. *Born* Durham 02.06.60
Welterweight
Manager J. Rushton
Previous Amateur Club Elmfield House

19.03.80 Kevin Walsh W RTD 3 Doncaster
29.04.80 Billy Ahearne L CO 1 Stockport
11.06.80 Martin Bridge W PTS 8 Morecambe
30.07.80 Gerry White L PTS 6 Doncaster
15.09.80 Kevin Walsh L PTS 6 Manchester
22.10.80 Robert Thornton W CO 3 Doncaster
25.11.80 Charlie Douglas W PTS 8 Doncaster
08.12.80 Phil Duckworth L PTS 8 Manchester
12.01.81 Johnny Francis W RSC 7 Manchester
09.02.81 Dave Goodwin W RSC 3 Manchester
25.03.81 Steve Davies W PTS 8 Doncaster
10.06.81 Phil Duckworth W PTS 8 Brodsworth
15.06.81 Steve McLeod L PTS 8 Manchester
21.09.81 Carl Bailey L CO 5 Manchester
30.03.82 Phil Duckworth W PTS 8 Leeds
28.04.82 Dave Douglas L PTS 8 Sheffield
17.05.82 Rocky Kelly L CO 2 Windsor
22.06.82 Gary Knight L RSC 7 Hornsey
07.09.82 Terry Marsh L PTS 8 Hornsey
16.10.82 P. J. Davitt L PTS 8 Killarney
28.10.82 John Andrews L RSC 5 Bloomsbury
07.12.82 R. W. Smith L CO 1 Kensington
20.01.83 Ian Chantler L RTD 1 Birkenhead
26.09.83 Gavin Stirrup L RSC 3 Manchester
24.10.83 Claude Rossi W CO 5 Nottingham
10.11.83 Nick Riozzi W PTS 6 Stafford
05.12.83 Malcolm Davies W CO 6 Nottingham
25.01.84 Nigel Thomas W CO 2 Stoke
20.02.84 Gunther Roomes L RSC 4 Mayfair
02.04.84 Danny Sullivan L CO 4 Mayfair
14.05.84 Steve Ward W PTS 6 Nottingham
21.05.84 Tommy Campbell L PTS 8 Aberdeen
Summary: 32 contests, won 14, lost 18

Henry Arnold
Burscough. *Born* Maghull 03.05.60
Lightweight
Manager R. Smith
Previous Amateur Club Burscough

15.06.84 Brian King W PTS 6 Liverpool
Summary: 1 contest, won 1

Alan Ash
Carshalton. *Born* London 15.04.62
L. Heavyweight
Manager C. Shorey
Previous Amateur Club Hillcrest

07.07.82 Chris Thorne W PTS 6 Newmarket
23.09.82 Eddie Vierling W PTS 6 Wimbledon
04.11.82 Jerry Golden W PTS 6 Wimbledon
07.02.83 John Moody L PTS 6 Brighton
28.03.83 John Elliott W RTD 3 Wolverhampton
06.04.83 Paul Newman L PTS 6 Mayfair
19.05.83 Paul Newman W RSC 5 Queensway
28.11.83 Harry Cowap W RTD 4 Southwark
06.02.84 Rolf Rocchigiani L PTS 6 Hamburg
17.04.84 Harry Cowap L PTS 8 Merton
Summary: 10 contests, won 6, lost 4

Peter Ashcroft
Liverpool. *Born* Liverpool 01.02.63
Welterweight
Manager C. Moorcroft
Previous Amateur Club Salisbury

10.05.84 Mark Simpson W PTS 6 Digbeth
Summary: 1 contest, won 1

Mohammed Aslam
Leeds. *Born* Pakistan 03.05.57
Welterweight
Manager (Self)
Previous Amateur Club Meanwood

12.05.83 Mike Calderwood L RSC 5 Morley
Summary: 1 contest, lost 1

Derek Atherton
Liverpool. *Born* Liverpool 23.10.61
L. Welterweight
Manager P. Dwyer
Previous Amateur Club Golden Gloves
Divisional Honours W Lancs Lightweight R/U 1983

18.01.83 Steve Harwood L RSC 5 Stoke
15.03.84 Chris McReedy L PTS 6 Kirkby
12.06.84 Gerard Treble L RSC 3 St Helens
Summary: 3 contests, lost 3

Ron Atherton
Liverpool. *Born* Liverpool 30.10.57
Welterweight
Manager P. Dwyer
Previous Amateur Club Golden Gloves

04.03.83 Robert Lloyd **L** CO 1 Queensferry
29.04.83 John Daly **L** PTS 6 Liverpool
17.06.83 Gary Lucas **L** RSC 2 Queensferry
07.11.83 Peter Flanagan **L** CO 3 Liverpool
Summary: 4 contests, lost 4

Stan Atherton
Liverpool. *Born* Liverpool 11.08.55
Welterweight
Manager (Self)
Previous Amateur Club Golden Gloves
National Honours Junior ABA Title 1972; Young England Rep.
Divisional Honours W Lancs Bantamweight R/U 1973; NW Counties Bantamweight Champion 1974; W Lancs Lightweight Champion 1975; W Lancs L. Welterweight Champion 1976; W Lancs Lightweight R/U 1977

02.03.78 Martin Bridge **W** PTS 6 Liverpool
15.03.78 Steve Early **L** PTS 6 Solihull
17.04.78 Martin Bridge DREW 6 Bradford
18.05.78 Dave Taylor **W** PTS 6 Liverpool
29.08.78 Eric Wood **L** PTS 6 Liverpool
28.09.78 Eric Wood **W** PTS 6 Liverpool
12.10.78 Najib Daho **W** PTS 6 Liverpool
12.02.79 Frank McCord **W** PTS 6 Manchester
22.02.79 Tommy Wright **W** PTS 6 Liverpool
15.03.79 Jess Harper **W** PTS 6 Caistor
22.03.79 George Schofield **L** CO 2 Liverpool
30.04.79 Tommy Wright **L** PTS 8 Barnsley
27.03.80 Terry Welch **L** PTS 8 Liverpool
10.02.81 Mohammed Ben **W** PTS 6 Nantwich
23.03.81 Gary Petty **L** PTS 6 Liverpool
13.04.81 Johnny Francis **L** PTS 8 Manchester
18.05.81 Steve MacLeod **L** RSC 6 Manchester
13.10.81 Frank McCord **L** RSC 2 Blackpool
30.11.82 Pat Belshaw DREW 6 Farnsworth
06.12.82 Peter Flanagan **L** PTS 6 Manchester
28.01.83 Michael Harris **L** PTS 6 Swansea
07.12.83 Edward Lloyd **L** PTS 6 Liverpool
14.02.83 Sam Church **W** PTS 6 Liverpool
05.03.84 Ray Murray **L** PTS 6 Liverpool
12.03.84 Ray Murray **L** PTS 6 Liverpool
06.04.84 Robert Harkin **L** RSC 4 Edinburgh
Summary: 26 contests, won 9, drew 2, lost 15

Alan Bagley
Birmingham. *Born* Birmingham 23.07.51
Heavyweight
Manager R. Gray
Previous Amateur Club Golden Gloves, Birmingham

11.09.78 Winston Allen **L** PTS 6 Birmingham
29.11.78 John Depledge **W** PTS 6 Evesham
31.01.79 Clive Beardsley **W** PTS 6 Stoke
19.02.79 Joe Awome **L** RSC 1 Birmingham
04.04.79 Joe Awome **L** RSC 4 Birmingham
07.06.84 Ian Priest **L** RSC 1 Dudley
Summary: 6 contests, won 2, lost 4

George Baigrie
Edinburgh. *Born* Edinburgh 19.08.62
Lightweight
Manager T. Gilmour
Previous Amateur Club McTaggart

10.10.83 Steve Swiftie **W** RSC 5 Glasgow
07.12.83 Willie Wilson **L** RSC 2 Stoke
27.02.84 Neville Fivey **L** PTS 6 Nottingham
13.03.84 Danny Knaggs DREW 6 Hull
06.04.84 Taffy Mills **W** RSC 4 Edinburgh
Summary: 5 contests, won 2, drew 1, lost 2

Devon Bailey
Derek Rowe (Photos) Ltd

Devon Bailey
Battersea. *Born* Jamaica 12.04.58
L. Heavyweight
Manager D. Bidwell
Previous Amateur Club Battersea
National Honours England Int.
Divisional Honours London L. Heavyweight Champion 1977–1979; ABA L. Heavyweight R/U 1980–1981

15.09.81 Gordon Stacey **W** RSC 3 Wembley
12.10.81 Eddie Cooper **W** PTS 6 Copthorne

12.12.81 Joe Gregory **W** PTS 6 Lewisham
12.01.82 Keith Bristol NC 4 Bethnal Green
22.02.82 Nye Williams **W** PTS 6 Mayfair
10.03.82 Cordwell Hylton **W** RSC 2 Birmingham
29.03.82 Keith Bristol **W** PTS 8 Copthorne
10.05.82 Joe Frater **W** CO 2 Copthorne
21.06.82 Jerry Golden **W** RSC 3 Copthorne
07.07.82 Ben Lawlor **W** CO 5 Newmarket
20.10.82 Carl Canwell L PTS 8 Strand
23.02.83 Cordwell Hylton **W** RSC 6 Mayfair
20.04.83 Davey Armstrong **W** RSC 2 Muswell Hill
14.10.83 Yombo Jo Araka DREW 8 Aix-en-Provence
06.02.84 Liam Coleman **W** RSC 7 Mayfair
Summary: 15 contests, won 12, drew 1, lost 1, NC 1

George Bailey

Bradford. *Born* Bradford 26.01.60
Bantamweight
Manager J. Celebanski
Previous Amateur Club St Patricks
Divisional Honours NE Counties L. Flyweight Champion 1977

29.09.77 Jackie Dinning DREW 4 Newcastle
10.10.77 Jackie Dinning L PTS 4 Marton
08.11.77 Jackie Dinning **W** PTS 4 Darlington
23.01.78 Eddie Glencross L PTS 6 Bradford
02.03.78 Jimmy Bott **W** PTS 6 Liverpool
20.03.78 Jimmy Bott DREW 6 Bradford
17.04.78 Jimmy Bott L PTS 8 Bradford
12.07.78 Jackie Dinning **W** PTS 6 Newcastle
04.09.78 Jimmy Bott L RSC 8 Wakefield
02.10.78 Joey Spring L PTS 6 Nantwich
31.10.78 Don Aageson L PTS 6 Wolverhampton
14.06.79 Bryn Jones **W** PTS 6 Dudley
03.09.79 Eddie Glencross L PTS 8 Glasgow
10.09.79 Kelvin Smart L RSC 4 Birmingham
09.10.79 Bryn Jones DREW 8 Wolverhampton
15.10.79 Billy Straub L PTS 8 Glasgow
06.11.79 Robert Hepburn L PTS 6 Stafford
21.11.79 John Griffiths L PTS 6 Evesham
28.04.80 Iggy Jano L PTS 8 Windsor
11.06.80 Peter Gabbitus L PTS 4 Morecambe
04.09.80 Carl Cleasby L PTS 4 Morecambe
16.09.80 Eddie McAllister **W** RSC 4 Southend
08.10.80 Pat Mallon **W** PTS 8 Stoke
07.11.80 Pat Mallon **W** PTS 6 Cambuslang
13.11.80 Steve Reilly **W** PTS 6 Stafford
02.02.81 Jimmy Bott L PTS 8 Nottingham
03.03.81 Gary Nickels L RTD 6 Wembley
06.04.81 Dave George L PTS 8 Bradford
04.05.81 Eddie Glencross L PTS 8 Glasgow
10.05.81 Jimmy Carson L PTS 8 Dublin
01.06.81 Carl Cleasby L PTS 8 Nottingham
30.09.81 Ken Coughlin **W** RSC 2 Evesham
09.10.81 Stuart Nicol L RSC 5 Cambuslang
16.11.81 Ivor Jones L PTS 6 Mayfair
24.11.81 Paddy Maguire **W** RSC 1 Wolverhampton
07.12.81 Stuart Nicol **W** PTS 8 Nottingham
16.02.82 Ivor Jones L PTS 6 Bethnal Green
13.09.82 Anthony Brown L RSC 3 Sheffield
19.10.82 Stuart Nicol **W** PTS 8 Wolverhampton
09.11.82 Hugh Russell L RSC 2 Belfast
01.12.82 Dave Pratt L PTS 6 Stafford
31.01.83 Eddie Morgan L PTS 8 Birmingham
01.03.83 Ray Gilbody L RSC 2 Kensington
22.03.83 Howard Williams **W** CO 1 Wolverhampton
08.04.83 John Farrell L RSC 7 Liverpool (*Vacant Central Area Bantamweight Title*)
09.05.83 Dave Pratt L PTS 8 Nottingham
16.05.83 Robert Dickie L RSC 3 Birmingham
10.10.83 Alex Cairney L PTS 6 Glasgow
27.10.83 Dai Williams L PTS 6 Ebbw Vale
Summary: 49 contests, won 13, drew 3, lost 33

Vince Bailey

Birmingham. *Born* Jamaica 01.03.62
L. Welterweight
Manager P. Lynch
Previous Amateur Club Austin

05.10.83 Dave Springer **W** PTS 6 Solihull
23.11.83 Mick Harkin L PTS 6 Solihull
19.01.84 John Faulkner **W** RSC 4 Digbeth
25.01.84 Albert Buchanan **W** PTS 6 Solihull
30.01.84 Tony McKenzie L RSC 1 Birmingham
02.05.84 Lenny Gloster L RSC 8 Solihull
Summary: 6 contests, won 3, lost 3

Mickey Baker

Worcester. *Born* Worcester 23.12.59
Lightweight
Manager (Self)
Previous Amateur Club Worcester

10.04.79 Selvin Bell **W** RTD 3 Wolverhampton
02.07.79 Bill Smith **W** CO 1 Wolverhampton
18.09.79 Brendan O'Donnell **W** RSC 4 Wolverhampton
29.10.79 Johnny Burns DREW 8 Wolverhampton
03.12.79 Tommy Thomas **W** RSC 1 Wolverhampton
21.01.80 Dai Davies **W** PTS 6 Wolverhampton
10.03.80 Tyrrel Wilson **W** PTS 8 Wolverhampton

CONTINUED OVERLEAF

29.05.80 Kid Murray **W** PTS 6 Wolverhampton
08.07.80 Dave Taylor **W** RSC 5 Wolverhampton
22.09.80 Billy Vivian **W** PTS 8 Wolverhampton
30.10.80 Eric Wood **L** DIS 6 Wolverhampton
09.03.81 Brian Snagg **W** PTS 8 Wolverhampton
13.04.81 Duncan Hamilton **W** RSC 8 Wolverhampton
09.07.81 Adey Allen **L** RSC 7 Dudley (*Midlands Area L. Welterweight Title Challenge*)
12.11.81 Eric Wood **W** PTS 8 Stafford
25.01.82 Paul Chance **L** PTS 10 Wolverhampton (*Vacant Midlands Area Lightweight Title*)
15.10.82 Dan M'Putu **W** RTD 3 Dunkirk
13.12.82 Andy Thomas **W** RTD 1 Wolverhampton
15.03.83 Winston Spencer **L** DIS 2 Wembley
20.09.83 Paul Chance **L** PTS 8 Dudley
27.03.84 Gary Williams **W** CO 3 Wolverhampton
27.04.84 George Feeney **L** PTS 10 Wolverhampton
Summary: 22 contests, won 15, drew 1, lost 6

Tony Baker

New Cross. *Born* Greenwich 06.08.56
Middleweight
Manager (Self)
Previous Amateur Club St Josephs

08.11.82 Terry Magee **L** PTS 6 Piccadilly
21.02.83 Steve Watt **L** PTS 6 Piccadilly
05.09.83 Gary Cable **W** PTS 6 Mayfair
23.09.83 Dennis Boy O'Brien **L** RSC 1 Longford
15.06.84 Dalton Jordan **W** RTD 2 Liverpool
Summary: 5 contests, won 2, lost 3

(Baba) Funso Banjo

West Ham. *Born* Nigeria 02.10.56
Southern Area Heavyweight Champion
Manager J. Quill
Previous Amateur Club Repton
Divisional Honours E Counties Heavyweight Champion 1978; E Counties Heavyweight R/U 1980

29.10.81 John Rafferty **W** PTS 6 Walthamstow
19.11.81 Eddie Cooper **W** CO 3 Morecambe
10.12.81 David Fry **W** CO 2 Walthamstow
04.02.82 Rocky Burton **W** RSC 2 Walthamstow
08.03.82 Andy Palmer **W** CO 1 Mayfair
01.04.82 Mick Chmilowskyj **W** RSC 6 Walthamstow
06.05.82 Tony Moore **W** PTS 8 Mayfair
13.10.82 Marco Vitagliano **W** PTS 8 Walthamstow
07.12.82 Mick Chmilowskyj **W** PTS 8 Kensington
08.02.83 Noel Quarless **W** RSC 3 Kensington
05.04.83 Ricky Keller **W** PTS 8 Kensington
08.11.83 Stewart Lithgo **W** PTS 8 Bethnal Green
13.03.84 Billy Thomas **W** PTS 8 Wembley
13.05.84 Hughroy Currie **W** PTS 10 Wembley (*Vacant Southern Area Heavyweight Title & Final Elim. British Heavyweight Title*)
Summary: 14 contests, won 14

(Rocklyn) Rocky Bantleman

Hayes. *Born* India 06.03.58
Featherweight
Manager (Self)
Previous Amateur Club Hayes

07.10.80 John Griffiths **W** PTS 6 Mayfair
03.11.80 Steve Pollard **L** CO 2 Mayfair
16.03.81 Jim Harvey **W** PTS 6 Mayfair
06.04.81 Robert Hepburn **W** RSC 5 Windsor
01.06.81 Alan Storey **W** PTS 7 Mayfair
08.02.82 Mike Wilkes **W** PTS 6 Piccadilly
25.03.82 Stuart Nicol **W** RSC 4 Glasgow
22.04.82 Steve Pollard **L** RSC 8 Piccadilly
19.10.82 Billy Hough **W** CO 2 Windsor
01.11.82 Brett Styles **W** PTS 6 Piccadilly
07.02.83 Stuart Nicol **W** RSC 3 Piccadilly
22.03.83 Billy Ruzgar **L** PTS 6 Bethnal Green
09.05.83 Brett Styles DREW 8 Piccadilly
Summary: 13 contests, won 9, drew 1, lost 3

Wayne Barker

Manchester. *Born* Salford 29.11.59
Middleweight
Manager N. Basso
Previous Amateur Club Cavendish
Divisional Honours E Lancs Welterweight R/U 1978

17.09.79 Jeff Aspell **W** PTS 6 Manchester
15.10.79 Jimmy Ellis **W** PTS 6 Manchester
23.10.79 Tommy Baldwin **W** RTD 3 Blackpool

27.10.79 Joey Saunders **W** PTS 6 Barnsley
15.11.79 Joey Saunders **W** RSC 4 Caister
19.11.79 Chris Glover **W** PTS 8 Stockport
27.11.79 Jimmy Ellis **W** PTS 8 Sheffield
10.12.79 Chris Glover **W** PTS 8 Manchester
07.01.80 Terry Matthews DREW 8 Manchester
21.01.80 Dennis Pryce **W** PTS 8 Nottingham
12.05.80 Leo Mulhearn **W** PTS 8 Manchester
03.06.80 Jimmy Batten L RSC 4 Kensington
31.08.81 Fulgencio Obelmejias L RSC 2 Caracas
05.11.81 Teddy Mann L DIS 6 Atlantic City
06.02.84 John Hargin **W** CO 4 Liverpool
19.03.84 Paul Murray **W** PTS 8 Manchester
04.06.84 Deano Wallace L RSC 6 Manchester
Summary: 17 contests, won 12, drew 1, lost 4

Newton Barnett
Camberwell. *Born* Jamaica 19.10.59
L. Middleweight
Manager K. March
Previous Amateur Club Fisher

03.10.83 Ian Martin L PTS 6 Eltham
21.11.83 Ian Martin L PTS 6 Eltham
30.11.83 Kevin Webb L PTS 6 Piccadilly
06.02.84 Cliff Eastwood **W** PTS 6 Mayfair
01.03.84 Tony Rabbetts DREW 6 Queensway
14.03.84 Danny Sullivan L PTS 6 Mayfair
17.04.84 Danny Sullivan L PTS 6 Merton
Summary: 7 contests, won 1, drew 1, lost 5

Billy Barton
Bridgend. *Born* Bridgend 29.11.62
Bantamweight
Manager T. Woodward
Previous Amateur Club Garw Valley
National Honours Welsh Flyweight Champion 1982; Welsh Int.

19.05.84 Steve Lucas **W** PTS 6 Bristol
Summary: 1 contest, won 1

Tony Batty
Walthamstow. *Born* London 12.05.64
Welterweight
Manager E. Fossey
Previous Amateur Club Waltham Forest

18.05.83 Dave Heaver L RSC 4 Bloomsbury
23.06.83 Dave Heaver L PTS 6 Bethnal Green
12.09.83 Jim Kelly L RSC 4 Glasgow
14.02.84 Joe Lynch L PTS 6 Southend
Summary: 4 contests, lost 4

Lateef Beachers
Bradford. *Born* Bradford 10.04.63
Welterweight
Manager J. Celebanski
Previous Amateur Club Bradford YMCA

16.04.84 Steve Ward DREW 6 Nottingham
09.05.84 Tucker Watts L CO 2 Leicester
Summary: 2 contests, drew 1, lost 1

Gerry Beard
Nottingham. *Born* Nottingham 18.10.56
Midlands Area Lightweight Champion
Manager R. Gray
Previous Amateur Club Clifton

14.10.80 John Sharkey L RSC 3 Wolverhampton
02.02.81 Lloyd Christie L PTS 4 Nottingham
10.02.81 Ray Smith **W** PTS 4 Wolverhampton
11.03.81 Julian Boustead L RSC 5 Evesham
15.04.81 Johnny Gwilliam **W** PTS 4 Evesham
27.04.81 Wayne Kline **W** PTS 4 Nottingham
08.06.81 Ken Rathbone **W** PTS 4 Bradford
24.09.81 Jimmy Bunclark L CO 5 Liverpool
09.11.81 Norman Morton DREW 6 Newcastle
16.11.81 Sam Omidi **W** PTS 6 Liverpool
01.12.81 Eric Wood DREW 8 Derby
07.12.81 Craig Walsh **W** PTS 6 Nottingham
08.01.82 Ken Foreman **W** RSC 6 Durham
16.02.82 Vernon Entertainer Vanriel L RTD 4 Bethnal Green
05.04.82 Eric Wood **W** PTS 6 Nottingham
19.04.82 Eddie Copeland L PTS 8 Mayfair
05.05.82 Walter Clayton L PTS 8 Solihull
20.05.82 Robbie Robinson L RSC 2 Preston
23.09.82 Jimmy Duncan L RSC 6 Liverpool
16.11.82 Tony Connolly **W** PTS 8 Bethnal Green
23.11.82 Joey Joynson L PTS 6 Wembley
18.01.83 Paul Huggins **W** PTS 8 Kensington
09.03.83 John Feeney L PTS 8 Solihull
21.03.83 Paul Huggins L RSC 3 Mayfair
08.11.83 Mo Hussein L RSC 4 Bethnal Green
06.02.84 Jim McDonnell L PTS 8 Bethnal Green
14.02.84 Adey Allen DREW 8 Wolverhampton
02.04.84 Jim McDonnell L PTS 8 Mayfair
16.04.84 Lee Halford **W** CO 8 Birmingham (*Vacant Midlands Area Lightweight Title*)
Summary: 29 contests, won 11, drew 3, lost 15

Clive Beardsley
I. J. Ball

Clive Beardsley

Melbourne. *Born* Derby 18.03.56
L. Heavyweight
Manager T. Sharp
Previous Amateur Club Melbourne
Divisional Honours M Counties Heavyweight R/U 1976–1977

19.09.77 Austin Okoye **L** PTS 6 Mayfair
27.09.77 Stan McDermott DREW 6 Wembley
18.10.77 Colin Flute **W** PTS 6 Wolverhampton
02.11.77 George Scott DREW 6 Newcastle
08.11.77 Brian Huckfield **L** PTS 6 W. Bromwich
14.11.77 Jimmy Evans **W** PTS 6 Reading
06.12.77 Bob Hennessey **L** PTS 6 Kensington
11.09.78 John Depledge **W** PTS 8 Bradford
31.01.79 Allan Bagley **L** PTS 6 Stoke
06.02.79 Joe Awome **L** RSC 2 Wembley
18.09.79 Roy Skeldon **L** CO 3 Wolverhampton
04.11.81 Jonjo Greene **W** RSC 8 Derby
01.12.81 Jerry Golden **W** PTS 6 Derby
20.01.82 Glenroy Taylor **W** PTS 6 Solihull
01.02.82 Jonjo Greene **W** PTS 6 Manchester
15.03.82 Paul Busette **W** RSC 5 Mayfair
23.03.82 Lee White **L** CO 2 Bethnal Green
11.05.82 Paul Heatley **W** RSC 7 Derby
24.05.82 Cordwell Hylton **L** RSC 4 Nottingham
19.10.82 Gary Jones **L** PTS 6 Wolverhampton
11.11.82 Al Stevens **W** PTS 6 Stafford
13.12.82 John Humphreys **L** PTS 6 Wolverhampton
23.02.83 Mick Morris **L** RSC 6 Chesterfield
Summary: 23 contests, won 10, drew 2, lost 11

Mervyn Bennett

Cardiff. *Born* Cardiff 20.02.60
Lightweight
Manager (Self)
Previous Amateur Club Llandaff
National Honours Welsh Featherweight Champion 1978; Welsh Int.; Euro. Junior Gold 1978
Divisional Honours Welsh Featherweight R/U 1980

06.01.81 Geoff Smart **W** RSC 6 Bethnal Green
26.01.81 Paddy Maguire **W** RSC 2 Edgbaston
07.04.81 Philip Morris **W** PTS 6 Newport
25.09.81 Alec Irvine **W** PTS 6 Nottingham
12.10.81 Richie Foster **W** PTS 8 Bloomsbury
19.11.81 Don George **L** PTS 10 Ebbw Vale (*Vacant Welsh Featherweight Title*)
26.10.82 Mick Rowley **L** PTS 8 Newport
24.11.82 Jimmy Duncan **L** PTS 8 Stoke
17.02.83 Kevin Pritchard **L** RSC 5 Coventry
18.04.83 Keith Foreman **L** RSC 6 Bradford
Summary: 10 contests, won 5, lost 5

Tommy Bennett

Sheffield. *Born* Jamaica 28.08.55
Welterweight
Manager B. Ingle
Previous Amateur Club Eckington

10.05.82 Andy Letts **W** PTS 4 Birmingham
21.05.82 Phil O'Hare **W** PTS 6 Sheffield
14.02.83 Mick Dono **W** PTS 6 Manchester
14.03.83 Steve Ward **W** RSC 3 Sheffield
18.04.83 Bobby Rimmer **L** PTS 6 Bradford
23.05.83 Mike Calderwood **W** PTS 6 Sheffield
09.11.83 Kevin Quinn **L** RTD 4 Sheffield
16.01.84 Tony Smith **L** PTS 6 Bradford
Summary: 8 contests, won 5, lost 3

Steve Benny (Jones)

Liverpool. *Born* Liverpool 17.05.60
Featherweight
Manager N. Basso
Previous Amateur Club St Helens

25.04.83 Les Walsh **L** RSC 2 Liverpool
20.06.83 Ian Murray **L** PTS 6 Manchester

18.01.84 Kenny Walsh **W** RSC 4 Stoke
23.01.84 Alex Cairney L RSC 3 Glasgow
13.02.84 Eugene Maloney L RSC 5 Eltham
Summary: 5 contests, won 1, lost 4

Tommy Bennett

Carlton Benoit

Hackney. *Born* Domenica 26.06.53
L. Heavyweight
Manager R. Colson
Previous Amateur Club London Transport
Divisional Honours NW London L. Heavyweight R/U 1975

10.05.76 Len Brittain **W** CO 5 Piccadilly
21.09.76 Roy Gumbs **W** PTS 6 Southend
12.10.76 Johnny Waldron L RTD 3 Wembley
02.12.76 Bob Pollard DREW 6 Southend
17.01.77 Johnny Cox **W** PTS 6 Mayfair
14.02.77 Reg Long **W** PTS 6 Bedford
16.03.77 Johnny Cox **W** PTS 8 Stoke
14.09.77 Danny McLoughlin **W** PTS 8 Sheffield
20.09.77 Johnny Cox **W** PTS 8 Southend
26.09.77 Winston Cousins L PTS 8 Manchester
02.11.77 Steve Fenton L CO 2 Southend
05.12.77 Brian Paul **W** PTS 8 Southend
15.02.78 Paul Kinsella **W** RTD 6 Cambridge
14.03.78 George Gray **W** PTS 6 Southend
20.03.78 Billy Knight **W** DIS 6 Mayfair
03.05.78 Tim Wood **W** PTS 8 Solihull
21.11.78 Steve Taylor **W** RSC 5 Cambridge
28.11.78 Tom Collins L CO 1 Sheffield
28.02.79 Eddie Fenton L RSC 3 Burslem
17.04.79 Ken Jones **W** PTS 8 Newcastle
13.05.79 Chris Lawson **W** RSC 2 Plymouth
23.10.79 Francis Hand **W** RSC 7 Blackpool
31.10.79 Karl Canwell L PTS 8 Burslem
27.11.79 Alek Penarski L PTS 8 Sheffield
28.04.80 Pat McCann **W** PTS 8 Windsor
22.09.80 Shaun Chalcraft L PTS 10 Lewisham
(Vacant Southern Area L. Heavyweight Title)
29.01.81 Hocine Tafer L RSC 5 Paris
19.06.81 Richard Caramanolis L PTS 8 Marseilles
29.10.81 Prince Mama Mohammed DREW 6 Glasgow
27.04.82 Lee White **W** PTS 6 Southend
06.05.82 Geoff Rymer **W** CO 6 Mayfair
19.05.83 Jerry Golden **W** RSC 4 Queensway
22.09.83 Karl Canwell L CO 7 Strand
Summary: 33 contests, won 20, drew 2, lost 11

Dominic Bergonzi

Battersea. *Born* Bethnal Green 09.09.58
Welterweight
Manager (Self)
Previous Amateur Club Kingston
National Honours England Int.
Divisional Honours NE London L. Welterweight R/U 1978; SW London Welterweight Champion 1979

03.06.80 George McGurk **W** RSC 2 Kensington
12.07.80 Paul Wetter **W** PTS 6 Wembley
16.09.80 Brian Anderson DREW 6 Wembley
18.11.80 Steve Freeman **W** RTD 5 Bethnal Green
06.01.81 Les Wint **W** PTS 8 Bethnal Green
09.02.81 Dennis Sheehan **W** PTS 8 Mayfair
31.03.81 P. J. Davitt **W** RTD 3 Wembley
06.05.81 Kid Murray **W** RSC 8 Solihull
26.05.81 John Wiggins **W** PTS 8 Bethnal Green
22.09.81 Tommy McCallum L RSC 2 Bethnal Green
20.10.81 P. J. Davitt L RSC 4 Bethnal Green
23.09.83 Steve Watt L RSC 5 Longford
08.11.83 John Bibby **W** DIS 3 Bethnal Green
01.03.84 Steve Watt L CO 3 Queensway
Summary: 14 contests, won 9, drew 1, lost 4

Michael Betts

Norwich. *Born* West Runton 11.05.64
L. Welterweight
Manager G. Holmes
Previous Amateur Club Watton & District

15.12.81 Thomas Leonard L PTS 4 Lewisham
24.01.82 Tony Wilkinson L RSC 2 Sunderland
18.03.82 Joey Morris L RSC 3 Caister
29.09.82 Dave Smithson DREW 4 Effingham Park
09.11.82 Michael Marsden W CO 3 Southend
01.02.83 Andy O'Rawe L PTS 4 Southend
14.02.83 Ron Shinkwin L PTS 4 Lewisham
16.03.83 Ron Shinkwin L PTS 6 Cheltenham
03.02.84 Davey Moore L RSC 3 Maidenhead
Summary: 9 contests, won 1, drew 1, lost 7

John Bibby

Bedford. *Born* Bedford 15.08.60
Welterweight
Manager A. Smith
Previous Amateur Club Sandy & District
Divisional Honours H Counties Welterweight R/U 1980; H Counties L. Welterweight Champion 1981

18.05.82 Andy Letts W RSC 1 Bethnal Green
07.09.82 Sam Omidi W PTS 6 Hornsey
16.11.82 Sam Omidi W PTS 6 Bethnal Green
26.04.83 Peter Ahmed W PTS 8 Bethnal Green
08.11.83 Dominic Bergonzi L DIS 3 Bethnal Green
15.03.84 John Langol L RSC 4 Leicester
Summary: 6 contests, won 4, lost 2

Mickey Bird

Chesterfield. *Born* Chesterfield 28.10.61
Welterweight
Manager W. Shinfield
Previous Amateur Club Target

23.02.83 Steve Ward W PTS 6 Chesterfield
21.03.83 Granville Allen L CO 2 Nottingham
23.06.83 Mickey Lerwill L RSC 5 Wolverhampton
05.09.83 Rob Williams W CO 3 Liverpool
12.09.83 Kid Sadler W PTS 6 Leicester
30.01.84 Tony Smith L PTS 6 Manchester
20.02.84 Frankie Moro L PTS 6 Bradford
12.03.84 Tony Brown L RSC 6 Liverpool
09.04.84 John McAllister L RSC 2 Glasgow
14.05.84 Tommy Campbell L PTS 8 Glasgow
06.06.84 Andy Sumner L RSC 3 Sheffield
Summary: 11 contests, won 3, lost 8

Carl Bishop

Northampton. *Born* Leeds 09.01.65
Welterweight
Manager J. Cox
Previous Amateur Club Northampton

19.09.83 Graeme Griffin L PTS 6 Nottingham
05.10.83 Graeme Griffin W PTS 6 Stoke
12.10.83 Joe Lynch L PTS 6 Evesham
09.11.83 Trevor Hopson L PTS 6 Southend
Summary: 4 contests, won 1, lost 3

Tony Blackstock

Nottingham. *Born* Leamington 26.05.64
Heavyweight
Manager J. Griffin
Previous Amateur Club Willenhall

05.04.82 Frank Robinson L PTS 4 Nottingham
26.04.82 Frank Robinson L CO 4 Leicester
10.02.83 Michael Fawcett W PTS 4 Walthamstow
12.03.83 Grant Wallis L PTS 4 Swindon
22.03.83 Deka Williams W RSC 4 Wolverhampton
16.09.83 Steve Abadom W PTS 4 Swindon
30.09.83 Al Malcolm L PTS 4 Leicester
Summary: 7 contests, won 3, lost 4

Willie Booth

Glasgow. *Born* Airdrie 05.09.56
Scottish Lightweight Champion & Former Scottish L. Welterweight Champion
Manager H. Hoey
Previous Amateur Club Clarkston
National Honours Scottish Int.
Divisional Honours Scottish Featherweight R/U 1974–1975

09.02.76 Delvin Whyte W PTS 4 Mayfair
23.02.76 Kenny Matthews W PTS 6 Glasgow
11.03.76 Ginger Bell W RSC 4 Hamilton
22.03.76 Dave Tuohey W PTS 6 Glasgow
05.04.76 Steve Elliston W RSC 3 Piccadilly
26.04.76 Kevin Doherty W PTS 6 Piccadilly
24.06.76 Dil Collins W PTS 8 Piccadilly
15.11.76 Ian Pickersgill W RSC 7 Glasgow
22.11.76 Billy Vivian L PTS 8 Piccadilly
18.03.77 Don Burgin W PTS 8 Holytown
02.05.77 Von Reid W RSC 3 Holytown
10.10.77 Bingo Crooks W PTS 8 Glasgow
14.11.77 Tommy Glencross W PTS 10 Glasgow
(*Scottish Lightweight Title Challenge*)
09.01.78 Billy Vivian W PTS 8 Piccadilly
16.01.78 Jeff Pritchard DREW 8 Birmingham
08.05.78 Tommy Dunn W RSC 5 Glasgow
31.10.78 Johnny Claydon L PTS 10 Hammersmith
(*Elim. British Lightweight Title*)

27.11.78 Mick Bell **W** RSC 8 Govan (*Vacant Scottish L. Welterweight Title*)
29.01.79 Tommy Davitt **L** RTD 3 Glasgow
17.04.79 Sylvester Gordon **W** PTS 8 Glasgow
18.06.79 George Peacock **L** PTS 10 Glasgow (*Scottish L. Welterweight Title Defence*)
08.10.79 Bingo Crooks **L** RTD 6 Glasgow
10.05.80 Paul Chance **L** PTS 10 Wolverhampton
21.04.80 Ricky Beaumont **L** RTD 4 Glasgow
07.06.80 Duncan Hamilton **W** PTS 10 Glasgow (*Scottish Lightweight Title Defence*)
28.06.80 Winston Spencer **L** PTS 8 Wembley
06.09.80 Langton Tinango **L** PTS 10 Salisbury
23.02.81 Peter Harrison **L** PTS 10 Glasgow (*Scottish Lightweight Title Defence*)
09.03.81 Norman Morton **W** PTS 8 Hamilton
13.04.81 Ricky Beaumont DREW 8 Glasgow
11.05.81 Vernon Entertainer Vanriel **L** PTS 8 Glasgow
08.06.81 George Metcalf **W** PTS 8 Motherwell
13.10.81 Winston Spencer **L** RSC 5 Kensington
19.04.82 Granville Allen **W** RSC 7 Glasgow
26.04.82 Ricky Beaumont **W** PTS 8 Piccadilly
31.05.82 Ian McLeod **W** PTS 10 Glasgow (*Vacant Scottish Lightweight Title*)
24.06.82 Robbie Robinson **L** PTS 10 Kirkby (*Elim. British Lightweight Title*)
01.10.82 John Muwanga **L** PTS 8 Helsinki
25.10.82 Ray Price **W** PTS 8 Airdrie
04.12.82 Rene Weller **L** PTS 10 Cologne
07.03.83 Des Gwilliam **W** PTS 8 Glasgow
25.04.83 Ray Cattouse **L** RSC 7 Southwark
15.09.83 Tony Sinnott **W** PTS 8 Liverpool
06.02.84 Brian Janssen **L** PTS 10 Brisbane
Summary: 44 contests, won 25, drew 2, lost 17

Tony Borg

Cardiff. *Born* Cardiff 17.12.64
Featherweight
Manager W. May
Previous Amateur Club Roath Youth
National Honours Schools Titles 1980–1981; NABC Title 1981; Welsh Featherweight Champion 1982; Welsh Int.

21.03.83 Kenny Watson **W** PTS 6 Piccadilly
21.04.83 Mick Hoolison **W** RSC 2 Piccadilly
14.06.83 Eddie Morgan **W** PTS 6 Newport
29.11.83 Steve James **W** PTS 6 Cardiff
26.01.84 Charlie Coke **L** RSC 5 Strand
16.04.84 Alex Cairney **W** CO 2 Glasgow
13.06.84 Steve James **L** PTS 8 Aberavon
Summary: 7 contests, won 5, lost 2

Mark Boswell

Canvey Island. *Born* Romford 25.01.62
Featherweight
Manager T. Mason
Previous Amateur Club Colvestone

17.11.83 Kenny Walsh **L** PTS 6 Basildon
31.05.84 Steve Lucas **L** PTS 6 Basildon
Summary: 2 contests, lost 2

Paul Boswell

Canvey Island. *Born* Rochford 15.01.65
Lightweight
Manager T. Mason
Previous Amateur Club Canvey Island

06.10.83 Teddy Anderson **L** PTS 6 Basildon
17.11.83 Carl Green **L** RSC 2 Basildon
07.06.84 Irish Tommy Kelliher **L** RSC 6 Piccadilly
Summary: 3 contests, lost 3

Julian Bousted

Plymouth. *Born* Torquay 19.03.62
Welterweight
Manager G. Bousted
Previous Amateur Club Newton Abbot

02.04.79 Wally Stocks **W** PTS 4 Piccadilly
21.05.79 Tommy Burling **W** PTS 4 Walworth
15.10.79 Terry Parkinson **W** CO 3 Mayfair
26.11.79 Joe Mills DREW 4 Birmingham
10.12.79 Walter Clayton DREW 4 Torquay
02.06.80 Mike Clemow **W** PTS 6 Plymouth
02.10.80 Colin Wake **L** CO 4 Hull
02.02.81 Lee McKenzie **L** PTS 6 Piccadilly
11.03.81 Gerry Beard **W** RSC 5 Evesham
28.04.81 Jimmy Woods **W** RSC 4 Leeds
08.05.81 Gary Petty DREW 8 Piccadilly
18.09.81 Dave Taylor **W** PTS 8 Swindon
04.12.81 Bobby Welburn **W** RSC 5 Bristol
10.10.82 Tyrell Wilson **W** PTS 8 Piccadilly
18.10.82 Delroy Pearce **W** PTS 8 Piccadilly
18.11.82 John McGlynn **W** RSC 8 Piccadilly
16.04.84 Phil Sheridan **W** RSC 6 Nottingham
19.05.84 Steve Tempro **W** PTS 8 Bristol
Summary: 18 contests, won 13, drew 3, lost 2

Peter Bowen

Wednesbury. *Born* Wolverhampton 19.10.55
Lightweight
Manager G. Riley
Previous Amateur Club Bilston Golden Gloves

14.02.84 Colin Anderson **L** PTS 6 Wolverhampton
14.03.84 Leroy James **W** RSC 2 Stoke
04.04.84 Dean Bramhald **W** PTS 6 Evesham
16.04.84 Dave Stokes **W** PTS 6 Birmingham
06.06.84 Jimmy Thornton **L** PTS 6 Sheffield
Summary: 5 contests, won 3, lost 2

Steve Boyle
Glasgow. *Born* Glasgow 28.11.62
Lightweight
Manager T. Gilmour
Previous Amateur Club Scottish National

19.05.83 Shaun Dooney **W** CO 3 Sunderland
06.06.83 Frankie Lake **W** RTD 3 Piccadilly
13.06.83 Mike McKenzie **W** PTS 6 Glasgow
19.09.83 Craig Walsh **W** PTS 6 Glasgow
17.10.83 Johnny Grant **W** PTS 6 Southwark
28.11.83 Robert Lloyd L PTS 6 Rhyl
07.12.83 Gary Lucas DREW 6 Stoke
27.02.84 Willie Wilson **W** RSC 3 Nottingham
26.03.84 Rocky Mensah DREW 8 Glasgow
11.06.84 Dave Haggarty **W** RSC 1 Glasgow
Summary: 10 contests, won 7, drew 2, lost 1

Dean Bramhald
Doncaster. *Born* Balby 25.05.63
Lightweight
Manager J. Rushton
Previous Amateur Club Elmfield House

25.01.84 Wayne Trigg L CO 3 Stoke
22.02.84 Andy De Abreu L PTS 6 Evesham
27.02.84 Billy Joe Dee **W** PTS 6 Nottingham
19.03.84 Billy Joe Dee L PTS 6 Bradford
27.03.84 Neville Fivey DREW 6 Wolverhampton
04.04.84 Peter Bowen L PTS 6 Evesham
12.04.84 Andy De Abreu L PTS 6 Piccadilly
09.05.84 Wayne Trigg DREW 4 Leicester
21.05.84 Doug Munro L PTS 6 Aberdeen
11.06.84 Glenn Tweedie L PTS 6 Glasgow
Summary: 10 contests, won 1, drew 2, lost 7

(Kevin) Sammy Brennan
Kirkby. *Born* Liverpool 01.04.60
Middleweight
Manager M. Goodall
Previous Amateur Club Holy Name
Divisional Honours W Lancs L. Heavyweight R/U 1979; W Lancs Middleweight R/U 1980

19.11.81 Deano Wallace **W** PTS 4 Liverpool
21.12.81 Joe Jackson **W** PTS 6 Bradford
25.01.82 Keith James **W** PTS 6 Bradford
01.03.82 Neville Wilson **W** PTS 8 Preston
22.03.82 Russell Humphreys **W** PTS 8 Bradford
20.05.82 Willie Wright **W** PTS 8 Preston
24.06.82 Terry Matthews **W** RSC 5 Kirkby
25.10.82 Nick Jenkins L RSC 4 Bradford
10.02.83 Graeme Ahmed **W** PTS 8 Sunderland
24.02.83 Dale Henderson **W** PTS 8 Liverpool
21.03.83 Jimmy Ellis L PTS 8 Bradford
20.04.83 Barry Ahmed DREW 8 South Shields
16.05.83 Jimmy Ellis DREW 10 Bradford (*Vacant Central Area Middleweight Title*)
09.12.83 Winston Burnett **W** PTS 8 Liverpool
30.01.84 Winston Burnett L PTS 8 Manchester
23.02.84 Stephane Ferrera L RSC 8 Nice
21.05.84 Brian Anderson L RTD 1 Bradford (*Central Area Middleweight Challenge*)
Summary: 17 contests, won 10, drew 2, lost 5

Graham Brett
Deptford. *Born* London 14.06.62
Featherweight
Manager F. Warren
Previous Amateur Club Westminster

20.04.83 Jimmy Young **W** CO 3 Muswell Hill
18.05.83 Charlie Coke L RSC 6 Bloomsbury
14.09.83 John Mwaimu **W** PTS 6 Muswell Hill
Summary: 3 contests, won 2, lost 1

Darwin Brewster
Cardiff. *Born* Cardiff 08.08.60
L. Middleweight
Manager W. May
Previous Amateur Club Roath Youth
National Honours ABA L. Middleweight Champion 1979; Welsh L. Middleweight Champion 1979–1980; Welsh Int.

13.10.80 Dave Arnott **W** RSC 4 Mayfair
08.12.80 Les Wint **W** PTS 6 Hastings
26.01.81 John Langol **W** PTS 6 Edgbaston
23.03.81 Brian Anderson DREW 6 Mayfair
08.06.81 Alan Mann **W** RSC 1 Motherwell
06.10.81 Carl Bailey **W** RSC 5 Liverpool
24.10.81 Hugo Samos **W** PTS 8 Calais
16.11.81 John Mugabi L RSC 6 Mayfair
10.12.81 Joe Jackson **W** PTS 8 Newport
19.12.81 Ace Russeki L PTS 8 Split
26.04.82 Pat Thomas **W** PTS 10 Cardiff
13.09.82 Brian Anderson L PTS 10 Sheffield (*Elim. British L. Middleweight Title*)
18.10.82 Chris Christian **W** PTS 8 Piccadilly
25.11.82 Graeme Ahmed **W** PTS 10 Sunderland
09.12.82 Steve Johnson **W** PTS 8 Bloomsbury
27.01.83 Marijan Benes L PTS 8 Rijeka
27.09.83 Chris Pyatt L PTS 8 Wembley
30.01.84 Helier Custos L PTS 8 Paris
02.05.84 Martin McEwan **W** PTS 8 Solihull
Summary: 19 contests, won 12, drew 1, lost 6

Keith Bristol
Clapham. *Born* Guyana 21.07.57
L. Heavyweight
Manager A. Lavelle
Previous Amateur Club St Anne's

16.09.80 Clint Jones L PTS 6 Southend
06.10.80 Lee White **W** PTS 6 Southwark
20.10.80 Tommy Jones **W** PTS 6 Birmingham

10.11.80 Clint Jones W PTS 6 Southwark
26.11.80 Gordon Stacey W CO 4 Wembley
01.12.80 Lee White L PTS 6 Bloomsbury
06.01.81 Lee White W PTS 6 Bethnal Green
16.02.81 Glenroy Taylor W RSC 4 Southwark
23.03.81 Ben Lawlor L RSC 5 Southwark
26.10.81 Paul Busette W RSC 5 Southwark
04.11.81 Rupert Christie W RSC 6 Derby
08.12.81 Paul Newman W RSC 1 Belfast
12.01.82 Devon Bailey NC 4 Bethnal Green
16.02.82 Lee White W PTS 6 Lewisham
22.03.82 Nye Williams W PTS 8 Mayfair
29.03.82 Devon Bailey L PTS 8 Copthorne
14.04.82 Shaun Chalcraft W CO 4 Strand
07.06.82 Tommy Kiely W PTS 8 Bloomsbury
13.08.82 Dennis Andries L PTS 10 Strand (*Southern Area L. Heavyweight Title Challenge*)
20.09.82 Cordwell Hylton NC 5 Wolverhampton
04.11.82 Chris Lawson W RTD 3 Wimbledon
14.12.82 Ben Lawlor W RSC 4 Belfast
19.01.83 Antonio Harris W PTS 8 Birmingham
02.03.83 Liam Coleman W PTS 6 Belfast
19.03.83 Rufino Angulo L RSC 6 Villeneuve-D'Ornon
22.09.83 Dennis Andries L CO 4 Strand (*Southern Area L. Heavyweight Title Challenge & Final Elim. British L. Heavyweight Title*)
Summary: 26 contests, won 17, lost 7, NC 2

Tony Britton
Lewisham. *Born* London 12.03.57
L. Middleweight
Manager D. Mancini
Previous Amateur Club Catford & District
Divisional Honours SE London Middleweight Champion 1979

04.06.79 Terry Matthews L PTS 6 Piccadilly
30.07.79 Ron Pearce W PTS 6 Mayfair
19.09.79 Terry Matthews W PTS 6 Mayfair
29.10.79 Steve Henty W PTS 6 Hove
12.11.79 Dennis Pryce L PTS 6 Mayfair
04.12.79 John Ridgman L PTS 6 Southend
04.02.80 Alan Cable W PTS 8 Hammersmith
11.02.80 Peter Bassey L PTS 6 Manchester
10.03.80 Martin McEwan L RSC 6 Mayfair
17.04.80 Paul Baekgaard W RSC 2 Copenhagen
20.05.80 Leo Mulhern W PTS 6 Southend
22.09.80 Chris Glover DREW 8 Mayfair
06.10.80 Mickey Mapp L PTS 6 Southwark
17.10.80 Torben Andersen L PTS 6 Copenhagen
08.12.80 Al Neville W PTS 6 Birmingham
21.01.81 Dennis Pryce W PTS 8 Solihull
16.03.81 Gary Cooper W PTS 6 Mayfair
13.04.81 Jimmy Cable L PTS 6 Southwark
11.05.81 Gary Cooper L PTS 8 Mayfair
28.10.81 Mickey Mapp DREW 8 Acton
15.12.81 Jimmy Cable L PTS 8 Lewisham
18.01.82 Curtis Marsh W PTS 8 Mayfair
02.04.82 Steve Dennis L PTS 8 Sydney
09.06.82 Peter Neal L PTS 8 Bristol
20.10.82 Richard Rodriguez L PTS 8 Paris
09.11.82 Nick Wilshire L RSC 4 Kensington
25.01.83 Jimmy Batten L PTS 8 Bethnal Green
04.03.83 Erwin Heiber L PTS 8 Cologne
15.03.83 Nick Wilshire L RSC 3 Wembley
25.04.83 Dennis Sheehan W PTS 8 Mayfair
16.05.83 Rob Wada W PTS 8 Mayfair
10.09.83 Agamil Yilderim W PTS 8 Cologne
22.11.83 Chris Pyatt L RSC 4 Wembley
13.02.84 Jack Sharp W PTS 8 Eltham
Summary: 34 contests, won 14, drew 2, lost 18

Graham Brockway
Pembroke Dock. *Born* Pembroke Dock 11.11.60
L. Welterweight
Manager R. Witts
Previous Amateur Club Pembroke

07.06.82 Bert Myrie L PTS 6 Piccadilly
02.11.82 Steve Ellwood L PTS 6 Hornsey
01.02.83 Mark Duffy L RSC 2 Southend
Summary: 3 contests, lost 3

Mickey Brooks
Hull. *Born* Hull 20.06.59
L. Welterweight
Manager M. Toomey
Previous Amateur Club North Hull
National Honours Junior ABA Title, 1976
Divisional Honours NE Counties Featherweight R/U 1977 & S/F 1978

16.04.84 Chris McReedy W PTS 6 Bradford
04.06.84 Les Remikie W PTS 6 Mayfair
15.06.84 Edward Lloyd W RSC 6 St Helens
30.06.84 Tony Dunlop L PTS 6 Belfast
Summary: 4 contests, won 3, lost 1

Andy Broughton
Sheffield. *Born* Sheffield 19.09.61
Lightweight
Manager B. Ingle
Previous Amateur Club Wybourn

03.12.80 Brian Lawrence W PTS 6 Sheffield
21.01.81 John Griffiths W PTS 6 Burslem
16.02.81 Keith Foreman W CO 6 Bradford
24.03.81 Ken Foreman L PTS 6 Sheffield
07.03.83 Chris Moorcroft W PTS 6 Liverpool
Summary: 5 contests, won 4, lost 1

Alex Brown
Derek Rowe (Photos) Ltd

Alex Brown

Willesden. *Born* Jamaica 20.10.59
Welterweight
Manager F. Warren
Previous Amateur Club All Stars

07.12.82 Alan Hardiman **L** CO 1 Southend
01.03.83 Delroy Pearce **W** PTS 6 Southend
28.03.83 Bobby Rimmer **L** RSC 3 Manchester
25.04.83 Cornelius Chisholm **W** PTS 6 Acton
10.05.83 John Ridgman **W** PTS 6 Southend
21.09.83 Glyn Mitchell DREW 6 Southend
03.10.83 Jim Hunter **W** PTS 6 Glasgow
06.12.83 Tim Moloney **L** PTS 6 Southend
19.01.84 Martin McGough **L** RSC 3 Digbeth
27.03.84 Dan Myers **W** PTS 6 Southend
03.04.84 Steve Ellwood **L** RSC 3 Lewisham
Summary: 11 contests, won 5, drew 1, lost 5

Anthony Brown

Islington. *Born* St. Helens 24.08.62
Bantamweight
Manager F. Warren
Previous Amateur Club St. Helens Star
National Honours NABC Title 1981; Young England Rep.
Divisional Honours W Lancs Featherweight R/U 1982

08.06.82 Billy Hough **W** PTS 6 Southend
07.09.82 Dave Khan **W** PTS 6 Crewe
13.09.82 George Bailey **W** RSC 3 Sheffield
14.10.82 Michael Marsden DREW 6 Nantwich
24.01.83 Danny Flynn **L** PTS 8 Glasgow
27.09.83 John Doherty **W** PTS 6 Stoke
26.10.83 Michael Marsden **W** RSC 2 Stoke
28.11.83 Alan Tombs **W** PTS 8 Bayswater
23.01.84 Danny Flynn **L** PTS 8 Glasgow
15.03.84 Hector Clottey **L** PTS 8 Kirkby
18.04.84 Mike Whalley **W** PTS 6 Stoke
25.04.84 Billy Hardy **L** RSC 5 Muswell Hill
Summary: 12 contests, won 7, drew 1, lost 4

Charlie Brown

Glasgow. *Born* Glasgow 31.10.59
Bantamweight
Manager H. Watt
Previous Amateur Club Clydeview

28.06.82 Chip O'Neill **W** PTS 6 Bradford
23.11.82 Duke McKenzie **L** RSC 1 Wembley
07.03.83 Chip O'Neill **W** RSC 3 Glasgow
25.04.83 Robert Dickie **L** RSC 4 Aberdeen
12.09.83 Gary Roberts **L** RSC 2 Glasgow
26.03.84 Gordon Stobie **W** PTS 6 Glasgow
Summary: 6 contests, won 3, lost 3

Tony Brown

Liverpool. *Born* Liverpool 10.08.61
Central Area L. Welterweight Champion
Manager N. Basso
Previous Amateur Club Litherland
National Honours Schools Titles 1976 – 1977; Junior ABA Title 1977
Divisional Honours W Lancs L. Welterweight R/U 1981

29.03.82 Paul Murray **W** PTS 6 Liverpool
05.04.82 Glen Crump **W** PTS 6 Manchester
22.04.82 Mickey Williams **W** RSC 3 Liverpool
10.05.82 Gary Petty **W** RSC 5 Liverpool
17.05.82 Cecil Williams **W** RSC 4 Manchester
03.06.82 Errol Dennis DREW 6 Liverpool
21.06.82 Errol Dennis **W** CO 3 Liverpool
06.07.82 Denny Garrison **W** PTS 6 Leeds
23.09.82 Ian Chantler **W** PTS 8 Liverpool
05.10.82 Ian Chantler **L** PTS 8 Liverpool
18.10.82 Steve Early **L** PTS 6 Edgbaston
06.12.82 Steve Early **L** PTS 8 Edgbaston
14.03.83 Walter Clayton **W** PTS 10 Sheffield (*Vacant Central Area L. Welterweight Title*)
20.04.83 Martin McGough **W** PTS 8 Solihull
03.10.83 Steve Tempro **W** PTS 8 Liverpool
13.10.83 Vernon Entertainer Vanriel **W** PTS 8 Bloomsbury
30.11.83 Tony Laing **L** PTS 8 Piccadilly
12.03.84 Mickey Bird **W** RSC 6 Liverpool
04.06.84 Tony Adams **L** RSC 2 Mayfair
Summary: 19 contests, won 13, drew 1, lost 5

Frank Bruno

Clapham. *Born* Hammersmith 16.11.61
Heavyweight
Manager T. Lawless
Previous Amateur Club Sir Philip Game
National Honours Young England Rep.; ABA Heavyweight Champion 1980

17.03.82 Lupe Guerra **W** CO 1 Kensington
30.03.82 Harvey Steichen **W** RSC 2 Wembley
20.04.82 Tom Stevenson **W** CO 1 Kensington
04.05.82 Ron Gibbs **W** RSC 4 Wembley
01.06.82 Tony Moore **W** RSC 2 Kensington
14.09.82 George Scott **W** RSC 1 Wembley
23.10.82 Ali Lukusa **W** CO 2 Berlin
09.11.82 Rudi Gauwe **W** CO 1 Kensington
23.11.82 George Butzbach **W** RTD 1 Wembley
07.12.82 Gilberto Acuna **W** RSC 1 Kensington
18.01.83 Stewart Lithgo **W** RTD 4 Kensington
08.02.83 Peter Mulendwa **W** CO 3 Kensington
01.03.83 Winston Allen **W** RSC 2 Kensington
05.04.83 Eddie Neilson **W** RSC 3 Kensington
03.05.83 Scott Le-Doux **W** RSC 3 Wembley
31.05.83 Barry Funches **W** RSC 5 Kensington
09.07.83 Mike Jameson **W** CO 2 Chicago
27.09.83 Bill Sharkey **W** CO 1 Wembley
11.10.83 Floyd Cummings **W** RSC 7 Kensington
06.12.83 Walter Santemore **W** CO 4 Kensington
13.03.84 Juan Figueroa **W** CO 1 Wembley
13.05.84 James Bonecrusher Smith **L** CO 10 Wembley
Summary: 22 contests, won 21, lost 1

Frank Bruno
Derek Rowe (Photos) Ltd

Dave Bryan

Rhyl. *Born* St. Asaph 01.03.60
Featherweight
Manager P. Dwyer
Previous Amateur Club Rhyl Star
National Honours Welsh Int.
Divisional Honours Welsh Featherweight R/U 1982

23.09.82 Mark Drew **W** PTS 4 Liverpool
05.10.82 Stuart Carmichael **W** PTS 6 Liverpool
01.11.82 Gary Lucas **W** PTS 6 Liverpool
20.01.83 Jimmy Bunclark DREW 6 Birkenhead
07.02.83 Kevin Pritchard **L** RSC 2 Liverpool
17.06.83 Mohammad Lovelock **W** PTS 6 Queensferry
17.02.84 Muhammad Lovelock **W** PTS 6 Rhyl
05.03.84 Ian Murray **W** PTS 6 Liverpool
12.03.84 Muhammad Lovelock **W** PTS 6 Liverpool
02.05.84 Michael Marsden **L** CO 7 Solihull
Summary: 10 contests, won 7, drew 1, lost 2

Denroy Bryan

Swindon. *Born* Birmingham 15.11.59
Heavyweight
Manager R. Porter
Previous Amateur Club Park Youth
Divisional Honours W Counties Heavyweight Champion 1981; W Counties S. Heavyweight Champion 1982 – 1983

16.09.83 Michael Armstrong **W** RSC 1 Swindon
14.11.83 Michael Armstrong **W** RSC 4 Nantwich
22.02.84 Glenn McCrory **L** PTS 6 Kensington
30.04.84 Dave Garside **L** PTS 8 Mayfair
Summary: 4 contests, won 2, lost 2

Billy Bryce

Hartlepool. *Born* 12.11.59
L. Middleweight
Manager (Self)
Previous Amateur Club Perth Green
Divisional Honours NE Counties L. Welterweight Champion 1979

06.10.80 Dave Finigan **W** PTS 6 Southwark
26.03.81 Charlie Douglas **W** PTS 6 Newcastle
27.04.81 Phil Duckworth **L** PTS 8 Newcastle
10.06.81 Kevin Durkin **L** PTS 8 Brodsworth
24.09.81 Liam Linnen **W** RSC 4 Hartlepool
26.10.81 Dudley McKenzie **L** PTS 8 Mayfair
24.11.81 Kevin Durkin DREW 8 Hartlepool
19.05.83 Terry Petersen **W** PTS 6 Sunderland

CONTINUED OVERLEAF

03.10.83 John Langol L RTD 3 Bradford
26.09.83 Phil O'Hare **W** PTS 8 Manchester
Summary: 10 contests, won 5, drew 1, lost 4

Albert Buchanan

Dundee. *Born* Dundee 11.02.58
Welterweight
Manager T. Gilmour
Previous Amateur Club Lochee
National Honours Scottish Lightweight Champion 1979; Scottish Int.

19.09.83 Paul Salih DREW 6 Glasgow
07.11.83 Stan Wall **W** RSC 1 Liverpool
22.11.83 Tony McKenzie L CO 3 Wolverhampton
25.01.84 Vince Bailey L PTS 6 Solihull
27.02.84 Peter Phillips **W** PTS 6 Glasgow
13.03.84 Paul Salih L PTS 6 Hull
Summary: 6 contests, won 2, drew 1, lost 3

Gary Buckle

Wednesbury. *Born* West Bromwich 08.10.61
Welterweight
Manager R. Gray
Previous Amateur Club Wednesbury

05.11.80 Kevin Johnson **W** PTS 6 Evesham
13.11.80 Kevin Johnson **W** PTS 4 Stafford
25.11.80 Steve Ward **W** PTS 6 Wolverhampton
28.01.81 Dave Goodwin L PTS 6 Stoke
10.02.81 Lloyd Christie L RSC 4 Wolverhampton
17.03.81 Errol Dennis **W** PTS 6 Wolverhampton
15.04.81 Errol Dennis **W** PTS 6 Evesham
06.05.81 P. J. Davitt L PTS 6 Solihull
01.06.81 Peter Stockdale **W** PTS 6 Wolverhampton
21.09.81 Paul Murray DREW 6 Wolverhampton
13.10.81 Paul Murray **W** PTS 6 Wolverhampton
11.11.81 Frank McCord L PTS 8 Evesham
25.01.82 Dave Taylor L PTS 8 Wolverhampton
21.02.82 Paul Murray L PTS 8 Nottingham
20.09.82 Davey Cox **W** PTS 6 Wolverhampton
06.10.82 Davey Cox **W** PTS 6 Stoke
18.10.82 Neville Wilson **W** PTS 8 Nottingham
10.11.82 John McGlynn L PTS 8 Evesham
29.11.82 Neville Wilson **W** PTS 8 Birmingham
13.12.82 Dan Myers **W** PTS 8 Wolverhampton
24.01.83 Dan Myers **W** PTS 8 Mayfair
21.02.83 Kid Murray **W** PTS 8 Nottingham
Summary: 22 contests, won 14, drew 1, lost 7

Jimmy Bunclark

Netherton. *Born* Bootle 25.06.61
Central Area Lightweight Champion
Manager N. Basso
Previous Amateur Club Netherton

05.03.80 Kevin Sheehan **W** RSC 1 Liverpool
10.03.80 Robert Wakefield **W** RSC 4 Manchester
19.05.80 Jackie Turner L PTS 8 Mayfair
18.09.80 Selvin Bell **W** RSC 6 Liverpool
30.10.80 Glyn Rhodes **W** RSC 7 Liverpool
10.11.80 Billy O'Grady L PTS 8 Southwark
05.03.81 Lloyd Christie **W** PTS 6 Liverpool
23.03.81 Dennis Sullivan L RSC 4 Liverpool
30.04.81 Brian Snagg L RSC 8 Liverpool
24.09.81 Gerry Beard **W** CO 5 Liverpool
15.02.82 Steve Parker **W** RSC 2 Liverpool
29.03.82 Ray Hood L RSC 2 Liverpool
22.04.82 Brian Snagg L RSC 3 Liverpool
23.09.82 Gary Lucas **W** PTS 6 Liverpool
11.10.82 Rocky Mensah L PTS 8 Manchester
26.10.82 Les Remikie **W** PTS 6 Bethnal Green
09.11.82 Damian Fryers L RSC 5 Belfast
20.01.83 Dave Bryan DREW 6 Birkenhead
07.02.83 Mark Drew **W** PTS 6 Liverpool
14.03.83 Glyn Rhodes **W** PTS 10 Sheffield (*Central Area Lightweight Title Challenge*)
23.05.83 Vince Vahey **W** RSC 1 Sheffield (*Central Area Lightweight Title Defence*)
05.09.83 Keith Foreman **W** CO 7 Liverpool
19.09.83 Ian McLeod L RSC 3 Glasgow
28.10.83 Ray Hood L RSC 8 Queensferry
30.04.84 Dave Haggarty L PTS 8 Rhyl
Summary: 25 contests, won 13, drew 1, lost 11

Nigel Burke

Newport. *Born* Newport 16.07.63
Lightweight
Manager M. Williams
Previous Amateur Club Maindee

22.02.84 Dave Stokes DREW 6 Evesham
17.04.84 Nicky Day L RSC 5 Piccadilly
Summary: 2 contests, drew 1, lost 1

Rory Burke

Ipswich. *Born* Ipswich 15.06.56
Featherweight
Manager G. Holmes
Previous Amateur Club Ipswich
Divisional Honours E Counties Lightweight Champion 1978 – 1981

05.08.81 Keith Foreman **W** RTD 2 Norwich
19.11.81 Russell Jones L PTS 6 Ebbw Vale
25.01.82 J. J. Barrett DREW 6 Bradford
16.02.82 Jimmy Duncan L PTS 6 Bloomsbury

18.03.82 John Pollard **W** PTS 6 Caister
26.05.82 Lee Graham **W** PTS 8 Piccadilly
20.09.82 David Miles **W** RTD 5 Mayfair
12.10.82 Clyde Ruan L RSC 7 Kensington
22.11.82 Andy Thomas L PTS 8 Mayfair
16.03.83 Stuart Shaw **W** RSC 4 Stoke
25.04.83 Paul Huggins L RSC 7 Mayfair (*Southern Area Featherweight Title Challenge*)
30.01.84 Najib Daho L PTS 8 Manchester
13.03.84 Alec Irvine **W** PTS 8 Wembley
13.05.84 Jim McDonnell L PTS 8 Wembley
Summary: 14 contests, won 6, drew 1, lost 7

Tony Burke

Croydon. *Born* Croydon 07.04.63
Middleweight
Manager H. Burgess
Previous Amateur Club Sir Philip Game

09.09.81 Chris Burchell L PTS 6 Morecambe
19.10.81 Bobby Williams L CO 3 Mayfair
10.12.81 Bobby Williams **W** PTS 6 Walthamstow
16.02.82 Chris Lewin **W** RSC 1 Bethnal Green
21.02.83 Terry Magee **W** PTS 6 Piccadilly
21.03.83 Roddy Crane **W** RSC 3 Piccadilly
20.04.83 Martin McEwan L RSC 2 Solihull
25.01.84 Shamus Casey **W** CO 1 Solihull
Summary: 8 contests, won 5, lost 3

Winston Burnett

Cardiff. *Born* Jamaica 04.05.59
L. Heavyweight
Manager M. Williams
Previous Amateur Club Llandaff

12.02.80 Mike Burton L PTS 4 Wembley
24.03.80 Mike Burton L PTS 4 Mayfair
27.05.80 Ray Pearce L PTS 6 Newport
20.10.80 Pharoah Bish **W** PTS 6 Birmingham
27.10.80 Prince Wilmot **W** PTS 6 Mayfair
10.11.80 Neville Wilson **W** PTS 6 Birmingham
19.01.81 John Humphreys DREW 6 Birmingham
27.01.81 Mark Kaylor L PTS 8 Kensington
16.02.81 Terry Christle L PTS 6 Mayfair
02.03.81 Peter Gorny L PTS 6 Piccadilly
16.03.81 Paddy Ryan **W** PTS 6 Mayfair
24.03.81 Mick Mills L PTS 8 Sheffield
30.03.81 Archie Salmon L PTS 8 Piccadilly
22.06.81 Henry Cooper **W** PTS 8 Glasgow
21.09.81 Billy Lauder DREW 8 Glasgow
06.10.81 Peter Gorny **W** PTS 8 Piccadilly
03.11.81 Mark Kaylor L RSC 6 Kensington
08.12.81 Steve Davies L PTS 8 Pembroke
23.02.82 Terry Christle L PTS 7 Belfast
08.03.82 Billy Lauder L PTS 8 Hamilton
15.03.82 Steve Johnson L RSC 5 Bloomsbury
22.06.82 Andy Straughn L PTS 6 Hornsey
31.08.82 Barry Ahmed L PTS 8 South Shields
07.10.82 Michael Madsen L PTS 6 Copenhagen
18.10.82 Nick Jenkins L PTS 8 Southwark
23.11.82 Cordwell Hylton L RSC 5 Wolverhampton
12.03.83 Nick Jenkins L PTS 6 Swindon
25.03.83 Jimmy Price L PTS 6 Bloomsbury
13.04.83 Paul Shell L PTS 6 Evesham
16.09.83 Cliff Curtis **W** PTS 6 Swindon
12.10.83 Deano Wallace L PTS 6 Evesham
01.11.83 Mickey Kidd L PTS 6 Dudley
09.12.83 Sammy Brennan L PTS 8 Liverpool
19.12.83 Dave Mowbray **W** RSC 4 Bradford
30.01.84 Sammy Brennan **W** PTS 8 Manchester
25.02.84 Paul Tchoue L RTD 4 Paris
02.04.84 Mickey Kidd L PTS 8 Mayfair
12.04.84 Alex Romeo **W** PTS 6 Piccadilly
17.04.84 Alex Romeo **W** PTS 6 Piccadilly
02.05.84 Romal Ambrose L PTS 8 Solihull
12.05.84 Willie Wright L PTS 8 Hanley
04.06.84 Chris Devine L PTS 6 Mayfair
Summary: 42 contests, won 11, drew 2, lost 29

Johnny Burns

Birmingham. *Born* Birmingham 25.02.59
Welterweight
Manager (Self)
Previous Amateur Club Sheldon Heath

22.01.79 Brendan O'Donnell **W** PTS 6 Wolverhampton
05.03.79 Gene McGarrigale **W** RSC 1 Wolverhampton
04.04.79 Mark Hill **W** CO 3 Birmingham
16.05.79 Selvin Bell **W** DIS 5 Wolverhampton
06.06.79 Barry Price DREW 6 Bedworth
02.07.79 Norman Morton L RSC 4 Wolverhampton
18.09.79 Dennis Sullivan L PTS 6 Wolverhampton
29.10.79 Mickey Baker DREW 8 Wolverhampton
21.01.80 Steve Ward **W** PTS 6 Wolverhampton
20.02.80 Kid Murray L PTS 6 Evesham
08.07.80 Steve Ward L PTS 6 Wolverhampton
30.10.80 Paul Chance L PTS 8 Wolverhampton
01.12.80 Jeff Pritchard **W** PTS 6 Wolverhampton
18.03.81 Duncan Hamilton L PTS 8 Stoke
12.11.81 Dai Davies **W** PTS 6 Stafford
25.11.81 Derek Nelson L PTS 6 Stoke
30.11.81 John Lindo L PTS 6 Birmingham
21.02.83 Valentino Maccarinelli L PTS 6 Edgbaston
10.02.84 Dan Myers L PTS 6 Dudley
Summary: 19 contests, won 7, drew 2, lost 10

(Wayne) Rocky Burton
Bedworth. *Born* Nuneaton 28.10.58
Heavyweight
Manager J. Griffin
Previous Amateur Club Golden Eagle

18.10.77 Tony Bennett **W** CO 1 Wolverhampton
30.11.77 Joey Williams **W** PTS 4 Wolverhampton
13.02.78 Eddie Vierling L RSC 2 Reading
06.03.78 Joey Williams L PTS 6 Wolverhampton
31.10.78 Reg Squire L RTD 2 Wolverhampton
27.11.78 Manny Gabriel L PTS 6 Kettering
31.01.79 Roy Skeldon L PTS 4 Stoke
15.03.79 Roy Skeldon L PTS 4 Dudley
21.03.79 Emmanuel Lucas **W** PTS 6 Stoke
28.03.79 Manny Gabriel L CO 1 Kettering
06.06.79 Emmanuel Lucas **W** PTS 6 Bedworth
26.09.79 Peter Les Reed **W** PTS 6 Stoke
17.12.79 John O'Neill **W** PTS 6 Wolverhampton
28.01.80 George Lewis **W** RSC 3 Edgbaston
18.02.80 Nigel Savery **W** PTS 6 Stockport
18.03.80 Gary Jones **W** PTS 6 Wolverhampton
27.03.80 Stan Carnall **W** PTS 6 Liverpool
21.04.80 Nigel Savery **W** RSC 4 Bradford
29.09.80 Terry O'Connor L RSC 6 Bedworth (*Vacant Midlands Area Heavyweight Title*)
25.11.80 Colin Flute **W** RSC 7 Bedworth
11.03.81 Steve Gee L PTS 8 Solihull
11.09.81 Paddy Finn L PTS 6 Edgbaston
10.11.81 Ricky James L CO 6 Bedworth (*Midlands Area Heavyweight Title Challenge*)
04.02.82 Funso Banjo L RSC 2 Walthamstow
20.09.82 Frank Robinson **W** PTS 6 Wolverhampton
20.10.82 Steve Howard **W** CO 1 Strand
11.11.82 Frank Robinson **W** PTS 6 Stafford
17.02.83 Ricky James L CO 3 Coventry (*Midlands Area Heavyweight Title Challenge*)
10.09.83 Thomas Classen L PTS 4 Cologne
01.11.83 Frank Robinson **W** RSC 5 Dudley
26.01.84 Martin Nee **W** RSC 3 Strand
Summary: 31 contests, won 17, lost 14

Gary Cable
Orpington. *Born* Penge 08.11.60
Middleweight
Manager D. Bidwell
Previous Amateur Club Fitzroy Lodge

24.01.83 Willie Wright L RSC 6 Mayfair
17.03.83 Dave Scott L CO 1 Marylebone
05.09.83 Tony Baker L PTS 6 Mayfair
06.10.83 Paul Morgan **W** RSC 3 Basildon
Summary: 4 contests, won 1, lost 3

Alex Cairney
Kirkintilloch. *Born* Lennoxtown 18.07.62
Featherweight
Manager T. Gilmour
Previous Amateur Club Kirkintilloch

05.09.83 Mick Hoolison **W** PTS 6 Glasgow
16.09.83 Paul Owen L PTS 6 Rhyl
05.10.83 Clinton Campbell **W** PTS 6 Stoke
10.10.83 George Bailey **W** PTS 6 Glasgow
07.11.83 Muhammad Lovelock L RSC 6 Liverpool
23.01.84 Steve Benny **W** RSC 3 Glasgow
16.04.84 Tony Borg L CO 2 Glasgow
18.06.84 Ian Murray L PTS 6 Manchester
Summary: 8 contests, won 4, lost 4

Mike Calderwood
Salford. *Born* Crumpsall 17.09.64
Welterweight
Manager J. Edwards
Previous Amateur Club Higher Blackley

14.02.83 Peter Flanagan L PTS 6 Manchester
11.04.83 Bobby Welburn DREW 6 Manchester
25.04.83 Colin Neagle L PTS 6 Liverpool
12.05.83 Mohammed Aslam **W** RSC 5 Morley
23.05.83 Tommy Bennett L PTS 6 Sheffield
20.06.83 Mick Dono L PTS 6 Manchester
09.04.84 Tony Kempson L RSC 5 Manchester
04.06.84 Chris Edge DREW 6 Manchester
Summary: 8 contests, won 1, drew 2, lost 5

Clinton Campbell
Stoke. *Born* Stoke 18.10.59
Featherweight
Manager F. Deakin
Previous Amateur Club Holden Lane

21.02.83 Andy Cassidy **W** PTS 4 Nottingham
02.03.83 Andy Cassidy **W** PTS 6 Evesham
16.03.83 Jim Paton L PTS 6 Stoke
13.04.83 Graham Kid Clarke L PTS 6 Evesham
09.05.83 Andy Cassidy **W** PTS 6 Nottingham
16.05.83 Carl Merrett L PTS 6 Birmingham
22.09.83 Graham Kid Clarke L PTS 6 Cardiff
05.10.83 Alex Cairney L PTS 6 Glasgow
18.10.83 Andy Green **W** PTS 6 Wolverhampton
27.03.84 Steve Cooke L PTS 6 Southend
06.04.84 John Maloney L PTS 6 Watford
Summary: 11 contests, won 4, lost 7

Davy Campbell
Enniskillen. *Born* Enniskillen 27.03.54
N. Ireland L. Welterweight Champion
Manager (Self)
Previous Amateur Club Enniskillen
National Honours Irish L. Welterweight Champion 1973; Irish Int.

16.12.77 Gene McGarrigale **W** CO 3 Enniskillen
03.02.78 George Kidd **W** RSC 4 Enniskillen
21.04.78 Granville Allen **L** PTS 8 Enniskillen
11.10.78 Benny Purdy **W** PTS 8 Belfast
01.12.78 Steve Early **L** RSC 2 Enniskillen
11.10.79 Vernon Entertainer Vanriel **W** PTS 6 Liverpool
29.10.79 Mike Clemow **W** PTS 6 Camborne
28.11.79 Hugh Smith **W** RSC 7 Solihull
25.02.80 Ray Heaney **W** RTD 7 Belfast (*Vacant N. Ireland Welterweight Title*)
04.03.80 Eddie Copeland **L** RSC 5 Wembley
10.11.80 Sid Smith **L** CO 2 Southwark
30.11.81 Larry Monaghan **L** RSC 2 Enniskillen
09.03.82 Gerry Maguire **W** PTS 6 Derry
22.04.82 Gerry Maguire **W** RSC 7 Enniskillen
28.09.82 Valentino Maccarinelli **W** PTS 6 Derry
20.01.83 Rocky Feliciello **W** PTS 6 Birkenhead
24.02.83 Tony Sinnott **L** CO 1 Liverpool
05.10.83 Damien Fryers **L** PTS 6 Belfast
28.10.83 Rocky Feliciello **L** PTS 8 Queensferry
28.11.83 Gunther Roomes **L** PTS 8 Southwark

Summary: 20 contests, won 11, lost 9

(Carlton) Sean Campbell
Farnborough. *Born* Jamaica 22.06.58
Welterweight
Manager (Self)
Previous Amateur Club Farnham
National Honours Schools Title 1973
Divisional Honours S Counties Welterweight Champion 1980 – 1981

16.02.82 Jimmy Smith **W** PTS 6 Lewisham
25.03.82 Mike McKenzie **L** PTS 6 Glasgow
22.04.82 John Daly **L** PTS 6 Piccadilly
08.06.82 Delroy Pearce **L** PTS 6 Southend
19.10.82 Tony Rabbetts DREW 6 Windsor
02.11.82 Tony Rabbetts **W** RSC 3 Hornsey
25.04.83 Glyn Mitchell **L** PTS 6 Piccadilly
01.02.84 Mickey Kilgallon **L** RSC 3 Bloomsbury

Summary: 8 contests, won 2, drew 1, lost 5

Tommy Campbell
Blantyre. *Born* Hamilton 11.05.63
Welterweight
Manager E. Coakley
Previous Amateur Club Blantyre MW
National Honours Scottish Int., Commonwealth Fed. Welterweight Champion 1983
Divisional Honours Scottish L. Welterweight R/U 1982; Scottish Welterweight Champion & ABA R/U 1983

30.01.84 Peter Foster **L** RTD 3 Glasgow
05.03.84 Tony Kempson **W** PTS 6 Glasgow
09.04.84 Peter Phillips **W** RSC 3 Glasgow
14.05.84 Mickey Bird **W** PTS 8 Glasgow
21.05.84 Robert Armstrong **W** PTS 8 Aberdeen

Summary: 5 contests, won 4, lost 1

Karl Canwell
Stoke Newington. *Born* London 20.04.57
L. Heavyweight
Manager G. Steene
Previous Amateur Club New Enterprise
Divisional Honours NW London Middleweight Champion 1977

05.09.77 Len Brittain **W** RSC 4 Mayfair
20.09.77 Wally Barnes **W** PTS 6 Southend
10.10.77 Joey Williams **W** PTS 6 Piccadilly
19.10.77 Steve Taylor **W** PTS 6 Bethnal Green
13.12.77 Pat Thompson **W** PTS 8 Southgate
24.01.78 Theo Josephs **W** RSC 4 Piccadilly
06.02.78 Bonny McKenzie **W** PTS 8 Piccadilly
27.02.78 Billy Knight **L** PTS 8 Mayfair
15.05.78 Victor Attivor **L** DIS 6 Mayfair
17.07.78 Tom Collins **W** RSC 6 Mayfair
18.09.78 Chris Lawson **W** RSC 5 Mayfair
30.09.78 Patrick Lyampemshya **W** CO 3 Lusaka
24.11.78 Tony Mundine **L** RSC 3 Brisbane
27.02.79 Lloyd James **W** RSC 6 Southend
05.03.79 Bonny McKenzie **L** PTS 8 Piccadilly
12.03.79 Bonny McKenzie **W** PTS 8 Mayfair
31.03.79 Chisanda Mutti **L** RTD 1 Lusaka
10.09.79 Harald Skog **W** CO 2 Oslo
31.10.79 Carlton Benoit **W** PTS 8 Burslem
17.10.80 Mustafa Wasajja **L** PTS 8 Copenhagen
09.03.81 Tom Collins **L** PTS 10 Bradford (*Elim. British L. Heavyweight Title*)
20.06.81 Chris Lawson **W** RSC 8 Wembley
26.03.82 Manfred Jassman **L** CO 3 Kiel
20.10.82 Devon Bailey **W** PTS 8 Strand
25.12.82 Jose Seyes **W** RSC 8 Izegem
04.02.83 Rufino Angulo **L** RSC 5 Bordeaux

CONTINUED OVERLEAF

28.02.83 Dennis Andries **L** CO 4 Strand (*Southern Area L. Heavyweight Title Challenge & Elim. British L. Heavyweight Title*)
22.09.83 Carlton Benoit **W** CO 7 Strand
Summary: 28 contests, won 18, lost 10

Charlie Carman
Norwich. *Born* Wisbech 14.08.62
L. Welterweight
Manager G. Holmes
Previous Amateur Club Parsons Drove
National Honours Schools Title 1978
Divisional Honours E Counties Featherweight Champion 1981

16.02.84 Nick Ellaway **L** PTS 6 Basildon
Summary: 1 contest, lost 1

(George) Gypsy Carman
Ipswich. *Born* Wisbech 23.11.64
L. Heavyweight
Manager G. Holmes
Previous Amateur Club Parsons Drove

30.01.84 Dave Mowbray **W** PTS 6 Manchester
16.02.84 Lennie Howard **L** RTD 1 Basildon
03.04.84 Gordon Stacey **W** PTS 6 Lewisham
07.06.84 Deka Williams **L** PTS 6 Dudley
Summary: 4 contests, won 2, lost 2

Stuart Carmichael
Hull. *Born* Hull 14.01.63
Featherweight
Manager B. Ingle
Previous Amateur Club St. Mary's, Hull
Divisional Honours NE Counties Featherweight R/U 1981; NE Counties Featherweight S/F 1982

21.06.82 Gordon Haigh **W** PTS 6 Hull
05.10.82 Dave Bryan **L** PTS 6 Liverpool
26.10.82 Carl Gaynor **W** PTS 6 Hull
18.11.82 John Doherty **L** PTS 6 Coventry
25.11.82 Jimmy Thornton **L** PTS 6 Morley
24.01.83 John Doherty **L** PTS 6 Bradford
17.02.83 John Doherty **L** PTS 6 Coventry
24.02.83 John Farrell **L** RSC 4 Liverpool
21.03.83 Ian Murray **W** PTS 6 Mayfair
29.03.83 Chris Moorcroft DREW 6 Hull
12.04.83 Terry Sullivan **W** RSC 5 Southend
05.09.83 Danny Flynn **L** PTS 8 Glasgow
12.09.83 Ian Murray **L** PTS 6 Leicester
19.09.83 Les Walsh **L** PTS 6 Manchester
14.11.83 John Doherty **W** RSC 7 Nantwich
06.12.83 Charlie Coke **L** PTS 6 Southend
03.02.84 Gary Nickels **L** PTS 8 Maidenhead
20.02.84 Steve Enright DREW 6 Bradford
19.03.84 Steve Enright **L** PTS 8 Bradford
09.04.84 Brian Hyslop **L** PTS 6 Glasgow
01.05.84 Gary Nickels **L** RSC 5 Bethnal Green
Summary: 21 contests, won 5, drew 2, lost 14

Young Tony Carroll
Liverpool. *Born* Liverpool 21.11.61
L. Welterweight
Manager M. Goodall
Previous Amateur Club Southern
Divisional Honours W Lancs L. Welterweight R/U 1982

18.10.82 John Daly **W** PTS 6 Blackpool
26.11.82 Dave Haggarty **L** PTS 6 Glasgow
09.12.83 Lee Halford **W** PTS 6 Liverpool
Summary: 3 contests, won 2, lost 1

Shamus Casey (West)
Alfreton. *Born* Pinxton 13.01.60
Middleweight
Manager B. Shamus
Previous Amateur Club South Normanton

25.01.84 Tony Burke **L** CO 1 Solihull
16.04.84 Ronnie Fraser **L** RSC 3 Nottingham
Summary: 2 contests, lost 2

Andy Cassidy
Nottingham. *Born* Nottingham 10.06.58
Featherweight
Manager J. Gill
Previous Amateur Club N.S.O.B.

21.02.83 Clinton Campbell **L** PTS 4 Nottingham
02.03.83 Clinton Campbell **L** PTS 6 Evesham
09.05.83 Clinton Campbell **L** PTS 6 Nottingham
25.05.83 Ian Murray **L** PTS 6 Rhyl
Summary: 4 contests, lost 4

Billy Cassidy
Smithfield. *Born* London 10.05.62
L. Heavyweight
Manager C. Hall
Previous Amateur Club New Enterprise
National Honours NABC Title 1981

18.10.82 Glenroy Taylor **W** PTS 6 Southwark
31.01.83 Jerry Golden **W** PTS 6 Southwark
25.04.83 Dwight Osbourne DREW 6 Southwark
17.10.83 Harry Cowap **L** PTS 8 Southwark
06.02.84 Glenroy Taylor **W** PTS 6 Bethnal Green
01.05.84 Theo Josephs **W** PTS 6 Bethnal Green
Summary: 6 contests, won 4, drew 1, lost 1

Trevor Cattouse
Balham. *Born* Stoke Newington 28.12.57
L. Heavyweight
Manager D. Bidwell
Previous Amateur Club Fitzroy Lodge

12.10.77 Pat Thompson L PTS 6 Stoke
19.10.77 Alan Tashy W PTS 6 Kingston
10.11.77 Joey Williams W PTS 6 Wimbledon
28.02.78 Ken Jones L PTS 8 Heathrow
13.03.78 Theo Josephs W PTS 8 Hove
20.04.78 Eddie Vierling L PTS 8 Piccadilly
03.05.78 Joe Jackson W PTS 8 Solihull
18.09.78 Eddie Vierling W RSC 4 Reading
12.10.78 Shaun Chalcraft L PTS 8 Wimbledon
23.11.78 Davey Mullings W RSC 4 Wimbledon
18.01.79 Clint Jones W PTS 8 Wimbledon
16.03.79 Eddie Vierling W CO 5 Thetford
10.04.79 Steve Lewin W PTS 6 Kensington
03.12.79 Roy Skeldon L PTS 8 Wolverhampton
16.01.80 Roy Skeldon W PTS 8 Stoke
21.01.80 Ken Jones L PTS 8 Mayfair
13.02.80 Steve Fenton W CO 5 Mayfair
24.03.80 Danny Lawford L RTD 2 Mayfair
11.06.80 Rupert Christie W PTS 8 Edgbaston
10.11.80 Rupert Christie DREW 8 Birmingham
21.11.80 Bonny McKenzie W PTS 8 Crawley
09.02.81 Danny Lawford DREW 8 Mayfair
11.05.81 Cordwell Hylton W PTS 8 Mayfair
21.05.81 John Odhiambo L RSC 2 Copenhagen
10.10.81 Richard Caramanolis L CO 2 Marseilles
21.12.81 Antonio Harris W PTS 8 Birmingham
16.02.82 Shaun Chalcraft W RTD 3 Lewisham
26.05.82 Tom Collins L CO 4 Leeds
(*British L. Heavyweight Title Challenge*)
23.09.82 Chris Lawson W PTS 8 Wimbledon
06.10.82 Glen McEwan W PTS 8 Solihull
04.12.82 Manfred Jassman L PTS 10 Cologne
31.01.83 Alex Tompkins DREW 8 Southwark
06.10.83 Michael Madsen L PTS 6 Copenhagen
31.10.83 Jonjo Greene W PTS 8 Mayfair
15.11.83 Louis Pergaud Ngatchou L RTD 2 Kassel
19.03.84 Jonjo Greene L PTS 8 Manchester
06.04.84 Nye Williams W PTS 8 Watford
25.05.84 Rufino Angulo L RSC 3 Toulouse
Summary: 38 contests, won 20, drew 3, lost 15

Shaun Chalcraft
Crawley. *Born* Redhill 12.03.57
Former Southern Area L. Heavyweight Champion
Manager P. Byrne
Previous Amateur Club Horley

16.01.78 Tony Burnett W PTS 6 Hove
13.02.78 Joey Williams W PTS 6 Walworth
17.04.78 Manny Gabriel W PTS 8 Hove
24.04.78 Joey Williams DREW 6 Walworth
17.07.78 Ken Jones L PTS 6 Mayfair
12.10.78 Trevor Cattouse W PTS 8 Wimbledon
23.11.78 Eddie Vierling W RSC 7 Wimbledon
18.01.79 Bonny McKenzie L PTS 8 Wimbledon
06.02.79 Johnny Waldron L PTS 8 Wembley
27.02.79 Danny Lawford L PTS 8 Southend
15.03.79 Bob Young W RTD 3 Wimbledon
24.04.79 Steve Taylor W RTD 7 Southend
29.05.79 Alex Tompkins L PTS 8 Southend
18.09.79 Joey Williams W PTS 8 Lewisham
29.10.79 Lloyd James W RSC 5 Hove
19.11.79 Alex Tompkins W PTS 8 Lewisham
28.01.80 Robert Amory W PTS 8 Rotterdam
24.04.80 Ken Jones W PTS 8 Queensway
22.09.80 Carlton Benoit W PTS 10 Lewisham
(*Vacant Southern Area L. Heavyweight Title*)
17.10.80 John Odhiambo L PTS 8 Copenhagen
20.01.81 Danny Lawford W PTS 8 Bethnal Green
23.03.81 Dennis Andries L PTS 10 Mayfair
(*Southern Area L. Heavyweight Title Defence*)
28.05.81 Pat McCann L PTS 8 Wimbledon
28.09.81 Alex Tompkins L PTS 8 Lewisham
16.02.82 Trevor Cattouse L RTD 3 Lewisham
14.04.82 Keith Bristol L CO 4 Strand
07.02.83 Jonjo Greene L RSC 5 Brighton
Summary: 27 contests, won 14, drew 1, lost 12

Gary Champion
Maidenhead. *Born* Dagenham 14.09.60
L. Welterweight
Manager G. Holmes
Previous Amateur Club West Ham
Divisional Honours E Counties Featherweight R/U 1978; E Counties L. Welterweight Champion 1980

22.02.83 Chris Harvey W PTS 6 Bethnal Green
22.03.84 Neil Patterson W PTS 6 Maidenhead
31.05.84 Ron Shinkwin L CO 6 Basildon
Summary: 3 contests, won 2, lost 1

Paul Chance

Wednesbury. *Born* Wednesbury 15.09.58
Former Undefeated Midlands Area Lightweight Champion
Manager (Self)
Previous Amateur Club Bilston Golden Gloves
National Honours Schools Title 1975; Junior ABA Title 1974 – 1975; Young England Rep.
Divisional Honours M Counties Bantamweight Champion 1976 – 1977

05.07.77 Malcolm McHugh **W** RSC 3 Wolverhampton
20.09.77 Don Aageson **W** RSC 2 Wolverhampton
18.10.77 Paul Clemit **W** PTS 8 Wolverhampton
31.10.77 Kenny Matthews **W** PTS 6 Birmingham
30.11.77 Tony Kerr **W** PTS 6 Wolverhampton
23.01.78 Gerry O'Neill **W** PTS 6 Wolverhampton
13.02.78 Kenny Matthews **W** CO 4 Birmingham
06.03.78 Steve Henderson **W** RSC 7 Wolverhampton
04.04.78 Gene McGarrigale **W** CO 1 Wolverhampton
18.04.78 Jeff Pritchard **W** PTS 8 Wolverhampton
18.09.78 Mark Bliss **W** PTS 8 Wolverhampton
31.10.78 George Sutton **W** PTS 8 Wolverhampton
22.01.79 Tommy Wright **W** PTS 8 Wolverhampton
05.03.79 Billy Rabbitt **W** RSC 4 Wolverhampton
10.04.79 Najib Daho **W** PTS 8 Wolverhampton
16.05.79 Mohammed Bounadka **W** PTS 8 Wolverhampton
18.09.79 Bingo Crooks **W** PTS 8 Wolverhampton
29.10.79 Des Gwilliam **W** PTS 10 Wolverhampton
(*Midlands Area Lightweight Title Challenge*)
21.01.80 Kevin Quinn **W** PTS 8 Wolverhampton
10.03.80 Willie Booth **W** PTS 10 Wolverhampton
29.05.80 Bingo Crooks **L** CO 9 Wolverhampton
(*Midlands Area Lightweight Title Defence*)
27.09.80 Winston Spencer **L** RSC 1 Wembley
30.10.80 Johnny Burns **W** PTS 8 Wolverhampton
01.12.80 Martin Galeozzie **W** RTD 6 Wolverhampton
13.04.81 Peter Harrison **W** PTS 8 Wolverhampton
28.04.81 Lance Williams **L** CO 8 Kensington
27.10.81 Tyrell Wilson **W** CO 2 Wolverhampton
24.11.81 Najib Daho **W** PTS 8 Wolverhampton
25.01.82 Mickey Baker **W** PTS 10 Wolverhampton
(*Vacant Midlands Area Lightweight Title*)
15.03.82 Lance Williams **L** PTS 10 Wolverhampton
24.05.82 Richard Nova **W** RSC 5 Wolverhampton
09.06.82 Chris Sanigar **L** RSC 8 Bristol
19.10.82 Lloyd Christie **L** RSC 1 Wolverhampton
21.03.83 John Lindo **W** PTS 8 Nottingham
28.03.83 Steve Tempro **W** PTS 8 Wolverhampton
27.04.83 Dan Myers **W** PTS 8 Wolverhampton
23.05.83 Gunther Roomes **L** RSC 6 Mayfair
20.09.83 Mickey Baker **W** PTS 8 Dudley
01.11.83 Ray Cattouse DREW 8 Dudley
10.02.84 George Feeney **L** PTS 12 Dudley
(*British Lightweight Title Challenge*)
Summary: 40 contests, won 31, drew 1, lost 8

Mick Chmilowskyj
Universal Pictorial Press

Ian Chantler (Ashton)
St. Helens. *Born* St. Helens 13.06.60
Welterweight
Manager P. Dwyer
Previous Amateur Club Lowe House

21.06.82 Elvis Morton W RSC 3 Liverpool
30.06.82 Kid Murray W PTS 6 Liverpool
23.09.82 Tony Brown L PTS 8 Liverpool
05.10.82 Tony Brown W PTS 8 Liverpool
18.10.82 Billy Ahearne W RSC 3 Blackpool
06.12.82 Lee Hartshorn L PTS 8 Manchester
20.01.83 Robert Armstrong W RTD 1 Birkenhead
28.01.83 Geoff Pegler L PTS 8 Swansea
14.02.83 Billy Ahearne W RSC 6 Liverpool
04.03.83 Danny Garrison W CO 5 Queensferry
25.03.83 Martin Patrick L PTS 8 Bloomsbury
29.04.83 Paul Mitchell L PTS 8 Liverpool
17.10.83 Gavin Stirrup L PTS 8 Manchester
06.12.83 Rocky Kelly L RSC 4 Kensington
06.04.84 Jim McIntosh L DIS 3 Edinburgh
12.06.84 Ray Murray W RSC 2 St. Helens
Summary: 16 contests, won 8, lost 8

Eddie Chatterton
Liverpool. *Born* Liverpool 08.06.59
L. Heavyweight
Manager B. Macdonald
Previous Amateur Club Golden Gloves

05.03.84 Paul Heatley DREW 6 Liverpool
30.04.84 Alan Price L PTS 6 Rhyl
Summary: 2 contests, drew 1, lost 1

(Clive) Cornelius Chisholm
Wolverhampton. *Born* Jamaica 05.12.59
Welterweight
Manager M. Sendell
Previous Amateur Club Wolverhampton

25.04.83 Alex Brown L PTS 6 Acton
27.09.83 John Daly W PTS 6 Stoke
12.10.83 Dan Myers W CO 6 Evesham
12.05.84 Terry Magee L RTD 3 Hanley
Summary: 4 contests, won 2, lost 2

Mick Chmilowskyj
Dagenham. *Born* Hackney 17.05.58
Heavyweight
Manager D. Mancini
Previous Amateur Club Dagenham
Divisional Honours NW London Heavyweight R/U 1976

03.12.79 Harry Pompey Allen W CO 2 Marylebone
04.02.80 Kenny March W RSC 2 Hammersmith
17.03.80 Colin Flute W RSC 2 Mayfair
01.04.80 David Fry L RSC 6 Wembley
08.12.80 Eddie Vierling W RSC 1 Piccadilly
16.02.81 Hughroy Currie L PTS 6 Southwark
13.04.81 Joe Christle W RSC 5 Southwark
14.09.81 Hughroy Currie W PTS 6 Mayfair
29.10.81 Eddie Cooper W CO 1 Walthamstow
26.01.82 Martin Nee L RSC 1 Hornsey
01.04.82 Funso Banjo L RSC 6 Walthamstow
18.10.82 Manny Gabriel W RSC 2 Southwark
07.12.82 Funso Banjo L PTS 8 Kensington
04.03.83 Werner Peltz L CO 4 Cologne
14.04.83 Hughroy Currie L CO 1 Basildon
Summary: 15 contests, won 8, lost 7

Errol Christie
Coventry. *Born* Leicester 29.06.63
Middleweight
Manager B. McCarthy
Previous Amateur Club Standard Triumph
National Honours Schools Titles 1976 – 1979; Junior ABA Titles 1979 – 1980; NABC Titles 1979 – 1981; Young England Rep./England Int.; ABA L. Middleweight Champion 1981; Euro. Junior Gold 1982
Divisional Honours M Counties L. Middleweight Champion 1982

18.11.82 Terry Matthews W RTD 3 Coventry
09.12.82 Jimmy Ellis W RSC 3 Bloomsbury
17.02.83 Harlein Holden W RSC 1 Coventry
21.04.83 Sam Leonard W CO 1 Letchworth
18.05.83 Lino Cajins W RSC 1 Bloomsbury
13.06.83 Vince Gajny W RSC 2 Coventry
24.09.83 Robert Thomas W PTS 6 New Jersey
28.09.83 Fred Reed W RSC 3 Detroit
15.10.83 Doug James W RSC 4 Coventry
01.02.84 Joel Bonnetaz W RSC 3 Bloomsbury
23.02.84 Dexter Bowman W RSC 2 Digbeth
25.04.84 Stacy McSwain W RSC 5 Muswell Hill
15.06.84 Stan White W RSC 5 Las Vegas
Summary: 13 contests, won 13

Errol Christie
Douglas Baton

Lloyd Christie
Wolverhampton. *Born* London 28.02.62
Welterweight
Manager M. Sendell
Previous Amateur Club Standard Triumph

19.01.81 Steve Tempro W CO 1 Birmingham
02.02.81 Gerry Beard W PTS 4 Nottingham
10.02.81 Gary Buckle W RSC 4 Wolverhampton
05.03.81 Jimmy Bunclark L PTS 6 Liverpool
17.03.81 Paul Clemit W RSC 1 Wolverhampton
24.03.81 Gary Brooks W CO 2 Bethnal Green
28.04.81 Colin Derrick L RSC 1 Kensington
22.06.81 George Peacock L RSC 6 Glasgow
07.10.81 Dennis Sullivan W CO 3 Solihull
19.11.81 Tony Willis L PTS 6 Liverpool
09.12.81 Colin Wake W RSC 7 Piccadilly
19.12.81 Jean-Marie Toutai L PTS 8 Dunkirk
21.02.82 Martin McGough W RSC 3 Birmingham
01.03.82 Robbie Robinson L PTS 8 Preston
05.04.82 Terry Marsh DREW 8 Bloomsbury
14.04.82 Gary Knight L RSC 5 Strand
25.06.82 John Muwanga L RTD 6 Hankoo
19.10.82 Paul Chance W RSC 1 Wolverhampton
26.10.82 Ricky Beaumont W PTS 8 Hull
08.12.82 Dave Allen L PTS 8 Piccadilly
24.01.83 Joey Frost W RSC 4 Bradford
16.02.83 Colin Power W RSC 6 Muswell Hill
24.02.83 Saad Skouma W PTS 8 Paris
11.03.83 Fred Coranson L PTS 6 Petite-Synthe
15.04.83 Jean-Marie Toutai L PTS 8 Bethune
19.05.83 Helier Custos W CO 8 Paris
09.02.84 Moussa Mukandjo L PTS 8 Geneva
24.02.84 John Munduga L RSC 6 Hamburg
10.05.84 Kostas Petrou L PTS 12 Digbeth
(*Midlands Area Welterweight Title Challenge & Final Elim. British Welterweight Title*)
Summary: 29 contests, won 14, drew 1, lost 14

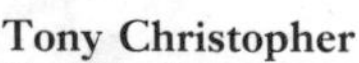
Tony Christopher
Coalville. *Born* Leicester 04.04.64
Lightweight
Manager J. Griffin
Previous Amateur Club Braunstone

30.09.83 Steve Swiftie W PTS 6 Leicester
Summary: 1 contest, won 1

Graham Kid Clarke
Derek Rowe (Photos) Ltd

Sam Church
Bradford. *Born* Bradford 04.03.59
L. Welterweight
Manager J. Celebanski
Previous Amateur Club Bradford Police

02.07.81 Phil O'Hare W PTS 4 Pudsey
07.10.82 Peter Phillips L PTS 6 Morley
25.10.82 Dave Markey W RSC 2 Airdrie
14.02.83 Stan Atherton L PTS 6 Liverpool
25.02.83 Gary Williams L RSC 2 Doncaster
13.06.83 Dave Foley L PTS 6 Doncaster
Summary: 6 contests, won 2, lost 4

Graham Kid Clarke
Cardiff. *Born* Cardiff 27.01.64
Bantamweight
Manager M. Williams
Previous Amateur Club St Josephs
National Honours Schools Title 1979

26.10.82 Howard Williams W PTS 6 Newport
23.11.82 Dave Pratt W PTS 6 Wolverhampton
06.12.82 Howard Williams W PTS 6 Bristol
13.04.83 Clinton Campbell W PTS 6 Evesham
22.09.83 Clinton Campbell W PTS 6 Cardiff
09.11.83 Dai Williams DREW 6 Evesham
01.03.84 Billy Hardy L PTS 8 Queensway
06.04.84 Billy Hardy L RSC 7 Watford
30.06.84 Roy Webb L PTS 8 Belfast
Summary: 9 contests, won 5, drew 1, lost 3

Walter Clayton

Sheffield. *Born* Sheffield 27.07.61
L. Welterweight
Manager B. Ingle
Previous Amateur Club St. Thomas's
National Honours Junior ABA Title 1977

22.10.79 Wally Stockings W RSC 4 Nottingham
27.10.79 Duncan Hamilton W PTS 6 Barnsley
10.12.79 Julian Boustead DREW 4 Torquay
09.01.80 Tyrrel Wilson W RTD 1 Burslem
22.01.80 Wally Stockings W RSC 5 Piccadilly
12.02.80 Norman Morton W PTS 8 Sheffield
13.03.80 Von Reid W RSC 6 Birkenhead
09.04.80 Vernon Entertainer Vanriel W PTS 8 Burslem
22.04.80 Mike Clemow W RSC 8 Sheffield
20.05.80 George Sutton W RSC 5 Southend
29.09.80 Dave Taylor W PTS 8 Chesterfield
03.12.80 Alan Burrows W PTS 6 Sheffield
09.03.81 Lance Williams L RSC 5 Mayfair
06.05.81 Martin Bolton W RSC 2 Chesterfield
10.05.81 Ray Heaney W RSC 3 Dublin
17.06.81 Eric Wood W DIS 4 Sheffield
07.09.81 Tony Carroll W PTS 8 Liverpool
23.09.81 Steve McLeod W RSC 4 Sheffield
26.10.81 Winston Spencer W PTS 8 Mayfair
16.11.81 Dave Sullivan W PTS 8 Liverpool
19.12.81 Dan M'Putu L CO 1 Dunkirk
17.03.82 Vernon Entertainer Vanriel DREW 8 Kensington
21.04.82 Tim Moloney DREW 8 Brighton
05.05.82 Gerry Beard W PTS 8 Solihull
21.05.82 Dave Finigan W RTD 3 Sheffield
28.06.82 Brian Baronet L PTS 8 Durban
14.11.82 P. J. Davitt L PTS 8 Navan
14.03.83 Tony Brown L PTS 10 Sheffield (*Vacant Central Area L. Welterweight Title*)
Summary: 28 contests, won 20, drew 3, lost 5

Steve Cleak

Porthcawl. *Born* Porth 10.06.57
Featherweight
Manager (Self)
Previous Amateur Club Llandaff
National Honours Welsh Int.

04.09.78 Pip Coleman L PTS 6 Barry
21.09.78 Ian Murray W PTS 6 Caerphilly
27.09.78 Alec Irvine W PTS 6 Evesham
15.11.78 Pip Coleman L RSC 2 Merthyr
11.12.78 Mick Whelan W PTS 6 Piccadilly
18.01.79 John Cooper DREW 6 Wimbledon
27.03.79 John Cooper L PTS 8 Southend
13.05.79 Terry McKeown L PTS 8 Glasgow
21.05.79 Gary Lucas L PTS 8 Piccadilly
04.06.79 John Cooper W PTS 8 Piccadilly
18.06.79 Gerry O'Neill L PTS 8 Piccadilly
24.09.79 Gary Lucas L PTS 8 Piccadilly
15.10.79 Selvin Bell W PTS 6 Windsor
05.11.79 Steve Henderson W PTS 8 Piccadilly
29.11.79 Mike Pickett W PTS 6 Ebbw Vale
13.12.79 John Cooper W PTS 8 Wimbledon
28.02.80 Glyn Davies W PTS 8 Ebbw Vale
19.03.80 Alec Irvine L PTS 8 Solihull
17.04.80 Lee Graham W PTS 8 Piccadilly
16.06.80 Steve Henderson W PTS 8 Piccadilly
01.07.80 Glyn Davies W RSC 5 Swindon
11.09.80 Paul Keers L RSC 4 Hartlepool
20.10.80 Roy Somer L PTS 8 Rotterdam
28.01.81 Mohammed Younis W PTS 8 Swindon
14.09.81 Mark West L RSC 6 Mayfair
03.11.81 Paul Huggins DREW 8 Kensington
09.02.82 Paul Huggins L CO 2 Kensington
10.03.82 Ian Murray L PTS 8 Birmingham
19.04.82 Jimmy Bott W PTS 8 Mayfair
24.04.82 Austin Owens L RTD 1 Southwark
07.02.83 Muhammad Lovelock W PTS 6 Brighton
21.02.83 Dave George W PTS 8 Glasgow
04.04.83 Ray Gilbody L DIS 6 Kensington
20.06.83 Mark West DREW 8 Piccadilly
Summary: 34 contests, won 16, drew 3, lost 15

Mark Cleverly

Southampton. *Born* Southampton 04.10.60
Heavyweight
Manager J. Bishop
Previous Amateur Club Southampton
Divisional Honours S Counties S. Heavyweight Champion 1982

07.03.83 Andrew Gerrard W PTS 6 Piccadilly
21.03.83 John Fallon W RSC 3 Piccadilly
21.04.83 Andrew Gerrard L PTS 6 Piccadilly
22.09.83 Barry Ellis L PTS 6 Strand
24.10.83 Dave Garside L PTS 6 Mayfair
Summary: 5 contests, won 2, lost 3

Danny Clinton

Tottenham. *Born* Hackney 08.02.61
L. Heavyweight
Manager H. Holland
Previous Amateur Club New Enterprise

09.05.84 Nigel Shingles L RSC 2 Mayfair
Summary: 1 contest, lost 1

Chris Coady

Manchester. *Born* Manchester 25.05.56
Middleweight
Manager J. Smith
Previous Amateur Club Manchester YMCA
Divisional Honours E Lancs L. Middleweight Champion 1975; E Lancs Middleweight Champion 1978

13.05.79 Redmond Everard **W** RSC 4 Edgbaston
04.06.79 Ron Pearce DREW 6 Liverpool
26.06.79 Davey Armstrong **L** PTS 6 Wembley
20.09.79 Redmond Everard **W** CO 4 Liverpool
08.10.79 George Danahar **L** PTS 8 Piccadilly
23.10.79 Paul Jones **W** RSC 3 Blackpool
19.11.79 Paul Jones **W** CO 2 Stockport
21.09.81 Brian Anderson **L** RTD 3 Manchester
13.10.81 Joey Frost **L** PTS 8 Blackpool
02.12.81 Leo Mulhern **W** CO 7 Manchester
01.02.82 Mick Morris **L** PTS 8 Manchester
06.03.82 Jimmy Ellis **L** RSC 3 Farnsworth
26.09.83 Cliff Curtis DREW 8 Manchester
17.10.83 Winston Wray **W** PTS 6 Manchester
05.12.83 Steve Johnson **L** RSC 5 Manchester
21.03.84 Stuart Robinson **L** PTS 6 Solihull
26.03.84 Stuart Robinson **L** PTS 6 Barnsley
14.05.84 Mike Farghaly **L** RSC 8 Manchester
15.06.84 Stuart Robinson **L** PTS 6 Liverpool
30.06.84 Chris Reid **L** RSC 2 Belfast
Summary: 20 contests, won 6, drew 2, lost 12

Charlie Coke

Croydon. *Born* Jamaica 23.01.59
Featherweight
Manager D. Read
Previous Amateur Club S.P.G.

27.04.83 Michael Marsden **L** PTS 6 Stoke
18.05.83 Graham Brett **W** RSC 6 Bloomsbury
06.12.83 Stuart Carmichael **W** PTS 6 Southend
26.01.84 Tony Borg **W** RSC 5 Strand
17.04.84 Muhammad Lovelock **W** PTS 6 Merton
Summary: 5 contests, won 4, lost 1

Ian Colbeck

Hartlepool. *Born* Darlington 27.03.62
Bantamweight
Manager T. Calligham
Previous Amateur Club Darlington

20.09.83 Kevin Downer **W** PTS 6 Mayfair
14.12.83 John Drummond **W** PTS 6 Stoke
25.01.84 Dave Boy McAuley **L** PTS 6 Belfast
Summary: 3 contests, won 2, lost 1

Liam Coleman
Jack Hickes

Liam Coleman

Leeds. *Born* Newry 23.09.60
N. Ireland L. Heavyweight Champion
Manager P. Byrne
Previous Amateur Club Market District
National Honours Schools Titles 1974 & 1977; Junior ABA Title 1977
Divisional Honours N Counties Middleweight Champion 1978

28.02.79 Mick Fellingham **W** PTS 6 Harrogate
24.04.79 Mick Fellingham **W** PTS 6 Glasgow
06.06.79 Joe Jackson **W** PTS 4 Bedworth
18.06.79 Steve Babbs **W** PTS 6 Piccadilly
24.10.79 George Lewis **W** PTS 8 Norwich
19.05.80 Roy Skeldon DREW 6 Bradford
24.09.80 Rupert Christie **L** PTS 8 Burslem
16.10.80 Alek Penarski **L** PTS 8 Bolton
29.10.80 Tommy Jones **W** PTS 6 Burslem
13.11.80 Tommy Taylor **L** PTS 8 Stafford
01.12.80 Cordwell Hylton **W** PTS 6 Wolverhampton
17.02.81 Trevor Kerr **W** PTS 10 Leeds (*Vacant N. Ireland L. Heavyweight Title*)
28.04.81 Greg Evans **W** PTS 8 Leeds
16.09.81 Dennis Andries **L** RSC 6 Burslem
20.10.81 Bonny McKenzie **W** PTS 8 Leeds
30.11.81 Trevor Kerr **W** RTD 6 Enniskillen (*N. Ireland L. Heavyweight Title Defence*)
30.03.82 Chris Lawson **L** PTS 8 Leeds

26.04.82 Antonio Harris **W** PTS 8 Edgbaston
07.06.82 Antonio Harris **L** PTS 10 Edgbaston (*Elim. British L. Heavyweight Title*)
02.03.83 Keith Bristol **L** PTS 6 Belfast
17.12.83 Patrick Lumumba **L** RTD 1 Mariehamn
06.02.84 Devon Bailey **L** RSC 7 Mayfair
28.04.84 Rolf Rocchigiani DREW 6 Hamburg
Summary: 23 contests, won 12, drew 2, lost 9

Tony Connolly

West Ham. *Born* London 17.06.61
Featherweight
Manager F. Warren
Previous Amateur Club St. Georges
National Honours Schools Title 1977; Junior ABA Titles 1977 – 1978; NABC Titles 1978 – 1979; Young England Rep.
Divisional Honours NE London Featherweight Champion 1980; London Lightweight Champion 1981

18.05.82 Bobby Finlay **W** RSC 4 Bethnal Green
28.09.82 Ray Plant **W** PTS 6 Bethnal Green
16.11.82 Gerry Beard **L** PTS 8 Bethnal Green
13.10.83 John Mwaimu **W** RSC 2 Bloomsbury
02.11.83 Billy Joe Dee **W** PTS 6 Bloomsbury
Summary: 5 contests, won 4, lost 1

Terry Connor

Forest Hill. *Born* London 20.04.62
Lightweight
Manager P. Oliphant
Previous Amateur Club Fisher
National Honours Junior ABA Title 1978; NABC Title 1978

17.02.83 Graeme Griffin **W** RSC 3 Coventry
25.04.83 Johnny Grant **L** PTS 6 Southwark
Summary: 2 contests, won 1, lost 1

James Cook

Peckham. *Born* Jamaica 17.05.59
Southern Area Middleweight Champion
Manager W. Wynter
Previous Amateur Club East Lane
Divisional Honours SE London Middleweight R/U 1977; SE London Middleweight Champion 1981 – 1982

20.10.82 Mick Courtney **W** PTS 6 Strand
01.11.82 Gary Gething **W** RSC 2 Piccadilly
19.01.83 Paul Shell **W** PTS 8 Birmingham
03.02.83 Jimmy Price **L** PTS 6 Bloomsbury
09.03.83 Willie Wright **W** PTS 8 Solihull
14.04.83 Dudley McKenzie **W** PTS 8 Basildon
16.05.83 Eddie Smith **W** RSC 6 Manchester
23.11.83 Vince Gajny **W** RTD 6 Solihull
05.06.84 T. P. Jenkins **W** RSC 9 Kensington (*Vacant Southern Area Middleweight Title*)
Summary: 9 contests, won 8, lost 1

Paul Cook

Bethnal Green. *Born* London 05.10.58
L. Welterweight
Manager A. Kasler
Previous Amateur Club West Ham
National Honours Junior ABA Title 1974
Divisional Honours NE London Lightweight R/U 1981

28.09.82 Dave Springer **W** RSC 2 Bethnal Green
16.11.82 Johnny Grant **W** RSC 2 Bethnal Green
21.02.83 Edward Lloyd **W** RSC 1 Mayfair
22.09.83 Bobby Welburn **W** RSC 4 Strand
06.02.84 Mo Hussein **L** CO 3 Bethnal Green
Summary: 5 contests, won 4, lost 1

James Cook

Tommy Cook
Larkhall. *Born* Larkhall 22.02.63
L. Welterweight
Manager E. Rea
Previous Amateur Club Lanark Welfare

15.02.82 Eddie Glass **W** PTS 6 Glasgow
22.02.82 Kevin Pritchard **W** PTS 6 Glasgow
08.03.82 Paul Wake **W** PTS 6 Hamilton
26.04.82 Ray Ross **W** PTS 6 Glasgow
07.06.82 Ray Ross **W** PTS 6 Glasgow
30.06.82 Ray Hood L PTS 8 Liverpool
25.10.82 Andy Thomas **W** PTS 8 Airdrie
29.11.82 Terry Smith L RTD 1 Southwark
31.01.83 Terry Smith L PTS 6 Southwark
07.03.83 John Daly **W** RSC 4 Glasgow
11.04.83 Dave Heaver **W** PTS 8 Glasgow
23.05.83 Ken Foreman L RSC 5 Glasgow
Summary: 12 contests, won 8, lost 4

James Cooke
Coventry. *Born* Coventry 25.10.57
Lightweight
Manager P. Lynch
Previous Amateur Club Tile Hill
National Honours Schools & Junior ABA Titles 1973 – 1974; Young England Rep.; Irish Featherweight Champion 1976
Divisional Honours ABA Featherweight R/U 1975

07.02.78 Philip Morris **W** RSC 5 Coventry
06.03.78 Mark Hill **W** CO 2 Wolverhampton
03.05.78 Eric Wood **W** PTS 8 Solihull
23.05.78 Jeff Pritchard DREW 8 Leicester
22.01.79 Brian Snagg **W** PTS 8 Wolverhampton
26.04.79 Benny Purdy **W** RTD 5 Liverpool
13.05.79 Jeff Pritchard **W** RSC 3 Edgbaston
10.09.79 Ceri Collins **W** RSC 8 Birmingham
29.10.79 Bingo Crooks **W** DIS 7 Wolverhampton
28.01.80 Tony Carroll **W** PTS 8 Edgbaston
13.06.83 Keith Foreman **W** PTS 6 Coventry
Summary: 11 contests, won 10, drew 1

Steve Cooke
Southend. *Born* Rochford 24.08.65
Lightweight
Manager M. Williamson
Previous Amateur Club Southend

06.12.83 Dave Springer **W** PTS 6 Southend
27.03.84 Clinton Campbell **W** PTS 6 Southend
01.05.84 Con Cronin DREW 6 Maidstone
14.05.84 Hugh Sugar Kelly L CO 1 Glasgow
Summary: 4 contests, won 2, drew 1, lost 1

Mickey Cotton
Doncaster. *Born* Sheffield 23.02.60
L. Welterweight
Manager K. Richardson
Previous Amateur Club Rotherham Baths

05.12.83 John Faulkner L PTS 6 Nottingham
16.04.83 Claude Rossi L RSC 2 Nottingham
11.06.84 Dave Kettlewell L CO 2 Manchester
Summary: 3 contests, lost 3

Mick Courtney
Chorleywood. *Born* London 27.04.59
L. Middleweight
Manager D. Smith
Previous Amateur Club Finchley
National Honours NABC Titles 1976 – 1977; Young England Rep./England Int.; Euro. Junior Silver 1978
Divisional Honours H Counties L. Middleweight Champion 1977; H Counties L. Middleweight R/U 1978 – 1979; NW London Middleweight Champion 1980

14.06.82 Joe Allotey L PTS 6 Mayfair
13.08.82 Joey Saunders **W** PTS 6 Strand
07.09.82 Phil Williams **W** RSC 4 Hornsey
14.09.82 Dennis Sheehan **W** PTS 8 Strand
20.10.82 James Cook L PTS 6 Strand
25.10.82 John McGlynn **W** PTS 8 Mayfair
29.11.82 Jack Sharp L PTS 6 Southwark
15.12.82 Arthur Davis **W** PTS 8 Queensway
07.04.83 Phil O'Hare **W** PTS 8 Strand
20.04.83 Martin Patrick DREW 8 Muswell Hill
04.10.83 Nigel Thomas **W** PTS 6 Bethnal Green
17.11.83 Randy Henderson **W** PTS 8 Basildon
16.02.84 Arthur Davis **W** RSC 6 Basildon
11.04.84 Cameron Lithgow **W** PTS 10 Kensington
Summary: 14 contests, won 10, drew 1, lost 3

Allan Coveley
Bethnal Green. *Born* Bethnal Green 16.08.61
Bantamweight
Manager B. McCarthy
Previous Amateur Club Repton
National Honours Junior ABA Title 1978; NABC Title 1980; English Int.
Divisional Honours NE London Bantamweight Champion 1981; London Bantamweight Champion 1982–1983; ABA Bantamweight R/U 1982

01.02.84 Billy Joe Dee **W** RSC 3 Bloomsbury
21.03.84 John Mwaimu **W** RSC 4 Bloomsbury
25.04.84 Bobby McDermott **W** PTS 6 Muswell Hill
Summary: 3 contests, won 3

Allan Coveley
Gloucester Photo Agency

Harry Cowap

Balham. *Born* Dublin 24.08.58
L. Heavyweight
Manager D. Mancini
Previous Amateur Club Battersea
Divisional Honours SW London Middleweight R/U 1982

13.10.82 Ian Lazarus W PTS 6 Walthamstow
26.10.82 Joey Williams W RSC 1 Bethnal Green
22.11.82 Glenroy Taylor W PTS 6 Mayfair
25.01.83 Dave Scott DREW 6 Bethnal Green
10.02.83 Glenroy Taylor W PTS 6 Walthamstow
09.03.83 Ian Lazarus W PTS 6 Solihull
21.03.83 Keith James L RTD 4 Mayfair
20.09.83 Romal Ambrose W PTS 8 Piccadilly
17.10.83 Billy Cassidy W PTS 8 Southwark
28.11.83 Alan Ash L RTD 4 Southwark
03.02.84 Alex Romeo W PTS 8 Maidenhead
22.03.84 Paul Shell W RTD 7 Maidenhead
17.04.84 Alan Ash W PTS 8 Merton
Summary: 13 contests, won 10, drew 1, lost 2

Davey Cox

Northampton. *Born* Hastings 07.10.59
Welterweight
Manager J. Cox
Previous Amateur Club Northampton

09.02.82 Errol Dennis L PTS 6 Wolverhampton
15.03.82 Errol Dennis W PTS 6 Wolverhampton
05.04.82 Errol Dennis L PTS 6 Nottingham
26.04.82 Mark Crouch W RSC 4 Leicester
24.05.82 Elvis Morton W PTS 6 Wolverhampton
07.09.82 Rocky Severino L PTS 6 Crewe
20.09.82 Gary Buckle L PTS 6 Wolverhampton
06.10.82 Gary Buckle L PTS 6 Stoke
10.11.82 Elvis Morton DREW 6 Evesham
13.12.82 Elvis Morton W PTS 6 Wolverhampton
19.01.83 Dave Heaver W PTS 6 Stoke
26.01.83 Dalton Jordan W PTS 6 Stoke
07.02.83 Tony Rabbetts DREW 6 Marylebone
15.02.83 Kid Murray L PTS 6 Wolverhampton
25.03.83 Tony Rabbetts L PTS 6 Bloomsbury
13.04.83 Mark Hill W PTS 6 Evesham
27.04.83 Mark Hill DREW 6 Wolverhampton
10.05.83 Tim Gladwish DREW 6 Southend
16.05.83 Lee Roy W RSC 6 Manchester
23.05.83 Mick Rowley L RSC 2 Mayfair
23.06.83 Steve Tempro L PTS 8 Wolverhampton
20.09.83 Gavin Stirrup L PTS 8 Dudley
12.10.83 Glyn Mitchell W RTD 6 Evesham
01.11.83 Mark Hill L PTS 6 Dudley
09.11.83 Andy O'Rawe L PTS 6 Southend
14.11.83 Jim Kelly L PTS 8 Glasgow
01.12.83 Roy Varden W CO 1 Dudley
05.12.83 Dave Heaver W CO 7 Nottingham
31.01.84 Tony Adams L CO 1 Kensington
15.03.84 Mick Dono L PTS 6 Kirkby
25.04.84 Mickey Kilgallon L RSC 5 Muswell Hill
Summary: 31 contests, won 11, drew 4, lost 16

Steve Craggs

Bedworth. *Born* Newcastle 06.08.64
Welterweight
Manager J. Griffin
Previous Amateur Club Bedworth Ex-Serv.

14.02.84 Mike Durvan W PTS 6 Wolverhampton
07.03.84 Nicky Day W PTS 6 Brighton
19.03.84 Tony Kempson W PTS 6 Bradford
31.03.84 Peter Flanagan W PTS 6 Derby
04.06.84 Granville Allen L PTS 8 Nottingham
Summary: 5 contests, won 4, lost 1

Roddy Crane

Newport. *Born* Clwyd 23.04.60
Middleweight
Manager (Self)
Previous Amateur Club Roath Youth
National Honours Welsh Int.

21.03.83 Tony Burke L RSC 3 Piccadilly
Summary: 1 contest, lost 1

Neil Crocker

Swansea. *Born* Swansea 03.02.61
L. Middleweight
Manager C. Breen
Previous Amateur Club Ragged School

08.09.83 Danny Sullivan **L** PTS 6 Queensway
06.10.83 Joe Lynch **L** CO 1 Basildon
19.12.83 Stephen Hibbs **W** RSC 1 Swansea
Summary: 3 contests, won 1, lost 2

Wayne Crolla

Manchester. *Born* Manchester 04.09.59
L. Middleweight
Manager J. Edwards
Previous Amateur Club Higher Blackley
Divisional Honours E Lancs Welterweight R/U 1979

07.12.81 Nick Riozzi **W** RSC 2 Manchester
01.02.82 Phil O'Hare **W** PTS 6 Manchester
08.02.82 Larry Monaghan **W** RTD 4 Manchester
15.02.82 Nick Riozzi **W** RSC 5 Liverpool
09.03.82 Phil O'Hare **W** PTS 6 Farnsworth
17.05.82 Glen Crump **L** RSC 4 Manchester
07.06.82 Phil O'Hare **W** PTS 6 Sheffield
28.09.82 Peter Bennett **L** RSC 3 Manchester
17.01.83 Alf Edwardes **W** PTS 6 Manchester
17.02.83 Paul Mitchell **W** PTS 6 Morley
29.03.83 Gary Petty **W** PTS 6 Hull
27.04.83 Geoff Pegler **W** PTS 8 Rhyl
25.05.83 Bert Myrie **W** PTS 8 Rhyl
20.06.83 Bert Myrie **W** PTS 8 Manchester
26.09.83 Gordon Pratt **L** PTS 8 Manchester
22.11.83 Jeff Standley **W** PTS 8 Manchester
13.02.84 Gordon Pratt **W** PTS 8 Manchester
18.04.84 Paul Mitchell **L** RSC 5 Stoke
(*Vacant Central Area L. Middleweight Title*)
18.06.84 John Ridgman **L** RSC 6 Manchester
Summary: 19 contests, won 14, lost 5

Con Cronin

Watford. *Born* Willesden 27.08.62
L. Welterweight
Manager G. Steene
Previous Amateur Club Islington

01.05.84 Steve Cooke DREW 6 Maidstone
09.05.84 Nicky Day DREW 6 Mayfair
Summary: 2 contests, drew 2

Mark Crouch

Epsom. *Born* Woking 20.09.61
L. Middleweight
Manager (Self)
Previous Amateur Club Epsom & Ewell

18.10.80 Kevin Johnson **W** PTS 6 Birmingham
21.11.80 Tommy Thomas **W** PTS 6 Crawley
12.01.81 Lee Hargie **W** RTD 3 Hove
19.01.81 Dave Finigan **L** PTS 6 Wimbledon
19.03.81 Gary Richards **W** PTS 6 Norwich
11.05.81 Delroy Pearce **L** PTS 6 Copthorne
22.09.81 Tommy Thomas **L** RTD 2 Southend
03.11.81 Ray Hood **L** CO 6 Southend
21.12.81 Kevin Johnson **L** PTS 6 Birmingham
16.02.82 Kevin Johnson **W** RSC 2 Birmingham
01.04.82 Danny Shinkwin **L** PTS 6 Walthamstow
26.04.82 Davey Cox **L** RSC 4 Leicester
21.06.82 Gary Brooks **L** PTS 6 Copthorne
23.09.82 Colin Neagle DREW 6 Wimbledon
04.11.82 Kevin Webb **W** PTS 6 Wimbledon
23.02.83 Colin Neagle **L** PTS 6 Mayfair
19.05.83 Kevin Webb **W** PTS 6 Queensway
Summary: 17 contests, won 7, drew 1, lost 9

Glen Crump

Sheffield. *Born* Sheffield 02.10.62
L. Middleweight
Manager B. Ingle
Previous Amateur Club St Thomas's

06.05.81 Dave Dunn **W** PTS 6 Chesterfield
01.06.81 Steve Brennan **W** PTS 6 Nottingham
09.07.81 Allan Jones **W** RSC 2 Dudley
23.09.81 Paul Goodwin **W** RTD 2 Sheffield
25.11.81 John Ridgman **L** RSC 3 Sheffield
05.04.82 Tony Brown **L** PTS 6 Manchester
17.05.82 Wayne Crolla **W** RSC 4 Manchester
07.06.82 Paul Costigan **W** RSC 7 Sheffield
06.12.82 Martin McGough **L** CO 6 Edgbaston
07.03.83 Winston Wray **W** RSC 4 Liverpool
Summary: 10 contests, won 7, lost 3

Hughroy Currie
Derek Rowe (Photos) Ltd

Terry Culshaw
Liverpool. *Born* Huyton 17.04.60
Welterweight
Manager R. Smith
Previous Amateur Club Huyton
Divisional Honours W Lancs Welterweight Champion 1983

15.06.84 Elvis Morton **W** RSC 6 Liverpool
Summary: 1 contest, won 1

(Trevor) Hughroy Currie
Catford. *Born* Jamaica 09.02.59
Heavyweight
Manager M. Hope
Previous Amateur Club Catford & District

16.02.81 Mick Chmilowskyj **W** PTS 6 Southwark
14.09.81 Mick Chmilowskyj **L** PTS 6 Mayfair
21.09.81 Paddy Finn **L** PTS 6 Wolverhampton
05.10.81 Steve Gee **W** PTS 6 Birmingham
12.10.81 Joe Christle **L** RSC 2 Bloomsbury
12.11.81 Jim Burns **DREW** 6 Stafford
05.05.82 Manny Gabriel **W** PTS 8 Solihull
18.05.82 Martin Herdman **L** RSC 4 Bethnal Green
18.10.82 Dave Garside **W** RTD 4 Southwark
22.02.83 Derek Simpkin **W** PTS 6 Bethnal Green
14.04.83 Mick Chmilowskyj **W** CO 1 Basildon
06.10.83 Adrian Elliott **W** RSC 5 Basildon
06.04.84 Alfredo Evangelista **W** PTS 8 Bilbao
13.05.84 Funso Banjo **L** PTS 10 Wembley
(Vacant Southern Area Heavyweight Title & Final Elim. British Heavyweight Title)
Summary: 14 contests, won 8, drew 1, lost 5

Cliff Curtis
Swindon. *Born* Chorley 15.11.61
Middleweight
Manager R. Porter
Previous Amateur Club Swindon

18.11.80 Mohammed Ben **W** PTS 6 Windsor
28.01.81 Dave Dunn **W** PTS 6 Swindon
11.03.81 Neville Wilson **W** PTS 6 Evesham
18.09.81 Gerry White **W** PTS 8 Swindon
22.10.81 Arthur Davis **L** PTS 6 Piccadilly
08.12.81 Mickey Harrison **W** PTS 6 Southend
26.01.82 Mickey Harrison **W** PTS 6 Hornsey
16.02.82 Keith James **L** PTS 6 Southend
08.03.82 Robbie Turner **W** PTS 6 Mayfair
01.04.82 George Danahar **L** RSC 6 Walthamstow
14.09.82 Martin Patrick **L** RTD 6 Southend
25.01.83 R. W. Smith **L** CO 2 Bethnal Green
16.04.83 Steve Ward **W** PTS 6 Bristol
16.05.83 Wayne Hawkins **L** PTS 6 Birmingham
16.09.83 Winston Burnett **L** PTS 6 Swindon
26.09.83 Chris Coady **DREW** 8 Manchester
06.10.83 John Mortensen **L** RTD 3 Copenhagen
Summary: 17 contests, won 8, drew 1, lost 8

Najib Daho

Najib Daho
Manchester. *Born* Morocco 13.01.59
Former Undefeated Central Area Lightweight Champion
Manager (Self)
Previous Amateur Club Manchester YMCA

17.05.77 Kevin Sheehan **W** RSC 2 Wolverhampton
31.05.77 Tony Zeni **L** PTS 6 Kensington
13.06.77 Roy Varden **L** PTS 6 Manchester
05.07.77 Winston Spencer **L** RSC 5 Wolverhampton
03.10.77 Paul Clemit **W** PTS 8 Barnsley
10.10.77 Don Burgin **W** PTS 8 Marton
24.10.77 Mick Bell **DREW** 8 Manchester
02.11.77 George McGurk **L** PTS 8 Newcastle
05.12.77 Mick Bell **W** PTS 8 Manchester

CONTINUED OVERLEAF

18.01.78 Steve Early L PTS 6 Solihull
12.10.78 Stan Atherton L PTS 6 Liverpool
24.10.78 Selvin Bell W PTS 6 Blackpool
02.11.78 Terry Welch W PTS 6 Liverpool
30.11.78 Tommy Wright W PTS 6 Caister
11.12.78 Vernon Penprase W PTS 8 Plymouth
18.12.78 Tommy Wright W PTS 8 Bradford
12.02.79 Jimmy Brown L PTS 8 Manchester
19.02.79 Martyn Galeozzie L DIS 8 Mayfair
01.03.79 Robbie Robinson L RSC 3 Liverpool
10.04.79 Paul Chance L PTS 8 Wolverhampton
17.04.79 Gerry Duffy W PTS 8 Glasgow
18.06.79 Brian Snagg W PTS 10 Manchester (*Vacant Central Area Lightweight Title*)
05.07.79 Barry Michael W PTS 8 Aberavon
12.09.79 Jimmy Brown W PTS 8 Liverpool
20.09.79 Brian Snagg W PTS 8 Liverpool
29.10.79 Lance Williams L PTS 8 Birmingham
04.12.79 Chris Sanigar W RSC 1 Wembley
09.02.80 Dan M'Putu L PTS 8 Dunkirk
14.03.80 Charm Chiteule W PTS 6 Glasgow
29.04.80 Billy Vivian W RSC 5 Piccadilly
15.05.80 Ken Buchanan L CO 7 Mayfair
01.11.80 Winston Spencer L RSC 5 Glasgow
24.11.81 Paul Chance L PTS 8 Wolverhampton
01.02.82 Alan Cooper W RTD 6 Manchester
08.12.82 Lee Graham W PTS 8 Piccadilly
21.03.83 Lee Halford W PTS 8 Piccadilly
17.05.83 Ian McLeod L PTS 8 Piccadilly
26.09.83 Mick Rowley W PTS 8 Manchester
22.11.83 Ray Hood W PTS 8 Manchester
30.01.84 Rory Burke W PTS 8 Manchester
19.03.84 Jackie Turner W RSC 5 Manchester
04.06.84 Keith Foreman W CO 5 Manchester
Summary: 42 contests, won 25, drew 1, lost 16

John Daly

Keighley. *Born* Keighley 27.12.58
Welterweight
Manager J. Celebanski
Previous Amateur Club Keighley
Divisional Honours NE Counties Featherweight S/F 1976; NE Counties L. Welterweight S/F 1978

06.04.82 Mike McKenzie W PTS 6 Leeds
22.04.82 Sean Campbell W PTS 6 Piccadilly
10.05.82 Mick Dono L PTS 6 Liverpool
31.05.82 Tyrell Wilson W PTS 6 Glasgow
18.10.82 Young Tony Carroll L PTS 6 Blackpool
25.10.82 Dave Haggarty L PTS 6 Airdrie
01.11.82 Stan Wall W PTS 6 Liverpool
18.11.82 Jeff Decker L CO 1 Coventry
07.01.83 Tony Wilkinson L PTS 6 Durham
07.03.83 Tommy Cook L RSC 4 Glasgow
29.04.83 Ron Atherton W PTS 6 Liverpool
15.09.83 Bobby Welburn W PTS 6 Liverpool
21.09.83 Frankie Lake W RTD 5 Southend
27.09.83 Cornelius Chisholm L PTS 6 Stoke
05.10.83 Peter Foster L RTD 4 Solihull
19.01.84 Billy Edwards W PTS 6 Digbeth
Summary: 16 contests, won 8, lost 8

Angelo D'Amore

Hendon. *Born* London 03.03.64
Lightweight
Manager D. Smith
Previous Amateur Club Finchley
National Honours NABC Title 1981

15.03.82 Paul Wake W PTS 6 Piccadilly
26.04.82 Craig Walsh W PTS 6 Piccadilly
18.05.82 Andy Thomas W PTS 6 Piccadilly
07.02.83 Bobby Welburn L PTS 6 Piccadilly
19.04.84 Teddy Anderson L PTS 6 Basildon
Summary: 5 contests, won 3, lost 2

George Danahar

Bethnal Green. *Born* London 27.11.56
L. Heavyweight
Manager (Self)
Previous Amateur Club Hove
Divisional Honours S Counties Middleweight R/U 1976; S Counties Middleweight Champion 1978

08.01.79 George Walker W PTS 6 Piccadilly
02.04.79 Joe Jackson W RTD 3 Piccadilly
23.04.79 Gordon George W PTS 6 Piccadilly
30.04.79 Russ Blanks W RTD 3 Mayfair
08.10.79 Chris Coady W PTS 8 Piccadilly
10.12.79 Peter Gorny W PTS 8 Piccadilly
17.03.80 Doug James W RSC 6 Mayfair
22.04.80 Herol Graham L PTS 8 Sheffield
30.04.80 Oscar Angus W PTS 8 Aylesbury
18.11.80 Davey Armstrong L RSC 2 Bethnal Green
20.10.81 Mark Kaylor L RSC 3 Bethnal Green
08.03.82 Kenny Feehan W PTS 6 Mayfair
01.04.82 Cliff Curtis W RSC 6 Walthamstow
21.04.82 Kenny Feehan W PTS 8 Brighton
27.09.82 Steve Johnson L PTS 6 Bloomsbury
29.11.82 Geoff Rymer W PTS 8 Brighton
10.02.83 John Joseph L PTS 8 Walthamstow
Summary: 17 contests, won 12, lost 5

Ranji Dastidar

Middlesbrough. *Born* Sedgefield 20.03.61
L. Middleweight
Manager J. Spensley
Previous Amateur Club North Ormesby
Divisional Honours NE Counties L. Middleweight S/F 1983

12.06.83 Jeff Standley L RSC 1 Middlesbrough
Summary: 1 contest, lost 1

Mark Davey

Wakefield. *Born* Rothwell 16.02.64
Lightweight
Manager V. Flynn
Previous Amateur Club Meanwood
National Honours NABC Titles 1980 – 1981

06.04.82 Kevin Howard **W** PTS 6 Leeds
13.05.82 Mike Bromby **W** PTS 6 Wakefield
26.05.82 Eric Wood **W** CO 3 Leeds
25.11.82 Peter Flanagan **W** PTS 6 Morley
24.01.83 Andy Thomas **W** RSC 3 Piccadilly
17.02.83 Les Remikie **W** PTS 8 Morley
11.04.83 Kevin Pritchard **W** PTS 8 Manchester
12.05.83 Kevin Pritchard **L** DIS 4 Morley
19.12.83 Keith Foreman **L** PTS 8 Bradford
Summary: 9 contests, won 7, lost 2

Floyd Davidson

Derby. *Born* Burton-on-Trent 26.12.62
Middleweight
Manager J. Griffin
Previous Amateur Club Burton

19.09.83 Jeff Standley **L** PTS 6 Nottingham
30.09.83 Dave Dunn **W** PTS 6 Leicester
10.11.83 John Elliott **L** RSC 1 Stafford
05.12.83 Mike Farghaly **L** RSC 2 Manchester
31.03.84 Dave Dunn **L** CO 2 Derby
09.05.84 Rex Weaver **L** PTS 6 Leicester
Summary: 6 contests, won 1, lost 5

Malcolm Davies

Shrewsbury. *Born* Welshampton 14.01.62
L. Middleweight
Manager R. Gray
Previous Amateur Club North Shropshire

18.10.83 Cecil Williams **W** PTS 6 Wolverhampton
07.11.83 Jeff Standley **L** PTS 6 Birmingham
05.12.83 Robert Armstrong **L** CO 6 Nottingham
27.03.84 Andy Whitehouse **W** CO 4 Wolverhampton
04.06.84 Elvis Morton **W** PTS 6 Nottingham
Summary: 5 contests, won 3, lost 2

Arthur Davis

Orpington. *Born* Erith 07.02.57
L. Middleweight
Manager D. Mancini
Previous Amateur Club Eltham & District
Divisional Honours SE London L. Middleweight Champion 1978; SE London L. Middleweight R/U 1981

12.10.81 Jimmy Ward **W** RSC 4 Copthorne
22.10.81 Cliff Curtis **W** PTS 6 Piccadilly
12.01.82 Richard Wilson **W** RSC 4 Bethnal Green
19.02.82 Terry Marsh **L** PTS 6 Bloomsbury
22.03.82 Mickey Mapp **W** RSC 7 Southwark
07.06.82 Colin Power **L** CO 3 Bloomsbury
14.09.82 Randy Henderson **W** PTS 8 Southend
20.10.82 Jimmy Cable **L** PTS 8 Strand
15.12.82 Mick Courtney **L** PTS 8 Queensway
24.01.83 Charlie Malarkey **L** CO 4 Glasgow
06.04.83 Jimmy Cable **L** RSC 5 Mayfair
17.10.83 Phil O'Hare **W** CO 2 Southwark
06.12.83 R. W. Smith **L** RSC 4 Kensington
16.02.84 Mick Courtney **L** RSC 6 Basildon
Summary: 14 contests, won 6, lost 8

(Patrick) P. J. Davitt

Stramullin. *Born* Dublin 19.08.58
Welterweight
Manager B. Eastwood
Previous Amateur Club Phoenix
National Honours Irish L. Welterweight Champion; Irish Int.

31.03.81 Dominic Bergonzi **L** RTD 3 Wembley
06.05.81 Gary Buckle **W** PTS 6 Solihull
20.10.81 Dominic Bergonzi **W** RSC 4 Bethnal Green
08.11.81 Dennis Sullivan **W** PTS 6 Navan
30.06.82 Judas Clottey **L** PTS 8 Liverpool
16.10.82 Robert Armstrong **W** PTS 8 Killarney
14.11.82 Walter Clayton **W** PTS 8 Navan
14.12.82 Patsy Quinn **W** PTS 10 Belfast
22.05.83 Dave Sullivan **W** RSC 7 Navan
16.11.83 Tommy McCallum **W** PTS 8 Belfast
04.04.84 Patsy Quinn **W** RTD 8 Belfast
05.06.84 Rocky Kelly **L** RSC 5 Kensington
Summary: 12 contests, won 9, lost 3

Tommy Davitt

Stramullin. *Born* Dublin 26.02.55
Welterweight
Manager (Self)
Previous Amateur Club Phoenix
National Honours Irish Featherweight Champion 1974; Irish Int.

04.10.76 Barry Price **L** PTS 8 Kensington
28.10.76 Barry Price **L** PTS 8 Mayfair
15.11.76 Lee Graham **W** PTS 6 Kensington
24.11.76 Albert Coley **W** RSC 4 Mayfair
30.11.76 Ricky Beaumont **L** PTS 6 Leeds
07.12.76 Ricky Beaumont **W** RSC 4 Kensington
25.01.77 Peter Neal **W** PTS 6 Piccadilly
07.02.77 Earl Noel **W** PTS 6 Mayfair
14.02.77 Billy Jeram **W** PTS 8 Walworth
25.02.77 Kevin Davies **L** PTS 8 Digbeth
22.03.77 Tommy Dunn **L** PTS 8 Bethnal Green

CONTINUED OVERLEAF

29.03.77 Earl Noel **W** PTS 6 Wembley
18.04.77 Barry Price **W** PTS 8 Walworth
09.05.77 Tommy Dunn L PTS 8 Mayfair
26.09.77 Barry Price **W** PTS 6 Piccadilly
10.10.77 Barry Price **W** PTS 8 Piccadilly
07.11.77 Billy Vivian **W** PTS 8 Piccadilly
18.11.77 Billy Vivian **W** PTS 8 Mayfair
30.01.78 Horace McKenzie L PTS 8 Glasgow
17.02.78 Dan M'Putu **W** PTS 8 Dunkirk
16.03.78 Hans Henrik Palm L PTS 6 Copenhagen
17.04.78 George Feeney **W** PTS 8 Mayfair
25.09.78 Sylvester Gordon DREW 8 Mayfair
27.11.78 Ray Cattouse L DIS 7 Mayfair
29.01.79 Willie Booth **W** RTD 3 Glasgow
05.02.79 Sylvester Gordon L PTS 8 Piccadilly
27.10.79 Juan Jose Giminez L PTS 8 Pesaro
12.11.79 Winston Spencer L PTS 8 Mayfair
18.02.80 Ricky Beaumont L PTS 8 Piccadilly
10.05.81 Carl Bailey **W** PTS 8 Dublin
24.09.81 Tony Sinnott L RSC 6 Liverpool
16.02.82 Dave Allen L PTS 8 Leeds
26.04.82 Sid Smith L RSC 1 Southwark
14.11.82 John Lindo DREW 8 Navan
12.04.83 Patsy Quinn L RSC 5 Belfast
Summary: 35 contests, won 16, drew 2, lost 17

Nicky Day

Southampton. *Born* Odstock 22.03.64
Lightweight
Manager J. Bishop
Previous Amateur Club Tidworth
Divisional Honours S Counties Lightweight Champion 1982

20.02.84 Colin Anderson DREW 6 Mayfair
07.03.84 Steve Craggs L PTS 6 Brighton
14.03.84 Neville Fivey **W** PTS 6 Mayfair
21.03.84 Mike Durvan L RSC 5 Mayfair
17.04.84 Nigel Burke **W** RSC 5 Piccadilly
27.04.84 Kenny Jinks L PTS 6 Wolverhampton
09.05.84 Con Cronin DREW 6 Mayfair
Summary: 7 contests, won 2, drew 2, lost 3

Andy De Abreu

Cardiff. *Born* Cardiff 28.09.64
Featherweight
Manager M. Williams
Previous Amateur Club Llandaff
National Honours NABC Champion 1983

22.02.84 Dean Bramhald **W** PTS 6 Evesham
04.04.84 Wayne Trigg **W** PTS 4 Evesham
12.04.84 Dean Bramhald **W** PTS 6 Piccadilly
15.06.84 Paul Owen **W** RSC 5 Liverpool
Summary: 4 contests, won 4

Dario De Abreu

Cardiff. *Born* Guyana 02.07.60
Welterweight
Manager M. Williams
Previous Amateur Club Llandaff

14.02.84 Trevor Hopson **W** PTS 6 Southend
07.06.84 Vince Stewart L PTS 6 Piccadilly
Summary: 2 contests, won 1, lost 1

Joe Dean (Campbell)

Huddersfield. *Born* Jamaica 21.06.59
L. Heavyweight
Manager T. Miller
Previous Amateur Club Slaithwaite

21.04.80 Redmond Everard **W** CO 3 Bradford
28.04.80 Mike Burton L PTS 6 Walworth
28.05.80 Paul Heatley **W** RSC 4 Cramlington
16.06.80 Joe Frater L PTS 6 Manchester
10.09.80 Jerry Golden **W** RSC 3 Liverpool
23.10.80 Brian Graham L PTS 8 Middlesbrough
15.12.80 Willie Wright L PTS 6 Bradford
28.01.81 Willie Wright L PTS 6 Stoke
09.02.81 Dave Turner DREW 6 Manchester
16.02.81 Tony Hoole **W** RSC 2 Bradford
03.03.81 Paul Heatley L PTS 6 Pudsey
16.03.81 Paul Heatley **W** PTS 6 Manchester
05.08.81 Chris Thorne L PTS 6 Norwich
28.09.81 Steve Babbs L PTS 6 Bradford
23.11.81 Keith James L PTS 6 Chesterfield
29.11.81 Barry Ahmed L RSC 6 Middlesbrough
03.10.83 Dave Mowbray DREW 6 Bradford
Summary: 17 contests, won 5, drew 2, lost 10

(Leaville) Ricky Deane (McIntosh)

Leicester. *Born* Jamaica 15.11.60
L. Welterweight
Manager (Self)
Previous Amateur Club Braunstone Vic.

11.10.82 Tommy Thomas **W** PTS 6 Bristol
22.11.82 Steve Ellwood L RSC 2 Lewisham
28.04.83 Kevin Sheehan L RSC 3 Leicester
07.06.83 Abdul Kareem L RSC 5 Southend
Summary: 4 contests, won 1, lost 3

Jeff Decker

Whitley Bay. *Born* North Shields 14.05.58
L. Welterweight
Manager L. Roberts
Previous Amateur Club St. Edwards
National Honours Young England Rep./England Int.; Euro. Junior Silver 1976
Divisional Honours N Counties Featherweight Champion 1976; NE Counties Featherweight Champion 1977; NE Counties L. Welterweight Champion 1980 – 1982

18.10.82 Tommy Thomas **W** PTS 6 Piccadilly

Jeff Decker
Douglas Baton

18.11.82 John Daly W CO 1 Coventry
24.01.83 John Murphy W RSC 5 Glasgow
07.03.83 Tyrell Wilson W PTS 8 Piccadilly
18.04.83 Tommy McCallum DREW 8 Glasgow
25.04.83 Ian McLeod DREW 8 Piccadilly
09.05.83 Tommy McCallum W PTS 8 Piccadilly
13.06.83 Ian McLeod L RSC 5 Glasgow
15.09.83 Alan Lamb W RSC 1 Liverpool
15.10.83 Peter Eubanks W PTS 8 Coventry
09.12.83 Tony Sinnott L RSC 5 Liverpool
23.02.84 Kostas Petrou L RSC 5 Digbeth
16.04.84 Lee McKenzie L RSC 2 Glasgow
Summary: 13 contests, won 7, drew 2, lost 4

(Mark) Billy Joe Dee (Dymell)

Derby. *Born* Pinxton 07.09.60
Lightweight
Manager W. Shinfield
Previous Amateur Club South Normanton

02.11.83 Tony Connolly L PTS 6 Bloomsbury
14.11.83 Muhammad Lovelock L RSC 1 Manchester
12.12.83 Shane Silvester L RSC 2 Birmingham
01.02.84 Allan Coveley L RSC 3 Bloomsbury
27.02.84 Dean Bramhald L PTS 6 Nottingham
19.03.84 Dean Bramhald W PTS 6 Bradford
28.03.84 Steve James L RSC 5 Aberavon
14.05.84 Les Walsh L CO 1 Manchester
07.06.84 Mickey Markie L PTS 6 Dudley
Summary: 9 contests, won 1, lost 8

Errol Dennis

Wolverhampton. *Born* Jamaica 26.04.56
Welterweight
Manager M. Sendell
Previous Amateur Club Bilston Golden Gloves

19.01.81 Mike Sullivan W PTS 6 Birmingham
26.01.81 Paul Murray L PTS 6 Edgbaston
02.02.81 Dennis Sheehan L RSC 3 Nottingham
11.03.81 Roger Ryder DREW 6 Evesham
17.03.81 Gary Buckle L PTS 6 Wolverhampton
24.03.81 George White W RSC 6 Bethnal Green
15.04.81 Gary Buckle L PTS 6 Evesham
27.04.81 Paul Kelly L RSC 3 Piccadilly
21.09.81 Steve Brennan L PTS 6 Wolverhampton
30.09.81 Kirk Davis W RSC 3 Evesham
06.10.81 Larry Monaghan L PTS 6 Piccadilly
02.11.81 Geoff Pegler L RSC 2 Nottingham
25.11.81 Dave Rylance W RSC 2 Stoke
02.12.81 Gary Knight L RSC 2 Burslem
09.02.82 Davey Cox W PTS 6 Wolverhampton
16.02.82 Paul Mitchell L PTS 6 Leeds
21.02.82 Cecil Williams W PTS 6 Nottingham
10.03.82 Rocky Severino W PTS 6 Burslem
15.03.82 Davey Cox L PTS 6 Wolverhampton
23.03.82 Paul Murray W PTS 6 Wolverhampton
05.04.82 Davey Cox W PTS 6 Nottingham
10.05.82 Elvis Morton W PTS 6 Birmingham
03.06.82 Tony Brown DREW 6 Liverpool
21.06.82 Tony Brown L CO 3 Liverpool
06.10.82 Steve Davies L CO 3 Stoke
01.12.82 Dave Maxwell W RSC 2 Stafford
15.12.82 Steve Ellwood L PTS 6 Queensway
17.01.83 Lee Hartshorn L PTS 8 Manchester
26.01.83 Steve Tempro W PTS 6 Stoke
07.02.83 Delroy Pearce L RSC 5 Marylebone
25.04.83 Tony Rabbetts L PTS 6 Acton
09.05.83 Kevin Sheehan L CO 3 Nottingham
Summary: 32 contests, won 12, drew 2, lost 18

Dave Dent

Camden Town. *Born* London 15.03.62
L. Welterweight
Manager T. Lawless
Previous Amateur Club St Pancras
National Honours England Int., Young England Rep. ABA L. Welterweight Champion 1983
Divisional Honours NW London Lightweight Champion 1980; NW London L. Welterweight Champion 1981–1982; London L. Welterweight Champion 1983

23.01.84 Lenny Gloster W PTS 6 Mayfair
13.03.84 Frankie Lake W RSC 4 Wembley
27.03.84 Lenny Gloster W PTS 6 Bethnal Green
19.04.84 Lenny Gloster W PTS 8 Basildon
Summary: 4 contests, won 4

Colin Derrick

Bethnal Green. *Born* London 08.06.60
Welterweight
Manager T. Lawless
Previous Amateur Club Repton
National Honours School Titles 1975 – 1976; Junior ABA Title 1977; NABC Title 1977; Young England Rep.
Divisional Honours ABA L. Welterweight R/U 1978; NE London L. Welterweight Champion 1979

22.01.80 Mike Clemow **W** RSC 4 Kensington
19.02.80 Chris Christian L PTS 6 Kensington
20.01.81 Jeff Aspell **W** RSC 3 Bethnal Green
10.02.81 Mick Miller **W** RSC 4 Bethnal Green
24.02.81 Kid Murray **W** PTS 8 Kensington
03.03.81 Terry Welch **W** RSC 1 Wembley
24.03.81 Mike Clemow **W** RSC 2 Bethnal Green
28.04.81 Lloyd Christie **W** RSC 1 Kensington
20.06.81 Dave Allen **W** PTS 6 Wembley
03.11.81 Carl Bailey **W** CO 2 Kensington
28.09.82 Sylvester Gordon **W** CO 3 Bethnal Green
26.10.82 Charlie Malarkey **W** RSC 8 Bethnal Green
(*Elim. British Welterweight Title*)
17.05.83 Joey Mack L PTS 8 Bethnal Green
Summary: 13 contests, won 11, lost 2

Chris Devine

Chesterfield. *Born* Huthwaite 17.08.59
L. Heavyweight
Manager (Self)
Previous Amateur Club St. Thomas's
National Honours Young England Rep.; Euro. Junior Bronze 1978
Divisional Honours M Counties L. Heavyweight Champion 1977

16.05.79 Peter Lygo **W** RSC 1 Sheffield
21.05.70 Bob Bleau **W** CO 2 Bradford
26.09.79 Stan Carnall **W** PTS 6 Sheffield
10.10.79 Glenn Adair L PTS 8 Torquay
29.09.80 Paul Newman **W** RSC 6 Chesterfield
06.05.81 Gordon Charlesworth **W** RSC 5 Chesterfield
17.06.81 Theo Josephs **W** RSC 1 Sheffield
09.07.81 Jim Burns **W** PTS 6 Dudley
11.11.82 Roy Skeldon L RSC 7 Stafford
23.02.83 Alex Romeo **W** PTS 8 Chesterfield
17.05.83 Nick Jenkins L PTS 6 Bethnal Green
04.06.84 Winston Burnett **W** PTS 6 Mayfair
Summary: 12 contests, won 9, lost 3

Gerry Devine

Glasgow. *Born* Paisley 30.11.58
Lightweight
Manager T. Gilmour
Previous Amateur Club Paisley
National Honours Scottish Int.
Divisional Honours Scottish L. Flyweight R/U 1976 & Flyweight R/U 1977

07.10.81 Paddy Maguire **W** RSC 2 Stoke
27.10.81 Steve Topliss L PTS 6 Wolverhampton
01.12.81 Stuart Shaw L CO 4 Derby
27.01.82 Dean Marsden L CO 5 Stoke
26.04.82 Dave Markey DREW 6 Glasgow
31.05.82 Ray Ross DREW 6 Glasgow
13.09.82 Dave Markey DREW 6 Glasgow
28.09.82 Dave Markey **W** RSC 3 Aberdeen
18.10.82 Keith Foreman L PTS 6 Glasgow
15.11.82 Mark Duffy **W** PTS 6 Glasgow
26.11.82 Craig Walsh DREW 6 Glasgow
16.03.83 Lee Halford L RSC 1 Stoke
26.03.84 Michael Marsden L CO 2 Glasgow
Summary: 13 contests, won 3, drew 4, lost 6

Robert Dickie

Swansea. *Born* Carmarthen 23.06.64
Bantamweight
Manager C. Breen
Previous Amateur Club Blaenau
National Honours Welsh Bantamweight Champion 1982; Welsh Int.

12.03.83 Billy Hough **W** PTS 6 Swindon
25.04.83 Charlie Brown **W** RSC 4 Aberdeen
16.05.83 George Bailey **W** RSC 3 Birmingham
27.05.83 Howard Williams **W** RSC 2 Swansea
13.06.83 Danny Flynn DREW 8 Glasgow
10.10.83 Danny Flynn L RSC 5 Glasgow
(*Vacant Scottish Bantamweight Title*)
14.05.84 Dave Pratt **W** PTS 8 Nottingham
Summary: 7 contests, won 5, drew 1, lost 1

Frank Dodson

Harrow. *Born* Guyana 04.06.57
Middleweight
Manager A. Lavelle
Previous Amateur Club All Stars
Divisional Honours NW London L. Heavyweight R/U 1982

01.02.83 Mark Kelly L PTS 6 Southend
Summary: 1 contest, lost 1

(Pat) John Doherty

Bradford. *Born* Bradford 12.07.62
Featherweight
Manager J. Celebanski
Previous Amateur Club Bradford YMCA

26.05.82 Taffy Mills L RSC 1 Leeds
07.10.82 John Lodge **W** RSC 4 Morley

18.10.82 Carl Gaynor **W** PTS 6 Blackpool
18.11.82 Stuart Carmichael **W** PTS 6 Coventry
24.01.83 Stuart Carmichael **W** PTS 6 Bradford
17.02.83 Stuart Carmichael **W** PTS 6 Coventry
09.03.83 John Mwaimu **W** RSC 2 Stoke
21.03.83 Muhammad Lovelock **W** PTS 6 Bradford
09.05.83 Les Walsh **W** PTS 6 Manchester
19.05.83 Ray Plant DREW 8 Sunderland
13.06.83 Steve Enright DREW 6 Doncaster
27.09.83 Anthony Brown L PTS 6 Stoke
15.10.83 Stuart Shaw **W** PTS 8 Coventry
27.10.83 Brett Styles **W** PTS 8 Ebbw Vale
14.11.83 Stuart Carmichael L RSC 7 Nantwich
09.02.84 Les Walsh DREW 8 Manchester
13.03.84 Joey Wainwright **W** PTS 8 Hull
18.04.84 Les Walsh **W** PTS 6 Stoke
07.06.84 Gary Nickels **W** PTS 8 Piccadilly
Summary: 19 contests, won 13, drew 3, lost 3

Pat Doherty

Croydon. *Born* Croydon 12.04.62
Featherweight
Manager F. Rix
Previous Amateur Club Sir Philip Game
Divisional Honours SE London Bantamweight R/U 1981

08.05.81 Gordon Haigh **W** PTS 6 Piccadilly
04.06.81 David Miles L PTS 6 Morecambe
28.09.81 Ray Cunningham **W** CO 1 Lewisham
15.12.81 Tony Whitmore **W** CO 2 Lewisham
10.03.82 Peter Jones **W** PTS 8 Solihull
01.06.82 Paul Huggins L RSC 5 Kensington
23.09.82 Steve Pollard **W** PTS 8 Wimbledon
04.11.82 Alan Tombs **W** RSC 2 Wimbledon
24.01.83 Lee Graham DREW 8 Piccadilly
21.02.83 Mark West DREW 8 Piccadilly
02.03.83 Keith Wallace L PTS 8 Belfast
12.12.83 Ian Murray **W** RSC 4 Bedworth
25.01.84 John Sharkey **W** RSC 4 Solihull
21.03.84 Mark West **W** RSC 8 Solihull
03.04.84 Paul Huggins **W** RSC 7 Lewisham
05.06.84 Clyde Ruan L PTS 12 Kensington (*Southern Area Featherweight Title Challenge & Final Elim. British Featherweight Title*)
Summary: 16 contests, won 10, drew 2, lost 4

Mick Dono (Donovan)

Liverpool. *Born* Liverpool 30.09.62
Welterweight
Manager N. Basso
Previous Amateur Club Salisbury

10.05.82 John Daly **W** PTS 6 Liverpool
26.05.82 Mark Duffy L PTS 6 Leeds
07.06.82 Vince Vahey **W** PTS 4 Sheffield
17.09.82 Vince Vahey L PTS 6 Liverpool
05.10.82 Stan Wall **W** PTS 6 Liverpool
14.10.82 Mark Duffy L PTS 6 Nantwich
22.11.82 Winston Ho-Shing **W** PTS 6 Liverpool
14.12.82 Damien Fryers L RSC 5 Belfast
20.01.83 Dave Taylor **W** PTS 6 Birkenhead
14.02.83 Tommy Bennett L PTS 6 Manchester
20.06.83 Mike Calderwood **W** PTS 6 Manchester
03.10.83 Phil O'Hare L PTS 6 Liverpool
13.10.83 Dean Scarfe L CO 6 Bloomsbury
15.03.84 Davey Cox **W** PTS 6 Kirkby
16.04.84 Sammy Sampson L RSC 6 Bradford
Summary: 15 contests, won 7, lost 8

Shaun Dooney

Darlington. *Born* Bradford 06.02.56
L. Welterweight
Manager T. Miller
Previous Amateur Club Newton Aycliffe

07.10.82 Gary Williams L RSC 1 Morley
18.04.83 Bobby McGowan L RSC 2 Bradford
19.05.83 Steve Boyle L CO 3 Sunderland
Summary: 3 contests, lost 3

Pat Doherty
Derek Rowe (Photos) Ltd

Johnny Dorey

Eltham. *Born* Bermondsey 24.10.59
Former Undefeated Southern Area Bantamweight Champion
Manager D. Mancini
Previous Amateur Club Eltham & District
Divisional Honours SE London Bantamweight R/U 1979; SE London Featherweight Champion 1980

24.09.81 Terry Allen W RSC 1 Hartlepool
26.10.81 Gordon Haigh W PTS 6 Southwark
09.12.81 Mike Wilkes W PTS 6 Piccadilly
01.02.82 Eddie Glencross DREW 6 Southwark
22.03.82 Billy Hough W RTD 3 Southwark
19.04.82 Robert Hepburn L PTS 6 Mayfair
06.05.82 Andy King W PTS 8 Mayfair
28.09.82 Ivor Jones L PTS 8 Bethnal Green
25.10.82 Steve Reilly W PTS 8 Mayfair
22.03.83 Ivor Jones W PTS 10 Bethnal Green (*Vacant Southern Area Bantamweight Title*)
19.09.83 Ray Somer DREW 8 Rotterdam
04.10.83 Dave George DREW 10 Bethnal Green
12.11.83 Franco Cherchi L PTS 8 Rome
23.01.84 Dave George L PTS 8 Mayfair
27.03.84 Peter Harris L RSC 6 Bethnal Green
Summary: 15 contests, won 7, drew 3, lost 5

Mark Duffy

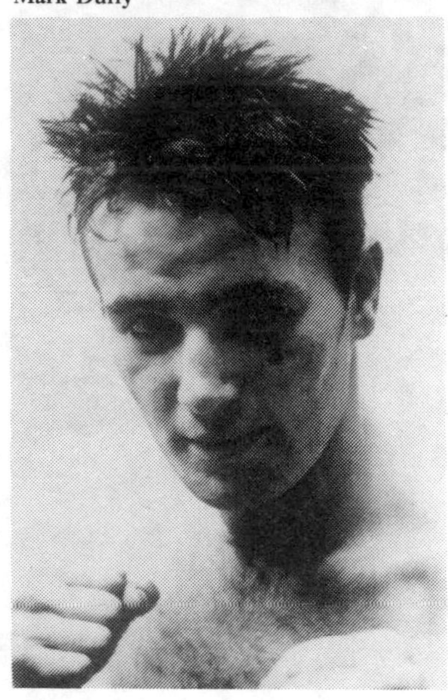

Alan Douglas (Smith)

Sheffield. *Born* London 30.08.62
Heavyweight
Manager B. Ingle
Previous Amateur Club Croft House
Divisional Honours NE Counties L. Heavyweight S/F 1980

23.02.83 Johnny Elliott L PTS 6 Chesterfield
21.03.83 Dwight Osbourne W RTD 2 Bradford
27.04.83 Deka Williams W RSC 6 Wolverhampton
03.10.83 Barry Ellis L PTS 6 Eltham
19.10.83 John Fallon L PTS 8 Hull
29.02.84 Eddie Fenton W PTS 6 Sheffield
19.03.84 Ian Priest W PTS 6 Bradford
26.03.84 Eddie Fenton W PTS 6 Leicester
06.06.84 Frank Robinson W PTS 8 Sheffield
Summary: 9 contests, won 6, lost 3

Dave Douglas

Larkhall. *Born* Bellshill 02.07.56
Former Scottish Welterweight Champion
Manager R. Watt
Previous Amateur Club Larkhall Welfare
National Honours Scottish Int.
Divisional Honours Scottish L Welterweight R/U 1976

18.10.78 Chris Sanigar L RSC 5 Glasgow
13.11.78 Tony Bogle W PTS 6 Glasgow
26.02.79 Pay Smythe W PTS 6 Glasgow
20.03.79 Gerry Maguire W PTS 6 Glasgow
23.04.79 Gerry Maguire W RSC 3 Glasgow
13.05.79 Peter Snowshall W RTD 4 Glasgow
03.09.79 Derek Nelson L PTS 8 Glasgow
26.09.79 Dave Allen L PTS 8 Sheffield
29.10.79 Chris Christian DREW 6 Birmingham
05.11.79 Jimmy Smith W PTS 6 Piccadilly
06.12.79 Liam Linnen W PTS 8 Glasgow
21.01.80 Chris Christian L PTS 6 Birmingham
18.02.80 Jeff Aspell W PTS 6 Birmingham
14.04.80 Tommy Wright W PTS 8 Motherwell
28.04.80 Neil Fannan DREW 6 Birmingham
02.06.80 Liam Linnen W RSC 9 Glasgow (*Vacant Scottish Welterweight Title*)
22.09.80 Gerry Young L RSC 3 Belfast
23.10.80 Dil Collins W PTS 8 Piccadilly
30.10.80 Tony Sinnott L PTS 8 Liverpool
07.11.80 Gary Newell W PTS 8 Cambuslong
13.11.80 Brian Anderson L RTD 5 Newcastle
26.01.81 Gary Pearce L PTS 8 Glasgow
12.05.81 Johnny Francis L PTS 8 Liverpool
09.11.81 Hugh Smith W PTS 10 Hamilton (*Scottish Welterweight Title Defence*)
29.11.81 Graeme Ahmed L PTS 8 Middlesbrough

28.04.82 Robert Armstrong **W** PTS 8 Sheffield
24.06.82 Joey Frost **W** RSC 4 Kirkby
07.10.82 Torben Andersen L CO 4 Copenhagen
03.10.83 Rocky Kelly **W** PTS 8 Glasgow
14.11.83 Paul Mitchell **W** PTS 8 Glasgow
30.01.84 Jim Kelly L CO 6 Glasgow (*Scottish Welterweight Title Defence*)
04.06.84 Tony Smith **W** PTS 8 Glasgow
Summary: 32 contests, won 18, drew 2, lost 12

Kevin Downer
Shoreditch. *Born* London 30.09.60
Bantamweight
Manager J. Barclay
Previous Amateur Club St. Monica's
Divisional Honours NE London Bantamweight R/U 1983

20.09.83 Ian Colbeck L PTS 6 Mayfair
21.11.83 Billy Hardy L PTS 6 Eltham
07.03.84 Gordon Stobie **W** PTS 6 Brighton
16.04.84 Shane Silvester L PTS 6 Birmingham
Summary: 4 contests, won 1, lost 3

Mark Drew
Liverpool. *Born* Liverpool 13.11.64
Lightweight
Manager (Self)
Previous Amateur Club Kirkby

17.09.82 Carl Gaynor **W** PTS 4 Liverpool
23.09.82 Dave Bryan L PTS 4 Liverpool
11.10.82 Joey Morris DREW 4 Manchester
07.02.83 Jimmy Bunclark L PTS 6 Liverpool
14.02.83 Terry Welch L CO 2 Liverpool
14.03.83 Bobby Rimmer L PTS 4 Manchester
Summary: 6 contests, won 1, drew 1, lost 4

John Drummond
Rhyl. *Born* East Fife 22.03.57
Bantamweight
Manager (Self)
Previous Amateur Club Rhyl Star
National Honours Welsh Int.

17.06.83 Carl Gaynor **W** PTS 6 Queensferry
24.11.83 Gordon Stobie **W** RSC 5 Kirkby
14.12.83 Ian Colbeck L PTS 6 Stoke
17.02.84 John Mwaimu **W** PTS 6 Rhyl
Summary: 4 contests, won 3, lost 1

Mickey Duddy
Derry. *Born* Derry 21.10.60
L. Welterweight
Manager C. Harkin
Previous Amateur Club St. Mary's Derry

22.09.81 Vince Griffin **W** RTD 3 Belfast
26.10.81 Gerry Maguire **W** PTS 6 Belfast
23.11.81 Mike Bromby L RSC 5 Glasgow
09.03.82 Ray Ross **W** PTS 8 Derry
20.04.82 Terry Smith L RSC 3 Kensington
12.04.83 Michael Harris L RSC 5 Belfast
16.11.83 Peppy Muir L RSC 2 Belfast
Summary: 7 contests, won 3, lost 4

Mark Duffy
Leeds. *Born* Leeds 08.05.61
L. Welterweight
Manager T. Callighan
Previous Amateur Club Market District

06.04.82 Mike Bromby DREW 6 Leeds
13.05.82 Frank Abercromby **W** RSC 1 Wakefield
26.05.82 Mick Dono **W** PTS 6 Leeds
14.10.82 Mick Dono **W** PTS 6 Nantwich
15.11.82 Gerry Devine L PTS 6 Glasgow
01.02.83 Graham Brockway **W** RSC 2 Southend
28.03.83 Gary Lucas **W** PTS 6 Manchester
29.04.83 Terry Welch L RTD 5 Liverpool
26.10.83 Mick Harkin DREW 6 Stoke
14.12.83 Mick Harkin L RSC 6 Stoke
Summary: 10 contests, won 5, drew 2, lost 3

Phil Duke
Plymouth. *Born* Plymouth 19.12.57
Lightweight
Manager D. Sullivan
Previous Amateur Club Devonport

22.03.83 Jim McDonnell L PTS 6 Bethnal Green
06.02.84 Steve Griffith L RSC 3 Bethnal Green
Summary: 2 contests, lost 2

Jimmy Duncan
Liverpool. *Born* Liverpool 21.10.56
Featherweight
Manager F. Warren
Previous Amateur Club St. Helens Star
Divisional Honours W Lancs L. Welterweight R/U 1974; W Lancs Featherweight Champion 1977; W Lancs Featherweight R/U 1978/1980; N Counties Featherweight Champion 1979; ABA Featherweight R/U 1981

16.02.82 Rory Burke **W** PTS 6 Bloomsbury
24.02.82 Andy Thomas **W** CO 2 Sheffield
09.03.82 Alan Cooper **W** RSC 2 Hornsey
23.03.82 Kevin Doherty **W** RSC 4 Nantwich
05.04.82 Ray Hood **W** PTS 8 Bloomsbury
07.06.82 Clyde Ruan L RSC 4 Bloomsbury
23.09.82 Gerry Beard **W** RSC 6 Liverpool
05.10.82 Barry McGuigan L RTD 4 Belfast
24.11.82 Mervyn Bennett **W** PTS 8 Stoke
24.11.83 Kevin Pritchard **W** PTS 8 Kirkby
15.03.84 Dev Hollywood **W** PTS 10 Kirkby
Summary: 11 contests, won 9, lost 2

Tony Dunlop
Belfast. *Born* Belfast 01.08.63
L. Welterweight
Manager P. Byrne
Previous Amateur Club Holy Family
National Honours Irish Lightweight Champion 1983; Irish Int.

30.06.84 Mickey Brooks **W** PTS 6 Belfast
Summary: 1 contest, won 1

Dave Dunn
Manchester. *Born* Rossendale 21.10.54
Middleweight
Manager T. Miller
Previous Amateur Club Lancs Constabulary

01.11.73 Dave Coombs L PTS 6 Liverpool
10.12.73 Dave Coombs L PTS 6 Liverpool
19.02.74 Al Stewart L CO 1 Blackpool
19.03.74 Tommy Naylor L RSC 3 Blackpool
19.12.77 Billy Nixon L PTS 6 Bradford
20.02.78 Billy Nixon L PTS 6 Bradford
02.03.78 Tony Hague L PTS 4 Caister
23.03.78 John Gilling L RSC 3 Sunderland
13.10.80 Gerry McGrath L RSC 3 Windsor
13.11.80 Nick Riozzi L PTS 6 Caister
12.01.81 Pat McCarthy **W** PTS 6 Manchester
19.01.81 Pat McCarthy **W** PTS 6 Bradford
28.01.81 Cliff Curtis L PTS 6 Swindon
12.02.81 Peter Stockdale DREW 4 Bolton
16.03.81 Steve Foster **W** PTS 6 Manchester
25.03.81 Mark Tobin DREW 4 Doncaster
02.04.81 Dale Henderson L PTS 6 Middlesbrough
06.05.81 Glen Crump L PTS 6 Chesterfield
12.05.81 Alex Gregal L PTS 6 Liverpool
17.06.81 Peter Bennett L RSC 4 Sheffield
24.01.82 Dave Rylance L PTS 6 Sunderland
30.09.83 Floyd Davidson L PTS 6 Leicester
20.02.84 Sammy Sampson L PTS 6 Bradford
31.03.84 Floyd Davidson **W** CO 2 Derby
21.05.84 Sammy Sampson L PTS 6 Bradford
18.06.84 Frankie Moro L RSC 6 Manchester
Summary: 26 contests, won 4, drew 2, lost 20

Mike Durvan
Penge. *Born* Paddington 27.09.63
L. Welterweight
Manager F. Rix
Previous Amateur Club Crystal Palace

17.11.83 Teddy Anderson **W** PTS 6 Basildon
14.02.84 Steve Craggs L PTS 6 Wolverhampton
21.03.84 Nicky Day **W** RSC 5 Mayfair
06.04.84 Ron Shinkwin **W** PTS 6 Watford
01.05.84 Gary Williams **W** PTS 6 Bethnal Green
Summary: 5 contests, won 4, lost 1

Calvin Earlington
Peckham. *Born* Jamaica 25.04.59
L. Heavyweight
Manager R. Colson
Previous Amateur Club Stowe
Divisional Honours NW London L. Heavyweight Champion 1982

29.09.82 Eddie Vierling **W** PTS 6 Effingham Park
19.05.83 Sam Reeson L PTS 6 Queensway
Summary: 2 contests, won 1, lost 1

Steve Early

Steve Early

Coventry. *Born* Coventry 07.05.56
Midlands Area L. Welterweight Champion
Manager (Self)
Previous Amateur Club St Elizabeths
National Honours School Title 1972; Junior ABA Title 1971; NABC Titles 1973 – 1974; Young England Rep.
Divisional Honours M Counties L. Welterweight Champion 1977

11.10.77 Kevin Sheehan **W** RSC 3 Coventry
18.01.78 Najib Daho **W** PTS 6 Solihull
23.01.78 Selvin Bell **W** RSC 2 Wolverhampton
07.02.78 Ian Pickersgill **W** RTD 1 Coventry
06.03.78 Joey Saunders **W** PTS 6 Wolverhampton
15.03.78 Stan Atherton **W** PTS 6 Solihull
18.04.78 Paul Clemit **W** PTS 8 Coventry
03.05.78 Paddy McAleese **W** PTS 8 Solihull
13.06.78 Eric Purkiss **W** RSC 2 Coventry
01.11.78 Dick Declerk **W** RSC 2 Izegem
20.11.78 George McGurk **W** RSC 5 Birmingham
01.12.78 Davy Campbell **W** RSC 2 Enniskillen
26.02.79 Frank McCord **W** CO 1 Edgbaston
19.11.79 Roger Guest **L** CO 1 Edgbaston
(*Vacant Midlands Area L. Welterweight Title*)
28.01.80 Sylvester Gordon **W** RSC 6 Edgbaston
10.03.80 Billy Waith **W** PTS 8 Wolverhampton
21.04.80 Chris Davies **W** RTD 3 Edgbaston
11.06.80 Tony Martey **W** PTS 8 Edgbaston
19.10.80 Dan M'Putu **W** PTS 10 Birmingham
26.01.81 Ken Buchanan **W** PTS 12 Edgbaston
(*Final Elim. British L. Welterweight Title*)
30.03.81 Didier Kowalski **W** RSC 7 Birmingham
02.06.81 Oscar Aparicio **L** RTD 6 Kensington
12.10.81 Roger Guest **W** RTD 4 Birmingham
16.02.82 Clinton McKenzie **L** RSC 4 Bloomsbury
(*British L. Welterweight Title Challenge*)
18.10.82 Tony Brown **W** PTS 6 Edgbaston
06.12.82 Tony Brown **W** PTS 8 Edgbaston
19.01.83 Dave McCabe **W** PTS 8 Birmingham
05.10.83 Adey Allen **W** PTS 10 Solihull
(*Midlands Area L. Welterweight Title Challenge*)
03.12.83 Gary Knight **L** PTS 8 Marylebone
Summary: 29 contests, won 25, lost 4

Cliff Eastwood

Epsom. *Born* Southend 13.11.65
L. Middleweight
Manager H. Holland
Previous Amateur Club Foley

01.03.83 Paul McHugh **W** PTS 4 Southend
25.04.83 Danny Williams **L** PTS 4 Acton
27.01.84 Daryl Lindsay **W** RSC 2 Longford
06.02.84 Newton Barnett **L** PTS 6 Mayfair
Summary: 4 contests, won 2, lost 2

Tom Eastwood

Epsom. *Born* Southend 24.05.62
Heavyweight
Manager H. Holland
Previous Amateur Club Foley

01.03.83 Andrew Gerrard **W** PTS 6 Southend
25.03.83 Andrew Gerrard **W** PTS 6 Bloomsbury
25.04.83 Steve Howard **W** PTS 6 Acton
Summary: 3 contests, won 3

Chris Edge

Dinnington. *Born* Chesterfield 29.03.58
Welterweight
Manager T. Miller
Previous Amateur Club Target

21.05.84 Bobby McGowan **W** DIS 2 Bradford
04.06.84 Mike Calderwood DREW 6 Manchester
Summary: 2 contests, won 1, drew 1

Alf Edwardes

Manchester. *Born* St. Vincent 20.10.57
L. Middleweight
Manager J. Gaynor
Previous Amateur Club Sharston

28.09.82 Billy Ahearne **L** PTS 6 Manchester
11.10.82 Phil O'Hare **L** PTS 6 Manchester
08.11.82 Gordon Pratt **L** PTS 6 Manchester
24.11.82 Dave Harrison **W** PTS 6 Stoke
30.11.82 Tommy Heffron **L** PTS 6 Farnsworth
07.01.83 Gordon Pratt **L** PTS 6 Durham
17.01.83 Wayne Crolla **L** PTS 6 Manchester
Summary: 7 contests, won 1, lost 6

Billy Edwards

Hoxton. *Born* Bethnal Green 07.05.61
Welterweight
Manager (Self)
Previous Amateur Club West Ham
Divisional Honours NE London Welterweight R/U 1982

01.09.83 Dave Haggarty **L** PTS 6 Bloomsbury

CONTINUED OVERLEAF

12.09.83 Gary Williams **W** RTD 3 Glasgow
02.11.83 Colin Neagle DREW 6 Bloomsbury
18.11.83 Frankie Lake L PTS 6 Sheffield
28.11.83 John Faulkner L PTS 6 Bayswater
19.01.84 John Daly L PTS 6 Digbeth
27.03.84 Mark Simpson **W** PTS 6 Southend
Summary: 7 contests, won 2, drew 1, lost 4

Craig Edwards
Shotton. *Born* Chester 04.11.61
Middleweight
Manager P. Dwyer
Previous Amateur Club Buckley

20.06.83 Winston Wray L RSC 1 Manchester
28.10.83 Mike Farghaly L CO 3 Queensferry
06.02.84 Terry Magee L RSC 3 Liverpool
26.03.84 Ronnie Fraser L PTS 6 Barnsley
Summary: 4 contests, lost 4

Earl Edwards
Clapham. *Born* Jamaica 01.11.53
Former Southern Area Middleweight Champion
Manager (Self)
Previous Amateur Club Hogarth
Divisional Honours SW London Middleweight R/U 1976/1979; SW London Middleweight Champion 1978

17.09.79 Doug James L PTS 6 Mayfair
24.10.79 Curtis Marsh **W** PTS 8 Norwich
26.11.79 Peter Simon **W** PTS 6 Hammersmith
10.12.79 Billy Hill L PTS 8 Manchester
20.12.79 Carl Daley L PTS 6 Queensway
16.01.80 Winston Davis L PTS 6 Solihull
05.02.80 Jimmy Ellis **W** PTS 8 Southend
12.02.80 Peter Simon DREW 8 Wembley
28.02.80 Carl Daley **W** RSC 5 Queensway
11.03.80 Harry Watson **W** CO 5 Piccadilly
17.03.80 Henry Cooper **W** CO 2 Birmingham
14.04.80 Joe Lally **W** PTS 8 Manchester
28.04.80 Vernon Scott L PTS 8 Windsor
13.10.80 Dave Owens **W** RSC 3 Windsor
18.11.80 Errol McKenzie **W** RSC 4 Windsor
16.02.81 Pierre Frank Winterstein L PTS 8 Paris
03.03.81 Davey Armstrong **W** RSC 2 Wembley
(*Vacant Southern Area Middleweight Title*)
15.03.81 Alex Blanchard L RSC 4 The Hague
23.03.82 Davey Armstrong L RSC 6 Bethnal Green
(*Southern Area Middleweight Title Defence*)
19.01.83 Mick Morris L RSC 8 Birmingham
17.03.83 T. P. Jenkins L CO 1 Marylebone
21.11.83 Jack Sharp L RSC 3 Eltham
Summary: 22 contests, won 10, drew 1, lost 11

Nick Ellaway
Rochford. *Born* Rochford 22.06.62
Welterweight
Manager T. Mason
Previous Amateur Club Rochford

20.09.83 Graeme Griffin L RSC 1 Mayfair
16.02.84 Charlie Carman **W** PTS 6 Basildon
19.04.84 Kevin Sanders **W** RSC 2 Basildon
31.05.84 Claude Rossi DREW 6 Basildon
Summary: 4 contests, won 2, drew 1, lost 1

Adrian Elliott
West Ham. *Born* Plaistow 19.10.57
Heavyweight
Manager T. Lawless
Previous Amateur Club Fairbairn House
National Honours England Int.; ABA Heavyweight Champion 1981 & S. Heavyweight Champion 1982
Divisional Honours NE London Heavyweight Champion 1980

25.01.83 Theo Josephs **W** RSC 6 Bethnal Green
22.03.83 Terry Mintus **W** PTS 8 Bethnal Green
06.10.83 Hughroy Currie L RSC 5 Basildon
13.05.84 Theo Josephs **W** RSC 4 Wembley
Summary: 4 contests, won 3, lost 1

John Elliott
Telford. *Born* Wellington 20.05.58
Middleweight
Manager R. Gray
Previous Amateur Club Sankeys

31.01.83 Paul Shell L PTS 6 Birmingham
23.02.83 Alan Douglas **W** PTS 6 Chesterfield
02.03.83 Paul Shell **W** PTS 6 Evesham
22.03.83 Paul Shell L PTS 6 Wolverhampton
28.03.83 Alan Ash L RTD 3 Wolverhampton
27.04.83 Dave Scott L PTS 6 Wolverhampton
16.05.83 Bobby Williams L CO 2 Birmingham
13.06.83 Paul Shell L PTS 8 Nottingham
20.09.83 Gary Gething L PTS 6 Dudley
10.10.83 Paul Shutt **W** CO 1 Birmingham
10.11.83 Floyd Davidson **W** RSC 1 Stafford
01.12.83 Dave Scott L PTS 6 Dudley
26.03.84 Blaine Longsden **W** PTS 8 Leicester
30.04.84 Winston Wray L PTS 6 Rhyl
09.05.84 Doug James L CO 4 Mayfair
11.06.84 Winston Wray L RSC 4 Manchester
Summary: 16 contests, won 5, lost 11

Adrian Elliott
Douglas Baton

Barry Ellis
Clapham. *Born* Islington 25.10.57
Heavyweight
Manager A. Lavelle
Previous Amateur Club All Stars
Divisional Honours NW London Heavyweight Champion 1983

22.09.83 Mark Cleverly **W** PTS 6 Strand
03.10.83 Alan Douglas **W** PTS 6 Eltham
12.12.83 Phil Simpson **W** CO 3 Bedworth
06.02.84 Glenn McCrory **L** RSC 1 Mayfair
01.03.84 Michael Armstrong **W** PTS 6 Queensway
17.04.84 Bob Young **DREW** 8 Merton
Summary: 6 contests, won 4, drew 1, lost 1

(Everard) Jimmy Ellis
Sheffield. *Born* Paddington 05.12.58
Middleweight
Manager B. Ingle
Previous Amateur Club Grassmoor
Divisional Honours M Counties Middleweight R/U 1979

12.09.79 Owen Slue **W** RSC 6 Burslem
26.09.79 Ron Pearce **W** RSC 4 Sheffield
15.10.79 Wayne Barker **L** PTS 6 Manchester
31.10.79 Gordon Stacey **W** RSC 4 Southend
27.11.79 Wayne Barker **L** PTS 8 Sheffield
04.12.79 Roy Commosioung **W** RSC 4 Southend
09.01.80 Richard Kenyon **W** RSC 4 Burslem
25.01.80 Malcolm Heath **L** PTS 6 Hull
05.02.80 Earl Edwards **L** PTS 8 Southend
05.03.80 Kenny Webber **L** PTS 8 Liverpool
10.03.80 Carl Bailey **W** PTS 8 Manchester
31.03.80 Peter Bassey **W** PTS 8 Cleethorpes
14.04.80 Kenny Webber **DREW** 8 Manchester
22.04.80 Mick Mills **W** RTD 6 Sheffield
14.05.80 Joe Jackson **W** PTS 8 Burslem
18.11.80 John Humphreys **L** PTS 6 Shrewsbury
25.11.80 Mike Burton **L** PTS 8 Norwich
16.02.81 Billy Hill **W** PTS 8 Bradford
24.03.81 Carl Daley **W** RSC 6 Sheffield
01.06.81 John Humphreys **DREW** 6 Wolverhampton
17.06.81 Steve Henty **W** RSC 7 Sheffield
09.07.81 Neville Wilson **W** RSC 3 Dudley
15.09.81 Mark Kaylor **L** RSC 5 Wembley
24.02.82 Ashley Jones **W** RSC 4 Sheffield
09.03.82 Chris Coady **W** RSC 3 Farnsworth
28.04.82 Mick Morris **W** CO 2 Sheffield
14.11.82 Terry Christle **L** CO 5 Navan
09.12.82 Errol Christie **L** RSC 3 Bloomsbury
14.02.83 Blaine Longsden **L** PTS 8 Manchester
21.03.83 Sammy Brennan **W** PTS 8 Bradford
16.05.83 Sammy Brennan **DREW** 10 Bradford
(*Vacant Central Area Middleweight Title*)
23.05.83 Brian Anderson **L** RSC 9 Sheffield
(*Vacant Central Area Middleweight Title*)
19.09.83 Blaine Longsden **L** PTS 8 Manchester
28.11.83 T. P. Jenkins **L** PTS 8 Southwark
Summary: 34 contests, won 17, drew 3, lost 14

Jimmy Ellis

Steve Ellwood
Derek Rowe (Photos) Ltd

Steve Ellwood

Camberwell. *Born* London 22.05.61
L. Welterweight
Manager B. McCarthy
Previous Amateur Club Lynn
National Honours Junior ABA Title 1976; NABC Title 1980
Divisional Honours SE London Lightweight Champion 1980; London L. Welterweight Champion 1981

26.04.82 Peter Flanagan **W** PTS 6 Southwark
02.11.82 Graham Brockway **W** PTS 6 Hornsey
22.11.82 Ricky Deane **W** RSC 2 Lewisham
15.12.82 Errol Dennis **W** PTS 6 Queensway
25.04.83 George Kerr **W** PTS 6 Piccadilly
22.09.83 Dennis Sullivan **W** PTS 8 Strand
23.02.84 Peter Foster **L** RSC 6 Digbeth
03.04.84 Alex Brown **W** RSC 3 Lewisham
Summary: 8 contests, won 7, lost 1

Steve Enright

Bradford. *Born* Limerick 26.12.53
Former Undefeated Central Area Bantamweight Champion
Manager T. Miller
Previous Amateur Club Halifax Star
Divisional Honours NE Counties Bantamweight Champion 1972

17.09.74 Ray Scott **W** PTS 6 Glasgow
21.10.74 Billy Smart **L** RSC 3 Nottingham
03.12.74 Ray Scott **W** PTS 6 Leeds
13.01.75 Gerry McBride **W** PTS 6 Nottingham
29.01.75 Richard Scarth **W** PTS 6 Stoke
06.03.75 Dave Tuohey DREW 6 Bradford
26.03.75 Dave Connell **L** PTS 6 Stoke
29.04.75 Dave Connell **L** PTS 6 Salford
22.09.75 Roger Doyle **L** PTS 6 Bedford
03.11.75 Frankie Wagstaff **W** PTS 6 Bedford
10.11.75 Dave Tuohey DREW 6 Bradford
02.12.75 Dave Tuohey **L** PTS 6 Leeds
10.12.75 Frankie Wagstaff **W** PTS 6 Bedford
26.04.76 Andy Dane **W** RSC 4 Nottingham
15.12.76 Don Aageson **W** PTS 6 Bradford
10.01.77 Wally Angliss **L** PTS 8 Walworth
02.02.77 George Sutton **L** RSC 2 Swansea
21.03.77 Lee Graham **L** RSC 5 Birmingham
21.04.77 Don Aageson **W** PTS 6 Liverpool
25.04.77 Tony Zeni **W** PTS 6 Northampton
16.05.77 Dave Wraxall **W** PTS 6 Manchester
26.05.77 Dave Wraxall **W** RSC 6 Bradford
14.06.77 Gary Davidson **L** RSC 6 Wembley
22.08.77 Alan Robertson **L** PTS 6 Stockton
02.11.77 Alan Robertson DREW 8 Newcastle
01.12.77 Tony Whitmore **W** PTS 6 Caister
18.01.78 Jimmy Brown **L** RSC 3 Stoke
13.02.78 Larry Richards **W** PTS 6 Manchester
20.02.78 Malcolm McHugh **W** PTS 6 Bradford
02.03.78 Larry Richards **L** PTS 6 Caister
20.03.78 Lawrence Devanney **L** PTS 8 Bradford
03.04.78 Larry Richards **W** PTS 6 Manchester
12.09.78 Gary Lucas **W** RSC 6 Birkenhead
18.09.78 Larry Richards DREW 6 Manchester
28.11.78 Doug Hill **L** PTS 6 Sheffield
18.12.78 Gary Lucas **W** PTS 6 Bradford
10.09.79 Carl Gaynor **W** PTS 6 Bradford
20.09.79 Chris Moorcroft **W** PTS 6 Liverpool
08.10.79 Ian Murray **W** PTS 6 Bradford
23.10.79 Ian Murray **L** PTS 6 Blackpool
05.12.79 Chris Moorcroft **W** PTS 6 Liverpool
10.12.79 Ian Murray **W** PTS 6 Manchester
17.12.79 Dave George **L** PTS 6 Bradford
24.01.80 John Feeney **L** PTS 8 Hartlepool
24.03.80 Jimmy Bott **W** PTS 10 Bradford
(*Vacant Central Area Bantamweight Title*)

20.10.80 Ivor Jones **W** PTS 8 Birmingham
26.11.80 Kelvin Smart L RSC 4 Solihull
19.10.81 Stuart Nicol L PTS 8 Glasgow
16.02.82 Jimmy Bott **W** PTS 8 Birmingham
28.04.82 Stuart Shaw L PTS 8 Burslem
24.05.82 John Farrell L PTS 6 Bradford
06.10.82 Stuart Shaw L RTD 5 Solihull
20.04.83 Ray Plant L PTS 8 South Shields
13.06.83 John Doherty DREW 6 Doncaster
24.10.83 Alec Irvine L RSC 5 Nottingham
20.02.84 Stuart Carmichael DREW 6 Bradford
29.02.84 Trevor Sumner L PTS 6 Sheffield
19.03.84 Stuart Carmichael **W** PTS 8 Bradford
Summary: 58 contests, won 27, drew 6, lost 25

Peter Eubanks

Brighton. *Born* Manchester 23.03.62
Lightweight
Manager J. Pook
Previous Amateur Club Newhaven & District
Divisional Honours S Counties Featherweight Champion 1980

20.10.80 Steve Farnsworth L PTS 6 Hove
16.02.81 David Miles L PTS 6 Piccadilly
02.03.81 Richie Foster L PTS 6 Brighton
23.03.81 Steve Henderson **W** PTS 6 Mayfair
30.03.81 Robert Hepburn **W** PTS 6 Piccadilly
27.04.81 Tony Davis **W** PTS 8 Brighton
15.06.81 Clyde Ruan L RSC 8 Piccadilly
03.08.81 Barry McGuigan **W** PTS 8 Brighton
08.12.81 Barry McGuigan L RSC 8 Belfast
08.02.82 Ian McLeod **W** PTS 8 Piccadilly
25.02.82 Rene Weller L PTS 8 Munich
22.04.82 Ian McLeod **W** PTS 8 Piccadilly
07.06.82 Winston Spencer L PTS 8 Piccadilly
22.09.82 Tony Willis L PTS 8 Mayfair
13.10.82 Vernon Entertainer Vanriel L PTS 8 Walthamstow
09.11.82 Mick Rowley **W** PTS 6 Belfast
06.04.83 Mick Rowley **W** RSC 6 Mayfair
15.10.83 Jeff Decker L PTS 8 Coventry
31.10.83 Bobby Welburn **W** RSC 1 Mayfair
26.01.84 Winston Spencer L RTD 5 Strand
Summary: 20 contests, won 9, lost 11

John Fallon

Hull. *Born* Hull 28.05.58
Heavyweight
Manager R. Tighe
Previous Amateur Club St Pauls
Divisional Honours NE Counties L. Heavyweight R/U 1978; NE Counties Heavyweight R/U 1981

26.05.82 Osbourne Taylor **W** RSC 1 Piccadilly
21.06.82 Eddie Cooper L RSC 1 Hull
29.11.82 Steve Howard **W** PTS 6 Brighton
20.12.82 Dave Garside **W** PTS 6 Bradford
10.02.83 John Westgarth L PTS 6 Walthamstow
16.03.83 Andrew Gerrard DREW 6 Cheltenham
21.03.83 Mark Cleverly L RSC 3 Piccadilly
22.05.83 Paddy Finn L RSC 6 Navan
15.09.83 Noel Quarless L PTS 8 Liverpool
19.10.83 Alan Douglas **W** PTS 8 Hull
Summary: 10 contests, won 4, drew 1, lost 5

Mike Farghaly

Manchester. *Born* Manchester 06.07.64
Middleweight
Manager N. Basso
Previous Amateur Club Sharston

19.09.83 Dave Mowbray **W** PTS 6 Manchester
28.10.83 Billy Edwards **W** CO 3 Queensferry
14.11.83 Dave Mowbray L RSC 1 Manchester
05.12.83 Floyd Davidson **W** RSC 2 Manchester
13.02.84 Dave Mowbray **W** RSC 2 Manchester
12.03.84 Paul Smith **W** PTS 8 Manchester
19.03.84 Kevin Shearon **W** RSC 3 Manchester
09.04.84 Paul Smith **W** RSC 3 Manchester
14.05.84 Chris Coady **W** RSC 8 Manchester
04.06.84 Harry Watson **W** CO 5 Manchester
18.06.84 Deka Williams **W** RSC 4 Manchester
Summary: 11 contests, won 10, lost 1

Peter Eubanks
Derek Rowe (Photos) Ltd

Steve Farnsworth
Sheffield. *Born* Sheffield 24.01.61
Former Central Area Featherweight Champion
Manager (Self)
Previous Amateur Club St. Vincent

09.09.80 Selvin Bell **W** PTS 6 Sheffield
15.09.80 Paul Huggins L PTS 6 Mayfair
29.09.80 Tony Manson **W** PTS 6 Chesterfield
13.10.80 Andy Thomas L PTS 6 Manchester
20.10.80 Peter Eubanks **W** PTS 6 Hove
03.12.80 Tony Manson **W** RSC 2 Sheffield
08.12.80 Martin Bolton **W** PTS 4 Hastings
21.01.81 Doug Hill L PTS 8 Burslem
02.02.81 Bryn Jones **W** PTS 6 Piccadilly
03.03.81 Ian Murray **W** PTS 6 Pudsey
17.03.81 Clyde Ruan L PTS 6 Southend
01.06.81 John Sharkey L RSC 3 Nottingham
15.09.81 Ray Plant L PTS 8 Sunderland
26.10.81 Steve Henderson **W** PTS 6 Mayfair
23.11.81 Ian Murray **W** PTS 10 Northwich (*Vacant Central Area Featherweight Title*)
22.03.82 Steve Henderson **W** PTS 8 Mayfair
21.05.82 Ray Plant **W** RSC 3 Sheffield
29.03.83 Steve Pollard L RSC 2 Hull (*Central Area Featherweight Title Defence*)

Summary: 18 contests, won 11, lost 7

John Farrell
Liverpool. *Born* Kirkby 18.06.58
Central Area Bantamweight Champion
Manager M. Goodall
Previous Amateur Club Holy Name
National Honours Young England Rep./England Int.
Divisional Honours W Lancs L. Flyweight R/U 1976; NW Counties Flyweight Champion 1977 – 1978; N Counties Bantamweight Champion 1979; W Lancs Bantamweight R/U 1980/1982

26.04.82 Ray Plant **W** PTS 6 Bradford
24.05.82 Steve Enright **W** PTS 6 Bradford
28.06.82 Jim Harvey **W** RSC 3 Bradford
20.09.82 Ian Murray **W** PTS 8 Bradford
18.10.82 Ian Murray **W** PTS 8 Blackpool
20.12.82 Keith Foreman L PTS 8 Bradford
24.02.83 Stuart Carmichael **W** RSC 4 Liverpool
08.04.83 George Bailey **W** RSC 7 Liverpool (*Vacant Central Area Bantamweight Title*)
09.12.83 Ray Gilbody DREW 10 Liverpool (*Central Area Bantamweight Title Defence*)

Summary: 9 contests, won 7, drew 1, lost 1

John Farrell
Douglas Baton

John Faulkner
Northampton. *Born* Northampton 05.12.61
L. Welterweight
Manager J. Cox
Previous Amateur Club Northampton

28.11.83 Billy Edwards **W** PTS 6 Bayswater
05.12.83 Mickey Cotton **W** PTS 6 Nottingham
12.12.83 Wayne Trigg **W** RSC 3 Birmingham
19.01.84 Vince Bailey L RSC 4 Digbeth
16.02.84 Ron Shinkwin L PTS 6 Basildon

Summary: 5 contests, won 3, lost 2

Michael Fawcett
West Ham. *Born* West Ham 22.10.61
Heavyweight
Manager (Self)
Previous Amateur Club New Enterprise

01.04.82 Glenroy Taylor **W** PTS 4 Walthamstow
13.09.82 Ian Lazarus **W** PTS 4 Brighton
10.02.83 Tony Blackstock L PTS 4 Walthamstow

Summary: 3 contests, won 2, lost 1

(Raffaele) Rocky Feliciello
Rhyl. *Born* St. Asaph 11.01.63
Welsh L. Middleweight Champion
Manager P. Dwyer
Previous Amateur Club Rhyl Star
Divisional Honours Welsh L. Middleweight R/U 1982

05.10.82 Rick Warrilow **W** RSC 5 Liverpool
01.11.82 John Davies **W** PTS 6 Liverpool
20.01.83 Davy Campbell L PTS 6 Birkenhead

07.02.83 Ian Henderson-Thynne W PTS 6 Liverpool
04.03.83 Bert Myrie W PTS 6 Queensferry
29.04.83 Blaine Longsden W PTS 6 Liverpool
17.06.83 Deano Wallace W RTD 5 Queensferry
28.10.83 Davy Campbell W PTS 8 Queensferry
24.11.83 John Andrews L RSC 5 Kirkby
17.02.84 John McGlynn W RSC 8 Rhyl
(*Vacant Welsh L. Middleweight Title*)
26.03.84 Paul Mitchell W PTS 8 Barnsley
02.05.84 Judas Clottey W PTS 8 Solihull
Summary: 12 contests, won 10, lost 2

Gary Felvus

Leeds. *Born* Los Angeles, USA 01.03.60
Lightweight
Manager T. Callighan
Previous Amateur Club Keighley
National Honours Young England Rep./England Int.
Divisional Honours NEC Featherweight Champion 1978; NE Counties Lightweight Champion 1980; ABA Lightweight R/U 1982

21.02.83 Willie Wilson W PTS 6 Nottingham
05.12.83 Muhammad Lovelock W PTS 6 Manchester
06.03.84 Edward Lloyd W PTS 8 Stoke
14.05.84 Willie Wilson W RSC 7 Nottingham
Summary: 4 contests, won 4

Gary Felvus

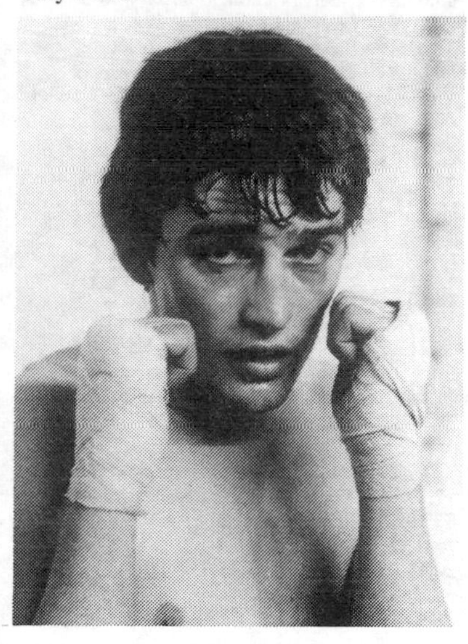

Eddie Fenton

Leicester. *Born* Leicester 12.01.54
Former Midlands Area L. Heavyweight Champion
Manager (Self)
Previous Amateur Club Thurmaston
Divisional Honours M Counties Middleweight R/U 1972

22.04.74 John Celebanski L PTS 6 Nottingham
29.04.74 John Depledge W PTS 6 Bristol
06.05.74 David Fry W RSC 4 Bedford
13.05.74 Lloyd Stewart W PTS 6 Nottingham
03.06.74 Lloyd Stewart W PTS 6 Manchester
24.06.74 Lloyd Stewart W PTS 6 Bedford
09.09.74 Tony Moore L PTS 6 Bedford
16.09.74 Dave Parris W CO 2 Birmingham
07.10.74 David Fry DREW 8 Bristol
14.10.74 John Celebanski W DIS 5 Bedford
23.10.74 Guinea Roger W PTS 8 Stoke
13.11.74 Steve Foley W PTS 8 Solihull
18.11.74 Neville Meade L RSC 5 Piccadilly
17.02.75 Tony Moore L PTS 6 Mayfair
04.03.75 John Depledge L RSC 3 Portsmouth
28.04.75 John Depledge W PTS 8 Kensington
14.05.75 Syd Paddock W CO 7 Camberley
24.06.75 Denton Ruddock L PTS 6 Piccadilly
24.09.75 David Fry W PTS 8 Solihull
10.10.75 Sid Falconer L PTS 8 Birmingham
10.11.75 Peter Freeman W PTS 8 Bradford
25.11.75 Eddie Neilson L RTD 3 Kensington
16.01.76 David Fry W PTS 8 Bournemouth
22.03.76 John Depledge W DIS 6 Nottingham
09.04.76 Garfield McEwan L PTS 10 Birmingham
(*Vacant Midlands Area Heavyweight Title*)
27.04.76 Paul Kinsella W RSC 4 Kensington
14.07.76 Danny McAlinden L RSC 4 Wolverhampton
27.09.76 Ishaq Hussien L PTS 8 Mayfair
14.12.76 Brian Huckfield NC 6 West Bromwich
10.02.77 Terry O'Connor L PTS 8 Coventry
23.02.77 Ishaq Hussien L RTD 3 Bradford
04.05.77 Garfield McEwan L PTS 8 Solihull
10.07.77 Tony Allen L RSC 8 Birmingham
05.09.77 Greg Evans L RSC 3 Mayfair
19.10.77 Roy John DREW 8 Kingston
12.12.77 Sid Falconer W PTS 8 Piccadilly
03.03.78 Ennio Cometti L CO 8 Milan
23.05.78 Tim Wood L PTS 8 Leicester
11.10.78 Gordon Ferris L CO 1 Belfast
20.11.78 Tim Wood L PTS 8 Evesham
28.02.79 Carlton Benoit W RSC 5 Burslem
28.03.79 Tim Wood W PTS 8 Evesham
02.05.79 Tony Allen W DIS 7 Solihull

CONTINUED OVERLEAF

(Midlands Area L. Heavyweight Title Challenge)
26.06.79 Ken Jones **W** RSC 8 Leicester
24.09.79 Danny Lawford L CO 1 Birmingham
27.11.79 Harry White L PTS 10 Wolverhampton
(Midlands Area L. Heavyweight Title Defence)
19.03.80 Harry White **W** PTS 10 Solihull
(Midlands Area L. Heavyweight Title Challenge
21.05.80 Howard Mills L CO 2 Coventry
08.07.80 Roy Skeldon L RSC 6 Wolverhampton
(Midlands Area L. Heavyweight Title Defence)
29.02.84 Alan Douglas L PTS 6 Sheffield
26.03.84 Alan Douglas L PTS 6 Leicester
12.04.84 Lee White DREW 6 Piccadilly
30.04.84 Lee White DREW 6 Mayfair
14.05.84 Lee White L PTS 6 Nottingham
Summary: 54 contests, won 22, drew 4, lost 27, NC 1

Paddy Finn
Dublin. *Born* Birmingham 30.04.60
Heavyweight
Manager P. Byrne
Previous Amateur Club Donore
National Honours Irish S. Heavyweight Champion 1981; Irish Int.

11.09.81 Rocky Burton **W** PTS 6 Edgbaston
21.09.81 Hughroy Currie **W** PTS 6 Wolverhampton
06.07.82 Noel Quarless **W** CO 2 Leeds
22.05.83 John Fallon **W** RSC 6 Navan
14.09.83 Anders Eklund L CO 1 Muswell Hill
Summary 5 contests, won 4, lost 1

Neville Fivey
Coventry. *Born* Belfast 28.02.64
Lightweight
Manager J. Jackson
Previous Amateur Club Bell Green

16.05.83 Mick Hoolison **W** PTS 6 Bradford
13.06.83 Joey Wainwright L RSC 4 Coventry
04.10.83 Mark Reefer L PTS 6 Bethnal Green
15.10.83 Mick Hoolison **W** PTS 6 Coventry
12.12.83 Kenny Walsh L PTS 6 Bedworth
27.02.84 George Baigrie **W** PTS 6 Nottingham
14.03.84 Nicky Day L PTS 6 Mayfair
27.03.84 Dean Bramhald DREW 6 Wolverhampton
Summary: 8 contests, won 3, drew 1, lost 4

Peter Flanagan
Manchester. *Born* Hyde 10.04.57
Welterweight
Manager N. Basso
Previous Amateur Club Mossley

18.05.81 Mike Dunlop **W** PTS 4 Manchester
15.06.81 Bobby Rimmer L RSC 2 Manchester
07.09.81 Peter Phillips **W** RSC 5 Liverpool
06.10.81 Ray Hood L RSC 5 Liverpool
04.11.81 Kenny Rathburn **W** PTS 6 Derby
23.11.81 Peter Phillips DREW 6 Nantwich
02.12.81 John Malone **W** PTS 6 Manchester
11.01.82 Savvy Amer **W** CO 2 Liverpool
01.02.82 Peter Phillips **W** RSC 2 Manchester
08.02.82 Tony Wilkinson L PTS 4 Manchester
05.04.82 Vince Griffin **W** RSC 2 Manchester
26.04.82 Steve Ellwood L PTS 6 Southwark
13.09.82 Phil Sheridan **W** CO 2 Manchester
11.10.82 Winston Ho-Shing L RSC 5 Manchester
25.11.82 Mark Davey L PTS 6 Morley
06.12.82 Stan Atherton **W** PTS 6 Manchester
14.02.83 Mike Calderwood **W** PTS 6 Manchester
29.03.83 Bobby Welburn **W** PTS 6 Hull
12.05.83 Bobby McGowan **W** RSC 5 Morley
23.05.83 Jimmy Thornton L RSC 3 Sheffield
16.09.83 Ken Foreman L PTS 8 Rhyl
07.11.83 Ron Atherton **W** CO 3 Liverpool
28.11.83 Vince Vahey L PTS 6 Rhyl
07.12.83 Tony McKenzie L PTS 6 Stoke
13.02.84 Lenny Gloster L RSC 6 Manchester
05.03.84 George Schofield DREW 6 Liverpool
31.03.84 Steve Craggs L PTS 6 Derby
30.04.84 Paul Kelly L RSC 4 Liverpool
Summary: 28 contests, won 13, drew 2, lost 13

Colin Flute
Tipton. *Born* Tipton 11.01.54
Heavyweight
Manager (Self)
Previous Amateur Club Bilston GG

18.10.77 Clive Beardsley L PTS 6 Wolverhampton
08.11.77 Bob Young L RSC 5 West Bromwich
17.04.78 Frank Caulfield DREW 6 Walworth
29.06.78 Terry O'Connor L PTS 8 Wolverhampton
12.07.78 Neil Malpass L RSC 6 Newcastle
27.09.78 Terry Chard L RSC 5 Evesham
31.10.78 Roy Skeldon **W** CO 4 Wolverhampton
20.11.78 Derek Simpkin L PTS 6 Birmingham
28.03.79 Glen Adair L PTS 6 Kettering

10.04.79 Roy Skeldon L PTS 4 Wolverhampton
16.05.79 Roy Skeldon L RSC 4 Wolverhampton
26.06.79 Steve Fenton L PTS 8 Leicester
26.09.79 Stewart Lithgo L RSC 4 Solihull
13.12.79 Martin Nee W PTS 6 Wolverhampton
17.03.80 Mick Chmilowskyj L RSC 2 Mayfair
14.05.80 Steve Gee L PTS 6 Burslem
22.09.80 Steve Gee L PTS 6 Birmingham
25.11.80 Rocky Burton L RSC 7 Bedworth
01.11.83 Alex Romeo W PTS 6 Dudley
01.12.83 Deka Williams W PTS 6 Dudley
10.02.84 Deka Williams L RSC 2 Dudley
07.06.84 Theo Josephs W PTS 6 Dudley
Summary: 22 contests, won 5, drew 1, lost 16

Danny Flynn
Edinburgh. *Born* Edinburgh 02.12.62
Scottish Bantamweight Champion
Manager T. Gilmour
Previous Amateur Club Meadowbank
National Honours Scottish Flyweight Champion 1980; Scottish Int.

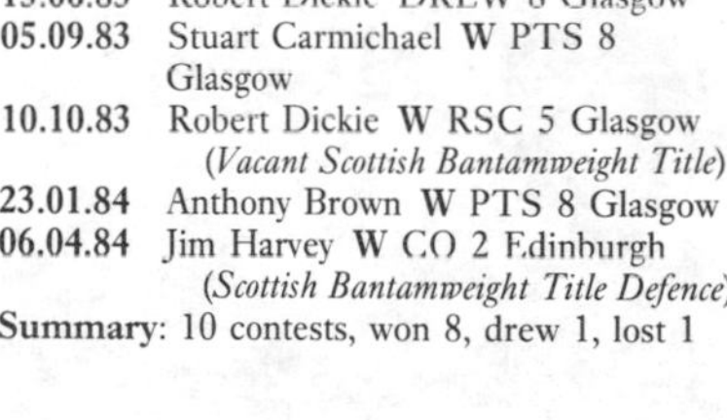

20.09.82 Chip O'Neill W RSC 2 Glasgow
08.12.82 Gary Roberts W RSC 6 Piccadilly
24.01.83 Anthony Brown W PTS 8 Glasgow
21.03.83 Michael Marsden W PTS 8 Glasgow
18.04.83 Dave George L PTS 8 Glasgow
13.06.83 Robert Dickie DREW 8 Glasgow
05.09.83 Stuart Carmichael W PTS 8 Glasgow
10.10.83 Robert Dickie W RSC 5 Glasgow (*Vacant Scottish Bantamweight Title*)
23.01.84 Anthony Brown W PTS 8 Glasgow
06.04.84 Jim Harvey W CO 2 Edinburgh (*Scottish Bantamweight Title Defence*)
Summary: 10 contests, won 8, drew 1, lost 1

Dave Foley
Doncaster. *Born* Carcroft 07.08.59
Middleweight
Manager J. Rushton
Previous Amateur Club Plant Works

16.05.83 Peter Phillips L PTS 6 Bradford
13.06.83 Sam Church W PTS 6 Doncaster
20.06.83 Kid Sadler L RSC 3 Manchester
25.01.84 Phil Sheridan DREW 6 Stoke
27.02.84 Lou Johnson W PTS 6 Nottingham
Summary: 5 contests, won 2, drew 1, lost 2

Danny Flynn
Scotsman/Evening News

Tyrone Forbes
Notting Hill. *Born* Paddington 31.07.59
Middleweight
Manager A. Lavelle
Previous Amateur Club All Stars
National Honours ABA Middleweight Champion 1983
Divisional Honours NW London Middleweight R/U 1982

23.05.84 Mickey Kidd W PTS 8 Mayfair
Summary: 1 contest, won 1

Keith Foreman
Hartlepool. *Born* Hartlepool 29.07.62
Lightweight
Manager T. Miller
Previous Amateur Club Hartlepool BW

16.02.81 Andy Broughton L CO 6 Bradford
02.07.81 Tony Whitmore W PTS 6 Pudsey
05.08.81 Rory Burke L RTD 2 Norwich
23.11.81 Tony Whitmore W PTS 6 Chesterfield

CONTINUED OVERLEAF

08.01.82 Ray Plant L PTS 6 Durham
24.01.82 Robert Hepburn W RTD 3 Sunderland
15.02.82 Brian Hyslop L PTS 6 Glasgow
18.03.82 Jim Harvey W PTS 6 South Shields
23.03.82 Hugh Russell L RSC 1 Belfast
31.08.82 Ray Plant L PTS 6 South Shields
26.09.82 Ian Murray W PTS 6 Middlesbrough
18.10.82 Gerry Devine W PTS 6 Glasgow
25.10.82 Ray Plant W PTS 6 Bradford
14.11.82 Richie Foster L CO 7 Navan
20.12.82 John Farrell W PTS 8 Bradford
10.02.83 Steve Pollard W PTS 8 Sunderland
21.02.83 Vince Vahey L PTS 8 Bradford
02.03.83 Seamus McGuinness L PTS 6 Belfast
11.04.83 Dave Haggarty DREW 8 Glasgow
18.04.83 Mervyn Bennett W RSC 6 Bradford
23.05.83 Dave Haggarty L PTS 8 Glasgow
06.06.83 Michael Harris L PTS 8 Piccadilly
13.06.83 James Cooke L PTS 6 Coventry
05.09.83 Jimmy Bunclark L CO 7 Liverpool
30.09.83 Les Remikie W PTS 8 Leicester
05.10.83 Peppy Muir L PTS 6 Belfast
19.10.83 Jackie Turner L PTS 8 Hull
14.11.83 Gary Lucas DREW 8 Nantwich
19.12.83 Mark Davey W PTS 8 Bradford
16.01.84 Gary Lucas L PTS 8 Bradford
27.02.84 Ian McLeod L PTS 8 Glasgow
01.05.84 Jim McDonnell L PTS 8 Bethnal Green
04.06.84 Najib Daho L CO 5 Manchester
Summary: 33 contests, won 12, drew 2, lost 19

Ken Foreman

Hartlepool. *Born* Hartlepool 29.07.62
J. Welterweight
Manager (Self)
Previous Amateur Club Hartlepool BW

13.11.80 Jim Harvey W PTS 4 Newcastle
25.11.80 Chris McCallum W PTS 6 Doncaster
15.12.80 Winston Ho-Shing W RSC 2 Bradford
26.01.81 Billy Laidman W PTS 6 Gosforth
16.02.81 Winston Ho-Shing W PTS 6 Bradford
09.03.81 Billy Laidman W PTS 6 Hamilton
24.03.81 Andy Broughton W PTS 6 Sheffield
02.04.81 Selvin Bell W PTS 6 Middlesbrough
11.05.81 Robert Wakefield W RSC 3 Bradford
08.06.81 Paul Wake W RSC 5 Bradford
29.06.81 Brian Snagg W PTS 8 Liverpool
16.08.81 Rene Weller L CO 2 Frankfurt
29.10.81 Chris McCallum L CO 6 Glasgow
08.01.82 Gerry Beard L RSC 6 Durham
23.05.83 Tommy Cook W RSC 5 Glasgow
16.09.83 Peter Flanagan W PTS 8 Rhyl
19.10.83 Bobby Welburn W PTS 6 Hull
14.11.83 Ray Hood W PTS 8 Nantwich
19.12.83 Tony Kempson W RTD 2 Bradford
16.01.84 Steve Tempro W PTS 8 Bradford
14.03.84 Ray Price W PTS 6 Mayfair
17.04.84 Mick Rowley L RSC 5 Piccadilly
Summary: 22 contests, won 18, lost 4

Tyrone Forbes
Gloucester Photo Agency

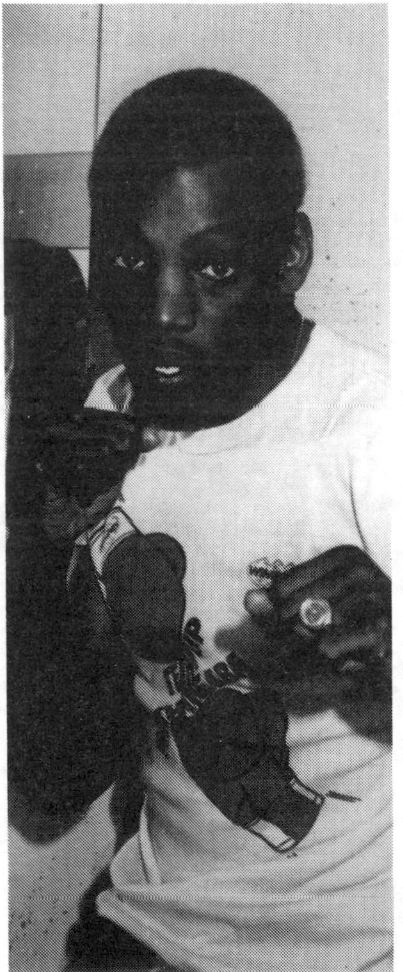

Keith Foreman

Paul Foster
Hartlepool. *Born* Hartlepool 19.03.62
L. Heavyweight
Manager D. Mancini
Previous Amateur Club Hartlepool BW

28.11.83 Lennie Howard **L** CO 2 Southwark
Summary: 1 contest, lost 1

Peter Foster
Birmingham. *Born* Jamaica 02.06.61
Welterweight
Manager P. Lynch
Previous Amateur Club Birmingham City

05.10.83 John Daly **W** RTD 4 Solihull
19.01.84 Joe Lynch **W** CO 1 Digbeth
30.01.84 Tommy Campbell **W** RTD 3 Glasgow
23.02.84 Steve Ellwood **W** RSC 6 Digbeth
10.05.84 Vince Stewart **W** RSC 6 Digbeth
Summary: 5 contests, won 5

Tommy Frankham
Kentish Town. *Born* Aylesbury 07.04.65
Lightweight
Manager D. Smith
Previous Amateur Club New Enterprise
National Honours Schools Title 1978
Divisional Honours NW London Lightweight R/U 1983

22.09.83 Kenny Watson **W** PTS 6 Strand
Summary: 1 contest, won 1

Ronnie Fraser
Birmingham. *Born* Birmingham 03.11.59
Middleweight
Manager E. Cashmore
Previous Amateur Club Nechells

12.12.83 Tucker Watts **L** PTS 6 Birmingham
14.02.84 Ian Martin **W** PTS 6 Wolverhampton
15.03.84 Tucker Watts **L** PTS 6 Leicester
21.03.84 Nigel Shingles **L** PTS 6 Solihull
26.03.84 Craig Edwards **W** PTS 6 Barnsley
16.04.84 Shamus Casey **W** RSC 3 Nottingham
Summary: 6 contests, won 3, lost 3

Steve Friel
Buncrana. *Born* Derry 24.06.60
L. Welterweight
Manager R. Barron
Previous Amateur Club Ring

27.02.84 Phil Sheridan **L** PTS 6 Birmingham
07.03.84 Ron Shinkwin **W** PTS 6 Brighton
21.03.84 John Andrews **L** RSC 2 Bloomsbury
10.05.84 Martin McGough **L** RSC 6 Digbeth
Summary: 4 contests, won 1, lost 3

Joey Frost
Liverpool. *Born* Liverpool 14.07.60
Central Area Welterweight Champion
Manager M. Goodall
Previous Amateur Club Bronte
National Honours Schools Title 1976; Junior ABA Titles 1976 – 1977; NABC Title 1978; Young England Rep.; England Int.; GB Rep.; ABA Welterweight Champion 1979
Divisional Honours W Lancs L. Welterweight Champion 1978; N Counties Welterweight Champion 1980; N Counties L. Middleweight Champion 1981

24.09.81 Kevin Walsh **W** CO 1 Liverpool
28.09.81 Jeff Aspell **W** RSC 1 Bradford
13.10.81 Chris Coady **W** PTS 8 Blackpool
21.12.81 Nigel Thomas **W** CO 2 Bradford
01.03.82 Horace McKenzie **W** PTS 8 Preston
20.05.82 Tommy McCallum **W** RSC 1 Preston
24.06.82 Dave Douglas **L** RSC 4 Kirkby
25.11.82 Peter Bennett **W** RSC 4 Morley (*Vacant Central Area Welterweight Title*)
24.01.83 Lloyd Christie **L** RSC 4 Bradford
24.02.83 Lee Hartshorn **W** RSC 5 Liverpool (*Central Area Welterweight Title Defence*)
15.06.84 Phil O'Hare **W** CO 6 Liverpool
Summary: 11 contests, won 9, lost 2

Joey Frost
Derek Rowe (Photos) Ltd

Damien Fryers

Belfast. *Born* Belfast 03.10.62
Welterweight
Manager B. Eastwood
Previous Amateur Club Holy Trinity
National Honours Irish Lightweight Champion 1981; Irish Int.

05.10.82 Elvis Morton **W** PTS 6 Belfast
09.11.82 Jimmy Bunclark **W** RSC 5 Belfast
14.12.82 Mick Dono **W** RSC 5 Belfast
25.01.83 Bobby Welburn **W** PTS 6 Belfast
02.03.83 Steve Ward **W** PTS 6 Belfast
12.04.83 Valentino Maccarinelli **W** RSC 4 Belfast
22.05.83 Sam Omidi **W** PTS 6 Navan
05.10.83 Davy Campbell **W** PTS 6 Belfast
Summary: 8 contests, won 8

Peter Gabbitus

Doncaster. *Born* Cantley 23.01.63
Featherweight
Manager J. Rushton
Previous Amateur Club Elmfield House
National Honours Schools Titles 1978 – 1979; Junior ABA Titles 1978 – 1979; NABC Title 1980

20.05.80 Iggy Jano **W** PTS 4 Southend
11.06.80 George Bailey **W** PTS 4 Morecambe
30.07.80 Brindley Jones **W** PTS 4 Doncaster
22.10.80 Steve Sammy Sims L PTS 4 Doncaster
25.11.80 Jim Harvey **W** PTS 4 Doncaster
19.01.81 Jim Harvey **W** PTS 4 Bradford
02.03.81 Paul Huggins L RSC 1 Brighton
10.06.81 Selvin Bell L PTS 6 Brodsworth
17.05.82 Lou Buttice **W** RSC 2 Windsor
28.06.82 Ian Murray **W** PTS 6 Bradford
07.09.82 Joey Joynson L RSC 2 Hornsey
19.01.83 Alan Tombs **W** RSC 2 Stoke
25.02.83 Paul Keers **W** RSC 4 Doncaster
10.10.83 Steve Topliss **W** PTS 8 Birmingham
Summary: 14 contests, won 10, lost 4

Carl Gaffney

Leeds. *Born* Leeds 15.04.64
Heavyweight
Manager T. Callighan
Previous Amateur Club Market District

12.05.84 Steve Abadom **W** RSC 3 Hanley
Summary: 1 contest, won 1

Vince Gajny

Stratford-on-Avon. *Born* Stratford-on-Avon 16.08.54
Middleweight
Manager J. Griffin
Previous Amateur Club Stratford
Divisional Honours M Counties L. Middleweight R/U 1978/1979; M Counties L. Middleweight Champion 1980

19.10.80 Clifton Wallace **W** PTS 6 Birmingham
05.11.80 Clifton Wallace DREW 6 Evesham
25.11.80 Neville Wilson **W** PTS 6 Bedworth
30.03.81 Steve Henty **W** PTS 6 Piccadilly
25.09.81 Kid Murray **W** PTS 6 Nottingham
30.09.81 Kid Murray **W** PTS 6 Evesham
07.10.81 Willie Wright **W** PTS 6 Stoke
20.10.81 Larry Monaghan **W** PTS 6 Leeds
10.11.81 Willie Wright **W** PTS 6 Bedworth
27.01.82 Dennis Sheehan **W** PTS 6 Stoke
09.02.82 Rob Wada **W** PTS 6 Wolverhampton
21.02.82 Deano Wallace **W** PTS 6 Nottingham
05.04.82 Russell Humphreys **W** PTS 8 Nottingham
20.09.82 Deano Wallace DREW 8 Wolverhampton
06.12.82 Nick Jenkins L RSC 7 Bristol
31.01.83 Jack Sharp **W** PTS 6 Southwark
16.04.83 Nick Jenkins **W** PTS 8 Bristol
13.06.83 Errol Christie L RSC 2 Coventry
20.09.83 Cameron Lithgow **W** PTS 8 Piccadilly
23.11.83 James Cook L RTD 6 Solihull
14.03.84 Cameron Lithgow L RSC 6 Mayfair
Summary: 21 contests, won 15, drew 2, lost 4

Danny Garrison

Wolverhampton. *Born* Wolverhampton 27.01.63
Welterweight
Manager M. Sendell
Previous Amateur Club Wolverhampton
National Honours Schools Titles 1976 – 1977; NABC Title 1980
Divisional Honours M Counties Lightweight Champion 1980

24.05.82 Steve Tempro **W** RSC 3 Wolverhampton
22.06.82 Alan Power **W** RTD 3 Hornsey
06.07.82 Tony Brown L PTS 6 Leeds
20.09.82 Tony Sinnott DREW 8 Bradford
13.10.82 Valentino Maccarinelli **W** CO 2 Evesham
02.11.82 Rocky Kelly L PTS 8 Hornsey
18.11.82 Dave Allen L RSC 5 Coventry
04.03.83 Ian Chantler L CO 5 Queensferry
Summary: 8 contests, won 3, drew 1, lost 4

Denny Garrison

Wolverhampton. *Born* Wolverhampton 27.01.63
L. Welterweight
Manager M. Sendell
Previous Amateur Club Bilston Golden Gloves

13.10.82 Andy Thomas L PTS 6 Evesham
24.11.82 Gary Lucas **W** PTS 6 Stoke
25.01.83 Johnny Grant L PTS 6 Bethnal Green
Summary: 3 contests, won 1, lost 2

Dave Garside
Douglas Baton

Dave Garside

Hartlepool. *Born* Hartlepool 14.03.63
Heavyweight
Manager D. Mancini
Previous Amateur Club Hartlepool BW
National Honours Young England Rep./England Int.
Divisional Honours ABA Heavyweight R/U 1981; N Counties Heavyweight Champion 1982

26.09.82 Eddie Cooper **W** PTS 6 Middlesbrough
18.10.82 Hughroy Currie L RTD 4 Southwark
29.11.82 Frank Robinson **W** PTS 6 Birmingham
20.12.82 John Fallon L PTS 6 Bradford
25.01.83 John Leitch **W** RSC 2 Belfast
23.02.83 John Westgarth **W** RTD 6 Mayfair
28.02.83 Frank Robinson **W** RSC 4 Birmingham
21.03.83 Theo Josephs **W** PTS 6 Bradford
11.04.83 Derek Simpkin **W** PTS 6 Gosforth
20.04.83 Steve Abadom **W** RSC 4 South Shields
22.09.83 Andrew Gerrard L PTS 8 Cardiff
24.10.83 Mark Cleverly **W** PTS 6 Mayfair
29.11.83 Andrew Gerrard L PTS 8 Cardiff
10.02.84 Al Malcolm **W** PTS 6 Dudley
14.03.84 Frank Robinson **W** PTS 8 Stoke
22.03.84 Grant Wallis **W** RSC 5 Maidenhead
30.04.84 Denroy Bryan **W** PTS 8 Mayfair
Summary: 17 contests, won 13, lost 4

Carl Gaynor

Manchester. *Born* Rochdale 05.06.61
Featherweight
Manager (Self)
Previous Amateur Club Ancoats

10.09.79 Steve Enright L PTS 6 Bradford
16.10.79 Ivor Jones L RSC 3 Lewisham
19.11.79 Kelvin Smart L RSC 3 Edgbaston
10.12.79 Chris Moorcroft L RSC 2 Manchester
10.09.80 Carl Mullings DREW 6 Liverpool
20.10.80 Paul Huggins L PTS 6 Hove
17.11.80 Ray Plant L PTS 6 Gosforth
15.12.80 David Miles L PTS 6 Merthyr
26.01.81 Ray Plant L PTS 6 Gosforth
11.03.81 Larry Richards L RSC 4 Burslem
29.04.81 Dave Smithson **W** PTS 6 Burslem
04.05.81 Brian Hyslop L RSC 5 Glasgow
08.06.81 Carl Campbell DREW 6 Bradford
15.06.81 Alan Burns **W** PTS 4 Manchester
29.06.81 Derek Groarke L CO 1 Liverpool
11.09.81 Don Aageson L PTS 6 Edgbaston
09.11.81 Steve Topliss L PTS 8 Derby
30.11.81 Steve Henderson L RSC 6 Birmingham
11.05.82 Eddie Toro L PTS 6 Derby
07.06.82 Kevin Hay **W** PTS 6 Sheffield
17.09.82 Mark Drew L PTS 4 Liverpool
18.10.82 John Doherty L PTS 6 Blackpool
26.10.82 Stuart Carmichael L PTS 6 Hull
29.11.82 Shaun Shinkwin L PTS 6 Southwark
07.01.83 Ray Plant L PTS 6 Durham
31.01.83 Shaun Shinkwin **W** PTS 6 Southwark
22.02.83 Joey Joynson L RSC 3 Bethnal Green
17.06.83 John Drummond L PTS 6 Queensferry
Summary: 28 contests, won 4, drew 2, lost 22

Steve Gee (Egege)

Birmingham. *Born* Bradford 01.04.61
Heavyweight
Manager E. Cashmore
Previous Amateur Club Nechells

15.04.80 Mike Creasey **W** RSC 5 Blackpool
29.04.80 Don Charles **W** RSC 2 Mayfair
14.05.80 Colin Flute **W** PTS 6 Burslem
22.09.80 Colin Flute **W** PTS 6 Birmingham
19.10.80 Jim Burns **W** RSC 3 Birmingham
30.10.80 Derek Simpkin DREW 6 Wolverhampton
10.11.80 Bob Hennessey L PTS 8 Birmingham
19.01.81 Martin Nee L RSC 5 Wimbledon
11.03.81 Rocky Burton **W** PTS 8 Solihull
25.03.81 Ian Scotting **W** PTS 8 Doncaster
28.04.81 Theo Josephs **W** PTS 8 Leeds
11.09.81 Jim Burns L PTS 8 Edgbaston
05.10.81 Hughroy Currie L PTS 6 Birmingham
08.11.81 Joe Christle L PTS 6 Navan
12.01.82 Martin Herdman **W** PTS 6 Bethnal Green
18.02.82 Noel Quarless L PTS 6 Liverpool

CONTINUED OVERLEAF

09.03.82 Martin Nee W PTS 8 Hornsey
30.03.82 Rudi Pika L PTS 8 Wembley
22.04.82 Joe Christle W RSC 6 Liverpool
22.06.82 Tommy Kiely W RSC 7 Hornsey
07.09.82 Stan McDermott L PTS 8 Hornsey
16.10.82 Mel Christle W RSC 6 Killarney
02.11.82 Martin Nee W RSC 5 Hornsey
14.11.82 Joe Christle DREW 6 Navan
22.11.82 Billy Aird L PTS 8 Lewisham
07.12.82 Theo Josephs W PTS 6 Southend
14.04.83 Winston Allen W PTS 8 Basildon
04.06.83 Mike Perkins L PTS 8 Atlantic City
03.09.83 Pierre Coetzer L PTS 8 Johannesburg
17.12.83 Anders Eklund L RSC 5 Mariehamn
28.01.84 Daniele Falconetti L PTS 6 Marsala
Summary: 31 contests, won 16, drew 2, lost 13

Dave George

Swansea. *Born* Swansea 13.11.59
Bantamweight
Manager P. Byrne
Previous Amateur Club Swansea Docks
National Honours Schools Titles 1973 & 1975; Welsh Flyweight Champion 1977 & Bantamweight Champion 1978 – 1979; Welsh Int.

03.10.79 Iggy Jano W CO 4 Reading
12.11.79 Alan Storey W PTS 6 Middlesbrough
17.12.79 Steve Enright W PTS 6 Bradford
25.02.80 Selvin Bell W PTS 8 Bradford
14.10.80 Jimmy Bott W PTS 8 Nantwich
29.10.80 Jimmy Bott W PTS 8 Burslem
01.12.80 Neil McLaughlin W PTS 8 Reading
06.04.81 George Bailey W PTS 8 Bradford
19.04.81 Gary Nickels W RSC 1 Ebbw Vale
(*Final Elim. British Flyweight Title*)
21.05.82 Antoine Montero L PTS 8 Geneva
14.09.82 Kelvin Smart L CO 6 Wembley
(*Vacant British Flyweight Title*)
25.01.83 Davy Larmour L RSC 6 Belfast
21.02.83 Steve Cleak L PTS 8 Glasgow
25.03.83 Franco Cherchi L PTS 8 Milan
18.04.83 Danny Flynn W PTS 8 Glasgow
04.10.83 Johnny Dorey DREW 10 Bethnal Green
23.01.84 Johnny Dorey W PTS 8 Mayfair
20.02.84 Ray Gilbody L RSC 2 Mayfair
(*Elim. British Bantamweight Title*)
Summary: 18 contests, won 11, drew 1, lost 6

Don George

Swansea. *Born* Swansea 04.11.57
Former Undefeated Welsh Featherweight Champion
Manager B. Walker
Previous Amateur Club Swansea Docks
National Honours Welsh Featherweight Champion 1976 – 1977 & Lightweight Champion 1979; Welsh Int.
Divisional Honours Welsh Featherweight R/U 1978

12.09.79 Paul Keers L PTS 6 Liverpool
22.10.79 Selvin Bell W PTS 6 Nottingham
28.01.80 Terry McKeown DREW 6 Glasgow
01.04.80 Austin Owens L PTS 8 Wembley
12.05.80 Ian Murray W RTD 7 Reading
19.05.80 Alan Storey W RTD 7 Piccadilly
24.09.80 Gary Lucas W PTS 8 Burslem
14.10.80 Steve Sammy Sims W PTS 8 Nantwich
17.03.81 Alan Cooper W PTS 8 Southend
02.05.81 Azumah Nelson L CO 5 Accra
14.09.81 Ian McLeod L PTS 8 Glasgow
19.11.81 Mervyn Bennett W PTS 10 Ebbw Vale
(*Vacant Welsh Featherweight Title*)
21.04.83 Mark West W PTS 8 Piccadilly
01.11.83 Jean Marc-Renard L CO 4 Izegem
Summary: 14 contests, won 8, drew 1, lost 5

Andrew Gerrard

Risca. *Born* Newport 29.05.63
Heavyweight
Manager W. May
Previous Amateur Club Newbridge

26.10.82 Frank Robinson W PTS 6 Newport
29.11.82 John Westgarth DREW 6 Newquay
26.01.83 Frank Robinson L PTS 6 Stoke
01.03.83 Tom Eastwood L PTS 6 Southend
07.03.83 Mark Cleverly L PTS 6 Piccadilly
16.03.83 John Fallon DREW 6 Cheltenham
25.03.83 Tom Eastwood L PTS 6 Bloomsbury
21.04.83 Mark Cleverly W PTS 6 Piccadilly
27.05.83 Scott Wilde W PTS 6 Swansea
14.06.83 Frank Robinson W RTD 3 Newport
22.09.83 Dave Garside W PTS 8 Cardiff
24.10.83 Horace Notice L PTS 6 Mayfair
29.11.83 Dave Garside W PTS 8 Cardiff
27.04.84 Horace Notice L RSC 2 Wolverhampton
13.06.84 Glenn McCrory L PTS 6 Aberavon
Summary: 15 contests, won 6, drew 2, lost 7

Gary Gething

Tredegar. *Born* Abergavenny 28.11.59
Middleweight
Manager J. Evans
Previous Amateur Club New Tredegar
National Honours Welsh L. Middleweight Champion 1982; Welsh Int.
Divisional Honours Welsh L. Middleweight R/U 1978

10.10.82 Bobby Williams **W** PTS 6 Piccadilly
01.11.82 James Cook **L** RSC 2 Piccadilly
14.06.83 Scott Wilde **W** PTS 6 Newport
20.09.83 John Elliott **W** PTS 6 Dudley
27.10.83 Bobby Williams **W** PTS 6 Ebbw Vale

Summary: 5 contests, won 4, lost 1

Ray Gilbody

St. Helens. *Born* Southport 21.03.60
Bantamweight
Manager M. Barrett
Previous Amateur Club St. Helens Star
National Honours Schools Titles 1975 – 1976; Junior ABA Title 1976; NABC Title 1977; Young England Rep.; England Int.; GB Rep.; ABA Flyweight Champion 1979 & Bantamweight Champion 1980/1982; Commonwealth Bronze 1982
Divisional Honours N Counties Bantamweight Champion 1981

01.03.83 George Bailey **W** RSC 2 Kensington
04.04.83 Steve Cleak **W** DIS 6 Kensington
03.05.83 Ray Somer **W** PTS 8 Wembley
11.10.83 Luis De La Sagra **W** RSC 8 Kensington
09.12.83 John Farrell DREW 10 Liverpool
(Central Area Bantamweight Title Challenge)
20.02.84 Dave George **W** RSC 2 Mayfair
(Elim. British Bantamweight Title)
23.05.84 Vicente Fernandez **W** RSC 2 Mayfair

Summary: 7 contests, won 6, drew 1

Ray Gilbody
Douglas Baton

Cliff Gilpin

Wolverhampton. *Born* Telford 26.04.59
Former Undefeated Midlands Area Welterweight & L. Middleweight Champion
Manager M. Sendell
Previous Amateur Club Wolverhampton
National Honours Young England Rep.
Divisional Honours M Counties Welterweight R/U 1978/1980; M Counties Welterweight Champion 1979

18.03.80 Richard Avery **W** PTS 6 Wolverhampton
09.04.80 Dave Taylor **W** PTS 6 Burslem
30.04.80 Gary Cooper **W** PTS 8 Wolverhampton
29.05.80 Tommy Wright **W** RSC 5 Wolverhampton
08.07.80 Brian Anderson **W** PTS 8 Wolverhampton
24.09.80 Nigel Thomas **W** PTS 8 Evesham
13.10.80 John Smith **W** PTS 8 Nottingham
18.11.80 Lee Hartshorn **W** PTS 8 Shrewsbury
01.12.80 Kid Murray **W** RTD 3 Wolverhampton
13.12.80 Jean-Marie Toutai **W** PTS 8 Dunkirk
17.03.81 Steve McLeod **W** RSC 5 Wolverhampton
28.05.81 Achille Mitchell **W** PTS 8 Edgbaston
13.10.81 Gary Cooper **W** PTS 8 Wolverhampton
18.11.81 Kirkland Laing **L** PTS 12 Solihull
(Final Elim. British Welterweight Title)
09.02.82 Derek McKenzie **W** RTD 3 Wolverhampton
26.04.82 Joey Singleton **L** PTS 8 Southwark
24.05.82 Lloyd Hibbert **W** RSC 6 Wolverhampton
(Vacant Midlands Area L. Middleweight Title)
15.10.82 Fred Coranson DREW 8 Dunkirk
20.10.82 Mick Mills **W** RSC 3 Strand
17.11.82 Joey Mack **W** PTS 10 Solihull
(Midlands Area Welterweight Title Challenge)
07.03.83 Cor Eversteyn **W** CO 1 Rotterdam
11.03.83 Eddy Mongelema **L** PTS 8 Petite-Synthe
05.04.83 Lloyd Honeyghan **L** PTS 12 Kensington
(Vacant British Welterweight Title)
12.09.83 Charlie Malarkey **W** RSC 9 Glasgow
(Final Elim. British Welterweight Title)

CONTINUED OVERLEAF

06.12.83 Lloyd Honeyghan **L** PTS 12 Kensington
(*British Welterweight Title Challenge*)
15.03.84 Franz Dorfer **W** CO 3 Vienna
04.06.84 Abdul Amoru Sanda **L** PTS 10 Accra
Summary: 27 contests, won 20, drew 1, lost 6

Carlo Giorno

Swindon. *Born* Swindon 02.02.61
Middleweight
Manager R. Porter
Previous Amateur Club Thamesdown

22.02.84 Stuart Robinson **L** PTS 6 Evesham
Summary: 1 contest, lost 1

Tim Gladwish

Hastings. *Born* Hastings 27.12.64
Welterweight
Manager D. Harris
Previous Amateur Club West Hill

10.05.83 Davey Cox DREW 6 Southend
23.06.83 Bob Thornton **W** PTS 6 Bethnal Green
01.09.83 Trevor Hopson **W** PTS 6 Bloomsbury
14.09.83 Mickey Kilgallon **L** PTS 4 Muswell Hill
03.10.83 Elvis Morton **W** RSC 3 Eltham
21.11.83 Kevin Webb DREW 6 Eltham
13.02.84 Sam Omidi **W** RSC 5 Eltham
Summary: 7 contests, won 4, drew 2, lost 1

Lenny Gloster

Peterborough. *Born* West Indies 19.11.56
Welterweight
Manager K. Whitney
Previous Amateur Club Focus
Divisional Honours E Counties Welterweight R/U 1975; E Counties Welterweight Champion 1977/1979 – 1983

09.11.83 Graeme Griffin **W** RSC 4 Evesham
01.12.83 Granville Allen **L** PTS 6 Dudley
23.01.84 Dave Dent **L** PTS 6 Mayfair
13.02.84 Peter Flanagan **W** RSC 6 Manchester
01.03.84 Steve Tempro **W** PTS 6 Queensway
12.03.84 Jimmy Thornton **W** PTS 6 Manchester
27.03.84 Dave Dent **L** PTS 6 Bethnal Green
19.04.84 Dave Dent **L** PTS 8 Basildon
02.05.84 Vince Bailey **W** RSC 8 Solihull
Summary: 9 contests, won 5, lost 4

Phil Glover

Doncaster. *Born* Doncaster 12.12.59
Featherweight
Manager J. Rushton
Previous Amateur Club None

21.03.83 Taffy Mills **L** PTS 4 Glasgow
Summary: 1 contest, lost 1

Jerry Golden

Manchester. *Born* Rochdale 08.03.56
L. Heavyweight
Manager (Self)
Previous Amateur Club Chelsea, Australia

25.09.79 Peter Simon **L** RSC 2 Hammersmith
16.01.80 Mickey Kidd **L** PTS 6 Stoke
21.01.80 Peter Bassey **L** RSC 4 Birmingham
31.03.80 Chuck Hirschmann DREW 4 Cleethorpes
10.09.80 Joe Dean **L** RSC 3 Liverpool
16.10.80 John Stone **W** DIS 5 Bolton
01.11.80 Terry Christle **L** RSC 2 Glasgow
09.01.81 Tony Hoole NC 3 Durham
21.01.81 John Vaughan **W** PTS 6 Burslem
12.02.81 Colin Nelson **L** PTS 6 South Shields
26.03.81 Brian Graham **W** CO 1 Newcastle
13.04.81 Dave Turner **L** PTS 6 Manchester
10.05.81 Trevor Kerr **L** PTS 8 Dublin
10.06.81 Leo Mulhern **L** RSC 8 Brodsworth
11.09.81 Antonio Harris **L** RSC 4 Edgbaston
19.10.81 Mal Kirk **L** RSC 4 Manchester
01.12.81 Clive Beardsley **L** PTS 6 Derby
09.03.82 John Stone **W** DIS 5 Farnsworth
22.03.82 Nigel Savery **L** PTS 6 Bradford
30.03.82 Nigel Savery **L** PTS 6 Leeds
19.04.82 Glenroy Taylor **W** PTS 6 Mayfair
10.05.82 Joey Williams DREW 6 Birmingham
24.05.82 Nigel Savery **W** CO 5 Bradford
21.06.82 Devon Bailey **L** RSC 3 Copthorne
13.09.82 Paul Shell **L** PTS 6 Manchester
18.10.82 Bernie Kavanagh **L** PTS 6 Blackpool
04.11.82 Alan Ash **L** PTS 6 Wimbledon
29.11.82 Glenroy Taylor **W** PTS 6 Southwark
31.01.83 Billy Cassidy **L** PTS 6 Southwark
24.02.83 Bernie Kavanagh **L** RSC 5 Liverpool
19.05.83 Carlton Benoit **L** RSC 4 Queensway
20.06.83 Paul Heatley **W** PTS 6 Manchester
22.09.83 Mal Kirk **L** RSC 2 Stockport
22.11.83 Steve Lewsam **W** RSC 5 Manchester
05.12.83 Mal Kirk **W** RSC 1 Manchester
17.12.83 Esa Veikkola **L** PTS 6 Mariehamn
30.01.84 Paul Shell DREW 6 Manchester
19.03.84 Blaine Longsden **L** RSC 3 Manchester

27.04.84 Deka Williams L PTS 6 Wolverhampton
06.06.84 Mick Mills L PTS 6 Sheffield
Summary: 40 contests, won 10, drew 3, lost 26, NC 1

Mark Good

Shirley. *Born* Norbury 10.04.61
L. Middleweight
Manager H. Burgess
Previous Amateur Club Fitzroy Lodge

04.11.82 Derek McKenzie L CO 3 Wimbledon
14.02.83 Kevin Webb L PTS 6 Lewisham
Summary: 2 contests, lost 2

Sylvester Gordon

Peckham. *Born* Jamaica 24.10.55
Welterweight
Manager (Self)
Previous Amateur Club Lynn
Divisional Honours SE London Welterweight R/U 1974; SE London L. Welterweight R/U 1977

18.04.77 Wayne Floyd L PTS 6 Piccadilly
26.04.77 Dai Davies W PTS 6 Piccadilly
23.05.77 Wayne Floyd L PTS 6 Hammersmith
02.06.77 Dai Davies W PTS 6 Piccadilly
10.10.77 Steve Holdsworth L PTS 6 Walworth
24.10.77 Martin Bridge L PTS 6 Piccadilly
07.11.77 Dai Davies W PTS 6 Piccadilly
15.11.77 Mick O'Mara DREW 6 Bethnal Green
12.12.77 Dave Taylor W PTS 8 Piccadilly
16.01.78 George Peacock L PTS 6 Birmingham
31.01.78 Cookie Roomes W PTS 6 Marylebone
21.02.78 Sylvester Mittee L RSC 5 Kensington
20.03.78 Paddy McAleese DREW 8 Piccadilly
23.05.78 Mick Bell W RSC 6 Leicester
20.06.78 Ray Cattouse L PTS 8 Piccadilly
11.09.78 Chris Walker L PTS 8 Birmingham
18.09.78 Carl Bailey W PTS 8 Manchester
25.09.78 Tommy Davitt DREW 8 Mayfair
15.11.78 Tony Martey L CO 7 Solihull
15.01.79 Joey Singleton L PTS 8 Nottingham
05.02.79 Tommy Davitt W PTS 8 Piccadilly
19.03.79 George Peacock L PTS 8 Piccadilly
17.04.79 Willie Booth L PTS 8 Glasgow
21.05.79 Joey Singleton L PTS 8 Walworth
17.10.79 Gary Pearce DREW 8 Piccadilly
30.10.79 Gary Pearce L PTS 8 Caerphilly
03.12.79 Sid Smith L RTD 5 Marylebone
28.01.80 Steve Early L RSC 6 Edgbaston
25.02.80 Herbie McLean W PTS 8 Glasgow
17.03.80 Ricky Beaumont L PTS 8 Piccadilly
01.10.80 Eirling Eng L PTS 4 Oslo
01.12.80 Eirling Eng L PTS 6 Oslo
13.12.80 Dan M'Putu L PTS 8 Dunkirk
16.02.81 Joey Singleton L PTS 8 Southwark
13.04.81 Billy Waith L PTS 8 Southwark
27.04.81 Hugh Smith W PTS 8 Piccadilly
19.05.81 Jimmy Connolly L PTS 8 Berne
19.11.81 Tim Moloney W RSC 2 Piccadilly
15.03.82 Dave Allen L PTS 8 Piccadilly
28.09.82 Colin Derrick L CO 3 Bethnal Green
06.12.82 Kostas Petrou L PTS 8 Edgbaston
07.04.83 Bert Myrie L RSC 1 Strand
10.10.83 Jim McIntosh L PTS 8 Glasgow
27.10.83 John McGlynn L CO 6 Ebbw Vale
Summary: 44 contests, won 11, drew 4, lost 29

(Leo) Lee Graham

Finchley. *Born* Birmingham 25.04.58
Featherweight
Manager (Self)
Previous Amateur Club Lynn

15.11.76 Tommy Davitt L PTS 6 Kensington
22.11.76 Michael Le Grange DREW 4 Southampton
07.02.77 Kevin Doherty DREW 6 Mayfair
22.02.77 Gary Davidson L PTS 6 Kensington
21.03.77 Steve Enright W RSC 5 Birmingham
29.03.77 Wally Angliss W RSC 5 Wembley
12.04.77 Mark Bliss L PTS 8 Kensington
31.05.77 Wayne Evans L PTS 8 Kensington
19.09.77 Alan Oag W CO 1 Glasgow
10.10.77 Kenny Matthews L PTS 8 Piccadilly
31.10.77 Pat Cowdell L PTS 8 Birmingham
29.11.77 Alan Buchanan DREW 8 Piccadilly
16.01.78 Eric Wood L PTS 8 Nottingham
24.01.78 Gerry Duffy L RSC 2 Piccadilly
28.02.78 Tony Whitmore DREW 6 Heathrow
06.03.78 Jeff Pritchard L PTS 8 Piccadilly
15.05.78 Tony Whitmore W RSC 3 Mayfair
23.05.78 Vernon Penprase L PTS 6 Islington
29.06.78 George Sutton DREW 8 Caerphilly
04.11.78 Charm Chiteule L DIS 5 Lusaka
29.01.79 Terry McKeown L PTS 6 Glasgow
05.02.79 John Cooper W PTS 8 Piccadilly
07.03.79 Wayne Evans L RSC 2 Solihull
03.04.79 Vernon Penprase L PTS 8 Caerphilly
19.04.79 Johnny Owen L PTS 8 Piccadilly
13.05.79 Vernon Penprase L PTS 8 Plymouth
15.10.79 Vernon Penprase L RTD 5 Piccadilly
15.11.79 Jimmy Brown L PTS 8 Manchester
03.12.79 John Feeney L PTS 8 Marylebone
31.03.80 Jim McKeown L PTS 8 Piccadilly
17.04.80 Steve Cleak L PTS 8 Piccadilly
20.11.80 Russell Jones W RSC 7 Piccadilly
02.02.81 Gary Lucas L PTS 8 Piccadilly

CONTINUED OVERLEAF

22.10.81 John Sharkey W RSC 2 Mayfair
09.12.81 Steve Henderson L CO 5 Piccadilly
08.02.82 Jim McKeown W RSC 6 Piccadilly
10.05.82 Steve Pollard DREW 8 Piccadilly
26.05.82 Rory Burke L PTS 8 Piccadilly
01.11.82 Alec Irvine W PTS 8 Piccadilly
18.11.82 Steve Henderson W PTS 8 Piccadilly
08.12.82 Najib Daho L PTS 8 Piccadilly
24.01.83 Pat Doherty DREW 8 Piccadilly
Summary: 42 contests, won 10, drew 7, lost 25

Johnny Grant

Enfield. *Born* Enfield 16.12.59
L. Welterweight
Manager M. Hope
Previous Amateur Club Enfield
National Honours Young England Rep.
Divisional Honours NW London L. Welterweight Champion 1979 – 1980

20.09.82 Dave Springer W PTS 6 Mayfair
13.10.82 Paul Keers W PTS 6 Walthamstow
25.10.82 Tyrell Wilson W RSC 6 Mayfair
16.11.82 Paul Cook L RSC 2 Bethnal Green
25.01.83 Denny Garrison W PTS 6 Bethnal Green
25.04.83 Terry Connor W PTS 6 Southwark
17.10.83 Steve Boyle L PTS 6 Southwark
28.11.83 Ricky Andrews L PTS 6 Southwark
15.03.84 Tony McKenzie L RSC 4 Leicester
Summary: 9 contests, won 5, lost 4

Andy Green

Birmingham. *Born* Birmingham 18.09.62
Lightweight
Manager E. Cashmore
Previous Amateur Club Castle Vale

18.10.83 Clinton Campbell L PTS 6 Wolverhampton
07.11.83 Wayne Trigg L PTS 4 Birmingham
10.02.84 Shane Silvester L RSC 5 Dudley
Summary: 3 contests, lost 3

Carl Green

Bradford. *Born* Jamaica 28.11.57
Lightweight
Manager J. Celebanski
Previous Amateur Club Springfield

17.11.83 Paul Boswell W RSC 2 Basildon
23.11.83 Ron Shinkwin L PTS 6 Solihull
Summary: 2 contests, won 1, lost 1

Jonjo Greene

Manchester. *Born* Linlithgo 24.05.62
L. Heavyweight
Manager J. Gaynor
Previous Amateur Club None

11.12.80 Paul Doyle W PTS 4 Bolton
30.03.80 Al Stevens L CO 4 Birmingham
04.05.80 Gary Jones L PTS 4 Glasgow
04.11.80 Clive Beardsley L RSC 8 Derby
02.12.80 Winston Richards W RTD 2 Manchester
08.12.80 John O'Neil L RSC 6 Pembroke
01.02.82 Clive Beardsley L PTS 6 Manchester
22.03.82 Glenroy Taylor W PTS 6 Southwark
29.03.82 Ian Lazarus L PTS 6 Piccadilly
26.04.82 Al Stevens W PTS 6 Edgbaston
07.06.82 Joe Frater W PTS 6 Sheffield
16.10.82 Ben Lawlor L PTS 8 Killarney
14.11.82 Ben Lawlor W RSC 2 Navan
02.12.82 Michael Madsen L RSC 4 Randers
07.02.83 Shaun Chalcraft W RSC 5 Brighton
28.03.83 Ian Lazarus L PTS 8 Manchester
07.04.83 John Moody L PTS 6 Strand
16.05.83 Alek Penarski W PTS 8 Manchester
31.10.83 Trevor Cattouse L PTS Mayfair
22.11.83 Bernie Kavanagh W PTS 8 Manchester
30.01.84 Freddie Rafferty DREW 8 Durban
19.03.84 Trevor Cattouse W PTS 8 Manchester
04.06.84 Bernie Kavanagh W RSC 8 Manchester
Summary: 23 contests, won 11, drew 1, lost 11

Jarvis Greenidge

Birmingham. *Born* Barbados 02.04.52
Former Midlands Area Featherweight Champion
Manager (Self)
Previous Amateur Club Birmingham Golden Gloves
Divisional Honours M Counties Featherweight Champion 1978 – 1979

09.10.79 Pat Devanney W PTS 6 Wolverhampton
17.10.79 Steve Sammy Sims W PTS 6 Evesham
30.10.79 John Henry W RSC 4 Bedworth
20.11.79 Paddy Graham L PTS 8 Belfast
03.12.79 Steve Parker L RTD 3 Wolverhampton
28.01.80 Paul Keers L PTS 8 Bradford
05.02.80 Steve Parker W PTS 6 Wolverhampton
21.02.80 Brian Snagg L PTS 8 Liverpool
10.03.80 Adey Allen W PTS 6 Wolverhampton
19.03.80 Steve Sammy Sims W PTS 8 Stoke
15.05.80 Tim Moloney L PTS 6 Mayfair
04.09.80 Glyn Rhodes L RSC 8 Morecambe
13.10.80 Kevin Sheehan W PTS 8 Nottingham
25.11.80 Paul Keers W RSC 7 Doncaster
08.12.80 Jimmy Flint L CO 2 Kensington
27.01.81 Charm Chiteule L DIS 7 Kensington

11.03.81 Steve Topliss W CO 3 Burslem
(*Vacant Midlands Area Featherweight Title*)
26.05.81 Billy O'Grady DREW 8 Bethnal Green
28.10.81 Clyde Ruan L PTS 8 Burslem
08.11.81 Richie Foster L PTS 8 Navan
25.01.82 John Sharkey L PTS 8 Glasgow
16.02.82 Clyde Ruan L PTS 8 Bristol
19.03.82 Alec Irvine L PTS 10 Nottingham
(*Midlands Area Featherweight Title Defence*)
20.04.82 Paul Huggins L RSC 2 Kensington
27.09.82 Dean Marsden L PTS 6 Birmingham
16.10.82 Richie Foster L PTS 8 Killarney
31.01.83 Steve Topliss L PTS 8 Birmingham
Summary: 27 contests, won 9, drew 1, lost 17

Steve Grieves

Leicester. *Born* Leicester 22.12.59
L. Middleweight
Manager B. Ridge
Previous Amateur Club Braunstone

28.04.83 Dave Harrison W PTS 6 Leicester
16.05.83 Dave Harrison DREW 6 Manchester
07.06.83 Dave Harrison W RSC 3 Southend
23.06.83 John Ridgman L RSC 1 Bethnal Green
Summary: 4 contests, won 2, drew 1, lost 1

Graeme Griffin (McMullen)

Corby. *Born* 11.06.64
Welterweight
Manager J. Griffin
Previous Amateur Club Corby Olympic

18.10.82 Glyn Mitchell L RSC 4 Nottingham
17.02.83 Terry Connor L RSC 3 Coventry
16.04.83 Ron Shinkwin L PTS 4 Bristol
28.04.83 Sammy Rodgers W PTS 4 Leicester
19.09.83 Carl Bishop W PTS 6 Nottingham
20.09.83 Nick Ellaway W RSC 1 Mayfair
05.10.83 Carl Bishop L PTS 6 Stoke
10.10.83 Mickey Lerwill W PTS 6 Birmingham
09.11.83 Lenny Gloster L RSC 4 Evesham
05.12.83 Ray Murray W PTS 6 Manchester
12.12.83 Ray Murray W PTS 6 Bedworth
30.01.84 Phil Sheridan W PTS 6 Birmingham
15.03.84 Andy Whitehouse W PTS 6 Leicester
26.03.84 Steve Tempro L PTS 6 Leicester
16.04.84 Mark Hill DREW 6 Birmingham
09.05.84 Dave Heaver W PTS 6 Leicester
Summary: 16 contests, won 9, drew 1, lost 6

Steve Griffith

Finchley. *Born* Finchley 09.03.65
Lightweight
Manager D. Smith
Previous Amateur Club New Enterprise
National Honours Schools Title 1978/1980/1981; NABC Title 1982

06.02.84 Phil Duke W RSC 3 Bethnal Green
27.03.84 Willie Wilson W PTS 6 Bethnal Green
19.04.84 Kenny Watson W PTS 6 Basildon
14.05.84 Brian Hyslop W PTS 6 Glasgow
31.05.84 Wayne Poultney W PTS 6 Basildon
Summary: 5 contests, won 5

Des Gwilliam

Birmingham. *Born* Birmingham 08.04.54
Former Midlands Area Lightweight Champion
Manager (Self)
Previous Amateur Club Rum Runner
National Honours NABC Titles 1970 – 1971; Young England Rep.; England Int.
Divisional Honours M Counties Lightweight Champion 1973; M Counties Lightweight R/U 1974; M Counties Lightweight Champion 1976

25.02.77 Marty Jacobs W RSC 6 Digbeth
07.04.77 Chris Glover DREW 6 Dudley
27.05.77 Barton McAllister L RTD 5 Digbeth
19.09.77 Barry Price DREW 8 Walworth
27.09.77 Cornelius Boza Edwards W RSC 6 Wembley
07.11.78 Hans-Henrik Palm L RSC 4 Randers
15.03.78 Joey Singleton L PTS 8 Solihull
18.04.78 Roy Varden L PTS 10 Coventry
(*Vacant Midlands Area L Welterweight Title*)
27.09.78 Bingo Crooks DREW 8 Solihull
31.10.78 Bingo Crooks W PTS 10 Wolverhampton
(*Vacant Midlands Area Lightweight Title*)
11.11.78 Dan M'Putu L PTS 8 Dunkirk
04.04.79 Dil Collins W PTS 8 Birmingham
02.07.79 Barry Price W PTS 8 Wolverhampton
29.10.79 Paul Chance L PTS 10 Wolverhampton
(*Midlands Area Lightweight Title Defence*)
28.02.80 Ricky Beaumont L RSC 7 Hull
26.03.80 Dil Collins W RSC 4 Evesham
30.04.80 Dave Taylor W PTS 8 Wolverhampton
20.10.80 Ken Buchanan L PTS 8 Birmingham
01.12.80 John Muwanga L PTS 6 Oslo
24.01.81 Didier Kowalski DREW 8 Paris

CONTINUED OVERLEAF

17.01.82 Andre Holyk DREW 8 Lyons
18.10.82 Tony Willis L PTS 8 Edgbaston
16.11.82 Vernon Entertainer Vanriel L PTS 8 Bethnal Green
07.03.83 Willie Booth L PTS 8 Glasgow
Summary: 24 contests, won 7, drew 5, lost 12

Dave Haggarty

Paisley. *Born* Paisley 23.02.62
L. Welterweight
Manager N. Sweeney
Previous Amateur Club Ferguslie

25.10.82 John Daly **W** PTS 6 Airdrie
26.11.82 Young Tony Carroll **W** PTS 6 Glasgow
21.02.83 Ray Ross **W** PTS 6 Glasgow
07.03.83 Tony Wilkinson **W** PTS 6 Glasgow
11.04.83 Keith Foreman DREW 8 Glasgow
23.05.83 Keith Foreman **W** PTS 8 Glasgow
01.09.83 Billy Edwards **W** PTS 6 Bloomsbury
03.10.83 Kevin Sheehan **W** RSC 2 Glasgow
14.11.83 Mick Rowley L RTD 4 Glasgow
30.01.84 Abdul Kareem **W** PTS 8 Glasgow
09.04.84 Jimmy Thornton **W** PTS 8 Glasgow
30.04.84 Jimmy Bunclark **W** PTS 8 Rhyl
11.06.84 Steve Boyle L RSC 1 Glasgow
Summary: 13 contests, won 10, drew 1, lost 2

Gordon Haigh

Hull. *Born* Hull 09.07.61
Featherweight
Manager (Self)
Previous Amateur Club Hull Fish Trades
Divisional Honours NE Counties Featherweight S/F 1980

23.03.81 Robert Carson **W** RSC 3 Glasgow
30.03.81 Stuart Nicol **W** PTS 6 Glasgow
13.04.81 Stuart Nicol L PTS 6 Glasgow
27.04.81 Robert Carson **W** RSC 1 Piccadilly
08.05.81 Pat Doherty L PTS 6 Piccadilly
11.06.81 Stuart Nicol L RSC 5 Hull
26.10.81 Johnny Dorey L PTS 6 Southwark
23.11.81 Mark Stoops DREW 4 Glasgow
04.12.81 Ray Cunningham **W** CO 4 Bristol
25.01.82 Terry Allen **W** RSC 1 Bradford
16.02.82 Mike Wilkes DREW 6 Bristol
06.04.82 Michael Marsden L PTS 4 Leeds
19.04.82 John Murphy L RSC 3 Glasgow
21.06.82 Stuart Carmichael L PTS 6 Hull
25.01.83 Seamus McGuinness L CO 1 Belfast
Summary: 15 contests, won 5, drew 2, lost 8

Lee Halford

Leicester. *Born* Leicester 09.11.58
Lightweight
Manager (Self)
Previous Amateur Club Highfields
Divisional Honours M Counties Lightweight R/U 1978

13.10.81 Ray Smyth **W** CO 2 Wolverhampton
20.10.81 Carl Ainsworth **W** RSC 4 Leeds
25.11.81 Kevin Howard **W** PTS 6 Stoke
25.01.82 Mick Rowley DREW 6 Piccadilly
19.03.82 Colin Harrison **W** PTS 6 Nottingham
07.04.82 Granville Allen **W** PTS 8 Evesham
27.04.82 Delroy Pearce L RSC 7 Southend
21.06.82 Kevin Pritchard L CO 2 Liverpool
27.09.82 Alan Tombs **W** PTS 6 Bloomsbury
26.10.82 Steve Pollard **W** PTS 8 Hull
01.12.82 Stuart Shaw L RSC 6 Stafford
(*Vacant Midlands Area Lightweight Title*)
02.03.83 Ray Price L PTS 6 Evesham
16.03.83 Gerry Devine **W** RSC 1 Stoke
21.03.83 Najib Daho L PTS 8 Piccadilly
16.05.83 Gary Lucas L PTS 8 Manchester
12.09.83 Jimmy Thornton **W** PTS 8 Leicester
09.12.83 Young Tony Carroll L PTS 6 Liverpool
29.02.84 Vince Vahey L PTS 8 Sheffield
16.04.84 Gerry Beard L CO 8 Birmingham
(*Vacant Midlands Area Lightweight Title*)
Summary: 19 contests, won 9, drew 1, lost 9

Dave Hall

Leyton. *Born* Germany 17.04.61
L. Middleweight
Manager A. Kasler
Previous Amateur Club West Ham
Divisional Honours NE London L. Middleweight R/U 1982

23.05.83 Rod Jones **W** PTS 6 Mayfair
13.06.83 Andy Roberts **W** CO 5 Nottingham
08.09.83 Tony Rabbetts **W** PTS 6 Queensway
31.10.83 Ian Martin L RSC 3 Mayfair
06.02.84 Dave Sullivan L RSC 3 Bethnal Green
Summary: 5 contests, won 3, lost 2

Dave Hallett

Plymouth. *Born* Torquay 04.09.60
Welterweight
Manager G. Bousted
Previous Amateur Club Riviera

25.01.84 Dave Heaver L PTS 6 Stoke
07.03.84 Mark Simpson L RSC 6 Brighton
03.04.84 Trevor Hopson L RSC 2 Lewisham
Summary: 3 contests, lost 3

Dave Hallett
Derek Rowe (Photos) Ltd

Steve Hanna

Belfast. *Born* Belfast 19.08.60
Featherweight
Manager (Self)
Previous Amateur Club St Oliver Plunkett
National Honours Irish Int.; Irish Featherweight Champion 1981

27.02.84 Shane Silvester **W** PTS 6 Birmingham
30.06.84 Keith Ward **L** PTS 6 Belfast
Summary: 2 contests, won 1, lost 1

Alan Hardiman

Hemel Hempstead. *Born* Wembley 16.09.52
Welterweight
Manager E. Fossey
Previous Amateur Club Hemel Hempstead
National Honours Schools Title 1969
Divisional Honours NW London Welterweight Champion 1971 – 1972

07.03.73 Kenny Davis **W** CO 1 Watford
14.03.73 Dave Taylor **W** RSC 4 Stoke
20.03.73 Roy Stevens **W** CO 2 Bethnal Green
27.03.73 Johnny Jennings **W** CO 5 Birmingham
30.04.73 Hughie Clarke **W** RSC 2 Kensington
11.06.73 Pat Marshall **W** RSC 5 Kensington
17.09.73 Mick Hinton **W** RSC 6 Kensington
29.10.73 Tony Bagshaw **L** CO 4 Walworth
04.12.73 Ray Fallone **W** PTS 8 Southend
10.12.73 Barton McAllister **W** PTS 8 Piccadilly
18.12.73 Graham Murphy **W** RSC 3 Shoreditch
07.01.74 John Smith **L** PTS 8 Piccadilly
07.04.74 Jim Devanney **L** RSC 6 Southend
16.05.74 Liam White **W** PTS 8 Walworth
03.06.74 Al Stewart **L** RTD 3 Manchester
09.09.74 Jim Devanney **L** RSC 4 Mayfair
07.10.74 George Salmon **L** PTS 10 Bristol
05.12.74 Roy Stevens **W** CO 2 Southend
06.01.75 Mick Evans **W** PTS 8 Hemel Hempstead
03.03.75 Mickey Ryce **W** PTS 8 Hemel Hempstead
02.09.75 Roy Commosioung **L** PTS 8 Hornsey
02.11.76 Mick Minter **W** PTS 8 Southend
17.11.76 Owen Robinson **W** PTS 6 Solihull
04.05.77 Jimmy King **W** RSC 3 Solihull
02.11.77 Dave Merrell **W** CO 3 Southend
14.11.77 Tim McHugh **L** PTS 8 Cambridge
30.01.79 Curtis Marsh **L** PTS 4 Southend
12.02.79 Gary Cooper DREW 6 Reading
27.02.79 Johnny Elliott **W** RSC 2 Southend
14.10.80 Gary Brooks **L** RSC 1 Nantwich
09.12.80 Pharoah Bish **L** PTS 6 Southend
11.03.81 Gerry McGrath **L** PTS 6 Burslem
22.09.81 Steve Henty **L** PTS 8 Southend
06.11.82 Neville Wilson DREW 6 Marylebone
07.12.82 Alex Brown **W** CO 1 Southend
15.12.82 Bert Myrie **W** RSC 4 Queensway
19.01.83 Phil O'Hare **L** PTS 6 Stoke
Summary: 37 contests, won 21, drew 2, lost 14

Billy Hardy

Sunderland. *Born* Sunderland 15.09.64
Bantamweight
Manager H. Holland
Previous Amateur Club Hylton Castle
National Honours Junior ABA Title 1981; Young England Rep.
Divisional Honours NE Counties Bantamweight Champion 1982 – 1983

21.11.83 Kevin Downer **W** PTS 6 Eltham
03.12.83 Brett Styles **W** PTS 6 Marylebone
27.01.84 Keith Ward **W** PTS 6 Longford
13.02.84 Johnny Mack **W** RSC 5 Eltham
01.03.84 Graham Kid Clarke **W** PTS 8 Queensway
27.03.84 Glen McLaggon **W** PTS 6 Battersea

CONTINUED OVERLEAF

06.04.84 Graham Kid Clarke **W** RSC 7 Watford
25.04.84 Anthony Brown **W** RSC 5 Muswell Hill
04.06.84 Roy Webb **L** PTS 6 Mayfair
Summary: 9 contests, won 8, lost 1

John Hargin
Corby. *Born* Glasgow 12.11.64
Middleweight
Manager K. Whitney
Previous Amateur Club Corby Olympic

09.11.83 Bert Myrie DREW 4 Evesham
23.01.84 Ian Martin DREW 6 Mayfair
06.02.84 Wayne Barker **L** CO 4 Liverpool
Summary: 3 contests, drew 2, lost 1

Mick Harkin
Birmingham. *Born* Birmingham 07.04.63
Welterweight
Manager G. Donaghy
Previous Amateur Club Small Heath

27.09.83 Mickey Lerwill DREW 6 Stoke
13.10.83 Andy O'Rawe **W** PTS 6 Bloomsbury
26.10.83 Mark Duffy DREW 6 Stoke
23.11.83 Vince Bailey **W** PTS 6 Solihull
07.12.83 Andy O'Rawe **L** PTS 6 Bloomsbury
14.12.83 Mark Duffy **W** RSC 6 Stoke
28.01.84 Robert Lloyd **W** PTS 6 Hanley
Summary: 7 contests, won 4, drew 2, lost 1

Robert Harkin
Renton. *Born* Glasgow 15.07.62
Welterweight
Manager R. Watt
Previous Amateur Club Clydeview

06.04.84 Stan Atherton **W** RSC 4 Edinburgh
11.06.84 Mike McKenzie **W** CO 3 Glasgow
Summary: 2 contests, won 2

Antonio Harris
Birmingham. *Born* Jamaica 08.06.59
Midlands Area L. Heavyweight Champion
Manager P. Lynch
Previous Amateur Club Nechells
National Honours Young England Rep./England Int.
Divisional Honours M Counties Heavyweight Champion 1980

30.03.81 Nigel Savery **W** PTS 6 Birmingham
28.05.81 Joe Jackson **W** PTS 6 Edgbaston
11.09.81 Jerry Golden **W** RSC 4 Edgbaston
25.09.81 Joe Jackson **W** RSC 2 Nottingham
05.10.81 Cordwell Hylton **L** PTS 8 Birmingham
12.10.81 Nye Williams **W** PTS 6 Birmingham
08.11.81 Ben Lawlor DREW 6 Navan
18.11.81 Steve Lewin **W** CO 5 Solihull
21.12.81 Trevor Cattouse **L** PTS 8 Birmingham
20.01.82 Roy Skeldon **W** PTS 10 Solihull
27.01.82 Ben Lawlor **L** PTS 6 Belfast
10.03.82 Roy Skeldon **W** PTS 10 Solihull (*Midlands Area L. Heavyweight Title Challenge*)
26.04.82 Liam Coleman **L** PTS 8 Edgbaston
07.06.82 Liam Coleman **W** PTS 10 Edgbaston (*Elim. British L. Heavyweight Title*)
18.10.82 Alek Penarski **W** RSC 3 Edgbaston
17.11.82 Roy Skeldon **W** PTS 8 Solihull
19.01.83 Keith Bristol **L** PTS 8 Birmingham
09.03.83 Tom Collins **L** RSC 6 Solihull (*British L. Heavyweight Title Challenge*)
16.09.83 Nick Jenkins **L** PTS 8 Swindon
19.01.84 Geoff Rymer **W** RTD 5 Digbeth
09.02.84 Enrico Scacchia DREW 8 Geneva
28.03.84 Nye Williams **W** PTS 8 Aberavon
07.05.84 Sakkie Horn **L** PTS 8 Johannesburg
Summary: 23 contests, won 13, drew 2, lost 8

Michael Harris
Swansea. *Born* Swansea 14.08.64
L. Welterweight
Manager C. Breen
Previous Amateur Club Gwent
National Honours Welsh Int.
Divisional Honours Welsh Welterweight R/U 1982

18.11.82 Frankie Lake **W** PTS 6 Piccadilly
23.11.82 Eddie Morgan **W** PTS 6 Wolverhampton
28.01.83 Stan Atherton **W** PTS 6 Swansea
21.02.83 Andy Letts **W** PTS 4 Edgbaston
12.04.83 Mickey Duddy **W** RSC 5 Belfast
16.04.83 Shaun Shinkwin **W** PTS 6 Bristol
25.04.83 Dave Savage **L** PTS 6 Aberdeen
27.05.83 Bobby Welburn **W** PTS 6 Swansea
06.06.83 Keith Foreman **W** PTS 8 Piccadilly
20.06.83 Jim Paton **W** PTS 8 Piccadilly
29.11.83 Colin Neagle **W** PTS 8 Cardiff
19.12.83 Gary Williams **W** PTS 8 Swansea
01.02.84 Kevin Pritchard **W** PTS 8 Bloomsbury
28.03.84 Colin Neagle **W** PTS 6 Aberavon
13.06.84 Ray Price **W** PTS 10 Aberavon (*Vacant Welsh L. Welterweight Title*)
Summary: 15 contests, won 14, lost 1

Peter Harris
Swansea. *Born* Swansea 23.08.62
Bantamweight
Manager C. Breen
Previous Amateur Club Gwent
Divisional Honours Welsh Featherweight R/U 1981

28.02.83 Dave Pratt **L** PTS 6 Birmingham
25.04.83 Jim Harvey DREW 6 Aberdeen

27.05.83 Brett Styles **W** PTS 8 Swansea
20.06.83 Danny Knaggs **W** PTS 6 Piccadilly
19.12.83 Kevin Howard **W** PTS 8 Swansea
06.02.84 Ivor Jones DREW 8 Bethnal Green
27.03.84 Johnny Dorey **W** RSC 6 Bethnal Green
13.06.84 Keith Wallace **W** PTS 10 Aberavon
Summary: 8 contests, won 5, drew 2, lost 1

Dave Harrison

Stoke. *Born* Stoke 24.06.64
L. Middleweight
Manager P. Brogan
Previous Amateur Club Stoke-on-Trent

16.09.81 Phil O'Hare **W** PTS 4 Burslem
28.10.81 John Malone **W** PTS 4 Burslem
20.01.82 John Malone **W** PTS 4 Burslem
10.03.82 Kevin Johnson **L** PTS 4 Burslem
07.09.82 Phil O'Hare DREW 6 Crewe
22.09.82 Phil O'Hare **L** PTS 6 Stoke
20.10.82 Elvis Morton **W** RSC 1 Stoke
24.11.82 Alf Edwardes **L** PTS 6 Stoke
28.02.83 Tony Rabbetts **L** PTS 6 Strand
28.03.83 Dave Heaver **W** PTS 6 Manchester
28.04.83 Steve Grieves **L** PTS 6 Leicester
16.05.83 Steve Grieves DREW 6 Manchester
07.06.83 Steve Grieves **L** RSC 3 Southend
Summary: 13 contests, won 5, drew 2, lost 6

Ian Harrison

Manchester. *Born* Stockport 14.01.59
L. Welterweight
Manager J. Edwards
Previous Amateur Club Higher Blackley

16.05.83 Dave Kettlewell DREW 6 Bradford
22.09.83 Dave Kettlewell **W** CO 2 Stockport
Summary: 2 contests, won 1, drew 1

(Brendan) Nipper Hartnett

Telford. *Born* Larne 10.01.62
L. Middleweight
Manager M. Sendell
Previous Amateur Club WSOB

23.06.83 Dan Myers **L** RTD 2 Wolverhampton
Summary: 1 contest, lost 1

Lee Hartshorn

Manchester. *Born* Ashton-under-Lyne 19.05.57
L. Middleweight
Manager N. Basso
Previous Amateur Club Mottram & Hattersley
Divisional Honours N Counties Welterweight Champion 1978

27.11.78 Don Hughes **W** PTS 6 Govan
17.01.79 Dave Allen **W** PTS 6 Burslem
22.01.79 John Chard **L** DIS 3 Mayfair
12.03.79 Tommy Baldwin **W** RSC 2 Manchester
19.03.79 Jess Harper **W** PTS 6 Bradford
02.04.79 Tony Hague **W** PTS 6 Manchester
10.04.79 Gary Newell **W** PTS 6 Wolverhampton
23.04.79 Carl North **W** CO 3 Bradford
02.05.79 John Kennedy **L** PTS 8 Solihull
21.05.79 Dennis Pryce **W** PTS 8 Manchester
18.06.79 Richard Avery **W** RTD 4 Manchester
05.07.79 Nigel Thomas **L** PTS 8 Aberavon
17.09.79 Dave Taylor **W** PTS 8 Manchester
15.10.79 Lloyd Lee **L** PTS 8 Windsor
23.10.79 Pat Smythe **W** PTS 8 Blackpool
29.11.79 Al Stewart **W** PTS 8 Liverpool
17.12.79 Terry Petersen **W** PTS 8 Bradford
02.02.80 Frankie Decaestecker **L** PTS 8 Torhut
11.02.80 Roy Varden **L** RTD 2 Manchester
27.03.80 Derek Nelson **W** PTS 8 Newcastle
28.04.80 Nigel Thomas **W** PTS 8 Piccadilly
22.09.80 Lloyd Hibbert **L** PTS 8 Wolverhampton
13.10.80 Tony Martey **L** PTS 8 Windsor
18.11.80 Cliff Gilpin **L** PTS 8 Shrewsbury
07.02.81 Dan M'Putu **L** PTS 8 Dunkirk
26.10.81 Joey Singleton **L** PTS 10 Southwark
(Central Area Welterweight Title Challenge)
08.11.82 Steve Tempro **W** PTS 6 Manchester
06.12.82 Ian Chantler **W** PTS 8 Manchester
17.01.83 Errol Dennis **W** PTS 8 Manchester
24.02.83 Joey Frost **L** RSC 5 Liverpool
(Central Area Welterweight Title Challenge)
22.03.83 Dan Myers **W** RSC 6 Wolverhampton
28.04.83 Chris Pyatt **L** RSC 3 Leicester
Summary: 32 contests, won 19, lost 13

Chris Harvey

Mile End. *Born* Stepney 21.05.59
L. Welterweight
Manager D. Mancini
Previous Amateur Club Repton

22.02.83 Gary Champion **L** PTS 6 Bethnal Green
17.03.83 Shaun Shinkwin **L** PTS 6 Marylebone
25.04.83 Ron Shinkwin **W** PTS 4 Southwark
16.05.83 Frankie Lake **L** PTS 6 Mayfair
Summary: 4 contests, won 1, lost 3

Jim Harvey
Glasgow. *Born* Canada 08.06.58
Bantamweight
Manager (Self)
Previous Amateur Club Argo

02.06.80 Bill Hay **W** PTS 4 Glasgow
13.11.80 Ken Foreman L PTS 4 Newcastle
25.11.80 Peter Gabbitus L PTS 4 Doncaster
01.12.80 Ray Plant **W** PTS 6 Middlesbrough
01.09.81 Ray Plant L PTS 6 Durham
19.01.81 Peter Gabbitus L PTS 4 Bradford
12.02.81 Ray Plant L PTS 6 South Shields
16.03.81 Rocky Bantleman L PTS 6 Piccadilly
30.11.81 Kenny Bruce L PTS 6 Enniskillen
08.12.81 Hugh Russell L RSC 5 Belfast
10.03.82 Eugene Maloney **W** PTS 6 Burslem
18.03.82 Keith Foreman L PTS 6 South Shields
05.04.82 Ian Murray **W** PTS 6 Glasgow
22.04.82 Hugh Russell L CO 1 Enniskillen
07.06.82 Stuart Nicol **W** RSC 2 Glasgow
28.06.82 John Farrell L RSC 3 Bradford
25.04.83 Peter Harris DREW 6 Aberdeen
23.05.83 Ray Plant **W** PTS 6 Glasgow
06.04.84 Danny Flynn L CO 2 Edinburgh (*Scottish Bantamweight Title Challenge*)
Summary: 19 contests, won 6, drew 1, lost 12

Steve Harwood
Leeds. *Born* Batley 18.04.64
Welterweight
Manager T. Calligban
Previous Amateur Club Homecharm

18.01.84 Derek Atherton **W** RSC 5 Stoke
07.03.84 Phil Jackson L DIS 2 Brighton
26.03.84 Tony Kempson **W** PTS 6 Barnsley
12.05.84 Mark Sperin L RSC 4 Hanley
Summary: 4 contests, won 2, lost 2

Steve Harwood

Wayne Hawkins
Wolverhampton. *Born* Walsall March 1964
Middleweight
Manager D. Alexander
Previous Amateur Club Bloxwich

02.03.83 Dave Scott L CO 4 Evesham
28.03.83 Rex Weaver **W** RSC 1 Wolverhampton
16.05.83 Cliff Curtis **W** PTS 6 Birmingham
23.06.83 Paul Murray **W** PTS 6 Wolverhampton
Summary: 4 contests, won 3, lost 1

Paul Heatley
Manchester. *Born* Manchester 25.12.58
L. Heavyweight
Manager (Self)
Previous Amateur Club None

09.04.80 Chuck Hirschmann L PTS 4 Liverpool
14.04.80 Joe Frater L RSC 5 Manchester
28.05.80 Joe Dean L RSC 4 Cramlington
07.07.80 Brian Graham L CO 2 Middlesbrough
11.12.80 Chuck Hirschmann DREW 4 Bolton
12.02.81 Joe Frater L PTS 6 Bolton
03.03.81 Joe Dean **W** PTS 6 Pudsey
16.03.81 Joe Dean L PTS 6 Manchester
22.06.81 Andy Peden L RSC 4 Glasgow
23.11.81 Osbourne Taylor **W** PTS 4 Chesterfield
07.12.81 Mal Kirk L RSC 4 Manchester
18.03.82 Barry Ahmed L RSC 2 South Shields
11.05.82 Clive Beardsley L RSC 7 Derby
20.06.83 Jerry Golden L PTS 6 Manchester
20.09.83 Deka Williams L PTS 6 Dudley
18.10.83 Wes Taylor L PTS 6 Wolverhampton
05.03.84 Eddie Chatterton DREW 6 Liverpool
12.03.84 Dougie Isles L RSC 4 Manchester
Summary: 18 contests, won 2, drew 2, lost 14

Dave Heaver
Doncaster. *Born* Ayr 27.12.57
L. Middleweight
Manager J. Rushton
Previous Amateur Club Langold

25.11.82 Peter Phillips L PTS 6 Morley
19.01.83 Davey Cox L PTS 6 Stoke
25.02.83 Bobby Rimmer L PTS 6 Doncaster
09.03.83 Elvis Morton **W** RSC 6 Stoke
28.03.83 Dave Harrison L PTS 6 Manchester
11.04.83 Tommy Cook L PTS 8 Glasgow
18.04.83 Gordon Pratt L PTS 6 Bradford
27.04.83 Robert Lloyd DREW 6 Rhyl
18.05.83 Tony Batty **W** RSC 4 Bloomsbury
13.06.83 Steve Metcalfe L PTS 6 Doncaster

23.06.83 Tony Batty **W** PTS 6 Bethnal Green
01.09.83 Dean Scarfe L RSC 2 Bloomsbury
26.09.83 Bobby Rimmer L RSC 3 Manchester
08.11.83 Vince Stewart L PTS 6 Bethnal Green
22.11.83 Phil Sheridan L PTS 6 Wolverhampton
05.12.83 Davey Cox L CO 7 Nottingham
25.01.84 Dave Hallett **W** PTS 6 Stoke
30.01.84 Dan Myers L RSC 4 Birmingham
04.04.84 Steve Ward L DIS 5 Evesham
17.04.84 Tony Rabbetts L PTS 6 Piccadilly
09.05.84 Graeme Griffin L PTS 6 Leicester
14.05.84 Rocky Mensah L PTS 6 Nottingham
Summary: 22 contests, won 4, drew 1, lost 17

Dale Henderson (Thynne)

Middlesbrough. *Born* Middlesbrough 11.07.57
L. Middleweight
Manager T. Miller
Previous Amateur Club Joe Walton's

02.04.81 Dave Dunn **W** PTS 6 Middlesbrough
27.04.81 Steve Heavisides **W** RSC 3 Newcastle
13.10.81 Nick Wilshire L RSC 2 Kensington
30.03.82 Kevin Durkin **W** PTS 8 Leeds
05.04.82 Kevin Durkin L PTS 8 Manchester
02.05.82 Dave Rylance **W** RTD 3 Middlesbrough
26.09.82 Colin Nelson **W** RSC 4 Middlesbrough
06.12.82 Tommy Heffron L PTS 6 Manchester
11.02.83 Torben Andersen L PTS 6 Copenhagen
24.02.83 Sammy Brennan L PTS 8 Liverpool
Summary: 10 contests, won 5, lost 5

Randy Henderson

Peckham. *Born* Jamaica 02.02.60
L. Middleweight
Manager H. Griver
Previous Amateur Club Broad Street
National Honours Young England Rep.
Divisional Honours NE London Welterweight R/U 1980

15.04.80 Dave Sullivan L PTS 6 Southend
15.05.80 Shaun Jones L PTS 6 Mayfair
16.09.80 Gerry White DREW 6 Southend
04.11.80 Ronnie Rathbone L PTS 6 Southend
25.11.80 Shaun Jones L PTS 6 Norwich
10.02.81 Dave Taylor L PTS 6 Nantwich
08.06.81 Dave Finigan L PTS 6 Moorgate
26.10.81 Dave Finigan **W** PTS 6 Southwark
23.11.81 Gary Knight **W** PTS 6 Bloomsbury
16.02.82 Gary Knight L PTS 6 Bloomsbury
01.04.82 Jimmy Smith **W** PTS 6 Walthamstow
14.09.82 Arthur Davis L PTS 8 Southend
19.10.82 Rocky Kelly L CO 8 Windsor
01.02.83 Vince Stewart **W** PTS 6 Southend
16.02.83 Martin Patrick L PTS 6 Muswell Hill
26.04.83 R. W. Smith L PTS 6 Bethnal Green
17.11.83 Mick Courtney L PTS 8 Basildon
Summary: 17 contests, won 4, drew 1, lost 12

Steve Henderson

Aylesbury. *Born* Lambeth 09.12.54
Featherweight
Manager D. Mancini
Previous Amateur Club Lynn
Divisional Honours SE London Featherweight Champion 1975

19.10.77 Eric Wood L PTS 4 Kingston
10.11.77 Tony Whitmore **W** PTS 6 Wimbledon
19.01.78 John Cooper L PTS 6 Wimbledon
06.03.78 Paul Chance L RSC 7 Wolverhampton
17.04.78 Wally Angliss **W** RSC 5 Mayfair
24.04.78 Tony Whitmore L PTS 6 Walworth
16.05.78 John Cooper L PTS 6 Aylesbury
11.10.78 Mohammed Younis L RTD 5 Stoke
05.11.79 Steve Cleak L PTS 8 Piccadilly
28.02.80 Winston Ho-Shing L RSC 5 Queensway
24.04.80 Robert Hepburn **W** RSC 6 Queensway
16.06.80 Steve Cleak L PTS 8 Piccadilly
23.03.81 Peter Eubanks L PTS 6 Mayfair
27.04.81 Richie Foster L PTS 6 Brighton
17.07.81 Rafael Blanco L PTS 6 Ostend
14.09.81 Alan Tombs L PTS 6 Mayfair
26.10.81 Steve Farnsworth L PTS 6 Mayfair
30.11.81 Carl Gaynor **W** RSC 6 Birmingham
09.12.81 Lee Graham **W** CO 5 Piccadilly
09.02.82 Mark West L PTS 8 Kensington
08.03.82 Ray Somer L PTS 8 Rotterdam
22.03.82 Steve Farnsworth L PTS 8 Mayfair
20.09.82 Alan Tombs L PTS 8 Mayfair
18.11.82 Lee Graham L PTS 8 Piccadilly
25.01.83 Thunder Clottey L RTD 3 Belfast
Summary: 25 contests, won 5, lost 20

Ian Henderson-Thynne

Middlesbrough. *Born* Middlesbrough 15.07.55
Middleweight
Manager (Self)
Previous Amateur Club Joe Walton's

25.11.82 Dave King **W** RSC 2 Sunderland
07.02.83 Rocky Feliciello L PTS 6 Liverpool
Summary: 2 contests, won 1, lost 1

Steve Henty
Brighton. *Born* Brighton 07.09.60
L. Middleweight
Manager R. Davies
Previous Amateur Club Hove

29.10.79 Tony Britton L PTS 6 Hove
23.04.80 Jeff Aspell L PTS 6 Hove
20.05.80 Adrian Clamp L DIS 5 Southend
16.06.80 Bobby Welburn W PTS 6 Piccadilly
14.07.80 Mick Miller DREW 6 Mayfair
21.11.80 Al Neville DREW 6 Crawley
09.03.81 Jimmy Cable L PTS 6 Copthorne
30.03.81 Vince Gajny L PTS 6 Piccadilly
27.04.81 Johnny Pincham W PTS 8 Brighton
17.06.81 Jimmy Ellis L RSC 7 Sheffield
22.09.81 Alan Hardiman W PTS 8 Southend
18.11.81 Dudley McKenzie L PTS 8 Solihull
24.11.81 Nick Wilshire L RSC 4 Wembley
13.09.82 Noel Blair L PTS 6 Brighton
06.11.82 John Andrews L PTS 8 Marylebone
29.11.82 Gary Petty W RSC 5 Brighton
09.12.82 Rocky Kelly L RSC 4 Bloomsbury
14.09.83 Martin Patrick L RSC 5 Muswell Hill
31.10.83 Paul Murray W PTS 6 Stoke
07.12.83 Martin Patrick L RSC 8 Bloomsbury
Summary: 20 contests, won 5, drew 2, lost 13

Robert Hepburn
Norwich. *Born* Aberdeen 30.07.58
Featherweight
Manager G. Holmes
Previous Amateur Club Lowestoft
Divisional Honours E Counties Bantamweight Champion 1977

06.04.79 John Henry W PTS 4 Norwich
26.06.79 Alec Irvine L PTS 6 Leicester
24.10.79 Stuart Crabb DREW 6 Norwich
06.11.79 George Bailey W PTS 6 Stafford
21.11.79 Don Aageson W PTS 6 Evesham
06.03.80 Ivor Jones L PTS 8 Wimbledon
17.03.80 Joey Wainwright L PTS 6 Piccadilly
10.04.80 Stuart Crabb W PTS 6 Norwich
24.04.80 Steve Henderson L RSC 6 Queensway
29.05.80 Gary Kittle L PTS 6 Wimbledon
03.06.80 Clyde Ruan L CO 2 Aylesbury
25.11.80 Wayne Williams W PTS 6 Norwich
19.03.81 Wayne Williams W RSC 4 Norwich
30.03.81 Peter Eubanks L PTS 6 Piccadilly
06.04.81 Rocky Bantleman L RSC 5 Windsor
02.07.81 Carl Cleasby W PTS 6 Pudsey
05.08.81 David Miles L PTS 6 Norwich
28.10.81 Eugene Maloney L RTD 3 Acton
24.01.82 Keith Foreman L RTD 3 Sunderland
16.02.82 Keith Wallace L RSC 2 Bloomsbury
23.03.82 Kevin Hay W PTS 6 Wolverhampton
19.04.82 Johnny Dorey W PTS 6 Mayfair
14.09.82 Peter Jones L PTS 6 Wembley
01.02.83 Michael Marsden L RSC 5 Southend
Summary: 24 contests, won 9, drew 1, lost 14

Godfrey Hibbert
Nottingham. *Born* Nottingham 23.10.59
Heavyweight
Manager W. Wigley
Previous Amateur Club NSOB

20.09.83 Frank Robinson L CO 4 Dudley
24.10.83 Frank Robinson L RSC 4 Nottingham
22.11.83 Al Malcolm L RSC 1 Wolverhampton
Summary: 3 contests, lost 3

Lloyd Hibbert
Birmingham. *Born* Birmingham 29.06.59
Welterweight
Manager (Self)
Previous Amateur Club Sheldon Heath
National Honours Schools Title 1974

31.01.79 Tommy Wright W PTS 6 Stoke
26.02.79 Gary Pearce W PTS 6 Edgbaston
05.03.79 Peter Snowshall W PTS 6 Wolverhampton
23.04.79 Johnny Elliott W PTS 8 Reading
16.05.79 Tommy Wright W PTS 8 Wolverhampton
02.07.79 Vic Jackson W PTS 8 Wolverhampton
26.09.79 Al Stewart W PTS 8 Stoke
17.10.79 Gary Cooper W PTS 8 Evesham
03.12.79 Nigel Thomas W PTS 8 Wolverhampton
22.09.80 Lee Hartshorn W PTS 8 Wolverhampton
21.01.81 Joey Singleton W PTS 8 Solihull
06.05.81 Roy Varden W RSC 7 Solihull
21.09.81 Tusikoleta Nkalankete W PTS 8 Wolverhampton
24.05.82 Cliff Gilpin L RSC 6 Wolverhampton
(*Vacant Midlands Area L. Middleweight Title*)
06.10.82 Joey Mack W PTS 8 Solihull
18.10.82 Tony Martey W PTS 8 Edgbaston
18.01.83 Lloyd Honeyghan L PTS 10 Kensington
(*Elim. British Welterweight Title*)
11.04.83 Charlie Malarkey L PTS 8 Glasgow
Summary: 18 contests, won 15, lost 3

Stephen Hibbs
Caerphilly. *Born* Caerphilly 03.06.64
L. Middleweight
Manager (Self)
Previous Amateur Club Lansbury Park

19.12.83 Neil Crocker L RSC 1 Swansea
Summary: 1 contest, lost 1

Mark Hill
Wednesbury. *Born* Wednesbury 17.06.59
L. Middleweight
Manager G. Riley
Previous Amateur Club Wednesbury

11.10.77 Larry Richards DREW 6 Coventry
31.10.77 Larry Richards DREW 4 Birmingham
22.11.77 Larry Richards L PTS 4 Wolverhampton
30.11.77 Larry Richards W PTS 4 Wolverhampton
01.02.78 Jimmy Brown L RSC 1 Evesham
06.03.78 James Cooke L CO 2 Wolverhampton
04.04.78 John Singlewood W RSC 3 Wolverhampton
18.04.78 Tony Whitmore W PTS 6 Wolverhampton
24.04.78 Gary Lucas W PTS 4 Glasgow
29.06.78 Larry Richards L PTS 6 Wolverhampton
11.10.78 Gary Collins L RSC 1 Stoke
04.04.79 Johnny Burns L CO 3 Birmingham
08.10.80 Barry Winter L RSC 3 Stoke
13.04.83 Davey Cox L PTS 6 Evesham
27.04.83 Davey Cox DREW 6 Wolverhampton
20.09.83 Dan Myers L RSC 2 Dudley
18.10.83 Roy Varden W PTS 6 Wolverhampton
01.11.83 Davey Cox W PTS 6 Dudley
16.04.84 Graeme Griffin DREW 6 Birmingham
Summary: 19 contests, won 6, drew 4, lost 9

Gary Hobbs
Acton. *Born* Stepney 15.09.56
Former Undefeated Southern Area Middleweight Champion
Manager H. Holland
Previous Amateur Club Hogarth
Divisional Honours SW London Middleweight Champion 1981

03.11.81 Casley McCallum W RSC 5 Southend
23.11.81 Prince Wilmot W RSC 2 Bloomsbury
02.12.81 Russell Humphreys W PTS 6 Burslem
26.01.82 Joe Jackson W PTS 6 Hornsey
09.03.82 Hugh Johnson L RSC 4 Hornsey
02.11.82 Deano Wallace W PTS 6 Hornsey
15.12.82 Conrad Oscar W PTS 8 Queensway
25.04.83 Deano Wallace W RSC 3 Acton
18.05.83 Dave Armstrong W RSC 1 Bloomsbury
(*Southern Area Middleweight Title Challenge*)
05.10.83 Mick Morris W RSC 7 Solihull
Summary: 10 contests, won 9, lost 1

Ray Hood
Liverpool. *Born* Queensferry 28.08.62
Welsh Lightweight Champion
Manager (Self)
Previous Amateur Club Buckley

09.06.81 Alan Tombs DREW 6 Southend
29.06.81 Vince Griffin W RSC 3 Liverpool
16.09.81 Jeff Smart W RTD 4 Burslem
23.09.81 Winston Ho-Shing L PTS 6 Sheffield
06.10.81 Peter Flanagan W RSC 5 Liverpool
13.10.81 Alan Cooper DREW 6 Nantwich
28.10.81 Delroy Pearce W PTS 6 Burslem
03.11.81 Mark Crouch W CO 6 Southend
16.11.81 Winston Ho-Shing W PTS 6 Liverpool
27.01.82 Eric Wood W PTS 6 Stoke
16.02.82 Aidan Wake W CO 4 Leeds
29.03.82 Jimmy Bunclark W RSC 2 Liverpool
05.04.82 Jimmy Duncan L PTS 8 Bloomsbury
03.06.82 Delroy Pearce W PTS 8 Liverpool
30.06.82 Tommy Cook W PTS 8 Liverpool
01.11.82 Andy Thomas W PTS 8 Liverpool
04.03.83 Andy Thomas W PTS 10 Queensferry
(*Vacant Welsh Lightweight Title*)
28.10.83 Jimmy Bunclark W RSC 8 Queensferry
14.11.83 Ken Foreman L PTS 8 Nantwich
22.11.83 Najib Daho L PTS 8 Manchester
15.03.84 Kevin Pritchard L PTS 8 Kirkby
06.04.84 Ian McLeod L RSC 2 Edinburgh
Summary: 22 contests, won 14, drew 2, lost 6

Mick Hoolison
Bradford. *Born* Blackpool 18.02.64
Featherweight
Manager J. Celebanski
Previous Amateur Club Bradford Police

25.02.83 Eddie Toro W RSC 2 Doncaster
21.04.83 Tony Borg L RSC 2 Piccadilly
16.05.83 Neville Fivey L PTS 6 Bradford
13.06.83 Taffy Mills L CO 5 Doncaster
05.09.83 Alex Cairney L PTS 6 Glasgow
15.09.83 Johnny Mack L PTS 6 Liverpool
15.10.83 Neville Fivey L PTS 6 Coventry
27.10.83 Steve James L RTD 3 Ebbw Vale
Summary: 8 contests, won 1, lost 7

Trevor Hopson
Derek Rowe (Photos) Ltd

Trevor Hopson
Billericay. *Born* Ilford 12.02.61
Welterweight
Manager E. Fossey
Previous Amateur Club Rayleigh Mill

01.09.83 Tim Gladwish L PTS 6 Bloomsbury
21.09.83 Joe Lynch **W** PTS 6 Southend
09.11.83 Carl Bishop **W** PTS 6 Southend
18.11.83 Joe Lynch L RTD 2 Sheffield
14.02.84 Dario De Abreu L PTS 6 Southend
03.04.84 Dave Hallet **W** RSC 2 Lewisham
01.05.84 Frankie Lake L PTS 6 Maidstone
Summary: 7 contests, won 3, lost 4

Billy Hough
Merthyr. *Born* Liverpool 23.07.63
Bantamweight
Manager G. Evans
Previous Amateur Club Rhondda

01.03.82 Steve King L RSC 3 Piccadilly
22.03.82 Johnny Dorey L RTD 3 Southwark
08.06.82 Anthony Brown L PTS 6 Southend
22.09.82 Dave Khan **W** RSC 2 Stoke
19.10.82 Rocky Bantleman L CO 2 Windsor
12.03.83 Robert Dickie L PTS 6 Swindon
14.06.83 Steve Reilly **W** PTS 4 Newport
Summary: 7 contests, won 2, lost 5

Kevin Howard
Sunderland. *Born* Sunderland 03.09.61
Featherweight
Manager F. Deans
Previous Amateur Club Sunderland

15.09.81 Selvin Bell **W** PTS 6 Sunderland
24.09.81 Eddie Glass **W** PTS 6 Hartlepool
09.10.81 Colin Harrison L PTS 6 Cambuslang
02.11.81 Colin Harrison DREW 6 South Shields
25.11.81 Lee Halford L PTS 6 Stoke
24.01.82 John Pollard DREW 6 Sunderland
08.02.82 Kevin Pritchard L PTS 6 Manchester
25.02.82 Colin Harrison L RSC 7 Hartlepool
06.04.82 Mark Davey L PTS 6 Leeds
21.05.82 Vince Vahey L PTS 6 Sheffield
31.08.82 Vince Vahey L PTS 6 South Shields
07.10.82 Karl Davey **W** RSC 2 Morley
25.11.82 Steve Pollard **W** PTS 6 Sunderland
10.02.83 John Sharkey **W** PTS 8 Sunderland
21.02.83 John Sharkey L RSC 5 Glasgow
19.12.83 Peter Harris L PTS 8 Swansea
23.01.84 John Murphy L PTS 8 Glasgow
16.04.84 John Sharkey L PTS 8 Glasgow
Summary: 18 contests, won 5, drew 2, lost 11

Lennie Howard
Chelmsford. *Born* Jamaica 05.01.59
L. Heavyweight
Manager H. Spriggs
Previous Amateur Club Barking
Divisional Honours E Counties L. Heavyweight Champion 1979/1982; NE London L. Heavyweight R/U 1983

28.11.83 Paul Foster **W** CO 2 Southwark
16.02.84 Gypsy Carman **W** RTD 1 Basildon
27.03.84 Alex Romeo **W** PTS 6 Bethnal Green
19.04.84 Robbie Turner **W** RSC 4 Basildon
Summary: 4 contests, won 4

Steve Howard
Battersea. *Born* London 07.07.58
Heavyweight
Manager D. Urry
Previous Amateur Club Wandsworth
Divisional Honours SW London Heavyweight R/U 1981

20.10.82 Rocky Burton L CO 1 Strand
29.11.82 John Fallon L PTS 6 Brighton
25.04.83 Tom Eastwood L PTS 6 Acton
Summary: 3 contests, lost 3

Lennie Howard
Gloucester Photo Agency

Paul Huggins

Hastings. *Born* Hastings 15.07.61
Former Southern Area Featherweight Champion
Manager F. Warren
Previous Amateur Club West Hill
National Honours Schools Title 1975
Divisional Honours S Counties Bantamweight R/U 1980

15.09.80 Steve Farnsworth **W** PTS 6 Mayfair
20.10.80 Carl Gaynor **W** PTS 6 Hove
08.12.80 Glyn Davies **W** PTS 8 Hastings
12.01.81 Richie Foster DREW 6 Hove
16.02.81 Glyn Davies **W** CO 1 Mayfair
02.03.81 Peter Gabbitus **W** RSC 1 Brighton
31.03.81 Jimmy Bott **W** RSC 3 Wembley
28.04.81 Gary Kittle **W** RSC 7 Kensington
02.06.81 Ian Murray **W** CO 2 Kensington
20.10.81 Selvin Bell **W** CO 3 Bethnal Green
03.11.81 Steve Cleak DREW 8 Kensington
09.02.82 Steve Cleak **W** CO 2 Kensington
02.03.82 Richie Foster **W** PTS 8 Kensington
20.04.82 Jarvis Greenidge **W** RSC 2 Kensington
01.06.82 Pat Doherty **W** RSC 5 Kensington
09.11.82 Barry McGuigan **L** RSC 5 Belfast (*Final Elim. British Featherweight Title*)
18.01.83 Gerry Beard **L** PTS 8 Kensington
21.02.83 Clyde Ruan **W** PTS 10 Mayfair (*Vacant Southern Area Featherweight Title*)
21.03.83 Gerry Beard **W** RSC 3 Mayfair
25.04.83 Rory Burke **W** RSC 7 Mayfair (*Southern Area Featherweight Title Defence*)
01.09.83 Kevin Pritchard **L** RSC 7 Bloomsbury
02.11.83 Terry Kemp **W** CO 2 Bloomsbury
07.12.83 Clyde Ruan **L** PTS 10 Bloomsbury (*Southern Area Featherweight Title Defence & Elim. British Featherweight Title*)
03.04.84 Pat Doherty **L** RSC 7 Lewisham
Summary: 24 contests, won 17, drew 2, lost 5

Mickey Hull

Chelmsford. *Born* Chelmsford 01.06.63
Lightweight
Manager T. Mason
Previous Amateur Club Barking
National Honours England Int.; Young England Rep.
Divisional Honours NE London Lightweight Champion 1983 & R/U 1982/1984

31.05.84 Eamonn Payne **W** PTS 6 Basildon
Summary: 1 contest, won 1

Paul Huggins
Derek Rowe (Photos) Ltd

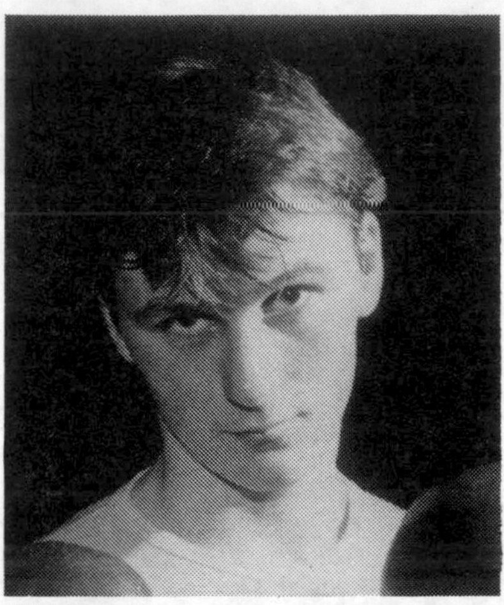

Mickey Hull
Douglas Baton

John Humphreys

Shrewsbury. *Born* Shrewsbury 09.01.59
L. Heavyweight
Manager R. Gray
Previous Amateur Club North Shropshire
National Honours Junior ABA Title 1975; NABC Title 1975; Young England Rep.; England Int.
Divisional Honours M Counties Middleweight R/U 1978

22.09.80 Clifton Wallace **W** PTS 6 Wolverhampton
13.10.80 Clifton Wallace **W** PTS 6 Nottingham
18.10.80 Willie Wright **W** PTS 6 Birmingham
18.11.80 Jimmy Ellis **W** PTS 6 Shrewsbury
01.12.80 Steve Bateman **W** RSC 4 Wolverhampton
19.01.81 Winston Burnett DREW 6 Birmingham
09.03.81 Willie Wright **W** PTS 6 Wolverhampton
13.04.81 Joe Jackson DREW 6 Wolverhampton
01.06.81 Jimmy Ellis DREW 6 Wolverhampton
25.01.82 Willie Wright **W** PTS 6 Wolverhampton
09.02.82 Willie Wright **W** PTS 6 Wolverhampton
24.02.82 Horace McKenzie DREW 8 Evesham
23.03.82 Peter Tidgewell **W** PTS 8 Wolverhampton
24.05.82 Terry Matthews **W** PTS 8 Wolverhampton
11.11.82 Eddy Mongelema L PTS 8 Dunkirk
13.12.82 Clive Beardsley **W** PTS 6 Wolverhampton
18.10.83 Romal Ambrose L PTS 8 Wolverhampton
Summary: 17 contests, won 11, drew 4, lost 2

Jim Hunter

Glasgow. *Born* Glasgow 18.10.60
Welterweight
Manager B. Watt
Previous Amateur Club Holyrood

09.02.81 Mike Dunlop L PTS 4 Glasgow
12.05.81 Kevin Walsh L RSC 6 Liverpool
08.06.81 Liam Linnen L PTS 6 Motherwell
03.10.83 Alex Brown L PTS 6 Glasgow
21.11.83 Peter Phillips L PTS 6 Glasgow
27.02.84 Mike McKenzie L RSC 3 Glasgow
Summary: 6 contests, lost 6

(Murad) Mo Hussein

West Ham. *Born* Hackney 17.11.62
Lightweight
Manager T. Lawless
Previous Amateur Club West Ham
National Honours Schools Title 1978
Divisional Honours NE London L. Welterweight Champion 1981; NE London L. Welterweight R/U 1982

18.05.82 Eddie Glass **W** RSC 4 Bethnal Green
28.09.82 Bobby Welburn **W** RSC 1 Bethnal Green
16.11.82 Ray Ross **W** RTD 3 Bethnal Green
25.01.83 Les Remikie **W** PTS 6 Bethnal Green
22.03.83 Robert Lloyd **W** PTS 6 Bethnal Green
17.05.83 Les Remikie **W** PTS 6 Bethnal Green
04.10.83 Ray Price **W** PTS 8 Bethnal Green
08.11.83 Gerry Beard **W** RSC 4 Bethnal Green
06.02.84 Paul Cook **W** CO 3 Bethnal Green
11.04.84 Glyn Rhodes **W** RSC 1 Kensington
Summary: 10 contests, won 10

Cordwell Hylton

Walsall. *Born* Jamaica 20.09.58
L. Heavyweight
Manager D. Alexander
Previous Amateur Club Bloxwich
Divisional Honours M Counties L. Heavyweight R/U 1979

22.09.80 Nigel Savery **W** PTS 6 Wolverhampton
30.10.80 Steve Fenton **W** CO 2 Wolverhampton

01.12.80 Liam Coleman L PTS 6 Wolverhampton
02.02.81 Steve Fenton W PTS 6 Nottingham
10.02.81 John O'Neill W RSC 6 Wolverhampton
16.03.81 Chris Lawson L RSC 5 Mayfair
13.04.81 Rupert Christie W RSC 5 Wolverhampton
11.05.81 Trevor Cattouse L PTS 8 Mayfair
05.10.81 Antonio Harris W PTS 8 Birmingham
30.11.81 Ben Lawlor W RSC 2 Birmingham
23.01.82 Chisanda Mutti L RSC 3 Berlin
16.02.82 Prince Mama Mohammed L PTS 8 Birmingham
10.03.82 Devon Bailey L RSC 2 Birmingham
24.05.82 Clive Beardsley W RSC 4 Nottingham
20.09.82 Keith Bristol NC 5 Wolverhampton
10.10.82 Alex Tompkins W PTS 8 Piccadilly
23.11.82 Winston Burnett W RSC 5 Wolverhampton
13.12.82 Steve Babbs L CO 1 Wolverhampton
15.02.83 Alek Penarski W RSC 4 Wolverhampton
23.02.83 Devon Bailey L RSC 6 Mayfair
28.03.83 Gordon Stacey W RSC 1 Birmingham
25.04.83 Alex Tompkins W PTS 8 Southwark
19.05.83 Richard Caramanolis L CO 4 Paris
03.12.83 Andy Straughn L PTS 8 Marylebone
25.01.84 Romal Ambrose W RSC 3 Solihull
07.06.84 Roy Skeldon L CO 7 Dudley
Summary: 26 contests, won 14, lost 11, NC 1

John Humphreys

Mark Hynes

Rugeley. *Born* Leicester 02.08.62
Welterweight
Manager F. Wolfindale
Previous Amateur Club Birmingham City

14.02.84 Elvis Morton L PTS 6 Wolverhampton
22.02.84 Elvis Morton W RSC 1 Evesham
14.03.84 Phil Sheridan L PTS 6 Stoke
Summary: 3 contests, won 1, lost 2

Brian Hyslop

Glasgow. *Born* Glasgow 08.06.61
Lightweight
Manager T. Gilmour
Previous Amateur Club Scottish National

04.05.81 Carl Gaynor W RSC 5 Glasgow
01.06.81 Stuart Shaw W CO 5 Nottingham
21.09.81 Selvin Bell W PTS 6 Glasgow
09.10.81 Alex Rodden W CO 2 Cambuslang
25.11.81 Steve Topliss L PTS 8 Stoke
15.02.82 Keith Foreman W PTS 6 Glasgow
08.03.82 Steve Pollard DREW 8 Hamilton
07.06.82 Ian Murray W PTS 8 Glasgow
09.04.84 Stuart Carmichael W PTS 6 Glasgow
14.05.84 Steve Griffith L PTS 6 Glasgow
Summary: 10 contests, won 7, drew 1, lost 2

Alec Irvine

Corby. *Born* Corby 14.09.54
Former Midlands Area Featherweight Champion
Manager (Self)
Previous Amateur Club Corby, Stewart & Lloyd

27.09.78 Steve Cleak L PTS 6 Evesham
24.10.78 Gary Nickels L PTS 6 Kensington
14.11.78 Gary Lucas L PTS 4 Birkenhead
20.02.79 John Henry W RSC 4 Wolverhampton
15.03.79 John Cooper L PTS 6 Caister
04.04.79 Jimmy Hancock DREW 6 Birmingham
17.04.79 Terry McKeown L PTS 8 Glasgow
17.05.79 John Cooper L PTS 8 Wimbledon
21.05.79 Mick Wheelan W PTS 6 Birmingham
26.06.79 Robert Hepburn W PTS 6 Edgbaston
12.09.79 Doug Hill L PTS 10 Burslem
(*Vacant Midlands Area Featherweight Title*)
15.11.79 Selvin Bell W PTS 6 Caister
05.02.80 Dave Laxen DREW 8 Southend
19.03.80 Steve Cleak W PTS 8 Solihull
29.04.80 Joey Wainwright W PTS 8 Piccadilly
11.06.80 Don Aageson L PTS 8 Edgbaston
18.10.80 Don Aageson W PTS 8 Birmingham
13.11.80 Ian Murray DREW 6 Caister
09.02.81 Jim McKeown L RSC 6 Glasgow
13.05.81 Neil Brown W CO 4 Leicester
25.09.81 Mervyn Bennett L PTS 6 Nottingham
23.11.81 George Sutton W RSC 3 Nottingham
07.12.81 John Sharkey L PTS 6 Nottingham

CONTINUED OVERLEAF

22.02.82 John Sharkey L RSC 5 Glasgow
19.03.82 Jarvis Greenidge W PTS 10 Nottingham
(Midlands Area Featherweight Title Challenge)
11.05.82 John Sharkey L PTS 8 Derby
01.11.82 Lee Graham L PTS 8 Piccadilly
29.11.82 Dean Marsden W RSC 4 Birmingham
28.02.83 Steve Topliss L PTS 10 Birmingham
(Midlands Area Featherweight Title Defence)
11.04.83 Paul Keers L PTS 8 Gosforth
09.05.83 Alan Tombs W PTS 8 Piccadilly
24.10.83 Steve Enright W RSC 5 Nottingham
07.11.83 Dave Pratt L PTS 8 Birmingham
06.12.83 Jim McDonnell L PTS 8 Kensington
10.02.84 Steve Topliss L PTS 10 Dudley
(Midlands Area Featherweight Title Challenge)
13.03.84 Rory Burke L PTS 8 Wembley
01.05.84 Mark Reefer L PTS 6 Bethnal Green
Summary: 37 contests, won 13, drew 3, lost 21

David Irving
Belfast. *Born* Belfast 20.02.62
L. Welterweight
Manager B. Eastwood
Previous Amateur Club Holy Family
National Honours Irish Int.; Irish L. Welterweight Champion 1982

25.01.84 Colin Neagle W RSC 1 Belfast
27.02.84 Tony McKenzie L RSC 3 Birmingham
04.04.84 John Murray W RSC 3 Belfast
05.06.84 Danny Shinkwin W CO 2 Kensington
30.06.84 Ray Price W RSC 4 Belfast
Summary: 5 contests, won 4, lost 1

Doug James
Derek Rowe (Photos) Ltd

Dougie Isles
Blackpool. *Born* Blackpool 26.09.63
L. Heavyweight
Manager G. Hill
Previous Amateur Club Fleetwood

12.03.84 Paul Heatley W RSC 4 Manchester
09.04.84 Winston Wray L RSC 1 Manchester
14.05.84 Stuart Robinson L RSC 2 Manchester
Summary: 3 contests, won 1, lost 2

Phil Jackson
Birmingham *Born* Nuneaton 05.09.62
Welterweight
Manager (Self)
Previous Amateur Club Nuneaton Boys

07.03.84 Steve Harwood W DIS 2 Brighton
Summary: 1 contest, won 1

Chris Jacobs
Swansea. *Born* Llanelli 28.04.61
Heavyweight
Manager C. Breen
Previous Amateur Club Trostre
National Honours Welsh S. Heavyweight Champion 1983

13.06.84 Tony Tricker W PTS 6 Aberavon
Summary: 1 contest, won 1

Doug James
Swansea. *Born* Swansea 31.03.58
Welsh Middleweight Champion
Manager D. Bidwell
Previous Amateur Club RAOB Swansea
National Honours Welsh Middleweight Champion 1979; Welsh Int.
Divisional Honours Welsh Middleweight R/U 1978

17.09.79 Earl Edwards W PTS 6 Mayfair
11.10.79 Joe Hannaford W RSC 2 Liverpool
30.10.79 Keith Roberts W RSC 5 Bedworth
06.11.79 Joe Jackson W PTS 8 Stafford
27.11.79 Clifton Wallace W PTS 6 Wolverhampton
04.02.80 Harry Watson W CO 1 Piccadilly
17.03.80 George Danahar L RSC 6 Mayfair
07.05.80 Peter Bassey DREW 8 Liverpool
12.08.80 Dave Owens W PTS 8 Gowertown
15.12.80 Carl Daley W RSC 2 Merthyr
25.01.82 Billy Lauder L PTS 8 Glasgow
15.03.82 Brian Anderson L PTS 8 Piccadilly
22.03.82 Kenny Feehan W CO 5 Swansea
18.05.82 Billy Lauder W RSC 4 Piccadilly
26.10.82 Mark Kaylor L RSC 2 Bethnal Green
28.01.83 Horace McKenzie W RSC 9 Swansea
(Vacant Welsh Middleweight Title)

25.04.83 Cameron Lithgow **W** RSC 8 Aberdeen
05.09.83 Brian Anderson **L** RSC 1 Mayfair
15.10.83 Errol Christie **L** RSC 4 Coventry
06.12.83 T. P. Jenkins **DREW** 8 Kensington
03.02.84 T. P. Jenkins **L** RSC 7 Maidenhead
09.05.84 John Elliott **W** CO 4 Mayfair
25.05.84 Pierre Jolly **L** PTS 8 Toulouse
Summary: 23 contests, won 13, drew 2, lost 8

Keith James

Norwich. *Born* Ipswich 11.12.57
Middleweight
Manager (Self)
Previous Amateur Club Hurstleigh
Divisional Honours E Counties Middleweight Champion 1977/1979/1981

23.11.81 Joe Dean **W** PTS 6 Chesterfield
25.01.82 Sammy Brennan **L** PTS 6 Bradford
16.02.82 Cliff Curtis **W** PTS 6 Southend
18.03.82 Rex Weaver **W** PTS 6 Caister
07.07.82 Willie Wright **W** PTS 8 Newmarket
28.09.82 T. P. Jenkins **DREW** 6 Bethnal Green
09.11.82 Peter Gorny **W** PTS 8 Southend
03.02.83 Mick Morris **W** PTS 8 Bloomsbury
28.02.83 Conrad Oscar **L** PTS 8 Strand
21.03.83 Harry Cowap **W** RTD 4 Mayfair
07.04.83 Conrad Oscar **W** PTS 8 Strand
Summary: 11 contests, won 8, drew 1, lost 2

Leroy James

Bradford. *Born* Bradford 26.09.62
Lightweight
Manager J. Celebanski
Previous Amateur Club Bradford YMCA

14.03.84 Peter Bowen **L** RSC 2 Stoke
Summary: 1 contest, lost 1

(Kendrick) Ricky James

Rugby. *Born* Jamaica 04.11.55
Midlands Area Heavyweight Champion
Manager J. Griffin
Previous Amateur Club Birmingham Golden Gloves
Divisional Honours M Counties Heavyweight Champion 1976 – 1978

13.06.78 Steve Fenton **L** PTS 6 Coventry
29.06.78 Roy Gregory **W** CO 2 Wolverhampton
27.09.78 Bob Young **W** CO 3 Solihull
24.10.78 Stan McDermott **W** CO 2 Kensington
20.11.78 Austin Okoye **W** RSC 6 Birmingham
21.05.79 Danny Lawford **L** PTS 8 Birmingham
25.06.79 Terry Mintus **W** PTS 8 Edgbaston
10.09.79 Gordon Ferris **L** PTS 8 Birmingham
23.10.79 Joe Awome **L** RSC 4 Wembley
19.11.79 Gordon Ferris **L** RSC 6 Edgbaston
30.04.80 Larry McDonald **L** PTS 8 Aylesbury
03.06.80 Stan McDermott **L** RSC 4 Kensington
17.03.81 Rudi Pika **L** PTS 6 Wembley
13.05.81 John Rafferty **W** CO 4 Leicester
25.09.81 Terry O'Connor **W** PTS 10 Nottingham
(*Midlands Area Heavyweight Title Challenge*)
10.11.81 Rocky Burton **W** CO 6 Bedworth
(*Midlands Area Heavyweight Title Defence*)
28.11.81 Al Syben **L** PTS 8 Brussels
26.04.82 Tony Moore **W** PTS 8 Leicester
30.08.82 Mike Koranacki **L** RSC 2 Johannesburg
02.12.82 Anders Eklund **L** RSC 3 Randers
17.02.83 Rocky Burton **W** CO 3 Coventry
(*Midlands Area Heavyweight Title Defence*)
22.09.83 John L. Gardner **L** RSC 6 Strand
Summary: 22 contests, won 10, lost 12

Steve James

Troedyrhiw. *Born* Merthyr 22.06.62
Featherweight
Manager D. James
Previous Amateur Club Courthouse
National Honours Welsh Int.; Welsh Featherweight Champion 1981

27.10.83 Mick Hoolison **W** RTD 3 Ebbw Vale
29.11.83 Tony Borg **L** PTS 6 Cardiff
22.02.84 Dave Pratt **L** PTS 8 Evesham
28.03.84 Billy Joe Dee **W** RSC 5 Aberavon
19.05.84 Andy Williams **W** PTS 6 Bristol
13.06.84 Tony Borg **W** PTS 8 Aberavon
Summary: 6 contests, won 4, lost 2

Brett Jefford

Basildon. *Born* London 08.03.60
L. Welterweight
Manager (Self)
Previous Amateur Club Berry Boys
National Honours Schools Title 1974; Junior ABA Title 1976
Divisional Honours E Counties Welterweight R/U 1980

10.02.83 Frankie Lake **W** PTS 6 Walthamstow
17.03.83 Jimmy Singleton **W** PTS 6 Marylebone
17.11.83 Rocky Mensah **W** RSC 3 Basildon
Summary: 3 contests, won 3

Nick Jenkins
Bristol. *Born* Bristol 19.12.57
L. Heavyweight
Manager R. Porter
Previous Amateur Club National Smelting
Divisional Honours W Counties L. Heavyweight Champion 1977/1979; W Counties L. Heavyweight R/U 1978/1981; W Counties Middleweight Champion 1980

16.02.82 Chris Thorne **W** RSC 4 Southend
28.04.82 Leo Mulhern **W** RSC 2 Sheffield
09.06.82 Phil Williams **W** RSC 2 Bristol
18.10.82 Winston Burnett **W** PTS 8 Southwark
25.10.82 Sammy Brennan **W** RSC 4 Bradford
06.12.82 Vince Gajny **W** RSC 7 Bristol
12.03.83 Winston Burnett **W** PTS 6 Swindon
16.04.83 Vince Gajny L PTS 8 Bristol
17.05.83 Chris Devine **W** PTS 6 Bethnal Green
16.09.83 Antonio Harris **W** PTS 8 Swindon
Summary: 10 contests, won 9, lost 1

(Tony) T. P. Jenkins
Brentford. *Born* Chiswick 15.08.59
Middleweight
Manager D. Mancini
Previous Amateur Club Old Actonians
National Honours England Int.
Divisional Honours SW London Middleweight Champion 1980/1982; SW London Middleweight R/U 1981

28.09.82 Keith James DREW 6 Bethnal Green
18.10.82 Tony Hart **W** RSC 3 Southwark
09.11.82 Bobby Williams **W** PTS 6 Kensington
29.11.82 Richard Wilson DREW 8 Southwark
31.01.83 Richard Wilson **W** RSC 4 Southwark
17.03.83 Earl Edwards **W** CO 1 Marylebone
25.04.83 Conrad Oscar **W** PTS 8 Southwark
17.05.83 Paul Murray **W** PTS 6 Bethnal Green
17.10.83 Cameron Lithgow **W** PTS 8 Southwark
28.11.83 Jimmy Ellis **W** PTS 8 Southwark
06.12.83 Doug James DREW 8 Kensington
03.02.84 Doug James **W** RSC 7 Maidenhead
22.03.84 Martin McEwan **W** PTS 8 Maidenhead
05.06.84 James Cook L RSC 9 Kensington (*Vacant Southern Area Middleweight Title*)
Summary: 14 contests, won 10, drew 3, lost 1

Kenny Jinks
West Bromwich. *Born* Tipton 11.04.65
Lightweight
Manager F. Wolfingdale
Previous Amateur Club Wednesfield

19.09.83 Paul Wright **W** RSC 3 Nottingham
05.10.83 John Murphy **W** RSC 2 Stoke
01.11.83 Willie Wilson **W** PTS 6 Dudley
01.12.83 Carl Merrett **W** PTS 6 Dudley
25.01.84 Carl Merrett **W** PTS 8 Stoke
27.03.84 Dave Pratt L RSC 1 Wolverhampton
27.04.84 Nicky Day **W** PTS 6 Wolverhampton
Summary: 7 contests, won 6, lost 1

Hugh Johnson
Small Heath. *Born* Jamaica 26.07.61
L. Heavyweight
Manager E. Cashmore
Previous Amateur Club Small Heath

11.09.81 Neville Wilson L RSC 1 Edgbaston
07.10.81 Russell Humphreys **W** PTS 6 Stoke
21.12.81 Neville Wilson L PTS 6 Birmingham
16.02.82 Rob Wada **W** PTS 6 Birmingham
09.03.82 Gary Hobbs **W** RSC 4 Hornsey
24.05.82 Joey Saunders **W** PTS 6 Nottingham
06.07.82 Leo Mulhern **W** PTS 6 Leeds
07.09.82 Mark Kelly **W** RSC 3 Crewe
06.10.82 Winston Davis L PTS 8 Stoke
16.03.83 Geoff Rymer **W** PTS 8 Cheltenham
22.03.83 Dave Scott L PTS 6 Wolverhampton
12.04.83 Geoff Rymer **W** PTS 8 Southend
Summary: 12 contests, won 8, lost 4

Kevin Johnson
Small Heath. *Born* Birmingham 16.10.61
Welterweight
Manager (Self)
Previous Amateur Club Nechells

30.04.80 Casley McCallum L RSC 4 Wolverhampton
15.09.80 Steve Davies L PTS 4 Manchester
13.10.80 Charlie Douglas DREW 6 Nottingham
18.10.80 Mark Crouch L PTS 6 Birmingham
05.11.80 Gary Buckle L PTS 6 Evesham
13.11.80 Gary Buckle L PTS 4 Stafford
26.11.80 Dave Goodwin L RSC 1 Stoke
16.02.81 Mike Clemow L PTS 6 Birmingham
21.09.81 Sam Boy Burton L PTS 6 Wolverhampton
13.10.81 Steve Brannan L PTS 6 Wolverhampton
04.12.81 Geoff Pegler L PTS 6 Bristol
21.12.81 Mark Crouch **W** PTS 6 Birmingham
16.02.82 Mark Crouch L RSC 2 Birmingham
10.03.82 Dave Harrison **W** PTS 4 Burslem

15.03.82 Dan Myers L RSC 5 Wolverhampton
29.11.82 Daryl Lindsay W RSC 4 Newquay
14.02.84 Frankie Lake DREW 6 Southend
21.03.84 Les Remikie L RSC 3 Mayfair
01.05.84 Mark Simpson L RSC 3 Maidstone
Summary: 19 contests, won 3, drew 2, lost 14

Lou Johnson

Nottingham. *Born* Nottingham 20.04.64
Middleweight
Manager J. Gill
Previous Amateur Club Radford Boys

05.12.83 Tucker Watts DREW 4 Nottingham
27.02.84 Dave Foley L PTS 6 Nottingham
06.03.84 Terry Magee L RSC 2 Stoke
Summary: 3 contests, drew 1, lost 2

Steve Johnson

Liverpool. *Born* Prescot 10.07.57
Middleweight
Manager F. Warren
Previous Amateur Club St. Helens Star
National Honours Young England Rep./England Int.
Divisional Honours W Lancs L. Middleweight Champion 1977; N Counties Middleweight Champion 1980 – 1981

26.01.82 Prince Wilmot W RSC 4 Hornsey
16.02.82 Steve Jarman W PTS 6 Southend
15.03.82 Winston Burnett W RSC 5 Bloomsbury
14.04.82 Dwight Osbourne W PTS 6 Strand
27.09.82 George Danahar W PTS 6 Bloomsbury
09.12.82 Darwin Brewster L PTS 8 Bloomsbury
24.11.83 Deano Wallace W RSC 3 Kirkby
05.12.83 Chris Coady W RSC 5 Manchester
09.02.84 Willie Wright W PTS 8 Manchester
Summary: 9 contests, won 8, lost 1

Gary Jones

Stirling. *Born* Cheltenham 02.06.54
L. Heavyweight
Manager T. Gilmour
Previous Amateur Club Stirling

03.09.79 Mick Fellingham DREW 6 Glasgow
10.09.79 Nigel Savery L PTS 6 Bradford
08.10.79 Mick Fellingham L PTS 6 Glasgow
12.11.79 Ernie Baister L RSC 5 Middlesbrough
06.12.79 Nigel Savery W PTS 6 Glasgow
21.01.80 Nigel Savery W PTS 6 Glasgow
18.02.80 Gordon George DREW 6 Birmingham
25.02.80 Ernie Baister W PTS 6 Glasgow
18.03.80 Rocky Burton L PTS 6 Wolverhampton
24.03.80 Gordon George W PTS 6 Glasgow
21.04.80 Rupert Christie L RSC 2 Edgbaston
31.08.80 Peter Tidgewell L PTS 8 Glasgow
04.05.81 Jonjo Greene W PTS 4 Glasgow
11.05.81 Mark Cumber L RSC 3 Glasgow
21.09.81 Andy Peden L PTS 6 Glasgow
09.10.81 Osbourne Taylor W PTS 4 Cambuslang
27.10.81 Jarlath McGough W DIS 6 Wolverhampton
09.11.81 Mal Kirk L PTS 6 Hamilton
23.11.81 Nye Williams L CO 2 Nantwich
25.01.82 Steve Babbs W PTS 6 Glasgow
16.02.82 Peter Tidgewell L PTS 6 Leeds
25.03.82 John Joseph L RSC 5 Glasgow
10.05.82 Nigel Savery L PTS 6 Liverpool
28.09.82 Geoff Rymer L PTS 6 Aberdeen
19.10.82 Clive Beardsley W PTS 6 Wolverhampton
15.11.82 Ian Lazarus L PTS 6 Glasgow
20.12.82 Bernie Kavanagh L RTD 3 Bradford
21.02.83 Geoff Rymer L PTS 6 Glasgow
20.04.83 Alex Romeo L CO 6 Solihull
Summary: 29 contests, won 9, drew 2, lost 18

Ivor Jones

Holloway. *Born* Hollyhead 08.04.56
Bantamweight
Manager C. Lake
Previous Amateur Club Cheveley
Divisional Honours H Counties L. Flyweight Champion 1974 – 1975; E Counties Bantamweight R/U 1977; E Counties Bantamweight Champion 1978 – 1979

16.10.79 Carl Gaynor W RSC 3 Lewisham
19.11.79 Stuart Crabb W RTD 3 Lewisham
22.01.80 Bryn Jones W PTS 6 Piccadilly
06.03.80 Robert Hepburn W PTS 8 Wimbledon
29.04.80 John Griffiths W RSC 6 Mayfair
29.05.80 Iggy Jano W PTS 8 Wimbledon
20.10.80 Steve Enright L PTS 8 Birmingham
22.09.81 Carl Cleasby W PTS 8 Bethnal Green
20.10.81 Steve Reilly W RSC 3 Bethnal Green
16.11.81 George Bailey W PTS 6 Mayfair
12.01.82 Joe Park W RSC 3 Bethnal Green
16.02.82 George Bailey W PTS 6 Bethnal Green
20.04.82 Davy Larmour L PTS 8 Kensington
04.05.82 Jimmy Bott L RSC 6 Wembley
01.06.82 Neil McLaughlin W CO 4 Kensington
28.09.82 Johnny Dorey W PTS 6 Bethnal Green

CONTINUED OVERLEAF

16.11.82 Jimmy Bott **L** PTS 8 Bethnal Green
22.03.83 Johnny Dorey **L** PTS 10 Bethnal Green
(*Vacant Southern Area Bantamweight Title*)
31.05.83 Gary Roberts **W** RSC 4 Kensington
06.02.84 Peter Harris DREW 8 Bethnal Green
Summary: 20 contests, won 14, drew 1, lost 5

Peter Jones

Gorseinon. *Born* Gorseinon 16.06.61
Bantamweight
Manager E. Thomas
Previous Amateur Club Penyrheol
National Honours Junior ABA Title 1978; ABA Bantamweight Title 1981; Welsh Flyweight Champion 1980 & Bantamweight Champion 1981; Welsh Int.

03.09.81 Mike Wilkes **W** RSC 4 Cardiff
29.11.81 Ray Plant **W** RSC 6 Middlesbrough
10.03.82 Pat Doherty **L** PTS 8 Solihull
19.03.82 Stuart Shaw **W** PTS 8 Nottingham
14.09.82 Robert Hepburn **W** PTS 6 Wembley
07.03.83 Ray Somer **W** PTS 8 Rotterdam
20.04.83 Mike Irungu **L** PTS 8 Muswell Hill
Summary: 7 contests, won 5, lost 2

Rod Jones

Telford. *Born* Paddington 09.02.61
Middleweight
Manager M. Sendell
Previous Amateur Club WSOB

23.05.83 Dave Hall **L** PTS 6 Mayfair
13.06.83 Elvis Morton **L** PTS 6 Nottingham
Summary: 2 contests, lost 2

Stanley Jones

Dyfed. *Born* Llandovery 15.01.64
L. Welterweight
Manager D. Davies
Previous Amateur Club Towy
Divisional Honours Welsh L. Welterweight R/U 1982

12.06.84 Frankie Lake **W** CO 5 Southend
Summary: 1 contest, won 1

Dalton Jordan

Leicester. *Born* Barbados 12.01.58
L. Middleweight
Manager M. Inskip
Previous Amateur Club Highfields

11.01.82 Paul Atherton **L** PTS 6 Liverpool
23.03.82 Paul Mitchell **L** PTS 6 Wolverhampton
30.03.82 Paul Costigan **L** PTS 6 Leeds
07.04.82 Cecil Williams **L** RSC 3 Evesham
28.04.82 John Andrews **L** PTS 4 Burslem
10.05.82 Chris Lewin **L** PTS 6 Birmingham
17.05.82 Blaine Longsden **L** PTS 6 Manchester
24.05.82 Dan Myers **W** RSC 5 Wolverhampton
17.09.82 Rick Warrilow **W** PTS 6 Liverpool
13.10.82 John Davies **L** CO 4 Evesham
24.11.82 Rocky Severino **W** PTS 6 Stoke
26.01.83 Davey Cox **L** PTS 6 Stoke
11.02.83 John Mortensen **L** CO 3 Copenhagen
11.04.83 Gordon Pratt **L** CO 2 Gosforth
04.06.84 Jeff Standley **W** PTS 6 Nottingham
15.06.84 Tony Baker **L** RTD 2 Liverpool
Summary: 16 contests, won 4, lost 12

John Joseph

Hayes. *Born* Grenada 31.01.58
L. Heavyweight
Manager (Self)
Previous Amateur Club Hayes
Divisional Honours NW London L. Heavyweight Champion 1979 – 1980

07.10.80 Bobby Williams **W** RSC 3 Piccadilly
16.02.81 Wayne McLaughlin **W** RSC 2 Piccadilly
16.03.81 Ray Pearce **W** RSC 4 Piccadilly
06.04.81 Gordon Stacey **L** RSC 2 Windsor
15.06.81 Mark Cumber **W** RSC 3 Piccadilly
21.09.81 Lee White **W** PTS 6 Piccadilly
09.12.81 Geoff Rymer **W** PTS 6 Piccadilly
15.03.82 Geoff Rymer **L** PTS 6 Piccadilly
25.03.82 Gary Jones **W** RSC 5 Glasgow
22.04.82 Peter Tidgewell **W** RSC 1 Piccadilly
08.06.82 Steve Jarman **W** RSC 2 Southend
01.11.82 Mal Kirk **W** RTD 4 Piccadilly
10.02.83 George Danahar **W** PTS 8 Walthamstow
22.03.83 John Moody **L** RSC 5 Bethnal Green
03.02.84 Sam Reeson **L** PTS 8 Maidenhead
Summary: 15 contests, won 11, lost 4

Theo Josephs

Halifax. *Born* Trinidad 29.03.55
L. Heavyweight
Manager T. Callighan
Previous Amateur Club Halifax Star
Divisional Honours NE Counties L. Heavyweight R/U 1977

06.10.77 Richie Smith **W** RSC 3 Liverpool
24.10.77 Alan Tashy **W** PTS 6 Piccadilly
23.11.77 Pat Thompson **L** PTS 6 Stoke
01.12.77 Danny McLoughlin **W** PTS 8 Caister
19.12.77 Pat Thompson **L** PTS 8 Bradford
18.01.78 George Gray **W** PTS 8 Stoke
24.01.78 Karl Canwell **L** RSC 4 Piccadilly
13.03.78 Trevor Cattouse **L** PTS 8 Hove

23.03.78 Howard Mills **L** PTS 8 Sunderland
24.04.78 Reg Long **L** PTS 8 Middlesbrough
08.05.78 Ron Green **L** PTS 6 Nottingham
18.07.78 Ron Green **L** PTS 8 Wakefield
18.09.78 Paul Busette **W** RSC 6 Manchester
28.09.78 Steve Hill **L** RSC 4 Liverpool
24.10.78 George Scott **L** PTS 6 Blackpool
30.11.78 Derek Simpkin **W** PTS 6 Caister
11.12.78 David Pearce **L** PTS 8 Plymouth
13.02.79 Reg Long **W** PTS 8 Wakefield
22.02.79 Ron McLean **W** RSC 5 Liverpool
20.03.79 Terry Chard **L** PTS 6 Mayfair
05.07.79 David Pearce **L** RSC 3 Aberavon
28.11.79 Tim Wood **W** PTS 8 Doncaster
03.03.80 Neil Malpass **L** PTS 8 Marton
19.03.80 Neil Malpass **L** PTS 8 Doncaster
28.04.81 Steve Gee **L** PTS 8 Leeds
17.06.81 Chris Devine **L** RSC 1 Sheffield
02.11.81 Jim Burns **L** PTS 8 Nottingham
16.02.82 Neil Malpass **L** RSC 8 Leeds
22.04.82 Noel Quarless **W** CO 1 Liverpool
03.06.82 Noel Quarless **L** PTS 6 Liverpool
13.09.82 Danny Lawford **L** PTS 8 Brighton
05.11.82 Anders Eklund **L** PTS 4 Copenhagen
07.12.82 Steve Gee **L** PTS 6 Southend
25.01.83 Adrian Elliott **L** RSC 6 Bethnal Green
21.02.83 Frank Robinson **W** PTS 6 Nottingham
21.03.83 Dave Garside **L** PTS 6 Bradford
21.04.83 Andy Straughn **L** RSC 3 Letchworth
30.11.83 Horace Notice **L** CO 1 Piccadilly
27.03.84 Glenroy Taylor **W** PTS 6 Bethnal Green
01.05.84 Billy Cassidy **L** PTS 6 Bethnal Green
13.05.84 Adrian Elliott **L** RSC 4 Wembley
07.06.84 Colin Flute **L** PTS 6 Dudley
Summary: 42 contests, won 12, lost 30

Mick Joyce

Doncaster. *Born* Livingstone 18.04.60
Welterweight
Manager K. Richardson
Previous Amateur Club Tom Hill YC

30.04.84 Grant Sutton **L** RSC 4 Liverpool
Summary: 1 contest, lost 1

Joey Joynson

Liverpool. *Born* Liverpool 15.06.62
Lightweight
Manager A. Smith
Previous Amateur Club Golden Gloves
National Honours Junior ABA Title 1979; Young England Rep.; England Int.
Divisional Honours W Lancs Lightweight Champion 1982

07.09.82 Peter Gabbitus **W** RSC 2 Hornsey
16.11.82 David Miles **W** RSC 2 Bethnal Green
23.11.82 Gerry Beard **W** PTS 6 Wembley
22.02.83 Carl Gaynor **W** RSC 3 Bethnal Green
25.04.83 Stuart Shaw **W** RSC 1 Mayfair
27.09.83 Alan Tombs **W** RSC 1 Wembley
22.11.83 Steve Pollard **W** PTS 8 Wembley
22.02.84 Gary Williams **W** RSC 1 Kensington
25.04.84 Elias Martinez **L** CO 5 Atlantic City
15.06.84 Mark Pearce **W** PTS 8 Liverpool
Summary: 10 contests, won 9, lost 1

(Keith) Abdul Kareem (Perez)

Walthamstow. *Born* Trinidad 20.10.60
Lightweight
Manager F. Warren
Previous Amateur Club New Enterprise

10.05.83 Ron Shinkwin **W** PTS 6 Southend
07.06.83 Ricky Deane **W** RSC 5 Southend
01.09.83 Gary Williams **W** PTS 6 Bloomsbury
14.11.83 Dave Savage **W** CO 6 Glasgow
18.11.83 Gary Williams **L** DIS 8 Sheffield
18.01.84 Willie Wilson **W** PTS 8 Stoke
30.01.84 Dave Haggarty **L** PTS 8 Glasgow
Summary: 7 contests, won 5, lost 2

Bernie Kavanagh

Liverpool. *Born* Liverpool 15.09.58
L. Heavyweight
Manager M. Goodall
Previous Amateur Club Golden Gloves
Divisional Honours NW Counties L. Heavyweight Champion 1980; N Counties L. Heavyweight Champion 1981; W Lancs L. Heavyweight R/U 1982

18.10.82 Jerry Golden **W** PTS 6 Blackpool
20.12.82 Gary Jones **W** RTD 3 Bradford
24.01.83 Mal Kirk **W** RSC 5 Bradford
24.02.83 Jerry Golden **W** RSC 5 Liverpool
16.05.83 Alex Romeo **L** RSC 1 Bradford
15.09.83 Eddie Cooper **L** RTD 2 Liverpool
22.11.83 Jonjo Greene **L** PTS 8 Manchester
20.02.84 Ian Lazarus **L** PTS 10 Bradford
(*Vacant Central Area L. Heavyweight Title*)
04.06.84 Jonjo Greene **L** RSC 8 Manchester
Summary: 9 contests, won 4, lost 5

Paul Keers

Bradford. *Born* Hartlepool 22.10.60
Lightweight
Manager (Self)
Previous Amateur Club Hartlepool US

05.04.79 Joey Spring **W** PTS 6 Liverpool
26.04.79 Bobby Breen **W** PTS 6 Liverpool
01.05.79 Austin Owens **L** PTS 6 Wembley
10.05.79 Glyn Davies DREW 6 Pontypool
18.06.79 Alan Storey **W** PTS 8 Bradford

CONTINUED OVERLEAF

05.07.79 Vernon Penprase L PTS 8 Aberavon
12.09.79 Don George **W** PTS 6 Liverpool
25.09.79 Gary Nickels **W** PTS 6 Wembley
08.10.79 Terry McKeown L PTS 8 Glasgow
03.12.79 Mohammed Younis **W** PTS 8 Wolverhampton
17.12.79 Selvin Bell L PTS 8 Bradford
08.01.80 Mohammed Younis **W** RTD 6 Windsor
28.01.80 Jarvis Greenidge **W** PTS 8 Bradford
03.03.80 Vernon Penprase L PTS 8 Piccadilly
27.03.80 Gary Lucas L PTS 8 Liverpool
12.05.80 Austin Owens DREW 8 Reading
02.06.80 Vernon Penprase L PTS 10 Plymouth
07.07.80 Charlie Parvin **W** RTD 5 Middlesbrough
11.09.80 Steve Cleak **W** RSC 4 Hartlepool
22.09.80 Wayne Evans **W** PTS 8 Birmingham
25.11.80 Jarvis Greenidge L RSC 7 Doncaster
24.02.81 Lance Williams L CO 1 Kensington
17.06.81 Glyn Rhodes L RSC 1 Sheffield
09.11.81 Winston Ho-Shing L CO 5 Hartlepool
20.09.82 Winston Ho-Shing **W** PTS 6 Bradford
13.10.82 Johnny Grant L PTS 6 Walthamstow
18.10.82 John McKinlay L PTS 6 Glasgow
25.10.82 Winston Ho-Shing L RSC 3 Bradford
25.11.82 Gary Williams L RSC 3 Morley
25.02.83 Peter Gabbitus L RSC 4 Doncaster
11.04.83 Alec Irvine **W** PTS 8 Gosforth
23.05.83 Dave Savage L RSC 5 Glasgow
06.02.84 Edward Lloyd L PTS 6 Liverpool
Summary: 33 contests, won 13, drew 2, lost 18

Irish Tommy Kelliher

Holloway. *Born* Tralee 22.06.60
L. Welterweight
Manager D. Smith
Previous Amateur Club Repton
Divisional Honours NE London Lightweight R/U 1983

14.05.84 Alastair Laurie L RSC 5 Glasgow
07.06.84 Paul Boswell **W** RSC 6 Piccadilly
Summary: 2 contests, won 1, lost 1

Hugh Sugar Kelly

Blantyre. *Born* Blantyre 27.06.61
Lightweight
Manager E. Coakley
Previous Amateur Club Blantyre MW
National Honours Scottish Int.
Divisional Honours Scottish Featherweight R/U 1982

30.01.84 Mickey Lerwill **W** PTS 6 Glasgow
05.03.84 Steve Swiftie **W** RSC 2 Glasgow
30.04.84 Doug Munro **W** CO 1 Glasgow
14.05.84 Steve Cooke **W** CO 1 Glasgow
21.05.84 Gary Williams L RSC 4 Aberdeen
Summary: 5 contests, won 4, lost 1

Jim Kelly

Wishaw. *Born* Craigneuk 27.07.62
Scottish Welterweight Champion
Manager E. Rea
Previous Amateur Club Lanark Welfare

13.09.82 Phil O'Hare L CO 5 Glasgow
25.10.82 Frank Abercromby **W** RSC 5 Airdrie
26.11.82 Phil O'Hare L PTS 6 Glasgow
23.05.83 Steve Metcalfe **W** PTS 6 Glasgow
13.06.83 Joe McGinley **W** RSC 1 Glasgow
12.09.83 Tony Batty **W** RSC 4 Glasgow
14.11.83 Davey Cox **W** PTS 8 Glasgow
30.01.84 Dave Douglas **W** CO 6 Glasgow (*Scottish Welterweight Title Challenge*)
05.03.84 Geoff Pegler **W** PTS 8 Glasgow
09.04.84 Frankie Moro L PTS 8 Glasgow
30.04.84 John McAllister L PTS 8 Glasgow
Summary: 11 contests, won 7, lost 4

Mark Kelly

Crewe. *Born* Crewe 08.08.59
Middleweight
Manager F. Deakin
Previous Amateur Club Crewe LMR

02.12.81 Willie Wright L PTS 6 Burslem
20.01.82 Willie Wright **W** PTS 6 Burslem
10.03.82 Willie Wright **W** PTS 6 Burslem
26.04.82 Deano Wallace L PTS 6 Edgbaston
07.09.82 Hugh Johnson L RSC 3 Crewe
09.12.82 Martin Patrick L PTS 6 Bloomsbury
01.02.83 Frank Dodson **W** PTS 6 Southend
28.02.83 Paul Mitchell **W** RTD 2 Strand
09.03.83 Phil O'Hare DREW 6 Stoke
28.03.83 Phil O'Hare L PTS 6 Manchester
12.04.83 Martin McEwan L CO 2 Southend
16.05.83 Phil O'Hare L RTD 4 Manchester
Summary: 12 contests, won 4, drew 1, lost 7

Paul Kelly

Doncaster. *Born* Doncaster 26.05.55
Welterweight
Manager K. Richardson
Previous Amateur Club Mexborough
National Honours Young England Rep.; England Int.; ABA Welterweight Champion 1974
Divisional Honours Combined Services L. Welterweight Champion 1975; ABA Welterweight R/U 1976; Combined Services Welterweight Champion 1976 – 1977; NEC L. Middleweight S/F 1980

08.12.80 Gerry McGrath L PTS 6 Piccadilly
23.02.81 Gerry Maguire **W** RSC 3 Glasgow
26.03.81 Dil Collins **W** PTS 6 Ebbw Vale

27.04.81 Errol Dennis W RSC 3 Piccadilly
25.01.82 Mike Clemow W PTS 8 Piccadilly
31.03.84 Claude Rossi W PTS 6 Derby
30.04.84 Peter Flanagan W RSC 4 Liverpool
Summary: 7 contests, won 6, lost 1

(Hamilton) Rocky Kelly

Acton. *Born* Liverpool 05.01.63
Southern Area Welterweight Champion
Manager H. Holland
Previous Amateur Club Hogarth
Divisional Honours SW London Welterweight Champion 1981

28.10.81 Dave Goodwin W CO 2 Acton
23.11.81 Alan Cable W RSC 5 Bloomsbury
16.02.82 Dave Sullivan W PTS 6 Bloomsbury
15.03.82 Gary Petty W CO 4 Bloomsbury
05.04.82 Mike Clemow W PTS 6 Bloomsbury
17.05.82 Robert Armstrong W CO 2 Windsor
07.06.82 Gary Knight L PTS 8 Bloomsbury
19.10.82 Randy Henderson W CO 8 Windsor
02.11.82 Danny Garrison W PTS 8 Hornsey
09.12.82 Steve Henty W RSC 4 Bloomsbury
03.02.83 Judas Clottey L PTS 8 Bloomsbury
25.01.83 Bert Myrie W CO 1 Acton
23.09.83 Gary Pearce W CO 1 Longford
03.10.83 Dave Douglas L PTS 8 Glasgow
06.12.83 Ian Chantler W RSC 4 Kensington
22.02.84 Chris Sanigur W PTS 10 Kensington
(*Vacant Southern Area Welterweight Title*)
27.03.84 Paul Murray W RTD 5 Battersea
05.06.84 P. J. Davitt W RSC 5 Kensington
Summary: 18 contests, won 15, lost 3

Tony Kempson

Blackpool. *Born* Manchester 01.05.60
Welterweight
Manager G. Hill
Previous Amateur Club Fleetwood

05.12.83 Gary Peel W PTS 6 Manchester
19.12.83 Ken Foreman L RTD 2 Bradford
30.01.84 Ray Murray L PTS 6 Manchester
06.02.84 Dennis Boy O'Brien L RSC 5 Mayfair
05.03.84 Tommy Campbell L PTS 6 Glasgow
12.03.84 Kevin Sanders W RSC 3 Manchester
19.03.84 Steve Craggs L PTS 6 Bradford
26.03.84 Steve Harwood L PTS 6 Barnsley
09.04.84 Mike Calderwood W RSC 5 Manchester
21.05.84 Andy Sumner L CO 4 Bradford
Summary: 10 contests, won 3, lost 7

George Kerr

Dundee. *Born* Dundee 03.03.60
L. Welterweight
Manager T. Gilmour
Previous Amateur Club Camperdown
National Honours Scottish Int.
Divisional Honours Scottish L. Welterweight R/U 1979 – 1980

18.04.83 Ray Ross W RSC 2 Glasgow
25.04.83 Steve Ellwood L PTS 6 Piccadilly
19.05.83 Tony Wilkinson W RSC 4 Sunderland
31.05.83 Terry Smith W RSC 3 Kensington
19.09.83 Jackie Turner L PTS 8 Glasgow
05.10.83 Granville Allen W PTS 8 Stoke
01.11.83 George Schofield L PTS 8 Liverpool
21.11.83 Sam Omidi W PTS 8 Glasgow
25.01.84 Martin McGough L PTS 8 Solihull
Summary: 9 contests, won 5, lost 4

Dave Kettlewell

Leeds. *Born* Leeds 15.08.63
L. Welterweight
Manager V. Flynn
Previous Amateur Club Meanwood

16.05.83 Ian Harrison DREW 6 Bradford
22.09.83 Ian Harrison L CO 2 Stockport
11.06.84 Mickey Cotton W CO 2 Manchester
Summary: 3 contests, won 1, drew 1, lost 1

Mickey Kidd (Neale)

Bedworth. *Born* Nuneaton 02.04.59
Middleweight
Manager C. Hall
Previous Amateur Club Newdigate

26.09.79 Barry Oakes W RSC 1 Stoke
30.10.79 Terry Matthews L PTS 6 Bedworth
27.11.79 Kendrick Edwards W PTS 6 Wolverhampton
17.12.79 Gary Newell W PTS 6 Wolverhampton
16.01.80 Jerry Golden W PTS 6 Stoke
21.04.80 Mike Copp W PTS 6 Mayfair
29.04.80 Mike Copp W PTS 6 Piccadilly
13.11.80 Al Neville W PTS 6 Stafford
25.11.80 Russell Humphreys W PTS 6 Bedworth
08.12.80 Russell Humphreys DREW 6 Nottingham
28.01.81 Winston Davis L RSC 2 Stoke
16.03.81 Willie Wright W DIS 6 Nottingham
15.04.81 Russell Humphreys L PTS 6 Evesham
27.04.81 Harry Watson DREW 6 Nottingham
13.05.81 Willie Wright W PTS 6 Leicester
01.06.81 Deano Wallace DREW 6 Wolverhampton

CONTINUED OVERLEAF

10.11.81 Alan Cable **W** PTS 6 Bedworth
23.11.81 Willie Wright **W** PTS 6 Nottingham
07.12.81 Deano Wallace **L** PTS 6 Nottingham
10.10.83 Dave Mowbray **W** RSC 1 Birmingham
24.10.83 Bert Myrie **W** PTS 6 Nottingham
01.11.83 Winston Burnett **W** PTS 6 Dudley
10.11.83 Deano Wallace **L** PTS 6 Stafford
07.12.83 Dennis Sheehan **W** PTS 8 Stoke
12.12.83 Harry Watson **W** PTS 6 Bedworth
02.04.84 Winston Burnett **W** PTS 8 Mayfair
23.05.84 Tyrone Forbes **L** PTS 8 Mayfair
Summary: 27 contests, won 18, drew 3, lost 6

Mickey Kilgallon
Peckham. *Born* London 26.07.65
Welterweight
Manager E. Fossey
Previous Amateur Club Peckham

23.06.83 Paul McHugh **W** RSC 2 Bethnal Green
14.09.83 Tim Gladwish **W** PTS 4 Muswell Hill
09.11.83 Gary Peel **W** RSC 6 Southend
07.12.83 Kenny Watson **W** RSC 5 Bloomsbury
01.02.84 Sean Campbell **W** RSC 3 Bloomsbury
21.03.84 Lee Roy **W** PTS 6 Bloomsbury
25.04.84 Davey Cox **W** RSC 5 Muswell Hill
Summary: 7 contests, won 7

Craig Killoran
Bracknell. *Born* Ascot 30.12.61
Bantamweight
Manager F. Turner
Previous Amateur Club Bracknell Boys

17.10.83 Dave Smith **W** PTS 4 Southwark
Summary: 1 contest, won 1

Andy King
Bridgend. *Born* Bridgend 16.06.62
Bantamweight
Manager D. Gardiner
Previous Amateur Club Garw Valley

14.09.81 Stuart Nicol **L** RSC 2 Glasgow
19.11.81 Ken Coughlin **W** CO 3 Ebbw Vale
10.12.81 Steve Reilly **W** PTS 6 Newport
25.01.82 Gary Nickels **L** PTS 8 Mayfair
06.05.82 Johnny Dorey **L** PTS 8 Mayfair
24.01.83 Duke McKenzie **L** RSC 2 Mayfair
Summary: 6 contests, won 2, lost 4

Brian King (Gambier)
Rhyl. *Born* Bow 07.12.64
Featherweight
Manager B. Lloyd
Previous Amateur Club None

30.04.84 Ian Murray DREW 6 Rhyl
15.06.84 Henry Arnold **L** PTS 6 Liverpool
Summary: 2 contests, drew 1, lost 1

Chris King
Rainham. *Born* Romford 12.09.63
L. Middleweight
Manager F. Turner
Previous Amateur Club St. Marys

14.04.83 Kevin Stevens **W** RSC 1 Basildon
16.05.83 Claude Rossi **W** PTS 6 Mayfair
17.10.83 Jeff Standley **W** PTS 6 Southwark
Summary: 3 contests, won 3

Steve King
Maesteg. *Born* Bettws 13.06.62
Featherweight
Manager D. Gardiner
Previous Amateur Club Garw Valley

01.03.82 Billy Hough **W** RSC 3 Piccadilly
09.03.82 Keith Wallace **L** RSC 3 Hornsey
24.01.83 Shaun Shinkwin **L** RSC 5 Mayfair
Summary: 3 contests, won 1, lost 2

Mal Kirk
Blackpool. *Born* Ashton 21.04.56
L. Heavyweight
Manager T. Callighan
Previous Amateur Club Mottram & Hattersley
Divisional Honours NW Counties Heavyweight Champion 1977; E Lancs L. Heavyweight R/U 1979

11.05.81 Dave Turner **W** PTS 6 Bradford
15.06.81 Tony Hoole **W** RSC 3 Manchester
21.09.81 Nigel Savery **W** RSC 4 Manchester
19.10.81 Jerry Golden **W** RSC 4 Manchester
09.11.81 Gary Jones **W** PTS 6 Hamilton
23.11.81 Chris Thorne **W** RSC 3 Chesterfield
07.12.81 Paul Heatley **W** RSC 4 Manchester
08.02.82 Reg Long **W** RSC 4 Manchester
22.02.82 Steve Goodwin **L** RSC 3 Bradford
30.04.82 Michael Madsen **L** RTD 3 Copenhagen
01.11.82 John Joseph **L** RTD 4 Piccadilly
24.01.83 Bernie Kavanagh **L** RSC 5 Bradford
22.09.83 Jerry Golden **W** RSC 2 Stockport
26.10.83 Geoff Rymer **W** PTS 6 Stoke
05.12.83 Jerry Golden **L** RSC 1 Manchester
09.02.84 Eddie Cooper **W** PTS 6 Manchester
12.06.84 Geoff Rymer **L** RSC 3 Southend
Summary: 17 contests, won 11, lost 6

Danny Knaggs
Hull. *Born* Hull 08.09.60
Featherweight
Manager R. Tighe
Previous Amateur Club St. Marys

20.06.83 Peter Harris **L** PTS 6 Piccadilly
05.09.83 Mike Whalley **L** CO 6 Liverpool
19.10.83 Ian Murray **W** PTS 6 Hull
13.03.84 George Baigrie DREW 6 Hull
Summary: 4 contests, won 1, drew 1, lost 2

Gary Knight (Colkett)
West Ham. *Born* Forest Gate 22.02.60
Welterweight
Manager E. Fossey
Previous Amateur Club West Ham

12.10.81 Dave Allen **W** PTS 6 Bloomsbury
23.11.81 Randy Henderson **L** PTS 6 Bloomsbury
02.12.81 Errol Dennis **W** RSC 2 Burslem
20.01.82 Peter Bennett **L** PTS 6 Burslem
16.02.82 Randy Henderson **W** PTS 6 Bloomsbury
15.03.82 Ron Pearce **W** CO 2 Bloomsbury
05.04.82 Noel Blair **W** RSC 4 Bloomsbury
14.04.82 Lloyd Christie **W** RSC 5 Strand
17.05.82 Dave Sullivan **W** PTS 8 Windsor
07.06.82 Rocky Kelly **W** PTS 8 Bloomsbury
22.06.82 Robert Armstrong **W** RSC 7 Hornsey
04.09.82 Dennis Sullivan DREW 8 Piccadilly
27.09.82 Gary Pearce **W** PTS 8 Bloomsbury
28.10.82 Geoff Pegler **W** PTS 8 Bloomsbury
16.02.83 Mick Rowley **W** PTS 8 Muswell Hill
25.03.83 Bert Myrie **W** PTS 8 Bloomsbury
20.04.83 Kevin Pritchard **W** PTS 8 Muswell Hill
23.06.83 Vernon Entertainer Vanriel **L** RSC 6 Bethnal Green
09.11.83 Sam Omidi **W** PTS 6 Southend
03.12.83 Steve Early **W** PTS 8 Marylebone
13.01.84 Mohammed Kawoya **L** PTS 6 Randers
28.04.84 Geoff Pegler **W** PTS 8 Aberavon
Summary: 22 contests, won 17, drew 1, lost 4

Tony Laing
Nottingham. *Born* Jamaica 22.09.57
L. Welterweight
Manager M. Duff
Previous Amateur Club Clifton
National Honours Junior ABA Title 1973; Young England Rep.

12.12.77 Bert Green DREW 6 Birmingham
20.03.78 Steve Ward **W** RSC 2 Mayfair
19.03.79 Jimmy Smith **W** RSC 4 Mayfair
15.03.82 Delroy Pearce **W** PTS 6 Mayfair
05.05.82 Sam Omidi **W** RSC 1 Solihull
06.10.82 Kostas Petrou **L** PTS 6 Solihull
01.03.83 Tony Adams **W** PTS 6 Kensington
24.10.83 Derek Nelson **W** RSC 3 Mayfair
30.11.83 Tony Brown **W** PTS 8 Piccadilly
11.04.84 Vernon Entertainer Vanriel **W** RSC 7 Kensington
Summary: 10 contests, won 8, drew 1, lost 1

Frankie Lake
Plymouth. *Born* Paignton 09.06.61
L. Welterweight
Manager D. Mahoney
Previous Amateur Club Ford

20.10.82 Shaun Robinson **W** PTS 6 Stoke
18.11.82 Michael Harris **L** PTS 6 Piccadilly
10.02.83 Brett Jefford **L** PTS 6 Walthamstow
21.02.83 Dave Smithson **L** PTS 8 Piccadilly
21.04.83 Jim Paton **L** PTS 8 Piccadilly
16.05.83 Chris Harvey **W** PTS 6 Mayfair
06.06.83 Steve Boyle **L** RTD 3 Piccadilly
21.09.83 John Daly **L** RTD 5 Southend
18.11.83 Billy Edwards **W** PTS 6 Southend
30.11.83 Tony Adams **L** RSC 2 Piccadilly
14.02.84 Kevin Johnson DREW 6 Southend
13.03.84 Dave Dent **L** RSC 4 Wembley
01.05.84 Trevor Hopson **W** PTS 6 Maidstone
12.06.84 Stanley Jones **L** CO 5 Southend
Summary: 14 contests, won 4, drew 1, lost 9

Alan Lamb

Alan Lamb

Lancaster. *Born* Lancaster 12.11.56
Former Undefeated Central Area L. Welterweight Champion
Manager H. Burgess
Previous Amateur Club Lancaster Lads
National Honours England Int.
Divisional Honours N Counties L. Welterweight Champion 1975; W Lancs L. Welterweight R/U 1976; W Lancs L. Welterweight Champion 1979

16.10.79 Gary Ball **W** RSC 6 Lewisham
19.11.79 Ray Ross **W** RSC 3 Lewisham
20.12.79 Dave Taylor **W** RSC 3 Queensway
15.04.80 Frank McCord **W** CO 1 Blackpool
11.06.80 Ceri Collins **W** RSC 6 Morecambe
14.07.80 Granville Allen **W** RSC 5 Mayfair
04.09.80 Messaoud Bouachiba **W** CO 1 Morecambe
13.11.80 Fred Roelandts **W** CO 2 Queensway
17.02.81 Eric Wood **W** PTS 8 Lewisham
30.04.81 Tony Carroll **W** PTS 10 Liverpool (*Vacant Central Area L. Welterweight Title*)
04.06.81 Patrizio Burini **W** RSC 3 Morecambe
09.09.81 Tim Moloney **W** RTD 7 Morecambe
19.11.81 Adey Allen **L** RSC 3 Morecambe
01.03.82 Dave Goodwin **W** RSC 4 Preston
03.06.82 Dave Taylor **W** PTS 10 Liverpool (*Central Area L. Welterweight Title Defence*)
30.06.82 Patsy Quinn **W** CO 4 Liverpool
13.09.82 George Peacock **W** PTS 10 Glasgow (*Elim. British L. Welterweight Title*)
08.04.83 Clinton McKenzie **L** PTS 12 Liverpool (*British L. Welterweight Title Challenge*)
15.09.83 Jeff Decker **L** RSC 1 Liverpool
Summary: 19 contests, won 16, lost 3

Billy Lauder

Bonnyrigg. *Born* Edinburgh 06.07.57
Middleweight
Manager (Self)
Previous Amateur Club Sparta
National Honours GB Rep.; ABA L. Middleweight Champion 1976; Euro. Junior Gold 1976

19.09.77 Dave Merrill **W** PTS 6 Glasgow
24.10.77 Vic Jackson **W** PTS 8 Doncaster
24.11.77 Brian Gregory **W** PTS 8 Doncaster
06.12.77 Joe Oke **W** PTS 8 Leeds
23.01.78 Ken Jones **L** PTS 6 Aberavon
13.02.78 Kenny Feehan **W** CO 2 Reading
27.02.78 Owen Robinson **W** PTS 8 Glasgow
10.04.78 Joey Mack **L** RSC 2 Birmingham
08.05.78 Charley Malarkey **L** PTS 10 Glasgow
20.06.78 Joe Oke **W** PTS 8 Piccadilly
02.10.78 Joe Lally **L** CO 6 Liverpool
19.02.79 Gerry Young **W** PTS 8 Belfast
19.03.79 Harry Watson **W** PTS 8 Glasgow
04.06.79 Chris Walker **W** PTS 8 Piccadilly
28.06.79 Torben Andersen **L** PTS 6 Randers
17.09.79 Harry Watson **W** PTS 8 Glasgow
22.10.79 Steve Hopkin **L** RTD 5 Mayfair
26.11.79 Gerry Young **W** PTS 8 Belfast
28.01.80 John Smith **W** PTS 8 Glasgow
14.04.80 Henry Cooper **W** PTS 8 Motherwell
28.04.80 Alex Blanchard **L** CO 4 Amsterdam
20.10.80 Malcolm Heath **W** RSC 6 Glasgow
26.11.80 Glen McEwan **L** CO 3 Solihull
23.02.81 Brian Anderson **L** RTD 3 Glasgow
21.09.81 Winston Burnett DREW 8 Glasgow
19.11.81 Mick Morris **L** RSC 7 Piccadilly
25.01.82 Doug James **W** PTS 8 Glasgow
25.02.82 Neil Fannan **W** PTS 8 Hartlepool
08.03.82 Winston Burnett **W** PTS 8 Hamilton
18.05.82 Doug James **L** RSC 4 Piccadilly
18.10.82 Mick Morris **L** RTD 6 Glasgow
22.11.83 Willie Wright **L** RSC 4 Manchester
06.04.84 Harry Watson **W** RSC 7 Edinburgh
18.06.84 Blaine Longsden **L** PTS 8 Manchester
Summary: 34 contests, won 19, drew 1, lost 14

Billy Lauder
Scotsman/Evening News

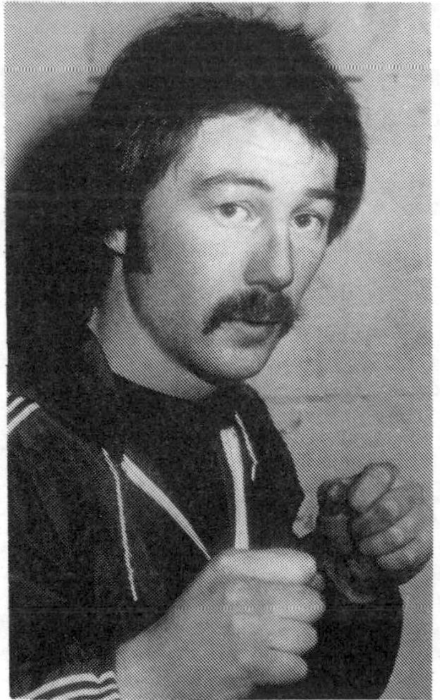

Alastair Laurie
Scotsman/Evening News

Alastair Laurie

Selkirk. *Born* Selkirk 27.04.63
L. Welterweight
Manager E. Coakley
Previous Amateur Club Selkirk
National Honours Scottish Int.; Scottish L. Welterweight Champion 1981–1982

30.04.84 Neil Patterson **W** PTS 6 Glasgow
14.05.84 Irish Tommy Kelliher **W** RSC 5 Glasgow
04.06.84 Rocky Mensah **W** PTS 8 Glasgow
Summary: 3 contests, won 3

Chris Lawson

Cardigan. *Born* Leeds 14.03.57
Former Welsh L. Heavyweight Champion
Manager (Self)
Previous Amateur Club Pembroke
National Honours GB Rep.; ABA L. Heavyweight Champion 1977; Welsh Middleweight Champion 1975 – 1976 & L. Heavyweight Champion 1977; Welsh Int.

23.01.78 Malcolm Worthington **W** CO 2 Aberavon
07.02.78 Ralph Green **W** RTD 2 Islington
20.03.78 Winston Cousins **W** PTS 6 Aberavon
22.05.78 Bonny McKenzie **L** PTS 8 Mayfair
10.07.78 Trevor Kerr **W** RSC 4 Aberavon
18.09.78 Karl Canwell **L** RSC 5 Mayfair
02.11.78 Steve Hill **W** RSC 2 Liverpool
29.11.78 Bonny McKenzie **W** PTS 10 Swansea
(*Vacant Welsh L. Heavyweight Title*)
17.01.79 Eddie Smith **L** RSC 4 Burslem
19.03.79 Ken Jones **W** PTS 10 Haverfordwest
(*Welsh L. Heavyweight Title Defence*)
13.05.79 Carlton Benoit **L** RSC 2 Plymouth
23.10.79 Alek Penarski **W** RSC 5 Blackpool
13.02.80 Danny Lawford DREW 8 Mayfair
17.03.80 Danny Lawford **W** PTS 8 Birmingham
15.04.80 Tom Collins **L** RSC 4 Blackpool
18.06.80 Dennis Andries **L** RSC 8 Burslem
12.08.80 Ken Jones **L** PTS 10 Swansea
(*Welsh L. Heavyweight Title Defence*)
22.09.80 Harry White **W** RSC 5 Wolverhampton
20.10.80 Rupert Christie **W** PTS 8 Birmingham
01.12.80 Roy Skeldon **L** PTS 8 Wolverhampton
11.12.80 Danny Lawford **L** RSC 2 Bolton
16.03.81 Cordwell Hylton **W** RSC 5 Mayfair
13.04.81 Tommy Taylor DREW 8 Wolverhampton
20.06.81 Karl Canwell **L** RSC 8 Wembley
21.09.81 Bonny McKenzie **L** PTS 10 Piccadilly
(*Vacant Welsh L. Heavyweight Title*)
02.11.81 Greg Evans **W** RSC 7 Piccadilly
08.12.81 Greg Evans **W** RSC 3 Pembroke
23.01.82 Manfred Jassman **L** CO 3 Berlin
30.03.82 Liam Coleman **W** PTS 8 Leeds
23.09.82 Trevor Cattouse **L** PTS 8 Wimbledon
04.11.82 Keith Bristol **L** RTD 3 Wimbledon
11.02.83 Michael Madsen **L** PTS 6 Copenhagen
19.05.83 Dennis Andries **L** CO 4 Queensway
22.09.83 Ian Lazarus **W** PTS 8 Stockport
27.09.83 Dave Scott **W** PTS 8 Stoke
27.10.83 Nye Williams **L** PTS 10 Ebbw Vale
(*Vacant Welsh L. Heavyweight Title*)
29.03.84 James Williams **L** PTS 10 Vancouver
22.05.84 Slobodan Kacar **L** CO 4 Pesaro
Summary: 38 contests, won 17, drew 2, lost 19

Dave Laxen

Ruislip. *Born* Hillingdon 19.09.56
Lightweight
Manager E. Fossey
Previous Amateur Club Ruislip
Divisional Honours NW London Lightweight R/U 1975; NW London Lightweight Champion 1976/1977/1979

09.04.79 Gerry Howland **W** PTS 6 Nottingham
24.04.79 Steve Briers DREW 6 Southend
13.05.79 Steve Briers **W** PTS 6 Plymouth
29.05.79 Joe Mills **W** RSC 5 Southend
06.06.79 Eric Regonesi DREW 6 Burslem
12.09.79 Bonnet Bryan **W** PTS 6 Burslem
25.09.79 Jeff Pritchard L PTS 8 Southend
29.10.79 Vernon Penprase L PTS 8 Camborne
04.12.79 Gary Lucas DREW 8 Southend
28.01.80 Tim Moloney L PTS 6 Hove
05.02.80 Alec Irvine DREW 8 Southend
27.02.80 Gary Lucas **W** PTS 8 Burslem
03.03.80 Steve Parker **W** PTS 6 Nottingham
11.03.80 Gary Lucas DREW 8 Nantwich
15.04.80 Wally Stockings L RSC 6 Southend
12.06.80 Danny Connolly L RSC 7 Cambridge
16.02.82 Eugene Maloney **W** PTS 6 Southend
15.03.82 Alan Tombs **W** RSC 2 Bloomsbury
27.04.82 Alan Tombs **W** RSC 7 Hornsey
07.06.82 Alan Tombs L RSC 8 Bloomsbury
13.08.82 David Miles L CO 7 Strand
28.04.83 Les Remikie L CO 4 Leicester
Summary: 22 contests, won 9, drew 5, lost 8

Ian Lazarus

Leeds. *Born* Jamaica 24.04.60
Central Area L. Heavyweight Champion
Manager T. Callighan
Previous Amateur Club Market District

27.01.82 Rob Wada L PTS 6 Stoke
24.02.82 Paul Shell **W** PTS 6 Evesham
29.03.82 Jonjo Greene **W** PTS 6 Piccadilly
13.09.82 Michael Fawcett L PTS 4 Brighton
13.10.82 Harry Cowap L PTS 6 Walthamstow
20.10.82 Alex Romeo **W** PTS 6 Stoke
09.11.82 Chris Thorne **W** PTS 6 Southend
15.11.82 Gary Jones **W** PTS 6 Glasgow
07.12.82 John Moody **W** RSC 2 Southend
09.03.83 Harry Cowap L PTS 6 Solihull
28.03.83 Jonjo Greene **W** PTS 8 Manchester
13.06.83 Andy Straughn DREW 8 Coventry
22.09.83 Chris Lawson L PTS 8 Stockport
18.11.83 Freddie Rafferty L RSC 4 Welborn SA
14.12.83 Alek Penarski L PTS 10 Stoke
20.02.84 Bernie Kavanagh **W** PTS 10 Bradford
(*Vacant Central Area L. Heavyweight Title*)
Summary: 16 contests, won 8, drew 1, lost 7

Mick Leachman

Dagenham. *Born* Hackney 17.01.60
L. Middleweight
Manager (Self)
Previous Amateur Club Beacon Youth

10.02.83 Valentino Maccarinelli DREW 6 Walthamstow
Summary: 1 contest, drew 1

Danny Lee

Greenock. *Born* Greenock 21.06.61
Bantamweight
Manager E. Coakley
Previous Amateur Club Kingston
National Honours Scottish L. Flyweight Champion 1979; Scottish Flyweight Champion 1981 & R/U 1980/1982; Scottish Bantamweight Champion 1983; Scottish Int.

14.05.84 Bobby McDermott **W** PTS 6 Glasgow
04.06.84 Gordon Stobie **W** PTS 6 Glasgow
Summary: 2 contests, won 2

Ian Lazarus
WRNS Pictures (Brian Worsnop) Ltd

John Leitch
Doagh. *Born* Antrim 07.07.55
Heavyweight
Manager (Self)
Previous Amateur Club Doagh

09.03.82 Eddie McDermott L RSC 2 Derry
22.04.82 Eddie McDermott L RSC 3 Enniskillen
25.01.83 Dave Garside L RSC 2 Belfast
Summary: 3 contests, lost 3

Mickey Lerwill
Telford. *Born* Telford 06.04.65
L. Welterweight
Manager M. Sendell
Previous Amateur Club WSOB

23.06.83 Mickey Bird W RSC 5 Wolverhampton
27.09.83 Mick Harkin DREW 6 Stoke
10.10.83 Graeme Griffin L PTS 6 Birmingham
18.01.84 Rocky Mensah L PTS 6 Stoke
30.01.84 Hugh Sugar Kelly L PTS 6 Glasgow
Summary: 5 contests, won 1, drew 1, lost 3

Andy Letts
Nottingham. *Born* Nottingham 22.05.60
Welterweight
Manager W. Wigley
Previous Amateur Club None

10.05.82 Tommy Bennett L PTS 4 Birmingham
18.05.82 John Bibby L RSC 1 Bethnal Green
21.02.83 Michael Harris L PTS 4 Edgbaston
28.02.83 Elvis Morton L PTS 4 Birmingham
Summary: 4 contests, lost 4

Chris Lewin
Streatham. *Born* London 15.07.58
Middleweight
Manager G. Davidson
Previous Amateur Club Hillcrest

16.02.82 Tony Burke L RSC 1 Bethnal Green
19.04.82 Joey Saunders L PTS 6 Mayfair
10.05.82 Dalton Jordan W PTS 6 Birmingham
22.02.83 Kevin Webb L PTS 6 Bethnal Green
Summary: 4 contests, won 1, lost 3

Steve Lewin
Streatham. *Born* London 08.04.57
L. Heavyweight
Manager (Self)
Previous Amateur Club Caius
Divisional Honours SW London Middleweight Champion 1977

15.09.77 Mohammed Akram W RSC 2 Bethnal Green
19.10.77 Peter Mullins W RSC 1 Bethnal Green
07.11.77 Dave Callen W RSC 4 Walworth
15.11.77 Steve Walker W PTS 6 Bethnal Green
29.11.77 Clifton Wallace L PTS 6 Bethnal Green
31.01.78 Joe Hannaford W RSC 3 Marylebone
13.03.78 John Breen W PTS 6 Walworth
04.04.78 Lloyd Gardner W PTS 6 Kensington
25.04.78 Tim McHugh W PTS 6 Kensington
26.09.78 Boyd Farrar W RSC 6 Wembley
07.11.78 Joey Williams W PTS 6 Wembley
21.11.78 Mick Fellingham W RSC 2 Wembley
23.01.79 Reg Squires L CO 2 Kensington
20.02.79 Mick Morris W PTS 6 Kensington
10.04.79 Trevor Cattouse L PTS 6 Kensington
15.05.79 Keith Bussey DREW 8 Wembley
18.02.80 Joey Williams W RSC 4 Lewisham
28.04.80 Bonny McKenzie L PTS 8 Southwark
29.05.80 Boyd Farrar W PTS 8 Wimbledon
16.09.80 Jimmy Harrington W RSC 3 Wembley
06.10.80 Ken Jones DREW 8 Southwark
24.02.81 Alex Tompkins L CO 6 Kensington
03.11.81 Billy Savage W RSC 5 Kensington
18.11.81 Antonio Harris L CO 5 Solihull
22.02.82 Danny Lawford L CO 1 Mayfair
17.04.84 Sam Reeson L PTS 8 Merton
Summary: 26 contests, won 16, drew 2, lost 8

Steve Lewsam
Grimsby. *Born* Cleethorpes 08.09.60
L. Heavyweight
Manager L. Slater
Previous Amateur Club Grimsby

22.11.82 Winston Wray W PTS 4 Liverpool
07.11.83 Wes Taylor W PTS 6 Birmingham
22.11.83 Jerry Golden L RSC 5 Manchester
Summary: 3 contests, won 2, lost 1

John Lindo
Bradford. *Born* Jamaica 23.02.61
L. Welterweight
Manager T. Miller
Previous Amateur Club Bradford Police

29.10.79 Tyrell Wilson L PTS 6 Birmingham
15.11.79 Glyn Rhodes W PTS 6 Liverpool
17.12.79 Winston Ho-Shing DREW 6 Bradford
24.01.80 Bill Smith W PTS 4 Hartlepool
06.02.80 Ronnie Rathbone DREW 6 Liverpool

CONTINUED OVERLEAF

25.02.80 Kevin Sheehan DREW 6 Bradford
14.03.80 Peter Harrison L PTS 6 Glasgow
22.04.80 Gary Lucas **W** PTS 6 Sheffield
19.05.80 Barry Winters L RSC 3 Bradford
09.09.80 Eric Wood L PTS 6 Mexborough
18.11.80 Winston Ho-Shing **W** RSC 3 Nantwich
11.12.80 Robert Wakefield L PTS 6 Bolton
22.01.81 George Schofield L CO 1 Liverpool
26.03.81 Steve Foster **W** RSC 1 Newcastle
06.04.81 Kevin Sheehan **W** RSC 5 Bradford
08.06.81 Ray Price L RSC 2 Bradford
16.11.81 Kevin Quinn L PTS 6 Liverpool
23.11.81 Dai Davies **W** RSC 5 Nantwich
30.11.81 Johnny Burns **W** PTS 6 Birmingham
01.02.82 Norman Morton DREW 8 Newcastle
18.02.82 Terry Welch **W** PTS 6 Liverpool
23.03.82 Patsy Quinn **W** CO 1 Belfast
26.04.82 Dave Taylor **W** PTS 8 Bradford
18.10.82 Tony Sinnott L PTS 8 Blackpool
14.11.82 Tommy Davitt DREW 8 Navan
25.11.82 Derek Nelson L RSC 4 Sunderland
21.03.83 Paul Chance L PTS 8 Nottingham
16.05.83 Steve Tempro L PTS 6 Manchester
Summary: 28 contests, won 11, drew 5, lost 12

Daryl Lindsay
Plymouth. *Born* Bournemouth 14.04.63
L. Middleweight
Manager D. Mahoney
Previous Amateur Club Oakmead

11.10.82 Paul McHugh L PTS 4 Bristol
29.11.82 Kevin Johnson L RSC 4 Newquay
27.01.84 Cliff Eastwood L RSC 2 Longford
Summary: 3 contests, lost 3

Cameron Lithgow
Swindon. *Born* Birmingham 24.05.60
L. Middleweight
Manager M. Barrett
Previous Amateur Club Park Yough
National Honours Junior ABA Title 1976; Young England Rep.; England Int.
Divisional Honours W Counties Welterweight R/U 1978; ABA L. Middleweight R/U 1979/1982

09.11.82 Dennis Sheehan **W** RSC 5 Kensington
07.12.82 Steve Davies **W** RSC 4 Kensington
15.03.83 Barry Ahmed **W** RTD 3 Wembley
05.04.83 Dave Scott **W** RSC 5 Kensington
25.04.83 Doug James L RSC 8 Aberdeen
31.05.83 Willie Wright DREW 6 Kensington
20.09.83 Vince Gajny L PTS 8 Piccadilly
17.10.83 T. P. Jenkins L PTS 8 Southwark
31.01.84 Bobby Williams **W** RSC 3 Kensington
14.03.84 Vince Gajny **W** RSC 6 Mayfair
11.04.84 Mick Courtney L PTS 10 Kensington
Summary: 11 contests, won 6, drew 1, lost 4

Edward Lloyd
Rhyl. *Born* St. Asaph 23.04.63
Lightweight
Manager B. Lloyd
Previous Amateur Club Rhyl Star
National Honours NABC Title 1979; Welsh Int.

07.02.83 Stan Atherton **W** PTS 6 Liverpool
14.02.83 Sammy Rodgers **W** RSC 4 Manchester
21.02.83 Paul Cook L RSC 1 Mayfair
27.04.83 Bobby Welburn **W** PTS 6 Rhyl
09.05.83 Jimmy Thornton L RSC 1 Manchester
16.09.83 Jim Paton L PTS 6 Rhyl
28.11.83 John Murphy L PTS 8 Rhyl
06.02.84 Paul Keers **W** PTS 6 Liverpool
06.03.84 Gary Felvus L PTS 8 Stoke
15.06.84 Mickey Brooks L RSC 6 St Helens
Summary: 10 contests, won 4, lost 6

Robert Lloyd
Rhyl. *Born* Prestatyn 04.08.60
L. Welterweight
Manager B. Lloyd
Previous Amateur Club Rhyl Star
National Honours Welsh Int.

17.02.83 Bobby McGowan **W** RSC 1 Morley
04.03.83 Ron Atherton **W** CO 1 Queensferry
22.03.83 Mo Hussein L PTS 6 Bethnal Green
27.04.83 Dave Heaver DREW 6 Rhyl
09.05.83 Terry Welch **W** PTS 6 Manchester
25.05.83 Kevin Sheehan **W** RSC 5 Rhyl
09.11.83 Glyn Rhodes L PTS 8 Sheffield
28.11.83 Steve Boyle **W** PTS 6 Rhyl
28.01.84 Mick Harkin L PTS 6 Hanley
06.02.84 George Schofield DREW 8 Liverpool
06.03.84 Lee Roy L PTS 6 Stoke
Summary: 11 contests, won 5, drew 2, lost 4

Cameron Lithgow
Derek Rowe (Photos) Ltd

John Lodge

Stockton. *Born* Middlesbrough 22.07.64
Featherweight
Manager T. Miller
Previous Amateur Club None

07.10.82 John Doherty L RSC 4 Morley
17.02.83 Michael Marsden L RSC 1 Morley
Summary: 2 contests, lost 2

Reg Long

Peterlee. *Born* Haswell 18.04.51
Former Northern Area L. Heavyweight Champion
Manager (Self)
Previous Amateur Club Peterlee

24.01.77 John McCullum L PTS 6 Glasgow
14.02.77 Carlton Benoit L PTS 6 Bedford
18.03.77 John McCullum W RSC 4 Holytown
18.04.77 Manny Gabriel NC 2 Bedford
24.04.77 Glenroy Taylor W CO 1 Birmingham
16.05.77 Manny Gabriel L PTS 6 Glasgow
30.05.77 Len Brittain W PTS 8 Marton
13.06.77 Winston Cousins L RSC 5 Manchester
22.08.77 Len Brittain W PTS 8 Stockton
29.09.77 Roy Gregory W RSC 5 Newcastle
08.11.77 Ralph Green W PTS 10 Darlington (*Vacant Northern Area L. Heavyweight Title*)
08.12.77 Francis Hands L RSC 7 Liverpool
07.02.78 Steve Taylor L PTS 8 Southend
24.04.78 Theo Josephs W PTS 8 Middlesbrough
03.05.78 Bonny McKenzie L RSC 7 Solihull
12.07.78 P. T. Grant W PTS 6 Newcastle
29.08.78 Steve Hill L PTS 8 Liverpool
04.12.78 George Scott DREW 8 Middlesbrough
13.02.79 Theo Josephs L PTS 8 Wakefield
13.05.79 Terry Chard W PTS 6 Glasgow
23.05.79 Joe Awome L RSC 2 Nottingham
12.11.79 George Scott L PTS 10 Middlesbrough (*Vacant Northern Area Heavyweight Title*)
11.12.79 Manny Gabriel L RSC 3 Milton Keynes
07.07.80 Stewart Lithgo L RSC 3 Middlesbrough
01.12.80 P. T. Grant DREW 6 Middlesbrough
27.01.81 Rudi Pika L RSC 3 Kensington
09.11.81 P. T. Grant L PTS 10 Newcastle (*Northern Area L. Heavyweight Title Defence*)
08.02.82 Mal Kirk L RSC 4 Manchester
19.05.83 Michael Armstrong L CO 1 Sunderland
Summary: 29 contests, won 9, drew 2, lost 17, NC 1

Blaine Longsden

Warrington. *Born* Warrington 30.10.61
Middleweight
Manager N. Basso
Previous Amateur Club Warrington

02.05.82 Robbie Bewick DREW 6 Middlesbrough
17.05.82 Dalton Jordan W PTS 6 Manchester
07.06.82 Joey Saunders W PTS 6 Sheffield
21.06.82 Bert Myrie W CO 3 Liverpool
13.09.82 Willie Wright L PTS 8 Manchester
28.09.82 Rob Wada W PTS 8 Manchester
08.11.82 Martin McEwan L PTS 8 Manchester
30.11.82 Martin McEwan L PTS 8 Farnsworth
17.01.83 Barry Ahmed W PTS 6 Manchester
14.02.83 Jimmy Ellis W PTS 8 Manchester
29.04.83 Rocky Feliciello L PTS 6 Liverpool
30.06.83 Paul Mitchell W RSC 8 Manchester
19.09.83 Jimmy Ellis W PTS 8 Manchester
26.09.83 Willie Wright L RTD 4 Manchester
19.03.84 Jerry Golden W RSC 3 Manchester
26.03.84 John Elliott L PTS 8 Leicester
30.04.84 Alex Romeo L PTS 8 Liverpool
18.06.84 Billy Lauder W PTS 8 Manchester
Summary: 18 contests, won 10, drew 1, lost 7

(Lorenzo) Muhammad Lovelock

Manchester. *Born* Manchester 17.06.57
Featherweight
Manager J. Gaynor
Previous Amateur Club Ardwick

08.03.82 Joey Morris L RSC 4 Manchester
25.11.82 Ray Plant L PTS 6 Sunderland
07.02.83 Steve Cleak L PTS 6 Brighton
21.03.83 John Doherty L PTS 6 Bradford
17.06.83 Dave Bryan L PTS 6 Queensferry
16.09.83 Carl Merrett L PTS 6 Swindon
03.10.83 Johnny Mack W RSC 1 Liverpool
07.11.83 Alex Cairney W RSC 6 Liverpool
14.11.83 Billy Joe Dee W RSC 1 Manchester
05.12.83 Gary Felvus L PTS 6 Manchester
17.02.84 Dave Bryan L PTS 6 Rhyl
12.03.84 Dave Bryan L PTS 6 Liverpool
27.03.84 Mark Reefer L PTS 6 Battersea
04.04.84 Roy Webb L PTS 6 Belfast
17.04.84 Charlie Coke L PTS 6 Merton
11.06.84 Ian Murray W PTS 6 Manchester
Summary: 16 contests, won 4, lost 12

Gary Lucas
Liverpool. *Born* Liverpool 29.07.60
Lightweight
Manager W. MacDonald
Previous Amateur Club Golden Gloves

24.04.78 Mark Hill **L** PTS 4 Glasgow
12.09.78 Steve Enright **L** RSC 6 Birkenhead
08.11.78 John Flynn **L** PTS 4 Stoke
14.11.78 Alec Irvine **W** PTS 4 Birkenhead
20.11.78 Gary Ball **W** PTS 6 Birmingham
11.12.78 Gary Ball **L** PTS 6 Birmingham
18.12.78 Steve Enright **L** PTS 6 Bradford
18.01.79 Selvin Bell **L** PTS 6 Liverpool
22.02.79 Larry Richards **W** PTS 6 Liverpool
22.03.79 Selvin Bell **L** PTS 6 Liverpool
19.04.79 Carl Mullings **W** PTS 6 Birkenhead
21.05.79 Steve Cleak **W** PTS 8 Piccadilly
18.06.79 Terry McKeown **L** RSC 4 Glasgow
24.09.79 Steve Cleak **W** PTS 8 Piccadilly
08.10.79 Mohammed Younis **W** RTD 5 Nantwich
19.11.79 Gerry O'Neill **L** PTS 8 Glasgow
04.12.79 Dave Laxen DREW 8 Southend
21.01.80 Gerry O'Neill **L** PTS 8 Birmingham
27.02.80 Dave Laxen **L** PTS 8 Burslem
03.03.80 Jim McKeown DREW 6 Piccadilly
11.03.80 Dave Laxen DREW 8 Nantwich
19.03.80 Jim McKeown **L** PTS 8 Stoke
27.03.80 Paul Keers **W** PTS 8 Liverpool
09.04.80 Steve Parker **W** PTS 8 Burslem
22.04.80 John Lindo **L** PTS 6 Sheffield
05.05.80 Jim McKeown **L** PTS 8 Glasgow
24.09.80 Don George **L** PTS 8 Burslem
13.10.80 Gerry O'Neill **L** PTS 8 Mayfair
08.12.80 Wayne Evans **L** PTS 8 Birmingham
02.02.81 Lee Graham **W** PTS 8 Piccadilly
13.05.81 Clyde Ruan **L** PTS 8 Piccadilly
01.06.81 Steve Pollard **W** PTS 8 Piccadilly
20.06.81 Barry McGuigan **L** RSC 4 Wembley
06.10.81 Ian McLeod **L** PTS 8 Piccadilly
20.01.82 Stuart Shaw **W** PTS 8 Burslem
29.03.82 Mick Rowley **L** PTS 8 Piccadilly
22.04.82 Barry McGuigan **L** CO 1 Enniskillen
23.09.82 Jimmy Bunclark **L** PTS 6 Liverpool
01.11.82 Dave Bryan **L** PTS 6 Liverpool
24.11.82 Denny Garrison **L** PTS 6 Stoke
28.03.83 Mark Duffy **L** PTS 6 Manchester
16.05.83 Lee Halford **W** PTS 8 Manchester
17.06.83 Ron Atherton **W** RSC 2 Queensferry
06.10.83 Gert Bo Jacobsen **L** CO 4 Copenhagen
14.11.83 Keith Foreman DREW 8 Nantwich
07.12.83 Steve Boyle DREW 6 Stoke
16.01.84 Keith Foreman **W** PTS 8 Bradford
Summary: 47 contests, won 15, drew 5, lost 27

Steve Lucas
Waltham Cross. *Born* Epping 24.10.64
Bantamweight
Manager J. Barclay
Previous Amateur Club Cheshunt
Divisional Honours H Counties Featherweight R/U 1983

19.05.84 Billy Barton **L** PTS 6 Bristol
31.05.84 Mark Boswell **W** PTS 6 Basildon
Summary: 2 contests, won 1, lost 1

Joe Lynch
Plymouth. *Born* Plymouth 13.11.64
Welterweight
Manager D. Mahoney
Previous Amateur Club Ford

21.09.83 Trevor Hopson **L** PTS 6 Southend
06.10.83 Neil Crocker **W** CO 1 Basildon
12.10.83 Carl Bishop **W** PTS 6 Evesham
18.11.83 Trevor Hopson **W** RTD 2 Sheffield
06.12.83 Vince Stewart **W** PTS 6 Southend
19.01.84 Peter Foster **L** CO 1 Digbeth
14.02.84 Tony Batty **W** PTS 6 Southend
21.03.84 Lee McKenzie **L** PTS 8 Mayfair
11.04.84 Tony Adams **L** RSC 3 Kensington
12.06.84 Bob McKenley **L** RSC 3 Southend
Summary: 10 contests, won 5, lost 5

John McAllister
Greenock. *Born* Greenock 24.03.60
Welterweight
Manager E. Coakley
Previous Amateur Club Kingston
National Honours Scottish Int. Scottish Lightweight Champion 1978; Scottish L. Welterweight Champion 1979–1980; Scottish Welterweight Champion 1982; ABA L. Welterweight R/U 1980

05.03.84 Peter Phillips **W** PTS 6 Glasgow
09.04.84 Mickey Bird **W** RSC 2 Glasgow
30.04.84 Jim Kelly **W** PTS 8 Glasgow
21.05.84 Tony Smith **W** PTS 8 Aberdeen
04.06.84 Steve Tempro **W** PTS 6 Glasgow
Summary: 5 contests, won 5

Dave Boy McAuley
Larne. *Born* Larne 15.06.61
Bantamweight
Manager P. Byrne
Previous Amateur Club St. Agnes
National Honours Irish Flyweight Champion 1980; Irish Int.

05.10.83 John Mwaimu DREW 6 Belfast
14.11.83 Dave Smith **W** CO 1 Belfast
25.01.84 Ian Colbeck **W** PTS 6 Belfast
27.02.84 Kenny Walsh DREW 6 Birmingham
Summary: 4 contests, won 2, drew 2

Dave McCabe
Scotsman/Evening News

Dave McCabe

Gartcosh. *Born* Glasgow 09.06.58
L. Welterweight
Manager (Self)
Previous Amateur Club Gartcosh
National Honours Scottish Int.
Divisional Honours Scottish L. Welterweight R/U 1977

17.10.77 Philip Morris **W** PTS 4 Glasgow
07.11.77 Gary Collins **W** RSC 3 Glasgow
14.11.77 Gene McGarrigale **W** RSC 5 Glasgow
24.11.77 Ian Pickersgill **W** PTS 6 Doncaster
12.12.77 Tony Carroll **W** PTS 6 Piccadilly
09.01.78 Billy Jeram **W** PTS 6 Piccadilly
30.01.78 Dai Davies **W** PTS 6 Glasgow
27.02.78 Albert Coley **W** PTS 6 Glasgow
13.03.78 Martin Bridge **W** PTS 8 Birmingham
20.03.78 Eric Wood **W** PTS 8 Glasgow
18.09.78 George Peacock **W** PTS 8 Glasgow
09.10.78 Tony Zeni **W** RSC 7 Piccadilly
23.10.78 Eric Wood **W** PTS 8 Glasgow
27.11.78 Eric Purkiss **W** PTS 8 Govan
22.01.79 Granville Allen **W** DIS 6 Wolverhampton
19.03.79 Martin Bridge **W** PTS 8 Glasgow
17.04.79 Bingo Crooks **W** PTS 8 Glasgow
03.09.79 Joe Phillips **W** RSC 9 Glasgow
08.01.80 Martyn Galleozzie **W** PTS 12 Windsor
(*Final Elim. British Lightweight Title*)
24.03.80 Ray Cattouse **L** RSC 8 Glasgow
(*Vacant British Lightweight Title*)
23.06.80 Derek Nelson **W** PTS 8 Glasgow
07.10.80 Chris Sanigar **W** PTS 8 Piccadilly
01.12.80 Ricky Beaumont **W** PTS 12 Hull
(*Final Elim. British Lightweight Title*)
23.03.81 Ray Cattouse **L** RSC 15 Glasgow
(*British Lightweight Title Challenge*)
20.07.81 Barry Michael **L** RSC 7 Melbourne
(*Commonwealth Lightweight Title Challenge*)
06.10.82 Patrizio Oliva **L** PTS 8 Gragnano
19.01.83 Steve Early **L** PTS 8 Birmingham
11.06.83 Brett Taylor **L** PTS 8 Wembley SA
Summary: 28 contests, won 22, lost 6

Tommy McCallum

Edinburgh. *Born* Edinburgh 03.03.58
Welterweight
Manager (Self)
Previous Amateur Club Leith Victoria
National Honours Scottish Lightweight Champion 1976 & Welterweight Champion 1980; Scottish Int.

02.06.80 Paul Wetter **W** PTS 6 Plymouth
13.10.80 Ronnie Rathbone **W** PTS 6 Mayfair
15.12.80 Paul Wetter **W** PTS 6 Merthyr
19.01.81 Kevin Durkin **W** PTS 8 Bradford
16.02.81 Jimmy Smith **W** PTS 8 Mayfair
11.05.81 Phil Duckworth **L** RSC 4 Bradford
22.09.81 Dominic Bergonzi **W** RSC 2 Bethnal Green
07.10.81 Roger Guest **W** PTS 8 Stoke
12.10.81 Kid Murray **L** PTS 6 Birmingham
23.11.81 Phil Duckworth **L** PTS 8 Nantwich
15.02.82 Phil Duckworth **L** PTS 8 Glasgow
02.03.82 Lloyd Honeyghan **L** PTS 6 Kensington
20.05.82 Joey Frost **L** RSC 1 Preston
18.04.83 Jeff Decker **DREW** 8 Glasgow
09.05.83 Jeff Decker **L** PTS 8 Piccadilly
06.06.83 Geoff Pegler **W** PTS 8 Piccadilly
20.09.83 Clinton McKenzie **L** CO 4 Mayfair
16.11.83 P. J. Davitt **L** PTS 8 Belfast
23.11.83 Harold Azeko **W** RSC 1 Solihull
17.02.84 George Schofield **W** PTS 8 Rhyl
21.03.84 Kostas Petrou **L** PTS 8 Solihull
11.06.84 Geoff Pegler **W** PTS 8 Glasgow
Summary: 22 contests, won 11, drew 1, lost 10

Tommy McCallum
Scotsman/Evening News

Frank McCord

Swansea. *Born* Swansea 06.08.56
Welterweight
Manager (Self)
Previous Amateur Club Gwent
National Honours Welsh Int.

29.03.77 Philip Morris **W** PTS 4 Ebbw Vale
18.04.77 Roger Doyle **W** PTS 6 Bedford
02.05.77 George Daines **W** PTS 4 Piccadilly
09.05.77 Winston Spencer **L** RTD 3 Mayfair
21.06.77 Eric Purkiss **L** PTS 6 Piccadilly
03.10.77 Dil Collins **L** DIS 6 Aberavon
17.10.77 Martin Bridge **L** RTD 5 Bedford
22.11.77 Eddie Porter **W** CO 4 Hemel Hempstead
14.12.77 Ian Pickersgill **W** CO 1 Swansea
13.03.78 Paddy McAleese **L** PTS 6 Birmingham
06.04.78 Mick Barker **W** CO 2 Ebbw Vale
10.04.78 Martin Bridge **L** PTS 6 Birmingham
17.04.78 Eric Purkiss **L** RSC 5 Piccadilly
19.06.78 Billy O'Grady DREW 6 Hove
27.06.78 Benny Purdy **W** RSC 4 Derry
18.09.78 Alan Burrows **L** PTS 6 Reading
03.10.78 Lloyd Lee **L** PTS 8 Aberavon
16.10.78 Harry Watson **W** PTS 6 Mayfair
28.10.78 Omar Sahli **L** PTS 6 Oslo
02.11.78 Al Stewart **W** RSC 3 Liverpool
05.12.78 Sid Smith **W** PTS 6 Kensington
11.12.78 Tommy Wright DREW 6 Plymouth
12.02.79 Stan Atherton **L** PTS 6 Manchester
26.02.79 Steve Early **L** CO 1 Edgbaston
05.04.79 Hugh Kelly **L** PTS 8 Belfast
10.05.79 Gary Pearce **L** PTS 8 Pontypool
06.06.79 Roy Varden **L** PTS 6 Bedworth
30.07.79 Tony Martey **L** RSC 4 Mayfair
22.01.80 John Mount **W** PTS 8 Piccadilly
28.02.80 Jeff Pritchard **L** PTS 8 Ebbw Vale
10.03.80 Chris Christian **L** PTS 8 Mayfair
15.04.80 Alan Lamb **L** CO 1 Blackpool
15.12.80 Mickey Durkin **L** PTS 6 Bradford
09.03.81 Jimmy Smith **W** PTS 6 Copthorne
07.04.81 Alan Burrows DREW 6 Newport
13.10.81 Stan Atherton **W** RSC 2 Blackpool
22.10.81 Dennis Pryce **L** PTS 8 Piccadilly
11.11.81 Gary Buckle **W** PTS 8 Evesham
01.02.82 Alan Cable **W** RSC 1 Copthorne
24.02.82 Mick Mills **L** CO 2 Sheffield
07.06.82 Billy Waith **L** PTS 10 Swansea (*Vacant Welsh Welterweight Title*)
28.09.82 Charlie Nash **L** PTS 8 Derry
12.10.82 Dave Sullivan **W** PTS 6 Kensington
26.10.82 Gunther Roomes **W** CO 1 Bethnal Green
22.11.82 Lloyd Honeyghan **L** CO 1 Mayfair
28.01.83 Kid Murray **L** PTS 8 Swansea
05.10.83 Kostas Petrou **L** PTS 8 Solihull
10.12.83 Billy Waith **L** PTS 10 Swansea (*Welsh Welterweight Title Challenge*)
22.02.84 Tony Adams **L** RSC 8 Kensington
Summary: 49 contests, won 17, drew 3, lost 29

Glenn McCrory

Anfield Plain. *Born* Stanley 23.09.64
Heavyweight
Manager D. Bidwell
Previous Amateur Club Consett Sports
National Honours Junior ABA Title 1981; Young England Rep.
Divisional Honours NE Counties L. Heavyweight S/F 1983

06.02.84 Barry Ellis **W** RSC 1 Mayfair
22.02.84 Denroy Bryan **W** PTS 6 Kensington
21.03.84 Steve Abadom **W** PTS 6 Mayfair
30.04.84 Frank Robinson **W** PTS 6 Mayfair
09.05.84 Frank Robinson **W** RSC 4 Mayfair
13.06.84 Andrew Gerrard **W** PTS 6 Aberavon
Summary: 6 contests, won 6

Bobby McDermott

Glasgow. *Born* Glasgow 13.02.60
Bantamweight
Manager E. Coakley
Previous Amateur Club Denniston
National Honours Scottish Flyweight Champion 1979

25.04.84 Allan Coveley **L** PTS 6 Muswell Hill
30.04.84 Gordon Stobie DREW 6 Glasgow
14.05.84 Danny Lee **L** PTS 6 Glasgow
Summary: 3 contests, drew 1, lost 2

Jim McDonnell
Camden Town. *Born* London 12.09.60
Lightweight
Manager T. Lawless
Previous Amateur Club St. Pancras
National Honours Young England Rep.; England Int.; ABA Lightweight Champion 1982; Commonwealth Silver 1982
Divisional Honours ABA Bantamweight R/U 1979 – 1980; London Bantamweight Champion 1981

22.03.83 Phil Duke **W** PTS 6 Bethnal Green
05.04.83 Willie Wilson **W** RSC 3 Kensington
26.04.83 Ray Plant **W** RSC 3 Bethnal Green
04.10.83 Steve Pollard **W** RSC 5 Bethnal Green
06.12.83 Alec Irvine **W** PTS 8 Kensington
23.01.84 Willie Wilson **W** CO 2 Mayfair
06.02.84 Gerry Beard **W** PTS 8 Bethnal Green
02.04.84 Gerry Beard **W** PTS 8 Mayfair
01.05.84 Keith Foreman **W** PTS 8 Bethnal Green
13.05.84 Rory Burke **W** PTS 8 Wembley
Summary: 10 contests, won 10

Glenn McCrory
Derek Rowe (Photos) Ltd

Jim McDonnell
David Thorne

(Donavon) Glen McEwan
Handsworth. *Born* Jamaica 17.08.58
Former Undefeated Midlands Area Middleweight Champion
Manager (Self)
Previous Amateur Club Rum Runner
National Honours Young England Rep.
Divisional Honours M Counties L. Middleweight Champion 1977

11.10.77 Mick Hinton **W** CO 2 Coventry
17.10.77 H. H. Thompson **W** RSC 3 Mayfair
21.11.77 Bonny McKenzie **W** PTS 8 Birmingham
05.01.78 Per Mullertz **W** PTS 6 Randers
21.02.78 Oscar Angus DREW 8 Wolverhampton
04.04.78 Wayne Bennett **W** PTS 8 Wolverhampton
13.06.78 Paul Shutt **W** RSC 2 Coventry
04.09.78 Dave Owens **W** CO 1 Wakefield
10.10.78 Mac Nicholson **W** RSC 5 Wolverhampton
22.11.78 Dennis Andries **L** RSC 7 Stoke
25.06.79 Prince Rodney **L** PTS 8 Edgbaston
24.09.79 Howard Mills **L** PTS 8 Mayfair
27.10.79 Damiano Lassandro **L** CO 2 Pesaro
12.02.80 Herol Graham **L** PTS 8 Sheffield
19.03.80 Romal Ambrose **W** CO 10 Solihull
(*Midlands Area Middleweight Title Challenge*)
15.04.80 Robbie Davies **W** CO 6 Blackpool
20.10.80 Romal Ambrose **W** CO 6 Birmingham
(*Midlands Area Middleweight Title Defence*)

CONTINUED OVERLEAF

26.11.80 Billy Lauder W CO 3 Solihull
21.01.81 Billy Savage W RSC 2 Solihull
24.04.81 Nicola Cirelli L CO 2 Milan
07.10.81 Howard Mills W PTS 8 Solihull
18.02.82 Roy Gumbs L RSC 13 Liverpool *(British Middleweight Title Challenge)*
28.09.82 Davey Armstrong W RSC 3 Bethnal Green *(Elim. British Middleweight Title)*
06.10.82 Trevor Cattouse L PTS 8 Solihull
01.03.83 Mark Kaylor L RSC 2 Kensington *(Final Elim. British Middleweight Title)*
Summary: 25 contests, won 15, drew 1, lost 9

Martin McEwan

Birmingham. *Born* Jamaica 24.06.55
Middleweight
Manager (Self)
Previous Amateur Club Rum Runner

21.02.78 Mick Morris L RSC 2 Wolverhampton
08.05.78 Dave Merrell W PTS 6 Nottingham
18.09.78 Mick Morris L CO 2 Wolverhampton
10.10.78 Kendrick Edwards W PTS 4 Wolverhampton
06.11.78 Kendrick Edwards W PTS 6 Stafford
22.11.78 Steve Fox W PTS 6 Stoke
29.11.78 Joe Jackson W PTS 6 Evesham
15.03.79 Ron Green W PTS 6 Dudley
19.04.79 Joe Hannaford W RSC 2 Birkenhead
21.05.79 Billy Hill W PTS 8 Bradford
25.06.79 Harry Watson W PTS 6 Edgbaston
11.09.79 Jimmy Harrington L PTS 6 Wembley
31.10.79 Redmond Everard W RSC 3 Burslem
10.12.79 Joe Jackson W PTS 6 Birmingham
05.02.80 Romal Ambrose L PTS 10 Wolverhampton *(Midlands Area Middleweight Title Challenge)*
10.03.80 Tony Britton W RSC 6 Mayfair
22.09.80 Peter Bassey L PTS 8 Birmingham
24.02.81 Mark Kaylor L RSC 6 Kensington
27.09.82 Winston Davis L PTS 6 Birmingham
16.10.82 Terry Christle L PTS 8 Killarney
08.11.82 Blaine Longsden W PTS 8 Manchester
30.11.82 Blaine Longsden W PTS 8 Farnsworth
07.12.82 Mick Mills L PTS 8 Southend
16.02.83 Jimmy Price L RSC 2 Muswell Hill
12.04.83 Mark Kelly W CO 2 Southend
20.04.83 Tony Burke W RSC 2 Solihull
07.06.83 Mick Mills L PTS 8 Southend
17.12.83 Tarmo Uusivirta L CO 2 Mariehamn
22.03.84 T. P. Jenkins L PTS 8 Maidenhead
02.05.84 Darwin Brewster L PTS 8 Solihull
Summary: 30 contests, won 16, lost 14

Joe McGinley

Paisley. *Born* Johnstone 08.08.60
Welterweight
Manager T. Gilmour
Previous Amateur Club Johnstone

13.06.83 Jim Kelly L RSC 1 Glasgow
Summary: 1 contest, lost 1

John McGlynn

Swansea. *Born* Swansea 03.10.62
L. Middleweight
Manager C. Breen
Previous Amateur Club Ragged School

07.06.82 Colin Neagle W CO 3 Swansea
28.09.82 Ray Ross W PTS 8 Derry
25.10.82 Mick Courtney L PTS 8 Mayfair
10.11.82 Gary Buckle W PTS 8 Evesham
18.11.82 Julian Bousted L RSC 8 Piccadilly
02.03.83 Steve Tempro W PTS 8 Evesham
27.10.83 Sylvester Gordon W CO 6 Ebbw Vale
01.12.83 Richard Wilson L PTS 8 Dudley
19.12.83 Bert Myrie W RSC 4 Swansea
17.02.84 Rocky Feliciello L RSC 8 Rhyl *(Vacant Welsh L. Middleweight Title)*
Summary: 10 contests, won 6, lost 4

Glen McEwan

Martin McEwan

Martin McGough

Coventry. *Born* Coventry 28.07.58
Welterweight
Manager P. Lynch
Previous Amateur Club Tile Hill
National Honours Junior ABA Title 1975; NABC Title 1975; Young England Rep.
Divisional Honours M Counties L. Welterweight Champion 1979

04.04.79 Terry Welch **W** PTS 6 Birmingham
28.05.81 Paul Murray **W** PTS 6 Edgbaston
11.09.81 Steve Tempro **W** RSC 4 Edgbaston
12.10.81 Granville Allen **W** CO 1 Birmingham
08.11.81 Dave Sullivan **W** PTS 6 Navan
18.11.81 Dennis Sullivan **L** RTD 2 Solihull
25.01.82 Paul Murray **W** RSC 4 Wolverhampton
21.02.82 Lloyd Christie **L** RSC 3 Birmingham
26.04.82 Peter Bennett **W** PTS 8 Edgbaston
07.06.82 Joey Mack **L** RTD 6 Edgbaston (*Midlands Area Welterweight Title Challenge*)
06.12.82 Glen Crump **W** CO 6 Edgbaston
20.04.83 Tony Brown **L** PTS 8 Solihull
19.01.84 Alex Brown **W** RSC 3 Digbeth
25.01.84 George Kerr **W** PTS 8 Solihull
10.05.84 Steve Friel **W** RSC 6 Digbeth
Summary: 15 contests, won 11, lost 4

Bobby McGowan

Leeds. *Born* 28.01.63
L. Welterweight
Manager V. Flynn
Previous Amateur Club Meanwood
National Honours Schools Title 1977

17.02.83 Robert Lloyd **L** RSC 1 Morley
18.04.83 Shaun Dooney **W** RSC 2 Bradford
12.05.83 Peter Flanagan **L** RSC 5 Morley
21.05.84 Chris Edge **L** DIS 2 Bradford
11.06.84 Alan Williams **L** DIS 1 Manchester
Summary: 5 contests, won 1, lost 4

Gerry McGrath

Paddington. *Born* Paddington 07.03.52
Welterweight
Manager L. Lake
Previous Amateur Club Fitzroy Lodge

28.04.80 Adrian Clamp **W** RSC 3 Windsor
29.05.80 Shaun Jones **W** PTS 6 Wimbledon
16.06.80 Gary Petty **W** RSC 1 Piccadilly
13.10.80 Dave Dunn **W** RSC 3 Windsor
04.11.80 Gary Brooks **W** RSC 3 Southend
08.12.80 Paul Kelly **W** PTS 6 Piccadilly
11.03.81 Alan Hardiman **W** PTS 6 Burslem
28.05.81 Alan Cable **W** PTS 8 Wimbledon
09.03.82 Terry Marsh **L** PTS 8 Hornsey
27.04.82 Colin Power **L** RTD 3 Hornsey
26.01.84 Steve Watt **L** RSC 2 Strand
Summary: 11 contests, won 8, lost 3

Seamus McGuinness

Belfast. *Born* Belfast 07.10.63
Lightweight
Manager B. Eastwood
Previous Amateur Club Immaculata

05.10.82 Eddie Morgan **W** PTS 6 Belfast
09.11.82 Craig Walsh DREW 6 Belfast
14.12.82 Jimmy Thornton **W** PTS 6 Belfast
25.01.83 Gordon Haigh **W** CO 1 Belfast
02.03.83 Keith Foreman **W** PTS 6 Belfast
12.04.83 Andy Thomas **W** RSC 2 Belfast
16.11.83 Anthony Abecheng **W** RSC 3 Belfast
Summary: 7 contests, won 6, drew 1

Paul McHugh

Leicester. *Born* Leicester 01.09.62
Welterweight
Manager B. Ridge
Previous Amateur Club Braunstone

10.10.82 Daryl Lindsay **W** PTS 4 Bristol
22.11.82 Kevin Webb **L** PTS 6 Lewisham

CONTINUED OVERLEAF

26.01.83 Elvis Morton L PTS 4 Stoke
01.03.83 Cliff Eastwood L PTS 4 Southend
23.06.83 Mickey Kilgallon L RSC 2 Bethnal Green
Summary: 5 contests, won 1, lost 4

Jim McIntosh

Edinburgh. *Born* Edinburgh 22.11.60
Welterweight
Manager T. Gilmour
Previous Amateur Club Meadowbank
National Honours Scottish Int.
Divisional Honours Scottish Featherweight R/U 1979 & Welterweight R/U 1981 – 1982

18.04.83 Tyrell Wilson **W** RSC 5 Glasgow
25.04.83 Lee McKenzie **W** PTS 8 Piccadilly
19.05.83 Gordon Pratt **W** PTS 8 Sunderland
10.10.83 Sylvester Gordon **W** PTS 8 Glasgow
27.02.84 Frankie Moro **W** PTS 8 Glasgow
06.04.84 Ian Chantler **W** DIS 3 Edinburgh
Summary: 6 contests, won 6

Jim McIntosh
Scotsman/Evening News

(Jerome) Joey Mack (McIntosh)

Birmingham. *Born* St. Kitts 14.12.48
Former Midlands Area Welterweight Champion
Manager D. Anderson
Previous Amateur Club Birmingham Golden Gloves
National Honours England Int.
Divisional Honours Combined Services Welterweight R/U 1972; M Counties L. Welterweight Champion 1975/1976

07.04.77 Gerry Young **L** PTS 8 Belfast
18.04.77 Tommy Joyce **L** PTS 8 Nottingham
17.05.77 Colin Ward **W** PTS 8 Wolverhampton
01.06.77 Les Pearson **W** RTD 1 Dudley
13.06.77 Carl Bailey **W** CO 2 Manchester
11.10.77 Henry Rhiney **W** RSC 7 Marylebone
26.12.77 Mario Guillotti **L** PTS 10 Rimini
14.01.78 Jo Kimpuani **L** PTS 10 Dunkirk
18.02.78 Clemente Tshinza **L** CO 1 Zele
10.04.78 Billy Lauder **W** RSC 2 Birmingham
08.05.78 Billy Waith **L** PTS 8 Birmingham
05.08.78 Gert Steyn **L** PTS 8 Empangani
20.10.78 Rogelio Zarza **W** PTS 8 Milan
17.11.78 Giovanni Molesini **L** CO 4 Milan
17.01.79 Carl Bailey **W** CO 3 Solihull
06.02.79 Mick Mills **W** RSC 3 Wembley
02.05.79 Achille Mitchell **W** CO 4 Solihull
(*Vacant Midlands Area Welterweight Title*)
30.10.79 Colin Jones **L** RSC 10 Caerphilly
(*Final Elim. British Welterweight Title*)
16.01.80 Salvo Nuclforo **W** PTS 8 Solihull
10.03.80 Roland Zenon **L** PTS 10 Paris
09.09.80 Herol Graham **L** PTS 8 Sheffield
18.10.80 Roy Varden **W** PTS 10 Birmingham
(*Midlands Area Welterweight Title Defence*)
01.12.80 Josef Nsubuga **L** PTS 8 Oslo
05.03.81 Hans Henrik Palm **L** PTS 8 Copenhagen
16.05.81 Michel Pagani **W** RSC 5 Calais
02.10.81 Frankie Dekaestecker **W** RSC 10 Bruges
17.10.81 Fred Coranson **L** PTS 8 Dunkirk
01.12.81 John F. Kennedy **W** PTS 10 Derby
(*Midlands Area Welterweight Title Defence*)
14.12.81 Tukisoleka N'Kalaankete **L** PTS 8 Paris
10.03.82 Gary Pearce **W** PTS 8 Solihull
05.05.82 Kirkland Laing **L** CO 7 Solihull
07.06.82 Martin McGough **W** RTD 6 Edgbaston
(*Midlands Area Welterweight Title Defence*)
13.09.82 Mick Mills **L** RSC 2 Sheffield
06.10.82 Lloyd Hibbert **L** PTS 8 Solihull

17.11.82 Cliff Gilpin L PTS 10 Solihull (*Midlands Area Welterweight Title Defence*)
19.01.83 Kostas Petrou L PTS 8 Birmingham
04.03.83 John Munduga L RSC 5 Cologne
17.05.83 Colin Derrick W PTS 8 Bethnal Green
13.06.83 Kostas Petrou L RSC 5 Coventry (*Vacant Midlands Area Welterweight Title*)
Summary: 39 contests, won 17, lost 22

Johnny Mack (Maguire)

Liverpool. *Born* Liverpool 07.04.64
Featherweight
Manager B. MacDonald
Previous Amateur Club Salisbury

05.09.83 John Mwaimu DREW 6 Liverpool
15.09.83 Mick Hoolison W PTS 6 Liverpool
22.09.83 Gordon Stobie DREW 6 Stockport
03.10.83 Muhammad Lovelock L RSC 1 Liverpool
13.02.84 Billy Hardy L RSC 5 Eltham
Summary: 5 contests, won 1, drew 2, lost 2

Bob McKenley

Islington. *Born* Manchester 10.01.59
Welterweight
Manager F. Warren
Previous Amateur Club Cavendish
National Honours ABA Welterweight Champion 1983; England Int.; Young England Rep.; Schools Titles 1972–1973; Junior ABA Title 1975; NABC Titles 1975–1976
Divisional Honours E Lancs Welterweight Champion 1979–1980; N Counties Welterweight Champion 1981–1983

12.06.84 Joe Lynch W RSC 3 Southend
Summary: 1 contest, won 1

Bob McKenley
Gloucester Photo Agency

(Patrick) Bonny McKenzie

Cardiff. *Born* Jamaica 14.07.55
Former Undefeated Welsh L. Heavyweight Champion
Manager (Self)
Previous Amateur Club Llandaff
National Honours Welsh L. Middleweight Champion 1975; Welsh Int.
Divisional Honours Welsh L. Middleweight R/U 1974

21.06.76 Joe Jackson W PTS 6 Piccadilly
11.08.76 Colin Breen W PTS 6 Cardiff
10.09.76 Tony Sibson L RSC 7 Digbeth
24.11.76 Al Neville W PTS 6 Battersea
01.12.76 Pat Brogan L PTS 8 Stoke
13.12.76 Eddie Burke L PTS 6 Piccadilly
14.02.77 Jimmy Pickard W PTS 8 Bedford
21.02.77 Roy Gumbs L PTS 8 Piccadilly
21.03.77 Eddie Vierling W RSC 1 Piccadilly
24.03.77 Tony Sibson L RSC 7 Leicester
19.09.77 Eddie Burke L PTS 8 Glasgow
03.10.77 Wayne Bennett L PTS 8 Aberavon
02.11.77 Kenny Feehan W RSC 5 Cardiff
21.11.77 Glen McEwan L PTS 8 Birmingham
29.11.77 Eddie Burke L PTS 8 Piccadilly
06.02.78 Karl Canwell L PTS 8 Piccadilly
03.05.78 Reg Long W RSC 7 Solihull
16.05.78 Ken Jones L PTS 8 Newport
22.05.78 Chris Lawson W PTS 8 Mayfair
20.06.78 Dennis Andries W PTS 8 Southend
18.07.78 Tony Sibson L PTS 8 Wakefield
27.09.78 Roy Gumbs L PTS 8 Stoke
29.11.78 Chris Lawson L PTS 10 Swansea (*Vacant Welsh L. Heavyweight Title*)
11.12.78 Oscar Angus W PTS 8 Piccadilly
18.01.79 Shaun Chalcraft W PTS 8 Wimbledon
19.02.79 David Pearce L PTS 8 Mayfair
03.03.79 Karl Canwell W PTS 8 Piccadilly
12.03.79 Karl Canwell L PTS 8 Mayfair
19.03.79 Eddie Smith W PTS 8 Piccadilly
24.04.79 Roy Gumbs L PTS 8 Piccadilly
13.05.79 Gordon Ferris L PTS 8 Edgbaston
06.06.79 Dennis Andries L PTS 8 Burslem
18.06.79 Alek Penarski DREW 8 Windsor
26.09.79 Eddie Smith L PTS 8 Solihull
15.10.79 Roy Gumbs L RSC 3 Mayfair
26.03.80 Cristiano Cavina L PTS 8 Rome
28.04.80 Steve Lewin W PTS 8 Southwark
10.05.80 Michel Pagani L DIS 3 Calais
14.08.80 Walter Celvo W PTS 8 Rimini
06.09.80 John Odhiambo L PTS 6 Aarhus
22.09.80 Danny Lawford L PTS 8 Mayfair
21.11.80 Trevor Cattouse L PTS 8 Crawley
29.09.80 Alek Blanchard L PTS 8 Rotterdam
02.03.81 David Pearce L PTS 8 Piccadilly
21.04.81 Richard Caramanolis L PTS 8 Marseilles

CONTINUED OVERLEAF

07.09.81 Hubert Zimmerman **L** PTS 8 Rotterdam
21.09.81 Chris Lawson **W** PTS 10 Piccadilly
(*Vacant Welsh L. Heavyweight Title*)
20.10.81 Liam Coleman **L** PTS 8 Leeds
06.11.81 Helmut Ulke **W** PTS 6 Kiel
23.01.82 Hocine Tafer **L** PTS 10 Grenoble
12.02.82 Fred Serres **L** PTS 10 Luxembourg
25.02.82 Manfred Jassman **L** PTS 8 Munich
14.04.82 Tommy Kiely **L** PTS 8 Strand
27.04.82 Ben Lawlor **W** DIS 4 Croydon
07.05.82 Guido Trane **L** PTS 8 Bologna
05.08.83 Rufino Angulo **L** PTS 8 Nimes
Summary: 56 contests, won 18, drew 1, lost 37

Dudley McKenzie

Croydon. *Born* Croydon 03.12.61
Middleweight
Manager G. Davidson
Previous Amateur Club Sir Philip Game
National Honours Schools Title 1975 – 1978; Junior ABA Titles 1977 – 1978; NABC Titles 1977 – 1978; Young England Rep.
Divisional Honours London L. Middleweight Champion 1980 – 1981

12.10.81 Casley McCallum **W** PTS 6 Copthorne
26.10.81 Billy Bryce **W** PTS 8 Mayfair
18.11.81 Steve Henty **W** PTS 8 Solihull
10.03.82 Neville Wilson **W** PTS 8 Birmingham
30.03.82 Willie Wright **W** PTS 6 Wembley
27.04.82 Mike Burton **W** PTS 6 Croydon
23.10.82 Tony Habermayer **W** PTS 8 Berlin
15.11.82 Winston Davis **W** CO 6 Glasgow
29.11.82 Paul Tchoue **L** PTS 8 Paris
14.04.83 James Cook **L** PTS 8 Basildon
Summary: 10 contests, won 8, lost 2

Dudley McKenzie
Derek Rowe (Photos) Ltd

Duke McKenzie

Croydon. *Born* Croydon 05.05.63
Flyweight
Manager M. Duff
Previous Amateur Club Battersea
National Honours Young England Rep.
Divisional Honours London Flyweight Champion 1981; SW London Bantamweight Champion 1982

23.11.82 Charlie Brown **W** RSC 1 Wembley
24.01.83 Andy King **W** RSC 2 Mayfair
27.02.83 Dave Pearson **W** RSC 2 Las Vegas
03.03.83 Gregorio Hernandez **W** RSC 3 Los Angeles
19.03.83 Lupe Sanchez **W** CO 2 Reno Nevada
18.10.83 Jerry Davis **W** RSC 2 Atlantic City
22.11.83 Alain Limarola **W** PTS 6 Wembley
15.01.84 David Capo **W** PTS 4 Atlantic City
23.05.84 Gary Roberts **W** CO 1 Mayfair
Summary: 9 contests, won 9

Horace McKenzie

Cardiff. *Born* Jamaica 18.02.57
Former Undefeated Welsh Welterweight Champion
Manager (Self)
Previous Amateur Club Llandaff
National Honours Junior ABA Title 1972; Welsh Int.

25.04.77 Ray Thomas **W** CO 2 Mayfair
02.06.77 Peter Rushfirth **W** RSC 1 Piccadilly
14.06.77 Mick Mills **L** RSC 4 Southend
18.07.77 Alan Jones **W** CO 4 Mayfair
21.09.77 Al Stewart **W** RSC 7 Solihull
11.10.77 Peter Neal DREW 8 Marylebone
02.11.77 Eric Purkiss **W** PTS 8 Cardiff
06.12.77 Colin Deans **W** RSC 7 Leeds
15.12.77 Louis Acaries **L** RSC 9 Paris
30.01.78 Tommy Davitt **W** PTS 8 Glasgow
13.02.78 Carl Bailey **W** PTS 8 Manchester
20.03.78 Tim McHugh **W** PTS 8 Aberavon
22.05.78 Roy Commosioung **W** PTS 8 Mayfair
10.07.78 Mike Copp **W** PTS 10 Aberavon
(*Vacant Welsh Welterweight Title*)
18.07.78 Prince Rodney **L** PTS 8 Wakefield
03.09.78 Joseph Nsubuga **L** PTS 8 Bergen
09.09.78 Raul Anon **W** PTS 8 La Carogne
03.10.78 Colin Jones **L** PTS 8 Aberavon
15.10.78 Fred Coranson **L** PTS 8 Dunkirk
07.12.78 Hans Henrik Palm **L** PTS 8 Copenhagen
08.01.79 Frank Albertus **W** PTS 8 Rotterdam
02.03.79 Clemente Tshinza **L** PTS 8 Bruges
13.05.79 Lloyd Lee **L** PTS 8 Edgbaston
18.06.79 Chris Walker **W** PTS 8 Piccadilly

19.11.79 Prince Rodney L PTS 8 Stockport
10.12.79 Roland Zenon L PTS 10 Paris
11.03.80 Gary Pearce W PTS 10 Piccadilly (*Welsh Welterweight Title Defence*)
12.05.80 Coenie Bekker L PTS 10 Cape Town
23.05.80 Luigi Minchillo L PTS 8 Pesaro
16.06.80 Roy Varden L PTS 8 Piccadilly
06.09.80 Jorgen Hansen L DIS 7 Aarhus
23.10.80 George Walker L PTS 8 Piccadilly
10.11.80 Claude Martin L PTS 8 St. Malo
21.01.81 Charlie Malarkey L PTS 8 Piccadilly
16.02.81 Colin Jones L RSC 7 Mayfair
30.03.81 Roy Varden L PTS 8 Piccadilly
05.05.81 Mick Mills L PTS 8 Southend
04.06.81 Luigi Minchillo L PTS 10 Milan
03.07.81 Richard Caramanolis L PTS 8 Marseilles
17.10.81 Jo Kimpuani L DIS 3 Dunkirk
25.11.81 Mick Mills L RSC 2 Sheffield
24.02.82 John Humphreys DREW 8 Evesham
01.03.82 Joey Frost L PTS 8 Preston
17.03.82 Jimmy Cable W CO 2 Kensington
07.05.82 Carlos Santos L RSC 6 Bologna
14.09.82 Nick Wilshire L RSC 5 Wembley
28.01.83 Doug James L RSC 9 Swansea (*Vacant Welsh Middleweight Title*)
10.11.83 John Langol L RSC 3 Stafford
Summary: 49 contests, won 16, drew 2, lost 31

Duke McKenzie
Douglas Baton

(Leroy) Lee McKenzie
Croydon. *Born* Croydon 21.07.61
L. Welterweight
Manager F. Rix
Previous Amateur Club Sir Philip Game
National Honours NABC Title 1978

25.11.80 Martin Bolton W PTS 6 Norwich
02.02.81 Julian Bousted W PTS 6 Piccadilly
17.02.81 Alan Cooper L PTS 6 Lewisham
09.04.81 Bobby Welburn W PTS 8 Piccadilly
15.06.81 Alan Cooper W PTS 6 Mayfair
09.09.81 Dave Sullivan W PTS 8 Morecambe
28.09.81 Alan Cooper W PTS 8 Lewisham
29.10.81 Sam Omidi W PTS 6 Walthamstow
10.12.81 Dave Finigan W PTS 6 Walthamstow
10.03.82 Kostas Petrou W PTS 8 Solihull
07.02.83 Ian McLeod L RSC 6 Piccadilly
25.04.83 Jim McIntosh L PTS 8 Piccadilly
09.11.83 Terry Marsh L PTS 8 Southend
21.03.84 Joe Lynch W PTS 8 Mayfair
26.03.84 Adey Allen W PTS 8 Glasgow
16.04.84 Jeff Decker W RSC 2 Glasgow
Summary: 16 contests, won 12, lost 4

Mike McKenzie
Perth. *Born* Perth 18.12.59
Welterweight
Manager (Self)
Previous Amateur Club Perth Railways

25.03.82 Sean Campbell W PTS 6 Glasgow
06.04.82 John Daly L PTS 6 Leeds
13.06.83 Steve Boyle L PTS 6 Glasgow
20.06.83 Elvis Morton DREW 6 Piccadilly
19.09.83 Kid Sadler L RSC 4 Manchester
22.11.83 Elvis Morton L PTS 6 Wolverhampton
27.02.84 Jim Hunter W RSC 3 Glasgow
11.06.84 Robert Harkin L CO 3 Glasgow
Summary: 8 contests, won 2, drew 1, lost 5

Tony McKenzie
Leicester. *Born* Leicester 04.03.63
L. Welterweight
Manager K. Squires
Previous Amateur Club Belgrave
National Honours Schools Title 1979
Divisional Honours M Counties L. Welterweight R/U 1981 – 1982

22.11.83 Albert Buchanan W CO 3 Wolverhampton
07.12.83 Peter Flanagan W PTS 6 Stoke
30.01.84 Vince Bailey W RSC 1 Birmingham
27.02.84 David Irving W RSC 3 Birmingham
15.03.84 Johnny Grant W RSC 4 Leicester
16.04.84 Danny Shinkwin L RSC 1 Birmingham
09.05.84 Ray Price W PTS 8 Leicester
Summary: 7 contests, won 6, lost 1

CONTINUED OVERLEAF

Terry McKeown
Barrhead. *Born* Barrhead 26.05.58
Lightweight
Manager T. Gilmour
Previous Amateur Club Paisley
National Honours Scottish Int.

18.09.78 Bobby Breen W PTS 6 Glasgow
09.10.78 Pip Coleman W PTS 6 Piccadilly
18.10.78 Bobby Breen W PTS 6 Glasgow
23.10.78 John Cooper W PTS 6 Glasgow
31.10.78 Larry Richards W PTS 6 Birmingham
27.11.78 Lance Williams W PTS 6 Govan
29.01.79 Lee Graham W PTS 6 Glasgow
26.02.79 Charm Chiteule L RSC 5 Mayfair
17.04.79 Alec Irvine W PTS 8 Glasgow
13.05.79 Steve Cleak W PTS 8 Glasgow
18.06.79 Gary Lucas W RSC 4 Glasgow
08.10.79 Paul Keers W PTS 8 Glasgow
03.11.79 Louis Loy L RSC 3 Glasgow
10.12.79 Vernon Penprase L PTS 8 Torquay
16.01.80 Selvin Bell W PTS 8 Solihull
28.01.80 Don George DREW 6 Glasgow
14.03.80 Gerry O'Neill L PTS 10 Glasgow
(*Vacant Scottish Featherweight Title*)
16.09.80 Austin Owens W RTD 2 Wembley
01.11.80 John Feeney L PTS 8 Glasgow
15.03.81 Roy Somer DREW 6 The Hague
04.05.81 Richie Foster W RSC 5 Glasgow
22.02.82 Vernon Penprase W PTS 12 Glasgow
(*Final Elim. British Featherweight Title*)
20.09.82 Steve Sammy Sims L CO 12 Glasgow
(*Vacant British Featherweight Title*)
26.11.82 Clyde Ruan L RSC 5 Glasgow
21.03.83 Ian McLeod L RSC 1 Glasgow
Summary: 25 contests, won 15, drew 2, lost 8

Ian McLeod
Scotsman/Evening News

John McKinlay
Glasgow. *Born* Glasgow 15.03.60
Lightweight
Manager T. Gilmour
Previous Amateur Club Noble Art
Divisional Honours Scottish Lightweight Champion 1980

18.10.82 Paul Keers W PTS 6 Glasgow
10.02.83 Tony Wilkinson L RSC 3 Sunderland
21.03.83 Gary Williams L PTS 6 Glasgow
Summary: 3 contests, won 1, lost 2

Glen McLaggon
Cardiff. *Born* Jamaica 22.12.59
Featherweight
Manager R. Elvin
Previous Amateur Club Ely Star
National Honours Welsh Featherweight Champion 1983

27.03.84 Billy Hardy L PTS 6 Battersea
Summary: 1 contest, lost 1

Ian McLeod
Edinburgh. *Born* Glasgow 23.05.58
Lightweight
Manager L. Roberts
Previous Amateur Club Sparta
National Honours Scottish Featherweight Champion 1977 – 1979; Scottish Int.; Euro. Junior Bronze 1976

23.03.81 Selvin Bell W PTS 6 Glasgow
13.04.81 Billy Smith W PTS 6 Glasgow
27.04.81 Steve Pollard W PTS 8 Piccadilly
11.05.81 Alan Storey W PTS 6 Glasgow
14.09.81 Don George W PTS 8 Glasgow
06.10.81 Gary Lucas W PTS 8 Piccadilly
23.11.81 Damien McDermott W RSC 7 Glasgow
08.02.82 Peter Eubanks L PTS 8 Piccadilly
25.03.82 Peter Harrison W PTS 8 Glasgow
22.04.82 Peter Eubanks L PTS 8 Piccadilly
31.05.82 Willie Booth L PTS 10 Glasgow
(*Vacant Scottish Lightweight Title*)
07.02.83 Lee McKenzie W RSC 6 Piccadilly
21.03.83 Terry McKeown W RSC 1 Glasgow
25.04.83 Jeff Decker DREW 8 Piccadilly
17.05.83 Najib Daho W PTS 8 Piccadilly
13.06.83 Jeff Decker W RSC 5 Glasgow
19.09.83 Jimmy Bunclark W RSC 3 Glasgow
21.11.83 Geoff Pegler W RSC 4 Glasgow
27.02.84 Keith Foreman W PTS 8 Glasgow
06.04.84 Ray Hood W RSC 2 Edinburgh
Summary: 20 contests, won 16, drew 1, lost 3

Chris McReedy (Davies)

Liverpool. *Born* Southport 28.03.61
Welterweight
Manager C. Moorcroft
Previous Amateur Club Long Lane

15.03.84 Derek Atherton W PTS 6 Kirkby
16.04.84 Mickey Brooks L PTS 6 Bradford
Summary: 2 contests, won 1, lost 1

Valentino Maccarinelli

Swansea. *Born* Swansea 16.10.59
Welterweight
Manager C. Breen
Previous Amateur Club Ragged School

27.04.82 Noel Blair W PTS 6 Southend
07.06.82 Jimmy Ward W PTS 6 Swansea
28.09.82 Davy Campbell L PTS 6 Derry
13.10.82 Danny Garrison L CO 2 Evesham
10.02.83 Mick Leachman DREW 6 Walthamstow
21.02.83 Johnny Burns W PTS 6 Edgbaston
02.03.83 Patsy Quinn L RSC 4 Belfast
12.04.83 Damien Fryers L RSC 4 Belfast
Summary: 8 contests, won 3, drew 1, lost 4

Terry Magee

Ammantord. *Born* Belfast 01.11.64
Middleweight
Manager B. Lloyd
Previous Amateur Club Sacred Heart

29.11.82 Robbie Turner W PTS 6 Brighton
08.12.82 Tony Baker W PTS 6 Piccadilly
07.02.83 Alex Romeo L PTS 6 Piccadilly
21.02.83 Tony Burke L PTS 6 Piccadilly
16.09.83 David Scere W PTS 6 Rhyl
28.11.83 Winston Wray W PTS 6 Rhyl
06.02.84 Craig Edwards W RSC 3 Liverpool
06.03.84 Lou Johnson W RSC 2 Stoke
12.05.84 Cornelius Chisholm W RTD 3 Hanley
Summary: 9 contests, won 7, lost 2

Charlie Malarkey

Glasgow. *Born* Glasgow 28.06.56
Scottish L. Middleweight Champion
Manager R. Watt
Previous Amateur Club Clydeview
Divisional Honours ABA & Scottish L. Middleweight Champion 1977

10.10.77 Albert Smith W PTS 6 Glasgow
14.11.77 Willie Turkington W RSC 8 Glasgow
08.12.77 Joe Lally L RSC 8 Liverpool
23.01.78 Brian Gregory L PTS 8 Bradford
27.02.78 Terry Schofield W PTS 8 Middlesbrough
20.03.78 Tony Burnett W PTS 8 Glasgow
08.05.78 Billy Lauder W PTS 10 Glasgow
19.06.78 Salvo Nuciforo L PTS 8 Glasgow
18.10.78 Carl Bailey W CO 3 Glasgow
13.11.78 Terry Petersen W PTS 8 Glasgow
08.01.79 Roy Commosioung W PTS 8 Piccadilly
26.02.79 Joe Oke W PTS 8 Glasgow
23.04.79 John Smith W PTS 12 Glasgow
(*Scottish L. Middleweight Title Challenge*)
08.10.79 Salvo Nuciforo W PTS 8 Piccadilly
27.10.79 Fred Coranson L PTS 8 Dunkirk
05.11.79 George Walker L PTS 8 Piccadilly
14.03.80 Prince Rodney W PTS 10 Glasgow
(*Elim. British L. Middleweight Title*)
05.05.80 Harry Watson W RSC 8 Glasgow
07.06.80 Steve Hopkin L RSC 5 Glasgow
(*Final Elim. British L. Middleweight Title*)
16.09.80 Jimmy Batten L RSC 4 Wembley
21.01.81 Horace McKenzie W PTS 8 Piccadilly
09.03.81 Achille Mitchell W PTS 8 Hamilton
30.03.81 Gerry Young W CO 4 Glasgow
14.09.81 Gary Pearce W PTS 8 Glasgow
29.10.81 Tony Martey W PTS 8 Glasgow
15.02.82 Kid Murray W RTD 5 Glasgow
18.03.82 Graeme Ahmed L PTS 8 South Shields
07.06.82 Mick Mills W PTS 8 Glasgow
28.09.82 Vic Jackson W PTS 8 Aberdeen
26.10.82 Colin Derrick L RSC 8 Bethnal Green
(*Elim. British Welterweight Title*)
24.01.83 Arthur Davis W CO 4 Glasgow
07.03.83 Dennis Pryce W PTS 8 Glasgow
11.04.83 Lloyd Hibbert W PTS 8 Glasgow
12.09.83 Cliff Gilpin L RSC 9 Glasgow
(*Final Elim. British Welterweight Title*)
Summary: 34 contests, won 24, lost 10

Charlie Malarkey

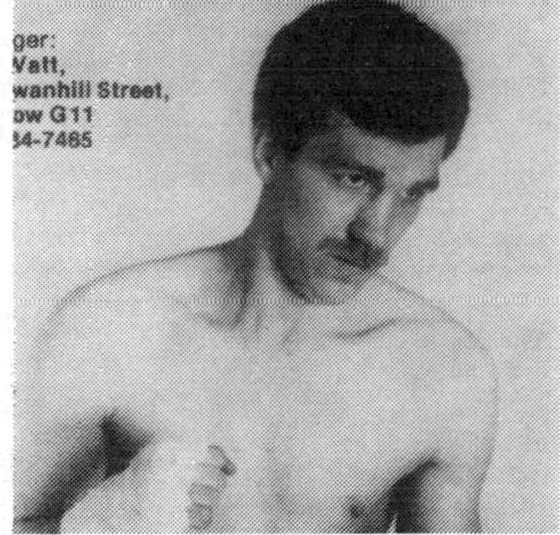

Al Malcolm

Birmingham. *Born* Birmingham 10.04.58
Heavyweight
Manager E. Cashmore
Previous Amateur Club Aston Villa
Divisional Honours M Counties S. Heavyweight Champion 1983

30.09.83 Tony Blackstock **W** PTS 4 Leicester
10.11.83 Grant Wallis **W** PTS 6 Stafford
22.11.83 Godfrey Hibbert **W** RSC 1 Wolverhampton
12.12.83 Frank Robinson L PTS 6 Birmingham
10.02.84 Dave Garside L PTS 6 Dudley
Summary: 5 contests, won 3, lost 2

Tommy Mallon

Doncaster. *Born* Coatbridge 24.10.61
Featherweight
Manager J. Rushton
Previous Amateur Club St Thomas'

07.06.84 Shane Silvester L RSC 5 Dudley
Summary: 1 contest, lost 1

Eugene Maloney

Walworth. *Born* London 29.05.56
Featherweight
Manager (Self)
Previous Amateur Club Hollington
Divisional Honours SE London Bantamweight R/U 1978

12.10.81 Steve Reilly **W** PTS 6 Bloomsbury
28.10.81 Robert Hepburn **W** RTD 3 Acton
23.11.81 Mike Wilkes L PTS 6 Bloomsbury
27.01.82 Hugh Russell L DIS 4 Belfast
16.02.82 Dave Laxen L PTS 5 Southend
10 03.82 Jim Harvey L PTS 6 Burslem
08.06.82 Shaun Shinkwin L PTS 4 Southend
13.02.84 Steve Benny **W** RSC 5 Eltham
Summary: 8 contests, won 3, lost 5

John Maloney

Barnet. *Born* Highgate 26.02.64
Featherweight
Manager D. Smith
Previous Amateur Club Finchley

26.01.84 John Mwaimu **W** RSC 5 Strand
02.04.84 Freddie Potter **W** RSC 2 Mayfair
06.04.84 Clinton Campbell **W** PTS 6 Watford
18.06.84 Mike Whalley L CO 1 Manchester
Summary: 4 contests, won 3, lost 1

John Maloney
Derek Rowe (Photos) Ltd

Neil Malpass

South Elmsall. *Born* South Elmsall 23.10.55
Central Area Heavyweight Champion
Manager T. Miller
Previous Amateur Club Hemsworth Colliery
Divisional Honours N Counties Heavyweight Champion 1976

10.02.77 Roy Johnson L PTS 4 Coventry
23.02.77 Keith Johnson **W** RSC 3 Bradford
28.02.77 John Clark **W** RSC 3 Mayfair
28.02.77 Henry Mears **W** RSC 3 Mayfair
28.02.77 Brian Paul **W** PTS 4 Mayfair
24.03.77 John Clark **W** RSC 4 Leicester
04.04.77 Alan Ward **W** CO 3 Luton
09.05.77 Derek Simpkin **W** PTS 6 Piccadilly
18.07.77 Tony Blackburn **W** RSC 3 Mayfair
19.09.77 Danny McAlinden **W** RSC 3 Mayfair
25.10.77 Kris Smith **W** CO 1 Kensington
08.11.77 Tommy Kiely L PTS 8 Wembley
12.12.77 Sean Reilly **W** RSC 3 Barnsley
19.01.78 Austin Okoye L CO 4 Wimbledon
20.02.78 Peter Freeman **W** CO 2 Bradford (*Central Area Heavyweight Title Challenge*)
27.02.78 Sean McKenna **W** CO 2 Sheffield

20.03.78 Paul Sykes **W** DIS 7 Bradford (*Central Area Heavyweight Title Defence*)
24.04.78 George Scott **L** PTS 8 Middlesbrough
01.06.78 Bob Pollard **L** PTS 8 Heathrow
12.07.78 Colin Flute **W** RSC 6 Newcastle
18.07.78 Paul Sykes DREW 10 Wakefield (*Central Area Heavyweight Title Defence*)
27.09.78 Bob Pollard **W** PTS 8 Rotherham
04.12.78 Christian Poncelet **W** RSC 3 Middlesbrough
16.06.79 Mike Schutte **L** PTS 8 Johannesburg
01.10.79 Billy Aird **L** PTS 10 Marylebone
28.11.79 Terry Mintus **L** DIS 5 Doncaster (*Central Area Heavyweight Title Defence*)
03.03.80 Theo Josephs **W** PTS 8 Marton
19.03.80 Theo Josephs **W** PTS 8 Doncaster
21.04.80 Joe Awome **W** RSC 8 Mayfair
28.04.80 Avenamar Peralta **W** PTS 8 Berlin
17.07.80 Alfredo Evangelista **L** PTS 8 Barcelona
27.09.80 Clarrie Hill **L** RSC 2 Wembley
18.11.80 Larry McDonald **L** DIS 1 Windsor
24.09.81 Bruce Grandham **W** CO 2 Liverpool
20.10.81 Terry Mintus **W** RSC 3 Leeds (*Central Area Heavyweight Title Challenge*)
16.02.82 Theo Josephs **W** RSC 8 Leeds
02.05.82 Stuart Lithgo **L** DIS 6 Middlesbrough
06.07.82 Stuart Lithgo **L** RSC 3 Leeds
05.02.83 Proud Kilimanjaro **L** PTS 10 Harare
24.06.83 Mary Konate **L** CO 2 Bamako
30.04.84 Proud Kilimanjaro **L** RSC 5 Glasgow
Summary: 41 contests, won 24, drew 1, lost 16

Neil Malpass

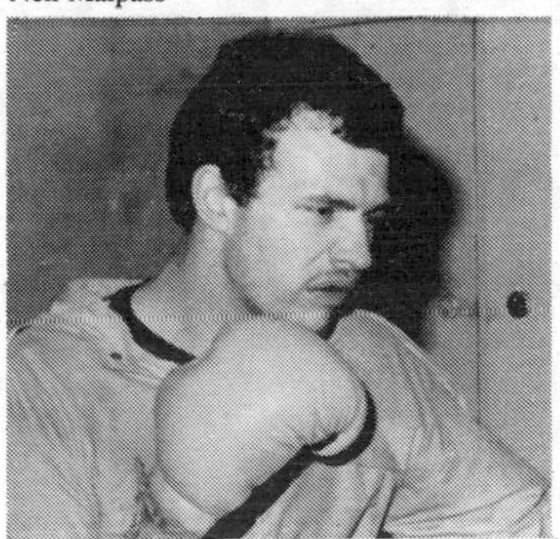

Mickey Markie

Kettering. *Born* Kettering 26.10.63
Featherweight
Manager C. Hall
Previous Amateur Club Keystone
Divisional Honours M Counties Featherweight R/U 1983 & Bantamweight Champion 1984

07.06.84 Billy Joe Dee **W** PTS 6 Dudley
Summary: 1 contest, won 1

Dean Marsden

Halifax. *Born* Leeds 06.12.60
Featherweight
Manager T. Callighan
Previous Amateur Club Market District

02.11.81 Stuart Shaw **W** PTS 6 Nottingham
27.01.82 Gerry Devine **W** CO 5 Stoke
27.09.82 Jarvis Greenidge **W** PTS 6 Birmingham
14.10.82 Alan Tombs **L** PTS 8 Nantwich
29.11.82 Alec Irvine **L** RSC 4 Birmingham
27.04.83 Alan Tombs **L** RSC 2 Stoke
Summary: 6 contests, won 3, lost 3

Dean Marsden
WRNS Pictures (Brian Worsnop) Ltd

Michael Marsden
WRNS Pictures (Brian Worsnop) Ltd

Michael Marsden

Leeds. *Born* Leeds 07.05.64
Featherweight
Manager T. Callighan
Previous Amateur Club Meanwood

10.11.81 Darren Craven **W** PTS 4 Bedworth
10.12.81 Danny Allen **W** CO 2 Walthamstow
27.01.82 Kevin Hay **W** PTS 4 Stoke
06.04.82 Gordon Haigh **W** PTS 4 Leeds
13.05.82 Mark Stoops **W** PTS 6 Wakefield
14.10.82 Anthony Brown DREW 6 Nantwich
09.11.82 Michael Betts L CO 3 Southend
01.02.83 Robert Hepburn **W** RSC 5 Southend
17.02.83 John Lodge **W** RSC 1 Morley
21.03.83 Danny Flynn L PTS 8 Glasgow
27.04.83 Charlie Coke **W** PTS 6 Stoke
30.09.83 Dave Pratt **W** PTS 8 Leicester
26.10.83 Anthony Brown L RSC 2 Stoke
26.03.84 Gerry Devine **W** CO 2 Glasgow
02.05.84 Dave Bryan **W** CO 7 Solihull
Summary: 15 contests, won 11, drew 1, lost 3

Terry Marsh

Basildon. *Born* Stepney 07.02.58
Former Undefeated Southern Area L. Welterweight Champion
Manager F. Warren
Previous Amateur Club Royal Navy
National Honours Schools Title 1974; Junior ABA Title 1973 – 1974; NABC Title 1976; Young England Rep.; England Int.; ABA Lightweight Champion 1978; Welterweight Champion 1980 & 1981
Divisional Honours London Lightweight Champion 1977; ABA L. Welterweight R/U 1979

12.10.81 Andrew Da Costa **W** PTS 6 Bloomsbury
28.10.81 Dave Sullivan **W** PTS 6 Acton
23.11.81 Kid Murray **W** PTS 6 Bloomsbury
08.12.81 Gary Brooks **W** PTS 6 Southend
19.02.82 Arthur Davis **W** PTS 6 Bloomsbury
09.03.82 Gerry McGrath **W** PTS 8 Hornsey
05.04.82 Lloyd Christie DREW 8 Bloomsbury
13.08.82 Dave Finigan **W** RSC 5 Strand
07.09.82 Robert Armstrong **W** PTS 8 Hornsey
11.10.82 Chris Sanigar **W** DIS 7 Bristol
19.02.83 Didier Kowalski **W** PTS 8 St Arnand
16.03.83 Andy Thomas **W** RSC 4 Cheltenham
26.04.83 Vernon Entertainer Vanriel **W** PTS 10 Bethnal Green
(*Vacant Southern Area L Welterweight Title*)
09.11.83 Lee McKenzie **W** PTS 8 Southend
16.04.84 Tony Sinnott **W** PTS 12 Bradford
(*Final Elim. British L. Welterweight Title*)
Summary: 15 contests, won 14, drew 1

Ian Martin

Croydon. *Born* Croydon 29.05.64
Middleweight
Manager F. Rix
Previous Amateur Club Clockhouse

03.10.83 Newton Barnett **W** PTS 6 Eltham
31.10.83 Dave Hall **W** RSC 3 Mayfair
21.11.83 Newton Barnett **W** PTS 6 Eltham
23.01.84 John Hargin DREW 6 Mayfair
03.02.84 Kevin Webb L PTS 6 Maidenhead
14.02.84 Ronnie Fraser L PTS 6 Wolverhampton
Summary: 6 contests, won 3, drew 1, lost 2

Dave Maxwell
Leicester. *Born* Leicester 29.11.62
L. Middleweight
Manager (Self)
Previous Amateur Club Belgrave

11.11.82 Clifton Wallace L PTS 6 Stafford
01.12.82 Errol Dennis L RSC 2 Stafford
21.02.83 Delroy Pearce L PTS 6 Mayfair
14.03.83 Gavin Stirrup L RSC 3 Manchester
Summary: 4 contests, lost 4

Carl Merrett
Newport. *Born* Newport 07.05.65
Lightweight
Manager M. Williams
Previous Amateur Club St. Joseph's

16.05.83 Clinton Campbell **W** PTS 6 Birmingham
16.09.83 Muhammad Lovelock **W** PTS 6 Swindon
09.11.83 Paul Wright **W** PTS 6 Evesham
01.12.83 Kenny Jinks L PTS 6 Dudley
10.12.83 Joey Wainwright DREW 6 Swansea
25.01.84 Kenny Jinks L PTS 8 Stoke
04.04.84 Rocky Mensah L PTS 8 Evesham
Summary: 7 contests, won 3, drew 1, lost 3

Steve Metcalfe
Rotherham. *Born* Rotherham 10.10.60
Welterweight
Manager T. Miller
Previous Amateur Club St. Thomas's

23.05.83 Jim Kelly L PTS 6 Glasgow
13.06.83 Dave Heaver **W** PTS 6 Doncaster
03.10.83 Kid Sadler L RSC 4 Bradford
Summary: 3 contests, won 1, lost 2

Mark Mills
Croydon. *Born* Caerphilly 20.06.58
Welterweight
Manager F. Rix
Previous Amateur Club New Addington
Divisional Honours SE London Welterweight Champion 1982 & R/U 1983

12.06.84 Andy O'Rawe **W** PTS 6 Southend
Summary: 1 contest, won 1

Mick Mills
Sheffield. *Born* Rotherham 21.03.56
L. Middleweight
Manager B. Ingle
Previous Amateur Club St. Thomas's
Divisional Honours NE Counties L. Middleweight Champion 1975; N Counties L. Middleweight Champion 1976

21.03.77 Dave Taylor **W** PTS 6 Stoke
05.04.77 Earl Noel **W** RSC 2 Southend
18.04.77 Bert Green **W** CO 1 Stafford
03.05.77 Johnny Hamm **W** RTD 5 Southend
14.06.77 Horace McKenzie **W** RSC 4 Southend
20.07.77 John Breen **W** RTD 2 Sheffield
14.09.77 Owen Robinson **W** RTD 4 Sheffield
20.09.77 Rocky Butler **W** RSC 2 Southend
02.11.77 Jim Moore **W** CO 1 Southend
05.12.77 Tim McHugh **W** RSC 2 Southend
13.12.77 Owen Robinson **W** PTS 8 Southgate
07.02.78 Henry Turkington **W** RSC 3 Southend
27.02.78 Albert Smith **W** PTS 8 Sheffield
14.03.78 Albert Smith **W** CO 2 Southend
11.04.78 John Smith **W** PTS 8 Sheffield
23.05.78 Joe Oke **W** CO 1 Southend
28.11.78 Esperno Postl **W** RSC 2 Sheffield
06.02.79 Joey Mack L RSC 3 Wembley
10.04.79 Salvo Nuciforo L RSC 5 Kensington
16.05.79 Prince Rodney L RSC 4 Sheffield (*Central Area L. Middleweight Title Challenge*)
12.02.80 Carl Bailey **W** RSC 5 Sheffield
09.04.80 Curtis Marsh L PTS 8 Burslem
22.04.80 Jimmy Ellis L RTD 6 Sheffield
04.11.80 Chris Christian L PTS 8 Southend
03.12.80 Dennis Pryce L PTS 8 Sheffield
03.02.81 Neil Fannan **W** RSC 6 Southend
10.02.81 Vic Jackson **W** PTS 8 Nantwich
24.03.81 Winston Burnett **W** PTS 8 Sheffield
05.05.81 Horace McKenzie **W** PTS 8 Southend
23.09.81 Steve Davies **W** RSC 2 Sheffield
03.11.81 Steve Goodwin **W** CO 2 Southend
25.11.81 Horace McKenzie **W** RSC 2 Sheffield
08.12.81 Curtis Marsh **W** CO 2 Southend
27.01.82 Terry Christle L CO 3 Belfast
24.02.82 Frank McCord **W** CO 2 Sheffield
06.04.82 Prince Rodney L RSC 4 Leeds (*Central Area L. Middleweight Title Challenge*)
07.06.82 Charlie Malarkey L PTS 8 Glasgow
13.09.82 Joey Mack **W** RSC 2 Sheffield
20.10.82 Cliff Gilpin L RSC 3 Strand
07.12.82 Martin McEwan **W** PTS 8 Southend
28.03.83 Willie Wright L CO 5 Manchester
07.06.83 Martin McEwan **W** PTS 8 Southend
21.07.83 Doug Sam L RSC 1 Brisbane
28.07.83 Michael Isaako L CO 1 Rotorua
06.06.84 Jerry Golden **W** PTS 6 Sheffield
Summary: 45 contests, won 31, lost 14

(Dave) Taffy Mills
Sunderland. *Born* Castletown 27.02.61
Featherweight
Manager T. Cumiskey
Previous Amateur Club Sunderland

26.05.82 John Doherty **W** RSC 1 Leeds
10.10.82 Brett Styles L RSC 2 Piccadilly

CONTINUED OVERLEAF

21.03.83 Phil Glover **W** PTS 4 Glasgow
13.06.83 Mick Hoolison **W** CO 5 Doncaster
06.04.84 George Baigrie L RSC 4 Edinburgh
Summary: 5 contests, won 3, lost 2

(Telford) Terry Mintus

Leeds. *Born* St. Kitts 21.04.48
Former Central Area Heavyweight Champion
Manager V. Flynn
Previous Amateur Club Market District
Divisional Honours NE Counties Heavyweight R/U 1974

28.04.75 Reg Smith **W** RSC 2 Kensington
08.09.75 Ishaq Hussien **W** PTS 6 Mayfair
04.11.75 Paul Kinsella L PTS 6 Wembley
18.11.75 Ishaq Hussien L PTS 6 Reading
02.12.75 David Fry DREW 6 Leeds
14.01.76 John Depledge **W** PTS 6 Bradford
20.01.76 Denton Ruddock L PTS 6 Kensington
24.02.76 Sean Reilly DREW 8 Manchester
10.03.76 Brian Huckfield DREW 8 Wolverhampton
05.04.76 John Depledge **W** PTS 6 Bradford
05.05.76 Derek Simpkin **W** RSC 6 Solihull
09.07.76 Alfio Righetti L CO 5 Rimini
21.09.76 Paul Kinsella **W** RSC 3 Southend
25.10.76 Ishaq Hussien L PTS 8 Mayfair
07.02.77 Derek Simpkin **W** PTS 8 Mayfair
01.06.77 Bunny Johnson L CO 1 Dudley
19.10.77 Tony Moore **W** PTS 8 Kingston
14.11.77 Les Stevens L PTS 8 Reading
06.04.78 Bjorn Rudi **W** PTS 6 Oslo
29.04.78 Rudi Gauwe L CO 4 Zele
12.10.78 Austin Okoye **W** RSC 8 Wimbledon
30.10.78 Sylvain Watbled L PTS 10 Paris
10.03.79 Jimmy Abbott L CO 4 Johannesburg
25.06.79 Ricky James L PTS 8 Edgbaston
25.09.79 Gordon Ferris L CO 6 Wembley
28.11.79 Neil Malpass **W** DIS 5 Doncaster (*Central Area Heavyweight Title Challenge*)
28.05.80 George Scott **W** PTS 10 Cramlington (*Elim. British Heavyweight Title*)
26.03.81 Neville Meade L RSC 3 Ebbw Vale (*Final Elim. British Heavyweight Title*)
12.09.81 Alfredo Evangelista L RSC 3 Oviavo
20.10.81 Neil Malpass L RSC 3 Leeds (*Central Area Heavyweight Title Defence*)
22.03.83 Adrian Elliott L PTS 8 Bethnal Green
Summary: 31 contests, won 12, drew 3, lost 16

Terry Mintus
Jack Hickes

Glyn Mitchell

Plymouth. *Born* Plymouth 15.08.62
Welterweight
Manager D. Mahoney
Previous Amateur Club Mayflower
Divisional Honours W Counties Lightweight R/U 1982

11.10.82 Ron Shinkwin **W** PTS 4 Bristol
18.10.82 Graeme Griffin **W** RSC 4 Nottingham
29.11.82 Jonathan Newall **W** PTS 4 Newquay
06.12.82 Sammy Rodgers DREW 6 Nottingham
19.01.83 Gary Williams L PTS 6 Stoke
24.01.83 Dave Smithson **W** PTS 6 Piccadilly
14.02.83 Dave Smithson DREW 8 Lewisham
25.04.83 Shaun Campbell **W** PTS 6 Piccadilly
06.06.83 Peter Phillips **W** PTS 6 Piccadilly
03.10.83 Alex Brown DREW 6 Southend
12.10.83 Davey Cox L RTD 6 Evesham
Summary: 11 contests, won 6, drew 3, lost 2

Paul Mitchell

Leeds. *Born* Leeds 30.09.60
Central Area L. Middleweight Champion
Manager T. Callighan
Previous Amateur Club Market District

25.01.82 Dan Myers L PTS 4 Wolverhampton

16.02.82 Errol Dennis **W** PTS 6 Leeds
23.03.82 Dalton Jordan **W** PTS 6 Wolverhampton
29.03.82 Dave King **W** RSC 4 Piccadilly
26.05.82 Jimmy Ward **W** PTS 6 Piccadilly
13.09.82 Robbie Turner **W** PTS 6 Brighton
26.09.82 Dennis Sheehan **W** PTS 6 Birmingham
14.10.82 John Ridgman **W** PTS 6 Nantwich
09.11.82 Alan Power **W** PTS 6 Southend
02.12.82 Torben Andersen **L** PTS 6 Randers
17.02.83 Wayne Crolla **L** PTS 6 Morley
28.02.83 Mark Kelly **L** RTD 2 Strand
29.04.83 Ian Chantler **W** PTS 8 Liverpool
18.05.83 Martin Patrick **W** PTS 8 Bloomsbury
20.06.83 Blaine Longsden **L** RSC 8 Manchester
14.11.83 Dave Douglas **L** PTS 8 Glasgow
26.03.84 Rocky Feliciello **L** PTS 8 Barnsley
18.04.84 Wayne Crolla **W** PTS 8 Stoke
(Vacant Central Area L. Middleweight Title)

Summary: 18 contests, won 11, lost 7

Paul Mitchell
WRNS Pictures (Brian Worsnop) Ltd

Sylvester Mittee

Bethnal Green. *Born* St. Lucia 29.10.56
Former Undefeated Southern Area L. Welterweight Champion
Manager F. Warren
Previous Amateur Club Repton
National Honours Junior ABA Title 1973; NABC Title 1975; England Int.; GB Rep.; ABA Lightweight Champion 1976
Divisional Honours London L. Welterweight Champion 1977

25.10.77 Earl Noel **W** RSC 2 Kensington
15.11.77 Rocky Butler **W** CO 2 Bethnal Green
29.11.77 Barton McAllister **W** RTD 3 Bethnal Green
21.02.78 Sylvester Gordon **W** RSC 5 Kensington
05.12.78 Ray Ross **W** RSC 2 Kensington
09.04.79 Chris Davies **W** RSC 2 Mayfair
29.05.79 Carl Bailey **W** CO 1 Kensington
09.10.79 Tony Martey **W** PTS 8 Kensington
11.12.79 Mick Bell **W** RSC 2 Milton Keynes
22.01.80 Colin Power **W** RSC 7 Kensington
(Elim. British L. Welterweight Title)
22.04.80 Des Morrison **L** PTS 12 Kensington
(Final Elim. British L. Welterweight Title)
27.09.80 Derek Nelson **W** RSC 2 Wembley
26.11.80 Juan Antonio Merlo **W** PTS 8 Wembley
31.03.81 Clinton McKenzie **L** PTS 15 Wembley
(British L. Welterweight Title Challenge)
20.10.81 Gary Pearce **W** CO 3 Bethnal Green
20.04.82 Chris Sanigar **W** RSC 9 Kensington
(Southern Area L. Welterweight Title Challenge & Elim. British L. Welterweight Title)
07.12.83 Judas Clottey **L** RSC 3 Bloomsbury
28.01.84 Judas Clottey **W** RSC 2 Hanley
21.03.84 Jerome Artis **W** CO 2 Bloomsbury
12.05.84 Ken Releford **W** RSC 3 Hanley

Summary: 20 contests, won 17, lost 3

Sylvester Mittee
Derek Rowe (Photos) Ltd

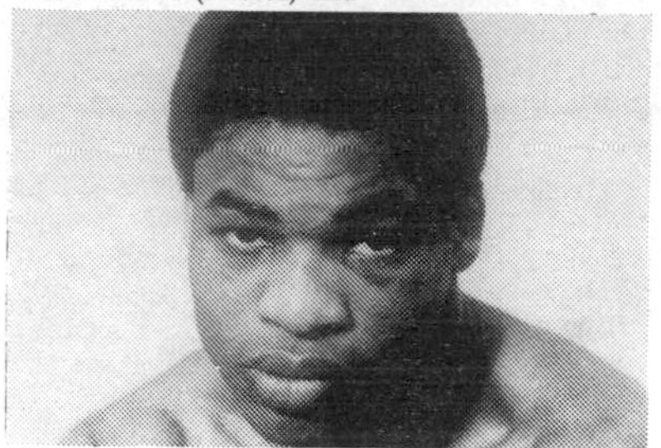

Tim Moloney

Brighton. *Born* Brighton 28.05.59
Welterweight
Manager R. Davies
Previous Amateur Club Newhaven & District
Divisional Honours S Counties Lightweight Champion 1978; S Counties L. Welterweight Champion 1979

17.09.79 Ray Price **W** PTS 4 Mayfair
08.10.79 Mike Clemow **W** PTS 6 Piccadilly
15.10.79 Wally Stockings **W** PTS 6 Mayfair
29.10.79 Tony Davis **W** PTS 4 Hove
03.12.79 Ray Price **W** PTS 6 Marylebone
28.01.80 Dave Laxen **W** PTS 6 Hove
03.03.80 Wally Stockings **W** PTS 6 Hove
17.03.80 Tony Davis **W** PTS 6 Mayfair
23.04.80 Danny Connolly **W** PTS 8 Hove
15.05.80 Jarvis Greenidge **W** PTS 6 Mayfair
27.05.80 Peter Harrison L PTS 8 Glasgow
03.06.80 Tommy Thomas **W** PTS 4 Aylesbury
20.10.80 Barry Price **W** PTS 8 Hove
12.01.81 Alan Cooper **W** PTS 8 Hove
16.02.81 Billy O'Grady DREW 8 Southwark
02.03.81 Duncan Hamilton **W** PTS 8 Brighton
01.06.81 Bobby Welburn **W** PTS 8 Piccadilly
09.09.81 Alan Lamb L RTD 7 Morecambe
29.10.81 Dennis Sullivan DREW 8 Walthamstow
19.11.81 Sylvester Gordon L RSC 2 Piccadilly
18.01.82 Jimmy Smith **W** PTS 8 Mayfair
04.02.82 Steve Tempro **W** PTS 8 Walthamstow
01.03.82 Peter Harrison **W** PTS 8 Piccadilly
08.03.82 Dave Allen DREW 8 Mayfair
21.04.82 Walter Clayton DREW 8 Brighton
06.12.83 Alex Brown **W** PTS 6 Southend
Summary: 26 contests, won 19, drew 4, lost 3

John Moody

Rayleigh. *Born* London 02.11.60
L. Heavyweight
Manager A. Kasler
Previous Amateur Club Bluehouse
National Honours England Int.
Divisional Honours E Counties Middleweight R/U 1979; E Counties Middleweight Champion 1980; E Counties L. Heavyweight Champion 1981

23.03.82 Dwight Osbourne **W** PTS 6 Bethnal Green
07.12.82 Ian Lazarus L RSC 2 Southend
07.02.83 Alan Ash **W** PTS 6 Brighton
28.02.83 Paul Newman **W** RSC 5 Strand
22.03.83 John Joseph **W** RSC 5 Bethnal Green
07.04.83 Jonjo Greene **W** PTS 6 Strand
26.04.83 Paul Shell **W** RTD 3 Bethnal Green
19.04.84 Paul Shell **W** CO 1 Basildon
31.05.84 Alex Romeo **W** RSC 3 Basildon
Summary: 9 contests, won 8, lost 1

Chris Moorcroft

Liverpool. *Born* Liverpool 26.06.56
Featherweight
Manager (Self)
Previous Amateur Club St. Philomena's

18.06.79 Jimmy Hancock **W** RSC 1 Manchester
20.09.79 Steve Enright L PTS 6 Liverpool
25.09.79 Stuart Crabb **W** PTS 6 Southend
31.10.79 John Cooper L CO 2 Southend
28.11.79 Kelvin Smart L PTS 6 Solihull
05.12.79 Steve Enright L PTS 6 Liverpool
10.12.79 Carl Gaynor **W** RSC 2 Manchester
16.01.80 Ian Murray L PTS 6 Liverpool
07.03.83 Andy Broughton L PTS 6 Liverpool
14.03.83 Vince Vahey L PTS 4 Sheffield
29.03.83 Stuart Carmichael DREW 6 Hull
11.04.83 Dave Pratt L RTD 4 Manchester
Summary: 12 contests, won 3, drew 1, lost 8

Colin Moorcroft

Liverpool. *Born* Liverpool 05.09.64
Flyweight
Manager (Self)
Previous Amateur Club Salisbury

07.03.83 Gary Roberts L CO 1 Liverpool
25.04.83 Howard Williams L RSC 3 Liverpool
Summary: 2 contests, lost 2

Davey Moore

Maidenhead. *Born* 11.01.64
L. Welterweight
Manager F. Turner
Previous Amateur Club Maidenhead
National Honours Young England Int.
Divisional Honours H Counties Lightweight Champion 1982–1983

03.02.84 Michael Betts **W** RSC 3 Maidenhead
Summary: 1 contest, won 1

Patsy Kid Moore (Moorehouse)

Perth. *Born* Perth 19.08.61
Middleweight
Manager D. Mahoney
Previous Amateur Club Perth Railways

17.03.81 Phil Williams **W** PTS 4 Wolverhampton
17.05.83 Mickey Williams L RSC 4 Piccadilly
Summary: 2 contests, won 1, lost 1

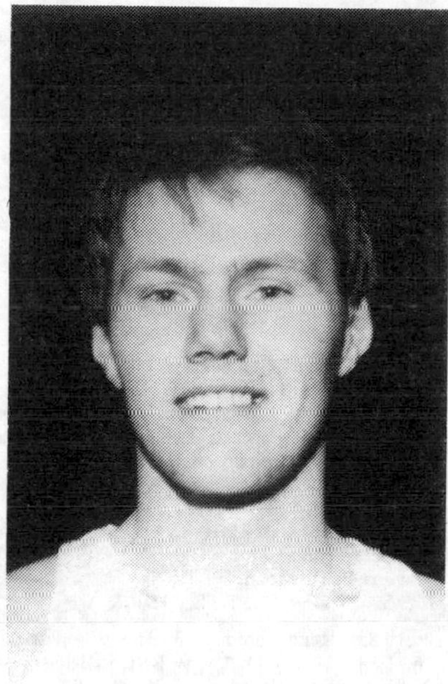

Davey Moore

Eddie Morgan

Corby. *Born* Kettering 26.06.63
Featherweight
Manager (Self)
Previous Amateur Club Corby Olympic

19.03.82 John Murphy **W** PTS 6 Nottingham
26.04.82 John Murphy L PTS 6 Glasgow
14.06.82 Shaun Shinkwin **W** PTS 6 Mayfair
05.10.82 Seamus McGuinness L PTS 6 Belfast
23.11.82 Michael Harris L PTS 6 Wolverhampton
06.12.82 Shaun Shinkwin DREW 6 Bristol
31.01.83 George Bailey **W** PTS 8 Birmingham
11.02.83 Gert Bo Jacobsen L RSC 3 Copenhagen
09.03.83 Shaun Shinkwin L PTS 6 Solihull
14.06.83 Tony Borg L PTS 6 Newport
05.09.83 John Sharkey L CO 3 Glasgow
Summary: 11 contests, won 3, drew 1, lost 7

Paul Morgan

Forest Hill. *Born* London 17.09.58
Middleweight
Manager (Self)
Previous Amateur Club Peckham

06.10.83 Gary Cable L RSC 3 Basildon
Summary: 1 contest, lost 1

Mick Morris

Wolverhampton. *Born* Jamaica 12.03.57
Middleweight
Manager M. Sendell
Previous Amateur Club Bilston GG

21.02.78 Martin McEwan **W** RSC 2 Wolverhampton
18.04.78 Dave Hunt **W** RSC 2 Wolverhampton
27.04.78 Richard Kenyon L CO 5 Doncaster
19.06.78 Richard Kenyon DREW 6 Manchester
18.09.78 Martin McEwan **W** CO 2 Wolverhampton
02.10.78 Clifton Wallace DREW 6 Nantwich
10.10.78 Romal Ambrose **W** RTD 2 Wolverhampton
30.10.78 Dave Merrell **W** RSC 4 Nottingham
15.11.78 Salvo Nuciforo L CO 7 Solihull
20.02.79 Steve Lewin L PTS 6 Kensington
26.02.79 Mike Copp **W** PTS 6 Edgbaston
05.03.79 Peter Gorny L PTS 6 Piccadilly
09.04.79 Keith Bussey L PTS 8 Mayfair
19.04.79 Les McAteer L PTS 8 Birkenhead
01.05.79 Jimmy Harrington DREW 6 Wembley
03.11.79 Eddie Burke L CO 2 Glasgow
21.02.80 Billy Hill L PTS 8 Liverpool
18.03.80 Clifton Wallace **W** PTS 6 Wolverhampton
01.04.80 Davey Armstrong L CO 1 Wembley
12.07.80 Jimmy Harrington **W** RTD 4 Wembley
16.10.80 Peter Bassey **W** PTS 8 Bolton
18.11.80 Steve Goodwin **W** PTS 8 Nantwich
16.01.81 Frank Winterstein L CO 2 Paris
16.03.81 Joe Jackson **W** PTS 6 Nottingham
06.11.81 Agamil Yilderin L PTS 6 Kiel
19.11.81 Billy Lauder **W** RSC 7 Piccadilly
27.11.81 Maurice Bufi L PTS 8 Brussels
01.02.82 Chris Coady **W** PTS 8 Manchester
09.02.82 Joe Jackson NC 3 Wolverhampton
18.02.82 Brian Anderson L PTS 8 Liverpool
09.04.82 Andre Mongelima L PTS 8 Luxembourg
28.04.82 Jimmy Ellis L CO 2 Sheffield
25.06.82 Tarmo Uusiverta L PTS 6 Hankoo
26.09.82 Barry Ahmed **W** PTS 8 Middlesbrough
07.10.82 Paul Tchoue L PTS 8 Paris

CONTINUED OVERLEAF

18.10.82 Billy Lauder W RTD 6 Glasgow
19.01.83 Earl Edwards W RSC 8 Birmingham
03.02.83 Keith James L PTS 8 Bloomsbury
16.02.83 Hendrik Seys W PTS 8 Hulste
23.02.83 Clive Beardsley W RSC 6 Chesterfield
00.03.83 Hendrik Seys W RTD 5 Hulste
28.03.83 Eddie Smith L CO 5 Manchester
19.05.83 Enrico Scacchia L PTS 8 Geneva
01.07.83 Jacques Chinon DREW 8 Paris
05.10.83 Gary Hobbs L RSC 7 Solihull
10.11.83 Enrico Scacchia L CO 2 Berne
24.02.84 Graciano Rocchigiani L PTS 4 Hamburg
27.03.84 Conrad Oscar W PTS 8 Battersea
07.05.84 Freddie Rafferty L PTS 8 Johannesburg
Summary: 49 contests, won 20, drew 4, lost 24, NC 1

(David) Taffy Morris

Darlington. *Born* Abergavenny 22.03.60
Welterweight
Manager T. Callighan
Previous Amateur Club Shildon

12.06.84 Grant Sutton W PTS 6 St Helens
Summary: 1 contest, won 1

Elvis Morton

Leicester. *Born* St. Kitts 09.01.62
Welterweight
Manager M. Inskip
Previous Amateur Club Granby

10.05.82 Errol Dennis L PTS 6 Birmingham
24.05.82 Davey Cox L PTS 6 Wolverhampton
21.06.82 Ian Chantler L RSC 3 Liverpool
05.10.82 Damien Fryers L PTS 6 Belfast
20.10.82 Dave Harrison L RSC 1 Stoke
10.11.82 Davey Cox DREW 6 Evesham
25.11.82 Gordon Pratt L PTS 6 Sunderland
06.12.82 Steve Tempro L PTS 6 Bristol
13.12.82 Davey Cox L PTS 6 Wolverhampton
26.01.83 Paul McHugh W PTS 4 Stoke
23.02.83 Andy Roberts L PTS 6 Chesterfield
28.02.83 Andy Letts W PTS 4 Birmingham
09.03.83 Dave Heaver L RSC 6 Stoke
16.04.83 Colin Neagle L PTS 6 Bristol
13.06.83 Rod Jones W PTS 6 Nottingham
20.06.83 Mike McKenzie DREW 6 Piccadilly
12.09.83 Spider Webb L PTS 6 Leicester
03.10.83 Tim Gladwish L RSC 3 Eltham
07.11.83 Phil Sheridan W PTS 6 Birmingham
22.11.83 Mike McKenzie W PTS 6 Wolverhampton
10.12.83 Colin Neagle L PTS 6 Swansea
14.02.84 Mark Hynes W PTS 6 Wolverhampton
22.02.84 Mark Hynes L RSC 1 Evesham
06.04.84 Danny Shinkwin W PTS 6 Watford
04.06.84 Malcolm Davies L PTS 6 Nottingham
15.06.84 Terry Culshaw L RSC 6 Liverpool
Summary: 26 contests, won 7, drew 2, lost 17

Dave Mowbray

Alfreton. *Born* Chesterfield 15.08.59
Middleweight
Manager W. Shinfield
Previous Amateur Club Alfreton

19.09.83 Mike Farghaly L PTS 6 Manchester
03.10.83 Joe Dean DREW 6 Bradford
10.10.83 Mickey Kidd L RSC 1 Birmingham
14.11.83 Mike Farghaly W RSC 1 Manchester
19.12.83 Winston Burnett L RSC 4 Bradford
30.01.84 Gypsy Carman L PTS 6 Manchester
13.02.84 Mike Farghaly L RSC 2 Manchester
Summary: 7 contests, won 1, drew 1, lost 5

(Gary) Peppy Muir

Belfast. *Born* Belfast 16.10.62
L. Welterweight
Manager B. Eastwood
Previous Amateur Club Ledley Hall & Army

05.10.83 Keith Foreman W PTS 6 Belfast
16.11.83 Mickey Duddy W RSC 2 Belfast
25.01.84 Kevin Pritchard L RTD 6 Belfast
Summary: 3 contests, won 2, lost 1

Doug Munro

Glasgow. *Born* Glasgow 17.02.65
L. Welterweight
Manager B. McEwan
Previous Amateur Club Carlton
National Honours Scottish Int.
Divisional Honours Scottish Lightweight R/U 1984

30.04.84 Hugh Sugar Kelly L CO 1 Glasgow
21.05.84 Dean Bramhald W PTS 6 Aberdeen
Summary: 2 contests, won 1, lost 1

John Murphy

Glasgow. *Born* Glasgow 15.03.62
Lightweight
Manager T. Gilmour
Previous Amateur Club Blantyre Miners
National Honours Scottish Int.

19.03.82 Eddie Morgan L PTS 6 Nottingham
19.04.82 Gordon Haigh W RSC 3 Glasgow
26.04.82 Eddie Morgan W PTS 6 Glasgow
20.09.82 Mike Bromby W CO 6 Glasgow
20.12.82 Bobby Welburn W PTS 6 Bradford
24.01.83 Jeff Decker L RSC 5 Glasgow
05.09.83 Craig Walsh W PTS 6 Glasgow
05.10.83 Kenny Jinks L RSC 2 Stoke
28.11.83 Edward Lloyd W PTS 8 Rhyl
23.01.84 Kevin Howard W PTS 8 Glasgow
Summary: 10 contests, won 7, lost 3

Ian Murray

Manchester. *Born* Manchester 23.05.51
Featherweight
Manager N. Basso
Previous Amateur Club Cavendish
Divisional Honours E Lancs Lightweight Champion 1972; E Lancs Featherweight Champion 1973; E Lancs Bantamweight Champion 1974 – 1975

11.06.75 Peter Scott **W** RSC 6 Bradford
22.09.75 Peter Scott **W** RSC 3 Manchester
10.11.75 John Chesters **W** PTS 6 Bradford
02.12.75 George Sutton L PTS 6 Piccadilly
05.01.76 George Sutton L CO 3 Piccadilly
28.01.76 John Chesters **W** PTS 6 Stoke
11.02.76 John Chesters **W** PTS 6 Bradford
21.09.76 Gary Davidson L RTD 5 Bethnal Green
15.11.76 Trevor Bromby **W** PTS 6 Nottingham
23.11.76 Johnny Owen L RSC 7 Treorchy
20.12.76 David Smith L PTS 6 Walworth
14.02.77 Jimmy Bott L PTS 6 Manchester
03.03.77 Jimmy Bott L PTS 6 Caister
30.03.77 Trevor Bromby **W** PTS 8 Barnsley
24.04.77 Paul Varden **W** PTS 6 Birmingham
10.05.77 Bryn Griffiths DREW 8 Merthyr
13.06.77 Jimmy Bott **W** PTS 6 Manchester
10.07.77 Paul Varden L PTS 6 Birmingham
21.09.77 Mohammed Younis L RSC 3 Solihull
12.04.78 Wally Angliss L PTS 8 Hammersmith
15.05.78 Dave Smith L PTS 8 Piccadilly
27.06.78 Neil McLaughlin L PTS 8 Derry
21.09.78 Steve Cleak L PTS 6 Caerphilly
09.10.78 Gary Nickels L PTS 6 Marylebone
23.10.78 Jimmy Bott **W** PTS 8 Manchester
04.12.78 Alan Storey DREW 4 Middlesbrough
18.01.79 Pip Coleman L RSC 8 Liverpool
18.06.79 Pip Coleman L PTS 8 Windsor
08.10.79 Steve Enright L PTS 6 Bradford
23.10.79 Steve Enright **W** PTS 6 Blackpool
10.12.79 Steve Enright L PTS 6 Manchester
16.01.80 Chris Moorcroft **W** PTS 6 Liverpool
22.01.80 Kelvin Smart L PTS 6 Caerphilly
14.03.80 Billy Straub L PTS 6 Glasgow
14.04.80 Billy Straub L PTS 8 Motherwell
12.05.80 Don George L RTD 7 Reading
13.10.80 Eddie Glass **W** PTS 6 Newcastle
13.11.80 Alec Irvine DREW 6 Caister
01.12.80 Mick Mason L PTS 8 Middlesbrough
26.01.81 Mick Mason L PTS 8 Gosforth
03.03.81 Steve Farnsworth L PTS 6 Pudsey
09.03.81 Carl Cleasby DREW 6 Bradford
23.03.81 Mark West L PTS 6 Mayfair
02.04.81 Ray Plant DREW 8 Middlesbrough
02.06.81 Paul Huggins L CO 2 Kensington
03.09.81 David Miles L PTS 8 Cardiff
02.11.81 Ray Plant L PTS 8 South Shields
23.11.81 Steve Farnsworth L PTS 10 Nantwich
(*Vacant Central Area Featherweight Title*)
08.02.82 Barry McGuigan L RSC 3 Mayfair
10.03.82 Steve Cleak **W** PTS 8 Birmingham
05.04.82 Jim Harvey L PTS 6 Glasgow
11.05.82 Steve Topliss L PTS 8 Derby
07.06.82 Brian Hyslop L PTS 8 Glasgow
28.06.82 Peter Gabbitus L PTS 6 Bradford
20.09.82 John Farrell L PTS 8 Bradford
26.09.82 Keith Foreman L PTS 6 Middlesbrough
18.10.82 John Farrell L PTS 8 Blackpool
15.11.82 Stuart Nicol L PTS 8 Glasgow
21.03.83 Stuart Carmichael L PTS 6 Mayfair
27.04.83 John Mwaimu **W** PTS 6 Stoke
25.05.83 Andy Cassidy **W** PTS 6 Rhyl
20.06.83 Steve Benny **W** PTS 6 Manchester
12.09.83 Stuart Carmichael **W** PTS 6 Leicester
19.10.83 Danny Knaggs L PTS 6 Hull
09.11.83 Trevor Sumner L RSC 5 Sheffield
12.12.83 Pat Doherty L RSC 4 Bedworth
05.03.84 Dave Bryan L PTS 6 Liverpool
09.04.84 Les Walsh **W** PTS 6 Manchester
30.04.84 Brian King DREW 6 Rhyl
11.06.84 Muhammad Lovelock L PTS 6 Manchester
18.06.84 Alex Cairney **W** PTS 6 Manchester
Summary: 71 contests, won 20, drew 6, lost 45

John Murray

Hull. *Born* Hull 13.08.60
Welterweight
Manager R. Tighe
Previous Amateur Club St. Pauls
Divisional Honours NE Counties Welterweight S/F 1983

25.05.83 Willie Wilson **W** PTS 6 Rhyl
13.03.84 Rocky Mensah L PTS 6 Hull
04.04.84 David Irving L RSC 3 Belfast
Summary: 3 contests, won 1, lost 2

(Ian) Kid Murray

Birmingham. *Born* Birmingham 05.12.59
Welterweight
Manager (Self)
Previous Amateur Club Sheldon Heath

06.06.79 Phil Lewis **W** PTS 6 Bedworth
14.06.79 Wally Stockings **W** PTS 6 Dudley
18.09.79 Steve Ward **W** PTS 6 Wolverhampton
26.09.79 Barry Price L PTS 8 Stoke
09.10.79 Tyrell Wilson **W** PTS 6 Wolverhampton
17.10.79 Jeff Pritchard L PTS 6 Evesham

CONTINUED OVERLEAF

14.11.79 Nigel Thomas L PTS 8 Stoke
21.11.79 Nigel Thomas L PTS 8 Evesham
27.11.79 Jimmy Smith W PTS 6 Wolverhampton
17.12.79 Dai Davies DREW 6 Wolverhampton
16.01.80 Jeff Aspell W PTS 8 Stoke
21.01.80 Dave Taylor W PTS 6 Wolverhampton
20.02.80 Johnny Burns W PTS 6 Evesham
10.03.80 Dave Taylor L PTS 6 Wolverhampton
18.03.80 Paul Wetter W PTS 6 Wolverhampton
26.03.80 Dennis Pryce L PTS 8 Evesham
21.04.80 Roy Varden L PTS 8 Edgbaston
29.05.80 Mickey Baker L PTS 6 Wolverhampton
11.06.80 Jeff Lee L PTS 8 Morecambe
12.08.80 Jeff Aspell L PTS 8 Gowertown
04.09.80 Dave Taylor W PTS 8 Morecambe
22.09.80 Jeff Lee L PTS 8 Lewisham
20.10.80 Jeff Aspell W RSC 5 Birmingham
13.11.80 Mike Clemow W PTS 8 Stafford
26.11.80 Tony Sinnott L PTS 8 Stoke
01.12.80 Cliff Gilpin L RTD 3 Wolverhampton
26.01.81 Adey Allen W PTS 8 Edgbaston
24.02.81 Colin Derrick L PTS 8 Kensington
16.03.81 Roger Guest W RSC 6 Nottingham
06.05.81 Dominic Bergonzi L RSC 8 Solihull
25.09.81 Vince Gajny L PTS 6 Nottingham
30.09.81 Vince Gajny L PTS 6 Evesham
12.10.81 Tommy McCallum W PTS 6 Birmingham
06.11.81 John Munduga L PTS 6 Kiel
23.11.81 Terry Marsh L PTS 6 Bloomsbury
21.12.81 Jimmy Smith W PTS 6 Birmingham
15.02.82 Charlie Malarkey L RTD 5 Glasgow
22.03.82 Peter Bennett L RSC 7 Birmingham
26.04.82 Roy Varden L PTS 6 Leicester
30.06.82 Ian Chantler L PTS 6 Liverpool
07.07.82 Paul Welch DREW 6 Newmarket
22.09.82 Lloyd Honeyghan L RSC 3 Mayfair
10.11.82 Dan Myers L PTS 6 Evesham
01.12.82 John Davies DREW 6 Stafford
06.12.82 John Davies L RSC 5 Edgbaston
28.01.83 Frank McCord W PTS 8 Swansea
08.02.83 Tony Adams L PTS 6 Kensington
15.02.83 Davey Cox W PTS 6 Wolverhampton
21.02.83 Gary Buckle L PTS 8 Nottingham
15.03.83 R. W. Smith L PTS 6 Wembley
08.04.83 Kostas Petrou L RTD 3 Liverpool

Summary: 51 contests, won 18, drew 3, lost 30

Paul Murray

Birmingham. *Born* Birmingham 08.01.61
L. Middleweight
Manager G. Donaghy
Previous Amateur Club Sheldon Heath

04.09.80 Gerry White W PTS 6 Morecambe
11.09.80 Graeme Ahmed L PTS 6 Hartlepool
29.09.80 Richard Wilson L PTS 6 Bedworth
08.10.80 Carl North W CO 2 Stoke
14.10.80 Steve McLeod W PTS 6 Wolverhampton
20.10.80 Steve Davies DREW 6 Birmingham
30.10.80 John Wiggins W PTS 6 Wolverhampton
07.11.80 Archie Salmon L PTS 6 Cambuslang
18.11.80 John Wiggins L PTS 6 Shrewsbury
26.11.80 Mike Clemow L PTS 8 Stoke
08.12.80 John Wiggins L PTS 6 Nottingham
26.01.81 Errol Dennis W PTS 6 Edgbaston
16.03.81 Dennis Sheehan DREW 6 Nottingham
15.04.81 Nigel Thomas DREW 8 Evesham
28.05.81 Martin McGough L PTS 6 Edgbaston
09.07.81 Roger Guest L CO 8 Dudley
21.09.81 Gary Buckle DREW 6 Wolverhampton
07.10.81 Kostas Petrou W RSC 5 Solihull
13.10.81 Gary Buckle L PTS 6 Wolverhampton
24.11.81 Nick Riozzi W PTS 6 Wolverhampton
25.01.82 Martin McGough L RSC 4 Wolverhampton
21.02.82 Gary Buckle W PTS 8 Nottingham
10.03.82 Ron Pearce L PTS 8 Solihull
23.03.82 Errol Dennis L PTS 6 Wolverhampton
29.03.82 Tony Brown L PTS 6 Liverpool
07.04.82 Dennis Sheehan W PTS 6 Evesham
28.04.82 Lee Roy W CO 3 Burslem
17.05.82 Paul Costigan L PTS 8 Manchester
24.05.82 Dennis Sheehan DREW 6 Nottingham
07.06.82 Kostas Petrou L PTS 6 Edgbaston
13.09.82 Paul Costigan W PTS 6 Manchester
18.10.82 Kostas Petrou L RSC 5 Edgbaston
15.02.83 Bert Myrie L PTS 6 Wolverhampton
21.02.83 Steve Tempro L DIS 3 Edgbaston
01.03.83 Chris Pyatt L RSC 2 Kensington
17.05.83 T. P. Jenkins L PTS 6 Bethnal Green
23.06.83 Wayne Hawkins L PTS 6 Wolverhampton
19.09.83 Bert Myrie W PTS 8 Nottingham
31.10.83 Steve Henty L PTS 6 Stoke
14.11.83 Kid Sadler L PTS 8 Manchester
14.12.83 John Andrews L PTS 6 Stoke
19.03.84 Wayne Barker L PTS 8 Manchester

27.03.84 Rocky Kelly L RTD 5 Battersea
Summary: 43 contests, won 12, drew 5, lost 26

Ray Murray

Manchester. *Born* Wythenshawe 21.01.55
Welterweight
Manager N. Basso
Previous Amateur Club Cavendish

08.09.75 Tommy Duffy L PTS 6 Glasgow
01.10.75 Tommy Duffy L PTS 6 Hamilton
15.10.75 Jimmy King L PTS 6 Birmingham
12.11.75 Tony Hudson L PTS 6 Bethnal Green
02.12.75 Barry White L PTS 6 Piccadilly
25.02.76 Von Reid L CO 2 Birmingham
31.01.77 Steve Laybourn L RSC 1 Bradford
05.12.83 Graeme Griffin L PTS 6 Manchester
12.12.83 Graeme Griffin L PTS 6 Bedworth
30.01.84 Tony Kempson W PTS 6 Manchester
13.02.84 Kevin Sanders W PTS 6 Manchester
29.02.84 Jimmy Thornton L PTS 6 Sheffield
05.03.84 Stan Atherton W PTS 6 Liverpool
12.03.84 Stan Atherton W PTS 6 Liverpool
30.04.84 Claude Rossi L PTS 6 Liverpool
12.06.84 Ian Chantler L RSC 2 St Helens
Summary: 16 contests, won 4, lost 12

John Mwaimu

Manchester. *Born* Tanzania 23.01.56
Bantamweight
Manager B. Robinson
Previous Amateur Club Bolton Lads

09.03.83 John Doherty L RSC 2 Stoke
27.04.83 Ian Murray L PTS 6 Stoke
05.09.83 Johnny Mack DREW 6 Liverpool
14.09.83 Graham Brett L PTS 6 Muswell Hill
05.10.83 Dave Boy McAuley DREW 6 Belfast
13.10.83 Tony Connolly L RSC 2 Bloomsbury
26.01.84 John Maloney L RSC 5 Strand
17.02.84 John Drummond L PTS 6 Rhyl
21.03.84 Allan Coveley L RSC 4 Bloomsbury
Summary: 9 contests, drew 2, lost 7

Dan Myers

Northampton. *Born* Northampton 05.10.59
Welterweight
Manager J. Cox
Previous Amateur Club Northampton

25.01.82 Paul Mitchell W PTS 4 Wolverhampton
15.03.82 Kevin Johnson W RSC 5 Wolverhampton
23.03.82 Lee Roy DREW 6 Nantwich
26.04.82 Cecil Williams DREW 6 Leicester
24.05.82 Dalton Jordan L RSC 5 Wolverhampton
04.09.82 Danny Shinkwin L PTS 6 Piccadilly
20.09.82 Neville Wilson L RSC 3 Wolverhampton
10.11.82 Kid Murray W PTS 6 Evesham
22.11.82 Sam Omidi W PTS 8 Lewisham
13.12.82 Gary Buckle L PTS 8 Wolverhampton
24.01.83 Gary Buckle L PTS 8 Mayfair
22.03.83 Lee Hartshorn L RSC 6 Wolverhampton
27.04.83 Paul Chance L PTS 8 Wolverhampton
23.06.83 Nipper Hartnett W RTD 2 Wolverhampton
20.09.83 Mark Hill W RSC 2 Dudley
12.10.83 Cornelius Chisholm L CO 6 Evesham
30.01.84 Dave Heaver W RSC 4 Birmingham
10.02.84 Johnny Burns W PTS 6 Dudley
16.02.84 Danny Sullivan L PTS 6 Basildon
22.03.84 Tony Rabbetts W PTS 6 Maidenhead
27.03.84 Alex Brown L PTS 6 Southend
Summary: 21 contests, won 9, drew 2, lost 10

Bert Myrie

Wolverhampton. *Born* Jamaica 21.05.56
L. Middleweight
Manager M. Sendell
Previous Amateur Club Wolverhampton

24.02.82 Noel Blair L PTS 6 Evesham
09.03.82 Jimmy Ward W RSC 3 Hornsey
23.03.82 John Andrews L CO 5 Nantwich
14.04.82 John Andrews L RSC 5 Strand
07.06.82 Graham Brockway W PTS 6 Piccadilly
21.06.82 Blaine Longsden L CO 3 Liverpool
07.09.82 Martin Patrick L PTS 6 Hornsey
13.09.82 John Ridgman L RSC 5 Sheffield
19.10.82 Jack Carswell W RSC 3 Wolverhampton
26.10.82 Gary Petty W CO 1 Hull
10.11.82 John Davies L RSC 1 Evesham
06.12.82 Peter Stockdale W CO 1 Nottingham
15.12.82 Alan Hardiman L RSC 4 Queensway
26.01.83 Dennis Sheehan L RSC 5 Stoke (*Vacant Midlands Area L. Middleweight Title*)
15.02.83 Paul Murray W PTS 6 Wolverhampton
04.03.83 Rocky Feliciello L PTS 6 Queensferry
25.03.83 Gary Knight L PTS 8 Bloomsbury
07.04.83 Sylvester Gordon W RSC 1 Strand
25.04.83 Rocky Kelly L CO 4 Acton

CONTINUED OVERLEAF

25.05.83 Wayne Crolla L PTS 8 Rhyl
20.06.83 Wayne Crolla L PTS 8 Manchester
19.09.83 Paul Murray L PTS 8 Nottingham
24.10.83 Mickey Kidd L PTS 6 Nottingham
09.11.83 John Hargin DREW 4 Evesham
19.12.83 John McGlynn L RSC 4 Swansea
Summary: 25 contests, won 7, drew 1, lost 17

Colin Neagle

Merthyr. *Born* Merthyr 18.02.59
Welterweight
Manager D. James
Previous Amateur Club Hoover

07.06.82 John McGlynn L CO 3 Swansea
23.09.82 Mark Crouch DREW 6 Wimbledon
26.10.82 Jonathan Newall **W** PTS 6 Newport
06.12.82 Peter Ahmed L RSC 2 Bristol
07.02.83 Lou Penfold **W** RSC 3 Marylebone
23.02.83 Mark Crouch **W** PTS 6 Mayfair
16.03.83 Andy Roberts **W** PTS 6 Stoke
16.04.83 Elvis Morton **W** PTS 6 Bristol
25.04.83 Mike Calderwood **W** PTS 6 Liverpool
17.05.83 Steve Watt L PTS 8 Piccadilly
23.06.83 Andy O'Rawe L RSC 4 Bethnal Green
15.10.83 Steve Tempro L PTS 6 Coventry
02.11.83 Billy Edwards DREW 6 Bloomsbury
29.11.83 Michael Harris L PTS 8 Cardiff
10.12.83 Elvis Morton **W** PTS 6 Swansea
25.01.84 David Irving L RSC 1 Belfast
28.03.84 Michael Harris L PTS 6 Aberavon
19.05.84 Danny Shinkwin **W** PTS 6 Bristol
Summary: 18 contests, won 8, drew 2, lost 8

Peter Neal

Abingdon. *Born* Abingdon 21.04.54
Former Undefeated Southern Area Welterweight Champion
Manager (Self)
Previous Amateur Club Abingdon
Divisional Honours H Counties L. Welterweight Champion 1974 – 1975

01.03.76 Mike Copp **W** RSC 6 Piccadilly
29.03.76 Mick Hampston DREW 6 Walworth
05.04.76 Johnny Pincham L PTS 6 Mayfair
29.09.76 Barry Price L PTS 6 Hammersmith
25.01.77 Tommy Davitt L PTS 6 Piccadilly
16.03.77 Steve Laybourn **W** CO 2 Solihull
21.03.77 George Kidd **W** PTS 6 Piccadilly
02.05.77 Tommy Joyce **W** CO 3 Walworth
23.05.77 Dave Proud L PTS 8 Walworth
11.10.77 Horace McKenzie DREW 8 Marylebone
14.11.77 Johnny Elliott **W** PTS 8 Reading
12.12.77 Johnny Pincham **W** PTS 12 Walworth
(*Vacant Southern Area Welterweight Title*)
31.01.78 Terry Petersen **W** PTS 8 Marylebone
22.03.78 Steve Angell **W** PTS 10 Mayfair
(*Southern Area Welterweight Title Defence*)
05.05.78 Marijan Benes L RSC 5 Frankfurt
28.02.79 Chris Walker **W** CO 8 Harrogate
23.04.79 Roy Commosioung **W** PTS 8 Reading
03.10.79 Henry Rhiney **W** PTS 12 Reading
(*Southern Area Welterweight Title Defence*)
01.07.80 Gary Pearce **W** PTS 8 Swindon
12.08.80 Colin Jones L RSC 5 Swansea
(*British Welterweight Title Challenge*)
04.12.80 Hans Henrik Palm L PTS 8 Randers
07.02.81 Fred Coranson L PTS 8 Dunkirk
08.04.81 Carlos Santos L PTS 8 Milan
09.06.82 Tony Britton **W** PTS 8 Bristol
18.10.82 Sid Smith L RSC 6 Southwark
(*Vacant Southern Area Welterweight Title*)
12.03.83 Billy Waith **W** PTS 8 Swindon
Summary: 26 contests, won 14, drew 2, lost 10

Martin Nee

Paddington. *Born* Galway 19.07.52
Heavyweight
Manager L. Lake
Previous Amaterur Club Stone Boys

28.02.77 Brian Paul L RSC 2 Mayfair
24.10.77 Jim Evans DREW 4 Hammersmith
10.11.77 John Clarke **W** RSC 4 Wimbledon
19.01.78 Alan Ward **W** PTS 4 Wimbledon
03.04.78 Bob Young L PTS 6 Piccadilly
24.04.78 George Gray **W** PTS 3 Barnsley
19.09.78 Bob Young **W** PTS 6 Southend
23.11.78 Bob Young L PTS 6 Wimbledon
01.12.78 Gordon Ferris L CO 4 Enniskillen
16.10.79 Kenny March L PTS 6 Lewisham
13.12.79 Colin Flute L PTS 6 Wimbledon
18.02.80 Ron McLean **W** CO 3 Lewisham
06.03.80 Les Dunn **W** PTS 6 Wimbledon
29.05.80 Ron McLean **W** PTS 8 Wimbledon
13.11.80 Derek Simpkin **W** PTS 8 Queensway
01.12.80 Derek Simpkin **W** PTS 6 Bloomsbury
19.01.81 Steve Gee **W** RSC 5 Wimbledon
17.02.81 Mel Christle L RSC 4 Lewisham
06.04.81 Bob Hennessey L RSC 2 Windsor
28.05.81 Denton Ruddock DREW 8 Wimbledon
05.08.81 Tony Moore L PTS 8 Norwich
26.01.82 Mick Chmilowskyj **W** RSC 1 Hornsey
09.03.82 Steve Gee L PTS 8 Hornsey
05.04.82 Joe Christle L RSC 1 Bloomsbury
02.11.82 Steve Gee L RSC 5 Hornsey

26.01.84 Rocky Burton L RSC 3 Strand
Summary: 26 contests, won 11, drew 2, lost 13

Eddie Neilson

Swindon. *Born* Birmingham 30.06.50
Heavyweight
Manager M. Williams
Previous Amateur Club Swindon BR
Divisional Honours W Counties Heavyweight Champion 1972

15.05.72 Sid Paddock W CO 2 Reading
22.05.72 Paul Cassidy W RSC 3 Piccadilly
06.06.72 Billy Wynter W PTS 6 Kensington
12.09.72 Bob French W RTD 1 Shoreditch
25.09.72 Shaun Dolan W RSC 2 Piccadilly
10.10.72 Joe Lewis W CO 2 Kensington
27.11.72 Dennis Avoth W PTS 8 Piccadilly
08.01.73 Lloyd Walford W RSC 4 Piccadilly
05.02.73 Brian Jewitt L RSC 2 Piccadilly
26.03.73 Woody Vuckovic W RTD 5 Bristol
30.04.73 Dennis Avoth W PTS 8 Piccadilly
05.06.73 Dave Hallinan W CO 2 Piccadilly
09.07.73 Joe Batten L CO 2 Mayfair
05.10.73 Roger Barlow W RSC 2 Cardiff
03.12.73 Vasco Fausthino L RSC 2 Bristol
11.02.74 Peter Freeman W RSC 4 Piccadilly
01.04.74 Tim Wood W CO 7 Piccadilly
23.04.74 Peter Freeman W CO 3 Kensington
06.05.74 Lloyd Walford W CO 4 Piccadilly
21.05.74 Dave Roden W RSC 2 Wembley
17.06.74 Pietro Zanola W RSC 2 Piccadilly
24.09.74 Vasco Fausthino W RTD 3 Reading
18.11.74 Paul Nilsen W RSC 3 Reading
15.12.74 Obie English W PTS 8 Piccadilly
06.01.75 Ngozika Ekwelum L RSC 2 Piccadilly
03.06.75 Mike Boswell W RSC 3 Kensington
04.08.75 John L. Johnson W PTS 8 Miami
25.11.75 Eddie Fenton W RTD 3 Kensington
12.12.77 P. T. Grant W RSC 3 Birmingham
22.11.78 Terry O'Connor W RSC 3 Stoke
27.02.79 Ishaq Hussien L RTD 5 Southend
16.02.82 Derek Simpkin W RSC 3 Bristol
19.04.82 Larry McDonald W CO 3 Bristol
09.06.82 Denton Ruddock W RSC 4 Bristol
09.12.82 Joe Bugner L RSC 5 Bloomsbury
05.04.83 Frank Bruno L RSC 3 Kensington
31.05.83 Rudi Pika L RSC 7 Kensington
Summary: 37 contests, won 29, lost 8

Derek Nelson

Sunderland. *Born* Sunderland 16.09.58
Welterweight
Manager (Self)
Previous Amateur Club Sunderland

23.03.78 Jim Fenwick W RSC 1 Sunderland
17.04.78 Peter Snowshall L PTS 6 Piccadilly
24.04.78 Norman Morton DREW 4 Middlesbrough
23.05.78 Peter Snowshall W PTS 6 Islington
12.07.78 Norman Morton L PTS 6 Newcastle
09.10.78 Selvin Bell W PTS 6 Middlesbrough
30.10.78 Roger Guest L PTS 6 Nottingham
27.11.78 Liam Linnen W PTS 6 Govan
04.12.78 Brendan O'Donnell W CO 4 Middlesbrough
15.01.79 Ian Pickersgill W PTS 6 Nottingham
26.02.79 Dai Davies L PTS 8 Middlesbrough
17.04.79 Liam Linnen W RSC 5 Glasgow
16.05.79 Dave Allen DREW 8 Sheffield
21.05.79 Dave Allen L PTS 6 Birmingham
18.06.79 Tony Bogle W PTS 8 Bradford
03.09.79 Dave Douglas W PTS 8 Glasgow
21.09.79 Andre Bayern W PTS 6 Zele
08.10.79 George Schofield W PTS 8 Bradford
22.10.79 Roger Guest L PTS 8 Piccadilly
31.10.79 Phil Lewis W CO 1 Burslem
19.11.79 Eric Purkiss L PTS 8 Piccadilly
24.01.80 Martin Bridge W CO 4 Hartlepool
04.02.80 Gary Pearce L PTS 8 Piccadilly
03.03.80 Kevin Quinn W PTS 8 Marton
27.03.80 Lee Hartshorn L PTS 8 Newcastle
31.05.80 Tony Carroll L PTS 8 Liverpool
23.06.80 Dave McCabe L PTS 8 Glasgow
27.09.80 Sylvester Mittee L RSC 2 Wembley
09.03.81 George Peacock L RSC 7 Hamilton
09.11.81 Gary Petty W PTS 8 Newcastle
25.11.81 Johnny Burns W PTS 6 Stoke
01.02.82 Peter Stockdale W RSC 6 Newcastle
29.03.82 Dave Allen W DIS 3 Piccadilly
25.11.82 John Lindo W RSC 4 Sunderland
24.10.83 Tony Laing L RSC 3 Mayfair
Summary: 35 contests, won 19, drew 2, lost 14

Lou Nelson

Stoke. *Born* Burton-on-Trent 11.07.60
Heavyweight
Manager F. Deakin
Previous Amateur Club Stoke-on-Trent

28.01.84 Ian Priest L RSC 3 Hanley
06.03.84 Ian Priest L CO 1 Stoke
Summary: 2 contests, lost 2

Paul Newman

Bognor Regis. *Born* Rustington 11.01.59
L. Heavyweight
Manager R. Davies
Previous Amateur Club Bognor Regis

28.01.80 Harry Pompey Allen W CO 2 Hove
03.03.80 John O'Neill DREW 6 Hove
19.05.80 John O'Neill L RSC 5 Mayfair
29.09.80 Chris Devine L RSC 6 Chesterfield
20.10.80 Gordon Stacey L RTD 1 Hove
19.01.81 Lee White L RTD 2 Wimbledon
23.03.81 Pharoah Bish W PTS 6 Mayfair
27.04.81 Glenroy Taylor W PTS 6 Brighton

CONTINUED OVERLEAF

11.05.81 Billy Warner **W** RSC 2 Copthorne
28.05.81 Lee White **W** PTS 8 Wimbledon
03.08.81 Gordon Stacey **L** RSC 6 Brighton
22.09.81 Trevor Kerr **L** RSC 7 Belfast
19.10.81 Clint Jones **W** PTS 8 Mayfair
26.10.81 Frank McCullagh **L** PTS 6 Belfast
08.12.81 Keith Bristol **L** RSC 1 Belfast
04.02.82 Paul Busette **L** PTS 8 Walthamstow
23.03.82 Frank McCullagh **L** PTS 6 Belfast
21.04.82 Lee White **W** PTS 6 Brighton
24.01.83 Geoff Rymer **W** PTS 6 Piccadilly
28.02.83 John Moody **L** RSC 5 Strand
06.04.83 Alan Ash **W** PTS 6 Mayfair
19.05.83 Alan Ash **L** RSC 5 Queensway
21.09.83 Geoff Rymer **L** PTS 8 Southend
07.03.84 Lee White **W** PTS 8 Brighton
27.03.84 Geoff Rymer **W** RSC 4 Southend
01.05.84 Geoff Rymer **L** RSC 4 Maidstone
Summary: 26 contests, won 11, drew 1, lost 14

Gary Nickels

Paddington. *Born* London 20.06.58
Featherweight
Manager T. Lawless
Previous Amateur Club Repton
National Honours Junior ABA Title 1975; NABC Title 1975; Young England Rep.; England Int.; ABA Flyweight Champion 1978
Divisional Honours H Counties Flyweight Champion 1976 – 1977

09.10.78 Ian Murray **W** PTS 6 Marylebone
24.10.78 Alec Irvine **W** PTS 6 Kensington
11.11.78 Terry Hanna **W** RSC 3 Marylebone
05.12.78 Pip Coleman **W** PTS 6 Kensington
13.02.79 John Cooper **W** PTS 8 Marylebone
19.03.79 Gary Ball DREW 8 Marylebone
25.09.79 Paul Keers **L** PTS 6 Wembley
04.03.80 Mike Pickett **W** PTS 6 Wembley

Gary Nickels
Derek Rowe (Photos) Ltd

22.04.80 Brindley Jones **W** PTS 6 Kensington
14.10.80 Billy Straub **W** PTS 8 Kensington
18.11.80 Jimmy Bott **W** PTS 8 Bethnal Green
08.12.80 Jimmy Bott **W** PTS 8 Kensington
03.03.81 George Bailey **W** RTD 6 Wembley
31.03.81 Neil McLaughlin **W** RTD 7 Wembley
19.11.81 Dave George **L** RSC 1 Ebbw Vale (*Final Elim. British Flyweight Title*)
25.01.82 Andy King **W** PTS 8 Mayfair
18.05.82 Mark West **L** PTS 8 Bethnal Green
12.12.83 Dave Pratt **L** PTS 8 Birmingham
03.02.84 Stuart Carmichael **W** PTS 8 Maidenhead
01.05.84 Stuart Carmichael **W** RSC 5 Bethnal Green
07.06.84 John Doherty **L** PTS 8 Piccadilly
Summary: 21 contests, won 15, drew 1, lost 5

Stuart Nicol

Cambuslang. *Born* Glasgow 18.10.61
Featherweight
Manager T. Gilmour
Previous Amateur Club Hoover
National Honours Scottish Int.

30.03.81 Gordon Haigh **L** PTS 6 Glasgow
13.04.81 Gordon Haigh **W** PTS 6 Glasgow
01.06.81 Paddy Maguire **W** RSC 3 Nottingham
11.06.81 Gordon Haigh **W** RSC 5 Hull
14.09.81 Andy King **W** RSC 2 Glasgow
09.10.81 George Bailey **W** RSC 5 Cambuslang
19.10.81 Steve Enright **W** PTS 8 Glasgow
23.11.81 Neil McLaughlin DREW 8 Glasgow
07.12.81 George Bailey **L** PTS 8 Nottingham
08.02.82 Hugh Russell **L** RSC 3 Mayfair
25.03.82 Rocky Bantleman **L** RSC 4 Glasgow
07.06.82 Jim Harvey **L** RSC 2 Glasgow
19.10.82 George Bailey **L** PTS 6 Wolverhampton
15.11.82 Ian Murray **W** PTS 8 Glasgow
07.02.83 Rocky Bantleman **L** RSC 3 Piccadilly
Summary: 15 contests, won 7, drew 1, lost 7

Horace Notice

Birmingham. *Born* West Bromwich 07.08.57
Heavyweight
Manager T. Lawless
Previous Amateur Club Nechells
National Honours ABA Heavyweight Champion 1983; England Int.
Divisional Honours ABA Heavyweight R/U 1982

24.10.83 Andrew Gerrard **W** PTS 6 Mayfair
30.11.83 Theo Josephs **W** CO 1 Piccadilly
27.04.84 Andrew Gerrard **W** RSC 2 Wolverhampton
Summary: 3 contests, won 3

Horace Notice
Gloucester Photo Agency

Dennis Boy O'Brien

Acton. *Born* Southall 15.05.64
L. Middleweight
Manager H. Holland
Previous Amateur Club Hogarth
Divisional Honours SW London L. Middleweight R/U 1983

08.09.83 Kevin Webb W CO 4 Queensway
23.09.83 Tony Baker W RSC 1 Longford
09.11.83 Bobby Rimmer W RSC 1 Southend
01.12.83 Nigel Pearce W RSC 3 Basildon
27.01.84 Phil O'Hare L PTS 6 Longford
06.02.84 Tony Kempson W RSC 5 Mayfair
27.03.84 Phil O'Hare L PTS 8 Battersea
Summary: 7 contests, won 5, lost 2

Terry O'Connor

Birmingham. *Born* Birmingham 07.07.53
Former Midlands Area Heavyweight Champion
Manager R. Gray
Previous Amateur Club Rum Runner
Divisional Honours M Counties Heavyweight R/U 1975

10.03.76 Barry Clough W PTS 6 Wolverhampton
17.03.76 Art Gibson W PTS 6 Solihull
29.03.76 Kenny Burrell W PTS 6 Mayfair
12.04.76 Kenny Burrell W PTS 6 Birmingham
26.05.76 Art Gibson W PTS 6 Wolverhampton
28.06.76 John Depledge W RSC 6 Luton
14.07.76 Alan Ward W RSC 2 Wolverhampton
29.08.76 Keith Johnson W PTS 6 Solihull
10.09.76 Brian Huckfield L PTS 8 Digbeth
27.10.76 Steve Carr W PTS 8 Wolverhampton
22.11.76 Kenny Burrell W PTS 6 Birmingham
20.12.76 Kris Smith L PTS 8 Walworth
10.02.77 Eddie Fenton W PTS 8 Coventry
08.03.77 George Gray W PTS 8 Wolverhampton
07.04.77 Danny McAlinden L RSC 1 Dudley
19.09.77 Les Stevens L PTS 8 Mayfair
30.09.77 George Butzbach L PTS 8 Hamburg
06.10.77 Bruce Grandham L RTD 4 Liverpool
06.12.77 Stan McDermott L RSC 5 Kensington
21.04.78 Gordon Ferris L PTS 8 Enniskillen
29.06.78 Colin Flute W PTS 8 Wolverhampton
12.07.78 George Scott DREW 8 Newcastle
07.09.78 Jimmy Abbott L PTS 8 Cape Town
06.11.78 Brian Huckfield L PTS 10 Stafford (*Vacant Midlands Area Heavyweight Title*)
22.11.78 Eddie Neilson L RSC 3 Stoke
17.01.79 Winston Allen W PTS 8 Solihull
10.02.79 Benito Eschriche W PTS 6 Zaragosa
05.03.79 Ishaq Hussien W PTS 6 Wolverhampton
06.04.79 Des Snoek W PTS 6 Brussels
17.05.79 Bob Hennessey L DIS 6 Wimbledon
30.05.79 Tommy Blythe W PTS 6 Oslo
10.11.79 Hennie Thoonen L PTS 8 Wimbledon
13.12.79 Tommy Kiely L PTS 8 Wimbledon
05.02.80 Larry McDonald L PTS 8 Wolverhampton
31.03.80 Rudi Lubbers L PTS 8 Rotterdam
02.07.80 Louis Hendricks DREW 8 Welkom
29.09.80 Rocky Burton W RSC 6 Bedworth (*Vacant Midlands Area Heavyweight Title*)
11.10.80 Felipe Rodriguez L PTS 8 Pontevedne
19.04.81 Mary Konate L RSC 2 Paris
01.07.81 Louis Acosta W PTS 8 Milan
25.09.81 Ricky James L PTS 10 Nottingham (*Midlands Area Heavyweight Title Defence*)
24.10.81 Alfredo Evangelista DREW 8 Madrid
14.11.81 Bennie Knoetze L RTD 5 Johannesburg
11.02.83 Anders Eklund L PTS 4 Copenhagen
Summary: 44 contests, won 20, drew 3, lost 21

Phil O'Hare

Manchester. *Born* Fallowfield 04.02.64
L. Middleweight
Manager B. Robinson
Previous Amateur Club Manchester YMCA

02.07.81 Sam Church L PTS 4 Pudsey
16.09.81 Dave Harrison L PTS 4 Burslem
21.09.81 Ken Rathburn L PTS 4 Manchester
19.10.81 Ken Rathburn W PTS 6 Manchester
01.02.82 Wayne Crolla L PTS 6 Manchester
09.03.82 Wayne Crolla L PTS 6 Farnsworth
23.03.82 Rocky Severino L PTS 6 Nantwich
28.04.82 Rocky Severino L PTS 6 Burslem
21.05.82 Tommy Bennett L PTS 6 Sheffield
07.06.82 Wayne Crolla L PTS 6 Sheffield
24.06.82 Charlie Douglas L PTS 6 Kirkby
07.09.82 Dave Harrison DREW 6 Crewe
13.09.82 Jim Kelly W CO 5 Glasgow
22.09.82 Dave Harrison W PTS 6 Stoke
11.10.82 Alf Edwardes W PTS 6 Manchester
26.11.82 Jim Kelly W PTS 6 Glasgow
19.01.83 Alan Hardiman W PTS 6 Stoke
28.02.83 Gary Pearce L PTS 6 Strand
09.03.83 Mark Kelly DREW 6 Stoke
28.03.83 Mark Kelly W PTS 6 Manchester
07.04.83 Mick Courtney L PTS 8 Strand
16.05.83 Mark Kelly W RTD 4 Manchester
26.09.83 Billy Bryce L PTS 8 Manchester
03.10.83 Mick Dono W PTS 6 Liverpool
17.10.83 Arthur Davis L CO 2 Southwark
05.12.83 John Andrews L CO 2 Manchester
27.01.84 Dennis Boy O'Brien W PTS 6 Longford
01.02.84 Martin Patrick L PTS 8 Bloomsbury
27.03.84 Dennis Boy O'Brien W PTS 8 Battersea
25.04.84 Martin Patrick L PTS 8 Muswell Hill
15.06.84 Joey Frost L CO 6 Liverpool
Summary: 31 contests, won 11, drew 2, lost 18

(Saled) Sam Omidi

Plymouth. *Born* Iran 22.11.59
Welterweight
Manager (Self)
Previous Amateur Club Mayflower

09.06.81 Tyrell Wilson DREW 6 Newport
09.09.81 Jimmy Woods DREW 6 Morecambe
20.10.81 Delroy Pearce W PTS 6 Plymouth
29.10.81 Lee McKenzie L PTS 6 Walthamstow
16.11.81 Gerry Beard L PTS 6 Liverpool
04.02.82 Jimmy Ward L PTS 6 Walthamstow
19.02.82 Alan Power L RSC 3 Bloomsbury
22.03.82 Dai Davies W PTS 6 Swansea
29.03.82 Winston McKenzie DREW 6 Copthorne
19.04.82 Peter Ahmed W CO 1 Bristol
05.05.82 Tony Laing L RSC 1 Solihull
07.09.82 John Bibby L PTS 6 Hornsey
28.09.82 Charlie Douglas L PTS 8 Aberdeen
11.10.82 Delroy Pearce L CO 4 Bristol
16.11.82 John Bibby L PTS 6 Bethnal Green
22.11.82 Dan Myers L PTS 8 Lewisham
08.04.83 Tony Sinnott L PTS 8 Liverpool
26.04.83 Gunther Roomes L RSC 3 Bethnal Green
22.05.83 Damien Fryers L PTS 6 Navan
09.11.83 Gary Knight L PTS 6 Southend
21.11.83 George Kerr L PTS 8 Glasgow
13.02.84 Tim Gladwish L RSC 6 Eltham
Summary: 22 contests, won 3, drew 3, lost 16

(Mike) Chip O'Neill

Sunderland. *Born* Sunderland 10.12.63
Flyweight
Manager T. Cumiskey
Previous Amateur Club Sunderland
National Honours Young England Rep.
Divisional Honours NE Counties Flyweight Champion 1981; NE Counties Bantamweight S/F 1982

28.06.82 Charlie Brown L PTS 6 Bradford
20.09.82 Danny Flynn L RSC 2 Glasgow
07.03.83 Charlie Brown L RSC 3 Glasgow
Summary: 3 contests, lost 3

Andy O'Rawe

Canvey Island. *Born* Ilford 08.09.63
L. Welterweight
Manager F. Warren
Previous Amateur Club Canvey Island
National Honours Junior ABA Title 1980; Young England Rep.
Divisional Honours E Counties Lightweight Champion 1982

01.02.83 Michael Betts W PTS 4 Southend
01.03.83 Tyrell Wilson W PTS 6 Southend

Andy O'Rawe
Douglas Baton

16.03.83 Tyrell Wilson **W** PTS 6 Cheltenham
10.05.83 Danny Williams **W** PTS 6 Southend
23.06.83 Colin Neagle **W** RSC 4 Bethnal Green
13.10.83 Mick Harkin **L** PTS 6 Bloomsbury
09.11.83 Davey Cox **W** PTS 6 Southend
07.12.83 Mick Harkin **W** PTS 6 Bloomsbury
12.06.84 Mark Mills **L** PTS 6 Southend
Summary: 9 contests, won 7, lost 2

Dwight Osbourne

Hammersmith. *Born* London 27.01.57
L. Heavyweight
Manager A. Pompey
Previous Amateur Club Fitzroy Lodge

22.09.81 Frank McCullagh **L** RSC 2 Belfast
08.11.81 Terry Christle **L** CO 5 Navan
23.03.82 John Moody **L** PTS 6 Bethnal Green
14.04.82 Steve Johnson **L** PTS 6 Strand
22.11.82 Prince Wilmot **W** RSC 5 Lewisham
21.03.83 Alan Douglas **L** RTD 2 Bradford
25.04.83 Billy Cassidy **DREW** 6 Southwark
Summary: 7 contests, won 1, drew 1, lost 5

Conrad Oscar

Lewisham. *Born* Domenica 25.04.60
Middleweight
Manager H. Holland
Previous Amateur Club Polytechnic
Divisional Honours NW London L. Middleweight Champion 1980

16.02.82 Mohammed Ben **W** RSC 2 Lewisham
22.03.82 Deano Wallace **DREW** 6 Southwark
26.04.82 Jack Sharp **W** PTS 6 Southwark
15.12.82 Gary Hobbs **L** PTS 8 Queensway
28.02.83 Keith James **W** PTS 8 Strand
07.04.83 Keith James **L** PTS 8 Strand
25.04.83 T. P. Jenkins **L** PTS 8 Southwark
27.03.84 Mick Morris **L** PTS 8 Battersea
Summary: 8 contests, won 3, drew 1, lost 4

Paul Owen

Rhyl. *Born* Preston 15.03.62
Featherweight
Manager B. Lloyd
Previous Amateur Club Rhyl Star
Divisional Honours E Lancs Bantamweight Champion 1980; E Lancs Featherweight R/U 1981

16.09.83 Alex Cairney **W** PTS 6 Rhyl
15.06.84 Andy De Abreu **L** RSC 5 Rhyl
Summary: 2 contests, won 1, lost 1

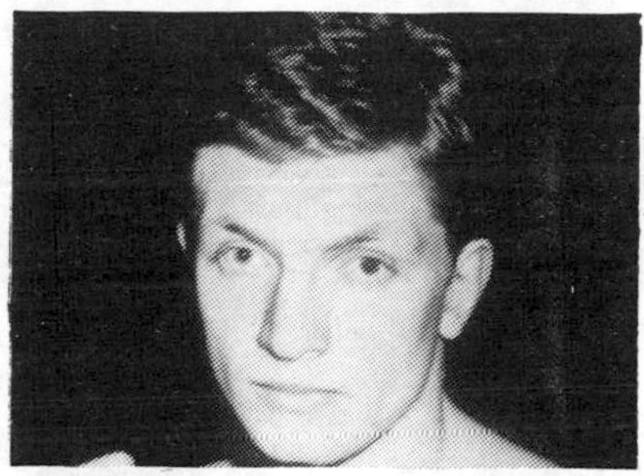

Martin Patrick
Gloucester Photo Agency

Jim Paton

Paisley. *Born* Paisley 12.09.62
L. Welterweight
Manager T. Gilmour
Previous Amateur Club Paisley

26.11.82 Ron Shinkwin **W** PTS 4 Glasgow
16.03.83 Clinton Campbell **W** PTS 6 Stoke
21.04.83 Frankie Lake **W** PTS 8 Piccadilly
19.05.83 Alan Storey **L** PTS 6 Sunderland
12.06.83 Alan Storey **W** PTS 6 Middlesbrough
20.06.83 Michael Harris **L** PTS 8 Piccadilly
16.09.83 Edward Lloyd **W** PTS 6 Rhyl
Summary: 7 contests, won 5, lost 2

Martin Patrick

Tottenham. *Born* London 17.10.60
L. Middleweight
Manager F. Warren
Previous Amateur Club New Enterprise
National Honours Young England Rep.
Divisional Honours NW London Welterweight R/U 1980; NW London L. Middleweight Champion 1981; ABA L. Middleweight R/U 1982

22.06.82 Neville Wilson **W** PTS 6 Hornsey
07.09.82 Bert Myrie **W** PTS 6 Hornsey
14.09.82 Cliff Curtis **W** RTD 6 Southend
27.09.82 Peter Stockdale **W** PTS 6 Bloomsbury
28.10.82 Joey Saunders **W** PTS 6 Bloomsbury
09.12.82 Mark Kelly **W** PTS 6 Bloomsbury
16.02.83 Randy Henderson **W** PTS 6 Muswell Hill
25.03.83 Ian Chantler **W** PTS 8 Bloomsbury
20.04.83 Mick Courtney **DREW** 8 Muswell Hill
18.05.83 Paul Mitchell **L** PTS 8 Bloomsbury
14.09.83 Steve Henty **W** RSC 5 Muswell Hill
07.12.83 Steve Henty **W** RSC 8 Bloomsbury
01.02.84 Phil O'Hare **W** PTS 8 Bloomsbury
25.04.84 Phil O'Hare **W** PTS 8 Muswell Hill
Summary: 14 contests, won 12, drew 1, lost 1

Neil Patterson

Darlington. *Born* Sedgfield 21.04.62
L. Welterweight
Manager T. Callighan
Previous Amateur Club Darlington
National Honours Young England Rep.
Divisional Honours NE Counties L. Flyweight Champion 1980

22.03.84 Gary Champion L PTS 6 Maidenhead
30.04.84 Alastair Laurie L PTS 6 Glasgow
Summary: 2 contests, lost 2

Eamonn Payne

Kings Lynn. *Born* Kings Lynn 18.02.62
Lightweight
Manager G. Holmes
Previous Amateur Club Kings Lynn
Divisional Honours E Counties L. Welterweight Champion 1983

31.05.84 Mickey Hull L PTS 6 Basildon
Summary: 1 contest, lost 1

Mark Pearce

Delroy Pearce

Tottenham. *Born* Jamaica 04.01.57
Welterweight
Manager (Self)
Previous Amateur Club Slough Boys

09.12.80 Lee Hargie L PTS 6 Southend
28.01.81 Mark Tobin W PTS 4 Swindon
09.03.81 Derek Paul L PTS 6 Copthorne
09.04.81 Craig Walsh L PTS 6 Piccadilly
11.05.81 Mark Crouch W PTS 6 Copthorne
20.10.81 Sam Omidi L PTS 6 Plymouth
28.10.81 Ray Hood L PTS 6 Burslem
16.11.81 Dai Davies W PTS 6 Mayfair
08.12.81 Geoff Pegler L PTS 6 Pembroke
16.02.82 Mike Clemow L PTS 6 Bristol
24.02.82 Phil Sheridan W PTS 6 Evesham
15.03.82 Tony Laing L PTS 6 Mayfair
19.04.82 Mike Clemow W PTS 6 Bristol
27.04.82 Lee Halford W RSC 7 Southend
03.06.82 Ray Hood L PTS 8 Liverpool
08.06.82 Sean Campbell W PTS 6 Southend
11.10.82 Sam Omidi W CO 4 Bristol
18.10.82 Julian Bousted L PTS 8 Piccadilly
07.02.83 Errol Dennis W RSC 5 Marylebone
14.02.83 Derek McKenzie L PTS 6 Lewisham
21.02.83 Dave Maxwell W PTS 6 Mayfair
01.03.83 Alex Brown L PTS 6 Southend
Summary: 22 contests, won 10, lost 12

Gary Pearce

Newport. *Born* Newport 25.06.60
Former Undefeated Welsh L. Middleweight Champion
Manager D. Gardiner
Previous Amateur Club Newport SC

25.09.78 Billy O'Grady DREW 6 Piccadilly
02.11.78 Mel Jones W RSC 2 Ebbw Vale
20.11.78 Jimmy Smith W PTS 6 Piccadilly
05.02.79 Peter Snowshall W PTS 6 Piccadilly
26.02.79 Lloyd Hibbert L PTS 8 Edgbaston
03.04.79 Alan Burrows W PTS 8 Caerphilly
10.05.79 Frank McCord W PTS 8 Pontypool
17.10.79 Sylvester Gordon DREW 8 Piccadilly
30.10.79 Sylvester Gordon W PTS 8 Caerphilly
29.11.79 Dil Collins W PTS 8 Ebbw Vale
04.02.80 Derek Nelson W PTS 8 Piccadilly
11.03.80 Horace McKenzie L PTS 10 Piccadilly
(*Welsh Welterweight Title Challenge*)
31.03.80 Roy Varden W PTS 8 Piccadilly
27.05.80 Richard Avery L PTS 10 Newport
01.07.80 Peter Neal L PTS 8 Swindon
30.07.80 Terry Welch W RSC 4 Doncaster
20.11.80 Chris Sanigar L PTS 8 Piccadilly

26.01.81 Dave Douglas W PTS 8 Glasgow
07.04.81 Terry Matthews W RSC 9 Newport (*Vacant Welsh L. Middleweight Title*)
13.05.81 Tony Martey W PTS 8 Piccadilly
21.05.81 Hans Henrik Palm L PTS 8 Copenhagen
14.09.81 Charlie Malarkey L PTS 8 Glasgow
20.10.81 Sylvester Mittee L CO 3 Bethnal Green
10.03.82 Joey Mack L PTS 8 Solihull
14.04.82 Colin Power L CO 6 Strand
27.09.82 Gary Knight L PTS 8 Bloomsbury
15.12.82 Vince Stewart L DIS 5 Queensway
28.02.83 Phil O'Hare W PTS 6 Strand
23.09.83 Rocky Kelly L CO 2 Longford
Summary: 29 contests, won 14, drew 2, lost 13

Mark Pearce

Cardiff. *Born* Cardiff 29.06.63
Featherweight
Manager M. Williams
Previous Amateur Club Llandaff
National Honours Welsh Int.

16.05.83 Young Yousuf W PTS 6 Birmingham
23.05.83 Dave Pratt W PTS 6 Mayfair
22.09.83 Dave Pratt DREW 6 Cardiff
01.12.83 Mark Reefer L PTS 6 Basildon
10.12.83 Mike Wilkes W PTS 6 Swansea
30.01.84 Dave Pratt L PTS 8 Birmingham
31.03.84 Steve Topliss L PTS 8 Derby
15.06.84 Joey Joynson L PTS 8 Liverpool
Summary: 8 contests, won 3, drew 1, lost 4

Nigel Pearce

Newport. *Born* Newport 16.10.64
L. Middleweight
Manager (Self)
Previous Amateur Club Newport Docks

01.12.83 Dennis Boy O'Brien L RSC 3 Basildon
Summary: 1 contest, lost 1

Mark Pearson

Cardiff. *Born* Cardiff 03.03.60
L. Heavyweight
Manager G. Evans
Previous Amateur Club Penarth
National Honours Welsh Int, Welsh L. Heavyweight Champion 1983
Divisional Honours Welsh Middleweight R/U 1980

14.02.84 Geoff Rymer L RSC 5 Southend
Summary: 1 contest, lost 1

Gary Peel

Manchester. *Born* Manchester 04.02.65
Welterweight
Manager J. Smith
Previous Amateur Club Wythenshawe YMCA

09.11.83 Mickey Kilgallon L RSC 6 Southend
05.12.83 Tony Kempson L PTS 6 Manchester
Summary: 2 contests, lost 2

Geoff Pegler

Swansea. *Born* Swansea 18.01.59
Welsh L. Welterweight Champion
Manager C. Breen
Previous Amateur Club Swansea Docks
Divisional Honours Welsh Welterweight R/U 1980

03.09.81 Mick Rowley L PTS 6 Cardiff
28.09.81 Winston Ho-Shing W PTS 6 Bradford
20.10.81 Tommy Thomas W PTS 4 Plymouth
02.11.81 Errol Dennis W RSC 2 Nottingham
22.11.81 Kostas Petrou L PTS 6 Evesham
04.12.81 Kevin Johnson W PTS 6 Bristol
08.12.81 Delroy Pearce W PTS 6 Pembroke
25.01.82 Gary Petty DREW 6 Glasgow
16.02.82 Winston McKenzie W PTS 8 Lewisham
27.05.83 Ray Price NC 1 Swansea (*Welsh L. Welterweight Title Challenge*)
06.06.83 Tommy McCallum L PTS 8 Piccadilly
08.09.83 Chris Sunigar L CO 3 Queensway
21.11.83 Ian McLeod L RSC 4 Glasgow
19.12.83 Ray Price W RTD 8 Swansea (*Welsh L. Welterweight Title Challenge*)
06.06.83 Tommy McCallum L PTS 8 Piccadilly
08.09.83 Chris Sanigar L CO 3 Queensway
21.11.83 Ian McLeod L RSC 4 Glasgow
19.12.83 Ray Price W RTD 8 Swansea (*Welsh L. Welterweight Title Challenge*)
05.03.84 Jim Kelly L PTS 8 Glasgow
24.04.84 Gary Knight L PTS 8 Aberavon
11.06.84 Tommy McCallum L PTS 8 Glasgow
Summary: 23 contests, won 9, drew 1, lost 12, NC 1

Alek Penarski

Alfreton. *Born* Chesterfield 18.05.53
Former Central Area L. Heavyweight Champion
Manager W. Shinfield
Previous Amateur Club Huthwaite

04.12.72 Steve Foley L RSC 3 Bedford
27.03.73 Barry Clough W PTS 6 Birmingham

CONTINUED OVERLEAF

Alek Penarski
Harry Goodwin

03.04.73 Nigel Williams L PTS 6 Blackpool
10.04.73 Johnny Wall L CO 3 Bethnal Green
06.06.73 Lloyd Stewart L CO 4 Blackpool
29.10.73 Pat Thompson L PTS 8 Walworth
30.01.74 Billy Baggott L CO 3 Wolverhampton
19.03.74 Pat Thompson L CO 5 Blackpool
29.10.74 Pat Thompson L PTS 8 Southend
10.03.75 Len Brittain W PTS 6 Nottingham
09.04.75 Len Brittain W PTS 6 Bradford
15.10.75 Len Brittain W PTS 8 Birmingham
16.02.76 Francis Hands L PTS 6 Manchester
09.03.76 Randy Barrett W PTS 6 Bradford
07.06.76 Danny McLoughlin W PTS 8 Manchester
25.10.76 Johnny Cox W RSC 7 Luton
31.01.77 Pat Thompson L PTS 8 Bradford
05.03.77 Pat Thompson W PTS 10 Liverpool (*Central Area L. Heavyweight Title Challenge*)
10.05.77 Walter Bimbo Pearce W PTS 8 Merthyr
16.12.77 Freddie De Kerpel L PTS 8 Grivegne
30.01.78 Tim Wood W PTS 8 Cleethorpes
06.04.78 Harald Skog L PTS 8 Oslo
24.10.78 Francis Hands L PTS 10 Blackpool (*Central Area L. Heavyweight Title Defence*)
19.01.79 Hocine Tafer L CO 5 Grenoble
18.06.79 Bonny McKenzie DREW 8 Windsor
23.10.79 Chris Lawson L RSC 5 Blackpool
27.11.79 Carlton Benoit W PTS 8 Sheffield
21.01.80 Danny Lawford L DIS 5 Nottingham
16.10.80 Liam Coleman W PTS 8 Bolton
12.02.81 Roy Skeldon W PTS 8 Bolton
23.11.81 Dennis Andries L PTS 10 Chesterfield
21.01.82 Richard Caramanolis L CO 1 Paris
18.10.82 Antonio Harris L RSC 3 Edgbaston
15.02.83 Cordwell Hylton L RSC 4 Wolverhampton
16.05.83 Jonjo Greene L PTS 8 Manchester
14.12.83 Ian Lazarus W PTS 10 Stoke
04.06.84 Sakkie Horn L RSC 8 Manchester
Summary: 37 contests, won 14, drew 1, lost 22

Lou Penfold

Brockley. *Born* Brixton 07.11.61
L. Welterweight
Manager (Self)
Previous Amateur Club Hollington

07.02.83 Colin Neagle L RSC 3 Marylebone
Summary: 1 contest, lost 1

Vernon Penprase

Devonport. *Born* Plymouth 20.05.58
Featherweight
Manager T. Penprase
Previous Amateur Club Devonport
National Honours Young England Rep.
Divisional Honours W Counties Bantamweight Champion 1977; W Counties Featherweight R/U 1978

23.05.78 Lee Graham W PTS 6 Islington
10.07.78 Billy Rabbitt W RTD 4 Aberavon

Vernon Penprase
Universal Pictorial Press

18.09.78 Eric Wood L PTS 6 Mayfair
03.10.78 Alan Oag W CO 5 Aberavon
11.12.78 Najib Daho L PTS 8 Plymouth
17.01.79 Lance Williams W PTS 6 Burslem
19.03.79 Glyn Williams W PTS 8 Haverfordwest
03.04.79 Lee Graham W PTS 8 Caerphilly
13.05.79 Lee Graham W PTS 8 Plymouth
13.06.79 Jeff Pritchard W PTS 8 Caerphilly
05.07.79 Paul Keers W PTS 8 Aberavon
15.10.79 Lee Graham W RTD 5 Mayfair
29.10.79 Dave Laxen W PTS 8 Camborne
10.12.79 Terry McKeown W PTS 8 Torquay
03.03.80 Paul Keers W PTS 8 Piccadilly
02.06.80 Paul Keers W PTS 10 Plymouth
12.08.80 George Sutton W PTS 8 Swansea
15.12.80 Steve Sammy Sims DREW 8 Merthyr
09.06.81 Steve Sammy Sims L PTS 10 Newport
(*Elim. British Featherweight Title*)
21.09.81 Jim McKeown W RSC 7 Glasgow
31.10.81 Daniel Londas L PTS 8 Chalons
22.02.82 Terry McKeown L PTS 12 Glasgow
(*Final Elim. British Featherweight Title*)
25.10.82 Mark West W PTS 8 Mayfair
23.11.82 John Feeney L PTS 8 Wembley
12.04.83 Barry McGuigan L RSC 2 Belfast
(*Vacant British Featherweight Title*)
Summary: 25 contests, won 17, drew 1, lost 7

Terry Petersen

Leeds. *Born* Highgate 10.07.51
Former Central Area Lightweight & Welterweight Champion
Manager (Self)
Previous Amateur Club St Patricks
Divisional Honours NE London L. Welterweight R/U 1973; N Counties Welterweight Champion 1974 – 1975

05.05.75 Tom Howard W RSC 2 Piccadilly
19.05.75 Hughie Clark W PTS 8 Piccadilly
10.06.75 Barton McAllister W PTS 8 Piccadilly
24.06.75 Hughie Clark W PTS 8 Piccadilly
08.09.75 Johnny Wall L PTS 8 Piccadilly
20.10.75 Brian Jones L PTS 8 Mayfair
27.10.75 Barton McAllister W PTS 6 Piccadilly
02.12.75 Jess Harper W PTS 10 Leeds
(*Central Area Lightweight Title Challenge*)
26.01.76 Hugh Smith W PTS 8 Glasgow
09.02.76 Gordon Kirk L PTS 8 Piccadilly
12.04.76 Hugh Smith W PTS 8 Birmingham
10.05.76 Jim Montague W PTS 8 Piccadilly
17.05.76 Billy Waith L PTS 8 Glasgow
19.06.76 Dick Van Der Westhuizen L PTS 8 Pretoria
27.09.76 Gordon Kirk L PTS 12 Piccadilly
(*Central Area Lightweight Title Defence*)
25.10.76 Jess Harper W RSC 7 Piccadilly
02.11.76 Colin Power L RSC 4 Southend
30.11.76 Jeff Gale W PTS 12 Leeds
(*Central Area Welterweight Title Challenge*)
19.02.77 Alois Carmeliet L CO 5 Zele
04.04.77 Henry Rhiney L RSC 7 Luton
13.06.77 Johnny Pincham W PTS 8 Piccadilly
20.06.77 John Smith DREW 8 Glasgow
08.10.77 Louis Acaries L PTS 8 Paris
06.12.77 Chris Glover W PTS 12 Leeds
(*Central Area Welterweight Title Defence*)
31.01.78 Peter Neal L PTS 8 Marylebone
23.02.78 Mike Copp DREW 8 Doncaster
15.04.78 Fred Coranson L CO 8 Petite Synthe
14.09.78 Hans Henrik Palm L PTS 8 Randers
13.11.78 Charlie Malarkey L PTS 8 Glasgow
23.01.79 Roy Varden L RSC 6 Piccadilly
19.02.79 Chris Glover W RSC 6 Piccadilly
(*Central Area Welterweight Title Defence*)
05.03.79 Carl Bailey L PTS 8 Barnsley
17.12.79 Lee Hartshorn L PTS 8 Bradford
04.02.80 Joey Singleton L PTS 10 Hammersmith
(*Central Area Welterweight Title Defence*)
02.06.80 Dennis Sullivan L PTS 8 Plymouth
13.11.80 Neil Fannan L PTS 8 Newcastle
19.05.83 Billy Bryce L PTS 6 Sunderland
Summary: 37 contests, won 14, drew 2, lost 21

Kostas Petrou

Birmingham. *Born* Birkenhead 17.04.59
Midlands Area Welterweight Champion
Manager P. Lynch
Previous Amateur Club Birmingham City
Divisional Honours M Counties Welterweight R/U 1981

07.10.81 Paul Murray L RSC 5 Solihull
11.11.81 Geoff Pegler W PTS 6 Evesham
30.11.81 Steve Tempro W PTS 6 Birmingham
25.01.82 Aiden Wake W PTS 6 Wolverhampton
24.02.82 Peter Ahmed W PTS 6 Evesham
10.03.82 Lee McKenzie L PTS 8 Solihull
26.04.82 Steve Tempro W RSC 3 Edgbaston
18.05.82 Lloyd Honeyghan L PTS 8 Bethnal Green
07.06.82 Paul Murray W PTS 6 Edgbaston
22.09.82 Gunther Roomes W PTS 6 Mayfair
06.10.82 Tony Laing W PTS 6 Solihull

CONTINUED OVERLEAF

Kostas Petrou
Fred Cicharski

18.10.82 Paul Murray W RSC 5 Edgbaston
17.11.82 Dave Taylor W RSC 2 Solihull
06.12.82 Sylvester Gordon W PTS 8 Edgbaston
19.01.83 Joey Mack W PTS 8 Birmingham
21.02.83 Geoff Pegler W PTS 8 Edgbaston
08.04.83 Kid Murray W RTD 3 Liverpool
20.04.83 Dennis Sullivan W RSC 4 Solihull
13.06.83 Joey Mack W RSC 5 Coventry (*Vacant Midlands Area Welterweight Title*)
05.10.83 Frank McCord W PTS 8 Solihull
23.02.84 Jeff Decker W RSC 5 Digbeth
21.03.84 Tommy McCallum W PTS 8 Solihull
10.05.84 Lloyd Christie W PTS 12 Digbeth (*Midlands Area Welterweight Title Defence & Final Elim. British Welterweight Title*)
29.06.84 Joseph Lala L PTS 8 Vereeniging
Summary: 23 contests, won 20, lost 3

Gary Petty
Hull. *Born* Hull 04.09.59
L. Middleweight
Manager (Self)
Previous Amateur Club Hull Fish Trades
Divisional Honours NE Counties L. Middleweight Champion 1978

21.04.80 Don Hughes W RSC 4 Glasgow
29.04.80 Dave Aspill W PTS 6 Piccadilly
16.06.80 Gerry McGrath L RSC 1 Piccadilly
09.09.80 Kevin Durkin L RTD 5 Mexborough
01.12.80 Charlie Douglas W PTS 6 Hull
08.12.80 Dil Collins W PTS 8 Piccadilly
21.01.81 Shaun Jones W RTD 5 Piccadilly
17.02.81 Archie Salmon L CO 2 Leeds
23.03.81 Stan Atherton W PTS 6 Liverpool
13.04.81 Kevin Durkin L PTS 6 Manchester
08.05.81 Julian Bousted DREW 8 Piccadilly
11.06.81 Steve Ward W PTS 6 Hull
07.09.81 Billy Ahearne L PTS 6 Liverpool
25.09.81 Dennis Sheehan L RSC 4 Nottingham
09.11.81 Derek Nelson L PTS 8 Newcastle
25.01.82 Geoff Pegler DREW 6 Glasgow
25.02.82 Phil Gibson L PTS 8 Hartlepool
08.03.82 Liam Linnen W PTS 8 Hamilton
15.03.82 Rocky Kelly L CO 4 Bloomsbury
19.04.82 Danny Shinkwin L PTS 6 Bristol
26.04.82 Charlie Douglas W PTS 6 Piccadilly
10.05.82 Tony Brown L RSC 5 Liverpool
21.06.82 Peter Stockdale W PTS 6 Hull
26.10.82 Bert Myrie L CO 1 Hull
29.11.82 Steve Henty L RSC 5 Brighton
29.03.83 Wayne Crolla L PTS 6 Hull
11.04.83 Gavin Stirrup L RSC 5 Manchester
Summary: 27 contests, won 10, drew 2, lost 15

Peter Phillips
Dinnington. *Born* Dinnington 16.12.62
Welterweight
Manager T. Miller
Previous Amateur Club Dinnington

12.02.81 Martin Tobin W PTS 4 Bolton
03.03.81 Mike Dunlop W RSC 4 Pudsey
25.03.81 Martin Tobin L PTS 4 Doncaster
06.04.81 Mike Bromby W PTS 6 Bradford
13.04.81 Mike Bromby W RSC 5 Manchester
02.07.81 John Malone W PTS 6 Pudsey
07.09.81 Peter Flanagan L RSC 5 Liverpool
23.11.81 Peter Flanagan DREW 6 Nantwich
01.02.82 Peter Flanagan L RSC 2 Manchester
20.05.82 J. J. Barrett L PTS 6 Preston
24.05.82 J. J. Barrett L RSC 5 Bradford
07.10.82 Sam Church W PTS 6 Morley
25.11.82 Dave Heaver W PTS 6 Morley
06.12.82 Pat Belshaw W PTS 6 Manchester
10.02.83 Gordon Pratt L PTS 6 Sunderland
17.02.83 Gordon Pratt W PTS 6 Morley
21.02.83 George Schofield L PTS 6 Bradford
16.05.83 Dave Foley W PTS 6 Bradford
06.06.83 Glyn Mitchell L PTS 6 Piccadilly
14.11.83 Tony Smith L PTS 6 Nantwich
21.11.83 Jim Hunter W PTS 6 Glasgow
19.12.83 Tony Smith L PTS 6 Bradford
27.02.84 Albert Buchanan L PTS 6 Glasgow
05.03.84 John McAllister L PTS 6 Glasgow
31.03.84 Jaswant Singh Ark L PTS 6 Derby
09.04.84 Tommy Campbell L RSC 3 Glasgow
Summary: 26 contests, won 11, drew 1, lost 14

Rudi Pika
Lawrence Lustig (Global Sports Photos)

Rudi Pika

Cardiff. *Born* Cardiff 15.03.62
Heavyweight
Manager M. Duff
Previous Amateur Club Prince of Wales
National Honours Schools Title 1975; Welsh Heavyweight Champion 1979 – 1980; Welsh Int.

26.11.80 David Fry **W** RSC 1 Wembley
08.12.80 Derek Simpkin **W** RSC 3 Kensington
27.01.81 Reg Long **W** RSC 3 Kensington
17.03.81 Ricky James **W** PTS 6 Wembley
20.06.81 Bob Young **W** RSC 1 Wembley
15.09.81 Bob Hennessey **W** PTS 8 Wembley
30.03.82 Steve Gee **W** PTS 8 Wembley
31.05.83 Eddie Neilson **W** RSC 7 Kensington
22.09.83 Winston Allen **W** PTS 8 Cardiff
13.05.84 Linwood Jones **W** PTS 6 Wembley
Summary: 10 contests, won 10

Ray Plant

South Shields. *Born* South Shields 12.04.56
Featherweight
Manager T. Conroy
Previous Amateur Club Perth Green

17.11.80 Carl Gaynor **W** PTS 6 Gosforth
01.12.80 Jim Harvey **L** PTS 6 Middlesbrough
09.01.81 Jim Harvey **W** PTS 6 Durham
26.01.81 Carl Gaynor **W** PTS 6 Gosforth
12.02.81 Jim Harvey **W** PTS 6 South Shields
02.04.81 Ian Murray DREW 8 Middlesbrough
15.09.81 Steve Farnsworth **W** PTS 8 Sunderland
02.11.81 Ian Murray **W** PTS 8 South Shields
29.11.81 Peter Jones **L** RSC 6 Middlesbrough
08.01.82 Keith Foreman **W** PTS 6 Durham
09.03.82 Kenny Bruce **L** RSC 4 Derry
26.04.82 John Farrell **L** PTS 6 Bradford
21.05.82 Steve Farnsworth **L** RSC 3 Sheffield
31.08.82 Keith Foreman **W** PTS 6 South Shields
28.09.82 Tony Connolly **L** PTS 6 Bethnal Green
25.10.82 Keith Foreman **L** PTS 6 Bradford
25.11.82 Muhammad Lovelock **W** PTS 6 Sunderland
07.01.83 Carl Gaynor **W** PTS 6 Durham
20.04.83 Steve Enright **W** PTS 8 South Shields
26.04.83 Jim McDonnell **L** RSC 3 Bethnal Green
19.05.83 John Doherty DREW 8 Sunderland
23.05.83 Jim Harvey **L** PTS 6 Glasgow
Summary: 22 contests, won 11, drew 2, lost 9

Steve Pollard

Hull. *Born* Hull 18.12.57
Central Area Featherweight Champion
Manager (Self)
Previous Amateur Club Kingston
Divisional Honours NE Counties Featherweight R/U 1976; NE Counties Lightweight R/U 1977/1980

28.04.80 Brindley Jones **W** PTS 6 Piccadilly
27.05.80 Pat Mallon **W** PTS 6 Glasgow
02.06.80 Andy Thomas **W** PTS 6 Piccadilly
02.10.80 Eddie Glass **W** PTS 6 Hull
03.11.80 Rocky Bantleman **W** CO 2 Piccadilly
01.12.80 Chris McCallum **W** PTS 6 Hull
17.02.81 Billy Laidman **W** PTS 6 Leeds
02.03.81 Bryn Jones **W** RSC 5 Piccadilly
30.03.81 John Sharkey **L** RSC 5 Glasgow
27.04.81 Ian McLeod **L** PTS 8 Piccadilly
01.06.81 Gary Lucas **L** PTS 8 Piccadilly
11.06.81 John Sharkey **W** PTS 8 Hull
08.03.82 Brian Hyslop DREW 8 Hamilton
22.04.82 Rocky Bantleman **W** RSC 8 Piccadilly
10.05.82 Lee Graham DREW 8 Piccadilly
26.05.82 Alan Tombs DREW 8 Piccadilly
23.09.82 Pat Doherty **L** PTS 8 Wimbledon
26.10.82 Lee Halford **L** PTS 8 Hull
25.11.82 Kevin Howard **L** PTS 6 Sunderland
10.02.83 Keith Foreman **L** PTS 8 Sunderland
29.03.83 Steve Farnsworth **W** RSC 2 Hull (*Central Area Featherweight Title Challenge*)
18.06.83 Andrea Blanco **W** PTS 8 Izegem
04.10.83 Jim McDonnell **L** RSC 5 Bethnal Green
22.11.83 Joey Joynson **L** PTS 8 Wembley
22.01.84 Jean Marc Renard **L** PTS 8 Izegem
Summary: 25 contests, won 12, drew 3, lost 10

Freddie Potter
Southampton. *Born* Southampton 26.02.62
Bantamweight
Manager J. Bishop
Previous Amateur Club Southampton
Divisional Honours S Counties Flyweight Champion 1980

02.04.84 John Maloney L RSC 2 Mayfair
Summary: 1 contest, lost 1

Wayne Poultney
Bedworth. *Born* Bedworth 06.02.60
Lightweight
Manager J. Jackson
Previous Amateur Club Bedworth

31.05.84 Steve Griffith L PTS 6 Basildon
Summary: 1 contest, lost 1

Dave Pratt
Leicester. *Born* Leicester 03.10.62
Featherweight
Manager M. Inskip
Previous Amateur Club Belgrave
Divisional Honours M Counties Featherweight Champion 1982

23.11.82 Graham Kid Clarke L PTS 6 Wolverhampton
01.12.82 George Bailey W PTS 6 Stafford
25.01.83 Billy Ruzgar W PTS 6 Bethnal Green
21.02.83 Shaun Shinkwin L PTS 6 Mayfair
28.02.83 Peter Harris W PTS 6 Birmingham
21.03.83 Young Yousuf W PTS 6 Nottingham
11.04.83 Chris Moorcroft W RTD 4 Manchester
15.04.83 Brett Styles L PTS 6 Piccadilly
09.05.83 George Bailey W PTS 8 Nottingham
23.05.83 Mark Pearce L PTS 6 Mayfair
22.09.83 Mark Pearce DREW 6 Cardiff
30.09.83 Michael Marsden L PTS 8 Leicester
07.11.83 Alec Irvine W PTS 8 Birmingham
12.12.83 Gary Nickels W PTS 8 Birmingham
30.01.84 Mark Pearce W PTS 8 Birmingham
22.02.84 Steve James W PTS 8 Evesham
27.03.84 Kenny Jinks W RSC 1 Wolverhampton
14.05.84 Robert Dickie L PTS 8 Nottingham
Summary: 18 contests, won 11, drew 1, lost 6

Gordon Pratt
Stockton. *Born* Stockton 16.11.57
Welterweight
Manager T. Miller
Previous Amateur Club Stockton

08.11.82 Alf Edwardes W PTS 6 Manchester
25.11.82 Elvis Morton W PTS 6 Sunderland
07.01.83 Alf Edwardes W PTS 6 Durham
10.02.83 Peter Phillips W PTS 6 Sunderland
17.02.83 Peter Phillips L PTS 6 Morley
11.04.83 Dalton Jordan W CO 2 Gosforth
18.04.83 Dave Heaver W PTS 6 Bradford
19.05.83 Jim McIntosh L PTS 8 Sunderland
26.09.83 Wayne Crolla W PTS 8 Manchester
22.11.83 Kid Sadler L PTS 8 Manchester
13.02.84 Wayne Crolla L PTS 8 Manchester
23.02.84 John Andrews L PTS 8 Digbeth
Summary: 12 contests, won 7, lost 5

Alan Price
Fishguard. *Born* Haverfordwest 30.01.59
L. Heavyweight
Manager B. Lloyd
Previous Amateur Club Royal Navy
Divisional Honours Welsh Heavyweight R/U 1983

30.04.84 Eddie Chatterton W PTS 6 Rhyl
Summary: 1 contest, won 1

Jimmy Price
Liverpool. *Born* Liverpool 21.10.60
Middleweight
Manager F. Warren
Previous Amateur Club Holy Name
National Honours England Int.; ABA L. Middleweight Champion 1980 & Middleweight Champion 1982; Commonwealth Gold 1982
Divisional Honours W Lancs L. Middleweight R/U 1978; N Counties L. Middleweight Champion 1979

03.02.83 James Cook W PTS 6 Bloomsbury
16.02.83 Martin McEwan W RSC 2 Muswell Hill

Jimmy Price
Douglas Baton

25.03.83 Winston Burnett **W** PTS 6 Bloomsbury
20.04.83 Willie Wright **W** PTS 6 Muswell Hill
18.05.83 John Langol **W** RSC 3 Bloomsbury
21.07.83 Bobby Bland **W** RSC 3 Atlantic City
14.09.83 Dennis Roberts **W** RSC 1 Muswell Hill
13.10.83 Sammy Floyd **W** RSC 4 Bloomsbury
02.11.83 Monty Oswald **W** RTD 3 Bloomsbury
24.11.83 Raymond Gonzalez **W** PTS 10 Kirkby
09.02.84 Manuel Jiminez **W** RTD 10 Manchester
28.03.84 Kenny Whetstone **W** RSC 4 Aberavon
25.04.84 Ayub Kalule L RSC 1 Muswell Hill
Summary: 13 contests, won 12, lost 1

Ray Price

Swansea. *Born* Swansea 16.07.61
Former Welsh L. Welterweight Champion
Manager C. Breen
Previous Amateur Club RAOB Swansea

30.04.79 Gerry Howland DREW 4 Barnsley
17.09.79 Tim Moloney L PTS 4 Mayfair
24.09.79 Bonnet Bryan **W** PTS 4 Mayfair
16.10.79 Kid Curtis **W** CO 2 West Bromwich
22.10.79 Billy Smith DREW 6 Mayfair
30.10.79 Phillip Morris DREW 6 Caerphilly
06.11.79 Neil Brown **W** PTS 6 Stafford
21.11.79 Neil Brown **W** PTS 6 Evesham
28.11.79 Shaun Durkin DREW 6 Doncaster
03.12.79 Tim Moloney L PTS 6 Marylebone
11.12.79 Young John Daly L PTS 6 Milton Keynes
17.03.80 Terry Parkinson **W** PTS 6 Mayfair
19.05.80 Colin Wake L PTS 6 Piccadilly
26.03.81 Billy Vivian L PTS 8 Ebbw Vale
07.04.81 Tyrell Wilson **W** PTS 6 Newport
11.05.81 Barry Price **W** PTS 8 Copthorne
08.06.81 John Lindo **W** RSC 2 Bradford
13.10.81 Robbie Robinson L CO 1 Blackpool
22.03.82 Geoff Pegler **W** PTS 10 Swansea (*Vacant Welsh L. Welterweight Title*)
25.10.82 Willie Booth L PTS 8 Airdrie
09.11.82 Tony Adams L RSC 1 Kensington
02.03.83 Lee Halford **W** PTS 6 Evesham
21.03.83 Gunther Roomes L RSC 1 Mayfair
27.05.83 Geoff Pegler NC 1 Swansea (*Welsh L. Welterweight Title Defence*)
04.10.83 Mo Hussein L PTS 8 Bethnal Green
19.12.83 Geoff Pegler L RTD 8 Swansea (*Welsh L. Welterweight Title Defence*)
30.01.84 Steve Tempro **W** PTS 8 Birmingham
14.03.84 Ken Foreman L PTS 6 Mayfair
09.05.84 Tony McKenzie L PTS 8 Leicester
13.06.84 Michael Harris L PTS 10 Aberavon (*Vacant Welsh L. Welterweight Title*)
30.06.84 David Irving L RSC 4 Belfast
Summary: 31 contests, won 11, drew 4, lost 15, NC 1

Ian Priest

Alfreton. *Born* Belper 05.10.62
Heavyweight
Manager B. Shinfield
Previous Amateur Club Target

28.01.84 Lou Nelson **W** RSC 3 Hanley
06.03.84 Lou Nelson **W** CO 1 Stoke
19.03.84 Alan Douglas L PTS 6 Bradford
07.06.84 Alan Bagley **W** RSC 1 Dudley
Summary: 4 contests, won 3, lost 1

Kevin Pritchard

Liverpool. *Born* Ipswich 26.09.61
Lightweight
Manager N. Basso
Previous Amateur Club Kirkby

21.12.81 J. J. Barrett **W** PTS 6 Bradford
11.01.82 Vince Griffin **W** RSC 1 Liverpool
08.02.82 Kevin Howard **W** PTS 6 Manchester
15.02.82 John Malone **W** PTS 6 Liverpool
22.02.82 Tommy Cook L PTS 6 Glasgow
08.03.82 Billy Laidman **W** PTS 6 Manchester
29.03.82 Tony Wilkinson **W** PTS 4 Liverpool
10.05.82 Colin Harrison DREW 8 Liverpool
26.05.82 Rocky Mensah **W** PTS 8 Leeds
07.06.82 Rocky Mensah **W** PTS 8 Sheffield
21.06.82 Lee Halford **W** CO 2 Liverpool
17.09.82 Rocky Mensah **W** CO 6 Liverpool
22.11.82 Glyn Rhodes L CO 5 Liverpool (*Vacant Central Area Lightweight Title*)
07.02.83 Dave Bryan **W** RSC 2 Liverpool
17.02.83 Mervyn Bennett **W** RSC 5 Coventry
07.03.83 Vince Vahey L PTS 8 Liverpool
14.03.83 Les Remikie **W** PTS 8 Manchester
11.04.83 Mark Davey L PTS 8 Manchester
20.04.83 Gary Knight L PTS 8 Muswell Hill
12.05.83 Mark Davey **W** DIS 4 Morley
01.09.83 Paul Huggins **W** RSC 7 Bloomsbury
06.10.83 Mohammed Kawoya L CO 2 Copenhagen
24.11.83 Jimmy Duncan L PTS 8 Kirkby
25.01.84 Peppy Muir **W** RTD 6 Belfast
01.02.84 Michael Harris L PTS 8 Bloomsbury
15.03.84 Ray Hood **W** PTS 8 Kirkby
10.05.84 Pat Cowdell L RSC 5 Digbeth
Summary: 27 contests, won 17, drew 1, lost 9

(Karl) Dennis Pryce

Wolverhampton. *Born* Jamaica 01.10.52
Welterweight
Manager (Self)
Previous Amateur Club Bilston Golden Gloves

27.05.77 Romal Ambrose **W** PTS 4 Digbeth
20.09.77 George Daines **W** PTS 4 Wolverhampton
19.10.77 Billy English **L** PTS 6 Bethnal Green
18.11.77 Andy Braidwood **L** PTS 6 Mayfair
22.11.77 Bert Green **W** PTS 6 Wolverhampton
12.12.77 Andy Braidwood **L** PTS 6 Walworth
13.02.78 Dave Maloney **W** PTS 6 Walworth
21.02.78 Roger Guest **W** PTS 4 Wolverhampton
17.04.78 Albert Hillman **L** PTS 8 Walworth
27.04.78 Dave Ward **W** PTS 8 Doncaster
12.09.78 Billy English **L** PTS 6 Wembley
27.09.78 John Chard **W** RSC 4 Evesham
02.10.78 Gary Newell **W** PTS 6 Nantwich
09.10.78 Gary Newell **W** PTS 6 Wolverhampton
30.10.78 Des Spence **W** PTS 6 Nottingham
16.11.78 Des Spence **W** CO 4 Liverpool
21.11.78 Gary Cooper DREW 6 Wolverhampton
11.12.78 Harry Watson **L** PTS 6 Birmingham
22.01.79 Colwyn Moore **W** PTS 6 Birmingham
31.01.79 Roy Varden DREW 8 Stoke
21.05.79 Lee Hartshorn **L** PTS 8 Manchester
12.09.79 Les Wint **W** PTS 8 Burslem
12.11.79 Tony Britton **W** PTS 6 Mayfair
20.11.79 John Breen DREW 8 Belfast
21.01.80 Wayne Barker **L** PTS 8 Nottingham
23.02.80 Dominique Fortemps **W** PTS 6 Moulinbeek
08.03.80 Claude Lancastre **L** PTS 8 St. Maur
26.03.80 Kid Murray **W** PTS 8 Evesham
18.06.80 Dave Allen **L** RTD 5 Burslem
06.09.80 Torben Andersen **L** PTS 6 Aarhus
04.10.80 Hugo Samo **L** PTS 8 Calais
03.12.80 Mick Mills **W** PTS 8 Sheffield
21.01.81 Tony Britton **L** PTS 8 Solihull
11.05.81 John Mugabi **L** CO 1 Mayfair
04.06.81 Tony Sinnott **W** DIS 2 Morecambe
02.07.81 Phil Duckworth **W** PTS 8 Pudsey
15.09.81 Graeme Ahmed **L** PTS 8 Sunderland
22.10.81 Frank McCord **W** PTS 8 Piccadilly
19.11.81 Tony Sinnott **W** PTS 8 Liverpool
02.12.81 John Ridgman **W** RSC 7 Burslem
14.05.82 Germain Lemaitre **L** PTS 10 St. Nazaire
25.06.82 Esperno Postl **W** PTS 6 Hankoo
18.10.82 Dennis Sheehan **W** PTS 6 Nottingham
11.11.82 Jo Kimpuani **L** PTS 8 Dunkirk
07.12.82 Billy Waith **W** CO 2 Kensington
20.12.82 Said Skouma **L** CO 6 Fumel
16.02.83 Frankie Decaestecker **L** CO 4 Hulste
07.03.83 Charlie Malarkey **L** PTS 8 Glasgow
Summary: 48 contests, won 25, drew 3, lost 20

Chris Pyatt
Douglas Baton

Chris Pyatt

Leicester. *Born* Islington 03.07.63
L. Middleweight
Manager S. Burns
Previous Amateur Club Belgrave
National Honours Schools Titles 1977/1979; Junior ABA Title 1980; Young England Rep.; England Int.; ABA Welterweight Champion 1982; Commonwealth Gold 1982
Divisional Honours ABA Welterweight R/U 1981

01.03.83 Paul Murray **W** RSC 2 Kensington
05.04.83 Billy Waith **W** RSC 8 Kensington
28.04.83 Lee Hartshorn **W** RSC 3 Leicester
27.09.83 Darwin Brewster **W** PTS 8 Wembley
08.10.83 Tyrone Demby **W** RSC 2 Atlantic City
22.11.83 Tony Britton **W** RSC 4 Wembley
22.02.84 Judas Clottey **W** PTS 8 Kensington
15.03.84 Pat Thomas **W** PTS 10 Leicester
09.05.84 Frankie Moro **W** CO 4 Leicester
23.05.84 Alfonso Redondo **W** RSC 3 Mayfair
Summary: 10 contests, won 10

Noel Quarless
Gordon Whiting

Noel Quarless

Liverpool. *Born* Liverpool 06.11.62
Heavyweight
Manager (Self)
Previous Amateur Club Salisbury
Divisional Honours W Lancs Heavyweight Champion 1980 – 1981

24.09.81 Phil Clarke **W** CO 1 Liverpool
19.11.81 John Rafferty **W** CO 1 Liverpool
20.01.82 Manny Gabriel L CO 1 Solihull
18.02.82 Steve Gee **W** PTS 6 Liverpool
30.03.82 Ian Scotting **W** CO 1 Leeds
22.04.82 Theo Josephs L CO 1 Liverpool
03.06.82 Theo Josephs **W** PTS 6 Liverpool
06.07.82 Paddy Finn L CO 2 Leeds
27.09.82 Stan McDermott **W** CO 3 Bloomsbury
08.02.83 Funso Banjo L RSC 3 Kensington
15.09.83 John Fallon **W** PTS 8 Liverpool
13.10.83 Anders Eklund **W** RSC 1 Bloomsbury
02.11.83 John L. Gardner **W** RSC 2 Bloomsbury
21.03.84 Conroy Nelson L DIS 7 Bloomsbury
11.04.84 Mark Lee L PTS 10 Kensington
13.05.84 Mark Lee L CO 1 Wembley
Summary: 16 contests, won 9, lost 7

Kevin Quinn

Manchester. *Born* Manchester 25.04.56
L. Welterweight
Manager N. Basso
Previous Amateur Club Sharston

14.04.75 Steve Gaze **W** RSC 3 Mayfair
24.04.75 Danny Fearon DREW 8 Ramsey
05.05.75 Charlie Wallace **W** CO 4 Manchester
13.05.75 Danny Fearon L RSC 4 Liverpool
11.06.75 Colin Power L RTD 3 Bradford
01.10.75 Hugh Smith L PTS 6 Hamilton
06.11.75 Jim McAllister **W** RSC 5 Blackpool
13.11.75 Winston McKenzie **W** PTS 6 Caister
02.12.75 John Sagar **W** PTS 8 Leeds
12.01.76 Steve Laybourn **W** PTS 6 Manchester
19.01.76 Steve Laybourn **W** RSC 1 Nottingham
27.01.76 John Sagar DREW 6 Doncaster
20.09.76 George Peacock **W** PTS 8 Glasgow
30.09.76 Al Stewart L RSC 1 Liverpool
03.11.76 Kevin Davies DREW 6 Caister
15.11.76 Kevin Davies L PTS 6 Nottingham
22.11.76 Vernon Entertainer Vanriel L RSC 2 Birmingham
08.05.78 Adey Allen **W** PTS 6 Manchester
19.06.78 Selvin Bell **W** PTS 6 Manchester
12.03.79 Shaun Stewart DREW 6 Manchester
02.04.79 Tony Carroll L PTS 8 Manchester
17.04.79 Hugh Smith L PTS 8 Glasgow
18.06.79 Shaun Stewart L PTS 8 Manchester
15.10.79 Phil Lewis **W** PTS 8 Manchester
15.11.79 Adey Allen L PTS 8 Caister
21.01.80 Paul Chance L PTS 8 Wolverhampton
03.03.80 Derek Nelson L PTS 8 Marton
27.03.80 Phil Lewis L RTD 3 Liverpool
31.05.80 Phil Lewis L RSC 6 Liverpool
26.11.80 Steve McLeod L RSC 4 Solihull
19.10.81 Dave Taylor L RSC 5 Manchester
16.11.81 John Lindo **W** PTS 6 Liverpool
08.03.82 Steve Tempro **W** PTS 6 Manchester
09.11.83 Tommy Bennett **W** RTD 4 Sheffield
Summary: 34 contests, won 14, drew 4, lost 16

(Danny) Patsy Quinn (McAllister)

Belfast. *Born* Belfast 08.09.60
Welterweight
Manager B. Eastwood
Previous Amateur Club Oliver Plunkett
National Honours Irish L. Welterweight Champion 1981; Irish Int.

08.12.81 Gerry Maguire **W** CO 2 Belfast
18.01.82 Eric Wood **W** PTS 6 Mayfair
27.01.82 Tyrell Wilson **W** RSC 5 Belfast

CONTINUED OVERLEAF

Patsy Quinn
A. McCullough

08.02.82 Winston Ho-Shing **W** RSC 7 Mayfair
23.02.82 Kevin Doherty **W** PTS 6 Belfast
23.03.82 John Lindo **L** CO 1 Belfast
22.04.82 Alan Cooper **W** RSC 2 Enniskillen
30.06.82 Alan Lamb **L** CO 4 Liverpool
14.12.82 P. J. Davitt **L** PTS 10 Belfast
02.03.83 Valentino Maccarinelli **W** RSC 4 Belfast
12.04.83 Tommy Davitt **W** RSC 5 Belfast
22.05.83 Dennis Sullivan **W** PTS 8 Navan
27.02.84 Granville Allen **L** RSC 3 Birmingham
04.04.84 P. J. Davitt **L** RTD 8 Belfast
Summary: 14 contests, won 9, lost 5

Tony Rabbetts
Heston. *Born* Watton 22.06.60
L. Middleweight
Manager H. Holland
Previous Amateur Club Hogarth

19.10.82 Sean Campbell DREW 6 Windsor
02.11.82 Sean Campbell **L** RSC 3 Hornsey
15.12.82 Kevin Webb **W** PTS 6 Queensway
07.02.83 Davey Cox DREW 6 Marylebone
28.02.83 Dave Harrison **W** PTS 6 Strand
25.03.83 Davey Cox **W** PTS 6 Bloomsbury
25.04.83 Errol Dennis **W** PTS 6 Acton
19.05.83 Danny Williams DREW 6 Queensway
08.09.83 Dave Hall **L** PTS 6 Queensway
27.01.84 Kevin Webb **L** PTS 8 Longford
01.03.84 Newton Barnett DREW 6 Queensway
22.03.84 Dan Myers **L** PTS 6 Maidenhead
17.04.84 Dave Heaver **W** PTS 6 Piccadilly
Summary: 13 contests, won 5, drew 4, lost 4

Tony Rahman
Newport. *Born* London 26.03.60
Featherweight
Manager (Self)
Previous Amateur Club Llandaff

08.11.83 Mark Reefer **L** RSC 4 Bethnal Green
27.03.84 Shane Silvester **L** PTS 6 Wolverhampton
16.04.84 Dave Adam **L** RSC 4 Glasgow
Summary: 3 contests, lost 3

Mark Reefer (Thompson)
Bethnal Green. *Born* Hackney 16.03.64
Featherweight
Manager D. Smith
Previous Amateur Club Beacon Youth
National Honours Schools Title 1979

04.10.83 Neville Fivey **W** PTS 6 Bethnal Green
08.11.83 Tony Rahman **W** RSC 4 Bethnal Green
01.12.83 Mark Pearce **W** PTS 6 Basildon
27.03.84 Muhammad Lovelock **W** PTS 6 Battersea
01.05.84 Alec Irvine **W** PTS 6 Bethnal Green
Summary: 5 contests, won 5

Sam Reeson
Battersea. *Born* London 05.01.63
L. Heavyweight
Manager A. Lavelle
Previous Amateur Club Battersea

19.05.83 Calvin Earlington **W** PTS 6 Queensway
17.10.83 Glenroy Taylor **W** PTS 6 Southwark
08.11.83 Alex Romeo **W** PTS 6 Bethnal Green
28.11.83 Geoff Rymer **W** PTS 8 Bayswater
12.12.83 Eddie Cooper **W** PTS 6 Bedworth
03.02.84 John Joseph **W** PTS 8 Maidenhead
27.03.84 Gordon Stacey **W** PTS 8 Battersea
17.04.84 Steve Lewin **W** PTS 8 Merton
Summary: 8 contests, won 8

Steve Reilly
Newport. *Born* Newport 06.03.60
Bantamweight
Manager (Self)
Previous Amateur Club St Josephs

22.09.80 Jimmy Carson **L** PTS 6 Belfast
13.11.80 George Bailey **L** PTS 6 Stafford
26.03.81 Tony Manson **W** PTS 6 Ebbw Vale
29.04.81 Cliff Storey **L** PTS 6 Burslem
22.09.81 Jimmy Carson **L** RSC 6 Belfast
12.10.81 Eugene Maloney **L** PTS 6 Bloomsbury

20.10.81 Ivor Jones L RSC 3 Bethnal Green
19.11.81 Dai Williams L PTS 6 Ebbw Vale
10.12.81 Andy King L PTS 6 Newport
15.03.82 Keith Wallace L RSC 2 Bloomsbury
26.04.82 Howard Williams L PTS 6 Cardiff
25.10.82 Johnny Dorey L PTS 8 Mayfair
14.06.83 Billy Hough L PTS 4 Newport
Summary: 13 contests, won 1, lost 12

Les Remikie

Leicester. *Born* Manchester 13.01.62
L. Welterweight
Manager F. Rix
Previous Amateur Club Belgrave
Divisional Honours M Counties Bantamweight Champion 1980; Midland Counties Lightweight Champion 1981 – 1982

26.10.82 Jimmy Bunclark L PTS 6 Bethnal Green
11.11.82 Sammy Rodgers W RSC 4 Stafford
01.12.82 Rocky Mensah W PTS 6 Stafford
25.01.83 Mo Hussein L PTS 6 Bethnal Green
17.02.83 Mark Davey L PTS 8 Morley
14.03.83 Kevin Pritchard L PTS 8 Manchester
28.04.83 Dave Laxen W CO 4 Leicester
17.05.83 Mo Hussein L PTS 6 Bethnal Green
30.09.83 Keith Foreman L PTS 8 Leicester
21.03.84 Kevin Johnson W RSC 3 Mayfair
04.06.84 Mickey Brooks L PTS 6 Mayfair
Summary: 11 contests, won 4, lost 7

Glyn Rhodes

Sheffield. *Born* Sheffield 22.10.59
Former Central Area Lightweight Champion
Manager (Self)
Previous Amateur Club St Thomas's

15.11.79 John Lindo L PTS 6 Liverpool
28.11.79 Mark Osbourne W PTS 4 Doncaster
10.12.79 Mike Clemow L PTS 6 Torquay
09.01.80 Steve Sammy Sims W RSC 6 Burslem
25.01.80 Shaun Durkin W PTS 6 Hull
05.02.80 John Cooper W PTS 6 Southend
12.02.80 Bill Smith W PTS 4 Sheffield
03.03.80 Kevin Sheehan L CO 1 Nottingham
24.03.80 Derek Groarke W RSC 4 Bradford
21.04.80 John Henry W RSC 5 Bradford
29.04.80 Jackie Turner L PTS 8 Mayfair
28.07.80 Billy Hay DREW 6 Fivemiletown
04.09.80 Jarvis Greenidge W RSC 8 Morecambe
15.09.80 Gary Ball DREW 6 Mayfair
07.10.80 Ceri Collins W RSC 8 Piccadilly
30.10.80 Jimmy Bunclark L RSC 7 Liverpool
01.12.80 Bobby Welburn L CO 1 Hull
22.01.81 Brian Snagg L PTS 8 Liverpool
09.03.81 Jimmy Brown W PTS 8 Mayfair
24.03.81 Eric Wood L PTS 8 Sheffield
29.04.81 Doug Hill W RTD 6 Burslem
11.05.81 Jackie Turner W RSC 2 Mayfair
17.06.81 Paul Keers W RSC 1 Sheffield
26.10.81 Lance Williams DREW 8 Mayfair
12.01.82 Vernon Entertainer Vanriel L CO 2 Bethnal Green
05.05.82 Lance Williams L RSC 7 Solihull
30.06.82 Brian Snagg W RTD 4 Liverpool
22.11.82 Kevin Pritchard W CO 5 Liverpool (*Vacant Central Area Lightweight Title*)
14.03.83 Jimmy Bunclark L PTS 10 Sheffield (*Central Area Lightweight Title Defence*)
09.11.83 Robert Lloyd W PTS 8 Sheffield
13.01.84 Frederic Geoffroy L RSC 5 Nemours
11.04.84 Mo Hussein L RSC 1 Kensington
Summary: 32 contests, won 16, drew 3, lost 13

John Ridgman

Boreham Wood. *Born* Boreham Wood 18.06.57
L. Middleweight
Manager D. Smith
Previous Amateur Club Brookside
Divisional Honours H Counties Welterweight Champion 1977 – 1979

29.10.79 Dave Sullivan W RTD 3 Camborne
19.11.79 Phil Pourou W RSC 5 Lewisham
04.12.79 Tony Britton W PTS 6 Southend
27.02.80 Vic Jackson L PTS 6 Burslem
09.12.80 Lawrence Hewitt W RSC 1 Southend
12.01.81 Bobby Williams W PTS 6 Hove
09.06.81 Tim McHugh L PTS 6 Southend
25.11.81 Glen Crump W RSC 3 Sheffield
02.12.81 Dennis Pryce L RSC 7 Burslem
13.09.82 Bert Myrie W RSC 5 Sheffield
14.10.82 Paul Mitchell L PTS 6 Nantwich
10.05.83 Alex Brown L PTS 6 Southend
23.06.83 Steve Grieves W RSC 1 Bethnal Green
22.02.84 R. W. Smith L RSC 3 Kensington
18.06.84 Wayne Crolla W RSC 6 Manchester
Summary: 15 contests, won 9, lost 6

Bobby Rimmer

Manchester. *Born* Manchester 22.11.59
L. Middleweight
Manager J. Gaynor
Previous Amateur Club Ardwick

15.06.81 Peter Flanagan W RSC 2 Manchester
06.10.81 Dave Goodwin L PTS 6 Liverpool
29.10.81 Charlie Douglas L PTS 6 Glasgow

CONTINUED OVERLEAF

22.03.82 Gunther Roomes L RSC 3 Southwark
25.02.83 Dave Heaver **W** PTS 6 Doncaster
14.03.83 Mark Drew **W** PTS 4 Manchester
28.03.83 Alex Brown **W** RSC 3 Manchester
18.04.83 Tommy Bennett **W** PTS 6 Bradford
26.09.83 Dave Heaver **W** RSC 3 Manchester
09.11.83 Dennis Boy O'Brien L RSC 1 Southend
Summary: 10 contests, won 6, lost 4

Nick Riozzi
Leicester. *Born* Leicester 29.10.60
L. Middleweight
Manager (Self)
Previous Amateur Club Belgrave

13.11.80 Dave Dunn **W** PTS 6 Caister
11.03.81 Lee Roy DREW 4 Burslem
13.05.81 Steve Brannan **W** PTS 6 Leicester
21.09.81 Peter Stockdale L PTS 6 Nottingham
13.10.81 Lee Roy **W** PTS 6 Nantwich
24.11.81 Paul Murray L PTS 6 Wolverhampton
07.12.81 Wayne Crolla L RSC 2 Manchester
15.02.82 Wayne Crolla L RSC 5 Liverpool
25.04.83 Gavin Stirrup L RTD 4 Liverpool
10.11.83 Robert Armstrong L PTS 6 Stafford
Summary: 10 contests, won 3, drew 1, lost 6

Andy Roberts
Stoke. *Born* Malaya 26.03.60
Welterweight
Manager R. Gray
Previous Amateur Club Holden Lane

23.02.83 Elvis Morton **W** PTS 6 Chesterfield
16.03.83 Colin Neagle L PTS 6 Stoke
13.04.83 Delroy Wallace **W** PTS 6 Evesham
13.06.83 Dave Hall L CO 5 Nottingham
Summary: 4 contests, won 2, lost 2

Gary Roberts
Wolverhampton. *Born* Willenhall 02.12.54
Midlands Area Flyweight Champion
Manager M. Sendell
Previous Amateur Club Wolverhampton
Divisional Honours M Counties Flyweight R/U 1978 – 1982

08.12.82 Danny Flynn L RSC 6 Piccadilly
07.03.83 Colin Moorcroft **W** CO 1 Liverpool
27.04.83 Cliff Storey **W** CO 1 Stoke (*Vacant Midlands Area Flyweight Title*)
31.05.83 Ivor Jones L RSC 4 Kensington
12.09.83 Charlie Brown **W** RSC 2 Glasgow
23.05.84 Duke McKenzie L CO 1 Mayfair
Summary: 6 contests, won 3, lost 3

Frank Robinson
Wednesbury. *Born* Birmingham 04.04.60
Heavyweight
Manager G. Riley
Previous Amateur Club West Bromwich College
Divisional Honours M Counties Heavyweight R/U 1980

05.04.82 Tony Blackstock **W** PTS 4 Nottingham
26.04.82 Tony Blackstock **W** CO 4 Leicester
20.09.82 Rocky Burton L PTS 6 Wolverhampton
26.10.82 Andrew Gerrard L PTS 6 Newport
11.11.82 Rocky Burton L PTS 6 Stafford
29.11.82 Dave Garside L PTS 6 Birmingham
06.12.82 John Westgarth L PTS 6 Nottingham
26.01.83 Andrew Gerrard **W** PTS 6 Stoke
15.02.83 Derek Simpkin **W** PTS 6 Wolverhampton
21.02.83 Theo Josephs L PTS 6 Nottingham
28.02.83 Dave Garside L RSC 4 Birmingham
14.06.83 Andrew Gerrard L RTD 3 Newport
20.09.83 Godfrey Hibbert **W** CO 6 Dudley
24.10.83 Godfrey Hibbert **W** RSC 4 Nottingham
01.11.83 Rocky Burton L RSC 5 Dudley
12.12.83 Al Malcolm **W** PTS 6 Birmingham
14.03.84 Dave Garside L PTS 8 Stoke
30.03.84 Glenn McCrory L PTS 6 Mayfair
09.05.84 Glenn McCrory L RSC 4 Mayfair
06.06.84 Alan Douglas L PTS 8 Sheffield
Summary: 20 contests, won 7, lost 13

Robbie Robinson
Liverpool. *Born* Liverpool 09.05.57
Lightweight
Manager (Self)
Previous Amateur Club St Ambrose
National Honours Young England Rep.
Divisional Honours ABA L. Flyweight R/U 1975; W Lancs Flyweight R/U 1976; NW Counties Bantamweight Champion 1977

24.01.78 Tony Whitmore **W** PTS 6 Piccadilly
30.01.78 Gerry O'Neill **W** PTS 6 Glasgow
28.02.78 Steve Holdsworth DREW 6 Heathrow
03.04.78 Albert Coley L PTS 6 Piccadilly
20.04.78 Dai Davies **W** PTS 6 Piccadilly
15.05.78 Barry Price **W** PTS 8 Manchester
23.05.78 Steve Ward **W** RSC 1 Leicester
25.09.78 Winston Spencer L PTS 8 Mayfair
01.03.79 Najib Daho **W** RSC 3 Liverpool
08.03.79 Andy Dane **W** RSC 3 Bangor
05.04.79 Tommy Wright **W** PTS 8 Liverpool
26.04.79 Alan Burrows L PTS 8 Liverpool
20.09.79 Tony Carroll L RSC 4 Liverpool
29.11.79 George Schofield **W** PTS 8 Liverpool

16.01.80 Lance Williams **W** PTS 8 Liverpool
21.02.80 George Metcalf **L** RTD 5 Liverpool
31.05.80 George Metcalf **W** RSC 6 Liverpool
18.09.80 Tony Carroll **W** PTS 8 Liverpool
22.01.81 George Feeney **L** CO 4 Liverpool
28.09.81 Dai Davies **W** RSC 3 Bradford
13.10.81 Ray Price **W** CO 1 Blackpool
21.12.81 Eric Wood **W** PTS 8 Bradford
25.01.82 Colin Wake **W** RSC 6 Bradford
01.03.82 Lloyd Christie **W** PTS 8 Preston
03.04.82 Davidson Andeh **L** CO 1 Lagos
20.05.82 Gerry Beard **W** RSC 2 Preston
26.04.82 Willie Booth **W** PTS 10 Kirkby
17.11.82 Tony Willis **L** RSC 5 Solihull
(*Elim. British Lightweight Title*)
08.04.83 Tony Willis **L** RTD 4 Liverpool
(*Elim. British Lightweight Title*)
Summary: 29 contests, won 19, drew 1, lost 9

Stuart Robinson

Birmingham. *Born* Birmingham 18.03.63
Middleweight
Manager P. Lynch
Previous Amateur Club Birmingham City
National Honours NABC Titles 1979–1980
Divisional Honours M Counties Middleweight Champion 1983

22.02.84 Carlo Giorno **W** PTS 6 Evesham
31.03.84 Chris Coady **W** PTS 6 Solihull
26.03.84 Chris Coady **W** PTS 6 Barnsley
14.05.84 Dougie Isles **W** RSC 2 Manchester
15.06.84 Chris Coady **W** PTS 6 Liverpool
Summary: 5 contests, won 5

Sammy Rodgers

Corby. *Born* Corby 23.10.61
Lightweight
Manager K. Whitney
Previous Amateur Club Corby Olympic

11.11.82 Les Remikie **L** RSC 4 Stafford
06.12.82 Glyn Mitchell **DREW** 6 Nottingham
24.01.83 Tony Wilkinson **L** PTS 6 Bradford
14.02.83 Edward Lloyd **L** RSC 4 Manchester
28.04.83 Graeme Griffin **L** PTS 4 Leicester
09.05.83 Willie Wilson **L** RSC 4 Nottingham
Summary: 6 contests, drew 1, lost 5

(Lamerick) Alex Romeo (Stevens)

Nottingham. *Born* Leicester 18.08.61
L. Heavyweight
Manager (Self)
Previous Amateur Club Granby
Divisional Honours M Counties Middleweight R/U 1982

06.10.82 Joey Saunders **W** PTS 6 Stoke
13.10.82 Paul Shell **L** PTS 6 Evesham
20.10.82 Ian Lazarus **L** PTS 6 Stoke
10.11.82 Willie Wright **W** PTS 6 Evesham
23.11.82 Steve Davies **W** PTS 6 Wolverhampton
29.11.82 Dave Scott **L** PTS 6 Birmingham
13.12.82 Rob Wada **W** PTS 6 Wolverhampton
31.01.83 Deano Wallace **L** PTS 6 Birmingham
07.02.83 Terry Magee **W** PTS 6 Piccadilly
23.02.83 Chris Devine **L** PTS 8 Chesterfield
20.04.83 Gary Jones **W** CO 6 Solihull
16.05.83 Bernie Kavanagh **W** RSC 1 Bradford
13.06.83 Nye Williams **L** RSC 2 Coventry
01.11.83 Colin Flute **L** PTS 6 Dudley
08.11.83 Sam Reeson **L** PTS 6 Bethnal Green
28.11.83 Glenroy Taylor **L** PTS 6 Southwark
03.02.84 Harry Cowap **L** PTS 8 Maidenhead
27.03.84 Lennie Howard **L** PTS 6 Bethnal Green
04.04.84 Roy Skeldon **L** PTS 6 Evesham
12.04.84 Winston Burnett **L** PTS 6 Piccadilly
17.04.84 Winston Burnett **L** PTS 6 Piccadilly
30.04.84 Blaine Longsden **W** PTS 8 Liverpool
31.05.84 John Moody **L** RSC 3 Basildon
Summary: 23 contests, won 8, lost 15

Gunther Roomes

Eltham. *Born* Lambeth 28.10.58
Welterweight
Manager T. Lawless
Previous Amateur Club Eltham & District
Divisional Honours London Welterweight Champion 1980

22.03.82 Bobby Rimmer **W** RSC 3 Southwark
04.05.82 Derek McKenzie **W** CO 1 Wembley
07.06.82 Mike Clemow **W** RSC 2 Piccadilly
22.09.82 Kostas Petrou **L** PTS 6 Mayfair
26.10.82 Frank McCord **L** CO 1 Bethnal Green
23.02.83 Derek McKenzie **W** RSC 7 Mayfair
21.03.83 Ray Pearce **W** RSC 1 Mayfair
26.04.83 Sam Omidi **W** RSC 3 Bethnal Green
23.05.83 Paul Chance **W** RSC 6 Mayfair
06.10.83 Dennis Sullivan **W** PTS 8 Basildon
28.11.83 Davy Campbell **W** PTS 8 Southwark
20.02.84 Robert Armstrong **W** RSC 4 Mayfair
12.04.84 Steve Tempro **W** RSC 6 Birmingham
Summary: 13 contests, won 11, lost 2

Colin Roscoe

Manchester. *Born* Chester 27.09.59
Lightweight
Manager N. Basso
Previous Amateur Club Ardwick

14.03.83 Dave Swann **L** RSC 2 Manchester
12.05.83 Jimmy Thornton **L** RSC 2 Morley
Summary: 2 contests, lost 2

Ray Ross

Ardglass. *Born* Killough 13.09.50
L. Welterweight
Manager (Self)
Previous Amateur Club Ardglass
National Honours Irish Lightweight Champion 1974; Irish Int.

05.03.75 Billy Boyd W RTD 1 Belfast
12.04.75 Pat Campbell W RSC 4 Belfast
28.04.75 Herbie McLean L PTS 6 Glasgow
21.05.75 Benny Purdy W RSC 5 Belfast
02.10.75 Charlie Nash L PTS 10 Derry (*Vacant N. Ireland Lightweight Title*)
17.11.75 Hugh Smith L RSC 6 Glasgow
04.03.76 Billy Surgeoner W RSC 3 Belfast
22.03.76 Herbie McLean L PTS 8 Glasgow
05.04.76 Tommy Dunn L RSC 7 Mayfair
24.05.76 Alan Richardson L RTD 5 Mayfair
09.11.76 Billy Vivian L PTS 6 Derry
28.01.77 Godfrey Butler W PTS 8 West Bromwich
24.03.77 Kevin Davies L PTS 8 Leicester
26.04.77 Jim Montague L PTS 10 Derry
26.07.77 Pat Campbell W PTS 6 Derry
05.08.77 Hogan Jimoh L RSC 6 Lagos
04.10.77 Benny Purdy L RSC 4 Belfast
03.02.78 Gene McGarrigale W PTS 6 Enniskillen
27.02.78 Ricky Beaumont L PTS 8 Sheffield
11.10.78 Billy Rabbitt W RSC 5 Belfast
11.11.78 Sid Smith L RSC 7 Marylebone
05.12.78 Sylvester Mittee L RSC 2 Kensington
27.06.79 Nigel Thomas L RSC 5 Derry
03.11.79 Hugh Smith L PTS 6 Glasgow
19.11.79 Alan Lamb L RSC 3 Lewisham
28.02.80 Jackie Turner L RSC 4 Hull
07.11.80 Duncan Hamilton L RTD 6 Cambuslang
09.03.82 Mickey Duddy L PTS 8 Derry
26.04.82 Tommy Cook L PTS 6 Glasgow
31.05.82 Gerry Devine DREW 6 Glasgow
07.06.82 Tommy Cook L PTS 6 Glasgow
13.09.82 Archie Durie L PTS 6 Glasgow
28.09.82 John McGlynn L PTS 8 Derry
16.11.82 Mo Hussein L RTD 3 Bethnal Green
14.02.83 George Schofield L PTS 6 Liverpool
21.02.83 Dave Haggarty L PTS 6 Glasgow
18.04.83 George Kerr L RSC 2 Glasgow
Summary: 37 contests, won 8, drew 1, lost 28

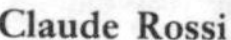
Claude Rossi

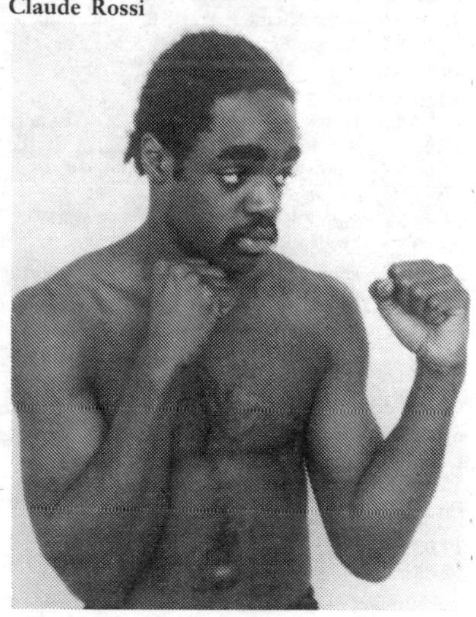

(Clive) Claude Rossi (Fearon)

Derby. *Born* London 03.04.62
Welterweight
Manager T. Sharpe
Previous Amateur Club Arboretum

16.05.83 Chris King L PTS 6 Mayfair
04.10.83 Danny Sullivan L PTS 6 Bethnal Green
24.10.83 Robert Armstrong L CO 5 Nottingham
31.03.84 Paul Kelly L PTS 6 Derby
16.04.84 Mickey Cotton W RSC 2 Nottingham
30.04.84 Ray Murray W PTS 6 Liverpool
31.05.84 Nick Ellaway DREW 6 Basildon
Summary: 7 contests, won 2, drew 1, lost 4

Mick Rowley

Merthyr. *Born* Australia 25.05.60
L. Welterweight
Manager G. Evans
Previous Amateur Club Rhondda

03.09.81 Geoff Pegler W PTS 6 Cardiff
21.09.81 Paul Clemit W RSC 3 Piccadilly
06.10.81 Craig Walsh W PTS 6 Piccadilly
02.11.81 Paul Wake W PTS 6 Piccadilly
25.01.82 Lee Halford DREW 6 Piccadilly
01.03.82 Eric Wood W RSC 3 Piccadilly
29.03.82 Gary Lucas W PTS 8 Piccadilly
22.09.82 Dave Taylor W PTS 8 Stoke
26.10.82 Mervyn Bennett W PTS 8 Newport
09.11.82 Peter Eubanks L PTS 6 Belfast
16.02.83 Gary Knight L PTS 8 Muswell Hill
06.04.83 Peter Eubanks L RSC 6 Mayfair
23.05.83 Davey Cox W RSC 2 Mayfair
26.09.83 Najib Daho L PTS 8 Manchester
14.11.83 Dave Haggarty W RTD 4 Glasgow
28.11.83 Vernon Entertainer Vanriel L PTS 8 Bayswater

19.01.84 Tony Willis L PTS 10 Digbeth
21.03.84 Vernon Entertainer Vanriel L PTS 8 Solihull
17.04.84 Ken Foreman W RSC 5 Piccadilly
Summary: 19 contests, won 11, drew 1, lost 7

(Leroy) Lee Roy (Maynard)

Burslem. *Born* Jamaica 08.10.59
Welterweight
Manager F. Deakin
Previous Amateur Club Stoke-on-Trent

21.01.81 Paul Goodwin L RSC 3 Burslem
11.03.81 Nick Riozzi DREW 4 Burslem
09.06.81 Alan Power L RSC 5 Southend
13.10.81 Nick Riozzi L PTS 6 Nantwich
10.11.81 Steve Brannan L PTS 6 Bedworth
23.03.82 Dan Myers DREW 6 Nantwich
28.04.82 Paul Murray L CO 3 Burslem
16.05.83 Davey Cox L RSC 6 Manchester
06.03.84 Robert Lloyd W PTS 6 Stoke
21.03.84 Mickey Kilgallon L PTS 6 Bloomsbury
18.04.84 Mark Sperin L PTS 6 Stoke
Summary: 11 contests, won 1, drew 2, lost 8

Clyde Ruan

Slough. *Born* St Kitts 21.04.60
Southern Area Featherweight Champion
Manager J. Barclay
Previous Amateur Club Slough Boys
National Honours Schools Title 1974
Divisional Honours H Counties Lightweight Champion 1979 – 1980

23.04.80 Stuart Crabb W PTS 6 Hove
30.04.80 Andy Thomas W PTS 4 Aylesbury
08.05.80 Larry Richards W PTS 6 Solihull
12.05.80 Brindley Jones W PTS 6 Reading
03.06.80 Robert Hepburn W CO 2 Aylesbury
18.06.80 Steve Sammy Sims W PTS 6 Burslem
18.11.80 Selvin Bell W PTS 6 Windsor
01.12.80 John Griffiths W PTS 6 Reading
21.01.81 Russell Jones DREW 6 Piccadilly
17.03.81 Steve Farnsworth W PTS 6 Southend
13.05.81 Gary Lucas W PTS 8 Piccadilly
15.06.81 Peter Eubanks W RSC 8 Piccadilly
28.10.81 Jarvis Greenidge W PTS 8 Burslem
16.02.82 Jarvis Greenidge W PTS 8 Bristol
15.03.82 Steve Topliss L PTS 8 Wolverhampton
07.06.82 Jimmy Duncan W RSC 4 Bloomsbury
12.10.82 Rory Burke W RSC 7 Kensington
26.11.82 Terry McKeown W RSC 5 Glasgow
21.02.83 Paul Huggins L PTS 10 Mayfair (*Vacant Southern Area Featherweight Title*)
21.04.83 John Sharkey W RSC 4 Letchworth
20.09.83 Mark West W PTS 10 Mayfair
07.12.83 Paul Huggins W PTS 10 Bloomsbury (*Southern Area Featherweight Title Challenge & Elim. British Featherweight Title*)
05.06.84 Pat Doherty W PTS 12 Kensington (*Southern Area Featherweight Title Defence & Final Elim. British Featherweight Title*)
Summary: 23 contests, won 20, drew 1, lost 2

Billy Ruzgar

Tottenham. *Born* Hackney 18.10.62
Bantamweight
Manager A. Kasler
Previous Amateur Club Lion

16.02.82 Ken Coughlin W RSC 1 Bethnal Green
01.04.82 Shaun Shinkwin W PTS 4 Walthamstow
26.10.82 Allen Terry W RSC 2 Bethnal Green
25.01.83 Dave Pratt L PTS 6 Bethnal Green
22.03.83 Rocky Bantleman W PTS 6 Bethnal Green
31.10.83 Gordon Stobie W PTS 6 Mayfair
Summary: 6 contests, won 5, lost 1

Geoff Rymer

Hull. *Born* Hull 05.10.59
L. Heavyweight
Manager (Self)
Previous Amateur Club Hull Fish Trades
National Honours Junior ABA Title 1975 – 1976; NABC Title 1975; Young England Rep.
Divisional Honours NE Counties Middleweight R/U 1978; NE Counties Middleweight Champion 1979; NE Counties L. Heavyweight R/U 1981

19.11.81 Scott Wilde W PTS 4 Piccadilly
09.12.81 John Joseph L PTS 6 Piccadilly
25.01.82 Joe Gregory W PTS 6 Piccadilly
10.03.82 Gordon Stacey W PTS 8 Burslem
15.03.82 John Joseph W PTS 6 Piccadilly
06.04.82 Peter Tidgewell W PTS 8 Leeds
26.04.82 Paul Busette W PTS 6 Piccadilly
06.05.82 Carlton Benoit L CO 6 Mayfair
21.06.82 Joe Frater L PTS 8 Hull
28.09.82 Gary Jones W PTS 6 Aberdeen
26.10.82 Malcolm Heath W RSC 4 Hull
05.11.82 Michael Madsen L PTS 6 Copenhagen
29.11.82 George Danahar L PTS 8 Brighton
24.01.83 Paul Newman L PTS 6 Piccadilly
21.02.83 Gary Jones W PTS 6 Glasgow
16.03.83 Hugh Johnson L PTS 8 Cheltenham
12.04.83 Hugh Johnson L PTS 8 Southend

CONTINUED OVERLEAF

21.09.83 Paul Newman W PTS 8 Southend
26.10.83 Mal Kirk L PTS 6 Stoke
18.11.83 Eddie Cooper W PTS 8 Sheffield
28.11.83 Sam Reeson L PTS 8 Bayswater
19.01.84 Antonio Harris L RTD 5 Digbeth
14.02.84 Mark Pearson W RSC 5 Southend
27.03.84 Paul Newman L RSC 4 Southend
01.05.84 Paul Newman W RSC 4 Maidstone
12.06.84 Mal Kirk W RSC 3 Southend
Summary: 26 contests, won 14, lost 12

(Lorenzo) Kid Sadler (Attkinson)

Manchester. *Born* Manchester 26.12.63
Welterweight
Manager N. Basso
Previous Amateur Club Collyhurst

20.06.83 Dave Foley W RSC 3 Manchester
12.09.83 Mickey Bird L PTS 6 Leicester
19.09.83 Mike McKenzie W RSC 4 Manchester
03.10.83 Steve Metcalfe W RSC 4 Bradford
19.10.83 Paul Salih W PTS 6 Hull
14.11.83 Paul Murray W PTS 8 Manchester
22.11.83 Gordon Pratt W PTS 8 Manchester
Summary: 7 contests, won 6, lost 1

Paul Salih

Hull. *Born* Hull 20.04.59
Welterweight
Manager R. Tighe
Previous Amateur Club St Pauls
National Honours Junior ABA Title 1974; NABC Title 1976

19.09.83 Albert Buchanan DREW 6 Glasgow
19.10.83 Kid Sadler L PTS 6 Hull
22.11.83 Billy Ahearne L PTS 6 Manchester
13.03.84 Albert Buchanan W PTS 6 Hull
Summary: 4 contests, won 1, drew 1, lost 2

Chris Sanigar
Universal Pictorial Press

(Cornel) Sammy Sampson

Preston. *Born* Jamaica 28.12.58
L. Middleweight
Manager M. Goodall
Previous Amateur Club Preston & Fulwood
Divisional Honours W Lancs L. Middleweight Champion 1983

20.02.84 Dave Dunn W PTS 6 Bradford
16.04.84 Mick Dono W RSC 6 Bradford
21.05.84 Dave Dunn W PTS 6 Bradford
Summary: 3 contests, won 3

Kevin Sanders

Peterborough. *Born* Chippenham 18.10.57
Welterweight
Manager K. Whitney
Previous Amateur Club Focus

13.02.84 Ray Murray L PTS 6 Manchester
12.03.84 Tony Kempson L RSC 3 Manchester
19.04.84 Nick Ellaway L RSC 2 Basildon
Summary: 3 contests, lost 3

Chris Sanigar

Bristol. *Born* Hackney 07.07.55
Former Southern Area L. Welterweight Champion
Manager (Self)
Previous Amateur Club Empire
National Honours England Int.
Divisional Honours ABA L. Welterweight R/U 1977; W Counties L. Welterweight Champion 1978

19.09.78 Eric Purkiss W PTS 6 Southend
25.09.78 Bob Bravado W RSC 5 Mayfair
18.10.78 Dave Douglas W RSC 5 Glasgow
04.11.78 Yotham Kunda W PTS 8 Lusaka
21.11.78 Dil Collins W RSC 7 Wolverhampton
29.01.79 Granville Allen W CO 3 Glasgow
20.02.79 Benny Purdy W RSC 3 Kensington
07.03.79 George McGurk L RSC 2 Solihull
31.03.79 Paysom Choolwe L PTS 8 Lusaka
23.04.79 Roy Varden DREW 8 Piccadilly
26.06.79 Lance Williams W PTS 8 Wembley
11.09.79 Adey Allen W PTS 6 Wembley
15.10.79 Chris Walker W PTS 8 Glasgow
04.12.79 Najib Daho L RSC 1 Wembley
19.02.80 Winston Spencer L PTS 8 Kensington
07.10.80 Dave McCabe L PTS 8 Piccadilly
03.11.80 Norman Morton W PTS 8 Piccadilly
20.11.80 Gary Pearce W PTS 8 Piccadilly
16.02.81 Wayne Floyd W DIS 3 Piccadilly
04.04.81 Dan M'Putu W RTD 4 Dunkirk
02.06.81 Sid Smith L RSC 3 Kensington
(*Vacant Southern Area L. Welterweight Title*)

29.08.81 Bruno Smili DREW 6 Via Reggio
30.11.81 Sid Smith **W** CO 4 Southwark
(Southern Area L. Welterweight Title Challenge)
30.01.82 Langton Tinago **L** PTS 10 Salisbury
21.02.82 Adey Allen **W** RSC 7 Birmingham
20.04.82 Sylvester Mittee **L** RSC 9 Kensington
(Southern Area L. Welterweight Title Defence & Elim. British L. Welterweight Title)
09.06.82 Paul Chance **W** RSC 8 Bristol
11.10.82 Terry Marsh **L** DIS 7 Bristol
28.03.83 Brian Janssen **L** RSC 7 Brisbane
08.09.83 Geoff Pegler **W** CO 3 Queensway
22.02.84 Rocky Kelly **L** PTS 10 Kensington
(Vacant Southern Area Welterweight Title)
Summary: 31 contests, won 18, drew 2, lost 11

Dave Savage
Glasgow. *Born* Glasgow 22.03.62
Lightweight
Manager O. Reilly
Previous Amateur Club Argo
National Honours Scottish Int.
Divisional Honours Scottish Featherweight R/U 1981 & Lightweight R/U 1982

11.04.83 Alan Storey **W** PTS 6 Glasgow
25.04.83 Michael Harris **W** PTS 6 Aberdeen
23.05.83 Paul Keers **W** RSC 5 Glasgow
03.10.83 Willie Wilson **W** RSC 7 Glasgow
14.11.83 Abdul Kareem **L** CO 6 Glasgow
Summary: 5 contests, won 4, lost 1

Dean Scarfe
Hackney. *Born* London 08.10.63
L. Middleweight
Manager E. Fossey
Previous Amateur Club Colvestone

21.07.83 Max Key **W** PTS 4 Atlantic City
06.08.83 Tony Torres **W** PTS 4 Florida
01.09.83 Dave Heaver **W** RSC 2 Bloomsbury
13.10.83 Mick Dono **W** CO 6 Bloomsbury
18.02.84 John Mortensen **W** RSC 2 Copenhagen
23.02.84 John Langol **W** CO 2 Digbeth
21.03.84 Judas Clottey **L** PTS 6 Bloomsbury
Summary: 7 contests, won 6, lost 1

David Scere (Jacobs)
Manchester *Born* Manchester 04.06.62
Middleweight
Manager N. Basso
Previous Amateur Club Higher Blackley

18.05.81 Steve Coleman **W** RSC 2 Manchester
15.06.81 Steve Coleman **W** CO 1 Manchester
29.06.81 Tim McHugh **W** PTS 6 Liverpool
19.11.81 Joey Saunders **L** PTS 4 Liverpool
16.09.83 Terry Magee **L** PTS 6 Rhyl
03.10.83 Paul Smith **W** PTS 6 Liverpool
17.10.83 Paul Smith **W** PTS 6 Manchester
Summary: 7 contests, won 5, lost 2

George Schofield
Liverpool. *Born* Liverpool 20.03.60
L. Welterweight
Manager P. Dwyer
Previous Amateur Club Golden Gloves

23.10.78 Kevin Sheehan **W** RTD 4 Manchester
06.11.78 Joe Mills **W** PTS 6 Piccadilly
04.12.78 Shaun Stewart **W** CO 1 Manchester
28.02.79 Lance Williams **L** PTS 6 Burslem
22.03.79 Stan Atherton **W** CO 2 Liverpool
13.05.79 Barry Price **W** PTS 6 Edgbaston
21.05.79 Tony Carroll **L** PTS 8 Manchester
08.10.79 Derek Nelson **L** PTS 8 Bradford
29.11.79 Robbie Robinson **L** PTS 8 Liverpool
18.09.80 Eric Wood **L** PTS 8 Liverpool
30.10.80 Barry Winter DREW 8 Liverpool
26.11.80 Steve Briers **W** PTS 6 Stoke
22.01.81 John Lindo **W** CO 1 Liverpool
30.04.81 Eric Wood **W** PTS 8 Liverpool
04.06.81 Ceri Collins **L** PTS 8 Morecambe
24.09.81 Brian Snagg **W** PTS 8 Liverpool
19.11.81 George Metcalf **L** CO 5 Liverpool
(Vacant Central Area Lightweight Title)
22.04.82 Winston McKenzie **W** PTS 8 Liverpool
07.06.82 Winston McKenzie **L** PTS 8 Liverpool
14.02.83 Ray Ross **W** PTS 6 Liverpool
21.02.83 Peter Phillips **W** PTS 6 Bradford
01.11.83 George Kerr **W** PTS 8 Liverpool
06.02.84 Robert Lloyd DREW 8 Liverpool
17.02.84 Tommy McCallum **L** PTS 8 Rhyl
05.03.84 Peter Flanagan DREW 8 Liverpool
Summary: 25 contests, won 13, drew 3, lost 9

Dave Scott
Telford. *Born* Wellington 26.02.62
Middleweight
Manager M. Sendell
Previous Amateur Club WSOB

29.11.82 Alex Romeo **W** PTS 6 Birmingham
17.01.83 Winston Wray **L** PTS 6 Manchester
25.01.83 Harry Cowap DREW 6 Bethnal Green
15.02.83 Al Stevens **W** RSC 2 Wolverhampton
02.03.83 Wayne Hawkins **W** CO 4 Evesham
17.03.83 Gary Cable **W** CO 2 Marylebone

CONTINUED OVERLEAF

22.03.83 Hugh Johnson W PTS 6 Wolverhampton
05.04.83 Cameron Lithgow L RSC 5 Kensington
27.04.83 John Elliott W PTS 6 Wolverhampton
12.06.83 Barry Ahmed W PTS 8 Middlesbrough
27.09.83 Chris Lawson L PTS 8 Stoke
23.11.83 Paul Shell W RSC 4 Solihull
01.12.83 John Elliott W PTS 6 Dudley
28.01.84 Willie Wright L RTD 5 Hanley
Summary: 14 contests, won 9, drew 1, lost 4

John Sharkey

Glasgow. *Born* Glasgow 24.11.59
Featherweight
Manager T. Gilmour
Previous Amateur Club Scottish National

15.09.80 Chris McCallum W RSC 3 Glasgow
14.10.80 Gerry Beard W RSC 3 Wolverhampton
09.02.81 Larry Richards DREW 4 Glasgow
18.03.81 Alex Rodden W RTD 4 Stoke
30.03.81 Steve Pollard W RSC 5 Glasgow
01.06.81 Steve Farnsworth W RSC 3 Nottingham
11.06.81 Steve Pollard L PTS 8 Hull
22.06.81 Selvin Bell W CO 5 Glasgow
21.09.81 George Sutton W CO 4 Glasgow
22.10.81 Lee Graham L RSC 12 Piccadilly
07.12.81 Alec Irvine W PTS 6 Nottingham
25.01.82 Jarvis Greenidge W PTS 8 Glasgow
22.02.82 Alec Irvine W RSC 5 Glasgow
11.05.82 Alec Irvine W PTS 8 Derby
27.09.82 Steve Topliss L PTS 8 Birmingham
10.02.83 Kevin Howard L PTS 8 Sunderland
21.02.83 Kevin Howard W RSC 5 Glasgow
11.03.83 Francis Tripp L PTS 10 St. Etienne
21.04.83 Clyde Ruan L RSC 4 Letchworth
05.09.83 Eddie Morgan W CO 3 Glasgow

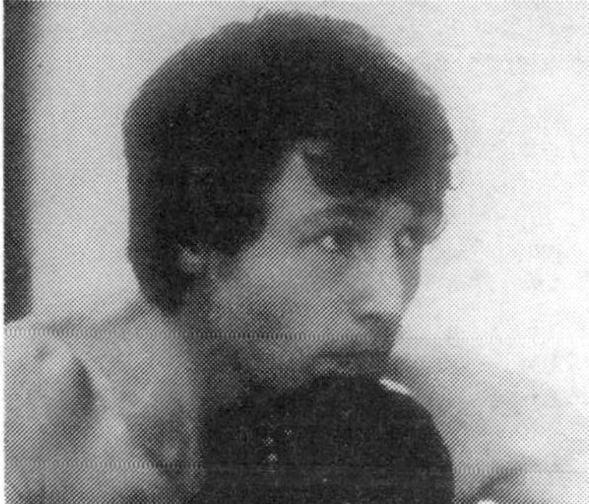

John Sharkey
Scotsman/Evening News

24.09.83 Jean Marc Renard L PTS 8 Oostrebeke
29.10.83 Guiseppe Louite L DIS 8 San Remo
22.11.83 Steve Topliss L PTS 8 Wolverhampton
25.01.84 Pat Doherty L RSC 4 Solihull
16.04.84 Kevin Howard W PTS 8 Glasgow
Summary: 25 contests, won 14, drew 1, lost 10

Jack Sharp

Eltham. *Born* London 17.06.60
L. Middleweight
Manager (Self)
Previous Amateur Club Eltham & District
National Honours Schools Title 1976
Divisional Honours SE London L. Middleweight R/U 1979

15.06.81 Jimmy Smith L PTS 6 Mayfair
03.08.81 Ian Baker W CO 2 Brighton
28.09.81 Jimmy Smith W PTS 6 Lewisham
26.10.81 Ashley Jones W RSC 4 Southwark
30.11.81 Casley McCallum W PTS 6 Southwark
16.02.82 Frank Campbell W RSC 1 Bethnal Green
23.03.82 Bobby Williams W PTS 6 Bethnal Green
26.04.82 Conrad Oscar L PTS 6 Southwark
18.10.82 Winston Davis L PTS 6 Southwark
29.11.82 Mick Courtney W PTS 6 Southwark
31.01.83 Vince Gajny L PTS 6 Southwark
21.11.83 Earl Edwards W RSC 3 Eltham
13.02.84 Tony Britton L PTS 8 Eltham
Summary: 13 contests, won 8, lost 5

Stuart Shaw

Nottingham. *Born* Huddersfield 14.10.59
Former Undefeated Midlands Area Lightweight Champion
Manager J. Gill
Previous Amateur Club Ruddington
Divisional Honours M Counties Featherweight R/U 1980 – 1981

01.06.81 Brian Hyslop L CO 5 Nottingham
25.09.81 Steve Topliss DREW 6 Nottingham
13.10.81 Steve Topliss L PTS 8 Wolverhampton
02.11.81 Dean Marsden L PTS 6 Nottingham
23.11.81 Alex Rodden W CO 4 Nottingham
01.12.81 Gerry Devine W CO 4 Derby
20.01.82 Gary Lucas L PTS 8 Burslem
19.03.82 Peter Jones L PTS 8 Nottingham
28.04.82 Steve Enright W PTS 8 Burslem
24.05.82 Brian Jones W PTS 6 Nottingham
14.06.82 Hugh Russell L PTS 8 Mayfair
30.06.82 Hector Clottey W PTS 8 Liverpool
07.09.82 Alan Tombs L PTS 8 Crewe

06.10.82 Steve Enright **W** RTD 5 Solihull
20.10.82 Alan Tombs L PTS 8 Stoke
01.12.82 Lee Halford **W** RSC 6 Stafford (*Vacant Midlands Area Lightweight Title*)
16.03.83 Rory Burke L RSC 4 Stoke
25.04.83 Joey Joynson L RSC 1 Mayfair
15.10.83 John Doherty L PTS 8 Coventry
Summary: 19 contests, won 7, drew 1, lost 11

Kevin Shearon

Boreham Wood. *Born* Hillingdon 10.11.59
Middleweight
Manager A. Kasler
Previous Amateur Club Brookside

08.09.83 Bobby Williams L PTS 6 Queensway
19.03.84 Mike Farghaly L RSC 3 Manchester
Summary: 2 contests, lost 2

Dennis Sheehan

Nottingham. *Born* Nottingham 09.09.59
Midlands Area L. Middleweight Champion
Manager (Self)
Previous Amateur Club NSOB

25.11.80 Steve Tempro **W** PTS 6 Wolverhampton
08.12.80 Peter Stockdale **W** RSC 2 Nottingham
02.02.81 Errol Dennis **W** RSC 3 Nottingham
09.02.81 Dominic Bergonzi L PTS 8 Mayfair
09.03.81 Dave Goodwin DREW 6 Wolverhampton
16.03.81 Paul Murray DREW 6 Nottingham
25.09.81 Gary Petty **W** RSC 4 Nottingham
13.10.81 R. W. Smith L PTS 6 Kensington
27.01.82 Vince Gajny L PTS 6 Stoke
21.02.82 Richard Wilson L RSC 4 Birmingham
07.04.82 Paul Murray L PTS 6 Evesham
26.04.82 Winston Davis L PTS 6 Leicester
24.05.82 Paul Murray DREW 6 Nottingham
13.08.82 Mickey Mapp **W** PTS 6 Strand
14.09.82 Mick Courtney L PTS 8 Southend
26.09.82 Paul Mitchell L PTS 6 Birmingham
06.10.82 Roy Varden **W** PTS 8 Stoke
18.10.82 Dennis Pryce L PTS 6 Nottingham
09.11.82 Cameron Lithgow L RSC 5 Kensington
26.01.83 Bert Myrie **W** RSC 5 Stoke (*Vacant Midlands Area L. Middleweight Title*)
22.02.83 Jimmy Batten L RSC 4 Bethnal Green
25.04.83 Tony Britton L PTS 8 Mayfair
16.05.83 Richard Wilson L PTS 8 Mayfair
07.12.83 Mickey Kidd L PTS 8 Stoke
15.03.84 Steve Ward L RSC 6 Leicester
Summary: 25 contests, won 7, drew 3, lost 15

Kevin Sheehan

Nottingham. *Born* Alfreton 18.02.58
Welterweight
Manager J. Gill
Previous Amateur Club Radford Boys

25.10.76 Young John Daly **W** PTS 4 Luton
30.11.76 Don Aageson L RSC 1 Dudley
03.03.77 Malcolm McHugh **W** RSC 3 Caister
15.03.77 Albert Coley DREW 4 Leeds
20.04.77 Cleveland Irvine **W** PTS 6 Manchester
17.05.77 Najib Daho L RSC 2 Wolverhampton
11.10.77 Steve Early L RSC 3 Coventry
12.10.78 Tony Vernon L PTS 6 Liverpool
23.10.78 George Schofield L RTD 4 Manchester
21.01.80 Dave Ramsden **W** RSC 1 Nottingham
28.01.80 Robert Wakefield **W** RSC 4 Bradford
25.02.80 John Lindo DREW 6 Bradford
03.03.80 Glyn Rhodes **W** CO 1 Nottingham
05.03.80 Jimmy Bunclark L RSC 1 Liverpool
13.10.80 Jarvis Greenidge L PTS 8 Nottingham
25.11.80 Terry Welch L CO 1 Wolverhampton
06.04.81 John Lindo L RSC 5 Bradford
28.04.83 Ricky Deane **W** RSC 3 Leicester
09.05.83 Errol Dennis **W** CO 3 Nottingham
25.05.83 Robert Lloyd L RSC 5 Rhyl
03.10.83 Dave Haggarty L RSC 2 Glasgow
Summary: 21 contests, won 8, drew 2, lost 11

Paul Shell (Sheldon)

Birmingham. *Born* Birmingham 03.03.54
L. Heavyweight
Manager G. Donaghy
Previous Amateur Club Sheldon Heath

24.02.82 Ian Lazarus L PTS 6 Evesham
10.03.82 Rob Wada L PTS 6 Nottingham
07.06.82 Al Stevens **W** DIS 1 Edgbaston
13.09.82 Jerry Golden **W** PTS 6 Manchester
13.10.82 Alex Romeo **W** PTS 6 Evesham
19.01.83 James Cook L PTS 8 Birmingham
31.01.83 John Elliott **W** PTS 6 Birmingham
02.03.83 John Elliott L PTS 6 Evesham
22.03.83 John Elliott **W** PTS 6 Wolverhampton
13.04.83 Winston Burnett **W** PTS 6 Evesham
26.04.83 John Moody L RTD 3 Bethnal Green
13.06.83 John Elliott **W** PTS 8 Nottingham
23.11.83 Dave Scott L RSC 4 Solihull
30.01.84 Jerry Golden DREW 6 Manchester
22.03.84 Harry Cowap L RTD 7 Maidenhead
19.04.84 John Moody L CO 1 Basildon
Summary: 16 contests, won 7, drew 1, lost 8

Phil Sheridan

Nottingham. *Born* Birmingham 18.09.63
Welterweight
Manager L. Anderson
Previous Amateur Club Sheldon Heath

24.02.82 Delroy Pearce **L** PTS 6 Evesham
13.09.82 Peter Flanagan **L** CO 2 Manchester
07.11.83 Elvis Morton **L** PTS 6 Birmingham
22.11.83 Dave Heaver **W** PTS 6 Wolverhampton
07.12.83 Steve Apollo **W** RSC 1 Stoke
25.01.84 Dave Foley DREW 6 Stoke
30.01.84 Graeme Griffin **L** PTS 6 Birmingham
27.02.84 Steve Friel **W** PTS 6 Birmingham
14.03.84 Mark Hynes **W** PTS 6 Stoke
16.04.84 Julian Boustead **L** RSC 6 Nottingham
Summary: 10 contests, won 4, drew 1, lost 5

Nigel Shingles

Brighton. *Born* Ramsgate 22.09.60
Middleweight
Manager A. Barron
Previous Amateur Club Patcham

21.03.84 Ronnie Fraser **W** PTS 6 Solihull
09.05.84 Danny Clinton **W** RSC 2 Mayfair
Summary: 2 contests, won 2

Ron Shinkwin
Derek Rowe (Photos) Ltd

Danny Shinkwin
Derek Rowe (Photos) Ltd

Danny Shinkwin

Boreham Wood. *Born* Watford 25.11.61
L. Welterweight
Manager J. Barclay
Previous Amateur Club Brookside
Divisional Honours H Counties Welterweight R/U 1981

01.04.82 Mark Crouch **W** PTS 6 Walthamstow
19.04.82 Gary Petty **W** PTS 6 Bristol

27.04.82 Eric Purkiss L PTS 6 Southend
04.09.82 Dan Myers W PTS 6 Piccadilly
06.04.84 Elvis Morton L PTS 6 Watford
16.04.84 Tony McKenzie W RSC 1 Birmingham
19.05.84 Colin Neagle L PTS 6 Bristol
05.06.84 David Irving L CO 2 Kensington
Summary: 8 contests, won 4, lost 4

Ron Shinkwin

Boreham Wood. *Born* Watford 27.11.64
L. Welterweight
Manager J. Barclay
Previous Amateur Club Brookside
Divisional Honours H Counties L. Welterweight Champion 1982

06.05.82 Vince Vahey L PTS 4 Mayfair
13.09.82 Shaun Robinson L PTS 4 Brighton
11.10.82 Glyn Mitchell L PTS 4 Bristol
26.11.82 Jim Paton L PTS 4 Glasgow
14.02.83 Michael Betts W PTS 4 Lewisham
16.03.83 Michael Betts W PTS 6 Cheltenham
21.03.83 Willie Wilson DREW 4 Nottingham
16.04.83 Graeme Griffin W PTS 4 Bristol
25.04.83 Chris Harvey L PTS 4 Southwark
10.05.83 Abdul Kareem L PTS 6 Southend
05.09.83 Ricky Andrews W PTS 6 Mayfair
06.10.83 T. Roy Smith DREW 6 Basildon
23.11.83 Carl Green W PTS 6 Solihull
16.02.84 John Faulkner W PTS 6 Basildon
07.03.84 Steve Friel L PTS 6 Brighton
06.04.84 Mike Durvan L PTS 6 Watford
31.05.84 Gary Champion W CO 6 Basildon
Summary: 17 contests, won 7, drew 2, lost 8

Shaun Shinkwin

Boreham Wood. *Born* Watford 30.11.62
Lightweight
Manager J. Barclay
Previous Amateur Club Brookside
Divisional Honours H Counties Bantamweight Champion 1981

01.04.82 Billy Ruzgar L PTS 4 Walthamstow
19.04.82 Vince Vahey L PTS 4 Bristol
10.05.82 Kevin Hay W PTS 6 Copthorne
08.06.82 Eugene Maloney W PTS 4 Southend
14.06.82 Eddie Morgan L PTS 6 Mayfair
13.10.82 Joe Donohoe L PTS 6 Walthamstow
22.11.82 Allen Terry W PTS 4 Lewisham
29.11.82 Carl Gaynor W PTS 6 Southwark
06.12.82 Eddie Morgan DREW 6 Bristol
24.01.83 Steve King W RSC 5 Mayfair
31.01.83 Carl Gaynor L PTS 6 Southwark
21.02.83 Dave Pratt W PTS 6 Mayfair
09.03.83 Eddie Morgan W PTS 6 Solihull
17.03.83 Chris Harvey W PTS 6 Marylebone
16.04.83 Michael Harris L PTS 6 Bristol
Summary: 15 contests, won 8, drew 1, lost 6

Paul Shutt

Paul Shutt

Leicester. *Born* Leicester 13.01.56
Middleweight
Manager (Self)
Previous Amateur Club Belgrave
Divisional Honours M Counties L. Middleweight R/U 1976

03.05.76 Jimmy Pickard W PTS 6 Birmingham
17.05.76 Joe Hannaford W RSC 5 Nottingham
07.06.76 Carlton Lyons W RSC 7 Manchester
30.09.76 Tim McHugh W PTS 8 Liverpool
25.10.76 Brian Gregory W RSC 5 Birmingham
03.11.76 Arthur Winfield W PTS 8 Caister
18.11.76 Dave Davies W PTS 8 Liverpool
28.01.77 Jim Devanney W RSC 7 West Bromwich
07.02.77 Steve Angell DREW 8 Mayfair
25.02.77 Achille Mitchell L RSC 6 Digbeth
12.12.77 George Salmon W PTS 8 Birmingham
16.01.78 H. H. Thompson W CO 2 Birmingham
31.01.78 Gilbert Cohen L CO 7 Paris
13.03.78 Dave Owens L RSC 2 Nottingham
17.04.78 Keith Bussey L CO 4 Walworth
13.06.78 Young McEwan L RSC 2 Coventry
21.02.79 Romal Ambrose L CO 7 Evesham
(*Vacant Midland Area Middleweight Title*)
10.04.79 Clifton Wallace W RSC 4 Wolverhampton
15.05.79 Steve Hopkin L RSC 2 Wembley
10.10.83 Johnny Elliott L CO 1 Birmingham
Summary: 20 contests, won 11, drew 1, lost 8

Shane Silvester
West Bromwich. *Born* West Bromwich 13.10.63
Bantamweight
Manager R. Gray
Previous Amateur Club Army

12.12.83 Billy Joe Dee W RSC 2 Birmingham
10.02.84 Andy Green W RSC 5 Dudley
27.02.84 Steve Hanna L PTS 6 Birmingham
14.03.84 Dave Smith W PTS 4 Stoke
27.03.84 Tony Rahman W PTS 6 Wolverhampton
16.04.84 Kevin Downer W PTS 6 Birmingham
07.06.84 Tommy Mallon W RSC 5 Dudley
Summary: 7 contests, won 6, lost 1

Derek Simpkin
Swadlincote. *Born* Hartshorne 09.02.53
Heavyweight
Manager (Self)
Previous Amateur Club Belgrave

24.06.74 John Depledge L PTS 6 Bedford
09.09.74 Barry Clough W RSC 2 Bedford
16.09.74 Tony Moore L RSC 5 Birmingham
23.10.74 Barry Clough DREW 6 Stoke
04.12.74 Bruce Woodward W CO 4 Stoke
10.12.74 John Depledge W PTS 6 Blackpool
13.01.75 Art Gibson W RSC 2 Mayfair
17.02.75 David Fry W RSC 6 Mayfair
26.02.75 Sid Paddock W PTS 6 Camberley
12.03.75 John Depledge W DIS 7 Solihull
24.03.75 Sid Paddock L PTS 6 Mayfair
09.04.75 John Depledge W PTS 6 Bradford
24.04.75 Bjorn Rudi W PTS 8 Ramsey
16.05.75 John Depledge W PTS 6 Birmingham
06.08.75 Neville Meade L RSC 3 Cardiff
25.11.75 Paul Kinsella L PTS 6 Kensington
12.12.75 Bjorn Rudi L PTS 8 Oslo
13.01.76 Garfield McEwan L PTS 8 Wolverhampton
03.02.76 David Fry L PTS 8 Southend
26.03.76 Brian Huckfield L PTS 8 Bournemouth
06.04.76 Paul Kinsella DREW 6 Kensington
05.05.76 Terry Mintus L RSC 6 Solihull
05.10.76 Brian Huckfield L RSC 5 Coventry
07.02.77 Terry Mintus L PTS 8 Mayfair
22.02.77 Peter Freeman L DIS 6 Wolverhampton
01.03.77 Kris Smith L PTS 8 Marylebone
18.04.77 Paul Kinsella W RTD 4 Mayfair
09.05.77 Neil Malpass L PTS 6 Mayfair
26.05.77 John Depledge W PTS 8 Bradford
08.09.77 Bruce Grandham L RSC 5 Liverpool
20.11.78 Colin Flute W PTS 6 Birmingham
30.11.78 Theo Josephs L PTS 6 Caister
19.03.79 Winston Allen L PTS 8 Bradford
16.10.79 Brian Huckfield L DIS 7 West Bromwich
30.10.80 Steve Gee DREW 6 Wolverhampton
13.11.80 Martin Nee L PTS 8 Queensway
01.12.80 Martin Nee L PTS 6 Bloomsbury
08.12.80 Rudi Pika L RSC 3 Kensington
16.02.82 Eddie Neilson L RSC 3 Bristol
15.02.83 Frank Robinson L PTS 6 Wolverhampton
22.02.83 Hughroy Currie L PTS 6 Bethnal Green
11.04.83 Dave Garside L PTS 6 Gosforth
Summary: 42 contests, won 13, drew 3, lost 26

Mark Simpson
Brighton. *Born* Coventry 16.04.62
Welterweight
Manager R. Davies
Previous Amateur Club None

07.03.84 Dave Hallett W RSC 6 Brighton
27.03.84 Billy Edwards L PTS 6 Southend
01.05.84 Kevin Johnson W RSC 3 Maidstone
10.05.84 Peter Ashcroft L PTS 6 Digbeth
Summary: 4 contests, won 2, lost 2

Phil Simpson
South Elmsall. *Born* Wakefield 25.11.57
Heavyweight
Manager K. Richardson
Previous Amateur Club Doncaster Plant Works
Divisional Honours NE Counties S. Heavyweight R/U 1983

12.12.83 Barry Ellis L CO 3 Bedworth
Summary: 1 contest, lost 1

Tony Sinnott
Gordon Whiting

Jimmy Singleton
Liverpool. *Born* Liverpool 21.01.61
L. Welterweight
Manager J. Singleton
Previous Amateur Club Rotunda

29.11.82 Dave Springer **W** PTS 6 Southwark
31.01.83 Dave Springer **W** CO 4 Southwark
17.03.83 Brett Jefford L PTS 6 Marylebone
Summary: 3 contests, won 2, lost 1

Tony Sinnott
Liverpool. *Born* Liverpool 20.09.58
L. Welterweight
Manager M. Goodall
Previous Amateur Club Glen Boys
Divisional Honours W Lancs L. Middleweight R/U 1977

18.09.80 Dave Sullivan **W** RTD 5 Liverpool
30.10.80 Dave Douglas **W** PTS 8 Liverpool
26.11.80 Kid Murray **W** PTS 8 Stoke
22.01.81 Dil Collins **W** RSC 2 Liverpool
05.03.81 Les Wint **W** PTS 8 Liverpool
30.04.81 Pat Smythe **W** RSC 3 Liverpool
04.06.81 Dennis Price L DIS 2 Morecambe
24.09.81 Tommy Davitt **W** RSC 6 Liverpool
19.11.81 Dennis Pryce L PTS 8 Liverpool
24.06.82 Barry Winter **W** CO 3 Kirkby
20.09.82 Danny Garrison DREW 8 Bradford
18.10.82 John Lindo **W** PTS 8 Blackpool
24.02.83 Davy Campbell **W** CO 1 Liverpool
08.04.83 Sam Omidi **W** PTS 8 Liverpool
15.09.83 Willie Booth L PTS 8 Liverpool
09.12.83 Jeff Decker **W** RSC 5 Liverpool
16.04.84 Terry Marsh L PTS 12 Bradford
(*Final Elim. British L. Welterweight Title*)
Summary: 17 contests, won 12, drew 1, lost 4

Roy Skeldon
Tipton. *Born* Tipton 15.12.52
Former Midlands Area L. Heavyweight Champion
Manager G. Riley
Previous Amateur Club None

20.09.72 Dave Parris DREW 6 Solihull
06.11.72 Steve Foley L RSC 2 Bedford
31.10.78 Colin Flute L CO 4 Wolverhampton
31.01.79 Rocky Burton **W** PTS 4 Stoke
15.03.79 Rocky Burton **W** PTS 4 Dudley
28.03.79 Ron Green **W** PTS 4 Evesham
10.04.79 Colin Flute **W** PTS 4 Wolverhampton
16.05.79 Colin Flute **W** RSC 4 Wolverhampton
02.07.79 Wally Barnes **W** RSC 4 Wolverhampton
18.09.79 Clive Beardsley **W** CO 3 Wolverhampton
29.10.79 Mick Fellingham **W** PTS 6 Wolverhampton
03.12.79 Trevor Cattouse **W** PTS 8 Wolverhampton
16.01.80 Trevor Cattouse L PTS 8 Stoke
19.05.80 Liam Coleman DREW 6 Bradford
08.07.80 Eddie Fenton **W** RSC 6 Wolverhampton
(*Midlands Area L. Heavyweight Title Challenge*)
01.12.80 Chris Lawson **W** PTS 8 Wolverhampton
12.02.81 Alex Tompkins L PTS 8 Bolton
06.05.81 Danny Lawford L PTS 8 Solihull
20.01.82 Antonio Harris L PTS 10 Solihull
10.03.82 Antonio Harris L PTS 10 Solihull
(*Midlands Area L. Heavyweight Title Defence*)
08.05.82 Kid Power L RSC 5 Salisbury
11.11.82 Chris Devine **W** RSC 7 Stafford
17.11.82 Antonio Harris L PTS 8 Solihull
07.03.83 Andy Straughn L RSC 3 Piccadilly
01.12.83 Romal Ambrose L RSC 4 Dudley
04.04.84 Alex Romeo **W** PTS 6 Evesham
07.06.84 Cordwell Hylton **W** CO 7 Dudley
Summary: 27 contests, won 14, drew 2, lost 11

Dave Smith
Hartlepool. *Born* Sherburn 07.06.64
Bantamweight
Manager D. Mancini
Previous Amateur Club Consett

17.10.83 Craig Killoran L PTS 4 Southwark
16.11.83 Dave Boy McAuley L CO 1 Belfast
14.03.84 Shane Silvester L PTS 4 Stoke
Summary: 3 contests, lost 3

Eddie Smith
Manchester. *Born* Jamaica 25.11.58
Middleweight
Manager M. Hope
Previous Amateur Club Collyhurst

01.04.76 Cyril Bishton **W** PTS 4 Liverpool
03.05.76 Peter Whittle **W** PTS 4 Southsea
07.06.76 Steve Heavisides **W** RSC 2 Manchester
13.09.76 Howard Mills **W** PTS 4 Manchester
11.10.76 Joe Jackson **W** PTS 4 Manchester
28.10.76 Al Neville L PTS 4 Mayfair
15.11.76 George Salmon **W** PTS 4 Nottingham
06.12.76 Owen Robinson **W** PTS 6 Manchester
17.01.77 Steve Stocks **W** PTS 4 Liverpool
14.03.77 Howard Mills L PTS 6 Manchester
21.03.77 Steve Fenton **W** RSC 6 Birmingham
20.04.77 Dave Merrell **W** CO 1 Manchester
09.05.77 Jimmy Pickard DREW 8 Liverpool
13.06.77 Jimmy Pickard L PTS 8 Manchester

CONTINUED OVERLEAF

08.09.77 Joe Lally **W** PTS 8 Liverpool
24.10.77 Bob Tuckett **W** PTS 8 Manchester
05.12.77 Jimmy Pickard **W** PTS 8 Manchester
18.01.78 Roy Gumbs **W** CO 8 Solihull
20.02.78 Joe Gregory **W** PTS 8 Nottingham
06.03.78 George Salmon **W** PTS 8 Manchester
24.04.78 H. H. Thompson **W** CO 4 Middlesbrough
08.05.78 Jimmy Pickard **L** PTS 8 Manchester
24.10.78 Tony Sibson **W** PTS 8 Kensington
17.01.79 Chris Lawson **W** RSC 4 Stoke
05.03.79 Tony Sibson **L** PTS 10 Wolverhampton
19.03.79 Bonny McKenzie **L** PTS 8 Piccadilly
26.09.79 Bonny McKenzie **W** PTS 8 Solihull
28.11.79 Tom Collins **L** PTS 8 Solihull
18.02.80 Eddie Burke **L** PTS 8 Stockport
27.03.80 Johnny Heard **W** RTD 5 Liverpool
29.04.80 Dave Owens **W** CO 1 Stockport
21.05.80 Chissanda Mutti **L** PTS 8 Coventry
26.09.80 Frank Wissenbach **L** DIS 4 Cologne
04.12.80 Frank Wissenbach **W** CO 8 Cologne
06.06.81 Rafael Zamora **W** RSC 3 Las Vegas
09.11.82 Mark Kaylor **L** RSC 3 Kensington
28.03.83 Mick Morris **W** CO 5 Manchester
16.05.83 James Cook **L** RSC 6 Manchester
Summary: 38 contests, won 25, drew 1, lost 12

Paul Smith

Sheffield. *Born* Sheffield 14.07.60
Middleweight
Manager B. Ingle
Previous Amateur Club Eckington

03.10.83 David Scere **L** PTS 6 Liverpool
17.10.83 David Scere **L** PTS 6 Manchester
09.11.83 Billy Ahearne **L** PTS 6 Sheffield
05.12.83 Billy Ahearne DREW 8 Manchester
30.01.84 Billy Ahearne **W** RSC 5 Manchester
12.03.84 Mike Farghaly **L** PTS 8 Manchester
09.04.84 Mike Farghaly **L** RSC 3 Manchester
Summary: 7 contests, won 1, drew 1, lost 5

R W Smith

(Robert) R. W. Smith

St Ives. *Born* Cambridge 02.10.62
L. Middleweight
Manager A. Smith
Previous Amateur Club Sandy & District
National Honours Schools Title 1978

26.05.81 Kirk Davis **W** RSC 3 Bethnal Green
20.06.81 Peter Sullivan **W** CO 1 Wembley
22.09.81 Ron Pearce **W** CO 2 Bethnal Green
13.10.81 Dennis Sheehan **W** PTS 6 Kensington
12.10.82 Mickey Mapp **W** PTS 6 Kensington
07.12.82 Robert Armstrong **W** CO 1 Kensington
25.01.83 Cliff Curtis **W** CO 2 Bethnal Green
15.03.83 Kid Murray **W** PTS 6 Wembley
26.04.83 Randy Henderson **W** PTS 6 Bethnal Green
03.05.83 Rob Wada **W** PTS 6 Wembley
11.10.83 Nigel Thomas **W** RSC 3 Kensington
06.12.83 Arthur Davis **W** RSC 4 Kensington
22.02.84 John Ridgman **W** RSC 3 Kensington
25.04.84 Dennis Fain **L** RSC 6 Atlantic City
Summary: 14 contests, won 13, lost 1

Sid Smith
Universal Pictorial Press

Sid Smith

Forest Hill. *Born* Lambeth 24.03.59
Former Southern Area L. Welterweight & Welterweight Champion
Manager D. Mancini
Previous Amateur Club Fitzroy Lodge
National Honours Junior ABA Titles 1974 – 1975; NABC Titles 1974 – 1975; Young England Rep.
Divisional Honours SE London L. Welterweight Champion 1977

13.03.78 Delvin Whyte **W** RSC 4 Walworth
17.04.78 Roger Guest **W** RTD 2 Walworth
25.04.78 Steve Ward **W** PTS 6 Kensington

09.10.78 Norman Morton W CO 4 Marylebone
11.11.78 Ray Ross W RSC 7 Marylebone
05.12.78 Frank McCord L PTS 6 Kensington
13.02.79 Eric Wood W PTS 8 Marylebone
19.03.79 Dai Davies W PTS 8 Marylebone
24.09.79 Eric Purkiss W PTS 8 Hammersmith
03.12.79 Sylvester Gordon W RTD 5 Marylebone
10.11.80 Davy Campbell W CO 2 Southwark
16.02.81 Tony Carroll W PTS 8 Southwark
02.06.81 Chris Sanigar W RSC 3 Kensington (*Vacant Southern Area L. Welterweight Title*)
26.10.81 Gary Brown W RSC 1 Southwark
30.11.81 Chris Sanigar L CO 4 Southwark (*Southern Area L. Welterweight Title Defence*)
22.03.82 Carl Bailey W CO 4 Southwark
26.04.82 Tommy Davitt W RSC 1 Southwark
18.10.82 Peter Neal W RSC 6 Southwark (*Vacant Southern Area Welterweight Title*)
29.11.82 Billy Waith W PTS 8 Southwark
01.03.83 Lloyd Honeyghan L CO 4 Kensington (*Southern Area Welterweight Title Defence & Elim. British Welterweight Title*)
Summary: 20 contests, won 17, lost 3

(Terry) T. Roy Smith

Tottenham. *Born* Finchley 09.07.62
Lightweight
Manager W. Wynter
Previous Amateur Club New Enterprise

06.10.83 Ron Shinkwin DREW 6 Basildon
27.03.84 Teddy Anderson DREW 6 Bethnal Green
Summary: 2 contests, drew 2

Terry Smith

Covent Garden. *Born* London 17.03.61
Lightweight
Manager D. Mancini
Previous Amateur Club Fitzroy Lodge
National Honours Schools Title 1975; Young England Rep.
Divisional Honours SE London Featherweight Champion 1979

30.11.81 Tony Davis W CO 1 Southwark
01.02.82 Chris McCallum W PTS 6 Southwark
22.03.82 Tyrell Wilson W RSC 1 Southwark
20.04.82 Mickey Duddy W RSC 3 Kensington
04.05.82 Rocky Mensah W PTS 6 Wembley
01.06.82 Kevin Doherty W RSC 3 Kensington
12.10.82 J. J. Barrett W PTS 6 Kensington
29.11.82 Tommy Cook W RTD 1 Southwark
31.01.83 Tommy Cook W PTS 6 Southwark
31.05.83 George Kerr L RSC 3 Kensington
Summary: 10 contests, won 9, lost 1

Tony Smith

Liverpool. *Born* Liverpool 12.10.61
Welterweight
Manager M. Goodall
Previous Amateur Club Golden Gloves

03.10.83 Paul Thompson W RSC 1 Bradford
14.11.83 Peter Phillips W PTS 6 Nantwich
09.12.83 Steve Tempro W PTS 6 Liverpool
19.12.83 Peter Phillips W PTS 6 Bradford
16.01.84 Tommy Bennett W PTS 6 Bradford
30.01.84 Micky Bird W PTS 6 Manchester
16.04.84 Jaswant Singh Ark L RSC 2 Bradford
21.05.84 John McAllister L PTS 8 Aberdeen
04.06.84 Dave Douglas L PTS 8 Glasgow
Summary: 9 contests, won 6, lost 3

Dave Smithson

South Norwood. *Born* Swindon 05.01.61
Lightweight
Manager H. Burgess
Previous Amateur Club Fitzroy Lodge

19.03.81 Neil Brown L PTS 6 Norwich
29.04.81 Carl Gaynor L PTS 6 Burslem
05.05.81 George White W PTS 6 Southend
16.02.82 Joshua Eshun W PTS 4 Lewisham
29.09.82 Michael Betts DREW 4 Effingham Park
24.01.83 Glyn Mitchell L PTS 6 Piccadilly
14.02.83 Glyn Mitchell DREW 8 Lewisham
21.02.83 Frankie Lake W PTS 8 Piccadilly
Summary: 8 contests, won 3, drew 2, lost 3

Winston Spencer

Walworth. *Born* Jamaica 03.10.56
Former Undefeated Southern Area Lightweight Champion
Manager G. Steene
Previous Amateur Club Lynn

14.02.77 Charlie Wallace W RTD 2 Walworth
21.02.77 Albert Coley L PTS 6 Nottingham
18.04.77 Pat Campbell W PTS 6 Walworth
09.05.77 Frank McCord W RTD 3 Mayfair
23.05.77 Pat Campbell W RSC 3 Hammersmith
05.07.77 Najib Daho W RSC 5 Wolverhampton
10.10.77 Johnny Gwilliam W CO 2 Mayfair

CONTINUED OVERLEAF

15.11.77 Wayne Floyd **W** RSC 7 Bethnal Green
25.04.78 Barry Price **W** PTS 8 Kensington
25.09.78 Robbie Robinson **W** PTS 8 Mayfair
20.11.78 Jeff Pritchard **W** RSC 6 Piccadilly
20.02.79 Eric Wood **W** CO 3 Kensington
19.03.79 George McGurk **W** DIS 2 Mayfair
24.09.79 Dil Collins **W** RSC 3 Mayfair
12.11.79 Tommy Davitt **W** PTS 8 Mayfair
19.02.80 Chris Sanigar **W** PTS 8 Kensington
22.04.80 Tony Carroll **L** PTS 8 Kensington
28.06.80 Willie Booth **W** PTS 8 Wembley
27.09.80 Paul Chance **W** RSC 1 Wembley
01.11.80 Najib Daho **W** RSC 5 Glasgow
31.03.81 George Feeney **L** RSC 9 Wembley (*Elim. British Lightweight Title*)
13.10.81 Willie Booth **W** RSC 5 Kensington
26.10.81 Walter Clayton **L** PTS 8 Mayfair
01.02.82 Billy O'Grady **W** RSC 6 Southwark (*Vacant Southern Area Lightweight Title*)
07.06.82 Peter Eubanks **W** PTS 8 Piccadilly
15.03.83 Mickey Baker **W** DIS 2 Wembley
01.12.83 Mohammed Kawoya **W** RSC 5 Copenhagen
26.01.84 Peter Eubanks **W** RTD 5 Strand
Summary: 28 contests, won 24, lost 4

Mark Sperin
Birmingham. *Born* Birmingham 08.12.60
Welterweight
Manager G. Donaghy
Previous Amateur Club Birmingham City
National Honours NABC Title 1977

18.04.84 Lee Roy **W** PTS 6 Stoke
12.05.84 Steve Harwood **W** RSC 4 Hanley
Summary: 2 contests, won 2

Gordon Stacey
Derek Rowe (Photos) Ltd

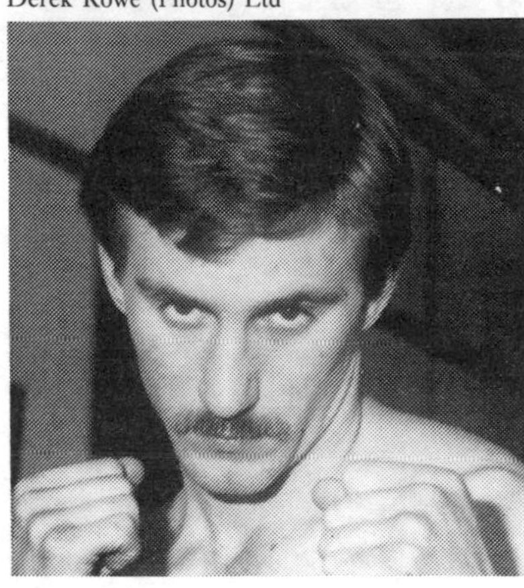

Dave Springer
Hayes. *Born* Barbados 05.09.54
Lightweight
Manager W. Wynter
Previous Amateur Club UER
Divisional Honours NW London Lightweight R/U 1974

20.09.82 Johnny Grant **L** PTS 6 Mayfair
28.09.82 Paul Cook **L** RSC 2 Bethnal Green
29.11.82 Jimmy Singleton **L** PTS 6 Southwark
31.01.83 Jimmy Singleton **L** CO 4 Southwark
05.10.83 Vince Bailey **L** PTS 6 Solihull
06.12.83 Steve Cooke **L** PTS 6 Southend
Summary: 6 contests, lost 6

Gordon Stacey
Battersea. *Born* Singapore 19.12.57
L. Heavyweight
Manager J. Simmons
Previous Amateur Club Devas
Divisional Honours SW London L. Heavyweight R/U 1978

21.11.78 Jimmy Harrington **L** RSC 1 Cambridge
18.01.79 Dave Reid **L** CO 2 Wimbledon
17.10.79 Mohammed Ali **W** CO 6 Piccadilly
31.10.79 Jimmy Ellis **L** RSC 4 Southend
22.09.80 Lenny Remice **L** PTS 4 Lewisham
20.10.80 Paul Newman **W** RTD 1 Hove
10.11.80 Billy Keen **W** PTS 6 Birmingham
26.11.80 Keith Bristol **L** CO 4 Wembley
03.02.81 John Vaughan **W** RSC 2 Southend
17.02.81 Pharoah Bish **W** RSC 3 Lewisham
02.03.81 Ben Lawlor **L** RSC 2 Brighton
06.04.81 John Joseph **W** RSC 2 Windsor
11.05.81 Ben Lawlor **L** PTS 8 Copthorne
11.06.81 Dave Turner **W** PTS 6 Southend
15.06.81 Steve Goodwin **W** PTS 6 Mayfair
03.08.81 Paul Newman **W** RSC 6 Brighton
15.09.81 Devon Bailey **L** RSC 3 Wembley
19.10.81 Steve Babbs **L** PTS 6 Mayfair
27.01.82 Frank McCullagh **L** RSC 2 Belfast
10.03.82 Geoff Rymer **L** PTS 8 Burslem
28.03.83 Cordwell Hylton **L** RSC 1 Birmingham
27.03.84 Sam Reeson **L** PTS 8 Battersea
03.04.84 Gypsy Carman **L** PTS 6 Lewisham
17.04.84 Gilbert Alexander **L** PTS 6 Merton
Summary: 24 contests, won 9, lost 15

Jeff Standley
Doncaster. *Born* Grimsby 06.01.60
L. Middleweight
Manager L. Slater
Previous Amateur Club Grimsby

19.03.81 Leo Mulhern **L** RSC 5 Doncaster
14.04.81 Brian Anderson **L** PTS 6 Manchester

12.06.83 Ranji Dastidar **W** RSC 1 Middlesbrough
19.09.83 Floyd Davidson **W** PTS 6 Nottingham
17.10.83 Chris King L PTS 6 Southwark
07.11.83 Malcolm Davies **W** PTS 6 Birmingham
22.11.83 Wayne Crolla L PTS 8 Manchester
04.06.84 Dalton Jordan L PTS 6 Nottingham
Summary: 8 contests, won 3, lost 5

Al Stevens
Quinton. *Born* Birmingham 01.07.56
L. Heavyweight
Manager (Self)
Previous Amateur Club Austin

29.05.80 Danny Cope L RSC 1 Wolverhampton
22.09.80 Joe Jackson L PTS 4 Wolverhampton
18.10.80 Steve Babbs **W** CO 2 Birmingham
09.03.81 Dave Turner **W** RSC 1 Wolverhampton
30.03.81 Jonjo Greene **W** CO 4 Birmingham
26.04.82 Jonjo Greene L PTS 6 Edgbaston
07.06.82 Paul Shell L DIS 1 Edgbaston
11.11.82 Clive Beardsley L PTS 6 Stafford
15.02.83 Dave Scott L RSC 2 Wolverhampton
Summary: 9 contests, won 3, lost 6

Kevin Stevens
Plymouth. *Born* Plymouth 28.10.57
L. Middleweight
Manager D. Sullivan
Previous Amateur Club Devonport
Divisional Honours W Counties L. Middleweight R/U 1981

14.04.83 Chris King L RSC 1 Basildon
Summary: 1 contest, lost 1

Vince Stewart
Tottenham. *Born* Jamaica 11.03.59
Welterweight
Manager W. Wynter
Previous Amateur Club Islington

13.03.81 Ron Pearce L PTS 6 Piccadilly
12.10.81 Jimmy Cable L PTS 6 Copthorne
21.06.82 Paul Welch L PTS 6 Copthorne
15.12.82 Gary Pearce **W** DIS 5 Queensway
01.02.83 Randy Henderson L PTS 6 Southend
08.11.83 Dave Heaver **W** PTS 6 Bethnal Green
06.12.83 Joe Lynch L PTS 6 Southend
10.05.84 Peter Foster L RSC 6 Digbeth
07.06.84 Dario De Abreu **W** PTS 6 Piccadilly
Summary: 9 contests, won 3, lost 6

Gavin Stirrup
Middleton. *Born* Middleton 20.04.63
L. Middleweight
Manager N. Basso
Previous Amateur Club Boarshaw

14.03.83 Dave Maxwell **W** RSC 3 Manchester
11.04.83 Gary Petty **W** RSC 5 Manchester
25.04.83 Nick Riozzi **W** RTD 4 Liverpool
09.05.83 John Langol L RSC 7 Manchester
20.09.83 Davey Cox **W** PTS 8 Dudley
26.09.83 Robert Armstrong **W** RSC 3 Manchester
17.10.83 Ian Chantler **W** PTS 8 Manchester
24.02.84 Steve Wonder **W** PTS 8 Marrickville
Summary: 8 contests, won 7, lost 1

Gordon Stobie
Darlington. *Born* Darlington 03.07.61
Bantamweight
Manager T. Callighan
Previous Amateur Club Darlington
Divisional Honours NE Counties Flyweight S/F 1980

13.06.83 Young Yousuf **W** PTS 6 Nottingham
22.09.83 Johnny Mack DREW 6 Stockport
31.10.83 Billy Ruzgar L PTS 6 Mayfair
24.11.83 John Drummond L RSC 5 Kirkby
07.03.84 Kevin Downer L PTS 6 Brighton
26.03.84 Charlie Brown L PTS 6 Glasgow
30.04.84 Bobby McDermott DREW 6 Glasgow
04.06.84 Danny Lee L PTS 6 Glasgow
Summary: 8 contests, won 1, drew 2, lost 5

Dave Stokes
Leicester. *Born* Leicester 22.12.61
Lightweight
Manager J. Dakin
Previous Amateur Club Belgrave
Divisional Honours M Counties L. Middleweight R/U 1982

22.02.84 Nigel Burke DREW 6 Evesham
16.04.84 Peter Bowen L PTS 6 Birmingham
Summary: 2 contests, drew 1, lost 1

Alan Storey
Sunderland. *Born* Sunderland 27.04.61
Lightweight
Manager (Self)
Previous Amateur Club Sunderland

09.10.78 Jackie Dinning **W** RSC 3 Middlesbrough
20.11.78 Jimmy Bott DREW 4 Birmingham
04.12.78 Ian Murray DREW 4 Middlesbrough

CONTINUED OVERLEAF

26.02.79 Pip Coleman W PTS 4 Middlesbrough
18.06.79 Paul Keers L PTS 8 Bradford
12.11.79 Dave George L PTS 6 Middlesbrough
19.11.79 Bobby Breen W PTS 6 Glasgow
26.11.79 Selvin Bell W PTS 6 Birmingham
03.12.79 Bryn Jones W RSC 3 Hull
10.12.79 Mike Pickett W PTS 6 Birmingham
25.02.80 Jim McKeown L PTS 6 Glasgow
03.03.80 Selvin Bell DREW 6 Marton
21.04.80 Charlie Parvin L PTS 8 Nottingham
28.04.80 Charlie Parvin L DIS 6 Birmingham
19.05.80 Don George L RTD 7 Piccadilly
11.05.81 Ian McLeod L PTS 6 Glasgow
01.06.81 Rocky Bantleman L PTS 6 Piccadilly
11.04.83 Dave Savage L PTS 6 Glasgow
19.05.83 Jim Paton W PTS 6 Sunderland
12.06.83 Jim Paton L PTS 6 Middlesbrough
Summary: 20 contests, won 7, drew 3, lost 10

Cliff Storey
Stoke. *Born* Bishop Auckland 13.04.60
Flyweight
Manager P. Brogan
Previous Amateur Club Royal Navy
Divisional Honours Combined Services Flyweight Champion 1979 – 1981

29.04.81 Steve Reilly W PTS 6 Burslem
16.09.81 Ray Cunningham W PTS 6 Burslem
28.10.81 Eddie Glencross W PTS 8 Burslem
10.03.82 Eddie Glencross W PTS 8 Burslem
09.03.83 Howard Williams W PTS 8 Stoke
27.04.83 Gary Roberts L CO 1 Stoke (*Vacant Midlands Area Flyweight Title*)
Summary: 6 contests, won 5, lost 1

Andy Straughn
Hitchin. *Born* Barbados 25.12.59
L. Heavyweight
Manager B. McCarthy
Previous Amateur Club Hitchin
National Honours Young England Rep.; England Int.; GB Rep.; ABA L. Heavyweight Champion 1979, 1980 & 1981

07.06.82 Joe Jackson W RSC 4 Bloomsbury
22.06.82 Winston Burnett W PTS 6 Hornsey
04.09.82 Joe Frater W RSC 3 Piccadilly
18.11.82 Eddie Cooper W RSC 2 Coventry
07.03.83 Roy Skeldon W RSC 3 Piccadilly
21.04.83 Theo Josephs W RSC 3 Letchworth
13.06.83 Ian Lazarus DREW 8 Coventry
03.12.83 Cordwell Hylton W PTS 8 Marylebone
15.04.84 Arthel Lawhorne L PTS 6 Detroit
03.05.84 Tim Bullock L PTS 6 Detroit
Summary: 10 contests, won 7, drew 1, lost 2

Brett Styles
Newport. *Born* Blaenau 28.09.61
Bantamweight
Manager D. Gardiner
Previous Amateur Club Cwmbran
National Honours Welsh Int.
Divisional Honours Welsh Bantamweight R/U 1981

10.10.82 Taffy Mills W RSC 2 Piccadilly
01.11.82 Rocky Bantleman L PTS 6 Piccadilly
15.04.83 Dave Pratt W PTS 6 Piccadilly
09.05.83 Rocky Bantleman DREW 8 Piccadilly
27.05.83 Peter Harris L PTS 8 Swansea
27.10.83 John Doherty L PTS 8 Ebbw Vale
03.12.83 Billy Hardy L PTS 8 Marylebone
10.12.83 Keith Ward L PTS 6 Swansea
Summary: 8 contests, won 2, drew 1, lost 5

Danny Sullivan
Finchley. *Born* Edmonton 15.01.60
L. Middleweight
Manager D. Smith
Previous Amateur Club Enfield
Divisional Honours NW London L. Middleweight Champion 1979; NW London Middleweight R/U 1981

08.09.83 Neil Crocker W PTS 6 Queensway
04.10.83 Claude Rossi W PTS 6 Bethnal Green
16.02.84 Dan Myers W PTS 6 Basildon
14.03.84 Newton Barnett W PTS 6 Mayfair
02.04.84 Robert Armstrong W CO 4 Mayfair
17.04.84 Newton Barnett W PTS 6 Merton
Summary: 6 contests, won 6

Dave Sullivan
Plymouth. *Born* Plymouth 01.06.59
L. Middleweight
Manager (Self)
Previous Amateur Club Mayflower
Divisional Honours W Counties Welterweight R/U 1979

29.10.79 John Ridgman L RTD 3 Camborne
22.01.80 Jeff Aspell W PTS 6 Caerphilly
12.02.80 Ronnie Rathbone L PTS 6 Sheffield
03.03.80 Steve Ward L PTS 6 Nottingham
15.04.80 Randy Henderson W PTS 6 Southend
02.06.80 Phil Duckworth L RSC 3 Plymouth
01.07.80 Jeff Aspell L PTS 6 Swindon
18.09.80 Tony Sinnott L RTD 5 Liverpool
10.02.81 Lloyd Honeyghan L PTS 6 Bethnal Green
11.03.81 John Wiggins W PTS 6 Evesham
23.03.81 Dave Taylor W PTS 6 Liverpool
09.09.81 Lee McKenzie L PTS 8 Morecambe

20.10.81 Billy Vivian **W** PTS 8 Plymouth
28.10.81 Terry Marsh **L** PTS 6 Acton
08.11.81 Martin McGough **L** PTS 6 Navan
16.11.81 Walter Clayton **L** PTS 8 Liverpool
16.02.82 Rocky Kelly **L** PTS 6 Bloomsbury
23.03.82 Lloyd Honeyghan **L** RSC 3 Bethnal Green
17.05.82 Gary Knight **L** PTS 8 Windsor
12.10.82 Frank McCord **L** PTS 6 Kensington
13.04.83 Peter Ahmed **L** PTS 8 Evesham
22.05.83 P. J. Davitt **L** RSC 7 Navan
06.02.84 Dave Hall **W** RSC 3 Bethnal Green
Summary: 23 contests, won 6, lost 17

Dennis Sullivan

Plymouth. *Born* Croydon 01.03.58
Welterweight
Manager (Self)
Previous Amateur Club Mayflower
National Honours NABC Title 1977
Divisional Honours W Counties L. Welterweight R/U 1977

18.09.79 Johnny Burns **W** PTS 6 Wolverhampton
08.10.79 Tommy Thomas **W** RSC 6 Piccadilly
29.10.79 Terry Welch **W** PTS 6 Camborne
10.12.79 Richard Avery **W** PTS 8 Torquay
16.01.80 Gary Cooper **L** PTS 6 Solihull
20.02.80 Granville Allen **L** PTS 8 Evesham
15.04.80 Vic Jackson **L** PTS 8 Southend
02.06.80 Terry Petersen **W** PTS 8 Plymouth
12.08.80 Richard Avery **L** PTS 8 Swansea
18.09.80 Al Stewart **W** RSC 7 Liverpool
16.10.80 Brian Anderson **L** PTS 8 Bolton
23.03.81 Jimmy Bunclark **W** RSC 4 Liverpool
07.10.81 Lloyd Christie **L** CO 3 Solihull
29.10.81 Tim Moloney DREW 8 Walthamstow
08.11.81 P. J. Davitt **L** PTS 6 Navan
18.11.81 Martin McGough **W** RTD 2 Solihull
04.09.82 Gary Knight DREW 8 Piccadilly
12.10.82 Tony Adams **L** RSC 1 Kensington
29.11.82 Bobby Welburn **W** PTS 8 Newquay
20.04.83 Kostas Petrou **L** RSC 4 Solihull
22.05.83 Patsy Quinn **L** PTS 8 Navan
22.09.83 Steve Ellwood **L** PTS 8 Strand
06.10.83 Gunther Roomes **L** PTS 8 Basildon
Summary: 23 contests, won 9, drew 2, lost 12

Terry Sullivan

Islington. *Born* London 10.10.58
Featherweight
Manager (Self)
Previous Amateur Club Gainsford
Divisional Honours NW London Flyweight R/U 1977

12.04.83 Stuart Carmichael **L** RSC 5 Southend
Summary: 1 contest, lost 1

Dave Summers

Glasgow. *Born* Bellshill 19.03.61
Heavyweight
Manager J. Murray
Previous Amateur Club Govan
National Honours Scottish Heavyweight Champion 1981, Scottish S. Heavyweight Champion 1983

05.03.84 Steve Abadom **W** PTS 4 Glasgow
Summary: 1 contest, won 1

Andy Sumner

Sheffield. *Born* Sheffield 17.08.63
L. Middleweight
Manager B. Ingle
Previous Amateur Club St Vincents

21.05.84 Tony Kempson **W** CO 4 Bradford
06.06.84 Mickey Bird **W** RSC 3 Sheffield
Summary: 2 contests, won 2

Trevor Sumner

Sheffield. *Born* Sheffield 26.08.63
Featherweight
Manager B. Ingle
Previous Amateur Club St Vincents

09.11.83 Ian Murray **W** RSC 5 Sheffield
14.11.83 Les Walsh **L** PTS 6 Manchester
05.12.83 Mike Whalley **L** CO 4 Manchester
29.02.84 Steve Enright **W** PTS 6 Sheffield
19.03.84 Les Walsh **L** PTS 8 Manchester
Summary: 5 contests, won 2, lost 3

Grant Sutton

Rhyl. *Born* St Asaph 12.11.63
Welterweight
Manager P. Dwyer
Previous Amateur Club Rhyl Star
National Honours Schools Title 1977

30.04.84 Mick Joyce **W** RSC 4 Liverpool
12.06.84 Taffy Morris **L** PTS 6 St Helens
Summary: 2 contests, won 1, lost 1

Dave Swann

Manchester. *Born* Manchester 30.11.57
Lightweight
Manager J. Edwards
Previous Amateur Club Fox

14.03.83 Colin Roscoe **W** RSC 2 Manchester
Summary: 1 contest, won 1

Steve Swiftie (Swift)
Halifax. *Born* Rotherham 08.06.60
Lightweight
Manager T. Miller
Previous Amateur Club St Thomas's

30.09.83 Tony Christopher L PTS 6 Leicester
10.10.83 George Baigrie L RSC 5 Glasgow
05.03.84 Hugh Sugar Kelly L RSC 2 Glasgow
Summary: 3 contests, lost 3

Dave Taylor
Bootle. *Born* Bootle 14.08.52
L. Welterweight
Manager (Self)
Previous Amateur Club Litherland

06.12.72 Bob Brown W CO 2 Manchester
08.01.73 Jess Harper L PTS 6 Manchester
19.02.73 Jess Harper L PTS 6 Manchester
14.03.73 Alan Hardiman L RSC 4 Stoke
07.06.76 Freddie Mills L RSC 3 Manchester
29.08.76 Barry White W CO 3 Solihull
21.03.77 Mick Mills L PTS 6 Stoke
05.04.77 Delvin Whyte DREW 4 Southend
18.04.77 Johnny Beauchamp DREW 6 Stafford
27.04.77 Johnny Gwilliam W PTS 4 Leicester
03.05.77 Rocky Butler L PTS 6 Southend
01.06.77 Roy Varden L PTS 6 Dudley
05.07.77 Roy Varden L PTS 8 Wolverhampton
20.07.77 John Kelly L PTS 6 Sheffield
08.09.77 Chris Glover L PTS 8 Liverpool
04.10.77 Tony Zeni L PTS 8 Southgate
31.10.77 Steve Holdsworth W PTS 6 Nantwich
14.11.77 Tony Zeni L RSC 3 Cambridge
05.12.77 John Kelly W PTS 4 Southend
12.12.77 Sylvester Gordon L PTS 8 Piccadilly
18.01.78 John Kelly DREW 8 Stoke
30.01.78 Eric Wood L PTS 6 Cleethorpes
27.02.78 John Kelly L PTS 8 Sheffield
06.03.78 Mick Bell L PTS 8 Manchester
27.04.78 Ian Pickersgill W RTD 1 Doncaster
08.05.78 Charlie Tonna W RSC 3 Birmingham
18.05.78 Stan Atherton L PTS 6 Liverpool
07.09.78 Tony Hague DREW 6 Liverpool
12.09.78 Martin Bridge L PTS 6 Birkenhead
02.11.78 Brian Snagg DREW 8 Liverpool
14.11.78 Dave Allen W PTS 8 Birkenhead
27.11.78 Vernon Entertainer Vanriel L PTS 8 Mayfair
18.01.79 Dai Davies W PTS 8 Liverpool
22.02.79 Jess Harper DREW 8 Liverpool
23.04.79 Martin Bridge L PTS 10 Bradford (*Vacant Central Area Lightweight Title*)
17.09.79 Lee Hartshorn L PTS 8 Manchester
30.10.79 Roy Varden L PTS 8 Bedworth
05.12.79 Richard Avery L PTS 6 Liverpool
20.12.79 Alan Lamb L RSC 3 Queensway
21.01.80 Kid Murray L PTS 6 Wolverhampton
28.01.80 Kevin Walsh W PTS 6 Bradford
11.02.80 Pat Smythe W PTS 6 Manchester
18.02.80 John Mount W RSC 4 Birmingham
10.03.80 Kid Murray W PTS 6 Wolverhampton
09.04.80 Cliff Gilpin L PTS 6 Burslem
30.04.80 Des Gwilliam L PTS 8 Wolverhampton
08.07.80 Mickey Baker L RSC 5 Wolverhampton
04.09.80 Kid Murray L PTS 8 Morecambe
29.09.80 Walter Clayton L PTS 8 Chesterfield
29.10.80 Alan Cooper L PTS 6 Burslem
18.11.80 Phil Duckworth L RSC 6 Nantwich
03.02.81 Paul Gibson L PTS 6 Southend
10.02.81 Randy Henderson W PTS 6 Nantwich
02.03.81 Colin Wake L PTS 8 Piccadilly
23.03.81 Dave Sullivan L PTS 6 Liverpool
09.06.81 Winston McKenzie W PTS 6 Southend
18.09.81 Julian Bousted L PTS 8 Swindon
19.10.81 Kevin Quinn W RSC 5 Manchester
19.11.81 Steve Tempro L PTS 8 Morecambe
07.12.81 Kevin Walsh W RSC 5 Manchester
11.01.82 Steve Tempro DREW 8 Liverpool
25.01.82 Gary Buckle W PTS 8 Wolverhampton
26.04.82 John Lindo L PTS 8 Bradford
03.06.82 Alan Lamb L PTS 10 Liverpool (*Central Area L. Welterweight Title Challenge*)
22.09.82 Mick Rowley L PTS 8 Stoke
17.11.82 Kostas Petrou L RSC 2 Solihull
20.01.83 Mick Dono L PTS 6 Birkenhead
Summary: 67 contests, won 18, drew 7, lost 42

Glenroy Taylor
Chiswick. *Born* Jamaica 22.09.55
L. Heavyweight
Manager D. Mancini
Previous Amateur Club None

10.02.75 Joe Hannaford L RTD 3 Bedford
05.05.75 Len Brittain L RSC 5 Piccadilly
23.06.75 Johnny Cox L DIS 3 Bedford
23.02.76 Pat Thompson L PTS 6 Nottingham
24.04.77 Reg Long L CO 1 Birmingham
15.03.78 Alan Butters L RTD 2 Stoke
18.04.78 George Gray L DIS 3 Coventry
16.02.81 Keith Bristol L RSC 4 Southwark
27.04.81 Paul Newman L PTS 6 Brighton
03.08.81 Frank McCullagh L PTS 6 Brighton

30.11.81 Kevin Woolnough L PTS 6 Southwark
20.01.82 Clive Beardsley L PTS 6 Solihull
25.01.82 Scott Wilde W RSC 2 Mayfair
01.02.82 Lee White L PTS 6 Southwark
22.03.82 Jonjo Greene L PTS 6 Southwark
01.04.82 Michael Fawcett L PTS 4 Walthamstow
19.04.82 Jerry Golden L PTS 6 Mayfair
18.10.82 Billy Cassidy L PTS 6 Southwark
04.11.82 Lee White L PTS 6 Wimbledon
22.11.82 Harry Cowap L PTS 6 Mayfair
29.11.82 Jerry Golden L PTS 6 Southwark
10.02.83 Harry Cowap L PTS 6 Walthamstow
17.10.83 Sam Reeson L PTS 6 Southwark
28.11.83 Alex Romeo W PTS 6 Southwark
06.02.84 Billy Cassidy L PTS 6 Bethnal Green
27.03.84 Theo Josephs L PTS 6 Bethnal Green
Summary: 26 contests, won 2, lost 24

Osbourne Taylor

Nottingham. *Born* Jamaica 10.04.55
Heavyweight
Manager (Self)
Previous Amateur Club None

15.11.78 David Pearce L RSC 1 Merthyr
25.11.80 Ian Scotting L RSC 1 Doncaster
09.10.81 Gary Jones L PTS 4 Cambuslang
23.11.81 Paul Heatley L PTS 4 Chesterfield
01.03.82 Mike Creasey L PTS 4 Preston
20.05.82 Mike Creasey DREW 4 Preston
26.05.82 John Fallon L RSC 1 Piccadilly
23.06.83 Deka Williams L RSC 3 Wolverhampton
Summary: 8 contests, drew 1, lost 7

Wes Taylor

Leicester. *Born* Jamaica 06.04.60
L. Heavyweight
Manager R. Gray
Previous Amateur Club Granby

18.10.83 Paul Heatley W PTS 6 Wolverhampton
07.11.83 Steve Lewsam L PTS 6 Birmingham
14.03.84 Deka Williams W PTS 6 Stoke
04.06.84 Eddie Cooper W RSC 3 Nottingham
Summary: 4 contests, won 3, lost 1

Steve Tempro

Leicester. *Born* Leicester 14.05.61
Welterweight
Manager (Self)
Previous Amateur Club Highfields

25.11.80 Dennis Sheehan L PTS 6 Wolverhampton
19.01.81 Lloyd Christie L CO 1 Birmingham
12.02.81 Alan Burns W CO 4 Bolton
03.03.81 Derek Groarke W PTS 6 Pudsey
16.03.81 Mark Virgin W RSC 6 Birmingham
11.09.81 Martin McGough L RSC 4 Edgbaston
20.10.81 Jimmy Woods W RTD 2 Leeds
19.11.81 Dave Taylor W PTS 8 Morecambe
30.11.81 Kostas Petrou L PTS 6 Birmingham
11.01.82 Dave Taylor DREW 8 Liverpool
04.02.82 Tim Moloney L PTS 8 Walthamstow
08.03.82 Kevin Quinn L PTS 6 Manchester
18.03.82 Phil Duckworth DREW 8 Caister
23.03.82 Granville Allen L PTS 8 Wolverhampton
29.03.82 Gerry White W PTS 6 Liverpool
26.04.82 Kostas Petrou L RSC 3 Edgbaston
24.05.82 Danny Garrison L RSC 3 Wolverhampton
06.10.82 Peter Ahmed L PTS 6 Solihull
19.10.82 Peter Ahmed L PTS 6 Wolverhampton
08.11.82 Lee Hartshorn L PTS 6 Manchester
06.12.82 Elvis Morton W PTS 6 Bristol
26.01.83 Errol Dennis L PTS 6 Stoke
21.02.83 Paul Murray W DIS 3 Edgbaston
02.03.83 John McGlynn L PTS 8 Evesham
16.03.83 Granville Allen W PTS 6 Stoke
28.03.83 Paul Chance L PTS 8 Birmingham
16.05.83 John Lindo W PTS 6 Manchester
23.06.83 Davey Cox W PTS 8 Wolverhampton
08.09.83 Steve Watt L CO 3 Queensway
03.10.83 Tony Brown L PTS 8 Liverpool
15.10.83 Colin Neagle W PTS 6 Coventry
09.12.83 Tony Smith L PTS 6 Liverpool
16.01.84 Ken Foreman L PTS 8 Bradford
30.01.84 Ray Price L PTS 8 Birmingham
01.03.84 Lenny Gloster L PTS 6 Queensway
26.03.84 Graeme Griffin W PTS 6 Leicester
12.04.84 Gunther Roomes L RSC 6 Piccadilly
19.05.84 Julian Bousted L PTS 8 Bristol
04.06.84 John McAllister L PTS 6 Glasgow
Summary: 39 contests, won 13, drew 2, lost 24

Andy Thomas (Bruton)

Swansea. *Born* Swansea 03.05.62
Lightweight
Manager C. Breen
Previous Amateur Club RAOB Swansea

30.04.80 Clyde Ruan L PTS 4 Aylesbury
19.05.80 John Henry W RSC 1 Birmingham
02.06.80 Steve Pollard L PTS 6 Piccadilly
13.10.80 Steve Farnsworth W PTS 6 Manchester
23.10.80 Eddie Glass W PTS 6 Middlesbrough
27.10.80 Geoff Smart W RSC 6 Mayfair

CONTINUED OVERLEAF

26.11.80 Selvin Bell DREW 6 Stoke
08.02.82 Colin Harrison L PTS 6 Piccadilly
24.02.82 Jimmy Duncan L CO 2 Sheffield
26.04.82 Brian Jones W PTS 6 Cardiff
18.05.82 Angelo D'Amore L PTS 6 Piccadilly
07.06.82 Tyrell Wilson W PTS 8 Swansea
28.09.82 Kenny Bruce L PTS 8 Derry
13.10.82 Denny Garrison W PTS 6 Evesham
01.11.82 Ray Hood L PTS 8 Liverpool
25.10.82 Tommy Cook L PTS 8 Airdrie
22.11.82 Rory Burke W PTS 8 Mayfair
13.12.82 Mickey Baker L RTD 1 Wolverhampton
24.01.83 Mark Davey L RSC 3 Piccadilly
04.03.83 Ray Hood L PTS 10 Queensferry (*Vacant Welsh Lightweight Title*)
16.03.83 Terry Marsh L RSC 4 Cheltenham
12.04.83 Seamus McGuinness L RSC 2 Belfast

Summary: 22 contests, won 8, drew 1, lost 13

Nigel Thomas

Llanelli. *Born* Swansea 07.04.60
Welterweight
Manager (Self)
Previous Amateur Club Gwent

03.10.77 Phillip Morris W PTS 4 Aberavon
17.10.77 Eddie Porter L RSC 2 Bedford
21.11.77 Derek Tew L PTS 4 Birmingham
16.01.78 Marty Crane W CO 1 Birmingham
24.01.78 Peter Snowshall L PTS 4 Piccadilly
06.03.78 Johnny Beauchamp W PTS 4 Piccadilly
06.04.78 Johnny Beauchamp W PTS 6 Ebbw Vale
20.04.78 Gary Collins L PTS 6 Mayfair
16.05.78 Johnny Beauchamp W PTS 6 Newport
10.07.78 Dai Davies L PTS 6 Aberavon
03.10.78 Dennis Powell W PTS 6 Aberavon
02.11.78 Brendan O'Donnell W PTS 6 Liverpool
14.11.78 Tony Carroll L PTS 6 Birkenhead
29.11.78 John Chard W CO 7 Swansea
04.12.78 Tony Carroll L PTS 6 Manchester
11.12.78 Roger Guest DREW 6 Birmingham
17.01.79 Shaun Stewart W PTS 6 Solihull
22.01.79 Roger Guest DREW 6 Birmingham
12.02.79 Jess Harper W PTS 6 Manchester
19.02.79 Roger Guest L PTS 8 Birmingham
04.04.79 Joe Mills W PTS 6 Birmingham
23.05.79 Mark Osbourne W PTS 4 Nottingham
18.06.79 Norman Morton DREW 8 Bradford
27.06.79 Ray Ross W RSC 5 Derry
05.07.79 Lee Hartshorn W PTS 8 Aberavon
25.09.79 John F. Kennedy L CO 2 Wembley
06.11.79 Gary Newell L PTS 6 Stafford
14.11.79 Kid Murray W PTS 8 Stoke
21.11.79 Kid Murray W PTS 8 Evesham
03.12.79 Lloyd Hibbert L PTS 8 Wolverhampton
28.02.80 Dil Collins W PTS 8 Ebbw Vale
10.03.80 Mickey Mapp L PTS 8 Mayfair
31.03.80 Kenny Webber L PTS 8 Cleethorpes
28.04.80 Lee Hartshorn L PTS 8 Piccadilly
19.05.80 Roy Varden L CO 6 Birmingham
16.06.80 Dave Ward L PTS 8 Manchester
24.09.80 Cliff Gilpin L PTS 8 Evesham
15.04.81 Paul Murray DREW 8 Evesham
21.09.81 Jimmy Smith W PTS 8 Piccadilly
04.11.81 John F. Kennedy L PTS 8 Derby
21.12.81 Joey Frost L CO 2 Bradford
02.03.82 Nick Wilshire L RSC 1 Kensington
04.10.83 Mick Courtney L PTS 6 Bethnal Green
11.10.83 R. W. Smith L RSC 3 Kensington
25.01.84 Robert Armstrong L CO 2 Stoke

Summary: 45 contests, won 18, drew 4, lost 23

Paul Thompson

Middlesbrough. *Born* Middlesbrough 09.02.57
L. Middleweight
Manager (Self)
Previous Amateur Club North Ormesby

03.10.83 Tony Smith L RSC 1 Bradford

Summary: 1 contest, lost 1

Bob Thornton

Leicester. *Born* Leicester 18.08.60
L. Welterweight
Manager (Self)
Previous Amateur Club Belgrave

22.09.80 Johnny Beauchamp L PTS 6 Birmingham
14.10.80 Barry Oliver DREW 4 Nantwich
22.10.80 Robert Armstrong L CO 3 Doncaster
23.06.83 Tim Gladwish L PTS 6 Bethnal Green

Summary: 4 contests, drew 1, lost 3

Jimmy Thornton

Sheffield. *Born* Sheffield 22.09.64
Lightweight
Manager B. Ingle
Previous Amateur Club Richmond
National Honours NABC Title 1981

25.11.82 Stuart Carmichael W PTS 6 Morley
14.12.82 Seamus McGuinness L PTS 6 Belfast
09.05.83 Edward Lloyd W RSC 1 Manchester
12.05.83 Colin Roscoe W RSC 2 Morley
23.05.83 Peter Flanagan W RSC 3 Sheffield
13.06.83 Gary Williams W RTD 5 Doncaster
12.09.83 Lee Halford L PTS 8 Leicester
29.02.84 Ray Murray W PTS 6 Sheffield

12.03.84 Lenny Gloster **L** PTS 6 Manchester
09.04.84 Dave Haggarty **L** PTS 8 Glasgow
06.06.84 Peter Bowen **W** PTS 6 Sheffield
Summary: 11 contests, won 7, lost 4

Alan Tombs

Hastings. *Born* Guildford 01.03.61
Bantamweight
Manager (Self)
Previous Amateur Club Onslow
Divisional Honours S Counties L. Welterweight Champion 1981

09.06.81 Ray Hood DREW 6 Southend
15.06.81 Mike Bromby **W** RSC 4 Piccadilly
14.09.81 Steve Henderson **W** PTS 6 Mayfair
12.10.81 Tony Davis **L** PTS 6 Copthorne
25.11.81 John Pollard **L** CO 4 Sheffield
01.02.82 Alun Thomas **W** PTS 6 Copthorne
15.03.82 Dave Laxen **L** RSC 2 Bloomsbury
27.04.82 Dave Laxen **L** RSC 7 Hornsey
26.05.82 Steve Pollard DREW 8 Piccadilly
07.06.82 Dave Laxen **W** RSC 8 Bloomsbury
22.06.82 Keith Wallace **L** RSC 4 Hornsey
07.09.82 Stuart Shaw **W** PTS 8 Crewe
20.09.82 Steve Henderson **W** PTS 8 Mayfair
27.09.82 Lee Halford **L** PTS 6 Bloomsbury
14.10.82 Dean Marsden **W** PTS 8 Nantwich
20.10.82 Stuart Shaw **W** PTS 8 Stoke
04.11.82 Pat Doherty **L** RSC 2 Wimbledon
19.01.83 Peter Gabbitus **L** RSC 2 Stoke
27.04.83 Dean Marsden **W** RSC 2 Stoke
09.05.83 Alec Irvine **L** PTS 8 Piccadilly
27.09.83 Joey Joynson **L** RSC 1 Wembley
28.11.83 Anthony Brown **L** PTS 8 Bayswater
Summary: 22 contests, won 9, drew 2, lost 11

Alex Tompkins

West Ham. *Born* Mile End 12.12.54
Former Southern Area Middleweight Champion
Manager D. Mancini
Previous Amateur Club West Ham
National Honours Junior ABA Title 1971

11.03.74 Joey Gammon **W** RSC 5 Kensington
28.04.74 Kevin Paddock **W** PTS 6 Southend
16.05.74 Mick Lock **W** RSC 2 Walworth
10.06.74 Alan Bursey **W** RSC 2 Walworth
16.09.74 Bob Murphy **L** PTS 6 Southampton
13.11.74 Randy Barrett **W** RSC 2 Solihull
05.12.74 Augustus Sims **W** RSC 2 Southend
10.02.75 Charlie Richardson **W** RSC 3 Kensington
18.02.75 Pat Brogan **W** PTS 6 Bethnal Green
05.05.75 Batman Austin **L** PTS 8 Bedford
14.07.75 Joe Lally **W** PTS 8 Mayfair
08.09.75 Batman Austin **L** PTS 8 Mayfair
22.09.75 Augustus Sims **W** RTD 4 Walworth
24.11.75 Joe Yekinni **W** PTS 8 Walworth
01.12.75 Trevor Francis **L** PTS 8 Mayfair
19.01.76 Claude Martin **L** PTS 10 Paris
23.02.76 Vernon Scott **L** PTS 8 Mayfair
03.05.76 Leroy Herriott **W** RTD 5 Walworth
18.10.76 Pat Brogan **W** RSC 5 Marylebone
25.10.76 Gareth Jones **W** RSC 1 Mayfair
07.12.76 Kevin Finnegan **L** PTS 8 Kensington
01.02.77 Billy Knight **W** RSC 4 Kensington
22.02.77 Peter Cain **W** CO 1 Kensington (*Southern Area Middleweight Title Challenge*)
12.04.77 Frankie Lucas **L** RSC 6 Kensington
18.07.77 Jan Magdziarz **L** RSC 5 Mayfair (*Southern Area Middleweight Title Defence*)
07.11.77 Keith Bussey **L** PTS 8 Walworth
29.05.79 Shaun Chalcraft **W** PTS 8 Southend
13.06.79 Ken Jones **L** PTS 8 Caerphilly
16.10.79 Keith Bussey **W** CO 8 Lewisham
19.11.79 Shaun Chalcraft **L** PTS 8 Lewisham
28.02.80 Vernon Scott **W** RSC 5 Queensway
18.11.80 Rupert Christie **W** RSC 6 Bethnal Green
24.02.81 Steve Lewin **W** CO 6 Kensington
21.05.81 Mustafa Wasajja **L** RTD 6 Copenhagen
28.09.81 Shaun Chalcraft **W** PTS 8 Lewisham
09.04.82 Pierre Kabassa **L** PTS 8 Luxembourg
10.10.82 Cordwell Hylton **L** PTS 8 Piccadilly
31.01.83 Trevor Cattouse DREW 8 Southwark
25.04.83 Cordwell Hylton **L** PTS 8 Southwark
Summary: 39 contests, won 22, drew 1, lost 16

Steve Topliss

Derby. *Born* Melbourne 19.11.58
Midlands Area Featherweight Champion
Manager R. Gray
Previous Amateur Club Melbourne
Divisional Honours M Counties Bantamweight Champion 1978

05.02.80 Don Aageson **W** PTS 6 Wolverhampton
11.03.80 Mike Pickett **W** PTS 6 Nantwich
29.05.80 Bryn Jones **W** PTS 6 Wolverhampton
16.10.80 Derek Groarke **W** PTS 6 Bolton
21.01.81 Don Aageson **L** RTD 3 Solihull
11.03.81 Jarvis Greenidge **L** CO 3 Burslem (*Vacant Midlands Area Featherweight Title*)
25.09.81 Stuart Shaw DREW 6 Nottingham
13.10.81 Stuart Shaw **W** PTS 8 Wolverhampton
27.10.81 Gerry Devine **W** PTS 6 Wolverhampton
04.11.81 Carl Gaynor **W** PTS 8 Derby

CONTINUED OVERLEAF

25.11.81 Brian Hyslop **W** PTS 8 Stoke
21.02.82 Mark West **W** PTS 6 Birmingham
15.03.82 Clyde Ruan **W** PTS 8 Wolverhampton
11.05.82 Ian Murray **W** PTS 8 Derby
27.09.82 John Sharkey **W** PTS 8 Birmingham
31.01.83 Jarvis Greenidge **W** PTS 8 Birmingham
28.02.83 Alec Irvine **W** PTS 10 Birmingham (*Midlands Area Featherweight Title Challenge*)
10.10.83 Peter Gabbitus L PTS 8 Birmingham
22.11.83 John Sharkey **W** PTS 8 Wolverhampton
10.02.84 Alec Irvine **W** PTS 10 Dudley (*Midlands Area Featherweight Title Defence*)
31.03.84 Mark Pearce **W** PTS 8 Derby
27.04.84 John Feeney L PTS 10 Wolverhampton
Summary: 22 contests, won 17, drew 1, lost 4

(Aderele) Eddie Toro (Adetoro)

Manchester. *Born* Manchester 27.08.57
Featherweight
Manager J. Gaynor
Previous Amateur Club Ardwick

11.05.82 Carl Gaynor **W** PTS 6 Derby
25.02.83 Mick Hoolison L RSC 2 Doncaster
Summary: 2 contests, won 1, lost 1

Gerard Treble

Runcorn. *Born* Liverpool 22.11.64
Lightweight
Manager C. Moorcroft
Previous Amateur Club Runcorn

12.06.84 Derek Atherton **W** RSC 3 St Helens
Summary: 1 contest, won 1

Tony Tricker

Norbury. *Born* Brixton 30.12.60
Heavyweight
Manager C. Shorey
Previous Amateur Club Battersea
Divisional Honours SW London S. Heavyweight Champion 1983

13.06.84 Chris Jacobs L PTS 6 Aberavon
Summary: 1 contest, lost 1

Wayne Trigg

Newtown. *Born* St Helens 25.03.66
Lightweight
Manager J. Griffin
Previous Amateur Club Newtown

28.04.83 Willie Wilson L RSC 3 Leicester
30.09.83 Colin Anderson L PTS 4 Leicester
07.11.83 Andy Green **W** PTS 4 Birmingham
12.12.83 John Faulkner L RSC 3 Birmingham
25.01.84 Dean Bramhald **W** CO 3 Stoke
15.03.84 Colin Anderson **W** RSC 2 Leicester
04.04.84 Andy De Abreu L PTS 4 Evesham
09.05.84 Dean Bramhald DREW 4 Leicester
Summary: 8 contests, won 3, drew 1, lost 4

Jackie Turner

Hull. *Born* Hull 30.09.59
Lightweight
Manager (Self)
Previous Amateur Club Hull FT
National Honours Schools Title 1973; Junior ABA Title 1976; NABC Titles 1976 – 1977; ABA Bantamweight Champion 1977 – 1978; Young England Rep.; Euro. Junior Bronze 1978
Divisional Honours NE Counties Featherweight Champion 1979

25.01.80 Alan Oag **W** PTS 6 Hull
13.02.80 Dai Davies **W** PTS 6 Mayfair
28.02.80 Ray Ross **W** RSC 4 Hull
24.03.80 Jeff Pritchard L PTS 8 Mayfair
29.04.80 Glyn Rhodes **W** PTS 8 Mayfair
19.05.80 Jimmy Bunclark **W** PTS 8 Mayfair
22.09.80 Jeff Pritchard **W** RSC 2 Mayfair
24.09.80 Peter Harrison L RSC 3 Solihull
08.12.80 Barry Price **W** PTS 8 Birmingham
09.02.81 Alan Cooper **W** DIS 3 Mayfair
02.03.81 Anton Varrips **W** RSC 5 Rotterdam
16.03.81 Eric Wood **W** PTS 8 Mayfair
11.05.81 Glyn Rhodes L RSC 2 Mayfair
14.09.81 Billy O'Grady **W** RSC 2 Mayfair
22.10.81 Rene Weller L RSC 3 Frankfurt
19.09.83 George Kerr **W** PTS 8 Glasgow
19.10.83 Keith Foreman **W** PTS 8 Hull
19.03.84 Najib Daho L RSC 5 Manchester
Summary: 18 contests, won 13, lost 5

Vernon Entertainer Vanriel
Derek Rowe (Photos) Ltd

Robbie Turner
Brighton. *Born* Cuckfield 03.01.64
L. Heavyweight
Manager D. Harris
Previous Amateur Club None

27.04.81 Ian Baker **W** RSC 4 Brighton
22.09.81 Joe Cameron **W** CO 1 Southend
04.02.82 Bobby Williams L CO 1 Walthamstow
08.03.82 Cliff Curtis L PTS 6 Mayfair
21.04.82 Paul Welch DREW 6 Brighton
13.09.82 Paul Mitchell L PTS 6 Brighton
29.11.82 Terry Magee L PTS 6 Brighton
19.04.84 Lennie Howard L RSC 4 Basildon
Summary: 8 contests, won 2, drew 1, lost 5

Glenn Tweedie
Loanhead. *Born* Edinburgh 20.09.62
Lightweight
Manager T. Gilmour
Previous Amateur Club Edinburgh City Transport

11.06.84 Dean Bramhald **W** PTS 6 Glasgow
Summary: 1 contest, won 1

Vince Vahey
Sheffield. *Born* Belfast 03.01.63
Lightweight
Manager B. Ingle
Previous Amateur Club Eckington

19.03.82 Steve Parker L PTS 6 Nottingham
19.04.82 Shaun Shinkwin **W** PTS 4 Bristol
06.05.82 Ron Shinkwin **W** PTS 4 Mayfair
21.05.82 Kevin Howard **W** PTS 6 Sheffield
07.06.82 Mick Dono L PTS 4 Sheffield
31.08.82 Kevin Howard **W** PTS 6 South Shields
17.09.82 Mick Dono **W** PTS 6 Liverpool
18.11.82 Rocky Mensah **W** PTS 6 Piccadilly
21.02.83 Keith Foreman **W** PTS 8 Bradford
07.03.83 Kevin Pritchard **W** PTS 8 Liverpool
14.03.83 Chris Moorcroft **W** PTS 4 Sheffield
23.05.83 Jimmy Bunclark L RSC 1 Sheffield (*Central Area Lightweight Title Challenge*)
28.11.83 Peter Flanagan **W** PTS 6 Rhyl
29.02.84 Lee Halford **W** PTS 8 Sheffield
Summary: 14 contests, won 11, lost 3

Vernon Entertainer Vanriel
Tottenham. *Born* Jamaica 10.07.55
L. Welterweight
Manager (Self)
Previous Amateur Club Poplar
Divisional Honours NE London L. Welterweight R/U 1975

15.03.76 Chris Walker L PTS 6 Mayfair
23.03.76 Eric Purkiss **W** PTS 6 Bethnal Green
31.03.76 Albert Coley DREW 6 Birmingham
05.04.76 Winston McKenzie **W** PTS 6 Mayfair
13.04.76 Kevin Doherty **W** PTS 6 Hornsey
10.05.76 Harry Watson L PTS 6 Mayfair
11.10.76 Tony Vernon **W** PTS 6 Nottingham
22.11.76 Kevin Quinn **W** RSC 2 Birmingham
11.01.77 Roy Varden **W** PTS 6 Wolverhampton
25.09.78 Young John Daly **W** RSC 5 Mayfair
30.10.78 Eric Wood **W** PTS 8 Birmingham
27.11.78 Dave Taylor **W** PTS 8 Mayfair
11.10.79 Davy Campbell L PTS 6 Liverpool
22.10.79 Norman Morton DREW 8 Mayfair
09.04.80 Walter Clayton L PTS 8 Burslem
15.09.80 Gerry O'Neill **W** PTS 8 Glasgow
11.05.81 Willie Booth **W** PTS 8 Glasgow
28.09.81 Kevin Doherty **W** PTS 8 Lewisham
29.10.81 Kevin Doherty **W** RSC 6 Walthamstow
10.12.81 Billy Vivian **W** RSC 2 Walthamstow
12.01.82 Glyn Rhodes **W** CO 2 Bethnal Green
16.02.82 Gerry Beard **W** RTD 4 Bethnal Green
17.03.82 Walter Clayton DREW 8 Kensington
13.10.82 Peter Eubanks **W** PTS 8 Walthamstow
16.11.82 Des Gwilliam **W** PTS 8 Bethnal Green
18.01.83 Sammy Young **W** RSC 1 Kensington
08.02.83 Gary Gibson L PTS 8 Kensington
26.04.83 Terry Marsh L PTS 10 Bethnal Green (*Vacant Southern Area L. Welterweight Title*)
23.06.83 Gary Knight **W** RSC 6 Bethnal Green
13.10.83 Tony Brown L PTS 8 Bloomsbury
28.11.83 Mick Rowley **W** PTS 8 Bayswater
21.03.84 Mick Rowley **W** PTS 8 Solihull
11.04.84 Tony Laing L RSC 7 Kensington
Summary: 33 contests, won 22, drew 3, lost 8

Roy Varden
Nuneaton. *Born* Nuneaton 19.01.58
Former Undefeated Midlands Area L. Welterweight Champion
Manager (Self)
Previous Amateur Club Nuneaton
National Honours Schools Title 1973

09.03.76 Dave Wraxall **W** PTS 6 Bradford
31.03.76 Steve Laybourn **W** RSC 4 Doncaster
09.04.76 Godfrey Butler L RSC 1 Birmingham
17.05.76 Dick Goodman **W** PTS 6 Nottingham

CONTINUED OVERLEAF

08.06.76 Tommy Singleton L PTS 6 Bradford
27.09.76 Kevin Doherty W PTS 6 Piccadilly
05.10.76 Albert Coley W PTS 6 Coventry
25.10.76 Tony Mattia W RSC 3 Birmingham
30.11.76 Tony Vernon W PTS 6 Dudley
11.01.77 Vernon Entertainer Vanriel L PTS 6 Wolverhampton
10.02.77 Delvin Whyte W PTS 6 Coventry
28.02.77 Young John Daly W PTS 4 Luton
08.03.77 Charlie Wallace W RSC 5 Wolverhampton
07.04.77 Albert Coley W CO 5 Dudley
17.05.77 Steve Butler W PTS 6 Wolverhampton
01.06.77 Dave Taylor W PTS 6 Dudley
13.06.77 Najib Daho W PTS 6 Manchester
05.07.77 Dave Taylor W PTS 8 Wolverhampton
22.08.77 Don Burgin L PTS 8 Stockton
20.09.77 Godfrey Butler W PTS 8 Wolverhampton
02.11.77 Kelvin Webber W PTS 8 Cardiff
22.11.77 Bingo Crooks W PTS 8 Wolverhampton
12.12.77 Jeff Pritchard W PTS 8 Birmingham
07.02.78 George McGurk W PTS 8 Coventry
15.03.78 Tommy Dunn W PTS 8 Solihull
18.04.78 Des Gwilliam W PTS 10 Coventry (*Vacant Midlands Area L. Welterweight Title*)
13.06.78 Trevor Roomes W RSC 8 Coventry
20.11.78 Carl Bailey L PTS 8 Birmingham
23.01.79 Terry Petersen W RSC 6 Piccadilly
31.01.79 Dennis Pryce DREW 8 Stoke
26.02.79 Carl Bailey L PTS 8 Edgbaston
23.04.79 Chris Sanigar DREW 8 Piccadilly
06.06.79 Frank McCord W PTS 8 Bedworth
02.07.79 Dil Collins W PTS 8 Wolverhampton
06.09.79 Hans Henrik Palm L RSC 7 Randers
30.10.79 Dave Taylor W PTS 8 Bedworth
11.02.80 Lee Hartshorn W RTD 2 Manchester
18.03.80 Granville Allen L PTS 8 Wolverhampton
31.03.80 Gary Pearce L PTS 8 Piccadilly
21.04.80 Kid Murray W PTS 8 Edgbaston
19.05.80 Nigel Thomas W CO 6 Birmingham
16.06.80 Horace McKenzie W PTS 8 Piccadilly
29.09.80 Gary Newell W PTS 8 Bedworth
18.10.80 Joey Mack L PTS 10 Birmingham (*Midlands Area Welterweight Title Challenge*)
25.11.80 Billy Waith L PTS 8 Bedworth
11.03.81 Billy Waith L PTS 8 Solihull
30.03.81 Horace McKenzie W PTS 8 Piccadilly
06.05.81 Lloyd Hibbert L RSC 7 Solihull
21.09.81 Roger Guest L RSC 2 Wolverhampton
26.04.82 Kid Murray W PTS 6 Leicester
06.10.82 Dennis Sheehan L PTS 8 Stoke
18.10.83 Mark Hill L PTS 6 Wolverhampton
09.11.83 Granville Allen W PTS 8 Evesham
01.12.83 Davey Cox L CO 1 Dudley
Summary: 54 contests, won 35, drew 2, lost 17

Rob Wada

Shrewsbury. *Born* Shrewsbury 16.03.59
Middleweight
Manager M. Sendell
Previous Amateur Club Shrewsbury

05.10.81 Prince Wilmot L PTS 6 Birmingham
12.11.81 Joey Saunders W PTS 6 Stafford
01.12.81 Joey Saunders W PTS 6 Derby
27.01.82 Ian Lazarus W PTS 6 Stoke
09.02.82 Vince Gajny L PTS 6 Wolverhampton
16.02.82 Hugh Johnson L PTS 6 Birmingham
21.02.82 Willie Wright W PTS 6 Nottingham
10.03.82 Paul Shell W PTS 6 Nottingham
07.04.82 Willie Wright L PTS 6 Evesham
28.09.82 Blaine Longsden L PTS 8 Manchester
13.10.82 Tony Hart L PTS 6 Evesham
13.12.82 Alex Romeo L PTS 6 Wolverhampton
03.05.83 R W Smith L PTS 6 Wembley
16.05.83 Tony Britton L PTS 8 Mayfair
Summary: 14 contests, won 5, lost 9

Billy Waith

Joey Wainwright

Hull. *Born* Hull 18.02.58
Lightweight
Manager (Self)
Previous Amateur Club St Pauls
National Honours England Int.; Young England Rep.
Divisional Honours N Counties Flyweight Champion 1976

18.02.80 Brindley Jones **W** PTS 6 Piccadilly
28.02.80 Jimmy Bott DREW 6 Hull
11.03.80 Brindley Jones **W** PTS 6 Piccadilly
17.03.80 Robert Hepburn **W** PTS 6 Piccadilly
31.03.80 John Griffiths **W** PTS 6 Piccadilly
29.04.80 Alec Irvine L PTS 8 Piccadilly
13.06.83 Neville Fivey **W** RSC 4 Coventry
10.12.83 Carl Merrett DREW 6 Swansea
13.03.84 John Doherty L PTS 8 Hull
Summary: 9 contests, won 5, drew 2, lost 2

Billy Waith

Cardiff. *Born* Cardiff 30.08.50
Welsh Welterweight Champion
Manager (Self)
Previous Amateur Club St Clare's
National Honours Junior ABA Title 1967; Welsh Int.

19.10.70 Mickey Vann **W** PTS 6 Aberavon
23.11.70 Alan Salter **W** PTS 6 Piccadilly
25.01.71 Mickey Lynch **W** PTS 6 Piccadilly
22.02.71 Nick Kennedy **W** PTS 6 Aberavon
05.04.71 Nero Luchman **W** RSC 3 Piccadilly
26.04.71 Arrow Abu **W** PTS 6 Aberavon
12.05.71 Arrow Abu **W** RSC 5 Caerphilly
07.06.71 Malcolm Lowe **W** PTS 6 Nottingham
14.06.71 Dave Tuohey L PTS 6 Piccadilly
22.06.71 Mickey Van Day **W** PTS 6 Piccadilly
05.07.71 Dave Grantley **W** PTS 6 Stockport
27.09.71 Gerry McBride **W** CO 4 Piccadilly
11.10.71 Young Silky **W** PTS 8 Piccadilly
01.11.71 Roger Howes **W** CO 4 Piccadilly
08.11.71 Marcel Clolus **W** RTD 4 Piccadilly
30.11.71 Young Silky **W** PTS 8 Leeds
24.01.72 Billy Hardacre **W** PTS 8 Piccadilly
21.02.72 Ali Messaoud **W** PTS 8 Piccadilly
28.03.72 Denny Flynn DREW 8 Wembley
10.04.72 Marius Cordier **W** RSC 7 Piccadilly
10.06.72 Andries Steyn L PTS 10 Johannesburg
24.10.72 Howard Hayes L PTS 10 Bethnal Green
(*Elim. British Featherweight Title*)
05.12.72 Alan Richardson DREW 8 Leeds
22.01.73 Jimmy Bell DREW 8 Piccadilly
26.03.73 Tommy Glencross **W** PTS 8 Swansea
14.05.73 Paul Bromley **W** PTS 8 Swansea
16.06.73 Arnold Taylor L PTS 10 Johannesburg
05.10.73 Tony Cunningham **W** PTS 8 Cardiff
19.11.73 Tony Cunningham **W** PTS 8 Glasgow
18.01.74 Angus McMillan **W** PTS 8 Solihull
07.05.74 Erik Nikkinen L PTS 8 Oslo
19.06.74 Jim Watt L PTS 12 Caerphilly
(*Final Elim. British Lightweight Title*)
25.11.74 Jim Montague **W** RSC 8 Glasgow
16.12.74 Jim Melrose **W** CO 6 Piccadilly
19.03.75 Jim Watt L PTS 10 Mayfair
21.04.75 Des Morrison L PTS 8 Mayfair
06.08.75 Dave Massey **W** RSC 5 Cardiff
22.09.75 Pat McCormack L PTS 8 Walworth
24.11.75 Jimmy Revie **W** PTS 8 Walworth
02.03.76 Dave Boy Green L RSC 11 Kensington
(*Final Elim. British L. Welterweight Title*)
08.04.76 Jorgen Hansen L PTS 8 Copenhagen
06.05.76 Peter Morris **W** PTS 8 Birmingham
17.05.76 Terry Petersen **W** PTS 8 Glasgow
24.06.76 Barton McAllister **W** PTS 8 Piccadilly
29.06.76 Jim Devanney **W** CO 3 Piccadilly
25.10.76 Achille Mitchell L PTS 8 Hammersmith
15.11.76 Hugh Smith **W** PTS 8 Glasgow
02.12.76 Louis Acaries L PTS 8 Paris
11.02.77 Everaldo Costa Azevedo L PTS 8 Milan
05.03.77 Jo Kimpouani L PTS 10 Dunkirk
15.03.77 Chris Walker **W** PTS 8 Leeds
24.03.77 Peter Morris **W** RSC 7 Leicester
04.07.77 Steve Angell **W** RSC 8 Usk
(*Final Elim. British Welterweight Title*)
30.07.77 Daniel Gonzalez L CO 7 Monte Carlo
13.02.78 Henry Rhiney L PTS 15 Barnsley
(*British Welterweight Title Challenge*)
08.05.78 Joey Mack **W** PTS 8 Birmingham
07.06.78 Roy Commosioung **W** PTS 8 Cardiff
01.08.78 Chris Clarke L PTS 10 Nova Scotia
18.08.78 Jose Ramon Gomez-Fouz DREW 8 Gijon
09.09.78 Andoni Amana L RTD 6 Mirande De Ebro
16.10.78 Henry Rhiney L PTS 8 Mayfair
28.10.78 Josef Nsubuga L PTS 8 Oslo
09.11.78 Hans Henrik Palm L PTS 8 Copenhagen
01.12.78 Carl Bailey **W** PTS 8 Minster
22.01.79 Chris Walker L PTS 8 Birmingham
10.02.79 Clemente Tshinza L PTS 8 Zele
15.02.79 Jorgen Hansen L PTS 8 Randers
31.03.79 Alois Carmeliet L PTS 8 Zele
25.04.79 Lloyd Lee L PTS 8 Burslem

CONTINUED OVERLEAF

18.06.79 Tony Martey **W** PTS 8 Windsor
11.12.79 Des Morrison **L** PTS 8 Milton Keynes
21.01.80 Colin Jones **L** CO 6 Mayfair
10.03.80 Steve Early **L** PTS 8 Wolverhampton
18.04.80 Roland Zenon **L** PTS 8 Paris
05.05.80 Richard Rodriguez **L** PTS 8 Paris
14.05.80 Dave Allen **W** PTS 8 Burslem
27.07.80 Nino La Rocca **L** RSC 3 Pietra Ligure
22.09.80 John Smith **W** PTS 8 Piccadilly
20.10.80 Fighting Mack **L** PTS 8 Rotterdam
25.11.80 Roy Varden **W** PTS 8 Bedworth
11.03.81 Roy Varden **W** PTS 8 Solihull
17.03.81 Jimmy Batten **L** PTS 8 Wembley
13.04.81 Sylvester Gordon **W** PTS 8 Southwark
02.05.81 Frankie Decaestecker **L** PTS 8 Zele
16.05.81 Perico Fernandez **W** PTS 8 Alicante
06.06.81 Dum Dum Pacheco DREW 8 Zaragoza
08.08.81 Frankie Decaestecker **L** PTS 8 Ostend
07.06.82 Frank McCord **W** PTS 10 Swansea
(*Vacant Welsh Welterweight Title*)
29.11.82 Sid Smith **L** PTS 8 Southwark
07.12.82 Dennis Pryce **L** CO 2 Kensington
12.03.83 Peter Neal **L** PTS 8 Swindon
05.04.83 Chris Pyatt **L** RSC 8 Kensington
10.12.83 Frank McCord **W** PTS 10 Swansea
(*Welsh Welterweight Title Defence*)
24.02.84 Jose Varela **L** RSC 3 Hamburg
Summary: 94 contests, won 47, drew 5, lost 42

George Walker

Tottenham. *Born* Jamaica 29.02.56
L. Middleweight
Manager A. Kasler
Previous Amateur Club Hogarth
National Honours NABC Title 1975; England Int.
Divisional Honours SW London L. Middleweight R/U 1976; London Welterweight Champion 1977; SW London Welterweight Champion 1978

21.11.78 Alan Worthington **W** PTS 6 Wolverhampton
08.01.79 George Danahar **L** PTS 6 Piccadilly
23.01.79 Harry Watson DREW 8 Piccadilly
05.02.79 Harry Watson **W** PTS 6 Nottingham
12.03.79 Billy English **W** PTS 8 Mayfair
19.03.79 Salvo Nuciforo **L** PTS 8 Mayfair
27.03.79 Herol Graham **L** PTS 8 Southend
23.04.79 Harry Watson **W** PTS 8 Piccadilly
25.09.79 Richard Kenyon **W** PTS 8 Southend
05.11.79 Charlie Malarkey **W** PTS 8 Piccadilly
04.12.79 Jimmy Batten **L** PTS 8 Wembley
09.02.80 Fred Coranson **L** PTS 8 Dunkirk
17.04.80 Terry Matthews **W** CO 3 Piccadilly
08.05.80 Kirkland Laing **L** PTS 8 Solihull
23.10.80 Horace McKenzie **W** PTS 8 Piccadilly
18.11.80 Jimmy Batten **L** PTS 8 Bethnal Green
10.02.81 Chris Christian DREW 8 Bethnal Green
10.04.81 Eckhard Dagge **L** PTS 10 Kiel
24.04.81 Nino La Rocca **L** CO 2 Milan
26.09.81 Armat Yilderin DREW 8 Cologne
12.01.82 Jimmy Cable **L** PTS 8 Bethnal Green
30.04.82 Frank Wissenbach **L** PTS 8 Cologne
09.06.82 Nick Wilshire **L** RSC 4 Bristol
18.01.83 Nick Wilshire **L** RSC 8 Kensington
Summary: 24 contests, won 8, drew 3, lost 13

Johnny Wall

Merthyr. *Born* Hereford 31.03.56
Former Welsh Lightweight Champion
Manager G. Evans
Previous Amateur Club Courthouse
National Honours Welsh Int.

28.01.75 Mark Bliss **W** PTS 6 Shoreditch
10.02.75 Billy Smart DREW 6 Mayfair
19.03.75 Billy Smart DREW 6 Mayfair
05.06.75 Danny Fearon **W** PTS 8 Hammersmith
14.07.75 Young Silky **W** PTS 8 Mayfair
06.08.75 Ray Holdcroft **W** RSC 7 Cardiff
08.09.75 Terry Petersen **W** PTS 8 Mayfair
17.09.75 Hughie Clark **W** RSC 2 Cardiff
17.11.75 Johnny Claydon **W** PTS 8 Mayfair
08.12.75 Barton McAllister **L** PTS 8 Merthyr
12.01.76 Johnny Claydon **L** PTS 10 Mayfair
13.04.76 Johnny Claydon **L** PTS 10 Southend
25.10.76 Ray Heaney **W** PTS 8 Mayfair
23.11.76 Martyn Galleozzie **L** PTS 10 Treorchy
19.01.77 George McGurk **W** PTS 8 Solihull
15.02.77 Martyn Galleozzie **W** PTS 10 Merthyr
(*Welsh Lightweight Title Challenge*)
10.05.77 Adolfo Osses **W** PTS 10 Merthyr
16.06.77 Billy Vivian **W** PTS 10 Ebbw Vale
(*Welsh Lightweight Title Defence*)
21.11.77 Dil Collins **W** PTS 10 Piccadilly
(*Welsh Lightweight Title Defence*)
20.03.78 Kelvin Webber **L** PTS 10 Aberavon
(*Welsh Lightweight Title Defence*)
24.04.78 Mick Bell **L** RSC 5 Glasgow
09.11.83 John Andrews **L** RSC 2 Southend
Summary: 22 contests, won 13, drew 2, lost 7

Stan Wall
Liverpool. *Born* Liverpool 18.10.60
L. Welterweight
Manager P. Dwyer
Previous Amateur Club St Ambrose

05.10.82 Mick Dono L PTS 6 Liverpool
01.11.82 John Daly L PTS 6 Liverpool
07.11.83 Albert Buchanan L RSC 1 Liverpool
Summary: 3 contests, lost 3

(Ron) Deano Wallace
Wolverhampton. *Born* Wolverhampton 04.01.62
Middleweight
Manager M. Sendell
Previous Amateur Club Wolverhampton

01.06.81 Mickey Kidd DREW 6 Wolverhampton
15.09.81 Barry Ahmed W PTS 6 Sunderland
30.09.81 Russell Humphreys W PTS 6 Evesham
19.11.81 Sammy Brennan L PTS 4 Liverpool
07.12.81 Mickey Kidd W PTS 6 Nottingham
21.02.82 Vince Gajny L PTS 6 Nottingham
15.03.82 Richard Wilson L PTS 8 Wolverhampton
22.03.82 Conrad Oscar DREW 6 Southwark
05.04.82 Joe Jackson W PTS 6 Nottingham
26.04.82 Mark Kelly W PTS 6 Edgbaston
10.05.82 Willie Wright W PTS 6 Birmingham
07.06.82 Willie Wright W PTS 6 Edgbaston
25.06.82 Ezio Grubiza W RSC 4 Hankoo
13.09.82 John Andrews W RSC 4 Sheffield
20.09.82 Vince Gajny DREW 8 Wolverhampton
01.10.82 Tarmo Uusivirta L CO 2 Helsinki
02.11.82 Gary Hobbs L PTS 6 Hornsey
31.01.83 Alex Romeo W PTS 6 Birmingham
11.03.83 Enrico Scacchia L CO 3 Geneva
25.04.83 Gary Hobbs L RSC 3 Acton
17.06.83 Rocky Feliciello L RTD 5 Queensferry
12.10.83 Winston Burnett W PTS 6 Evesham
10.11.83 Mickey Kidd W PTS 6 Stafford
24.11.83 Steve Johnson L RSC 3 Kirkby
04.06.84 Wayne Barker W RSC 6 Manchester
Summary: 25 contests, won 13, drew 3, lost 9

Delroy Wallace
Telford. *Born* Jamaica 02.10.58
Welterweight
Manager M. Sendell
Previous Amateur Club Wolverhampton

13.04.83 Andy Roberts L PTS 6 Evesham
Summary: 1 contest, lost 1

Grant Wallis
Swindon. *Born* Wroughton 15.04.58
Heavyweight
Manager R. Porter
Previous Amateur Club Park Youth

13.03.83 Tony Blackstock W PTS 4 Swindon
10.11.83 Al Malcolm L PTS 6 Stafford
22.03.84 Dave Garside L RSC 5 Maidenhead
Summary: 3 contests, won 1, lost 2

Craig Walsh
Bradford. *Born* Birmingham 28.09.61
Lightweight
Manager J. Celebanski
Previous Amateur Club Bradford YMCA
National Honours Young England Rep.
Divisional Honours NE Counties Lightweight Champion 1979

17.02.81 Colin Harrison W PTS 6 Leeds
09.04.81 Delroy Pearce W PTS 6 Piccadilly
28.04.81 Winston Ho-Shing W PTS 6 Leeds
09.09.81 Terry Parkinson W RSC 5 Morecambe
06.10.81 Mick Rowley L PTS 6 Piccadilly
07.10.81 Gerry Beard L PTS 6 Nottingham
26.04.82 Angelo D'Amore L PTS 6 Piccadilly
09.11.82 Seamus McGuinness DREW 6 Belfast
26.11.82 Gerry Devine DREW 6 Glasgow
05.09.83 John Murphy L PTS 6 Glasgow
29.09.83 Steve Boyle L PTS 6 Glasgow
Summary: 11 contests, won 4, drew 2, lost 5

Kenny Walsh
Bradford. *Born* Bradford 30.10.64
Bantamweight
Manager J. Celebanski
Previous Amateur Club Bradford YMCA

17.11.83 Mark Boswell W PTS 6 Basildon
12.12.83 Neville Fivey W PTS 6 Bedworth
18.01.84 Steve Benny L RSC 4 Stoke
27.02.84 Dave Boy McAuley DREW 6 Birmingham
Summary: 4 contests, won 2, drew 1, lost 1

Les Walsh
Manchester. *Born* Manchester 01.11.60
Featherweight
Manager J. Edwards
Previous Amateur Club Boarshaw

25.04.83 Steve Benny W RSC 2 Liverpool
09.05.83 John Doherty L PTS 6 Manchester
19.09.83 Stuart Carmichael W PTS 6 Manchester
14.11.83 Trevor Sumner W PTS 6 Manchester

CONTINUED OVERLEAF

09.02.84 John Doherty DREW 8 Manchester
19.03.84 Trevor Sumner W PTS 8 Manchester
09.04.84 Ian Murray L PTS 6 Manchester
18.04.84 John Doherty L PTS 6 Stoke
14.05.84 Billy Joe Dee W CO 1 Manchester
18.06.84 Dave Adam L PTS 6 Manchester
Summary: 10 contests, won 5, drew 1, lost 4

Keith Ward
Cwmbran. *Born* Merthyr 26.11.63
Bantamweight
Manager G. Evans
Previous Amateur Club Tre-Ivor
National Honours Welsh Bantamweight Champion 1983; Welsh Int.

10.12.83 Brett Styles W PTS 6 Swansea
27.01.84 Billy Hardy L PTS 6 Longford
30.06.84 Steve Hanna W PTS 6 Belfast
Summary: 3 contests, won 2, lost 1

Steve Ward
Nottingham. *Born* Nottingham 12.08.56
L. Middleweight
Manager J. Gill
Previous Amateur Club NSOB

14.09.77 Peter Snowshall W PTS 6 Cambridge
20.09.77 Steve Holdsworth L PTS 6 Southend
20.03.78 Tony Laing L RSC 2 Mayfair
10.04.78 Gary Collins W PTS 6 Nottingham
17.04.78 Adey Allen L PTS 6 Mayfair
25.04.78 Sid Smith L PTS 6 Kensington
23.05.78 Robbie Robinson L RSC 1 Leicester
18.09.79 Kid Murray L PTS 6 Wolverhampton
15.10.79 Kevin Walsh W PTS 6 Manchester
15.11.79 Kevin Walsh L PTS 6 Caister
28.11.79 Mike Clemow W PTS 6 Solihull
21.01.80 Johnny Burns L PTS 6 Wolverhampton
03.03.80 Dave Sullivan W PTS 6 Nottingham
11.03.80 Lee Town L PTS 6 Southend
14.04.80 Paul Wetter W PTS 6 Mayfair
21.04.80 Paul Wetter W PTS 6 Nottingham
08.05.80 Jimmy Smith W PTS 6 Solihull
19.05.80 Jeff Aspell L RSC 3 Birmingham
12.06.80 Adrian Clamp L PTS 6 Cambridge
08.07.80 Johnny Burns W PTS 6 Wolverhampton
09.09.80 Johnny Francis L RSC 3 Sheffield
13.11.80 Kevin Durkin L PTS 6 Caister
25.11.80 Gary Buckle L PTS 6 Wolverhampton
27.04.81 Steve Brannan L PTS 6 Nottingham
11.06.81 Gary Petty L PTS 6 Hull
23.02.83 Mickey Bird L PTS 6 Chesterfield
02.03.83 Damien Fryers L PTS 6 Belfast
14.03.83 Tommy Bennett L RSC 3 Sheffield
16.04.83 Cliff Curtis L PTS 6 Bristol
15.03.84 Dennis Sheehan W RSC 6 Leicester
04.04.84 Dave Heaver W DIS 5 Evesham
16.04.84 Lateef Beachers DREW 6 Nottingham
14.05.84 Robert Armstrong L PTS 6 Nottingham
Summary: 33 contests, won 11, drew 1, lost 21

Harry Watson
Doncaster. *Born* Kirkcaldy 17.03.55
Middleweight
Manager (Self)
Previous Amateur Club Huthwaite
National Honours England Int.; Young England Rep.
Divisional Honours M Counties L. Welterweight R/U 1972; ABA Welterweight R/U 1973; M Counties Welterweight Champion 1975

10.05.76 Vernon Entertainer Vanriel W PTS 6 Mayfair
01.06.76 Johnny Pincham W PTS 6 Kensington
22.09.76 Kirkland Laing L RSC 5 Mayfair
02.11.76 Barton McAllister W PTS 8 Cambridge
14.02.77 Clinton McKenzie L RTD 4 Mayfair
15.02.78 Bob Bravado W CO 1 Cambridge
16.10.78 Frank McCord L PTS 6 Mayfair
11.12.78 Dennis Pryce W PTS 6 Birmingham
15.01.79 Joey Saunders W PTS 6 Nottingham
23.01.79 George Walker DREW 8 Piccadilly
05.02.79 George Walker L PTS 6 Nottingham
19.03.79 Billy Lauder L PTS 8 Glasgow
23.04.79 George Walker L PTS 8 Piccadilly
18.06.79 Gordon George W PTS 6 Piccadilly
25.06.79 Martin McEwan L PTS 6 Edgbaston
17.09.79 Billy Lauder L PTS 8 Glasgow
22.10.79 Winston Davis L PTS 6 Nottingham
05.11.79 Peter Gorny L PTS 6 Piccadilly
12.11.79 Winston Davis W PTS 8 Mayfair
04.02.80 Doug James L CO 1 Piccadilly
11.03.80 Earl Edwards L CO 5 Piccadilly
05.05.80 Charlie Malarkey L RSC 8 Glasgow
09.09.80 Winston Davis L CO 7 Mexborough
30.03.81 Winston Davis L PTS 6 Cleethorpes
27.04.81 Mickey Kidd DREW 6 Nottingham
06.05.81 Brian Anderson L RSC 2 Chesterfield
12.12.83 Mickey Kidd L PTS 6 Bedworth
06.04.84 Billy Lauder L RSC 7 Edinburgh
04.06.84 Mike Farghaly L CO 5 Manchester
Summary: 29 contests, won 8, drew 2, lost 19

Kenny Watson

South Norwood. *Born* London 22.02.58
Lightweight
Manager F. Rix
Previous Amateur Club Battersea
Divisional Honours SW London Featherweight R/U 1980; SW London Lightweight Champion 1982

21.03.83 Tony Borg L PTS 6 Piccadilly
22.09.83 Tommy Frankham L PTS 6 Strand
07.12.83 Mickey Kilgallon L RSC 5 Bloomsbury
16.02.84 Teddy Anderson L PTS 6 Basildon
19.04.84 Steve Griffith L PTS 6 Basildon
31.05.84 Teddy Anderson W PTS 6 Basildon
Summary: 6 contests, won 1, lost 5

Steve Watt

Steve Watt

Hayes. *Born* Glasgow 26.01.59
Welterweight
Manager D. Gunn
Previous Amateur Club Hayes
National Honours Scottish Int.
Divisional Honours NW London L. Middleweight R/U 1979; NW London Welterweight Champion 1981; London Welterweight Champion 1982

21.02.83 Tony Baker W PTS 6 Piccadilly
17.05.83 Colin Neagle W PTS 8 Piccadilly
08.09.83 Steve Tempro W CO 3 Queensway
23.09.83 Dominic Bergonzi W RSC 5 Longford
26.01.84 Gerry McGrath W RSC 2 Strand
01.03.84 Dominic Bergonzi W CO 3 Queensway
Summary: 6 contests, won 6

(Mark) Tucker Watts

Leicester. *Born* Leicester 10.04.60
Middleweight
Manager M. Inskip
Previous Amateur Club Granby

05.12.83 Lou Johnson DREW 4 Nottingham
12.12.83 Ronnie Fraser W PTS 6 Birmingham
15.03.84 Ronnie Fraser W PTS 6 Leicester
26.03.84 Winston Wray L RSC 2 Leicester
09.05.84 Lateef Beachers W CO 2 Leicester
Summary: 5 contests, won 3, drew 1, lost 1

Rex Weaver

Leicester. *Born* Burbage 22.02.62
Middleweight
Manager C. Gunns
Previous Amateur Club Nuneaton

18.03.82 Keith James L PTS 6 Caister
18.10.82 Joey Saunders L RSC 4 Nottingham
28.03.83 Wayne Hawkins L RSC 1 Birmingham
09.05.84 Floyd Davidson W PTS 6 Leicester
Summary: 4 contests, won 1, lost 3

Kevin Webb

Grove Park. *Born* Greenwich 16.04.63
L. Middleweight
Manager A. Lavelle
Previous Amateur Club Bournemouth Corinthians

16.02.82 Mark Virgin L PTS 4 Bristol
04.11.82 Mark Crouch L PTS 6 Wimbledon
22.11.82 Paul McHugh W PTS 6 Lewisham
15.12.82 Tony Rabbetts L PTS 6 Queensway
14.02.83 Mark Good W PTS 6 Lewisham
22.02.83 Chris Lewin W PTS 6 Bethnal Green
07.03.83 Mickey Williams W PTS 6 Piccadilly
06.04.83 Mickey Williams W PTS 6 Mayfair
19.05.83 Mark Crouch L PTS 6 Queensway
08.09.83 Dennis Boy O'Brien L CO 4 Queensway
21.11.83 Tim Gladwish DREW 6 Eltham
30.11.83 Newton Barnett W PTS 6 Piccadilly
27.01.84 Tony Rabbetts W PTS 8 Longford
03.02.84 Ian Martin W PTS 6 Maidenhead
Summary: 14 contests, won 8, drew 1, lost 5

Roy Webb

Larne. *Born* Banbridge 26.02.62
Bantamweight
Manager P. Byrne
Previous Amateur Club Holy Family
National Honours Irish Int.; Irish Bantamweight Champion 1981; Irish Featherweight Champion 1983

25.01.84 Dai Williams W CO 2 Belfast
04.04.84 Muhammad Lovelock W PTS 6 Belfast
04.06.84 Billy Hardy W PTS 6 Mayfair
30.06.84 Graham Kid Clarke W PTS 8 Belfast
Summary: 4 contests, won 4

(John) Spider Webb (Mills)

Manchester. *Born* Manchester 17.03.64
Welterweight
Manager N. Basso
Previous Amateur Club Collyhurst
Divisional Honours E Lancs Welterweight R/U 1982

12.09.83 Elvis Morton **W** PTS 6 Leicester
Summary: 1 contest, won 1

Bobby Welburn

Hull. *Born* Hull 11.02.60
L. Welterweight
Manager (Self)
Previous Amateur Club Hull Fish Trades

21.04.80 Bryan McConnell **L** PTS 6 Glasgow
28.04.80 Phillip Morris **W** PTS 6 Piccadilly
05.05.80 Barry Winter **L** RSC 2 Glasgow
02.06.80 Joe Mills DREW 6 Piccadilly
16.06.80 Steve Henty **L** PTS 6 Piccadilly
15.09.80 Joe McNamee **W** RSC 2 Glasgow
02.10.80 Steve Freeman **W** PTS 6 Hull
20.10.80 Alex Gregal **W** RSC 5 Glasgow
03.11.80 Richard White **W** PTS 6 Piccadilly
01.12.80 Glyn Rhodes **W** CO 1 Hull
09.04.81 Lee McKenzie **L** PTS 8 Piccadilly
01.06.81 Tim Moloney **L** PTS 8 Piccadilly
11.06.81 Eric Wood **W** PTS 8 Hull
04.12.81 Julian Bousted **L** RSC 5 Bristol
28.09.82 Mo Hussein **L** RSC 1 Bethnal Green
29.11.82 Dennis Sullivan **L** PTS 8 Newquay
20.12.82 John Murray **L** PTS 6 Bradford
25.01.83 Damien Fryers **L** PTS 6 Belfast
07.02.83 Angelo D'Amore **W** PTS 6 Piccadilly
29.03.83 Peter Flanagan **L** PTS 6 Hull
11.04.83 Mike Calderwood DREW 6 Manchester
27.04.83 Edward Lloyd **L** PTS 6 Rhyl
27.05.83 Michael Harris **L** PTS 6 Swansea
15.09.83 John Daly **L** PTS 6 Liverpool
22.09.83 Paul Cook **L** RSC 4 Strand
19.10.83 Ken Foreman **L** PTS 6 Hull
31.10.83 Peter Eubanks **L** RSC 1 Mayfair
Summary: 27 contests, won 8, drew 2, lost 17

Terry Welch

Liverpool. *Born* Liverpool 13.02.59
L. Welterweight
Manager (Self)
Previous Amateur Club Golden Gloves

12.09.78 Selvin Bell **W** PTS 6 Birkenhead
19.09.78 Johnny Beauchamp **W** PTS 6 Southend
27.10.78 Gerry Maguire **W** RSC 5 Belfast
02.11.78 Najib Daho **L** PTS 6 Liverpool
21.11.78 Johnny Waring **L** PTS 6 Wolverhampton
21.12.78 Joe Mills **L** PTS 6 Liverpool
17.01.79 Tony Zeni **W** PTS 6 Burslem
13.02.79 Tommy Wright **L** PTS 8 Wakefield
22.03.79 Dave Allen **W** PTS 6 Liverpool
04.04.79 Martin McGough **L** PTS 6 Birmingham
21.05.79 Lance Williams **L** PTS 8 Manchester
25.09.79 Peter Snowshall **W** CO 6 Southend
08.10.79 Norman Morton **W** PTS 8 Bradford
29.10.79 Dennis Sullivan **L** PTS 6 Camborne
15.11.79 Hugh Smith **L** PTS 8 Liverpool
05.12.79 Johnny Mount **W** PTS 8 Liverpool
05.03.80 George McGurk **W** PTS 6 Liverpool
27.03.80 Stan Atherton **W** PTS 8 Liverpool
30.07.80 Gary Pearce **L** RSC 4 Doncaster
25.11.80 Kevin Sheehan **W** CO 1 Wolverhampton
03.03.81 Colin Derrick **L** RSC 1 Wembley
18.02.82 John Lindo **L** PTS 6 Liverpool
10.03.82 Granville Allen **L** PTS 8 Nottingham
14.02.83 Mark Drew **W** CO 2 Liverpool
29.04.83 Mark Duffy **W** RTD 5 Liverpool
09.05.83 Robert Lloyd **L** PTS 6 Manchester
Summary: 26 contests, won 13, lost 13

Mark West

Newhaven. *Born* Brighton 12.02.60
Featherweight
Manager D. Harris
Previous Amateur Club Newhaven & District
National Honours Young England Rep.
Divisional Honours S Counties Flyweight Champion 1978 – 1979

20.10.80 Carl Cleasby **W** PTS 6 Hove
02.03.81 Pat Mallon **W** PTS 6 Brighton
23.03.81 Ian Murray **W** PTS 6 Mayfair
14.09.81 Steve Cleak **W** RSC 6 Mayfair
09.02.82 Steve Henderson **W** PTS 8 Kensington
21.02.82 Steve Topliss **L** PTS 6 Birmingham
18.05.82 Gary Nickels **W** PTS 8 Bethnal Green
25.10.82 Vernon Penprase **L** PTS 8 Mayfair
21.02.83 Pat Doherty DREW 8 Piccadilly
21.04.83 Don George **L** PTS 8 Piccadilly
20.06.83 Steve Cleak DREW 8 Piccadilly
20.09.83 Clyde Ruan **L** PTS 10 Mayfair
21.03.84 Pat Doherty **L** RSC 8 Solihull
Summary: 13 contests, won 6, drew 2, lost 5

John Westgarth
Newcastle. *Born* Malta 23.12.59
Heavyweight
Manager D. Mahoney
Previous Amateur Club West End Boys
Divisional Honours N Counties S. Heavyweight Champion 1982

29.11.82 Andrew Gerrard DREW 6 Newquay
06.12.82 Frank Robinson **W** PTS 6 Nottingham
10.02.83 John Fallon **W** PTS 6 Walthamstow
23.02.83 Dave Garside L RTD 6 Mayfair
Summary: 4 contests, won 2, drew 1, lost 1

Mike Whalley
Manchester. *Born* Manchester 01.05.60
Featherweight
Manager J. Edwards
Previous Amateur Club Collyhurst

05.09.83 Danny Knaggs **W** CO 6 Liverpool
05.12.83 Trevor Sumner **W** CO 4 Manchester
18.04.84 Anthony Brown L PTS 6 Stoke
18.06.84 John Maloney **W** CO 1 Manchester
Summary: 4 contests, won 3, lost 1

Lee White
Morden. *Born* Mitcham 29.06.62
Heavyweight
Manager T. Lavelle
Previous Amateur Club Rosehill
National Honours NABC Title 1980

06.10.80 Keith Bristol L PTS 6 Southwark
23.10.80 Nigel Savery **W** PTS 6 Middlesbrough
01.12.80 Keith Bristol **W** PTS 6 Bloomsbury
15.12.80 Nye Williams L PTS 6 Merthyr
06.01.81 Keith Bristol L PTS 6 Bethnal Green
19.01.81 Paul Newman **W** RTD 2 Wimbledon
17.02.81 Ben Lawlor L PTS 6 Lewisham
19.03.81 Vernon Scott L PTS 8 Norwich
28.05.81 Paul Newman L PTS 8 Wimbledon
05.08.81 Joe Jackson L PTS 8 Norwich
21.09.81 John Joseph L PTS 6 Piccadilly
12.10.81 Jarlath McGough L PTS 6 Birmingham
01.02.82 Glenroy Taylor **W** PTS 6 Southwark
08.02.82 Joe Gregory **W** PTS 6 Mayfair
16.02.82 Keith Bristol L PTS 6 Lewisham
23.03.82 Clive Beardsley **W** CO 2 Bethnal Green
21.04.82 Paul Newman L PTS 6 Brighton
27.04.82 Carlton Benoit L PTS 6 Southend
23.09.82 Joey Williams **W** PTS 6 Wimbledon
04.11.82 Glenroy Taylor **W** PTS 6 Wimbledon
07.03.84 Paul Newman L PTS 8 Brighton
12.04.84 Eddie Fenton DREW 6 Piccadilly
30.04.84 Eddie Fenton DREW 6 Mayfair
14.05.84 Eddie Fenton **W** PTS 6 Nottingham
Summary: 24 contests, won 9, drew 2, lost 13

Andy Whitehouse
Doncaster. *Born* Worksop 02.05.63
L. Middleweight
Manager J. Rushton
Previous Amateur Club Plant Works

15.03.84 Graeme Griffin L PTS 6 Leicester
27.03.84 Malcolm Davies L CO 4 Wolverhampton
Summary: 2 contests, lost 2

Scott Wilde
Bournemouth. *Born* Isle of Man 19.03.61
L. Heavyweight
Manager D. Mahoney
Previous Amateur Club Paignton

19.11.81 Geoff Rymer L PTS 4 Piccadilly
25.01.82 Glenroy Taylor L RSC 2 Mayfair
27.05.83 Andrew Gerrard L PTS 6 Swansea
14.06.83 Gary Gething L PTS 6 Newport
Summary: 4 contests, lost 4

Mike Wilkes
Merthyr. *Born* Merthyr 28.08.59
Featherweight
Manager D. James
Previous Amateur Club Hoover

09.06.81 Ken Coughlin **W** PTS 6 Newport
03.09.81 Peter Jones L RSC 4 Cardiff
23.11.81 Eugene Maloney **W** PTS 6 Bloomsbury
09.12.81 Johnny Dorey L PTS 6 Piccadilly
18.01.82 Hugh Russell L PTS 6 Mayfair
08.02.82 Rocky Bantleman L PTS 6 Piccadilly
16.02.82 Gordon Haigh DREW 6 Bristol
10.12.83 Mark Pearce L PTS 6 Swansea
Summary: 8 contests, won 2, drew 1, lost 5

Tony Wilkinson
Sunderland. *Born* Sunderland 27.11.64
L. Welterweight
Manager T. Cumiskey
Previous Amateur Club Sunderland
National Honours Schools Title 1981; Junior ABA Title 1981

24.01.82 Michael Betts **W** RSC 2 Sunderland
08.02.82 Peter Flanagan **W** PTS 4 Manchester
08.03.82 Dave Markey **W** RSC 3 Hamilton
18.03.82 Shaun Stewart **W** RSC 3 South Shields
29.03.82 Kevin Pritchard L PTS 4 Liverpool
07.01.83 John Daly **W** PTS 6 Durham

CONTINUED OVERLEAF

24.01.83 Sammy Rodgers W PTS 6 Bradford
10.02.83 John McKinlay W RSC 3 Sunderland
07.03.83 Dave Haggarty L PTS 6 Glasgow
19.05.83 George Kerr L RSC 4 Sunderland
Summary: 10 contests, won 7, lost 3

Alan Williams

Liverpool. *Born* Liverpool 02.08.62
L. Middleweight
Manager C. Moorcroft
Previous Amateur Club Salisbury
Divisional Honours W Lancs Welterweight R/U 1983

11.06.84 Bobby McGowan W DIS 1 Manchester
Summary: 1 contest, won 1

Andy Williams

Pontnewynydd. *Born* Newport 10.10.65
Lightweight
Manager J. Evans
Previous Amateur Club Pontnewynydd
National Honours Schools Titles 1980–1981
Divisional Honours Welsh Lightweight R/U 1983

19.05.84 Steve James L PTS 6 Bristol
Summary: 1 contest, lost 1

Bobby Williams

Southampton. *Born* Jamaica 18.10.58
Middleweight
Manager J. Bishop
Previous Amateur Club Southampton

07.10.80 John Joseph L RSC 3 Piccadilly
01.12.80 Pharaoh Bish W PTS 6 Reading
12.01.81 John Ridgman L PTS 6 Hove
19.10.81 Tony Burke W CO 3 Mayfair
10.12.81 Tony Burke L PTS 6 Walthamstow
04.02.82 Robbie Turner W CO 1 Walthamstow
01.03.82 Kenny Feehan W PTS 6 Piccadilly
23.03.82 Jack Sharp L PTS 6 Bethnal Green
10.10.82 Gary Gething L PTS 6 Piccadilly
09.11.82 T. P. Jenkins L PTS 6 Kensington
16.05.83 John Elliott W CO 2 Birmingham
08.09.83 Kevin Shearon W PTS 6 Queensway
27.10.83 Gary Gething L PTS 6 Ebbw Vale
31.01.84 Cameron Lithgow L RSC 3 Kensington
Summary: 14 contests, won 6, lost 8

Cecil Williams

Birmingham. *Born* St Kitts 18.03.55
L. Middleweight
Manager (Self)
Previous Amateur Club Birmingham City

21.02.82 Errol Dennis L PTS 6 Nottingham
07.04.82 Dalton Jordan W RSC 3 Evesham
26.04.82 Dan Myers DREW 6 Leicester
17.05.82 Tony Brown L RSC 4 Manchester
08.11.82 Tommy Heffron L RSC 1 Manchester
18.10.83 Malcolm Davies L PTS 6 Wolverhampton
Summary: 6 contests, won 1, drew 1, lost 4

(David) Dai Williams

Swansea. *Born* Cefn Hengoed 17.07.63
Bantamweight
Manager D. Gardiner
Previous Amateur Club Gelligaer
National Honours Welsh Flyweight Champion 1981; Welsh Int.

14.09.81 Eddie Glencross L DIS 2 Glasgow
12.11.81 Steve Reilly W PTS 6 Ebbw Vale
27.10.83 George Bailey W PTS 6 Ebbw Vale
09.11.83 Graham Kid Clarke DREW 6 Evesham
21.11.83 Gabriel Kuphey W PTS 6 Glasgow
25.01.84 Roy Webb L CO 2 Belfast
Summary: 6 contests, won 3, drew 1, lost 2

Danny Williams

Romney Marsh. *Born* Hastings 21.05.59
Welterweight
Manager D. Harris
Previous Amateur Club Romney Marsh
Divisional Honours H Counties L. Welterweight R/U 1978

25.04.83 Cliff Eastwood W PTS 4 Acton
10.05.83 Andy O'Rawe L PTS 6 Southend
19.05.83 Tony Rabbetts DREW 6 Queensway
Summary: 3 contests, won 1, drew 1, lost 1

(Derek) Deka Williams

West Bromwich. *Born* West Bromwich 23.04.60
L. Heavyweight
Manager F. Wolfingdale
Previous Amateur Club None

22.03.83 Tony Blackstock L RSC 4 Wolverhampton
27.04.83 Alan Douglas L RSC 6 Wolverhampton
23.06.83 Osbourne Taylor W RSC 3 Wolverhampton
20.09.83 Paul Heatley W PTS 6 Dudley
01.12.83 Colin Flute L PTS 6 Dudley
10.02.84 Colin Flute W RSC 2 Dudley
14.03.84 Wes Taylor L PTS 6 Stoke
27.04.84 Jerry Golden W PTS 6 Wolverhampton
07.06.84 Gypsy Carman W PTS 6 Dudley
18.06.84 Mike Farghaly L RSC 4 Manchester
Summary: 10 contests, won 5, lost 5

Gary Williams
Doncaster. *Born* Doncaster 23.03.59
Lightweight
Manager J. Rushton
Previous Amateur Club Bentley MW

07.10.82 Shaun Dooney **W** RSC 1 Morley
25.10.82 Joey Morris DREW 6 Bradford
25.11.82 Paul Keers **W** RSC 3 Morley
19.01.83 Glyn Mitchell **W** PTS 6 Stoke
25.02.83 Sam Church **W** RSC 2 Doncaster
21.03.83 John McKinlay **W** PTS 6 Glasgow
13.06.83 Jimmy Thornton **L** RTD 5 Doncaster
01.09.83 Abdul Kareem **L** PTS 6 Bloomsbury
12.09.83 Billy Edwards **L** RTD 3 Glasgow
18.11.83 Abdul Kareem **W** DIS 8 Sheffield
19.12.83 Michael Harris **L** PTS 8 Swansea
22.02.84 Joey Joynson **L** RSC 1 Kensington
27.03.84 Mickey Baker **L** CO 3 Wolverhampton
01.05.84 Mike Durvan **L** PTS 6 Bethnal Green
21.05.84 Hugh Sugar Kelly **W** RSC 4 Aberdeen
Summary: 15 contests, won 7, drew 1, lost 7

Howard Williams
Merthyr. *Born* Merthyr 11.07.58
Bantamweight
Manager D. James
Previous Amateur Club Tre-Ivor

26.04.82 Steve Reilly **W** PTS 6 Cardiff
26.10.82 Graham Kid Clarke **L** PTS 6 Newport
06.12.82 Graham Kid Clarke **L** PTS 6 Bristol
09.03.83 Cliff Storey **L** PTS 8 Stoke
22.03.83 George Bailey **L** CO 1 Wolverhampton
25.04.83 Colin Moorcroft **W** RSC 3 Liverpool
27.05.83 Robert Dickie **L** RSC 2 Swansea
Summary: 7 contests, won 2, lost 5

Mickey Williams
Stepney. *Born* London 23.05.56
Middleweight
Manager H. Burgess
Previous Amateur Club Broad Street

22.04.82 Tony Brown **L** RSC 3 Liverpool
07.03.83 Kevin Webb **L** PTS 6 Piccadilly
06.04.83 Kevin Webb **L** PTS 6 Mayfair
17.05.83 Patsy Kid Moore **W** RSC 4 Piccadilly
Summary: 4 contests, won 1, lost 3

Nye Williams
Derek Rowe (Photos) Ltd

Nye Williams
Gilwen. *Born* Gilwen 25.06.60
Welsh L. Heavyweight Champion
Manager W. G. Davies
Previous Amateur Club Semtex
National Honours Welsh L. Heavyweight Champion 1978 – 1979; Welsh Int.

15.12.80 Lee White **W** PTS 6 Merthyr
16.02.81 Paul Busette **W** PTS 6 Mayfair
09.06.81 Phil Williams **W** RSC 1 Newport
03.09.81 Nigel Savery **W** PTS 6 Cardiff
12.10.81 Antonio Harris **L** PTS 6 Birmingham
23.11.81 Gary Jones **W** CO 2 Nantwich
22.02.82 Devon Bailey **L** PTS 6 Mayfair
22.03.82 Keith Bristol **L** PTS 8 Mayfair
26.04.82 Steve Goodwin **W** RSC 4 Bradford
09.06.82 Paul Busette **W** RSC 5 Bristol
13.06.83 Alex Romeo **W** RSC 2 Coventry
27.10.83 Chris Lawson **W** PTS 10 Ebbw Vale (*Vacant Welsh L. Heavyweight Title*)
28.03.84 Antonio Harris **L** PTS 8 Aberavon
06.04.84 Trevor Cattouse **L** PTS 8 Watford
Summary: 14 contests, won 9, lost 5

Rob Williams
Manchester. *Born* Manchester 11.08.62
Welterweight
Manager N. Basso
Previous Amateur Club Cavendish

05.09.83 Mickey Bird **L** CO 3 Liverpool
Summary: 1 contest, lost 1

CONTINUED OVERLEAF

Tony Willis
David Thorne

Tony Willis

Liverpool. *Born* Liverpool 17.06.60
Lightweight
Manager P. Lynch
Previous Amateur Club Rotunda
National Honours Schools Title 1976; Junior ABA Title 1977; Young England Rep.; England Int.; GB Rep., ABA L. Welterweight Champion 1980 & 1981; Olympic Bronze 1980
Divisional Honours N Counties Featherweight Champion 1978; E Lancs Lightweight Champion 1979

28.09.81 Winston McKenzie **W** RSC 1 Lewisham
13.10.81 Eric Wood **W** PTS 8 Blackpool
19.11.81 Lloyd Christie **W** PTS 6 Liverpool
18.02.82 Tony Carroll **W** RSC 5 Liverpool
07.06.82 Peter Bennett **W** RSC 3 Edgbaston
22.09.82 Peter Eubanks **W** PTS 8 Mayfair
18.10.82 Des Gwilliam **W** PTS 8 Edgbaston
17.11.82 Robbie Robinson **W** RSC 5 Solihull (*Elim. British Lightweight Title*)
06.12.82 Charlie Nash **W** RSC 3 Edgbaston
21.02.83 Judas Clottey **W** RSC 5 Edgbaston
08.04.83 Robbie Robinson **W** RTD 4 Liverpool (*Elim. British Lightweight Title*)
01.09.83 Carlos Amaya **W** RSC 7 Bloomsbury
02.11.83 Terry Medley **W** RSC 1 Bloomsbury
03.12.83 George Feeney **L** RSC 1 Marylebone (*British Lightweight Title Challenge*)
19.01.84 Mick Rowley **W** PTS 10 Digbeth
Summary: 15 contests, won 14, lost 1

Nick Wilshire

Bristol. *Born* Bristol 03.11.61
L. Middleweight
Manager M. Duff
Previous Amateur Club National Smelting
National Honours Schools Title 1978; Junior ABA Title 1978; NABC Title 1979; Young England Rep.; England Int.; GB Rep.; ABA Middleweight Champion 1979; World Junior Silver 1979; Euro Junior Gold 1980
Divisional Honours ABA L. Middleweight R/U 1980

28.04.81 Steve Davies **W** PTS 8 Kensington
02.06.81 Les Wint **W** RSC 4 Kensington
15.09.81 Vic Jackson **W** PTS 6 Wembley
13.10.81 Dale Henderson **W** RSC 2 Kensington
03.11.81 Mickey Mapp **W** CO 3 Kensington
24.11.81 Steve Henty **W** RSC 4 Wembley
09.02.82 Steve Davies **W** RTD 3 Kensington
02.03.82 Nigel Thomas **W** RSC 1 Kensington
17.03.82 Dominic Delorme **W** RSC 3 Kensington
09.06.82 George Walker **W** RSC 4 Bristol
30.06.82 Jose Serna **W** CO 2 Las Vegas
14.09.82 Horace McKenzie **W** RSC 5 Wembley
30.09.82 Harry Truman **W** RSC 4 Las Vegas
07.10.82 Warren Hardy **W** RSC 2 Los Angeles
09.11.82 Tony Britton **W** RSC 4 Kensington
23.11.82 Fred Boynton **W** RTD 4 Wembley
18.01.83 George Walker **W** RSC 8 Kensington
08.02.83 Jose Mirales **W** RSC 2 Kensington
15.03.83 Tony Britton **W** RSC 3 Wembley
03.05.83 Jimmy Cable **L** PTS 10 Wembley
23.06.83 Rodolfo Gutierrez **W** RSC 1 Los Angeles
08.07.83 Pedro Guerrero **W** RSC 4 Los Angeles
27.09.83 Reg Ford **W** CO 1 Wembley
22.10.83 Danny Chapman **W** RSC 4 Atlantic City
12.11.83 Bruce Jackson **W** RSC 4 Tampa
22.11.83 Bruce Johnson **W** CO 3 Wembley
31.01.84 Jose Vallejo **W** RSC 3 Kensington
22.02.84 Jimmy Cable **L** PTS 12 Kensington (*Vacant British L. Middleweight Title*)
13.05.84 John Langol **W** RSC 6 Wembley
05.06.84 Wo Lamani Wo **W** RTD 7 Kensington
Summary: 30 contests, won 28, lost 2

Richard Wilson

Nuneaton. *Born* Nuneaton 13.03.60
L. Middleweight
Manager (Self)
Previous Amateur Club Nuneaton
National Honours Schools Titles 1973, 1975, 1976; NABC Title 1977; Young England Rep.

29.09.80 Paul Murray **W** PTS 6 Bedworth
20.01.81 Steve Davies **W** PTS 6 Bethnal Green

16.02.81 Dave Finigan **W** PTS 6 Southwark
13.04.81 John Wiggins **W** PTS 6 Wolverhampton
27.10.81 Neville Wilson **W** PTS 6 Wolverhampton
12.01.82 Arthur Davis L RSC 4 Bethnal Green
21.02.82 Dennis Sheehan **W** RSC 4 Birmingham
15.03.82 Deano Wallace **W** PTS 8 Wolverhampton
29.11.82 T. P. Jenkins DREW 8 Southwark
31.01.83 T. P. Jenkins L RSC 4 Southwark
21.04.83 Derek McKenzie **W** PTS 8 Letchworth
16.05.83 Dennis Sheehan **W** PTS 8 Mayfair
01.12.83 John McGlynn **W** PTS 8 Dudley
Summary: 13 contests, won 10, drew 1, lost 2

Tyrell Wilson

Newport. *Born* Jamaica 11.01.59
Welterweight
Manager W. May
Previous Amateur Club St Michael's

10.09.79 George White **W** PTS 6 Birmingham
24.09.79 Steve Parker L PTS 6 Birmingham
04.10.79 Phillip Morris **W** PTS 6 Ebbw Vale
09.10.79 Kid Murray L PTS 6 Wolverhampton
29.10.79 John Lindo **W** PTS 6 Birmingham
20.12.79 Wally Stockings DREW 6 Queensway
09.01.80 Walter Clayton L RSC 1 Burslem
18.02.80 Danny Connolly L PTS 6 Mayfair
10.03.80 Mickey Baker L PTS 8 Wolverhampton
24.03.80 Danny Connolly L PTS 6 Mayfair
07.04.81 Ray Price L PTS 6 Newport
09.06.81 Sam Omidi DREW 6 Newport
30.09.81 Shaun Stanley **W** PTS 6 Evesham
27.10.81 Paul Chance L CO 2 Wolverhampton
10.12.81 Steve Brannan **W** RSC 3 Newport
27.01.82 Patsy Quinn L RSC 5 Belfast
22.03.82 Terry Smith L RSC 1 Southwark
26.04.82 Dai Davies **W** PTS 6 Cardiff
31.05.82 John Daly L PTS 6 Glasgow
07.06.82 Andy Thomas L PTS 8 Swansea
20.09.82 Colin Harrison **W** RTD 4 Glasgow
10.10.82 Julian Bousted L PTS 8 Piccadilly
25.10.82 Johnny Grant L RSC 6 Mayfair
01.03.83 Andy O'Rawe L PTS 6 Southend
07.03.83 Jeff Decker L PTS 8 Piccadilly
16.03.83 Andy O'Rawe L PTS 6 Cheltenham
18.04.83 Jim McIntosh L RSC 5 Glasgow
Summary: 27 contests, won 7, drew 2, lost 18

(Peter) Willie Wilson

Nottingham. *Born* Ashington 13.08.56
Lightweight
Manager J. Gill
Previous Amateur Club Army

21.02.83 Gary Felvus L PTS 6 Nottingham
21.03.83 Ron Shinkwin DREW 4 Nottingham
05.04.83 Jim McDonnell L RSC 3 Kensington
28.04.83 Wayne Trigg **W** RSC 3 Leicester
09.05.83 Sammy Rodgers **W** RSC 4 Nottingham
25.05.83 John Murray L PTS 6 Rhyl
03.10.83 Dave Savage L RSC 7 Glasgow
01.11.83 Kenny Jinks L PTS 6 Dudley
07.12.83 George Baigrie **W** RSC 2 Stoke
18.01.84 Abdul Kareem L PTS 8 Stoke
23.01.84 Jim McDonnell L CO 2 Mayfair
27.02.84 Steve Boyle L RSC 3 Nottingham
27.03.84 Steve Griffith L PTS 6 Bethnal Green
14.05.84 Gary Felvus L RSC 7 Nottingham
Summary: 14 contests, won 3, drew 1, lost 10

Winston Wray

Bolton. *Born* Jamaica 30.10.60
Middleweight
Manager N. Basso
Previous Amateur Club Bolton Lads
Divisional Honours NW Counties L. Heavyweight Champion 1982

22.11.82 Steve Lewsam L PTS 4 Liverpool
30.11.82 John Stone **W** RSC 2 Farnsworth
17.01.83 Dave Scott **W** PTS 6 Manchester
07.03.83 Glen Crump L RSC 4 Liverpool
27.04.83 John Langol L PTS 6 Rhyl
20.06.83 Billy Edwards **W** RSC 1 Manchester
17.10.83 Chris Coady L PTS 6 Manchester
28.11.83 Terry Magee L PTS 6 Rhyl
26.03.84 Tucker Watts **W** RSC 2 Leicester
09.04.84 Dougie Isles **W** RSC 1 Manchester
30.04.84 John Elliott **W** PTS 6 Rhyl
11.06.84 John Elliott **W** RSC 4 Manchester
Summary: 12 contests, won 7, lost 5

Paul Wright

Nottingham. *Born* Nottingham 11.12.56
Featherweight
Manager J. Gill
Previous Amateur Club Nottingham SOB

19.09.83 Kenny Jinks L RSC 3 Nottingham
09.11.83 Carl Merrett L PTS 6 Evesham
Summary: 2 contests, lost 2

Willie Wright

Birmingham. *Born* Birmingham 16.11.61
Middleweight
Manager G. Donaghy
Previous Amateur Club Nechells

26.03.80 Don Hughes **W** PTS 6 Evesham
21.04.80 Casley McCallum **W** PTS 6 Edgbaston

CONTINUED OVERLEAF

24.09.80 Steve Bateman W PTS 6 Evesham
29.09.80 Robbie Smith W PTS 6 Bedworth
08.10.80 Joe Jackson L PTS 6 Stoke
14.10.80 Tommy Taylor L PTS 6 Wolverhampton
18.10.80 John Humphreys L PTS 6 Birmingham
05.11.80 Joe Frater L PTS 6 Evesham
18.11.80 Russell Humphreys L PTS 6 Shrewsbury
15.12.80 Joe Dean W PTS 6 Bradford
28.01.81 Joe Dean W PTS 6 Stoke
10.02.81 Steve Bateman W PTS 6 Wolverhampton
09.03.81 John Humphreys L PTS 6 Wolverhampton
16.03.81 Mickey Kidd L DIS 6 Nottingham
13.05.81 Mickey Kidd L PTS 6 Manchester
28.05.81 Russell Humphreys W PTS 6 Edgbaston
07.10.81 Vince Gajny L PTS 6 Stoke
27.10.81 Russell Humphreys L PTS 6 Wolverhampton
02.11.81 Joey Saunders W PTS 6 Nottingham
10.11.81 Vince Gajny L PTS 6 Bedworth
23.11.81 Mickey Kidd L PTS 6 Nottingham
02.12.81 Mark Kelly W PTS 6 Burslem
20.01.82 Mark Kelly L PTS 6 Burslem
25.01.82 John Humphreys L PTS 6 Wolverhampton
09.02.82 John Humphreys L PTS 6 Wolverhampton
21.02.82 Rob Wada L PTS 6 Nottingham
10.03.82 Mark Kelly L PTS 6 Burslem
15.03.82 Russell Humphreys L PTS 8 Wolverhampton
30.03.82 Dudley McKenzie L PTS 6 Wembley
07.04.82 Rob Wada W PTS 6 Evesham
26.04.82 Danny Cope W CO 6 Leicester
10.05.82 Deano Wallace L PTS 6 Birmingham
20.05.82 Sammy Brennan L PTS 8 Preston
07.06.82 Deano Wallace L PTS 6 Edgbaston
07.07.82 Keith James L PTS 8 Newmarket
13.09.82 Blaine Longsden W PTS 8 Manchester
10.11.82 Alex Romeo L PTS 6 Evesham
24.01.83 Gary Cable W RSC 6 Mayfair
09.03.83 James Cook L PTS 8 Solihull
28.03.83 Mick Mills W CO 5 Manchester
20.04.83 Jimmy Price L PTS 6 Muswell Hill
31.05.83 Cameron Lithgow DREW 6 Kensington
26.09.83 Blaine Longsden W RTD 4 Manchester
22.11.83 Billy Lauder W RSC 4 Manchester
28.01.84 Dave Scott W RTD 5 Hanley
09.02.84 Steve Johnson L PTS 8 Manchester
12.05.84 Winston Burnett W PTS 8 Hanley
Summary: 47 contests, won 19, drew 1, lost 27

Bob Young

Croydon. *Born* Jamaica 01.08.52
Heavyweight
Manager D. Read
Previous Amateur Club Croydon
Divisional Honours SE London L. Heavyweight R/U 1975–1976

20.07.77 Pat Thompson L PTS 6 Sheffield
05.09.77 Billy Warner DREW 6 Hove
19.09.77 Billy Warner W PTS 6 Mayfair
08.11.77 Colin Flute W RSC 5 West Bromwich
05.12.77 George Scott L RSC 3 Marton
07.02.78 Brian Paul W PTS 6 Southend
20.03.78 Guinea Roger W PTS 6 Piccadilly
03.04.78 Martin Nee W PTS 6 Piccadilly
15.05.78 Paul Kinsella W RSC 3 Glasgow
19.09.78 Martin Nee L PTS 6 Southend
27.09.78 Ricky James L CO 3 Solihull
23.11.78 Martin Nee W PTS 6 Wimbledon
21.02.79 Danny Lawford L RSC 5 Cambridge
15.03.79 Shaun Chalcraft L RTD 3 Wimbledon
04.10.79 Winston Allen W PTS 6 Ebbw Vale
06.03.80 Austin Okoye L PTS 8 Wimbledon
22.09.80 Jim Burns W RSC 2 Wolverhampton
03.01.81 Rudi Gauwe L CO 5 Zele
09.03.81 Andy Palmer W RSC 2 Mayfair
20.06.81 Rudi Pika L RSC 1 Wembley
25.01.82 Andy Palmer L CO 2 Mayfair
17.04.84 Barry Ellis DREW 8 Merton
Summary: 22 contests, won 10, drew 2, lost 10

Jimmy Young

Manchester. *Born* Manchester 23.07.61
Lightweight
Manager B. Robinson
Previous Amateur Club Ancoats

20.04.83 Graham Brett L CO 3 Muswell Hill
Summary: 1 contest, lost 1

(Mohammed) Young Yousuf

Walsall. *Born* Pakistan 26.11.59
Featherweight
Manager G. Riley
Previous Amateur Club West Bromwich College
Divisional Honours M Counties Bantamweight Champion 1979

21.03.83 Dave Pratt L PTS 6 Nottingham
16.05.83 Mark Pearce L PTS 6 Birmingham
13.06.83 Gordon Stobie L PTS 6 Nottingham
Summary: 3 contests, lost 3

Active British Based Boxers: British Record Only

Includes the *British record only* of all boxers active since 01.01.84 who made their debuts outside of the U.K. and who were not born in Britain. Boxers shown in this section could be in the U.K. on a temporary basis.

Hector Clottey

Liverpool. *Born* Lambeth 03.08.60
Bantamweight
Manager M. Atkinson

30.06.82 Stuart Shaw L PTS 8 Liverpool
31.01.84 John Feeney L PTS 8 Kensington
15.03.84 Anthony Brown W PTS 8 Kirkby
Summary: 3 contests, won 1, lost 2

Judas Clottey

Liverpool. *Born* Ghana 24.08.58
Welterweight
Manager C. Atkinson

30.06.82 P. J. Davitt W PTS 8 Liverpool
09.12.82 John Andrews DREW 6 Bloomsbury
03.02.83 Rocky Kelly W PTS 8 Bloomsbury
21.02.83 Tony Willis L RSC 5 Edgbaston
07.12.83 Sylvester Mittee W RSC 3 Bloomsbury
28.01.84 Sylvester Mittee L RSC 2 Hanley
22.02.84 Chris Pyatt L PTS 8 Kensington
21.03.84 Dean Scarfe W PTS 6 Bloomsbury
02.05.84 Rocky Feliciello L PTS 8 Solihull
Summary: 9 contests, won 4, drew 1, lost 4

Eddie Cooper

Bradford. *Born* Nigeria 16.06.55
L. Heavyweight
Manager J. Celebanski

12.10.81 Devon Bailey L PTS 6 Copthorne
29.10.81 Mick Chmilowskyj L CO 1 Walthamstow
19.11.81 Funso Banjo L CO 3 Morecambe
22.03.82 Prince Mohammed L PTS 8 Bradford
05.04.82 Prince Mohammed L RSC 5 Glasgow
21.06.82 John Fallon W RSC 1 Hull
26.09.82 Dave Garside L PTS 6 Middlesbrough
13.10.82 Gilberto Acuna L CO 3 Walthamstow
18.11.82 Andy Straughn L RSC 2 Coventry
20.04.83 Michael Armstrong L PTS 6 South Shields
12.06.83 Steve Abadom L PTS 6 Middlesbrough
15.09.83 Bernie Kavanagh W RTD 2 Liverpool
18.11.83 Geoff Rymer L PTS 8 Sheffield
12.12.83 Sam Reeson L PTS 6 Bedworth
09.02.84 Mal Kirk L PTS 6 Manchester
04.06.84 Wes Taylor L RSC 3 Nottingham
Summary: 16 contests, won 2, lost 14

John Langol

Birmingham. *Born* Uganda 06.02.55
L. Middleweight
Manager (Self)

26.01.81 Darwin Brewster L PTS 6 Birmingham
30.03.81 Carl Bailey W PTS 8 Birmingham
27.04.83 Winston Wray W PTS 6 Rhyl
09.05.83 Gavin Stirrup W RSC 7 Manchester
18.05.83 Jimmy Price L RSC 3 Bloomsbury
03.10.83 Billy Bryce W RTD 3 Bradford
10.11.83 Horace McKenzie W RSC 3 Stafford
22.11.83 Jimmy Cable L RSC 1 Wembley
23.02.84 Dean Scarfe L CO 2 Digbeth
15.03.84 John Bibby W RSC 4 Leicester
13.05.84 Nick Wilshire L RSC 6 Wembley
Summary: 11 contests, won 6, lost 5

(Peter) Rocky Mensah

Bradford. *Born* Ghana 20.07.60
L. Welterweight
Manager J. Celebanski

26.04.82 J. J. Barrett W PTS 6 Bradford
04.05.82 Terry Smith L PTS 6 Wembley
26.05.82 Kevin Pritchard L PTS 8 Leeds
07.06.82 Kevin Pritchard L PTS 8 Manchester
28.06.82 J. J. Barrett W PTS 8 Bradford
17.09.82 Kevin Pritchard L CO 6 Liverpool
11.10.82 Jimmy Bunclark W PTS 8 Manchester
18.11.82 Vince Vahey L PTS 6 Piccadilly
01.12.82 Les Remikie L PTS 6 Stafford
17.11.83 Brett Jefford L RSC 3 Basildon
18.01.84 Mickey Lerwill W PTS 6 Stoke
13.03.84 John Murray W PTS 6 Hull
26.03.84 Steve Boyle DREW 8 Glasgow
04.04.84 Carl Merrett W PTS 8 Evesham
14.05.84 Dave Heaver W PTS 6 Nottingham
04.06.84 Alastair Laurie L PTS 8 Glasgow
Summary: 16 contests, won 7, drew 1, lost 8

Frankie Moro (Tahiru)

Liverpool. *Born* Ghana 04.02.57
Welterweight
Manager T. Miller

20.02.84 Mickey Bird W PTS 6 Bradford
27.02.84 Jim McIntosh L PTS 8 Glasgow
09.04.84 Jim Kelly W PTS 8 Glasgow
09.05.84 Chris Pyatt L CO 4 Leicester
18.06.84 Dave Dunn W RSC 6 Manchester
Summary: 5 contests, won 3, lost 2

75 Years of *Boxing News*

by Harry Mullan (Editor of *Boxing News*)

Whenever I'm tempted to write a paragraph or two in criticism of one of our referees, it's helpful to remind myself that there, but for the grace of God and the formation of the British Boxing of Control, go I.

In the days before the Board was formed in 1929, it was commonplace for the editor of *Boxing*, as it then was, or his staff to be invited by promoters to officiate at their bills.

Thus it could have been Harry Mullan rather than Harry Gibbs trying to decide what to do when there's just been a double knockdown in the last round of a championship fight, when at least one of the blows was probably a foul, and both fighters were in any case too badly cut to continue.

The system though, did have its perks as well as its nightmares. My predecessor, Gilbert Odd, one of the handful of journalists from those days who is still working, relates with relish how a promoter at Woolwich Baths once paid him a hefty £5 bonus for having the presence of mind to award a draw in a fiercely-fought local derby between the Woolwich favourite and his neighbour from Plumstead.

'If you'd given it either way there'd have been a riot', the promoter told him. 'They'd have torn the hall apart and put me out of business.'

Gilbert, then a poorly paid junior reporter, pocketed the fiver and thanked him for his generosity. He somehow forgot to explain that the reason he'd scored it a draw was that he'd been so terrified by the thought of having to give a verdict that he had completely forgotten to keep a running scorecard, and so had not the slightest idea who was ahead anyway.

The paper does not have quite that degree of power anymore: nowadays we quibble about other peoples' verdicts rather than giving them ourselves.

But the influence has grown, probably out of proportion to the paper's size and circulation. This year, we celebrate our 75th birthday, which makes *Boxing News* comfortably the oldest publication in the world devoted solely to the sport. *Ring* claims seniority, but we had been enlightening the sporting masses at a penny a copy for well over a decade before Nat Fleisher's brainchild first appeared.

Competitors have surfaced briefly, and have gone under just as quickly. After 75 years, it would be hard for any newcomer to oust BN from its position as the game's 'Bible'.

Even Hitler couldn't put us out of business. Gilbert Odd, who joined the staff in 1922, had two spells as editor, and still a regular contributor in his eighties, remembers being bombed out of his EC4 office halfway through production and finishing the week's issue in a room 'borrowed' from a Fleet Street daily.

It's had two titles – *Boxing* being relaunched as *Boxing News* in 1946 – and a succession of owners. Vivian Brodsky, whose *War Facts Press* made him an invaluable aide to Propaganda Minister Beaverbrook during the Second World War, had probably the longest spell in the publisher's chair.

After his death, and that of his wife Paula a few years later, the paper passed briefly to Rupert Murdoch's subsidiary City Magazines, before being taken over again by Williams Publishing, itself a subsidiary of Warner Brothers, the movie makers.

Since 1974 it has been owned jointly by David Kaye, once the 'Kaye' of Kaye Cards, and Richard Kravitz, a New Yorker who has long been a London resident.

For most of the British public, boxing experts are bylines in Fleet Street tabloids, and the people who swear by Colin Hart, Peter Moss, and the rest of the chaps have probably never heard of our publication.

But the trade knows us, here and abroad. I was amused last year to be allocated a ring-apron position at Caesar's Palace for the biggest fight of the year, Hagler v Duran, just a couple of weeks after a boxing promoter had denied us admittance to one of the small halls back home.

The views and ratings of *Boxing News* are read with attention by matchmakers, commissioners, journalists, and broadcasters throughout the world. Reg Gutteridge, who contributes an occasional column to our paper, likes to tell how he was introduced to an American in a New York hotel elevator, and got the reaction: 'Reg Gutteridge? Ain't you the guy who writes for *Boxing News*?' *Sic transit gloria.*

The first issue appeared on 11 September 1909, predating even the Lonsdale Belt. It was founded by a sports-minded aristocrat, Lord Camrose, and edited by a colourful Scot called John Murray, whose prodigious output filled the paper's columns almost single-handed.

Volume 1, Number 1 sold out within two hours, forcing Murray to print an apology to all the disappointed would-be readers in the next issue. The demand proved that the paper was needed, and at a penny a copy the sales were remarkable.

Murray's first editorial said:

> *Boxing* is not offered to its public with an apology. We claim it is wanted, and wanted badly. It will stand for good clean sport. Its success or failure is in the hands of those who believe in sport of that character.

Murray's words set the standards which his successors in the editorial chair – only nine in 75 years – have tried to uphold.

We aim to be impartial, although inevitably, we come into frequent conflict with boxing's establishment; with promoters, administrators and amateur officialdom. I don't believe the paper would be doing its job if we always chose the safe and uncontroversial course; the function of a critic is to criticise, not to acquiesce.

Daily papers, where boxing rates low editorial priority, have only perhaps a dozen column inches in which to preview or report the major shows, so comment has necessarily to be limited. Also, their readers are general sports fans rather than boxing addicts, and so would not be greatly interested in detailed analysis of the quality of matches and the true worth of opponents.

That's where we come in; our readers buy the paper because they WANT to know so much more than their daily paper can tell them, echoing John Murray's words again.

The reader who seeks only to know Frank Bruno's taste in music or clothes can find out from a Sunday glossy: but the real fan, who wants to know whether Bonecrusher Smith's best punch is his left hook or his right uppercut, or how many times Juan Figueroa has been stopped, or which of Eddie Neilson's eyes is the more cut-prone, will find out from *Boxing News*.

Murray's declaration that 'we will stand for good clean sport' means, at least in my interpretation, that we must never tolerate mismatches, or sloppy administration, or any relaxation of the safeguards on the boxers' health and well-being.

There have been times when that interpretation has brought us into conflict with the Board of Control as well as the promoters, and to the outsider it might seem that our relationships with the Board are frosty. Not so: boxing is a small, tightly-knit family, and as in all families a good row is necessary now and again to clear the tensions built by too-close an association.

The Board is not perfect, any more than *Boxing News* is perfect or infallible, but its honesty and efficiency far outstrip most of its fellows. My own feelings about boxing are often ambiguous, and I believe that it can only be justified when its administration is above reproach.

That precondition is generally fulfilled, in this country at least: and on those happily rare occasions when it's not, we're quick to spotlight the short-coming. That's the way a free press should operate in a healthy society, and I'd like to think that the Board recognises the unique role that *Boxing News* plays in British boxing.

We're working towards the same goal: the 'good clean sport' defined by John Murray in our very first issue, and it's as worthwhile a traget now as it was all those years ago.

British Champions, 1891 – 1928: Championship Records

Includes complete Championship records for every Champion who lost his Title or retired prior to the inception of the BBBC (1929). The section includes Champions from 1891 only, when the National Sporting Club was founded and the Marquess of Queensberry Rules were revised. Champions who remained undefeated are listed and there is a separate list of British boxers who were not national Champions but contested International Titles during the above period.

CHAMPIONSHIP CONTEST CODE
B = British Title; BE = British Empire Title; C = Commonwealth Title; EU = European Title; W = World Title

† British Championship contests carrying Lonsdale Belt status
* Contests which are not universally recognised to have constituted a Championship match.

Titleholder Birthplace	Birth Death	Date	Opponent	Result	Venue	Titles	Weight
Charlie Allum	*b* 1876	16.11.03	Charlie Knock	W CO 9	London	B	Welter
(*Notting Hill*)	*d* 1918	23.04.06	Pat O'Keefe	L CO 6	London	B†	Middle
Joe Barrett	*b* 1878	25.02.98	Joe Elms	W PTS 12	Birmingham	B*	Bantam
(Joe Burrett)	*d* 1953						
(*Canning Town*)							
Johnny Basham	*b* 1890	14.12.14	Johnny Summers	W CO 14	London	B†	Welter
(*Newport*)	*d* 1947	20.04.15	Albert Badoud	L CO 9	Liverpool	EU	Welter
		10.05.15	Tom McCormick	W RSC 13	London	B†	Welter
		01.05.16	Eddie Beattie	W RSC 19	London	B†	Welter
		02.09.19	Francois Charles	W PTS 20	London	EU*	Welter
		13.11.19	Matt Wells	W PTS 20	London	B BE	Welter
		12.04.20	Fred Kay	W PTS 20	London	BE	Welter
		09.06.20	Ted Kid Lewis	L CO 9	London	B BE EU	Welter
		19.11.20	Ted Kid Lewis	L CO 19	London	B EU	Welter
		31.05.21	Gus Platts	W PTS 20	London	B EU	Middle
		14.10.21	Ted Kid Lewis	L CO 12	London	B EU	Middle
Joe Beckett	*b* 1892	25.02.18	Dick Smith	L PTS 20	London	B†	L. Heavy
(*Southampton*)	*d* 1965	27.02.19	Bombardier Billy Wells	W CO 5	London	B BE	Heavy
		17.06.19	Frank Goddard	W CO 2	London	B	Heavy
		04.12.19	Georges Carpentier	L CO 1	London	EU	Heavy
		05.03.20	Dick Smith	W CO 5	London	B*	Heavy
		10.05.20	Bombardier Billy Wells	W CO 3	London	B*	Heavy
		17.07.20	Tommy Burns	W RTD 7	London	BE	Heavy
		12.09.21	Boy McCormick	W RSC 12	London	B*	Heavy
		10.04.22	George Cook	W DIS 6	London	BE	Heavy
		14.03.23	Dick Smith	W CO 17	London	B	Heavy
Tom Berry	*b* 1890	09.03.25	Sid Pape	W PTS 20	London	B†	L. Heavy
(*Poplar*)	*d* 1943	31.01.27	Dave Magill	W PTS 20	Manchester	BE	L. Heavy
		25.04.27	Gipsy Daniels	L PTS 20	London	B† BE	L. Heavy
Bill Beynon	*b* 1891	02.06.13	Digger Stanley	W PTS 20	London	B†	Bantam
(*Taibach*)	*d* 1932	27.10.13	Digger Stanley	L PTS 20	London	B†	Bantam

Titleholder Birthplace	Birth Death	Date	Opponent	Result	Venue	Titles	Weight
Bandsman Blake	*b* 1893	03.03.14	Bombardier				
(Jack Blake)	*d* 1961		Billy Wells	L CO 4	London	B*	Heavy
(*Great Yarmouth*)		22.05.16	Pat O'Keefe	W PTS 20	London	B†	Middle
		28.01.18	Pat O'Keefe	L CO 2	London	B†	Middle
Jack Bloomfield	*b* 1899	27.06.21	Ted Kid Lewis	L PTS 20	London	B	Middle
(Jack Blumenfeld)	*d* 1961	01.05.22	Harry Drake	W RTD 9	London	B†	L. Heavy
(*Islington*)		26.03.23	Horace Jones	W RTD 5	London	BE	L. Heavy
		17.05.23	Dave Magill	W RTD 13	London	BE	L. Heavy
		21.11.23	Frank Goddard	L DIS 2	London	B*	Heavy
Joe Bowker	*b* 1883	15.12.02	Harry Ware	W PTS 15	London	B†	Bantam
(Tommy Mahon)	*d* 1955	25.05.03	Andrew Tokell	W PTS 15	London	B†	Bantam
(*Salford*)		03.10.03	Bill King	W PTS 15	London	B†	Bantam
		30.05.03	Owen Moran	W PTS 20	London	B†	Bantam
		17.10.04	Frankie Neil	W PTS 20	London	W	Bantam
		20.03.05	Pedlar Palmer	W CO 12	London	B†	Feather
		23.10.05	Spike Robson	W PTS 20	London	B†	Feather
		28.05.06	Jim Driscoll	L PTS 15	London	B†	Feather
		01.06.07	Jim Driscoll	L CO 17	London	B†	Feather
		07.03.10	Jean Audony	W CO 8	London	EU	Bantam
		17.10.10	Digger Stanley	L CO 8	London	B† EU W*	Bantam
Hamilton	*b* 1901	08.01.23	Seaman Hall	L PTS 20	Edinburgh	B EU	Light
Johnny Brown	*d* 1983	03.07.24	Ted Kid Lewis	L PTS 20	London	B*	Welter
(John Fleming)		08.10.25	Harry Mason	WPTS 20	London	B	Welter
(*Hamilton*)		19.11.25	Harry Mason	L PTS 20	London	B	Welter
Johnny Brown	*b* 1902	26.11.23	Bugler Lake	W PTS 20	London	B† BE EU	Bantam
(Phil Hackman)	*d* 1975	23.02.25	Harry Corbett	W RTD 16	London	B† BE	Bantam
(*Stepney*)		19.10.25	Mick Hill	W CO 12	London	B† BE	Bantam
		29.08.28	Teddy Baldock	L RSC 2	London	B BE	Bantam
Dick Burge	*b* 1865	25.05.91	Jem Carney	W DIS 11	London	B	Light
(*Cheltenham*)	*d* 1918	27.06.92	Lackie				
			Thompson	W CO 2	London	B	Light
		04.05.94	Harry Nickless	W CO 28	London	B	Light
		26.11.94	Ted Pritchard	L CO 2	London	B	Middle
		26.11.95	Jem Smith	L DIS 9	London	B	Heavy
		01.06.96	George Lavigne	L CO 17	London	W	Light
		31.05.97	Tom Causer	L RTD 7	London	B	Light
		08.10.97	Tom Causer	W CO 1	London	B	Light
Tom Causer		31.05.97	Dick Burge	W RTD 7	London	B	Light
(*Bermondsey*)		08.10.97	Dick Burge	L CO 1	London	B	Light
Elky Clark	*b* 1898	31.03.24	Kid Kelly	W RSC 20	London	B†	Fly
(*Glasgow*)	*d* 1956	06.09.24	Jim Hanna	W RSC 10	Glasgow	BE	Fly
		21.11.24	Michel				
			Montreuil	L PTS 20	Glasgow	EU	Fly
		31.01.25	Michel				
			Montreuil	W PTS 20	Glasgow	EU	Fly
		30.04.25	Young Johnny				
			Brown	W RSC 20	London	EU	Fly
		19.04.26	George Kid				
			Socks	W RSC 20	London†	B BE EU	Fly
		07.10.26	Francois				
			Morracchini	W PTS 20	London	EU	Fly
		21.01.27	Fidel La Barba	L PTS 12	New York	W	Fly
George Crisp	*b* 1874	19.02.97	Jem Smith	W DIS 5	Newcastle	B	Heavy
(*Newcastle*)							
Johnny Curley	*b* 1897	30.03.25	George				
(*Lambeth*)	*d* 1982		McKenzie	W PTS 20	London	B†	Feather
		29.03.26	Harry Corbett	W PTS 20	London	B†	Feather
		01.11.26	Billy Hindley	W PTS 20	Manchester	B	Feather
		24.01.27	Johnny Cuthbert	L PTS 20	London	B†	Feather

CONTINUED OVERLEAF

Titleholder Birthplace	Birth Death	Date	Opponent	Result	Venue	Titles	Weight
Will Curley	*b* 1876	02.11.99	George Dixon	L PTS 25	New York	W*	Feather
(*Newcastle*)	*d* 1973	22.01.00	Nat Smith	W PTS 20	Newcastle	B*	Feather
		21.01.01	Jack Roberts	L CO 7	London	B	Feather
Gipsy Daniels	*b* 1902	25.04.27	Tom Berry	W PTS 20	London	B BE	L. Heavy
(Danny Thomas)	*d* 1967						
(*Newport*)							
Tony Diamond	*b* 1861	25.02.98	Dido Plumb	W PTS 12	Birmingham	B	Middle
(*Birmingham*)							
Jim Driscoll	*b* 1880	28.05.06	Joe Bowker	W PTS 15	London	B†	Feather
(*Cardiff*)	*d* 1925	01.06.07	Joe Bowker	W CO 17	London	B†	Feather
		24.02.08	Charlie Griffin	W PTS 15	London	BE	Feather
		19.02.09	Abe Attell	ND 10	New York	W*	Feather
		14.02.10	Arthur Hayes	W RSC 6	London	B†	Feather
		18.04.10	Spike Robson	W CO 15	London	B†	Feather
		30.01.11	Spike Robson	W RSC 11	London	B†	Feather
		03.06.12	Jean Poesy	W CO 12	London	EU W*	Feather
		27.01.13	Owen Moran	DREW 20	London	B† EU W*	Feather
		20.10.19	Charles Ledoux	L RTD 16	London	EU	Bantam
Llew Edwards	*b* 1894	31.05.15	Owen Moran	W DIS 10	London	B†	Feather
(*Porth*)	*d* 1965	18.12.15	Jim Hill	W RTD 13	Sydney	BE	Feather
Arthur Evernden	*b* 1886	23.01.11	Young Joseph	W DIS 3	London	B	Welter
(*Chatham*)		17.06.12	Johnny Summers	L RSC 13	London	B†	Welter
		11.10.13	Johnny Summers	L PTS 20	Sydney	BE	Welter
Joe Fox	*b* 1892	22.11.15	Jimmy Berry	W RSC 16	London	B†	Bantam
(*Leeds*)	*d* 1965	17.04.16	Tommy Harrison	W PTS 20	London	B†	Bantam
		25.06.17	Joe Symonds	W RSC 18	London	B†	Bantam
		31.10.21	Mike Honeyman	W PTS 20	London	B†	Feather
Frank Goddard	*b* 1891	25.05.19	Jack Curphey	W RTD 10	London	B†	Heavy
(*Clapham*)	*d* 1957	17.06.19	Joe Beckett	L CO 2	London	B	Heavy
		21.11.23	Jack Bloomfield	W DIS 2	London	B*	Heavy
		29.04.24	Jack Stanley	W CO 6	London	B*	Heavy
		18.03.26	Phil Scott	L CO 3	London	B	Heavy
Jack Goldswain	*b* 1878	3.04.06	Jabez White	W PTS 20	London	B†	Light
(*Bermondsey*)	*d* 1954	11.02.07	Pat Daly	W CO 5	London	B†	Light
		23.11.08	Johnny Summers	L RSC 14	London	B†	Light
		13.03.09	Curley Watson	L 6	London	B*	Welter
		22.05.09	Curley Watson	W 6	London	B*	Welter
		11.06.09	Curley Watson	L RTD 6	London	B*	Welter
		21.03.10	Young Joseph	L DIS 11	London	B†	Welter
Harry Greenfield	*b* 1873	11.01.97	Fred Johnson	W CO 13	London	B*	Feather
(*Camden Town*)	*d* 1946	03.05.97	Larry Barnes	W CO 8	Birmingham	B*	Feather
		29.05.99	Ben Jordan	L CO 9	London	B† W*	Feather
Tom Gummer	*b* 1894	29.03.20	Jim Sullivan	W RTD 14	London	B†	Middle
(*Kimberworth*)	*d* 1982	07.12.20	Ercole Balzac	L CO 9	Paris	EU	Middle
		28.03.21	Gus Platts	L RTD 6	Sheffield	B	Middle
Iron Hague	*b* 1885	19.04.09	Gunner Moir	W CO 1	London	B† EU	Heavy
(William Hague)	*d* 1951	11.02.10	P. O. Curran	W CO 15	Plymouth	B*	Heavy
(*Mexborough*)		21.02.10	Jewey Smith	W PTS 20	Sheffield	B*	Heavy
		26.05.10	Sgt Sunshine	W PTS 20	Liverpool	B*	Heavy
		15.08.10	Pte W. Smith	W PTS 20	Sheffield	B*	Heavy
		07.11.10	Cpl Brown	W CO 18	Sheffield	B*	Heavy
		05.12.10	Jewey Smith	W PTS 20	Sheffield	B*	Heavy
		02.01.11	Sgt Sunshine	W CO 9	Mexborough	B*	Heavy

Titleholder Birthplace	Birth Death	Date	Opponent	Result	Venue	Titles	Weight
		30.01.11	Bill Chase	W CO 6	London	B†	Heavy
		24.04.11	Bombardier Billy Wells	L CO 6	London	B† EU	Heavy
Seaman Hall (James Hall) (*Peebles*)	*b* 1892 *d* 1953	18.09.22	Ernie Rice	W PTS 20	Liverpool	B EU	Light
		08.01.23	Hamilton Johnny Brown	W PTS 20	Edinburgh	B EU	Light
		17.05.23	Harry Mason	L DIS 13	London	B EU	Light
Charlie Hardcastle (*Barnsley*)	*b* 1894	04.06.17	Alf Wye	W CO 1	London	B†	Feather
		05.11.17	Tancy Lee	L CO 4	London	B†	Feather
Jack Harrison (*Rushden*)	*b* 1888 *d* 1971	20.05.12	Pat McEnroy	W PTS 20	London	B†	Middle
Tommy Harrison (*Stoke*)	*b* 1892 *d* 1931	17.04.16	Joe Fox	L PTS 20	London	B†	Bantam
		24.10.21	Charles Ledoux	W PTS 20	Hanley	EU	Bantam
		24.04.22	Charles Ledoux	L PTS 20	Liverpool	EU	Bantam
		26.06.22	Jim Higgins	W CO 13	Liverpool	B BE	Bantam
		09.10.22	Charles Ledoux	L RSC 18	Hanley	EU	Bantam
		26.02.23	Bugler Lake	L PTS 20	London	B† BE	Bantam
Dennis Haugh (*Tipperary*)		09.06.13	Sid Ellis	W CO 1	London	B*	L. Heavy
		10.11.13	Dan Voyles	W RSC 8	London	B*	L. Heavy
		19.01.14	Dick Smith	W PTS 15	London	B*	L. Heavy
		09.03.14	Dick Smith	L PTS 20	London	B	L. Heavy
Jimmy Higgins (*Hamilton*)	*b* 1897 *d* 1964	23.02.20	Harold Jones	W RSC 13	London	B†	Bantam
		26.04.20	Vince Blackburn	W PTS 20	London	BE	Bantam
		31.05.20	Charles Ledoux	L CO 11	London	EU	Bantam
		29.11.20	Billy Eynon	W PTS 20	London	B†	Bantam
		31.01.21	Ernie Symonds	W PTS 20	London	B†	Bantam
		26.06.22	Tommy Harrison	L CO 13	Liverpool	B BE	Bantam
Mike Honeyman (*Woolwich*)	*b* 1896 *d* 1944	26.01.20	Billy Marchant	W PTS 20	London	B†	Feather
		31.05.20	Arthur Wyns	L RTD 10	London	EU	Feather
		25.10.20	Tancy Lee	W RTD 19	London	B†	Feather
		31.10.21	Joe Fox	L PTS 20	London	B†	Feather
Johnny Hughes		25.04.98	Jim Curran	W PTS 20	London	B*	Light
Ernie Izzard (*Herne Hill*)	*b* 1905	24.11.24	Jack Kirk	W PTS 20	London	B†	Light
		27.04.25	Teddy Baker	W PTS 20	London	B†	Light
		22.06.25	Harry Mason	L RSC 9	London	B	Light
Andrew Jeptha (*Cape Town South Africa*)	*b* 1879	11.02.07	Curley Watson	L PTS 20	London	B	Welter
		25.03.07	Curley Watson	W CO 4	London	B	Welter
		08.08.07	Joe White	L PTS 15	Cardiff	B	Welter
		18.11.07	Curley Watson	L PTS 15	London	B†	Welter
Fred Johnson (*Hackney*)		27.06.92	George Dixon	L CO 14	New York	W*	Feather
		29.04.95	Charlie Beadling	W CO 4	Newcastle	B	Feather
		11.01.97	Harry Greenfield	L CO 13	London	B*	Feather
		22.02.97	Ben Jordan	L RSC 13	London	B†	Feather
Percy Jones (*Porthcawl*)	*b* 1892 *d* 1922	26.01.14	Bill Ladbury	W PTS 20	London	B† EU W*	Fly
		26.03.14	Eugene Criqui	W PTS 20	Liverpool	EU W*	Fly
		15.05.14	Joe Symonds	L RTD 18	Plymouth	B EU W*	Fly
		19.10.14	Tancy Lee	L RTD 14	London	B† EU	Fly
Ben Jordan (*Bermondsey*)	*b* 1873 *d* 1945	22.02.97	Fred Johnson	W RSC 13	London	B†	Feather
		29.11.97	Tommy White	W CO 19	London	B†	Feather
		04.04.98	Eddie Curry	W RTD 17	London	B†	Feather
		01.07.98	George Dixon	L PTS 25	New York	W	Feather
		29.05.99	Harry Greenfield	W CO 9	London	B† W*	Feather

CONTINUED OVERLEAF

Titleholder Birthplace	Birth Death	Date	Opponent	Result	Venue	Titles	Weight
		10.10.99	Eddie Santry	L CO 15	New York	W*	Feather
		20.10.02	Jack Roberts	W CO 5	London	B†	Feather
		12.12.04	Pedlar Palmer	W PTS 15	London	B†	Feather
Young Joseph	*b* 1885	19.10.08	Cpl Baker	W PTS 15	London	B†	Welter
(Aschel Joseph)	*d* 1952	21.03.10	Jack Goldswain	W DIS 11	London	B†	Welter
(*Aldgate*)		27.06.10	Harry Lewis	L RTD 7	London	W*	Welter
		19.12.10	Battling Lecroix	W PTS 20	Paris	EU	Welter
		23.01.11	Arthur Evernden	L DIS 3	London	B	Welter
		05.05.11	Robert Eustache	W PTS 15	Paris	EU	Welter
		23.10.11	Georges Carpentier	L RTD 10	London	EU	Welter
		11.04.12	Johnny Summers	L PTS 20	Liverpool	B	Welter
Charlie Knock	*b* 1880	16.11.03	Charlie Allum	L CO 9	London	B	Welter
(*Stratford*)		21.05.06	Curley Watson	W RSC 17	London	B	Welter
		17.12.06	Curley Watson	L PTS 10	London	B	Welter
		18.04.08	Curley Watson	L PTS 10	London	B	Welter
Bill Ladbury	*b* 1891	02.06.13	Sid Smith	W RSC 11	London	B EU W*	Fly
(*New Cross*)	*d* 1916	26.01.14	Percy Jones	L PTS 20	London	B EU W*	Fly
Bugler Lake	*b* 1902	26.02.23	Tommy Harrison	W PTS 20	London	B BE	Bantam
(Harry Lake)	*d* 1970						
(*Devonport*)		30.07.23	Charles Ledoux	W PTS 20	London	EU	Bantam
		26.11.23	Johnny Brown	L PTS 20	London	B BE EU	Bantam
Tancy Lee	*b* 1882	19.10.14	Percy Jones	W RTD 14	London	B† EU	Fly
(James Lee)	*d* 1941	25.01.15	Jimmy Wilde	W RSC 17	London	B† EU	Fly
(*Paisley*)		18.10.15	Joe Symonds	L RSC 16	London	B† W*	Fly
		26.06.16	Jimmy Wilde	L RSC 11	London	B† EU W	Fly
		05.11.17	Charlie Hardcastle	W CO 4	London	B†	Feather
		21.10.18	Joe Conn	W CO 7	London	B†	Feather
		24.02.19	Danny Morgan	W PTS 20	London	B†	Feather
		24.12.19	Louis de Ponthieu	L CO 17	Paris	EU	Feather
		25.10.20	Mike Honeyman	L RTD 19	London	B†	Feather
Ted Kid Lewis	*b* 1894	06.10.13	Alec Lambert	W RSC 17	London	B† EU	Feather
(Gershon	*d* 1970	02.02.14	Paul Til	W DIS 12	London	EU	Feather
Mendelhoff)		31.08.15	Jack Britton	W PTS 12	Boston	W	Welter
(*Aldgate*)		27.09.15	Jack Britton	W PTS 12	Boston	W*	Welter
		26.10.15	Joe Mandot	W PTS 12	Boston	W*	Welter
		02.11.15	Milburn Saylor	W PTS 12	Boston	W*	Welter
		23.11.15	Jimmy Duffy	W CO 1	Boston	W*	Welter
		28.12.15	Willie Ritchie	ND 10	New York	W	Welter
		17.01.16	Kid Graves	ND 10	Milwaukee	W*	Welter
		20.01.16	Jack Britton	ND 10	New York	W*	Welter
		15.02.16	Jack Britton	ND 10	New York	W*	Welter
		01.03.16	Harry Stone	W PTS 20	New Orleans	W*	Welter
		24.04.16	Jack Britton	L PTS 20	New Orleans	W	Welter
		17.10.16	Jack Britton	L PTS 12	Boston	W	Welter
		14.11.16	Jack Britton	DREW 12	Boston	W	Welter
		26.03.17	Jack Britton	ND 10	Cincinatti	W*	Welter
		19.05.17	Jack Britton	ND 10	Toronto	W*	Welter
		06.06.17	Jack Britton	ND 10	St. Louis	W*	Welter
		14.06.17	Jack Britton	ND 10	New York	W*	Welter
		25.06.17	Jack Britton	W PTS 20	Dayton	W	Welter
		04.07.17	Johnny Griffiths	ND 15	Akron	W*	Welter
		31.08.17	Albert Badoud	W CO 1	New York	EU*	Welter

Titleholder Birthplace	Birth Death	Date	Opponent	Result	Venue	Titles	Weight
		24.10.17	Battling Ortega	DREW 4	Emeryville	W*	Welter
		13.11.17	Johnny McCarthy	W RSC 4	San Francisco	W*	Welter
		17.05.18	Johnny Tillman	W PTS 20	Denver	W	Welter
		04.07.18	Johnny Griffiths	ND 20	Akron	W*	Welter
		23.09.18	Benny Leonard	ND 8	Newark	W	Welter
		10.03.19	Johnny Griffiths	ND 8	Memphis	W*	Welter
		17.03.19	Jack Britton	L CO 9	Canton	W	Welter
		28.07.19	Jack Britton	ND 8	New Jersey	W*	Welter
		01.09.19	Mike O'Dowd	ND 10	New York	W*	Middle
		11.03.20	Johnny Bee	W CO 4	London	B	Middle
		09.06.20	Johnny Basham	W CO 9	London	B BE EU	Welter
		19.11.20	Johnny Basham	W CO 19	London	B EU	Welter
		07.02.21	Jack Britton	L PTS 15	New York	W	Welter
		27.06.21	Jack Bloomfield	W PTS 20	London	B	Middle
		14.10.21	Johnny Basham	W CO 12	London	B EU	Middle
		11.05.22	Georges Carpentier	L CO 1	London	EU W	Heavy L. Heavy
		19.06.22	Frankie Burns	W CO 11	London	BE	Middle
		20.11.22	Roland Todd	W PTS 20	London	B†	Middle
		15.02.23	Roland Todd	L PTS 20	London	B BE EU	Middle
		03.07.24	Hamilton Johnny Brown	W PTS 20	London	B*	Welter
		26.11.24	Tommy Milligan	L PTS 20	Edinburgh	B BE	Welter
Boy McCormick (Noel McCormick) (*India*)	*b* 1899 *d* 1939	28.04.19	Harold Rolph	W DIS 11	London	B†	L. Heavy
		12.09.21	Joe Beckett	L RSC 12	London	B*	Heavy
		30.04.26	Phil Scott	L RTD 10	Manchester	B	Heavy
Tom McCormick (*Dundalk*)	*b* 1890 *d* 1916	10.01.14	Johnny Summers	W PTS 20	Sydney	B BE	Welter
		24.01.14	Waldemar Holberg	W DIS 6	Melbourne	W	Welter
		14.02.14	Johnny Summers	W CO 1	Sydney	B BE	Welter
		21.03.14	Matt Wells	L PTS 20	Sydney	B BE W	Welter
		10.05.15	Johnny Basham	L RSC 13	London	B†	Welter
George McKenzie (*Leith*)	*b* 1900 *d* 1941	02.06.24	Harry Leach	W PTS 20	London	B†	Feather
		15.12.24	Harry Leach	W PTS 20	London	B†	Feather
		30.03.25	Johnny Curley	L PTS 20	London	B†	Feather
Bob Marriott (*Bermondsey*)		10.04.19	Raymond Vittet	W DIS 3	London	EU	Light
		23.06.19	Johnny Summers	W DIS 10	London	B†	Light
		17.05.20	Georges Papin	L PTS 20	Paris	EU	Light
Tommy Milligan (Tommy Mulligan) (*Wishaw*)	*b* 1904 *d* 1970	26.11.24	Ted Kid Lewis	W PTS 20	Edinburgh	B BE	Welter
		08.06.25	Bruno Frattini	W PTS 20	London	EU	Middle
		12.07.26	George West	W RSC 14	London	B BE	Middle
		07.10.26	Ted Moore	W RSC 14	London	B BE	Middle
		27.01.27	Ted Moore	W RSC 14	London	B BE	Middle
		30.06.27	Mickey Walker	L CO 10	London	W	Middle
		14.03.28	Alex Ireland	L DIS 9	Edinburgh	B BE	Middle
		06.08.28	Frank Moody	L CO 1	Glasgow	B	Middle
Gunner Moir (James Moir) (*Lambeth*)	*b* 1869 *d* 1939	29.10.06	Jack Palmer	W DIS 9	London	B† EU	Heavy
		25.02.07	Tiger Smith	W CO 1	London	B†	Heavy
		02.12.07	Tommy Burns	L CO 10	London	W	Heavy
		19.04.09	Iron Hague	L CO 1	London	B† EU	Heavy
		10.09.13	Bombardier Billy Wells	L CO 5	London	B	Heavy

Titleholder Birthplace	Birth Death	Date	Opponent	Result	Venue	Titles	Weight
Tommy Noble	*b* 1897	25.11.18	Joe Symonds	W PTS 20	London	B†	Bantam
(*Bermondsey*)	*d* 1966	30.06.19	Walter Ross	L RSC 10	London	B†	Bantam
Pat O'Keefe	*b* 1883	02.01.03	Jack Kingsland	W PTS 3	London	B	Welter
(*Bromley-by Bow*)	*d* 1960	19.03.06	Mike Crawley	W PTS 15	London	B†	Middle
		23.04.06	Charlie Allum	W CO 6	London	B†	Middle
		28.05.06	Tom Thomas	L PTS 15	London	B†	Middle
		04.08.13	Bombardier Billy Wells	L CO 15	London	B*	Heavy
		19.01.14	Georges Carpentier	L CO 5	Nice	EU	Heavy
		23.02.14	Harry Reeve	W PTS 20	London	B†	Middle
		27.04.14	Nicol Simpson	W PTS 20	London	B	Middle
		25.05.14	Jim Sullivan	W PTS 20	London	B†	Middle
		21.02.16	Jim Sullivan	W PTS 20	London	B*	Middle
		22.05.16	Bandsman Blake	L PTS 20	London	B†	Middle
		28.01.18	Bandsman Blake	W CO 2	London	B†	Middle
Jack Palmer	*b* 1878	23.09.01	Jack Scales	L CO 4	Newcastle	B*	Heavy
(Jack Liddell)	*d* 1928	14.04.02	Joe White	W CO 11	Newcastle	B*	Middle
(*Newcastle*)		23.06.02	Dave Peters	W CO 7	Merthyr	B*	Middle
		13.09.02	Slouch Dixon	W CO 5	Newcastle	B*	Middle
		02.05.03	Ben Taylor	W CO 12	Newcastle	B	Heavy
		18.12.05	Geoff Thorne	W CO 4	London	B†	Heavy
		29.10.06	Gunner Moir	L DIS 9	London	B† EU	Heavy
		10.02.08	Tommy Burns	L CO 4	London	W	Heavy
Pedlar Palmer	*b* 1876	25.11.95	Billy Plimmer	W DIS 14	London	B† W*	Bantam
(Tom Palmer)	*d* 1949	12.10.96	Johnny Murphy	W PTS 20	London	W*	Bantam
(*Canning Town*)		25.01.97	Ernie Stanton	W RSC 14	London	W*	Bantam
		18.10.97	Dave Sullivan	W PTS 20	London	W*	Bantam
		12.12.98	Billy Plimmer	W RSC 20	London	B† W	Bantam
		17.09.99	Billy Rochford	W RSC 3	London	W*	Bantam
		22.09.99	Terry McGovern	L CO 1	New York	W	Bantam
		28.05.00	Harry Ware	W PTS 15	London	B†	Bantam
		12.11.00	Harry Ware	L PTS 20	London	B†	Bantam
		18.03.01	Harry Harris	L PTS 20	London	W	Bantam
		12.12.04	Ben Jordan	L PTS 15	London	B†	Feather
		20.03.05	Joe Bowker	L CO 12	London	B†	Feather
Gus Platts	*b* 1891	21.02.21	Ercole Balzac	W RTD 7	Sheffield	EU	Middle
(*Sheffield*)	*d* 1943	28.03.21	Tom Gummer	W RTD 6	Sheffield	B	Middle
		31.05.21	Johnny Basham	L PTS 20	London	B EU	Middle
Billy Plimmer	*b* 1869	02.04.91	Jem Stevens	W RTD 15	London	B†	Bantam
(*Aston*)	*d* 1929	09.05.92	Tommy Kelly	W PTS 10	New York	W*	Bantam
		22.08.93	George Dixon	W CO 4	New York	W*	Bantam
		28.05.95	George Corfield	W CO 7	London	B† W*	Bantam
		25.11.95	Pedlar Palmer	L DIS 14	London	B† W*	Bantam
		12.12.98	Pedlar Palmer	L RSC 17	London	B† W*	Bantam
Dido Plumb	*b* 1872	25.02.98	Tony Diamond	L PTS 12	Birmingham	B	Middle
	d 1920	14.04.02	Jem Ryan	W CO 2	London	B*	Middle
Ted Pritchard		12.03.91	Jack Burke	W CO 3	London	B	Middle
(*Lambeth*)		27.07.91	Jem Smith	W CO 3	London	B	Heavy
		26.11.94	Dick Burge	W CO 2	London	B	Middle
		10.05.95	Jem Smith	L CO 2	London	B	Heavy
Harry Reeve	*b* 1893	23.02.14	Pat O'Keefe	L PTS 20	London	B†	Middle
(*Stepney*)	*d* 1958	10.10.16	Dick Smith	W PTS 20	London	B†	L. Heavy
Ernie Rice	*b* 1896	11.04.21	Ben Callicott	W CO 7	London	B†	Light
(*Hull*)	*d* 1979	09.05.21	Georges Papin	W CO 10	London	EU	Light
		18.09.22	Seaman Hall	L PTS 20	Liverpool	B EU	Light

Titleholder Birthplace	Birth Death	Date	Opponent	Result	Venue	Titles	Weight
		21.11.23	Harry Mason	L PTS 20	London	B EU	Light
		11.02.26	Harry Mason	L DIS 5	London	B*	Light
		17.09.28	Sam Steward	L CO 12	London	B	Light
Jack Roberts	*b* 1873	21.01.01	Will Curley	WCO 7	London	B†	Feather
(*Drury Lane*)		20.10.02	Ben Jordan	L CO 5	London	B†	Feather
Spike Robson	*b* 1877	23.10.05	Joe Bowker	L PTS 20	London	B†	Feather
(Frank Robson) (*South Shields*)	*d* 1957	29.01.06	Johnny Summers	L PTS 20	London	B†	Feather
		17.12.06	Johnny Summers	W DIS 4	London	B†	Feather
		01.04.08	Joe Gans	L CO 3	Philadelphia	W*	Light
		18.04.10	Jim Driscoll	L CO 15	London	B†	Feather
		30.01.11	Jim Driscoll	L RSC 11	London	B†	Feather
Walter Ross	*b* 1898	30.06.19	Tommy Noble	W RSC 10	London	B†	Bantam
(*Manchester*)							
Jack Scales	*b* 1874	07.01.01	Cloggy Saunders	W CO 2	London	B*	Heavy
		23.09.01	Jack Palmer	W CO 4	Newcastle	B*	Heavy
		25.06.02	Ben Taylor	W PTS 10	London	B*	Heavy
		13.10.02	Slouch Dixon	W CO 7	London	B*	Heavy
		08.11.02	Charlie Wilson	L CO 3	London	B*	Heavy
Dick Smith	*b* 1886	19.01.14	Dennis Haugh	L PTS 15	London	B*	L. Heavy
(*Woolwich*)	*d* 1950	09.03.14	Dennis Haugh	W PTS 20	London	B†	L. Heavy
		31.05.15	Bombardier Billy Wells	L CO 9	London	B*	Heavy
		21.02.16	Bombardier Billy Wells	L CO 3	London	B*	Heavy
		05.06.16	Harry Curzon	W PTS 20	London	B†	L. Heavy
		26.08.16	Bombardier Billy Wells	L RTD 9	Newcastle	B*	Heavy
		10.10.16	Harry Reeve	L PTS 20	London	B†	L. Heavy
		25.02.18	Joe Beckett	W PTS 20	London	B†	L. Heavy
		19.07.19	Georges Carpentier	L CO 8	Paris	EU	Heavy
		05.03.20	Joe Beckett	L CO 5	London	B*	Heavy
		14.03.23	Joe Beckett	L CO 17	London	B	Heavy
Jem Smith	*b* 1863	27.07.91	Ted Pritchard	L CO 3	London	B	Heavy
(*Cripplegate*)	*d* 1931	10.05.95	Ted Pritchard	W CO 2	London	B	Heavy
		26.11.95	Dick Burge	W DIS 9	London	B	Heavy
		19.02.97	George Crisp	L DIS 5	Newcastle	B	Heavy
Sid Smith	*b* 1889	25.09.11	Stoker Hoskyne	W PTS 20	London	B*	Fly
(*Bermondsey*)	*d* 1948	19.10.11	Louis Ruddick	W PTS 20	Liverpool	B	Fly
		04.12.11	Joe Wilson	W PTS 20	London	B†	Fly
		19.09.12	Curley Walker	W PTS 20	London	B*	Fly
		11.04.13	Eugene Criqui	W PTS 20	Paris	EU W*	Fly
		02.06.13	Bill Ladbury	L RSC 11	London	B EU W*	Fly
Digger Stanley	*b* 1883	20.10.05	Jimmy Walsh	L PTS 15	Chelsea,	W	Bantam
(George Stanley)	*d* 1919	13.12.06	Ike Bradley	W PTS 20	Liverpool	W*	Bantam
(*Norwich*)		24.05.09	Jimmy Walsh	DREW 15	London	W*	Bantam
		17.10.10	Joe Bowker	W CO 8	London†	B EU W*	Bantam
		05.12.10	Johnny Condon	W PTS 20	London	B* W*	Bantam
		14.09.11	Ike Bradley	W PTS 20	Liverpool	B* W*	Bantam
		22.04.12	Charles Ledoux	W PTS 20	London	EU W*	Bantam
		23.06.12	Charles Ledoux	L CO 7	Dieppe	EU W*	Bantam
		21.10.12	Alex Lafferty	W PTS 20	London	B†	Bantam
		02.06.13	Bill Beynon	L PTS 20	London	B†	Bantam
		27.10.13	Bill Beynon	W PTS 20	London	B†	Bantam
		20.04.14	Curley Walker	L DIS 13	London	B†	Bantam

Titleholder Birthplace	Birth Death	Date	Opponent	Result	Venue	Titles	Weight
Jim Sullivan	*b* 1886	14.11.10	Tom Thomas	W PTS 20	London	B†	Middle
(*Bermondsey*)	*d* 1949	08.06.11	Billy Papke	L RTD 9	London	W*	Middle
		29.02.12	Georges Carpentier	L CO 2	Monte Carlo	EU	Middle
		25.05.14	Pat O'Keefe	L PTS 20	London	B†	Middle
		21.02.16	Pat O'Keefe	L PTS 20	London	B*	Middle
		29.03.20	Tom Gummer	L RTD 14	London	B†	Middle
Johnny Summers	*b* 1882	29.01.06	Spike Robson	W PTS 20	London	B†	Feather
(Johnny Somers)	*d* 1946	19.03.06	Arthur Hayes	W PTS 20	London	B†	Feather
(*Custom House*)		01.10.06	Boss Edwards	W PTS 20	London	B†	Feather
		17.12.06	Spike Robson	L DIS 4	London	B†	Feather
		23.11.08	Jack Goldswain	W RSC 14	London	B†	Light
		08.11.09	Freddie Welsh	L PTS 20	London	B†	Light
		25.01.11	Harry Lewis	L CO 4	London	W*	Welter
		11.04.12	Young Joseph	W PTS 20	Liverpool	B	Welter
		17.06.12	Arthur Evernden	W RSC 13	London	B†	Welter
		09.12.12	Sid Burns	W PTS 20	London	B†	Welter
		11.06.13	Sid Burns	W PTS 20	Sydney	BE	Welter
		11.10.13	Arthur Evernden	W PTS 20	Sydney	BE	Welter
		10.01.14	Tom McCormick	L PTS 20	Sydney	B BE	Welter
		14.02.14	Tom McCormick	L CO 1	Sydney	B BE	Welter
		14.12.14	Johnny Basham	L CO 14	London	B†	Welter
		23.06.19	Bob Marriott	L DIS 10	London	B†	Light
Joe Symonds	*b* 1894	15.05.14	Percy Jones	W RTD 18	Plymouth	B EU W*	Fly
(Hubert Toms)	*d* 1953	18.10.15	Tancy Lee	W RSC 16	London	B† W*	Fly
(*Plymouth*)		14.02.16	Jimmy Wilde	L RSC 12	London	B† W	Fly
		25.06.17	Joe Fox	L RSC 18	London	B†	Bantam
		25.11.18	Tommy Noble	L PTS 20	London	B†	Bantam
Tom Thomas	*b* 1880	28.05.06	Pat O'Keefe	W PTS 15	London	B†	Middle
(*Penycraig*)	*d* 1911	30.04.08	Mike Crawley	W CO 5	London	B	Middle
		01.06.08	Tiger Smith	W CO 4	London	B†	Middle
		17.11.08	Jack Costello	W CO 6	Swansea	B	Middle
		05.10.09	Jack Kingsland	W RTD 11	Pontypridd	B	Middle
		20.12.09	Charlie Wilson	W CO 2	London	B†	Middle
		14.11.10	Jim Sullivan	L PTS 20	London	B†	Middle
Roland Todd	*b* 1900	20.11.22	Ted Kid Lewis	L PTS 20	London	B	Middle
(*Kensington*)	*d* 1969	15.02.23	Ted Kid Lewis	W PTS 20	London	B BE EU	Middle
		30.11.24	Bruno Frattini	L PTS 20	Milan	EU	Middle
		16.02.27	Frank Moody	L PTS 15	London	B* BE*	Middle
Andrew Tokell	*b* 1878	13.02.02	Harry Ware	W PTS 20	London	B	Bantam
(*Gateshead*)		12.05.02	Jim Williams	W PTS 20	London	B†	Bantam
		08.09.02	Harry Ware	L DIS 8	London	B	Bantam
		27.02.03	Harry Forbes	L PTS 10	Detroit	W	Bantam
		25.05.03	Joe Bowker	L PTS 15	London	B†	Bantam
Curley Walker	*b* 1894	19.09.12	Sid Smith	L PTS 20	London	B*	Fly
(Con Walker)	*d* 1973	20.04.14	Digger Stanley	W DIS 13	London	B†	Bantam
(*Lambeth*)							
Harry Ware	*b* 1875	28.05.00	Pedlar Palmer	L PTS 15	London	B†	Bantam
(*Mile End*)		12.11.00	Pedlar Palmer	W PTS 20	London	B†	Bantam
		13.02.02	Andrew Tokell	L PTS 20	London	B	Bantam
		08.09.02	Andrew Tokell	W DIS 8	London	B	Bantam
		15.12.02	Joe Bowker	L PTS 15	London	B†	Bantam
Curley Watson	*b* 1883	21.05.06	Charlie Knock	L RSC 17	London	B	Welter
(Robert Watson)	*d* 1909	17.12.06	Charlie Knock	W PTS 10	London	B	Welter
(*Chatham*)		11.02.07	Andrew Jeptha	W PTS 20	London	B	Welter

Titleholder Birthplace	Birth Death	Date	Opponent	Result	Venue	Titles	Weight
		25.03.07	Andrew Jeptha	L CO 4	London	B	Welter
		18.11.07	Andrew Jeptha	W PTS 15	London	B†	Welter
		18.04.08	Charlie Knock	W PTS 10	London	B	Welter
		21.05.08	Joe White	L PTS 20	Liverpool	B	Welter
		13.03.09	Jack Goldswain	W 6	London	B*	Welter
		22.05.09	Jack Goldswain	L 6	London	B*	Welter
		11.06.09	Jack Goldswain	W RTD 6	London	B*	Welter
Bombardier	*b* 1887	24.04.11	Iron Hague	W CO 6	London	B† EU	Heavy
Billy Wells	*d* 1967	18.12.11	Fred Storbeck	W CO 11	London	BE	Heavy
(William Wells)		06.12.12	George Rodel	W CO 2	London	BE	Heavy
(*Mile End*)		01.06.13	Georges Carpentier	L CO 4	Ghent	EU	Heavy
		30.06.13	Packey Mahoney	W CO 13	London	B†	Heavy
		04.08.13	Pat O'Keefe	W CO 15	London	B*	Heavy
		10.09.13	Gunner Moir	W CO 5	London	B*	Heavy
		08.12.13	Georges Carpentier	L CO 1	London	EU	Heavy
		14.01.14	Gunner Rawles	W RTD 10	Belfast	B*	Heavy
		03.03.14	Bandsman Blake	W CO 4	London	B*	Heavy
		30.04.14	Bandsman Rice	W PTS 20	Liverpool	B*	Heavy
		30.06.14	Colin Bell	W CO 2	London	BE	Heavy
		24.02.15	Bandsman Rice	W CO 6	Belfast	B*	Heavy
		31.05.15	Dick Smith	W CO 9	London	B*	Heavy
		27.12.15	Bandsman Rice	W CO 1	Liverpool	B*	Heavy
		21.02.16	Dick Smith	W CO 3	London	B*	Heavy
		31.03.16	P.O. Curran	W CO 5	Plymouth	B*	Heavy
		26.08.16	Dick Smith	W RTD 9	Newcastle	B*	Heavy
		18.12.16	Dan Voyles	W RSC 2	London	B†	Heavy
		27.02.19	Joe Beckett	L CO 5	London	B BE	Heavy
		10.05.20	Joe Beckett	L CO 3	London	B*	Heavy
Matt Wells	*b* 1886	27.02.11	Freddie Welsh	W PTS 20	London	B† EU	Light
(*Walworth*)	*d* 1953	11.11.12	Freddie Welsh	L PTS 20	London	B† EU	Light
		28.02.14	Ray Bronson	W RSC 7	Sydney	W*	Welter
		21.03.14	Tom McCormick	W PTS 20	Sydney	B* BE W	Welter
		01.06.15	Mike Glover	L PTS 12	Boston	W	Welter
		13.11.19	Johnny Basham	L PTS 20	London	B BE	Welter
Freddie Welsh	*b* 1886	23.08.09	Henri Piet	W RTD 12	Mountain Ash	EU	Light
(Freddie Thomas)	*d* 1927						
(*Pontypridd*)		08.11.09	Johnny Summers	W PTS 20	London	B†	Light
		27.02.11	Matt Wells	L PTS 20	London	B† EU	Light
		11.11.12	Matt Wells	W PTS 20	London	B† EU	Light
		16.12.12	Hughie Mehegan	W PTS 20	London	BE	Light
		10.02.13	Paul Brevieres	W RTD 3	Cardiff	EU	Light
		03.03.13	Raymond Vittet	W RSC 10	Sheffield	EU	Light
		07.07.14	Willie Ritchie	W PTS 20	London	W	Light
		31.03.16	Benny Leonard	ND 10	New York	W*	Light
		04.07.16	Ad Wolgast	W DIS 11	Colorado	W*	Light
		28.07.16	Benny Leonard	ND 10	New York	W*	Light
		04.09.16	Charlie White	W PTS 20	Colorado	W	Light
		28.05.17	Benny Leonard	L CO 9	New York	W	Light
Jabez White	*b* 1876	20.11.99	Harry Greenfield	W CO 8	London	B†	Light
(*Birmingham*)	*d* 1966						
		23.12.01	Jim Curran	DREW 20	Birmingham	B	Light

CONTINUED OVERLEAF

Titleholder Birthplace	Birth Death	Date	Opponent	Result	Venue	Titles	Weight
		21.04.02	Bill Chester	W CO 6	London	B†	Light
		05.05.05	Jimmy Britt	L RSC 20	San Francisco	W*	Light
		23.04.06	Jack Goldswain	L PTS 20	London	B†	Light
Joe White		14.04.02	Jack Palmer	L CO 11	Newcastle	B*	Middle
(*Cardiff*)		08.08.07	Andrew Jeptha	W PTS 15	Cardiff	B	Welter
		21.05.08	Curley Watson	W PTS 20	Liverpool	B	Welter
Jimmy Wilde	*b* 1892	30.03.14	Eugene Husson	W CO 6	London	EU*	Fly
(*Tylorstown*)	*d* 1969	16.04.14	Albert Bouzonnie	W CO 6	Liverpool	EU*	Fly
		11.05.14	Georges Gloria	W CO 9	London	EU*	Fly
		25.01.15	Tancy Lee	L RSC 17	London	B† EU	Fly
		14.02.16	Joe Symonds	W RSC 12	London	B† W	Fly
		24.04.16	Johnny Rosner	W RTD 11	Liverpool	W	Fly
		26.06.16	Tancy Lee	W RSC 11	London	B† EU W	Fly
		31.07.16	Johnny Hughes	W CO 10	London	B EU W	Fly
		18.12.16	Young Zulu Kid	W CO 11	London	W	Fly
		11.03.17	George Clark	W RSC 4	London	B† EU W	Fly
		29.04.17	Dick Heasman	W RSC 2	London	B†	Fly
		18.06.23	Pancho Villa	L CO 7	New York	W	Fly

Undefeated Champions

Charlie Allum, British Welterweight Champion, 1903 – 1905; **Joe Beckett**, British Heavyweight Champion, 1919 – 1923 and British Empire Heavyweight Champion, 1919 – 1923; **Jack Bloomfield**, British L. Heavyweight Champion, 1922 – 1924 and British Empire L. Heavyweight Champion, 1923 – 1924; **Joe Bowker**, British Featherweight Champion, 1905; **Johnny Brown**, European Bantamweight Champion, 1923 – 1924; **Dick Burge**, British Lightweight Champion, 1897 – 1898; **Elky Clark**, British, British Empire and European Flyweight Champion, 1924 – 1927; **George Crisp**, British Heavyweight Champion, 1897 – 1898; **Gipsy Daniels**, British and British Empire L. Heavyweight Champion, 1927; **Tony Diamond**, British Middleweight Champion, 1898 – 1899; **Jim Driscoll**, British Featherweight Champion, 1906 and 1913. British Empire Featherweight Champion, 1908 – 1913 and European Featherweight Champion, 1913; **Llew Edwards**, British and British Empire Featherweight Champion, 1915 – 1917; **Joe Fox**, British Bantamweight Champion, 1915 – 1918. British Featherweight Champion, 1921 – 1923; **Jack Harrison**, British Middleweight Champion, 1912 – 1913; **Ben Jordan**, British Featherweight Champion, 1897 – 1905; **Tancy Lee**, British Featherweight Champion, 1917 – 1919; **Ted Kid Lewis,** British Featherweight Champion, 1913 – 1914, European Featherweight Champion, 1914 and European Welterweight Champion, 1920; **Boy McCormick**, British L. Heavyweight Champion, 1919 – 1920; **Bob Marriott**, British Lightweight Champion, 1919 – 1920; **Tommy Milligan**, British and British Empire Welterweight Champion, 1924 – 1925 and European Middleweight Champion, 1925; **Pat O'Keefe**, British Welterweight Champion, 1903. British Middleweight Champion, 1918; **Ted Pritchard**, British Middleweight Champion, 1891 – 1894; **Harry Reeve**, British L. Heavyweight Champion, 1916 – 1917; **Spike Robson**, British Featherweight Champion, 1906 – 1907; **Walter Ross**, British Bantamweight Champion, 1919; **Dick Smith**, British L. Heavyweight Champion, 1918 – 1919; **Jim Sullivan**, British Middleweight Champion, 1910 – 1912; **Roland Todd**, British and British Empire Middleweight Champion, 1923 – 1926; **Freddie Welsh**, British, British Empire and European Lightweight Champion, 1912 – 1914; **Joe White**, British Welterweight Champion, 1907 – 1908; **Jimmy Wilde**, British and European Flyweight Champion, 1916 – 1923.

British Boxers (not National Champions) Versus Foreign Opposition in Championship Contests (1891 – 1928)

Boxer	Date	Opponent	Result	Venue	Titles	Weight
Frankie Ash	30.05.24	Pancho Villa	L PTS 15	New York	W	Fly
Peter Brown	04.05.10	Harry Lewis	L CO 3	Paris	W*	Welter
Ben Callicott	05.12.21	Arthur Wyns	L CO 17	London	EU	Feather
Joe Conn	26.07.20	Arthur Wyns	L RTD 14	London	EU	Feather
Walter Croot	06.12.97	Jimmy Barry	L CO 20	London	W	Bantam
P. O. Curran	18.01.11	Bill Lang	W DIS 1	London	BE	Heavy
Fred Davies	12.09.22	Piet Hobin	L PTS 15	Brussels	EU	Welter
Fred Dyer	09.10.15	Les D'Arcy	L CO 6	Sydney	W*	Middle
Danny Frush	17.08.21	Johnny Kilbane	L CO 7	Cleveland	W	Feather
	15.08.22	Johnny Dundee	L CO 9	New York	W*	Feather
	24.06.24	Fred Bretonnel	L RTD 8	Paris	EU	Light
Freddie Jacks	26.05.21	Johnny Kilbane	ND 10	Cleveland	W	Feather
	25.06.23	Jack Bernstein	L CO 5	Philadelphia	W*	J. Light
Ernie Jarvis	19.12.27	Frenchie Belanger	L PTS 12	Toronto	W*	Fly
Jim Kendrick	19.02.10	Johnny Coulon	L PTS 10	New Orleans	W	Bantam
	06.03.10	Johnny Coulon	L CO 19	New Orleans	W	Bantam
Billy Mack	23.04.23	Piet Hobin	W DIS 11	Liverpool	EU*	Welter
	03.12.23	Piet Hobin	L PTS 15	Antwerp	EU*	Welter
Billy Matthews	12.06.22	Arthur Wyns	W PTS 20	Liverpool	EU*	Feather
	02.12.22	Eugene Criqui	L RTD 17	Paris	EU*	Feather
Charlie Mitchell	25.01.94	James J. Corbett	L CO 3	Jacksonville	W	Heavy
Ted Moore	26.06.24	Harry Greb	L PTS 15	New York	W	Middle
Owen Moran	01.01.08	Abe Attell	DREW 20	San Francisco	W	Feather
	07.09.08	Abe Attell	DREW 23	San Francisco	W	Feather
	04.07.11	Ad Wolgast	L CO 13	San Francisco	W	Light
Billy Porcher	06.03.23	Piet Hobin	L PTS 15	Paris	EU	Welter
Bandsman Rice	12.02.13	Georges Carpentier	L CO 2	Paris	EU	L. Heavy
Jewey Smith	18.08.08	Tommy Burns	L CO 5	Paris	W	Heavy

British Champions, 1929 – 1982: Career Records

Includes the records of all British Champions or British boxers who have won National or International Titles since the formation of the BBBC. It does not include Champions still active (for their records *see* Current British Champions, including ex-Champions Still Active). The records show Championship contests listed separately while non-Championship opponents are shown in sequence by result. Championship venues are listed by town (for a more detailed location of contest *see* A Championship Diary of All Title Bouts Contested by British Boxers, 1929 – 1984). The status of disputed World Championship contests are shown in a note at the end of the entry.

Championship Contest Code:
B British Title; BE British Empire Title; C Commonwealth Title; EU European Title; W World Title

George Aldridge

British Middleweight Champion, 1962 – 1963
Born 01.02.36 *From* Market Harborough *Pro Career* 1956 – 1963 (52 contests, won 36, drew 2, lost 14)

CHAMPIONSHIP CONTESTS (3)

26.11.62	John Cowboy McCormack	W CO 6	Manchester	B	Middleweight Title
06.02.63	Laszlo Papp	L RSC 15	Vienna	EU	Middleweight Title
28.05.63	Mick Leahy	L RSC 1	Nottingham	B	Middleweight Title

NON CHAMPIONSHIP CONTESTS (49)

WON PTS (18)	**1957** Jacob Dempsey, John Stansfield, Joe Walcott, Alan Dean. **1958** Les Allen, Ted Buck. **1959** Ted Buck, Derek Liversidge. **1960** Johnny Melfah, Johnny Cunningham, Maxie Smith. **1961** Malcolm Worthington, Sandy Luke, Harry Scott. **1962** Ray Drayton, Harry Scott, Pat O'Grady, Phil Edwards
WON CO (4)	**1957** Tommy Turner, Danny Wall. **1961** Egon Thomson. **1962** Fred Elderfield
WON RSC/RTD (12)	**1956** Frank Davis. **1957** Jack Whittaker, Johnny Hunt, Bonny Garraway. **1958** John Woollard, Ronnie Vale. **1959** Jimmy Lynas. **1960** Teddy Haynes. **1961** Brian Husband, Pat O'Grady. **1962** Orlando Paso. **1963** Dave Wakefield
WON DIS (1)	**1957** Jacky Scott
DREW (2)	**1956** Paddy Delargy. **1961** Giancarlo Garbelli
LOST PTS (5)	**1957** Jacky Scott. **1958** Attu Clottey, Martin Hansen, Freddie Cross. **1961** Harry Scott
LOST CO (2)	**1962** Nino Benvenuti. **1963** Jackie Harwood
LOST RSC/RTD (3)	**1957** Len Mullen. **1959** Attu Clottey. **1960** Cowboy McCormack
LOST DIS (2)	**1959** Johnny Read. **1961** Chris Christensen

Terry Allen

British Flyweight Champion, 1951 – 1952. Undefeated British Flyweight Champion, 1952 – 1954. European & World Flyweight Champion, 1950
Born 18.06.24 *From* Islington (birthname – Edward Govier) *Pro Career* 1942 – 1954 (74 contests, won 60, drew 1, lost 13)

George Aldridge

Terry Allen

CHAMPIONSHIP CONTESTS (11)

30.09.48	Rinty Monaghan	DREW 15	Belfast	B, BE, EU, W	Flyweight Titles
25.04.50	Honore Pratesi	**W** PTS 15	London	EU, W	Flyweight Titles
01.08.50	Dado Marino	L PTS 15	Honolulu	W	Flyweight Title
30.10.50	Jean Sneyers	L PTS 15	Nottingham	EU	Flyweight Title
11.06.51	Vic Herman	**W** PTS 15	Leicester	B	Flyweight Title
01.11.51	Dado Marino	L PTS 15	Honolulu	W	Flyweight Title
17.03.52	Teddy Gardner	L PTS 15	Newcastle	B, BE, EU	Flyweight Titles
21.10.52	Eric Marsden	**W** RSC 6	London	B	Flyweight Title
27.10.53	Yoshio Shirai	L PTS 15	Tokyo	W	Flyweight Title
16.02.54	Eric Marsden	**W** DIS 5	London	B	Flyweight Title
10.09.54	Nazzareno Giannelli	L PTS 15	Milan	EU	Flyweight Title

NON CHAMPIONSHIP CONTESTS (63)

WON PTS (39)	**1942** Jim Thomas. **1943** Les Johnson, Tommy Burney, Ronnie Bishop, Roy Ball, Jack McKenzie, Mickey Jones. **1944** Jackie Evans, Tommy Burney, Mickey Jones, George Shamar, Hassan Ramadhin. **1945** Christo Kyrisco, Hassan Saada, Sapper Johnstone, Phil Milligan, Mustapha Ezzatt (3). **1946** Les Johnson, Frank Tierney, Billy Hazelgrove. **1947** Pinchie Thompson, Alf Hughes, Johnny Summers, Les Johnson, Frank Tierney. **1948** Jackie Bryce, Charlie Wilson, Tommy Farricker. **1949** Billy Hazelgrove, Dickie O'Sullivan, Rinty Monaghan, Jackie Foster, Norman Tennant. **1950** Peter Fay. **1951** Jimmy Pearce, Henry Carpenter. **1952** Jimmy Pearce
WON CO (10)	**1943** Ronnie Kingston, George Howell. **1944** Roy Ball, Ahmed Mahu, Chehata Hafez. **1945** Abdul Nassan (2), Sayed Mustapha, Hassan Robbou. **1948** Jimmy Gill
WON RSC/RTD (6)	**1943** Doug Claxton, Billy Hazelgrove. **1944** Joe Josephs. **1946** Billy Davies. **1947** Adam McCulloch, Tommy Whittle
WON DIS (1)	**1948** Dickie O'Sullivan
LOST PTS (4)	**1948** Jackie Bryce. **1949** Honore Pratesi. **1952** Maurice Sandeyron. **1953** Gaetano Annaloro
LOST CO (2)	**1946** Alex Murphy. **1954** Dai Dower
LOST RSC/RTD (1)	**1947** Rinty Monaghan

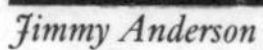
Jimmy Anderson

Vic Andreetti

Jimmy Anderson

Undefeated British J. Welterweight Champion, 1968 – 1969
Born 01.10.42 *From* Waltham Cross *Pro Career* 1964 – 1971 (37 contests, won 27, drew 1, lost 9)

CHAMPIONSHIP CONTESTS (3)

Date	Opponent	Result	Venue		Title
20.02.68	Jimmy Revie	W RSC 9	London	B	J. Lightweight Title
08.10.68	Brian Cartwright	W PTS 15	London	B	J. Lightweight Title
25.02.69	Colin Lake	W RSC 7	London	B	J. Lightweight Title

NON CHAMPIONSHIP CONTESTS (34)

WON PTS (2)	**1964** Ali Juma. **1967** Hiroshi Shoji
WON CO (4)	**1966** Joe Okezie. **1967** Gaetano Dos Santos, Santos Martins II. **1971** Bobby Hughes
WON RSC/RTD (18)	**1964** Dick Sauva, Billy Seasman, Manley Brown. **1965** Terry Cook, Peter Lavery, Terry Halpin, John Adebesi, Mick Greaves. **1966** Ali Juma, Winston Laud, Peter Lavery, Dixie Dean, Brian Smyth, Brian Cartwright, Johnny Mantle. **1967** Kid Durango, Tei Dovie. **1968** Hugh Baxter
DREW (1)	**1969** Bill Whittenburg
LOST PTS (3)	**1965** Brian Smyth. **1968** Howard Winstone. **1969** Johnny Famechon
LOST CO (1)	**1967** Rafiu King
LOST RSC/RTD (1)	**1971** Brian Hudson
LOST DIS (4)	**1964** Sugar Ray Johnson (2). **1967** Bobby Fisher. **1969** Colin Lake

Vic Andreetti

Undefeated British J. Welterweight Champion, 1969
Born 29.01.42 *From* Hoxton *Pro Career* 1961 – 1969 (67 contests, won 51, drew 3, lost 13)

CHAMPIONSHIP CONTESTS (5)

Date	Opponent	Result	Venue		Title
30.11.65	Maurice Cullen	L PTS 15	Wolverhampton	B	Lightweight Title
25.04.67	Maurice Cullen	L PTS 15	Newcastle	B	Lightweight Title
27.02.68	Des Rea	L PTS 15	London	B	J. Welterweight Title
17.02.69	Des Rea	W PTS 15	Nottingham	B	J. Welterweight Title
13.10.69	Des Rea	W CO 4	Nottingham	B	J. Welterweight Title

NON CHAMPIONSHIP CONTESTS (62)

WON PTS (31)	**1961** Tommy Kansas, Colin Mannock, Teddy Carter (2), Tommy Tiger, Dave Parsons, Stan Bishop, Alex McMillan, Billy Secular. **1962** Jimmy

Evan Armstrong

Bobby Arthur

	Norcott, Junior Cassidy, Ron Jones, Chris Elliott, Johnny Cooke. **1963** Terry Edwards, Floyd Robertson, Spike McCormack. **1964** Spike McCormack, Chris Elliott, John White, Harry Edwards. **1965** Joe Tetteh, Rafiu King, Tony Perez, Mohamed Ben Said, Ivan Whiter. **1966** Terry Edwards, Al Rocca (2), Phil Lundgren. **1969** Victor Paul
WON CO (4)	**1961** Ken Pugh, Tony Icke. **1963** Belarmino Fragoso. **1964** Johnny McKenna
WON RSC/RTD (14)	**1961** Joe Jacobs, Ronnie Brown. **1962** Phil McGrath, Johnny Kidd, Billy Secular, Danny O'Brien, Victor Teixeira, Jaime Aparici. **1964** Harry Edwards, Brian Brazier. **1965** Joe Brown. **1966** Jose Medrazo. **1968** Malcolm McKenzie, Billy Seasman
DREW (3)	**1962** Terry Edwards (2). **1963** Chris Elliott
LOST PTS (8)	**1961** Sammy McSpadden (2). **1962** Alex McMillan. **1963** Maurice Cullen. **1964** Maurice Cullen. **1966** Al Rocca. **1969** Ermanno Fasoli, Boerge Krogh
LOST RSC/RTD (2)	**1967** Eddie Perkins. **1969** Ramon Carrasco

Evan Armstrong

British Featherweight Champion, 1971 – 1972. Undefeated British Featherweight Champion, 1973 – 1974. Commonwealth Featherweight Champion, 1974
Born 15.02.43 *From* Ayr *Pro Career* 1963 – 1974 (54 contests, won 39, drew 1, lost 14)

CHAMPIONSHIP CONTESTS (10)

09.06.69	Alan Rudkin	L RTD 11	Manchester	B	Bantamweight Title
05.07.71	Jimmy Revie	**W** CO 12	London	B	Featherweight Title
06.09.71	Toro George	L PTS 15	Melbourne	C	Featherweight Title
15.02.72	Jose Legra	L PTS 15	London	EU	Featherweight Title
18.04.72	Howard Hayes	**W** RSC 6	Nottingham	B	Featherweight Title
25.09.72	Tommy Glencross	L PTS 15	Glasgow	B	Featherweight Title
17.09.73	Tommy Glencross	**W** RSC 3	Glasgow	B	Featherweight Title
05.04.74	Bobby Dunne	**W** RSC 8	Brisbane	C	Featherweight Title
08.07.74	Alan Richardson	**W** RSC 11	London	B, C	Featherweight Titles
07.12.74	David Kotey	L RSC 10	Accra	C	Featherweight Title

NON CHAMPIONSHIP CONTESTS (44)

WON PTS (9)	**1964** Dele Majeke, Con Mount Bassie, Ali Juma. **1965** Peter Lavery, Johnny Adabesi. **1966** Bobby Davies. **1969** Billy Hardacre. **1971** Abdou Fakyh. **1973** Bingo Crooks

CONTINUED OVERLEAF

WON CO (7)	**1963** Candido Sawyer. **1964** Dele Majeke, Mick Greaves. **1965** Johnny Adabesi. **1966** Jackie Brown. **1969** Reg Gullefer. **1974** Vernon Sollas
WON RSC/RTD (18)	**1964** Billy Williams, Mick Carney. **1965** Tommy Burgoyne, Tony Riley, George Bowes, Johnny Mantle. **1966** Tei Dovie, Monty Laud, Oye Turpin, Angel Chinea, Orizu Obilaso. **1967** Benny Lee, Jim McCann. **1968** Pornchai Poppraigam, Patrick Mambwe, Jose Bisbal. **1970** Jimmy Bell. **1972** Howard Hayes
DREW (1)	**1967** Patrick Mambwe
LOST PTS (5)	**1964** Brian Cartwright. **1965** Tony Riley. **1966** Brian Cartwright. **1968** Joe Medel. **1970** Jose Legra
LOST CO (1)	**1972** Arnold Taylor
LOST RSC/RTD (3)	**1964** Bobby Fisher. **1968** Jesus Castillo, Bob Allotey

Bobby Arthur

British Welterweight Champion, 1972 – 1973
Born 25.07.47 *From* Coventry *Pro Career* 1967 – 1976 (41 contests, won 26, lost 15)

CHAMPIONSHIP CONTESTS (3)

31.10.72	John H. Stracey	W DIS 7	London	B	Welterweight Title
05.06.73	John H. Stracey	L CO 4	London	B	Welterweight Title
25.09.73	Larry Paul	L CO 10	Wolverhampton	B	L. Middleweight Title

NON CHAMPIONSHIP CONTESTS (38)

WON PTS (19	**1967** Mike Keeney, Johnny Adolphi, Frank Dolan, Ronnie Van Der Walt. **1968** Len Gregory, Johnny Brown, Peter Quinn, Jackie Turpin, Osmo Kanerva. **1969** Jackie Turpin. **1970** Chris Jobson. **1971** Ernest Musso, Chris Jobson, Frank Young. **1972** Les Pearson, Jose Medrazo. **1975** John Smith (2). **1976** Jim Moore
WON RSC/RTD (6)	**1967** Pat Walsh. **1968** Rod Griffiths, Ronnie Van Der Walt, Ivan Drew. **1970** Gus Farrell. **1971** Stoffel Steyn
LOST PTS (9)	**1969** Maurice Cullen. **1970** Angel Garcia, Jorgen Hansen, Les Pearson, Jose Duran. **1971** Chris Jobson. **1974** Jeff Gale. **1975** George Warusfel. **1977** Les Pearson
LOST CO (3)	**1970** Spider Kelly. **1975** Tom Imrie. **1976** Alois Carmeliet
LOST RSC/RTD (1)	**1975** Jim Devanney

Eddie Avoth

British L. Heavyweight Champion, 1969 – 1971. Commonwealth L. Heavyweight Champion, 1970–1971
Born 02.05.45 *From* Cardiff *Pro Career* 1963 – 1972 (53 contests, won 44, lost 9)

CHAMPIONSHIP CONTESTS (6)

19.06.67	Young John McCormack	L RSC 7	London	B	L. Heavyweight Title
13.01.69	Young John McCormack	W RTD 11	London	B	L. Heavyweight Title
28.06.69	Yvan Prebeg	L PTS 15	Zagreb	EU	L. Heavyweight Title
06.04.70	Young John McCormack	W DIS 8	Nottingham	B	L. Heavyweight Title
23.10.70	Trevor Thornbury	W RTD 6	Brisbane	C	L. Heavyweight Title
24.01.71	Chris Finnigan	L RSC 15	London	B, C	L. Heavyweight Titles

NON CHAMPIONSHIP CONTESTS (47)

WON PTS (23)	**1963** Dave Arnold, Terry Phillips, Ray Fallone, Joe Somerville. **1964** Sid Brown (2), Jack Powell, Louis Onwuna, Fitzroy Lindo, Tony French. **1965** Joe Bell. **1966** Charlie Wilson, Ernie Fields, Johnny Halafihi. **1967** Guinea Roger. **1968** John Hendrickson (2), Stanford Bulla. **1969** Lloyd Walford, Bunny Johnson. **1970** Emile Okee Griffith. **1971** Guinea Roger, Kosie Smith
WON CO (5)	**1964** Dave Arnold, Jimmy Stewart, Louis Onwuna, George Palin. **1969** Lou Gutierrez

WON RSC/RTD (13)	**1964** Henry Turkington, Gary Chippendale. **1965** Roy Thomas, Sid Brown, Fitzroy Lindo. **1966** Lloyd Walford (2), Charlie Wilson, Steve Richards, Clarence Prince, Johnny Ould. **1967** John Hendrickson. **1968** Curtis Bruce
LOST PTS (4)	**1963** Joe Somerville. **1966** Derek Richards. **1970** Mike Quarry. **1971** Sarel Aucamp
LOST RSC/RTD (2)	**1967** Ernie Field. **1972** Bunny Johnson

Teddy Baldock

Undefeated British Bantamweight Champion, 1928 and 1929 – 1931. Undefeated British Empire Bantamweight Champion, 1928–1931. World Bantamweight Champion, 1927
Born 23.05.07 *From* Poplar *Died* 1971 *Pro Career* 1921 – 1931 (80 contests, won 72, drew 3, lost 5)

CHAMPIONSHIP CONTESTS (4)

05.05.27	Archie Bell	**W** PTS 15	London	W	Bantamweight Title
06.10.27	Willie Smith	L PTS 15	London	W	Bantamweight Title
29.08.28	Johnny Brown	**W** RSC 2	London	B, BE	Bantamweight Titles
16.05.29	Alf Kid Pattenden	**W** PTS 15	London	B, BE	Bantamweight Titles

NON CHAMPIONSHIP CONTESTS (76)

WON PTS (31)	**1921** Young Makepeace (2). **1922** Johnny O'Brien (2). **1923** Arthur Webb (2), Young Riley, Percy Faithful. **1924** Young Bill Lewis (2), Dod Oldfield (2), Harry Hill. **1925** Ernie Jarvis, Frankie Ash, Tiny Smith, Antoine Merlo. **1926** Frankie Ash, Francois Morrachini, Micky Gill, Tommy Atova, Johnny Eriksen, San Sanchez, Tommy Lorenzo, Billy Reynolds, Ralph Nischio, Pierre de Caluwe. **1928** Phil Lolosky. **1930** Lew Pinkus, Alf Kid Pattenden. **1931** Terence Morgan
WON CO (12)	**1923** Johnny Faithful. **1924** Young Bowler. **1925** Johnny Murton. **1926** Arthur de Champlaine. **1927** Johnny Brown, Feux Friedmann, Len Oldfield, Len Fowler. **1928** Pierre Calloir, Phil Lolosky. **1930** Jimmy Docherty. **1931** Gideon Potteau
WON RSC/RTD (24)	**1923** Johnny O'Brien, Young Stoneham, Kid Roberts, Joe Goddard. **1924**Arthur Cowley, Kid Hughes, Vic Wakefield. **1925** Fred Hinton (2), Willie Evans (2), Johnny Haydn, Frankie Kestrell, Jim Haddon, Billy Shaw, Ernie Veitch. **1926** Alf Barber, Tiny Smith, Joe Clifford. **1928** Bugler Lake, Mick Hill. **1929** Van Paemal, Gideon Potteau. **1930** Charlie Rowbotham

CONTINUED OVERLEAF

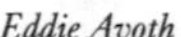
Eddie Avoth

Teddy Baldock

WON DIS (2)	**1926** Billy Marlow. **1930** Emile Pladner
DREW (3)	**1923** Kid Socks. **1926** Jackie Cohen. **1927** Johnny Cuthbert
LOST PTS (2)	**1930** Benny Sharkey. **1931** Dick Corbett
LOST RSC/RTD (1)	**1931** Al Brown
LOST DIS (1)	**1926** Kid Nicholson

NOTE:
The Lonsdale Belt was not issued for the British Championship Contest versus Johnny Brown. Both World Championship Contests, versus Archie Bell and Willie Smith, were for the GB version of the Title.

Ron Barton

Undefeated British L. Heavyweight Champion, 1956
Born 25.02.33 *From* West Ham *Pro Career* 1954 – 1961 (31 contests, won 26, lost 5)

CHAMPIONSHIP CONTESTS (2)

13.03.56	Albert Finch	**W** RTD 8	London	B	L. Heavyweight Title
19.06.56	Gordon Wallace	L PTS 15	London	BE	L. Heavyweight Title

NON CHAMPIONSHIP CONTESTS (29)

WON PTS (7)	**1954** Roy Johnson, Wally Curtis, Brian Anders. **1955** Arthur Howard. **1956** Alessandro D'Ottavio. **1959** Neville Rowe, Redvers Sangoe
WON CO (7)	**1954** Jim Lindley, Gerry McNally, Ken Gardner, Ron Crookes, Sammy Mercier. **1955** Ramon Martinez, Austin Jones
WON RSC/RTD (9)	**1954** Joe Odeyemi, Eric Metcalfe, Wally Beckett, Jimmy Davis. **1955** Luigi Dominico, Don Ellis, Mel Brown. **1959** Andre Verburgh, Gordon Corbett
WON DIS (2)	**1955** Yvon Durelle. **1961** Jimmy Attoh
LOST PTS (2)	**1955** Alessandro D'Ottavio. **1959** Billy Smith
LOST CO (1)	**1961** Stan Cullis
LOST RSC/RTD (1)	**1960** Stan Cullis

Jackie Kid Berg

British Lightweight Champion, 1934 – 1936. World J. Welterweight Champion, 1930 – 1931
Born 28.06.09 *From* Stepney (birthname – Judah Bergman) *Pro Career* 1924–1945 (192 contests, won 157, drew 9, lost 26)

CHAMPIONSHIP CONTESTS (15)

18.02.30	Mushy Callahan	**W** RTD 10	London	W	J. Welterweight Title
04.04.30	Joe Glick	**W** PTS 10	New York	W	J. Welterweight Title
29.05.30	Al Delmont	**W** RSC 4	Newark	W	J. Welterweight Title
12.06.30	Herman Perlick	**W** PTS 10	New York	W	J. Welterweight Title
03.09.30	Buster Brown	**W** PTS 10	Newark	W	J. Welterweight Title
18.09.30	Joe Glick	**W** PTS 10	New York	W	J. Welterweight Title
10.10.30	Billy Petrolle	**W** PTS 10	New York	W	J. Welterweight Title
23.01.31	Goldie Hess	**W** PTS 10	Chicago	W	J. Welterweight Title
31.01.31	Herman Perlick	**W** PTS 10	New York	W	J. Welterweight Title
10.04.31	Billy Wallace	**W** PTS 10	Detroit	W	J. Welterweight Title
24.04.31	Tony Canzoneri	L CO 3	Chicago	W	J. Welterweight & Lightweight Titles
10.09.31	Tony Canzoneri	L PTS 15	New York	W	J. Welterweight & Lightweight Titles
29.10.34	Harry Mizler	**W** RTD 10	London	B	Lightweight Title
11.01.36	Laurie Stevens	L PTS 12	Johannesburg	BE	Lightweight Title
24.04.36	Jimmy Walsh	L RSC 9	Liverpool	B	Lightweight Title

NON CHAMPIONSHIP CONTESTS (177)

WON PTS (73)	**1924** Billy Clarke, Albert Hicks, Young Clancy, Jimmy Wooder, Fred Patten, Arthur Lloyd. **1925** Billy Streets, Sid Carter, Fred Green (2),

Ron Barton

Jackie Kid Berg

	Johnny Britton, Johnny Curley, Van Dyke. **1926** Andre Routis, Mick Hill, Harry Corbett, Phil Bond. **1927** Joe Claes, Vittorio Venturi, Lucien Vinez. **1928** Freddie Mueller, Pedro Amador, Johnny Mello, Alf Mancini. **1929** Lucien Vinez, Bruce Flowers (3), Herman Perlick, Mushy Callahan, Spug Myers, Phil McGraw, Eddie Elkins, Art Delucca. **1930** Tony Canzoneri, Jack Phillipe, Henry Perlick, Kid Chocolate. **1931** Ray Keiser, Tony Herrera, Phil Griffin, Johnny McNamara. **1932** Buster Brown, Mike Sarko, Kid Chocolate. **1934** Jackie Flynn. **1935** Peter McKinley. **1937** Ivor Pickens, Alby Day, Leo Phillips. **1938** Larry Anzalone, Vince Pimpinella, Frankie Wallace, Johnny Horstmann (2), Ray Napolitano, Johnny McHale (3), Pete Cara, Joey Greb, Frankie Cavanna. **1939** Pete Galiano, Tippy Larkin, Johnny Rohrig, Joey Greb, Paddy Roche. **1940** Harry Davis, George Reynolds. **1941** Harry Craster, Harry Charman, Harry Mizler. **1945** Jimmy Brunt
WON CO (11)	**1924** Teddy Pullen. **1925** Norman Radford. **1927** Jack Kirk. **1929** Tommy Gerval. **1931** Teddy Watson. **1933** Louis Saerens. **1935** Harry Brown. **1938** Silvio Zangrillo. **1939** Marine Bunker. **1945** Eric Dolby, Johnny McDonald
WON RSC/RTD (48)	**1924** Young Gordon, Charlie Harwood, Syd Lyons, Harry Miller, Teddy Shepherd, Bert Saunders, Billy Colebourne. **1925** Albert Colcombe, Arthur Lloyd, Billy Streets, Kid Lewis, Billy Shepherd, Jack Slattery, Joe Samuels, George Green, Johnny Cuthbert. **1926** Henri Hebrans, Paul Gay, Billy Gilmore. **1927** Walter Wright, Paul Fritsch, Bob Miller, Robert Sirvain. **1928** Mickey Waters. **1929** Joe Trabon, Harry Wallace. **1931** Tony Lambert, Maurius Baudry. **1933** George Rose, Eugene Drouhin, Harry Wallace. **1934** Joe Kerr, Nicolas Wilke, Alf Bastin. **1935** Gustave Humery, Pat Butler. **1937** George Purchase, Harry Mason, Pat Haley, Jake Kilrain, Charlie Chetwin. **1939** Paddy Roche. **1940** Paddy Roche, Dick Bradshaw, Harry Davis. **1941** Joe Connolly. **1942** Paddy Roche, Joe Connolly
WON DIS (14)	**1925** George Davis, Ernie Swash. **1926** Andre Routis, Emile Saerens. **1927** Alf Simmons, Raymond Jansin. **1928** Jackie Donn, Spug Myers. **1929** George Balduc, Tony Caragliano. **1934** Len Wickwar. **1937** Pat Haley. **1940** Eddie Ryan. **1941** Eric Boon
DREW (9)	**1924** Billy Clarke, Jimmy Wooder. **1926** Harry Corbett. **1928** Billy Petrolle. **1929** Stanislaus Loayza. **1932** Sammy Fuller. **1937** Louis Saerens, Jack Lewis. **1938** Augie Aurellano

CONTINUED OVERLEAF

LOST PTS (15)	**1925** Johnny Cuthbert (2). **1926** Harry Corbett. **1932** Sammy Fuller. **1933** Cleto Locatelli, Tony Falco. **1934** Cleto Locatelli. **1935** Gustave Humery (2). **1938** Red Cochrane. **1939** Baby Breeze, Mike Piskin. **1941** Ernie Roderick, George Odwell. **1943** Gordon Woodhouse
LOST CO (1)	**1939** Pedro Montanez
LOST RSC/RTD (6)	**1928** Billy Petrolle. **1934** Jimmy Stewart. **1936** Aldo Spoldi. **1937** George Odwell. **1939** Milt Aaron. **1941** Arthur Danahar

NOTE:
It is debatable whether the World Championship Contests held in America for the J. Welterweight Title are valid but they are listed in *The Ring* Record Book and as such are shown. The Lonsdale Belt was not issued for the British Championship Contests versus Harry Mizler and Jimmy Walsh.

Jack Bodell

British Heavyweight Champion, 1969 – 1970 and 1971 – 1972. Commonwealth Heavyweight Champion, 1971 – 1972. European Heavyweight Champion, 1971
Born 11.08.40 *From* Swadlincote *Pro Career* 1962 – 1972 (71 contests, won 58, lost 13)

CHAMPIONSHIP CONTESTS (6)

13.06.67	Henry Cooper	L RSC 2	Wolverhampton	B, BE	Heavyweight Titles
13.10.69	Carl Gizzi	W PTS 15	Nottingham	B	Heavyweight Title
24.03.70	Henry Cooper	L PTS 15	London	B, C	Heavyweight Titles
27.09.71	Joe Bugner	W PTS 15	London	B, C, EU	Heavyweight Titles
17.12.71	Jose Urtain	L RSC 2	Madrid	EU	Heavyweight Title
27.06.72	Danny McAlinden	L CO 2	Birmingham	B, C	Heavyweight Titles

NON CHAMPIONSHIP CONTESTS (65)

WON PTS (22	**1962** Mick Cowan, Joe Louis, Jack Whittaker, Jimmy Blanche. **1963** Dave Ould. **1964** Ron Redrup. **1965** Ron Gray, Freddie Mack, Billy Daniels. **1966** Jo Juvillier, Guiseppe Migliari, Renato Moraes, Sante Amonti. **1967** Ray Patterson, Sonny Moore, Rocky Campbell (2). **1968** Johnny Prescott. **1969** Joe Roman. **1970** Jimmy Richards. **1971** Manuel Ramos, Bill Drover
WON CO (7)	**1962** Rupert Bentley. **1963** Rupert Bentley. **1965** Rudolph Vaughan, Al Roye, Benito Canal. **1969** John Jordon. **1971** Jack O'Halloran
WON RSC/RTD (24)	**1962** Ossie Nelson, Jimmy Leach, Roy Seward (2), Brian Stannard, John Hendrickson. **1963** Jack Whittaker. **1965** Al Roye, Eric Fearon, Ray Shiel, Buddy Turman, Johnny Halafihi, Levi Forte, Yvan Prebeg, Mariano Echevarria. **1966** Bill Nielson, Ski Goldstein, Giorgio Masteghin, Bob Stallings. **1968** Lion Ven, Brian London, Mel Turnbow, Carl Gizzi. **1969** Billy Walker
WON DIS (3)	**1963** Ron Gray. **1965** Dave Ould. **1969** Roosevelt Eddie
LOST PTS (1)	**1964** Joe Erskine
LOST CO (1)	**1971** Jerry Quarry
LOST RSC/RTD (6)	**1962** Joe Louis. **1963** Stoffel Willemse, Renato Moraes. **1964** Freddie Mack, Hubert Hilton. **1966** Thad Spencer, Piero Tomasoni

Eric Boon

British Lightweight Champion, 1938 – 1944
Born 28.12.19 *From* Chatteris *Died* 1981 *Pro Career* 1935 – 1952 (122 Contests, won 93, drew 5, lost 23, no contest 1)

CHAMPIONSHIP CONTESTS (5)

15.12.38	Dave Crowley	W CO 13	London	B	Lightweight Title
23.02.39	Arthur Danahar	W RSC 14	London	B	Lightweight Title
09.12.39	Dave Crowley	W CO 7	London	B	Lightweight Title
12.08.44	Ronnie James	L CO 10	Cardiff	B	Lightweight Title
09.12.47	Ernie Roderick	L PTS 15	London	B	Welterweight Title

NON CHAMPIONSHIP CONTESTS (117)

WON PTS (28)	**1935** Teddy Royal, Teddy Softly, Young Higgins, Boy Bessell, Charlie Smith. **1936** Charlie Smith, Len Ash (2), Charlie Wise, Jack Watkins (2), George Cunningham. **1937** Dave James, Chucky Robinson, Bob Barlow, George Kelly, Jack Lilley, Bryn Morris (2). **1938** Alex Jackson, Johnny Softley, Jimmy Walsh, Mitsos Grispos. **1941** Dave Finn. **1942** Jake Kilrain. **1943** Billy Jones. **1944** Jimmy Molloy. **1947** Maurice Ouezmann
WON CO (37)	**1935** Yorkie Perkins. **1936** Terry Ellis, Young Hawes, Young Griffo, Joe Page, Jack Roberts, Teddy Larkham, Nat Williams. **1937** Billy Bennett, Billy Griffiths, Mike Sullivan, Spin Anson, Bobby Lyons, Albert Heasman, Harry Mackenzie, Bob Rowlands, Llew Thomas. **1938** George Reynolds, Tommy Dowlais, Jack Hardiman, Dodo Williams, Boyo Rees, Len Lemaux, Billy Masters, George Reynolds. **1939** Johnny McGrory, Len Wickwar. **1942** Norman Snow, Dick Wheeler, Jake Kilrain. **1946** Cyril Wills, Mick Magee, Billy Stevens, Laurie Stevens, Tiger Burns. **1947** Alf James (2)
WON RSC/RTD (23)	**1935** Young Snowball, Ginger Daniels, Charlie Smith. **1936** Bert Whall, Bobby Lyons, Nick Lucas. **1937** Al Church, Tony Butcher, Jocker Johnson, Ron Porter, Wilf Dexter, Charlie Wise. **1938** Johnny Ward, Matt Moran, Raymond Renard, Eric Dolby. **1939** Boyo Rees. **1946** Paddy Burgin, Jean Wanes, Maurice Ouezmann. **1947** Maurice Ouezmann. **1948** Omar Kouidri
WON DIS (2)	**1937** Con Flynn. **1938** Mac Perez
DREW (5)	**1935** Young Higgins. **1936** Fred Dyer, Jack Kershaw. **1937** Bert Chambers, Angus McGregor
LOST PTS (6)	**1935** Steve Yates, Kid Savage. **1936** Ginger Brant. **1940** Ernie Roderick. **1943** Harry Mizler. **1947** Giel de Roode
LOST CO (4)	**1943** Tommy Armour. **1948** Robert Villemain, Johnny Greco, Robert Takeshita
LOST RSC/RTD (8)	**1937** Harry Brooks, Johnny Softley. **1945** Henry Hall. **1946** Arthur Danahar. **1948** Beau Jack. **1952** George Barnes, Pran Mikus, Pat Ford
LOST DIS (3)	**1941** Jackie Kid Berg. **1942** Frank Duffy. **1949** Fernando Jannilli
NC (1)	**1948** Gwyn Williams

Jack Bodell

Eric Boon

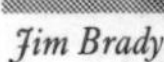

Jim Brady

Jackie Brown (Edinburgh)

Jim Brady

British Empire Bantamweight Champion, 1941 – 1945
Born 1920 *From* Dundee *Died* 1980 *Pro Career* 1932 – 1947 (169 contests, won 104, drew 15, lost 50)

CHAMPIONSHIP CONTESTS (3)

01.01.41	Kid Tanner	**W** PTS 15	Dundee	BE	Bantamweight Title
05.08.41	Jackie Paterson	**W** PTS 15	Glasgow	BE	Bantamweight Title
12.09.45	Jackie Paterson	L PTS 15	Glasgow	BE	Bantamweight Title

NON CHAMPIONSHIP CONTESTS (167)

WON PTS (61) — **1932** Willie Vogan, Jim Hill, Dan Conlin. **1933** Freddie Tennant (2), Joe Bradley, Bobby Magee (2), Paddy Docherty, Tommy Steele, Scabby Adair, Jackie Ryan, Mickey Summers, Arthur Burke. **1934** Jim Campbell, Johnny McManus, George Pull, Johnny Buckley. **1935** George Pull (2), Freddie Tennant, Tommy Stewart, Dave Finn. **1936** Jim McInally, Johnny Ryan, Johnny Peters, Willie Smith. **1937** Billy McHugh, Len Hampston, Benny Jones. **1938** Jackie Brown, Pat McStravick, George Marsden, Gaston Van Den Bos. **1939** Alex Knight, Len Beynon, Balthazar Sangchilli, Paul Jones, Tommy Burns. **1940** Tommy Stewart, Kid Tanner. **1941** Joe Hardy, Nel Tarleton, Syd Worgan (2). **1942** Dick Corbett, Jim Hayes, Syd Worgan, Tony Roberts. **1943** Sammy Reynolds, Syd Worgan, Sgt Calvert. **1944** Phil Milligan, Tommy Davies, Sammy Reynolds. **1945** Len Davies, Ken Barrett, Tim Mahoney, Harry McAuley. **1947** Sammy Reynolds, Harry Croker

WON CO (15) — **1934** Phil Milligan. **1936** Arthur Smith. **1937** Young Chocolate, Dixie Kid. **1938** Pat Palmer, Rafael Valdez, Johnny Griffiths. **1940** Mickey O'Neil. **1941** Billy Cakewell, Billy Tansey, Billy Walker. **1943** Tony Roberts. **1944** Jimmy Dunn, Des Wright. **1946** Dick Perriam

WON RSC/RTD (26) — **1933** Alf Middleton, Mick McAdam, Jim Spalding, Paddy Docherty. **1934** Johnny Brown. **1935** Harry Orton. **1938** Young Gonzales. **1939** Gary Roche, Ken Barrett. **1940** Young Chocolate. **1941** Billy Cakewell, Cyclone Kelly (2), George Pull. **1942** Benny Isaacs (2), Freddie Cotton, Wilf Parkin, Eddie McCoy, Phil Milligan. **1943** Billy Doherty, Frank Bonser, Tommy Hyams. **1945** Ken Barrett. **1947** Ginger Todd, Frankie Williams

DREW (15) — **1933** Jackie Ryan, Alf Middleton, Benny Lynch. **1934** Freddie Tennant. **1935** Jimmy Warnock, Bobby Magee. **1936** George Marsden, Jack Gubbins, Tut Walley. **1937** Aurel Toma. **1939** Jim Hayes. **1942** Bobby Watson, Jim Hayes. **1944** Ben Duffy. **1945** Ben Duffy

LOST PTS (39)	**1933** Mickey Malone, Benny Lynch, Freddie Tennant, Jimmy Knowles. **1934** Benny Lynch (2), Joe Mendiola, Peter Miller, George Pull, Jimmy Albin. **1935** Joe Mendiola, Mickey Summers. **1936** Tut Walley (2), Syd Parker. **1937** Len Hampston, Jimmy Warnock, Len Beynon, Aurel Toma. **1939** Jim Hayes. **1941** Jackie Paterson, Tom Smith. **1943** Tommy McGlinchey, Len Davies, Al Phillips, Peter Kane, Ben Duffy (2). **1944** Al Phillips (2), Tommy McGlinchey, Ben Duffy. **1945** Jimmy Stubbs, Paul Dogniaux. **1946** Jackie Hughes, Frank Kenny, Phil Milligan. **1947** Stan Rowan, Sammy Reynolds
LOST RSC/RTD (7)	**1933** Snowball Frame. **1935** Len Hampston. **1940** Phil Milligan. **1945** Danny Webb, Al Phillips. **1946** Cliff Curvis. **1947** Teddy O'Neil
LOST DIS (3)	**1933** Frank O'Neil. **1936** Jack Gubbins. **1938** George Marsden

Jackie Brown

British & British Empire Flyweight Champion, 1962 – 1963
Born 02.03.35 *From* Edinburgh *Pro Career* 1958 – 1966 (44 contests, won 32, drew 1, lost 10, no contest 1)

CHAMPIONSHIP CONTESTS (3)

27.02.62	Brian Cartwright	W PTS 15	Birmingham	B	Flyweight Title
10.12.62	Orizu Obilaso	W PTS 15	London	BE	Flyweight Title
02.05.63	Walter McGowan	L CO 12	Paisley	B, BE	Flyweight Titles

NON CHAMPIONSHIP CONTESTS (41)

WON PTS (19)	**1959** Eddie Barraclough, Malcolm McLeod, John Agwu. **1960** Eddie Barraclough, John Agwu, Pancho Bhatachaji, Alberto Younsi, Mario D'Agata, Johnny Morrissey. **1961** Brian Cartwright, Ollie Wyllie, Walter McGowan. **1962** Brian Bissmire. **1963** Kid Solomon. **1964** Tommy Burgoyne, Glyn Davies. **1965** Glyn Davies. **1966** Terry Gale, Carl Taylor
WON CO (1)	**1960** Billy Walker
WON RSC/RTD (9)	**1958** Mark Quinn. **1959** Frankie Spencer, Alex Ambrose, Derek Lloyd. **1962** Ben Laiache. **1963** Alex O'Neill. **1965** Baby John, Don Weller, Ramon Casal
WON DIS (1)	**1965** Jim McCann
DREW (1)	**1964** Johnny Caldwell
LOST CO (5)	**1961** Freddie Gilroy, Piero Rollo. **1962** Risto Luukkonen. **1965** Ron Jones. **1966** Evan Armstrong
LOST RSC/RTD (4)	**1960** Derek Lloyd. **1963** Felix Brami. **1966** Bob Allotey, George Bowes
NC (1)	**1961** Eddie Barraclough

Jackie Brown

British Flyweight Champion, 1929 – 1930 and 1931 – 1935. Undefeated European Flyweight Champion, 1931 – 1932. World Flyweight Champion, 1932 – 1935
Born 29.11.09 *From* Manchester *Died* 1971 *Pro Career* 1926 – 1939 (135 contests, won 103, drew 8, lost 24)

CHAMPIONSHIP CONTESTS (13)

13.10.29	Bert Kirby	W CO 3	W. Bromwich	B	Flyweight Title
03.03.30	Bert Kirby	L CO 3	London	B	Flyweight Title
02.02.31	Bert Kirby	W PTS 15	Manchester	B	Flyweight Title
04.05.31	Lucien Popescu	W PTS 15	Manchester	EU	Flyweight Title
15.06.31	Emile Degand	W PTS 15	London	EU	Flyweight Title
06.07.31	Vincenzo Savo	W PTS 15	Manchester	EU	Flyweight Title
19.09.32	Jim Maharg	W DIS 8	Manchester	B, EU	Flyweight Titles
31.10.32	Young Perez	W RSC 13	Manchester	W	Flyweight Title
12.06.33	Valentin Angelmann	W PTS 15	London	W	Flyweight Title
11.12.33	Ginger Foran	W PTS 15	Manchester	B, W	Flyweight Titles
18.06.34	Valentin Angelmann	DREW 15	Manchester	W	Flyweight Title
09.09.35	Benny Lynch	L RTD 2	Manchester	B, W	Flyweight Titles
31.05.37	Johnny King	L CO 13	Manchester	B	Bantamweight Title

CONTINUED OVERLEAF

NON CHAMPIONSHIP CONTESTS (122)

WON PTS (55)	**1926** Dick Manning. **1927** Joe Fleming, Harry Yates, Freddie Webb, Jack Cantwell, Young Siki. **1928** Young Fitz, Ernie Barker (2), Jim Crawford (2), Fred Morgan, Martin Gallagher, Freddie Webb, Joe Fleming, Arthur Evitt, Jean Locatelli, Harry Yates, Jerry O'Neill, Tommy Brown, Dickie Inkles, Kid Hughes. **1929** George Greaves, Phineas John (2). **1930** Emile Degand, Rene Chalange. **1931** Young Colignon, Benny Thackaray, George Aziz. **1932** Benny Thackaray, Emile Degand (2), Len Beynon. **1933** Young Perez, Valentin Angelmann, Jimmy Knowles. **1934** Aurel Toma. **1935** Henri Barrass, Maurice Filhol, Ernst Weiss. **1936** Johnny Cusick, Len Hampston, Rafael Valdez, Len Beynon. **1937** Bobby Hindes. **1938** Joe Skelly, Pat Palmer, Freddie Tennant, Jim Hayes, Pierce Ellis. **1939** Syd Parker, Jim Hayes, Teddy O'Neill, Benny Jones
WON CO (13)	**1930** Percy Dexter. **1935** Orlando Magliozzi, George Marsden, Eric Jones, Tommy Pardoe, Ellis Ashurst. **1936** Petit Biquet, Jackie Ryan, Nipper Fred Morris, Tucker Winch, Ted Green, Jim McInally. **1937** Van Meensal
WON RSC/RTD (24)	**1927** Ben Doyle, Jim Crawford. **1928** Siki Coulton. **1929** Boy Edge, Walter Lemon, Tony Roberti, Jim Campbell, Harry Hill. **1930** Kid Hughes. **1931** Ottavio Gori, Percy Dexter. **1932** Jean Cuart, George Marsden, Johnny Regan, Bob Fielding. **1933** Billy Bryon. **1935** Jackie Quinn, Syd Rose, Bert Kirby. **1937** Juanito Hernandez, Pat Palmer. **1938** Joe Skelly, Dave Keller, Ginger Murphy
WON DIS (2)	**1927** Young Fagill. **1931** Jim Maharg
DREW (7)	**1927** Ernie Hendricks. **1928** Glovers Nipper (2), Fred Morgan, Cuthbert Taylor. **1935** Benny Lynch, Kid Francis
LOST PTS (16)	**1927** Tommy Brown, Freddie Webb, Glovers Nipper. **1928** Dickie Inkles (2), Phineas John. **1930** Billy James. **1932** Mickey McGuire. **1933** Etienne Mura, Midget Wolgast. **1936** Johnny Cusick. **1938** Jim Hayes, Jim Brady, Joe Connolly. **1939** Tucker Smith, Kid Tanner
LOST RSC/RTD (1)	**1935** Johnny King
LOST DIS (4)	**1932** Tucker Winch. **1933** Dave Crowley, Mickey McGuire. **1937** Len Hampston

Jackie Brown (Manchester)

Ken Buchanan

NOTE:
The Lonsdale Belt was not issued for the British Championship Contests versus Bert Kirby (13.10.29) and Benny Lynch. All of the above World Championship Contests were for the IBU/NBA version of the Title.

Ken Buchanan

Undefeated British Lightweight Champion, 1968 – 1971 and 1973 – 1974. Undefeated European Lightweight Champion, 1974 – 1975. World Lightweight Champion, 1970 – 1972
Born 28.06.45 *From* Edinburgh *Pro Career* 1965–1982 (69 contests, won 61, lost 8)

CHAMPIONSHIP CONTESTS (13)

19.02.68	Maurice Cullen	W CO 11	London	B	Lightweight Title
29.01.70	Miguel Velazquez	L PTS 15	Madrid	EU	Lightweight Title
12.05.70	Brian Hudson	W CO 5	London	B	Lightweight Title
26.09.70	Ismael Laguna	W PTS 15	San Juan	W	Lightweight Title
12.02.71	Ruben Navarro	W PTS 15	Los Angeles	W	Lightweight Title
13.09.71	Ismael Laguna	W PTS 15	New York	W	Lightweight Title
26.06.72	Roberto Duran	L RSC 13	New York	W	Lightweight Title
29.01.73	Jim Watt	W PTS 15	Glasgow	B	Lightweight Title
01.05.74	Antonio Puddu	W CO 6	Cagliari	EU	Lightweight Title
16.12.74	Leonard Taverez	W RSC 14	Paris	EU	Lightweight Title
27.02.75	Guts Ishimatsu	L PTS 15	Tokyo	W	Lightweight Title
25.07.75	Giancarlo Usai	W RSC 12	Cagliari	EU	Lightweight Title
06.12.79	Charlie Nash	L PTS 12	Copenhagen	EU	Lightweight Title

NON CHAMPIONSHIP CONTESTS (56)

WON PTS (30)	**1965** Junior Cassidy. **1966** Tommy Tiger (2), Chris Elliott, Junior Cassidy, Ivan Whiter, Mick Laud, Antonio Paiva, Al Keen, Phil Lundgren. **1967** John McMillan, Tommy Garrison, Winston Laud, Rene Roque, Spike McCormack. **1968** Leonard Taverez, Ivan Whiter, Angel Garcia. **1969** Frankie Narvaez, Jose Luis Torcida. **1970** Leonard Taverez, Chris Fernandez, Donato Paduano. **1972** Al Ford. **1973** Hector Matta, Frankie Otero. **1974** Jose Peterson. **1979** Ben Benitez, Eloy de Souza. **1980** Des Gwilliam
WON CO (3)	**1973** Miguel Araujo. **1974** Joe Tetteh. **1980** Najib Daho
WON RSC/RTD (19)	**1965** Brian Tonks, Vic Woodhall, Billy Williams, Joe Okezie. **1966** Manley Brown, Brian Smyth. **1967** Franco Brondi, Al Rocca. **1968** Ameur Lamine. **1969** Mike Cruz, Jerry Graci, Vincenzo Pitardi. **1971** Carlos Hernandez. **1972** Andries Steyn, Carlos Ortiz, Chang Kil-Lee. **1973** Chu Chu Malave, Frankie Otero. **1974** Winston Noel
LOST PTS (4)	**1981** Steve Early, Langton Tinago, Lance Williams. **1982** George Feeney.

NOTE:
The World Championship Contests versus Ismael Laguna (twice) and Roberto Duran were for the WBA version of the Title, whilst the World Championship Contest versus Guts Ishimatsu was for the WBC version. When Buchanan defeated Ruben Navarro the Title was not in dispute.

Pat Butler

Undefeated British Welterweight Champion, 1934 – 1936
Born 16.05.13 *From* Mountsorrel *Pro Career* 1931 – 1936 (111 contests, won 63, drew 4, lost 43, no contest 1)

CHAMPIONSHIP CONTESTS (1)

17.12.34	Harry Mason	W PTS 15	Leicester	B	Welterweight Title

NON CHAMPIONSHIP CONTESTS (110)

WON PTS (27)	**1931** Jack Richards, Bart McDonald, Frank Hullett, Len Kirk, George Siddons, Tommy Allen, Bob Grey. **1932** Jack Kirby, George Lovell,

CONTINUED OVERLEAF

Pat Butler

Alex Buxton

	Billy Mellows, Jack Lawrence, Tommy Kirk. **1933** Pat O'Connor, Chris Lovell, George Lawley, Frank Matthews, Bill Downey, Len Wickwar, Syd Raiteri. **1934** Mick Miller (2), Harry Gregory, Fred Mitchell, Ernie Roderick, Len Tiger Smith, Harry Mason. **1935** Eddie Gott
WON CO (11)	**1931** Fred Collis, Harry Austin, Sam Brewin. **1932** Alf Hewlett, Len Williams. **1933** Fred Taylor, Jack Glover, Kid Haycock. **1934** Fred Cook, Harry Fenn, Len Wickwar
WON RSC/RTD (21)	**1931** Bob Grey. **1932** Jack Kirby (2), Alf Mosley, George Lovell, Bert Sales. **1933** Billy Wood, Len Kirk, Cliff Hodgetts, Roy Boulton, Billy Peters, Billy Jackson, Peter Nolan, Roy Hilton, Jim Learoyd. **1934** Cyclone Warriner, Jack Moody, Tom Cartwright, Paddy Peters. **1935** Fred Clements, George Swadling
WON DIS (3)	**1934** Pat Cowley, Fred Mitchell. **1935** Panther Purchase
DREW (4)	**1931** George Lovell (2). **1932** Bob Parkin. **1934** Leo Phillips
LOST PTS (30)	**1931** Jack Tranter, George Siddons, Tommy Allen. **1932** Pat Haley, Len Wickwar, Johnny Gudge, Norman Snow (2), Tiger Bert Ison, Arnold Kid Sheppard, Horace Barber. **1933** Len Wickwar (2), Arnold Kid Sheppard, Horace Barber, George Daly, Ginger Sadd, Tommy Marren. **1934** Chuck Parker (2), Pat Haley, Len Tiger Smith, Chris Dawson, Dave McCleave. **1935** George Bunter, Jack Kid McCabe, George Rose, Ginger Sadd, Roy Mills, Kid Davies
LOST RSC/RTD (12)	**1932** Fred Webster. **1934** Charlie Baxter, Johnny Quill. **1935** Paul Schaefer, Ernie Roderick, Jimmy Stewart, Jack McLeod, Jean Morin, Mick Miller, Jackie Kid Berg, Eric Dolby. **1936** Harry Woodward
LOST DIS (1)	**1932** Arnold Kid Sheppard
NC (1)	**1934** Huib Huizenarr

NOTE:
The Lonsdale Belt was not issued for the British Championship Contest versus Mason.

Alex Buxton

British L. Heavyweight Champion, 1953–1955
Born 10.05.25 *From* Watford *Pro Career* 1942–1963 (125 Contests, Won 78, Drew 4, Lost 43)

CHAMPIONSHIP CONTESTS (4)

26.10.53	Dennis Powell	W RSC 10	Nottingham	B	L. Heavyweight Title
09.11.54	Albert Finch	W CO 8	Birmingham	B	L. Heavyweight Title
26.04.55	Randy Turpin	L CO 2	London	B, BE	L. Heavyweight Titles
26.11.56	Randy Turpin	L RSC 5	Leicester	B	L. Heavyweight Title

NON CHAMPIONSHIP CONTESTS (121)

WON PTS (23)	**1943** Joe Orsatelli. **1946** Alby Hollister, Len Harrison. **1947** Tommy Ward, Young Milo, Alabama Kid, Jack Johnson, Gus Jansen. **1948** Alabama Kid, Lucien Krawczyk. **1949** Jimmy Davis, Des Jones, Koffi Kiteman, George Dilkes. **1950** George Angelo. **1951** Kid Marcel, Bert Sanders (2), Henry Hall. **1952** Bobby Dawson, Bernardo Pacini. **1953** Allen Williams, Johnny Barton
WON CO (23)	**1945** Jack Kirkham, Frank Duff, Les Sloane, Vic Calteaux. **1946** Ritchie Sands, Alby Hollister. **1947** Bede Welsh, Colin Hoddy, Ritchie Sands. **1949** Jim Wellard, Ollie Williams, Billy Colouilias, Des Jones, Tom Bodell, Norman Twigger. **1950** Ron Grogan, Joe Rood, Jimmy Ingle, Jimmy Davis. **1951** Joe Maseko. **1952** Ron Crookes. **1956** Max Resch, Terence Murphy
WON RSC/RTD (28)	**1943** Manuel Sulley, Charlie Smith. **1945** Fred Manuels. **1946** George Dilkes, Johnny Houlston. **1947** Max Cameron, Ritchie Sands. **1948** Ron Grogan. **1949** Chris Adcock, Jackie Wilson, Reg Hoblyn. **1950** Alby Hollister, Gaston Chambraud, Widmor Milandri, George Casson, Allan Cooke. **1951** Ted Mason, Richard Armagh, Jackie Marr, Burl Charity. **1952** Reg Spring, Bruce Crawford. **1953** Emile Delmine, Peter Muller. **1954** Bruno Tripodi. **1956** Kit Pompey. **1957** Italo Scortichini. **1959** Noel Trigg
WON DIS (2)	**1945** Jack Day. **1948** Bert Sanders
DREW (4)	**1946** Tommy Davies. **1957** Italo Scortichini. **1959** Gunter Hase. **1960** Franz Szuzina
LOST PTS (34)	**1942** Norman Bell. **1943** Billy Hughes, Johnny Boyd. **1946** Dave Sands. **1947** O'Neill Bell, George Allen, Dave Sands. **1948** Ross Pippett. **1949** Vince Hawkins. **1951** Ron Pudney. **1953** Hans Stretz. **1954** Wim Snoek, Franco Festucci, Charles Humez. **1955** Gustav Scholz, Olle Bengtsson. **1956** Willi Besmanoff, Hans Stretz. **1957** Gerhard Hecht, Gustav Scholz. **1958** Hanswerner Wohlers, Rocco Mazzola, Freddie Cross. **1959** Max Resch. **1960** Erich Walter, Horst Niche, Karl Mildenberger, Manfred Hass, Helmutt Ball. **1961** Marcel Pigou, Ottavio Panunzi, Gerry McNally. **1962** Piero Tomasoni. **1963** Bob Nicolson
LOST RSC/RTD (7)	**1943** Billy Hughes, Vince Hawkins. **1946** Jack Johnson. **1952** Randy Turpin, Bobby Dawson, Andre de Keersgieter. **1957** Willie Armstrong

Chic Calderwood

Undefeated British & British Empire L. Heavyweight Champion, 1960 – 1966
Born 09.01.37 *From* Craigneuk *Died* 1966 *Pro Career* 1957 – 1966 (55 contests, won 44, drew 1, lost 9, no contest 1)

CHAMPIONSHIP CONTESTS (9)

28.01.60	Arthur Howard	W RSC 13	Paisley	B	L. Heavyweight Title
09.06.60	Johnny Halafihi	W RSC 12	Glasgow	BE	L. Heavyweight Title
12.02.62	Stan Cullis	W CO 4	London	B, BE	L. Heavyweight Titles
04.06.62	Johnny Halafihi	W PTS 15	Newcastle	BE	L. Heavyweight Title
28.09.62	Giulio Rinaldi	L PTS 15	Rome	EU	L. Heavyweight Title
30.07.63	Ron Redrup	W RTD 11	Blackpool	B, BE	L. Heavyweight Titles
11.11.64	Bob Nicolson	W RTD 7	Paisley	B	L. Heavyweight Title
17.08.66	Piero Del Papa	NC 6	Lignano	EU	L. Heavyweight Title
15.10.66	Jose Torres	L CO 2	San Juan	W	L. Heavyweight Title

CONTINUED OVERLEAF

Chic Calderwood

Johnny Caldwell

NON CHAMPIONSHIP CONTESTS (46)

WON PTS (14)	**1958** Jackie Scott, Joe Walcott, Neville Rowe, Ted Williams. **1959** Harry Dodoo, Ron Redrup. **1960** Willie Pastrano, Sonny Ray. **1963** Ray Shiel, Tommy Fields, Von Clay. **1964** Freddie Cross. **1965** Johnny Persol. **1966** Dick Hall
WON CO (3)	**1957** Jimmy Teasdale. **1958** Stan Cullis. **1959** Yolande Pompey
WON RSC/RTD (21)	**1957** Johnny Summers, John Hunt, Gordon Corbett. **1958** Jackie Scott, Johnny Cole, Clark Mellor, Billy Ellaway, Dave Mooney, Neville Rowe. **1959** Redvers Sangoe, Burke Emery, Charlie Forrest, Sam Langford, Jack Whittaker. **1960** Joey Armstrong, Rolf Peters. **1961** Dave Rent. **1964** Alan Harmon. **1965** Otha Brown. **1966** Derek Richards, Alfredo Vogrig
DREW (1)	**1961** Jim Cooper
LOST PTS (4)	**1961** Von Clay, Henry Hank. **1963** Eddie Cotton, Gustave Scholz
LOST CO (1)	**1965** Freddie Mack
LOST RSC/RTD (2)	**1965** John Cowboy McCormack. **1966** Jose Menno

Johnny Caldwell

Undefeated British Flyweight Champion, 1960 – 1961. British & British Empire Bantamweight Champion, 1964 – 1965. World Bantamweight Champion, 1961 – 1962
Born 07.05.38 *From* Belfast *Pro Career* 1958 – 1965 (35 contests, won 29, drew 1, lost 5)

CHAMPIONSHIP CONTESTS (7)

08.10.60	Frankie Jones	**W** CO 3	Belfast	B	Flyweight Title
30.05.61	Alphonse Halimi	**W** PTS 15	London	W	Bantamweight Title
31.10.61	Alphonse Halimi	**W** PTS 15	London	W	Bantamweight Title
18.01.62	Eder Jofre	L RTD 10	Sao Paulo	W	Bantamweight Title
20.10.62	Freddie Gilroy	L RTD 9	Belfast	B, BE	Bantamweight Titles
05.03.64	George Bowes	**W** RSC 7	Belfast	B, BE	Bantamweight Titles
22.03.65	Alan Rudkin	L RSC 10	Nottingham	B, BE	Bantamweight Titles

NON CHAMPIONSHIP CONTESTS (28)

WON PTS (13)	**1958** Moncef Fehri, Dennis Adams, Esteban Martin. **1959** Henri

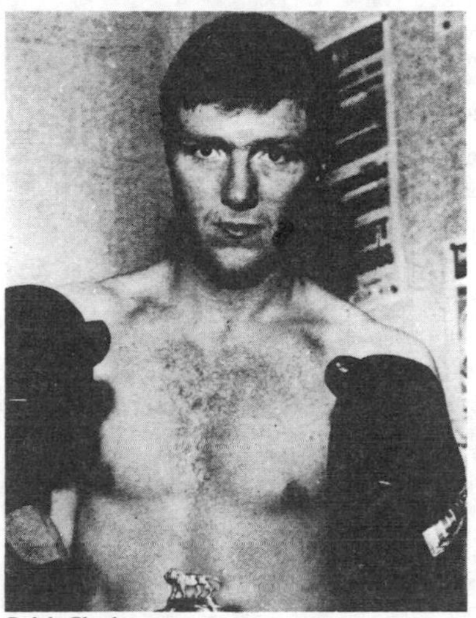

Ralph Charles

Dave Charnley

	Schmid, Pierre Rossi, Giacomo Spano, Salvatore Manca. **1960** Risto Luukkonen, Rene Libeer. **1961** Pierre Vetroff. **1962** Federico Scarponi. **1964** Rafael Fernandez, Orizu Obilaso
WON CO (5)	**1958** Billy Downer, Eddie Barraclough, Juanito Cid. **1960** Young Martin. **1961** Juan Cardenas
WON RSC/RTD (7)	**1958** Michael Lamora. **1959** Simon Carnezzo, Francesco Carreno, Salvatore Manca. **1960** Christian Marchand. **1961** Angelo Rampin, Jacques Jacob
DREW (1)	**1964** Jackie Brown
LOST PTS (1)	**1965** Monty Laud
LOST RSC/RTD (1)	**1963** Michel Atlan

NOTE:
The World Championship Contests versus Alphonse Halimi were for the GB/EBU version of the Title.

Ralph Charles

Undefeated British & British Empire/Commonwealth Welterweight Champion, 1968 – 1972.
European Welterweight Champion, 1970 – 1971
Born 05.02.43 *From* West Ham *Pro Career* 1963 – 1972 (43 contests, won 39, lost 4)

CHAMPIONSHIP CONTESTS (7)

20.02.68	Johnny Cooke	W PTS 15	London	B, BE	Welterweight Titles
11.11.69	Chuck Henderson	W CO 5	London	B, BE	Welterweight Titles
20.11.70	Johann Orsolics	W CO 12	Vienna	EU	Welterweight Title
04.06.71	Roger Menetrey	L CO 7	Geneva	EU	Welterweight Title
05.09.71	Jeff White	W RSC 5	Brisbane	C	Welterweight Title
07.12.71	Bernie Terrell	W RSC 8	London	B, C	Welterweight Titles
28.03.72	Jose Napoles	L CO 7	London	W	Welterweight Title

NON CHAMPIONSHIP CONTESTS (36)

WON PTS (4)	**1964** Darkie Smith. **1965** Joe Falcon. **1966** Harry Edwards. **1967** Dick Duffy

CONTINUED OVERLEAF

WON CO (2)	**1963** Bill Rowan, Johnny Brown
WON RSC/RTD (27)	**1964** Maurice Lloyd, George Onwuka, Terry Phillips, Johnny Fuller, Wally Williams. **1965** Ivan Whiter, Panther Cyril, Bob Sempey, Darkie Smith. **1966** George Onwuka, Peter McLaren, Jack Sylveer, Sammy McSpadden. **1967** Ron Van Der Walt, Ricky Porter, Abder Faradji. **1968** Joey Durelle. **1969** Larry Brown, Ivan Whiter, Len Gibbs, Luis Vinales, Nat Jacobs, Andre L'Homme, Lionel Cuypers. **1970** Dave Hilton, Johnny Kramer. **1971** Bobby Williams
WON DIS (1)	**1971** Dorman Crawford
LOST PTS (1)	**1970** Raul Soriano
LOST RSC/RTD (1)	**1966** Ernest Musso

Dave Charnley

Undefeated British Lightweight Champion, 1957 – 1964. British Empire Lightweight Champion, 1959 – 1962. Undefeated European Lightweight Champion, 1960 – 1961
Born 10.10.35 *From* Dartford *Pro Career* 1954 – 1964 (61 contests, won 48, drew 1, lost 12)

CHAMPIONSHIP CONTESTS (11)

09.04.57	Joe Lucy	W PTS 15	London	B	Lightweight Title
09.07.57	Willie Toweel	L PTS 15	London	BE	Lightweight Title
12.05.59	Willie Toweel	W CO 10	London	BE	Lightweight Title
02.12.59	Joe Brown	L RTD 5	Houston	W	Lightweight Title
29.03.60	Mario Vecchiatto	W RTD 10	London	EU	Lightweight Title
21.02.61	Fernand Nollett	W PTS 15	London	EU	Lightweight Title
18.04.61	Joe Brown	L PTS 15	London	W	Lightweight Title
05.07.61	Ray Nobile	W RTD 4	Rome	EU	Lightweight Title
20.11.61	Darkie Hughes	W CO 1	Nottingham	B, BE, EU	Lightweight Titles
04.08.62	Bunny Grant	L PTS 15	Kingston	BE	Lightweight Title
20.05.63	Maurice Cullen	W PTS 15	Manchester	B	Lightweight Title

NON CHAMPIONSHIP CONTESTS (50)

WON PTS (15)	**1954** Roy Paine. **1955** Johnny Mann, Teddy Best, Leo Molloy. **1956** Sammy McCarthy, Alby Tissong. **1957** Ron Hinson. **1958** Don Jordan, Joey Lopes. **1960** Saveur Benamou. **1961** Gene Gresham, Lenny Matthews. **1962** Jose Stable. **1963** Jethro Cason. **1964** Kenny Lane
WON CO (7)	**1954** Percy James. **1955** Andy Monaghan, Nye Ankara, Neville Tetlow. **1960** Paul Armstead. **1961** L. C. Morgan. **1963** Joe Brown
WON RSC/RTD (16)	**1954** Malcolm Ames, Pat McCoy. **1955** Stan Skinkiss, Jackie Butler, Kurt Ernest. **1956** Johnny Butterworth, Fernand Coppens, Johnny Miller. **1957** Willie Lloyd, Johnny Gonsalves, Joe Woussem. **1958** Tony Garcia, Peter Waterman, Jimmy Croll. **1959** Jimmy Brown. **1962** J. D. Ellis
WON DIS (3)	**1955** Denny Dawson, Jeff Walters. **1959** Billy Spider Kelly
DREW (1)	**1955** Willie Lloyd
LOST PTS (7)	**1955** Guy Gracia. **1956** Willie Lloyd. **1958** Carlos Ortiz. **1959** Guy Gracia. **1962** Doug Vaillant. **1963** Tito Marshall. **1964** Brian Curvis
LOST RSC/RTD (1)	**1964** Emile Griffith

Johnny Clark

Undefeated British & European Bantamweight Champion, 1973 – 1974
Born 10.09.47 *From* Walworth *Pro Career* 1966 – 1974 (43 contests, won 39, drew 1, lost 3)

CHAMPIONSHIP CONTESTS (5)

21.04.70	Alan Rudkin	L RSC 12	London	B, C	Bantamweight Titles
25.01.72	Alan Rudkin	L PTS 15	London	B, C	Bantamweight Titles
20.02.73	Paddy Maguire	W PTS 15	London	B	Bantamweight Title
17.04.73	Franco Zurlo	W PTS 15	London	EU	Bantamweight Title
15.01.74	Salvatore Fabrizio	W PTS 15	London	EU	Bantamweight Title

Johnny Clark

Ronnie Clayton

NON CHAMPIONSHIP CONTESTS (38)

WON PTS (9)	**1967** Simon Tiger, Ron Elliott. **1968** John McCluskey. **1969** Karim Young, Manuel Arnal. **1971** Michel Jamet. **1973** Hiro Hamada (2). **1974** Luigi Tessarin
WON CO (1)	**1968** Sammy Abbey
WON RSC/RTD (26)	**1966** Peter Drew, Simon Tiger. **1967** Tommy Burgoyne (2), Tommy Connor, Billy Hardacre, Winston Van Guylenburg, Wellington Vilella, Brian Bissmire, Sammy McNorthey, Orizu Obilaso. **1968** Billy Brown, Marc Vandomme. **1969** Giancarlo Centa, Achene Saifi, Karim Young, Claude Lapinte, Ulf Danielsson, Jackie Burke. **1970** Felipe Gonzales, Antoine Porcel. **1971** Ben Salah Abdesselem, John Kellie. **1972** Norbert Barriere, Carlos Zayas. **1974** Chuck Spencer
DREW (1)	**1966** Tommy Connor
LOST RSC/RTD (1)	**1971** John Kellie

Ronnie Clayton

British Featherweight Champion, 1947 – 1954. British Empire Featherweight Champion, 1947 – 1951. European Featherweight Champion, 1947 – 1948
Born 09.02.23 *From* Blackpool *Pro Career* 1941 – 1954 (114 contests, won 80, drew 8, lost 26)

CHAMPIONSHIP CONTESTS (13)

11.09.47	Tiger Al Phillips	**W** PTS 15	Liverpool	B, BE, EU	Featherweight Titles
22.03.48	Ray Famechon	L PTS 15	Nottingham	EU	Featherweight Title
11.04.49	Johnny Molloy	**W** PTS 15	Nottingham	B, BE	Featherweight Titles
11.08.49	Eddie Miller	**W** CO 12	Liverpool	BE	Featherweight Title
18.11.49	Ray Famechon	L PTS 15	Manchester	EU	Featherweight Title
28.11.50	Jim Kenny	**W** PTS 15	London	B, BE	Featherweight Titles

CONTINUED OVERLEAF

26.02.51	Tiger Al Phillips	W PTS 15	Nottingham	B, BE	Featherweight Titles
30.04.51	Roy Ankrah	L PTS 15	London	BE	Featherweight Title
25.02.52	Roy Ankrah	L RTD 13	Nottingham	BE	Featherweight Title
21.04.52	Ray Famechon	L RTD 5	Nottingham	EU	Featherweight Title
30.06.52	Dai Davies	W RSC 5	Abergavenny	B	Featherweight Title
12.05.53	Freddie King	W CO 4	London	B	Featherweight Title
01.06.54	Sammy McCarthy	L RTD 8	London	B	Featherweight Title

NON CHAMPIONSHIP CONTESTS (101)

WON PTS (25) — **1941** Al Sinclair, Jim Hines, Billy Mayne (2). **1942** Frank Walker, Ronnie Bishop, Tommy Plowright, Les Johnson (2), Tony Roberts, Willie Smith. **1943** Frank Bonser. **1945** Jim McCann. **1946** Paddy Dowdall, Bert Jackson, Cliff Morris, Ben Duffy. **1947** Ben Duffy. **1949** Stan Gossip, Jackie Turpin, Manuel Ortiz. **1950** Jim McCann. **1952** Francis Bonnardel. **1954** Charlie Tucker, Tommy Higgins

WON CO (17) — **1941** Red O'Brien, Kid Wood, Billy Todd, Mickey Jones, Ginger McDermott. **1942** Dick Hughes, Micky O'Neil, Pat Palmer. **1943** Eddie Petrin, George Thomas. **1944** Tony Roberts, Jim Dunn. **1945** Willie Grey. **1946** Joe Kay. **1947** George Pook, Joe Carter. **1951** Louis de Santiago

WON RSC/RTD (29) — **1941** Al Sinclair, Jim Hines, Jim Alexander. **1942** Jack Kiley, Billy Hodgson, Willie Grey, Willie Smith, Billy Jenkins. **1943** George Thomas, Eddie Middle, Frank Bonser, Joe Docherty. **1944** Johnny Rawlings, Freddie Cotton, Wilf Parkin, Jackie Chambers, Bobby Hindes, Danny Nagle, Jim McCann. **1945** Frank Benson, Charlie Meikle. **1946** Billy Innes, Frank Kenny, Fred Morris. **1947** Enzo Corregioli. **1948** Jackie Hughes. **1951** Danny O'Sullivan. **1952** Marcel Auclair. **1953** Billy Spider Kelly

WON DIS (2) — **1950** Jackie Hughes. **1951** Guido Ferracin

DREW (8) — **1941** Al Sinclair. **1944** Danny Woods. **1946** Pierce Ellis. **1947** Paul Dogniaux, Jean Machterlinck (2). **1948** Cliff Anderson. **1950** Luis de Santiago

LOST PTS (17) — **1941** Norman Lewis. **1942** Frank Walker. **1943** Gus Foran, Joe Curran. **1946** Eric Powell, Tom Smith. **1947** Ray Famechon. **1948** Johnny Molloy, Ben Duffy, Jean Machterlinck. **1949** Tommy Burns, Tony Lombard. **1950** Tiger Al Phillips. **1951** Bernard Pugh. **1952** Jim Kenny, Sammy McCarthy. **1953** Vic Toweel

LOST RSC/RTD (3) — **1944** Jackie Paterson. **1951** Louis Van Hoeck. **1952** Tommy Collins

Don Cockell

British L. Heavyweight Champion, 1950–1952. Undefeated European L. Heavyweight Champion, 1951 – 1952. Undefeated British & British Empire Heavyweight Champion, 1953 – 1956
Born 22.09.28 *From* Battersea *Died* 1983 *Pro Career* 1946–1956 (79 contests, won 64, drew 1, lost 14)

CHAMPIONSHIP CONTESTS (7)

17.10.50	Mark Hart	W CO 14	London	B	L. Heavyweight Title
27.03.51	Albert Yvel	W RSC 6	London	EU	L. Heavyweight Title
16.10.51	Albert Finch	W CO 7	London	B, EU	L. Heavyweight Titles
10.06.52	Randy Turpin	L RSC 11	London	B, BE	L. Heavyweight Titles
12.05.53	Johnny Williams	W PTS 15	London	B, BE	Heavyweight Titles
30.01.54	Johnny Arthur	W PTS 15	Johannesburg	BE	Heavyweight Title
16.05.55	Rocky Marciano	L RSC 9	San Fransisco	W	Heavyweight Title

NON CHAMPIONSHIP CONTESTS (72)

WON PTS (25) — **1946** Harry O'Grady, Paddy Roche, Reg Spring, Jim Carroll. **1947** Hal Anthony, Ginger Sadd, Paddy Roche, Reg Spring. **1948** Johnny Williams, Gene Fowler (2), Johnny Barton. **1949** Lloyd Barnett, Mark Hart, Paddy Slavin, Bert Gilroy, Don Mogard. **1950** Georges Rogiers,

Don Cockell

John Conteh

	Lloyd Barnett. **1951** Freddie Beshore. **1952** Renato Tontini. **1953** Harry Matthews, Uber Bacilieri. **1954** Roland la Starza, Harry Matthews
WON CO (17)	**1946** Trevor Lowder (2), Ron Baker, Jim Salles, Frank Johnson. **1947** Jim Carroll, Hal Anthony, Ronnie Croud, Matt Hardy. **1948** Jimmy Carroll, George Barrett, Trevor Burt, Henry Palmer, Doug Richards. **1949** Gabriel Bigotte. **1951** Lloyd Marshall, Nick Barone
WON RSC/RTD (16)	**1946** Sid Watts, Frank Baldwin, Harry Lawrence, Battling Igo. **1947** Trevor Burt, Reg Spring. **1948** Koffi Kiteman, Battling Igo, Dave Goodwin. **1949** Charlie Collett. **1950** Andre le Franc, Jimmy Carroll. **1952** Paddy Slavin, Frank Bell. **1953** Tommy Farr. **1954** Harry Matthews
WON DIS (1)	**1950** Lloyd Marshall
DREW (1)	**1948** Jimmy Carroll
LOST PTS (4)	**1946** Jock Taylor. **1948** Reg Spring, Johnny Barton. **1950** Aaron Wilson
LOST CO (3)	**1947** Jock Taylor. **1950** Aaron Wilson. **1956** Kitione Lave
LOST RSC/RTD (4)	**1947** Dave Goodwin. **1948** Johnny Williams. **1951** Jimmy Slade. **1955** Nino Valdes
LOST DIS (1)	**1949** Jimmy Carroll

John Conteh

Undefeated British, Commonwealth & European L. Heavyweight Champion, 1973 – 1974.
Undefeated World L. Heavyweight Champion, 1974 – 1977
Born 27.05.51 *From* Liverpool *Pro Career* 1971 – 1980 (39 contests, won 34, drew 1, lost 4)

CHAMPIONSHIP CONTESTS (12)

13.03.73	Rudiger Schmidtke	W RSC 12	London	EU	L. Heavyweight Title
22.05.73	Chris Finnegan	W PTS 15	London	B, C, EU	L. Heavyweight Titles
23.10.73	Baby Boy Rolle	W PTS 15	Nottingham	C	L. Heavyweight Title
12.03.74	Tom Bogs	W RTD 6	London	EU	L. Heavyweight Title

CONTINUED OVERLEAF

21.05.74	Chris Finnegan	W RSC 6	London	B, C, EU	L. Heavyweight Titles
01.10.74	Jorge Ahumada	W PTS 15	London	W	L. Heavyweight Title
11.03.75	Lonnie Bennett	W RSC 5	London	W	L. Heavyweight Title
09.10.76	Alvaro Yaqui Lopez	W PTS 15	Copenhagen	W	L. Heavyweight Title
05.03.77	Len Hutchins	W RSC 3	Liverpool	W	L. Heavyweight Title
17.06.78	Mate Parlov	L PTS 15	Belgrade	W	L. Heavyweight Title
18.08.79	Matthew Saad Muhammad	L PTS 15	Atlantic City	W	L. Heavyweight Title
29.03.80	Matthew Saad Muhammad	L RSC 4	Atlantic City	W	L. Heavyweight Title

NON CHAMPIONSHIP CONTESTS (27)

WON PTS (6) — **1971** Tony Burwell. **1973** Dave Matthews. **1974** Les Stevens. **1975** Willie Taylor. **1978** Joe Cokes. **1979** Ivy Brown

WON CO (5) — **1971** Okacha Boubekeur. **1972** Larry Sykes, Ruben Figueroa, Johnny Hudgins. **1978** Leonardo Roger

WON RSC/RTD (14) — **1971** Pierre Minier, Frank Bullard, Emile Okee Griffith. **1972** Wilhelm Jankow, Joe Gholston, Billy Aird, Johnny Mac, Ferenc Cristofczak, Bill Drover, Sam McGill. **1973** Terry Daniels, Vicente Rondon, Fred Lewis. **1980** James Dixon

DREW (1) — **1979** Jesse Burnett

LOST PTS (1) — **1972** Eddie Duncan

NOTE:
All of the above World Championship Contests were for the WBC version of the Title.

Johnny Cooke

British & British Empire Welterweight Champion, 1967 – 1968
Born 17.12.34 *From* Bootle *Pro Career* 1960 – 1971 (93 contests, won 52, drew 7, lost 34)

CHAMPIONSHIP CONTESTS (6)

28.07.64	Brian Curvis	L RTD 5	Porthcawl	B, BE	Welterweight Titles
13.02.67	Brian McCaffrey	W PTS 15	Manchester	B	Welterweight Title
09.05.67	Shaun Doyle	W PTS 15	Liverpool	B	Welterweight Title
16.08.67	Carmelo Bossi	L RSC 12	San Remo	EU	Welterweight Title
16.10.67	Lennox Beckles	W PTS 15	Liverpool	BE	Welterweight Title
20.02.68	Ralph Charles	L PTS 15	London	B, BE	Welterweight Titles

NON CHAMPIONSHIP CONTESTS (87)

WON PTS (44) — **1960** Junior Cassidy, Mickey Driscoll, Alex McMillan. **1961** Spike McCormack, Jimmy Gibson, Peter Heath, Byron Hollingsworth, Roy Jacobs, Ebe Mensah, Brian Jones, Chico Velez. **1962** Dave Coventry, Guy Gracia, Boswell St Louis, Nat Jacobs. **1963** Johnny Kramer, Al Sharpe, Joe Shaw, Jan de Vos, Jackie Harwood, Wally Swift. **1964** Jimmy McGrail. **1965** Tony Smith, Jackie Harwood, Jim Swords (2), Paul Armstead, Giuilio Nervino. **1966** Bo Petterson, Aldo Battista, Stig Walterson, Peter Cobblah, Sugar Bill Robinson, Ske Mullen. **1967** Bo Petterson. **1968** Fred Powney, Bob Cofie, Don Davis. **1969** Peter Cragg. **1970** Gus Farrell, Des Rea, Alan Tottoh, Tommy Gray. **1971** Dick Duffy

WON CO (2) — **1960** John Bacon. **1961** Dave Higgins

WON RSC/RTD (3) — **1960** Ken Pugh, Sammy Etiolaja. **1966** Peter Schmidt

DREW (7) — **1960** Dave Coventry. **1961** Epiphane Akono. **1964** Tony Smith. **1968** Len Gibbs. **1969** Roger Menetrey. **1971** Robert Gallois, Gielie Buitendag

LOST PTS (25) — **1961** Maurice Cullen. **1962** Maurice Cullen, Vic Andreetti. **1963** Mauri Backman, Wally Swift. **1964** Sammy McSpadden, Tony Smith. **1965** Bo Hogberg. **1966** Ernest Musso, Jackie Harwood. **1968** Chuck Henderson, Oblitey Commey, Mark Rowe. **1969** Lennox Beckles, Robert Gallois, Fighting Mack. **1970** Tony Ortiz, Marcel Cerdan, Donato

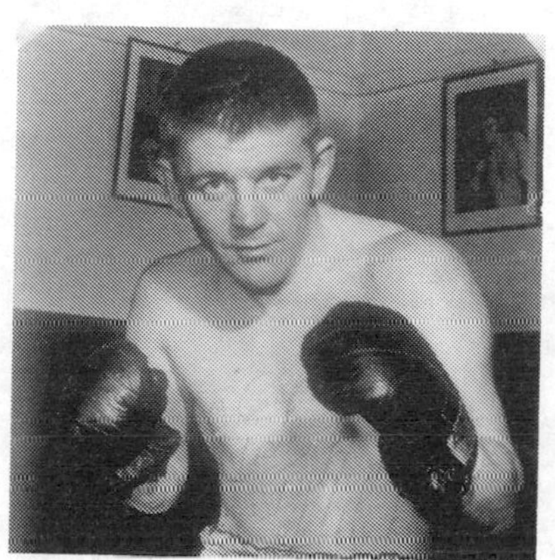
Johnny Cooke

Henry Cooper

	Paduano, Les Pearson, Eric Blake. **1971** Antonio Torres, Garibaldi Pereira, Jorgen Hansen, Les Pearson
LOST CO (1)	**1965** Willie Ludick
LOST RSC/RTD (5)	**1962** J. D. Ellis. **1963** Joe Shaw. **1964** Lucien Fernandes. **1966** Jo Gonzales, Obletey Commey

Henry Cooper

Undefeated British Heavyweight Champion, 1959 – 1960 and British Heavyweight Champion, 1970 – 1971. British Empire/Commonwealth Heavyweight Champion 1959 – 1971. Undefeated European Heavyweight Champion, 1964, 1968 – 1969 and European Heavyweight Champion, 1970 – 71

Born 03.05.34 *From* Bellingham *Pro Career* 1954 – 1971 (55 contests, won 40, drew 1, lost 14)

CHAMPIONSHIP CONTESTS (19)

19.02.57	Joe Bygraves	L CO 9	London	BE	Heavyweight Title
19.05.57	Ingemar Johansson	L CO 5	Stockholm	EU	Heavyweight Title
17.09.57	Joe Erskine	L PTS 15	London	B	Heavyweight Title
12.01.59	Brian London	**W** PTS 15	London	B, BE	Heavyweight Titles
26.08.59	Gawie de Klerk	**W** RSC 5	Porthcawl	BE	Heavyweight Title
17.11.59	Joe Erskine	**W** RSC 12	London	B, BE	Heavyweight Titles
21.03.61	Joe Erskine	**W** RTD 5	London	B, BE	Heavyweight Titles
02.04.62	Joe Erskine	**W** RSC 9	Nottingham	B, BE	Heavyweight Title
26.03.63	Dick Richardson	**W** CO 5	London	B, BE	Heavyweight Titles
24.02.64	Brian London	**W** PTS 15	Manchester	B, BE, EU	Heavyweight Titles
15.06.65	Johnny Prescott	**W** RTD 10	Birmingham	B, BE	Heavyweight Titles
21.05.66	Cassius Clay	L RSC 6	London	W	Heavyweight Title
13.06.67	Jack Bodell	**W** RSC 2	Wolverhampton	B, BE	Heavyweight Titles
07.11.67	Billy Walker	**W** RSC 6	London	B, BE	Heavyweight Titles
18.09.68	Karl Mildenberger	**W** DIS 8	London	EU	Heavyweight Title
13.03.69	Piero Tomasoni	**W** CO 5	Rome	EU	Heavyweight Title
24.03.70	Jack Bodell	**W** PTS 15	London	B, C	Heavyweight Titles
10.11.70	Jose Urtain	**W** RSC 9	London	EU	Heavyweight Title

CONTINUED OVERLEAF

16.03.71 Joe Bugner	L PTS 15 London	B, C, EU	Heavyweight Titles

NON CHAMPIONSHIP CONTESTS (36)

WON PTS (8)	**1955** Cliff Purnell, Joe Bygraves. **1957** Hans Kalbfell. **1958** Zora Folley. **1960** Roy Harris, Alex Miteff. **1962** Wayne Bethea. **1967** Boston Jacobs
WON CO (5)	**1954** Harry Painter, Denny Ball. **1955** Uber Bacilieri. **1965** Chip Johnson. **1966** Jefferson Davis
WON RSC/RTD (12)	**1954** Dinny Powell, Eddie Keith. **1955** Colin Strauch, Joe Crickmar, Ron Harmon. **1956** Maurice Mols, Brian London, Gianni Luise. **1958** Dick Richardson. **1962** Tony Hughes. **1965** Dick Wipperman. **1966** Hubert Hilton
WON DIS (1)	**1955** Hugh Ferns
DREW (1)	**1958** Heinz Neuhaus
LOST PTS (3)	**1955** Joe Erskine. **1964** Roger Rischer. **1965** Amos Johnson
LOST CO (2)	**1961** Zora Folley. **1966** Floyd Patterson
LOST RSC/RTD (3)	**1955** Uber Bacilieri. **1956** Peter Bates. **1963** Cassius Clay
LOST DIS (1)	**1958** Erich Schoeppner

NOTE:
The World Championship Contest versus Cassius Clay was for the WBC version of the Title.

Dick Corbett

British Bantamweight Champion, 1931 – 1932 and Undefeated British Bantamweight Champion, 1934. British Empire Bantamweight Champion, 1930 – 1932 and Undefeated British Empire Bantamweight Champion, 1934
Born 28.09.08 *From* Bethnal Green *Died* 1943 (birthname – Dick Coleman) *Pro Career* 1926 – 1943 (183 contests, won 130, drew 17, lost 36)

CHAMPIONSHIP CONTESTS (5)

22.05.30 Willie Smith	**W** PTS 15 London	BE	Bantamweight Title
21.12.31 Johnny King	**W** PTS 15 Manchester	B, BE	Bantamweight Titles
10.10.32 Johnny King	L PTS 15 Manchester	B, BE	Bantamweight Titles
12.02.34 Johnny King	**W** PTS 15 Manchester	B, BE	Bantamweight Titles
20.08.34 Johnny King	DREW 15 London	B, BE	Bantamweight Titles

NON CHAMPIONSHIP CONTESTS (178)

WON PTS (88)	**1926** Bert Freeman (2), Arthur Cunningham, Bert Gallard, Kid Rich. **1927** Bert Kirby, Fred Hinton, Billy Gibson, Harry Scott, Kid Rich (2), Johnny Edwards, Jim Haddon, Vic Wakefield, Jack Ellis, Tiny Smith. **1928** Vic Wakefield, Eddie Pinn, Terence Morgan, Young Jackie Brown, George Williams, Lew Pinkus. **1929** Minty Rose, Kid Socks, Lew Pinkus, Francois Moracchini, Willie Metzner, Johnny Green, Pinkey Silverburg, Herb Barker, Archie Cowan. **1930** Emile Pladner, Kid Pattenden, Benny Sharkey. **1931** Petit Biquet, Jean Locatelli, Willie Smith, Teddy Baldock. **1932** Bob Lamb, Dave Crowley, Benny Sharkey. **1934** Billy Gannon, Francois Machtens, Jim Cowie, Dave Finn, Phineas John. **1935** Doug Kestrell, Spike Robinson, Cuthbert Taylor, Harry Edwards (2), Tommy Rogers, Fred Todkill, Benny Sharkey. **1936** Cuthbert Taylor (2), Billy Charlton, Dave Crowley, Maurice Holtzer, Stan Jehu (2), Benny Caplan, Dick Titley, Phineas John, Johnny Peters. **1937** Ginger Roberts, George Marsden, Robert Disch, Tommy Hyams, Johnny Cusick. **1938** Benny Caplan, Frank Hill, Young Beckett, Mistos Grispos, Jack Carrick, Fred Morris. **1939** Johnny Softley, Mistos Grispos, Joe Connolly. **1941** George Williams, Mick Carney. **1942** Warren Kendall, Eric Dolby, Gordon Ashun
WON CO (3)	**1928** Johnny Croxon. **1935** Teddy Rollins. **1936** Jean Locatelli
WON RSC/RTD (29)	**1926** Kid Roberts, Harry Williams, Young Dennis, Phil Durley, Bill Huntley. **1927** Tommy Hughes, Frank Wiggins, Kid Rich, Billy Boulger, Digger Pugh. **1928** Johnny Croxon, Kid O'Connor, Andre Gleizes, Joe Chapman, Lew Sullivan, Teddy Bennett, Leopold

	Cortvrant, Francois Vandeleene. **1929** Reg Cameron, Wyndham Blake. **1932** Young Johnny Brown. **1933** Tony Butcher, Fred Davidson, Terence Morgan, Arley Hollingsworth. **1934** Jim Maharg. **1935** Danny Thomas, Frank Barron. **1936** Peter Clarke
WON DIS (7)	**1926** Billy Gibson. **1928** Joe Greenwood. **1930** Jules Badson. **1932** Johnny Peters. **1933** Tommy Hyams. **1935** Hal Cartwright. **1940** Len Beynon
DREW (16)	**1926** Young Riley (3). **1927** Harry Hill. **1928** Andre Gleizes. **1929** Packy McFarland, Petey Sarron. **1930** Young Johnny Brown. **1932** Dick Burke. **1933** Francois Machtens. **1934** Johnny King. **1935** Ronnie James. **1937** Len Lemaux. **1939** Frank Kenny. **1941** Warren Kendall
LOST PTS (29)	**1927** Bert Kirby (3), Billy Moss. **1928** Johnny Croxon, Lew Pinkus, Billy Boulger. **1929** Packy McFarland, Nipper Pat Daly. **1931** Willie Smith. **1933** Billy Gannon, Louis Botes, Bobby Leitham, Dave Crowley. **1934** Seaman Tommy Watson. **1935** Johnny McGrory. **1937** Jimmy Walsh, Jim Spider Kelly, Billy Charlton, Benny Caplan, Billy Murdoch. **1938** Len Beynon. **1939** Ronnie James. **1940** Freddie Simpson, Tom Smith, Benny Caplan, Dave Finn. **1942** Jim Brady. **1943** Jimmy Watson
LOST RSC/RTD (2)	**1927** Harry Hill. **1940** Len Beynon
LOST DIS (4)	**1927** Billy Boulger. **1929** Billy Boulger. **1937** Billy Charlton. **1943** Ronnie James

NOTE:
The Lonsdale Belt was not issued for the British Championship Contest versus Johnny King (20.08.34). The British Empire Title Contests versus Willie Smith and Johnny King (21.12.31, 10.10.32) were not generally recognised to have been Championship matches.

Harry Corbett

British Featherweight Champion, 1928 – 1929
Born 14.02.04 *From* Bethnal Green *Died* 1957 (birthname Henry Coleman) *Pro Career* 1921 – 1936 (214 contests, won 139, drew 25, lost 47, no contest 3)

CHAMPIONSHIP CONTESTS (6)

23.02.25	Johnny Brown	L RTD 16	London	B, BE, EU	Bantamweight Titles
29.03.26	Johnny Curley	L PTS 20	London	B	Featherweight Title
12.03.28	Johnny Cuthbert	W PTS 20	London	B	Featherweight Title
18.03.29	Johnny Cuthbert	DREW 15	London	B	Featherweight Title

CONTINUED OVERLEAF

Dick Corbett

Harry Corbett

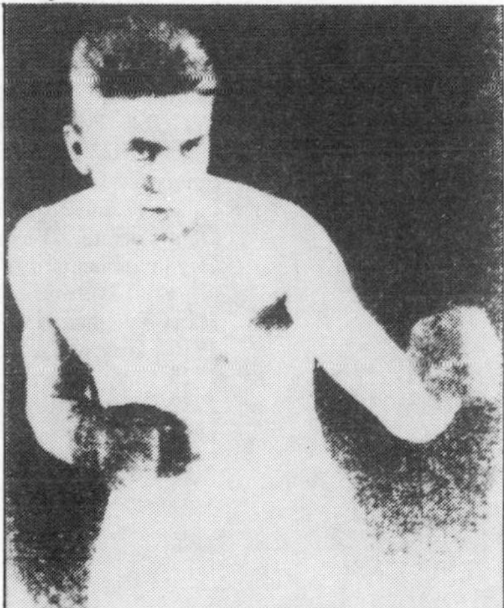

 Harry Corbett

16.05.29	Johnny Cuthbert	L PTS 15	London	B	Featherweight Title
10.10.31	Bep Van Klaveren	L PTS 15	Bristol	EU	Lightweight Title

NON CHAMPIONSHIP CONTESTS (208)

WON PTS (84)	**1921** Barney Brown, Albert Krught, Joe Gibson, Arthur Spenceley. **1922** Jack Langston, Bobby Ward, Ben Treloar, Wally Trainor (2), Harry Reynolds, Teddy Benton, Jimmy Spiers, Young Sullivan, Wag Bennett, Arthur Lloyd (2), Harry Miller, George Lindsay, Pat Crawford (2), Harry Ford, Phil Myers (2), Frank Morgan, Sid Franks, Len Jay. **1923** Harry Miller, Mike Branstone (3), Albert Hicks, Harry Pullen (2), Teddy Maybury, Bert Marsh, Charlie Rogers, Wal Jordan, Albert Jeal. **1924** Albert Hicks, Teddy Murton, Harry Pullen, Mick Hill, Billy Colbourne, Viaud Appolton, Len Fowler, Johnny Brown. **1925** Len Oldfield, Albert Malaise, Johnny Cuthbert, Battling Van Dyk, Andre Routis, Jack Dando. **1926** Jackie Kid Berg, Mick Hill, Knud Larsen. **1927** Jack Hyams, Sam Steward (2), Battling Van Dyk, Jan Scheffers. **1928** Horace Barber, Archie Sexton, Billy Streets, Jim Elzeur. **1929** Johnny McMillan, Johnny Curley. **1930** Camille Desmet, Charlie Tonner. **1931** Haydn Williams, Lucien Lelding, Peter Ronaldson, Harry White, Jack Sheppard, Cecil Kid Como, Alf Howard. **1932** Chuck Parker. **1933** Ernie Higley (2), Flutey Green. **1934** Young Connolly, Jerry Sands, Tuck Mason, Buster Osborne, Ernie Higley
WON CO (12)	**1921** Young Clark. **1922** Jim Robinson. **1924** Len Fowler. **1925** Victor Ferrand. **1927** Phil Bond. **1931** Sam Walters. **1933** Tommy Lee, Billy Mack. **1934** China White, Young Jordan (2), Sol Severns
WON RSC/RTD (37)	**1921** Arthur Krught, Harold Burchell. **1922** Arthur King, Arthur Selby, Young Riley, Jack Hinton. **1923** Ted Treloar, Arthur Lloyd (2), Harry Hart. **1924** Billy Colbourne, Frankie Ash. **1925** Bugler Lake, Young Bull, Jules de Keyser, Antoine Ascensio, Raymond Perrier, Edouard Vleetschower, Albert Marchant. **1926** Johnny Britton, Billy Matthews, Deaf Burke. **1927** Louis Seferre, Teddy Baker, Louis Saerens, Nick Peranic, Paul Loukemanns. **1928** Gustave Humery, Victor Crauc, Jack Kirby. **1929** Len White. **1930** Alf Howard, Pierre Godaert, Ralph Morris. **1931** Cleto Locatelli. **1934** Kid Brooks, Flutey Green
WON DIS (5)	**1923** Bert Marsh. **1927** Billy Palmer, Henri Scillie. **1929** Lou Bloom. **1932** Phil Richards
DREW (24)	**1922** Teddy Conway, Harry Pullen, Joe Chalk, Harry Hart. **1923** George Nolan, Len Jay, Charlie Rogers. **1925** Battling Van Dyk. **1926** Jackie Kid Berg, Edouard Mascart, Battling Van Dyk, Johnny Cuthbert. **1927** Louis Saerens, Jack Donn, Frank McAloran. **1928** Francois Lingles, Jose Martinez. **1930** Len Tiger Smith. **1931** Haydn Williams, Panther Purchase, Len Tiger Smith. **1933** Billy Peters, Jerry Sands. **1934** Ginger Sadd
LOST PTS (37)	**1921** Billy Pinn, Harry Mason. **1922** Teddy Benton, Billy Pinn, Dudley Harris. **1923** Harry Hart. **1924** Kid Nicholson, Billy Hindley, George Spiers, Johnny Cuthbert. **1925** Jules Alveral. **1926** Jackie Kid Berg, Knud Larsen, Edouard Mascart, Johnny Cuthbert, Francois Sybille. **1928** Dom Volante, Al Brown (2). **1929** Jack Hyams, Norman Gillespie. **1930** Haydn Williams, Fred Webster. **1931** Jack Sheppard, Panther Purchase (2), Fred Webster (2), George Rose, Tommy Speirs, Moe Moss. **1932** Harry Vaughan. **1934** Sol Severns, Con Flynn. **1935** Dick Connors. **1936** Harry Kid Lightfoot, Charlie Bint
LOST CO (1)	**1925** Camille Desmet
LOST RSC/RTD (2)	**1922** Johnny Murton. **1930** Alf Mancini
LOST DIS (3)	**1921** Albert Krught. **1926** Johnny Cuthbert. **1927** Young Clancy
NC (3)	**1922** Dan Trainer. **1933** Curly Merrett. **1934** Benny Hinton

Harry Crossley

British L. Heavyweight Champion, 1929 – 1932
Born 04.05.01 *From* Mexborough *Died* 1948 *Pro Career* 1924 – 1934 (84 contests, won 56, drew 8, lost 19, no decision 1)

CHAMPIONSHIP CONTESTS (2)

25.11.29	Frank Moody	**W** PTS 15	London	B	L. Heavyweight Title
23.05.32	Jack Petersen	L PTS 15	London	B	L. Heavyweight Title

NON CHAMPIONSHIP CONTESTS (82)

WON PTS (25)	**1924** Cyril Devine. **1925** Percy Stobart. **1926** George Slack, Rocky Knight. **1927** Eugene Steppe, Jack Hankinson, Charlie Chetwynd. **1928** Daniel Marrouget, Harry Robinson, Ernest Guhring. **1929** Frank Fowler, Gipsy Daniels. **1930** Reg Meen, Gipsy Daniels, Frank Fowler. **1931** Georges Gardebois, Bob Carvill. **1932** Tom Toner, Albert Harvey, Gipsy Daniels. **1933** Arthur Meurant, Gipsy Daniels, Paul Swiderski, Maurice Griselle, Charlie Smith
WON CO (10)	**1926** Ike Clark. **1927** Stoker Stubbs, Joe Mullins, Harry Chaplain. **1928** Harry Foster . **1930** Jean Taneh, Dick Power. **1931** Emile Egrel, Kid Moose. **1932** Arthur Vermant
WON RSC/RTD (19)	**1925** Billy Marsden, Billy Cook. **1926** Jim Slater. **1927** George Slack, Jack Phoenix, Bill Trinder, Tom Fowler, Charlie Chetwynd, Stoker Miller. **1928** Jim Shaw, Eddie Ritchie, Louis Maurlea. **1929** Primo Ubaldo, Bob Carvill. **1930** Bobby Shields, P. O. Stubbs. **1931** Frank Fowler, Steve McCall. **1933** Jack Marshall
WON DIS (1)	**1930** Bob Carvill
DREW (8)	**1927** Rocky Knight. **1928** Con O'Kelly, Rudi Wagner, Heine Muller, Jack Stanley. **1930** Len Johnson, Thyse Petersen
LOST PTS (14)	**1925** Mick Hennesey, Jim McDonald. **1926** Dick Power, Bill Trinder. **1927** George Clough. **1928** Ludwig Haymann (2), Don Shortland. **1929** Jack Stanley, Len Johnson, Larry Gains. **1930** Ernest Pistulla. **1931** Reg Meen. **1933** Walter Neusel
LOST CO (2)	**1931** Don McCorkindale. **1934** Larry Gains
LOST RSC/RTD (2)	**1931** Jimmy Tarante. **1934** Jack Petersen
ND (1)	**1930** Georges Gardebois

Dave Crowley

British Lightweight Champion, 1938
Born 04.05.10 *From* Clerkenwell *Died* 1974 *Pro Career* 1929 – 1946 (180 contests, won 128, drew 11, lost 41)

CONTINUED OVERLEAF

Harry Crossley

Dave Crowley

CHAMPIONSHIP CONTESTS (5)

17.12.34	Nel Tarleton	L PTS 15	London	B	Featherweight Title
03.09.36	Mike Belloise	L CO 9	New York	W	Featherweight Title
23.06.38	Jimmy Walsh	W PTS 15	Liverpool	B	Lightweight Title
15.12.38	Eric Boon	L CO 13	London	B	Lightweight Title
09.12.39	Eric Boon	L CO 7	London	B	Lightweight Title

NON CHAMPIONSHIP CONTESTS (175)

WON PTS (81)	**1929** George Green, Tommy Cann, Alf Patten, Arthur Everitt, Jimmy Mellish, Harry Brown, George Willis. **1930** Young Siki (2), Eddie Bolton, Jim Wise, Len Lemaux, Alf Harris, Tucker Winch, Jack Landon, Harry Paulding (2), Teddy Lewis (2), Billy Jones. **1931** Jack Connell, Harry Paulding, Pat Cassidy, Billy Jones (2), Len Beynon, Harry Connolly (2), Boy Edge, Bert Kirby (2), Emile Degand. **1932** Praxille Gyde, Frankie Ash, Jerry O'Neill, Jackie Rees, Bill Lewis. **1933** Dick Corbett, Bill Lewis. **1934** Tommy Rogers. **1935** Tony Butcher, Ginger Foran, Francois Machtens, Johnny Peters. **1936** Al Gillette, Harry Mizler, Cuthbert Taylor. **1937** George Reynolds, Jimmy Walsh, George Odwell. **1938** Doug Kestrell, Harry Mizler, Pancho Martinez, Mistos Grispos, Johnny Softley. **1940** Freddie Simpson. **1941** Johnny Cunningham, Freddie Simpson, Harry Lazar, Douglas Bygrave. **1942** Eric Dolby. **1943** Sam Darkie Sullivan. **1944** Ken Barrett (2), Bob Ramsey, Jack Carrick, Jimmy Jury, Jackie Rankin, Eric Dolby, Johnny Russell, Syd Worgan, Ben Duffy, John McManus. **1945** Len Davies, George Pook, Hal Cartwright, Al Phillips (2), Johnny Price, Jimmy Smith, Jackie Rankin
WON CO (11)	**1930** Johnny Edwards. **1931** Harry Paulding, Ron Summerton. **1932** Dickie Inkles. **1933** Billy Hazel. **1934** Johnny King, Gilbert Johnstone. **1935** Kid Farlo. **1941** Tiny Ryan. **1944** Eric Dolby. **1945** Hal Cartwright
WON RSC/RTD (25)	**1930** Johnny Merrick, Dick Furness, George Wells, Tommy Brown. **1931** Johnny Stanton, Jack Ellis, Bud Walley, George Marsden, Harry Paulding, Arley Hollingsworth. **1932** Tommy Brown, Werner Riethdorf, Danny Andrews. **1933** Billy Boulger. **1934** Albert Roothooft, August Gyde, Nicolas Wilke. **1935** Van Oosterhout. **1936** Tommy Rogers, Billy Murdoch. **1939** Griff Williams. **1942** Johnny McGrory. **1944** Phil Close, Jimmy Jury. **1945** George Pook
WON DIS (10)	**1932** Johnny Peters. **1933** Jackie Brown. **1936** Ronnie James. **1937** Petey Sarron, Jack Carrick. **1939** Ronnie James. **1942** Len Beynon. **1943** Jim Watson, Terry McStravick, Al Phillips
DREW (1)	**1929** George Crain, George Green, Pat Cassidy. **1930** Billy Jones, Tucker Winch. **1934** Francois Machtens. **1935** Benny Caplan. **1936** Benny Sharkey, Mike Belloise. **1940** Johnny Cunningham. **1944** George Pook
LOST PTS (27)	**1930** Billy Jones, Fred Green. **1931** Andrew Devine. **1932** Johnny King. **1933** Johnny King, Len Beynon, Al Brown, Jimmy Walsh, Dick Corbett. **1934** Freddie Miller. **1935** Benny Caplan, Benny Sharkey. **1936** Dick Corbett. **1938** Johnny McGrory. **1940** Dave Finn. **1941** Harry Lazar (2). **1942** Tom Smith, Dave Finn. **1944** Syd Worgan, Ben Duffy. **1945** Dave Finn (3), Al Phillips, Tom Smith. **1946** Billy Biddles
LOST CO (3)	**1933** Seaman Tommy Watson. **1942** Jackie Rankin. **1943** Laurie Buxton
LOST RSC/RTD (2)	**1929** Fred Davidson. **1942** Ronnie James
LOST DIS (5)	**1931** Bert Kirby. **1933** Jimmy Walsh. **1935** Johnny McGrory. **1943** Ben Duffy. **1944** Johnny Russell

NOTE:
The World Championship Contest versus Mike Bellose was for the New York version of the Title.

Maurice Cullen

British Lightweight Champion, 1965 – 1968
Born 30.12.37 *From* Shotton *Pro Career* 1959 – 1970 (55 contests, won 45, drew 2, lost 8)

CHAMPIONSHIP CONTESTS (6)

20.05.63	Dave Charnley	L PTS 15	Manchester	B	Lightweight Title

08.04.65	Dave Coventry	**W** PTS 15	Liverpool	B	Lightweight Title
30.11.65	Vic Andreetti	**W** PTS 15	Wolverhampton	B	Lightweight Title
06.06.66	Terry Edwards	**W** RSC 5	Newcastle	B	Lightweight Title
25.04.67	Vic Andreetti	**W** PTS 15	Newcastle	B	Lightweight Title
19.02.68	Ken Buchanan	L CO 11	London	B	Lightweight Title

NON CHAMPIONSHIP CONTESTS (49)

WON PTS (32)	**1959** Ricky McMasters. **1960** John McNally, Love Allotey, Tommy Tiger, Jimmy Gibson, Dave Stone. **1961** Phil McGrath, Ebe Mensah, Johnny Cooke, Spike McCormack, Byron Hollingsworth, Guy Gracia, Roy Jacobs. **1962** Spike McCormack, Brian Jones, Dave Coventry, Johnny Cooke, Ben Said. **1963** Vic Andreetti. **1964** Vic Andreetti, Harry Edwards. **1965** Rafiu King, Bunny Grant. **1966** Angel Garcia, Oblitey Commey. **1967** Olli Maki, Mike Cruz. **1969** Tommy Carson, Boerge Krogh, Peter Quinn, Bobby Arthur. **1970** Victor Paul
WON CO (1)	**1960** Pat Loughran
WON RSC/RTD (8)	**1959** John Bacon. **1960** Colin Salcombe, Dick Kiernan, John Davis. **1963** Billy Kid Davis. **1964** Joe Tetteh. **1966** Roger Younsi, Valerio Nunez
DREW (2)	**1960** Dick Kiernan, Ebe Mensah
LOST PTS (5)	**1960** Spike McCormack. **1962** Sammy McSpadden. **1963** Carlos Ortiz. **1968** Joao Henrique. **1969** Eddie Perkins
LOST CO (1)	**1967** Lloyd Marshall

Brian Curvis

Undefeated British & British Empire Welterweight Champion, 1960 – 1966
Born 14.08.37 *From* Swansea (birthname Brian Nancurvis) *Pro Career* 1959 – 1966 (41 contests, won 37, lost 4)

CHAMPIONSHIP CONTESTS (10)

09.05.60	George Barnes	**W** PTS 15	Swansea	BE	Welterweight Title
21.11.60	Wally Swift	**W** PTS 15	Nottingham	B, BE	Welterweight Titles
08.05.61	Wally Swift	**W** PTS 15	Nottingham	B, BE	Welterweight Titles

CONTINUED OVERLEAF

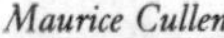

Maurice Cullen

Brian Curvis

31.10.61	Mick Leahy	W CO 8	London	B, BE	Welterweight Titles
20.02.62	Tony Mancini	W RSC 5	London	B, BE	Welterweight Titles
12.02.63	Tony Smith	W RSC 10	London	B, BE	Welterweight Titles
28.07.64	Johnny Cooke	W RTD 5	Porthcawl	B, BE	Welterweight Titles
22.09.64	Emile Griffith	L PTS 15	London	W	Welterweight Title
25.11.65	Sammy McSpadden	W RSC 12	Cardiff	B, BE	Welterweight Titles
25.04.66	Jean Josselin	L RTD 13	Paris	EU	Welterweight Title

NON CHAMPIONSHIP CONTESTS (31)

WON PTS (11)	**1959** Peter Cobblah, Bob Roberts. **1960** Albert Carroll, Al Sharpe. **1961** Luis Folledo. **1962** Guy Sumlin. **1963** Sugar Cliff. **1964** Dave Charnley. **1965** Vince Shomo, Gaspar Ortega. **1966** Tito Marshall
WON CO (2)	**1959** Jack Burley. **1963** Maurice Auzel
WON RSC/RTD (15)	**1959** Harry Haydock, Terry Banning, Reg Fisher, Ron Jackson, Ron Richardson. **1960** Paddy Graham, Terry Burnett, Michel Lombardet, Emile Vlaemynck, Johnny Gorman. **1961** Nino Borra, Maurice Devilliers. **1965** Isaac Logart. **1966** Jose Stable, Des Rea
WON DIS (1)	**1962** Ralph Dupas
LOST PTS (1)	**1965** Willie Ludick
LOST RSC/RTD (1)	**1962** Guy Sumlin

Cliff Curvis

Undefeated British Welterweight Champion, 1952 – 1953. British Empire Welterweight Champion, 1952

Born 20.11.27 *From* Swansea (birthname Cliff Nancurvis) *Pro Career* 1944 – 1953 (55 contests, won 42, drew 1, lost 12)

CHAMPIONSHIP CONTESTS (4)

13.09.50	Eddie Thomas	L PTS 15	Swansea	B	Welterweight Title
24.07.52	Wally Thom	W CO 9	Liverpool	B, BE	Welterweight Titles
08.12.52	Gerald Dreyer	L PTS 15	Johannesburg	BE	Welterweight Title
22.03.53	Gilbert Lavoine	L DIS 10	Paris	EU	Welterweight Title

NON CHAMPIONSHIP CONTESTS (51)

WON PTS (29)	**1945** Vernon Ball, Tommy Plowright, Cliff Anderson, Mickey Colbert. **1946** Cliff Morris, Billy Comerford, Louis Orsini, Eric Powell, Ben Duffy, Frankie Williams, Bert Jackson, Germain Perez, Billy Marlow, Tom Smith. **1947** Johnny Russell, Tommy Davies, Andre Famechon, Jan Nicholaas, Paddy Dowdall, Josef Preys. **1948** Andre Famechon. **1949** Titi Clavel, Job Roos. **1950** Ernie Roderick, Gwyn Williams, Giel de Roode. **1951** Constant Reypens, Titi Clavel. **1952** Danny Womber
WON CO (5)	**1944** Bryn Collins. **1945** Tommy Plowright. **1948** Claude Dennington. **1949** Eddie Cardew. **1951** Billy Rattray
WON RSC/RTD (6)	**1945** Curly Roberts. **1946** Jim Brady. **1947** Ronnie James. **1948** Ivor Germain. **1950** Ric Sanders, Harry Bos
WON DIS (1)	**1951** Danny Womber
DREW (1)	**1951** Kay Kalio
LOST PTS (3)	**1948** Peter Fallon. **1949** Billy Thompson. **1950** Charles Humez
LOST CO (2)	**1946** Al Phillips. **1949** Gwyn Williams
LOST RSC/RTD (2)	**1949** Harry Hughes, Leandre Mateos
LOST DIS (2)	**1946** Frankie Williams. **1951** Wally Thom

Johnny Cusick

British & British Empire Featherweight Champion, 1939 – 1940

Born 27.01.16 *From* Manchester *Pro Career* 1932 – 1949 (73 contests, won 60, drew 3, lost 10)

CHAMPIONSHIP CONTESTS (2)

28.06.39	Jim Spider Kelly	W RSC 12	Belfast	B, BE	Featherweight Titles
01.02.40	Nel Tarleton	L PTS 15	Liverpool	B, BE	Featherweight Titles

Cliff Curvis

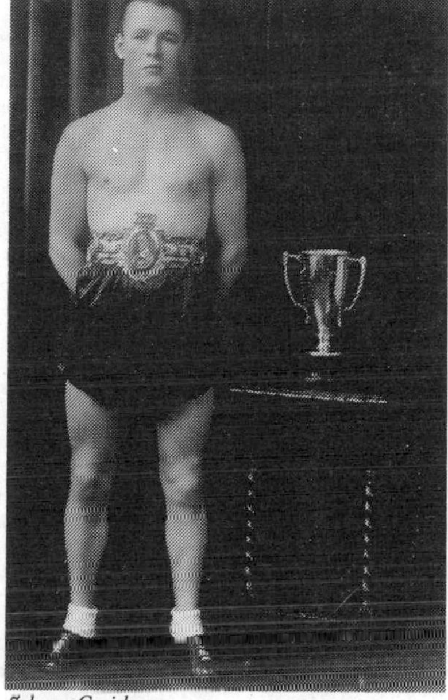

Johnny Cusick

NON CHAMPIONSHIP CONTESTS (71)

WON PTS (49)	**1932** Tim Gregory. **1933** Joe Skelly. **1934** Stan Brown, Boy Egerton, Jake Chadwick, Cyclone Kelly. **1935** Matty Matthews, Arley Hollingsworth, Chris Dillon, Syd Rose, Nipper Mack, George Marsden, Eric Jones, Bob Healey, Billy Miller, Tommy Tune. **1936** Billy Miller, George Marsden, Mog Mason, Nipper Fred Morris, Jackie Brown, Bobby Hindes, Johnny King, Johnny Truesdale, Benny Sharkey, Len Beynon, Harry Edwards. **1937** Tommy Burns, Ginger Roberts, Johnny Kilburn, Frank McCudden, Alex Alston, Benny Caplan, Frank Harsene, Billy Charlton, Jim Spider Kelly. **1938** Jim Spider Kelly, Johnny McGrory, Johnny King, Billy Charlton. **1939** Frank Parkes (2), Bernard Leroux. **1940** Ginger Roberts, Al Lyttle. **1942** Gunboat Jack. **1947** Jimmy Stubbs, Ben Duffy. **1949** Billy Barton
WON CO (3)	**1936** Len Hampston. **1937** Dick Titley, Al Capone
WON RSC/RTD (6)	**1936** Ellis Ashurst, Bobby Magee, Ken Barrett. **1937** Harry Edwards. **1939** Eugene Peyre. **1947** Billy Marlow
WON DIS (1)	**1936** Kayo Morgan
DREW (3)	**1935** Laddie Hines. **1936** Jim McInally. **1942** Cpl Briggs
LOST PTS (6)	**1935** Johnny Roberts. **1936** Jackie Brown. **1937** Dick Corbett. **1938** Benny Caplan. **1939** Tom Smith. **1947** Arthur Machtelinck
LOST CO (1)	**1938** Freddie Miller
LOST DIS (2)	**1938** Benny Sharkey. **1947** Frankie Williams

Johnny Cuthbert

British Featherweight Champion, 1927 – 1928 and 1929 – 1931. British Lightweight Champion, 1932 – 1934
Born 09.07.05 *From* Sheffield *Pro Career* 1921 – 1934 (154 contests, won 110, drew 14, lost 30)

CONTINUED OVERLEAF

CHAMPIONSHIP CONTESTS (10)

24.01.27	Johnny Curley	W PTS 20	London	B	Featherweight Title
12.03.28	Harry Corbert	L PTS 20	London	B	Featherweight Title
18.03.29	Harry Corbett	DREW 15	London	B	Featherweight Title
16.05.29	Harry Corbett	W PTS 15	London	B	Featherweight Title
22.05.30	Dom Volante	W PTS 15	London	B	Featherweight Title
06.11.30	Nel Tarleton	DREW 15	Liverpool	B	Featherweight Title
15.12.30	Al Foreman	DREW 15	London	B, BE	Lightweight Titles
01.10.31	Nel Tarleton	L PTS 15	Liverpool	B	Featherweight Title
11.08.32	Jim Hunter	W CO 10	Glasgow	B	Lightweight Title
18.01.34	Harry Mizler	L PTS 15	London	B	Lightweight Title

NON CHAMPIONSHIP CONTESTS (144)

WON PTS (67)	**1921** Young Hazeltine. **1922** Billy Moss (2), George Wright. **1923** Tiny Smith, Kid Nicholson. **1924** Elky Clark, Walter Stanton, Ted Williams, Kid Anthony, Teddy Murton, Tommy Dowd, Harry Corbett, Billy Hindley. **1925** Charlie Stone, Mick Hill, Young Bull, Jackie Kid Berg (2), Johnny Britton, Jack Dando, Johnny Curley (2), Bugler Lake, Frank Carberry, Norman Radford, Billy Matthews. **1926** Tom Bailey, Wattie Price, Kid Kelly, Jack Slattery, Battling Van Dyk, Jack Jones, Johnny Curley, Fred Green, Harry Corbett, Falgere. **1927** Francois Sybille, Young Johnny Brown (2), Jack Hyams (2), Billy Brown, Edouard Mascart. **1928** Vincent Cerdan, Dom Volante, Eddie Donoghue, Johnny McMillan. **1928** Edouard Mascart, Paul Noack. **1930** Benny Valgar, Aine Gyde, Nobby Baker, Len Tiger Smith, Teddy Brown. **1931** Guy Bonaguere, Chuck Parker. **1932** Chuck Parker, Dom Volante, Norman Dale, Tommy Bland. **1933** Jim Learoyd, Jimmy Stewart, Francois Machtens, Tommy Spiers, Tony Butcher, Joe Kerr
WON CO (11)	**1923** Clarence Booth. **1926** Frank McAloran. **1927** Gustave Humery. **1929** Billy Evans, Billy Streets, Nipper Pat Daly, Peter Cuthbertson. **1930** Len Tiger Smith, Kid Simende. **1931** Frank McAloran, Tommy John
WON RSC/RTD (21)	**1921** H. Millwards. **1923** Jim Hague, Joe Kileen. **1924** Young Fred Welsh, Leo Kelly, Young Lundy. **1926** Jack Cooper, Mick Hill, Bugler Lake, Kej Oslen, Victor Steverlinck. **1927** Willie Minchel, Young Clancy, Horace Barber, Mur Santos. **1928** Fred Merryweather, Cockney Buxton. **1929** Jim Travis. **1930** Roy Beresford. **1933** Little Minor, Ginger Jones
WON DIS (7)	**1923** Johnny Lowry. **1925** Billy Colbourne. **1926** Harry Corbett. **1928** Gustave Humery, Antoine Ascensio. **1931** Al Brown. **1933** Ettore Mortale
DREW (11)	**1923** Harry Leach. **1924** Albert Colcombe. **1925** Jack Cooper. **1926** Frank Carberry, Francois Sybille (2), Harry Corbett. **1927** Teddy Baldock. **1928** Andre Routis, Al Brown. **1929** Benny Valgar
LOST PTS (20)	**1922** Tiny Smith. **1923** Harry Leach, Tom Bailey, Kid Kelly. **1924** Tony Thomas, Tommy Murray. **1925** Bugler Lake, Harry Corbett, Joe Fox. **1926** Frank Harvey. **1927** Knud Larsen (2), Young Johnny Brown. **1929** Dom Volante. **1930** Kid Nicholson. **1932** Cleto Locatelli. **1933** Francois Machtens, Walter Deckman, Jake Kilrain. **1934** Seaman Tommy Watson
LOST CO (4)	**1925** Ernie Swash. **1931** Douglas Parker. **1933** Gustave Humery. **1934** Freddie Miller
LOST RSC/RTD (2)	**1925** Jackie Kid Berg. **1928** Gustave Humery
LOST DIS (1)	**1925** Johnny Brown

NOTE:
The Lonsdale Belt was not issued for the British Championship Contests versus Jim Hunter and Harry Mizler.

Johnny Cuthbert

Dai Dower

Dai Dower

Undefeated British Flyweight Champion, 1955 – 1957. Undefeated British Empire Flyweight Champion, 1954 – 1957. European Flyweight Champion, 1955
Born 26.06.33 *From* Abercynon *Pro Career* 1953 – 1958 (37 contests, won 34, lost 3)

CHAMPIONSHIP CONTESTS (6)

19.10.54	Jake Tuli	W PTS 15	London	BE	Flyweight Title
08.02.55	Eric Marsden	W PTS 15	London	B, BE	Flyweight Titles
08.03.55	Nazzareno Giannelli	W PTS 15	London	EU	Flyweight Title
03.10.55	Young Martin	L CO 12	Nottingham	EU	Flyweight Title
06.12.55	Jake Tuli	W PTS 15	London	BE	Flyweight Title
30.03.57	Pascuel Perez	L CO 1	Buenos Aires	W	Flyweight Title

NON CHAMPIONSHIP CONTESTS (31)

WON PTS (17)	**1953** Colin Clitheroe, Mickey Roche (2), Henry Carpenter, Joe Murphy. **1954** Ogli Tettey (2), Henk Van Der Zee, Alex Bollaert. **1955** Jean Kidy, Robert Mouginot. **1956** Henri Schmid, Robert Meunier, Roberto Tartari, Stanis Sobolak, Pipo Dionisio. **1958** Eric Brett
WON CO (3)	**1953** Alf Smith. **1954** Terry Allen. **1955** Willibald Koch
WON RSC/RTD (9)	**1953** Vernon John, Ron Hughes, Pete Hallberg, Colin Clitheroe, Jimmy Quinn, Joe Cairney. **1954** Franco Lombardozzi, Hilaire Gaviano. **1955** Pierre Gress
WON DIS (1)	**1954** Emile Delphanque
LOST PTS (1)	**1958** Pat Supple

Terry Downes

British Middleweight Champion, 1958 – 1959. Undefeated British Middleweight Champion, 1959 – 1962. World Middleweight Champion, 1961 – 1962
Born 09.05.36 *From* Paddington *Pro Career* 1957 – 1964 (44 contests, won 35, lost 9)

CHAMPIONSHIP CONTESTS (8)

30.09.58	Phil Edwards	W RSC 13	London	B	Middleweight Title
15.09.59	John Cowboy McCormack	L DIS 8	London	B	Middleweight Title

CONTINUED OVERLEAF

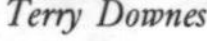

Terry Downes

Richard Dunn

03.11.59	John Cowboy McCormack	W RSC 8	London	B	Middleweight Title
05.07.60	Phil Edwards	W RTD 12	London	B	Middleweight Title
14.01.61	Paul Pender	L RSC 7	Boston	W	Middleweight Title
11.07.61	Paul Pender	W RTD 9	London	W	Middleweight Title
07.04.62	Paul Pender	L PTS 15	Boston	W	Middleweight Title
30.11.64	Willie Pastrano	L RSC 11	Manchester	W	L. Heavyweight Title

NON CHAMPIONSHIP CONTESTS (36)

WON PTS (7)	**1957** Lew Lazar. **1958** Tuzo Portuguez, Pat McAteer. **1960** Joey Giardello. **1962** Don Fullmer, Sugar Ray Robinson. **1964** Ed Zaremba
WON CO (6)	**1957** Peter Longo, George Lavery. **1959** Andre Davier. **1960** Orlando di Pietro, Richard Bouchez. **1963** Rudi Nehring
WON RSC/RTD (18)	**1957** Jim Lynas, Allan Dean, Sammy Hamilton, John Woollard, Derek Liversidge, Eddie Phillips, Hamouda Bouraoui. **1958** Serge Leveque, Dennis Booty, Ben Salah Farhat, Constant Alcantara, Mohamed Taibi. **1960** Carlos Vanneste. **1961** Willie Greene, Tony Montano. **1962** Phil Moyer. **1963** Jimmy Beecham, Mike Pusateri
LOST PTS (1)	**1957** Les Allen
LOST RSC/RTD (4)	**1957** Dick Tiger. **1958** Freddie Cross, Spider Webb. **1959** Michel Diouf

Richard Dunn

British & Commonwealth Heavyweight Champion, 1975 – 1976. European Heavyweight Champion, 1976
Born 19.01.45 *From* Bradford *Pro Career* 1969 – 1977 (45 contests, won 33, lost 12)

CHAMPIONSHIP CONTESTS (5)

30.09.75	Bunny Johnson	W PTS 15	London	B, C	Heavyweight Titles
04.11.75	Danny McAlinden	W CO 2	London	B, C	Heavyweight Titles
06.04.76	Bernd August	W RSC 3	London	EU	Heavyweight Title
25.05.76	Mohammad Ali	L RSC 5	Munich	W	Heavyweight Title
12.10.76	Joe Bugner	L CO 1	London	B, C, EU	Heavyweight Titles

NON CHAMPIONSHIP CONTESTS (40)

WON PTS (15)	**1969** Del Phillips, Billy Aird, John Cullen, Lloyd Walford. **1970** Obe Hepburn, Billy Wynter. **1971** Brian Jewitt, Bunny Johnson, Dennis Forbes,

Joe Erskine

Tommy Farr

	Carl Gizzi. **1972** Roger Tighe, Ray Patterson. **1973** Roy Williams, Billy Aird. **1974** Tim Wood
WON CO (8)	**1970** Dennis Forbes. **1972** Ron Oliver, Larry Renaud. **1973** John Griffin, Larry Beilfuss. **1975** Terry Krueger
WON RSC/RTD (8)	**1969** Jack Cotes (2), George Dulaire. **1970** Obe Hepburn. **1971** Cliff Field. **1974** Obie English. **1975** Neville Meade, Rocky Campbell
WON DIS (1)	**1973** Rufus Brassell
LOST PTS (1)	**1970** Billy Aird
LOST CO (6)	**1969** Danny McAlinden. **1971** Rocky Campbell. **1973** Bunny Johnson. **1974** Ngozika Ekwelum, Jose Urtain. **1977** Kallie Knoetze
LOST RSC/RTD (3)	**1970** Billy Aird, George Dulaire. **1974** Jimmy Young

Joe Erskine

British Heavyweight Champion, 1956 – 1958. British Empire Heavyweight Champion, 1957 – 1958
Born 26.01.34 *From* Cardiff *Pro Career* 1954 – 1964 (54 contests, won 45, drew 1, lost 8)

CHAMPIONSHIP CONTESTS (8)

27.08.56	Johnny Williams	W PTS 15	Cardiff	B	Heavyweight Title
17.09.57	Henry Cooper	W PTS 15	London	B	Heavyweight Title
25.11.57	Joe Bygraves	W PTS 15	Leicester	BE	Heavyweight Title
21.02.58	Ingemar Johansson	L RTD 13	Gothenberg	EU	Heavyweight Title
03.06.58	Brian London	L CO 8	London	B, BE	Heavyweight Titles
17.11.59	Henry Cooper	L RSC 12	London	B, BE	Heavyweight Titles
21.03.61	Henry Cooper	L RTD 5	London	B, BE	Heavyweight Titles
02.04.62	Henry Cooper	L RSC 9	Nottingham	B, BE	Heavyweight Titles

NON CHAMPIONSHIP CONTESTS (46)

WON PTS (27)	**1954** Frank Walshaw, Mick Cowan, Denny Ball (2), Jim Moran, Dennis Lockton, Morry Bush, Cliff Purnell. **1955** Cliff Purnell, Joe Crickmar, Peter Bates, Ansel Adams, Uber Bacillieri, Henry Cooper. **1956** Marcel Limage, Gunther Nurnberg, Dick Richardson. **1957** Peter Bates. **1958** Max Brianto. **1959** Willie Pastrano, Dick Richardson, Bruno Scarabellin. **1961** Ulli Ritter. **1962** Mariano Echevarria. **1963** Freddie Mack. **1964** Jack Bodell, Johnny Prescott

CONTINUED OVERLEAF

WON CO (2)	**1954** Alf Price. **1955** Baby de Voogd
WON RSC/RTD (11)	**1954** Tommy Rodgers, Joe Farley, Eddie Keith, Frank Walker. **1955** Hugh McDonald, Simon Templar, Antonio Crosia, Al Bernard. **1960** Jose Gonzalez. **1962** Alex Barrow. **1963** Ray Cillien
WON DIS (2)	**1954** Frank Walker. **1961** Geo Chuvalo
DREW (1)	**1954** Dinny Powell
LOST PTS (2)	**1963** Karl Mildenberger. **1964** Billy Walker
LOST RSC/RTD (1)	**1957** Nino Valdes

Tommy Farr

Undefeated British & British Empire Heavyweight Champion, 1937 – 1938
Born 12.03.14 *From* Tonypandy *Pro Career* 1926 – 1953 (122 contests, won 78, drew 13, lost 29, no decision 2)

CHAMPIONSHIP CONTESTS (3)

04.02.35	Eddie Phillips	L PTS 15	Mountain Ash	B	L. Heavyweight Title
15.03.37	Ben Foord	W PTS 15	London	B, BE	Heavyweight Titles
30.08.37	Joe Louis	L PTS 15	New York	W	Heavyweight Title

NON CHAMPIONSHIP CONTESTS (119)

WON PTS (52)	**1926** Jack Jones. **1927** Cliff Smith. **1928** Young Hazell. **1929** Tom Thomas, Herbie Hill, Tom Herbert, Kid Evans, Tom Howley, Billy Jones, Cliff Llewellyn. **1930** Emlyn Jones, Steve Donoghue, Herb Morse. **1931** Jack Powell. **1932** Charlie Bundy. **1933** Bunny Eddington (2), Jerry Daley, Charlie Bundy, Billy Thomas, Tony Arpino, George Smith, Tiger Ellis, Ernie Simmons, Randy Jones, Tom Benjamin, Seaman Harvey, Leo Evans. **1934** Jim Winters, Charlie Belanger, Charlie Bundy, Eddie Pierce. **1935** Eddie Wenstob (2), Pavesi Presidio, George Brennan (2), Renus de Boer. **1936** Tommy Loughran, Peter Van Goole, Bob Olin, Charlie Rutz. **1937** Max Baer. **1939** Red Burman. **1951** Gerry McDermott, Steve McCall, Robert Eugene, Georges Rogiers. **1952** Giorgio Milan, Georges Rogiers, Joe Weidin, Al Hoosman
WON CO (11)	**1934** Kid Scott, Pat McAuliffe. **1935** Arthur Novell, Pavesi Presidio, Frank Moody. **1936** Jim Wilde. **1937** Joe Zeeman, Walter Neusel. **1939** Manuel Abrew. **1950** Jan Klein, Piet Wilde
WON RSC/RTD (13)	**1929** Eddie Worton. **1930** Billy Thomas. **1933** Randy Jones, Gunner Bennett, Jack O'Brien, Charlie Chetwynd, Jack Marshall, Steve McCall. **1934** Seaman Harvey. **1935** Manuel Abrew. **1939** Larry Gains. **1940** Zachy Nicholas. **1951** Dennis Powell
WON DIS (1)	**1930** Jack Powell
DREW (13)	**1927** Kid Denham, S. Hewers. **1928** Young Grocutt. **1929** Len Jones, Idris Pugh, Trevor Herbert (2). **1930** Billy Pritchard. **1931** Bryn Powell. **1932** Jerry Daley. **1934** Ernie Simmons. **1935** Frank Moody. **1936** Jim Wilde
LOST PTS (20)	**1927** Alby Davies. **1928** Evan Lane, Young Grocutt. **1929** Kid Spurdle, Idris Pugh. **1930** Lew Haydn, Walt Saunders. **1932** Albert Donovan. **1933** Billy Thomas. **1934** Eddie Phillips, Jack Casey, Charlie Belanger, Dave Carstens. **1938** James J. Bradock, Max Baer, Lou Nova. **1939** Red Burman. **1950** Lloyd Marshall. **1951** Al Hoosman. **1952** Werner Wiegand
LOST CO (1)	**1951** Frank Bell
LOST RSC/RTD (5)	**1928** Evan Lane, Albie Davies. **1933** Eddie Steele. **1938** Josh Sullivan. **1953**Don Cockell
LOST DIS (1)	**1934** Eddie Phillips
ND (2)	**1927** Dai Davies, Young Howe

NOTE:
The Lonsdale Belt was not issued for the British Championship Contest versus Eddie Phillips.

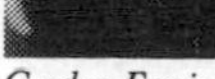

Gordon Ferris

Albert Finch

Gordon Ferris

British Heavyweight Champion, 1981
Born 21.11.52 *From* Enniskillen *Pro Career* 1977 – 1982 (26 contests, won 20, lost 6)

CHAMPIONSHIP CONTESTS (2)

30.03.81	Billy Aird	W PTS 15	Birmingham	B	Heavyweight Title
12.10.81	Neville Meade	L CO 1	Birmingham	B	Heavyweight Title

NON CHAMPIONSHIP CONTESTS (24)

WON PTS (8)	**1978** Terry O'Connor. **1979** Austin Okoye, Bonny McKenzie, Ricky James. **1980** Billy Aird, Tommy Kiely. **1981** Larry McDonald. **1982** Barry Funches
WON CO (7)	**1977** Keith Johnson. **1978** Tony Monaghan, Eddie Fenton, Martin Nee. **1979** Stan McDermott, Terry Mintus. **1980** Mohammed Galoul
WON RSC/RTD (4)	**1979** Ricky James, Austin Okoye. **1981** Dwain Bonds. **1982** Stuart Lithgo
LOST PTS (2)	**1978** Robert Desnouck. **1979** Stan McDermott
LOST CO (1)	**1982** David Pearce
LOST RSC/RTD (2)	**1978** George Scott. **1980** Sylvain Watbled

Albert Finch

British Middleweight Champion, 1949 – 1950
Born 16.05.26 *From* Croydon *Pro Career* 1945 – 1958 (103 contests, won 72, drew 9, lost 21, no contest 1)

CHAMPIONSHIP CONTESTS (6)

20.06.49	Dick Turpin	L PTS 15	Birmingham	B, BE	Middleweight Titles
24.04.50	Dick Turpin	W PTS 15	Nottingham	B	Middleweight Title
17.10.50	Randy Turpin	L CO 5	London	B	Middleweight Title
16.10.51	Don Cockell	L CO 7	London	B, EU	L. Heavyweight Titles
09.11.54	Alex Buxton	L CO 8	Birmingham	B	L. Heavyweight Titles
13.03.56	Ron Barton	L RTD 8	London	B	L. Heavyweight Title

CONTINUED OVERLEAF

NON CHAMPIONSHIP CONTESTS (96)

WON PTS (49)	**1945** Gordon Griffiths, Ted Barter, Jim Hockley, Jack Lewis (2), Jim Laverick. **1946** Jim Hockley (2), Paddy Roche (2), Billy Cottrell, Frank Hayes (2), Johnny Blake, Jimmy Stewart, Harry Groves, Alby Hollister, Tommy Braddick. **1947** Ginger Sadd, Jimmy Ingle, Freddie Price, Al Marson, Geoff Heath. **1948** Randy Turpin, George Dilkes, Bert Sanders, Mark Hart. **1949** Des Jones, Bert Hyland, Bert Sanders, George Ross, Albert Heyen. **1950** Joe Beckett, Eli Elandon, Albert Heyen. **1951** Reg Spring, Jackie Harris, Don Mogard, Paddy Slavin. **1952** Garnett Denny, Brian Anders. **1953** Johnny Barton, Charles Colin, Jimmy Davis. **1954** Joe Bygraves. **1955** Charles Colin. **1956** Serge Leveque. **1957** Terence Murphy, Tony Dove
WON CO (3)	**1945** Cyril Johnson. **1949** Bob Cleaver, Jimmy Ingle
WON RSC/RTD (18)	**1946** Billy Cottrell, Paddy Roche. **1947** Bert Hyland, Pat Mulcahy. **1948** Jock Taylor, Duggie Myers. **1950** Juan Torrecillas, Dick Turpin. **1951** Johnny McGowan, Dave Williams, Bill Wood. **1952** Gene Fowler, Michel Lapourielle. **1953** Dave Williams, Billy Dean. **1954** Arthur Howard, Marcel Limage. **1956** Andre Cottyn
WON DIS (1)	**1957** Jim Cooper
DREW (9)	**1945** Eddie Starrs. **1950** Allan Cooke, Mel Brown, Cyrille Delannoit. **1953** Arthur Howard. **1955** Fred Powell. **1956** Uwe Janssen. **1958** Jack Whittaker, Ron Redrup
LOST PTS (10)	**1946** Vince Hawkins, Mark Hart. **1947** Mark Hart. **1949** Luc Van Dam, Bert Hyland. **1950** Baby Day. **1953** Wim Snoek, Dennis Powell. **1957** Erich Schoeppner, Willie Armstrong
LOST CO (3)	**1952** George Walker. **1957** Manuel Burgo. **1958** Noel Trigg
LOST RSC/RTD (2)	**1946** Harry Watson. **1953** Gerhard Hecht
LOST DIS (1)	**1952** George Walker
NC (1)	**1947** Jack Johnson

Chris Finnegan

British L. Heavyweight Champion, 1971 – 1973 and Undefeated British L. Heavyweight Champion, 1975. Commonwealth L. Heavyweight Champion, 1971 – 1973. European L. Heavyweight Champion, 1972

Born 05.06.44 *From* Iver *Pro Career* 1968 – 1975 (37 contests, won 29, drew 1, lost 7)

CHAMPIONSHIP CONTESTS (12)

27.08.70	Tom Bogs	L PTS 15	Copenhagen	EU	Middleweight Title
24.01.71	Eddie Avoth	W RSC 15	London	B, C	L. Heavyweight Titles
05.05.71	Conny Velensek	DREW 15	Berlin	EU	L. Heavyweight Title
01.02.72	Conny Velensek	W PTS 15	Nottingham	EU	L. Heavyweight Title
06.06.72	Jan Lubbers	W CO 8	London	EU	L. Heavyweight Title
26.09.72	Bob Foster	L CO 14	London	W	L. Heavyweight Title
14.11.72	Rudiger Schmidtke	L RSC 12	London	EU	L. Heavyweight Title
13.03.73	Roy John	W PTS 15	London	B, C	L. Heavyweight Titles
22.05.73	John Conteh	L PTS 15	London	B, C, EU	L. Heavyweight Titles
21.05.74	John Conteh	L RSC 6	London	B, C, EU	L. Heavyweight Titles
03.06.75	Johnny Frankham	L PTS 15	London	B	L. Heavyweight Title
14.10.75	Johnny Frankham	W PTS 15	London	B	L. Heavyweight Title

NON CHAMPIONSHIP CONTESTS (25)

WON PTS (10)	**1969** Dervan Airey, Liam Dolan, Ronnie Hough, Harry Scott. **1970** Guerrino Scattolin. **1971** Hal Carroll. **1972** Ronnie Wilson. **1973** Mike Quarry. **1974** Harold Richardson, Victor Attivor
WON RSC/RTD (14)	**1968** Mick Fleetham, Dick Griffiths. **1969** Larry Brown, Brendan Ingle. **1970** Francisco Ferri, Ray Brittle, Hans Dieter Schwartz, Dervan Airey, Clarence Cassius. **1971** Pete Riccitelli, Bob Benoit, Roger Rouse. **1972** Jerry Evans. **1973** Brian Kelly
LOST RSC/RTD (1)	**1969** Danny Ashie

Kevin Finnegan

British Middleweight Champion, 1974 – 1975 and 1977. Undefeated British Middleweight Champion, 1979 – 1980. European Middleweight Champion, 1974 – 1975 and 1980
Born 18.04.48 *From* Iver *Pro Career* 1970 – 1980 (47 contests, won 35, drew 1, lost 11)

CHAMPIONSHIP CONTESTS (11)

11.02.74	Bunny Sterling	W PTS 15	London	B	Middleweight Title
27.05.74	Jean-Claude Bouttier	W PTS 15	Paris	EU	Middleweight Title
07.05.75	Gratien Tonna	L PTS 15	Monte Carlo	EU	Middleweight Title
04.11.75	Alan Minter	L PTS 15	London	B	Middleweight Title
14.09.76	Alan Minter	L PTS 15	London	B	Middleweight Title
31.05.77	Frankie Lucas	W RSC 11	London	B	Middleweight Title
08.11.77	Alan Minter	L PTS 15	London	B	Middleweight Title
06.11.79	Tony Sibson	W PTS 15	London	B	Middleweight Title
07.02.80	Gratien Tonna	W PTS 12	Paris	EU	Middleweight Title
14.05.80	Georg Steinherr	DREW 12	Munich	EU	Middleweight Title
10.09.80	Matteo Salvemini	L PTS 12	San Remo	EU	Middleweight Title

NON CHAMPIONSHIP CONTESTS (36)

WON PTS (18)	**1971** Gerald Gooding, Clive Cook, Dick Duffy, Pat Dwyer. **1972** Harry Scott, Tom Bell, Eric Blake, Carlos Marks. **1973** Pat McCann, Alvin Anderson, Frank Young. **1974** Frank Reiche. **1976** Oscar Angus (2), Alex Tompkins. **1977** Karl Vinson. **1978** Bobby Patterson. **1979** Abel Cordova
WON CO (2)	**1973** Ronnie Hough. **1976** Freddie de Kerpel
WON RSC/RTD (10)	**1970** Bill Deasy, Maurice Thomas. **1971** Dave Ivory, Mick O'Neill. **1972** Dave Cranswick, Len Gibbs. **1973** Leon Washington, Bob Murphy. **1974** Eddie Mazon. **1976** Danny McCafferty
LOST PTS (1)	**1978** Ayub Kalule
LOST RSC/RTD (5)	**1971** Ronnie Hough. **1972** Don McMillan. **1978** Marvin Hagler (2). **1979** Charlie Weir

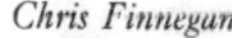

Chris Finnegan

Kevin Finnegan

Ben Foord

British & British Empire Heavyweight Champion, 1936 – 1937
Born 21.01.13 *From* Vrede, South Africa *Died* 1942 *Pro Career* 1932 – 1940 (59 contests, won 40, drew 4, lost 15)

CHAMPIONSHIP CONTESTS (2)

17.08.36	Jack Petersen	W RSC 3	Leicester	B, BE	Heavyweight Titles
15.03.37	Tommy Farr	L PTS 15	London	B, BE	Heavyweight Titles

NON CHAMPIONSHIP CONTESTS (57)

WON PTS (17)	**1932** Bill Horn. **1933** Clyde Chastain (2), Vince Parille, Charlie Smith, Hans Schonrath, Jack London. **1935** Jack London, Harry Staal, Larry Gains. **1936** Roy Lazer, Tommy Loughran, Larry Gains. **1938** Jim Wilde. **1939** Butch Everett, James J. Britt. **1940** Tom Porter
WON CO (15)	**1932** Billy Miller, Dick Manz, Battling Jack Grayling, Jack Vaney, Alec Storbeck. **1934** Eddie Phillips, Willie Storm, Alf Luxton. **1935** Frank Borrington (2), Gunner Bennett, Frank Moody, Guardsman Brown. **1936** George Cook, Manuel Abrew
WON RSC/RTD (5)	**1932** Ben Oosthuizen. **1933** Tommy Tucker. **1935** Harry Staal, Jack Pettifer, Pancho Villar
WON DIS (2)	**1934** Bill Horn. **1938** Manuel Abrew
DREW (4)	**1932** Bill Horn, Dave Carstens. **1934** Pavesi Presidio. **1935** Eddie Wenstob
LOST PTS (8)	**1932** Johnny Squires. **1933** Clyde Chastain. **1935** Norman Baines, Gunner Barlund, Roy Lazer. **1936** Walter Neusel. **1938** Max Schmeling. **1940** Tommy Bensch
LOST CO (2)	**1938** Eddie Phillips, George James
LOST RSC/RTD (3)	**1934** Jack Petersen. **1935** Maurice Strickland. **1937** Max Baer

NOTE:
The Lonsdale Belt was not issued for the British Championship Contest versus Jack Petersen.

Al Foreman

Undefeated British Lightweight Champion, 1930 – 1932. British Empire Lightweight Champion, 1930 – 1933. Undefeated British Empire Lightweight Champion, 1933 – 1934
Born 03.11.04 *From* Bow *Died* 1954 (birthname Albert Harris) *Pro Career* 1920 – 1934 (164 contests, won 133, drew 11, lost 20)

CHAMPIONSHIP CONTESTS (5)

21.05.30	Fred Webster	W CO 1	London	B, BE	Lightweight Titles
20.10.30	George Rose	W CO 6	Manchester	B, BE	Lightweight Titles
15.12.30	Johnny Cuthbert	DREW 15	London	B, BE	Lightweight Titles
24.04.33	Jimmy Kelso	L PTS 15	Sydney	BE	Lightweight Title
22.05.33	Jimmy Kelso	W DIS 3	Sydney	BE	Lightweight Title

NON CHAMPIONSHIP CONTESTS (159)

WON PTS (43)	**1920** Sgnt Stanton, Harry Jackson, Johnny Morelli, Sam Butcher, Tom Weller, Bob Pierce, Sam Wooten. **1921** Harry Bell, George Handley, Tom Cherry, Young Pucker, Arthur Partridge, George Marston, Barney Brown, Bill Dobson. **1922** Young Pucker, Young Partridge, Billy Palmer, Harry Pullen, Arthur Partridge, Johnny Murton, Gus Legge. **1923** Kid Russell. **1924** Kid Gagnon, Kid Lewis. **1925** Freddie Jacks. **1926** Bud Mangino, Izzy Cooper, Harry Brooks, Joe Souza. **1927** Joe Williams, Frankie Fink, Armando Santiago. **1928** Jimmy Hackley. **1929** Silvio Mireault. **1930** Maurice Holtzer. **1931** Selwyn Davies, Norman Dale. **1932** Jim Learoyd, Selwyn Davies, Bert Osborne, Bobby Blay. **1933** Jimmy Bland
WON CO (65)	**1920** Private Saunders, Private Abel, Private Stewart, Ace Scott, Arthur Johnson, Harry Fuller, Jimmy Ryan, Danny Morgan, Bill Kennedy. **1921** Bill Shepherd, Jim Smith, Alex Brown, Bill Perry, Ted Treloar,

Ben Foord

Al Foreman

	Jack Josephs, Barney Brown. **1922** Sid Whatley, Bill Wooder, Tommy Hughes, George Nolan. **1923** George Neilan. **1924** Georges Gerardin, Billy Hines, Eddie de Simon. **1925** Andy Bowen, Joe Rivers, Billy Miske, Kid Julien, Patsy McNulty, Tony Cortez, Walter Vance, Bill Kline. **1926** Dick Houle, Goldie Ahearn, Jimmy Monroe, Arthur Robilo, Young Phillips. **1927** Ruby Stein, Mike Ballerino, Joe Williams, Armand Shackles, Babe Picato. **1928** Don Davis, Tommy Mitchell, Ruby Levine, Bill Kline, George Chabot. **1929** Johnny Dundee, Frank Erne, Frisco Bautista. **1930** Roy Beresford, Douglas Parker, Len Tiger Smith, Harry Brooks, Sam Hatchett, Mickey Genaro. **1931** Aine Gyde, Heinrich Muller. **1932** Fred Chandler, Tommy McMillan, Tommy Little, Lew Pinkus. **1933** Cecil Kid Como, Bobby Watson, Bobby Allen
WON RSC/RTD (18)	**1921** Bob Finch, Harry Bell, Tommy Burns, George Ratty, Young Pucker. **1922** Frank Morgan, Jimmy Sherratt, Len Kemp. **1923** Fred Bullions. **1927** Russ Klump, Billy Herald. **1928** Leo Kid Roy. **1930** Pete Zivic. **1931** Guiseppe Branca, Joe Cadman, Harry Berry. **1932** Glyn Mainwaring, Jim Travis
WON DIS (4)	**1921** Charlie Duggan. **1922** Kid Davis. **1927** Carl Tremaine. **1928** Jimmy Hackley
DREW (10)	**1921** Barney Brown, Sam Wooten, Albert Hicks, Billy Palmer. **1922** Ernie Izzard, Johnny Brown, Billy Palmer, Battling Van Dyk. **1925** Lew Haywood. **1929** Phil McGraw
LOST PTS (16)	**1921** Bill Owen. **1922** Tom Cherry (2), George Marston. **1923** Billy Palmer, Fred Bullions, Silvio Mireault. **1924** Silvio Mireault, Leo Kid Roy, Ted Cassette. **1927** Louis Kid Kaplan. **1928** Jimmy Hackley. **1929** Billy Townsend. **1932** Nel Tarleton. **1933** Jimmy Kelso. **1934** Petey Sarron
LOST RSC/RTD (2)	**1923** Johnny Curley. **1933** Joe Ghnouly
LOST DIS (1)	**1923** Billy Palmer

NOTE:
The Lonsdale Belt was not issued for the British Championship Contest versus Fred Webster.

Johnny Frankham

Jack Gardner

Johnny Frankham

British L. Heavyweight Champion, 1975
Born 06.06.48 *From* Reading *Pro Career* 1970 – 1976 (40 contests, won 28, drew 1, lost 1)

CHAMPIONSHIP CONTESTS (2)

03.06.75	Chris Finnegan	**W** PTS 15	London	B	L. Heavyweight Title
14.10.75	Chris Finnegan	L PTS 15	London	B	L. Heavyweight Title

NON CHAMPIONSHIP CONTESTS (38)

WON PTS (22)	**1970** John Newman, Clarence Cassius, Keith Drewett (2). **1971** Phil Matthews, Keith Drewett (2), Bob Tuckett, Guinea Roger, Dave Hawkes, Brian Jewitt, Ba Sounkalo. **1972** Karl Zurheide, Ruben Figueroa, Herschel Jacobs, Wendell Joseph. **1973** Devil Green, Bob Tuckett. **1974** Danny Fontillio. **1975** Phil Matthews, Armand Xhonneux. **1976** Danny Fontillio
WON RSC/RTD (5)	**1970** Fred Drinnan. **1971** Dervan Airey, Eddie Owens. **1973** Tommy Hicks, Tom Jensen
DREW (1)	**1972** Eddie Duncan
LOST PTS (9)	**1972** Tom Bethea, Roy John. **1973** Pat McCann, Tom Bogs. **1974** Pat McCann, Kosie Smith, Tom Jensen. **1975** Freddie de Kerpel, Phil Martin
LOST RSC/RTD (1)	**1970** Geoff Shaw

Jack Gardner

British & British Empire Heavyweight Champion, 1950 – 1952. European Heavyweight Champion, 1951
Born 06.11.26 *From* Market Harborough *Died* 1978 *Pro Career* 1948 – 1956 (34 contests, won 28, lost 6)

CHAMPIONSHIP CONTESTS (4)

14.11.50	Bruce Woodcock	**W** RTD 11	London	B, BE	Heavyweight Titles
27.03.51	Joe Weidin	**W** PTS 15	London	EU	Heavyweight Title
23.09.51	Hein Ten Hoff	L PTS 15	Berlin	EU	Heavyweight Title
11.03.52	Johnny Williams	L PTS 15	London	B, BE	Heavyweight Titles

NON CHAMPIONSHIP CONTESTS (30)

WON PTS (4)	**1949** Stephane Olek. **1950** Johnny Williams. **1954** Ansel Adams. **1955** Kitione Lave
WON CO (8)	**1948** Ron Raynor. **1949** Matt Hardy, Gene Fowler, Bill Brennan, Tommy Brown, Charlie Collett. **1950** Robert Eugene. **1955** Johnny Williams

Teddy Gardner

Freddie Gilroy

WON RSC/RTD (14)	**1948** Hugh O'Reilly, Harry Bedford. **1949** Nick Fisher, Les Pam, Johnny Morkus, Frank Ronan, Ken Shaw, Frank Walker, Prosper Beck, Nisse Andersson, Robert Eugene. **1953** Uber Bacilieri. **1954** Frank Bell, Lucien Touzard
LOST PTS (2)	**1950** Vern Escoe. **1951** Cesar Brion
LOST RSC/RTD (2)	**1949** Vern Escoe. **1956** Joe Bygraves

Teddy Gardner

Undefeated British & European Flyweight Champion, 1952. British Empire Flyweight Champion, 1952
Born 27.1.22 *From* West Hartlepool *Died* 1977 *Pro Career* 1934 – 1952 (71 contests, won 56, drew 5, lost 10)

CHAMPIONSHIP CONTESTS (5)

13.12.49	Danny O'Sullivan	L RTD 9	London	B	Bantamweight Title
18.02.52	Louis Skena	W CO 6	Newcastle	EU	Flyweight Title
17.03.52	Terry Allen	W PTS 15	Newcastle	B, BE, EU	Flyweight Titles
30.06.52	Otello Belardinelli	W PTS 15	Hartlepool	EU	Flyweight Title
08.09.52	Jake Tuli	L RSC 12	Newcastle	BE	Flyweight Title

NON CHAMPIONSHIP CONTESTS (66)

WON PTS (42)	**1934** Kid Ashcroft. **1939** Billy Charnock, Harry Godfrey (2), Matt English, Frank Lobley, Harry Parkes. **1940** Wally Knightley, Barney Cullen. **1943** Pat Palmer. **1944** Mickey Jones, Billy Hamilton. **1945** Vernon Ball, Baby Bassett, The Steamboat, Battling Siki, Buddy Yasmin. **1946** Jeff Smith, Jack Mussen, Joe Collins. **1947** Jack Mussen, Len Shaw. **1948** Jackie Horseman, Jimmy Gill, Bunty Doran, Jackie Paterson, Gaston Van Den Bos, Sammy Reynolds. **1949** Jimmy Stewart, Eddie Carson, Norman Lewis, Stan Rowan. **1950** Hannes Schneider, Henry Carpenter, Black Pico, Dickie O'Sullivan. **1951** Honore Pratesi, Louis Skena, Kalla Persson, Joe Murphy, Vic Herman. **1952** Maurice Sandeyron
WON CO (1)	**1938** Jack Herbert
WON RSC/RTD (10)	**1938** Tommy Scott. **1939** Carlo Aldini. **1940** Matt English. **1946** Jackie Rees, Stan Mace. **1947** Joe Josephs. **1950** Billy Ashton, Robert Mouginot. **1951** Charles Bohbot, Joe Cairney
DREW (5)	**1934** Kid Morris, Johnny Mustard. **1945** Young Tarley. **1946** Tommy Burns. **1950** Henry Carpenter
LOST PTS (5)	**1934** Kid Morris. **1938** Kid Rich. **1948** Gus Foran, Bunty Doran. **1949** Jimmy Green

CONTINUED OVERLEAF

LOST CO (1) — **1935** Johnny Curry
LOST RSC/RTD (2) — **1939** Paddy Gill. **1950** Fernando Gagnon

Freddie Gilroy

Undefeated British & British Empire Bantamweight Champion, 1959 – 1962. European Bantamweight Champion, 1959 – 1960
Born 07.03.36 *From* Belfast *Pro Career* 1957 – 1962 (31 contests, won 28, lost 3)

CHAMPIONSHIP CONTESTS (8)

10.01.59	Peter Keenan	W RSC 11	Belfast	B, BE	Bantamweight Titles
03.11.59	Piero Rollo	W PTS 15	London	EU	Bantamweight Title
05.12.59	Bernie Taylor	W CO 5	Belfast	BE	Bantamweight Title
19.03.60	Billy Rafferty	W RSC 13	Belfast	B, BE, EU	Bantamweight Titles
25.10.60	Alphonse Halimi	L PTS 15	London	W	Bantamweight Title
27.05.61	Pierre Cossemyns	L RTD 9	Brussels	EU	Bantamweight Title
03.03.62	Billy Rafferty	W CO 12	Belfast	B, BE	Bantamweight Titles
20.10.62	Johnny Caldwell	W RTD 9	Belfast	B, BE	Bantamweight Titles

NON CHAMPIONSHIP CONTESTS (23)

WON PTS (9)	**1957** Jackie Tiller. **1958** Kimpo Amarfio, Geo Bowes, Jose Martinez. **1959** Al Asuncion, Mario D'Agata. **1961** Ugo Milan, Billy Calvert. **1962** Rene Libeer
WON CO (8)	**1957** Derek McReynolds, Danny McNamee, Jim Creswell, Terry McHale, Archie Downie. **1958** Pierre Cossemyns. **1959** Charles Sylla. **1961** Jackie Brown
WON RSC/RTD (5)	**1957** Jose Alvarez, George O'Neill. **1958** Johnny Morrissey. **1959** Jacques Colomb. **1961** Boualem Belouard
LOST PTS (1)	**1960** Ignacio Pina

NOTE:
The World Championship Contest versus Alphonse Halimi was for the GB/EBU version Title.

Tommy Glencross

British Featherweight Champion, 1972 – 1973
Born 31.07.47 *From* Glasgow *Pro Career* 1967 – 1978 (48 contests, won 31, drew 1, lost 16)

CHAMPIONSHIP CONTESTS (4)

17.05.72	Jose Legra	L PTS 15	Birmingham	EU	Featherweight Title
25.09.72	Evan Armstrong	W PTS 15	London	B	Featherweight Title
12.05.73	Gitano Jiminez	L PTS 15	Gijon	EU	Featherweight Title
17.09.73	Evan Armstrong	L RSC 3	Glasgow	B	Featherweight Title

NON CHAMPIONSHIP CONTESTS (44)

WON PTS (22)	**1967** Roger Adolph, Bernard Nicholls, Billy Hardacre, Sonny McNorthy. **1968** Ossie O'Connor, Frank Fitzgerald. **1969** Gerry McBride, Roger Howes. **1970** Kenny Cooper, Billy Hardacre (2), Valentin Loren. **1971** Tony Cunningham (2), Sammy Lockhart. **1972** Jean-Claude Demarthe. **1976** Barton McAllister (2), Tommy Wright, John Gillan, Billy Belnavis, Alun Trembath
WON CO (1)	**1972** Valentin Loren
WON RSC/RTD (7)	**1967** Frank Fitzgerald. **1969** Billy Surgenor, Jimmy Allen. **1970** Pat Pain. **1971** Tony Cunningham, Sammy Lockhart. **1976** Martyn Galleozzie
DREW (1)	**1972** Jimmy Bell
LOST PTS (6)	**1970** Bob Allotey. **1973** Bingo Crooks, Billy Waith. **1974** Charlie Nash. **1977** Willie Booth, Granville Allen
LOST RSC/RTD (6)	**1974** Bingo Crooks. **1976** Vernon Sollas, Cecillo Lastra. **1977** Colin Power, Cornelius Boza-Edwards. **1978** Joey Singleton
LOST DIS (1)	**1977** Granville Allen

Dave Boy Green

Undefeated British & European L. Welterweight Champion, 1976 – 1977. European Welterweight Champion, 1979

Born 02.06.53 *From* Chatteris *Pro Career* 1974 – 1981 (41 contests, won 37, lost 4)

CHAMPIONSHIP CONTESTS (6)

01.06.76	Joey Singleton	**W** RSC 6	London	B	L. Welterweight Title
07.12.76	Jean-Baptiste Piedvache	**W** RTD 9	London	EU	L. Welterweight Title
14.06.77	Carlos Palomino	L CO 11	London	W	Welterweight Title
23.01.79	Henry Rhiney	**W** RSC 5	London	EU	Welterweight Title
28.06.79	Jorgen Hansen	L CO 3	Randers	EU	Welterweight Title
31.03.80	Sugar Ray Leonard	L CO 4	Landover	W	Welterweight Title

NON CHAMPIONSHIP CONTES (35)

WON PTS (8)	**1975** George Salmon, Angus McMillan. **1976** Jim Montague, Jimmy Heair. **1977** Mario Guilloti, Andy Price. **1979** Dick Ecklund. **1981** Jose-Ramon Gomez Fouz
WON CO (6)	**1974** Yotham Kunda. **1975** Dave Coombs, Tommy Joyce, Brian Jones. **1976**George McGurk. **1978** Roy Johnson
WON RSC/RTD (20)	**1975** Derek Simpson, Barton McAllister, Al Stewart, Alan Salter. **1976** Billy Waith, Giuseppe Minotti, Herbie McLean, Ernesto Bergamesco, Jean-Pierre Younsi, Ugo Dipietro, Ramiro Bolanos. **1977** John H. Stracey. **1978** Aundra Love, Sammy Masias. **1979** Lawrence Hafey, Rafael Rodriguez, Steve Michelarya. **1980** Mario Mendez. **1981** Gary Holmgren, Danny Long
LOST RSC/RTD (1)	**1981** Reg Ford

NOTE:
The World Championship Contest versus Carlos Palomino was for the WBC version of the Title.

Henry Hall

British Welterweight Champion, 1948 – 1949

Born 06.09.22 *From* Sheffield *Died* 1979 *Pro Career* 1945 – 1952 (66 contests, won 43, drew 3, lost 20)

CONTINUED OVERLEAF

Tommy Glencross

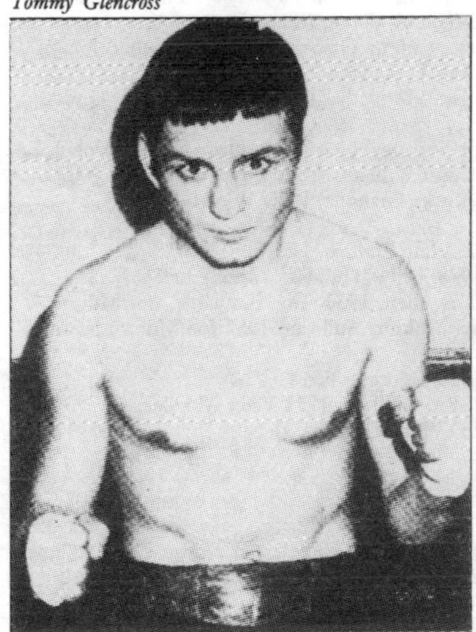

Dave Boy Green

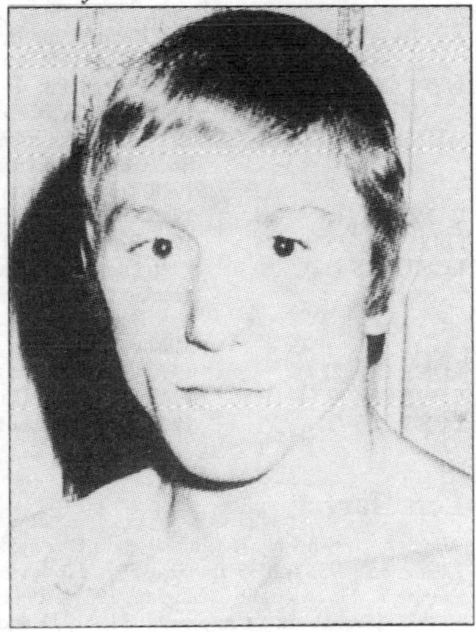

Henry Hall

Len Harvey

CHAMPIONSHIP CONTESTS (2)

08.11.48	Ernie Roderick	W PTS 15 London	B	Welterweight Title
15.11.49	Eddie Thomas	L PTS 15 London	B	Welterweight Title

NON CHAMPIONSHIP CONTESTS (64)

WON PTS (24)	**1945** Bob Moorcroft, Dick Shields, George Odwell. **1946** John Watters, Billy Walker, Jack Phillips. **1947** Omar Kouidri, Dave Edwards, Cyril Gallie, Gwyn Williams. **1948** Jo Goreux, Billy Exley, Tommy Armour. **1949** Tony Janiro. **1950** Sammy Wilde, Jimmy Davis, Johnny Nuttall, Rod Deamer, Joe Beckett, Tommy Davies. **1951** Ron Cooper, Johnny Nuttall, Jackie Wilson, Ron Pudney
WON CO (5)	**1945** Johnny Pitt. **1946** Jock Kennedy, Tony Byrne. **1947** Pat Quinn. **1948** Willie Whyte
WON RSC/RTD (12)	**1945** Mick McCann, Joe Yeardley, George Fordham, Jim Thornhill, Eric Boon, Bob Moorcroft, Gwyn Williams. **1946** Cyril Wills, Dick Johnson. **1948** Yrjoe Piitulainen, Rocky Gianolla, Willy Wimms
WON DIS (1)	**1946** Ginger Roberts
DREW (3)	**1951** Ron Pudney. **1952** Eddie Phillips, Jeff Tite
LOST PTS (12)	**1946** Ginger Stewart. **1948** Eddie Thomas, Tommy Armour. **1949** Frankie Cortese. **1950** Les Allen. **1951** Eric McQuade, Bos Murphy, Alex Buxton, Jimmy Davis, Johnny Sullivan. **1952** Joe Munro, Sammy Milsom
LOST CO (2)	**1946** Ginger Stewart. **1950** George Dilkes
LOST RSC/RTD (3)	**1949** Emmanuel Clavel, Ric Sanders. **1951** Peter Mueller
LOST DIS (2)	**1946** Gwyn Williams. **1947** Harry Lazar

Len Harvey

British & British Empire Middleweight Champion, 1929 – 1933. Undefeated British L. Heavyweight Champion, 1933 – 1935 and British L. Heavyweight Champion, 1938 – 42. Undefeated British Empire L. Heavyweight Champion, 1939 – 1942. World L. Heavyweight Champion, 1939 – 1942. British Heavyweight Champion, 1933 – 1934 and Undefeated British Heavyweight Champion,

1938 – 1942. British Empire Heavyweight Champion, 1934 and Undefeated British Empire Heavyweight Champion, 1939 – 1942
Born 11.07.07 *From* Callington *Died* 1976 *Pro Career* 1920–1942 (134 contests, won 112, drew 9, lost 13)

CHAMPIONSHIP CONTESTS (21)

29.04.26	Harry Mason	DREW 20	London	B	Welterweight Title
16.05.29	Alex Ireland	**W** CO 7	London	B, BE	Middleweight Titles
21.10.29	Jack Hood	**W** PTS 15	London	B, BE	Middleweight Titles
18.12.29	Jack Hood	DREW 15	London	B, BE	Middleweight Titles
22.05.30	Steve McCall	**W** RTD 9	London	B, BE	Middleweight Titles
22.06.31	Jack Hood	**W** PTS 15	London	B, BE	Middleweight Titles
21.03.32	Jock McAvoy	**W** PTS 15	Manchester	B, BE	Middleweight Titles
04.07.32	Marcel Thil	L PTS 15	London	W	Middleweight Title
12.12.32	Jack Casey	**W** PTS 15	Newcastle	B, BE	Middleweight Titles
10.04.33	Jock McAvoy	L PTS 15	Manchester	B, BE	Middleweight Titles
12.06.33	Eddie Phillips	**W** PTS 15	London	B	L. Heavyweight Title
30.11.33	Jack Petersen	**W** PTS 15	London	B	Heavyweight Title
08.02.34	Larry Gains	**W** PTS 15	London	BE	Heavyweight Title
04.06.34	Jack Petersen	L RTD 12	London	B, BE	Heavyweight Titles
29.01.36	Jack Petersen	L PTS 15	London	B, BE	Heavyweight Titles
09.11.36	John Henry Lewis	L PTS 15	London	W	L. Heavyweight Title
07.04.38	Jock McAvoy	**W** PTS 15	London	B	L. Heavyweight Title
01.12.38	Eddie Phillips	**W** DIS 4	London	B	Heavyweight Title
10.03.39	Larry Gains	**W** RTD 13	London	BE	Heavyweight Title
10.07.39	Jock McAvoy	**W** PTS 15	London	B, BE, W	L. Heavyweight Titles
20.06.42	Freddie Mills	L CO 2	London	B, BE, W	L. Heavyweight Titles

NON CHAMPIONSHIP CONTESTS (113)

WON PTS (46)	**1920** Young King, Stanleys Nipper, Kid Roberts. **1921** Young Jinks (5), Young Richards, Callicotts Nipper, Johnny Cotter. **1922** Young Callicott, Jack Palmer. **1923** Bill Lewis, Fred Bicknell, Young Jinks, Kid Socks, Pop Humphries, Bill Riley. **1924** Pop Humphries, Bill Riley, Bill Davies, Young Clancy, Ernie Jarvis, Young Fred Welsh, Albert Hicks, Billy Streets, Bert Saunders, Sid Cannon. **1925** Karel Veldt, Paul Leukemanns (2), Edourd Baudry. **1926** Nol Steenhorst. **1927** Maurice Prunier, Piet Brand, Marcel Thil. **1928** Emile Egrel. **1930** Dave Shade, George Slack. **1932** George Slack, Jack Casey, Len Johnson, Seaman Harvey. **1935** Marcel Lauriot, Eddie Phillips
WON CO (20)	**1920** Young Mac. **1921** Young Richards. **1924** Wal Jordan. **1925** Walter Maloney, Johnny Thomas, Peter Bianchi, Harry Gent, Glyn Davies. **1926** Billy Bird, Billy Mattick. **1927** Joe Rolfe, Charlie Screve, Billy Farmer, Primo Ubaldo. **1930** Francois Stevens, Charlie McDonald. **1931** Rene Devos, Jerry Daley, Fred Shaw. **1933** Carmelo Candel
WON RSC/RTD (28)	**1922** Young O'Neill, Johnny Cotter, Bob Williams. **1924** Matt George, Tim Rowley, Young Dando. **1925** Seaman Harrod, Harry Kent, Laurie Guard, Fred Bullions, Terry Donlan, Bill Handley, Henri Dupont. **1926** Nol Steenhorst, Andy Newton. **1927** Emile Egrel, Jack Etienne. **1928** Antoine Forr, Auguste Langagne (2), Johnny Sullivan, Len Frick, Antoine Dubois. **1929** Frank Moody. **1930** Henri Vandevever. **1932** Theo Saas, Glen Moody. **1937** Manuel Abrew
WON DIS (5)	**1927** Joe Bloomfield, Piet Brand. **1928** Kid Nitram, George West. **1934** Jim Tarante
DREW (7)	**1920** Young Paul. **1923** Young Callicott. **1924** Young Dando. **1926** Alf Mancini, Johnny Brown. **1933** Eddie Phillips. **1934** Walter Neusel
LOST PTS (7)	**1920** Young Fern. **1922** Young Callicott. **1926** Johnny Sullivan. **1927** Len Johnson. **1931** Vince Dundee (2), Ben Jeby

NOTE:
The Lonsdale Belt was not issued for the British Championship Contests versus Harry Mason, Jack Hood (22.06.31) and Jack Petersen (30.11.33, 04.06.34, 29.01.36). The World Championship Contests versus Jock McAvoy and Freddie Mills were for the GB version of the Title, whilst the World Championship Contest versus Marcel Thil was for the IBU version.

Vince Hawkins

Charlie Hill

Vince Hawkins

British Middleweight Champion, 1946 – 1948
Born 15.04.23 *From* Eastleigh *Pro Career* 1940 – 1950 (86 contests, won 75, drew 1, lost 10)

CHAMPIONSHIP CONTESTS (4)

29.05.45	Ernie Roderick	L PTS 15	London	B	Middleweight Title
28.10.46	Ernie Roderick	**W** PTS 15	London	B	Middleweight Title
26.01.48	Bos Murphy	L PTS 15	London	BE	Middleweight Title
28.06.48	Dick Turpin	L PTS 15	Birmingham	B, BE	Middleweight Titles

NON CHAMPIONSHIP CONTESTS (82)

WON PTS (36)	**1940** Teddy Catlin. **1941** Spike Robson, Teddy Catlin, Freddie Baxter, John Byles. **1948** Les Campbell (3), George Bennett (3). **1943** Jack Beech, Jim Duffy, Paddy Roche, Frank Duffy. **1944** Ginger Sadd, Tommy Davies (2), Jackie Wilson (2), Johnny Clements, Jack Lewis, Johnny Kilburn. **1945** Lefty Flynn, Bert Gilroy, Glen Moody, Tommy Jones. **1946** Mark Hart, George Dilkes, Albert Finch, Joe Brun. **1947** Jim Ingle, Widmer Milandri. **1948** Bert Sanders, Jean Stock. **1949** Alex Buxton
WON CO (11)	**1941** Billy Smith, Phil Shaw, Kid Doyle (2). **1942** Benny Green, Tony Ward. **1943** Trevor Burt, Ivor Jones. **1944** Charlie Knock, Charlie Parkin. **1947** Augustine Mendicote
WON RSC/RTD (27)	**1941** Jock Kennedy, Joe Prince, Cpl Rodell, Joe Boyle. **1942** Teddy Harwood, Les Campbell. **1943** Jack Kenny, Harry O'Grady (2), Ron Lindley, Harry Maywood, Alex Buxton, Charlie Parkin, Jackie Potts. **1944** Ron Lindley, Paddy Roche, Charlie Knock, Pat O'Connor, Jack Moran (2), Johnny Clements, Dave McCleave. **1945** Jim Laverick, Jack Lewis (2). **1946** Taffy Williams. **1947** Jimmy Bray
DREW (1)	**1944** Tommy Davies
LOST PTS (5)	**1947** Gus Degouve. **1948** Randy Turpin. **1949** Cyrille Delannoit, George Angelo. **1950** Dick Turpin
LOST RSC/RTD (2)	**1947** Dick Turpin. **1950** George Casson

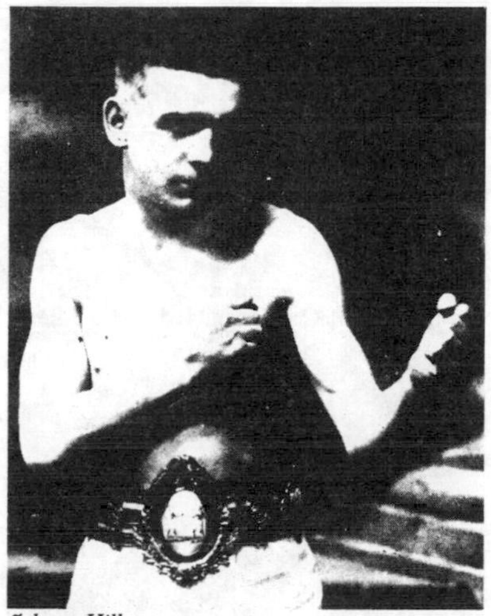

Johnny Hill

Jack Hood

Charlie Hill

British Featherweight Champion, 1956 – 1959
Born 20.06.30 *From* Cambuslang *Pro Career* 1953 – 1959 (36 contests, won 31, lost 5)

CHAMPIONSHIP CONTESTS (5)

04.02.56	Billy Spider Kelly	W PTS 15	Belfast	B	Featherweight Title
07.10.57	Jimmy Brown	W CO 10	Nottingham	B	Featherweight Title
09.12.57	Percy Lewis	L RSC 10	Nottingham	BE	Featherweight Title
02.07.58	Chic Brogan	W RTD 11	Glasgow	B	Featherweight Title
13.04.59	Bobby Neill	L RSC 9	Nottingham	B	Featherweight Title

NON CHAMPIONSHIP CONTESTS (31)

WON PTS (16)	**1953** Art Belec, Bob Hodgson, Tommy Higgins. **1954** Freddie King, Gene Caffrey, Henk Klok, Chic Brogan. **1955** Flaviano Ciancarelli, Jacques Bataille, Denny Dawson, Ken Lawrence, Jesus Rubio. **1956** Flaviano Ciancarelli. **1957** Denny Dawson, Alf Drew. **1958** Joe Quinn
WON CO (4)	**1953** Ray Hillyard, Andy Monaghan, Jim Fisher, Michael Feeney
WON RSC/RTD (8)	**1953** Peter Fay. **1954** Billy Smith, Bobby Dodoo, Eddie McNally, Steve Trainor, Jacques Lesseine. **1956** Ken Lawrence, Aime Devisch
LOST RSC/RTD (2)	**1956** Bobby Neill. **1957** Joe Quinn
LOST DIS (1)	**1953** Andy Monaghan

Johnny Hill

Undefeated British Flyweight Champion, 1927 – 1929. European Flyweight Champion, 1928 – 1929. Undefeated World Flyweight Champion, 1928 – 1929
Born 14.12.05 *From* Edinburgh *Died* 1929 *Pro Career* 1926 – 1929 (23 contests, won 18, drew 3, lost 1, no contest 1)

CHAMPIONSHIP CONTESTS (5)

23.05.27	Alf Barber	W RSC 14	London	B	Flyweight Title
19.03.28	Emile Pladner	W PTS 15	London	EU	Flyweight Title
29.08.28	Newsboy Brown	W PTS 15	London	W	Flyweight Title
07.02.29	Emile Pladner	L CO 6	Paris	EU	Flyweight Title
21.03.29	Ernie Jarvis	W PTS 15	London	B	Flyweight Title
29.06.29	Ernie Jarvis	W DIS 10	Glasgow	B	Flyweight Title

CONTINUED OVERLEAF

NON CHAMPIONSHIP CONTESTS (17)

WON PTS (4)	**1926** Henri Poutrain. **1927** Tiny Smith, Petit Biquet, Emile Pladner
WON CO (1)	**1926** Arthur Cunningham
WON RSC/RTD (7)	**1926** Billy Huntley, Frank Maurier, Young Jackie Brown. **1927** Young Denain, Phil Lolosky, Jim Hanna, Francois Morrachini
WON DIS (1)	**1927** Petit Biquet
DREW (3)	**1926** Billy James, Tiny Smith. **1927** Phil Lolosky
NC (1)	**1926** Mark Lesnick

NOTE:
The Lonsdale Belt was not issued for the British Championship Contest versus Ernie Jarvis. The World Championship Contest versus Newsboy Brown was for the GB/Californian version of the Title.

Jack Hood

Undefeated British Welterweight Champion, 1926 – 1934. Undefeated European Welterweight Champion, 1933
Born 17.12.02 *From* Birmingham *Pro Career* 1921–1935 (81 contests, won 66, drew 7, lost 6, no contest 1, no decision 1)

CHAMPIONSHIP CONTESTS (8)

31.05.26	Harry Mason	W PTS 20	London	B	Welterweight Title
22.07.26	Harry Mason	W PTS 20	London	B	Welterweight Title
25.06.28	Alf Mancini	W PTS 15	Birmingham	B	Welterweight Title
21.10.29	Len Harvey	L PTS 15	London	B	Middleweight Title
18.12.29	Len Harvey	DREW 15	London	B, BE	Middleweight Titles
22.06.31	Len Harvey	L PTS 15	London	B, BE	Middleweight Titles
13.03.33	Stoker Reynolds	W CO 9	Birmingham	B	Welterweight Title
22.05.33	Adrien Aneet	W DIS 3	Birmingham	EU	Welterweight Title

NON CHAMPIONSHIP CONTESTS (73)

WON PTS (38)	**1923** Kid Swaffer, Harry Bradley, Reg Norman. **1924** Bill Green, Fred Brown, Jack Whitehouse, Jim Tyler, Joe Boswell, Jim Carroll, Horace Probert. **1925** Walter Funke, Frank Lane, Jim Cox, Edouard Verret, Len Johnson, Piet Brand. **1926** Edouard Verret, Alex Ireland, Sailor Darden, Paul Doyle, Harry Galfund. **1927** Young Jack Dempsey, Maurice Prunier, Johnny Sullivan, Leo Darton, Jack Etienne, Marcel Thil, Auguste Langagne. **1928** KO Screve, Len Johnson, Louis Wustenrad. **1929** Leo Wax. **1931** Jack Casey, Sandy McKenzie. **1932** Charlie McDonald. **1933** Huib Huizenaar. **1934** Len Tiger Smith. **1935** Charlie Baxter
WON CO (7)	**1923** Bill Dyer. **1924** Fred Ellis, Jack Trentfield. **1928** Joe Briscot. **1930** Jack Hyams. **1931** Andre Dhainaut, Orlando Leopardi
WON RSC/RTD (15)	**1921** W. G. Brown. **1923** Jack Franklin, Sam Sherwood. **1925** Joe Boswell, Billy Mack, Gaston Paumelle, Joe Rolfe, Nipper Plant, Armand Baudoux. **1927** Nol Steenhorst. **1928** Georges Rouquet, Rene Dumondin, Bruno Frattini. **1930** Jack Haynes. **1931** Henri Mouha
WON DIS (1)	**1925** Billy Mattick
DREW (6)	**1925** Andy Newton, Sonny Bird. **1926** Jimmy Jones. **1930** Dave Shade (2). **1931** Vince Dundee
LOST PTS (3)	**1925** Edouard Verret. **1930** Harry Mason. **1934** Len Tiger Smith
LOST RSC/RTD (1)	**1932** Marcel Thil
ND (1)	**1926** Jack McVey
NC (1)	**1928** Joe Bloomfield

NOTE:
The Lonsdale Belt was not issued for the British Championship Contests versus Alf Mancini, Len Harvey (22.06.31) and Stoker Reynolds.

Maurice Hope

Undefeated British L. Middleweight Champion, 1974 – 1977. Undefeated Commonwealth L. Middleweight Champion, 1976 – 1979. Undefeated European L. Middleweight Champion, 1976 – 1978. World L. Middleweight Champion, 1979 – 1981
Born 06.12.51 Antigua, W.I. *From* Hackney *Pro Career* 1973 – 1982 (35 contests, won 30, drew 1, lost 4)

CHAMPIONSHIP CONTESTS (14)

05.11.74	Larry Paul	W CO 8	Wolverhampton	B	L. Middleweight Title
10.06.75	Bunny Sterling	L RSC 8	London	B	Middleweight Title
30.09.75	Larry Paul	W RSC 4	London	B	L. Middleweight Title
20.04.76	Tony Poole	W RSC 12	London	B, C	L. Middleweight Titles
01.10.76	Vito Antuofermo	W RSC 15	Rome	EU	L. Middleweight Title
15.03.77	Eckhard Dagge	DREW 15	Berlin	W	L. Middleweight Title
07.05.77	Frank Wissenbach	W PTS 15	Hamburg	EU	L. Middleweight Title
08.11.77	Joel Bonnetaz	W CO 5	London	EU	L. Middleweight Title
04.03.79	Rocky Mattioli	W RTD 8	San Remo	W	L. Middleweight Title
25.09.79	Mike Baker	W RSC 7	London	W	L. Middleweight Title
12.07.80	Rocky Mattioli	W RSC 11	London	W	L. Middleweight Title
26.11.80	Carlos Herrera	W PTS 15	London	W	L. Middleweight Title
24.05.81	Wilfred Benitez	L CO 12	Las Vegas	W	L. Middleweight Title
30.03.82	Luigi Minchillo	L PTS 12	London	EU	L. Middleweight Title

NON CHAMPIONSHIP CONTESTS (21)

WON PTS (4)	**1973** John Smith, Pat Brogan. **1974** Mike Manley. **1978** Melvin Dennis
WON CO (4)	**1974** Mick Hussey, John Smith. **1975** Jurgen Voss. **1978** Vincenzo Ungaro
WON RSC/RTD (12)	**1973** Len Gibbs, Arthur Winfield. **1974** Mike Manley, Dave Davies, Top Cat Jackson. **1975** Don Cobbs. **1976** Carl Speare, Mimouin Mohatar, Kevin White, Tim McHugh. **1977** Tony Lopes. **1978** Alphonso Haymon
LOST PTS (1)	**1973** Mickey Flynn

NOTE:
All of the above World Championship Contests were for the WBC version of the Title.

Maurice Hope

Alf Howard

Alf Howard

European Lightweight Champion, 1930
Born 1907 *From* Liverpool *Died* 1959 *Pro Career* 1923 – 1937 (87 contests, won 62, drew 3, lost 22)

CHAMPIONSHIP CONTESTS (2)

16.01.30	Francois Sybille	W DIS 8	Liverpool	EU	Lightweight Title
18.06.30	Francois Sybille	L CO 9	Brussels	EU	Lightweight Title

NON CHAMPIONSHIP CONTESTS (84)

WON PTS (18)	**1923** Jack Stroyan. **1924** Young Fitzpatrick, Dom Volante (2), Bert Jones, Billy Foster. **1925** Danny O'Donnell, Jim Martin, Tom Ritchie, Jack Hamlett, Young Sharkey. **1926** Harry Hill, Joe Samuels. **1927** Ossie Jones, Jack McFarlane. **1928** Frank Carberry. **1930** Harry Mason, Jack Hyams
WON CO (18)	**1925** Frank Phillips. **1926** Young Knock, Walter Malone, Harry Gent. **1927** Charlie Baxter. **1928** Nash Shakespeare, Alf Butters, Charlie Baxter, Henri Battonet. **1929** Billy Jones, Ivor Davies. **1930** Ashton Jones, Sandy McKenzie, Joe Bracke. **1931** Jack Haynes, Billy Viner, George Rose (2)
WON RSC/RTD (24)	**1925** Billy Wilkie, Kid Maskery. **1926** Joe Samuels, Danny Ramsey. **1927** Fred Fox, Jim Dagnall. **1928** Ossie Jones (2), Johnny Seeley, Cal Barton, Charlie Tonner. **1929** Harry Fenn, Charlie Tonner, Fred Green, Ernie Izzard, Ralph Morris, Willie McDermott, Haydn Williams, Louis Saerens, Jan Scheffers. **1930** Fritz Ensel, Fred Webster. **1931** Alex Thake, Harry Jenkins
WON DIS (1)	**1932** Willie Hamilton
DREW (3)	**1924** Billy Foster. **1925** Tommy Hassell (2)
LOST PTS (10)	**1924** Jim Martin. **1927** Harry Gent. **1929** Benny Valger. **1930** Camille Desmet, Haydn Williams. **1931** Gustave Roth, Harry Corbett, Jim Winters. **1932** Barney Keiswetter. **1937** Charlie Parkin
LOST CO (3)	**1924** Jack Hamlett. **1929** Eugene Julien. **1930** Gene Drouhin
LOST RSC/RTD (8)	**1926** George Willis, Billy Walker. **1928** Eugene Julien. **1930** Harry Corbett. **1931** Jim Winters. **1932** Stoker Reynolds. **1933** Charlie Baxter. **1937** Charlie Parkin

Alex Ireland

British and British Empire Middleweight Champion, 1928 – 1929
Born 11.02.01 *From* Leith *Died* 1966 *Pro Career* 1922 – 1929 (47 contests, won 34, drew 3, lost 10)

CHAMPIONSHIP CONTESTS (3)

14.03.28	Tommy Milligan	W DIS 9	Edinburgh	B, BE	Middleweight Titles
17.09.28	Frank Moody	W PTS 15	Edinburgh	B, BE	Middleweight Titles
16.05.29	Len Harvey	L CO 7	London	B, BE	Middleweight Titles

NON-CHAMPIONSHIP CONTESTS (44)

WON PTS (21)	**1922** Pat McAllister, Billy Pritchard, Ted Coveney, Dave Gordon, Bob Lowrie, Seaman Hall, Billy Mack. **1923** Van't Hoff, Jimmy Cox (2), Maurice Prunier. **1924** Jack Dunn, Joe Rolfe, Nol Steenhorst. **1925** Simon Rosman, Willie Baker, Johnny Squires, Bruno Frattini (2). **1927** Bert Molina, Tom Berry
WON CO (3)	**1922** Jim Prendy, Johnny Windsor. **1924** Fred Newberry
WON RSC/RTD (7)	**1922** Willie Devlin, Joe Davis. **1923** Tommy Moran, Bob Lowrie. **1924** Harry Moody. **1927** Laurie Raiteri. **1928** John Schut
WON DIS (1)	**1927** Jack Elliott
DREW (3)	**1923** Billy Mack, Billy Pritchard. **1925** Billy Mack
LOST PTS (8)	**1922** Billy Mack. **1923** Johnny Brown. **1924** Tommy Milligan, Joe Bloomfield. **1926** Jack Hood, Johnny Brown, Harry Mason. **1929** Steve McCall
LOST DIS (1)	**1924** Johnny Brown

NOTE:
The Lonsdale Belt was not issued for the British Championship Contests versus Tommy Milligan and Frank Moody.

Ronnie James

Undefeated British Lightweight Champion, 1944 – 1947
Born 08.10.17 *From* Swansea *Died* 1977 *Pro Career* 1933 – 1947 (116 contests, won 95, drew 5, lost 16)

CHAMPIONSHIP CONTESTS (2)

12.08.44	Eric Boon	**W** CO 10	Cardiff	B	Lightweight Title
04.09.46	Ike Williams	L CO 9	Cardiff	W	Lightweight Title

NON-CHAMPIONSHIP CONTESTS (114)

WON PTS (37) — **1933** Bert Rees. **1934** Iswlyn Howells, Evan Evans, Nick Cantwell, Young Britton, Pete McCamley, Wyn Lewis. **1935** Arley Hollingsworth, Tucker Winch, Les Greenaway, Jim Knowles, Fred Bailey, Joe Horridge, Harry Daly, Len Beynon (2). **1936** Jackie Wilson, Bob Lamb, Johnny Peters, Teddy Hayes, Frankie Simms. **1937** Cuthbert Taylor. **1938** Danny Mack, Mitsos Grispos, Mac Perez. **1939** Dick Corbett, Dennis Chadwick, Jimmy Vaughan. **1940** Freddie Simpson. **1941** Harry Lazar, Johnny Ward. **1942** Jimmy Molloy. **1944** Johnny Russell. **1945** Dick Shields, Gwyn Williams. **1946** Maurice Ouezmann, Pat Cunnane

WON CO (23) — **1933** Harry Sullivan, Idris Pugh, Johnny Griffiths. **1934** Llew Edwards. **1935** Ernie Gaze, Eric Jones, Teddy Rollins, Jim Connolly. **1936** Phineas John, Boyo Burns, Harold Kid Lewis. **1937** Joe Riley. **1938** Matt Powell, Tommy Hyams, Johnny McGrory. **1939** Kid Brooks, Johnny Sayers, Benny Caplan. **1940** Joe Slack. **1941** Freddie Simpson. **1942** Jimmy Watson. **1943** Eric Dolby. **1945** Cyril Wills

WON RSC/RTD (28) — **1933** Syd Williams, Dave Collins, Tubby Evans. **1934** Kid Davis, Frank Sweetman. **1935** Terence Morgan, Stan Croft, Fred Morris. **1936** Danny Thomas, Tudor Thomas, Willie Williams. **1936** Tommy Fox. **1938** Billy Masters, Charlie Curry. **1939** Johnny Jones, Jack Carrick, Dave Finn, Al Binney. **1942** Danny Mack, Dave Crowley, Tom Smith, Freddie Simpson. **1943** John Lookie, Lefty Flynn, Jimmy Watson, Dick Shields. **1944** Jimmy Watson. **1947** Mick Gibbons

CONTINUED OVERLEAF

Alex Ireland

Ronnie James

WON DIS (6)	**1935** Jack Collins. **1937** Doug Kestrell. **1940** Dave Finn. **1943** Dick Corbett. **1945** Jimmy Molloy. **1947** Tommy Burns
DREW (5)	**1933** Reggie Morgan, Idris Pugh, Chick Jones. **1935** Dick Corbett. **1936** Dick Corbett
LOST PTS (9)	**1936** Balthazar Sangchilli, Billy Charlton. **1937** Arnold Legrand. **1939** Dave Finn. **1943** Lefty Flynn (2). **1944** Arthur Danahar (2). **1945** Arthur Danahar
LOST RSC/RTD (1)	**1947** Cliff Curvis
LOST DIS (5)	**1936** Dave Crowley. **1938** Freddie Miller, Dave Crowley. **1940** Eric Dolby. **1944** Gwyn Williams

NOTE:
The World Championship Contest versus Ike Williams was for the NBA version of the Title.

(Frank) Bunny Johnson

British & Commonwealth Heavyweight Champion, 1975. Undefeated British L. Heavyweight Champion, 1977 - 1981.
Born 10.5.47 Jamaica *From* Birmingham *Pro Career* 1968 - 1981 (73 contests, won 55, drew 1, lost 17)

CHAMPIONSHIP CONTESTS (6)

13.01.75	Danny McAlinden	W CO 9	London	B, C	Heavyweight Titles
30.09.75	Richard Dunn	L PTS 15	London	B, C	Heavyweight Titles
08.03.77	Tim Wood	W CO 1	Wolverhampton	B	L. Heavyweight Title
26.11.77	Aldo Traversaro	L RSC 11	Genoa	EU	L. Heavyweight Title
13.05.79	Rab Affleck	W CO 4	Glasgow	B	L. Heavyweight Title
27.02.80	Dennis Andries	W PTS 15	Burslem	B	L. Heavyweight Title

NON CHAMPIONSHIP CONTESTS (67)

WON PTS (21)	**1968** Paul Brown, Billy Wynter, Guinea Roger, Lloyd Walford (2). **1969** Peter Boddington, Dennis Avoth. **1970** Dennis Avoth, Billy Aird. **1971** Dick Hall, Jerry Judge. **1972** Rocky Campbell, Brian Jewett, Roger Tighe, Guinea Roger, Billy Aird. **1973** Les Stevens. **1974** Oliver Wright. **1975** Pedro Agosta, Ray Anderson. **1979** Dennis Andries.
WON CO (11)	**1968** Roy Ferguson. **1969** Hans Jacobsen. **1970** Maxie Smith, Rocky Campbell. **1973** Richard Dunn. **1974** Koli Vailea. **1975** Young Sekona. **1976** Peter Brisland. **1977** Terry Mintus. **1978** Sylvain Watbled. **1981** Fetaki Namoa.
WON RSC/RTD (19)	**1968** Peter Thomas, Bernard Pollard, Tommy Woods, George Dulaire. **1969** Billy Wynter, Terry Daly. **1970** Guinea Roger. **1971** Brian Jewett, Peter Boddington. **1972** Eddie Avoth, Roger Russell. **1973** Guinea Roger, Morrie Jackson. **1974** Cookie Wallace. **1975** Angel Oquendo, Obie English. **1976** Phil Martin. **1977** Harry White. **1981** Mike Quarry.
DREW (1)	**1976** Billy Aird
LOST PTS (7)	**1969** Riger Tighe, Eddie Avoth. **1971** Richard Dunn, Dennis Avoth. **1979** Lottie Mwale, Sylvain Watbled. **1980** John Odihambo
LOST CO (2)	**1968** Guinea Roger. **1969** Roger Tighe
LOST RSC/RTD (6)	**1976** Duane Bobick. **1978** Dave Conteh. **1979** Mustapha Wassaja, James Scott. **1981** Tony Mundine, Steve Aczel

Frank Johnson

Undefeated British Lightweight Champion, 1952 – 1953 and British Lightweight Champion, 1955 – 1956. British Empire Lightweight Champion, 1953
Born 27.11.28 *From* Manchester *Died* 1970 (birthname Frank Williamson) *Pro Career* 1946 – 1957 (58 contests, won 47, lost 11)

CHAMPIONSHIP CONTESTS (7)

25.07.52	Tommy McGovern	W PTS 15	Manchester	B	Lightweight Title
23.01.53	Frank Flannery	W RSC 10	Melbourne	BE	Lightweight Title

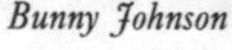

Bunny Johnson

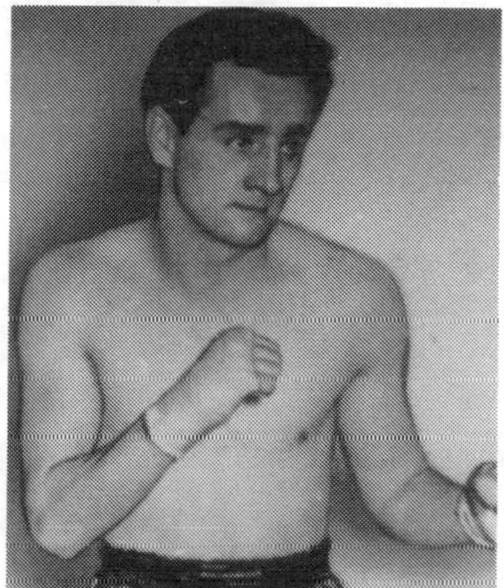

Frank Johnson

28.08.53	Pat Ford	L PTS 15	Melbourne	BE	Lightweight Title
09.10.53	Pat Ford	L CO 13	Melbourne	BE	Lightweight Title
26.04.55	Joe Lucy	W PTS 15	London	B	Lightweight Title
13.04.56	Joe Lucy	L RSC 8	Manchester	B	Lightweight Title
17.12.56	Peter Waterman	L RTD 10	Birmingham	B	Welterweight Title

NON CHAMPIONSHIP CONTESTS (51)

WON PTS (19)	**1947** Tony McGowan, Billy Ellis, Con Bailey, Charlie White. **1948** Jim Dwyer. **1949** Eddie Magee, Dave Watson (2), Charlie Neeson, Dai Davies. **1952** Allan Tanner, Elis Ask, Tom Bailey. **1954** Bola Lawal, Alby Tissong, Johhny Butterworth. **1955** Johnny Mann, Guy Gracia. **1956** Pierre Wouters
WON CO (8)	**1946** Mickey Donovan. **1947** Billy Speers, Ron Perry, Van Robertson. **1949** Hal Crosby. **1951** Steve Walsh, Terry Riley. **1952** Jim Findlay
WON RSC/RTD (17)	**1947** Ronnie Sinclair, Paddy Burke, Mickey Green, Jimmy Green. **1949** Kid Tanner, Jim Gifford. **1950** Jock Bonas, Bobby Dodoo. **1951** Stan Salter, Jim Kenny, Teddy Odus, Jackie Keough. **1952** Tommy Barnham. **1956** Jimmy Croll, Albert Carroll, Ziyaris Taki. **1957** Ray Corbett
LOST PTS (6)	**1948** Tom Bailey. **1953** Joe Lucy. **1955** Solly Cantor, Gordon Goodman. **1956** Sammy McCarthy. **1957** Sandy Manuel
LOST RSC/RTD (1)	**1957** Boswell St Louis

Frankie Jones

British Flyweight Champion, 1957 – 1960. British Empire Flyweight Champion, 1957
Born 12.02.33 *From* Plean *Pro Career* 1955 – 1960 (25 contests, won 17, lost 8)

CHAMPIONSHIP CONTESTS (4)

31.07.57	Len Reece	W CO 11	Porthcawl	B, BE	Flyweight Titles
23.10.57	Dennis Adams	L CO 3	Glasgow	BE	Flyweight Title
05.02.59	Alex Ambrose	W PTS 15	Glasgow	B	Flyweight Title
08.10.60	Johnny Caldwell	L CO 3	Belfast	B	Flyweight Title

NON CHAMPIONSHIP CONTESTS (21)

WON PTS (11)	**1955** Kenny Langford, Bobby Robinson, Eddie O'Connor. **1956** Malcolm McLeod, Vic Glenn, Dick Currie. **1957** Jose Ogazon, Christian Marchand.

CONTINUED OVERLEAF

Frankie Jones

Peter Kane

	1958 Malcolm McLeod, Dennis Adams. **1959** George McDade
WON RSC/RTD (4)	**1956** Dave Moore. **1957** Len Reece, Malcolm McLeod. **1960** Eddie Barraclough
LOST PTS (3)	**1958** Terry Toole. **1959** Derek Lloyd. **1960** Ron Ponty Davies
LOST CO (2)	**1958** George Bowes. **1960** Ramon Arias
LOST RSC/RTD (1)	**1958** Pancho Bhatachaji

Peter Kane

World Flyweight Champion, 1938 – 1943. European Bantamweight Champion, 1947 – 1948
Born 28.02.18 *From* Goldborne *Pro Career* 1934 – 1948 (97 contests, won 87, drew 2, lost 7, no contest 1)

CHAMPIONSHIP CONTESTS (7)

13.10.37	Benny Lynch	L CO 13	Glasgow	B, W	Flyweight Titles
22.09.38	Jackie Jurich	W PTS 15	Liverpool	W	Flyweight Title
19.06.43	Jackie Paterson	L CO 1	Glasgow	B, BE, W	Flyweight Titles
19.09.47	Theo Medina	W PTS 15	Manchester	EU	Bantamweight Title
15.12.47	Joe Cornelis	W PTS 15	Manchester	EU	Bantamweight Title
20.02.48	Guido Ferracin	L PTS 15	Manchester	EU	Bantamweight Title
16.07.48	Guido Ferracin	L RTD 5	Manchester	EU	Bantamweight Title

NON CHAMPIONSHIP CONTESTS (90)

WON PTS (31)	**1936** Joe Curran, Tiny Bostock, Ernst Weiss, Willy McCamley, Valentin Angelmann. **1937** Valentin Angelmann, Fortunato Ortega, Ernst Weiss. **1938** Georges Bataille, Bernard Leroux. **1939** Raoul Degryse, Gino Cattaneo, Balthazar Sangchilli, El Houssine. **1940** Jim Hayes. **1941** Terry O'Neil, Jimmy Stubbs. **1942** Joe Curran, Sammy Reynolds (2), Norman Lewis, Hugh Cameron. **1943** Willie Grey, Gus Foran, Jim Brady, Sammy Reynolds. **1946** Jean Jouas. **1947** Bunty Doran, Joe Cornelis, Dado Marino. **1948** Sammy Reynolds
WON CO (20)	**1935** Nipper Carroll, Jackie Burns, Jackie Shea, Charlie Reed, Billy Charnock. **1936** Willie Smith, Praxille Gyde, Herbie Hill, Enrico Urbinati, Al Hopp, Pat Warburton. **1937** Paul Schaffer, Maurice Huguenin. **1938** Hubert Offermans. **1941** Tommy McGlinchey. **1942** Joe Curran. **1943** Johnny Summers. **1946** Norman Lewis. **1947** Tommy Madine, Albert Braedt

WON RSC/RTD (32)	**1934** Joe Jacobs. **1935** Kid Patterson, Charlie Powell, Bobby Doyle, Billy Charnock, Frank Bonser, Jackie Forshaw, Clarrie Gill. **1936** Jim Laird, Cyclone Kelly, Jim Maharg, Jimmy Stewart, Pedrito Ruiz, Eugene Huat, Gaston Van Den Bos. **1937** Pierre Louis, Poppi Decico, Phil Milligan, Petit Biquet, Jimmy Warnock. **1938** George Bataille. **1939** Albert Legrand, Pierre Louis. **1941** Jimmy Stubbs. **1942** Willie Grey, Eddie Petrin, Frank Bonser, Paddy Ryan. **1946** Ron Bissell. **1947** Len Coffin, Theo Medina. **1948** Bunty Doran
WON DIS (1)	**1946** Jackie Hughes
DREW (2)	**1938** Benny Lynch. **1948** Amleto Falcinelli
LOST PTS (2)	**1941** Jimmy Lyden. **1948** Stan Rowan
LOST RSC/RTD (1)	**1940** Jackie Rankin
NC (1)	**1943** Willie Grey

Peter Keenan

British Bantamweight Champion, 1951 – 1953 and 1954 – 1959. British Empire Bantamweight Champion, 1955 – 1959. European Bantamweight Champion, 1951 – 1952 and 1953
Born 08.08.28 *From* Glasgow *Pro Career* 1948 – 1959 (66 contests, won 54, drew 1, lost 11)

CHAMPIONSHIP CONTESTS (17)

09.05.51	Danny O'Sullivan	W CO 6	Glasgow	B	Bantamweight Title
27.06.51	Bobby Boland	W RSC 12	Glasgow	B	Bantamweight Title
05.09.51	Luis Romero	W PTS 15	Glasgow	EU	Bantamweight Title
26.01.52	Vic Toweel	L PTS 15	Johannesburg	BE, W	Bantamweight Titles
21.05.52	Jean Sneyers	L CO 5	Glasgow	EU	Bantamweight Title
28.01.53	Frankie Williams	W RSC 7	Paisley	B	Bantamweight Title
16.06.53	Maurice Sandeyron	W PTS 15	Glasgow	EU	Bantamweight Title
03.10.53	John Kelly	L PTS 15	Belfast	B, EU	Bantamweight Titles
21.09.54	John Kelly	W CO 6	Paisley	B	Bantamweight Title
11.12.54	George O'Neill	W PTS 15	Belfast	B	Bantamweight Title
28.03.55	Bobby Sinn	W PTS 15	Sydney	BE	Bantamweight Title
14.09.55	Jake Tuli	W CO 14	Glasgow	BE	Bantamweight Title
22.10.56	Kevin James	W RSC 2	Sydney	BE	Bantamweight Title
22.05.57	John Smillie	W RSC 6	Glasgow	B, BE	Bantamweight Titles
02.04.58	Graham Van Der Walt	W PTS 15	Paisley	BE	Bantamweight Title
16.10.58	Pat Supple	W PTS 15	Paisley	BE	Bantamweight Title
10.01.59	Freddie Gilroy	L RSC 11	Belfast	B, BE	Bantamweight Titles

NON CHAMPIONSHIP CONTESTS (49)

WON PTS (24)	**1948** Dennis Sale, Billy Hazelgrove, Jimmy Gill. **1949** Jackie Fairclough, Vic Herman, Raoul Degryse. **1950** Jean Sneyers, Maurice Sandeyron, Vic Herman, Bunty Doran, Louis Skena. **1951** Jesus Rubio, Amleto Falcinelli. **1953** Stan Rowan. **1954** Robert Meunier, Eddie Carson, Vic Herman. **1955** Dante Bini, Pierre Cossemyns. **1956** Federico Scarponi. **1957** Roberto Tartari, Rudy Edwards, Alfred Schweer. **1958** Billy Peacock
WON CO (5)	**1948** Al Hutt, Ken Jepson, Pat McNally. **1950** Dickie O'Sullivan, Tommy Proffitt
WON RSC/RTD (11)	**1948** Dennis Reed. **1949** Johnny Bartles, Micky McLaughlin, Chris Hardy, Charlie Squire, Jackie Briers, Joe Murphy, Theo Nolten. **1951** Armand Deianna. **1953** Ron Johnson. **1958** Dick Currie
WON DIS (1)	**1949** Emile Famechon
DREW (1)	**1951** Maurice Sandeyron
LOST PTS (4)	**1955** Andre Valignat, Roberto Spina, Emile Chemama. **1958** Alphonse Halimi
LOST CO (1)	**1956** Al Asuncion
LOST RSC/RTD (2)	**1952** Amleto Falcinelli. **1958** Derry Treanor

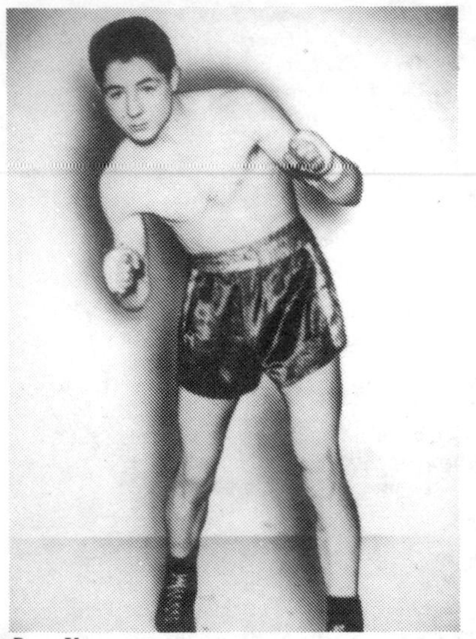

Peter Keenan

Billy Spider Kelly

Billy Spider Kelly

British Featherweight Champion, 1955 – 1956. British Empire Featherweight Champion, 1954 – 1955
Born 21.04.32 *From* Belfast *Pro Career* 1950 – 1962 (83 contests, won 56, drew 4, lost 23)

CHAMPIONSHIP CONTESTS (5)

02.10.54	Roy Ankrah	**W** PTS 15	Belfast	BE	Featherweight Title
22.01.55	Sammy McCarthy	**W** PTS 15	Belfast	B, BE	Featherweight Titles
27.05.55	Ray Famechon	L PTS 15	Dublin	EU	Featherweight Title
19.11.55	Hogan Bassey	L CO 8	Belfast	BE	Featherweight Title
04.02.56	Charlie Hill	L PTS 15	Belfast	B	Featherweight Title

NON CHAMPIONSHIP CONTESTS (78)

WON PTS (38)	**1950** Peter Walmsley (2). **1951** Bob O'Hara, Nel Blackburn, Len Shaw, Bobby Dodoo, Harry Croker, Pat M'Coy, Arthur Jarrett, Jock Bonas. **1952** Roy Bennett, Charlie Simpkins, Harry Croker, Dan Collie, Bobby Dodoo, Gene Caffrey, Jackie Horseman, Teddy Odus, George Lamont. **1953** Denny Dawson, Tommy Miller, Hugh Mackie, John Griffen, Al Young, Eddie McCormick, Hogan Bassey. **1954** Jacques Legendre, Juan Alvarez. **1955** Teddy Peckham, Flaviano Ciancarelli, Louis Poncy. **1956** Salvatore Vangi, Syd Greb. **1957** Jimmy Brown. **1958** George Martin. **1959** Barney Beale, Ron Hinson. **1960** Sammy Etiolaja
WON CO (5)	**1951** Pat McCusker, Jackie Molloy, Jim O'Brien, Pepi Smith. **1952** Jack Walton
WON RSC/RTD (10)	**1951** Maurice Gordon, Jackie Molloy, John Griffen, Joe King. **1952** Brian Jelley, Bernard Fairbanks, Eddie Moran. **1953** Rufus Cobbson, Tommy Higgins. **1954** Altidoro Polidori
WON DIS (1)	**1954** Juan Cardenas
DREW (4)	**1952** Jim Travers. **1957** Fernand Nollet. **1959** Guy Gracia. **1962** Spike McCormack
LOST PTS (9)	**1951** Don McTaggart. **1952** Tommy Miller. **1954** Roy Ankrah. **1956** Percy Lewis. **1957** Willie Toweel. **1958** Ron Hinson. **1960** Johnny Van Rensburg, Darkie Hughes. **1961** Brian Jones

LOST CO (2)	**1957** Johnny Mann. **1961** Dave Coventry
LOST RSC/RTD (8)	**1951** Hugh Mackie. **1953** Ronnie Clayton. **1956** Charlie Tucker. **1957** Boswell St Louis. **1958** Guy Gracia, Louis Van Hoeck. **1960** Teddy Best, Peter Heath
LOST DIS (1)	**1959** Dave Charnley

Jim Spider Kelly

British & British Empire Featherweight Champion, 1938 – 1939
Born 25.02.12 *From* Londonderry *Pro Career* 1928 – 1948 (150 contests, won 105, drew 12, lost 33)

CHAMPIONSHIP CONTESTS (2)

23.11.38	Benny Caplan	W PTS 15 Belfast	B, BE	Featherweight Titles
28.06.39	Johnny Cusick	L RSC 12 Belfast	B, BE	Featherweight Titles

NON CHAMPIONSHIP CONTESTS (148)

WON PTS (79)	**1928** Jim Sharpe. **1929** Young Taggart, Young Harden, George Ballantyne. **1930** Dan Wyper, Arthur Norton, Alf Barrett. **1931** Percy Dexter, Billy Warnock, Jim Corbett, Young Harden, Johnny Grant. **1932** Jack McCleary, Johnstone Chambers (2), Mickey Summers, Joe Frame, Arthur Grant, Alf Barrett, Kid Socks, Jack Bunting. **1933** Pat Cassidy, Nipper McFarlane, Joe Croft, Jackie Quinn, Jim Driscoll, Arthur Killeen, Frank Markey, Battling Croft, Andy Byrne. **1934** Jack Bunting, Albert Lindley, Jim Travers, Billy Smith, Jack Garland, Fran Barron, Stan Jehu, Angus McGregor. **1935** Alex Alston, Jack Lillie, Dan McGoldrick, Freddie Miller, Johnny Truesdale, Bob Croxton, Chuck Flanagan, Joe Calo. **1936** Lynton O'Neill, Kid Dawson, Benny Thackaray, Dan Gallagher, Fred Todhill, Gustave Ansini, Ventura Hernandez. **1937** Nel Tarleton, Dick Corbett, Jim Palmer, Billy Charlton. **1938** Tommy Burns, Johnny McGrory, Norman Denny, Frank McCudden, Tommy Hyams, Jackie Hurst. **1939** Billy Charlton, Benny Caplan. **1940** Frank Kenny, Taffy Davies, Dennis Cohill, Tommy Cullen, Fred Morris. **1941** Vic Andrews, Angus McGregor, Mick Magee, Ken Seeley. **1942** Jim Hamilton, Jim McCann. **1943** Mick Magee. **1947** Jim Coates, Dempsey Brady
WON CO (6)	**1929** Jim Sharpe, Dickie Mack. **1935** Al Pedlar. **1936** Joe Doyle. **1938** Dan McAllister. **1947** Frankie Brown
WON RSC/RTD (16)	**1928** Hugh Britton. **1929** Jim McSarley. **1931** Jackie Quinn. **1932** Jim Haycock, Willie Vint. **1933** Johnny Regan. **1935** Kid McLean. **1936** Spike Robinson, Frank McAloran. **1937** George Williams. **1940** Vic Andrews, Billy Baxter. **1941** Vic Andrews. **1942** Mickey Quinn. **1946** Nick Weldridge, Joe Scott
WON DIS (3)	**1933** Bert Cantor. **1934** Jimmy Barr. **1947** Gerry Smyth
DREW (12)	**1930** Ted Rosbottom. **1932** Fred Hardy. **1933** Fred Carpenter, Jackie Quinn, Frank Markey. **1934** Spike Robinson. **1935** Benny Sharkey. **1937** Ginger Roberts. **1939** Tom Smith. **1942** Jimmy Smith. **1943** Jimmy Smith. **1947** Jackie King
LOST PTS (18	**1928** Ted Rosbottom, Frank Traynor. **1929** Jackie Quinn. **1932** Jack Bunting, Peter McKinlay. **1933** Jack Bunting, Stan Jehu, Frank Markey. **1934** Norman Milton, Tommy Rogers. **1937** Ginger Foran, Johnny McGrory, Johnny Cusick. **1938** Johnny Cusick. **1939** Len Beynon, Nel Tarleton. **1943** Jimmy Ingle. **1947** Tommy McMenemy
LOST CO (4)	**1929** Tom Wonder. **1933** Bert Cantor. **1946** Stan Hawthorne. **1948** Paddy Trainor
LOST RSC/RTD (9)	**1931** Little Minor. . **1933** Ted Sullivan, Albert Lindley. **1940** Jim Keery, Al Lyttle. **1944** Freddie Price. **1947** Jim Coates, Jackie King, Paddy Dowdall
LOST DIS (1)	**1941** Angus McGregor

Jim Spider Kelly

John Kelly

John Kelly

British & European Bantamweight Champion, 1953 – 1954
Born 17.01.32 *From* Belfast *Pro Career* 1951 – 1957 (28 contests, won 24, lost 4)

CHAMPIONSHIP CONTESTS (3)

03.10.53	Peter Keenan	W PTS 15	Belfast	B, EU	Bantamweight Titles
27.02.54	Robert Cohen	L CO 3	Belfast	EU	Bantamweight Title
21.09.54	Peter Keenan	L CO 6	Paisley	B	Bantamweight Title

NON CHAMPIONSHIP CONTESTS (25)

WON PTS (8)	**1952** Mickey King, Jim Dwyer, Hogan Bassey, Tommy Marsden, Dennis Wild, Neville Tetlow. **1953** Jean Kidy. **1955** Aime Devisch
WON CO (4)	**1952** Ron Perry, Jimmy Jennings. **1953** Ron Perry. **1957** Teddy Barker
WON RSC/RTD (10)	**1951** Peter Morrison. **1952** Billy Baker, Tony Kay, Alf Clarke, Len Shaw, Jackie Fairclough. **1953** Johnny Haywood, Tommy Proffitt, Bunty Doran. **1955** Laurie McShane
WON DIS (1)	**1953** Glyn David
LOST CO (2)	**1954** Pierre Cossemyns. **1955** Teddy Peckham

Jake Kilrain

British Welterweight Champion, 1963 – 1939
Born 1914 *From* Bellshill (birthname Harry Owens) *Pro Career* 1931 – 1949 (132 contests, won 102, drew 4, lost 26)

CHAMPIONSHIP CONTESTS (3)

02.06.36	Dave McCleave	W CO 8	Glasgow	B	Welterweight Title
21.02.38	Jack Lord	W PTS 15	Manchester	B	Welterweight Title
23.03.39	Ernie Roderick	L CO 7	Liverpool	B	Welterweight Title

NON CHAMPIONSHIP CONTESTS (129)

WON PTS (51)	**1931** Joe Mack, D. Yardley, Dave Bates, Kid Harvey, Jack Fisher, Sonny Love, Pat McGuire. **1932** Harry Small, Frank Higgins, Charlie McDonald, Peter Kerr, Bobby Turnbull, Ralph Townsley, Tommy Taylor, Kid Williams, Joe Kerr, Matt Callaghan, Bob Coyle, Seaman Hall, Billy Armour, Al Kenny, Jim Boyle. **1933** Jim Christie, Pat Haley, Billy Gilmore, Jim Lush, Eddie Beattie, Alex Tennant, Tommy Taylor, Johnny Cuthbert, Jim Learoyd. **1935** Harry Brown, Frankie Brown, Billy Graham, Panther Purchase. **1936** Panther Purchase, Billy Graham, Jean Debeaumont, Chuck Parker, Paul Schaefer. **1937** Sonny Jones, Frank Erne. **1938** Jimmy Purcell, Armand Alassindrini. **1939** Felix Wouters. **1942** George Odwell. **1943** Johnny Kilburn. **1946** Jock McCusker, Johnny Clements, Willie Whyte. **1949** Willie Whyte
WON CO (20)	**1931** J. Gallagher, M. Lorimer, Billy Mack. **1932** Phil Mallory, Harry McQuade, Jerry Smith, Sid Webster, Bobby Reid. **1933** Boyo Rees, Eric Harkness, Tommy Speirs, Jim Clamp, Charlie Donnelly. **1934** Joe Davis. **1935** Len Wickwar, Ted Turner. **1936** Mick Miller. **1939** Tommy Jones. **1945** Dennis Skidmore. **1946** George Dilkes
WON RSC/RTD (25)	**1931** Joe Mack. **1932** J. Wilson, George Lewthwaite, Johnny Smith, Bobby Lees, Alex Tennant, Con Evans. **1933** Joe Brophy, Snowball Reynolds, Pat O'Connor, Alistair McInroy, Tommy Sinclair, Joe Kerr. **1935** Billy Hughes, Herbie Nurse, J. P. Boyle, Harry Mason. **1938** Bob Moorcroft, Jack Phillips. **1942** Billy Mack, Johnny Kilburn. **1946** Eddie Starrs, Jack Sean Clancy. **1947** Tommy Armour. **1948** Johnny McKenna
WON DIS (4)	**1933** Alphonse Heintz. **1936** Seaman Jim Lawlor, Sonny Jones, Norman Snow
DREW (4)	**1935** Joe Kerr, Mick Miller. **1936** Paul Schaefer. **1937** Lefty Flynn
LOST PTS (10)	**1931** J. Donnolly. **1932** Jim Boyle, Tommy Speirs. **1935** Leo Phillips. **1936** Ernie Roderick. **1937** Jimmy Purcell. **1940** Tommy Armour. **1942** Lefty Flynn, Eric Boon. **1948** Doug Miller
LOST CO (2)	**1942** Eric Boon, Jackie Wilson
LOST RSC/RTD (8)	**1934** Boyo Rees. **1937** Ernie Roderick, Jackie Kid Berg. **1938** Johnny Clements. **1940** Arthur Danahar. **1942** Arthur Danahar. **1943** Pat O'Connor. **1946** Harry Lazar
LOST DIS (5)	**1931** C. Mack. **1932** Curley Mitchell, Jock McFarlane. **1935** Fred Lowbridge, Freddie Price

NOTE:
The Lonsdale Belt was not issued for the British Championship Contest versus Dave McCleave.

Johnny King

British Bantamweight Champion, 1932 – 1934 and 1935 – 1947. British Empire Bantamweight Champion, 1932 – 1934
Born 08.01.12 *From* Manchester *Died* 1963 *Pro Career* 1926 – 1947 (214 contests, won 151, drew 14, lost 48, no contest 1)

CHAMPIONSHIP CONTESTS (11)

21.12.31	Dick Corbett	L PTS 15	Manchester	B, BE	Bantamweight Titles
10.10.32	Dick Corbett	W PTS 15	Manchester	B, BE	Bantamweight Titles
12.06.33	Bobby Leitham	W PTS 15	London	BE	Bantamweight Title
03.07.33	Al Brown	L PTS 15	Manchester	W	Bantamweight Title
12.02.34	Dick Corbett	L PTS 15	Manchester	B, BE	Bantamweight Titles
20.08.34	Dick Corbett	DREW 15	London	B, BE	Bantamweight Titles
27.05.35	Len Hampston	W PTS 15	Manchester	B	Bantamweight Title
06.05.36	Nel Tarleton	L PTS 15	Liverpool	B	Featherweight Title
31.05.37	Jackie Brown	W CO 13	Manchester	B	Bantamweight Title
22.06.38	Len Hampston	W DIS 3	Leeds	B	Bantamweight Title
10.02.47	Jackie Paterson	L CO 7	Manchester	B	Bantamweight Title

CONTINUED OVERLEAF

Jake Kilrain

Johnny King

NON CHAMPIONSHIP CONTESTS (203)

WON PTS (72) **1926** Jim Costello, Sid Longworth, Joe Murray. **1927** Young Sutton, Sid Longworth, Jim Costello, Willie Walsh, Joe Melia (2), Young Fenn, Tom McLeish (3), Tommy Ross, Young Leach. **1928** Tich Cain, Asa Hilditch, Boy Knowles, Dom Randolph, Joe Melia. **1929** Harold Henthorne, Frank Cooley, Dot Boxall, Eddie Sherry (3), Bill Hagan, Paddy Dowling, Jack Keelars, Reg Hall, Moe Mizler. **1930** Boy Edge, Alex Farries, Arthur Tomlinson, Fred Bebbington (2), Jackie Quinn, Spike Bradley, Little Minor. **1931** Petit Biquet (2). **1932** Stan Jehu, Dick Burke, Joe Myers, Harold Lewis, Dave Crowley, Alfredi Magnolfi, Stan Davies. **1933** Stan Davies, Dave Crowley, Jackie Quinn. **1934** Len Beynon(2), Stan Jehu, George Marsden, Joe Horridge. **1935** Dominic Bernasconi, Charles Vercammen, Nel Tarleton, George Williams, Simon Chavez, Joe Parisia. **1936** Gil Johnston, Boyo Burns, Jimmy Lester. **1937** Gus Ansini, Alex Alston, Joe Green, Benny Sharkey. **1938** Frank Kenny. **1939** Phineas John. **1943** Syd Worgan

WON CO (27) **1928** Jim Coupe (2), Jim Speight. **1929** Eddie Conway, Jim Coupe. **1930** George Greaves, Tommy Brown. **1931** Johnny Gibson, Billy Shinfield, Bert Kirby, Al Miller. **1932** Joe Myers, Harold Lewis. **1933** Jean Locatelli, Pat Gorman, Benny Thackaray (2), Syd Rose, John Barrett, Teddy Higgins. **1934** Mog Mason. **1935** Giovanni Sili. **1936** Charles Vercammen. **1937** Johnny Ryan, Young Chocolate. **1938** Hal Bagwell, Raphael Valdez

WON RSC/RTD (42) **1928** Asa Hilditch. **1929** Alf Shaw, Fred Morgan. **1930** Martin Gallagher, Boy Edge, Young Siki, Ted Griffin. **1931** Tommy Barber, Jack Kirk, Arley Hollingsworth, Alf Grisdale, Benny Thackaray, Pat Gorman, Frank Markey, Ray Martinet. **1932** Arly Hollingsworth, Tommy Kirk. **1933** Jim O'Neil, Henri Poutrain, Tucker Winch, Ted Higgins, Johnny Peters. **1934** Stan Davies, Marcel Sartos, Al Lindley, Ellis Ashurst, Phineas John. **1935** Joe Horridge, Michel Escargdella, Len Beynon, Fran Barron, Jackie Brown. **1936** Fred Todkill, Spike Robinson, Tom Steele. **1937** George Marsden, Spike Robinson, Tommy Burns. **1938** John McManus. **1939** Jackie Hurst, John McManus, George Marsden

WON DIS (5)	**1931** Lew Sullivan. **1932** Johnny Peters. **1937** Alex Alston. **1938** Harry Edwards. **1944** Nel Tarleton
DREW (13)	**1926** Jim Costello. **1927** Wilf Duckworth. **1928** Willie Walsh. **1929** Harold Henthorne. **1930** Billy James, Young Perez. **1931** Benny Thackaray. **1934** Dick Corbett, Johnny Holt. **1935** Nel Tarleton. **1937** George Marsden. **1942** Fred Barry. **1943** Ben Duffy
LOST PTS (35)	**1926** Sid Longworth (2). **1927** Sid Longworth, Harry Stafford. **1928** Harold Henthorne. **1929** Paddy Dowling, Bert Kirby. **1930** Tommy Brown, Billy James. **1931** Benny Thackaray. **1933** Francois Machtens. **1934** Len Beynon, George Marsden. **1935** George Williams. **1936** K. O. Morgan, Benny Sharkey, Johnny Cusick, Ginger Foran. **1937** Alex Alston, George Marsden. **1938** George Williams, Johnny McGrory, Dan McAllister, Paul Dogniaux, Freddie Miller, Gus Ansini, Johnny Cusick. **1939** Tom Smith, Frank Parkes, Frank Kenny, Billy Charlton. **1940** Jackie Rankin. **1944** Nel Tarleton. **1946** Frank Kenny. **1947** Teddy O'Neil
LOST CO (3)	**1933** Dominic Bernasconi. **1934** Dave Crowley. **1945** Eddie Miller
LOST RSC/RTD (4)	**1926** Sid Longworth. **1928** Harold Henthorne. **1929** Billy Yates. **1939** Len Beynon
LOST DIS (1)	**1934** Benny Thackaray
NC (1)	**1930** Ted Griffin

NOTE:
The Lonsdale Belt was not issued for the British Championship Contests versus Dick Corbett (20.08.34) and Nel Tarleton, whilst the Contests for the British Empire Bantamweight Title versus Dick Corbett (21.12.31 and 10.10.32) were not generally recognised to have been Championship matches.

Bert Kirby

British Flyweight Champion, 1930 – 1931
Born 1908 *From* Birmingham *Pro Career* 1926 – 1938 (185 contests, won 109, drew 14, lost 59, no contest 1)

CHAMPIONSHIP CONTESTS (3)

13.10.29	Jackie Brown	L CO 3	West Bromwich	B	Flyweight Title
03.03.30	Jackie Brown	W CO 3	London	B	Flyweight Title
02.02.31	Jackie Brown	L PTS 15	Manchester	B	Flyweight Title

NON CHAMPIONSHIP CONTESTS (182)

WON PTS (66)	**1927** Private Morpeth, Harry Scott, Phil Durley (2), Johnny Edwards, Moe Mizler (2), Billy Clarke, Lew Mosby, Dick Corbett (3), George Greaves, Billy James, Dod Oldfield, Jack Swann, Kid Watson. **1928** Harry Hill, Jimmy Hadden, Minty Rose, Terry Morgan, Tiny Smith, Johnny Croxon. **1929** Cuthbert Taylor, Billy James (2), Harry Hill, Kid Canard, Tucker Winch, Jimmy Hadden, Boy Edge, Walter Lemmon, Johnny King. **1930** Freddie Morgan, Young Siki, Minty Rose, Billy Yates, Terence Morgan, Percy Dexter (2), Frankie Ash, Moe Mizler. **1931** Young Siki, Jim Maharg. **1932** Carlo Cavagnoli (2), Reg Hall, Billy Bryan, Harry Connolly, Tommy Rogers, Percy Dexter, Joe Mendolig, Jerry O'Neill, Kid McNally, George Marsden. **1933** Boy Edge, Willie Smith, Fran Barron, Bobby Morgan (2), Fred Bebbington (2), Carlo Cavagnoli. **1935** Harry Edwards. **1936** Cyclone Kelly, Jerry O'Neill
WON CO (15)	**1926** Young Kilby. **1927** Johnny Fitzsimmons, Bill Huntley. **1928** Johnny Croxon. **1929** Johnny Edwards, Arthur Norton, Jim Ireland, Evan Lane. **1930** Walter Lemmon. **1931** Dickie Inkles. **1932** Harold Kid Lewis, Teddy Rollins. **1933** Teddy Rollins. **1934** Kid Leyland, Charlie Hazel
WON RSC/RTD (19)	**1927** Kid Davis, Jack Gliteman, Teddy Benton, Kid Rees, Billy Reynolds, Kid Rich, Tiny Smith. **1928** Jim Campbell. **1929** Bud Walley. **1930** Young Siki, George Aziz, Martin Gallagher. **1931** Bud Walley (2), Cachet Yvet. **1932** Kid McNally. **1933** Willie Smith, Kurt Aust. **1936** Tommy Fletcher

CONTINUED OVERLEAF

WON DIS (8)	**1928** Ernie Jarvis. **1929** Harry Hill, Ernie Jarvis. **1930** Terence Morgan. **1931** Dave Crowley. **1932** Billy Yates, Billy Bryan. **1938** Young Chocolate
DREW (14)	**1927** Billy James, Billy Boulger. **1928** Tiny Smith, Frankie Ash. **1929** Phineas John. **1930** Bob Rimmer. **1932** Praxille Gyde, Jimmy Jones. **1933** Ellis Ashurst. **1934** Peter Miller, George Marsden. **1935** Jim Devlin. **1936** George Pull, Freddie Tennant
LOST PTS (41)	**1927** Dick Corbett, Billy James, Billy Reynolds, Harry Hill. **1928** Petit Biquet (2), Nipper Pat Daly. **1929** Phineas John, Billy James. **1930** Boy Edge. **1931** Dick Burke, Len Beynon, Jim Campbell, Dave Crowley (2). **1932** Jimmy Turner, Harry Connolly, Billy Bryan (2). **1933** Tut Whalley (2). **1933** George Marsden, Mickey McGuire (2), Ellis Ashurst, Percy Dexter, Benny Lynch, Tommy Pardoe. **1934** Tommy Pardoe, Doug Kestrell, Jackie Quinn, Harry Edwards. **1935** Pat Palmer, Billy Nash, Charlie Hazel, Spider Armstrong. **1936** Syd Parker, Tommy Rose, Jimmy Lester, Freddie Tennant. **1938** Hal Bagwell
LOST CO (4)	**1930** Rene Chalange. **1931** Johnny King. **1934** Eric Jones, Johnny Ryan
LOST RSC/RTD (8)	**1931** Tom Cowley, Valentin Angelmann. **1932** Ginger Foran. **1934** Bobby Magee, Billy Miller. **1935** Jackie Brown. **1937** Tommy Fletcher, Mog Mason
LOST DIS (6)	**1928** Johnny Edwards. **1930** Bob Rimmer. **1932** Bud Walley, Tucker Winch. **1933** Herbie Hill. **1935** Eric Jones
NC (1)	**1933** Tut Whalley

NOTE:
The Lonsdale Belt was not issued for the British Championship Contest versus Jackie Brown (13.10.29).

Mick Leahy

British Middleweight Champion, 1963 – 1964
Born 12.03.35 *From* Coventry *Pro Career* 1956 – 1965 (71 contests, won 46, drew 7, lost 18)

CHAMPIONSHIP CONTESTS (5)

31.10.61	Brian Curvis	L CO 8	London	B, BE	Welterweight Titles
28.05.63	George Aldridge	W RSC 1	Nottingham	B	Middleweight Title
22.10.63	Gomeo Brennan	L PTS 15	London	BE	Middleweight Title
09.10.64	Laszlo Papp	L PTS 15	Vienna	EU	Middleweight Title
14.12.64	Wally Swift	L PTS 15	Nottingham	B	Middleweight Title

NON CHAMPIONSHIP CONTESTS (66)

WON PTS (30)	**1957** Don Doherty, Bob Roberts, Terry Gill, Johnny Melfah, Peter Smith . **1958** Johnny Melfah, Boswell St Louis, Santos Martins. **1959** Paddy Graham, Eddie Bee, Don Barnes, Sandy Manuel, George Barnes. **1960** Al Sharpe, Bob Cofie, Boswell St Louis, Larry Baker, Johnny Melfah, Ola Michael. **1961** Jimmy McGrail, Cecil Shorts, Tanos Lambrianides. **1962** Orlando Paso (2), Sandy Luke, Harry Scott. **1963** Wally Swift, Gil Diaz. **1964** Larry Carney, Sugar Ray Robinson
WON CO (4)	**1956** Des Wilkins. **1957** Ray Corbett. **1959** Brian Sheehan, Billy Todd
WON RSC/RTD (11)	**1956** Steve Gee, Richard Mensah, Sammy Royals. **1957** Tex Williams, Bob Batey, Peter Goldie, Jackie Butler. **1958** Sam Lamptney. **1959** Jack Walsh, Clive Stewart (2)
DREW (7)	**1957** Ray Corbett, Ron Richardson. **1958** Boswell St Louis. **1961** Teddy Wright. **1962** Wilf Greaves, Gomeo Brennan, Wally Swift
LOST PTS (10)	**1958** Sandy Manuel. **1959** Bruno Ravaglia, Joe Ngidi, George Barnes, Tuna Scanlon. **1960** Tanos Lambrianides. **1962** Wally Swift. **1964** Tuna Scanlon. **1965** Nino Benvenuti, Jupp Elze
LOST CO (1)	**1957** Tommy Tagoe
LOST RSC/RTD (3)	**1958** Jimmy Croll, Leo Molloy. **1964** Dante Pelaez

Bert Kirby

Mick Leahy

Brian London

British & British Empire Heavyweight Champion, 1958 – 1959
Born 19.06.34 *From* Blackpool (birthname Brian Harper) *Pro Career* 1955 – 1970 (58 contests, won 37, drew 1, lost 20)

CHAMPIONSHIP CONTESTS (6)

03.06.58	Joe Erskine	**W** CO 8	London	B, BE	Heavyweight Titles
12.01.59	Henry Cooper	L PTS 15	London	B, BE	Heavyweight Titles
01.05.59	Floyd Patterson	L CO 11	Indianapolis	W	Heavyweight Title
29.08.60	Dick Richardson	L RTD 8	Porthcawl	EU	Heavyweight Title
24.02.64	Henry Cooper	L PTS 15	Manchester	B, BE, EU	Heavyweight Titles
06.08.66	Muhammad Ali	L CO 3	London	W	Heavyweight Title

NON CHAMPIONSHIP CONTESTS (52)

WON PTS (10)	**1955** Robert Eugene. **1957** Kitione Lave, Howie Turner. **1962** Young Jack Johnson, Von Clay. **1963** Tom McNeeley, Don Warner. **1965** Billy Walker. **1967** James Woody, Zora Folley
WON CO (13)	**1955** Frank Walshaw, Hugh McDonald, Dinny Powell, Prosper Beck. **1956** Trevor Snell, Werner Wiegand. **1957** Robert Duquesne, Willi Schagen, Peter Bates. **1960** Pete Rademacher. **1962** Howard King. **1963** Bill Nielsen. **1965** Roger Rischer
WON RSC/RTD (12)	**1955** Dennis Lockton, Paddy Slavin, Jose Gonzales, Simon Templar, Basil Kew. **1956** Jim Cooper, Jose Peyre, George Naufaha. **1958** Willie Pastrano. **1961** Billy Hunter. **1964** Chip Johnson. **1965** Giorgio Masteghin
WON DIS (1)	**1966** Amos Johnson
DREW (1)	**1969** Henry Clark
LOST PTS (7)	**1957** Heinz Neuhaus. **1958** Willie Pastrano. **1962** Sante Amonti. **1963** Ingemar Johansson. **1964** Johnny Prescott. **1966** Thad Spencer. **1967** Jerry Quarry

CONTINUED OVERLEAF

Brian London

Jack London

LOST CO (1)	**1969** Jerry Quarry
LOST RSC/RTD (7)	**1956** Henry Cooper. **1959** Nino Valdes. **1961** Eddie Machen. **1968** Roberto Davilla, Jack Bodell. **1969** Jim Fletcher. **1970** Joe Bugner

Jack London

British & British Empire Heavyweight Champion, 1944 – 1945
Born 23.06.13 *From* West Hartlepool *Died* 1964 (birthname Jack Harper) *Pro Career* 1931 – 1949 (141 contests, won 95, drew 5, lost 39, no contest 2)

CHAMPIONSHIP CONTESTS (2)

15.09.44	Freddie Mills	W PTS 15	Manchester	B, BE	Heavyweight Titles
17.07.45	Bruce Woodcock	L CO 6	London	B, BE	Heavyweight Titles

NON CHAMPIONSHIP CONTESTS (139)

WON PTS (39)	**1931** Jack Wharton, Jim Williams. **1932** Dick Bartlett, Paul McGuire, Guardsman Gater. **1933** Charlie McDonald, Eddie Strawer, Bert Ikin, Al Conquest, Tony Arpino, Seaman Rowles. **1934** Frank Borrington, Jack Strongbow, Alex Bell (2), Italo Colonello. **1935** Frank Borrington, Jack Casey, Johnny Rice, Eddie Steele. **1936** Eddie Houghton, Roy Lazer, Maurice Strickland, Obie Walker, Hans Stronrath. **1937** Bob Carvill. **1938** Hans Stronrath, Harry Staal, Al Delaney. **1939** George James. **1941** Tom Reddington, Tommy Martin. **1944** George James. **1946** Nick Wolmarans. **1947** Al Robinson, Piet Wilde. **1949** Reg Andrews (2), Don Mogard
WON CO (30)	**1931** Barney Stockton, Phil Henry, Corp. Ingledew, Jim Williams, Tom Powell. **1932** Corp. Dorry, Dick Bartlett, Bill Brennan. **1933** Bob Shields. **1935** Jack Pettifer, Helmuth Hartkopp, Jack Strongbow, Syd Hauxwell. **1936** Frank Borrington. **1937** Pancho Villar, George Bennett, Jim Wilde, Manuel Abrew. **1938** Joe Zeman, Charlie Bundy, George Cook. **1939** Al Delaney, Jean Verbeeren. **1941** Larry Gains (2). **1942** Larry Gains. **1943** Al Robinson. **1946** Joe Foord. **1947** Jan Klein, Jim Britt
WON RSC/RTD (21)	**1932** Joe Morrison, Jim Ainsley, Tom Powell, Jack Strongbow. **1933** Dick Bartlett, Jack Morris, Battling Sullivan (2), Con Van Lewen. **1934**

	Johnny Rice. **1935** George Slack, Charlie Smith, Syd Hauxwell. **1938** Alf Luxton. **1939** Tom Reddington. **1940** Al Robinson. **1942** Jim Wilde. **1943** Jim Wilde. **1945** Ken Shaw. **1947** Fernand Honore. **1949** Prosper Beck
WON DIS (4)	**1931** Battling Manners. **1933** Johnny Rice. **1936** Pat Marrinan. **1938** Harry Lister
DREW (5)	**1932** Frank Bagley (2). **1933** George Slack, Gipsy Daniels. **1934** Jack Pettifer
LOST PTS (26)	**1931** Chris Rock, Eddie Strawer, Tommy Moore, Jack Smith (2), Tom Powell, Willie Duncan, Frank Bagley. **1932** Jack Clancy, Charlie McDonald. **1933** Gipsy Daniels, Len Johnson, Ben Foord. **1934** Charlie Smith, George Slack (2). **1935** Ben Foord. **1936** Tommy Loughran. **1937** Harry Staal, Buddy Baer. **1939** Tommy Martin. **1941** Freddie Mills. **1945** Jock Porter. **1946** Olle Tandberg. **1947** Ken Shaw. **1949** Piet Wilde
LOST CO (4)	**1933** Larry Gains. **1934** Pierre Charles, Charlie Belanger. **1949** Aaron Wilson
LOST RSC/RTD (4)	**1932** Jack O'Malley. **1933** Jack Casey, Gipsy Daniels. **1949** Verne Escoe
LOST DIS (4)	**1934** Bert Melzow, Charlie Belanger. **1935** Alex Bell. **1938** Al Delaney
NC (2)	**1933** Les Saunders. **1936** Larry Gains

Joe Lucy

British Lightweight Champion, 1953 – 1955 and 1956 – 1957
Born 09.02.30 *From* Mile End *Pro Career* 1950 – 1957 (37 contests, won 27, lost 10)

CHAMPIONSHIP CONTESTS (6)

29.09.53	Tommy McGovern	W PTS 15	London	B	Lightweight Title
12.02.55	Johnny Van Rensburg	L PTS 15	Johannesburg	BE	Lightweight Title
26.04.55	Frank Johnson	L PTS 15	London	B	Lightweight Title
13.04.56	Frank Johnson	W RSC 8	Manchester	B	Lightweight Title
26.06.56	Sammy McCarthy	W RSC 13	London	B	Lightweight Title
09.04.57	Dave Charnley	L PTS 15	London	B	Lightweight Title

NON CHAMPIONSHIP CONTESTS (31)

WON PTS (18)	**1950** Jimmy Blackburn, Laurie Henry, Johnny Hudson, Vince Marshall. **1951** Ronnie Wormall, Mickey O'Neill, Alan Tanner, Luigi Male, Selwyn Evans, Billy Elliott. **1952** Laurie Buxton, Owen Trainor. **1953** Tommy McGovern, Louis Carrara, Frank Johnson, Roy Bennett. **1954** Joseph Janssens. **1956** Leo Molloy
WON CO (2)	**1952** Emmett Kenny. **1956** Gordon Goodman
WON RSC/RTD (4)	**1951** Stan Parkes, Billy Shaw, Johnny Flannigan. **1952** Ted Ansell
LOST PTS (6)	**1951** Gerald Dreyer. **1952** Tommy Barnham, Hocine Khalfi. **1954** Johnny Butterworth. **1955** Duilio Loi. **1956** Guy Gracia
LOST RSC/RTD (1)	**1954** Johnny Butterworth

Benny Lynch

Undefeated British & World Flyweight Champion, 1935 – 1938
Born 02.04.13 *From* Glasgow *Died* 1946 *Pro Career* 1931 – 1938 (110 contests, won 82, drew 15, lost 13)

CHAMPIONSHIP CONTESTS (4)

09.09.35	Jackie Brown	W RTD 2	Manchester	B, W	Flyweight Titles
16.09.36	Pat Palmer	W CO 8	Glasgow	B, W	Flyweight Titles
19.01.37	Small Montana	W PTS 15	London	W	Flyweight Title
13.10.37	Peter Kane	W CO 13	Glasgow	B, W	Flyweight Titles

NON CHAMPIONSHIP CONTESTS (106)

WON PTS (47)	**1931** Peter Sherry, Billy Leggatt, Jim McKenzie, Young O'Brien, Mick Cassidy, Peter Sherry, Pat Sweeney. **1932** Young Hardie, Jack Riley,

CONTINUED OVERLEAF

Joe Lucy

Benny Lynch

	Kid Murray, Jimmy Barr, Scotty Deans, Jim O'Driscoll, Young Griffo, Tiger Naughton (2), Joe Aitken, Jim Jeffries, Paddy Docherty (3), Freddie Tennant, Alec Farries (2), Tommy Higgins. **1933** Dan Conlin, Jim Brady, Walter Lemmon, Freddie Tennant (2), Alec Farries, Jim Maharg, Bert Kirby. **1934** Jim Brady (2), Carlo Cavagnoli, Jim Campbell (2), Maurice Huguenin, Valentin Angelmann, Pedrito Ruiz, Sandy McEwan. **1935** Bobby Magee, Gaston Maton, Harry Orton, Phil Milligan. **1937** Fortunato Ortega
WON CO (10)	**1932** Scotty Deans. **1933** Willie Vogan. **1934** Freddie Webb, Peter Miller (2), Johnny Griffiths. **1935** Charlie Hazel. **1936** Syd Parker, Eric Jones. **1938** Jackie Jurich
WON RSC/RTD (20)	**1931** Young McColl, Jim Devanney. **1932** Charlie Deacon, George McLeod. **1933** Billy Warnock, Billy Hughes, Alec Farries, Joe Cowley, Boy McIntosh. **1934** George Lowe, Evan Evans, Billy Johnstone. **1935** Tommy Pardoe. **1936** Mickey McGuire, Pat Warburton, Phil Milligan. **1937** Len Hampston, Roy Underwood, Georges Bataille. **1938** Maurice Filhol
WON DIS (1)	**1934** Tut Whalley
DREW (15)	**1931** Young Donnelly, Jim Boag. **1932** Young McManus, Tommy Higgins, Tony Fleming, Joe Aitken, Young Beattie, Paddy Docherty, Freddie Tennant. **1933** Joe Aitken, Paddy Docherty, Jim Brady, Bob Fielding. **1935** Jackie Brown. **1938** Peter Kane
LOST PTS (11)	**1931** Packy Boyle, Young O'Brien, Paddy Docherty, Young McAdam. **1932** Tommy Higgins, Young Griffo, Freddie Tennant. **1933** Jimmy Knowles. **1936** Jimmy Warnock. **1937** Jimmy Warnock. **1938** K. O. Morgan
LOST CO (1)	**1938** Aurel Toma
LOST DIS (1)	**1937** Len Hampston

NOTE:

The Lonsdale Belt was not issued for the British Championship Contest versus Jackie Brown. The World Championship Contests versus Jackie Brown and Pat Palmer were for the GB/NBA version of the Title and it was not until Lynch defeated Small Montana that the Title became undisputed.

Danny McAlinden

Les McAteer

Danny McAlinden

British & Commonwealth Heavyweight Champion, 1972 – 1975
Born 01.06.47 Newry *From* Coventry *Pro Career* 1969 – 1981 (45 contests, won 31, drew 2, lost 12)

CHAMPIONSHIP CONTESTS (3)

27.06.72	Jack Bodell	W CO 2	Birmingham	B, C	Heavyweight Titles
13.01.75	Bunny Johnson	L CO 9	London	B, C	Heavyweight Titles
04.11.75	Richard Dunn	L CO 2	London	B, C	Heavyweight Titles

NON CHAMPIONSHIP CONTESTS (41)

WON PTS (3)	**1971** Lou Bailey, Rahman Ali, Carl Gizzi
WON CO (10)	**1969** Richard Dunn. **1970** Henri Ferjules, Sylvester Dullaire, J. D. McAuley. **1971** Bill Drover, Chuck Olivera. **1972** Willie Moore. **1973** Vern McIntosh. **1975** Richie Yates, Harmut Sasse
WON RSC/RTD (17)	**1969** John Cullen, Dennis Avoth, Obe Hepburn, Phil Smith. **1970** Tommy Clark, Billy Wynter, Edmund Stewart, Mose Harrell, Tommy Hicks. **1971** Roberto Davila, Dick Gosha. **1973** Tony Ventura. **1975** Rodell Dupree. **1976** Eddie Fenton. **1977** Terry O'Connor, Sean McKenna. **1980** David Fry
DREW (2)	**1970** Ray Patterson. **1971** Tommy Hicks
LOST PTS (4)	**1970** Jack O'Halloran. **1974** Pat Duncan. **1979** George Scott. **1980** Tony Moore
LOST RSC/RTD (6)	**1972** Larry Middleton. **1973** Morris Jackson. **1976** Tony Moore. **1977** Neil Malpass. **1978** Tommy Kiely. **1981** Denton Ruddock

Les McAteer

British Middleweight Champion, 1969 – 1970
Born 19.08.45 *From* Birkenhead *Pro Career* 1965 – 1972 (37 contests, won 25, drew 2, lost 10)

CHAMPIONSHIP CONTESTS (4)

26.02.68	Johnny Pritchett	L PTS 15	Nottingham	B, BE	Middleweight Titles
14.07.69	Wally Swift	W RTD 11	Nottingham	B, BE	Middleweight Titles
02.04.70	Tom Bogs	L RTD 11	Aarhus	EU	Middleweight Title
12.05.70	Mark Rowe	L RSC 14	London	B, C	Middleweight Titles

CONTINUED OVERLEAF

NON CHAMPIONSHIP CONTESTS (33)

WON PTS (12)	**1965** Steve Richards, Tom Bell. **1966** Henry Turkington, Len Gibbs. **1967** Fabio Bettini, Jackie Harwood, Al Sharpe. **1968** Clarence Cassius, Harry Scott. **1969** Willie Ludick. **1971** Eric Blake, Cyclone Barth
WON CO (5)	**1965** Benny Bell, Louis Onwuna, Sammy Robinson, Mickey Pearce. **1968** Jim Swords
WON RSC/RTD (6)	**1965** Chris McAuley, Jimmy Stewart, Chris Sammy. **1966** Louis Onwuna, Johnny Kramer. **1968** George Johnson
WON DIS (1)	**1966** Vince Martinez
DREW (2)	**1967** Bo Pettersen. **1971** Jan Kies
LOST PTS (5)	**1967** Ben Lachemi. **1969** Wally Swift, Tom Bogs. **1971** Pierre Fourie. **1972** Tom Jensen
LOST CO (2)	**1971** Jan Kies. **1972** Pat Dwyer

Pat McAteer

Undefeated British Middleweight Champion, 1955 – 1958. British Empire Middleweight Champion, 1955 – 1958

Born 17.03.32 *From* Birkenhead *Pro Career* 1952 – 1958 (57 contests, won 49, drew 2, lost 6)

CHAMPIONSHIP CONTESTS (7)

16.06.55	Johnny Sullivan	W DIS 9	Liverpool	B, BE	Middleweight Titles
12.11.55	Mike Holt	W PTS 15	Johannesburg	BE	Middleweight Title
08.10.56	Lew Lazar	W RSC 4	Nottingham	B, BE	Middleweight Titles
04.02.57	Charles Humez	L RSC 8	Paris	EU	Middleweight Title
04.05.57	Jimmy Elliott	W CO 6	Johannesburg	BE	Middleweight Title
05.09.57	Martin Hansen	W PTS 15	Liverpool	B, BE	Middleweight Titles
27.03.58	Dick Tiger	L CO 9	Liverpool	BE	Middleweight Title

NON CHAMPIONSHIP CONTESTS (50)

WON PTS (22)	**1952** Dudley Cox. **1953** Eddie Phillips, Ernie Vickers, Rocco King, Jimmy Longton, Bob Cleaver, Richard Armah. **1954** Bert Sanders, Tom Meli, Leo Starosch, Martin Hansen, Gino Rossi, Gaston Meulenbroucq, Gino Menozzi, Les Allen. **1955** Andre De Keersgeter, Andre Drille, Franz Szuzina. **1956** Tino Albanese, Billy Ellaway, Jerry Luedee. **1957** Marcel Pigou
WON CO (7)	**1952** Art Lewis. **1953** Ron Grogan. **1954** George Dilkes, George Roe, Harry Mino. **1955** Emile Delmine. **1956** Willie Armstrong
WON RSC/RTD (15)	**1952** Jack Thomas, Stan Prescott, Frankie Webb, Tommy Hilton. **1953** Tom Johnston, Bobby Rhodes, Rocco King. **1954** Bert Sanders, Arthur Acha, Jean Mollekens, Frans Wahl, Gino Rossi, Mario Salvoldi. **1955** Heinz Sanger. **1957** Leen Jansen
DREW (2)	**1957** Dick Tiger. **1958** Hanswerner Wohlers
LOST PTS (3)	**1956** Jimmy Elliott, Tiberio Mitri. **1958** Terry Downes
LOST RSC/RTD (1)	**1956** Spider Webb

Jock McAvoy

Undefeated British Middleweight Champion, 1933 – 1945. Undefeated British Empire Middleweight Champion, 1933 – 1939. British L. Heavyweight Champion, 1937 – 1938

Born 20.11.08 *From* Rochdale *Died* 1971 (birthname Joe Bamford) *Pro Career* 1927 – 1945 (147 contests, won 133, lost 14)

CHAMPIONSHIP CONTESTS (12)

21.03.32	Len Harvey	L PTS 15	Manchester	B, BE	Middleweight Titles
10.04.33	Len Harvey	W PTS 15	Manchester	B, BE	Middleweight Titles
09.10.33	Archie Sexton	W CO 10	Manchester	B, BE	Middleweight Titles
14.01.35	Marcel Thil	L PTS 15	Paris	EU	L. Heavyweight Title
24.06.35	Al Burke	W PTS 15	Manchester	B, BE	Middleweight Titles
13.03.36	John Henry Lewis	L PTS 15	New York	W	L. Heavyweight Title

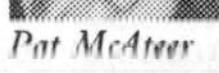

Pat McAteer

Jack McAvoy

23.04.36	Jack Petersen	L PTS 15	London	B, BE	Heavyweight Titles
27.04.37	Eddie Phillips	W CO 14	London	B	L. Heavyweight Title
25.10.37	Jack Hyams	W RTD 11	Manchester	B, BE	Middleweight Titles
07.04.38	Len Harvey	L PTS 15	London	B	L. Heavyweight Title
22.05.39	Ginger Sadd	W PTS 15	Manchester	B, BE	Middleweight Titles
10.07.39	Len Harvey	L PTS 15	London	B, BE, W	L. Heavyweight Titles

NON CHAMPIONSHIP CONTESTS (135)

WON PTS (38) **1929** Jack Ogden, Griff Williams, Billy Chew. **1930** Fred Oldfield, Fred Blything, George Porter, Farmer Jackson, Jimmy Cox (2), Joe Rostron, Joe Lowther. **1931** Shocker Bowman, Charlie McDonald, Sonny Doke (2), Fred Shaw. **1932** Seaman Harvey, Jack Etienne, Carmelo Candel, George Brown, Hans Seifried. **1933** Jack Hyams, Oddone Piazza, George Brown, Jack Forster. **1934** Eddie Pierce, Ernie Simmons. **1935** Garcia Lluch, Marcel Lauriot, Al McCoy. **1936** Anson Green, Rienus de Boer. **1937** Cheo Morejan, Dai Jones. **1938** Joe Quigley. **1939** Jack Hyams. **1941** Jack Hyams. **1945** Tommy Davies

WON CO (53) **1927** Billy Longworth, Bill Lee, Tommy Walsh. **1929** Teddy Cox, Frank Ormerod, Jack Ogden, Tiger Ennis. **1930** Marine Davies, Sid Aldridge, Jack Ogden, Andy Ross, Jack Wilkinson, Ted Lewis, Dai Beynon, Eddie Strawer (2), Shocker Bowman, Jim Pearson, Patsy Flynn, Jim Johnson. **1931** Charlie Keeling, Johnny Seamark, Jack Bottomley, Jerry Daley, Bill Adair, Red Pullen. **1932** Jack Marshall, Bill Hood, Sandy McKenzie, Phil Green, Tommy Moore. **1933** Les Ward, Red Pullen, Leonard Steyaert. **1934** Al Burke, Eddie Maguire, Teddie Phillips, Charlie Parkin, Jack Etienne, Kid Tunero. **1935** Babe Risco. **1936** Jim Smith, Bob Simpkins, Bill Wainwright. **1938** Bill Hardy, Jack Strongbow, Marcel Lauriot, Frank Hough. **1939** Emile Lebrize. **1940** Charlie Parkin. **1941** Jim Berry. **1945** George Howard, Johnny Clements

WON RSC/RTD (35) **1927** Bert Hilditch. **1929** Teddy Hay, Eric Bargh, Jack Jukes, Seaman Douglas, Jack Harrison, Ted Abbott, Lud Gresvig, Billy Horner. **1930** Fred Oldfield, Soldier Jones, Billy Delahaye, Tate Evans, Bill Green. **1931** Dick Burt, Con Van Leuwen, Jack O'Brien, Joe Lowther, Alf Pegazzano, Paul Maguire, Sonny Doke. **1932** Edwin John, Billy Thomas,

CONTINUED OVERLEAF

	Tom Benjamin, Billy Roberts, Ted Coveney, Milhail Fubeq. **1933** Glen Moody. **1936** Albert Barjolin. **1937** Alban Mulrooney, Vasile Serbanesco. **1938** Jack Strongbow, Jack Robinson. **1939** Tino Rolando. **1940** Jim Berry
WON DIS (1)	**1931** Jack Hyams
LOST PTS (4)	**1930** Jim Pearson, Joe Rostron. **1940** Freddie Mills, Eddie Maguire
LOST RSC/RTD (2)	**1928** Billy Chew. **1942** Freddie Mills
LOST DIS (2)	**1931** Paul Maguire. **1932** Jack Casey

NOTE:
The Lonsdale Belt was not issued for the British Championship Contest versus Jack Petersen, whilst the World Championship Contest versus Len Harvey was for the GB version of the title.

Sammy McCarthy

British Featherweight Champion, 1954 – 1955
Born 05.11.31 *From* Stepney *Pro Career* 1951 – 1957 (53 contests, won 44, drew 1, lost 8)

CHAMPIONSHIP CONTESTS (4)

16.02.54	Jean Sneyers	L PTS 15	London	EU	Featherweight Title
01.06.54	Ronnie Clayton	W RTD 8	London	B	Featherweight Title
22.01.55	Billy Spider Kelly	L PTS 15	Belfast	B, BE	Featherweight Titles
26.06.56	Joe Lucy	L RSC 13	London	B	Lightweight Title

NON CHAMPIONSHIP CONTESTS (49)

WON PTS (17)	**1951** Jackie Horseman. **1952** Jim McCann, Denny Dawson, Johnny Molloy, Jim Kenny, Charlie Simpkins, George Stewart, Ronnie Clayton. **1953** Amleto Falcinelli, Jacques Legendre. **1954** Teddy Peckham, Joe Woussem, Roy Ankrah. **1955** Lucien Meraint. **1956** Frank Johnson, Johnny Mann (2)
WON CO (5)	**1951** Hector Macrow, Roy Groome, Jackie Leonard. **1955** Andre Younsi, Willi Swoboda
WON RSC/RTD (20)	**1951** Peter Morrison, Teddy Odus, Zeke Brown. **1952** Jackie Lucraft, Hugh Mackie, Laurie McShane, Pat Kelly, Freddie King, Jackie Turpin, Jan Maas. **1953** Eugene Servais, Louis Cabo, Gene Caffrey. **1954** Enrico Macale, Pierre Richard. **1955** Teddy Peckham, Jesus Rubio, Juan Alvarez. **1956** Johnny Miller, Jacques Dumnesnil
WON DIS (1)	**1953** Ken Lawrence
DREW (1)	**1951** Freddie Hicks
LOST PTS (5)	**1953** Hogan Bassey, Ray Famechon. **1955** Jean Sneyers. **1956** Dave Charnley. **1957** Guy Gracia

Dave McCleave

British Welterweight Champion, 1936
Born 1911 *From* Smithfield *Pro Career* 1934 – 1945 (115 contests, won 84, drew 3, lost 28)

CHAMPIONSHIP CONTESTS (2)

23.04.36	Chuck Parker	W PTS 15	London	B	Welterweight Title
02.06.36	Jake Kilrain	L CO 8	Glasgow	B	Welterweight Title

NON CHAMPIONSHIP CONTESTS (113)

WON PTS (48)	**1934** Chuck Parker, Jimmy Walker, Pat Butler, Stoker Reynolds, Harry Mason, Ernie Roderick, Panther Purchase. **1935** Bob Nelson, George Rose, Billy Bird, Roy Mills, Leo Phillips. **1936** Ginger Sadd, George Bunter, Tommy Bland, George Daly, Sven Suvio. **1937** Bert Bevan, Ginger Sadd, Harry Gains, Jim Mount. **1938** Dai Jones (2), Paul Schaefer, Mohammed Fahmy, Tom Curran, Freddie Mills. **1939** Paul Schaefer, Eddie Maguire. **1940** A/C Meadows, Paul Schaefer, Jack Lewis, Johnny Clements. **1941** Johnny Blake (3), Eddie Maguire. **1942** H. Moy, Charlie Parkin, Reg Gregory, Paddy Roche, Tommy Davies, Trevor Burt. **1943** Jim Berry, Tommy Smith, Paddy Roche. **1944** Jim Berry, Dick Turpin, Bert Gilroy

Sammy McCarthy

Dave McCleave

WON CO (11) **1935** George Rose, Jim Reinenberg. **1936** George Bunter Frank Davey. **1938** Moe Moss. **1940** Albert O'Brien, Elfryn Morris. **1941** Charlie Parkin. **1942** Sid Williams, Charlie Parkin (2)

WON RSC/RTD (15) **1934** Tommy Marren. **1935** Jim Toohig. **1936** Harry Ainsworth, Bob Simpkins. **1937** Dan Sullivan. **1938** Charlie Parkin, Jack Powell. **1941** Jim Johnson. **1942** Ted Barter, Charlie Knock, George Gale, Charlie Parkin. **1943** Charlie Parkin. **1944** Charlie Parkin. **1945** Trevor Burt

WON DIS (9) **1935** Ernie Molde. **1936** Johnny Rust. **1937** Alban Mulrooney. **1938** Moe Moss. **1939** Eddie Maguire, Jack Powell. **1941** Ray McIntyre. **1943** Bert Gilroy. **1944** Jim Berry

DREW (3) **1935** Leo Phillips. **1936** Paul Schaefer. **1937** Stafford Barton

LOST PTS (6) **1935** Ernie Roderick, Ginger Sadd. **1936** Ernie Roderick. **1937** Ben Valentine. **1939** Jack Hyams. **1941** Jack Hyams

LOST CO (9) **1936** Jack Lord. **1937** Stafford Barton. **1938** George Davis. **1939** Freddie Mills (2), Ernie Roderick, Stafford Barton. **1940** Dick Turpin. **1942** Johnny Blake

LOST RSC/RTD (11) **1937** Eddie Maguire. **1938** Hein Weisner, George Davis. **1941** Jim Laverick, Ron Lindley, Paddy Lyons, Ginger Sadd. **1942** Pat O'Connor, Jack Hyams. **1943** Jim Berry. **1944** Vince Hawkins

LOST DIS (1) **1935** Johnny Quill

NOTE:
The Lonsdale Belt was not issued for the British Championship Contests versus Chuck Parker and Jake Kilrain.

John McCluskey

Undefeated British Flyweight Champion, 1967 – 1975. Commonwealth Flyweight Champion, 1970 – 1971
Born 23.01.44 *From* Hamilton *Pro Career* 1965 – 1975 (38 contests, won 23, lost 15)

CONTINUED OVERLEAF

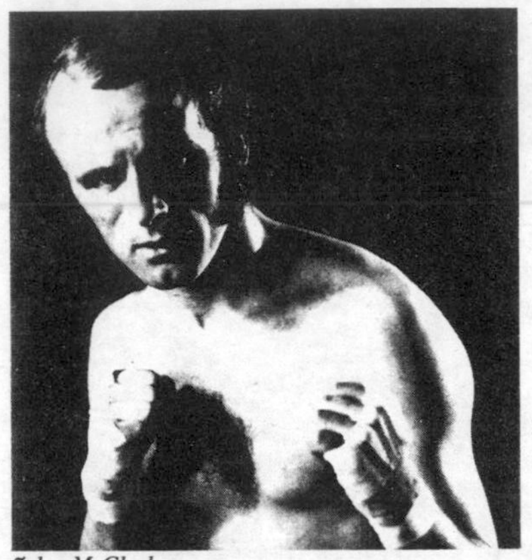
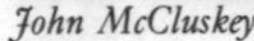
John McCluskey

John Cowboy McCormack

CHAMPIONSHIP CONTESTS (9)

16.01.67	Tony Barlow	**W** CO 8	Manchester	B	Flyweight Title
26.06.68	Fernando Atzori	L CO 4	Naples	EU	Flyweight Title
07.05.69	Tony Barlow	**W** RSC 13	Solihull	B	Flyweight Title
04.04.70	Franco Zurlo	L PTS 15	Zurich	EU	Bantamweight Title
16.06.70	Harry Hayes	**W** PTS 15	Melbourne	C	Flyweight Title
19.03.71	Fernando Atzori	L PTS 15	Zurich	EU	Flyweight Title
06.08.71	Henry Nissen	L RTD 8	Melbourne	C	Flyweight Title
26.12.72	Fritz Chervet	L PTS 15	Zurich	EU	Flyweight Title
14.10.74	Tony Davies	**W** RSC 1	Swansea	B	Flyweight Title

NON CHAMPIONSHIP CONTESTS (29)

WON PTS (12)	**1965** Baby John. **1966** Simon Tiger, Tommy Connor, Winston Van Guylenburg. **1967** Manolin Alvarez, Lachy Linares, Jan Persson. **1968** Fabian Bellanco. **1969** Mike Buttle, Fritz Chervet. **1971** Colin Miles. **1974** John Kellie
WON CO (1)	**1968** Kid Miller
WON RSC/RTD (6)	**1965** Tony Barlow. **1966** Tommy Connor, Tony Barlow. **1969** Glyn Davies, Arturo Leon. **1970** John Kellie
LOST PTS (6)	**1967** Fernando Atzori. **1968** Johnny Clark, Fritz Chervet. **1970** Paul Ferreri, Tony Moreno. **1974** Patrick Mambwe
LOST RSC/RTD (4)	**1971** Dave Needham. **1972** Paddy Maguire. **1974** Helenio Ferreira. **1975** Wayne Evans

John Cowboy McCormack

British Middleweight Champion, 1959. European Middleweight Champion, 1961 – 1962
Born 09.01.35 *From* Maryhill *Pro Career* 1957 – 1966 (45 contests, won 38, lost 7)

CHAMPIONSHIP CONTESTS (6)

15.09.59	Terry Downes	**W** DIS 8	London	B	Middleweight Title
03.11.59	Terry Downes	L RSC 8	London	B	Middleweight Title
17.10.61	Harko Kokmeyer	**W** PTS 15	London	EU	Middleweight Title
06.01.62	Heini Freytag	**W** PTS 15	Frankfurt	EU	Middleweight Title
08.02.62	Chris Christensen	L DIS 4	Copenhagen	EU	Middleweight Title
26.11.62	George Aldridge	L CO 6	Manchester	B	Middleweight Title

NON CHAMPIONSHIP CONTESTS (39)

WON PTS (17)	**1957** Dudley Cox. **1958** Johnny Read, Attu Clottey, Len Mullen, Jim

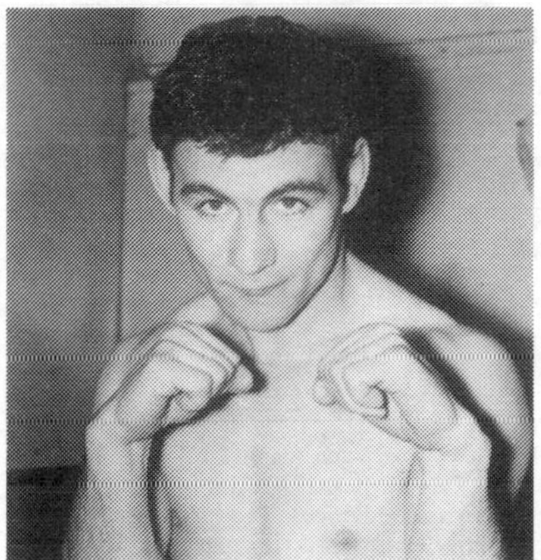

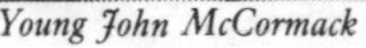

Young John McCormack *Pat McCormack*

	Lynas, Martin Hansen, Jean Ruellet. **1959** Orlando Paso, Michel Diouf, Gene Johns. **1960** Giancarlo Garbelli, George Benton. **1961** Phil Edwards, Michel Diouf, Sandy Luke. **1962** Henry Hank, Ike White
WON CO (5)	**1957** Cliff Garvey, Jack Willis, Frank Davis. **1958** Harry Dodoo. **1964** Malcolm Worthington
WON RSC/RTD (13)	**1957** Eddie Williams, Bonnie Garraway, Wally Scott, Eddie Lennon, Evie Vorster. **1958** Vincent O'Kine. **1959** Paddy Delargy, Remo Carati. **1960** Tommy Tagoe, George Aldridge. **1964** Joe Louis. **1965** Bernard Quellier, Chic Calderwood
LOST PTS (2)	**1960** Gustav Scholz. **1966** Young John McCormack
LOST RSC/RTD (2)	**1957** Jim Lynas. **1963** Harry Scott

Young John McCormack

British L. Heavyweight Champion, 1967 – 1969
Born 11.12.44 *From* Dublin *Pro Career* 1963 – 1970 (42 contests, won 33, drew 1, lost 8)

CHAMPIONSHIP CONTESTS (5)

19.06.67	Eddie Avoth	W RSC 7	London	B	L. Heavyweight Title
22.11.67	Derek Richards	W CO 7	Solihull	B	L. Heavyweight Title
12.02.68	Bob Dunlop	L RSC 7	Sydney	BE	L. Heavyweight Title
13.01.69	Eddie Avoth	L RTD 11	London	B	L. Heavyweight Title
06.04.70	Eddie Avoth	L DIS 8	Nottingham	B	L. Heavyweight Title

NON CHAMPIONSHIP CONTESTS (37)

WON PTS (5)	**1965** Malcolm Worthington, Gerry Hassett. **1966** John Cowboy McCormack. **1967** Lion Ven. **1968** Lloyd Walford
WON CO (3)	**1963** Terry Phillips. **1964** John James. **1967** Daniel Levillier
WON RSC/RTD (22)	**1963** Roy Burke, Joe Somerville, Patrick Onwuna. **1964** Gary Chippendale, Roy Thomas, Billy Allport, Ivor Evans, Roy Sewards (2), Dave Wakefield, Jack Grant. **1965** Roy Sewards, Ivor Evans, Bob Nicolson. **1966** Derek Richards, Victor Chapelle. **1967** Valerie Mahau. **1968** Guinea Roger, John Hendrickson. **1969** Lloyd Walford, Guinea Roger, Cosimo Bruno
WON DIS (1)	**1963** Derek Cowper
DREW (1)	**1964** Derek Richards
LOST PTS (2)	**1966** Lion Ven. **1969** Tom Bogs
LOST RSC/RTD (3)	**1964** George Hollister. **1965** Orlando Paso. **1969** Guinea Roger

Pat McCormack

British L. Welterweight Champion, 1974
Born 28.04.46 Dublin *From* Brixton *Pro Career* 1968 – 1975 (49 contests, won 30, drew 1, lost 18)

CHAMPIONSHIP CONTESTS (3)

26.03.74	Des Morrison	W CO 11	London	B	L. Welterweight Title
21.11.74	Joey Singleton	L PTS 15	Liverpool	B	L. Welterweight Title
15.12.75	Pat Thomas	L CO 13	London	B	Welterweight Title

NON CHAMPIONSHIP CONTESTS (46)

WON PTS (4)	**1968** Tommy Tiger. **1969** Tommy Tiger. **1971** Jimmy Fairweather. **1975** Billy Waith
WON CO (4)	**1968** Barry Coley. **1972** Giele Buitendag. **1974** Vasco Armstrong. **1975** Giele Buitendag
WON RSC/RTD (20)	**1968** Winston Thomas, Lloyd Wallace, Victor Paul, Tony Cunningham, Ray Fallone. **1969** Victor Paul, Lex Hunter. **1970** Paul Bromley, Enzo Petrigua, Boerge Krogh (2), Tomasso Marocco, Teddy Cooper. **1971** Phil Dykes. **1972** David Pesenti, Phil Dykes. **1973** Jorgen Hansen, Erkki Meronen. **1974** Tony Bagshaw. **1975** Kevin White
WON DIS (1)	**1974** Joseph Sossou
DREW (1)	**1972** Gert Steyn
LOST PTS (3)	**1971** Stoffel Steyn. **1972** Amos Talbot. **1975** Gert Craemer
LOST CO (3)	**1969** Peter Quinn. **1971** Johnny Gant. **1973** Giele Buitendag
LOST RSC/RTD (8)	**1969** Ricky Porter. **1971** Joe Tetteh. **1972** Amos Talbot, Jorgen Hansen. **1973** Hector Thompson. **1974** Laurits Jensen, Kristian Hoydhal. **1975** Tony Petronelli
LOST DIS (2)	**1971** Bruno Meggiolaro. **1973** Jorgen Hansen

Tommy McGovern

British Lightweight Champion, 1951 – 1952
Born 05.02.24 *From* Bermondsey *Pro Career* 1947 – 1953 (65 contests, won 44, drew 4, lost 17)

CHAMPIONSHIP CONTESTS (4)

11.07.50	Billy Thompson	L PTS 15	Hanley	B	Lightweight Title
28.08.51	Billy Thompson	W CO 1	London	B	Lightweight Title
20.03.52	Jorgen Johansen	DREW 15	Copenhagen	EU	Lightweight Title
25.07.52	Frank Johnson	L PTS 15	Manchester	B	Lightweight Title

NON CHAMPIONSHIP CONTESTS (61)

WON PTS (33)	**1947** Ben Mendells, Charlie Harris, Joe Poccia, Zach Taylor, Don Murray, Clyde English, Joe Murray, Jimmy Warren, Pete Manchio, Tony Labua. **1948** Billy Barton, George Daly, Freddie Smith. **1949** Bert Hornby, Freddie Smith, Jim Keery, Al Wilburn. **1950** Chris Jenkins, Elis Ask, Frank Parkes, Peter Fallon, Alberto Diori, Mickey O'Neill, Tommy Barnham. **1951** Frank Parkes, Emmett Kenny, Allan Tanner. **1952** Cliff Anderson, Emmett Kenny, Frank Parkes, Ricky McCullough, Tom Bailey. **1953** John Mahlangu
WON CO (3)	**1947** Fox Williams. **1948** Morry Jones, Tommy Barton
WON RSC/RTD (7)	**1948** Johnny Fitzpatrick. **1949** George Daly, Ben Duffy. **1950** Chris Jenkins, Morty Kelleher. **1951** Des Garrod, Maurice Mancini
DREW (3)	**1949** Vernon Ball, Jimmy Toweel. **1953** Solly Cantor
LOST PTS (15)	**1947** Phil Terranova, Jimmy Warren, Arthur King, Ritchie Shinn. **1948** Ben Duffy, Claude Dennington. **1949** Solly Cantor, Harry Hughes, Arthur King. **1951** Allan Tanner, Roy Ankrah. **1952** Hoacine Khalfi. **1953** Joe Lucy (2), Jacques Prigent

Walter McGowan

Undefeated British Flyweight Champion, 1963 – 1966. Undefeated British Empire Flyweight Champion 1963 – 1970. World Flyweight Champion, 1966. British & British Empire Bantamweight Champion, 1966 – 1968
Born 13.10.42 *From* Hamilton *Pro Career* 1961 – 1969 (40 contests, won 32, drew 1, lost 7)

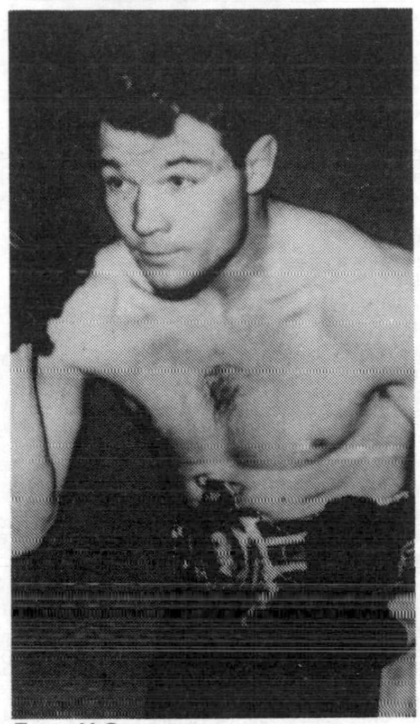

Tommy McGovern

Walter McGowan

CHAMPIONSHIP CONTESTS (9)

02.05.63	Jackie Brown	W CO 12	Paisley	B, BE	Flyweight Titles
12.09.63	Kid Solomon	W RSC 9	Paisley	BE	Flyweight Title
24.04.64	Salvatore Burruni	L PTS 15	Rome	EU	Flyweight Title
03.12.65	Tommaso Galli	DREW 15	Rome	EU	Bantamweight Title
14.06.66	Salvatore Burruni	W PTS 15	London	W	Flyweight Title
06.09.66	Alan Rudkin	W PTS 15	London	B, BE	Bantamweight Titles
30.12.66	Chartchai Chionoi	L RSC 9	Bangkok	W	Flyweight Title
19.09.67	Chartchai Chionoi	L RSC 7	London	W	Flyweight Title
13.05.68	Alan Rudkin	L PTS 15	Manchester	B, BE	Bantamweight Titles

NON CHAMPIONSHIP CONTESTS (31)

WON PTS (16)	**1961** Eddie Barraclough, Brian Bissmire. **1962** Danny Lee. **1963** Bernard Jubert, Ric Magramo. **1964** Risto Luukkonen, Natalio Jiminez. **1965** Felix Brami, Benny Lee. **1966** Ernesto Miranda. **1967** Osamu Miyashita, Giancarlo Centa, Antoine Porcel. **1968** Messaoud Boussabova. **1969** Umberto Simbola, Antonio Chiloiro
WON CO (1)	**1962** Jacques Jacob
WON RSC/RTD (11)	**1961** George McDade. **1962** Rene Libeer, Ray Jutras. **1963** Ray Perez. **1964** Luis Rodriguez. **1965** Mick Hussey. **1966** Nevio Carbi, Jose Bisbal. **1968** Gerard Macrez, Marc Van Domme. **1969** Michel Houdeau
LOST PTS (1)	**1961** Jackie Brown
LOST RSC/RTD (2)	**1965** Joe Medel, Ron Jones

NOTE:
All of the above World Championship Contests were for the WBC version of the Title

Johnny McGrory

Undefeated British & British Empire Featherweight Champion, 1936 – 1938
Born 25.04.15 *From* Glasgow *Pro Career* 1933 – 1943 (102 contests, won 71, drew 8, lost 23)

CHAMPIONSHIP CONTESTS (2)

24.09.36	Nel Tarleton	**W** PTS 15	Liverpool	B	Featherweight Title
26.12.36	Willie Smith	**W** PTS 12	Johannesburg	BE	Featherweight Title

NON CHAMPIONSHIP CONTESTS (100)

WON PTS (47)	**1933** Alex Adams, Mick Malone, Jim Driscoll, Frank Markey, Jim Cowie, Arley Hollingsworth, Phineas John, George Morris, Dave Finn. **1934** Charlie Jordan, Tony Butcher, Sammy Haines, Tommy Fox, Benny Sharkey, Billy Hazel, Stan Jehu, Len Beynon, Young Beckett, Johnny Peters, Joe Horridge, Joe Connolly. **1935** Harry Daly, Dick Corbett, Doug Kestrell, Hal Cartwright, Pancho Martinez. **1936** Simon Chavez, KO Morgan, Gustave Ansini. **1937** Arnold Lagrand, Jim Spider Kelly. **1938** Johnny King, Billy Charlton, Dan McAllister, Jackie Hurst, Jack Carrick, Dave Crowley. **1939** Johnny Jenkins, Johnny Walters. **1941** Peter Brown, Les McCarthy, Dave Finn. **1942** Doug Bygrave, Griff Williams, Cuthbert Taylor (3)
WON CO (7)	**1933** Freddie Smith, Freddie Warnock. **1934** Albert Roothooft, Jim Cowie. **1935** Gilbert Johnston, Boyo Burns. **1938** Tommy Bruce
WON RSC/RTD (8)	**1934** Jackie Bishop, Bobby Morgan. **1935** Teddy Hayes, Johnny McMillan. **1936** Lucien Biquet, Benny Sharkey, Joe Green, Billy Gannon
WON DIS (7)	**1933** Alf Barrett. **1935** Dave Crowley. **1936** Ginger Foran. **1939** Hal Cartwright, Charlie Fox, Len Beynon. **1942** Jimmy Watson
DREW (8)	**1933** Fred Hardy. **1934** Benny Caplan. **1937** George Williams. **1938** Benny Caplan. **1939** Dave Finn, Len Wickwar. **1940** Joe Connolly. **1942** Johnny Ward
LOST PTS (12)	**1934** Gilbert Johnston, Benny Caplan. **1935** Joe Connolly. **1937** Benny Sharkey. **1938** Jim Spider Kelly, Johnny Cusick, Jack Carrick. **1939** Tommy Hyams, Charlie Fox. **1940** Harry Lazar. **1941** Ivor Thomas. **1943** Tommy Hyams
LOST CO (4)	**1935** KO Morgan. **1937** Ginger Foran. **1938** Ronnie James. **1939** Eric Boon
LOST RSC/RTD (6)	**1935** Phil Zwick. **1936** Jackie Wilson. **1940** Tommy Hyams, Eddie Ryan. **1941** Ginger Stewart. **1942** Dave Crowley
LOST DIS (1)	**1942** Jimmy Watson

Paddy Maguire

British Bantamweight Champion, 1975 – 1977
Born 26.09.48 *From* Belfast *Pro Career* 1969 – 1977 (35 contests, won 26, drew 1, lost 8)

CHAMPIONSHIP CONTESTS (7)

20.02.73	Johnny Clark	L PTS 15	London	B	Bantamweight Title
10.12.74	Dave Needham	L PTS 15	Nottingham	B	Bantamweight Title
07.03.75	Paul Ferreri	L RSC 8	Melbourne	C	Bantamweight Title
20.10.75	Dave Needham	**W** RSC 14	London	B	Bantamweight Title
16.01.76	Daniel Trioulaire	DREW 15	Cluses	EU	Bantamweight Title
28.09.77	Franco Zurlo	L RTD 8	Sardinia	EU	Bantamweight Title
29.11.77	Johnny Owen	L RSC 11	London	B	Bantamweight Title

NON CHAMPIONSHIP CONTESTS (28)

WON PTS (10)	**1969** Bernard Nicholls, Gerry McBride. **1971** Colin Miles. **1972** Guy Caudron, Barry Sponagle. **1974** Antonio Tenza, Achene Saifi. **1976** Jose Luis Del Flores, Alun Trembath, Raoul Ramirez
WON CO (6)	**1970** Al Hutcheon, Kamara Diop. **1972** Ben Salah Abdesselem. **1973** Frankie Taberner. **1976** Charlie Parvin, John Kellie

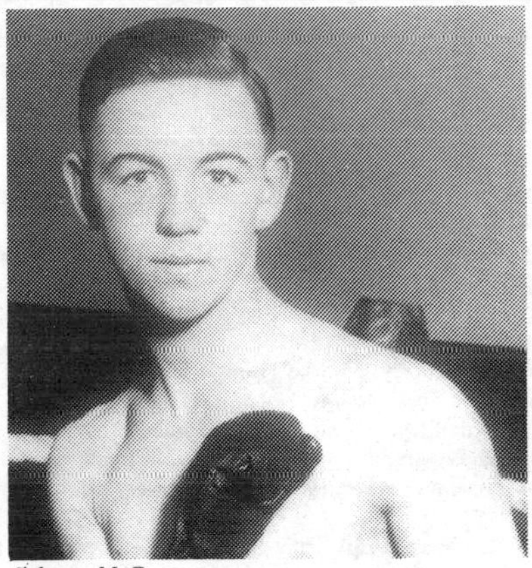

Johnny McGrory

Paddy Maguire

WON RSC/RTD (9)	**1970** Joey Lando, Glyn Davies, Dionisio Bisbal. **1971** Karim Young. **1972** John Mitchell, John McCluskey, Michel Jamet. **1976** Les Pickett. **1977** George Sutton
LOST PTS (1)	**1977** Helenio Ferreira
LOST RSC/RTD (2)	**1971** Bob Allotey. **1977** Alberto Sandoval

Harry Mason

Undefeated British Lightweight Champion, 1923 – 1928. Undefeated European Lightweight Champion, 1923. British Welterweight Champion, 1925 – 1926 and 1934
Born 27.03.03 London *From* Leeds *Died* 1977 *Pro Career* 1920 – 1937 (207 contests, won 140, drew 14, lost 51, no decision 2)

CHAMPIONSHIP CONTESTS (11)

17.05.23	Seaman Hall	W DIS 13	London	B, EU	Lightweight Titles
21.11.23	Ernie Rice	W PTS 20	London	B, EU	Lightweight Titles
22.06.25	Ernie Izzard	W RSC 9	London	B	Lightweight Title
08.10.25	Hamilton Johnny Brown	L PTS 20	London	B	Welterweight Title
19.11.25	Hamilton Johnny Brown	W PTS 20	London	B	Welterweight Title
11.02.26	Ernie Rice	W DIS 5	London	B	Lightweight Title
29.04.26	Len Harvey	DREW 20	London	B	Welterweight Title
31.05.26	Jack Hood	L PTS 20	London	B	Welterweight Title
22.07.26	Jack Hood	L PTS 20	London	B	Welterweight Title
11.06.34	Len Tiger Smith	W DIS 14	Birmingham	B	Welterweight Title
17.12.34	Pat Butler	L PTS 15	Leicester	B	Welterweight Title

NON CHAMPIONSHIP CONTESTS (196)

WON PTS (102)	**1920** Young Bull, Jack Lloyd, Alf Perry. **1921** George Smith, Charlie Baynard, Young Bull, Young Corbett, Young Humphries, Ted Murton, Albert Hicks, Charlie Duggan, Les Kemp, Nat Green. **1922** Jack Wayland, Phil Bond, Jack Alexander, Teddy Baker (2), Jack Dando, Benny Lee, Mike Blake, Harry Whybrow, Jim Jeffords, Harry Barton, Harry Jones, Johnny Gibbons, Fred Bullions, Arthur Abbott, Bill Handley, Jack Kirk, Charlie Webb, Joe Conn, Mike Honeyman, Francis Rossi, Harry Salkend, Fred Archer. **1923** Bob Jackson, Ben Callicot, Bill Handley, Jack Kirk, Seaman Hall. **1924** Harry Brown, Herb Brodie, Paul Fritsch, Danny Morgan, Phil Waters, Tom McInnes, Alf Simmons. **1925** Sonny Bird, Jack Kirk, Edouard Baudry, Frank Lane. **1926** Alex Ireland. **1927** Billy Mattick, Archie Walker, Alf Mancini, Leo Geeraerts.

CONTINUED OVERLEAF

	1928 Billy Bird. **1929** Len Shepherd (2), Oscar Jacobson, Leo Genet, Harry Gadd, Archie Sexton.. **1930** Henri Mouha, Jack Hood, Charles Ollivon, Jackie Brady, Alf Mancini, Jack Casey, Jack Hyams, Steve McCall. **1931** Stoker Reynolds, George Rose. **1932** Paul McGuire, Billy Bird, Jack Powell, Seaman Froggatt. **1933** Jack Forster, Al Bowden, Jim Abbott, Billy Bird, Stoker Reynolds, Fred Webster, Wal Dinsey, John Summers, Charlie Baxter. **1934** Gaston Deveux, George Willis, George Purchase, Danny Evans. **1935** Joe Kelso, George Willis, Chris Dawson, Jack Moody (2), Jim Boyle, Fred Clements. **1936** Tab Davies, Harry Ainsworth, Ron Barber, Billy Strange
WON CO (4)	**1921** Dan Bowling. **1922** Billy Simpson. **1928** Billy Richards. **1930** Julius de Kessler
WON RSC/RTD (21)	**1921** George Hewitt, Harry Halberry, George Humphries, Tony Francis. **1922** George Senior, Jack Wayland, George Nolan, Jim Corp. **1927** Billy Mattick. **1928** Young Ziland, Jack Donn. **1929** Horace Burkell. **1930** Albert Shoppone, Ona Westmoet, Jack Haynes. **1933** Tuck Mason, Les Ward. **1934** Tommy Taylor. **1935** Chuck Parker, Eddie Gott. **1936** Ron Barber
WON DIS (7)	**1922** Walter Rossi. **1928** Leo Wax. **1930** Ernie Rice, Camille Desmet. **1935** Chris Dawson. **1936** Buster Osborne, George Davis
DREW (13)	**1921** George Hewitt. **1922** Walter Rossi, Seaman Hall. **1923** Mike Honeyman. **1925** Lucien Vinez. **1931** Arie Van Vliet, Haydn Williams, Jim Winters. **1932** George Rose, Glen Moody, Joe Rostron. **1933** Danny Evans. **1934** Moe Moss
LOST PTS (33)	**1921** Alf Hancock, Dan Bowling. **1922** Jack Kirk. **1923** Henri Dupont. **1924** Johnny Clinton, Red Herring. **1927** Tommy Freeman. **1928** Tommy Fairhall, Jack Carroll. **1929** Jack Spar. **1930** Joe Dundee, Alf Howard, Steve McCall, Sandy McKenzie. **1931** Fred Webster. **1932** Fred Webster, George Rose. **1933** Joe Rostron, Fred Webster. **1934** Pat Haley, George Bunter, George Purchase, Pat Butler, Dave McCleave. **1935** Len Wickwar, Ginger Sadd, Jim Lawlor. **1936** Len Wickwar, John Rust (2), Jack Lewis, Alban Mulrooney, Jack Powell
LOST CO (5)	**1922** Alf Simmons. **1924** Dave Caplan. **1928** Wes Ketchell. **1933** Moe Moss. **1936** Bob Scally
LOST RSC/RTD (6)	**1932** Dai Beynon, Del Fontaine. **1935** Charlie Parkin, Jake Kilrain. **1936** Tommy Martin. **1937** Jackie Kid Berg
LOST DIS (3)	**1929** Charlie McDonald. **1931** Jack Casey. **1934** Henri Baumas
ND (2)	**1924** Sid Barbarian, Billy McCann

NOTE:
The Lonsdale Belt was only issued for the British Championship Contests versus Ernie Izzard and Jack Hood (2) and the Contest versus Ernie Rice (11.02.26) was not generally recognised to have been a Championship match

Reggie Meen

British Heavyweight Champion, 1931 – 1932
Born 1907 *From* Desborough *Pro Career* 1927 – 1939 (103 contests, won 57, drew 3, lost 43)

CHAMPIONSHIP CONTESTS (2)

16.11.31	Charlie Smith	**W** PTS 15	Leicester	B	Heavyweight Title
12.07.32	Jack Petersen	L CO 2	London	B	Heavyweight Title

NON CHAMPIONSHIP CONTESTS (101)

WON PTS (6)	**1930** Gipsy Daniels. **1931** Harry Crossley, Maurice Griselle, Joe Woods (2). **1932** Bob Carvill
WON CO (38)	**1927** Stanley Glen, Tom Fowler. **1928** Joe Gordon, Horace Hampton. **1929** Fred Davies, Will Lancaster, Battling Sullivan, George Tootles, Frank Berwick, Charlie Chetwynd, Eddie Steele, Arthur Evans, Joe Mullins, Alf Noble, George Slack, Bob Shields. **1930** Albert Nakin, Jack Stanley, Bill Trinder, Dick Power, Dan Shortland. **1931** Frank

Fowler, Jack Humbeek, Peter Van Goole, Epifano Islas. **1933** Frank Barrington, Rene Morris, Kid Scott. **1934** Max Hodgetts, Frank Hawkins. **1935** Dick Holland, Ted Glover, Leo Wax. **1936** Paddy Donovan, Jack Stanley, Guardsman Wilkinson. **1937** Jack Stanley, Sam Godfrey

WON RSC/RTD (10)	**1928** Frank Brown, Steve Taylor, Dan McCarthy. **1929** Willie McMahon. **1930** Marc Noben. **1931** Joe Mullins. **1932** Charlie Smith. **1933** Maurice Griselle. **1935** Bob Stone. **1936** Chick Knight
WON DIS (2)	**1929** Joe Mullins. **1934** Eddie Steele
DREW (3)	**1928** Harry Reeve. **1930** Georges Gardebois. **1933** Ernst Guhring
LOST PTS (11)	**1928** Andrew Newton. **1929** Eddie Steele. **1930** Georges Gardebois, Harry Crossley, Charlie Smith. **1932** George Cook. **1933** Charlie Smith, Gipsy Daniels, Vincenz Hower. **1934** Jim Winters. **1935** Tommy Allen
LOST CO (12)	**1927** Joe Mullins (2). **1928** Ted Sandwina. **1931** Maurice Griselle. **1932** Don McCorkindale. **1933** Jack Pettifer, Pierre Charles. **1934** Jack Petersen, Alf Luxton, Bob Carvill. **1937** Ron Lindley, Max Hodgetts
LOST RSC/RTD (12)	**1930** Gipsy Daniels, Charlie Smith, Primo Carnera. **1931** Hans Schonrath. **1932** Hein Muller. **1933** Walter Neusel. **1934** Frank Barrington. **1936** Bill Wainwright. **1937** Jack Casey. **1938** Tony Arpino. **1939** Zachy Nicholas, Jack Beech
LOST DIS (7)	**1928** Eddie Ritchie. **1929** Frank Berwick. **1933** Larry Gains, Ted Mason. **1934** Jack Casey, Archie Norman, Bert Ikin

NOTE:
The Lonsdale Belt was not issued for the British Championship Contest versus Charlie Smith

Freddie Mills

Undefeated British & British Empire L. Heavyweight Champion, 1942 – 1950. Undefeated European L. Heavyweight Champion, 1947 – 1950. World L. Heavyweight Champion, 1942 – 1946 and 1948 – 1950

Born 26.06.19 *From* Bournemouth *Died* 1965 *Pro Career* 1936 – 1950 (100 contests, won 76, drew 6, lost 18)

CONTINUED OVERLEAF

Harry Mason

Reggie Meen

Freddie Mills

Alan Minter

CHAMPIONSHIP CONTESTS (8)

20.06.42	Len Harvey	W CO 2	London	B, BE, W	L. Heavyweight Titles
15.09.44	Jack London	L PTS 15	Manchester	B, BE	L. Heavyweight Titles
14.05.46	Gus Lesnevich	L RSC 10	London	W	L. Heavyweight Title
08.09.47	Paul Goffaux	W RTD 4	London	EU	L. Heavyweight Title
17.02.48	Paco Bueno	W CO 2	London	EU	L. Heavyweight Title
26.07.48	Gus Lesnevich	W PTS 15	London	W	L. Heavyweight Title
02.06.49	Bruce Woodcock	L CO 14	London	B, BE	Heavyweight Titles
24.01.50	Joey Maxim	L CO 10	London	W	L. Heavyweight Title

NON CHAMPIONSHIP CONTESTS (92)

WON PTS (21) — **1937** Jack McKnight (2), Red Pullen, Jack Alder, Harry Lister, Albert Johnson. **1938** Jim Greaves, Tommy Taylor, Jack Lewis, Charlie Parkin, Tom Curran, Butcher Gascoigne. **1939** Paul Schaeffer, Eddie Maguire, Charlie Parkin. **1940** Jim Berry, Ginger Sadd, Jock McAvoy. **1941** Tom Reddington, Jack London. **1947** Stephane Olek

WON CO (26) — **1936** Reg Davis, Fred Lennington, Jim Riley, Jack Scott (2), Slogger Wilson, George Bradby. **1937** Billy Brown, Terry Warren, Kid Anthony, Billy Fuller. **1938** Moe Moss, Seaman Long, Yorkie Bentley. **1939** Dave McCleave (2), Charlie Parkin, Elfryn Morris. **1941** Jim Wilde. **1943** Al Robinson. **1944** Al Delaney. **1946** John Nilsson. **1947** Willie Quentemeyer, Enrico Bertola, Nick Wolmarans. **1948** Johnny Ralph

WON RSC/RTD (25) — **1936** Stan Nelson. **1937** Harry Frolic, Fred Clements. **1938** Ginger Dawkins, Billy James, Ted Barter, Harry Vine, Charlie Parkin, Fred Clements. **1939** Yorkie Bentley, Johnny Blake. **1940** Stafford Barton, Ben Valentine, Ernie Simmons. **1941** Ginger Sadd, Trevor Burt, Jack Hyams, Jack Powell, Tommy Martin. **1942** Tom Reddington, Jock McAvoy, Al Robinson. **1944** Bert Gilroy. **1945** Ken Shaw. **1948** Ken Shaw

DREW (6) — **1936** Stan Nelson, George Heskett. **1937** Jim Greaves, Ginger Dawkins. **1939** Nat Franks, Eddie Maguire

LOST PTS (9) — **1937** George Davis, Jack Lewis. **1938** Dave McCleave. **1939** Butcher

	Gascoigne, Elfryn Morris, Ginger Sadd, Eddie Maguire. **1941** Tom Reddington. **1946** Bruce Woodcock
LOST CO (2)	**1937** George Davis. **1947** Lloyd Marshall
LOST RSC/RTD (2)	**1936** Eddie Gill. **1946** Joe Baksi
LOST DIS (1)	**1941** Jack Hyams

NOTE:
The World Championship Contest versus Len Harvey was for the GB version of the Title.

Alan Minter

Undefeated British Middleweight Champion, 1975 – 1977 and 1977 – 1978. European Middleweight Champion, 1977 and Undefeated European Middleweight Champion, 1978 – 1979. World Middleweight Champion, 1980
Born 17.08.51 *From* Crawley *Pro Career* 1972 – 1981 (49 contests, won 39, lost 9, no contest 1)

CHAMPIONSHIP CONTESTS (12)

04.11.75	Kevin Finnegan	W PTS 15	London	B	Middleweight Title
27.04.76	Billy Knight	W RSC 2	London	B	Middleweight Title
14.09.76	Kevin Finnegan	W PTS 15	London	B	Middleweight Title
04.02.77	Germano Valsecchi	W CO 5	Milan	EU	Middleweight Title
21.09.77	Gratien Tonna	L RSC 8	Milan	EU	Middleweight Title
08.11.77	Kevin Finnegan	W PTS 15	London	B	Middleweight Title
19.07.78	Angelo Jacopucci	W CO 12	Bellaria	EU	Middleweight Title
07.11.78	Gratien Tonna	W RTD 6	London	EU	Middleweight Title
16.03.80	Vito Antuofermo	W PTS 15	Las Vegas	W	Middleweight Title
28.06.80	Vito Antuofermo	W RTD 8	London	W	Middleweight Title
27.09.80	Marvin Hagler	L RSC 3	London	W	Middleweight Title
15.09.81	Tony Sibson	L CO 3	London	EU	Middleweight Title

NON CHAMPIONSHIP CONTESTS (37)

WON PTS (12)	**1973** Pat Dwyer, Harry Scott, Frank Young, Octavio Romero. **1974** Tony Byrne, Shako Mamba. **1975** Tony Allen, Larry Paul. **1977** Emile Griffith. **1979** Rudy Robles, Doug Demmings. **1981** Ernie Singletary
WON CO (3)	**1973** Mike McCluskie. **1975** Henry Cooper, Peter Wulf
WON RSC/RTD (15)	**1972** Maurice Thomas, John Lowe, Anton Schnedl, Ron Hough. **1973** Pat Brogan, Gabe Bowens, King George Aidoo, Eddie Burns. **1976** Trevor Francis, Frank Reiche, Tony Licata, Sugar Ray Seales. **1978** Sandy Torres. **1979** Renato Garcia, Monty Betham
LOST PTS (1)	**1981** Mustafa Hamsho
LOST RSC/RTD (5)	**1973** Don McMillan, Jan Magdziarz (2). **1974** Ricky Ortiz. **1977** Ronnie Harris
NC (1)	**1974** Jan Magdziarz

Harry Mizler

British Lightweight Champion, 1934
Born 22.01.13 *From* Stepney *Pro Career* 1933 – 1943 (81 contests, won 63, drew 2, lost 16)

CHAMPIONSHIP CONTESTS (4)

18.01.34	Johnny Cuthbert	W PTS 15	London	B	Lightweight Title
04.08.34	Billy Quinlan	W PTS 15	Swansea	B	Lightweight Title
29.10.34	Jackie Kid Berg	L RTD 10	London	B	Lightweight Title
19.10.36	Jimmy Walsh	L PTS 15	London	B	Lightweight Title

NON CHAMPIONSHIP CONTESTS (77)

WON PTS (36)	**1933** Jim Bird, Evan Lane, Norman Dale. **1934** Jules Steyaert (2), Edourd Jamsin, Joe Kerr, Norman Dale, Tiger Defer, Nicolas Wilke. **1935** Francois Machtens, Robert Disch, Sonny Lee, Boyo Rees, Norman Snow. **1936** Raymond Renard, Alby Day, Jackie Flynn. **1937** Robert Disch, Jimmy Walsh, Dave Finn, Douglas Kestrell, Al Roth. **1938** Harry Craster, Leo Phillips, George Daly, Bert Chambers. **1939** Norman

CONTINUED OVERLEAF

Harry Mizler

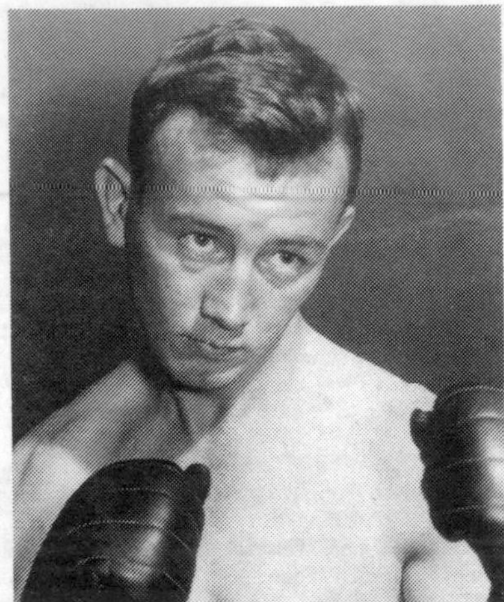
Tommy Molloy

	Snow, George Odwell. **1941** Harry Craster, Paddy Roche, Eddie Ryan. **1942** Frank Duffy. **1943** Frank Duffy, Eric Boon. **1944** Jimmy Thornhill
WON CO (6)	**1933** Jim Travis, Nobby Baker, Jim Gordon, Norman Snow. **1936** Jose Mico. **1940** Albert O'Brien
WON RSC/RTD (14)	**1933** Bob Lamb, Albert Heasman, Len Burrows, Harry Sankey, Aine Gyde, Alec Law. **1934** Jack Garland. **1935** George Reynolds, Gustave Humery. **1936** Antoine Aarts. **1937** Dodo Williams. **1938** Rex Whitney. **1941** Pat Howard. **1942** Tommy Harlow
WON DIS (5)	**1935** Peter Clarke. **1936** Raymond Renard. **1937** Petey Sarron, Frank Hill. **1942** Jim Wellard
DREW (2)	**1938** Hans Drescher. **1940** Jackie Potts
LOST PTS (11)	**1934** Jimmy Walsh. **1936** Dave Crowley. **1937** Petey Sarron. **1938** Dave Crowley, Harry Craster, Hans Drescher. **1941** Jackie Kid Berg. **1942** Charlie Parkin, Arthur Danahar, Jim Wellard. **1943** Harry Lazar
LOST RSC/RTD (3)	**1941** Ernie Roderick. **1943** Arthur Danahar, Jimmy Molloy

NOTE:
The Lonsdale Belt was not issued for the British Championship Contests versus Johnny Cuthbert, Billy Quinlan and Jackie Kid Berg.

Tommy Molloy

British Welterweight Champion, 1958 – 1960
Born 02.02.34 *From* Birkenhead *Pro Career* 1955 – 1963 (43 contests, won 34, drew 2, lost 6, no contest 1)

CHAMPIONSHIP CONTESTS (3)

15.07.58	Jimmy Newman	**W** PTS 15	London	B	Welterweight Title
14.10.59	Albert Carroll	**W** RSC 12	Liverpool	B	Welterweight Title
01.02.60	Wally Swift	L PTS 15	Nottingham	B	Welterweight Title

NON CHAMPIONSHIP CONTESTS (40)

WON PTS (19)	**1955** Johnny Delmore, Peter Cobblah (2), Ken Ashwood, Phil Mellish. **1956** Teddy Barrow, Jack Armstrong, Jeff Dudu, Joe Rufus, Roy Baird, Eddie Phillips, Peter Smith. **1957** Syd Greb, Leo Molloy, Joe Janssens, Fritz Van Kempen, Paul King. **1958** Tommy Tagoe. **1963** Fitzroy Lindo.

WON CO (4)	**1955** Stan Barnett, Andy Baird, Eric Billington, Ken Regan
WON RSC/RTD (8)	**1955** Cliff Lawrence, Derek Clark, Johnny Finnigan, Tim McLeary, Bobby Johnson. **1956** Jimmy Newman, Tony Barrett. **1959** Ron Jackson
WON DIS (1)	**1962** Nat Jacobs
DREW (2)	**1957** Jimmy Newman. **1959** Paddy Graham
LOST PTS (2)	**1959** Brian Husband. **1961** Cliff Brown
LOST RSC/RTD (2)	**1960** Duilio Loi, Hippolyte Annex
LOST DIS (1)	**1958** Johnny Melfah
NC (1)	**1957** Jimmy Croll

(John) Rinty Monaghan

Undefeated British, British Empire & European Flyweight Champion, 1948 – 1950. Undefeated World Flyweight Champion, 1947 – 1950
Born 21.08.20 *From* Belfast *Died* 1984 *Pro Career* 1935 – 1949 (66 contests, won 51, drew 6, lost 9)

CHAMPIONSHIP CONTESTS (4)

20.10.47	Dado Marino	**W** PTS 15	London	W	Flyweight Title
23.03.48	Jackie Paterson	**W** CO 7	Belfast	B, BE, W	Flyweight Titles
05.04.49	Maurice Sandeyron	**W** PTS 15	Belfast	EU, W	Flyweight Titles
30.09.49	Terry Allen	DREW 15	Belfast	B, BE, EU, W	Flyweight Titles

NON CHAMPIONSHIP CONTESTS (62)

WON PTS (29)	**1934** Jim Pedlow. **1935** Young Finnegan. **1936** Sam Ramsey, Young Joseph, Young Kelly, Joe Duffy. **1937** Mike Gibbons (2), Sam Ramsey (2), Ted Meikle (2). **1938** Cyclone Kelly (2), Joe McCluskey, Joe Keily, Joe Curran. **1939** Sammy Reynolds, Tommy Steward, Billy Ashton, Seaman Chetty. **1940** Tommy Stewart. **1942** Joe Meikle. **1945** Joe Collins, Tommy Burney. **1946** Tommy Burney, Alex Murphy. **1947** Emile Famechon. **1949** Otello Belardinelli
WON CO (10)	**1935** Vic Large. **1937** George Lang, Tommy Allen. **1938** Alf Hughes, Spider Allen, Peter Peters, Ivor Neil. **1939** Joe Curran. **1944** Joe Meikle. **1945** Bunty Doran
WON RSC/RTD (8)	**1936** Young Josephs. **1937** Ted Meikle, Frank Benson, Paddy Toole. **1938** Pat Murphy. **1946** Jackie Paterson. **1947** Terry Allen. **1948** Charlie Squire
WON DIS (1)	**1946** Sammy Reynolds
DREW (5)	**1934** Sam Ramsey. **1936** Sam Ramsey, Jack MacKenzie, Young Josephs. **1943** Harry Rodger
LOST PTS (7)	**1937** Jim Keery. **1938** Tommy Stewart. **1940** Paddy Ryan, Jimmy Gill. **1943** Ike Weir. **1945** Joe Curran. **1949** Terry Allen
LOST CO (1)	**1938** Jackie Paterson
LOST DIS (1)	**1947** Dado Marino

NOTE:
The contest for the World Title versus Dado Marino was for the NBA version of the title as the BBBC were constrained by a court injunction, but full recognition was attained when Monaghan beat Jackie Paterson.

Frank Moody

British & British Empire Middleweight Champion, 1927 – 1928. British L. Heavyweight Champion, 1927 – 1929
Born 27.08.1900 *From* Pontypridd *Died* 1963 *Pro Career* 1914 – 1936 (204 contests, won 129, drew 15, lost 51, no decision 9)

CHAMPIONSHIP CONTESTS (5)

16.02.27	Roland Todd	**W** PTS 15	London	B, BE	Middleweight Titles
27.11.27	Ted Moore	**W** PTS 20	London	B	L. Heavyweight Title
06.08.28	Tommy Milligan	**W** CO 1	Glasgow	B	Middleweight Title
17.09.28	Alex Ireland	L PTS 15	Edinburgh	B, BE	Middleweight Titles
25.11.29	Harry Crossley	L PTS 15	London	B	L. Heavyweight Title

CONTINUED OVERLEAF

NON CHAMPIONSHIP CONTESTS (199)

WON PTS (51)	**1914** Kid Evans. **1915** Young Jones, Sid Doyle. **1916** Gomer Perkins, Young Riley, Jack Tucker. **1917** Gomer Perkins, Steve Kavanagh (2), Mog Pugh, Jim Hogan, Jack Mignot. **1918** Jim Jones, Luntry Price, Johnny Vaughan, Harry Higgins (2), Willie Galley, Eddie Stevens, Dick Hillson, Bert Dyke, Idris Jenkins. **1919** Archie Northrope, Gus Platts (3), Arthur Tracey, Albert Brown, Ike Clark. **1920** Alf Craig, Gus Platts. **1921** Albert Croucher, Fred Davies. **1922** George Pembridge. **1923** Albert Lloyd, Arthur Townley, Gipsy Daniels, Fred Davies, Caveman Fisher. **1924** Pal Reed (2), George Robinson, Tommy Robson, Jock Malone. **1925** Chief Halbran, Larry Estridge, Lew Chester. **1926** Benny Ross, Lou Scozza, Del Fontaine. **1930** Gipsy Daniels
WON CO (36)	**1916** Johnny Eamer. **1918** Tom Tees, Gunboat Baker. **1919** Jim Watts. **1920** Gunboat Baker, Johnny Bee. **1921** Peter Jackson, Albert Croucher. **1922** Felix Leonard, Sid Pape. **1923** Sid Pape, Ted Coolidge, Leo Leonard, Jackie Clarke. **1924** Pierre Nicolas, Pat McCarthy. **1925** Bing Conley, Kid Norfolk, Vince Lopez. **1926** Caveman Fisher, Tony Marullo, Kid Carter, Johnny Roberts, Bob Preston, Dick Daniels, Jack Morrison, Ray Thompson, Harry Jackson, Joe Bloomfield. **1927** Van't Hof, Jack Stanley, Tom Berry, Raoul Paillaux. **1929** Leon Jacovacci. **1935** Jack McKenzie, Arthur Novell
WON RSC/RTD (35)	**1917** Billy Jones. **1918** Ernie Thomas, Charlie Lane, Jack Simpson, Dick Beland. **1919** Wyn Price, Jim Culverhouse, Kid Carter (2), Eddie Beattie, Willie Brooks, Llew Probert. **1920** Eddie Beattie, Ike Clarke (2), Sid Burns. **1921** Jim Falcus. **1922** Fred Newberry, Fred Davies, Peter Jackson, Bert O'Neill. **1923** Leon Jacovacci, Larry Gains, Rocky Knight, George Cook, Jack Ford, Arthur Cotter. **1924** Lou Bogash. **1927** Frank Fowler, Dave Magill, Max Gornic. **1928** Abel Argotte, Hamilton Johnny Brown. **1930** Theo Saas. **1935** Jack Marshall
WON DIS (4)	**1918** Freddie Jacks, Willie Farrell. **1920** Ike Clarke. **1921** Ted Moore
DREW (15)	**1916** Jack Tucker, Jim Rice. **1917** Chris Langdon, Jim Jones, Billy Moore. **1918** Dick Moss. **1919** Willie Brooks, Roland Todd, Jerry Shea. **1924** Allentown Joe Gans. **1928** George Cook. **1929** Pierre Gandon. **1930** Ernst Pistulla. **1931** Steve McCall. **1935** Tommy Farr
LOST PTS (32)	**1914** Young Carver. **1916** Gomer Perkins, Jim Carver, Jim Rice (2), Jack Tucker, Chris Langdon. **1917** Young Tucker, Billy Simpson. **1918** Idris Jones, Kid Plested, Kid Doyle. **1919** Joe Attwood, Llew Probert, Willie Brooks. **1920** Jerry Shea, Rene Devos, Fred Davies. **1921** Ted Moore. **1922** Bermondsey Billy Wells, Ted Moore, Dave Magill. **1923** Ted

Rinty Monaghan

Frank Moody

	Moore. **1924** Lou Bogash (2), Allentown Joe Gans. **1925** Tiger Flowers. **1926** Maxie Rosenbloom, Dave Shade, George Courtney. **1927** Gipsy Daniels, Michel Bonaglia
LOST CO (9)	**1915** Charlie Stone. **1919** Joe Attwood, Bermondsey Billy Wells. **1920** Ted Kid Lewis, Roland Todd. **1924** Harry Greb. **1926** Martin Burke. **1935** Ben Foord, Tommy Farr
LOST RSC/RTD (7)	**1917** Billy Simpson. **1918** Ernie Rice, Archie Northrope. **1924** Jack Delaney. **1926** George Courtney. **1929** Len Harvey. **1936** Frank Hough
LOST DIS (1)	**1918** Idris Jones
ND (9)	**1924** Joe Jackson, Jock Malone, Jeff Smith, Allentown Joe Gans. **1925** Homer Robertson. **1926** Dave Shade, Lou Bogash, Pal Reed, Tony Robson

NOTE:
The Lonsdale Belt was not issued for the British Championship Contests versus Roland Todd, Tommy Milligan and Alec Ireland. The British Empire Title Contest versus Roland Todd was not generally recognised to have been a Championship match.

Des Morrison

British L. Welterweight Champion, 1973 – 1974
Born 01.02.50 Jamaica *From* Bedford *Pro Career* 1970 – 1982 (50 contests, won 36, drew 2, lost 12)

CHAMPIONSHIP CONTESTS (6)

27.11.73	Joe Tetteh	W PTS 15	London	B	L. Welterweight Title
26.03.74	Pat McCormack	L CO 11	London	B	L. Welterweight Title
11.11.76	Joey Singleton	L PTS 15	Manchester	B	L. Welterweight Title
19.10.77	Colin Power	L RSC 10	London	B	L. Welterweight Title
06.01.81	Clinton McKenzie	L RSC 14	London	B	L. Welterweight Title
11.06.82	Obisia Nwankpa	L RSC 10	Aba	C	L. Welterweight Title

NON CHAMPIONSHIP CONTESTS (44)

WON PTS (17)	**1970** Lex Wilson, Tony Burnett (2), Ray Fallone, Danny Turpin, Leroy Mack. **1971** Pat Marshall. **1972** Alan Reid, Mickey Flynn, Des Rea. **1973** Tommy Joyce, Des Rea, Ricky Porter. **1975** Billy Waith. **1976** Derek Simpson. **1979** Billy Waith. **1980** Sylvester Mittee
WON CO (2)	**1971** Lex Wilson. **1979** Louis Acaries
WON RSC/RTD (16)	**1970** Pat Walsh (2). **1971** Alan Reid, Ron Woods. **1972** Robin Polak, Phil Dykes, Frank Young. **1974** Steve Angell. **1976** Tom Imrie, Kenny

CONTINUED OVERLEAF

Des Morrison

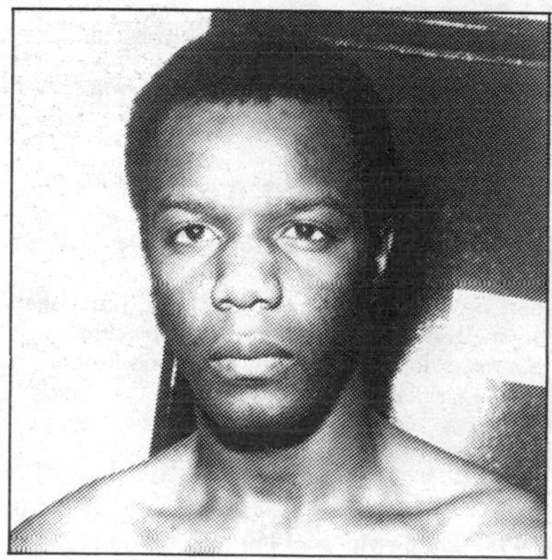

Dave Needham

	Webber, Colin Power. **1977** Barton McAllister. **1978** Tony Martey, Chris Glover, Joey Singleton. **1980** Otis Hooper
DREW (2)	**1970** Harry Adams. **1973** Kevin White
LOST PTS (6)	**1971** Dusty Smith. **1972** Ricky Porter. **1974** Jorgen Hansen. **1975** Tony Poole. **1979** Clinton McKenzie, Kirkland Laing
LOST CO (1)	**1982** Frank Ropis

Dave Needham

British Bantamweight Champion, 1974–1975. British Featherweight Champion, 1978 – 1979
Born 15.08.51 *From* Nottingham *Pro Career* 1971 – 1980 (39 contests, won 30, drew 1, lost 8)

CHAMPIONSHIP CONTESTS (8)

10.12.74	Paddy Maguire	W PTS 15	Nottingham	B	Bantamweight Title
11.04.75	Daniel Trioulaire	Drew 15	Barentin	EU	Bantamweight Title
20.10.75	Paddy Maguire	L RSC 14	London	B	Bantamweight Title
20.04.78	Alan Richardson	W PTS 15	London	B	Featherweight Title
16.12.78	Robert Castanon	L RTD 5	Leon	EU	Featherweight Title
18.09.79	Pat Cowdell	W PTS 15	Wolverhampton	B	Featherweight Title
06.11.79	Pat Cowdell	L PTS 15	London	B	Featherweight Title
29.05.80	Pat Cowdell	L RTD 12	Wolverhampton	B	Featherweight Title

NON CHAMPIONSHIP CONTESTS (31)

WON PTS (16)	**1971** Roger Howes, Karim Young, Billy Hardacre, Michel Jamet. **1972** Billy Hardacre (2), Paddy Graham, Colin Miles. **1973** Jesus Nieves, John Mitchell, John Kellie, Hiro Hamada. **1975** Earl Large. **1977** Pasqualino Morbidelli. **1978** Alan Robertson. **1979** George Sutton
WON CO (2)	**1971** Jimmy Killeen. **1977** Vernon Sollas
WON RSC/RTD (8)	**1971** Sammy Abbey, Al Hutcheon, Dave Tuohy, John McCluskey. **1972** Jean-Pierre Flambeau, Francois Payelle, Dionisio Bisbal. **1973** Eddie Rivera
WON DIS (1)	**1974** Bashew Sibaca
LOST PTS (1)	**1976** Arnold Taylor
LOST RSC/RTD (3)	**1976** Alan Richardson. **1977** Jeff Pritchard. **1980** Charm Chiteule

Bobby Neill

British Featherweight Champion, 1959–1960
Born 10.10.33 *From* Edinburgh *Pro Career* 1955 – 1960 (35 contests, won 28, lost 7)

CHAMPIONSHIP CONTESTS (3)

13.04.59	Charlie Hill	W RSC 9	Nottingham	B	Featherweight Title
27.09.60	Terry Spinks	L RSC 7	London	B	Featherweight Title
22.11.60	Terry Spinks	L CO 14	London	B	Featherweight Title

NON CHAMPIONSHIP CONTESTS (32)

WON PTS (4)	**1955** Percy James. **1956** Denny Dawson, Ken Lawrence. **1960** Alberto Serti
WON CO (5)	**1955** Eddie McCormick. **1956** Billy Ashcroft. **1958** Arthur Devlin. **1959** Terry Spinks. **1960** Jimmy Carson
WON RSC/RTD (17)	**1955** Denny Dennis, Albert Stokes, George Clay, Peter Fay, Jim Fisher. **1956** Freddie Reardon, Juan Alvarez, Matt Fulton, Ray Famechon, Charlie Hill. **1957** Dos Santos, Edouard Roelandt. **1958** Con Mount Bassie, Owen Reilly, George Dormer, Aime Devisch. **1960** Germain Vivier
WON DIS (1)	**1958** Andy Hayford
LOST PTS (1)	**1957** Victor Pepeder
LOST CO (1)	**1957** Jimmy Brown
LOST RSC/RTD (3)	**1957** Arthur Donnachie. **1959** Davey Moore. **1960** Johnny Kidd

Bobby Neill

John O'Brien

John O'Brien

British Empire Featherweight Champion, 1967
Born 20.02.37 *From* Glasgow *Died* 1979 *Pro Career* 1956–1971 (46 contests, won 29, lost 17)

CHAMPIONSHIP CONTESTS (5)

07.12.59	Percy Lewis	L CO 2	Nottingham	BE	Featherweight Title
09.12.63	Howard Winstone	L PTS 15	London	B, EU	Featherweight Titles
03.02.67	Floyd Robertson	W RTD 12	Accra	BE	Featherweight Title
24.11.67	Johnny Famechon	L RSC 11	Melbourne	BE	Featherweight Title
24.03.69	Jimmy Revie	L RSC 5	London	B	Featherweight Title

NON CHAMPIONSHIP CONTESTS (41)

WON PTS (15)	**1956** Alan McGregor, Jackie Tiller, John Bamborough. **1957** Len Harvey, George Mason, Gil Neil. **1958** George Dormer. **1959** Con Mount Bassie, Johnny Howard, Eric Brett, Terry Spinks. **1969** Arnold Taylor. **1970** Don Johnson. **1971** Anthony Morodi (2)
WON CO (2)	**1957** Tommy Houston. **1965** Jesus Saucedo
WON RSC/RTD (11)	**1957** Jack Richards. **1962** Andy Doherty, Phil Lundgren. **1963** George Bowes, Con Mount Bassie, Bobby Fisher. **1964** Dennis Adjei. **1968** Daniel Vermandeer, Ray Opoku. **1970** Paul Rourre, Gilberto Biondi
LOST PTS (8)	**1958** Roy Jacobs (2), George Dormer, Chic Brogan. **1959** Ayree Jackson. **1963** Lino Mastellaro. **1971** Jeff White, Manny Santos
LOST RSC/RTD (5)	**1962** Kenny Field, George Bowes. **1965** Rafiu King, Mario Diaz. **1971** Manny Santos

Danny O'Sullivan

British Bantamweight Champion, 1949 – 1951
Born 06.01.23 *From* Kings Cross *Pro Career* 1947 – 1951 (43 contests, won 33, drew 1, lost 9)

CHAMPIONSHIP CONTESTS (4)

13.12.49	Teddy Gardner	W RTD 9	London	B	Bantamweight Title
25.04.50	Luis Romero	L RSC 13	London	EU	Bantamweight Title
02.12.50	Vic Toweel	L RTD 10	Johannesburg	BE, W	Bantamweight Titles
09.05.51	Peter Keenan	L CO 6	Glasgow	B	Bantamweight Title

CONTINUED OVERLEAF

NON CHAMPIONSHIP CONTESTS (39)

WON PTS (15)	**1947** Freddie Hicks, Johnny Kent. **1948** Kid Tanner, Amleto Falcinelli, Jimmy Webster, Jean Jouas, Georges Mousse, Tino Cardinale. **1949** Len Shaw, Jackie Paterson, Ronnie Draper, Fernando Gagnon. **1950** Alvaro Nuvoloni, Francis Bonnardel. **1951** Alex Sinnaeve
WON CO (5)	**1947** Ron Bissell. **1948** Tommy Cummings, Jackie McCall. **1949** Bunty Doran, Michel Verhamme
WON RSC/RTD (12)	**1947** Wally Basquille, Mickey Jones, Jimmy Green, Ernie Ormerod. **1948** Johhny Boom, Len Jones, Tommy Madine. **1949** Guido Ferracin, Jackie Sutton. **1950** Jackie Hughes. **1951** Jim McCann, Eddie Magee
DREW (1)	**1951** Tony Lombard
LOST PTS (3)	**1948** Stan Rowan. **1950** Ray Fitton, Bobby Boland
LOST CO (1)	**1948** Jackie Paterson
LOST RSC/RTD (1)	**1951** Ronnie Clayton
LOST DIS (1)	**1949** Mickey McKay

Johnny Owen

Undefeated British Bantamweight Champion, 1977 – 1980. Undefeated Commonwealth Bantamweight Champion, 1978–1980. Undefeated European Bantamweight Champion, 1980

Born 07.01.56 *From* Merthyr *Died* 1980 *Pro Career* 1976 – 1980 (28 contests, won 25, drew 1, lost 2)

CHAMPIONSHIP CONTESTS (8)

29.11.77	Paddy Maguire	W RSC 11	London	B	Bantamweight Title
06.04.78	Wayne Evans	W RSC 10	Ebbw Vale	B	Bantamweight Title
02.11.78	Paul Ferreri	W PTS 15	Ebbw Vale	C	Bantamweight Title
03.03.79	Juan Francisco Rodriguez	L PTS 15	Almeira	EU	Bantamweight Title
13.06.79	Dave Smith	W RTD 12	Caerphilly	B, C	Bantamweight Titles
28.02.80	Juan Francisco Rodriguez	W PTS 12	Ebbw Vale	EU	Bantamweight Title
28.06.80	John Feeney	W PTS 15	London	B, C	Bantamweight Titles
19.09.80	Lupe Pintor	L CO 12	Los Angeles	W	Bantamweight Title

Danny O'Sullivan

Johnny Owen

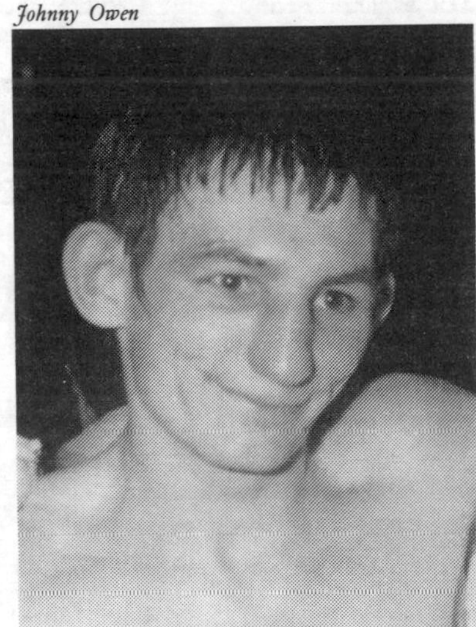

NON CHAMPIONSHIP CONTESTS (20)

WON PTS (11)	**1976** George Sutton. **1977** Neil McLaughlin (2), George Sutton (2). **1978** Antonio Medina, Dave Smith. **1979** Lee Graham, Guy Caudron, Neil McLaughlin, Davey Vasquez
WON RSC/RTD (8)	**1976** Ian Murray. **1977** John Kellie, Terry Hanna. **1978** Alan Oag, Davy Larmour, Wally Angliss. **1979** Jose Luis Garcia. **1980** Glyn Davies
DREW (1)	**1976** Neil McLaughlin

NOTE:
The World Championship Contest versus Lupe Pintor was for the WBC version of the Title.

Jackie Paterson

British Flyweight Champion, 1939 – 1948. British Empire Flyweight Champion 1940 – 1948. World Flyweight Champion, 1943 – 1948. British Bantamweight Champion, 1947 – 1949. British Empire Bantamweight Champion, 1945 – 1949. European Bantamweight Champion, 1946
Born 05.09.20 *From* Springfield *Died* 1966 *Pro Career* 1938 – 1950 (92 contests, won 64, drew 3, lost 25)

CHAMPIONSHIP CONTESTS (13)

30.09.39	Paddy Ryan	W CO 13	Glasgow	B	Flyweight Title
11.03.40	Kid Tanner	W PTS 15	Manchester	BE	Flyweight Title
03.02.41	Paddy Ryan	W CO 8	Nottingham	B, BE	Flyweight Titles
05.08.41	Jim Brady	L PTS 15	Glasgow	BE	Bantamweight Title
19.06.43	Peter Kane	W CO 1	Glasgow	B, BE, W	Flyweight Titles
12.09.45	Jim Brady	W PTS 15	Glasgow	BE	Bantamweight Title
19.03.46	Theo Medina	W DIS 8	London	EU	Bantamweight Title
10.07.46	Joe Curran	W PTS 15	Glasgow	B, BE, W	Flyweight Titles
30.10.46	Theo Medina	L CO 4	Glasgow	EU	Bantamweight Title
10.02.47	Johnny King	W CO 7	Manchester	B	Bantamweight Title
20.10.47	Norman Lewis	W CO 5	London	B, BE	Bantamweight Titles
23.03.48	Rinty Monaghan	L CO 7	Belfast	B, BE, W	Flyweight Titles
24.03.49	Stan Rowan	L PTS 15	Liverpool	B, BE	Bantamweight Titles

NON CHAMPIONSHIP CONTESTS (79)

WON PTS (19)	**1938** Joe Kiely, Mickey O'Neill. **1939** Raoul Degryse, Joe Curran. **1940** Kid Tanner. **1941** Jim Brady, Phil Milligan, Jimmy Stubbs, Kid Tanner, Teddy O'Neil. **1942** Phil Milligan, Norman Lewis. **1943** Gus Foran, Jim Hayes. **1944** Ben Duffy (2). **1945** Jackie Grimes. **1947** Corrado Conti, Al Chavez
WON CO (17)	**1938** Rinty Monaghan. **1939** Jack Kiley, Tut Whalley, Eric Jones. **1940** Jimmy Stewart (2). **1941** Billy Clinton, Billy Hazelgrove, Dudley Lewis. **1942** Billy Tansey, Eddie Petrin, Jim Hayes. **1943** George Pook. **1946** Jimmy Webster. **1947** Emilio Cacciatori. **1948** Danny O'Sullivan. **1949** Mustapha Mustaphaoui
WON RSC/RTD (19)	**1938** Pat McStravick, Billy Nash, Phil Milligan. **1939** Gavino Matta, Freddie Tennant. **1940** Wally Knightley, Young Chocolate. **1941** Billy Hazelgrove, Kid Tanner, Jimmy Lyden. **1942** Joe Hardy (2), Frank Bonser. **1943** Phil Milligan, Tiger Al Phillips, George Williams. **1944** Ronnie Clayton. **1945** Sammy Reynolds. **1948** Fernando Rosa
DREW (3)	**1938** Tommy Stewart. **1939** Tut Whalley, Valentin Angelmann
LOST PTS (12)	**1939** Charlie Brown. **1943** Len Davies. **1945** Gus Foran, Theo Medina. **1946** Bunty Doran. **1947** Cliff Anderson. **1948** Teddy Gardner, Ronnie Draper. **1949** Danny O'Sullivan, Manuel Ortiz, Vic Toweel. **1951** Willie Myles
LOST CO (3)	**1944** Ben Duffy. **1948** Jean Machterlinck. **1950** Eddie Carson
LOST RSC/RTD (5)	**1938** Joe Curran. **1942** Frank Bonser. **1944** Danny Webb. **1946** Rinty Monaghan. **1947** Stan Rowan
LOST DIS (1)	**1938** Joe Curran

NOTE:
Paterson was stripped of the World Flyweight Title in July, 1947 for failure to make the weight against Dado Marino. The NBA gave their recognition to Rinty Monaghan, but the BBBC were constrained by a court injunction.

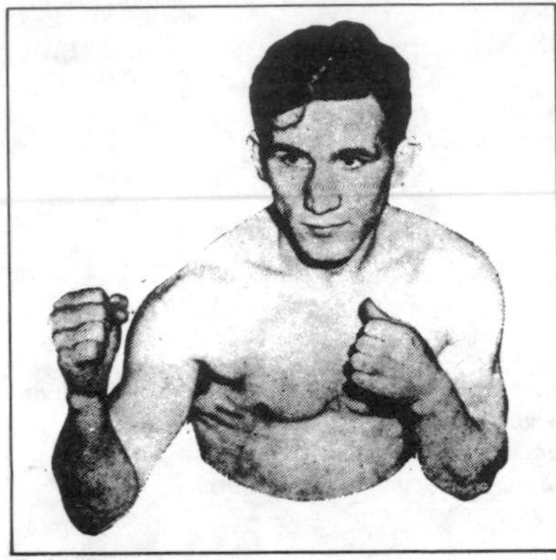
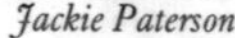
Jackie Paterson

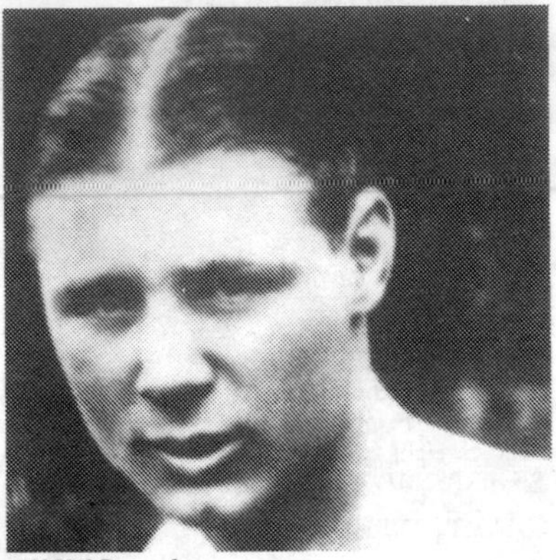
Alf Kid Pattenden

Alf Kid Pattenden

British Bantamweight Champion, 1928 – 1929
From Mile End *Pro Career* 1926 – 1931 (66 contests, won 38, drew 4, lost 24)

CHAMPIONSHIP CONTESTS (3)

04.06.28	Kid Nicholson	**W** CO 12	London	B	Bantamweight Title
25.11.28	Young Johnny Brown	**W** RTD 12	London	B	Bantamweight Title
16.05.29	Teddy Baldock	L PTS 15	London	B, BE	Bantamweight Titles

NON CHAMPIONSHIP CONTESTS (63)

WON PTS (16)	**1926** Danny Dando, Tiny Smith, Young Brooks, Peter Howard, Frankie Ash, Kid Brooks, Nel Tarleton. **1927** Kid Nicholson, Johnny Brown. **1928** Jean Jullian, Young Johnny Brown, Gideon Putteau, Jean Gregaire, Leo Cortvant. **1931** Phil Lolosky, Frank Markey
WON CO (5)	**1926** Billy Lowe. **1929** Jack Bates, Jack Mordy. **1930** Jimmy Rowbottom. **1931** Albert Marchant
WON RSC/RTD (13)	**1926** Billy Clark, Johnny Murton. **1927** Billy Sullivan, Bert Mills, Harry Stein, Len Fowler, Young Jackie Brown, Kid Socks, Young Stanley. **1929** Tiny Smith, Andre Steverlinch, Jack Kirby. **1931** Tom Upton
WON DIS (2)	**1930** Leo Koortvriens. **1930** Lew Pinkus
DREW (4)	**1927** Peter Howard, Archie Bell. **1929** Lew Pinkus. **1930** Lew Pinkus
LOST PTS (20)	**1927** Milton Cohen, Archie Bell, Len Fowler. **1929** Nel Tarleton, Henri Poutrain, Nipper Pat Daly, Len Tiger Smith. **1930** Charlie Rowbottom, Dick Corbett, Frank Markey, Selwyn Davies, Jack Garland, Bert Taylor, Teddy Baldock. **1931** Bill Rewston, Kid Farlo, Francois Machtens, Phineas John, Joe Bull, Arley Hollingsworth
LOST RSC/RTD (2)	**1930** Douglas Parker. **1931** Johnny Peters
LOST DIS (1)	**1930** Jimmy Rowbottom

Larry Paul

British L. Middleweight Champion, 1973 – 1974
Born 19.04.52 *From* Wolverhampton *Pro Career* 1973 – 1978 (40 contests, won 30, drew 1, lost 9)

CHAMPIONSHIP CONTESTS (5)

25.09.73	Bobby Arthur	**W** CO 10	Wolverhampton	B	L. Middleweight Title
24.04.74	Kevin White	**W** PTS 15	Wolverhampton	B	L. Middleweight Title
05.11.74	Maurice Hope	L CO 8	Wolverhampton	B	L. Middleweight Title
30.09.75	Maurice Hope	L RSC 4	London	B	L. Middleweight Title
25.10.77	Jimmy Batten	L RSC 4	London	B	L. Middleweight Title

Larry Paul

Jack Petersen

NON CHAMPIONSHIP CONTESTS (35)

WON PTS (11)	**1973** Antonio Torres, Don McMillan, Joe Yekinni, Frank Young. **1974** Jan Magdziarz. **1975** Mike Manley, Carl Speare (2), Wolfgang Gans. **1977** Wayne Bennett. **1978** Joe Jackson
WON CO (4)	**1973** Pat Dwyer, Ron Hough, Pat Brogan. **1974** Mickey Flynn
WON RSC/RTD (11)	**1973** Les Avoth, Dave Cranswick. **1974** Alan Tottoh, Tom Imrie. **1975** Poul Knudsen, Frank Reiche, Colin Davies. **1976** Danny McCafferty, Joe Oke, Errol McKenzie, Peter Morris
WON DIS (2)	**1976** Mickey Flynn. **1977** Pat Thomas
DREW (1)	**1974** Trevor Francis
LOST PTS (2)	**1975** Alan Minter. **1976** Rocky Mattioli
LOST CO (3)	**1976** Jean Mateo, Ayub Kalule. **1977** Frank Wissenbach
LOST RSC/RTD (1)	**1976** Radames Cabrera

Jack Petersen

Undefeated British L. Heavyweight Champion, 1932 – 1933. British Heavyweight Champion, 1932 – 1933 and 1934 – 1936. British Empire Heavyweight Champion, 1934 – 1936
Born 02.09.11 *From* Cardiff *Pro Career* 1931 – 1937 (38 contests, won 33, lost 5)

CHAMPIONSHIP CONTESTS (11)

23.05.32	Harry Crossley	W PTS 15	London	B	L. Heavyweight Title
12.07.32	Reggie Meen	W CO 2	London	B	Heavyweight Title
26.01.33	Jack Pettifer	W CO 12	London	B	Heavyweight Title
12.07.33	Jack Doyle	W DIS 2	London	B	Heavyweight Title
30.11.33	Len Harvey	L PTS 15	London	B	Heavyweight Title
04.06.34	Len Harvey	W RTD 12	London	B, BE	Heavyweight Titles
10.09.34	Larry Gains	W RTD 13	London	BE	Heavyweight Title
17.12.34	George Cook	W PTS 15	London	B, BE	Heavyweight Titles
29.01.36	Len Harvey	W PTS 15	London	B, BE	Heavyweight Titles
23.04.36	Jock McAvoy	W PTS 15	London	B, BE	Heavyweight Titles
17.08.36	Ben Foord	L RSC 3	Leicester	B, BE	Heavyweight Titles

NON CHAMPIONSHIP CONTESTS (27)

WON PTS (8)	**1931** George Porter, George Brown (2), Jack Stratton, Leo Bandias, Gunner Bennett. **1933** Ernst Guhring, George Cook
WON CO (9)	**1931** Alf Noble, Jim Campbell. **1932** Jack Newitt, Dick Power, George Slack, Charlie Smith. **1933** Hein Muller. **1934** Charlie Smith, Reggie Meen

WON RSC/RTD (6)	**1931** Bill Partridge, Jeff Wilson, Tom Wailes. **1933** Hans Schonrath. **1934** Harry Crossley, Ben Foord
WON DIS (1)	**1932** Tom Toner
LOST RSC/RTD (3)	**1935** Walter Neusel (2). **1937** Walter Neusel

NOTE:
The Lonsdale Belt was not issued for the British Championship Contests versus Len Harvey (30.11.33/04.06.34/29.01.36), Jock McAvoy and Ben Foord.

Tiger Al Phillips

British Empire & European Featherweight Champion, 1947
Born 25.01.20 *From* Aldgate *Pro Career* 1938–1951 (89 contests, won 72, drew 3, lost 14)

CHAMPIONSHIP CONTESTS (6)

23.02.45	Nel Tarleton	L PTS 15	Manchester	B, BE	Featherweight Titles
18.03.47	Cliff Anderson	W PTS 15	London	BE	Featherweight Title
27.05.47	Ray Famechon	W DIS 8	London	EU	Featherweight Title
01.07.47	Cliff Anderson	W DIS 8	London	BE	Featherweight Title
11.09.47	Ronnie Clayton	L PTS 15	Liverpool	B, BE, EU	Featherweight Titles
26.02.51	Ronnie Clayton	L PTS 15	Nottingham	B, BE	Featherweight Titles

NON CHAMPIONSHIP CONTESTS (83)

WON PTS (32)	**1939** Henry Dove, Dave Clemo, Jackie Barr, Wally Smith. **1942** Frankie Jackson, Len Davies, Ben Duffy, Tommy Hyams. **1943** Kid Tanner, Joe Davis, Jim Brady, Len Davies (2), Tommy McGlinchey (2). **1944** Tommy McGlinchey (2), Jim Brady (2), Ben Duffy (2), Tommy Davies, Kid Tanner. **1945** Johnny Price, Dave Crowley. **1947** Jean Mougin. **1948** Frankie Williams. **1949** Tony Lombard (2), Bernard Pugh. **1950** Tom Bailey, Ronnie Clayton
WON CO (10)	**1938** Charlie Hall (2), Tony Maselli, Harry Ruff. **1941** Basil Magee. **1943** George Pook. **1944** George Pook. **1945** Danny Webb. **1946** Cliff Curvis. **1950** Ron Cooper
WON RSC/RTD (22)	**1938** Steve Watson, Dick Conway, Tommy Dawson, Darkie Benilq. **1939** Red McDonald, Tommy Morgan, George Willoughby, Sid Walters. **1942** Syd Worgan, Ben Duffy. **1943** Jimmy Smith, Don Cameron. **1944** Tommy McGlinchey, Bobby Hindes, Tommy Davies, Bert Jackson. **1945** Jackie Grimes, Ben Duffy, Jim Brady. **1946** Paul Dogniaux, Roger Tison, Rene Megret
WON DIS (5)	**1938** Sonny Smith. **1942** Bobby Hindes. **1944** Len Davies. **1945** Jimmy Stubbs. **1948** Alvaro Cerasani
DREW (3)	**1941** Gordon Ashun. **1943** Jim Hayes. **1944** Syd Worgan
LOST PTS (7)	**1945** Dave Crowley (2), Tommy McGlinchey. **1947** Josef Preys. **1948** Johnny Molloy, Ray Famechon. **1949** Tony Lombard
LOST CO (1)	**1938** Red McDonald
LOST RSC/RTD (2)	**1941** Tom Granton. **1943** Jackie Paterson
LOST DIS (1)	**1944** Dave Crowley

Eddie Phillips

British L. Heavyweight Champion, 1935 – 1937
Born 1909 *From* Bow *Pro Career* 1928 – 1945 (57 contests, won 47, drew 4, lost 6)

CHAMPIONSHIP CONTESTS (4)

13.06.33	Len Harvey	L PTS 15	London	B	L. Heavyweight Title
04.02.35	Tommy Farr	W PTS 15	Mountain Ash	B	L. Heavyweight Title
27.04.37	Jock McAvoy	L CO 14	London	B	L. Heavyweight Title
01.12.38	Len Harvey	L DIS 4	London	B	Heavyweight Title

Tiger Al Phillips

Eddie Phillips

NON CHAMPIONSHIP CONTESTS (53)

WON PTS (17)	**1930** Jack Mansfield, Jack Delaney, Ted Giles, Sid Butler, Jim Carr. **1931** Ted Mason, Jack Stratton. **1932** Bob Carvill, Louis Weustenrad, Eddie Steele. **1934** Tommy Farr. **1935** Eddie Wenstob. **1936** Ernie Simmons (2), Jim Wilde. **1937** Arno Kolblin. **1945** Olle Tandberg
WON CO (10)	**1930** Reg Palmer. **1931** Tony Arpino, George Porter, Marine Trinder. **1932** Jack Newitt. **1934** Alf Luxton. **1936** Louis Weustenrad. **1938** Ben Foord, Jack Doyle. **1939** Jack Doyle
WON RSC/RTD (17)	**1928** Len Davies. **1930** Bert Pridgeon, Roy Webb. **1931** Alf Noble, Billy Allick, Jeff Wilson, Lucien Delleau, Dave Minter. **1932** Jack Marshall, Leo Bandias, Billy Allick, Bill Hudson, Jim Shaw, Jack O'Malley. **1933** Peter Van Goole. **1937** Bert Ikin, Alex Bell
WON DIS (2)	**1934** Tommy Farr. **1935** Eddie Wenstob
DREW (4)	**1929** Reg Palmer. **1933** Len Harvey. **1934** Charlie Belenger. **1935** Charlie Bundy
LOST PTS (1)	**1935** Len Harvey
LOST CO (2)	**1932** Bill Partridge. **1934** Ben Foord

NOTE:
The Lonsdale Belt was not issued for the British Championship Contest versus Tommy Farr.

Dennis Powell

British L. Heavyweight Champion, 1953
Born 12.12.24 *From* Four Crosses *Pro Career* 1947 – 1954 (68 contests, won 42, drew 4, lost 22)

CHAMPIONSHIP CONTESTS (2)

26.03.53	George Walker	W RTD 11	Liverpool	B	L. Heavyweight Title
26.10.53	Alex Buxton	L RSC 10	Nottingham	B	L. Heavyweight Title

NON CHAMPIONSHIP CONTESTS (66)

WON PTS (23)	**1947** Tommy Paddock, Jack Darlington. **1948** Jack O'Hara, Maxwell Ijeh, Nick Fisher, Tommy Paddock, Allan Cooke, Len Bennett. **1949**

CONTINUED OVERLEAF

	Gerry McDermott, Frank Walker, Gene Fowler, Derek Alexander, Jimmy Carroll, Jackie Marr. **1950** Mark Hart, Bernardo Pacini. **1951** Billy Wood, Jackie Harris, Victor D'Haes. **1952** Don Scott, Paddy Slavin, Garnett Denny. **1953** Albert Finch
WON CO (9)	**1948** Danny O'Brien, Nick Fisher, Harry Naylor. **1949** Doug Brock, Doug Richards (2), Tom North, Jack Farr, George James
WON RSC/RTD (8)	**1947** Dick Freeman. **1948** Tom Bodell. **1949** Joe Quigley, Tommy Davies. **1950** Jan Declercq. **1952** Billy Wood, Dennis Lockton. **1954** Johnny Barton
WON DIS (1)	**1952** George Walker
DREW (4)	**1947** Derek Alexander. **1948** Fred Edwards, Allan Cooke. **1949** Paddy Slavin
LOST PTS (11)	**1948** Jeff Morris, Fred Edwards, Johnny Barton (2), Tommy Whelan (2), Derek Alexander, Jimmy Carroll. **1950** Paddy Slavin, Mark Hart. **1952** Garnett Denny
LOST CO (4)	**1946** Tommy Smyth. **1948** Gerry McDermott, Tom North, Jimmy Carroll
LOST RSC/RTD (6)	**1949** Jimmy Carroll. **1950** Mel Brown, Willi Schagen (2). **1951** Tommy Farr. **1954** Polly Smith

Johnny Pritchett

Undefeated British Middleweight Champion, 1965 – 1969. Undefeated British Empire Middleweight Champion, 1967 – 69

Born 15.02.43 *From* Bingham *Pro Career* 1963 – 1969 (34 contests, won 32, drew 1, lost 1)

CHAMPIONSHIP CONTESTS (6)

08.11.65	Wally Swift	**W** RSC 12	Nottingham	B	Middleweight Title
21.03.66	Nat Jacobs	**W** RTD 13	Nottingham	B	Middleweight Title
20.02.67	Wally Swift	**W** PTS 15	Nottingham	B	Middleweight Title
09.10.67	Milo Calhoun	**W** RTD 8	Manchester	BE	Middleweight Title
26.02.68	Les McAteer	**W** PTS 15	Nottingham	B, BE	Middleweight Titles
20.02.69	Carlos Duran	L DIS 13	Rome	EU	Middleweight Title

NON CHAMPIONSHIP CONTESTS (28)

WON PTS (10)	**1964** Roy Thomas. **1965** Joe Bell, Johnny Angel, Willie Hart. **1966** Fabio Bettini, Freddie Thomas. **1967** Wilbert McClure. **1968** Wilfredo Hurst, Len Gibbs, Doug Huntley
WON CO (2)	**1964** Darkie Smith. **1965** Francois Martinera
WON RSC/RTD (15)	**1963** Les Ferdinand, Maurice Lloyd. **1964** Gary Chippendale, Dave Arnold, Sid Brown, George Palin, John West, Paddy Delargy. **1965** Gary Chippendale, Willie Fisher. **1966** Jose Torres, Johnny Kramer, Jim Swords, Lat Phonso. **1967** Henry Turkington
DREW (1)	**1967** Milo Calhoun

Des Rea

British J. Welterweight Champion, 1968 – 1969

Born 08.01.44 *From* Belfast *Pro Career* 1964 – 1974 (69 contests, won 28, drew 5, lost 36)

CHAMPIONSHIP CONTESTS (4)

27.02.68	Vic Andreetti	**W** PTS 15	London	B	J. Welterweight Title
21.08.68	Bruno Arcari	L RSC 6	San Remo	EU	L. Welterweight Title
17.02.69	Vic Andreetti	L PTS 15	Nottingham	B	J. Welterweight Title
13.10.69	Vic Andreetti	L CO 4	Nottingham	B	J. Welterweight Title

NON CHAMPIONSHIP CONTESTS (65)

WON PTS (20)	**1964** Tommy Tiger. **1965** Ron Rowley, Manley Brown, Ivan Drew, Ivan Whiter, John McMillan, Bob Sempey, Rory O'Shea. **1966** Joe Falcon, Fred Powney. **1967** Mick Laud (2). **1968** Lex Hunter. **1970** Alan Moore.

	1971 Chris Jobson, Jimmy Fairweather. **1972** Teddy Meho, Amos Talbot, Tommy Joyce. **1973** Alan Reid
WON CO (1)	**1970** Gus Farrell
WON RSC/RTD (5)	**1965** Chris McAuley. **1968** Amos Talbot. **1970** Chuck Henderson. **1972** Mickey Flynn. **1973** Mick Laud
WON DIS (1)	**1964** Kenny Hinds
DREW (5)	**1965** Brian McCaffrey. **1967** Chris Jobson. **1973** Mick Laud, Kenny Webber, Les Pearson
LOST PTS (20)	**1965** John McMillan. **1966** Shaun Doyle. **1967** Peter Cobblah. **1968** Paul Armstead. **1969** Barry Calderwood. **1970** Johnny Cooke, Bernie Terrell. **1971** Jorgen Hansen, Stoffel Steyn. **1972** Gielie Butendag, Mickey Flynn, Alan Tottoh, Charlie Cooper, Des Morrison. **1973** Pat Thomas, Ronnie du Preez, Frank Young, Des Morrison, Jim Melrose. **1974**Tony Poole
LOST CO (1)	**1974** Kristian Haydahl
LOST RSC/RTD (12)	**1966** Jose Stable, Brian Curvis. **1968** Jose Napoles. **1970** Brendan Jackson, Alan Tottoh. **1971** Joseph Bessala, Barry Calderwood. **1972** John H. Stracey. **1973** Alan Reid, Pat Thomas, Max Hebeisen. **1974** Pat Thomas

Willie Reilly

Undefeated British Lightweight Champion, 1972
Born 25.03.47 *From* Glasgow *Pro Career* 1968 – 1972 (23 contests, won 13, drew 3, lost 7)

CHAMPIONSHIP CONTESTS (1)

01.02.72	Jim Watt	W RSC 10	Nottingham	B	Lightweight Title

NON CHAMPIONSHIP CONTESTS (22)

WON PTS (8)	**1968** Geoff Williams, Malcolm Lowe. **1969** Frank Fitzgerald, Roger Howes. **1970** Gary Yean, Johnny Cheshire. **1971** Paul Bink. **1972** Herbie McLean

CONTINUED OVERLEAF

Dennis Powell

Johnny Pritchett

WON RSC/RTD (4)	**1968** Paul Swinscoe, Winston Van Guylenburg. **1969** Sonny McNorthey. **1970** Brian Hudson
DREW (3)	**1968** Malcolm McNeill. **1971** Paul Moore, Boerge Krogh
LOST PTS (4)	**1969** Hugh Baxter. **1970** Reg Gullefer, Kokkie Olivier. **1971** Al Ford
LOST CO (1)	**1969** Billy Hardacre
LOST RSC/RTD (2)	**1969** Young Silky. **1971** Jim Watt

Jimmy Revie

British Featherweight Champion, 1969 – 1971
Born 08.07.47 *From* Stockwell *Pro Career* 1966 – 1975 (44 contests, won 37, lost 7)

CHAMPIONSHIP CONTESTS (6)

20.02.68	Jimmy Anderson	L RSC 9	London	B	J. Lightweight Title
24.03.69	John O'Brien	**W** RSC 5	London	B	Featherweight Title
08.09.70	Alan Rudkin	**W** PTS 15	London	B	Featherweight Title
25.01.71	Jose Legra	L PTS 15	London	EU	Featherweight Title
05.07.71	Evan Armstrong	L CO 12	London	B	Featherweight Title
25.03.75	Vernon Sollas	L CO 4	London	B	Featherweight Title

NON CHAMPIONSHIP CONTESTS (38)

WON PTS (12)	**1968** Bobby Davies, Colin Lake (2). **1969** Tommaso Galli, Miguel Herrera, Ould Makloufi. **1972** Simon Rawlings. **1973** George McGurk. **1974** George McGurk (2), Bingo Crooks, Vernon Sollas
WON CO (2)	**1969** Messaoud Boussaboua. **1973** Billy Hardacre
WON RSC/RTD (20)	**1966** Brian Gullefer, Sammy Rodgers, Johnny Pearce, Johnny Ratcliffe, Vic Woodhall. **1967** Joe Okezie, Billy Williams, George Evans, George O'Neill, Ayree Jackson, Ray Opoku, Hugh Baxter, Peter Lavery. **1968** Ola Alolade. **1969** George O'Neill, Ola Alolade. **1970**Antonio Chiloiro. **1972** Dennis Flynn. **1974** Mario Stango. **1975** George McGurk
WON DIS (1)	**1972** Johnny Cheshire
LOST PTS (1)	**1975** Billy Waith
LOST RSC/RTD (2)	**1970** Ben Tahar. **1974** Mario Stango

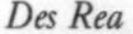

Des Rea

Willie Reilly

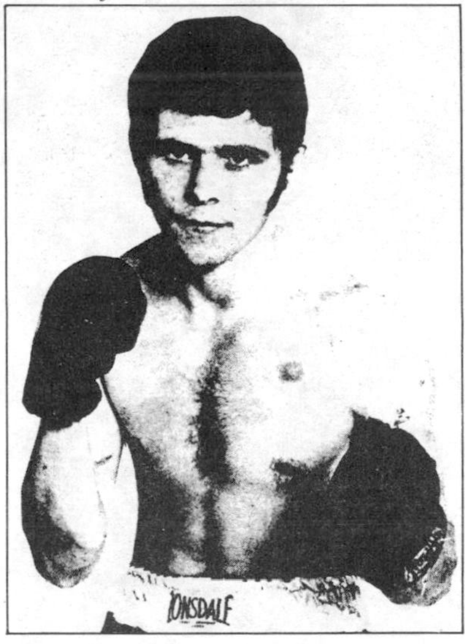

Henry Rhiney

British Welterweight Champion, 1976 – 1979. European Welterweight Champion, 1978 – 1979
Born 28.11.51 Jamaica *From* Luton *Pro Career* 1973 – 1980 (57 contests, won 32, drew 6, lost 19)

CHAMPIONSHIP CONTESTS (5)

07.12.76	Pat Thomas	W RSC 8	Luton	B	Welterweight Title
13.02.78	Billy Waith	W PTS 15	Barnsley	B	Welterweight Title
02.12.78	Josef Pachler	W CO 10	Dornbirn	EU	Welterweight Title
23.01.79	Dave Boy Green	L RSC 5	London	EU	Welterweight Title
04.04.79	Kirkland Laing	L RSC 10	Birmingham	B	Welterweight Title

NON CHAMPIONSHIP CONTESTS (52)

WON PTS (21)	**1973** Ray Thorogood, Keith Nugent, Mick Evans, Brian Gregory, Liam White. **1974** Jim Devanney, Liam White, Tommy Joyce, John Smith, Alan Reid, Trevor Francis. **1975** John Smith (2), Kevin White. **1976** Mickey Flynn (2), John Smith. **1977** Sinclair Christie. **1978** Sinclair Christie, Mickey Morse, Billy Waith
WON CO (1)	**1974** Jim Devanney
WON RSC/RTD (6)	**1975** Kevin White (2). **1976** Mickey Ryce. **1977** Terry Petersen, Mickey Flynn, Brian Gregory
WON DIS (1)	**1974** Peter Cain
DREW (6)	**1973** Terry Davies. **1974** Mickey Flynn. **1975** Trevor Francis (2), Clemente Tshinza, Claude Martin
LOST PTS (14)	**1973** Derek Simpson, Jeff Gale. **1974** Pat Thomas (2). **1975** Clemente Tshinza. **1976** James Vrij, Josef Pachler. **1977** Steve Angell, Pat Thomas. **1978** Harold Volbrecht. **1979** Peter Neal, Hans Henrik Palm. **1980** Andoni Amana, Torben Andersen
LOST CO (1)	**1975** Germain Le Maitre
LOST RSC/RTD (2)	**1974** Les Pearson. **1977** Joey Mack

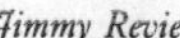
Jimmy Revie

Henry Rhiney

Alan Richardson

British Featherweight Champion, 1977 – 1978
Born 04.11.48 *From* Fitzwilliam *Pro Career* 1971 – 1978 (27 contests, won 17, drew 1, lost 9)

CHAMPIONSHIP CONTESTS (6)

08.07.74	Evan Armstrong	L RSC 11	London	B, C	Featherweight Titles
15.03.77	Vernon Sollas	W RSC 8	Leeds	B	Featherweight Title
17.06.77	Eddie Ndukwu	L RSC 12	Lagos	C	Featherweight Title
03.10.77	Les Pickett	W PTS 15	Aberavon	B	Featherweight Title
09.12.77	Eddie Ndukwu	L RTD 9	Lagos	C	Featherweight Title
20.04.78	Dave Needham	L PTS 15	London	B	Featherweight Title

NON CHAMPIONSHIP CONTESTS (21)

WON PTS (10)	**1971** Arrow Abu, Bingo Crooks. **1972** Bingo Crooks, Sammy Vernon, Neil Gauci. **1973** John Mitchell, Billy Hardacre. **1975** Danny Fearon, Colin Miles. **1976** John Mitchell
WON RSC/RTD (5)	**1972** Dave Tuohey. **1973** Barry Harris. **1976** Ray Ross, Gerry Duffy, Dave Needham
DREW (1)	**1972** Billy Waith
LOST PTS (4)	**1972** Billy Hardacre. **1973** Billy Hardacre. **1975** Fernand Roelands. **1978** Les Pickett
LOST RSC/RTD (1)	**1975** Vernon Sollas

Dick Richardson

European Heavyweight Champion, 1960 – 1962
Born 01.06.34 *From* Newport *Pro Career* 1954 – 1963 (47 contests, won 31, drew 2, lost 14)

CHAMPIONSHIP CONTESTS (7)

27.05.57	Joe Bygraves	DREW 15	Cardiff	BE	Heavyweight Title
27.03.60	Hans Kalbfell	W RSC 13	Dortmund	EU	Heavyweight Title
29.08.60	Brian London	W RTD 8	Porthcawl	EU	Heavyweight Title
18.02.61	Han Kalbfell	W PTS 15	Dortmund	EU	Heavyweight Title
24.02.62	Karl Mildenberger	W CO 1	Dortmund	EU	Heavyweight Title
17.06.62	Ingemar Johansson	L CO 8	Gothenburg	EU	Heavyweight Title
26.03.63	Henry Cooper	L CO 5	London	B, BE	Heavyweight Titles

NON CHAMPIONSHIP CONTESTS (40)

WON PTS (5)	**1954** Johnny Hall. **1955** Prosper Beck. **1958** Bob Baker, Garvin Sawyer. **1959** Bert Whitehurst
WON CO (7)	**1954** Peter Green, **1955** Sammy Clarke, Morry Bush, Emile Degreef, Robert Eugene, Alain Cherville. **1958** Hans Friedrich
WON RSC/RTD (14)	**1955** Johnny McLeavy, Sid Cain, Jim Cooper, Denny Ball, Jean Serres, Peter Bates, Bobby Warmbrunn. **1956** Werner Weigand, Marcel Limage, Gunter Nurnberg, Kurt Schiegl. **1957** Gianni Luise, Hans Kalbfell. **1958** Maurice Mols
WON DIS (1)	**1956** Ezzard Charles
DREW (1)	**1954** Bernie Jelley
LOST PTS (7)	**1954** Jim Cooper. **1956** Joe Erskine. **1957** Willie Pastrano, Bob Baker. **1959** Joe Erskine, Mike de John. **1961** Howard King
LOST RSC/RTD (2)	**1956** Nino Valdes. **1958** Henry Cooper
LOST DIS (3)	**1955** Hugh Ferns. **1958** Cleveland Williams. **1960** Mike de John

Ernie Roderick

British Welterweight Champion, 1939 – 1948. European Welterweight Champion, 1946 – 1947.
British Middleweight Champion, 1945 – 1946
Born 25.01.14 *From* Liverpool *Pro Career* 1931 – 1950 (140 contests, won 112, drew 4, lost 24)

CHAMPIONSHIP CONTESTS (11)

23.03.39	Jake Kilrain	W CO 7	Liverpool	B	Welterweight Title

Alan Richardson

Dick Richardson

25.05.39	Henry Armstrong	L PTS 15	London	W	Welterweight Title
13.07.40	Norman Snow	W PTS 15	Northampton	B	Welterweight Title
29.09.41	Arthur Danahar	W PTS 15	London	B	Welterweight Title
29.05.45	Vince Hawkins	W PTS 15	London	B	Middleweight Title
04.06.46	Omar Kouidri	W PTS 15	London	EU	Welterweight Title
28.10.46	Vince Hawkins	L PTS 15	London	B	Middleweight Title
01.02.47	Robert Villemain	L RTD 9	Paris	EU	Welterweight Title
08.09.47	Gwyn Williams	W PTS 15	London	B	Welterweight Title
09.12.47	Eric Boon	W PTS 15	London	B	Welterweight Title
08.11.48	Henry Hall	L PTS 15	London	B	Welterweight Title

NON CHAMPIONSHIP CONTESTS (129)

WON PTS (58) **1931** Tony Butcher, Young Martin, Jackie Fraser, Tommy Eustace, Tommy Bailey. **1932** Billy Quinlan, Alec Law. **1933** Jim Hunter. **1934** Jack Daly, Charlie Baxter. **1935** Jack Powell, Billy Graham (2), Roy Mills, Dave McCleave, Pat Haley, George Bunter, Harry Lister, Jimmy Stewart. **1936** Jack McCleod, Ivor Pickens, Jake Kilrain, Panther Purchase, Dave McCleave, George Daly, Paul Schaeffer, Lefty Flynn. **1937** Stafford Barton, Paul Schaeffer, Ercole Buratti, Nestor Charlier, Lefty Flynn, Frank Erne, Jean Morin. **1938** Jack McCabe, Cleto Locatelli, Jim Purcell, Dai Jones, Charlie Parkin, Kid Janas, Al Baker (2). **1939** Paddy Roche, Lionel Gibbs. **1940** Jackie Potts, Harry Craster, Eric Boon. **1941** Ray McIntyre, Jackie Kid Berg. **1942** Ginger Sadd. **1943** Jackie Potts, Tommy Davies. **1944** Tommy Davies, Johnny Clements. **1945** George Odwell, Tommy Davies, Johnny Clements. **1947** Tino Clarari

WON CO (23) **1932** Jerry Smith. **1933** Alec Law, Packey McFarland, Jackie Flynn. **1935** Jim Boyle, Frank McCall, Willie Hamilton, Len Tiger Smith, George Rose, Walter Saunders. **1937** George Bunter, Kid Silver. **1938** Reg Gregory, Jack McKnight, Roy Mills, Gustave Humery. **1939** Dave McCleave, Charlie Parkin. **1940** Jimmy Griffiths, Taffy Williams. **1941** Paddy Roche. **1944** Billy Mawson. **1945** Jim Wellard

CONTINUED OVERLEAF

Ernie Roderick

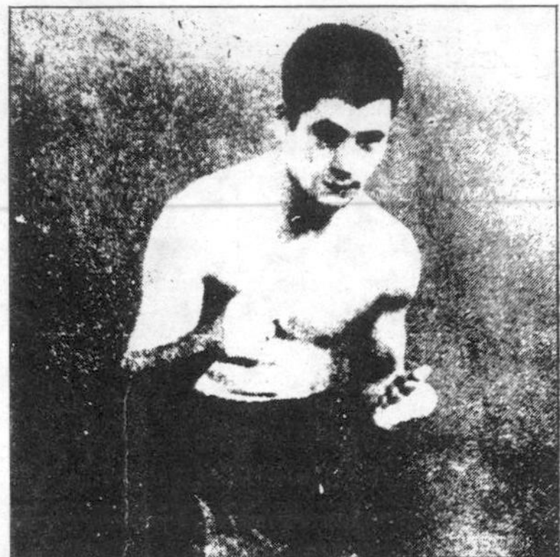
Stan Rowan

WON RSC/RTD (21)	**1932** Jerry Smith. **1933** Bryn Edwards, Herbie Fraser. **1934** Henry Baumas. **1935** Jack Moody, Pat Butler. **1936** Cock Moffitt. **1937** Jake Kilrain, Cyril Pluto, Johnny Rust, Jim Purcell. **1938** Jack Powell, Tommy Smith, Johnny Clements. **1939** Gaspard de Ridder. **1941** Jack Sean Clancy, Ron Lindley, Harry Mizler. **1942** Jim Heruhy. **1943** Stafford Barton, Paddy Roche
WON DIS (3)	**1934** Panther Purchase, Jack Lord. **1938** Ben Donners
DREW (4)	**1933** Tommy John, Bobby Blay. **1935** Pat Haley. **1946** Jimmy Ingle
LOST PTS (16)	**1932** Jimmy Stewart. **1933** Cyril Pluto. **1934** Bob Nelson, Pat Butler, Dave McCleave, Charlie Baxter. **1936** Sonny Jones. **1937** Jimmy Walsh. **1939** Arthur Danahar. **1943** Pat O'Connor, Lefty Flynn. **1945** Bert Hyland. **1946** Jean Walzach. **1948** Eddie Thomas. **1949** Eddie Thomas. **1950** Cliff Curvis
LOST RSC/RTD (1)	**1933** Bobby Delaney
LOST DIS (3)	**1934** Billy Bird, Jack Lord, Tommy Taylor

Stan Rowan

Undefeated British Bantamweight Champion, 1949. British Empire Bantamweight Champion, 1949
Born 06.09.24 *From* Liverpool *Pro Career* 1942 – 1953 (67 contests, won 46, drew 5, lost 16)

CHAMPIONSHIP CONTESTS (2)

24.03.49	Jackie Paterson	**W** PTS 15 Liverpool	B, BE	Bantamweight Titles
12.11.49	Vic Toweel	L PTS 15 Johannesburg	BE	Bantamweight Title

NON CHAMPIONSHIP CONTESTS (65)

WON PTS (28)	**1942** Eddie Douglas, Frankie Kelly, Alf Roe, Dennis Collins, Jim Healy, Ronnie Bishop. **1943** Young Josephs, Jackie Hodder, Tich Gravell, Jack Mackenzie. **1946** Barney McVeigh, Norman Lewis, Jackie Hughes, Eddie Dumazel. **1947** Tucker Smith, Ritchie McCulloch, Jim Brady, Joe Cornelis, Charlie Brown. **1948** Black Bond, Bunty Doran, Danny O'Sullivan, Theo Medina, Peter Kane. **1949** Amleto Falcinelli (2). **1952** Jackie Briers, Tommy Icke
WON CO (6)	**1942** Jimmy Mack. **1943** Fred Bridges. **1946** Joe Collins, Len Coffin. **1947** Mickey Francis, Joe Curran
WON RSC/RTD (10)	**1946** Ritchie McCulloch, Mickey Jones, Jimmy Webster, Tommy Madine, Mickey Colbert. **1947** Teddy Peckham, Alex Sinnaeve, Jackie Paterson. **1948** Fernand Van Houche, Louis Fernandez
WON DIS (1)	**1952** Glyn Evans

Mark Rowe

Alan Rudkin

DREW (5) **1942** Frankie Kelly, Johnny Rawlings. **1947** Johnny Boom. **1948** Ronnie Draper. **1949** Mickey McKay

LOST PTS (7) **1946** Johnny Boom. **1947** Tsuneshi Maruo, Guido Ferracin. **1949** Teddy Gardner. **1950** Jim Kenny, Lou Alter. **1953** Peter Keenan

LOST CO (1) **1944** Frank Bonser

LOST RSC/RTD (7) **1948** Georges Mousse. **1949** Bunty Doran, Bobby Boland. **1950** Lou Alter, Peter Guichan. **1952** Tommy Proffit, Ken Lawrence

Mark Rowe

British & Commonwealth Middleweight Champion, 1970

Born 12.07.47 *From* Camberwell *Pro Career* 1966 – 1973 (47 contests, won 38, drew 1, lost 8)

CHAMPIONSHIP CONTESTS (3)

12.05.70	Les McAteer	**W** RSC 14	London	B, C	Middleweight Titles
08.09.70	Bunny Sterling	L RSC 4	London	B, C	Middleweight Titles
17.04.73	Bunny Sterling	L PTS 15	London	B	Middleweight Title

NON CHAMPIONSHIP CONTESTS (44)

WON PTS (9) **1967** Hugh Lynch. **1968** Johnny Cooke. **1969** Dramane Ouedrago, Doug Huntley. **1970** Dick Duffy. **1971** Sauro Soprani. **1972** Jimmy Mitchell, Carlos Marks. **1973** Gerard Cola

WON CO (5) **1967** Willie Fisher. **1968** Johnny Kramer. **1971** Dramane Ouedrago, William Poitrimol. **1972** Skip Yeaton

WON RSC/RTD (22) **1966** Chris Jobson, Dave Wakefield. **1967** Derek Cowper, Joe Falcon, Ernest Musso, Roger Van Laere, Tom Bell, Jackie Cailliau. **1968** Henry Turkington, Larry Brown, Nat Jacobs, Len Gibbs. **1969** Pascal di Benedetto, Jimmy Ramos, Bob Herrington, Lionel Cuypers, Matt Donovan. **1970 Pat Dwyer, Danny Perez. 1971** Ronnie Hough. **1972** Werner Mundt. **1973** Tony Berrios

WON DIS (1) **1968** Assane Fakyh

DREW (1) **1971** Fate Davis

LOST PTS (2) **1966** Hugh Lynch. **1970** Tom Bethea

LOST RSC/RTD (4) **1967** Pat Dwyer. **1968** Nojeen Adigun. **1971** Tom Bethea. **1972** Howard Sharpe

Alan Rudkin

British Bantamweight Champion, 1965 – 1966 and Undefeated British Bantamweight Champion, 1968 – 1972. British Empire Bantamweight Champion, 1965 – 1966 and 1968 – 1969. Undefeated Commonwealth Bantamweight Champion, 1970 – 1972. European Bantamweight Champion, 1971
Born 18.11.41 *From* Liverpool *Pro Career* 1962 – 1972 (50 contests, won 42, lost 8)

CHAMPIONSHIP CONTESTS (13)

22.03.65	Johnny Caldwell	**W** RSC 10	Nottingham	B, BE	Bantamweight Titles
30.11.65	Fighting Harada	L PTS 15	Tokyo	W	Bantamweight Title
06.09.66	Walter McGowan	L PTS 15	London	B, BE	Bantamweight Titles
27.04.67	Ben Ali	L PTS 15	Barcelona	EU	Bantamweight Title
13.05.68	Walter McGowan	**W** PTS 15	Manchester	B, BE	Bantamweight Titles
08.03.69	Lionel Rose	L PTS 15	Melbourne	BE, W	Bantamweight Titles
09.06.69	Evan Armstrong	**W** RTD 11	Manchester	B	Bantamweight Title
12.12.69	Reuben Olivares	L RSC 2	Los Angeles	W	Bantamweight Title
21.04.70	Johnny Clark	**W** RSC 12	London	B, C	Bantamweight Titles
08.09.70	Jimmy Revie	L PTS 15	London	B	Featherweight Title
16.02.71	Franco Zurlo	**W** RTD 11	London	EU	Bantamweight Title
10.08.71	Augustin Senin	L PTS 15	Bilbao	EU	Bantamweight Title
25.01.72	Johnny Clark	**W** PTS 15	London	B, C	Bantamweight Titles

NON CHAMPIONSHIP CONTESTS (37)

WON PTS (24)	**1962** Carl Taylor, Eddie Barraclough. **1963** Eddie Barraclough (2), Danny Wells, Brian Cartwright, Pierre Vetroff. **1964** Danny Lee, Orizu Obilaso, Baby John, Brian Cartwright (2). **1965** Ben Ali, Ray Assis. **1966** Felipe Gonzales, Edmundo Esparza, Raul Vega, Jose Bisbal, Bob Allotey, Bobby Davies. **1968** Pornchai Poppraigam, Billy Brown, Manny Elias. **1971** Hugo Bidyeran
WON CO (3)	**1962** Dickie Hanna, Gerry Jones. **1967** Ron Jones
WON RSC/RTD (8)	**1962** Tommy Burgoyne, Danny Wells. **1964** Don Weller. **1965** Jose Cejudo, Michel Lamora. **1967** Yoshiichi Tzuganezawa. **1968** Rudy Corona. **1969** Karim Young
WON DIS (1)	**1963** Brian Bissmire
LOST RSC/RTD (1)	**1962** Carl Taylor

Phil Scott

Undefeated British Heavyweight Champion, 1926 – 1931. British Empire Heavyweight Champion, 1926 – 1931
Born 03.01.1900 *From* Marylebone (birthname Phil Suffling) *Died* 1983 *Pro Career* 1919 – 1931 (85 contests, won 65, drew 4, lost 14, no contest 2)

CHAMPIONSHIP CONTESTS (6)

27.01.26	George Cook	**W** DIS 17	Edinburgh	BE	Heavyweight Title
18.03.26	Frank Goddard	**W** CO 3	London	B	Heavyweight Title
30.04.26	Boy McCormick	**W** RTD 10	Manchester	B	Heavyweight Title
14.06.26	Harry Persson	L CO 11	London	EU	Heavyweight Title
10.07.26	Tom Heeney	**W** PTS 20	Southampton	BE	Heavyweight Title
13.06.31	Larry Gains	L CO 2	Leicester	BE	Heavyweight Title

NON CHAMPIONSHIP CONTESTS (79)

WON PTS (29)	**1919** Piper Taylor, P. O. Prizeman. **1920** Tom Ireland, Jim Rideout, Sid Pape. **1921** Jim Rideout, Jack Tyrell, Sid Pape, Ivor Powell. **1923** Sid Pape, Harry Gold, Charlie Penwill, Gipsy Daniels. **1924** Albert Lloyd, Tom Berry, Jack Humbeek, George Cook, Tom Heeney, Horace Jones. **1925** Paul Samson-Koerner, Tom Berry (2), Gipsy Daniels. **1927** Franz Diener, Pierre Charles. **1928** Pierre Charles, Roberto Roberti. **1929** Ludwig Haymann, Vittorio Campolo
WON CO (14)	**1919** Gunner Poole, Gunner Gazzard. **1920** E. V. Grimes, Ted Hayes, Victor Scott. **1922** Jack Tyrell. **1923** Ike Ingleton. **1924** Marcel Nilles. **1925** Jack Stanley (2). **1926** Marcel Luneau, Leon Sabel. **1927** Harry Reeve, Helmuth Siewert

WON RSC/RTD (13)	**1920** Peter Rocca, Nick Birch. **1921** Jack Hobbs, George Lewis. **1922** Billy Naish, Joe Dixon, Jack Rollings. **1923** Bob Spiller, Jack Hankinson. **1924** O. Ahaus, Andre Anderson, Kid Moose. **1927** Monte Munn
WON DIS (5)	**1926** Armand de Carolis. **1927** Riccardo Bartozolle, Yale Okun. **1929** Ted Sandwina, Otto Von Porat
DREW (4)	**1919** Piper Taylor, P. O. Prizeman. **1921** Piet Van Der Veer. **1924** Harry Reeve
LOST PTS (6)	**1920** Sid Pape, Fred Sale. **1921** Sid Pape, Piet Van Der Veer. **1924** Gipsy Daniels. **1927** Johnny Risco
LOST CO (5)	**1920** Harry Drake. **1922** Albert Lloyd. **1925** Paolino Uzcudun. **1927** Knute Hansen. **1930** Young Stribling
LOST DIS (1)	**1930** Jack Sharkey
NC (2)	**1920** Jack Stanley, Alf Bright

NOTE:
The Lonsdale Belt was not issued for any of the above British Championship Contests and the European Heavyweight Title Contest versus Harry Persson was not generally recognised to have been a Championship match.

Joey Singleton

British L. Welterweight Champion, 1974 – 1976
Born 06.06.51 *From* Kirkby *Pro Career* 1973 – 1982 (40 contests, won 27, drew 2, lost 11)

CHAMPIONSHIP CONTESTS (5)

21.11.74	Pat McCormack	W PTS 15	Liverpool	B	L. Welterweight Title
30.09.75	Alan Salter	W RSC 9	London	B	L. Welterweight Title
11.11.75	Des Morrison	W PTS 15	Manchester	B	L. Welterweight Title
01.06.76	Dave Boy Green	L RSC 6	London	B	L. Welterweight Title
17.04.80	Jorgen Hansen	L PTS 12	Copenhagen	EU	L. Welterweight Title

NON CHAMPIONSHIP CONTESTS (35)

WON PTS (18)	**1973** Barton McAllister, Angus McMillan, Jess Harper, Jimmy Fairweather, Noel McIvor. **1975** Alan Salter. **1978** Des Gwilliam, Mick Bell. **1979** Sylvester Gordon (2), Carl Bailey (2), Achille Mitchell. **1980**

CONTINUED OVERLEAF

Phil Scott

Joey Singleton

	Terry Petersen. **1981** Sylvester Gordon, Lee Hartshorn. **1982** Tony Martey, Cliff Gilpin
WON CO (1)	**1974** Jim Melrose
WON RSC/RTD (5)	**1978** Tommy Glencross, George McGurk, Kevin Davies. **1980** Martyn Galleozzie. **1982** Cor Eversteyn
DREW (2)	**1976** Carlos Foldes. **1981** Frankie Decaestecker
LOST PTS (5)	**1976** George Turpin, Colin Power. **1979** Hans Henrik Palm. **1980** Kirkland Laing. **1981** Lloyd Hibbert
LOST RSC/RTD (4)	**1973** Jim Montague. **1976** Charlie Nash. **1978** Des Morrison. **1982** Frank Ropis

Vernon Sollas

British Featherweight Champion, 1975 – 1977
Born 14.08.54 *From* Edinburgh *Pro Career* 1973 – 1977 (32 contests, won 24, drew 1, lost 7)

CHAMPIONSHIP CONTESTS (3)

25.03.75	Jimmy Revie	W CO 4	London	B	Featherweight Title
25.02.76	Elio Cotena	L CO 14	London	EU	Featherweight Title
15.03.77	Alan Richardson	L RSC 8	Leeds	B	Featherweight Title

NON CHAMPIONSHIP CONTESTS (29)

WON PTS (4)	**1973** Bashew Sibaca. **1974** Tommy Wright, Billy Belnavis. **1976** George Turpin
WON CO (1)	**1973** Martyn Galleozzie
WON RSC/RTD (18)	**1973** John O'Rawe, Billy Belnavis, Albert Amatler, Mickey Piner, John Mitchell, Jo Jo Jackson. **1974** Colin Miles, Phil Hudson, Bashew Sibaca. **1975** Alan Richardson, Alberto Reyes, James Martinez, Chamaco Reyes. **1976** Francisco Villegas, Bingo Crooks, Tommy Glencross, Rodolfo Moreno, Arnold Taylor
DREW (1)	**1974** Tommy Wright
LOST PTS (1)	**1974** Jimmy Revie
LOST CO (2)	**1974** Evan Armstrong. **1977** Dave Needham
LOST RSC/RTD (2)	**1973** George McGurk. **1977** Les Pickett

Terry Spinks

British Featherweight Champion, 1960 – 1961
Born 28.02.38 *From* Canning Town *Pro Career* 1957 – 1962 (49 contests, won 41, drew 1, lost 7)

CHAMPIONSHIP CONTESTS (3)

27.09.60	Bobby Neill	W RSC 7	London	B	Featherweight Title
22.11.60	Bobby Neill	W CO 14	London	B	Featherweight Title
02.05.61	Howard Winstone	L RTD 10	London	B	Featherweight Title

NON CHAMPIONSHIP CONTESTS (46)

WON PTS (27)	**1957** Jerry Parker (3), Ivan McCready, Pancho Bhatachaji, Malcolm McLeod. **1958** George McDade, Alex Bollaert, Eric Brett, Henri Schmid, Pierre Cossemyns, Eddie O'Connor, Mohamed Zarzi, Pat Supple. **1959** Con Mount Bassie, Pierre Cossemyns, Eric Brett, George Dormer. **1960** Junior Cassidy, Johnny Kidd, Dave Croll. **1961** Kimpo Amarfio, Con Mount Bassie. **1962** Eugene le Cozannet, Ron Jones, Jean Biosca, Billy Kid Davis
WON CO (2)	**1958** Attai Ben Aissa. **1959** Sugar Ray
WON RSC/RTD (9)	**1957** Jim Loughrey, Billy Kane, Pat Glancy, George McDade, Stanis Sobolak. **1958** Malcolm McLeod, Terry Toole. **1959** Eddie Burns. **1962** Johnny Mantle
WON DIS (1)	**1961** Dave Hilton
DREW (1)	**1960** Roy Jacobs
LOST PTS (3)	**1959** Derry Treanor, John O'Brien. **1962** Billy Kid Davis
LOST CO (1)	**1959** Bobby Neill
LOST RSC/RTD (2)	**1958** Billy Rafferty. **1962** Bobby Fisher

Vernon Sollas

Terry Spinks

Bunny Sterling

British Middleweight Champion, 1970 – 1974 and Undefeated British Middleweight Champion, 1975. Commonwealth Middleweight Champion, 1970 – 1972. European Middleweight Champion, 1976

Born 01.01.48 Jamaica *From* Finsbury Park *Pro Career* 1966 – 1977 (57 contests, won 35, drew 4, lost 18)

CHAMPIONSHIP CONTESTS (14)

08.09.70	Mark Rowe	W RSC 4	London	B, C	Middleweight Titles
13.11.70	Kahu Mahanga	W PTS 15	Melbourne	C	Middleweight Title
21.01.71	Tony Mundine	DREW 15	Sydney	C	Middleweight Title
22.03.71	Johann Louw	W PTS 15	Edmonton	C	Middleweight Title
20.12.71	Jean-Claude Bouttier	L CO 14	Paris	EU	Middleweight Title
14.04.72	Tony Mundine	L RSC 15	Brisbane	C	Middleweight Title
19.09.72	Phil Matthews	W CO 5	Manchester	B	Middleweight Title
17.01.73	Don McMillan	W RSC 11	Solihull	B	Middleweight Title
17.04.73	Mark Rowe	W PTS 15	London	B	Middleweight Title
07.11.73	Elio Calcabrini	L PTS 15	San Remo	EU	Middleweight Title
11.02.74	Kevin Finnegan	L PTS 15	London	B	Middleweight Title
10.06.75	Maurice Hope	W RSC 8	London	B	Middleweight Title
20.02.76	Frank Reiche	W RSC 13	Hamburg	EU	Middleweight Title
04.06.76	Angelo Jacopucci	L PTS 15	Milan	EU	Middleweight Title

NON CHAMPIONSHIP CONTESTS (43)

WON PTS (18) **1966** Fess Parker, Tony Dowling. **1967** Fess Parker, Mike Keeney, Darkie Smith, Al Sharpe, Henry Turkington. **1968** Larry Brown, Bo Pettersson. **1970** Harry Scott. **1971** Bill Douglas, Luis Rodriguez, Tom Bogs. **1973** Dave Adkins. **1974** Tom Jensen, Poul Knudsen, Victor Attivor, Rudiger Schmidtke

CONTINUED OVERLEAF

WON RSC/RTD (9) — **1967** Dave Derbyshire, Ted Sherwood, Joe Somerville. **1968** Jim Swords, Johnny Kramer. **1970** Denny Pleace, Mario Almanzo. **1972** Tom Bethea. **1977** Frank Reiche

DREW (3) — **1968** Klaus Stokmann. **1969** Max Cohen. **1972** Roy Lee

LOST PTS (13) — **1966** Joe Devitt, Willie Turkington, Fess Parker. **1967** Dick Duffy, Wally Swift. **1968** Johnny Kramer. **1969** Wally Swift, Harry Scott, Dick Duffy. **1973** Maxie Smith. **1974** Tom Bogs. **1977** Rudi Koopmans, Mustapha Wassaja

Sam Steward

British Lightweight Champion, 1928 – 1929

Born 1906 *From* Lewisham *Pro Career* 1923 – 1936 (116 contests, won 79, drew 19, lost 18)

CHAMPIONSHIP CONTESTS (2)

17.09.28	Ernie Rice	**W** CO 12	London	B	Lightweight Title
02.05.29	Fred Webster	L PTS 15	London	B	Lightweight Title

NON CHAMPIONSHIP CONTESTS (114)

WON PTS (54) — **1923** Ted Smith, Tony Francis (2), Teddy Munns, Harry Kemp, Jack Hall, Kid Diamond, Johnny Thomas, Johnny Lewis. **1924** Jimmy Berry, George Salter (2), Walter McLean, Kid Lewis, Frankie Brown, Stoker Everett, Bill Softley, Johnny Page, Jim Thake. **1925** Bob Ballantyne, A/M Finney, Steve Dallegan, Billy Ward. **1926** Fred Bullions, Jack Kirk, Arthur Tyrell, Jack Donn, Fred Tilston, Bill Softley, Frank Robossee. **1927** Teddy Baker, Battling Van Dyk, Pop Newman, Ernie Izzard, Jack Hyams, Sapper Hill. **1928** Haydn Williams, Alf Butters, Jack Hyams (2), Jan Scheffers. **1929** Tom Daly, Billy Gilmore, Frank Carberry (2), Aine Gyde, Harry Fenn. **1930** Walter Wright, Fred Bullions, Aine Gyde. **1931** Aine Gyde, Vic Carter, Fred Bullions. **1936** Billy Reynolds

WON CO (6) — **1924** Arthur Connor, Cpl Pendrich, Fred Mottram. **1928** Ike Bradley, George Rose. **1930** Gaston Devaux

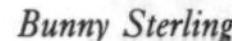

Bunny Sterling

Sam Steward

WON RSC/RTD (16)	**1923** Harry Kemp. **1924** Jim Richardson. **1925** Billy Adair, Bill Duckworth, Mike Honeyman. **1926** Johnny Bishop. **1927** Arthur Debeve, Teddy Baker, Austin O'Connor, Jimmy Welsh. **1928** Pop Newman, Charlie Evans, Albert Holmes, Aine Gyde. **1929** Pierre Godart. **1930** Jim Hocking
WON DIS (2)	**1927** Harry Fenn. **1929** Benny Valger
DREW (19)	**1923** Jack Hall. **1925** Reg Caswell, Walter Wright. **1926** Reg Caswell, Ted Marchant, Jack Donn, Cockney Buxton, George Gogah, Archie Sexton. **1927** Archie Sexton, Jan Scheffers. **1928** Albert Holmes, Billy Brown, Lucien Vinez. **1929** Harry Fenn (2). **1930** Johnny Curley. **1931** Jack Sheppard, Dick Stubbings
LOST PTS (12)	**1923** Johnny Thomas. **1924** Harry Broad, Frankie Brown. **1925** Reg Caswell. **1926** Jack Donn. **1927** Harry Corbett. **1929** Fred Webster. **1930** Louis Saarens, Haydn Williams, Peter Nolan. **1931** Johnny Sheehan, Dick Stubbings
LOST RSC/RTD (5)	**1924** Billy Bird. **1926** Billy Palmer. **1931** Jack Hudson. **1935** Bert Francis. **1936** Fred Bullions

NOTE:
The Lonsdale Belt was not issued for either of the above British Championship Contests.

John H. Stracey

Undefeated British Welterweight Champion, 1973 – 1975. Undefeated European Welterweight Champion, 1974 – 1975. World Welterweight Champion, 1975 – 1976
Born 22.09.50 *From* Bethnal Green *Pro Career* 1969 – 1978 (51 contests, won 45, drew 1, lost 5)

CHAMPIONSHIP CONTESTS (7)

31.10.72	Bobby Arthur	L DIS 7	London	B	Welterweight Title
05.06.73	Bobby Arthur	W CO 4	London	B	Welterweight Title
27.05.74	Roger Menetrey	W RSC 8	Paris	EU	Welterweight Title
29.04.75	Max Hebeisen	W RSC 6	London	EU	Welterweight Title
06.12.75	Jose Napoles	W RSC 6	Mexico City	W	Welterweight Title
20.03.76	Hedgemon Lewis	W RSC 10	London	W	Welterweight Title
22.06.76	Carlos Palomino	L RSC 12	London	W	Welterweight Title

NON CHAMPIONSHIP CONTESTS (44)

WON PTS (6)	**1970** David Pesenti. **1971** Dante Pelaez, Ait Bouzid Elmenceur. **1972** Ricky Porter. **1973** Danny McAloon, Jose Peterson
WON CO (6)	**1969** Santos Martins, Ronnie Clifford. **1971** Yvon Mariolle. **1972** Yvon Mariolle. **1973** Otho Tyson. **1974** Vernon Mason
WON RSC/RTD (26)	**1969** Ray Opoku, Bryn Lewis. **1970** Tommy Carson, Tei Dovie, Bernard Martin, Harri Pittulainen, Billy Seasman, Willie Rea, Ferdinand Ahumibe. **1971** Dave Wyatt, Guy Vercoutter. **1972** Bernie Terrell, Des Rea, Antonio Torres, Joe Yekinni, Les Pearson, David Melendez. **1973** Irish Pat Murphy, Jose Melendez, Urban Baptiste, Marc Gervais. **1974** Jackie Tillman, Tony Garcia, Ernie Lopez. **1975** Ruben Vasquez. **1978** George Warusfel
WON DIS (2)	**1971** Teddy Cooper. **1975** Keith Averett
DREW (1)	**1971** Frankie Lewis
LOST PTS (1)	**1972** Marshall Butler
LOST RSC/RTD (2)	**1973** Cubby Jackson. **1977** Dave Boy Green

NOTE:
All of the above World Championship Contests were for the WBC version of the Title

Johnny Sullivan

British & British Empire Middleweight Champion, 1954 – 1955
Born 19.12.32 Horden *From* Preston (birthname John Hallmark) *Pro Career* 1948 – 1960 (97 contests, won 68, drew 3, lost 26)

CONTINUED OVERLEAF

John H. Stracey

Johnny Sullivan

CHAMPIONSHIP CONTESTS (2)

14.09.54	Gordon Hazell	W CO 1	London	B, BE	Middleweight Titles
16.06.55	Pat McAteer	L DIS 9	Liverpool	B, BE	Middleweight Titles

NON CHAMPIONSHIP CONTESTS (95)

WON PTS (31)	**1948** Wilf Stacey. **1949** Fred Holmes, Eric Roberts, Bobby Graham, Gordon Ashun. **1950** Roy Davies, Rees Moore. **1951** Jackie Whitehouse, Bob Cleaver (2), Ron Cooper, Henry Hall. **1952** Bert Sanders, Jackie Marr, George Roe, Gilbert Stock, Bob Cleaver. **1953** Richard Armah. **1954** Arthur Acha, Leo Starosch, Titi Clavel, Martin Hansen, Jan Hagenaar. **1955** Karl Bucher, Abe Quartey, Jean Ruellet. **1956** Jackie King, Tony Johnson, Jackie Labua, Willie Troy. **1957** Arthur Howard
WON CO (15)	**1950** Jackie Socks, Joe Black, Gerry Hames, Alf Marsh, Sam McKnight, Tony Dwyer, Jackie King, Billy Clarke, Al Murphy. **1951** Sammy Milsom, Tommy Harlow, Ron Grogan. **1953** Ron Crookes. **1954** Gaston Meulenbrucq. **1955** Andre de Keersgieter
WON RSC/RTD (20)	**1949** Eric Billington, John Reeves. **1950** Johnny Cross, Joe Elliott, Gordon Ashun, Eddie Parsons. **1951** Freddie Webb, Tom Johnston. **1952** Les Allen, Jean Invernizzi, Mike Gillo, Billy Fifield, Gus Rubicini, Irvin Schulz. **1953** Duggie Miller, Michael Stack, Tony Liversage, Wally Beckett, Bruce Crawford. **1954** Gordon Hazell
WON DIS (1)	**1951** Bos Murphy
DREW (3)	**1949** Eric Roberts. **1951** Ron Pudney, George Roe
LOST PTS (19)	**1949** Eric Billington, Ossie Hall. **1950** Roy Davies (2), Rees Moore. **1951** John Nuttall, George Roe. **1952** Les Allen, Gordon Wallace. **1953** Gordon Hazell, Jimmy King. **1954** Martin Hansen. **1955** Hans Stretz. **1956** Rocky Castellani, Joey Giambra (2), Randy Sandy. **1957** Sam Langford, Johnny Halafihi
LOST RSC/RTD (5)	**1955** Artie Towne, Eduard Lausse. **1956** Rory Calhoun. **1957** Yolande Pompey. **1960** Sixto Rodriguez
LOST DIS (1)	**1952** George Roe

Wally Swift

British Welterweight Champion, 1960. British Middleweight Champion, 1964 – 1965
Born 10.08.36 *From* Nottingham *Pro Career* 1957 – 1969 (88 contests, won 68, drew 3, lost 17)

CHAMPIONSHIP CONTESTS (9)

01.02.60	Tommy Molloy	**W** PTS 15	Nottingham	B	Welterweight Title
21.11.60	Brian Curvis	L PTS 15	Nottingham	B, BE	Welterweight Titles
08.05.61	Brian Curvis	L PTS 15	Nottingham	B, BE	Welterweight Titles
14.12.64	Mick Leahy	**W** PTS 15	Nottingham	B	Middleweight Title
08.11.65	Johnny Pritchett	L RSC 12	Nottingham	B	Middleweight Title
20.02.67	Johnny Pritchett	L PTS 15	Nottingham	B	Middleweight Title
09.09.67	Sandro Mazzinghi	L RTD 6	Milan	EU	L. Middleweight Title
26.03.68	Carlos Duran	L DIS 10	Birmingham	EU	Middleweight Title
14.07.69	Les McAteer	L RTD 11	Nottingham	B, BE	Middleweight Titles

NON CHAMPIONSHIP CONTESTS (79)

WON PTS (53)	**1957** Willie Smith, Cliff Lawrence, Terry Tulley, Billy Wooding. **1958** Fitzroy Lindo, Tommy Keeley, Joe Somerville, Terry Burnett, Harry Haydock. **1959** Phil Williams, Brian Husband (2), Ritchie Edwardson, Terry Banning, Willie Toweel. **1960** Virgil Akins, Emile Vlaemynck, Larry Baker, Assane Fakyh, Henri Cabelduc. **1961** Tony Smith, Boswell St Louis, Albert Carroll, Mauri Backman. **1962** Billy Tarrant, Ahmed Sebbane, Tanos Lambrianides, Orlando Paso, Harry Scott, Mick Leahy, Tony Smith, Maxie Smith. **1963** Dennis Read, Wilson Harris, Johnny Cooke, Jim Swords, Johnny Angel. **1964** Felipe Playeto, Joe Bell, Harry Scott. **1965** Charley Austin, Daniel Leuillier, Nat Jacobs. **1966** Freddie Thomas, Al Sharpe, Horst Wiesorek, Manfred Graus. **1967** Len Gibbs, Bob Cofie, Bunny Sterling. **1968** Len Gibbs. **1969** Bunny Sterling, Les McAteer
WON CO (3)	**1962** Sammy Cowan. **1966** James Shelton. **1967** Ade Ajasco
WON RSC/RTD (10)	**1958** Tommy Saxon, Peter Cobblah. **1959** Ray Corbett. **1961** Bob Cofie. **1962** Johnny Kramer, Bob Roberts. **1964** Nelis Oostrum. **1965** Jim Lloyd. **1966** Reinhard Dampmann. **1966** Freddie Thomas
DREW (3)	**1959** Boswell St Louis. **1962** Mick Leahy. **1963** Johnny Angel
LOST PTS (6)	**1958** Albert Carroll. **1959** Tony Smith. **1961** Fortunato Manca. **1962** Chris Christensen. **1963** Mick Leahy, Johnny Cooke
LOST RSC/RTD (2)	**1963** Teddy Haynes. **1968** Tom Bogs
LOST DIS (2)	**1956** Santos Martins. **1961** Albert Carroll

Nel Tarleton

British Featherweight Champion, 1931 – 1932, 1934 – 1936 & Undefeated British Featherweight Champion, 1940 – 1945. Undefeated British Empire Featherweight Champion, 1940 – 1945
Born 14.01.06 *From* Liverpool *Died* 1956 *Pro Career* 1926 – 1945 (143 contests, won 115, drew 8, lost 20)

CHAMPIONSHIP CONTESTS (12)

06.11.30	Johnny Cuthbert	Drew 15	Liverpool	B	Featherweight Title
01.10.31	Johnny Cuthbert	**W** PTS 15	Liverpool	B	Featherweight Title
10.11.32	Seaman Tommy Watson	L PTS 15	Liverpool	B	Featherweight Title
26.07.34	Seaman Tommy Watson	**W** PTS 15	Liverpool	B	Featherweight Title
21.09.34	Freddie Miller	L PTS 15	Liverpool	W	Featherweight Title
12.12.34	Dave Crowley	**W** PTS 15	London	B	Featherweight Title
12.06.35	Freddie Miller	L PTS 15	Liverpool	W	Featherweight Title
06.05.36	Johnny King	**W** PTS 15	Liverpool	B	Featherweight Title
24.09.36	Johnny McGrory	L PTS 15	Liverpool	B	Featherweight Title
01.02.40	Johnny Cusick	**W** PTS 15	Liverpool	B, BE	Featherweight Titles
02.11.40	Tom Smith	**W** PTS 15	Liverpool	B, BE	Featherweight Titles
23.02.45	Tiger Al Phillips	**W** PTS 15	Manchester	B, BE	Featherweight Titles

NON CHAMPIONSHIP CONTESTS (131)

WON PTS (63)	**1926** George Sankey, Young Wilson. **1927** Mick Hill, Dom Volante (2), Jerome Vanpaemel (2), Peter Howard, Kid Socks. **1928** Billy Hindley, Kid Carter, Jim Mackenzie, Dom Volante, Robert Obrecht, Kid

CONTINUED OVERLEAF

Wally Swift

Nel Tarleton

	Nicholson, Billy Streets, Julian Verbist, Lew Pinkus. **1929** Alf Kid Pattenden, Billy Evans, Jack Kirby, Andre Beghin, Henri Poutrain (2), Robert Tassain, Archie Bell, Jackie Cohen, Pinkie Silverberg. **1930** Micky Greb, Tom Dexter. **1931** Ginger Jones, Jack Garland, Doug Parker, Albert Barker, Nick Bensa. **1932** Young Josephs, Francois Machtens, Al Foreman, Benny Sharkey. **1933** Dan McGarry, August Gyde, Jimmy Kelso. **1934** Norman Dale, Harry Brooks. **1935** Norman Milton, Jimmy Walsh, Harry Edwards. **1936** Joe Connelly, Raymond Renard, Marius Baudry. **1937** Frank Harsen. **1938** Arnie Lagrand. **1939** Josef Preys, Jim Spider Kelly. **1940** Billy Walker. **1941** Bobby Watson, Billy Walker. **1942** Syd Worgan (2). **1943** Syd Worgan. **1944** Ben Duffy, George Pook, Johnny King
WON CO (12)	**1926** Pat Malone, Les Tarrant. **1927** Frank Marcel, Bert Saunders, Arthur Lloyd. **1928** Young Denain, Don Jones. **1930** Frankie Marchesi. **1931** Angelo Agatensi. **1932** Doug Parker (2). **1942** Pancho Ford
WON RSC/RTD (29)	**1926** Joe Martin, Leo Kelly, Kid Fitzpatrick, Chris Cairney, Victor Crauc, Bert Mills. **1927** Maurice Prudholme, Jack Kirby, Alf Barber. **1928** Louis Lepesant, Robert Douillet, Billy Boulger, Henri Pelemans, Robert Obrecht, Rene Boitaert. **1929** Mick Hill, Bugler Lake. **1930** Rene Boitaert, Phil Claret. **1931** Ernest Mignard, Louis Laseaux, Albert Barker. **1932** Tom Dexter. **1933** Leon Mestre, Alec Law. **1934** Nick Bensa, Georges Covaci. **1935** Hal Cartwright. **1936** George Williams
WON DIS (4)	**1926** Kid Brooks. **1928** Don Jones. **1938** Fred Morris. **1939** Billy Charlton
DREW (7)	**1927** Peter Howard, Enrico Venturi. **1928** Julian Verbist. **1930** Jimmy Slavin. **1932** Al Brown. **1933** Tod Morgan. **1935** Johnny King
LOST PTS (15)	**1926** Arthur Boddington, Dom Volante, Alf Kid Pattenden. **1927** Jack Ellis, Johnny Brown. **1929** Al Ridgeway. **1930** Joey Scalfaro. **1933** Young Llew Edwards. **1934** Sonny Lee. **1935** Johnny King. **1937** Jim Spider Kelly. **1941** Tom Smith, Jim Brady. **1943** Len Davies, Ben Duffy
LOST DIS (1)	**1944** Johnny King

NOTE:
The Lonsdale Belt was not issued for the British Championship Contest versus Johnny King. Both the World Championship contests versus Freddie Miller were for the NBA version of the Title.

Wally Thom

British Welterweight Champion, 1951 – 1952 and 1953 – 1956. British Empire Welterweight Champion, 1951 – 1952. European Welterweight Champion, 1954 – 1955
Born 14.06.26 *From* Birkenhead *Died* 1980 *Pro Career* 1949 – 1956 (54 contests, won 42, drew 1, lost 11)

CHAMPIONSHIP CONTESTS (7)

16.10.51	Eddie Thomas	**W** PTS 15	London	B, BE	Welterweight Titles
24.07.52	Cliff Curvis	L CO 9	Liverpool	B, BE	Welterweight Titles
24.09.53	Peter Fallon	**W** PTS 15	Liverpool	B	Welterweight Title
26.08.54	Gilbert Lavoine	**W** RSC 10	Liverpool	EU	Welterweight Title
19.10.54	Lew Lazar	**W** CO 6	London	B, EU	Welterweight Titles
23.06.55	Idrissa Dione	L PTS 15	Liverpool	EU	Welterweight Title
05.06.56	Peter Waterman	L RTD 5	London	B	Welterweight Title

NON CHAMPIONSHIP CONTESTS (47)

WON PTS (20)	**1949** Rex Bryan, Cal Johnson. **1950** Bob Burniston, Rees Moore, Laurie Buxton, Kay Kalio, Danny McKay, Jimmy Molloy. **1951** Willie Whyte, Alf Danahar, Titi Clavel. **1952** Giel de Roode, Kay Kalio, Bob Cleaver. **1953** Billy Wells, Bernie Newcombe, Kit Pompey. **1954** Mickey O'Neill. **1955** Somidez Yonkitrat, Jean Ruellet
WON CO (8)	**1949** Eph Taylor, Jesse Birtwhistle. **1950** Alf Marsh, Jackie King. **1951** Giel de Roode. **1952** Terry Ratcliffe. **1953** Danny Malloy. **1955** Andre de Keersgieter
WON RSC/RTD (9)	**1949** Phil Mellish, Jack Humphries, Gordon Ashun. **1950** Roy Davies, Micky Talbot, Eddie Cardew. **1954** George Happe, Attu Clottey. **1955** Louis Trochon
WON DIS (1)	**1951** Cliff Curvis
DREW (1)	**1952** Danny Womber
LOST PTS (3)	**1953** Peter Fallon, Hector Constance. **1954** Kid Dussart
LOST RSC/RTD (5)	**1951** Jimmy Molloy. **1952** Hector Constance. **1954** Vincent O'Kine. **1955** Jimmy King, Benny Nieuwenhuizen

Eddie Thomas

British Welterweight Champion, 1949 – 1951. British Empire & European Welterweight Champion, 1951
Born 27.07.26 *From* Merthyr *Pro Career* 1946 – 1954 (48 contests, won 40, drew 2, lost 6)

CHAMPIONSHIP CONTESTS (6)

15.11.49	Henry Hall	**W** PTS 15	London	B	Welterweight Title
13.09.50	Cliff Curvis	**W** PTS 15	Swansea	B	Welterweight Title
27.01.51	Pat Patrick	**W** CO 13	Johannesburg	BE	Welterweight Title
19.02.51	Michele Palermo	**W** PTS 15	Carmarthen	EU	Welterweight Title
13.06.51	Charles Humez	L PTS 15	Porthcawl	EU	Welterweight Title
16.10.51	Wally Thom	L PTS 15	London	B, BE	Welterweight Titles

NON CHAMPIONSHIP CONTESTS (42)

WON PTS (24)	**1946** Jackie Simpson, Reg Quinlan, Bob Ramsey, Dick Shields, Ginger Ward. **1947** Bill Cadby, Jean Wanes. **1948** Henry Hall, Jack Phillips, Ernie Roderick, Gwyn Williams. **1949** Billy Exley, Billy Graham, Job Roos, Ernie Roderick. **1950** Constant Reypens, Bruno Marostegan, Henri Hecquard, Gilbert Ussin. **1951** Antonio Monzon, Giel de Roode. **1953** George Roe, Kit Pompey. **1954** Terry Ratcliffe
WON CO (3)	**1947** Jimmy Brunt. **1948** Willie Whyte. **1951** Eric McQuade
WON RSC/RTD (9)	**1946** Don Chiswell. **1947** Billy Walker, Kid Marcel, Willy Wimms. **1948**

CONTINUED OVERLEAF

Wally Thom

Eddie Thomas

	Chris Adcock, Giel de Roode. **1949** Stan Hawthorne. **1950** Emile Delmine. **1953** Roy Baird
DREW (2)	**1950** Titi Clavel. **1953** Bunty Adamson
LOST PTS (3)	**1948** Gwyn Williams. **1954** Bunty Adamson, Ron Duncombe
LOST RSC/RTD (1)	**1947** Yrjoe Piitulainen

Billy Thompson

British Lightweight Champion, 1947 – 1951. European Lightweight Champion, 1948 – 1949
Born 20.10.25 *From* Hickleton Main *Pro Career* 1945 – 1953 (63 contests, won 46, drew 4, lost 13)

CHAMPIONSHIP CONTESTS (11)

16.10.47	Stan Hawthorne	W RSC 3	Liverpool	B	Lightweight Title
17.02.48	Roberto Proietti	W PTS 15	London	EU	Lightweight Title
26.07.48	Pierre Montane	DREW 15	London	EU	Lightweight Title
01.10.48	Arthur King	L RTD 7	Manchester	BE	Lightweight Title
17.01.49	Josef Preys	W PTS 15	Birmingham	EU	Lightweight Title
18.05.49	Harry Hughes	W RSC 5	Glasgow	B, EU	Lightweight Titles
05.07.49	Kid Dussart	L DIS 6	London	EU	Lightweight Title
31.01.50	Roberto Proietti	L PTS 15	London	EU	Lightweight Title
11.07.50	Tommy McGovern	W PTS 15	Hanley	B	Lightweight Title
23.02.51	Pierre Montane	L CO 12	Manchester	EU	Lightweight Title
28.08.51	Tommy McGovern	L CO 1	London	B	Lightweight Title

NON CHAMPIONSHIP CONTESTS (52)

WON PTS (19)	**1945** Billy Cunningham. **1946** Syd Worgan, Ben Duffy (2), Battling Hai, Josef Preys, Claude Dennington (2), Jimmy Jury, Ginger Roberts, Alf Edwards, Paul Renucci. **1947** Josef Preys, Andre Famechon (2). **1948** Andre Gonnet. **1949** Cliff Curvis. **1951** Jackie Braddock. **1952** Duggie du Preez
WON CO (5)	**1945** Billy Cunningham. **1946** Don Cameron, Billy Biddles. **1947** John Ingle. **1949** Morrie Jones
WON RSC/RTD (14)	**1945** Ken Barratt, Charlie Fox. **1946** Jackie Grimes, Jack Carrick, Jim Watson, Dan McAllister, Harry Hughes, Jimmy Jury. **1947** Gerry Smyth, Bert Hornby. **1950** Billy Humphries. **1951** Tommy Hinson. **1952** Tommy Hinson. **1953** Johnny Fish
WON DIS (3)	**1946** Billy Biddles, Dave Finn. **1950** Guiseppe Colasanti
DREW (3)	**1947** Tommy Barnham. **1949** Josef Preys. **1953** Alf Danahar
LOST PTS (7)	**1946** Stan Hawthorne, Andre Famechon. **1948** Andre Famechon, Solly

Billy Thompson

Dick Turpin

	Cantor. **1950** Ginger Roberts. **1951** Gerald Dreyer. **1953** Roy Baird
LOST DIS (1)	**1949** Jim Keery

Dick Turpin

British Middleweight Champion, 1948 – 1950. British Empire Middleweight Champion, 1948 – 1949 *Born* 26.11.20 *From* Leamington Spa *Pro Career* 1937 – 1950 (99 contests, won 74, drew 6, lost 18, no contest 1)

CHAMPIONSHIP CONTESTS (5)

18.05.48	Bos Murphy	**W** CO 1	Coventry	BE	Middleweight Title
28.06.48	Vince Hawkins	**W** PTS 15	Birmingham	B, BE	Middleweight Titles
20.06.49	Albert Finch	**W** PTS 15	Birmingham	B, BE	Middleweight Titles
06.09.49	Dave Sands	**L** CO 1	London	BE	Middleweight Title
24.04.50	Albert Finch	**L** PTS 15	Nottingham	B	Middleweight Title

NON CHAMPIONSHIP CONTESTS (94)

WON PTS (40)	**1937** Frank Guest, Trevor Burt. **1938** Walter Rankin, Trevor Burt, Sid Fitzhugh, Johnny Clarke, Jack McKnight. **1939** Walter Rankin, Mick Miller, Jack Hammer, George Robey, Jimmy Griffiths, Wally Pack, Jack Milburn, Nat Franks, Harry Ainsworth, Charlie Parkin, Ben Valentine (2). **1940** Ginger Sadd, Jim Berry, Tommy Davies, Paddy Roche, Pat O'Connor. **1946** Paddy Roche. **1947** Ron Cooper (2), Jim Wellard, Jim Hockley, Des Jones, Bert Sanders (2), Johnny Boyd, Billy Stevens, Freddie Price. **1948** Mark Hart, Bert Sanders. **1949** Ron Cooper. **1950** Vince Hawkins, Ron Pudney
WON CO (9)	**1937** Frank Guest, Ray Chadwick. **1938** Trevor Burt. **1940** Dave McCleave, Albert O'Brien. **1946** Jack Lord, Trevor Burt, Johnny Boyd. **1947** Frank Hayes
WON RSC/RTD (21)	**1937** Eric Lloyd, Eddie Harris, Phil Proctor. **1938** Bill Blythling, Frank Smith. **1939** Johnny Thornton, George Robey. **1940** Maurice Dennis, Tommy Smith. **1946** Johnny Blake, Art Owen, Billy Mayne. **1947** Tommy Braddock, Gordon Griffiths, Norman Rees, Billy Stevens, Tommy Davies, Vince Hawkins, Art Owen. **1948** Dougie Miller. **1949** George Ross
WON DIS (1)	**1949** Robert Charron
DREW (6)	**1938** Bob Hartley, Alf Bishop. **1939** George Robey. **1940** Eddie Maguire. **1947** Bert Sanders. **1948** Tiberio Mitri
LOST PTS (9)	**1938** Charlie Parkin. **1939** Butcher Gascoigne, Jimmy Griffiths, George

CONTINUED OVERLEAF

	Howard. **1940** Eddie Maguire. **1944** Dave McCleave. **1946** Johnny Boyd. **1949** Tiberio Mitri. **1950** Baby Day
LOST CO (3)	**1937** Trevor Burt. **1947** George Howard. **1949** Marcel Cerdan
LOST RSC/RTD (4)	**1940** Ginger Sadd. **1946** Johnny Best. **1950** Cyrille Delannoit, Albert Finch
NC (1)	**1937** Eddie Harris

Randy Turpin

Undefeated British Middleweight Champion, 1950 – 1954. Undefeated British Empire Middleweight Champion, 1952 – 1954. European Middleweight Champion, 1951 – 1954. World Middleweight Champion, 1951. Undefeated British L. Heavyweight Champion, 1952 – 1953, 1955 and 1956 – 1958. Undefeated British Empire L. Heavyweight Champion, 1952 – 1956
Born 07.06.28 *From* Leamington Spa *Died* 1966 *Pro Career* 1946 – 1958 (73 contests, won 64, drew 1, lost 8)

CHAMPIONSHIP CONTESTS (12)

17.10.50	Albert Finch	W CO 5	London	B	Middleweight Title
27.02.51	Luc Van Dam	W CO 1	London	EU	Middleweight Title
10.07.51	Sugar Ray Robinson	W PTS 15	London	W	Middleweight Title
12.09.51	Sugar Ray Robinson	L RSC 10	New York	W	Middleweight Title
10.06.52	Don Cockell	W RSC 11	London	B, BE	L. Heavyweight Titles
21.10.52	George Angelo	W PTS 15	London	BE	Middleweight Title
09.06.53	Charles Humez	W PTS 15	London	EU	Middleweight Title
21.10.53	Carl Bobo Olson	L PTS 15	New York	W	Middleweight Title
02.05.54	Tiberio Mitri	L RSC 1	Rome	EU	Middleweight Title
26.04.55	Alex Buxton	W CO 2	London	B, BE	L. Heavyweight Titles
26.11.56	Alex Buxton	W RSC 5	Leicester	B	L. Heavyweight Title
11.06.57	Arthur Howard	W PTS 15	Leicester	B	L. Heavyweight Title

NON CHAMPIONSHIP CONTESTS (61)

WON PTS (13)	**1946** Des Jones. **1947** Bert Sanders, Jury VII, Mark Hart. **1948** Vince Hawkins, Alby Hollister. **1949** Dougie Miller. **1950** Gilbert Stock, Gus Degouve. **1953** Dougie Miller. **1954** Olle Bengtsson. **1955** Polly Smith. **1958** Wim Snoek
WON CO (16)	**1946** Bill Blythling. **1947** Jimmy Davis, Dai James, Bert Hyland, Tommy Davies, Leon Fouquet. **1948** Freddie Price. **1950** Eli Elandon, Jose Alamo. **1951** Eduardo Lopez, Billy Brown, Jan de Bruin. **1952** Jacques Hairabedian. **1953** Victor D'Haes. **1955** Jose Gonzalez. **1956** Jacques Bro
WON RSC/RTD (22)	**1946** Gordon Griffiths. **1947** Johnny Best, Frank Dolan, Ron Cooper, Jimmy Ingle. **1948** Gerry McCready. **1949** Jackie Jones, Mickey Laurent, Cyrille Delannoit, Jean Wanes, Roy Wouters, Pete Mead. **1950** Richard Armah. **1951** Jean Stock, Jackie Keough. **1952** Alex Buxton. **1956** Alessandro D'Ottavio. **1957** Ahmed Boulgroune, Sergio Berchi, Uwe Janssen. **1958** Eddie Wright, Redvers Sangoe
WON DIS (4)	**1949** William Poli. **1950** Tommy Yarosz. **1953** Walter Cartier. **1955** Ray Schmidt
DREW (1)	**1947** Mark Hart
LOST PTS (2)	**1948** Albert Finch. **1956** Hans Stretz
LOST CO (2)	**1955** Gordon Wallace. **1958** Yolande Pompey
LOST RSC/RTD (1)	**1948** Jean Stock

Jimmy Walsh

British Lightweight Champion,1936 – 1938
Born 1913 *From* Chester *Died* 1964 *Pro Career* 1931 – 1940 (88 contests, won 67, drew 2, lost 18, no contest 1)

CHAMPIONSHIP CONTESTS (3)

24.04.36	Jackie Kid Berg	W RSC 9	Liverpool	B	Lightweight Title
19.10.36	Harry Mizler	W PTS 15	London	B	Lightweight Title
23.06.38	Dave Crowley	L PTS 15	Liverpool	B	Lightweight Title

Randy Turpin

Jimmy Walsh

NON CHAMPIONSHIP CONTESTS (85)

WON PTS (43)	**1932** Billy Walsh, Tom Manley, Ted Westry, Joe Baldesara. **1933** Jim Hurst, Dave Crowley, Freddie Irving, Louis Botes, Benny Sharkey, Aine Gyde. **1934** Harry Mizler, Bobby Turnbull, Edouard Jamsin (2), Frankie Brown, Maurice Holtzer. **1935** Jimmy Stewart, Louis Saerens, Billy Smith, Frankie Brown, Carlo Orlandi, Joe Kerr, Francois Machtens, Tommy Steele. **1936** Dave Finn, Boyo Rees (2), Harry Craster, Fred Lowbridge. **1937** Alby Day, Robert Disch, Dick Corbett, Joe Connolly, Les McCarthy, Ernie Roderick, Albert Esser. **1938** Johnny Kilburn, Patsy Quinn, Jack Carrick, Dave Finn. **1939** Johnny Softley, Johnny Jenkins. **1940** A/C Murdoch
WON CO (5)	**1932** Archie Wilkie. **1933** Len Wickwar, Jack Richardson. **1937** Jackie Flynn. **1938** Jim Cameron
WON RSC/RTD (11)	**1932** Nat Williams. **1933** Johnny McMillan. **1934** Bobby Mack, Nicolas Wilke. **1935** Jimmy Clough. **1936** Fred Lowbridge, Billy Hughes, Benny Caplan, Aldo Linz, George Daly. **1939** Dennis Cahill
WON DIS (6)	**1933** Billy Quinlan, Dave Crowley. **1934** Maurice Holtzer. **1935** Wesley Ramey, George Daly. **1937** George Reynolds
DREW (2)	**1933** Tony Butcher. **1935** Joe Connolly
LOST PTS (17)	**1931** Frankie Brown. **1932** Alf Barrett. **1933** Benny Sharkey, Sonny Lee. **1934** Seaman Tommy Watson, Freddie Miller. **1935** Freddie Miller, George Daly, Nel Tarleton, Joe Connolly, Frank Barton. **1937** Dave Crowley, Harry Mizler, George Odwell, Phil Zwick, Len Wickwar. **1938** Eric Boon
NC (1)	**1939** Tommy Jones

NOTE:
The Lonsdale Belt was not issued for the British Championship Contest versus Jackie Kid Berg.

Peter Waterman

Undefeated British Welterweight Champion, 1956 – 1958. Undefeated European Welterweight Champion, 1958
Born 08.12.34 *From* Clapham *Pro Career* 1952 – 1958 (46 contests, won 41, drew 2, lost 3)

CONTINUED OVERLEAF

Peter Waterman

Seaman Tommy Watson

CHAMPIONSHIP CONTESTS (4)

05.06.56	Wally Thom	**W** RTD 5	London	B	Welterweight Title
17.12.56	Frank Johnson	**W** RTD 10	Birmingham	B	Welterweight Title
30.05.57	Emilio Marconi	DREW 15	Rome	EU	Welterweight Title
28.01.58	Emilio Marconi	**W** RSC 14	London	EU	Welterweight Title

NON CHAMPIONSHIP CONTESTS (42)

WON PTS (7)	**1952** Laurie Davies. **1954** Santos Martin, Boswell St Louis. **1955** Sandy Manuel. **1956** Kid Gavilan, Idrissa Dione. **1957** Ben Buker II
WON CO (8)	**1952** Wally Webb. **1953** Tommy Organ, Bert Middleton. **1954** Bernie Newcombe. **1955** Teun Brommer, Raphael de Silva, Billy Wooding. **1957** Ernest Zetmann
WON RSC/RTD (22)	**1953** Tony Brazil, Ron Ball, Johnny Hunt. **1954** Patsy Guttridge, Algar Smith, Peter Smith, Johnny Carrington, Jack Thornbury. **1955** Jackie Keough, Paul King, Gilbert Ussin, Roy Baird, Boswell St Louis, George Happe, Valere Benedetto, Roger Facqueur. **1956** Bruno Marostegan. **1957** Jimmy Croll, Siegmund Jarych, Michel Francois, Nick Moos
WON DIS (1)	**1955** Peter King
DREW (1)	**1953** Jack Armstrong
LOST PTS (2)	**1956** Kid Gavilan. **1957** Boswell St Louis
LOST RSC/RTD (1)	**1958** Dave Charnley

Seaman Tommy Watson

British Featherweight Champion, 1932 – 1934
Born 02.06.08 *From* Newcastle *Died* 1971 *Pro Career* 1927 – 1935 (115 contests, won 105, drew 1, lost 9)

CHAMPIONSHIP CONTESTS (4)

10.11.32	Nel Tarleton	**W** PTS 15	Liverpool	B	Featherweight Title
19.05.33	Kid Chocolate	L PTS 15	New York	W	Featherweight & J. Lightweight Titles
21.03.34	Johnny McMillan	**W** PTS 15	Glasgow	B	Featherweight Title
26.07.34	Nel Tarleton	L PTS 15	Liverpool	B	Featherweight Title

NON CHAMPIONSHIP CONTESTS (111)

WON PTS (79)	**1927** Tom Pinkney, Billy Graham, Tom Slattery. **1928** Tommy Hall (2), Sig Morris, Fred Fox, Johnny Gordon (2), Ernie Beresford, L/S Clarke, Joe Batten, Billy Handley, Piper Connor, A/B Pledger, George Rumsey, Harry Pitt, Billy Jones, Harry Best, Horace Barber, Harry White, Charlie Chew (2), Tommy Little, Billy Reynolds, Frank Warne. **1929** Stoker Little. **1930** Johnny Quill (2), L/C Grainger, Jack Wright, George Swinbourne, Trevor Gregory, Horace Barber, A/B Castle, Jim Hocking, Sid Raiteri, Billy Streets, Harry Brooks, Aine Gyde, Roy Beresford, Jack Garland, Joe Cadman, Jim Briley, Francois Machtens. **1931** Jim Hocking, Doug Parker (2), Nobby Baker, Teddy Brown, Julian Verbist, Benny Sharkey Francois Machtens, Ernie Bicknell, Peter Cuthbertson. **1932** Battling Sandjack, Boyo Rees, Selwyn Davies, Francois Machtens, Phineas John, Billy Wyper. **1933** Fidel la Barba, August Gyde, Bobby Lawrence, Benny Sharkey. **1934** Johnny Cuthbert, Billy Gannon, Aine Gyde, Jimmy Walsh, Francois Machtens, Dick Corbett, Con Flynn, Camille Desmet, Harry Brooks, Norman Snow. **1935** Sonny Lee, Tommy Spiers, Jules Stayaert, Nobby Baker
WON CO (8)	**1927** Ted Power (2), L/C Davies. **1930** Nash Shakespeare, Jim Travis. **1933** Dave Crowley. **1934** Jim Cowie, George Odwell
WON RSC/RTD (15)	**1928** Billy Graham, Harry Atkin, Don Jeal, L/S Ellesmore, Billy Brown. **1930** Slosh Saunders, Ted Byrne, Nipper Pat Daly, Jack Garland. **1931** Jim Travis, Victor Cohen, Bert Swaddle, Doug Parker. **1932** Ginger Jones. **1935** Frankie Brown
WON DIS (1)	**1932** Luigi Quadrini
DREW (1)	**1930** Joe Cadman
LOST PTS (3)	**1928** George Rose. **1930** George Rose. **1935** Freddie Miller
LOST CO (1)	**1935** Freddie Miller
LOST RSC/RTD (2)	**1931** Dom Volante. **1935** George Daly
LOST DIS (1)	**1933** Sonny Lee

NOTE:
The World J. Lightweight Title Contest versus Kid Chocolate is not generally recognised to have been a Championship match but it is listed in *The Ring* Record Book and as such is shown, whilst the same bout also contested the Featherweight Title which was for the New York version.

Jim Watt

British Lightweight Champion, 1972 – 1973 Undefeated British Lightweight Champion, 1975 – 1977. Undefeated European Lightweight Champion, 1977 – 1979. World Lightweight Champion, 1979 – 1981
Born 18.07.48 *From* Glasgow *Pro Career* 1968 – 1981 (46 contests, won 38, lost 8)

CHAMPIONSHIP CONTESTS (16)

01.02.72	Willie Reilly	L RSC 10	Nottingham	B	Lightweight Title
03.05.72	Tony Riley	W RSC 12	Solihull	B	Lightweight Title
29.01.73	Ken Buchanan	L PTS 15	Glasgow	B	Lightweight Title
27.01.75	Johnny Cheshire	W RSC 7	Glasgow	B	Lightweight Title
03.05.75	Jonathan Dele	L PTS 15	Lagos	C	Lightweight Title
21.02.77	Johnny Claydon	W RSC 10	Glasgow	B	Lightweight Title
05.08.77	Andre Holyk	W RSC 1	Glasgow	EU	Lightweight Title
16.11.77	Jeronimo Lucas	W RSC 10	Solihull	EU	Lightweight Title
17.02.78	Perico Fernandez	W PTS 15	Madrid	EU	Lightweight Title
18.10.78	Antonio Guinaldo	W RTD 5	Glasgow	EU	Lightweight Title
17.04.79	Alfredo Pitalua	W RSC 12	Glasgow	W	Lightweight Title
03.11.79	Roberto Vasquez	W RSC 9	Glasgow	W	Lightweight Title
14.03.80	Charlie Nash	W RSC 4	Glasgow	W	Lightweight Title
07.06.80	Howard Davis	W PTS 15	Glasgow	W	Lightweight Title
01.11.80	Sean O'Grady	W RSC 12	Glasgow	W	Lightweight Title
20.06.81	Alexis Arguello	L PTS 15	London	W	Lightweight Title

CONTINUED OVERLEAF

NON CHAMPIONSHIP CONTESTS (30)

WON PTS (9)	**1969** Victor Paul, Tommy Tiger. **1971** David Pesenti. **1973** Johnny Cheshire, Angus McMillan. **1974** Kokkie Oliver, Billy Waith. **1975** Billy Waith. **1978** Billy Vivian
WON CO (3)	**1968** Santos Martins. **1970** Sammy Lockhart. **1976** George Turpin
WON RSC/RTD (14)	**1968** Alex Gibson. **1969** Winston Thomas. **1970** Victor Paul, Bryn Lewis, Ronnie Clifford. **1971** Henri Nesi, Willie Reilly, Leonard Tavarez. **1972** Noel McIvor. **1973** Noel McIvor. **1974** Andries Steyn. **1976** Jimmy Revie, Hector Diaz, Franco Diana
LOST PTS (2)	**1974** Anthony Morodi. **1975** Andre Holyk
LOST RSC/RTD (2)	**1970** Victor Paul. **1976** Johnny Claydon

NOTE:
All of the above World Championship Contests were for the WBC version of the Title.

Fred Webster

British Lightweight Champion, 1929 – 1930
Born 18.06.08 *From* Kentish Town *Died* 1971 *Pro Career* 1928 – 1934 (65 contests, won 46, drew 5, lost 14)

CHAMPIONSHIP CONTESTS (2)

02.05.29	Sam Steward	W PTS 15	London	B	Lightweight Title
21.05.30	Al Foreman	L CO 1	London	B, BE	Lightweight Titles

NON CHAMPIONSHIP CONTESTS (63)

WON PTS (32)	**1928** Charles Ernst. **1929** George Rose, Sam Steward, Harry Fenn. **1930** Walter Wright, Charlie Mack, Harry Brooks, Harry Corbett. **1931** Jim Learoyd, Vic Carter, Camille Desmet (2), Harry Fenn, Phil Richards, Harry Corbett (2), Harry Mason, Harry Brooks (2), Leo Phillips. **1932** Billy Bird (3), Harry Mason, Evan Lane, Moe Moss (2), Johnny Quill. **1933** Harry Mason, Chuck Parker, Leo Phillips. **1934** Fred Cook
WON CO (2)	**1931** Billy Jones. **1932** Billy Thomas
WON RSC/RTD (7)	**1928** Jimmy Duggan. **1931** Harold Higginson, Charlie Mack, Johnny Hudson. **1932** Pat Butler, George Willis. **1933** George Rose
WON DIS (4)	**1930** Haydn Williams. **1931** Len Tiger Smith (2). **1933** Moe Moss
DREW (5)	**1929** Jack Hyams. **1931** Eugene Drouhin, Solly Schwartz. **1934** Harry Brooks, Chuck Parker
LOST PTS (5)	**1930** George Rose. **1933** Tommy Taylor, Charlie Baxter, Harry Mason, Johnny Quill

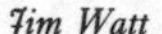
Jim Watt

Fred Webster

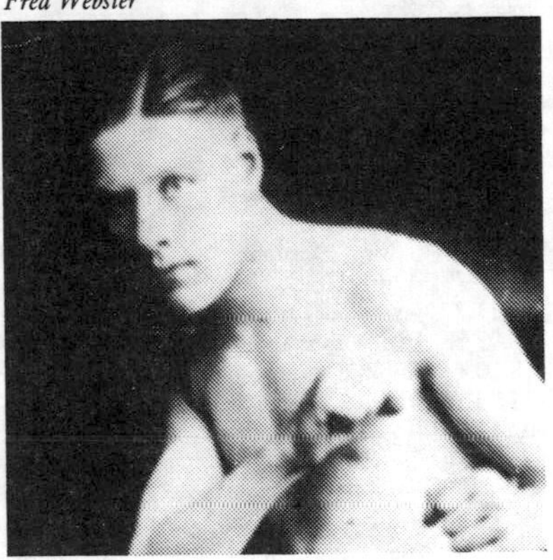

LOST CO (3)	**1929** Justo Suarez, Felix Sposito. **1934** Johnny Rust
LOST RSC/RTD (2)	**1930** Alf Howard. **1934** Johnny Rust
LOST DIS (3)	**1931** Cleto Locatelli. **1932** Stoker Reynolds, George Rose

NOTE:
The Lonsdale Belt was not issued for either of the above British Championship Contests.

Johnny Williams

British & British Empire Heavyweight Champion, 1952 – 1953
Born 25.12.26 *From* Rugby *Pro Career* 1946 – 1956 (75 contests, won 60, drew 4, lost 11)

CHAMPIONSHIP CONTESTS (4)

11.03.52	Jack Gardner	W PTS 15	London	B, BE	Heavyweight Titles
13.10.52	Johnny Arthur	W RTD 7	Leicester	BE	Heavyweight Title
12.05.53	Don Cockell	L PTS 15	London	B, BE	Heavyweight Titles
27.08.56	Joe Erskine	L PTS 15	Cardiff	B	Heavyweight Title

NON CHAMPIONSHIP CONTESTS (71)

WON PTS (21)	**1946** Billy Rhodes, Tom Smith, Joe Williams, Jim Hollies, Joe Burt. **1947** Wally With, Doug Richards. **1948** Des Jones, Bobby Ogg, Jock Taylor, Fred Vorster. **1949** Nisse Andersson, Piet Wilde, Stephane Olek. **1950** Lloyd Barnett, Vern Escoe. **1951** Aaron Wilson, Omelio Agramonte. **1953** Ansel Adams, Al Bernard. **1954** Hugo Salfeld
WON CO (15)	**1946** Mike Gearing, Harry O'Grady. **1947** Ted Barter, Trevor Burt, Jimmy Carroll. **1948** Matt Locke, Gene Fowler, Billy Wood. **1950** Piet Wilde. **1951** Reg Andrews. **1952** Werner Wiegand. **1953** Fred Powell. **1954** Gerhard Hecht. **1955** Hennie Quentemeyer, Kitone Lave
WON RSC/RTD (22)	**1946** Tom Smith, Tommy Bostock. **1947** Art Owen, Joe Kerry, Paddy Roche, Bernard O'Neill, Jimmy Carroll, George Barratt. **1948** Allan Cooke, Billy Phillips, Sid Falconer, Don Cockell, Reg Spring. **1949** Nick Wolmarans, Ken Shaw, Paddy Slavin. **1950** George Kaplan. **1951** Joe Weidin. **1952** Jimmy Rousse. **1954** Jack Hobbs, Francis Coeuret. **1955** Lucien Touzard
DREW (4)	**1946** Jim Greaves. **1947** Johnny Houlston. **1951** Heinz Neuhaus. **1956** Willi Hoepner
LOST PTS (3)	**1947** Reg Spring. **1948** Don Cockell. **1950** Jack Gardner
LOST CO (2)	**1953** Heinz Neuhaus. **1955** Jack Gardner
LOST RSC/RTD (4)	**1950** Pat Comiskey, Bill Weinberg. **1956** Tommy Jackson, Joe Bygraves

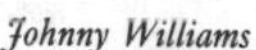
Johnny Williams

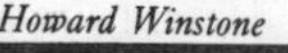
Howard Winstone

Tim Wood

Bruce Woodcock

Howard Winstone

Undefeated British Featherweight Champion, 1961 – 1968. Undefeated European Featherweight Champion, 1963 – 1967. World Featherweight Champion, 1968
Born 15.04.39 *From* Merthyr Tydfil *Pro Career* 1959 – 1968 (67 contests, won 61, lost 6)

CHAMPIONSHIP CONTESTS (17)

0205.62	Terry Spinks	W RTD 10	London	B	Featherweight Title
10.04.62	Derry Treanor	W RSC 14	London	B	Featherweight Title
30.05.62	Harry Carroll	W RTD 6	Cardiff	B	Featherweight Title
31.01.63	Johnny Morrissey	W RSC 11	Glasgow	B	Featherweight Title
09.07.63	Alberto Serti	W RTD 14	Cardiff	EU	Featherweight Title
20.08.63	Billy Calvert	W PTS 15	Porthcawl	B, EU	Featherweight Titles
09.12.63	John O'Brien	W PTS 15	London	B, EU	Featherweight Titles
12.05.64	Lino Mastallaro	W RTD 8	London	EU	Featherweight Title
22.01.65	Yves Desmarets	W PTS 15	Rome	EU	Featherweight Title
07.09.65	Vicente Saldivar	L PTS 15	London	W	Featherweight Title
07.03.66	Andrea Silanos	W RSC 15	Sassari	EU	Featherweight Title
06.09.66	Jean de Keers	W RSC 3	London	EU	Featherweight Title
07.12.66	Lennie Williams	W RSC 8	Aberavon	B, EU	Featherweight Titles
15.06.67	Vicente Saldivar	L PTS 15	Cardiff	W	Featherweight Title
14.10.67	Vicente Saldivar	L RTD 12	Mexico City	W	Featherweight Title
23.01.68	Mitsunori Seki	W RSC 9	London	W	Featherweight Title
24.07.68	Jose Legra	L RSC 5	Porthcawl	W	Featherweight Title

NON CHAMPIONSHIP CONTESTS (50)

WON PTS (30)	**1959** Billy Graydon, Peter Sexton, Tommy Williams, Jackie Bowers, Jake O'Neale, Ollie Wylie, Hugh O'Neill, Billy Calvert. **1960** Robbie Wilson, Con Mount Bassie, Phil Jones, Jean Renard, Roy Jacobs. **1961** Floyd Robertson, Ayree Jackson, Gene Fossmire, Olli Maki. **1962** Dos Santos, Dennis Adjei, George Bowes. **1963** Juan Cardenas, Miguel Kimbo. **1964** Rafiu King, Jose Bisbal, Baby Luis, Boualem Belouard. **1965** Don Johnson, Jose Legra. **1967** Richie Sue. **1968** Jimmy Anderson
WON RSC/RTD (17)	**1959** Billy Calvert, Joe Taylor. **1960** George O'Neill, Colin Salcombe,

	Terry Rees, Gordon Blakey, George Carroll, Noel Hazard, Sergio Milan, Jean Renard. **1962** Billy Kid Davis, Freddie Dobson, Teddy Rand. **1963** Gracieux Lamperti. **1964** Phil Lundgren. **1965** Lalo Guerrero, Brian Cartwright
WON DIS (1)	**1966** Don Johnson
LOST PTS (1)	**1964** Don Johnson
LOST RSC/RTD (1)	**1962** Leroy Jeffery

NOTE:
The World Championship Contest versus Mitsunori Seki was for the GB/EBU version of the Title, whilst the World Championship Contest versus Jose Legra was for the WBC version.

Tim Wood

British L. Heavyweight Champion, 1976 – 1977
Born 10.08.51 Camden Town *From* Leicester *Pro Career* 1972 – 1979 (31 contest, won 19, drew 1, lost 11)

CHAMPIONSHIP CONTESTS (2)

28.04.76	Phil Martin	W PTS 15	London	B	L. Heavyweight Title
08.03.77	Bunny Johnson	L CO 1	Wolverhampton	B	L. Heavyweight Title

NON CHAMPIONSHIP CONTESTS (29)

WON PTS (11)	**1972** Ade Ajasco. **1973** Billy Wynter, Woody Vuckovic, Dennis Avoth, Bill Drover. **1975** Victor Attivor, Baby Boy Rolle, Sid Falconer. **1976** Danny Fontillio. **1978** Eddie Fenton (2)
WON CO (1)	**1972** Peter Freeman
WON RSC/RTD (6)	**1972** Kenny Burrell. **1973** Boston Blackie. **1975** Guinea Roger. **1976** Johnny Wall. **1979** Wilson Perez, Steve Fenton
DREW (1)	**1973** Charlie White
LOST PTS (8)	**1974** Les Stevens, Richard Dunn. **1975** Roy John. **1977** Victor Attivor. **1978** Alek Penarski, Carlton Benoit. **1979** Eddie Fenton, Theo Josephs
LOST CO (1)	**1974** Eddie Neilson
LOST RSC/RTD (1)	**1976** Harry White

Bruce Woodcock

British & British Empire Heavyweight Champion, 1945 – 1950. Undefeated European Heavyweight Champion, 1946 – 1950
Born 18.01.21 *From* Doncaster *Pro Career* 1942 – 1950 (39 contests, won 35, lost 4)

CHAMPIONSHIP CONTESTS (6)

17.07.45	Jack London	W CO 6	London	B, BE	Heavyweight Titles
29.07.46	Albert Renet	W CO 6	Manchester	EU	Heavyweight Title
17.03.47	Stephane Olek	W PTS 15	Manchester	EU	Heavyweight Title
26.03.49	Johnny Ralph	W CO 3	Johannesburg	BE	Heavyweight Title
02.06.49	Freddie Mills	W CO 14	London	B, BE, EU	Heavyweight Titles
14.11.50	Jack Gardner	L RTD 11	London	B, BE	Heavyweight Titles

NON CHAMPIONSHIP CONTESTS (33)

WON PTS (2)	**1942** Charley Bundy. **1946** Freddie Mills
WON CO (8)	**1942** Jack Robinson. **1943** Arnold Hayes. **1944** Tom Reddington, Bert Gilroy, Al Delaney. **1946** Gus Lesnevich, Georges Martin. **1948** Lee Oma.
WON RSC/RTD (19)	**1942** Fred Clark, Tommy Moran, Len Munden, Don Burton, George Davis, George Hinchcliffe. **1943** George Muir, Glen Moody (2), Martin Thornton. **1944** Ken Shaw, Joe Quigley, George Markwick. **1945** Cal Rooney, Martin Thornton, Jock Porter. **1946** George James, Bert Gilroy, Nisse Andersson
WON DIS (1)	**1948** Lee Savold
LOST CO (1)	**1946** Tami Mauriello
LOST RSC/RTD (2)	**1947** Joe Baksi. **1950** Lee Savold

A Championship Diary of all Title Bouts Contested by British Boxers, 1929 – 1984

A complete record in diary format with individual summaries of all Championship contests that British boxers have participated in since the inception of the BBBC (1929). Note that all Champions or winners of vacant Titles are stated first. Non-British boxers are given their country of naturalisation.

1929

07.02.29 ***Johnny Hill, L CO 6 Emile Pladner (France), European Flyweight Title***
VELADROME D'HIVER, PARIS, FRANCE Pladner, a great puncher, immediately made the body his target and although the little Scot was able to defend for a while he had been floored three times by the end of the second round. Gamely holding up until the sixth, he was again floored and then bowled over for the full count

18.03.29 ***Harry Corbett, DREW 15 Johnny Cuthbert, British Featherweight Title***
NATIONAL SPORTING CLUB, LONDON History was made under Lonsdale Rules with the first draw and the first championship bout over fifteen rounds. Cuthbert did all the forcing, but the Bethnal Green boy boxed cleverly on the retreat nullifying most of the attacks. Corbett was over twice but, that apart, was in no real difficulties

21.03.29 ***Johnny Hill, W PTS 15 Ernie Jarvis, British Flyweight Title***
ALBERT HALL, LONDON For the first eight rounds Hill did little more than take punishment until he shook the challenger with a short jolt to the jaw. The Scot again hurt Jarvis in the tenth and started to use the left hand, but with the Londoner still coming forward, the verdict did not please the paying public

02.05.29 ***Sam Steward, L PTS 15 Fred Webster, British Lightweight Title***
ALBERT HALL, LONDON The challenger boxed off Steward with an immaculate left lead round after round, whilst for his part the champion tried desperately without any great success to get inside. Webster lasted the better of the pair and further increased the tempo to run out a clear winner

16.05.29 ***Alex Ireland, L CO 7 Len Harvey, British & British Empire Middleweight Titles***
OLYMPIA, LONDON Harvey was the complete master of the situation with the champion constantly troubled. Ireland was outboxed and outpunched continuously before being floored in the sixth, with the full count tolled over his prostrate body just one round later

16.05.29 ***Harry Corbett, L PTS 15 Johnny Cuthbert, Vacant British Featherweight Title***
OLYMPIA, LONDON With their recent contest still fresh in the memory, when the BBBC formed the opinion that Corbett should retain his belt but the title be declared vacant, Corbett was even more disappointing this time, allowing Cuthbert to force the pace from start to finish. Corbett failed to bring his superior skills into play and was adjudged the loser

16.05.29 ***Alf Kid Pattenden, L PTS 15 Teddy Baldock, British Bantamweight Title (Baldock defended British Empire Bantamweight Title)***
OLYMPIA, LONDON Baldock, with his extra reach, accrued a fair lead, but his fellow East Ender fought ferociously and actually battered him through the ropes on two occasions. Both men stood toe to toe in a remarkable battle of endurance with the loser being acclaimed as the gamest of bantam cocks

29.06.29 ***Johnny Hill, W DIS 10 Ernie Jarvis, British Flyweight Title***
CARTYNE GREYHOUND TRACK, GLASGOW Once again Jarvis put up a tremendous struggle in his bid to gain the title, but in the tenth round he unfortunately delivered a right to the body which went low. At that time Hill seemed to be losing his grip on the title and the Londoner was certainly the stronger of the pair when ruled out

13.10.29 ***Jackie Brown, W CO 3 Bert Kirby, Vacant British Flyweight Title***
THE RINK, WEST BROMWICH The fight was originally a final eliminator, but when Johnny Hill died it was amended to decide the vacant title. Kirby was the harder hitter, but Brown kept up a fast pace, punching rapidly with both hands. Following a collision of heads the Brummie staggered back whereupon the champion elect drove a straight right clean to the point of the jaw which terminated the action

16.05.29. Len Harvey (right) stabbing out the left with Alex Ireland once again on the receiving end.

17.10.29 *Frankie Genaro (USA), W PTS 15 Ernie Jarvis, World Flyweight Title (NBA/IBU version)*

ALBERT HALL, LONDON The contest was not sanctioned by the BBBC and only came about when Johnny Hill, the British champion who was due to meet Genaro, suddenly died. The American brilliantly used a variety of quality punches to confuse Jarvis, who never once stopped coming forward, although as early as the second round he was badly cut over the left eye. In the last third of the fight Jarvis frantically strived for a winning punch with the champion in desperate straits

21.10.29 *Len Harvey, W PTS 15 Jack Hood, British & British Empire Middleweight Titles*

HOLBORN STADIUM, LONDON Both men boxed well with left leads, but Harvey earned the decision by his cleaner punching and aggression. Hood put in a grandstand finish but his punches lacked real sting and the middleweight champion boxed with clockwork precision to carry off the verdict

25.11.29 *Frank Moody, L PTS 15 Frank Crossley, British L. Heavyweight Title*

HOLBORN STADIUM, LONDON The Northerner waged a well-planned defensive battle by allowing the older man to do all the forcing and being content to counter-punch whenever the opportunity arose. Moody was the aggressor, but could not nail his challenger and did not score with enough solid blows to warrant the decision

18.12.29 *Len Harvey, DREW 15 Jack Hood, British & British Empire Middleweight Titles*

OLYMPIA, LONDON The exchanges were far more open than in their previous meeting, with Harvey gaining an early ascendancy. Despite being cut, Hood's brilliant left hand work began to wipe off some of the arrears from the eighth round onwards, with the title holder recovering well by the fourteenth

1930

16.01.30 *Francois Sybille (Belgium), L DIS 8 Alf Howard, European Lightweight Title*

THE STADIUM, LIVERPOOL The Englishman was put down heavily by a body punch in the third, but continued to be the aggressor with scything hooks. Sybille was warned on several occasions to keep his punches up and finally, in the eighth round, when he caught the incoming Howard with another low blow the referee disqualified him

18.02.30 ***Mushy Callahan (USA), L RTD 10 Jackie Kid Berg, World J. Welterweight Title***

ALBERT HALL, LONDON Berg set up an attack that lasted in its ferocity almost the whole contest by pounding the Yank all over the ring. Callahan desperately wanted to keep his title and in a last ditch effort he met the East Ender in a real 'slug-fest' of a round before reeling back to his corner in a state of collapse – never to fight again

03.03.30 ***Jackie Brown, L CO 3 Bert Kirby, British Flyweight Title***

HOLBORN STADIUM, LONDON After two disappointing rounds Kirby measured Brown with a smashing right hand counter and followed up with a terrific left hook to the jaw. Brown, by now virtually defenceless, took another heavy right to the mouth and was counted out after going headlong through the ropes

04.04.30 ***Jackie Kid Berg, W PTS 10 Joe Glick (USA), World J. Welterweight Title***

MADISON SQUARE GARDEN, NEW YORK, USA Berg won well despite being struck twice by palpably low blows and suffering from other tricks of the trade. On both occasions the champion was sent to the boards, but got up to punch Glick about the ring without unduly worrying about the effects of the low punches

21.05.30 ***Fred Webster, L CO 1 Al Foreman, British Lightweight Title & Vacant British Empire Lightweight Title***

PREMIERLAND, LONDON Foreman immediately went on the attack and banged over a left hook to the jaw before springing at Webster with a terrific right to the temple which dropped him in a heap. After scrambling up, Webster was put down again by a right and left to the jaw, the count being a formality

22.05.30 ***Len Harvey, W RSC 9 Steve McCall, British & British Empire Middleweight Titles***

OLYMPIA, LONDON The Scot was sent reeling into the ropes from the first punch of the contest, but was always trying to fight back from that point, although having to play second fiddle. McCall attacked almost recklessly in the ninth and was dropped for three long counts before the referee stepped in

22.05.30 ***Dick Corbett, W PTS 15 Willie Smith (S. Africa), Vacant British Empire Bantamweight Title***

OLYMPIA, LONDON Corbett produced a top drawer display of boxing that delighted the connoisseur. Having the longer reach of the two he used it to outbox the South African comprehensively. Smith tried all he knew to land a finisher, but the Englishman could not be caught and was returned a good winner on points

22.05.30 ***Johnny Cuthbert, W PTS 15 Dom Volante, British Featherweight Title***

OLYMPIA, LONDON Volante fought at top speed but the champion was able to evade and parry whilst in the main getting his counters to work effectively. When the challenger tired Cuthbert began to meet him halfway and although the Liverpudlian put in a great twelfth round he was being chased all around the ring at the finish

29.05.30 ***Jackie Kid Berg, W RSC 4 Al Delmont (USA), World J. Welterweight Title***

DREAMLAND PARK, NEWARK, USA The Britisher put Delmont under terrific stress with his fists buzzing continuously as he fought in the usual whirlwind style that had already endeared him to the Stateside fans. By round four the referee had seen enough and pulled Berg away from the unfortunate American

12.06.30 ***Jackie Kid Berg, W PTS 10 Herman Perlick (USA), World J. Welterweight Title***

QUEENSBORO STADIUM, NEW YORK, USA Berg was not at his best and was on the verge of a knockout in the fifth when the American got home with some heavy blows. The Englishman came back to batter Perlick all over the ring and the remaining rounds saw the American in the sorest straits possible before the final gong saved him

18.06.30 ***Alf Howard, L CO 9 Francois Sybille (Belgium), European Lightweight Title***

BRUSSELS, BELGIUM Although floored by a blow to the body in the opening round, Howard by his persistent aggression was out in front until the sixth. Sybille by then had realised the Englishman was tiring rapidly and opened up, dropping him four times for long counts, before another deadly hook to the midsection ended the contest

03.09.30 ***Jackie Kid Berg, W PTS 10 Buster Brown (USA), World J. Welterweight Title***

DREAMLAND PARK, NEWARK, USA Brown stood no chance against the machine-gun fire of Kid Berg's battery and was under constant pressure. Although losing his temper on occasions the American finally settled down, with Berg appearing to take every round

18.09.30 ***Jackie Kid Berg, W PTS 10 Joe Glick (USA), World J. Welterweight Title***

QUEENSBORO STADIUM, NEW YORK, USA The slashing perpetual motion Kid Berg and the American waged war for the second time in six months with the title on the line. Again the result was as before and again Glick used every trick in his repertoire to bring down the champion but without success

18.02.30. Both Mushy Callahan (right) and Jackie Kid Berg spar for an opening prior to the bout developing into a ferocious affair.

10.10.30 ***Jackie Kid Berg, W PTS 10 Billy Petrolle (USA), World J. Welterweight Title***
MADISON SQUARE GARDEN, NEW YORK, USA In a fierce battle Petrolle occasionally went low, but the Englishman continued to fight in his usual whirlwind fashion. Berg generally outspeeded his challenger and although the American had the reputation of being a deadly puncher he was rarely able to land with any telling effect

20.10.30 ***Al Foreman, W CO 6 George Rose, British & British Empire Lightweight Titles***
BELLE VUE, MANCHESTER In the early part of the contest Rose cleverly kept out of danger by making good use of an excellent left lead. The third round saw him decked and an uppercut put him down on the bell to end the fifth. Coming out for action in the sixth, Foreman hammered his unfortunate challenger with a right to the jaw and it was all over

06.11.30 ***Johnny Cuthbert, DREW 15 Nel Tarleton, British Featherweight Title***
THE STADIUM, LIVERPOOL Cuthbert advanced continuously but was generally smothered, although a hard right knocked the Liverpudlian's gum shield out in the sixth. In the main Tarleton's defence showed to good effect when being content to jab his man off, but Cuthbert's persistent attacking deserved better

15.12.30 ***Al Foreman, DREW 15 Johnny Cuthbert, British & British Empire Lightweight Titles***
OLYMPIA, LONDON A wicked left hook to the jaw floored Cuthbert after only 15 seconds, but he bounded up to fight off the big hitting lightweight champion who was intent on destruction. In the eighth round again the Sheffield blade was floored, this time twice, but fought back so well that at the end of the contest a drawn result was given

1931

23.01.31 ***Jackie Kid Berg, W PTS 10 Goldie Hess (USA), World J. Welterweight Title***
THE STADIUM, CHICAGO, USA A slashing fight all the way saw both men hitting out at top speed as fiercely as able in an effort to destroy the opposition. Berg got on top from the third round but the American rallied near the end despite being dropped, to put together all he had. The Kid weathered the storm to come back hard himself

31.01.31 ***Jackie Kid Berg, W PTS 10 Herman Perlick (USA), World J. Welterweight Title***
MADISON SQUARE GARDEN, NEW YORK, USA Despite being hit in the groin on the off, Berg just bored in relentlessly. The champion started with an injured shoulder, but won at least four rpunds by wide margins with Perlick fighting hard to stay in the fight

02.02.31 ***Bert Kirby, L PTS 15 Jackie Brown, British Flyweight Title***
BELLE VUE, MANCHESTER Unlike their previous two contests for the flyweight crown, both of which ended in the third round, the rubber went all the way. After fifteen scintillating rounds of a closely fought contest the referee adjudged Brown the winner

10.04.31 ***Jackie Kid Berg, W PTS 10 Billy Wallace (USA), World J. Welterweight Title***
OLYMPIA, DETROIT, USA Wallace took the first three rounds by repeatedly jerking the Englishman's head back and landing a corking right to the jaw. From the fourth Berg got into his stride when driving the challenger to the ropes to batter him heavily and at the end of the final round Wallace was extremely unsteady on his feet

24.04.31 ***Jackie Kid Berg, L CO 3 Tony Canzoneri (USA), World J. Welterweight Title. (Canzoneri Defended World Lightweight Title)***
THE STADIUM, CHICAGO, USA Both fighters smashed away at each other giving and taking heavy punches until Canzoneri saw an opening for his right which caught the Englishman flush on the jaw, dropping him in a heap. Berg gamely tried to struggle to his feet but just failed to beat the count

04.05.31 ***Lucien Popescu (Rumania), L PTS 15 Jackie Brown, European Flyweight Title***
BELLE VUE, MANCHESTER At the weigh-in, the European champion was overweight and flatly refused to go to the scales again. The fight went ahead and Brown completely overwhelmed Popescu to run out an easy points winner. Brown was later awarded the Title in accordance with the IBU ruling

13.06.31 ***Phil Scott, L CO 2 Larry Gains (Canada), British Empire Heavyweight Title***
TIGERS GROUND, LEICESTER Setting up an early attack, Scott drove his challenger to the ropes, but was caught by a left to the jaw and was floored for nine. In the second round Scott appeared to

10.09.31. *Jackie Kid Berg is put down by a low blow in the eighth round against the hard hitting Tony Canzoneri, but gets up to fight on.*

have shaken off the effects of the knockdown to open up with rights and lefts before Gains sent in the two punches which spelt 'finis'

15.06.31 ***Jackie Brown, W PTS 15 Emile Degand (Belgium), European Flyweight Title***

OLYMPIA, LONDON Brown forced from the start, getting home with heavy rights to the jaw, but the Belgian proved a tough nut to crack by coming back with several sharp rallies. The Mancunian started to tire around the eleventh but Degand was unable to take advantage

22.06.31 ***Len Harvey, W PTS 15 Jack Hood, British & British Empire Middleweight Titles***

ALBERT HALL, LONDON The early part of the bout was fought mainly at close quarters with both men clinching at the first move. During the fifth Harvey unfortunately dropped low, but sent Hood down and almost through the ropes during the tenth. By now Harvey was attacking with regularity and although Hood fought back desperately, his punches lacked venom

06.07.31 ***Jackie Brown, W PTS 15 Vincenzo Savo (Italy), European Flyweight Title***

BELLE VUE, MANCHESTER Savo proved a sturdy little fighter with a real wallop in both hands and caught the champion several times. When Brown resorted to his scientific boxing he proved the complete master, but the Italian continually took the fight to his man and often puzzled the Mancunian

10.09.31 ***Tony Canzoneri (USA), W PTS 15 Jackie Kid Berg, World J. Welterweight & Lightweight Titles***

POLO GROUNDS, NEW YORK, USA Twice the Kid was floored in the opening round, but got back into his whirlwind stride to be in front until being floored with a low blow in the eighth. With the no foul rule operating Berg just beat the count and despite a cut eye was trading blows at the finish, only to go down on a wafer thin decision

01.10.31 ***Johnny Cuthbert, L PTS 15 Nel Tarleton, British Featherweight Title***

ANFIELD FOOTBALL GROUND, LIVERPOOL In the first round Tarleton was unfortunate to have the referee step on his foot and with Cuthbert setting up several bustling attacks he had to box his way out of trouble. As the contest progressed Cuthbert was dropped for a couple of counts as the Liverpudlian boxed on brilliantly for a points victory

10.10.31 ***Bep Van Klaveren (Holland), W PTS 15 Harry Corbett, European Lightweight Title***

COLSTON HALL, BRISTOL Van Klaveren opened up fast with his favourite punch being a left hook to the jaw. The Englishman was boxing cleverly but not taking advantage by countering when the occasion arose, and the Dutchman was able to keep up the pressure to finish a mile in front

16.11.31 ***Reggie Meen, W PTS 15 Charlie Smith, Vacant British Heavyweight Title***

GRANBY HALLS, LEICESTER In the sixth round Meen dropped the Londoner for seven and then smashed him through the ropes, but could not finish the job and let him off the hook. Smith was able to keep out of the way of any further big punches but was well outpointed by the finish

21.12.31 ***Dick Corbett, W PTS 15 Johnny King, British Empire Bantamweight Title & Vacant British Bantamweight Title***

BELLE VUE, MANCHESTER Corbett's evasive tactics were the order of the day as he made the young challenger miss consistently. Whilst King was frequently hitting the air, the champion was piling up the points with stinging jabs to the face and short punches to the body

1932

21.03.32 ***Len Harvey, W PTS 15 Jock McAvoy, British & British Empire Middleweight Titles***

BELLE VUE, MANCHESTER In the fifth round the challenger crashed out of the ring, before getting back and charging into Harvey. The contest was fairly even up to the thirteenth but in that fateful round McAvoy was badly hurt again, and although not going down became an easy target for the rest of the fight

23.05.32 ***Harry Crossley, L PTS 15 Jack Petersen, British L. Heavyweight Title***

HOLBORN STADIUM, LONDON In the early stages Crossley dictated affairs with an unerring straight left and when the challenger did get inside he was too inexperienced to take advantage. Later in the contest however, the champion took two long counts when tiring but fought on courageously

04.07.32 ***Marcel Thil (France), W PTS 15 Len Harvey, World Middleweight Title (IBU version)***

WHITE CITY, LONDON In a contest fought mainly at close range, Harvey had great difficulty in understanding the Swiss referee's instructions. The British champion easily won the early part of bout, but then for some unknown reason, allowed Thil to assume the initiative

12.07.32 ***Reggie Meen, L CO 2 Jack Petersen, British Heavyweight Title***

WIMBLEDON STADIUM, LONDON The light heavyweight champion completely eclipsed the heavier man attacking him from the off with rare abandon. Petersen finished the job with a magnificent right to the jaw, which gave Meen no chance to beat the count

12.07.32. Reggie Meen sprawls on the canvas to be counted out following a tremendous right to the jaw delivered by the new Champion, Jack Petersen.

11.08.32 ***Johnny Cuthbert, W RSC 10 Jim Hunter, Vacant British Lightweight Title***

WHITE CITY, GLASGOW Johnny Cuthbert bewildered the Scot with a variety of punches and in the eighth put him on the deck with a right to the jaw. That was the beginning of the end, with Hunter down twice more before being dispatched for the full count

19.09.32 ***Jackie Brown, W DIS 8 Jim Maharg, British & European Flyweight Titles***

BELLE VUE, MANCHESTER Brown boxed confidently from long range and was just too much for the Scot to handle. Eventually Maharg resorted to holding in an effort to avoid further punishment, but the writing was on the wall and when he landed a very low blow, the referee immediately disqualified him

10.10.32 ***Dick Corbett, L PTS 15 Johnny King, British & British Empire Bantamweight Titles***

BELLE VUE, MANCHESTER In a return match, once again the action was hectic, but this time the Mancunian got through when mixing his punches well and confusing the champion. At the time Corbett fought back well, but could never find a rhythm for any period and the decision, although close, was well received

31.10.32 ***Young Perez (Tunisia), L RSC 13 Jackie Brown, World Flyweight Title (IBU/NBA version)***

BELLE VUE, MANCHESTER Coming into the fatal thirteenth, after both men had taken hard knocks during a fluctuating contest, Brown connected with a left-right which left the Tunisian spreadeagled on the canvas. When arising Perez was met by a tremendous barrage of punches before the referee pulled the challenger off

10.11.32 ***Nel Tarleton, L PTS 15 Seaman Tommy Watson, British Featherweight Title***

THE STADIUM, LIVERPOOL The seaman used both hands to head and body whereas the champion was content to box him off with rapid fire jabs. Watson proved how tough he was by coming back even harder in the later stages when forcing the brilliant Tarleton to fight his kind of fight

12.12.32 ***Len Harvey, W PTS 15 Jack Casey, British & British Empire Middleweight Titles***

ST. JAMES' HALL, NEWCASTLE Casey made the running with the champion's best punches having little effect on his chin. Many times blows to the point of the jaw thudded in to no avail, whereupon Harvey recognised that he was not going to win inside the distance and nullified his opponent's aggression to run out an easy winner

1933

26.01.33 ***Jack Petersen, W CO 12 Jack Pettifer, British Heavyweight Title***
OLYMPIA, LONDON Although flooring the challenger in the first, it took another eleven rounds before Petersen could get his rival where he wanted him. A left-right and a left hook smashed the giant senseless to the canvas, but until that moment the Welshman had been given a tough battle and finished with cuts around both eyes

13.03.33 ***Jack Hood, W CO 9 Stoker Reynolds, British Welterweight Title***
EMBASSY RINK, BIRMINGHAM Although extremely game Reynolds appeared to be fighting out of his class and went down heavily from a one-two in the seventh round. After handing out a thorough shellacking Hood finally capsized his challenger with a short right to the jaw

10.04.33 ***Len Harvey, L PTS 15 Jock McAvoy, British & British Empire Middleweight Titles***
BELLE VUE, MANCHESTER After five rounds of negative fighting the referee asked for more action and McAvoy responded by sustained attacks mainly to the body, whereas the champion was content to back pedal in an effort to counterpunch. The Rochdale Thunderbolt, by dint of his forcing the contest, fully deserved the title

24.04.33 ***Al Foreman, L PTS 15 Jimmy Kelso (Australia), British Empire Lightweight Title***
SYDNEY, AUSTRALIA The hard-punching Foreman was unable to keep the Australian challenger down and was outmanoeuvred over the distance to lose his Empire title. The Englishman, reckoned to be one of the heaviest one-hit fighters around, neared the end of his career

19.05.33 ***Kid Chocolate (Cuba), W PTS 15 Seaman Tommy Watson, World Featherweight Title (New York version) & World J. Lightweight Title***
MADISON SQUARE GARDEN, NEW YORK, USA From first to last bell the contest was fought at a tremendous pace with fortunes fluctuating. Both men shipped severe punishment throughout, with Chocolate firing in hooks and uppercuts only for the Englishman to keep marching forward. In a fight that struck a valiant blow for British boxing, the decision was close but just

22.05.33 ***Adrien Aneet (Belgium), L DIS 3 Jack Hood, European Welterweight Title***
EMBASSY RINK, BIRMINGHAM For two and half rounds Hood completely outboxed the European champion, being well on the way to total supremacy. In his desperation to land a telling punch Aneet wildly went low with an intended body blow and was promptly ruled out

22.05.33 ***Jimmy Kelso (Australia), L DIS 3 Al Foreman, British Empire Lightweight Title***
SYDNEY, AUSTRALIA Foreman rewon the title he had dropped to the Aussie only a month previously when the referee disqualified Kelso for a low blow infringement. The third man had no alternative as the Londoner was in no fit state to continue

12.06.33 ***Jackie Brown, W PTS 15 Valentin Angelmann (France), World Flyweight Title (IBU/NBA version)***
OLYMPIA, LONDON The exchanges were fast and furious with the really effective work coming from Brown, but the Frenchman was no easy proposition and was always dangerous with his short-arm blows. There were some brilliant toe to toe exchanges and Angelmann, realising he had to score a kayo to win, tried everything in vain during the last round, but was being totally outpunched at the finish

12.06.33 ***Johnny King, W PTS 15 Bobby Leitham (Canada), British Empire Bantamweight Title***
OLYMPIA, LONDON The Britisher boxed well within himself using the ring to great effect, whilst the extremely rugged Canadian made the body his target. Leitham was outboxed all along with only his great strength saving him from going down inside the distance, and although he made a grand rally over the last three rounds, the verdict was a formality

13.06.33 ***Len Harvey, W PTS 15 Eddie Phillips, Vacant British L. Heavyweight Title***
OLYMPIA, LONDON The man from Bow put Harvey down early on but the champion went on to build up a points lead whilst avoiding Phillip's efforts to end the contest summarily. From the thirteenth round however Harvey was forced to fight tooth and nail as the challenger made his supreme effort

03.07.33 ***Al Brown (Panama), W PTS 15 Johnny King, World Bantamweight Title***
BELLE VUE, MANCHESTER The contest was one of two halves. The first saw King attacking incessantly, but being countered effectively and being dumped on the canvas on no less than six occasions. The second half, from the ninth, saw the Englishman's strength gain him the ascendancy, but he could not put the beanpole fighter down

12.07.33 ***Jack Petersen, W DIS 2 Jack Doyle, British Heavyweight Title***
WHITE CITY, LONDON After being warned during the first interval to keep his punches up, Doyle repeatedly hit Petersen below the belt in the second round and was promptly disqualified. The Irishman's purse money was confiscated and he was suspended for six months

09.10.33. A prostrate Archie Sexton is counted out after being hammered to the floor by the 'Rochdale Thunderbolt,' Jock McAvoy.

09.10.33 ***Jock McAvoy, W CO 10 Archie Sexton, British & British Empire Middleweight Titles***

BELLE VUE, MANCHESTER The Londoner was content to use the left lead sparingly in an effort to draw McAvoy on to the counter punch. For his part Jock made the body a target and in the tenth caught Sexton with a left to the body followed by a sweeping right uppercut to the point which terminated any further action

30.11.33 ***Jack Petersen, L PTS 15 Len Harvey, British Heavyweight Title***

ALBERT HALL, LONDON At long range Petersen was the master, so Harvey tied him up at close quarters where he could score points at will. However the referee spotted the consistent holding and gave the Cornishman a final warning. The bout went all the way resulting in a narrow victory for Harvey, who in twelve months had thus won three National Titles

11.12.33 ***Jackie Brown, W PTS 15 Ginger Foran, British & World Flyweight Titles (IBU/NBA version of World Title)***

BELLE VUE, MANCHESTER Over fifteen fierce rounds both fighters gave their all in a bruising confrontation. In the twelfth round Foran had been thumped and battered almost helpless over the ropes, but lasted out to finish with a flourish

1934

18.01.34 ***Johnny Cuthbert, L PTS 15 Harry Mizler, British Lightweight Title***

ALBERT HALL, LONDON The Londoner repeatedly stabbed back Cuthbert's head with his immaculate straight left, although the champion never stopped trying to unload with powerful rights. The pattern was maintained and by the last third of the contest Mizler had gained the ascendancy which he was to keep

08.02.34 ***Larry Gains (Canada), L PTS 15 Len Harvey, British Empire Heavyweight Title***

ALBERT HALL, LONDON It was the challenger who dictated the exchanges with a brilliant exhibition of fistic strategy. Gains never looked like dropping Harvey, who was content to sneak points using his superior speed and by keeping the Canadian off balance

12.02.34 ***Johnny King, L PTS 15 Dick Corbett, British & British Empire Bantamweight Titles***

BELLE VUE, MANCHESTER Once again Corbett employed his crafty tactics to the utmost when winning at least ten of the fifteen rounds. He even decked King in the tenth round and the champion

21.09.34. Nel Tarleton (left) slips the southpaw right of Freddie Miller and leads with a left to the American's stomach.

seemed unable to come to terms with his opponent's style. The Londoner evaded all efforts at a pay-off punch to run out an easy points winner

21.03.34 *Seaman Tommy Watson, W PTS 15 Johnny McMillan, British Featherweight Title*

KELVIN HALL, GLASGOW Watson was a comfortable winner over the course, well outpointing his rival. Only in the eleventh and twelfth rounds did the Scot come close to bothering Watson with punches from both hands, but the Geordie always had the fight under control to finish a firm winner

04.06.34 *Len Harvey, L RTD 12 Jack Petersen, British & British Empire Heavyweight Titles*

WHITE CITY, LONDON The fifth round saw the first action of the contest when Petersen cut loose to completely close the champion's eye. Although later in the fight the Welshman himself was gashed, Harvey just could not see the punches coming and fought a brilliant rearguard battle to stem the tide. By the twelfth he was all in and under tremendous pressure with no chance of winning, and he retired at the end of the round

11.06.34 *Harry Mason, W DIS 14 Len Tiger Smith, Vacant British Welterweight Title*

EMBASSY RINK, BIRMINGHAM Smith was a rough tough customer but for round after round Mason was far too clever and elusive for him, by fiddling about inside whilst steadily picking up points. The Tiger eventually lost his head and crashed in a low blow during the penultimate round, whereupon he was immediately led to his corner and disqualified

18.06.34 *Jackie Brown, DREW 15 Valentin Angelmann (France), World Flyweight Title (IBU/NBA version)*

BELLE VUE, MANCHESTER The Frenchman fought on aggressive lines throughout, throwing heavy ammunition at Brown continuously. Jackie showed bags of courage but Angelmann would not be denied and at the finish the result could not be believed by the majority of spectators

26.07.34 *Seaman Tommy Watson, L PTS 15 Nel Tarleton, British Featherweight Title*

ANFIELD FOOTBALL GROUND, LIVERPOOL Tarleton won back his title in fine fashion, by concentrating more on aggression in an effort to frustrate the champion's greater strength. Left hooks and right crosses with two-handed attacks to the body were the instruments of the Liverpudlian's great victory

04.08.34 ***Harry Mizler, W PTS 15 Billy Quinlan, British Lightweight Title***
VETCH FIELD, SWANSEA Quinlan gradually pulled back Mizler's early lead, but in the last round the Londoner jerked himself together and scored with a crisp variety of blows which had the Welshman in some difficulty. The decision was close and if the challenger had punched correctly the result could have been reversed

20.08.34 ***Dick Corbett, DREW 15 Johnny King, British & British Empire Bantamweight Titles***
CLAPTON STADIUM, LONDON Corbett was soon on the defensive in this fourth title meeting between the pair. Once again King did all the attacking and staggered the champion heavily in the fifth, but was never able to put him away. The referee's decision appeared to favour the Londoner

10.09.34 ***Jack Petersen, W RTD 13 Larry Gains (Canada), British Empire Heavyweight Title***
WHITE CITY, LONDON Petersen boxed with far more restraint in this contest, putting a curb on his impetuous nature, and the pace he set coupled with his hitting power took its toll on Gains. At the end of the thirteenth round the Canadian staggered back to his corner battered and bleeding to be retired

21.09.34 ***Freddie Miller (USA), W PTS 15 Nel Tarleton, World Featherweight Title (NBA version)***
ANFIELD FOOTBALL GROUND, LIVERPOOL Miller kept up the pressure over the duration to win well in an exhilarating contest during which the Englishman showed good skills. Tarleton was downed in the sixth but came back and lasted well despite being nearly out on his feet at the finish

29.10.34 ***Harry Mizler, L RTD 10 Jackie Kid Berg, British Lightweight Title***
ALBERT HALL, LONDON The contest developed into a grim dour struggle when Mizler sustained damage to both hands early on. The fury of Berg's attacks increased and the champion was punished steadfastly, with only his fighting instinct saving him from being destroyed. At the end of the tenth round Mizler was retired by his corner when the situation had become irreversible

12.12.34 ***Nel Tarleton, W PTS 15 Dave Crowley, British Featherweight Title***
EMPIRE POOL, WEMBLEY Crowley had to do most of the attacking against a master of defence who had a far longer reach and positively looked down on his challenger. Both boys boxed cleanly throughout, with Tarleton negating the Londoner's assaults whilst picking up enough points to gain a narrow decision

17.12.34 ***Harry Mason, L PTS 15 Pat Butler, British Welterweight Title***
GRANBY HALLS, LEICESTER Thwarted early on in the contest by the experienced champion, Butler increased the tempo from the sixth round with an aggressive blend of fighting. Cutting loose again in the tenth, the challenger, in an effort to finish the contest, eventually ran out of steam and Mason put in a grandstand finish, which although eye-catching was not enough

17.12.34 ***Jack Petersen, W PTS 15 George Cook (Australia), British & British Empire Heavyweight Titles***
ALBERT HALL, LONDON Petersen's display was ordinary to say the least, and if it had not been for a last ditch attack he could well have lost the decision. Cook defeated all the Welshman's efforts to put him out for the count and showed up Petersen's lack of a finishing punch at this level

1935

14.1.35 ***Marcel Thil (France), W PTS 15 Jock McAvoy, European L. Heavyweight Title***
PALAIS DES SPORTS, PARIS, FRANCE With his peculiar crouching style Thil proved a most awkward opponent for the Englishman, who badly damaged his right hand early on. The contest developed into a tremendous slugging match with neither man giving ground. Only two knockdowns late in the fight, one of which McAvoy could genuinely have claimed a disqualification on, made sure that Thil retained his title

04.02.35 ***Eddie Phillips, W PTS 15 Tommy Farr, Vacant British L. Heavyweight Title***
THE PAVILION, MOUNTAIN ASH Farr boxed well in the early rounds, but fell away the further the bout progressed. Phillips forced the issue, boxing well in control with good left hand leads and the Welshman eventually finished a long way behind on the referee's scorecard

27.05.35 ***Johnny King, W PTS 15 Len Hampston, Vacant British Bantamweight Title***
BELLE VUE, MANCHESTER The former champion boxed effectively from long range trying to nullify Hampston's explosive punching power. The Yorkshireman worked hard trying to get to close quarters, but tired in the later rounds and despite a last ditch rally the verdict went to King

12.06.35 ***Freddie Miller (USA), W PTS 15 Nel Tarleton, World Featherweight Title (NBA version)***
STANLEY GREYHOUND TRACK, LIVERPOOL The contest looked over in the first round when Tarleton was dropped by a body punch, but he got up and survived a rough passage for five more

rounds. The Liverpudlian then surprised Miller with his body punching to take the middle stages and the American had to pull out all the stops to gain the decision with a sizzling late effort

24.06.35 ***Jock McAvoy, W PTS 15 Al Burke (Australia), British & British Empire Middleweight Titles***

BELLE VUE, MANCHESTER The Australian champion had qualified to fight for the title but appeared more intent on staying the distance. McAvoy, still troubled by the right hand, was able to force the pace without ever looking to knock over Burke, and cruised to a comprehensive points victory

09.09.35 ***Jackie Brown, L RTD 2 Benny Lynch, British & World Flyweight Titles (IBU/NBA version of World Title)***

BELLE VUE, MANCHESTER Somehow Jackie Brown survived the first round after Lynch had put him on the boards twice for short counts. Coming out for the second, Brown tried to take the play away from his challenger but was down twice more before sagging to the canvas defenceless under the Scots heavier punching

09.09.35. Jackie Brown loses his titles after being floored several times by Benny Lynch and being deemed by the referee not to be in a position to defend himself any further.

1936

11.01.36 ***Laurie Stevens (S. Africa), W PTS 12 Jackie Kid Berg, Vacant British Empire Lightweight Title***

THE WANDERERS CRICKET GROUND, JOHANNESBURG, S. AFRICA The South African boxed mainly on the defensive in the early stages, whilst Berg appeared to hit with the open glove. Stevens was later seen to greater advantage when attacking with the Englishman hard put to defend himself, although staging desperate rallies, and the bout ended with the pair swapping punches

29.01.36 ***Jack Petersen, W PTS 15 Len Harvey, British & British Empire Heavyweight Titles***

EMPIRE POOL, WEMBLEY A beautifully timed right had Harvey down in the opening minute, from which he never fully recovered. Displaying much of his former speed, Petersen assumed the initiative for the entire contest and was good value for his win

13.03.36 ***John Henry Lewis (USA), W PTS 15 Jock McAvoy, World L. Heavyweight Title***

MADISON SQUARE GARDEN, NEW YORK, USA McAvoy, the smaller man by far, tried to work close, but was punched off tigerishly by the world

champion who appeared relaxed at distance. Once the Englishman had found a way through, the fight became fairly hectic with both men grimly trying to land the 'coup de grace' and John Henry was just out in front at the finish

23.04.36 *Jack Petersen, W PTS 15 Jock McAvoy, British & British Empire Heavyweight Titles*
EMPRESS HALL, LONDON Despite having clear advantages in height and reach Petersen did not really know how to handle his bustling opponent, other than left-hand him off. McAvoy was out of distance before any real damage was inflicted, until in the fifteenth he was floored for a long count but he held on desperately

23.04.36 *Dave McCleave, W PTS 15 Chuck Parker, Vacant British Welterweight Title*
EMPRESS HALL, LONDON After a tough fight McCleave proved too much of a boxer for the Yorkshireman and although hard pressed at times never wavered. Parker took a lot of punishment but came back for more and made a great effort in the fifteenth, still looking for the one punch payoff, before losing clearly on points

24.04.36 *Jackie Kid Berg, L RSC 9 Jimmy Walsh, British Lightweight Title*
THE STADIUM, LIVERPOOL Early in the fight Walsh showed the sign of what was to come when he put the Londoner down with a solid body punch. Berg was floored a further four times before he twisted an ankle at the end of the eighth round. The former great champion was then rescued by the referee when in no position to defend himself

06.05.36 *Nel Tarleton, W PTS 15 Johnny King, British Featherweight Title*
THE STADIUM, LIVERPOOL Tarleton once again proved himself a master of defence and counter-punching, when beating his smaller challenger. King was dropped three times in all, but was always looking to take the fight to the champion and with both eyes badly damaged he staged a magnificent grandstand finish to the delight of the fans

02.06.36 *Dave McCleave, L CO 8 Jake Kilrain, British Welterweight Title*
SHAWFIELD PARK, GLASGOW Kilrain staked everything on a two-fisted non-stop attack in an effort to lift the title. He had the titleholder down for two counts prior to the eventful eighth and in that round caught McCleave with a couple of heavy body shots, one of which laid him senseless

17.08.36. Ben Foord (right) swings wildly in the first round of his contest against Jack Petersen.

17.08.36 ***Jack Petersen, L RSC 3 Ben Foord (S. Africa), British & British Empire Heavyweight Titles***

THE TIGERS GROUND, LEICESTER From the first gong the South African, Foord, waded in with crude clubbing punches in windmill fashion which Petersen seemed unable to avoid. A vicious right from distance split the champion's left eyebrow in the second and a round later another terrific right knocked him flat on his back. On courageously rising he was smashed into a gory mess before the referee wisely led him back to his corner

03.09.36 ***Mike Belloise (USA), W CO 9 Dave Crowley, World Featherweight Title (New York version)***

MADISON SQUARE GARDEN, NEW YORK, USA Crowley had recently drawn with the American and immediately took up the offensive with exchanges more than lively. The Englishman was more than holding his own until Belloise drove in a terrific left to the body which ended the contest

16.09.36 ***Benny Lynch, W CO 8 Pat Palmer, British & World Flyweight Titles (GB/NBA version of World Title)***

SHAWFIELD PARK, GLASGOW The game London challenger took the fight to the great Scot for several rounds before the champion's heavy punching began to take its toll. The seventh saw Palmer saved by the gong but there was to be no respite and Lynch measured his man with a left hook to the jaw for the full count

24.09.36 ***Nel Tarleton, L PTS 15 Johnny McGrory, British Featherweight Title***

THE STADIUM, LIVERPOOL Attacking strongly from the start McGrory pressured the older man incessantly before putting him down in the seventh round with a peach of a right uppercut. Amazingly enough Tarleton got up at the count of nine and lasted the distance only to go down finally on points

19.10.36 ***Jimmy Walsh, W PTS 15 Harry Mizler, British Lightweight Title***

EMPRESS HALL, LONDON In a classic contest Mizler had to rely on all his defensive ability to prevent him from succumbing to the Deeside man's diverse attacks. Walsh eventually gained a clear-cut victory, when carrying the fight non-stop to his opponent and boxing in really clever fashion

09.11.36 ***John Henry Lewis (USA), W PTS 15 Len Harvey, World L. Heavyweight Title***

EMPIRE POOL, WEMBLEY Harvey shocked everybody by going straight on to the attack, but early in the fight badly damaged his right hand. John Henry by now had slipped into top gear, counter-punching brilliantly, with the Englishman always running second best. For survival the British champion fought a tough close range contest and finished with a badly cut eye before going down

26.12.36 ***Johnny McGrory, W PTS 12 Willie Smith (S. Africa), Vacant British Empire Featherweight Title***

CITY HALL, JOHANNESBURG, S. AFRICA McGrory scored first blood by putting the home man down in the third and cutting his left eye, but the South African cleverly avoided further trouble despite his injury and countered well to keep in the fight. The Scot continuously punched away with great vigour and when he dropped Smith in the closing minute his victory was assured

1937

19.01.37 ***Benny Lynch, W PTS 15 Small Montana (Philippines), Undisputed World Flyweight Title***

EMPIRE POOL, WEMBLEY This brilliant flyweight battle developed into a keenly contested battle of wits between two well-matched fighters who knew the game inside out. The pattern of the contest was set early on with Montana using his speed around the ring with Lynch in deadly pursuit, and the final bell saw the opponents locked in embrace

15.03.37 ***Ben Foord (S. Africa), L PTS 15 Tommy Farr, British & British Empire Heavyweight Titles***

HARRINGAY ARENA, LONDON Foord's timing badly let him down and he found it extremely difficult to land a punch on the elusive Welshman. The challenger made the South African miss consistently and was content to pile up scoring shots to win in a canter

27.04.37 ***Eddie Phillips, L CO 14 Jock McAvoy, British L. Heavyweight Title***

EMPIRE POOL, WEMBLEY Phillips appeared tense and overawed even though he had all the physical advantages. The Rochdale Thunderbolt assumed the initiative early on and until Phillips realised his title was slipping, had things all his own way. Phillips in his new role as aggressor, unfortunately ran straight into a corking right and was counted out

31.05.37 ***Johnny King, W CO 13 Jackie Brown, British Bantamweight Title***

BELLE VUE, MANCHESTER Brown delighted the crowd by attacking two-fistedly and ignoring the counters, but began to run out of steam by the eighth. The former flyweight champion took a terrible shellacking for the next five rounds before catapulting off the ropes in the thirteenth only to run into a tremendous right on the point which ended the contest summarily

30.08.37 ***Joe Louis (USA), W PTS 15 Tommy Farr, World Heavyweight Title***

YANKEE STADIUM, NEW YORK, USA Few people gave the challenger much chance, but Farr surprised all of his critics when boxing brilliantly not only to stay the distance but to thwart the

30.08.37. The irrepressible Tommy Farr (left) never allowed the great Joe Louis much scope by constantly using the jab to keep the great man from setting up attacks.

'Brown Bomber' and come mighty close to gaining the verdict. Louis was taken out of his stride round after round by the Welshman's clever defence and ability to box inside

13.10.37 ***Benny Lynch, W CO 13 Peter Kane, British & World Flyweight Titles***
SHAWFIELD PARK, GLASGOW For twelve rounds Kane stalked forward in an effort to wear down the Scot, despite being canvassed in the first session. Lynch, for his part, played a waiting game and in the twelfth round smashed his challenger down with a left hook. The thirteenth saw the Golborne youngster battered to the floor and finally counted out following a fusillade of blows

25.10.37 ***Jock McAvoy, W RTD 11 Jack Hyams, British & British Empire Middleweight Titles***
BELLE VUE, MANCHESTER A battle of wits saw Hyams content to use the left lead as a scoring weapon. In the sixth round however McAvoy opened up a cut under the challenger's left eye and from then on it was just a matter of time before it became impossible for the Londoner to stem the incessant flow of punches

1938

21.02.38 ***Jake Kilrain, W PTS 15 Jack Lord, British Welterweight Title***
BELLE VUE, MANCHESTER The Northern Area title holder from Bolton put up a titanic struggle in a contest which had plenty of drama. Lord was decked three times and the champion twice, but Kilrain finally proved too strong for his challenger, fully deserving the referee's verdict

07.04.38 ***Jock McAvoy, L PTS 15 Len Harvey, British L. Heavyweight Title***
HARRINGAY ARENA, LONDON Harvey was forced to use the right hand far more than normal, when his left was damaged, whereas McAvoy fought his normal battle of aggression. The champion would often be tied up inside with Harvey using the right to good effect but when the decision was announced there was great controversy as to its accuracy

22.06.38 ***Johnny King, W DIS 3 Len Hampston, British Bantamweight Title***
THE RUGBY GROUND, HEADINGLEY While it lasted, the fight developed into a real battle with the Batley boy stalking forward tossing in heavy right handers, and King aiming to outbox his rival comprehensively. In the third King was downed by a terrific right to the jaw and upon rising

Hampston swung a left well below the belt which led to his immediate disqualification

23.06.38 ***Jimmy Walsh, L PTS 15 Dave Crowley, British Lightweight Title***
ANFIELD FOOTBALL GROUND, LIVERPOOL Walsh boxed well below normal form and Crowley made the most of his good fortune. The Chester man was handicapped by a cut left eye from the seventh onwards which slowed him effectively and despite a late effort he was defeated comprehensively

22.09.38 ***Peter Kane, W PTS 15 Jackie Jurich (USA), Vacant World Flyweight Title***
ANFIELD FOOTBALL GROUND, LIVERPOOL The little Californian boxed brilliantly, but his punches lacked the power of Kane's and the longer the fight progressed the more pronounced it became. Jurich was never going to halt the Englishman who kept up relentless pressure and dumped the American on the boards half a dozen times, but could not keep him down for good

23.11.38 ***Jim Spider Kelly, W PTS 15 Benny Caplan, Vacant British & British Empire Featherweight Titles***
KINGS HALL, BELFAST Kelly forced throughout with the Londoner's clever boxing on the retreat making a grand contest. Eventually the vicious body punches got to Caplan and he fell to his knees in the fourteenth. The last round went to the Irishman who used the body drives to pave the way home

01.12.38 ***Len Harvey, W DIS 4 Eddie Phillips, Vacant British Heavyweight Title***
HARRINGAY ARENA, LONDON Harvey outboxed the challenger for the first three rounds and at the beginning of the fourth dropped his man with a great left hook. The East Ender surprised everybody by fighting back to floor the champion, but as Harvey arose he was unfortunately struck low and Phillips was led back to his corner

5.12.38 ***Dave Crowley, L CO 13 Eric Boon, British Lightweight Title***
HARRINGAY ARENA, LONDON Up to the eleventh round it had been rather one-sided with Boon's left eye in a terrible state, but the tide turned for the youngster when he finally dropped Crowley with a right to the body. In the thirteenth Crowley, after arising from another count, was finally flattened by a heavy right to the jaw

1939

23.02.39 ***Eric Boon, W RSC 14 Arthur Danahar, British Lightweight Title***
HARRINGAY ARENA, LONDON In one of the great classics of the ring, Danahar completely outboxed Eric Boon for seven scintillating rounds. From

22.09.38. Peter Kane (left) gets home with a left to the body of Jackie Jurich who misses with his left lead.

then on however the Londoner was floored on nine separate occasions and although fighting back at times with immense courage, the referee eventually decided he had shipped enough punishment

10.03.39 ***Len Harvey, W RTD 13 Larry Gains (Canada), Vacant British Empire Heavyweight Title***

HARRINGAY ARENA, LONDON The contest unfortunately deteriorated into one long clinch, with the busiest man being the referee. Harvey fought his usual tactical fight, nullifying the veteran Canadian's efforts, and at the end of the thirteenth round Gains retired due to a badly damaged left eye, having finally come to the end of his tether

23.03.39 ***Jake Kilrain, L CO 7 Ernie Roderick, British Welterweight Title***

ANFIELD FOOTBALL GROUND, LIVERPOOL Kilrain boxed well below par with the Liverpudlian on top throughout. Jake, determinedly making a last ditch effort in the seventh, was struck down by a mighty right cross and although he rose to one knee he was counted out in that position

22.05.39 ***Jock McAvoy, W PTS 15 Ginger Sadd, British & British Empire Middleweight Titles***

BELLE VUE, MANCHESTER Sadd showed fleetness of foot coupled with an orthodox straight left and plenty of courage to travel the distance. McAvoy was the aggressor and was always trying hard to break through the East Anglian's excellent defence, which held firm

25.05.39 ***Henry Armstrong (USA), W PTS 15 Ernie Roderick, World Welterweight Title***

HARRINGAY ARENA, LONDON 'Homicide Hank', the American World champion, raised the pace of the contest round after round throwing punches from all angles. Roderick fought on stubbornly, but had great difficulty stemming the tide, let alone being able to attack on his own accord, and finished well beaten, but cheered to the rafters for his courageous stand

28.06.39 ***Jim Spider Kelly, L RSC 12 Johnny Cusick, British & British Empire Featherweight Titles***

KINGS HALL, BELFAST The titleholder did all the early attacking, but missed repeatedly and was countered effectively. By the tenth round Kelly had burnt himself out and Cusick went to work with a vengeance, before the referee finally called a halt two rounds later

23.02.39. Skilful Arthur Danahar (right) trades lefts with the heavy hitting Eric Boon.

01.02.40. Johnny Cusick (left) tries evasive action against Nel Tarleton in an effort to set up his own left-handed attacks.

10.07.39 *Len Harvey, W PTS 15 Jock McAvoy, British & Vacant British Empire L. Heavyweight Titles (British version of Vacant World L. Heavyweight Title)*

WHITE CITY, LONDON As in previous fights, McAvoy made the running with Harvey evading trouble by keeping at a distance, and when inside fiddling the points. The final two rounds went to the 'Thunderbolt' on sheer power, but he could not quite make up the leeway and Harvey just about got home

30.09.39 *Jackie Paterson, W CO 13 Paddy Ryan, Vacant British Flyweight Title*

CARTYNE GREYHOUND TRACK, GLASGOW The contest was ended prematurely in the unlucky thirteen round when a near perfect left hook to the jaw left Ryan prostrate on the canvas. It is almost certain that had the Mancunian got up he would have won, because Paterson's right leg became seized with cramp and he had to be carried back to his corner

09.12.39 *Eric Boon, W CO 7 Dave Crowley, British Lightweight Title*

HARRINGAY ARENA, LONDON Crowley stood up to the champion's raw power well until midway through the seventh, when he received a heavy right to the shoulder, which bowled him over. Boon was declared the winner when the Londoner could not get up, being counted out after damaging an ankle

1940

01.02.40 *Johnny Cusick, L PTS 15 Nel Tarleton, British & British Empire Featherweight Titles*

THE STADIUM, LIVERPOOL Tarleton, with height and reach advantages, proved far too good for the young Mancunian. Following a battle of wits, the brilliant skills of the older man by twelve years, saw him returned a decisive points winner in front of an ecstatic crowd

11.03.40 *Jackie Paterson, W PTS 15 Kid Tanner (B. Guiana), Vacant British Empire Flyweight Title*

BELLE VUE, MANCHESTER Fifteen rounds of spirited fighting saw both battlers give and take with no quarter asked for or given. The capacity crowd watched Paterson add to his British title, but the coloured whirlwind Kid Tanner took him desperately close and the winner proved his right to challenge for the World title

13.07.40 ***Ernie Roderick, W PTS 15 Norman Snow, British Welterweight Title***
THE RUGBY GROUND, NORTHAMPTON The local man gave the big crowd something to shout about when he staggered the Liverpudlian with a terrific left hook to midriff in the third round. Roderick somehow weathered the storm by using his great ringcraft to edge out the challenger in a tense struggle

02.11.40 ***Nel Tarleton, W PTS 15 Tom Smith, British & British Empire Featherweight Titles***
THE STADIUM, LIVERPOOL It was a hard merciless fight, with Smith trying to wear down the old man by setting up non-stop attacks although being floored in the first. Tarleton eventually took the upper hand and stayed in front, drawing on his greater experience to stave off the aggressive challenger

1941

01.01.41 ***Jim Brady, W PTS 15 Kid Tanner (B. Guiana), Vacant British Empire Bantamweight Title***
DENS PARK, DUNDEE Fighting in a snowstorm, it took the Kid several rounds to warm up, but by the twelfth both fighters were on even terms, albeit Brady being badly cut. The Scot then got on top and although Tanner belted in some great punches he began to weaken and the decision rendered was close, but just

03.02.41 ***Jackie Paterson, W CO 8 Paddy Ryan, British & British Empire Flyweight Titles***
ICE RINK, NOTTINGHAM Ryan was hammered throughout, coming in for some especially rough treatment and having his eye cut during the fifth. Paterson really cut loose in the sixth putting the challenger down for nine and repeated the dose in the eighth before the referee decided he had seen enough

05.08.41 ***Jim Brady, W PTS 15 Jackie Paterson, British Empire Bantamweight Title***
HAMPDEN PARK, GLASGOW Despite being dropped in the first round, Brady repeatedly made the challenger miss to come back with double handed attacks of his own. Paterson got on top, but eventually eased up after cutting both of the champion's eyes and this allowed Brady to go all out in the last two sessions to gain an extremely narrow decision

29.09.41 ***Ernie Roderick, W PTS 15 Arthur Danahar, British Welterweight Title***
ALBERT HALL, LONDON Roderick nearly lost this

29.09.41. The left hand of Arthur Danahar (left) holds Ernie Roderick up momentarily, but the Liverpudlian would not be denied.

20.06.42. Freddie Mills (left) drives Len Harvey to the ropes prior to putting the Champion through them and out for the count.

19.06.43. The referee completes the count out after only 61 seconds with Peter Kane helpless at the hands of Jackie Paterson.

one when he floored the Londoner dramatically with a misguided blow to the body, but it was Danahar himself who waved the Liverpudlian on. The contest was even until the tenth, but Danahar began to tire and in the thirteenth was savagely floored twice. He got up courageously to box on and last the distance

1942

20.06.42 ***Len Harvey, L CO 2 Freddie Mills, British & British Empire L. Heavyweight Titles (British version of World L. Heavyweight Title)***

WHITE HART LANE, LONDON Three years out of the ring had taken its toll of a once great fighter and Harvey was counted out after falling from the ring. Mills' efforts had been nullified in the first, but coming out for the second he went in throwing punches from every angle until enforcing the count out

1943

19.06.43 ***Jackie Paterson, W CO 1 Peter Kane, British & British Empire Flyweight Titles (Kane defended World Flyweight Title)***

HAMPDEN PARK, GLASGOW The fight lasted just 61 seconds, but in that time Kane was floored several times including the count out. From the opening bell, the World champion leapt into the fray only to be countered by the southpaw's right hand, which left him open for the Scot's superior hitting power with the left

1944

12.08.44 ***Eric Boon, L CO 10 Ronnie James, British Lightweight Title***

ARMS PARK, CARDIFF The challenger swamped Boon before battering him to the canvas for a long count in the third. This became the pattern of things to come as the 'Boy' took twelve further counts, but surprised everybody by knocking James over in the seventh. The fight ended prematurely when Boon took a terrific punch to the head and crashed over to be counted out

15.09.44 Jack London (left) and Freddie Mills appear to be sizing each other up in the early stages of their bout for the vacant Heavyweight title.

23.02.45. Nel Tarleton (right) tries to find a way through the continental style guard of Al Phillips, the 'Aldgate Tiger.'

15.09.44 ***Jack London, W PTS 15 Freddie Mills, Vacant British & British Empire Heavyweight Titles***
BELLE VUE, MANCHESTER Mills was outweighed by over three stones, but for the duration of the contest he hurled himself non-stop at his giant opponent in an effort to bring him down. London resolutely stood his ground and took a lot of energy out of the light-heavyweight champion with heavy body blows to secure his victory

1945

23.02.45 ***Nel Tarleton, W PTS 15 Tiger Al Phillips, British & British Empire Featherweight Titles***
BELLE VUE, MANCHESTER The Aldgate Tiger attacked furioulsy aiming to blast Tarleton into oblivion and for eleven rounds the champion was forced to fight a rearguard action. In the twelfth the challenger was suddenly struck down with cramp and Tarleton was able to coast from thereon to take a narrow decision

29.05.45 ***Ernie Roderick, W PTS 15 Vince Hawkins, Vacant British Middleweight Title***
ALBERT HALL, LONDON The challenger had age and weight as an advantage but after receiving damage to his left eye in the fifth, found the going tough. In the ninth round a left to the body and chin felled Hawkins for a long count, but although he fought back well, he could not match the skills of Roderick, winning only two rounds on the referee's scorecard

17.07.45 ***Jack London, L CO 6 Bruce Woodcock, British & British Empire Heavyweight Titles***
WHITE HART LANE, LONDON London was sadly out of distance upstairs, apart from a punch that bloodied the Doncaster man's nose, so he began to concentrate more on the body. Although having fair success it left him open to a right hander that dumped him and when he rose Woodcock drove in two more piledriving rights to the jaw which left London an ex-titleholder

12.09.45 ***Jim Brady, L PTS 15 Jackie Paterson, British Empire Bantamweight Title***
HAMPDEN PARK, GLASGOW Paterson did most of the early forcing, landing solid punches to the body, before toppling Brady over and cutting his left eye in the third. A thunderstorm broke during the seventh and this nullified both mens' efforts, but they came back in hectic fashion to stage a grandstand finish

1946

19.03.46 ***Jackie Paterson, W DIS 8 Theo Medina (France), Vacant European Bantamweight Title***

ALBERT HALL, LONDON After a fairly even seven rounds the swarthy French gypsy suddenly found the range, having the little Scot down three times before landing a very low blow, which left the referee no choice but to award the contest to the prostrate Paterson

14.05.46 ***Gus Lesnevich (USA), W RSC 10 Freddie Mills, World L. Heavyweight Title***

HARRINGAY ARENA, LONDON The challenger, after being floored four times in the second came back with a tremendous display of guts to batter Lesnevich, but in the tenth round the American smashed Mills to the canvas twice more, rendering the gallant Britisher unable to continue

04.06.46 ***Ernie Roderick, W PTS 15 Omar Kouidri (France), Vacant European Welterweight Title***

HARRINGAY ARENA, LONDON Roderick was a good winner over the stipulated distance giving the Algerian a boxing lesson with the use of the traditional straight left. The older man never gave Kouidri a chance to establish himself and finished as fit as a fiddle in the process

10.07.46 ***Jackie Paterson, W PTS 15 Joe Curran, British, British Empire & World Flyweight Titles***

HAMPDEN PARK, GLASGOW The little challenger from Liverpool was well outpointed by the Scot who surprised most of the public by making the weight, let alone finishing the contest

29.07.46 ***Bruce Woodcock, W CO 6 Albert Renet (France), Vacant European Heavyweight Title***

BELLE VUE, MANCHESTER After quickly solving the Frenchman's awkward southpaw stance, the Doncaster man began to score at will, downing his opponent twice prior to the finish. Renet was eventually cut down by a terrific right hand to the jaw for the full count

04.09.46 ***Ike Williams (USA), W CO 9 Ronnie James, World Lightweight Title (NBA version)***

NINIAN PARK, CARDIFF The first World title bout ever staged in Wales was won on a knockout in the ninth round by the heavy hitting champion Ike Williams, who destroyed the game challenger, having him down on six occasions prior to the

04.09.46. The Welsh challenger Ronnie James (left) bobs and weaves in an effort to avoid Ike Williams' superior punching power.

'coup de grace' and proving himself one of the hardest hitters to come out of the lightweights

28.10.46 ***Ernie Roderick, L PTS 15 Vince Hawkins, British Middleweight Title***
ALBERT HALL, LONDON The fighting fireman from Eastleigh became the new British champion when dethroning Ernie Roderick over fifteen rounds. The older man had to give ground, bringing all his skill and generalship into play to survive the course

30.10.46 ***Jackie Paterson, L CO 4 Theo Medina (France), European Bantamweight Title***
HAMPDEN PARK, GLASGOW The Scot lost his title when, after throwing a wild punch at Medina, he fell to the boards and being unable to regain his feet was counted out. The 45,000 crowd had already witnessed Paterson canvassed on four occasions from punches to the midriff, which eventually took their toll

1947

01.02.47 ***Ernie Roderick, L RTD 9 Robert Villemain (France), European Welterweight Title***
PALAIS DES SPORTS, PARIS, FRANCE Roderick was forced to surrender the title in the ninth round due to a badly cut eye. During the early stages he boxed well, having the Frenchman down in the second, but by the fifth the stronger Villemain took over with effective punching to head and body with the end coming as no real surprise

10.02.47 ***Johnny King, L CO 7 Jackie Paterson, British Bantamweight Title***
BELLE VUE, MANCHESTER Despite a magnificent display of courage the holder, King, who had great difficulty in making the weight, finally succumbed to the first punch thrown in the seventh round. He had previously been sent down for long counts in the three preceding rounds at the hands of the heavy punching Scot

17.03.47 ***Bruce Woodcock, W PTS 15 Stephane Olek (France), European Heavyweight Title***
BELLE VUE, MANCHESTER Woodcock was found wanting in this contest, although being a clear winner on points over the French Pole, and occasionally was even forced back on his heels, with the challenger getting a rousing reception at the finish

18.03.47 ***Tiger Al Phillips, W PTS 15 Cliff Anderson (British Guiana), Vacant British Empire Featherweight Title***
ALBERT HALL, LONDON An uproar ensued when the Aldgate Tiger was awarded the decision after being on the deck for three counts of nine in the fourth round. The crowd voiced their feelings long after the contest had ended

27.05.47 ***Tiger Al Phillips, W DIS 8 Ray Famechon (France), Vacant European Featherweight Title***
ALBERT HALL, LONDON The contest suddenly erupted in the sixth when the Frenchman began to land with heavy body punches. Phillips was forced to take five counts in the seventh round before the Frenchman was disqualified after landing a low blow

01.07.47 ***Tiger Al Phillips, W DIS 8 Cliff Anderson (British Guiana), British Empire Featherweight Title***
OLYMPIA, LONDON Once again the Aldgate Tiger was involved in amazing scenes when defending his title against the man he had beaten for the vacant crown. This time he was on the canvas four times before Anderson connected with another heavy blow which unfortunately turned into a kidney punch, leaving Phillips unconscious, but still champion

08.09.47 ***Ernie Roderick, W PTS 15 Gwyn Williams, British Welterweight Title***
HARRINGAY ARENA, LONDON The Liverpudlian won the contest going away, using his greater experience to the full and forcing the young Welshman to take a count in the sixth. Williams played second fiddle for the remainder of an interesting if unspectacular bout

08.09.47 ***Freddie Mills, W RTD 4 Paul Goffaux (France), Vacant European L. Heavyweight Title***
HARRINGAY ARENA, LONDON The Frenchman was forced to surrender in the fourth, having taken five earlier counts. Mills was cumbersome at first, but once under heavy pressure, Goffaux had no defence and the referee stepped in to save him from further punishment

11.09.47 ***Ronnie Clayton, W PTS 15 Tiger Al Phillips, Vacant British Featherweight Title (Phillips defended British Empire and European Featherweight Titles***
ANFIELD FOOTBALL GROUND, LIVERPOOL Young Ronnie Clayton took three titles in one go when brilliantly outpointing Al Phillips. The tough Londoner fought a resolute fight, but was bettered in the art of boxing by speed and heavier hitting, showing obvious signs of wear and tear at the finish

19.09.47 ***Theo Medina (France), L PTS 15 Peter Kane, European Bantamweight Title***
BELLE VUE, MANCHESTER The contest was a war of attrition fought mainly at close quarters with no holds barred, and both fighters hooking heavily to head and body. Kane, being the most adept at defence, won commandingly with the Frenchman a gallant loser

09.12.47. The man from Chatteris, Eric Boon (left), looks to counter as Ernie Roderick leads with a left to the body.

16.10.47 ***Billy Thompson, W RSC 3 Stan Hawthorne, Vacant British Lightweight Title***

ANFIELD FOOTBALL GROUND, LIVERPOOL The man from Hickleton Main forced Hawthorne to take so much punishment in the third that the referee stepped in to save the game fighter from further distress. Earlier in the contest Hawthorne had been sent to the canvas on three occasions and never fully recovered

20.10.47 ***Jackie Paterson, W CO 5 Norman Lewis, British & British Empire Bantamweight Titles***

HARRINGAY ARENA, LONDON Lewis was on the canvas in the first round, but got up to reach the fifth whereupon, after taking a count, he received a short right which knocked him out. The Glasgow man thus retained his titles with the minimum amount of fuss

20.10.47 ***Rinty Monaghan, W PTS 15 Dado Marino (Hawaii), Vacant World Flyweight Title (NBA version)***

HARRINGAY ARENA, LONDON The singing Irishman won the title sequestrated from Jackie Paterson when he tantalised and outpointed the rather pedestrian Dado Marino. The Hawaiian tended to conduct his campaign from the centre of the ring, but was picked off with snappy point scoring punches for most of the fight

09.12.47 ***Ernie Roderick, W PTS 15 Eric Boon, British Welterweight Title***

HARRINGAY ARENA, LONDON Ernie Roderick again proved his skill, building up a good points lead, but came mighty close to not finishing the contest. Boon attacked non stop over the last four rounds, with the champion shaken, dropped once and apparently all in at the end

15.12.47 ***Peter Kane, W PTS 15 Joe Cornelis (Belgium), European Bantamweight Title***

BELLE VUE, MANCHESTER In a tame contest the Englishman won readily against a rather docile challenger. The fight really never got going with Kane obviously carrying the heavier dig and content just to do enough

1948

26.01.48 ***Bos Murphy (New Zealand), W PTS 15 Vince Hawkins, Vacant British Empire Middleweight Title***

ALBERT HALL, LONDON Murphy cleverly outpointed the fighting fireman mainly by the use of his good left hook to the body. Hawkins missed his chance when he floored his opponent in the first round, but was unable to take advantage and the opportunity was lost

17.02.48 ***Freddie Mills, W CO 2 Paco Bueno (Spain), European L. Heavyweight Title***
HARRINGAY ARENA, LONDON The Englishman only needed five minutes for this demolition job on a challenger who was not really up to championship standard. Once Mills had found the range he hammered the head and body before a right to the jaw dropped Bueno for the full count

17.02.48 ***Roberto Proietti (Italy), L PTS 15 Billy Thompson, European Lightweight Title***
HARRINGAY ARENA, LONDON A great all action contest was well won by the British champion who attacked non stop with Proietti standing his ground and fighting back in true tradition. Thompson continually kept up the pressure allowing the champion no time to settle whilst mixing heavy punches with great variety

20.02.48 ***Peter Kane, L PTS 15 Guido Ferracin (Italy), European Bantamweight Title***
BELLE VUE, MANCHESTER The Italian titleholder outspeeded Kane from start to finish giving as neat a display of footwork as one would wish to see. Every time the champion came forward he was hit by countless punches which if carrying any power would have made it unnecessary for the referee to use his scorecard

22.03.48 ***Ronnie Clayton, L PTS 15 Ray Famechon (France), European Featherweight Title***
ICE RINK, NOTTINGHAM The Frenchman proved himself a master box-fighter at the expense of Ronnie Clayton, who fought his usual type of all-action campaign. Famechon kept in front all the way even though the British boy would not be completely subdued

23.03.48 ***Jackie Paterson, L CO 7 Rinty Monaghan, British, British Empire & Undisputed World Flyweight Titles***
KINGS HALL, BELFAST Paterson was belted to the canvas in round two but Monaghan was unable to finish the fight there and then, biding his time. In the seventh round the little Scot, on rising from a count of nine, went down again to be counted out in a sitting position

18.05.48 ***Bos Murphy (New Zealand), L CO 1 Dick Turpin, British Empire Middleweight Title***
HIGHFIELD ROAD, COVENTRY Murphy, defending his newly acquired title made the mistake of forcing and was cleverly manoeuvred on to a perfect right to the chin, which ended the contest. He had previously paid a visit to the canvas, taking a count of seven in the process

28.06.48 ***Vince Hawkins, L PTS 15 Dick Turpin, British Middleweight Title (Turpin defended British Empire Middleweight Title)***
VILLA PARK, BIRMINGHAM Dick Turpin, already the Empire titleholder, became the first coloured British champion when he dethroned Hawkins to gain a clear cut victory. Hawkins attacked incessantly but the Leamington man brilliantly countered, leaving his opponent battered and bruised

06.07.48 ***Maurice Sandeyron (France), DREW 15 Dickie O'Sullivan, European Flyweight Title***
OLYMPIA, LONDON It could only have been the Frenchman's lack of punch which enabled the fight to go the distance and O'Sullivan came back strongly in the later rounds to share the verdict

16.07.48 ***Guido Ferracin (Italy), W RTD 5 Peter Kane, European Bantamweight Title***
BELLE VUE, MANCHESTER In the fourth Kane received bad cuts following a clash of heads, and coming out for the next round with impaired vision was put on the canvas. Although making a great effort he blindly staggered up only to be retired by his corner

26.07.48 ***Gus Lesnevich (USA), L PTS 15 Freddie Mills, World L. Heavyweight Title***
WHITE CITY, LONDON Virtually from the first bell Lesnevich had his eye cut and in a gruelling struggle he paid two long visits to the canvas. Mills put in a grandstand last round, driving his opponent before him, and was a most popular winner

26.07.48 ***Billy Thompson, DREW 15 Pierre Montane (France), European Lightweight Title***
WHITE CITY, LONDON The Frenchman appeared a clear winner to all but the referee, outsmarting the Britisher throughout the bout. Thompson appeared jaded and did not strike any rhythm but worked well to the body in the later stages

01.10.48 ***Arthur King (Canada), W RTD 7 Billy Thompson, Vacant British Empire Lightweight Title***
BELLE VUE, MANCHESTER Thompson fought a game fight before he was retired suffering from cuts. King appeared to be well on the way to winning, having taken the English boy's best punches and showing superior ringcraft

08.11.48 ***Maurice Sandeyron (France), W PTS 15 Dickie O'Sullivan, European Flyweight Title***
HARRINGAY ARENA, LONDON The Frenchman confirmed his superiority over O'Sullivan, but this time collected the verdict. Sandeyron won every round, although all credit must be given to the game little Londoner who fought an uphill battle to the very end

26.07.48. The magnificent Freddie Mills (left) smashes into Gus Lesnevich on his way to taking the American's title.

08.11.48 ***Ernie Roderick, L PTS 15, Henry Hall, British Welterweight Title***
HARRINGAY ARENA, LONDON The new champion was decked twice during the contest, but in the earlier stages he had stabbed away with the straight left to pile up the points. In the last few rounds Roderick fought back in tremendous fashion, cutting his opponent's left eye in a thrilling climax

1949

17.01.49 ***Billy Thompson, W PTS 15 Josef Preys (Belgium), European Lightweight Title***
EMBASSY RINK, BIRMINGHAM Billy Thompson retained his title after fifteen rounds of an uninspiring bout. The main exchanges were at close quarters with both contestants warned frequently for holding

24.03.49 ***Jackie Paterson, L PTS 15 Stan Rowan, British & British Empire Bantamweight Titles***
ANFIELD FOOTBALL GROUND, LIVERPOOL Stan Rowan cleverly outboxed the champion to get on top by the middle stages. Paterson was lifted clear off his feet by a terrific uppercut in the eleventh before going down to a convincing defeat

26.03.49 ***Bruce Woodcock, W CO 3 Johnny Ralph (S. Africa), British Empire Heavyweight Title***
JOHANNESBURG, S. AFRICA It was all one way traffic with the Englishman flooring Ralph seven times before a right cross terminated the contest in the third

05.04.49 ***Rinty Monaghan, W PTS 15 Maurice Sandeyron (France), World Flyweight Title (Sandeyron defended European Flyweight Title)***
KINGS HALL, BELFAST The bout was dictated by the Irishman, who was content to keep Sandeyron at bay with constant use of the straight left. The Frenchman was never able to get inside and the fight developed into a brilliant battle of wits

11.04.49 ***Ronnie Clayton, W PTS 15 Johnny Molloy, British & British Empire Featherweight Titles***
ICE RINK, NOTTINGHAM Ronnie Clayton put a second notch on the Lonsdale belt by brilliantly outpointing the man from St. Helens, having him down twice for long counts. Molloy fought back in gritty fashion in an uphill struggle

18.05.49 *Billy Thompson, W RSC 5 Harry Hughes, British and European Lightweight Titles*

CELTIC PARK, GLASGOW Knocked down four times before being rescued by the referee, Hughes was always travelling second best. Constantly outgunning his challenger Thompson was more like his real self for this defence

02.06.49 *Bruce Woodcock, W CO 14 Freddie Mills, British, British Empire & European Heavyweight Titles*

WHITE CITY, LONDON The Doncaster man stood up well against an early barrage of ferocious hitting, and then put Mills down for counts on six occasions. This laid the foundation for victory in the fourteenth when three tremendous right handers put the challenger on one knee for the full count

20.06.49 *Dick Turpin, W PTS 15 Albert Finch, British & British Empire Middleweight Titles*

ST. ANDREWS, BIRMINGHAM Gaining a clear points verdict the champion, mainly by his greater ability as a box-fighter, was always in command. Turpin only fought when he needed to, being quite content to cruise to victory in a rather tame affair

05.07.49 *Billy Thompson, L DIS 6 Kid Dussart (Belgium), European Lightweight Title*

OLYMPIA, LONDON A dramatic contest saw Thompson on the floor three times before being disqualified in the sixth. After a warning for going low, he immediately dropped the Kid with another body shot and the referee called a halt to the proceedings

11.08.49 *Ronnie Clayton, W CO 12 Eddie Miller (Australia), British Empire Featherweight Title*

THE STADIUM, LIVERPOOL A surprise ending to this brilliantly fought battle of wits came with the rapidly tiring Australian out in front. Miller got caught with a solid left hook to the body and a cracking right to the head which left him in a heap on the boards

06.09.49 *Dick Turpin, L CO 1 Dave Sands (Australia), British Empire Middleweight Title*

HARRINGAY ARENA, LONDON Turpin took just 2 mins 45 seconds to lose to the Aborigine wonder boy, Dave Sands. The Englishman was down for two long counts, before being finished with a left to the solar plexus and a stunning right on the point

02.06.49 Fiery Freddie Mills (right) opens up with a smashing right-hander as Bruce Woodcock looks to counter with the left hook.

30.09.49 ***Rinty Monaghan, DREW 15 Terry Allen, British , British Empire, European & World Flyweight Titles***
KINGS HALL, BELFAST Having put the champion on the deck in the second, Allen was still rather fortunate to get a share of the honours. Monaghan, if not at his best, at least forced the contest, whilst the challenger was content to cruise along

12.11.49 ***Stan Rowan, L PTS 15 Vic Toweel (S. Africa), British Empire Bantamweight Title***
JOHANNESBURG, S. AFRICA The dynamic Toweel was on the attack from start to finish, landing punches at the rate of six to one. Rowan stood up to his task in the manner befitting a champion to finish the course

15.11.49 ***Henry Hall, L PTS 15 Eddie Thomas, British Welterweight Title***
HARRINGAY ARENA, LONDON The only real excitement in this contest came when the Welshman put Hall down from a punch to the hip in the thirteenth round, an offence for which he could have been ruled out. Thomas kept just in front by the use of his extra quality, but was made to work hard

18.11.49 ***Ray Famechon (France), W PTS 15 Ronnie Clayton, European Featherweight Title***
BELLE VUE, MANCHESTER Ray Famechon won this tremendous contest with superior skill. Until the eleventh the Englishman had a chance of pulling it all out of the fire, by dint of purposeful aggression, but the man from across the Channel poured it on to run out a brilliant winner

13.12.49 ***Danny O'Sullivan, W RTD 9 Teddy Gardner, Vacant British Bantamweight Title***
ALBERT HALL, LONDON Gardner was forced to retire at the end of the ninth round with a badly cut eyelid, having earlier proved himself to be a true craftsman. O'Sullivan bided his time, finally inflicting heavy damage following a blistering offensive

1950

24.01.50 ***Freddie Mills, L CO 10 Joey Maxim (USA), World L. Heavyweight Title***
EARLS COURT, LONDON The challenger got well on top, subjecting Mills to heavy punishment inside and the end came following a quick right to the jaw followed up with a body punch. Mills sunk slowly to the canvas and after a sterling effort to rise he was counted out

31.01.50 ***Roberto Proietti (Italy), W PTS 15 Billy Thompson, European Lightweight Title***
EMPRESS HALL, LONDON Unhandicapped by a cut over the right eye sustained in the third, Proietti dictated the contest, nullifying the Englishman's attacks whilst building up a good points margin

24.04.50 ***Dick Turpin, L PTS 15 Albert Finch, British Middleweight Title***
ICE RINK, NOTTINGHAM In what transpired as a victory by the narrowest of possible margins, Turpin lost his change of winning a Lonsdale Belt outright. Finch was cut around the eyes and took two counts, but was adjudged the winner and new champion

25.04.50 ***Terry Allen, W PTS 15 Honore Pratesi (France), Vacant European & World Flyweight Titles***
HARRINGAY ARENA, LONDON In an extremely hard fought bout the Islington barrow boy boxed at long range with Pratesi desperately trying to fight inside, but generally thwarted

25.04.50 ***Luis Romero (Spain), W RSC 13 Danny O'Sullivan, European Bantamweight Title***
HARRINGAY ARENA, LONDON Luis Romero battered the English challenger to the canvas on no less than thirteen occasions before the referee stepped in to save a game fighter from further punishment and a lost cause

11.07.50 ***Billy Thompson, W PTS 15 Tommy McGovern, British Lightweight Title***
THE STADIUM, HANLEY Billy Thompson and his stable partner McGovern put on an all action contest, which was ultimately decided by the champion's aggression over the distance

01.08.50 ***Terry Allen, L PTS 15 Dado Marino (Hawaii), World Flyweight Title***
HONOLULU, HAWAII By the seventh round both fighters were bleeding freely, but Marino, although the older man by nine years, had the inspiration of fighting in front on his home fans who drove him on to a close victory

13.09.50 ***Eddie Thomas, W PTS 15 Cliff Curvis, British Welterweight Title***
ST HELENS GROUND, SWANSEA Although the challenger was floored for a count of eight in the sixth and finished the contest with a badly cut left eye, he worried Thomas considerably, but the man from Merthyr hit that little bit harder to obtain the verdict

17.10.50 ***Don Cockell, W CO 14 Mark Hart, Vacant British L. Heavyweight Title***
HARRINGAY ARENA, LONDON The first nine rounds were of a monotonous pattern with Cockell in pursuit of the lighter hitting Croydon man. The champion elect finally got to grips with Hart who

was put down four times before being despatched in the 14th following a remorseless barrage of punches

17.10.50 ***Albert Finch, L CO 5 Randy Turpin, British Middleweight Title***

HARRINGAY ARENA, LONDON The dynamic punching of Turpin disposed of the title holder, having him on the deck three times from vicious punches to both head and body. The lights went out for Finch in the fifth when the Leamington destroyer sledge-hammered a right to the jaw which laid him out cold

30.10.50 ***Terry Allen, L PTS 15 Jean Sneyers (Belgium), European Flyweight Title***

ICE RINK, NOTTINGHAM In a brilliant closely fought contest Sneyers proved a top class box-fighter when standing up to Allen's aggression. The crowd were stunned by the decision but it was close enough to go either way

14.11.50 ***Bruce Woodcock, L RTD 11 Jack Gardner, British & British Empire Heavyweight Titles***

EARLS COURT, LONDON The young challenger immediately took the fight to Woodcock and sustained the pressure right up to the retirement. The champion pounded in right handers throughout but to no avail and by the end of the eleventh was a spent force

28.11.50 ***Ronnie Clayton, W PTS 15 Jim Kenny, British & British Empire Featherweight Titles***

EMPRESS HALL, LONDON Game Kenny was unfortunate to sustain hand damage which restricted him considerably. After being smashed out of the ring in the fourth he made a supreme effort in returning, but was never in the hunt from thereon, the decision being a formality

02.12.50 ***Vic Toweel (S. Africa), W RTD 10 Danny O'Sullivan, British Empire & World Bantamweight Titles***

WEMBLEY STADIUM, JOHANNESBURG, S. AFRICA Floored time and again, the game Britisher was given a standing ovation from the large crowd after being rescued by the referee. During the tenth round he had been put down five times before dropping on his stool from sheer exhaustion

25.04.50. At the end of a hard bout, Terry Allen has his hand raised by the referee when adjudged the winner over a disconsolate Honore Pratesi.

1951

27.01.51 ***Eddie Thomas, W CO 13 Pat Patrick (S. Africa), Vacant British Empire Welterweight Title***

WEMBLEY STADIUM, JOHANNESBURG, S. AFRICA The Welshman dictated the fight from the opening gong with spearing lefts and rights to the head. The finishing blow was a crushing left hook which caught Patrick flush on the jaw

19.02.51 ***Michele Palermo (Italy), L PTS 15 Eddie Thomas, European Welterweight Title***

MARKET HALL, CARMARTHEN The 40-year-old Italian continuously bustled forward only to be caught by every punch in the book. Thomas dealt out two floorings and generally punished his opponent at will

23.02.51 ***Pierre Montane (France), W CO 2 Billy Thompson, Vacant European Lightweight Title***

BELLE VUE, MANCHESTER Thompson had to visit the scales three times before making the weight and this obviously drained him. Montane, whilst never having things all his own way, finally delivered the winning punch, a right to the jaw

26.02.51 ***Ronnie Clayton, W PTS 15 Tiger Al Phillips, British, & British Empire Featherweight Titles***

ICE RINK, NOTTINGHAM The Blackpool man retained his titles against the Aldgate Tiger winning decisively on points, but at no time did Phillips stop trying. Floored twice he finished a very game loser indeed

27.02.51 ***Randy Turpin, W CO 1 Luc Van Dam (Holland), Vacant European Middleweight Title***

HARRINGAY ARENA, LONDON It took the Leamington man just 48 seconds to collect another title. After no preliminary action Turpin shot a left hook to the jaw followed by a swift chopping right which spelt 'finis'

27.03.51 ***Jo Weidin (Austria), L PTS 15 Jack Gardner, European Heavyweight Title***

EARLS COURT, LONDON Gardner relied mainly on an accurate left jab to secure this win, when more use of the right cross could have ended the fight prematurely. Weidin gamely kept going despite eye damage

27.03.51 ***Don Cockell, W RSC 6 Albert Yvel (France), Vacant European L. Heavyweight Title***

EARLS COURT, LONDON After six rounds of lusty punching, Cockell whipped in some hefty rib benders following up with head punches and with blood spurting from Yvel's mouth, the referee leapt in to save him from further punishment

30.04.51 ***Ronnie Clayton, L PTS 15 Roy Ankrah (Gold Coast), British Empire Featherweight Title***

EARLS COURT, LONDON One of the greatest all action contests produced for many years saw the British champion surrender his title. The further the bout went the more furious Ankrah fought giving Clayton no respite with an incessant barrage of leather disrupting any planned offensive

09.05.51 ***Danny O'Sullivan, L CO 6 Peter Keenan, British Bantamweight Title***

FIRHILL PARK, GLASGOW The Londoner, obviously weak, took eight long counts before the finishing blow deprived him of his title. Keenan, compact at the weight, just bided his time until the champion was no more than a punch bag

11.06.51 ***Terry Allen, W PTS 15 Vic Herman, Vacant British Flyweight Title***

GRANBY HALLS, LEICESTER The champion outspeeded the bagpipe-playing Scot all the way, never allowing him an opportunity to take control. Right on the bell Allen was downed, but had done more than enough to take the verdict

13.06.51 ***Eddie Thomas, L PTS 15 Charles Humez (France), European Welterweight Title***

CONEY BEACH ARENA, PORTHCAWL Humez gave a great display of two handed hitting when taking Thomas' newly won title. The Welshman was cut over the right eye, and never able to get into the contest

27.06.51 ***Peter Keenan, W RSC 12 Bobby Boland, British Bantamweight Title***

FIRHILL PARK, GLASGOW In one of the goriest battles witnessed, the game challenger was stopped after being on the canvas twice in the earlier rounds. Keenan was also cut, but appeared to be ahead at the closure

10.07.51 ***Sugar Ray Robinson (USA), L PTS 15 Randy Turpin, World Middleweight Title***

EARLS COURT, LONDON A great fistic upset resulted in Turpin wresting the title with a brilliant display of strength and science. Whatever the American tried, Randy came back harder. The large crowd were estatic when the only possible decision was given

28.08.51 ***Billy Thompson, L CO 1 Tommy McGovern, British Lightweight Title***

GREYHOUND STADIUM, WANDSWORTH The challenger took only 45 seconds and two punches to collect the crown. His stablemate, drawn by weight problems, had no answer to any form of attack and had been dumped by a right to the head before going down again to be counted out

10.07.51. In one of the greatest fistic upsets of all time Randy Turpin (left) took the great Sugar Ray Robinson's World Middleweight title.

05.09.51 ***Luis Romero (Spain), L PTS 15 Peter Keenan, European Bantamweight Title***

FIRHILL PARK, GLASGOW The British champion, cheered on by 30,000 fans, overwhelmed his aggresive opponent by sheer artistry. Romero, the heavier puncher of the two, ran into counter punches frequently, finally being outboxed, outfought, but still always looking to finish by the short route

12.09.51 ***Randy Turpin, L RSC 10 Sugar Ray Robinson (USA), World Middleweight Title***

POLO GROUNDS, NEW YORK, USA After beginning to forge ahead Turpin cut the American up badly. In the tenth Robinson, with a last ditch effort opened up in violent fashion, pounding away at will until the referee felt it was time to rescue the champion with only a few seconds remaining to the bell

23.09.51 ***Jack Gardner, L PTS 15 Hein Ten Hoff (W. Germany), European Heavyweight Title***

WALDBUHNE STADIUM, BERLIN, W. GERMANY Gardner was outreached and outpunched by the German who opened up a two-inch cut on his left eyebrow in the second. From then on only the Englishman's gameness kept him upright when being constantly out-jabbed and crossed with the right

16.10.51 ***Don Cockell, W CO 7 Albert Finch, British & European L. Heavyweight Titles***

HARRINGAY ARENA, LONDON The challenger was put down twice from rib benders prior to the fateful seventh, the finish coming within 45 seconds when a left hook and a right to the ribs completed the job for the Don with maximum efficiency

16.10.51 ***Eddie Thomas, L PTS 15 Wally Thom, British & British Empire Welterweight Titles***

HARRINGAY ARENA, LONDON The Liverpool southpaw fought from the first to last bell, gaining the title on a disputed decision. Thomas did not open up until it was too late and gave Thom a rare pounding from the eleventh round onwards

01.11.51 ***Dado Marino (Hawaii), W PTS 15 Terry Allen, World Flyweight Title***

HONOLULU, HAWAII Marino, a 35–year–old grandfather, beat the Englishman to the punch throughout, to gain the unanimous verdict by a wide margin. Both contestants finished wearily with Allen having no alibi for his defeat

1952

26.01.52 ***Vic Toweel (S. Africa), W PTS 15 Peter Keenan, British Empire & World Bantamweight Titles***

RAND STADIUM, JOHANNESBURG, S. AFRICA The champion, making his third defence at altitude, immediately waded into the little Scot, uppercutting and hooking him from head to body. Keenan survived two first round knockdowns to last the distance courageously, being under pressure throughout

18.02.52 ***Teddy Gardner, W CO 6 Louis Skena (France), Vacant European Flyweight Title***

ST JAMES' HALL, NEWCASTLE After several rounds of a nip and tuck affair Gardner dropped the Frenchman with a tremendous left hook to the solar plexus. Skena tried to get up several times before being counted out

25.02.52 ***Roy Ankrah (Gold Coast), W RTD 13 Ronnie Clayton, British Empire Featherweight Title***

ICE RINK, NOTTINGHAM Clayton was always that little bit behind, but put up a truly game performance. Near the end of the thirteenth the 'black flash' waded in with some heavy shots to the body which left the Englishman in no state to continue after the bell came to his rescue

11.03.52 ***Jack Gardner, L PTS 15 Johnny Williams, British & British Empire Heavyweight Titles***

EARLS COURT, LONDON Over fifteen punishing rounds Williams sneaked the points verdict and title from his great rival. Gardner with weight advantage was badly cut up but forced the fight without ever gaining control

17.03.52 ***Teddy Gardner, W PTS 15 Terry Allen, Vacant British Empire & European Flyweight Titles (Allen defended British Flyweight Title)***

ST JAMES'S HALL, NEWCASTLE Following this all-action contest Gardner was awarded the verdict and with it Allen's British flyweight title. There had been little in it, with the Geordie touching down for a short count early on, but presenting a difficult target, and scoring well throughout

20.03.52 ***Jorgen Johansen (Denmark), DREW 15 Tommy McGovern, European Lightweight Title***

K.B. HALLE, COPENHAGEN, DENMARK Tommy McGovern appeared to have won handsomely, despite damaging a left hand in the sixth. The Dane sustained a cut left eye early on which hampered his work, but he was in the main always travelling second best

10.06.52. The fight is almost over for Don Cockell as he finds himself on the seat of his pants once again at the hands of Randy Turpin.

21.04.52 ***Ray Famechon (France), W RTD 5 Ronnie Clayton, European Featherweight Title***
ICE RINK, NOTTINGHAM A badly cut eye sustained in the fifth, signalled the end of Clayton's game challenge. The French master continuously used the left lead and when inside, brought up heavy rights with great effect

21.05.52 ***Peter Keenan, L CO 5 Jean Sneyers (Belgium), European Bantamweight Title***
FIRHILL PARK, GLASGOW The champion appeared well ahead at the time of the unfortunate ending which was precipitated by his tearing a cartilage in the right knee. Keenan sank to the boards in agony hanging to the middle rope, only to be counted out

10.06.52 ***Don Cockell, L RSC 11 Randy Turpin, British & Vacant British Empire L. Heavyweight Titles***
WHITE CITY, LONDON The Don went down fighting, trying to make light of his weight problems. Turpin was just too tigerish, having his man down on three occasions, before the referee rescued Cockell 70 seconds into the eleventh

30.06.52 ***Ronnie Clayton, W RSC 5 Dai Davies, British Featherweight Title***
MARKET HALL, ABERGAVENNY Davies, who had difficulty in making the weight, was dropped in the second and was well on the way to a decisive defeat. The referee called a halt in the fifth due to the deep gash by the side of the Welshman's left eye

30.06.52 ***Teddy Gardner, W PTS 15 Otello Belardinelli (Italy), European Flyweight Title***
GREYHOUND STADIUM, WEST HARTLEPOOL On a warm evening the local boy successfully defended his title, being a clear winner by dint of his clever boxing. The champion's left leads found the Italian's face with utmost regularity, whilst never being in any difficulties himself

24.07.52 ***Wally Thom, L CO 9 Cliff Curvis, British & British Empire Welterweight Titles***
THE STADIUM, LIVERPOOL The Welshman scored a brilliant kayo win after having Thom down on four other occasions. Wally's eye was cut in the sixth, but he was fighting back gamely, until being blasted out with the left hook in the first all-southpaw British title bout

25.07.52 ***Tommy McGovern, L PTS 15 Frank Johnson, British Lightweight Title***
BELLE VUE, MANCHESTER After reigning for less than a year McGovern lost his title by a wide margin of points in a clean and lively contest when he was outboxed all the way. The new champion also had the upper hand with punching power, having Tommy down twice

08.09.52 ***Teddy Gardner, L RSC 12 Jake Tuli (S. Africa), British Empire Flyweight Title***
ST JAMES'S HALL, NEWCASTLE Following two counts Gardner was defenceless sitting on the middle rope before being rescued by the referee. The tireless little Zulu fought non-stop throughout, becoming champion in only his eleventh contest

13.10.52 ***Johnny Williams, W RTD 7 Johnny Arthur (S. Africa), British Empire Heavyweight Title***
GRANBY HALLS, LEICESTER The young South African made a courageous stand but was outclassed and was eventually retired when suffering a damaged right eye. Williams was extremely effective at range but was never inclined to fight inside

21.10.52 ***Randy Turpin, W PTS 15 George Angelo (S. Africa), Vacant British Empire Middleweight Title***
HARRINGAY ARENA, LONDON In a tedious affair, Angelo was content to backpedal for safety. It was not until the last third of the contest that Turpin finally tried to end matters, having the visitor down in the thirteenth, but he was not able to land the finisher

21.10.52 ***Terry Allen, W RSC 6 Eric Marsden, Vacant British Flyweight Title***
HARRINGAY ARENA, LONDON The man from St Helens was put down from a punch to the sciatic nerve, which temporarily paralysed him and left the referee no choice but to stop the contest. Prior to that Marsden, although taking an early count, was more than holding his own

08.12.52 ***Cliff Curvis, L PTS 15 Gerald Dreyer (S. Africa), British Empire Welterweight Title***
RAND STADIUM, JOHANNESBURG, S. AFRICA Into the sixth round and ahead on points Curvis dropped Dryer with a cracking left uppercut to the chin, which broke his hand into the bargain. The referee interrupted the count to order the Welshman to a neutral corner which allowed the challenger to recover and go on to win over the distance

1953

23.01.53 ***Frank Johnson, W RSC 10 Frank Flannery (Australia), Vacant British Empire Lightweight Title***
THE STADIUM, MELBOURNE, AUSTRALIA Johnson's correct punching was the dominant factor throughout. He completely outboxed the Aussie, having him down six times before the referee came to Flannery's aid

09.06.53. Charles Humez (right) looks bloodied and stunned as Randy Turpin puts together a series of heavy blows.

28.01.53 ***Peter Keenan, W RSC 7 Frankie Williams, British Bantamweight Title***
ICE RINK, PAISLEY After receiving a cut eye in the second, Keenan became a fighting fury, having his game challenger down twice before the deciding round. In the seventh Williams was sent to the boards time and again without taking a count before the referee intervened

22.03.53 ***Gilbert Lavoine (France), W DIS 10 Cliff Curvis, Vacant European Welterweight Title***
THE MUTUALITE, PARIS, FRANCE The only real excitement in the contest came during the second round when Curvis floored the Frenchman for a count of four. The Welshman was finally disqualified for persistent wrestling

26.03.53 ***Dennis Powell, W RTD 11 George Walker, Vacant British L. Heavyweight Title***
THE STADIUM, LIVERPOOL A most gruelling contest saw both men floored twice and bleeding profusely with the finish only a matter of time. By the eleventh Walker had virtually no vision and was reeling around the ring before the corner signalled his retirement

12.05.53 ***Johnny Williams, L PTS 15 Don Cockell, British & British Empire Heavyweight Titles***
HARRINGAY ARENA, LONDON Cockell surprised everyone when taking the fight to the champion who seemed remarkably subdued. Even when half blinded, the challenger stormed in to the attack, being an extremely popular winner

12.05.53 ***Ronnie Clayton, W CO 4 Freddie King, British Featherweight Title***
HARRINGAY ARENA, LONDON While it lasted, it was a brilliant battle of wits with ability in abundance. The end came with a short right flush on the jaw leaving King slithering all over the ring to be counted out

09.06.53 ***Randy Turpin, W PTS 15 Charles Humez (France), European Middleweight Title***
WHITE CITY, LONDON Turpin won this fight, billed in some quarters for the World title, with the greatest of ease. The Englishman's beautiful left carved up Humez's face into a bloody mess with the Frenchman still coming in for more

16.06.53 ***Peter Keenan, W PTS 15 Maurice Sandeyron (France), Vacant European Bantamweight Title***
FIRHILL PARK, GLASGOW Keenan turned in a great display to outbox and outclass a clever, crafty opponent, who although behind on points throughout, remained dangerous until the final bell. From the fourth onwards Sandeyron bled profusely from a cut over the right eye

28.08.53 ***Frank Johnson, L PTS 15 Pat Ford (Australia), British Empire Lightweight Title***
MELBOURNE STADIUM, AUSTRALIA Johnson delighted the fans with his boxing skills, but the young challenger forced the pace all the way and was always threatening with heavy punches from both hands. At the end of fifteen rounds Ford was awarded an extremely close decision

24.09.53 ***Wally Thom, W PTS 15 Peter Fallon, Vacant British Welterweight Title***
THE STADIUM, LIVERPOOL In gaining a clear cut victory, Thom rewon the title he had held previously, but although punching the harder was downed for a nine count. Fallon carried a bad cut from the second round, which subdued him throughout

29.09.53 ***Joe Lucy, W PTS 15 Tommy McGovern, Vacant British Lightweight Title***
EARLS COURT, LONDON After fifteen hard fought rounds, Lucy, who had stood his ground, won by a fairly substantial margin. McGovern just could not resolve the right hand lead and was constantly hit by the counters, finishing with cuts around both eyes

03.10.53 ***Peter Keenan, L PTS 15 John Kelly, British and European Bantamweight Titles***
KINGS HALL, BELFAST The Belfast southpaw annexed the little Scot's titles, never presenting a fixed target, jabbing and moving continuously. From the eighth round the champion's eye began to close and from then on he fought a losing battle

09.10.53 ***Pat Ford (Australia), W CO 13 Frank Johnson, British Empire Lightweight Title***
MELBOURNE, AUSTRALIA The Aussie was faster than Johnson, who fought determinedly to regain his title but was handed a terrific shellacking in the twelfth. In the following round Ford crossed Johnson's left with his right, repeated the dose and the British champion crashed down without any hope of rising

21.10.53 ***Carl Bobo Olson (USA), W PTS 15 Randy Turpin, Vacant World Middleweight Title***
MADISON SQUARE GARDEN, NEW YORK, USA Randy Turpin proved to be just a shell of the former great fighter, allowing the American to bull away inside and control the bout. Turpin was downed twice, with only extreme gameness keeping him in contention

26.10.53 ***Dennis Powell, L RSC 10 Alex Buxton, British L. Heavyweight Title***
ICE RINK, NOTTINGHAM When the contest was terminated, Powell was so far behind on points that he could not have gained the verdict over the distance. A terrible gash near the left eye made it impossible to continue with only his wonderful courage still intact

27.10.53 ***Yoshio Shirai (Japan), W PTS 15 Terry Allen, World Flyweight Title***
KORAKUEN STADIUM, TOKYO, JAPAN The champion appeared to hit with open gloves and when Allen got set to work the body he was immediately pulled off by the referee. After fairly even exchanges the challenger tired near the end with Shirai beginning to get on top

1954

30.01.54 ***Don Cockell, W PTS 15 Johnny Arthur (S. Africa), British Empire Heavyweight Title***
RAND STADIUM, JOHANNESBURG, S. AFRICA Giving away six inches in height the British champion boxed rings around Arthur, although receiving a cut left eye in the fifth round. The South African tried to open up in the latter rounds, getting floored by a left hook in the fourteenth, but he got up to last the distance

16.02.54 ***Terry Allen, W DIS 5 Eric Marsden, British Flyweight Title***
HARRINGAY ARENA, LONDON A careless blow delivered midway into the fifth robbed Eric Marsden of the chance to become the new champion. He was apparently well in control and had Allen on the floor twice before the unfortunate incident

16.02.54 ***Jean Sneyers (Belgium), W PTS 15 Sammy McCarthy, European Featherweight Title***
HARRINGAY ARENA, LONDON The champion gave a wonderful exhibition of boxing skill to convincingly outpoint the Englishman. Sneyers continuously outboxed the 'Smiler,' whose only resort was pluck and courage

27.02.54 ***John Kelly, L CO 3 Robert Cohen (France), European Bantamweight Title***
KINGS HALL, BELFAST 20,000 Irishmen watched their idol smashed to the canvas six times before the 'coup de grace'. The end mercifully came 30 seconds into the third with a barrage of punches leaving Kelly battered, broken and out to the world

02.05.54 ***Randy Turpin, L RSC 1 Tiberio Mitri (Italy), European Middleweight Title***
STADIO TORINO, ROME, ITALY With the first real punch of the contest Turpin was caught under the right ear with a left hook. He fell heavily and although stumbling upright before the full count, was led back to his corner after just 65 seconds

01.06.54 ***Ronnie Clayton, L RTD 8 Sammy McCarthy, British Featherweight Title***
WHITE CITY, LONDON Clayton was an open

target for the East Ender's jabs and retired at the end of the eighth suffering from loss of vision. He had been comprehensively beaten and the contest was in danger of becoming totally one sided

26.08.54 ***Gilbert Lavoine (France), L RSC 10 Wally Thom, European Welterweight Title***

THE STADIUM, LIVERPOOL The end came with Lavoine being hammered, offering no resistance in a neutral corner, doubled up and capsizing under a torrent of blows. Thom had gradually gained control from the early rounds, despite eye damage, and he drained the champion's strength with heavy body shots

10.09.54 ***Nazzareno Giannelli (Italy), W PTS 15 Terry Allen, Vacant European Flyweight Title***

PALAZZO DEL CHIACCIO, MILAN, ITALY After fifteen hard rounds the Italian was awarded a very close decision. Allen had been handicapped by a badly cut left eye from the ninth round, but floored Giannelli at the end of the twelfth before the bell came to the rescue

14.09.54 ***Johnny Sullivan, W CO 1 Gordon Hazell, Vacant British & British Empire Middleweight Titles***

HARRINGAY ARENA, LONDON The fight was all over after 2 minutes 22 seconds. Soon sampling some very heavy blows, Hazell was hit with a ramrod left to the face and a long right which caught him flush on the temple ending the contest instantly

21.09.54 ***John Kelly, L CO 6 Peter Keenan, British Bantamweight Title***

ICE RINK, PAISLEY The Irishman seemed a spent force and in the sixth round Keenan switched his attack from body to head, putting Kelly down for a nine count. When he rose a barrage of punches connected before a left hook to the jaw enforced the full count

02.10.54 ***Roy Ankrah (Gold Coast), L PTS 15 Billy Spider Kelly, British Empire Featherweight Title***

KINGS HALL, BELFAST 'Spider' Kelly, by winning this contest, became the first man to win a title previously held by his father. Ankrah fought the only way he knew, but the challenger used every countering trick possible to gain a close decision

19.10.54 ***Wally Thom, W CO 6 Lew Lazar, British & European Welterweight Titles***

HARRINGAY ARENA, LONDON The challenger started fast and kept up brisk attacks forcing

10.09.54. The Italian Nazzareno Giannelli (left) smartly ducks a straight right thrown by the onrushing Terry Allen.

Thom onto the defensive. In the fateful sixth, Lazar was lured onto a counter punch which came following an exchange of hooks and he was bowled over for the full count

19.10.54 ***Jake Tuli (S. Africa), L PTS 15 Dai Dower, British Empire Flyweight Title***
HARRINGAY ARENA, LONDON With a brilliant display of boxing the young man from the Welsh valleys won clearly and comprehensively over the distance. Dower rattled up the points with accurate left leads making the Zulu miss, whilst tying him up effectively at close quarters

09.11.54 ***Alex Buxton, W CO 8 Albert Finch, British L. Heavyweight Title***
EMBASSY SPORTSDROME, BIRMINGHAM Both fighters bled virtually from the start and in round six a collision of heads split the champion's left eye. The decisive eighth saw Buxton mounting an attack which dropped Finch, who took two further long counts before being put away

11.12.54 ***Peter Keenan, W PTS 15 George O'Neill, British Bantamweight Title***
KINGS HALL, BELFAST O'Neill did remarkably well to stay the course after being floored twice and cut severely over both eyes. Keenan was the master throughout, making constant use of his left hand which piled up the points

1955

22.01.55 ***Sammy McCarthy, L PTS 15 Billy Spider Kelly, British Featherweight Title (Kelly defended British Empire Featherweight Title)***
KINGS HALL, BELFAST The 'Spider' mastered the British champion at every phase of the game when adding to his Empire title. Kelly's victory was superbly executed whilst McCarthy fought in a very limited fashion

08.02.55 ***Dai Dower, W PTS 15 Eric Marsden, Vacant British Flyweight Title (Dower defended British Empire Flyweight Title)***
HARRINGAY ARENA, LONDON Dower harried the St Helens boy for the full fifteen rounds with superb left hand leading, crossing the right occasionally and all the time weaving forward leaving no real target. Marsden was consistently beaten to the punch and outspeeded throughout

12.02.55 ***Johnny Van Rensburg (S. Africa), W PTS 15 Joe Lucy, Vacant British Empire Lightweight Title***
RAND STADIUM, JOHANNESBURG, S. AFRICA The result was in dispute right up to the final bell, the decision being split. By the tenth Lucy had wiped out any deficit, but the South African staged a late rally which brought him back into the fray

08.03.55 ***Nazzareno Giannelli (Italy), L PTS 15 Dai Dower, European Flyweight Title***
EARLS COURT, LONDON Dower easily outpointed the Italian veteran who backpedaled continuously. The contest was all about the Welshman chasing and stabbing home the left hand which lacked any real power and Giannelli feeling his 30 years

28.03.55 ***Peter Keenan, W PTS 15 Bobby Sinn (Australia), Vacant British Empire Bantamweight Title***
THE STADIUM, SYDNEY, AUSTRALIA The British champion won every round, giving the Aussie a severe drubbing. From the off Keenan jabbed, hooked and crossed with Sinn having no answer except to get inside where he was tied up easily

26.04.55 ***Alex Buxton, L CO 2 Randy Turpin, British L. Heavyweight Title (Turpin defended British Empire L. Heavyweight Title)***
HARRINGAY ARENA, LONDON After a non-action first round, Randy finished the fight with deadly accuracy, using a terrific short left to body and a right to the jaw. Buxton buckled at the knees sinking to the canvas with blood spurting from his mouth, minus his British title

26.04.55 ***Joe Lucy, L PTS 15 Frank Johnson, British Lightweight Title***
HARRINGAY ARENA, LONDON Adopting a non-stop attack from start to finish, the Mancunian re-won the title he never lost in the ring. Lucy boxed in the main on the retreat and was downed by a right beneath the ribs in the thirteenth

16.05.55 ***Rocky Marciano (USA), W RSC 9 Don Cockell, World Heavyweight Title***
KEZAR STADIUM, SAN FRANSISCO, USA Giving one of the gamest displays of all time, the Britisher stayed on his feet throughout the 'Rock's' tremendous onslaught. He was knocked down twice in the ninth, and the referee would not allow the carnage to carry on, stopping it with Cockell still upright

27.05.55 ***Ray Famechon (France), W PTS 15 Billy Spider Kelly, European Featherweight Title***
DONNYBROOK BUS DEPOT, DUBLIN, EIRE Kelly was content to duck and weave using counters, but the more experienced champion soon realised the Irishman was susceptible to body punches. 'Spider' came right back in the middle stages but Famechon paced himself beautifully

16.06.55 ***Johnny Sullivan, L DIS 9 Pat McAteer, British & British Empire Middleweight Titles***
THE STADIUM, LIVERPOOL McAteer boxed with supreme coolness, using his best punch, the left hook, freely and countering to great effect. Sullivan charged forward incessantly without inflicting real damage, the end coming when two

27.05.55. The ebullient Irishman Billy Spider Kelly (left) tries to ward off body punches thrown by Ray Famechon.

blows went low and the referee awarded the contest to 'Patmac'

23.06.55 ***Wally Thom, L PTS 15 Idrissa Dione (France), European Welterweight Title***

THE STADIUM, LIVERPOOL The French Senegalese turned out a real surprise package winning clearly on points. Thom fought on in grim fashion after a fourth round knockdown carrying two badly cut eyes and finishing with a fractured left hand into the bargain

14.09.55 ***Peter Keenan, W CO 14 Jake Tuli (S. Africa), British Empire Bantamweight Title***

CATHKIN PARK, GLASGOW Keenan was downed three times in the opening round collecting two cut eyes plus nose damage, before fighting back well in the twelfth to floor Tuli for eight. The Zulu was all in during the thirteenth and the contest was ended with a perfect left hook

03.10.55 ***Dai Dower, L CO 12 Young Martin (Spain), European Flyweight Title***

ICE RINK, NOTTINGHAM The Spaniard, with the tenacity of a bull, moved forward throwing punches incessantly, mainly concentrating on the body. Dower was put down nine times in all before being knocked out by a crushing left hook to the stomach

12.11.55 ***Pat McAteer, W PTS 15 Mike Holt (S. Africa), British Empire Middleweight Title***

RAND STADIUM, JOHANNESBURG, S. AFRICA Holt started strongly and meted out a lot of punishment, but 'Patmac', using his cleverer boxing, nulified the attacks using a heavy right whenever required. Although the decision was a formality, the Englishman sustained a broken left hand for his pains

19.11.55 ***Billy Spider Kelly, L CO 8 Hogan Bassey (Nigeria), British Empire Featherweight Title***

KINGS HALL, BELFAST By dint of brilliant boxing 'Spider' Kelly was a proverbial mile in front coming into the eighth. With a gaping eye wound bleeding profusely Bassey suddenly unleashed a crashing right hook to the jaw which stretched the champion prostrate on the canvas

06.12.55 ***Dai Dower, W PTS 15 Jake Tuli (S. Africa), British Empire Flyweight Title***

HARRINGAY ARENA, LONDON Showing all his old brilliance, Dower survived the handicap of two damaged eyes and a fourth round knockdown to give a superb exhibition of delightful boxing. The little Welshman was a clear winner over a very tough and determined challenger

1956

04.02.56 ***Billy Spider Kelly, L PTS 15 Charlie Hill, British Featherweight Title***
KINGS HALL, BELFAST A new champion was crowned, followed by a riot costing many casualties. Kelly should have taken complete control, but was content to cruise along casually as the Scot was downed twice and badly cut above the left eye. Hill resolutely stuck to his task and was adjudged the winner

13.03.56 ***Ron Barton, W RTD 8 Albert Finch, Vacant British L. Heavyweight Title***
HARRINGAY ARENA, LONDON Barton became the new champion when the old campaigner retired with a severly gashed left eye. It had been an exciting bout while it had lasted, but Finch finally shot his bolt after giving his all in the seventh

13.04.56 ***Frank Johnson, L RSC 8 Joe Lucy, British Lightweight Title***
BELLE VUE, MANCHESTER Beleaguered by weight problems, the Mancunian did not have anything left to offer after being floored twice and badly cut. It still took Lucy eight rounds to do the job, but with Johnson tottering and the blood flowing, the referee finally stepped in

05.06.56 ***Wally Thom, L RTD 5 Peter Waterman, British Welterweight Title***
HARRINGAY ARENA, LONDON The challenger appeared to be biding his time after putting Thom on the boards and opening up eye wounds. Wally made a game fight back but was being hit at will before his corner pulled him out

19.06.56 ***Gordon Wallace (Canada), W PTS 15 Ron Barton, Vacant British Empire L. Heavyweight Title***
CLAPTON STADIUM, LONDON In a real upset Ron Barton was clubbed and dropped twice by the wild-swinging Canadian. The British champion strangely did not have any answer to the uncompromising attacks, appearing subdued throughout

26.06.56 ***Joe Lucy, W RSC 13 Sammy McCarthy, British Lightweight Title***
EMPIRE POOL, WEMBLEY The referee stopped the bout when he considered the deficit was too great between the contestants. After one of the tamest title fights ever witnessed Lucy was presented with the Lonsdale Belt outright

27.08.56 ***Joe Erskine, W PTS 15 Johnny Williams, Vacant British Heavyweight Title***
MAINDY STADIUM, CARDIFF A hard fought unre-

13.03.56. Ron Barton (left) fends off Albert Finch with a left lead and looks to unload a heavy right on his wily opponent.

lenting contest between the two Welshmen kept the fans sitting tight despite the torrential rain. Erskine finished the bout badly cut over both eyes with his brilliant evasive ability getting him through

08.10.56 ***Pat McAteer, W RSC 4 Lew Lazar, British & British Empire Middleweight Titles***

ICE RINK, NOTTINGHAM Lazar was put down three times in the fateful fourth and the fight was stopped when his right eye was completely glazed. The punch that decided the contest was a left swing which caught the Londoner smack on the eyeball

22.10.56 ***Peter Keenan, W RSC 2 Kevin James (Australia), British Empire Bantamweight Title***

THE STADIUM, SYDNEY, AUSTRALIA Conceding height and reach, the champion carefully drew the lead during the first. In the second round Keenan produced heavy rights to spreadeagle the Australian four times in all before the referee had seen enough

26.11.56 ***Randy Turpin, W RSC 5 Alex Buxton, Vacant British L. Heavyweight Title***

GRANBY HALLS, LEICESTER Whilst only a shell of his former self, Turpin still had too much power for his old opponent. Down in the first, Buxton was rescued by the referee after suffering the ignominy of five further counts during the decisive round

17.12.56 ***Peter Waterman, W RTD 10 Frank Johnson, British Welterweight Title***

EMBASSY SPORTSDROME, BIRMINGHAM In a titanic seesaw struggle, Waterman was downed in the fourth and cut badly in the sixth. Amazingly he was still able to subdue the challenger who was pulled out by his corner when blinded with damage to both eyes

1957

04.02.57 ***Charles Humez (France), W RSC 8 Pat McAteer, European Middleweight Title***

PALAIS DES SPORTS, PARIS, FRANCE The turning point came during the fourth round, when McAteer sustained a split left eye. Prior to that he was out in front, but the injury worsened, leaving him half blinded before being rescued by the referee

19.02.57 ***Joe Bygraves (Jamaica), W CO 9 Henry Cooper, British Empire Heavyweight Title***

EARLS COURT, LONDON Cooper, who had not boxed for several months, seemed ring rusty and when badly cut showed obvious caution. The Jamaican giant began to concentrate on the body and a heavy right knocked the Londoner down, setting him up for the finishing blow

30.03.57 ***Pascuel Perez (Argentine), W CO 1 Dai Dower, World Flyweight Title***

SAN LORENZO DE ALMAGRO STADIUM, BUENOS AIRES, ARGENTINA 85,000 wildly excited patriots saw the Britisher demolished in 2 minutes 48 seconds. After the preliminaries Perez set Dower up with a left-right to the jaw and it was all over

09.04.57 ***Joe Lucy, L PTS 15 Dave Charnley, British Lightweight Title***

HARRINGAY ARENA, LONDON Up to the twelfth round the contest was fairly mundane, but once the Dartford boilermaker had connected to Lucy's ribs, there was no doubting the result. The champion was decked six times in all with the final bell coming to his rescue

04.05.57 ***Pat McAteer, W CO 6 Jimmy Elliott (S. Africa), British Empire Middleweight Title***

RAND STADIUM, JOHANNESBURG, S. AFRICA Tragedy followed this fight as the challenger never regained consciousness and died the next day. Until the finishing blows there had been no knockdowns, but when floored Elliott had banged his head and struggled up at eight, only to slump face down

19.05.57 ***Ingemar Johansson (Sweden), W CO 5 Henry Cooper, European Heavyweight Title***

STOCKHOLM, SWEDEN The finish came suddenly after Cooper had exposed his chin to the big Swede. A short right on the point, which had a paralysing effect, finished it, but up to that moment the referee had scored both fighters even

22.05.57 ***Peter Keenan, W RSC 6 John Smillie, British & British Empire Bantamweight Titles***

FIRHILL PARK, GLASGOW The cut eye bogey, which the champion had encountered more than once, struck again in the opening round. For five rounds Keenan fell further behind until two decisive 'out of the blue' knockdowns forced the referee to rescue his compatriot who was seemingly on his way to victory

27.05.57 ***Joe Bygraves (Jamaica), DREW 15 Dick Richardson, British Empire Heavyweight Title***

MAINDY STADIUM, CARDIFF Both fighters absorbed plenty of punishment in a gruelling brawl. The Marquis of Queensberry rules did not seem to count on occasion, but it was all action and if uncompromising at times the result was about right

30.05.57 ***Emilio Marconi (Italy), DREW 15 Peter Waterman, European Welterweight Title***

FORO ITALICO, ROME, ITALY In a mauling contest

09.04.57. A thudding right from Dave Charnley (right) knocks Joe Lucy off balance during a hectic session in the twelfth round.

the Italian octopus held on to his title as Waterman appeared to make up any lost ground from the middle stages, despite sustaining eye damage. Marconi tired in the latter rounds with the Englishman well on top

11.06.57 ***Randy Turpin, W PTS 15 Arthur Howard, British L. Heavyweight Title***

GRANBY HALLS, LEICESTER Howard wasted a glorious chance of success when putting the once great Randy on the canvas three times. Turpin won the fight going away on points, but the 'Islington Tiger' came mighty close to gaining a decisive victory

09.07.57 ***Willie Toweel (S. Africa), W PTS 15 Dave Charnley, British Empire Lightweight Title***

EMPRESS HALL, LONDON Although the margin of victory was decisive, the British challenger appeared more chastised than hurt at the end of the contest. There were no knockdowns and the Springbok again proved himself a boxing master adept at all facets of the game

31.07.57 ***Frankie Jones, W CO 11 Len Reece, Vacant British & British Empire Flyweight Titles***

CONEY BEACH ARENA, PORTHCAWL Way out in front, the game Welshman began to run out of steam, the end coming with a flurry of blows and ending with a left hook. Frankie Jones had been on the canvas himself earlier, but hung on with great courage

05.09.57 ***Pat McAteer, W PTS 15 Martin Hansen, British & British Empire Middleweight Titles***

THE STADIUM, LIVERPOOL 'Patmac' won the first four rounds then ran into some difficulty, but coasted the contest from the eighth onwards. Both men were cut, but there were no knockdowns to record

17.09.57 ***Joe Erskine, W PTS 15 Henry Cooper, British Heavyweight Title***

HARRINGAY ARENA, LONDON Erskine won a lack-lustre fight narrowly with the challenger failing in his third championship bout of the year. Neither man did any significant work and each round was rather close for comfort, but Cooper forced too little to capture the crown

07.10.57 ***Charlie Hill, W CO 10 Jimmy Brown, British Featherweight Title***

ICE RINK, NOTTINGHAM The game Scot was floored in the second and by the tenth round had gradually been set up for the kill. Nobody in the hall could have envisaged what happened next as Hill suddenly landed four right handers that smashed the Irishman down for the full count

23.10.57 ***Frankie Jones, L CO 3 Dennis Adams (S. Africa), British Empire Flyweight Title***

KELVIN HALL, GLASGOW In a contest of brawn versus brain, the former prevailed. Jones decided to fight it out after flooring the challenger in the first and this proved his undoing, when after he had been floored three times a terrific right to the jaw ended the proceedings

25.11.57 ***Joe Bygraves (Jamaica), L PTS 15 Joe Erskine, British Empire Heavyweight Title***

GRANBY HALLS, LEICESTER The British champion relieved big Joe of his titles with the utmost of ease, giving a superb display of boxing. Unfortunately Erskine did not possess a damaging punch otherwise the contest would have been concluded well inside the distance

09.12.57 ***Percy Lewis (Trinidad), W RSC 10 Charlie Hill, Vacant British Empire Featherweight Title***

ICE RINK, NOTTINGHAM Another fantastic display of courage from the little Scot had the fans on their seats. This time in opposition to Percy Lewis, a southpaw, Hill hit the deck nine times in all before the referee decided to rescue him

1958

28.01.58 ***Emilio Marconi (Italy), L RSC 14 Peter Waterman, European Welterweight Title***

HARRINGAY ARENA, LONDON The referee pulled the Italian out at the end of the penultimate round with a terrible left eye wound. By that time Marconi could not win on points, but at least had the satisfaction of putting the challenger down twice in the eleventh in a contest where there were far too many warnings for holding

21.02.58 ***Ingemar Johansson (Sweden), W RTD 13 Joe Erskine, European Heavyweight Title***

MASSHALLEN, GOTHENBURG, SWEDEN Erskine, although losing emphatically, showed great courage and took the Swede's much publicised artillery without showing any sign of crumbling. The fleet footed displays normally associated with the 'Tiger Bay' boy were missing and both eyes were damaged badly before he was pulled out

28.01.58. Peter Waterman (right) throws a heavy right hand which the Italian Emilio Marconi adroitly gets underneath.

27.03.58 ***Pat McAteer, L CO 9 Dick Tiger (Nigeria), British Empire Middleweight Title***
THE STADIUM, LIVERPOOL Leading by the proverbial mile, McAteer decided to mix it with the teak tough Tiger. The contest immediately changed direction with the champion finally destroyed by a vicious left hook which sent him down without any hope of rising

02.04.58 ***Peter Keenan, W PTS 15 Graham Van Der Walt (S. Africa), British Empire Bantamweight Title***
ICE RINK, PAISLEY Keenan outboxed and outmanoeuvred the tough little South African, winning hands down. Van Der Walt never gave up trying and was always dangerous, but the Scot, using straighter punches, brought his man up short on countless occasions

03.06.58 ***Joe Erskine, L CO 8 Brian London, British & British Empire Heavyweight Titles***
WHITE CITY, LONDON Brian London won the title once held by his father, when he kayoed the crestfallen Erskine. When the Welshman's eye went, London was transformed into a fighting fury, smashing his opponent twice to the canvas where he was counted out on one knee

02.07.58 ***Charlie Hill, W RTD 11 Chic Brogan, British Featherweight Title***
CATHKIN PARK, GLASGOW The challenger did some good work in the earlier rounds although cut in the opener. Brogan's tendency to swing, enabled Hill to establish his class and pick his punches better. The fight was terminated with the challenger's eye deteriorating rapidly in the eleventh

15.07.58 ***Tommy Molloy, W PTS 15 Jimmy Newman, Vacant British Welterweight Title***
ICE RINK, STREATHAM Molloy won a comfortable if hard-earned victory from a fight which fell below the championship standard. Both fighters sustained eye injuries but the Liverpudlian's better variety of punches finally won the day

30.09.58 ***Terry Downes, W RSC 13 Phil Edwards, Vacant British Middleweight Title***
HARRINGAY ARENA, LONDON After a feeling-out first round, crashing, bashing Terry Downes set about systematic destruction of his more experienced rival. By the twelfth Edwards had nothing left and a round later when he was offering no real resistance, the referee stopped the massacre

16.10.58 ***Peter Keenan, W PTS 15 Pat Supple (Canada), British Empire Bantamweight Title***
ICE RINK, PAISLEY Successfully defending his title once again, Keenan came from behind gradually to overhaul the early lead built up by his young rival. Although put down in the final round the champion deserved the decision with his greater experience being a deciding factor

1959

10.01.59 ***Peter Keenan, L RSC 11 Freddie Gilroy, British & British Empire Bantamweight Titles***
KINGS HALL, BELFAST Battered to the canvas on three occasions prior to the eleventh, Keenan was again floored three times by savage crippling blows that left him powerless to defend himself. Gilroy was crowned to the strains of 'When Irish Eyes Are Smiling'

12.01.59 ***Brian London, L PTS 15 Henry Cooper, British & British Empire Heavyweight Titles***
EARLS COURT, LONDON Giving a tantalizing superb display of left hand boxing, Henry Cooper wrested the titles from Brian London by a margin the length of Blackpool Pier. Both men suffered bad eye injuries and although London took terrific punishment there were no knockdowns

05.02.59 ***Frankie Jones, W PTS 15 Alex Ambrose, British Flyweight Title***
KELVIN HALL, GLASGOW Jones produced one of his best displays in gaining a clear-cut victory over his fellow countryman. Ambrose was well beaten in every phase of the game, but was never disgraced and gamely battled on to the end

13.04.59 ***Charlie Hill, L RSC 9 Bobby Neill, British Featherweight Title***
ICE RINK, NOTTINGHAM In another familiar display of red-masked courage Charlie Hill's title was hooked loose when he visited the canvas on no less than 10 occasions. Neill just could not keep down the wonderfully game Hill, with the referee finishing the job for him

01.05.59 ***Floyd Patterson (USA), W CO 11 Brian London, World Heavyweight Title***
INDIANAPOLIS, USA The tenth was the beginning of the end, when the challenger was put down for the first time in his career. The decisive round saw Patterson raining blow after blow until a lightning left hook ended matters promptly

12.05.59 ***Willie Toweel (S. Africa), L CO 10 Dave Charnley, British Empire Lightweight Title***
EMPIRE POOL, WEMBLEY The end was predictable when Toweel sustained a bad cut in the ninth, but until then it had been an evenly fought affair. The Englishman really got to work in the tenth landing blow upon blow to the South African's head until a right over the top ended the contest

15.09.59. John Cowboy McCormack (right) looks apprehensive as the crashing, bashing Champion Terry Downes hurtles in once again.

26.08.59 ***Henry Cooper, W RSC 5 Gawie De Klerk (S. Africa), British Empire Heavyweight Title***

CONEY BEACH ARENA, PORTHCAWL After making a slow start the British champion gradually got his left hand working in piston-like fashion. In the fifth Cooper unleashed a dynamic left hook following a 'Break' which floored the South African, who on rising was put down again before the referee ended the carnage

15.09.59 ***Terry Downes, L DIS 8 John Cowboy McCormack, British Middleweight Title***

EMPIRE POOL, WEMBLEY Downes displayed such superiority over his challenger, but still lost his crown after the bow-legged Scot had been floored six times. The finish came after a blow under the elbows had put McCormack down and earned a borderline disqualification for the champion following a previous warning

14.10.59 ***Tommy Molloy, W RSC 12 Albert Carroll, British Welterweight Title***

THE STADIUM, LIVERPOOL Until the eleventh round Carroll was apparently cruising to a comfortable win. Molloy at last cut loose from his tormenter, flooring him twice before the referee called a halt to a sensational finish

03.11.59 ***Piero Rollo (Italy), L PTS 15 Freddie Gilroy, European Bantamweight Title***

EMPIRE POOL, WEMBLEY Gilroy added to his titles when gaining a comfortable and convincing points victory. The earlier rounds paved the way for victory, but when he could have cruised along the Irishman was quite prepared to mix it

03.11.59 ***John Cowboy McCormack, L RSC 8 Terry Downes, British Middleweight Title***

EMPIRE POOL, WEMBLEY The Paddington express regained his title after just 49 days in a sensational contest. Despite terrible facial damage he smashed the Scot to the floor on half a dozen occasions, before the referee saved McCormack from serious injury

17.11.59 ***Henry Cooper, W RSC 12 Joe Erskine, British & British Empire Heavyweight Titles***

EARLS COURT, LONDON One of the best heavyweight fights for years saw Cooper retaining his titles with a first-class demolition job on the Welshman. Floored four times in the twelfth, Erskine was counted out lying backwards over the bottom rope

02.12.59 ***Joe Brown (USA), W RTD 5 Dave Charnley, World Lightweight Title***
SAM HOUSTON COLISEUM, HOUSTON, USA The British challenger was just getting into his stride, when a clash of heads saw him stagger away with an eye swelling and dripping blood. Charnley's handlers immediately signalled surrender with no hope of repairing the damage

05.12.59 ***Freddie Gilroy, W CO 5 Bernie Taylor (S. Africa), British Empire Bantamweight Title***
KINGS HALL, BELFAST Taylor was beginning to soak up more than enough punishment before being despatched. Caught against the ropes the challenger stopped a vicious barrage of short hooks with his chin, and a body attack left him on the canvas, the count a formality

07.12.59 ***Percy Lewis (Trinidad), W CO 2 John O'Brien, British Empire Featherweight Title***
ICE RINK, NOTTINGHAM Following a bright first round when the challenger took up an offensive, Lewis got down to some better boxing and a long swinging left toppled O'Brien off balance. Beating the count looked a formality, but the Scot somehow stayed down on one knee

1960

28.01.60 ***Chic Calderwood, W RSC 13 Arthur Howard, Vacant British L. Heavyweight Title***
ICE RINK, PAISLEY The game but outclassed 'Islington Tiger' made a brave final stand in the thirteenth, before the referee decided he had taken too much punishment. Calderwood had dominated the proceedings throughout with a mixture of science and deadly two handed punching

01.02.60 ***Tommy Molloy, L PTS 15 Wally Swift, British Welterweight Title***
ICE RINK, NOTTINGHAM Whilst the champion posed and waited, Swift speared his left hand to the head with great accuracy. Molloy, with a look of desperation as the fight drew to a close tried hard to get inside, but to no avail

19.03.60 ***Freddie Gilroy, W RSC 13 Billy Rafferty, British, British Empire & European Bantamweight Titles***
KINGS HALL, BELFAST With his face cut grotesquely Rafferty was led back to his corner by the referee. Down in the first and hit with some tremendous punches, the tough Scot had closed Gilroy's eye when coming more into the fight, but the Irishman seemed to have the proverbial bit in hand

27.03.60 ***Dick Richardson, W RSC 13 Hans Kalbfell (W. Germany), Vacant European Heavyweight Title***
WESTFALENHALLE, DORTMUND, W. GERMANY In a bruising battle Richardson suffered a bad eye injury before coming through in sensational fashion. Kalbfell was floored for eight in the thirteenth round, but upon rising was immediately flattened with his corner claiming that no 'box on' instructions had been given

29.03.60 ***Mario Vecchiatto (Italy), L RTD 10 Dave Charnley, European Lightweight Title***
EMPIRE POOL, WEMBLEY Charnley started rather slowly, but gradually increased the tempo and after sinking several hooks into the Italian's midsection, floored him in the tenth with a short right to the jaw. Upon rising Vecchiatto was put down again signifying his retirement when up on one knee

09.05.60 ***George Barnes (Australia), L PTS 15 Brian Curvis, British Empire Welterweight Title***
VETCH FIELD, SWANSEA 14,000 fans watched the young local rest the title from Barnes in a gruelling struggle. Despite being cut and running out of steam near the finish, Curvis boxed like a real champion keeping the fight at distance whilst using his hard right to great effect

09.06.60 ***Chic Calderwood, W RSC 12 Johnny Halafihi (Tonga), Vacant British Empire L. Heavyweight Title***
FIRHILL PARK, GLASGOW The Tongan took the lead in the early rounds putting Calderwood down but the punch of the fight was a right cross that floored Halafihi in the tenth. Two rounds later his left eye was closed, forcing the referee to step in

05.07.60 ***Terry Downes, W RTD 12 Phil Edwards, British Middleweight Title***
EMPIRE POOL, WEMBLEY In a hard non-stop battle, Edwards punched himself to a standstill trying to contain the tigerish ferocity of the Londoner. Although hurt on occasions, Downes would not take a backward step and after a thorough demolition job, the challenger was retired

29.08.60 ***Dick Richardson, W RTD 8 Brian London, European Heavyweight Title***
CONEY BEACH ARENA, PORTHCAWL Brian London was unlucky to collect bad cuts after having built up a big lead. The bout will unfortunately be better remembered by the after-fight brawl that ensued in the ring, leaving bodies strewn all over the canvas

27.09.60 ***Bobby Neill, L RSC 7 Terry Spinks, British Featherweight Title***
ALBERT HALL, LONDON Both challenger and champion came out of a clinch in the seventh

08.10.60. The right does the trick for Johnny Caldwell as Frankie Jones goes crashing to the canvas in round three.

carrying cuts and as the bell ended the round the referee directed Neill to his corner. Prior to the ending Spinks was just about in front with his speedy leading countering the champion's aggression

08.10.60 ***Frankie Jones, L CO 3 Johnny Caldwell, British Flyweight Title***
KINGS HALL, BELFAST The little Scot met the challenger head on, but it soon became obvious that the match would not go the distance. Caldwell's attacks were concentrated on the body, but in the third he switched and two long rights to the chin finished the contest promptly

25.10.60 ***Alphonse Halimi (France), W PTS 15 Freddie Gilroy, Vacant World Bantamweight Title (EBU version)***
EMPIRE POOL, WEMBLEY Amid tremendous excitement Freddie Gilroy was floored heavily in the thirteenth only to be rescued by the bell. Until then the Irishman had forced the contest with plenty to spare and although Halimi had a good penultimate round, Gilroy seemed dreadfully unlucky to drop the decision

21.11.60 ***Wally Swift, L PTS 15 Brian Curvis, British Welterweight Title (Curvis defended British Empire Welterweight Title)***
ICE RINK, NOTTINGHAM Swift survived two knockdowns in the eighth to fight on gamely only to lose the decision eventually. The local man could not match Curvis for variety and enterprise, allied to some tremendous left hand punching

22.11.60 ***Terry Spinks, W CO 14 Bobby Neill, British Featherweight Title***
EMPIRE POOL, WEMBLEY Spinks boxed brilliantly to drift into a long lead by dint of straight accurate punches from both hands. Utterly exhausted, the Scot came out for the fourteenth, but was floored three times before failing to beat the count

1961

14.01.61 ***Paul Pender (USA), W RSC 7 Terry Downes, World Middleweight Title***
THE ARENA, BOSTON, USA There was a shock for the Englishman in the first when he was put down, but he recovered well and was beginning to get to Pender with his body attacks. Unfortunately Downes received a deep nose wound which ultimately necessitated twelve stitches and brought the fight to an end

18.02.61 ***Dick Richardson, W PTS 15 Hans Kalbfell (Germany), European Heavyweight Title***
WESTFALENHALLE, DORTMUND, W. GERMANY At the end of fifteen torrid rounds Richardson well deserved his victory against a wonderfully game challenger. Both men were badly cut and Kalbfell took two counts, with only tremendous courage getting him through

21.02.61 ***Dave Charnley, W PTS 15 Fernand Nollet (France), European Lightweight Title***
ICE RINK, STREATHAM Incredibly the French challenger was not only standing at the finish but had given the Englishman a rather hard tussle. There were no knockdowns, but in the thirteenth Charnley sustained a cut right eye, which held up well

21.03.61 ***Henry Cooper, W RTD 5 Joe Erskine, British & British Empire Heavyweight Titles***
EMPIRE POOL, WEMBLEY Cooper retained his titles when the Welshman was retired suffering from a badly damaged left eye. Until then both fighters had boxed extremely well but Cooper always looked dangerous with the left hook

18.04.61 ***Joe Brown (USA), W PTS 15 Dave Charnley, World Lightweight Title***
EARLS COURT, LONDON The American gave a classic display of counter-punching, but Charnley forced the contest all the way and appeared to have won the title. Brown was content to wait for his challenger who threw punches non-stop, but suffered quite an amount of facial damage in the process

02.05.61 ***Terry Spinks, L RTD 10 Howard Winstone, British Featherweight Title***
EMPIRE POOL, WEMBLEY In a battle of the 'golden boys' Winstone became the new titleholder by dint of his brilliant boxing. The Welshman pumped in lefts and rights in rapid succession without reply throughout and although not floored Spinks was exhausted, but had given his all when retired

08.05.61 ***Brian Curvis, W PTS 15 Wally Swift, British & British Empire Welterweight Titles***
ICE RINK, NOTTINGHAM Curvis won all the way, having the game Swift on the floor twice, but could not put sufficient punches together to halt him. The local man put up game resistance and was always trying to fight back

27.05.61 ***Pierre Cossemyns (Belgium), W RTD 9 Freddie Gilroy, Vacant European Bantamweight Title***
PALAIS DES SPORTS, BRUSSELS, BELGIUM Six times Gilroy was battered to the canvas before his corner threw the towel in. In the earlier rounds the Irishman had put Cossemyns down twice, but later it became apparent that the Belgian had the heavier armoury, which ultimately proved decisive

30.05.61 ***Alphonse Halimi (France), L PTS 15 Johnny Caldwell, World Bantamweight Title (EBU version)***
EMPIRE POOL, WEMBLEY The little Irishman won all the way and when they came out for the final bell he only had to remain standing to win the title. Instead of sitting back Caldwell met Halimi at his own game with some cracking punches, one of which put him down for a long count

05.07.61 ***Dave Charnley, W RTD 4 Ray Nobile (Italy), European Lightweight Title***
FLAMINIO STADIUM, ROME, ITALY Over four rounds of controlled power Charnley outclassed the Italian, but although on the floor several times Nobile never took an official count. At the beginning of the fifth, the challenger remained on his stool, officially retiring with a damaged thumb

11.07.61 ***Paul Pender (USA), L RTD 9 Terry Downes, World Middleweight Title***
EMPIRE POOL, WEMBLEY With both eyes cut and fighting only in sustained rallies Pender relinquished his title on the stool. Downes, although cut himself, waged a great campaign varying his work from boxing to fighting with regularity, and had the American under constant pressure

13.08.61 ***Salvatore Burruni (Italy), W RSC 6 Derek Lloyd, European Flyweight Title***
SAN REMO, ITALY The British challenger was battered to defeat after weight-making difficulties, being smashed to the floor on three occasions. Lloyd provided an easy target for Burruni's merciless attacks, and the end came with him cornered and without any defence

17.10.61 ***John Cowboy McCormack, W PTS 15 Harko Kokmeyer (Holland), Vacant European Middleweight Title***
EMPIRE POOL, WEMBLEY Over fifteen dull, rather one-sided rounds, McCormack made heavy weather of what appeared to be an easy task. Kokmeyer was floored twice with the Scot not possessing the armoury to finish it conclusively

31.10.61 ***Johnny Caldwell, W PTS 15 Alphonse Halimi (France), World Bantamweight Title (EBU version)***
EMPIRE POOL, WEMBLEY This return contest was decidedly closer with Caldwell retaining his titles when working that much harder than the Frenchman. Halimi held at every opportunity, pinning his faith in one punch, whereas Caldwell fired in the majority of quality blows

31.10.61 ***Brian Curvis, W CO 8 Mick Leahy, British & British Empire Welterweight Titles***
EMPIRE POOL, WEMBLEY Leahy was on the attack throughout, in an attempt to take Curvis out of

30.05.61. Another great straight left from Johnny Caldwell (right) goes straight through Alphonse Halimi's guard.

his stride, but the champion was never really ruffled. In the eighth the Irishman was set up by a vicious body assault and was despatched by a left hook to the jaw

20.11.61 ***Dave Charnley, W CO 1 Darkie Hughes, British, British Empire & European Lightweight Titles***

ICE RINK, NOTTINGHAM In the quickest finish of any British title fight, a record 30 seconds, the Dartford boilermaker showed just why he considered the contest a mismatch. After squaring up Charnley unleashed his right hook, putting down Hughes three times which included the count out

1962

06.01.62 ***John Cowboy McCormack, W PTS 15 Heini Freytag (W. Germany), European Middleweight Title***

FRANKFURT, W. GERMANY The contest developed into a non-incident lacklustre affair with Freytag more and more out of his depth. With the German cut up, but still throwing punches, McCormack was content to take no chances and the result was a formality

18.01.62 ***Eder Jofre (Brazil), W RTD 10 Johnny Caldwell, Undisputed World Bantamweight Title***

IBIRAPUERA STADIUM, SAO PAULO, BRAZIL The first four rounds were uneventful, but once Jofre had put down the Irishman in the fifth with a punch seemingly below the belt, the writing was on the wall. Down again in the tenth and in real trouble, Caldwell's manager threw in the towel

08.02.62 ***John Cowboy McCormack, L DIS 4 Chris Christensen (Denmark), European Middleweight Title***

K.B. HALL, COPENHAGEN, DENMARK Looking to have matters all his own way McCormack floored the Dane with a short right, who upon rising was sent crashing, this time out to the world. The referee then disqualified the champion for not waiting the 'box on' instruction

12.02.62 ***Chic Calderwood, W CO 4 Stan Cullis, British & British Empire L. Heavyweight Titles***

NATIONAL SPORTING CLUB, LONDON The Bristolian was not in the same class as Calderwood, who was never in any trouble. Put down twice Cullis was in no real position to defend himself when rising and the referee counted on to 'ten'

20.02.62 ***Brian Curvis, W RSC 5 Tony Mancini, British & British Empire Welterweight Titles***

ALBERT HALL, LONDON Mancini gave a lesson in the art of skilful defensive boxing, but unfortunately it was not enough to deter the purposeful Curvis indefinitely. The champion won every round on aggression and retained his title when the Londoner was badly cut

24.02.62 ***Dick Richardson, W CO 1 Karl Mildenberger (W. Germany), European Heavyweight Title***

WESFALENHALLE, DORTMUND, W. GERMANY Richardson sensationally retained his title by knocking out the challenger after 2 minutes 35 seconds of the first round. A terrific right cross caught Mildenberger high up on the cheek leaving him exposed and Richardson finished the job with great efficiency

27.02.62 ***Jackie Brown, W PTS 15 Brian Cartwright, Vacant British Flyweight Title***

EMBASSY SPORTSDROME, BIRMINGHAM Over fifteen rather fluctuating rounds the little Scot just about got home, finishing the stronger of the two. Cartwright was cut early on and this affected his performance considerably

03.03.62 ***Freddie Gilroy, W CO 12 Billy Rafferty, British & British Empire Bantamweight Titles***

KINGS HALL, BELFAST During the early session the fight developed into a gruelling slugging fiesta, but later Gilroy began to right jab his way into a clear lead. After being floored three times, Rafferty was finally chopped down in the twelfth by a short right to the head

02.04.62 ***Henry Cooper, W RSC 9 Joe Erskine, British & British Empire Heavyweight Titles***

ICE RINK, NOTTINGHAM The plucky Welsh challenger was stopped on cuts in a contest that at one time seemed heading for an upset. Erskine boxed extremely well, whilst Cooper was only just beginning to find some kind of form before the unfortunate finish

07.04.62 ***Terry Downes, L PTS 15 Paul Pender (USA), World Middleweight Title***

THE GARDENS, BOSTON, USA Despite giving it everything that he had, Downes still came away minus his title. Pender negated all of the Englishman's attacks by clutching and using his left hand to score a narrow points victory. It would have been rather different if the referee had shown more control

10.04.62 ***Howard Winstone, W RSC 14 Derry Treanor, British Featherweight Title***

EMPIRE POOL, WEMBLEY Treanor forced the fight all the way, but could not land with clean punches and was stopped with a cut eye. The champion met his rushes with a steady stream of left jabs and uppercuts but lacked the stopping punch to be more decisive

30.05.62 ***Howard Winstone, W RTD 6 Harry Carroll, British Featherweight Title***

MAINDY STADIUM, CARDIFF With as brilliant an exhibition of left hand attacking as one would wish to see, Winstone scored a near faultless victory. His outclassed challenger was forced to retire after being punched from pillar to post, with his eye injuries worsening

04.06.62 ***Chic Calderwood, W PTS 15 Johnny Halafihi (Tonga), British Empire L. Heavyweight Title***

ST JAMES'S HALL, NEWCASTLE The pattern of the fight was set early on with Calderwood leading with fast lefts followed up by hard rights. Halafihi sustained bad eye damage, but was still in there fighting, even with the Scot coasting to a comfortable victory

17.06.62 ***Dick Richardson, L CO 8 Ingemar Johansson (Sweden), European Heavyweight Title***

ULLEVI STADIUM, GOTHENBURG, SWEDEN In a rather one-sided affair Johansson prodded the Welshman throughout with the left lead, looking to set him up for the right. The end came when a short right exploded on Richardson's chin, and after taking another right he was counted out

04.08.62 ***Dave Charnley, L PTS 15 Bunny Grant (Jamaica), British Empire Lightweight Title***

KINGSTON, JAMAICA There was little argument about the way Charnley lost his title. The young inexperienced local boy held the upper hand throughout and Charnley finished the contest with cuts over both eyes

28.09.62 ***Guilio Rinaldi (Italy), W PTS 15 Chic Calderwood, Vacant European L. Heavyweight Title***

PALAZZO DELLO SPORT, ROME, ITALY The Scot outboxed Rinaldi for the majority of the contest and appeared desperately unlucky not to have won. Calderwood had the Italian down in the first, but was unable to repeat the dose

20.10.62 ***Freddie Gilroy, W RTD 9 Johnny Caldwell, British & British Empire Bantamweight Titles***

KINGS HALL, BELFAST Gilroy retained his titles in a bruising contest, with the challenger having cuts over both eyes and eventually succumbing to some heavy left hand hitting. The champion had downed his rival earlier and although cut himself proved the stronger of the pair

17.06.62. Ingemar Johansson (right) gets smartly under Dick Richardson's straight left and looks set to throw his famed 'Ingo's Bingo'.

26.11.62 ***George Aldridge, W CO 6 John Cowboy McCormack, Vacant British Middleweight Title***

BELLE VUE, MANCHESTER Weight-making difficulties obviously hampered McCormack who winced almost every time Aldridge landed. The Market Harborough man had made the body his target by the sixth round and a right to the ribs, following two previous floorings, finished the bout

10.12.62 ***Jackie Brown, W PTS 15, Orizu Obilaso (Nigeria), Vacant British Empire Flyweight Title***

NATIONAL SPORTING CLUB, LONDON After being put down for a count of nine in the second, the British titleholder gave a masterly exhibition of jab and run. Obilaso was incapable of finding any solutions and was decisively outpointed in a one-sided contest

1963

31.01.63 ***Howard Winstone, W RSC 11 Johnny Morrissey, British Featherweight Title***

KELVIN HALL, GLASGOW Winstone, by virtue of classic left hand artistry and superb ringcraft, won practically every round prior to the closure. After taking three counts, two in the fatal eleventh, the referee decided Morrissey had shipped enough punishment

06.02.63 ***Laszlo Papp (Hungary), W RSC 15 George Aldridge, European Middleweight Title***

CITY HALL, VIENNA, AUSTRIA The Hungarian stopped Aldridge with only 36 seconds of the contest remaining when the British champion had just about come to the end of his tether, following two counts, one of them a standing four. Papp paced himself admirably, but the Englishman was right in the fight up to the eleventh round

12.02.63 ***Brian Curvis, W RSC 10 Tony Smith, British & British Empire Welterweight Titles***

ALBERT HALL, LONDON The referee intervened in the tenth round after Smith had been floored for the sixth time. He had resisted well until then, even having Curvis down in the second, before the Welshman discovered his vulnerable mid section with smashing left hooks

26.03.63 ***Henry Cooper, W CO 5 Dick Richardson, British & British Empire Heavyweight Titles***

EMPIRE POOL, WEMBLEY Cooper was cut right at the start, but showed the better boxing throughout whilst the Welshman was looking to rough it up. The end came following three left hooks to the

09.12.63. John O'Brien (left) looks in a mess as the brilliant Howard Winstone lets go with another burst of punching.

jaw, a body blow and then another brilliant left hook to the point

02.05.63 ***Jackie Brown, L CO 12 Walter McGowan, British & British Empire Flyweight Titles***

ICE RINK, PAISLEY From the fifth round onwards, it became apparent that the title would change hands, with McGowan getting on top. In the twelfth Brown was rocked with smashing lefts and rights to the head and was finished off by a left hook flush on the jaw

20.05.63 ***Dave Charnley, W PTS 15 Maurice Cullen, British Lightweight Title***

BELLE VUE, MANCHESTER The Dartford destroyer was given the run around by an opponent with tremendous speed of foot, but by his unflagging pursuit Charnley scored the greater number of points mainly at short range. Cullen was down in the thirteenth, although it counted as more of a slip than a punch

28.05.63 ***George Aldridge, L RSC 1 Mick Leahy, British Middleweight Title***

ICE RINK, NOTTINGHAM The fight was all over in one minute 45 seconds, when the referee stepped in to save Aldridge from further punishment. Leahy had floored the champion for five and was freely hitting him on the ropes at the finish

09.07.63 ***Alberto Serti (Italy), L RTD 14 Howard Winstone, European Featherweight Title***

MAINDY STADIUM, CARDIFF Producing a flawless display of left hand work Winstone forced the referee to come to the aid of the Italian, who had no real answer and was defenceless. If the Welshman had any semblance of a punch Serti would have been kayoed

30.07.63 ***Chic Calderwood, W RTD 11 Ron Redrup, British & British Empire L. Heavyweight Titles***

EMPRESS BALLROOM, BLACKPOOL Calderwood never appeared likely to lose this contest, but lacked the sparkle to drop the Londoner. In his vain but abortive attempt to wrest the titles, Redrup was finally pulled out suffering from a cut eye and swollen forehead

20.08.63 ***Howard Winstone, W PTS 15 Billy Calvert, British & European Featherweight Titles***

CONEY BEACH ARENA, PORTHCAWL In the most difficult defence of his titles the worried and bruised Welshman had to go fifteen rounds for the first time. Calvert brought into the fray a determination, relentless punching and an ability to work close to Winstone which produced a close and interesting contest

12.09.63 ***Walter McGowan, W RSC 9 Kid Solomon (Jamaica), British Empire Flyweight Title***
ICE RINK, PAISLEY McGowan won practically every round, but sustained a nasty gash under the left eye in the process. Putting on the pressure in the ninth McGowan opened up by dropping Solomon twice, who was then rescued by the referee

22.10.63 ***Gomeo Brennan (Bahamas), W PTS 15 Mick Leahy, Vacant British Empire Middleweight Title***
EMPIRE POOL, WEMBLEY Gomeo Brennan became the new champion when out-pointing the Irishman over fifteen hard, but uneventful rounds. It was the man from the Bahamas who took the eye in the closing rounds with his more methodical punching just about earning him the decision

09.12.63 ***Howard Winstone, W PTS 15 John O'Brien, British & European Featherweight Titles***
NATIONAL SPORTING CLUB, LONDON Both fighters threw a similar amount of leather, but whereas O'Brien hardly reached the target, the Welshman's fists unerringly found the challenger time and time again. This was the pattern of the whole fifteen rounds, proving once again Winstone was the master craftsman

1964

24.02.64 ***Henry Cooper, W PTS 15 Brian London, British, British Empire & Vacant European Heavyweight Titles***
BELLE VUE, MANCHESTER Cooper won this contest by the proverbial mile with his left hand again being the architect of victory. London on the other hand had to get to close quarters to achieve any form of success and took a fair amount of punishment in the process

05.03.64 ***Johnny Caldwell, W RSC 7 George Bowes, Vacant British & British Empire Bantamweight Titles***
ABC CINEMA, BELFAST Making the running from the off Caldwell handed out a lesson in boxing artistry, jabbing and hooking with brilliant combination punching. When he finally appeared to be getting into the fight, Bowes suffered cuts which brought proceedings to a halt

24.04.64 ***Salvatore Burruni (Italy), W PTS 15 Walter McGowan, European Flyweight Title***
PALAZZO DELLO SPORT, ROME, ITALY Although well beaten by the more experienced Italian, McGowan put up an excellent performance in a fast clean, sportsmanlike contest. Burruni pressed with fierce attacks, but could never completely dominate

12.05.64 ***Howard Winstone, W RTD 8 Lino Mastallaro (Italy), European Featherweight Title***
EMPIRE POOL, WEMBLEY Mastallaro was just not in Winstone's class and was on the receiving end of numerous rapier like jabs and solid body punches. Floored for seven in the fifth round he was later given a standing count before signalling that he wished to retire

28.07.64 ***Brian Curvis, W RTD 5 Johnny Cooke, British & British Empire Welterweight Titles***
CONEY BEACH ARENA, PORTHCAWL The veteran from Liverpool charged in square on whilst Curvis was able to counter punch to great effect. Cooke's face soon showed signs of battle and in a one-sided contest he pulled out summarily with a badly swollen left eye

22.09.64 ***Emile Griffith (USA), W PTS 15 Brian Curvis, World Welterweight Title***
EMPIRE POOL, WEMBLEY The gallant Welshman was always travelling second best going further behind as the bout progressed. Curvis was floored three times before bravely finishing the course, but Griffith, handing out a boxing lesson, further emphasised the class gap between the two contestants

09.10.64 ***Laszlo Papp (Hungary), W PTS 15 Mick Leahy, European Middleweight Title***
CITY HALL, VIENNA, AUSTRIA In a tough gruelling fight, the Hungarian did not have matters all his own way. Papp floored the challenger twice and was well on the way to victory, but Leahy put in a grandstand finish over the last third of the contest to run the champion close

11.11.64 ***Chic Calderwood, W RTD 7 Bob Nicolson, Vacant British L. Heavyweight Title***
ICE RINK, PAISLEY Up to the dramatic end, the Farnborough man had given a fairly good account of himself and there was not a great deal between them. Calderwood finally put it together with good right hands and floored Nicolson twice but the bell came to his rescue before he was retired

30.11.64 ***Willie Pastrano (USA), W RSC 11 Terry Downes, World L. Heavyweight Title***
BELLE VUE, MANCHESTER A most dramatic finish saw Pastrano holding on to his title, after Downes had battered and mauled him incessantly throughout, with the end seemingly in sight. Suddenly the American produced an attack in the eleventh which had the challenger down twice, whereupon the referee stopped the contest

14.12.64 ***Mick Leahy, L PTS 15 Wally Swift, British Middleweight Title***
ICE RINK, NOTTINGHAM Never ruffled by the

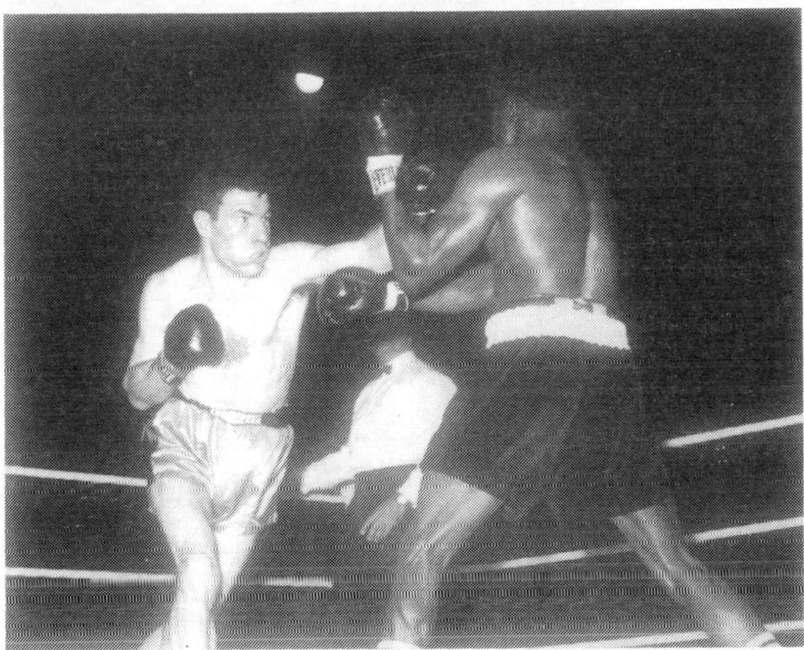

22.09.64. The gallant Brian Curvis (left) throws a powerful left which gets through Emile Griffith's defence.

agressive champion, Swift's ringcraft was always superior and he used both hands in punishing fashion. Leahy was rocked throughout with heavy punches and was outboxed convincingly

1965

22.01.65 ***Howard Winstone, W PTS 15 Yves Desmarets (France), European Featherweight Title***
PALAZZO DELLO SPORT, ROME, ITALY Winstone rarely had to elevate the contest beyond exhibition pace as he jabbed and hooked in clusters without return. The challenger for his part was content to back-pedal just to go the distance

22.03.65 ***Johnny Caldwell, L RSC 10 Alan Rudkin, British & British Empire Bantamweight Titles***
ICE RINK, NOTTINGHAM From the third round Rudkin began to forge ahead, with the Irishman gradually becoming more exhausted. The end saw Caldwell in distress and sustaining facial damage before being pulled out by the third man

08.04.65 ***Maurice Cullen, W PTS 15 Dave Coventry, Vacant British Lightweight Title***
THE STADIUM, LIVERPOOL Over fifteen gripping rounds Cullen boxed coolly and confidently, using his immaculate piston-like left to great effect. Coventry chased hard with aggression in abundance, but could never get the contest going his way

15.06.65 ***Henry Cooper, W RTD 10 Johnny Prescott, British & British Empire Heavyweight Titles***
ST ANDREWS, BIRMINGHAM The game Prescott was retired at the end of the tenth after being floored three times and out of his depth, but he never stopped trying. Cooper hardly put a foot wrong and was streets ahead when the contest was concluded

07.09.65 ***Vicente Saldivar (Mexico), W PTS 15 Howard Winstone, World Featherweight Title***
EARLS COURT, LONDON Many thought that Winstone would try to outbox the champion, but instead he elected to fight. This proved his undoing when he tired in the latter stages and Saldivar, who had pressured throughout, got on top to take the decision after a blistering battle

03.12.65. Walter McGowan (left) appears to be on the receiving end of Tommaso Galli's right as he lets go with his own two-handed attack.

08.11.65 ***Wally Swift, L RSC 12 Johnny Pritchett, British Middleweight Title***
ICE RINK, NOTTINGHAM The end came with Swift labouring under the severe handicap of a badly cut left eye and the challenger making it his target. Prior to the finish Pritchett was probably just ahead in a closely fought contest

25.11.65 ***Brian Curvis, W RSC 12 Sammy McSpadden, British & British Empire Welterweight Titles***
SOPHIA GARDENS, CARDIFF Curvis floored McSpadden in the first and outclassed him from thereon, but was unable to produce a finishing blow. The Scot came forward hooking continuously only to be met by well placed counters, and when his strength began to wane he became an open target

30.11.65 ***Maurice Cullen, W PTS 15 Vic Andreetti, British Lightweight Title***
CIVIC HALL, WOLVERHAMPTON In one of the finest boxer versus fighter combinations seen for many a day, Cullen comfortably retained his title. The champion set the pattern early on with the stabbing left hand leads going to work, whilst Andreetti was always looking to work inside

30.11.65 ***Fighting Harada (Japan), W PTS 15 Alan Rudkin, World Bantamweight Title***
BUDOKAN HALL, TOKYO, JAPAN A great performance by the British champion, who just failed in his attempt to wrest the title when losing by a close margin. Harada had Rudkin down in the first round but thereafter never looked likely to repeat the trick, with both boxers showing grim determination to stay the course

03.12.65 ***Tommaso Galli (Italy), DREW 15 Walter McGowan, European Bantamweight Title***
PALAZZO DELLO SPORT, ROME, ITALY With McGowan mainly on the offensive the decision seemed inexplicable and even the locals pelted the ring with refuse. The Scot not only forced the contest but landed the better scoring blows as well as bamboozling Galli at times with his skill

1966

07.03.66 ***Howard Winstone, W RSC 15 Andrea Silanos (Italy), European Featherweight Title***
TERDI THEATRE, SASSARI, ITALY The Sardinian was put on the canvas in the last round and when he got up the referee stopped the fight. Winstone had been in control from the beginning never giving Silanos any openings, and when the home fighter was badly cut his became a lost cause

21.03.66 ***Johnny Pritchett, W RTD 13 Nat Jacobs, British Middleweight Title***
ICE RINK, NOTTINGHAM Pritchett took control from the fifth onwards, but the game challenger was always dangerous until wilting under incessant punishment. By the thirteenth Jacobs was glad to hear the bell as he reeled under heavy head punches and the corner wisely retired him

25.04.66 ***Jean Josselin (France), W RTD 13 Brian Curvis, Vacant European Welterweight Title***
PALAIS DES SPORTS, PARIS, FRANCE From the fifth round Curvis visibly tired whilst the Frenchman bored in relentlessly. It was apparent that the British champion had no answer to the constant onslaught, being forced to back-pedal for long periods and it came as no surprise when he failed to come out for the fourteenth

21.05.66 ***Muhammad Ali (USA), W RSC 6 Henry Cooper, World Heavyweight Title (WBC version)***
HIGHBURY STADIUM, LONDON Until the fatal sixth, Cooper appeared to be just in front, but became transformed into a fighting tornado when Ali had delivered a sweeping right which cut the Britisher badly. He forced the American to retreat, but Ali fired in punches like tracers, and the referee stepped in quickly

06.06.66 ***Maurice Cullen, W RSC 5 Terry Edwards, British Lightweight Title***
ST JAMES'S HALL, NEWCASTLE By dint of terrific speed and left hand work Cullen moved way out in front. The champion then put Edwards down for two long counts and with the Brummie never looking likely to recover, the third man stepped in

14.06.66 ***Salvatore Burruni (Italy), L PTS 15 Walter McGowan, World Flyweight Title (WBC version)***
EMPIRE POOL, WEMBLEY After fifteen hard rounds, there could only be one winner – McGowan, who had boxed like a little master. Using his speed, jabbing in clusters and banging the right home, he left Burruni chasing shadows all night. The Italian's only opportunity came when the Scot sustained a badly cut eye

06.08.66 ***Muhammad Ali (USA), W CO 3 Brian London, World Heavyweight Title (WBC version)***
EARLS COURT, LONDON London allowed the American totally to dominate proceedings whilst in the main covering up. The third round saw Ali going to work and finishing the job with a short

21.05.66. Henry Cooper, with his face a bloody mess, is on the verge of being stopped by the ubiquitous Muhammad Ali.

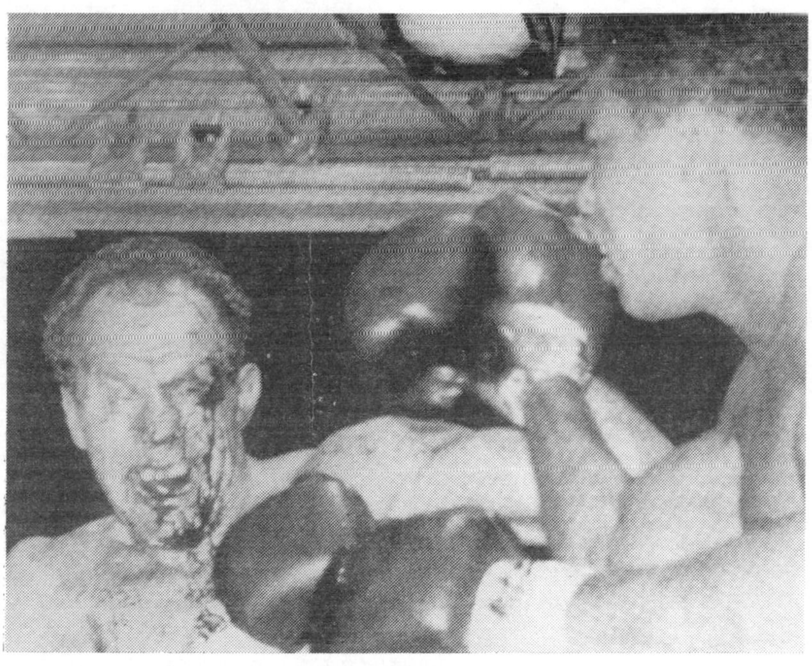

right followed by a steady stream of punches, until London collapsed on the canvas to be counted out

17.08.66 ***Piero Del Papa (Italy), NC 6 Chic Calderwood, European L. Heavyweight Title***
LIGNANO, ITALY The contest was stopped by torrential rain which made the ring too slippery. Until the closure it had been fairly even, although both fighters sustained badly cut eyes in the process

06.09.66 ***Alan Rudkin, L PTS 15 Walter McGowan, British & British Empire Bantamweight Titles***
EMPIRE POOL, WEMBLEY What a pity that there had to be a loser in this great contest. In the early rounds Rudkin set a fast pace, but over the last half of the battle the challenger, now boxing brilliantly, began to claw back the deficit. It was desperately close at the finish

06.09.66 ***Howard Winstone, W RSC 3 Jean de Keers (Belgium), European Featherweight Title***
EMPIRE POOL, WEMBLEY Winstone was just getting into his stride when the Belgium sustained a badly cut eye and the bout was terminated. De Keers had no earthly hope of outboxing the Welshman and was beginning to ship a lot of left leads

15.10.66 ***Jose Torres (USA), W CO 2 Chic Calderwood, World L. Heavyweight Title***
BITHORN STADIUM, SAN JUAN, PUERTO RICA Following a quiet opening round, Torres surprised in the second when he caught Calderwood with a tremendous right cross to the jaw which laid the Scot out cold

07.12.66 ***Howard Winstone, W RSC 8 Lennie Williams, British & European Featherweight Titles***
WYVERN SPORTING CLUB, ABERAVON Winstone outclassed his opponent with brilliant boxing which nullified all the attacks that were mustered. The champion got off to a fast start and the fight ended summarily when Williams was tottering around the ring unsteadily

30.12.66 ***Walter McGowan, L RSC 9 Chartchai Chionoi (Thailand), World Flyweight Title (WBC version)***
KITTIKACHORN STADIUM, BANGKOK, THAILAND An accidental head butt in the second round eventually cost McGowan his title in a hard contest. Neither fighter was ever in complete control, but Chionoi appeared to hit harder and with the Scot bleeding profusely the referee stopped the fight

1967

16.01.67 ***John McCluskey, W CO 8 Tony Barlow, Vacant British Flyweight Title***
FREE TRADE HALL, MANCHESTER In a thrill-a-minute battle the little Scot displayed great ringcraft. Barlow was down in the sixth and two rounds later McCluskey got him on the ropes with a short right to the point terminating the bout

03.02.67 ***Floyd Robertson (Ghana), L RTD 12 John O'Brien, British Empire Featherweight Title***
ACCRA, GHANA Floyd Robertson surrendered the title on his stool after being beaten all the way. O'Brien pressured from the off and it became obvious that the champion's weight-reducing had weakened him considerably

13.02.67 ***Johnny Cooke, W PTS 15 Brian McCaffrey, Vacant British Welterweight Title***
BELLE VUE, MANCHESTER A truly magnificent contest was decided by just a quarter of a point with both fighters finishing battered and bruised. Cooke, although down in the thirteenth, weathered the storm with clever boxing which negated McCaffrey's aggression

20.02.67 ***Johnny Pritchett, W PTS 15 Wally Swift, British Middleweight Title***
ICE RINK, NOTTINGHAM In one of the finest contests one could wish to see, neither boxer gave nor expected any quarter. There were furious exchanges with plenty of action and the fight swung precariously in the balance, but the referee had no hesitation in raising Pritchett's hand at the closure

21.03.67 ***Karl Mildenberger (W. Germany), W RSC 8 Billy Walker, European Heavyweight Title***
EMPIRE POOL, WEMBLEY Mildenberger was never in real danger against the belligerent brave Billy Walker and early on decided to back up and allow the blond bomber to come forward. This policy reaped dividends as the Englishman was badly cut up, took a standing count and was ultimately rescued by the referee

25.04.67 ***Maurice Cullen, W PTS 15 Vic Andreetti, British Lightweight Title***
ST JAMES'S HALL, NEWCASTLE Cullen produced a slick left hand display and countless times rocked the challenger's head back when building up an unassailable lead. Despite a badly cut left eye, which was damaged in the third, the champion's adroit footwork kept him out of trouble

27.04.67 ***Mimoun Ben Ali (Spain), W PTS 15 Alan Rudkin, European Bantamweight Title***
BARCELONA, SPAIN The superior speed and mobility of Rudkin was gradually worn down by

the Spaniard's experience and harder punching ability. After a fast start when he looked to make short work of Ali the Liverpudlian faded towards the end

09.05.67 ***Johnny Cooke, W PTS 15 Shaun Doyle, British Welterweight Title***

THE STADIUM, LIVERPOOL Doyle gave a fearless and courageous do-or-die effort against the stylish champion right up to the final bell. Pacing the fight well, Cooke clearly outwitted the tough challenger and was good value with his correct hitting

13.06.67 ***Henry Cooper, W RSC 2 Jack Bodell, British & British Empire Heavyweight Titles***

MOLINEUX GROUNDS, WOLVERHAMPTON A clinical annihilation was completed when Cooper trapped the challenger on the ropes pounding him with the famous left hook. Finally Bodell broke free but was punched across the ring and was draped over the bottom rope

15.06.67 ***Vicente Saldivar (Mexico), W PTS 15 Howard Winstone, World Featherweight Title***

NINIAN PARK, CARDIFF The Welshman carried the fight to Saldivar right up to the halfway stage. Still boxing superbly Winstone began to tire and the bull-like Mexican powered forward, downing him in the fourteenth. Fighting like a tornado Saldivar just about finished in front after a wonderfully close contest

19.06.67 ***Young John McCormack, W RSC 7 Eddie Avoth, Vacant British L. Heavyweight Title***

NATIONAL SPORTING CLUB, LONDON At the time of the stoppage the Irishman was well behind on points, after starting quite well. Avoth then began to exhibit a fine uppercut coupled with good jabbing and it was a great disappointment when he collected a badly cut left eye, which ended the contest summarily

16.08.67 ***Carmelo Bossi (Italy), W RSC 12 Johnny Cooke, European Welterweight Title***

SAN REMO, ITALY All the British champion had to offer was a big heart and stacks of courage in an abortive attempt to wrest the crown. Bossi was able to land with a wide variety of punches, bemusing Cooke completely at times, but the Liverpudlian stuck to his task manfully

19.09.67. Walter McGowan (right), bleeding profusely from face wounds, makes a desperate effort to nail Chartchai Chionoi.

09.09.67 ***Sandro Mazzinghi (Italy), W RTD 6 Wally Swift, European L. Middleweight Title***

MILAN, ITALY Until the stoppage Swift looked good when fighting inside to nullify the Italian's longer reach. Unfortunately during one of the exchanges the Nottingham man's eye gushed blood after colliding with Mazzinghi's head and the referee signalled the end immediately

19.09.67 ***Chartchai Chionoi (Thailand), W RSC 7 Walter McGowan, World Flyweight Title (WBC version)***

EMPIRE POOL, WEMBLEY McGowan got off to a great start with top drawer boxing. As the bout progressed he collected bad cuts but was smashing Chionoi all over the ring for a couple of rounds, until the referee decided to halt the proceedings

09.10.67 ***Milo Calhoun (Jamaica), L RTD 8 Johnny Pritchett, British Empire Middleweight Title***

BELLE VUE, MANCHESTER Punching with great power, Pritchett was the complete master. Bruised severely around the face, Calhoun sustained a badly lacerated nose in the eighth and was retired upon reaching his corner

14.10.67 ***Vicente Saldivar (Mexico), W RTD 12 Howard Winstone, World Featherweight Title***

MEXICO CITY Saldivar was held at bay by effective jabbing for eleven rounds, but in the twelfth an obviously tiring Winstone was put down for a long count. He was then battered from pillar to post, receiving damage to both eyes before the towel was thrown in

16.10.67 ***Johnny Cooke, W PTS 15 Lennox Beckles (Guyana), Vacant British Empire Welterweight Title***

THE STADIUM, LIVERPOOL It was Beckles who provided all the class in what proved to be a great disappointment. Cooke was the aggressor throughout, but the majority of his work was negated by the Guyanan who appeared desperately unlucky to lose

07.11.67 ***Henry Cooper, W RSC 6 Billy Walker, British & British Empire Heavyweight Titles***

EMPIRE POOL, WEMBLEY The West Ham 'bomber' was stopped due to a bad cut at the side of the right eye. Although neither fighter had been on the deck, Cooper jabbed and moved effectively whereas Walker did not land many telling punches

22.11.67 ***Young John McCormack, W CO 7 Derek Richards, British L. Heavyweight Title***

MIDLAND SPORTING CLUB, SOLIHULL The long spell of inactivity caught up with Richards, whose challenge was brushed aside with consummate ease by the Irishman. Two heavy jaw punches completed the task with the challenger draped across the bottom rope, too dazed to beat the count

24.11.67 ***John O'Brien, L RSC 11 Johnny Famechon (Australia), British Empire Featherweight Title***

THE STADIUM, MELBOURNE, AUSTRALIA There was nothing to chose between the two fighters until Famechon cut loose, inflicting heavy facial damage. At the end of the round the referee decided O'Brien was too badly cut to continue and stopped the bout

1968

23.01.68 ***Howard Winstone, W RSC 9 Mitsunori Seki (Japan), Vacant World Featherweight Title (EBU/GB version)***

ALBERT HALL, LONDON After a rather lackadaisical start Winstone began to get into gear with his better boxing, when the bout was suddenly halted on Seki sustaining a cut eye. The finish appeared to be rather premature, but the stocky Jap was beginning to be opened up

12.02.68 ***Bob Dunlop (Australia), W RSC 7 Young John McCormack, Vacant British Empire L. Heavyweight Title***

THE STADIUM, SYDNEY, AUSTRALIA In a bruising battle McCormack went behind as Dunlop found the range for his heavier punches. The fight was stopped in the seventh with the Irishman against the ropes helpless under a tremendous barrage of leather

19.02.68 ***Maurice Cullen, L CO 11 Ken Buchanan, British Lightweight Title***

ANGLO AMERICAN SPORTING CLUB, LONDON Cullen was forced to come out fighting as the challenger got through with his clever box-fighting tactics. The Geordie was eventually made to pay dearly and Buchanan put him down five times, including the full count

20.02.68 ***Johnny Cooke, L PTS 15 Ralph Charles, British & British Empire Welterweight Titles***

ALBERT HALL, LONDON The young East Londoner was full of enterprise from the first round and attacked the ring-wise champion with both fists. A hard contest saw Charles holding on to his earlier lead as Cooke battled away with great urgency in a late bid to retain his titles

20.02.68 ***Jimmy Anderson, W RSC 9 Jimmy Revie, Vacant British J. Lightweight Title***

ALBERT HALL, LONDON This hard-hitting affair saw both men scorning defence in an effort to land the decisive punch. Anderson was put down in the seventh, but came back to floor Revie twice

23.01.68. *Howard Winstone (left) moves inside the right hand of Mitsunori Seki in an effort to land solidly.*

in a dramatic ninth round before the referee stepped in

26.02.68 ***Johnny Pritchett, W PTS 15 Les McAteer, British & British Empire Middleweight Titles***
ICE RINK, NOTTINGHAM McAteer, in trying to emulate his uncle Pat, gave the champion the fight of his life, with his ability to take good punches and use penetrating left leads. Pritchett, with heavy body attacks, just proved too strong for his game challenger over the distance

27.02.68 ***Des Rea, W PTS 15 Vic Andreetti, Vacant British J. Welterweight Title***
YORK HALL, LONDON In a cracking contest both men fought toe to toe with Rea gaining the very close decision. Andreetti had started throwing plenty of leather but the Irishman never backed off, biding his time and coming strongly over the last few rounds

26.03.68 ***Carlos Duran (Italy), W DIS 10 Wally Swift, European Middleweight Title***
EMBASSY SPORTSDROME, BIRMINGHAM Wally Swift lost this contest apparently for misuse of the head with no prior warnings given. The Italian was fairly negative and the Nottingham boy seemed to be just out in front with Duran's eye bleeding badly when the end came

13.05.68 ***Walter McGowan, L PTS 15 Alan Rudkin, British & British Empire Bantamweight Titles***
BELLE VUE, MANCHESTER Rudkin decided to dictate matters early by setting a fast pace and not allowing the Scot any freedom. Both fighters finished badly cut, with McGowan fighting furiously in a vain bid to retain his titles

26.06.68 ***Fernando Atzori (Italy), W CO 4 John McCluskey, European Flyweight Title***
PALAZZETTO DELLO SPORT, NAPLES, ITALY The British champion appeared suspect to fast counter-attacks with his defence often being pierced. Atzori put McCluskey down in the second and again in the fourth when the referee carried on counting with the Scot upright after rising from a heavy right to the jaw

24.07.68 ***Howard Winstone, L RSC 5 Jose Legra (Cuba), World Featherweight Title (WBC version)***
CONEY BEACH ARENA, PORTHCAWL With the fight only seconds old Winstone was caught cold by a bolo punch which put him down and closed his eye. Moments later he was floored again and it became one way traffic until the fifth when Legra's dominance finally forced the referee to act

21.08.68 ***Bruno Arcari (Italy), W RSC 6 Des Rea, European L. Welterweight Title***
SAN REMO, ITALY The champion demolished his rival flooring him twice in the sixth round with right handers and forcing the referee to intervene. Arcari was much faster than Rea and landed at will throughout, although the game challenger fought back well at times

18.09.68 ***Karl Mildenberger (W. Germany), L DIS 8 Henry Cooper, European Heavyweight Title***
EMPIRE POOL, WEMBLEY Having put the German down, Cooper was way out in front, when following several warnings Mildenberger was disqualified. Coming out of a clinch it was apparent that the Englishman was too badly cut to continue and the referee deemed the damage to have been caused by a butt

08.10.68 ***Jimmy Anderson, W PTS 15 Brian Cartwright, British J. Lightweight Title***
ALBERT HALL, LONDON The clever Brummie held up Anderson with defensive boxing of a high quality, but the champion earned the close verdict by sheer aggression. Both men were badly marked at the finish, with Cartwright proving his mettle

1969

13.01.69 ***Young John McCormack, L RTD 11 Eddie Avoth, British L. Heavyweight Title***
WORLD SPORTING CLUB, LONDON The Welshman came more into the fight after the fifth round, and was beginning to make up McCormack's early lead. The champion's whirlwind tactics slowed appreciably and when he sustained a badly cut eye the contest was terminated by the corner

17.02.69 ***Des Rea, L PTS 15 Vic Andreetti, British J. Welterweight Title***
ICE RINK, NOTTINGHAM Andreetti proved a worthy winner with his ability to pace himself over the distance. Rea had taken command early on, but the Hoxton boy came back strongly from the eleventh round to win this all-action fiercely contested battle

20.02.69 ***Carlos Duran (Italy), W DIS 13 Johnny Pritchett, European Middleweight Title***
PALAZZO DELLO SPORT, ROME, ITALY In one of the most amazing scenes ever witnessed in a boxing ring the Italian's title was saved by an act of providence. Pritchett had forced the fight all

08.03.69. Alan Rudkin (right) adroitly moves inside the left hand of Lionel Rose to set up his own attack.

the way, but in the thirteenth, with Duran cut up and well beaten, the referee disqualified the Englishman for an alleged butt

25.02.69 ***Jimmy Anderson, W RSC 7 Colin Lake, British J. Lightweight Title***
ALBERT HALL, LONDON The challenger was brushed aside by the heavy hitting Anderson and although fighting a defensive rearguard action was never able to match the titleholder's power. Lake was put down twice and was being punished freely with only a timely intervention saving him from a count out

08.03.69 ***Lionel Rose (Australia), W PTS 15 Alan Rudkin, World Bantamweight Title (Rudkin defended British Empire Bantamweight Title)***
KOOYONG STADIUM, MELBOURNE, AUSTRALIA Rudkin began to get right back into contention following eye damage during the middle rounds. After an extremely closely fought affair the Aborigine held on to win a hotly disputed decision

13.03.69 ***Henry Cooper, W CO 5 Piero Tomasoni (Italy), European Heavyweight Title***
PALAZZO DELLO SPORT, ROME, ITALY Urged on by the crowd, Tomasoni put Cooper down twice from dubious groin punches after being floored himself in the opening round. Fuming with anger, Cooper, stepped in with a terrific left hook which sunk the local without trace

24.03.69 ***Jimmy Revie, W RSC 5 John O'Brien, Vacant British Featherweight Title***
WORLD SPORTING CLUB, LONDON The fourth round was the turning point when the Londoner closed O'Brien's left eye and hit him with some heavy shots on the blind side. Revie appeared in full ascendancy and damage to the Scot's other eye bought the contest abruptly to a halt

07.05.69 ***John McCluskey, W RSC 13 Tony Barlow, British Flyweight Title***
MIDLAND SPORTING CLUB, SOLIHULL Barlow never stopped trying to attack, but in the main he was on the receiving end. The weary challenger was hit with heavy combination punches in the thirteenth and was rescued by the referee after he had risen from a count of eight

09.06.69 ***Alan Rudkin, W RTD 11 Evan Armstrong, British Bantamweight Title***
BELLE VUE, MANCHESTER Rudkin gave a masterly display when winning by the proverbial mile over his game challenger. Armstrong had no answer to the brilliant box-fighting Liverpudlian and was retired bleeding badly from facial injuries

28.06.69 ***Yvan Prebeg (Yugoslavia), W PTS 15 Eddie Avoth, Vacant European L. Heavyweight Title***
SALATA STADIUM, ZAGREB, YUGOSLAVIA In a hard fought battle the more experienced Prebeg came through. Avoth's strength and resistance staved off any possible knockdowns and the Welshman cut Prebeg's left eye, but mainly the contest was decided at distance with the Yugoslav claiming superiority

14.07.69 ***Les McAteer, W RTD 11 Wally Swift, Vacant British & British Empire Middleweight Titles***
ICE RINK, NOTTINGHAM Despite a great fighting stand by the ex-champion, McAteer bided his time with quality punches and eventually cut up Swift so badly that the corner retired him. In the third round a crunching left-right floored the veteran but he fought back well

13.10.69 ***Jack Bodell, W PTS 15 Carl Gizzi, Vacant British Heavyweight Title***
ICE RINK, NOTTINGHAM In a contest that lacked skill, endevour was certainly not missing and although neither boxer really punched his weight there were plenty of thrills. Bodell became the new champion by a mere point following a bruising battle

13.10.69 ***Vic Andreetti, W CO 4 Des Rea, British J. Welterweight Title***
ICE RINK, NOTTINGHAM This time, Andreetti was clearly the master from the start, with the challenger only a shadow of his former self. Rea was downed for nine in the fourth and on rising was floored again by a short right for the full count

11.11.69 ***Ralph Charles, W CO 5 Chuck Henderson, British & British Empire Welterweight Titles***
ALBERT HALL, LONDON The outclassed challenger was caught up in a whirlwind from the second round after Charles had been badly cut on the right eye. The champion hurled himself at Henderson who somehow stayed on his feet until finally crashing over for the full count in round five

12.12.69 ***Ruben Olivares (Mexico), W RSC 2 Alan Rudkin, World Bantamweight Title***
INGLEWOOD FORUM, LOS ANGELES, USA In a brief but savage encounter, Rudkin was floored four times before the referee terminated the contest. Olivares, a pocket battleship of a fighter, took the challenger's best blows and came right back with murderous punches which finally crushed his opponent

1970

29.01.70 ***Miguel Velazquez (Spain), W PTS 15 Ken Buchanan, Vacant European Lightweight Title***
MADRID, SPAIN A below-form Buchanan got caught by punches he would normally have

12.05.70. The end is near for Brian Hudson as he tries to get up after being felled by Ken Buchanan in the fifth.

avoided and took a count in the ninth. Velazquez did most of the forcing whilst the Scot favoured a stabbing left hand, but did not work hard enough to warrant the decision

24.03.70 ***Jack Bodell, L PTS 15 Henry Cooper, British Heavyweight Title (Cooper defended Commonwealth Heavyweight Title)***

EMPIRE POOL, WEMBLEY Down three times, brave Bodell defied all Cooper's attempts to knock him out, finishing in some distress with damage around both eyes. Cooper won by a wide margin of points against his outclassed rival

02.04.70 ***Tom Bogs (Denmark), W RSC 11 Les McAteer, European Middleweight Title***

VEJLBY, RISSKOVHALLEN, AARHUS, DENMARK McAteer was dropped three times from the Dane's lightning fast left-right combinations and was eventually stopped on rubbery legs following a standing count. Bogs outboxed and out thought the British champion throughout but the Liverpudlian displayed great courage

04.04.70 ***Franco Zurlo (Italy), W PTS 15 John McCluskey, European Bantamweight Title***

HALLENSTADION, ZURICH, SWITZERLAND The Italian controlled the early part of the fight and was never in any difficulty. The contest later developed into a fierce punching affair and Zurlo won quite handsomely even though he sustained a partially closed right eye

06.04.70 ***Eddie Avoth, W DIS 8 Young John McCormack, British L. Heavyweight Title***

ICE RINK, NOTTINGHAM A most unsatisfactory ending saw McCormack tossed out of the ring for illegal use of the head after previous warnings. Avoth had set out to dominate with straight punches, but the challenger bored in continuously, which eventually led to his dismissal

21.04.70 ***Alan Rudkin, W RSC 12 Johnny Clark, British & Vacant Commonwealth Bantamweight Titles***

ALBERT HALL, LONDON Over the first half of the contest, fought at breakneck speed, Rudkin had to give ground. By the eighth round it was a weary challenger who somehow stumbled through four more rounds with only his great fighting spirit left, before the referee rightly rescued him

12.05.70 ***Les McAteer, L RSC 14 Mark Rowe, British & Commonwealth Middleweight Titles***

EMPIRE POOL, WEMBLEY A drama packed battle saw McAteer countering superbly and the challenger chasing non-stop. It was not until the fourteenth round that Rowe finally got on top, with the tired McAteer being smashed to the floor three times before the referee saved him from further punishment

12.05.70 ***Ken Buchanan, W CO 5 Brian Hudson, British Lightweight Title***

EMPIRE POOL, WEMBLEY A sensational start saw Buchanan put his challenger on the floor in the first round, but Hudson got up to fight on bravely, always trying to go forward. Launching an all-out attack in the fifth the champion torpedoed in a perfect right to the jaw which poleaxed his game rival for the full count

16.06.70 ***John McCluskey, W PTS 15 Harry Hayes (Australia), Vacant Commonwealth Flyweight Title***

CHEVRON HOTEL, MELBOURNE, AUSTRALIA McCluskey won all the way over an opponent who only fought spasmodically. The Scot was the aggressor throughout and both fighters were suffering from cuts at the finish

27.08.70 ***Tom Bogs (Denmark), W PTS 15 Chris Finnegan, European Middleweight Title***

COPENHAGEN, DENMARK In a desperately close fight Bogs only began to take control when Finnegan's eye was gashed in the thirteenth. Until then the inexperienced ex-Olympic champion had jabbed and countered effectively whilst proving his strength at close quarters

08.09.70 ***Mark Rowe, L RSC 4 Bunny Sterling, British & Commonwealth Middleweight Titles***

EMPIRE POOL, WEMBLEY Sterling became the first immigrant to win a British title under the 10-year residential rule. Rowe did all the attacking, but picked up serious cuts around both eyes and desperately attacked the Jamaican in an effort to end it summarily before the referee had to call a halt

08.09.70 ***Jimmy Revie, W PTS 15 Alan Rudkin, British Featherweight Title***

EMPIRE POOL, WEMBLEY Revie peppered his outreached challenger with southpaw jabs throughout and dominated the early exchanges but Rudkin came on strong in the last third to make it close

26.09.70 ***Ismael Laguna (Panama), L PTS 15 Ken Buchanan, World Lightweight Title (WBA version)***

HIRAM BITHORN STADIUM, SAN JUAN, PUERTO RICA A split decision enabled Buchanan to gain a superb victory despite being badly marked. The Scot opened fast and then finished strongly with crisp punching, but it was his counter to the jab which earned the points over the classy Laguna

23.10.70 ***Eddie Avoth, W RTD 6 Trevor Thornbury (Australia), Vacant Commonwealth L. Heavyweight Title***

FESTIVAL HALL, BRISBANE, AUSTRALIA The fight was halted when Thornbury could not continue owing to an inch-long gash over the left eye, but Avoth appeared well ahead at the closure. The injury was caused by a stinging right hook in the third round

10.11.70 ***Jose Urtain (Spain), L RSC 9 Henry Cooper, European Heavyweight Title***

EMPIRE POOL, WEMBLEY Although hitting Urtain with some solid left hooks, Cooper never looked likely to floor the Spaniard. Cooper won the fight by using the trusted left jab, which turned the champion's face into a bloody mess, leaving the referee no alternative but to stop the contest in the ninth

13.11.70 ***Bunny Sterling, W PTS 15 Kahu Mahanga (N. Zealand), Commonwealth Middleweight Title***

THE STADIUM, MELBOURNE, AUSTRALIA The London-based Jamaican gave an excellent display of ringcraft to beat Mahanga, who was willing enough, but lacked all-round skill. Sterling jabbed accurately, moved well and worked to the body with a variety of punches, all of which were effective

20.11.70 ***Johann Orsolics (Austria), L CO 12 Ralph Charles, European Welterweight Title***

STADHALLE, VIENNA, AUSTRIA An extremely tough championship battle produced plenty of heavy artillery throughout and both men sustained nasty eye wounds. In round twelve Orsolics complained of a foul blow, dropped his hands, and Charles put him down for the full count

1971

21.01.71 ***Bunny Sterling, DREW 15 Tony Mundine (Australia), Commonwealth Middleweight Title***

WHITE CITY STADIUM, SYDNEY, AUSTRALIA Sterling built up a good lead in the early rounds and although fading temporarily came back strongly during the closing stages. Mundine, who was cut early on, often landed heavy punches, but the champion was able to back off avoiding any further trouble

24.01.71 ***Eddie Avoth, L RSC 15 Chris Finnegan, British & Commonwealth L. Heavyweight Titles***

WORLD SPORTING CLUB, LONDON Finnegan took command from the off, was quicker to the punch and was able to absorb the Welshman's best blows. Both men showed great courage with the end coming in the final round when Avoth, reeling under a battery of punches, was rescued by the referee

25.01.71 ***Jose Legra (Spain), W PTS 15 Jimmy Revie, European Featherweight Title***
ANGLO AMERICAN SPORTING CLUB, LONDON The Cuban exile gave the British champion a painful boxing lesson and decked him twice into the bargain. Revie for his part was occasionally able to get through with good punches, although often being made to pay for his temerity

12.02.71 ***Ken Buchanan, W PTS 15 Ruben Navarro (Mexico), World Lightweight Title***
OLYMPIC AUDITORIUM, LOS ANGELES, USA By the tenth Buchanan had assumed full control with his speed being generally too much for the game challenger. Prior to the tenth Navarro had given a good account before being handed out an artistic points beating

16.02.71 ***Franco Zurlo (Italy), L RTD 11 Alan Rudkin, European Bantamweight Title***
ALBERT HALL, LONDON Rudkin, with solid carefully picked blows, gradually wore down the Italian, whose main weapon was a long sweeping punch. Both men suffered from facial damage, but at the end of the eleventh, with the challenger in complete control, Zurlo retired on his stool

16.03.71 ***Henry Cooper, L PTS 15 Joe Bugner, British, Commonwealth & European Heavyweight Titles***
EMPIRE POOL, WEMBLEY Henry Cooper announced his retirement after controversially losing his titles by a narrow decision, after an unexciting contest. Bugner for all his caution had shown a good left early on and in finishing strongly emphasised his physical advantages, whereas Cooper's punches appeared to lack their old spark

19.03.71 ***Fernando Atzori (Italy), W PTS 15 John McCluskey, European Flyweight Title***
HALLENSTADION, ZURICH, SWITZERLAND McCluskey, although not hitting as hard as the Italian, landed more often in a thrilling contest and appeared to have won. Atzori was always looking to knock the Scot out and succeeded in putting him down for a count, but could not keep him on the deck

22.03.71 ***Bunny Sterling, W PTS 15 Johann Louw (Canada), Commonwealth Middleweight Title***
EDMONTON, CANADA The champion unanimously outpointed Louw and although not looking too good earlier on, he produced a storming finish to win well. There were no knockdowns, and both fighters suffered facial damage with Sterling absorbing the hard-hitting Canadian's punches well

05.05.71 ***Conny Velensek (W. Germany), DREW 15 Chris Finnegan, European L. Heavyweight Title***
DEUTSCHANDHALLE, BERLIN, W. GERMANY Velensek rumbled forward like a tank, but the challenger began to counter well and by the eleventh the German was a beaten man. Finnegan unfortunately lacked a stopping punch, but was still smashing away at his defenceless opponent for round after round only to be amazed by the diabolical decision rendered

11.05.71 ***Joe Bugner, W PTS 15 Jurgen Blin (W. Germany), European Heavyweight Title***
EMPIRE POOL, WEMBLEY Despite winning, Bugner failed to dominate a far smaller man and although his punches were the more correct, Blin's sheer quantity nearly made it. Bugner boxed apathetically and it was just as well the German did not possess a stopping punch

04.06.71 ***Ralph Charles, L CO 7 Roger Menetrey (France), European Welterweight Title***
ICE STADIUM, GENEVA, SWITZERLAND Charles dominated his game opponent for six action-packed rounds, belting the Frenchman to the point of exhaustion, but Menetrey came out swinging desperately in the seventh, scoring two knockdowns including the count out

05.07.71 ***Jimmy Revie, L CO 12 Evan Armstrong, British Featherweight Title***
WORLD SPORTING CLUB, LONDON Revie looked a winner throughout the early stages, but after his hand let him down the challenger got right back in the fight. Armstrong now had the title in his grasp and booming right hands put Revie down twice in the twelfth including the final count out

06.08.71 ***John McCluskey, L RTD 8 Henry Nissen (Australia), Commonwealth Flyweight Title***
ST KILDA'S TOWN HALL, MELBOURNE, AUSTRALIA The champion was rocked constantly with heavy punches and ultimately took a count. Both fighters were cut, but McCluskey seemed on the verge of exhaustion when retired by his corner.

10.08.71 ***Alan Rudkin, L PTS 15 Agustin Senin (Spain), European Bantamweight Title***
THE BULLRING, BILBAO, SPAIN The rugged Spaniard had Rudkin down four times with powerful lefts before the champion settled down to a rearguard action. Senin constantly pressed forward and appeared too strong for the game Liverpudlian

05.09.71 ***Ralph Charles, W RSC 5 Jeff White (Australia), Commonwealth Welterweight Title***
MILTON STADIUM, BRISBANE, AUSTRALIA Charles

used every punch at his disposal to outclass his opponent, flooring the Aussie three times in all. White appeared to be without hope and when he crashed to the floor in round five the referee had seen enough

06.09.71 ***Toro George (N. Zealand), W PTS 15 Evan Armstrong, Commonwealth Featherweight Title***

MELBOURNE, AUSTRALIA Over fifteen hard exciting rounds Armstrong was unable to floor his rival, who consistently closed in with two-handed attacks to the body. George was just too big, but the Scot never stopped trying to land the big one and occasionally had the New Zealander holding on grimly

13.09.71 ***Ken Buchanan, W PTS 15 Ismael Laguna (Panama), World Lightweight Title (WBA version)***

MADISON SQUARE GARDEN, NEW YORK, USA An aggressive Buchanan, despite a terrible eye wound, hammered out a unanimous decision over the former champion. Laguna got off to a good start, but by the middle stages began to wane and Buchanan battled right back with hard scoring punches amid great excitement

27.09.71 ***Joe Bugner, L PTS 15 Jack Bodell, British, Commonwealth & European Heavyweight Titles***

EMPIRE POOL, WEMBLEY Bodell took charge from the first round and built up a massive points margin. Bugner was beaten out of sight and was inept throughout when surrendering his three titles

07.12.71 ***Ralph Charles, W RSC 8 Bernie Terrell, British & Commonwealth Welterweight Titles***

ALBERT HALL, LONDON Some of Charles shots were borderline and one that had Terrell on the floor was palpably low. In the eighth the champion, his right eye leaking blood, poured the punches in until a left hook floored the game challenger, who upon rising and shipping more punishment was rescued by the referee

17.12.71 ***Jack Bodell, L RSC 2 Jose Urtain (Spain), European Heavyweight Title***

PALACIO DE DEPORTES, MADRID, SPAIN Bodell was well in command during the first round, prodding out his southpaw right lead to keep the clubbing Spaniard out. The second brought disaster, with Bodell exposing his fragile jaw and Urtain blasting him to the floor three times before the referee stopped it

13.09.71. The brilliant Scot Ken Buchanan (left) easily avoids the scything punches of former Champion Ismael Laguna.

20.12.71 ***Jean-Claude Bouttier (France), W CO 14 Bunny Sterling, European Middleweight Title***
PALAIS DES SPORTS, PARIS, FRANCE The British titleholder boxed brilliantly to have a clear lead after twelve rounds but tired rapidly and was smashed to the canvas three times in the thirteenth. The fourteenth round saw Bouttier cut Sterling down with a right to the head which rendered him senseless

1972

25.01.72 ***Alan Rudkin, W PTS 15 Johnny Clark, British & Commonwealth Bantamweight Titles***
ALBERT HALL, LONDON Rudkin jabbed and countered his challenger who sought to attack mainly the body. Clark, with the heavier punch, had the Liverpudlian tottering from hooks in the fourth, but the older man put in the stronger finish to save his titles

01.02.72 ***Willie Reilly, W RSC 10 Jim Watt, Vacant British Lightweight Title***
ICE RINK, NOTTINGHAM The blond Watt was getting on top before collecting a gashed right eyebrow, forcing the referee to stop the contest, thus giving Reilly a rather hollow victory. Watt had gone in pursuit of the Wembley-based Scot following a slow start and was beginning to land with heavy punches prior to the unfortunate ending

01.02.72 ***Conny Velensek (W. Germany), L PTS 15 Chris Finnegan, European L. Heavyweight Title***
ICE RINK, NOTTINGHAM Finnegan won by a clear margin in a grim contest, marked by the strength of the German. Velensek finished still standing but looking as though he had gone through a mincer

15.02.72 ***Jose Legra (Spain), W PTS 15 Evan Armstrong, European Featherweight Title***
ALBERT HALL, LONDON The raw-boned challenger gave everything, but Legra was in control with flashy counters and general ringcraft. Armstrong suffered facial damage from the eleventh but he still marched forward with Legra's class nullifying a good deal of his effort

28.03.72 ***Jose Napoles (Cuba), W CO 7 Ralph Charles, World Welterweight Title***
EMPIRE POOL, WEMBLEY Charles stepped out of his class on this occasion and was comfortably beaten by a supreme champion, who picked his punches brilliantly. Once Napoles decided to go to work the British champion was despatched by a series of arcing combinations, with the count just a formality

14.04.72 ***Bunny Sterling, L RSC 15 Tony Mundine (Australia), Commonwealth Middleweight Title***
MILTON TENNIS COURTS, BRISBANE, AUSTRALIA Sterling was battered to defeat with only thirty seconds remaining after being down four times in all. Mundine continually came forward, brushing aside the Jamaican's flashy ringwork, with his fists constantly pounding the target

18.04.72 ***Evan Armstrong, W RSC 6 Howard Hayes, British Featherweight Title***
ICE RINK, NOTTINGHAM The fight looked likely to develop into a classic prior to Hayes receiving bad eye injuries, which bought about the closure. Armstrong rammed home some heavy head punches, which inflicted the damage after the challenger had produced good early work

03.05.72 ***Jim Watt, W RSC 12 Tony Riley, Vacant British Lightweight Title***
MIDLAND SPORTING CLUB, SOLIHULL The Midlander fought gamely but never looked likely to shake the dominant Watt, who repeatedly jerked his head back with southpaw leads. The referee called a halt when Riley sustained a cut left eye and was being punished freely if not outclassed

17.05.72 ***Jose Legra (Spain), W PTS 15 Tommy Glencross, European Featherweight Title***
PRINCES' HALL, BIRMINGHAM Glencross came mighty close to lifting the title, but the exiled Cuban put in an eye-catching rally over the last couple of rounds to gain the narrow verdict. The Scot proved himself a worthy challenger in a contest that was rather too negative to be exciting

06.06.72 ***Chris Finnegan, W CO 8 Jan Lubbers (Holland), European L. Heavyweight Title***
ALBERT HALL, LONDON Lubbers was worn down, being hurt badly by body blows and finally he keeled over in the eighth following a short right to the jaw. Finnegan for his part pressured the Dutchman from the beginning and opened up with a vengeance in the penultimate round

26.06.72 ***Ken Buchanan, L RSC 13 Roberto Duran (Panama), World Lightweight Title (WBA version)***
MADISON SQUARE GARDEN, NEW YORK, USA The Panamanian continuously ran roughshod over the stylish Scot who had been pounded to the canvas in the first. The champion boxed well, but could never take the play away from Duran and the referee stopped the fight with Buchanan in pain from a blow to the abdomen

27.06.72 ***Jack Bodell, L CO 2 Danny McAlinden, British & Commonwealth Heavyweight Titles***
VILLA PARK, BIRMINGHAM Bodell was counted

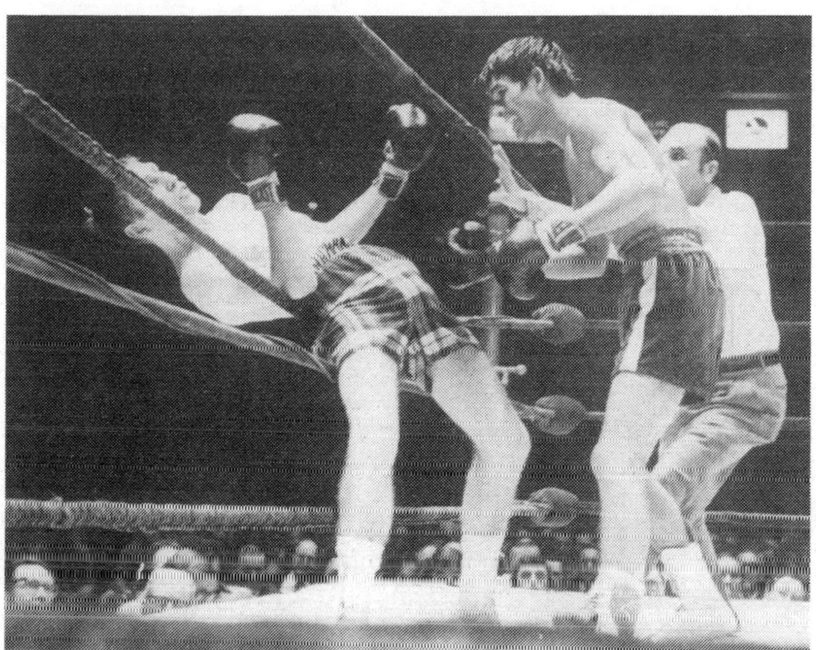

26.06.72. The hard hitting Roberto Duran hammers Ken Buchanan through the ropes prior to the finish in the 13th round.

out flat on his face after being put down four times in all. The fight was a wild swinging affair with both men on the floor together on one occasion, until McAlinden ended it amidst a barrage of crushing hammer-like blows

16.09.72 ***Paul Ferreri (Australia), W PTS 15 John Kellie, Vacant Commonwealth Bantamweight Title***

FRANKSTON, AUSTRALIA Ferreri easily outpointed the Scot, proving his mastery at every facet, although Kellie did stage a desperate rally in the final round. The Aussie was far too fast and knew too many ropes for his opponent who to his credit never stopped trying

19.09.72 ***Bunny Sterling, W CO 5 Phil Matthews, British Middleweight Title***

BELLE VUE, MANCHESTER Matthews, for all his power, just could not cope with the all-round class of the ring-wise champion. Once Sterling got to work the writing was on the wall and in the fifth the challenger just crumpled up following a left hook to the body

25.09.72 ***Evan Armstrong, L PTS 15 Tommy Glencross, British Featherweight Title***

ANGLO AMERICAN SPORTING CLUB, LONDON Waging a shrewd campaign, Glencross just about deserved the points verdict in his favour. Armstrong, with his usual attacking style, was out in front over the first third, but the challenger came back with the right jab and worked the body well on occasions

26.09.72 ***Bob Foster (USA), W CO 14 Chris Finnegan, World L. Heavyweight Title***

EMPIRE POOL, WEMBLEY Foster's terrific hitting ultimately clinched victory in a never-to-be-forgotten contest. Finnegan, always a moving target, dug in some great body shots and although floored in the tenth he got up to trade blows until the final right-hand exploded on his jaw

10.10.72 ***Jurgen Blin (W. Germany), L CO 8 Joe Bugner, European Heavyweight Title***

ALBERT HALL, LONDON Bugner finally delivered a positive showing to knock out the champion with a chopping blow delivered in the region of the left ear. The blond Adonis was on top all the way, flooring Blin in the first and battering him continuously thereafter

30.10.72 ***Charkey Ramon (Australia), W RSC 8 Pat Dwyer, Vacant Commonwealth L. Middleweight Title***

FESTIVAL HALL, MELBOURNE, AUSTRALIA The

gallant Dawyer, forever under pressure, made a comeback to floor the Aussie in the sixth. Then Ramon, using his own right handers, forced Dwyer to take a standing count in the seventh before the referee rescued his rival amid a hail of leather in the following round

31.10.72 ***Bobby Arthur, W DIS 7 John H. Stracey, Vacant British Welterweight Title***
ALBERT HALL, LONDON At no stage did Arthur appear to look like winning whilst spending most of the time holding and retreating. Under constant pressure throughout he finally succumbed to a body punch, going down clutching his abdomen, and in a most unsatisfactory ending the referee disqualified Stracey

14.11.72 ***Chris Finnegan, L RSC 12 Rudiger Schmidtke (W. Germany), European L. Heavyweight Title***
EMPIRE POOL, WEMBLEY When way out in front Finnegan became desperate when his nose was split by a straight right hand. The German had not relished Finnegan's earlier attacks by constantly laying off, but was galvanised into action at the sign of damage, forcing the referee to stop the contest

26.12.72 ***Fritz Chervet (Switzerland), W PTS 15 John McCluskey, European Flyweight Title***
HALLENSTADION, ZURICH, SWITZERLAND The little Scot was convincingly outpointed by Chervet and took two standing counts along the route. McCluskey was always trying to nail Chervet, but the Swiss fighter was in control throughout with his heavier artillery being decisive

1973

16.01.73 ***Joe Bugner, W PTS 15 Rudi Lubbers (Holland), European Heavyweight Title***
ALBERT HALL, LONDON Once again Bugner was hesitant, when making hard work of outpointing the Dutchman. Lubbers was able to mess the British champion about inside and often when Joe had his challenger in trouble he would stand off

17.01.73 ***Bunny Sterling, W RSC 11 Don McMillan, British Middleweight Title***
MIDLAND SPORTING CLUB, SOLIHULL The Scot fought under the handicap of a gashed left eye

29.01.73. Jim Watt (left) looks set to counter the advancing Ken Buchanan who looks menacing.

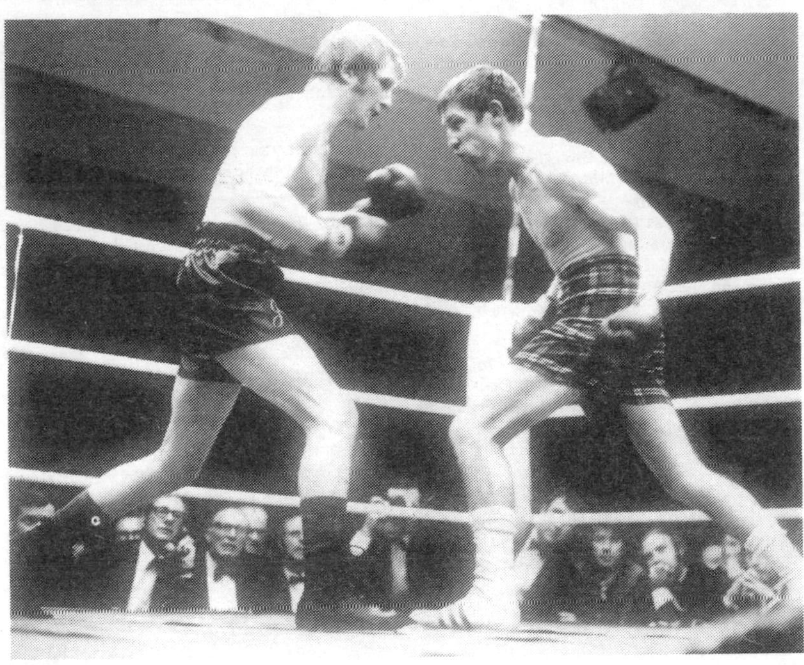

from the first round, but it was doubtful whether that made a great difference. Sterling whipped in punches, moved away from counters, tied up McMillan when needed and remained totally unruffled

29.01.73 ***Jim Watt, L PTS 15 Ken Buchanan, British Lightweight Title***

ST ANDREWS SPORTING CLUB, GLASGOW A real battle saw Buchanan regain his old title by taking an early lead and piling up points with his left. Watt made it a tough fight from the middle rounds onward and both finished with facial damage

20.02.73 ***Johnny Clark, W PTS 15 Paddy Maguire, Vacant British Bantamweight Title***

ALBERT HALL, LONDON This great fight between two fine bantam cocks had the fans out of their seats. Maguire was the aggressor throughout but Clark outboxed him and when the Irishman was put down in the thirteenth from a body shot he had to pull out all the stops to finish the full fifteen

13.03.73 ***Rudiger Schmidtke (W. Germany), L RSC 12 John Conteh, European L. Heavyweight Title***

EMPIRE POOL, WEMBLEY Conteh jabbed and hooked to build up a good lead before cutting loose in the sixth when administering three counts. In the twelfth the Liverpudlian smashed a bleeding Schmidtke all over the ring until the referee gave him a standing count prior to rescuing him

13.03.73 ***Chris Finnegan, W PTS 15 Roy John, British & Commonwealth L. Heavyweight Titles***

EMPIRE POOL, WEMBLEY The plucky Welsh challenger was clearly outpointed and took a long count in the twelfth, but despite all that he stuck to his guns. Finnegan was in control from the moment he found the range, but John never allowed him to relax

17.04.73 ***Bunny Sterling, W PTS 15 Mark Rowe, British Middleweight Title***

ALBERT HALL, LONDON Sterling scored a convincing points victory but the challenger made things interesting by trying to swing the fight his way with one punch. The Jamaican was just too elusive and skilful for the plodding Rowe, who finished well marked facially

17.04.73 ***Johnny Clark, W PTS 15 Franco Zurlo (Italy), Vacant European Bantamweight Title***

ALBERT HALL, LONDON In an interesting, often fiercely fought, contest Clark's solid left jabbing controlled most of the early exchanges, with the Italian making a late rally. With his long reach Zurlo was always dangerous, but a cut eye received in the second round hampered his progress

12.05.73 ***Gitano Jiminez (Spain), W PTS 15 Tommy Glencross, Vacant European Featherweight Title***

THE BULLRING, GIJON, SPAIN Glencross was soundly outpointed by the taller Spaniard who exploited his long jabs and hooks to hand out a comprehensive beating. The Britisher also collected warnings for ducking, whilst trying to avoid heavy head punches

22.05.73 ***Chris Finnegan, L PTS 15 John Conteh, British & Commonwealth L. Heavyweight Titles (Conteh defended European L. Heavyweight Title)***

EMPIRE POOL, WEMBLEY In one of the greatest light-heavyweight battles for years Conteh won beyond doubt, but the champion made great efforts to stay on to the end. Despite facial damage Finnegan drew on extra reserves to rally strongly, but the Liverpudlian picked his punches brilliantly

05.06.73 ***Bobby Arthur, L CO 4 John H. Stracey, British Welterweight Title***

ALBERT HALL, LONDON Arthur was determined to prove a worthy champion and for the first three rounds he jabbed well with good left leads. Early in the fourth he unfortunately essayed the jab, but Stracey moved inside with a perfect right leaving the referee to complete the formalities

17.09.73 ***Tommy Glencross, L RSC 3 Evan Armstrong, British Featherweight Title***

ST ANDREWS SPORTING CLUB, GLASGOW Until a roundhouse right split his left eye, Glencross was boxing well to have the challenger in some distress on occasions. On the bell to end the third round the referee followed the champion back to his corner, calling a halt and declaring Armstrong the winner

25.09.73 ***Larry Paul, W CO 10 Bobby Arthur, Vacant British L. Middleweight Title***

CIVIC CENTRE, WOLVERHAMPTON Arthur set the younger man all sorts of problems in the early rounds, but in the eighth the writing was on the wall when he was dropped by a booming right hander. The finish came with Paul following up a two-fisted attack in the tenth and ending proceedings with a sweeping right to the chin

02.10.73 ***Joe Bugner, W PTS 15 Bepi Ros (Italy), European Heavyweight Title***

ALBERT HALL, LONDON The British champion was unable to sink or even floor the roly-poly Italian, although winning beyond dispute. Ros, game and durable, was able to withstand Bugner's best efforts, leaving him content to control from long range

23.10.73 ***John Conteh, W PTS 15 Baby Boy Rolle (Bahamas), Commonwealth L. Heavyweight Title***

ICE RINK, NOTTINGHAM After damaging his left hand early on Conteh recognised that he could not knock the challenger over and was content to cruise to victory. Rolle had nothing to offer apart from wild swinging punches and the contest developed into a boring affair

07.11.73 ***Elio Calcabrini (Italy), W PTS 15 Bunny Sterling, Vacant European Middleweight Title***

SAN REMO, ITALY Another outrageous Continental decision saw Calcabrini awarded the verdict after being well and truly outboxed over the duration. Even allowing for the fact that Sterling had received an amazing amount of warnings, the decision had appeared to be a formality

27.11.73 ***Des Morrison, W PTS 15 Joe Tetteh, Vacant British L. Welterweight Title***

SHOREDITCH TOWN HALL, LONDON In a contest of immigrants Morrison from Jamaica beat Tetteh from Ghana by a narrow points verdict to the strain of bongo drums. Morrison was put down twice in the eleventh round, but managed to get up to outlast the older man

1974

15.01.74 ***Johnny Clark, W PTS 15 Salvatore Fabrizio (Italy), European Bantamweight Title***

ALBERT HALL, LONDON Making every effort to nullify the champion's superior skill, Fabrizio parried and hustled throughout. Clark banged in solid punches mixed with skilful boxing, but the Italian was tough and forever fighting back to lose narrowly over the distance

11.02.74 ***Bunny Sterling, L PTS 15 Kevin Finnegan, British Middleweight Title***

ANGLO AMERICAN SPORTING CLUB, LONDON Finnegan emulated his brother when becoming British titleholder. Until the tenth round Sterling appeared to have his opponent's measure, but the challenger fought on in determined spirits whereas the Jamaican faded badly

12.03.74 ***John Conteh, W RTD 6 Tom Bogs (Denmark), European L. Heavyweight Title***

EMPIRE POOL, WEMBLEY Despite the ignominy of being floored for a count of eight in the first round, Conteh well and truly beat the Dane, mainly using ramrod left jabs with good rights over the top. The tough Bogs was battered non-stop in the sixth and with his eye cut badly, was retired at the end of the round

26.03.74 ***Des Morrison, L CO 11 Pat McCormack, British L. Welterweight Title***

ALBERT HALL, LONDON Morrison, although boxing gamely to inflict heavy punishment on his challenger, finally wilted himself. In a tremendous all action contest McCormack threw leather incessantly, continuously coming forward being prepared to do or die in the attempt and finally landed the finisher

05.04.74 ***Bobby Dunne (Australia), L RSC 8 Evan Armstrong, Commonwealth Featherweight Title***

FESTIVAL HALL, BRISBANE The Aussie made the mistake of trading punches with Armstrong after boxing well at long range. Once the Scot got to work launching vicious two-handed attacks the writing was on the wall and Dunne was dropped in the seventh before being rescued in the following round when under extreme pressure

24.04.74 ***Larry Paul, W PTS 15 Kevin White, British L. Middleweight Title***

CIVIC HALL, WOLVERHAMPTON Paul was never able to relax against his aggresive and determined opponent, relying ultimately on his better skills to secure the decision. The champion boxed far more defensively than previously but cut White up in the process, mainly with counter punches

01.05.74 ***Antonio Puddu (Italy), L CO 6 Ken Buchanan, European Lightweight Title***

SANTA ELIA STADIUM, CAGLIARI, ITALY The Italian absorbed a steady beating from the start and in the sixth, bleeding badly, he was punched defenceless to be counted out on his feet. Buchanan, with streams of left jabs and crosses was in a different class to the game Puddu, who did well to go so far

21.05.74 ***John Conteh, W RSC 6 Chris Finnegan, British, Commonwealth & European L. Heavyweight Titles***

EMPIRE POOL, WEMBLEY Finnegan appeared to be narrowly in front by the sixth, with both men fighting forcibly, but following a clash of heads he pulled away with blood streaming down his face. The referee had no hesitation in calling the contest off and declaring Conteh the winner

27.05.74 ***Jean-Claude Bouttier (France), L PTS 15 Kevin Finnegan, European Middleweight Title***

ROLAND GARROS STADIUM, PARIS, FRANCE Bouttier finished marked around both eyes, and in the main was on the receiving end of a well-merited decision. Finnegan stayed cool throughout to outbox the Frenchman convincingly, even flooring him in the thirteenth round

27.05.74 ***Roger Menetrey (France), L RSC 8 John H. Stracey, European Welterweight Title***

ROLAND GARROS STADIUM, PARIS, FRANCE Menetrey was almost crushed before the referee rescued him from further punishment. Reaching his opponent easily with the jab, Stracey was able to open up the Frenchman who, in relying on round-arm punches, was outboxed, outpunched and utterly demoralised

01.10.74. A smashing right hand over the top delivered by John Conteh (right) halts Jorge Ahumada in his tracks.

29.05.74 ***Joe Bugner, W RTD 9 Mario Baruzzi (Italy), European Heavyweight Title***
COPENHAGEN, DENMARK This mediocre contest ended when Baruzzi refused to come out for the tenth following damage to his right eye. Bugner had been in control throughout, only exerting pressure when required, and the Italian was badly hurt in the ninth although remaining upright

08.07.74 ***Evan Armstrong, W RSC 11 Alan Richardson, British & Commonwealth Featherweight Titles***
WORLD SPORTING CLUB, LONDON A bloody battle saw Armstrong retain his title after flooring the challenger in the eleventh. Richardson had moved out in front despite a seventh round knock-down, but the champion mustered all his strength to pull the iron out of the fire when it mattered most

01.10.74 ***John Conteh, W PTS 15 Jorge Ahumada (Argentine), Vacant World L. Heavyweight Title (WBC version)***
EMPIRE POOL, WEMBLEY Over fifteen gruelling rounds Conteh gave a great display of both skill and courage to counter the non-stop charge of the man from the Pampas. Round after round Ahumada threw menacing punches at the Britisher, who used every punch in the book to run out a brilliant winner

14.10.74 ***John McCluskey, W RSC 1 Tony Davies, British Flyweight Title***
TOP RANK SUITE, SWANSEA The impetuous challenge of Davies was contemptuously laid aside in just 125 seconds. In that time he was smashed to the canvas twice before being rescued by the referee. McCluskey, who had waited five years for a challenger, was too heavy a hitter for the young Welshman

05.11.74 ***Larry Paul, L CO 8 Maurice Hope, British L. Middleweight Title***
CIVIC CENTRE, WOLVERHAMPTON Maurice Hope, the Antiguan-born southpaw having only his eleventh contest, catapulted the champion onto the ropes with a salvo of blows and finally ended it with a perfect left cross to the jaw. Paul, badly cut in the first, had fought gamely enough, but appeared weak at the weight

21.11.74 ***Pat McCormack, L PTS 15 Joey Singleton, British L. Welterweight Title***
THE STADIUM, LIVERPOOL Over fifteen thrilling rounds the local boy Singleton came good when maintaining a fantastic pace to jab, move and outdistance himself from his opponent. McCor-

mack had put his opponent down in the first, but from then on could not keep up in the sprint to the finish

07.12.74 ***Evan Armstrong, L RSC 10 David Kotey (Ghana), Commonwealth Featherweight Title***

ACCRA, GHANA The fight was recognised as a final eliminator for the World title and the Ghanaian was just too much for the British champion. Following a clinical beating Armstrong was put down midway through the tenth and the referee stopped the count at eight, declaring Kotey the winner

10.12.74 ***Dave Needham, W PTS 15 Paddy Maguire, Vacant British Bantamweight Title***

ICE RINK, NOTTINGHAM Despite the handicap of bad cuts, Needham fought his way to a thrilling victory. Neither man stopped punching and surprisingly there was only one knockdown, which came in the third, when Maguire was toppled over

16.12.74 ***Ken Buchanan, W RSC 14 Leonard Tavarez (France), European Lightweight Title***

PARC DES EXPOSITIONS, PARIS, FRANCE Although cut in the second, Buchanan kept firmly in control with good left jabs and occasionally cut loose with combinations. Tavarez had come to the end of his tether by the penultimate round and following two standing counts, the referee pulled the Scot away

1975

13.01.75 ***Danny McAlinden, L CO 9 Bunny Johnson, British & Commonwealth Heavyweight Titles***

WORLD SPORTING CLUB, LONDON Bunny Johnson became Britain's first black heavyweight champion when McAlinden, after being dropped for nine, finally sank down for the full count. Johnson himself was floored in the fourth but throughout easily jabbed and countered the lumbering Irishmen, who had both eyes cut into the bargain

27.01.75 ***Jim Watt, W RSC 7 Johnny Cheshire, Vacant British Lightweight Title***

ST ANDREWS SPORTING CLUB, GLASGOW Cheshire was rescued by the referee after being floored twice for long counts in the sixth. Watt had been rather sluggish in the earlier rounds but once he stepped into his southpaw rhythm his opponent's work became ragged

19.02.75 ***Steve Aczel (Australia), W RSC 3 Maxie Smith, Vacant Commonwealth L. Heavyweight Title***

BELLE VUE, MANCHESTER The Britisher was on the floor five times before the referee finally halted the carnage. Hungarian-born Aczel produced an exciting brand of power hitting which simply crushed Smith, who was only able to land a few blows of his own

27.02.75 ***Guts Ishimatsu (Japan), W PTS 15 Ken Buchanan, World Lightweight Title (WBC version)***

METROPOLITAN GYM, TOKYO, JAPAN Buchanan, boxing in the classic orthodox style, scored well at times, but could not ward off the champion's two-fisted attacks indefinitely. Both fighters got through with solid punches and although the Scot's left eye was closed from the fifth onwards, the margin of defeat was extremely close

01.03.75 ***Joe Bugner, W RSC 4 Dante Cane (Italy), European Heavyweight Title***

BOLOGNA, ITALY Bugner retained his title when stopping the large Italian, who had sustained a badly cut left eye. Cane often bulled forward landing many crude blows, but by the closure had shot his bolt and was being punished freely

07.03.75 ***Paul Ferreri (Australia), W RSC 8 Paddy Maguire, Commonwealth Bantamweight Title***

FESTIVAL HALL, MELBOURNE, AUSTRALIA The rugged Maguire constantly bored in forcing the Aussie against the ropes, but Ferreri's tight defence and brilliant counter-punching kept him well in front. The fight was stopped with the Irishman under pressure from a stream of jabs and crosses

11.03.75 ***John Conteh, W RSC 5 Lonnie Bennett (USA), World L. Heavyweight Title (WBC version)***

EMPIRE POOL, WEMBLEY Conteh had begun to beat the American to the punch prior to the contest being stopped, when Bennett sustained a badly gashed left eye. Both fighters matched skills throughout with solid punches in an effort to attain mastery, but Conteh produced the blows that counted

25.03.75 ***Vernon Sollas, W CO 4 Jimmy Revie, Vacant British Featherweight Title***

ALBERT HALL, LONDON Sollas dominated from the beginning, picking his shots deliberately, and the Londoner was never allowed to use his reach advantage. Revie was counted out after being floored for the third time following a volley of solid punches to the jaw

11.04.75 ***Daniel Trioulaire (France), DREW 15 Dave Needham, European Bantamweight Title***

BARENTIN, FRANCE The Frenchman's main tactic was to hustle Needham, but his right hand punching lacked real power and the Nottingham man should have stamped his authority on the contest. Although the better craftsman, he was frequently taken out of his stride and seemed strangely subdued in the middle rounds

29.04.75 ***John H. Stracey, W RSC 6 Max Hebeison (Switzerland), European Welterweight Title***

ALBERT HALL, LONDON Stracey finally nailed his slippery opponent in the sixth following a sweeping left uppercut that went through Hebeison's guard. He followed up with a left-right to the jaw which flattened the Swiss challenger, who upon rising at the count of nine was rescued by the referee

03.05.75 ***Jonathan Dele (Nigeria), W PTS 15 Jim Watt, Vacant Commonwealth Lightweight Title***

NATIONAL STADIUM, LAGOS Dele carried the fight to the Scot throughout, never allowing the southpaw to find a rhythm. Watt was dropped briefly in the second, but staged a fine defensive battle and despite being under pressure fought back well during the twelfth

07.05.75 ***Kevin Finnegan, L PTS 15 Gratien Tonna (France) European Middleweight Title***

LOUIS II STADIUM, MONTE CARLO In a gruelling, bloody contest Finnegan lost his title. Tonna was outskilled early on, but came back hitting solidly to swamp the champion and surprised many by outjabbing him over the last few rounds

13.05.75 ***Billy Moeller (Australia), W PTS 15 Jimmy Bell, Vacant Commonwealth J. Lightweight Title***

ST MARYS CLUB, SYDNEY, AUSTRALIA An interesting, rather than exciting bout, between two southpaws, saw the Aussie eke out a close decision. Moeller's left hook was probably the deciding factor when both men strove to gain supremacy

03.06.75 ***Johnny Frankham, W PTS 15 Chris Finnegan, Vacant British L. Heavyweight Title***

ALBERT HALL, LONDON The fight was decided by Frankham's stubborn countering when under pressure from the former champion's relentless aggression. There were no knockdowns, but each man was rocked occasionally in a great battle of swaying fortunes

10.06.75 ***Bunny Sterling, W RSC 8 Maurice Hope, Vacant British Middleweight Title***

NATIONAL SPORTING CLUB, LONDON Hope stepped out of his division only to be remorselessly thrashed over eight one-sided rounds. Although

06.12.75. John H. Stracey (left), well on the way to victory against the ageing Jose Napoles, seen here on the receiving end of a left jab.

on the offensive earlier, the light-middleweight champion was systematically broken up, having little effect with his own punches, until the referee had seen enough

01.07.75 ***Muhammad Ali (USA), W PTS 15 Joe Bugner, World Heavyweight Title***

INDEPENDENCE STADIUM, KUALA LUMPUR It was a disappointing display by Bugner, whose tactics once again erred on the side of caution. The Englishman absorbed Ali's best shots throughout and even fought back well on limited occasions, but was never really able to penetrate the American's guard

25.07.75 ***Ken Buchanan, W RSC 12 Giancarlo Usai (Italy), European Lightweight Title***

CAGLIARI FOOTBALL STADIUM, SARDINIA Usai pressed the Scot strongly, but fell apart in the eleventh when a vicious uppercut to the body badly hurt him. The climax saw Buchanan hammering his defenceless target, who took a compulsory eight count, before slumping against the ropes with nothing left to offer

30.09.75 ***Bunny Johnson, L PTS 15 Richard Dunn, British & Commonwealth Heavyweight Titles***

EMPIRE POOL, WEMBLEY Richard Dunn upset the odds, making good use of his physical advantages when pounding and prodding his way to victory. There were no knockdowns, but the big Yorkshireman pressurised Johnson over the last third to run out a clear winner

30.09.75 ***Joey Singleton, W RSC 9 Alan Salter, British L. Welterweight Title***

EMPIRE POOL, WEMBLEY The bout was stopped when Salter received a cut left eyebrow and was too far behind on points. Singleton outsmarted the challenger throughout, popping in the jab relentlessly and banging in solid punches to the target

30.09.75 ***Maurice Hope, W RSC 4 Larry Paul, British L. Middleweight Title***

EMPIRE POOL, WEMBLEY There were some stunning rallies whilst the fight lasted and both fighters suffered eye damage in the furious exchanges. Hope's aggression finally won through and Paul was hammered against the ropes before the referee duly called a halt to the proceedings

14.10.75 ***Johnny Frankham, L PTS 15 Chris Finnegan, British L. Heavyweight Title***

ALBERT HALL, LONDON This thriller even surpassed their last one, with Finnegan forging ahead from the tenth round and Frankham boxing as well as he knew but not having his rival's staying power. Both fighters finished with cuts, but there were no knockdowns in a match that had all the ingredients

20.10.75 ***Dave Needham, L RSC 14 Paddy Maguire, British Bantamweight Title***

WORLD SPORTING CLUB, LONDON Dave Needham lost his title when he received further damage to his already badly ravaged eyebrows and the referee was left with no alternative. Maguire landed the more solid blows, but Needham had taken everything and banged back with plenty of his own

04.11.75 ***Richard Dunn, W CO 2 Danny McAlinden, British & Commonwealth Heavyweight Titles***

EMPIRE POOL, WEMBLEY The wild swinging ex-champion was an easy target for Dunn and was down twice, before succumbing following some solid left handers. McAlinden was counted out on one knee with blood coming from a mouth wound

04.11.75 ***Alan Minter, W PTS 15 Kevin Finnegan, Vacant British Middleweight Title***

EMPIRE POOL, WEMBLEY Minter finished the stronger of the two by outpunching his rival in some gruelling exchanges over the last two rounds. Prior to that Finnegan had fought solidly for long periods and the contest was in the main evenly balanced

11.11.75 ***Joey Singleton, W PTS 15 Des Morrison, British L. Welterweight Title***

BELLE VUE, MANCHESTER Too much of Morrison's aggression appeared ineffectual and Singleton put the verdict beyond reach by going in to outhustle his man over the last five rounds. Earlier the Liverpudlian had conducted the contest from long range with effective hit-and-run tactics

06.12.75 ***Jose Napoles (Cuba), L RSC 6 John H. Stracey, World Welterweight Title (WBC version)***

PLAZA DE TOROS, MEXICO CITY Both fighters had been downed prior to the finish, when Napoles under a terrific battery of punches was rescued by the referee. Earlier the World champion had thrown his best punches to no avail, with Stracey walking through with the left jab and opening up the Cuban, who became a broken shell of a once great fighting machine

15.12.75 ***Pat Thomas, W CO 13 Pat McCormack, Vacant British Welterweight Title***

MANOR PLACE BATHS, LONDON Pat Thomas became Britain's first immigrant welterweight titleholder following one of the roughest title bouts imaginable. McCormack fought bravely, but was finally worn down, and took two counts before a cluster of blows, finished off by a straight right to the jaw, put him on the canvas for the final time

28.04.76. Phil Martin (right) unleashes a heavy battery of punches to put Tim Wood on the rack.

1976

16.01.76 ***Daniel Trioulaire (France), DREW 15 Paddy Maguire, European Bantamweight Title***

GYMNASE DE LA SARDAGNE, CLUSES, FRANCE A hard unrelenting bout saw the Irishman working well to the body throughout with Trioulaire sneaking in rights. Maguire had his man down in the twelfth from a good body shot and appeared to have justified the decision

20.02.76 ***Bunny Sterling, W RSC 13 Frank Reiche (W. Germany), Vacant European Middleweight Title***

ALSTERDORF SPORTHALLE, HAMBURG, W. GERMANY Sterling produced a peach of a right hander out of the blue when under a good deal of pressure. The German toppled over, but the fight was stopped before the count was completed. Reiche had handed out two counts previously and was just beginning to get on top

25.02.76 ***Elio Cotena (Italy), W CO 14 Vernon Sollas, European Featherweight Title***

YORK HALL, LONDON The Scot boxed competently for the first ten rounds, but from then on faded badly and was lucky to survive the thirteenth with all his strength drained. Cotena leapt out in the penultimate round immediately flooring Sollas, who on arising was dumped again and counted out in a standing position

20.03.76 ***John H. Stracey, W RSC 10 Hedgemon Lewis (USA), World Welterweight Title (WBC version)***

EMPIRE POOL, WEMBLEY Stracey hammered the American challenger to defeat in an all-action contest, after surviving a shaky first round. Lewis found the aggressive persistence of the new champion just too much to handle, eventually disintegrating from the overwhelming onslaught

06.04.76 ***Richard Dunn, W RSC 3 Bernd August (W. Germany), Vacant European Heavyweight Title***

ALBERT HALL, LONDON Despite some shaky moments Dunn came right back to batter the German to a standstill, having him down three times in all, before the referee halted the carnage. August finished with both eyes closed and was on the verge of complete annihilation

09.04.76 ***Marco Scano (Italy), W CO 2 Pat Thomas, Vacant European Welterweight Title***

PALAZZO DELLO SPORT, CAGLIARI, ITALY Thomas was counted out on his feet as he climbed up from the third knockdown of the round. He had previously been on the floor after only thirty seconds and had then tried an offensive before finally succumbing to Scano's heavy rights

20.04.76 ***Maurice Hope, W RSC 12 Tony Poole, British & Vacant Commonwealth L. Middleweight Titles***

YORK HALL, LONDON Following a gritty display Tony Poole was finally halted due to a badly gashed left eye. Hope was firmly in front and had hit the challenger with every punch in the book, but the Kettering lad kept marching through the destruction

27.04.76 ***Alan Minter, W RSC 2 Billy Knight, British Middleweight Title***

ALBERT HALL, LONDON The referee called a halt to the contest with Knight propped in a neutral corner being hammered unmercifully and carrying a long cut over the right eye. Minter had put his rival down three times and although marked himself kept up enough pressure to make sure he did not have to travel the distance

28.04.76 ***Tim Wood, W PTS 15 Phil Martin, Vacant British L. Heavyweight Title***

WORLD SPORTING CLUB, LONDON Both fighters finished with eye damage in a lacklustre bout, with Wood, mainly due to a late rally, getting the verdict. Martin was hammered all round the ring but was not put down and the decision appeared to favour the new champion

25.05.76 ***Muhammad Ali (USA), W RSC 5 Richard Dunn, World Heavyweight Title***

OLYMPIAHALLE, MUNICH, W. GERMANY Dunn had been dropped five times before the referee decided he had seen enough. The fight was hopelessly one-sided as the American picked his spot against a rival who charged in recklessly and was duly countered with punches pouring in from both hands

01.06.76 ***Joey Singleton, L RSC 6 Dave Boy Green, British L. Welterweight Title***

ALBERT HALL, LONDON Officially the contest was stopped due to cuts, but there was no way Singleton could have taken much more. He had not gone down, but Green had hammered away non-stop in an exciting bloody battle that electrified the crowd

04.06.76 ***Bunny Sterling, L PTS 15 Angelo Jacopucci (Italy), European Middleweight Title***

PALAZZO DELLO SPORT, MILAN, ITALY The Italian outreached Sterling and for long spells his jab controlled the contest. The Britisher tried to make a real effort in the last third, but weight-reducing was in evidence as he began to fade under Jacopucci's offensive

22.06.76 ***John H. Stracey, L RSC 12 Carlos Palomino (USA), World Welterweight Title (WBC version)***

EMPIRE POOL, WEMBLEY Stracey fought an uphill battle from the third round and eventually went down for two counts as the result of persistent body punching. The Londoner was outjabbed and outpunched as he failed to get his form together

14.09.76 ***Alan Minter, W PTS 15 Kevin Finnegan, British Middleweight Title***

ALBERT HALL, LONDON Here was a contest that could have gone either way with Finnegan having Minter nearly out on his feet in an unforgettable last round. Prior to that Minter had inflicted serious eye damage, but it was the former champion who produced more of the quality punches throughout

22.09.76 ***Pat Thomas, W PTS 15 Trevor Francis, British Welterweight Title***

ANGLO AMERICAN SPORTING CLUB, LONDON The first British title bout at the weight between immigrants produced a dreary affair, which was notable for several cautions handed out for holding. Francis did not show enough aggression to take the title whilst Thomas was content to feel his way back after recent poor results

01.10.76 ***Vito Antuofermo (Italy), L RSC 15 Maurice Hope, European L. Middleweight Title***

PALAZZO DELLO SPORT, ROME, ITALY Antuofermo was finally reduced to a bloody wreck after taking two standing counts and being on the verge of total destruction. Hope, the master at range, was often unsettled by the champion's bull-like rushes, although keeping his cool throughout

09.10.76 ***John Conteh, W PTS 15 Alvaro Lopez (USA), World L. Heavyweight Title (WBC version)***

THE FORUM, COPENHAGEN, DENMARK Albeit winning well, Conteh used his suspect right rather sparingly and victory in the main was achieved by the use of his solid left hand lead, backed up with strong left hooks. Lopez gamely pressed forward but could never break the Englishman's classy defence

12.10.76 ***Richard Dunn, L CO 1 Joe Bugner, British, Commonwealth & European Heavyweight Titles***

EMPIRE POOL, WEMBLEY As the opening bell sounded Bugner crashed in with a solid right to the jaw and following up floored the big Yorkshireman for five. Lefts and rights had him down again and upon rising Dunn was subjected to a barrage of punches, before being finally smashed down flat on his back

07.12.76 ***Dave Boy Green, W RTD 9 Jean-Baptiste Piedvache (France), Vacant European L. Welterweight Title***

ALBERT HALL, LONDON Piedvache finally retired with his left eye closed completely, but prior to that he had given the Fen Tiger one hell of a battle. Green persisted with his solid probing left and both men banged away freely to the body in a gruelling struggle

07.12.76 ***Pat Thomas, L RSC 8 Henry Rhiney, British Welterweight Title***

CAESARS PALACE, LUTON Rhiney fought with great enthusiasm against a lethargic champion who never got going. Thomas was eventually downed twice in the eighth before the referee stopped the contest after deciding that he was not fit to continue

1977

01.02.77 ***Jimmy Batten, W RTD 7 Albert Hillman, Vacant British L. Middleweight Title***

ALBERT HALL, LONDON Batten fought with great skill and determination to halt his fellow Londoner who never really looked likely to win at any stage. Retiring due to bad left eye damage, Hillman had given his all but to no avail

04.02.77 ***Germano Valsecchi (Italy), L CO 5 Alan Minter, European Middleweight Title***

NUOVO PALAZZO DELLO SPORT, MILAN, ITALY Minter bombed away throughout, often beating the Italian to the punch, and it was only a matter of time when the finisher would be applied. Valsecchi eventually took two standing counts before being rendered useless

21.02.77 ***Jim Watt, W RSC 10 Johnny Claydon, British Lightweight Title***

ST ANDREWS SPORTING CLUB, GLASGOW The southpaw punch of Watt was too much for the Londoner to handle and the referee intervened rather belatedly after Claydon had been sunk for the fourth time during the tenth. The challenger was on the deck earlier, but showed great spirit when fighting back.

05.03.77 ***John Conteh, W RSC 3 Len Hutchins (USA), World L. Heavyweight Title (WBC version)***

THE STADIUM, LIVERPOOL Conteh's finishing left hook was tremendous, but he had already taken the American apart earlier with solid jabs and right handers over the top. Hutchins complained of a clash of heads in the first which left him with terrible eye damage, but it was deemed accidental and the champion finished the job clinically

03.10.77. Alan Richardson (left) finds the answer to Les Pickett's aggression with an old fashioned straight left

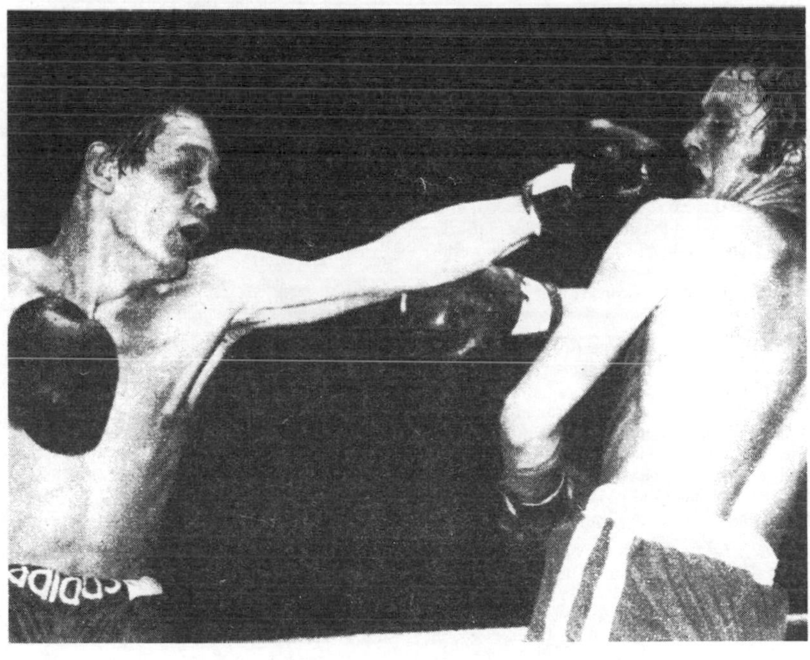

08.03.77 ***Tim Wood, L CO 1 Bunny Johnson, British L. Heavyweight Title***
CIVIC HALL, WOLVERHAMPTON It took just ten seconds for Johnson to win a second title when demolishing the Leicester boy in record time. A right to the jaw send Wood crashing to the canvas with the back of his head hitting the floor and the referee formally completed the count

15.03.77 ***Ekhard Dagge (W. Germany), DREW 15 Maurice Hope, World L. Middleweight Title (WBC version) – (Hope defended European L. Middleweight Title)***
DEUTSCHLANDHALLE, BERLIN, W. GERMANY The German was several inches taller than Hope and landed the harder punches of the fight, but the Britisher maintained a higher workrate. There were no knockdowns, although Dagge sustained eye damage administered by the southpaw's right jab

15.03.77 ***Vernon Sollas, L RSC 8 Alan Richardson, British Featherweight Title***
TOWN HALL, LEEDS The gritty Yorkshireman fought a brave controlled fight, sapping Sollas' strength with body shots and keeping the jab going whenever caught himself. The Scot suddenly drained of energy and the end came with him on the ropes taking punches and offering no return

07.05.77 ***Maurice Hope, W PTS 15 Frank Wissenbach (W. Germany), European L. Middleweight Title***
CONGRESS CENTRE, HAMBURG, W. GERMANY Hope generally dominated, but although winning clearly it was unexciting stuff. Right jabs had Wissenbach bleeding throughout, but he was most elusive and the only time the champion looked likely to halt him was in the eleventh round

31.05.77 ***Kevin Finnegan, W RSC 11 Frankie Lucas, Vacant British Middleweight Title***
ALBERT HALL, LONDON In a tough, bloody affair Finnegan re-won the title he never lost in the ring when Lucas was stopped with a bad gash over the right eye. Finnegan had just edged in front at the closure and ended the contest with a closed right eye

14.06.77 ***Carlos Palomino (USA), W CO 11 Dave Boy Green, World Welterweight Title (WBC version)***
EMPIRE POOL, WEMBLEY Every round was bitterly contested with fortunes swaying until the tenth when Green's eye suddenly closed. In the eleventh a left hook poleaxed the Englishman who, prior to that, had victory in his grasp as Palomino was thumped about and cut up facially

17.06.77 ***Eddie Ndukwu (Nigeria), W RSC 12 Alan Richardson, Vacant Commonwealth Featherweight Title***
NATIONAL STADIUM, LAGOS, NIGERIA The referee called a halt when Richardson got up shakily after being dropped twice in the twelfth. He had been down twice previously and although his left eye had closed was marginally ahead at the time

05.08.77 ***Jim Watt, W RSC 1 Andrew Holyk (France), Vacant European Lightweight Title***
ST ANDREWS SPORTING CLUB, GLASGOW In just 82 seconds the French champion was led back to his corner after sustaining an ugly gash on the right eyebrow, following an exchange. Holyk had backed off immediately with blood flowing down his face and it was debated whether an accidental head clash had caused the damage

21.09.77 ***Alan Minter, L RSC 8 Gratien Tonna (France), European Middleweight Title***
PALAZZO DELLO SPORT, MILAN, ITALY After surviving an onslaught in the second, Minter had the Frenchman wilting in the suceeding rounds. Tonna then opened up a vertical cut on Minter's forehead with a wild clubbing right with the Englishman well on his way to victory

28.09.77 ***Franco Zurlo (Italy), W RTD 8 Paddy Maguire, European Bantamweight Title***
FORT VILLAGE, SARDINIA, ITALY After riding out an early storm, Zurlo's right hand counters and left hooks eventually found Maguire's face with utmost regularity. The Irishman still bustled forward non-stop but his corner finally pulled him out when a deep gash appeared over his eye

03.10.77 ***Alan Richardson, W PTS 15 Les Pickett, British Featherweight Title***
AFAN LIDO, ABERAVON Following fifteen unforgettable rounds of action the challenger failed narrowly to wrest the title. Richardson boxed brilliantly over the first half of the contest, but Pickett came right back in a storming finish, producing a magnificent effort

19.10.77 ***Colin Power, W RSC 10 Des Morrison, Vacant British L. Welterweight Title***
YORK HALL, LONDON The ninth round turned into one of the greatest single rounds of title fighting as Morrison was down three times and between knockdowns Power himself was on the verge of destruction. The tenth saw the Jamaican battered around the ring before being rescued by the referee

25.10.77 ***Jimmy Batten, W RSC 4 Larry Paul British L. Middleweight Title***
ALBERT HALL, LONDON At the finish Paul was propped up in his opponent's corner taking a steady flow of punches. Batten had floored the former champion with a short right to the point

earlier on but had to ride out a desperate rally himself before settling for victory

08.11.77 ***Maurice Hope, W CO 5 Joel Bonnetaz (France), European L. Middleweight Title***
EMPIRE POOL, WEMBLEY The Frenchman was clinically taken apart by the accurate punches of Maurice Hope. Bonnetaz was dropped in the third and destroyed two rounds later by a left-right combination, which left him being counted out on all fours in Hope's corner

08.11.77 ***Kevin Finnegan, L PTS 15 Alan Minter, British Middleweight Title***
EMPIRE POOL, WEMBLEY Once again these two world-class opponents fought out an absorbing championship battle and once more Finnegan found himself a narrow loser. This time, mainly due to his last round effort, Minter shaded the decision with both men tired to the point of exhaustion

16.11.77 ***Jim Watt, W RSC 10 Jeronimo Lucas (Spain), European Lightweight Title***
MIDLAND SPORTING CLUB, SOLIHULL Lucas fought a rearguard action, but was ultimately dismantled by the cultured southpaw punches of the champion. Watt cut the Spaniard up badly, belting him to head and body before inflicting a standing count which quickly bought a timely intervention from the third man

26.11.77 ***Aldo Traversaro (Italy), W RSC 11 Bunny Johnson, Vacant European L. Heavyweight Title***
PALAZZO DELLO SPORT, GENOA, ITALY Following a great start Johnson inexplicably retreated behind his jab and the fight developed into a scrambling uninspired affair. Traversaro opened up a big points gap and in the tenth badly hurt the Jamaican, who was rescued a round later after taking three standing counts

29.11.77 ***Paddy Maguire, L RSC 11 Johnny Owen, British Bantamweight Title***
NATIONAL SPORTING CLUB, LONDON Owen countered cleverly, picking off the Irishman with neat rights and stepping up the punishment as the fight went on. Both men were cut, but Maguire was fast running out of ideas and when his eye injury worsened the referee called it a day.

06.12.77 ***Charlie Magri, W RSC 7 Dave Smith, Vacant British Flyweight Title***
ALBERT HALL, LONDON The referee led Smith back to the corner after he had been decked five times in all and had no real answer to his opponent's driving aggression. Magri hit far too hard for his rival and Smith simply could not keep him at bay for any concerted period of time

09.12.77 ***Eddie Ndukwu (Nigeria), W RTD 8 Alan Richardson, Commonwealth Featherweight Title***
NATIONAL STADIUM, LAGOS, NIGERIA The Nigerian retained his title when Richardson was retired by his corner due to worsening eye damage following a clash of heads. Ndukwu worked the injury over throughout and in the fourth round had put the Englishman down for two short counts

1978

13.02.78 ***Henry Rhiney, W PTS 15 Billy Waith, British Welterweight Title***
CIVIC HALL, BARNSLEY When retaining his British title Rhiney answered the critics, who maintained that his stamina and character were suspect. In what was more of a scientific battle than a war of attrition Rhiney proved himself a master boxer

17.02.78 ***Jim Watt, W PTS 15 Perico Fernandez (Spain), European Lightweight Title***
SPORTS PALACE, MADRID, SPAIN The Scot survived a first-round knockdown to well and truly overwhelm the local man. Fernandez received three standing counts and spent most of the contest backed against the ropes with Watt on the offensive picking openings

27.02.78 ***Colin Power, W RSC 7 Chris Walker, British L. Welterweight Title***
TOP RANK SUITE, SHEFFIELD Power was less than impressive prior to the seventh when boxing without real authority and getting caught by punches he should have avoided. All of this changed however when the champion unleashed some heavy rights to floor Walker three times before the referee finally counted the challenger out

28.02.78 ***Charlie Nash, W RSC 12 Johnny Claydon, Vacant British Lightweight Title***
TEMPLEMORE SPORTS COMPLEX, DERRY The fight was halted on a technicality when, at the end of twelve completed rounds, the referee's score-card gave Nash a ten point lead. Unfortunately Claydon was very strong at the time, and had badly gashed the Irishman's right eyebrow in the ninth to put himself very much in contention

03.03.78 ***Alfredo Evangelista (Spain), W PTS 15 Billy Aird, European Heavyweight Title***
LEON, SPAIN Making a magnificent challenge, Aird showed the home crowd good old fashioned British courage coupled with skill and ability. Evangelista, by far the heavier and younger man, probably would not have gained the verdict if the contest had been fought outside Spain

06.04.78 ***Johnny Owen, W RSC 10 Wayne Evans, British Bantamweight Title***
LEISURE CENTRE, EBBW VALE The end of the contest was signalled when Evans slid to the floor as Owen slammed away with both hands. The seventh and eighth rounds were rough for the challenger who had to take an eight count as well as damaging his right hand, before he succumbed.

20.04.78 ***Alan Richardson, L PTS 15 Dave Needham, British Featherweight Title***
WORLD SPORTING CLUB, LONDON Needham bled from the first round and was dropped in the ninth, but due to his corner's resolute work he was still able to fight aggresively. Richardson damaged his hand but tended to land the better quality single punches in a bitterly fought battle

05.06.78 ***Jean-Baptiste Piedvache (France), L RTD 11 Colin Power, European L. Welterweight Title***
PALAIS DES SPORTS, PARIS, FRANCE It was a hard gruelling contest for Power until the ninth when he really got on top. Piedvache was hit with everything during that session and also in the tenth was worked over non-stop, before a right to the chin smashed all the fight from him and the towel fluttered in

17.06.78 ***Mate Parlov (Yugoslavia), W PTS 15 John Conteh, World L. Heavyweight Title (WBC version)***
RED STAR STADIUM, BELGRADE, YUGOSLAVIA Conteh fought a frustrating campaign, finding the champion a difficult target with his height and lean-back style prevailing in the earlier rounds. The Englishman used the right sparingly, collected public warnings and in general did not live up to expectations, although he appeared to beat Parlov handily

19.07.78 ***Alan Minter, W CO 12 Angelo Jacopucci (Italy), Vacant European Middleweight Title***
MUNICIPAL STADIUM, BELLARIA, ITALY Following a shaky start Minter asserted himself steadily and Jacopucci was forced to take a count in the seventh. By the tenth the local challenger was fading and the finish came when three right hooks followed by a crushing left put him down. The aftermath of battle was soured by the tragic news that Jacopucci passed away two days later when suffering from a brain haemorrhage

09.09.78 ***Colin Power, L RSC 12 Fernando Sanchez (Spain), European L. Welterweight Title***
THE BULL RING, MIRANDA DE EBRO, SPAIN To call the stoppage premature understated the fact that Power, although taking a standing count, had weathered the storm and was fighting back. Prior to that the Spaniard's appetite for taking punishment was amazing as he was steadily outboxed, outpunched and facially was a complete mess

12.09.78 ***Jimmy Batten, W RTD 13 Tony Poole, British L. Middleweight Title***
CONFERENCE CENTRE, WEMBLEY Poole was an open target for the champion's counters and eventually retired with severe nose damage. Earlier the Northampton man had wobbled Batten on several occasions and at the end of the seventh floored him with a left hook to the body, but the Londoner got up to draw ahead with the left jab working well

11.10.78 ***Clinton McKenzie, W RSC 10 Jim Montague, Vacant British L. Welterweight Title***
MAYSFIELD LEISURE CENTRE, BELFAST With the minimum of inconvenience Montague was dismantled clinically and he finished dazed in his own corner. McKenzie put the Irishman down four times before the referee jumped between them with the victim helpless and being hammered against the ropes

18.10.78 ***Jim Watt, W RTD 5 Antonio Guinaldo (Spain), European Lightweight Title***
KELVIN HALL, GLASGOW The Spaniard surrendered in mid-battle obviously out of his depth, having been dropped and subjected to painful body shots. From the off Watt got down to business and had pursued Guinaldo with a vengeance until the unsatisfactory ending

24.10.78 ***John L. Gardner, W RTD 5 Billy Aird, Vacant British & Commonwealth Heavyweight Titles***
ALBERT HALL, LONDON Aird was cut around both eyes and pummelled without any let up, before retiring himself. The new champion lacked the power to floor his rival, but with superb conditioning had pounded away with non-stop barrages and clusters of blows that disheartened if not destroyed

02.11.78 ***Johnny Owen, W PTS 15 Paul Ferreri (Australia), Vacant Commonwealth Bantamweight Title***
LEISURE CENTRE, EBBW VALE Owen stormed in front not to be denied, jabbing at range and walking through the counters to smash home his own hurtful punches. The best blows Ferreri landed almost went unnoticed as the Welshman's terrific work rate saw him buzzing non-stop to victory

07.11.78 ***Alan Minter, W RTD 6 Gratien Tonna (France), European Middleweight Title***
EMPIRE POOL, WEMBLEY The Frenchman was pounded to a standstill when outboxed, outpunched and outgamed by the heavy hitting Minter. Tonna tried for a disqualification win prior to

17.06.78. A menacing John Conteh (left) moves in on the southpaw Mate Parlov in an effort to regain his old title.

getting cut on the right eye and was taking severe body belts before quitting

21.11.78 ***Gilbert Cohen, (France) W CO 3 Jimmy Batten, Vacant European L. Middleweight Title***

CONFERENCE CENTRE, WEMBLEY Batten boxed without inspiration for two rounds and the Frenchman just cuffed away ineffectually. The third session saw Cohen connecting with jarring right uppercuts before unleashing a left hook and a sweeping right hander which dumped the Englishman for the full count

02.12.78 ***Josef Pachler (Austria), L CO 10 Henry Rhiney, European Welterweight Title***

THE STADTHALIE, DORNBIRN, AUSTRIA After a good start Rhiney appeared to go into his shell, allowing the champion to dominate with aggresive tactics. In the tenth however he caught Pachler with two hooks to the head and then nailed him flush on the jaw with a perfect right uppercut

16.12.78 ***Roberto Castanon (Spain), W RTD 5 Dave Needham, European Featherweight Title***

LEON, SPAIN Needham could not match the Spaniard for power, but was outboxing him handily before collecting facial damage and a standing count. In the fifth the Britisher traded blows with Castanon in a do-or-die effort, but with his face covered in blood the cornermen finally pulled him out

1979

23.01.79 ***Henry Rhiney, L RSC 5 Dave Boy Green, European Welterweight Title***

ALBERT HALL, LONDON Apart from the third round, Rhiney was never able to withstand the aggression of the challenger. Green drew on his greater strength to bull the Luton man before him and in the fifth heavy hooks imposed a standing count before the referee leapt in

06.02.79 ***Clinton McKenzie, L PTS 15 Colin Power, British L. Welterweight Title***

CONFERENCE CENTRE, WEMBLEY One of the finest all-action contests for years saw both fighters display bravery of the highest order. There were no knockdowns and the pace never slackened with each man punching hard enough to win

03.03.79 ***Juan Francisco Rodriguez (Spain), W PTS 15 Johnny Owen, European Bantamweight Title***

THE BULLRING, ALMERIA, SPAIN Following the decision it appeared that Owen had been robbed, after pressuring continuously. Rodriguez fought sporadically and in the main was forced backwards doing little work other than defend

04.03.79 ***Rocky Mattioli (Italy), L RTD 8 Maurice Hope, World L. Middleweight Title (WBC version)***

SAN REMO, ITALY Hope floored the Italian within the opening ten seconds and from then on dominated totally. The end became ominous as Mattioli was battered and cut up conclusively before being retired slumped on his stool when complaining of a damaged hand

04.04.79 ***Henry Rhiney, L RSC 10 Kirkland Laing, British Welterweight Title***

ARDEN SPORTING CLUB, BIRMINGHAM A dejected and weary champion was led back to his corner by the referee after being floored six times. Rhiney had lost his desire and it was Laing who proved his worth, especially when letting the punches flow

10.04.79 ***Tony Sibson, W RSC 5 Frankie Lucas, Vacant British Middleweight Title***

ALBERT HALL, LONDON From the moment Lucas was cut badly, one could sense that Sibson would not let him off the hook. The referee eventually stopped the contest after he had been floored three times and was sagging on the bottom rope

17.04.79 ***Jim Watt, W RSC 12 Alfredo Pitalua (Colombia), Vacant World Lightweight Title (WBC version)***

KELVIN HALL, GLASGOW Watt countered solidly, jabbing brilliantly on the retreat and when the Colombian flagged in the later stages he finished him off with ruthless efficiency. The seventh round saw Pitalua put down by a near perfect left hook but he survived until a sustained burst of punches forced the referee to intervene

01.05.79 ***Franco Udella (Italy), L PTS 12 Charlie Magri, European Flyweight Title***

EMPIRE POOL, WEMBLEY The young man from Stepney won beyond doubt with a controlled performance against the chunky experienced Udella. Magri jabbed accurately throughout and as the Italian tired he put in a driving finish to force him continuously against the ropes

13.05.79 ***Bunny Johnson, W CO 4 Rab Affleck, British L. Heavyweight Title***

ST ANDREWS SPORTING CLUB, GLASGOW Following a cautious start Johnson cut loose to inflict eye damage on his opponent, before flattening him with vicious punches to the head. The crowd were stunned as Affleck was counted out prostrate in the champion's corner

13.06.79 ***Johnny Owen, W RTD 12 Dave Smith, British & Commonwealth Bantamweight Titles***

DOUBLE DIAMOND CLUB, CAERPHILLY Although it was fairly one-sided, Smith put up a terrific battle before retiring with his left eye completely closed. Owen was supreme, producing a steady volume of punches to head and body, but the challenger to his credit was never floored

26.06.79 ***John L. Gardner, W RSC 6 Paul Sykes, British & Commonwealth Heavyweight Titles***

EMPIRE POOL, WEMBLEY Gardner obeyed his corner to the letter by boxing calmly and not rushing in. Showing a sound defence and after weathering early storms, he remorselessly battered Sykes until the referee had seen enough

27.06.79 ***Charlie Nash, W PTS 12 Andre Holyk (France), Vacant European Lightweight Title***

TEMPLEMORE SPORTS COMPLEX, DERRY Although comprehensively outboxed Holyk chased his man doggedly in every round, vainly hoping to land the finisher. Nash, boxing brilliantly on the retreat with the southpaw jab highly effective, scored a flawless points win

28.06.79 ***Dave Boy Green, L CO 3 Jorgen Hansen (Denmark), European Welterweight Title***

RANDERSHALLEN, RANDERS, DENMARK The Englishman recklessly abandoned all defence in an effort to crush the veteran Hansen, after flooring him in the second. Walking into a cracking couple of rights, Green was put low and on rising was clubbed down for the full count

29.07.79 ***Kenny Bristol (Guyana), W PTS 15 Pat Thomas, Vacant Commonwealth L. Middleweight Title***

GEORGETOWN, GUYANA A boring contest saw Thomas hold the centre of the ring slipping the leads for several rounds before realising that he would have to get on the offensive. Chasing hard, he was often restrained by Bristol when inside, to become the victim of a debatable decision

18.08.79 ***Matthew Saad Muhammad (USA), W PTS 15 John Conteh, World L. Heavyweight Title (WBC version)***

RESORT HOTEL, ATLANTIC CITY, USA Muhammad fought on from the fifth suffering from appalling cuts with the Britisher boxing superbly behind the left jab and opening up a good lead. Unfortunately Conteh was battered throughout the thirteenth and floored twice in the penultimate round before losing out on the judges scoring

11.09.79 ***Jimmy Batten, L RSC 9 Pat Thomas, British L. Middleweight Title***

CONFERENCE CENTRE, WEMBLEY The referee

10.04.79. A determined Frankie Lucas (left) storms into the attack during his great contest against Tony Sibson.

pulled the Welshman off Batten in the ninth with the Londoner completely handicapped by a grotesque swelling over the right eye. He had become defenceless against the left hook and was being pounded non-stop along the ropes

11.09.79 ***Colin Power, L PTS 15 Clinton McKenzie, British L. Welterweight Title***
CONFERENCE CENTRE, WEMBLEY As in their previous contest it was difficult to score, with Power punching solidly but the challenger throwing the flashier combinations. The champion took the early rounds and McKenzie the middle section with both men going hard at the finish

18.09.79 ***Dave Needham, W PTS 15 Pat Cowdell, British Featherweight Title***
CIVIC HALL, WOLVERHAMPTON When entering the fifteenth round it seemed that Cowdell was only moments away from being crowned champion after controlling the pace and snapping in crisp jabs throughout. To his credit Needham stayed in the fight after a bad start with his strength being predominant

25.09.79 ***Maurice Hope, W RSC 7 Mike Baker (USA), World L. Middleweight Title (WBC version)***
EMPIRE POOL, WEMBLEY The American challenger was handed a monotonous clubbing with Hope putting him down heavily before the referee saved him from further punishment. Amazingly Baker did well to survive for so long when often shipping all the punches that came his way

03.11.79 ***Jim Watt, W RSC 9 Roberto Vasquez (USA), World Lightweight Title (WBC version)***
KELVIN HALL, GLASGOW A totally outclassed Vasquez was hammered to defeat and finally rescued by the referee as he was being battered by a barrage of solid punches without reply. Although not flooring his challenger Watt had handed out a systematic beating and was composed nearly to the point of arrogance

06.11.79 ***Tony Sibson, L PTS 15 Kevin Finnegan, British Middleweight Title***
ALBERT HALL, LONDON Fortunes swayed constantly, but ultimately the crafty ex-champion edged the decision as wild man Sibson missed too often with the final punches. By the fifth Finnegan's left eye had gone, but boxing at range using jabs and counters he held Sibson up long enough to take the nod

06.11.79 ***Dave Needham, L PTS 15 Pat Cowdell, British Featherweight Title***
ALBERT HALL, LONDON There were no mistakes this time even if Cowdell's work rate appeared extremely low during the middle rounds.

Needham always forced with his industry and was ever threatening but the challenger came back strongly at the finish matching him punch for punch

30.11.79 ***Hogan Jimoh (Nigeria), W RSC 8 Johnny Claydon, Commonwealth Lightweight Title***
LAGOS, NIGERIA Claydon was stopped on his feet when taking heavy punishment, although earlier he had produced some good work. Hard rights had shaken Jimoh up, but he came right back to floor the Englishman just prior to the closure

04.12.79 ***Charlie Magri, W PTS 12 Manuel Carrasco (Spain), European Flyweight Title***
EMPIRE POOL, WEMBLEY The extremely brave Spaniard was thrashed in twelve one-sided rounds and to his credit remained upright. Magri never let up before damaging his own right hand in the fifth and cruising along from thereon

06.12.79 ***Charlie Nash, W PTS 12 Ken Buchanan, European Lightweight Title***
BRONDBYHALLEN, COPENHAGEN, DENMARK On conclusion the contest appeared to have gone either way, but it was the Irishman who retained his title. Buchanan proved that he still had the stamina for a title bout whilst Nash, although boxing competently, never set the crowd alight

11.12.79 ***Pat Thomas, W CO 7 Dave Proud, British L. Middleweight Title***
BLETCHLEY LEISURE CENTRE, MILTON KEYNES Proud displayed immense raw-boned courage before being dispatched by a perfect left hook midway through the seventh. Prior to that Thomas had cut his challenger up badly and put him down three times during a desperate third round

1980

07.02.80 ***Kevin Finnegan, W PTS 12 Gratien Tonna (France), Vacant European Middleweight Title***
STADE PIERRE DE COUBERTIN, PARIS, FRANCE This was a memorable victory for Finnegan who came back from two counts in the third to smash away ferociously at the Frenchman. Tonna finished damaged facially after being on the receiving end of sharp cutting punches and was generally bemused throughout

08.02.80 ***Ray Amoo (Nigeria), W PTS 15 Neil McLaughlin, Vacant Commonwealth Flyweight Title***
LAGOS, NIGERIA The game Irishman fought bravely, but was mainly on the end of the African champion's punches. Amoo won clearly with McLaughlin being warned several times for holding in the later stages

19.02.80 ***Pat Cowdell, W RTD 11 Jimmy Flint, British Featherweight Title***
ALBERT HALL, LONDON Flint was comprehensively outboxed and outpunched from the moment Cowdell got his jab working effectively. The Londoner also ran into heavy counters which eventually left him in no fit state to continue and he was retired wisely by his corner

27.02.80 ***Bunny Johnson, W PTS 15 Dennis Andries, British L. Heavyweight Title***
ADULT BALLROOM, BURSLEM A dreary affair saw Johnson retain his title even allowing for the fact that few scoring punches were thrown. Andries eventually settled for wrestling the champion to the floor frequently over the last three rounds

28.02.80 ***Juan Francisco Rodriguez (Spain), L PTS 12 Johnny Owen, European Bantamweight Title***
THE LEISURE CENTRE, EBBW VALE The Spaniard was methodically worn down by Owen who won beyond argument mainly by the use of a jarring left jab. Rodriguez, although coming back well on occasions, finished in an exhausted state

04.03.80 ***Tony Sibson, W PTS 15 Chisanda Mutti (Zambia), Vacant Commonwealth Middleweight Title***
EMPIRE POOL, WEMBLEY Sibson landed the crisper punches, although having to settle for a points victory when his early onslaught failed to bring the Zambian down. Having an upright style, Mutti always posed problems with his extra reach and was also often dangerous with an occasional chopping right hand

14.03.80 ***Jim Watt, W RSC 4 Charlie Nash, World Lightweight Title (WBC version)***
KELVIN HALL, GLASGOW With an awesome display of controlled aggression Watt floored the challenger three times with precise punching before the referee stepped in. The battle of southpaws had earlier seen Nash floor the Scot with a powerful right before receiving a badly cut left eye himself

16.03.80 ***Vito Antuofermo (Italy), L PTS 15 Alan Minter, World Middleweight Title***
CAESARS PALACE, LAS VEGAS, USA Minter fought consistently and produced the better work during a hard contest, with the Italian-American always swinging away but often getting countered heavily. Both men were cut and Antuofermo was awarded a dubious knockdown when Minter was pushed over in the penultimate round

24.03.80 ***Ray Cattouse, W RSC 8 Dave McCabe, Vacant British Lightweight Title***
ST ANDREWS SPORTING CLUB, GLASGOW The Scot appeared to have a clear lead going into the sixth round, but Cattouse came out mixing right uppercuts to head and body. McCabe showed visible signs of flagging and was continuously

forced to the ropes before his left eye split following some close quarter fighting in the eighth

29.03.80 ***Matthew Saad Muhammad (USA), W RSC 4 John Conteh, World L. Heavyweight Title (WBC version)***
RESORTS INTERNATIONAL HOTEL, ATLANTIC CITY, USA Conteh was smashed to conclusive defeat before the referee intervened, following the fifth knockdown. The Englishman had tried to keep Muhammad at distance, but was hurt and then finally destroyed once the American found the range

31.03.80 ***Sugar Ray Leonard, W CO 4 Dave Boy Green, World Welterweight Title (WBC version)***
CAPITAL CENTRE, LANDOVER, USA A thundering left hook spelt the end for Green and his head cracked against the boards leaving only the formality of the court. Leonard had thrown rapid punches throughout which frequently found their way through the Englishman's defence but Green was always looking to make a fight of it

01.04.80 ***Kirkland Laing, L RSC 9 Colin Jones, British Welterweight Title***
CONFERENCE CENTRE, WEMBLEY After eight rounds of chasing Jones finally saw his opportunity and took it well with the big right hand, and although Laing did not sink, the referee had no alternative than to stop the contest. Prior to the dramatic end the champion had built up a wide points margin

17.04.80 ***Jorgen Hansen (Denmark), W PTS 12 Joey Singleton, European Welterweight Title***
BRONDBYHALLEN, COPENHAGEN, DENMARK Despite a two-inch gash over the right eye, Singleton boxed a crafty fight which enabled him to last the distance. Hansen for his part was content on keeping one punch ahead, but was never able to get set for his big right

22.04.80 ***John L. Gardner, W RTD 9 Rudi Gauwe (Belgium), Vacant European Heavyweight Title***
ALBERT HALL, LONDON The Belgian finally surrendered after sinking to his knees following the after effects of being put down by a right under the heart. Gardner with relentless pressure had punched Gauwe to a standstill and demoralised him long before the finish

27.09.80. The fearsome looking Marvin Hagler (right) blasts a right hand through the defences of Alan Minter shortly before the finish.

14.05.80 ***Kevin Finnegan DREW 12, Georg Steinherr (W. Germany), European Middleweight Title***

OLYMPIAHALLE, MUNICH, W. GERMANY Following twelve bitterly fought rounds, Finnegan appeared lucky to hold on to his crown. Steinherr dealt out terrific punishment early on and cut his opponent up badly, but the Englishman clawed his way back doggedly

29.05.80 ***Pat Cowdell, W RTD 12 Dave Needham, British Featherweight Title***

CIVIC HALL, WOLVERHAMPTON Cowdell won ownership of the Lonsdale Belt in record time, when Needham was retired with a badly swollen face. The ex-titleholder had tried to walk through the leather, but was picked off with stabbing punches to the head time and again

07.06.80 ***Jim Watt, W PTS 15 Howard Davis (USA), World Lightweight Title (WBC version)***

IBROX PARK, GLASGOW With a brilliantly executed points victory, Watt proved his right to the title and was only a punch away from halting his challenger in the penultimate round. Davis threw more punches than the Scot, but lacked any accuracy whilst the champion's fists were better placed and carried more authority

28.06.80 ***Charlie Magri, W RSC 3 Giovanni Camputaro (Italy), European Flyweight Title***

EMPIRE POOL, WEMBLEY The Italian grimly hung on to Magri at every opportunity in an effort to avoid punishment. Eventually Camputaro was tagged by two heavy right hands and was defenceless on the ropes, which bought about the referee's intervention

28.06.80 ***Johnny Owen, W PTS 15 John Feeney, British & Commonwealth Bantamweight Titles***

EMPIRE POOL, WEMBLEY A cracker of a fight saw both men giving and taking solid shots with Owen forever coming forward, whilst the challenger favoured the counter punch. Feeney was never allowed to take the initiative. Although occasionally landing good punches, he was swamped by the champion's workrate

28.06.80 ***Alan Minter, W RTD 8 Vito Antuofermo (Italy), World Middleweight Title***

EMPIRE POOL, WEMBLEY The Italian-American fought the only way he knew, hurling himself at Minter round after round before finishing in a bloody mess to be retired by his corner. Minter picked Antuofermo off throughout with heavy combinations and was never in difficulty himself, whilst coasting to the inevitable victory

04.07.80 ***Obisia Nwankpa (Nigeria), W PTS 15 Clinton McKenzie, Commonwealth L. Welterweight Title***

NATIONAL STADIUM, LAGOS, NIGERIA The British champion took the fight to Nwankpa nearly every round, but was countered steadily and was often guilty of incorrect hitting. Neither man was floored and McKenzie really turned it on over the last three rounds in an effort to pull the contest his way

12.07.80 ***Maurice Hope, W RSC 11 Rocky Mattioli (Italy), World L. Middleweight Title (WBC version)***

EMPIRE POOL, WEMBLEY Following a successful eye operation Hope bounded back into action with a brilliant victory over the tough Italian, who was saved by the referee with only his courage intact. Mattioli would not succumb to Hope's cutting punches even when being hit with almost every shot in the book

12.08.80 ***Colin Jones, W RSC 5 Peter Neal, British Welterweight Title***

EISTEDDFOD PAVILION, SWANSEA Colin Jones crushed his challenger unmercifully with a special brand of destructive hitting which left Neal a grotesque mess facially. Shrugging off the punches the challenger could not be faulted for his courage, but was on a hiding to nothing when the referee rescued him

27.08.80 ***Guiseppe Martinese (Italy), W RTD 10 Clinton McKenzie, Vacant European L. Welterweight Title***

SENEGALIA, ITALY McKenzie was retired after taking steady punishment from the ninth round onwards, during which he sustained a badly gashed right eye. Prior to the eighth however the Britisher appeared to dominate, before tiring badly and allowing Martinese to gain control, with his long leads inflicting the damage

10.09.80 ***Kevin Finnegan, L PTS 12 Matteo Salvemini (Italy), European Middleweight Title***

ARISTON CINEMA, SAN REMO, ITALY Despite flooring his opponent in the fourth, Finnegan began to show signs of coming to the end of his career when he was bulled to defeat, and suffered bad eye damage. Salvemini was strong and awkward, but lacked the class of the champion, with his youth being the deciding factor

16.09.80 ***Pat Thomas, W RSC 15 Steve Hopkin, British L. Middleweight Title***

CONFERENCE CENTRE, WEMBLEY The young challenger showed plenty of raw courage as well as possessing a good punch in giving Thomas all the trouble he could handle. Eventually the referee stopped the contest with Hopkins badly cut following an accidental clash of heads

19.09.80 *Lupe Pintor (Mexico), W CO 12 Johnny Owen, World Bantamweight Title (WBC version)*
OLYMPIC AUDITORIUM, LOS ANGELES, USA For the first eight rounds Owen stayed on top of the Mexican, but the turning point came when he was floored at the end of the ninth. From then on it was one way traffic with Pintor finally delivering the finishing punch – a long right hand following a further knockdown. Tragically Owen never regained consciousness

27.09.80 *Alan Minter, L RSC 3 Marvin Hagler (USA), World Middleweight Title*
EMPIRE POOL, WEMBLEY Minter walked straight into the American and was facially cut to ribbons before he could even get into the contest. The referee rescued the champion in the third from Hagler's clinical fists with cuts both under and over each eye which eventually needed 15 stitches

01.11.80 *Jim Watt, W RSC 12 Sean O'Grady (USA), World Lightweight Title (WBC version)*
KELVIN HALL, GLASGOW A tenth round clash of heads turned the course of the fight for Watt, who although ahead on points was himself suffering from an eye wound. The aftermath saw O'Grady stopped with his face masked in blood from a terrible forehead wound which made it almost impossible for him to see

26.11.80 *Maurice Hope, W PTS 15 Carlos Herrera (Argentine), World L. Middleweight Title (WBC version)*
EMPIRE POOL, WEMBLEY During fifteen hard-fought rounds Hope pulled out all the stops to hang on to his title in a great contest. Herrera proved himself to be a tough handful by carrying the fight to Maurice and hurting him often, although never able to consolidate

28.11.80 *John L. Gardner, W CO 5 Lorenzo Zanon (Italy), European Heavyweight Title*
CAMPIONE D'ITALIA, ITALY The Italian was disposed of by a display of power punching by Gardner, who delivered the finishing blow, a solid right leaving the count out just a formality. Prior to that Zanon had scored well using his longer reach, but had looked vulnerable when under body attacks

08.12.80 *Matteo Salvemini (Italy), L CO 7 Tony Sibson, European Middleweight Title*
ALBERT HALL, LONDON Sibson took the champion apart with a venomous display of punching, flooring him twice in the fourth round before catching up with him finally in the seventh. Salvemini, his left eye cut, was hammered around the ring and dropped face first by a mighty right to the head

14.12.80 *Francisco Leon (Spain), L PTS 12 Charlie Nash, European Lightweight Title*
BURLINGTON Hotel, DUBLIN, EIRE The Irishman knew far too much for the limited Leon who although battling constantly was picked off and left chasing shadows. Nash was content to counter his fellow southpaw when it seemed that sustained aggression could have brought about an inside-the-distance win

1981

06.01.81 *Clinton McKenzie, W RSC 14 Des Morrison, British L. Welterweight Title*
YORK HALL, LONDON A titanic struggle saw McKenzie come through a tremendous eighth round with bad eye damage to eventually force the challenger to be rescued by the referee. Morrison had given his all and been dropped twice prior to the finish

02.02.81 *Roy Gumbs, W RSC 3 Howard Mills, Vacant British Middleweight Title*
NATIONAL SPORTING CLUB, LONDON The contest was won in the second round when Mills was dropped and never fully recovered. Gumbs again opened up to drop his man for a further three counts a round later before the referee had seen enough

24.02.81 *Charlie Magri, W RSC 2 Enrique Rodriguez Cal (Spain), European Flyweight Title*
ALBERT HALL, LONDON The Spaniard was floored four times by body punches before being rescued from Magri's attack. Whilst the contest lasted it was totally one-sided and although Rodriguez Cal's credentials were good it was an obvious mismatch

03.03.81 *Colin Jones, W RSC 9 Mark Harris (Guyana), Vacant Commonwealth Welterweight Title*
CONFERENCE CENTRE, WEMBLEY After encountering stubborn resistance early on, Colin Jones finally got through with devastating effect to floor his rival three times and force the closure. Harris had shown great spirit to keep in the fight, despite being floored earlier

08.03.81 *Rafael Limon (Mexico), L PTS 15 Cornelius Boza-Edwards, World J. Lightweight Title (WBC version)*
STOCKTON, CALIFORNIA, USA The British-based Ugandan met the champion head on in a brilliant slugging feast and not only floored him in the fifth, but generally outpunched him. Limon later resorted to low blows and with both men marked the Mexican was consistently beaten at his own brand of aggressive tactics

20.06.81. A sleek Alexis Arguello (left) looks poised to set up another attack against Jim Watt.

23.03.81 ***Ray Cattouse, W RSC 15 Dave McCabe, British Lightweight Title***
ST ANDREWS SOCIAL CLUB, GLASGOW Cattouse retained his title after a torrid all-action contest that seesawed throughout. In the ninth McCabe had been floored, but fought back well only to be overwhelmed in the final round before the referee rescued him

24.03.81 ***Pat Thomas, L PTS 15 Herol Graham, British L. Middleweight Title***
CITY HALL, SHEFFIELD The contest was dominated by the new champion who made Thomas look pedestrian at times, whilst he glided around the ring. Graham landed effectively over the course and in the main slipped most blows that came his way

30.03.81 ***Gordon Ferris, W PTS 15 Billy Aird, Vacant British Heavyweight Title***
ASTON SPORTS CENTRE, BIRMINGHAM Ferris probably won the title on the strength of his better start, but when the Liverpudlian finally got to work he looked the likely winner. Both men were cut but gave their all in a tough uncompromising showing and both remained vertical

31.03.81 ***Clinton McKenzie, W PTS 15 Sylvester Mittee, British L. Welterweight Title***
CONFERENCE CENTRE, WEMBLEY The exuberant McKenzie matched his work rate against the one-punch power of Mittee and used accurate combinations to suppress his rival. Mittee was always dangerous with heavy punches, but McKenzie had courage in abundance plus the will to win

28.04.81 ***Colin Jones, W RSC 9 Kirkland Laing, British & Commonwealth Welterweight Titles***
ALBERT HALL, LONDON Laing boxed brilliantly in the early stages and in the eighth round floored the Welshman twice with punches that appeared to go low. Coming out purposefully in the ninth, Jones smashed away at his rival, dropping him with a terrific left hook to the chin and although Laing got up at nine the referee immediately stopped the bout

10.05.81 ***Charlie Nash, L CO 6 Joey Gibilisco (Italy), European Lightweight Title***
DALYMOUNT PARK DUBLIN, EIRE Nash never got going, taking standing counts in rounds two and four, before being counted out in the sixth following a further knockdown. There were signs that Gibilisco had spent himself, but the writing

was on the wall once the Irishman had picked up a split right eyebrow

14.05.81 ***Tony Sibson, W PTS 12 Andoni Amana (Spain), European Middleweight Title***

THE BULLRING, BILBAO, SPAIN The Spaniard took two counts and was generally outpunched with the decision never really in doubt. Sibson continually came forward, but picked up a cut over the right eye with Amana making desperate efforts to get into the contest without success

24.05.81 ***Maurice Hope, L CO 12 Wilfred Benitez (Puerto Rico), World L. Middleweight Title (WBC version)***

CAESARS PALACE, LAS VEGAS, USA The champion was fighting a losing battle by the sixth round, but refused to give ground until the inevitable right hander stretched him prostrate on the canvas. Although cutting up his rival, Hope suffered severe body shots with Benitez dumping him prior to the count out

30.05.81 ***Cornelius Boza-Edwards, W RTD 13 Bobby Chacon (USA), World J. Lightweight Title (WBC version)***

SHOWBOAT CASINO, LAS VEGAS, USA Chacon was often troubled by the southpaw stance but the pair punched it out for ten rounds before he began to falter. Boza then got right on top until finally at the end of the thirteenth, completely exhausted and badly cut up, Chacon was retired by his corner

17.06.81 ***Valerio Nati (Italy), W PTS 12 John Feeney, European Bantamweight Title***

CERVIA, ITALY The Italian was strong but limited, being caught repeatedly by short punches inside and was dropped in the second. Although Feeney boxed well throughout, his work rate was not high enough to match Nati, who would not be subdued

20.06.81 ***Jim Watt, L PTS 15 Alexis Arguello (Nicaragua), World Lightweight Title (WBC version)***

EMPIRE POOL, WEMBLEY Watt staged a clever defensive campaign but it was never going to be enough to win with the knowledge that he could not outspeed the Nicaraguan. The Scot was floored in the seventh, but eventually his rear-guard action wore down Arguello, who was content to box to victory

20.07.81 ***Barry Michael (Australia), W RSC 7 Dave McCabe, Commonwealth Lightweight Title***

DALLAS BROOKES CENTRE, MELBOURNE, AUSTRALIA The Scot was floored five times in all and was totally outgunned as the English-born Michael used the body as his main target. The final flooring meant an automatic stoppage on the three knockdown ruling

29.08.81 ***Cornelius Boza-Edwards, L CO 5 Rolando Navarette (Philippines), World J. Lightweight Title (WBC version)***

STADIO DE PINI, VIA REGGIO, ITALY From the moment Boza-Edwards received a terrible eye wound, he was forced to try and end the contest quickly. He had previously been well on top but Navarette dropped him half blinded by his own blood twice in the fourth, before finishing the job with a vicious right to the jaw

15.09.81 ***Tony Sibson, W CO 3 Alan Minter, European Middleweight Title***

EMPIRE POOL, WEMBLEY Terrific hooks from both hands paved the way for the two knockdowns Minter was to suffer in the third round. A left dropped him and on rising he found Sibson swarming all over him, thudding in heavy punches to the head until the ex-champion was finally battered to the floor

22.09.81 ***John Feeney, W RSC 8 Dave Smith, Vacant British Bantamweight Title***

YORK HALL, LONDON Contesting his third British championship, Dave Smith once again found the going tough and was reeling against the ropes before the referee finally rescued him. Feeney proved too powerful and aggressive for the gallant Londoner, whose punching power unfortunately did not match his skill

12.10.81 ***Gordon Ferris, L CO 1 Neville Meade, British Heavyweight Title***

ASTON VILLA LEISURE CENTRE, BIRMINGHAM Neville Meade became the oldest man to gain the heavyweight crown when kayoing the champion after just two minutes 45 seconds. The jab paved the way, before an explosive right caught Ferris high on the temple to send him face downwards

13.10.81 ***Antonio Guinaldo (Spain), L PTS 12 Clinton McKenzie, European L. Welterweight Title***

ALBERT HALL, LONDON It was a relatively easy job for Clinton until the tenth round when things began to warm up. Guinaldo finished facially damaged and unbowed, but had been under terrific pressure before fighting back to force a great finish

29.10.81 ***Roy Gumbs, W RSC 6 Eddie Burke, British Middleweight Title***

KELVIN HALL, GLASGOW Gumbs ruthlessly crushed the Scot who was knocked down on four separate occasions, before the referee rescued him when his right eye was pouring blood. Burke had found it difficult to counter the champion's sharper punching, but always fought back when under pressure

24.11.81 ***Tony Sibson, W CO 10 Nicola Cirelli, European Middleweight Title***

EMPIRE POOL, WEMBLEY Frustrated at range and

tagged by both hands, Sibson finally put it together in the ninth with a blistering attack. A left hook dropped Cirelli in the tenth, who upon rising was belted incessantly with left hooks until his legs gave way for the count out to be completed

25.11.81 ***Kenny Bristol (Guyana), L PTS 15 Herol Graham, Commonwealth L. Middleweight Title***

CITY HALL, SHEFFIELD Showing a clever defence, Bristol was never in any real danger of losing inside the distance, but did not have the armoury himself to end the contest conclusively. Graham was merely content to jab and move for a decisive win but the fight lacked lustre

12.12.81 ***Salvador Sanchez (Mexico), W PTS 15 Pat Cowdell, World Featherweight Title (WBC version)***

THE ASTRODOME, HOUSTON, USA The Britisher boxed magnificently, but suffered a badly cut eyebrow in the ninth which eventually necessitated 20 stitches and undoubtedly affected his overall performance. Sanchez, recognised as one of the great champions, finally floored Cowdell in the last round, but the split decision proved the challenger's class

1982

16.02.82 ***Clinton McKenzie, W RSC 4 Steve Early, British L. Welterweight Title***

BLOOMSBURY CREST HOTEL, LONDON The fourth round saw McKenzie in dominating form with the challenger beginning to tire rapidly and being dropped for eight, before the referee saved him. Early lacked the variety to bother the Londoner and the contest became rather one-sided

18.02.82 ***Roy Gumbs, W RSC 13 Glen McEwan, British Middleweight Title***

THE STADIUM, LIVERPOOL Although looking menacing in the early rounds, Gumbs was continually frustrated by his opponent's shifty style. Both men were cut by the twelfth round with McEwan having made his major effort before exhaustion set in and he was rescued by the referee after visiting the canvas twice during the thirteenth

24.02.82 ***Herol Graham, W RSC 9 Chris Christian, British & Commonwealth L. Middleweight Titles***

CITY HALL, SHEFFIELD Graham imposed himself upon Christian by staying at close quarters and firing in punches, but avoiding any real damage to himself. The London-based fighter was only dropped once mainly due to his amazing courage and proved his ability to absorb punishment

24.02.82 ***Joey Gibilisco (Italy), DREW 12 Ray Cattouse, European Lightweight Title***

CAMPOBASSO, ITALY Over twelve torrid rounds Cattouse, despite being floored in the first, came back to take the champion's best punches and deliver plenty of his own. Gibilisco was punched out by the ninth and the Englishman began to cut back any leeway by swarming all over his rival until the final bell

5.03.82 ***Tom Collins, W PTS 15 Dennis Andries, Vacant British L. Heavyweight Title***

BLOOMSBURY CREST HOTEL, LONDON Collins sealed his victory with a knockdown in each of the last two rounds, after starting the bout in a lethargic manner. He gradually settled down to box behind the left jab with Andries clubbing in wild punches and only occasionally getting home

17.03.82 ***Carlos Hernandez (Spain), L RTD 4 Cornelius Boza-Edwards, European J. Lightweight Title***

ALBERT HALL, LONDON Hernandez walked out of the contest near the end of the fourth round without being decked or in any apparent difficulties. The Spaniard had fought well early on and Boza-Edwards was just as perplexed as the crowd at the walk out

30.03.82 ***Luigi Minchillo (Italy), W PTS 12 Maurice Hope, European L. Middleweight Title***

EMPIRE POOL, WEMBLEY The Italian never took a backward step and every time Hope landed, he would come right back. Maurice was in the contest with every chance until the tenth round, but faded and Minchillo came close to a stoppage win before the final bell rang

30.03.82 ***Salvatore Melluzzo (Italy), L RSC 10 Pat Cowdell, European Featherweight Title***

EMPIRE POOL, WEMBLEY Even allowing for the fact that Cowdell boxed well below form he was still a class above the Italian, who was restricted to bull-like charges. In the sixth round a cut was opened over Melluzzo's right eyebrow and when he received another cut under the same eye the referee pulled him out

02.04.82 ***Paul Ferreri (Australia), W RSC 13 John Feeney, Commonwealth Bantamweight Title***

CONCERT HALL, SYDNEY, AUSTRALIA Ferreri was far too experienced for the Englishman and wore him down with effective body punches. Although Feeney occasionally worked well with the jab he eventually ran out of steam and was rescued by the referee

12.10.82. In one of the great British Championship fights, George Feeney (left) and Ray Cattouse fought almost to a standstill.

04.05.82 ***Tony Sibson, W RSC 10 Jacques Chinon (France), European Middleweight Title***

EMPIRE POOL, WEMBLEY This contest did little to enhance Sibson's reputation, but once he had cut the French challenger under the left eye in the seventh round the writing was on the wall. Chinon collected a standing count in the tenth before the referee decided he had seen enough

26.05.82 ***Tom Collins, W CO 4 Trevor Cattouse, British L. Heavyweight Title***

ASTORIA CENTRE, LEEDS Cattouse tried to pressure the more skilful champion into a slugging bout and even when put down in the first round, he kept on coming forward. Into the fourth and Collins opened up with a vengeance throwing a whole series of punches, but it was a right to the jaw that led to the count out

11.06.82 ***Obisia Nwankpa (Nigeria), W RSC 10 Des Morrison, Commonwealth L. Welterweight Title***

ABA, NIGERIA The humidity eventually got to Morrison who was saved by the referee when under heavy punishment in the tenth. Nwankpa finally caught up with the challenger, who wilted as the Nigerian poured in the punches

30.06.82 ***Guiseppe Fossati (Italy) W PTS 12 John Feeney, European Bantamweight Title***

SICILY, ITALY Fossati quickly gained control with heavy rights and then left hooks to floor the challenger in the fourth round. On several occasions he looked set to repeat the dose, but Feeney showed commendable courage to keep going against the odds

14.09.82 ***Colin Jones, W CO 2 Sakaria Ve (Fiji), Commonwealth Welterweight Title***

EMPIRE POOL, WEMBLEY The Welshman stalked Ve during the first, obviously weighing his man up, but the round was fairly uneventful. Jones then went to work in the second with left hooks backing up the challenger along the ropes, before he fell down to be counted out

14.09.82 ***Kelvin Smart, W CO 6 Dave George, Vacant British Flyweight Title***

EMPIRE POOL, WEMBLEY Smart dominated from the moment he realised his fellow Welsh opponent did not have the power to keep him away and had resorted to purely defensive measures. In the sixth George was hurt by two left hooks before a body shot ended the contest summarily

18.09.82 ***Charlie Magri, W CO 2 Enrique Rodriquez Cal (Spain), European Flyweight Title***
CATTLE MARKET, AVILES, SPAIN In the first round Magri belted his opponent to the floor and it was noticeable that the Spaniard's left eye had been split. The referee appeared to give a long count, but in the second round Rodriguez Cal was put down for five before another barrage enforced the count out

20.09.82 ***Steve Sammy Sims, W CO 12 Terry McKeown, Vacant British Featherweight Title***
ST ANDREWS SPORTING CLUB, GLASGOW A brave attempt ended in the twelfth round when the Scot succumbed under a series of hooks to the head and was counted out on his haunches. McKeown had a big lead prior to the eighth, but from then on Sims just marched through the punches to whittle away the margin

30.09.82 ***Herol Graham, W PTS 15 Hunter Clay (Nigeria), Commonwealth L. Middleweight Title***
SPORTS STADIUM, LAGOS, NIGERIA Despite continuous infringements of the regulations by the Nigerian, Graham steadily outboxed him over the duration. In the fourth however, Clay dropped the champion with body punches, but was put down himself in the ninth and thirteenth and then floored four times during the final round

12.10.82 ***Ray Cattouse, L RSC 14 George Feeney, British Lightweight Title***
ALBERT HALL, LONDON The fight of the year saw George Feeney rip the title away from the proud champion, who was reeling under a savage attack with his eye bleeding profusely, before being rescued by the referee. Rally upon rally had ensued to thunderous applause, but it was Cattouse who wilted.

12.10.82 ***Clinton McKenzie, L DIS 2 Robert Gambini (France), European L. Welterweight Title***
ALBERT HALL, LONDON Gambini opened up with southpaw jabs and crosses, but the Croydon man came right back and was getting into his stride by the end of the first round. The end came suddenly when McKenzie threw body punches followed by a low right which left the referee no alternative but to disqualify him

30.10.82 ***Pat Cowdell, W RSC 12 Sepp Iten (Switzerland), European Featherweight Title***
ZURICH, SWITZERLAND It did not take long for Cowdell to sort out his challenger's southpaw stance and then to use every punch in the book as the contest progressed. Iten was eventually floored in the eleventh when he was trapped in a corner and then rescued a round later by the referee as he was about to go down again

05.11.82 ***Hans Henrik Palm (Denmark), L RSC 2 Colin Jones, European Welterweight Title***
K.B. HALLE, COPENHAGEN, DENMARK The first round saw Jones the fighter out-jabbing the Danish master boxer and in the second the same pattern persisted. Suddenly Palm was caught by a mighty left hook to the jaw and although beating the count he was put down again, only to rise in the face of a further onslaught before the referee saved him

1983

25.01.83 ***John Feeney, L DIS 13 Hugh Russell, British Bantamweight Title***
ULSTER HALL, BELFAST The defending champion was disqualified for persistent misuse of the head with the contest still in the balance. The marked difference in height between Feeney and Russell was probably the real reason their heads clashed on occasions, with the Irishman unfortunately picking up eye damage in the second round

03.02.83 ***Steve Muchoki (Kenya), L RSC 9 Keith Wallace, Commonwealth Flyweight Title***
BLOOMSBURY CREST HOTEL, LONDON Muchoki by dint of his elegant jab appeared to be in front prior to the eighth, but early in that round a right uppercut badly hurt him and he was lucky to last out. The ninth started with Wallace banging in another uppercut followed by a variety of heavy punches before the referee drew the contest to a halt

08.02.83 ***Roy Gumbs, W RSC 5 Ralph Hollett (Canada), Vacant Commonwealth Middleweight Title***
SPORTSPLEX, DARTMOUTH, NOVA SCOTIA It seemed that the British champion was well on the way to defeat when floored in the third and hammered incessantly to the body a round later. Round five saw Gumbs strike back with a solid right to the jaw, followed up by a two-handed attack, leaving Hollett hanging over the middle strand defenceless

11.02.83 ***Marvin Hagler (USA), W RSC 6 Tony Sibson, World Middleweight Title***
CENTRUM ARENA, WORCESTER, USA Midway through six one-sided rounds the referee waved Sibson back to his corner after he had been floored for the second time. Hagler confused the Britisher throughout with his switch hitting and his extra reach made it difficult for Sibson to get close enough to unleash his hooks

02.03.83 ***Hugh Russell, L PTS 12 Davy Larmour, British Bantamweight Title***
KINGS HALL, BELFAST Both Irishmen were cut facially, and it was Larmour who produced the

artillery when it counted. He put Russell over for eight in the fifth round and when the champion later tried to mix it, he was shaken up by fierce right hand shots to the head

09.03.83 ***Tom Collins, W RSC 6 Antonio Harris, British L. Heavyweight Title***

MIDLANDS SPORTING CLUB, SOLIHULL Collins suddenly got home with a vicious right in the sixth round, which dropped the challenger for seven. Upon rising Harris was battered against the ropes before being rescued by the referee. Harris had been hurt on earlier occasions, but the contest was fairly even at the closure

15.03.83 ***Eleoncio Mercedes (Dominican Republic), L RSC 7 Charlie Magri, World Flyweight Title (WBC version)***

EMPIRE POOL, WEMBLEY The defending champion was stopped due to a deep cut over the left eye in an exciting bout that brought the house down. Magri never looked to lose this one, as he went forward constantly, ripping in body shots and taking Mercedes' best punches, before the clash of heads ended the contest

19.03.83 ***Colin Jones, DREW 12 Milton McCrory (USA), Vacant World Welterweight Title (WBC version)***

RENO NEVADA, USA During the first five rounds McCrory boxed with the jab and move routine to go well in front as the Welshman looked to land big hooks. Once Jones had got to the American it was obvious he could knock him out, but he spent too much time getting set as McCrory used the ring and literally ran from any trouble

29.03.83 ***Roy Gumbs, W RSC 4 Ralph Hollett (Canada), Commonwealth Middleweight Title***

METRO CENTRE, HALIFAX, NOVA SCOTIA The Canadian had no real answer to the left hand and was nailed by a whole series of blows to the head during the third. Gumbs opened up further in the fourth with a vengeance letting fly with jabs, hooks and uppercuts before the referee intervened

05.04.83 ***Lloyd Honeyghan, W PTS 12 Cliff Gilpin, Vacant British Welterweight Title***

ALBERT HALL, LONDON Gilpin produced a blitzing attack from the off and dropped the Londoner in the second for a short count. Once he had weathered the storm however, Honeyghan fought his way back, to get on top with some solid left hooks, before a magnificent last round sent the fans delirious

19.03.83 Colin Jones (left) appears to be landing with a left hook as he closes in on Milton McCrory with an effort to land the finisher.

07.04.83 ***Loris Stecca (Italy), W RSC 5 Steve Sammy Sims, Vacant European Featherweight Title***
SASSARI, ITALY The Italian's sharp punches inflicted a cut by the side of Sims right eye which obviously affected his vision, but he fought back well at times. Although Stecca poured the leather in, the Welshman never once took a backward step and was beginning to get through, prior to the referee ending the contest

08.04.83 ***Clinton McKenzie, W PTS 12 Alan Lamb, British L. Welterweight Title***
THE STADIUM, LIVERPOOL The determined challenger was never once off his feet, although he finished up with facial damage. McKenzie's blows generally had more snap, whilst Lamb manfully struck to his jab and move tactics, with both men sharing in some tremendous rallies before the champion clearly retained his title

12.04.83 ***Barry McGuigan, W RSC 2 Vernon Penprase, Vacant British Featherweight Title***
ULSTER HALL, BELFAST From the opening bell McGuigan was totally dominant, using his jab to open up his opponent. The second round had barely started when a left hook dropped Penprase, who upon rising was pursued relentlessly before a right to the head sent him sprawling again

23.05.83 ***Herol Graham, W CO 2 Clemente Tshinza (Belgium), Vacant European L. Middleweight Title***
CITY HALL, SHEFFIELD The Belgium-based boxer from Zaire was down twice before Graham drove in further combinations which dropped him for the full count in his own corner. Tshinza had only offered up spoiling tactics, which were never going to be enough to hold up his younger rival

13.08.83 ***Milton McCrory (USA), W PTS 12 Colin Jones, Vacant World Welterweight Title (WBC version)***
DUNES HOTEL, LAS VEGAS, USA Once again McCrory ran from the dynamic fists of the Welshman, but it was he who scored the only knockdown of the contest with a left uppercut in the first round. Jones fought his way back with relentless pressure to wipe out any arrears with the decision split

14.09.83 ***Roy Gumbs, L CO 5 Mark Kaylor, British & Commonwealth Middleweight Titles***
ALEXANDRA PAVILION, LONDON The challenger showed a confidence that bordered on arrogance, but in the fourth round he began to take a hammering, and eventually was put down. The fifth saw Kaylor moving in to the attack, cutting Gumbs, whilst ripping in heavy punches to head and body that enforced a count out

22.09.83 ***Neville Meade, L RSC 9 David Pearce, British Heavyweight Title***
ST DAVIDS HALL, CARDIFF Once Pearce had weathered the early storms, he effectively waited for the older man to run out of steam. In the eighth Meade was floored, only to come under heavy fire again in the next round before he was rescued by the referee after being battered against the ropes

27.09.83 ***Charlie Magri, L RSC 6 Frank Cedeno (Philippines), World Flyweight Title (WBC version)***
EMPIRE POOL, WEMBLEY Magri mixed his punches well in the early stages, but unfortunately found that his best blows had little effect on the Filipino. The sixth round was dominated by Cedeno who floored the Britisher three times before the referee intervened

11.10.83 ***Prince Rodney, W RSC 6 Jimmy Batten, Vacant British L. Middleweight Title***
ALBERT HALL, LONDON The new champion was nearly always on top and close to finishing the contest as early as the third round. Batten however showed great courage, the end coming when he was floored and cut on the cheek, only to get up to be dropped again, before the referee stopped the contest

16.11.83 ***Barry McGuigan, W CO 6 Valerio Nati (Italy), Vacant European Featherweight Title***
KINGS HALL, BELFAST For the first three rounds Nati had reasonable success and fought on level terms, but from then on he was systematically taken apart. McGuigan began to use every punch in the book and in the sixth attacked non-stop with volleys of blows before putting the Italian down for keeps

16.11.83 ***Davy Larmour, L RSC 3 John Feeney, British Bantamweight Title***
KINGS HALL, BELFAST The Irishman was the aggressor for the first two rounds and clearly won them both, but in the end it was these tactics which bought about his downfall. Feeney finally connected with a great left hook which dumped Larmour for five and on arising he was being belted along the ropes, before being rescued

03.12.83 ***George Feeney, W RSC 1 Tony Willis, British Lightweight Title***
REGENT CREST HOTEL, LONDON Southpaw Willis was caught by a right-left-right to the head and floored for a count of seven before crashing down again in his own corner. This immediately prompted the referee to stop the contest in favour of Feeney who had come into the ring the underdog. The finish came after just two minutes of the first round

06.12.83 ***Lloyd Honeyghan, W PTS 12 Cliff Gilpin, British Welterweight Title***
ALBERT HALL, LONDON Honeyghan was superior throughout, with the challenger never able to rise to the heights as in their previous contest. Gilpin was outmanoevred constantly, but was not floored and gamely lasted the distance, ending up with a badly swollen eye as a souvenir

07.12.83 ***Antoine Montero (France), W CO 8 Keith Wallace, European Flyweight Title***
BLOOMSBURY CREST HOTEL, LONDON Wallace lacked sparkle, possible due to difficulties making the weight, and was counted out after a body punch. He had collected a standing count in the seventh, but was still in front prior to the summary conclusion, with Montero suffering from a cut right eye

09.12.83 ***Herol Graham, W RSC 8 Germain Lemaitre (France), European L. Middleweight Title***
LA SOUCOPOUP STADIUM, ST NAZAIRE, FRANCE An unexciting contest saw Graham win when the French challenger was stopped at the beginning of the eight after sustaining a badly damaged left eye. Earlier Lemaitre had concentrated on survival and had exposed Graham's inability to finish

28.12.83 ***Walter Giorgetti (Italy), W PTS 12 John Feeney, European Bantamweight Title***
CAMPOBASSO, ITALY Unfortunately Feeney was put down by an overarm right in the opening minutes and the Italian stayed in command from thereon. Girgetti often pinned the challenger against the ropes for long periods, and even when breaking free Feeney was subjected to further punishment

1984

25.1.84 ***Kelvin Smart, L. RTD. 7. Hugh Russell, British Flyweight Title***
KINGS HALL, BELFAST Russell became the first man to win both flyweight and bantamweight titles in reverse order when the champion was retired on his stool, unable to see out of his left eye. In the earlier rounds however, Smart had looked dangerous, but the little Irishman began to get right on top with good counters and then, totally bemused his rival when going all out in the seventh.

16.1.84 ***Tom Collins, L PTS 12 Dennis Andries, British L. Heavyweight Title***
LYCEUM BALLROOM, LONDON The champion appeared to pose far too frequently, which allowed Andries to come forward throwing wild punches. Collins had begun to pull back the deficit by the tenth, but then tired and a strong finish by the hungry challenger saw him home, rather by quantity than quality, in a ring that measured less than regulation size.

10.2.84 ***George Feeney, W PTS 12 Paul Chance, British Lightweight Title***
TOWN HALL, DUDLEY The game Chance proved his mettle in a gruelling bout, when he withstood the heavier punches of the North Easterner. Feeney was unable to finish his rival off and Chance, even when hurt, responded determinedly with the crowd right behind him, to fight back in inspired fashion.

22.2.84 ***Jimmy Cable, W PTS 12, Nick Wilshire, Vacant British L. Middleweight Title***
ALBERT HALL, LONDON In winning the title, Cable boxed brilliantly on the retreat, firing in the jab backed up by right uppercuts. Wilshire to his credit, never stopped coming forward and occasionally had his man in trouble, but was never able to pin his elusive opponent down for any length of time.

25.2.84 ***Louis Acaries (France) L PTS 12 Tony Sibson, European Middleweight Title***
BERCY STADIUM, PARIS, FRANCE The Frenchman fought an extraordinary contest, allowing Sibson to keep on the offensive throughout and build up a good lead by the use of a solid left hand. Acaries was negative from start to finish and gave the impression of being more intent on survival than throwing punches of his own, in an effort to stem the tide.

30.3.84 ***Lucien Rodriguez (France) W PTS 12 David Pearce, European Heavyweight Title***
LIMOGES, FRANCE Apart from a couple of moments during the sensational eighth round, Pearce was comprehensively outboxed and continually on the receiving end of scoring, if not hurtful punches. During the eighth however, the Welshman downed Rodriguez twice and had him bleeding ominously, but the champion got up to box his way out of any further trouble.

06.04.84 ***Dennis Andries W PTS 12 Tom Collins, British L. Heavyweight Title***
TOWN HALL, WATFORD This return contest saw Collins start well and finish strongly, with Andries at his best during the middle stanzas. Collins used the left hand to better effect on this occasion, but as before the champion never stopped coming forward and it was his heavier punching that ultimately swung the bout his way.

14.5.84. ***Stewart Lithgo, W CO 11 Steve Aczel (Australia), Vacant Commonwealth Cruiserweight title***
BRISBANE, AUSTRALIA – In a battle for the newly

05.06.84. Barry McGuigan looks down on an outclassed Eguia who is paying one of his three visits to the canvas before being counted out.

instigated cruiserweight title, the Australian set up furious attacks for the first eight rounds, but then ran out of gas as Lithgo's more controlled punches began to assume authority. Aczel had tired completely by the eleventh and finally succumbed to a shock count out defeat.

25.05.84 ***Jimmy Cable, W RSC 11 Said Skouma (France), Vacant European L. Middleweight Title***

TOULOUSE, FRANCE What a magnificent gutsy performance by Cable as he came off the deck three times plus taking a standing count, to force the referee to save the Frenchman from further punishment. Skouma had been floored at the end of the tenth and in the penultimate round although a mile ahead on points, he collected a standing count before a right to the head put him down enforcing the stoppage.

05.06.84 ***Barry McGuigan, W CO 3 Esteban Eguia (Spain), European Featherweight Title***

ALBERT HALL, LONDON – A one sided contest saw the brilliant McGuigan totally demolish his game challenger who was counted out face downwards in the third after being poleaxed by two left hooks and a right. In the second round the end had clearly looked in sight when Eguia was floored twice, but he showed great courage battling against all the odds in trying to fight back.

Britain's Ex-Boxers' Associations Come of Age

Ron Olver (a leading boxing historian and former Assistant Editor of 'Boxing News')

There can be no doubt that the ever-growing number of Ex-Boxers' Associations (EBAs) has proved to be one of the most important happenings in the history of the sport, and I am particularly proud of my own contribution in helping to make this possible.

My interest started in 1967, when browsing through a copy of *Boxing News*, I thought how little news there was about boxers whose careers had ended. What had happened to the men we had admired so much, who had been household names in their particular eras?

From time to time *Boxing News* published the complete records of some of the former stars, and it was surprising how many letters were received from appreciative fans. Some wrote that the boxers so featured lived near them, and were able to confirm that they were well or otherwise.

This gave me the idea of using these letters as a basis for a regular column, so that the fans could read about their old favourites. My editor was agreeable, purely as an experiment, and as there was no extra space available, whatever I wrote about the old-timers had to be included on my regular page 'Telefight News'.

Anyway, it was a start, and in August 1967 appeared 16 paragraphs under the heading 'Old-Timers Corner,' and involving Arnold Kid Sheppard, Len Wickwar and Kid Kelly. The response to this new feature was encouraging, and it soon developed into a regular item.

In those early days a typical reader's letter was as follows: 'It's great to have news of former boxers who were active before the last war. Please carry on with the good work.' That one was from Norman Jones, a keen collector of boxing memorabilia, who a few years later was to be instrumental in helping to form the Leicester EBA. He was appointed the secretary, a position he still holds, and we have become good friends.

At the time 'Old-Timers Corner' first appeared, I shouldn't think there were more than half a dozen EBAs throughout the country, but I know these included Leeds (formed 1952), Birmingham (1956) and Sunderland (1959).

There was no such body in London, but in 1967 Ernie Woodman had organised a get-together, which was attended by many boxers, including some champions. Then, just as action seemed imminent, Ernie moved to Hove owing to business commitments, and indeed helped to form the Sussex EBA in 1974. Today he is their chairman.

So the London project was temporarily shelved, and it wasn't until 1971 that former fighter Alf Paolozzi came to see me. He said he was prepared to have another go at trying to form an Association in London, and would I help with the publicity.

Naturally I was delighted. There was a meeting of a few enthusiasts, and in my column dated 19 November 1971, appeared the following:

> 'Apparently the get-together at Charlie Webster's Tollington Arms went very well, and I have had letters from some of those who attended . . . great stuff, and thanks are due to Alf Paolozzi and his henchmen for their efforts. I have kept nagging away in this column, hoping that a London branch would be formed, and am delighted that this has now materialized.'

So London was in business, with the inspired choice of Jack Powell, former Sheffield middleweight, as secretary. Jack has held this position ever since, and the continued success of LEBA is due in no small part to him and his wife Mary, who do all the administration from their own home.

In the 1960s there were formations in Kent, Manchester and North Staffs, but the floodgates opened in the 1970s, when no less than 20 new Associations came into being. This was really sensational, and I found that I was receiving so many letters that it was difficult to include all the news in my column.

However, at long last I was granted a full page, which is now entitled 'With The Ex-Boxers.' I am receiving enough letters to fill two pages, am vice-president of several Associations, and member of most others.

At this juncture I would like to explain that the EBAs have three common aims: (a) for former boxers to get together – champions and six-rounders, all are equal; (b) to help members in need; and (c) to help charities.

Frankly, raising money for charity was something I had not anticipated. I did not think enough money would be raised to make this possible, but I sadly underestimated these ex-fighters. Functions were arranged, like darts matches and social evenings, and the proceeds went to EBA funds, and also to local charities.

Amazing, when one realises that the appointed officers and committees operate on a voluntary basis, giving their time and energy for free. Also, help is invariably given, not only to members, but to any former boxer who is known to be in need. This can take the form of cash, gifts or maybe just visits to homes or hospitals.

Senior Citizens are particularly well looked after. LEBA have a draw when four of the older generation benefit financially each month, and most Associations are able to subsidise them on occasions like the Annual Outings (LEBA go to Brighton) and other varied functions.

Several branches, including LEBA, Slough and Reading have had sponsored greyhound meetings, a favourite way of raising funds, but one which requires a tremendous amount of organisation.

An attendance of between 200 and 400 at LEBA's monthly meetings tells its own story, and there has been a large increase in the exchange visits. For instance, during the summer months, LEBA play host to three or four other EBAs who enjoy a Sunday coach trip to London. Leeds and Leicester are regulars, and this year came the first-ever visit from Tyneside. Many other branches exchange visits throughout the year.

At their Annual Dinners, LEBA present the Dave Crowley Memorial Belt to the Best Boxer of the Year, as voted by members. In 1983 it went to Barry McGuigan.

In 1979 the British Boxing Board of Control celebrated its 50th Anniversary with a Banquet. Secretary Ray Clarke asked me for the addresses of the larger Associations, as it had been decided to invite their representatives. This was indeed gratifying, especially to me, because it meant status and recognition for the good work being carried out.

Today important people have become members and others have attended meetings. Member of Parliament Greville Janner is president of Leicester EBA, House of Commons Speaker Bernard Weatherill attended a Croydon meeting, as did Board Secretary Ray Clarke. Jerry Dunn, Chief Inspector of the Board of Control, often travels around the country to EBA meetings, spreading the word of good fellowship in his speeches, and the local Mayors pay regular visits.

Presidents include Pat Floyd (LEBA), in my opinion the greatest amateur heavyweight of all-time; top referee Roland Dakin (Reading), flyweight star Tut Whalley (North Staffs), fine boxer and referee Frank Parkes (Nottingham), title contender Tom Smith (Sunderland), former welter champ Cliff Curvis (Swansea), top middleweight Glen Moody (Wales) and former middleweight champion Pat McAteer (Wirrall).

At the end of this article is an EBA Directory which I have compiled, and which is as up-to-date as possible. Officers come up for election every year, in some cases two years, so changes do occur from time to time.

In most cases the approximate membership is stated. However, some members belong to more than one body, and in some cases there are lady members. There are also Honorary Members and Associate Members, which is quite normal, but obviously the hard core come from former boxers, most of whom were active in the 1930s and 1940s.

Therefore it is inevitable that the numbers will be depleted as the years go by, unless boxers who have retired in recent years begin to show more interest. I sincerely hope so, in order that there should be continuity in the good work carried out. There are towns and cities which produced a crop of prominent boxers, but which still do not have an EBA.

So my aim is for even more formations, but with the realisation that not everyone has the time or the inclination to devote to helping to organise them. It just needs a few dedicated individuals, and this can happen, proof being the vast number of EBAs already in being. Rest assured that I will do all I can to help anyone who is interested. I'd like to end this article as I began – there can be no doubt that the ever-growing number of Ex-Boxers' Associations has proved to be one of the most important happenings in the history of the sport.

Directory of Ex-Boxers' Associations

Birmingham
Founded 1956. Members 250. HQ 128 Jenkins Street, Small Heath. Meetings held first Friday of each month. *Officials* Bernard Watton (P and C); Terry Burton (VC); George Hunt (T); Norman Gibbons (PRO and W); Reg Shakespear(S), 128 Jenkins Street, Small Heath, Birmingham.

Bournemouth
Founded 1980. Members 40. HQ Cherries Supporters Club, Dean Court. Meetings second Sunday of each month. *Officials* Lt. Col Jack Longbottom (P); Al Porter (C); George Wellman (VC); Ev Turner (T); Les Smith (WO); Harry Legge (S and PRO), 41 St Swithuns Road, Bournemouth.

Cork
Founded 1973. Members 40. HQ Acra House, Maylor Street, Cork. Meetings first Wednesday of each month. *Officials* Paddy Martin (P and C); Ray Donnelly (T); John Cronin (VC); Tim O'Sullivan (S), Acra House, Maylor Street, Cork.

Croydon
Founded 1982. Members 110. HQ Prince of Wales, Parchmore Road, Thornton Heath. Meetings last Sunday in each month (except December). *Officials* Marvin Hart (P); Pat Stribling (C); Tom Powell (VC); Ralph Griffiths (T); Gilbert Allnutt (S), 25 Melrose Avenue, London SW16.

Eastern Area
Founded 1973. Members 35. HQ West End Public House, Brown Street, Norwich. Meetings first Sunday in each month. *Officials* Jack Wakefield (P); Len Dunthorne (C); Clive Campling (VC); Alf Carter (T); Donny Eastick (S), 12 Cranworth Gardens, Norwich.

Furness
Founded 1971. Members 100. HQ Capital Palace Hotel, Dalkeith Street, Barrow. Meetings every Wednesday. *Officials* William Robinson (P); Frank Hill (C); Tommy Robson (VC); Matt Bowness (T); Ron Gelling (S), c/o Risedale School, Risedale Road, Barrow.

Ipswich
Founded 1970. Members 22. HQ Duke of York, Woodridge Road, Ipswich. Meetings first Thursday of each month. *Officials* A. Kingham (P); George Whitfield (C); Frank Webb (VC); Doug Perkins (PRO and WO), Reg Gooch (S and T), 6 Howe Avenue, Ipswich.

Irish
Founded 1973. Members 200. HQ National Boxing Stadium, S.C. Road, Dublin 8. Meetings every Sunday (winter) and every fortnight (summer). *Officials* Roy O'Sullivan (P); Gerry O'Colmain (C); Willie Duggan (VC); Tom Clancy (T); Charlie Mooney and Dick Donnelly (PROs), Denis Morrison (S), 55 Philipsburgh Terrace, Marino, Dublin 3.

Kent
Founded 1968. Members 100. HQ Royal Naval Club Luton Road, Chatham. Meetings second Sunday of every month. *Officials* Teddy Bryant (P); Stoker Tim Cole (C); John Scully (T); Ray Lambert (PRO); Mick Smith (S), 14 Downsview, Chatham.

Leeds
Founded 1952. Members 60. HQ The Nelsons Sports Centre. Meetings first Sunday of each month. *Officials* Johnny Durkin (P); Jim Windsor and Alex Steene (Hon P); Benny Marsh (C); Bert Corris (VC and PRO); Vernon Appleyard (T); Les Pollard (S), 50 Rossefield Terrace, Bramley, Leeds.

Leicester
Founded 1972. Members 150. HQ Belgrave WMC, Checketts Road, Leicester. Meetings first Tuesday of each month. *Officials* Greville Janner QC, MP (P); Mick Greaves (C); Jim Knight (VC and T); Norman Jones (S), 60 Dumbleton Avenue, Leicester.

London
Founded 1971. Members 600. HQ Michael Sobell Sports Centre, Hornsey Road, London Meetings first Sunday of each month. *Officials* Pat Floyd (P and C); Jimmy Frew (VC); George Howard (T); Stephen Powell (PRO); Jack Powell (S), 36 St. Peters Street, London N1.

Manchester
Founded 1968. Members 130. HQ Smithfield Vaults, Swan Street, Manchester 3. Meetings first Sunday of each month. *Officials* Jackie Braddock (P); Tommy Proffitt (C); Jack Edwards (VC); Art Dykes (T); Bert Daly (PRO and WO); Jack Jamieson (S), 5 Magpie Walk, Bradford.

Merseyside (Liverpool)
Founded 1973. Members 125. HQ Queen Hotel, Derby Square, Liverpool. Meetings every fifth Sunday from 1 July 1984. *Officials* Johnny Cooke (P); Terry Riley (C); Jim Jenkinson (R); Tommy Bailey (T); Rupert Rice (PRO); Jerry Costello (WO); Billy Davies, Jun (S), 7 Rockford Walk, Kirkby, Liverpool.

Northamptonshire
Founded 1981. Members 102. HQ RAFA Club, Grove Road, Northampton. Meetings first Sunday of each month. *Officials* Harry Brown (P and WO); Fred Stoner (C); Cliff Brown (VC); Eddie Forrestal (T); Cyril Green (PRO); Bill Evans (S), 36 Palmerston Road, Northampton.

Northern Federation
Founded 1974. Member Associations Furness, Irish, Leeds, Manchester, Merseyside, Nottingham, Notts & Derby, Preston, St Helens, Sefton, Southport, Wirral. Annual Gala at Pontins, Ainsdale, every October. President selected from different Association each year. Meetings at different Associations each year. *Official* John Holmes (S), 41 Higher End Park, Sefton, Bootle 10, Merseyside.

Northern Ireland
Founded 1970. Members 30. *Officials* Desmond Marrinan (P); Billy Barnes (C); Billy Warnock (VC); Al Lyttle (T); Tom Meli (PRO); Terry Milligan (WO); Jackie Briers (S), 9 Benview Drive, Belfast 14.

North Staffs and South Cheshire
Founded 1969. Members 50. HQ Marquis of Granby, Market Place, Burslem. Meetings first Tuesday of each month. *Officials* Tut Whalley (P), Sam Pearson (C), Billy Tudor (VC and PRO), Albert Lithgoe (T), Albert Birke (S), 199 Campbell Road, Stoke-on-Trent.

Nottingham
Founded 1979. Members 150. HQ The Fox Inn, Parliament Street, Nottingham. Meetings first Sunday of each month. *Officials* Frank Parkes (P), Harold Roe (C) Stan Jackson (VC), George Austin (T), Jack Aslin (PRO), Johnny and Mrs Carrington (WO), Jimmy Thompson (S), 27 Ainsley Road, Western Boulevard., Nottingham.

Notts and Derby
Founded 1973. Members 15. HQ Three Horse Shoes Inn, Pinxton, Notts. *Officials* Billy Shinfield (P); Billy Strange (C); Bill Perry (VC); Arthur Connah (T); Dick Johnson (S and PRO), 13 Church Street, East Pinxton, Notts.

Plymouth
Founded 1982. HQ Exmouth Road Social Club, Exmouth Road, Devonport, Plymouth. Meetings last Sunday of each month. *Officials* George Borg (P); Flash Acton (C); Tony Penprase (VC); Joe Finch (T); Buck Taylor (S), 15 Greenbank Avenue, St Judes, Plymouth.

Preston
Founded 1973. HQ London Road Labour Club, Preston. Members 85. *Officials* Cyril Maudsley (P); Ronnie Riley (C); Tom Benson (VC); Jimmy Powell (T); Frank Casey (PRO and WO); Ted Sumner (S), 21 Clovelly Avenue, Ashton, Preston.

Reading
Founded 1977. Members 90. HQ The Dove, Orts Road, Reading. Meetings second Sunday of each month. *Officials* Roland Dakin (P), Jack Price (C); Alf Warwick (VC); George Pitman (T); Ron Draper (WO), Pat Burke (S), 45 Rosedale Crescent, Earley, Reading.

St Helens
Founded 1983. Members 30. HQ Exchange Vaults, Cooper Street, St Helens. Meetings every other Sunday. *Officials* John Turnbull (P); Vinty Matthews (C); Bold Thomas (VC) John Sines (T); Jonty Pilkington (PRO and WO); Eric Marsden (S), 59 Chadwick Road, Haresfinch, St Helens.

Scottish
Founded 1974. Members 40. HQ Dorchester Hotel, Saucihall Street, Glasgow. Meetings first Sunday

of each month. *Officials* Sam Stewart (P); No permanent chairman; Peter Keenan (VC); Frank O'Donnell (T); George Dougan (S), 10 Garrioch Crescent, Glasgow G20.

Sefton
Founded 1975. Members 12. HQ St Benets Parochial Club, Netherton. *Officials* Tom Reilly (P); Jimmy Duffy (C); Jerry Costello (VC); Alf Lunt (T); Harry Bennett (PRO), John Holmes (S), 41 Higher End Park, Sefton, Bottle 10, Merseyside.

Sheffield
Founded 1974. Members 50. HQ Foresters Inn, Division Street, Sheffield. Meetings first Tuesday of each month. *Officials* Gordon Morrison (P); Charlie Simpson (C); Neil Hawcroft (VC and S), 14 Guildford Close, Norfolk Park, Sheffield 2; H. Hainley (T).

Slough
Founded 1973. Members 40. HQ Dolphin Hotel, Slough. Meetings last Sunday of each month. *Officials* Bernard Hart (P); Gerry McNally (C); Robin Green and Mick Cavanagh (VC); Paul Yacomine (T); Pete Davis (Projects Officer); Cyril Thomas (PRO), Joe Prince (S), 40 Oldway Lane, Cippenham.

Southport
Founded 1974. Members 32. HQ Mount Pleasant Hotel, Southport. Meetings first Wednesday in each month. *Officials* Jack Coney (P); Sammy Mulligan (C and WO); Dudley Coney (VC); Johnny 'Al' Coney (T); Stan Heyes (PRO); Eddie Monahan (S), 127A Lord Street, Southport.

Square Ring
Founded 1978. Members 30. HQ Torquay Social Club. Annual Reunion, but no regular meetings. *Officials.* A. Parker (P); Bill Ellery (C); P. Robson (VC); Paul King (WO); V. Best (S and T), 180B Lichfield Ave., Barton, Torquay.

Sunderland
Founded 1959. Members 150. HQ Sunderland Catholic Club, Tatham Street, Sunderland. Meetings first Sunday of each month. *Officials* Tom Smith (P), Bert Ingram (C); Billy Simmons (VC); Massie Wakinshaw (T); Tom Crome (PRO); Ernie Britton (WO); Dave Wooton (S), 85 Torquay Road, Thorney Close, Sunderland.

Sussex
Founded 1974. Members 550. HQ Sussex Cricketer, Sussex County Cricket Ground. Meetings second Sunday of each month. *Officials* Bill Parish (P); Ernie Woodman (C); Sid Starr (VC); Ken Wittey (T); Derek Leney (PRO); Bill Wigzell (S), 35 Mile Oak Road, Southwick, Brighton.

Swansea
Founded 1983. Members 100. HQ Villiers Arms, Neath Road, Hafod, Swansea. Meetings first Monday of each month. *Officials* Cliff Curvis (P); Terry Collins (C); Geoffrey Ford (T); Grey Phillips (S and PRO); 67 Tirpenny Street, Morriston, Swansea.

Tramore.
Founded 1981. Members 55. HQ Market Street Gym, Tramore, and Robinsons Bar, Main Street, Tramore. Meetings second Thursday of each month. *Officials* J. Walsh (P); T. Flynn (C); A. Roche (VC); W. Hutchinson (T); N. Graham and P. O'Reilly (PROs); Pete Graham (S), 2 Riverstown, Tramore, Co. Waterford, Ireland.

Tyneside.
Founded 1970. Members 50. HQ Swan Inn, Haworth, Gateshead. Meetings last Sunday of each month. *Officials* James Ramshaw (P); Maxie Walsh (C); Gordon Smith (VC); Mal Dinning (T); Eddie Shippen (PRO); Billy Charlton (S), 335 Whitehall Road, Bensham, Gateshead-on-Tyne.

Welsh
Founded 1976. Members 100. HQ Rhydyfelin Labour Club, Pontypridd. Meetings first Monday of each month. *Officials* Glen Moody (P); Doug Kestrell (C); Syd Worgan (S); Stan Bateman (VC); Llew Miles (T and PRO), 21 Edward Street, Miskin, Mountain Ash.

Wirral (Birkenhead)
Founded 1973. Members 230. HQ Wirral Boxers, Argyle Street, Birkenhead. Meetings Tuesday of every week. *Officials* Pat McAteer (P); Bob Nelson (VC); Charlie Hayes (T); Tony Valenti (S), Terry Carson (C, PRO and WO), 59 Whetstone Lane, Birkenhead.

Abbreviations:
P–President; C–Chairman; VC–Vice Chairman; T–Treasurer; S–Secretary; PRO–Public Relations Officer; WO–Welfare Officer; R–Registrar

Leading British Based Boxers, 1946–1982: Career Summary

Includes British-based boxers since the Second World War who retired prior to 1983, never having won a National Championship, but who won and drew more contests than they lost. Area Champions and National Title challengers are listed automatically.

CAREER RECORD CODE
C = Contests; W = Won; L = Lost; D = Drawn

ø Challenger for National or International Championship.

Name	Domicile	Born	Weight	Career	Record C	W	L	D
Bunty Adamson	Banbridge	03.06.30	Welter	1950–1955	43	36	6	1
Clem A'Court	Morden	21.09.31	Bantam	1953–1954	15	8	6	1
Rab Affleck ø	Irvine	30.01.53	L. Heavy	1974–1979	20	15	5	0
Roy Agland	Tiryberth	02.10.26	Middle	1950–1954	13	11	2	0
Ray Ako	Liverpool	26.02.45	L. Heavy	1965–1969	13	10	2	1
Derek Alexander	Willenhall	09.11.28	L. Heavy	1946–1953	36	22	13	1
Les Allen	Bedworth	06.09.29	Middle	1947–1958	94	64	23	7
Tony Allen	Birmingham	11.06.54	L. Heavy	1974–1980	29	18	11	0
Jim Allsopp	Bangor	09.08.27	Middle	1949–1951	20	14	5	1
Alex Ambrose ø	Glasgow	22.04.36	Fly	1957–1963	40	25	13	2
Billy Ambrose	Stepney	21.09.29	Welter	1948–1952	37	32	4	1
Brian Anders	Brighton	27.07.29	L. Heavy	1949–1956	44	22	20	2
Billy Andrews	West Ham	17.04.28	Middle	1948–1954	15	10	4	1
Reg Andrews	Deal	19.03.19	Heavy	1942–1953	54	36	13	5
Steve Angell	Hemel Hempstead	25.04.51	Welter	1973–1978	33	22	10	1
Tommy Armour	Belfast	18.02.16	Welter	1936–1952	184	139	40	5
Willie Armstrong	Port Glasgow	25.01.30	Middle	1951–1958	53	32	19	2
Billy Ashcroft	Wigan	16.07.32	Feather	1951–1957	39	25	9	5
Billy Ashton	Wigan	07.08.19	Fly	1937–1950	49	25	22	2
Gordon Ashun	Liverpool	10.03.21	Welter	1939–1950	97	50	42	5
Dennis Avoth	Cardiff	25.10.47	Heavy	1967–1973	25	19	6	0
Joe Awome	Golders Green	25.07.53	Heavy	1979–1980	12	9	3	0
Neville Axford	Bermondsey	05.09.36	Welter	1959–1961	15	12	3	0
Tony Bagshaw	Hull	16.03.47	Welter	1969–1974	26	14	10	2
Hal Bagwell	Gloucester	18.12.20	Light	1938–1949	71	63	5	3
Tom Bailey	Liverpool	26.12.25	Feather	1947–1953	78	49	25	4
Roy Baird	Birmingham	24.06.27	Welter	1950–1956	40	25	14	1
Allan Ball	Cardiff	24.09.47	L. Heavy	1967–1970	10	6	4	0
Gerry Banwell	Tonyrefail	01.05.42	Middle	1962–1966	22	13	9	0
Colin Barber	Sutton-in-Ashfield	01.11.35	Bantam	1953–1956	34	27	6	1
Johnny Barclay	Ickenham	13.09.25	Bantam	1950–1952	16	11	4	1
Roger Barlow	Coventry	25.01.51	L. Heavy	1971–1978	18	12	5	1
Tony Barlow ø	Manchester	10.06.41	Fly	1963–1969	39	21	14	4
Johnny Barnham	Fulham	06.06.32	Bantam	1952–1955	12	5	4	3
Tommy Barnham	Fulham	25.04.19	Light	1937–1952	93	74	15	4
Tony Barrett	Pimlico	16.12.33	Welter	1952–1957	25	16	8	1
Johnny Barton	Lancaster	31.03.24	L. Heavy	1943–1959	65	34	29	2
Tommy Barton	Mile End		Light	1947–1949	15	11	4	0
Peter Bates	Sheffield	02.04.43	Heavy	1953–1963	52	33	15	4
Barney Beale	Lambeth	01.01.35	Light	1955–1960	39	24	13	2
Roy Beaman	Brixton	12.07.38	Bantam	1959–1962	24	18	6	0
Ricky Beaumont	Hull	06.11.56	L. Welter	1976–1982	25	18	6	1

Name	Domicile	Born	Weight	Career	Record			
					C	W	L	D
Ron Bebbington	West Ham	25.08.28	Middle	1948–1951	24	16	6	2
Joe Beckett	Hempnall	02.11.21	Middle	1946–1950	46	33	9	4
Wally Beckett	Carshalton	23.11.31	Middle	1950–1956	57	38	17	2
Frank Bell	Barnoldswick	12.10.26	Heavy	1949–1956	31	17	13	1
Jimmy Bell ø	Kilmarnock	06.04.56	Feather	1968–1975	48	34	10	4
Mick Bell	Leicester	24.07.58	L. Welter	1977–1979	21	9	8	4
Billy Belnavis	Wolverhampton	29.12.49	Light	1970–1976	50	13	33	4
Len Bennett	Bethnal Green	1922	Heavy	1939–1953	73	47	22	4
Roy Bennett	Salford	07.09.33	Light	1951–1959	34	24	9	1
Wayne Bennett	Tredegar	10.10.55	Middle	1975–1978	17	10	6	1
Johnny Berry	Harlesden	14.04.35	Middle	1957–1961	25	18	6	1
Albert Bessell	Bristol		Feather	1933–1950	81	59	15	7
Teddy Best	Cardiff	24.09.33	Light	1953–1963	56	26	28	2
Billy Biddles	Birmingham	06.04.22	Light	1944–1949	47	31	13	3
Eric Billington	Golborne	02.01.31	Welter	1947–1955	93	58	30	5
Johnny Black	Preston	23.04.28	Fly	1948–1953	48	33	12	3
Eric Blake	Leatherhead	30.08.46	Middle	1969–1973	22	13	9	0
Tommy Blears	Bolton	21.09.28	Feather	1949–1953	43	26	14	3
Mark Bliss	Cheshunt	23.04.54	Feather	1974–1978	17	10	6	1
Peter Boddington	Coventry	01.10.42	Heavy	1967–1971	20	17	3	0
Bobby Boland ø	Dundee	01.04.29	Bantam	1946–1956	74	47	22	5
Jock Bonas	Hickleton Main	15.01.26	Feather	1943–1954	86	62	21	3
Johnny Boom	Stratford	14.01.20	Bantam	1937–1949	86	53	26	7
Dennis Booty	Covent Garden	01.06.33	Middle	1956–1958	18	13	5	0
George Bowes ø	Hesleden	01.10.36	Bantam	1957–1967	62	42	16	4
John Bowler	Luton	13.10.37	Middle	1958–1961	18	10	6	2
Johnny Boyd	Peterborough	20.08.22	Middle	1943–1949	54	32	20	2
Jackie Braddock	Manchester	07.08.27	Welter	1946–1956	49	30	16	3
Don Braithwaite	Caerphilly	18.02.37	Fly	1959–1962	27	13	11	3
Jimmy Bray	Liverpool	15.11.24	Middle	1942–1949	34	20	14	0
Brian Brazier	Croydon	09.01.42	Light	1963–1966	14	9	5	0
Eric Brett	Retford	09.09.38	Feather	1956–1961	57	27	26	4
Jimmy Brewer	Kings Cross	03.03.26	Bantam	1950–1955	48	29	12	7
Martin Bridge	Bradford	06.11.59	L. Welter	1977–1980	28	11	13	4
Jackie Briers	Belfast	03.05.26	Fly	1946–1953	42	26	15	1
Peter Brisland	Southampton	17.11.49	L. Heavy	1972–1976	17	11	5	1
Ray Brittle	Twickenham	19.11.48	L. Heavy	1968–1971	15	12	3	0
Doug Brock	Newcastle	24.04.23	Middle	1946–1949	29	16	12	1
Chic Brogan ø	Clydebank	08.01.32	Feather	1950–1959	42	22	19	1
Jim Brogden	Manchester	31.12.26	Welter	1951–1956	37	20	15	2
Alf Brown	Nuneaton	1920	Heavy	1943–1948	22	14	6	2
Charley Brown	Belfast	1918	Bantam	1937–1951	63	44	18	1
Jackie Brown	Belfast	19.03.31	Middle	1948–1951	34	22	9	3
Jimmy Brown ø	Belfast	22.11.34	Feather	1955–1964	41	29	11	1
Phil Bryant	Cardiff	28.04.51	Feather	1971–1972	7	7	0	0
Jackie Bryce	Airdrie	05.10.26	Fly	1945–1951	39	22	15	2
Alan Buchanan	Edinburgh	09.01.49	Feather	1973–1978	23	17	4	2
Manuel Burgo	North Shields	21.01.34	Heavy	1955–1958	22	18	4	0
Tommy Burgoyne	Demmy	19.08.38	Bantam	1960–1967	53	15	36	2
Eddie Burke ø	Woodside	16.11.54	Middle	1976–1981	19	16	3	0
Terry Burnett	Cardiff	13.11.36	Welter	1956–1960	28	18	8	2
Bob Burniston	Barry	18.12.20	Welter	1947–1952	31	16	15	0
Eddie Burns	Liverpool	27.10.34	Feather	1955–1960	49	25	21	3
Jeff Burns	Swansea	16.05.48	Middle	1972–1976	20	11	9	0
Tommy Burns	Stockton	1914	Feather	1934–1952	103	66	32	5
Alan Burton	Battersea	22.04.48	Heavy	1970–1972	10	9	1	0
Keith Bussey	Camberwell	24.02.56	L. Heavy	1976–1979	24	19	2	3
Godfrey Butler	Birmingham	05.07.54	Light	1976–1977	17	9	8	0
Jackie Butler	Preston	24.04.36	Light	1952–1958	60	42	15	3

LEADING BRITISH BASED BOXERS, 1946–1982: CAREER SUMMARY

Name	Domicile	Born	Weight	Career	Record C	W	L	D
Johnny Butterworth	Rochdale	15.05.32	Light	1951–1960	55	35	16	4
Alan Buxton	Watford	28.02.27	Light	1949–1953	30	17	11	2
Bert Buxton	Norwich		Welter	–1949	30	16	11	3
Laurie Buxton	Watford	02.11.24	Light	1939–1952	126	57	61	8
Pat Byrne	Glasgow	30.12.36	Middle	1958–1959	7	6	1	0
Tony Byrne	Liverpool	23.03.51	Middle	1973–1974	7	4	3	0
Gene Caffrey	Glasgow	26.06.27	Feather	1948–1954	85	35	38	12
Mick Cain	Canvey Island	15.09.46	Middle	1966–1972	20	16	3	1
Peter Cain	Notting Hill	27.03.51	Middle	1973–1977	23	15	7	1
Joe Cairney	Coatbridge	17.11.26	Fly	1945–1954	38	22	13	3
Barry Calderwood	Manchester	23.09.44	Middle	1961–1971	52	26	22	4
Bill Calvert ø	Sheffield	16.10.33	Feather	1958–1965	49	24	21	4
Don Cameron	Glasgow	13.04.20	Welter	1938–1949	54	27	22	5
Hugh Cameron	Glasgow		Fly	1938–1947	43	20	20	3
Rocky Campbell	Leicester	02.10.43	Heavy	1965–1975	43	22	18	3
Clive Campling	Norwich	10.02.31	Light	1948–1957	31	25	4	2
Eddie Cardew	Holloway	19.04.27	Welter	1946–1953	56	28	24	4
Jimmy Cardew	Holloway	26.12.30	Bantam	1947–1957	70	39	28	3
Mick Carney	Wakefield	18.08.37	Feather	1963–1967	27	11	10	6
Frank Carpenter	Coventry	14.08.43	Heavy	1972	9	7	2	0
Henry Carpenter	Peckham	28.12.25	Fly	1948–1953	49	34	11	4
Jack Carrick	Hull	25.03.14	Light	1932–1946	114	75	28	11
Johnny Carrington	Nottingham	05.10.28	Light	1946–1954	106	60	35	11
Albert Carroll ø	Bethnal Green	09.06.35	Welter	1952–1962	56	38	17	1
Billy Carroll	Doncaster	18.06.21	Middle	1946–1952	40	25	14	1
George Carroll	Covent Garden	01.10.35	Feather	1956–1965	41	28	10	3
Harry Carroll ø	Cardiff	22.09.39	Feather	1958–1964	25	22	1	2
Jimmy Carroll	Stockport	24.02.23	L. Heavy	1946–1952	48	20	23	5
Tony Carroll	Liverpool	04.06.54	L. Welter	1977–1982	23	15	8	0
Eddie Carson	Edinburgh	14.04.25	Bantam	1945–1956	91	60	26	5
Jimmy Carson	Belfast	25.02.32	Bantam	1954–1963	32	16	15	1
Jimmy Carson	Belfast	25.08.58	Bantam	1980–1982	7	5	1	1
Joe Carter	Mitcham	06.03.21	Feather	1946–1950	25	16	8	1
Brian Cartwright ø	Birmingham	28.12.37	Bantam	1960–1969	83	53	26	4
Joe Cassidy	Glasgow	05.12.22	Welter	1946–1951	33	24	9	0
George Casson	North Shields	03.03.26	Middle	1947–1950	33	22	8	3
Vic Chandler	Bermondsey	05.01.42	Light	1964–1967	21	13	4	4
Peter Cheevers	Streatham	26.06.42	Light	1961–1964	22	18	3	1
Johnny Cheshire ø	Ayr	11.09.47	Light	1969–1974	31	20	10	1
Gary Chippendale	Bristol	15.09.39	Middle	1963–1972	33	18	15	0
Chris Christian ø	Stoke Newington	08.12.58	L. Middle	1979–1982	18	8	7	3
Terry Clark	West Ham	14.03.44	Welter	1966–1968	16	12	3	1
Johnny Claydon ø	West Ham	10.12.53	L. Welter	1973–1980	25	15	9	1
Bob Cleaver	Attleborough	04.12.25	Middle	1946–1954	83	35	41	7
Colin Clitheroe	Preston	26.05.32	Fly	1950–1956	33	22	9	2
Billy Cobb	Chesterfield	06.01.31	Light	1952–1957	44	26	14	4
Len Coffin	Chester	25.12.23	Bantam	1944–1947	16	11	5	0
Johnny Cole	Stepney	04.08.34	L. Heavy	1957–1961	26	18	8	0
Pip Coleman	Swansea	17.04.58	Bantam	1978–1980	14	7	7	0
Charlie Collett	Watford	06.03.23	Heavy	1939–1950	75	48	25	2
Ernie Comley	Birmingham		L. Heavy	1949–1953	19	14	5	0
Billy Connor	St. Helens	09.02.32	Light	1951–1955	22	14	7	1
Tommy Connor	Glasgow	18.08.40	Bantam	1963–1968	27	12	13	2
Allan Cooke	Worksop		L. Heavy	1938–1950	68	46	20	2
Henry Cooper	Larkhall	29.01.53	Middle	1973–1981	25	15	9	1
Jim Cooper	Bellingham	03.05.34	Heavy	1954–1964	31	16	14	1
Kenny Cooper	Birmingham	20.10.43	Feather	1967–1970	18	13	5	0
Ron Cooper	Poplar	25.11.24	Light	1949–1952	22	15	3	4

Name	Domicile	Born	Weight	Career	Record			
					C	W	L	D
Ron Cooper	Pyle	05.02.28	Middle	1943–1952	57	20	31	6
Roy Coote	Falmouth	14.05.24	Light	1945–1954	55	34	20	1
Eddie Copeland	Manchester	04.04.57	Light	1979–1982	11	10	1	0
Ray Corbett	Birmingham	09.02.34	Welter	1950–1959	50	24	23	3
Joe Corcoran	Huddersfield	09.05.29	Welter	1949–1952	37	17	17	3
Dai Corp	Cardiff	15.08.40	Bantam	1961–1963	15	9	5	1
Charlie Cosgrove	Belfast	07.03.34	Welter	1955–1957	15	14	1	0
George Cottle	Bermondsey	12.10.39	Welter	1958–1962	24	18	6	0
Dave Coventry ø	Liverpool	18.06.40	Light	1959–1964	43	36	6	1
Sammy Cowan	Belfast	24.09.37	Light	1954–1964	52	27	22	3
Peter Cragg	Letchworth	16.11.45	Welter	1966–1970	32	25	7	0
Bruce Crawford	Thornaby	09.12.28	Middle	1949–1954	50	38	11	1
Terry Crimmins	Cardiff	28.09.40	Bantam	1959–1965	31	25	5	1
Dave Croll	Dundee	20.02.36	Feather	1954–1962	48	28	14	6
Jimmy Croll	Dundee	29.01.34	Welter	1951–1960	59	35	18	6
Ron Crookes	Sheffield	11.04.29	Middle	1949–1955	61	33	22	6
Bingo Crooks	Wolverhampton	01.10.51	Light	1971–1980	56	22	28	6
Freddie Cross	Nuneaton	01.05.35	Middle	1956–1965	33	24	8	1
Johnny Cross	Horwich	25.06.30	Light	1947–1953	61	29	26	6
Terry Cullen	Shotton	28.02.30	Welter	1947–1956	53	31	19	3
Stan Cullis ø	Bristol	10.06.39	L. Heavy	1956–1966	31	18	12	1
Johnny Cunningham	Huddersfield	10.09.36	Middle	1957–1961	26	15	10	1
Joe Curran ø	Liverpool	27.04.15	Fly	1932–1948	154	84	64	6
Dick Currie	Dalmarnock	05.09.33	Fly	1955–1958	16	11	5	0
Steve Curtis	Cardiff	26.12.48	Bantam	1968–1969	7	4	2	1
George Daly	Blackfriars	14.11.14	Light	1930–1951	152	114	31	7
Jim Daly	Canning Town	28.05.38	Welter	1958–1963	20	13	7	0
Alf Danahar	Bethnal Green	15.03.23	Welter	1946–1955	56	30	21	5
Arthur Danahar ø	Bethnal Green	02.06.18	Light	1938–1947	74	66	8	0
Glyn David	Caerau	02.02.29	Fly	1946–1953	36	17	16	3
Gary Davidson	Bermondsey	04.04.53	Bantam	1976–1979	17	15	1	1
Billy Davies	Birmingham	08.01.20	Light	1946–1950	40	29	10	1
Bobby Davies	West Ham	05.08.41	Feather	1961–1968	53	24	24	5
Chris Davies	Cardiff	13.10.56	Welter	1976–1980	18	11	7	0
Colin Davies	Aberfan	17.04.50	Middle	1972–1975	16	11	5	0
Dai Davies ø	Skewen	10.07.22	Feather	1948–1954	54	27	20	7
Dave Davies	Bangor	09.04.48	L. Middle	1972–1979	30	14	13	3
Eric Davies	Stourbridge	01.11.29	Welter	1950–1957	35	21	12	2
Glyn Davies	Merthyr	11.03.43	Bantam	1962–1981	67	29	32	6
Kevin Davies	Nottingham	08.08.54	Light	1976–1978	13	9	3	1
Len Davies	Swansea		Feather	1937–1952	90	56	31	3
Robbie Davies	Birkenhead	1948	Middle	1977–1980	15	11	4	0
Ron Ponty Davies	Cardiff	19.10.37	Fly	1957–1960	8	8	0	0
Ronnie Davies	Brighton	08.05.46	Welter	1965–1970	20	12	6	2
Roy Davies	Spratton	11.10.28	Welter	1946–1952	106	53	41	12
Terry Davies	Cardiff	1955	L. Middle	1973–1975	6	4	1	1
Tommy Davies	Cwmgorse	1920	Middle	1938–1951	80	47	27	6
Tommy Davies	Nantyalgo	01.05.20	Feather	1941–1949	51	32	16	3
Tony Davies ø	Caerphilly	30.05.52	Bantam	1972–1974	8	7	1	0
Billy Kid Davis	Bow	11.04.43	Feather	1960–1964	30	22	7	1
Dave Davis	Darlington	02.02.27	L. Heavy	1947–1951	35	25	6	4
Harry Davis	Bethnal Green	04.08.15	Welter	1933–1949	142	81	47	14
Jimmy Davis	Bethnal Green	13.06.26	Middle	1945–1954	92	66	21	5
Stan Davis	Walworth	18.02.26	Welter	1947–1949	25	20	5	0
Denny Dawson	Sheffield	05.03.27	Feather	1948–1958	106	54	45	7
George Dawson	Builth Wells	20.05.25	Heavy	1946–1951	26	16	10	0
Bobby Day	Lancaster	23.03.40	Light	1961–1964	13	8	5	0
Rod Deamer	Paddington	22.08.26	Middle	1948–1953	33	24	8	1
Billy Dean	Greenwich	19.04.28	L. Heavy	1949–1957	35	20	15	0

Name	Domicile	Born	Weight	Career	Record C	W	L	D
Dixie Dean	Covent Garden	13.11.42	Feather	1963–1966	13	8	3	2
Colin Deans	Jarrow	27.12.56	Welter	1977	10	6	2	2
Claude Dennington	Peckham	05.08.23	Light	1945–1954	38	19	14	5
Garnett Denny	Belfast	19.07.31	Heavy	1947–1960	79	55	18	6
Jim Devanney	Bradford	10.09.49	L. Middle	1973–1977	36	18	13	5
Lawrie Devanney	Bradford	14.01.51	Feather	1974–1978	23	13	9	1
Arthur Devlin	Millwall	28.07.35	Feather	1956–1958	23	16	6	1
George Dilkes	South Elmsall	15.05.26	Middle	1944–1955	78	50	28	0
Ken Diston	Hendon	15.05.28	Bantam	1948–1953	32	17	15	0
Billy Dixon	Walker	19.09.29	Light	1948–1951	31	23	4	4
Freddie Dobson	Manchester	07.02.39	Feather	1959–1964	30	19	11	0
Arthur Donnachie	Greenock	06.10.33	Light	1956–1959	22	15	7	0
Bunty Doran	Belfast	16.12.22	Bantam	1938–1953	109	84	20	5
George Dormer	East Ham	08.02.35	Bantam	1955–1961	30	16	13	1
Eddie Douglas	Liverpool	20.10.22	Fly	1942–1948	28	18	6	4
Tony Dove	Battersea	23.11.32	L. Heavy	1954–1960	31	17	13	1
Johnny Downes	Manchester	29.06.15	Welter	1940–1951	53	27	24	2
Shaun Doyle ø	Barnsley	01.01.45	Welter	1963–1967	27	20	6	1
Ronnie Draper	Southampton	21.12.23	Bantam	1945–1951	57	36	17	4
Alf Drew	Hackney	03.05.32	Feather	1955–1958	26	13	10	3
Keith Drewett	Battersea	21.11.43	L. Heavy	1970–1972	12	6	6	0
Ben Duffy	Jarrow	20.04.20	Feather	1942–1950	163	76	75	12
Dick Duffy	Cardiff	06.10.45	Middle	1965–1971	58	35	20	3
Frank Duffy	Liverpool	03.10.16	Middle	1941–1952	68	36	26	6
Gerry Duffy	Dunfermline	04.12.53	Feather	1974–1979	16	12	3	1
Ron Duncombe	Jersey	29.09.29	Middle	1953–1956	24	14	8	2
Tommy Dunn	Reading	30.09.54	Light	1974–1979	36	19	14	3
Pat Dwyer ø	Liverpool	02.05.46	Middle	1965–1973	51	38	11	2
Jim Dwyer	Glasgow	11.06.29	Bantam	1948–1952	42	25	17	0
Alf Edwards	Smethwick		Light	1937–1947	42	36	4	2
Harry Edwards	Smethwick	28.04.36	Light	1957–1966	41	25	14	2
Phil Edwards ø	Cardiff	12.05.36	Middle	1952–1962	71	59	8	4
Terry Edwards ø	Smethwick	17.07.39	Light	1959–1966	43	27	11	5
Fred Elderfield	Hammersmith	25.06.38	Middle	1959–1962	13	12	1	0
Billy Ellaway	Liverpool	09.10.32	Middle	1950–1958	73	51	21	1
Chris Elliott	Leicester	21.02.41	Feather	1958–1967	83	44	31	8
Dave Elms	Brighton	04.07.28	L. Heavy	1951–1952	14	11	3	0
Roy Enifer	Poplar	23.07.40	Heavy	1963–1970	21	15	5	1
Glyn Evans	Askern	12.02.32	Feather	1949–1958	57	39	14	4
Greg Evans	Liverpool	08.07.52	L. Heavy	1976–1982	20	10	10	0
Kevin Evans	Hemel Hempstead	02.05.53	Light	1973–1976	30	16	11	3
Selwyn Evans	Newbridge	28.08.28	Light	1947–1953	53	26	19	8
Wayne Evans ø	Waterlooville	13.05.55	Feather	1974–1980	15	13	2	0
Billy Exley	Newcastle	12.11.20	Welter	1946–1951	40	25	14	1
Jackie Fairclough	Preston	12.08.29	Fly	1946–1953	71	52	15	4
Peter Fallon ø	Birkenhead	08.07.28	Welter	1943–1954	100	71	25	4
Gus Farrell	Dublin	25.09.45	Welter	1966–1971	23	13	10	0
Tommy Farricker	Manchester	05.07.13	Fly	1935–1950	63	30	27	6
Peter Fay	Bournemouth	12.01.28	Bantam	1948–1955	87	45	31	11
Steve Fenton	Leicester	19.07.57	L. Heavy	1976–1981	29	16	12	1
Hugh Ferns	Greenock	04.12.29	Heavy	1951–1955	23	14	8	1
Dennis Fewkes	Nottingham	07.12.33	L. Heavy	1950–1956	43	23	18	2
Cliff Field	Dunstable	03.06.43	Heavy	1968–1971	15	11	4	0
Kenny Field	Hoxton	28.02.39	Feather	1960–1963	23	17	5	1
Jim Findlay	Motherwell	24.06.29	Light	1948–1953	35	23	11	1
Dave Finn	Stepney	22.04.15	Light	1930–1946	170	89	64	17
Johnny Fish	Harlow	15.06.32	Welter	1950–1958	56	34	15	7
Bobby Fisher	Wishaw	02.12.38	Feather	1961–1968	31	19	11	1

Name	Domicile	Born	Weight	Career	Record C	W	L	D
Nick Fisher	Nantyalgo	09.03.27	L. Heavy	1946–1954	34	19	14	1
Reg Fisher	Leyton	18.04.31	Welter	1952–1960	39	23	14	2
Willie Fisher	Craigneuk	14.03.40	Middle	1961–1967	32	20	12	0
Ray Fitton	Manchester	18.09.27	Feather	1947–1954	57	33	16	8
Johnny Fitzgerald	Blackheath	27.09.47	Feather	1967–1972	10	8	2	0
Micky Flanagan	Birkenhead	28.11.26	Light	1949–1955	38	24	12	2
Johnny Flannigan	Whitburn	23.04.28	Light	1948–1951	42	31	10	1
Jimmy Flint	Wapping	06.11.52	Feather	1973–1981	30	27	3	0
Mickey Flynn	Manchester	21.03.45	Welter	1967–1977	54	24	27	3
Gus Foran	Liverpool	15.10.19	Bantam	1939–1951	81	53	27	1
Mickey Forrester	West Ham	12.04.27	Feather	1948–1952	28	16	10	2
Ernie Fossey	Islington	02.09.30	Light	1950–1959	52	32	17	3
Jackie Foster	Belfast	13.07.25	Fly	1946–1953	56	30	15	11
Trevor Francis ø	Basingstoke	27.12.50	L. Middle	1972–1977	39	21	12	6
Peter Freeman	Bolton	17.11.46	Heavy	1972–1978	24	14	10	0
Tony French	Woking	01.11.41	Middle	1958–1965	44	27	16	1
Bob Frost	West Ham	18.06.26	Welter	1947–1953	46	30	15	1
Matt Fulton	Coabridge	23.10.34	Feather	1954–1958	26	18	6	2
Jeff Gale	Leeds	17.02.54	Welter	1973–1976	14	10	4	0
Terry Gale	Cardiff	02.05.40	Bantam	1964–1968	21	10	9	2
Martyn Galleozzie	Merthyr	12.03.54	Light	1972–1980	32	16	14	2
Cyril Gallie	Cardiff	19.01.20	Welter	1944–1948	22	15	7	0
Des Garrod	Paddington	09.06.25	Light	1947–1954	41	24	11	6
Neil Gauci	Cardiff	16.12.52	Feather	1971–1974	15	8	6	1
Tommy Gibbons	Hanwell	04.05.37	L. Heavy	1959–1960	9	6	3	0
Len Gibbs	St. Pancras	01.03.42	L. Middle	1964–1973	45	20	21	1
Billy Gibson	Fishburn	05.04.30	Bantam	1951–1956	45	17	22	6
Jimmy Gibson	Dunfermline	08.03.39	Light	1960–1963	24	15	8	1
Cliff Giles	Linton	05.01.30	Bantam	1949–1957	67	31	29	7
Tim Giles	Stepney	28.05.33	Middle	1955–1958	18	12	6	0
Jimmy Gill	Mabelthorpe	05.10.19	Fly	1931–1950	116	70	35	11
Ronnie Gill	Bethnal Green	14.02.32	Light	1949–1954	31	22	7	2
Terry Gill	West Ham	02.04.36	Welter	1956–1960	30	22	6	2
John Gillan	Aberdeen	14.02.48	Light	1975–1976	4	3	1	0
Tommy Gillen	Hayes	01.03.33	Bantam	1953–1955	17	9	8	0
Bert Gilroy	Airdrie	10.05.18	L. Heavy	1933–1949	117	84	26	7
Carl Gizzi ø	Rhyl	14.05.44	Heavy	1964–1971	43	31	12	0
Johnny Gleed	Poplar	26.01.38	L. Heavy	1960–1965	11	7	4	0
Ian Glenn	Doagh	17.09.51	Heavy	1975–1980	7	2	5	0
Vic Glenn	Stepney	30.11.28	Fly	1952–1956	17	9	6	2
Chris Glover	Liverpool	19.01.57	L. Middle	1976–1980	28	15	11	2
Terry Gooding	Cardiff	15.04.31	L. Heavy	1954–1956	14	12	2	0
Gordon Goodman	Christchurch	11.06.27	Light	1949–1957	69	51	12	6
Dave Goodwin	Shirebrook	03.11.23	L. Heavy	1939–1949	89	70	17	2
Paul Gormley	Canterbury	10.07.37	L. Heavy	1958–1961	22	16	6	0
Stan Gossip	Hull	25.05.23	Feather	1948–1950	35	19	13	3
Billy Graham	Manchester	10.05.55	Middle	1974–1976	14	12	2	0
Paddy Graham	Belfast	05.05.32	Light	1953–1962	53	33	19	1
Paddy Graham	Belfast	27.06.47	Feather	1968–1979	29	16	12	1
Jack Grant	Chesterfield	28.05.40	L. Heavy	1962–1965	22	14	8	0
Malcolm Grant	Glasgow	11.07.32	Bantam	1956–1957	7	5	2	0
P. T. Grant	Newcastle	14.06.55	L. Heavy	1975–1982	11	4	6	1
Billy Gray	Walsall	17.05.44	Heavy	1964–1969	24	18	5	1
George Gray	Bradford	30.07.52	L. Heavy	1970–1978	75	36	36	3
Tommy Gray	Southend	22.04.50	Middle	1969–1972	33	18	14	1
Mick Greaves	Leicester	04.02.39	Feather	1960–1965	37	23	12	2
Ron Greb	Liverpool	26.05.30	Light	1950–1956	31	21	10	0
Syd Greb	Liverpool	11.01.32	Welter	1953–1960	33	14	14	5
Jimmy Green	Warrington	25.11.26	Bantam	1945–1952	67	44	19	4

LEADING BRITISH BASED BOXERS, 1946–1982: CAREER SUMMARY

Name	Domicile	Born	Weight	Career	Record C	W	L	D
John Griffen	Belfast	13.03.26	Feather	1949–1954	29	17	12	0
Ron Grogan	Paddington	28.08.25	Middle	1945–1953	53	27	25	1
Roger Guest	Dudley	07.03.58	L. Welter	1977–1981	29	12	15	2
Peter Guichan	Glasgow	08.12.26	Feather	1948–1952	29	18	10	1
Reg Gullefer	Dagenham	24.05.43	Feather	1965–1970	21	18	3	0
Pat Guttridge	Bow	23.12.32	Welter	1953–1955	24	12	11	1
Billy Hall	Sheffield	03.05.48	Light	1973	7	6	1	0
Sammy Hamilton	Belfast	07.05.29	Middle	1951–1958	35	20	14	1
Francis Hands	Liverpool	13.11.51	L. Heavy	1975–1979	20	13	6	1
Martin Hansen ø	Liverpool	17.07.25	Middle	1949–1959	64	41	18	5
George Happe	Bethnal Green	19.05.31	Welter	1951–1958	41	23	14	4
Billy Hardacre	Liverpool	11.11.45	Light	1965–1974	55	32	21	2
Ron Harman	Brighton	01.11.32	Heavy	1952–1956	19	15	3	1
Jess Harper	Manchester	01.07.52	L. Welter	1972–1979	28	10	17	1
Colin Harrison	Rotherham	25.06.30	Light	1952–1958	20	17	2	1
Mark Harrison	West Hartlepool	01.05.28	Fly	1946–1953	44	21	20	3
Peter Harrison	Cambuslang	10.04.51	Light	1980–1982	13	7	6	0
Vic Harrison	Liverpool	18.02.28	L. Heavy	1950–1955	14	10	4	0
Mark Hart ø	Croydon	29.05.24	Middle	1945–1953	59	43	13	3
Willie Hart	Glasgow	21.12.39	Middle	1961–1966	22	15	6	1
Danny Harvey	Glasgow	05.10.31	Welter	1952–1956	25	18	7	0
Jackie Harwood	Bolton	09.01.44	Middle	1960–1967	30	22	6	2
Gerry Hassett	Belfast	19.02.33	Welter	1950–1969	67	45	22	0
Dave Hawkes	Farnham	30.03.47	L. Heavy	1968–1973	20	15	5	0
Stan Hawthorne ø	North Shields	06.07.23	Light	1945–1951	75	60	11	4
Howard Hayes ø	Doncaster	22.11.49	Feather	1970–1974	21	18	2	1
Jim Hayes	Leeds		Bantam	1932–1950	149	89	45	15
Teddy Haynes	Birmingham	27.07.36	Middle	1958–1965	30	21	9	0
Johnny Haywood	Nottingham	21.04.29	Bantam	1946–1955	49	23	22	4
Gordon Hazell ø	Bristol	19.03.28	Middle	1949–1955	46	31	13	2
Jim Healy	Manchester		Feather	1941–1950	37	20	15	2
Eddie Hearn	Battersea	02.04.29	Heavy	1953–1957	20	13	7	0
Peter Heath	Coventry	09.04.34	Light	1958–1962	29	17	6	6
Chuck Henderson ø	Peterlee	02.12.42	Welter	1965–1970	27	20	6	1
Harry Herbert	Bethnal Green	11.10.28	Feather	1949–1953	29	22	4	3
Vic Herman ø	Glasgow	12.02.29	Fly	1947–1954	57	38	16	3
Stan Hibbert	Battersea		Light	1946–1949	39	20	17	2
Freddie Hicks	Bermondsey	22.01.27	Feather	1945–1956	71	38	22	11
Ken Hignett	Bootle	16.02.36	Light	1958–1960	19	10	8	1
Doug Hill	Stoke	18.03.56	Feather	1978–1981	18	12	4	2
Albert Hillman ø	Farnborough	02.01.55	L. Middle	1974–1980	30	19	10	1
Alf Hines	West Ham	09.02.29	L. Heavy	1949–1952	18	12	5	1
Dennis Hinson	Dagenham	25.05.33	Light	1954–1959	30	20	9	1
Ron Hinson	Dagenham	27.05.31	Light	1952–1961	50	34	13	3
Tommy Hinson	Dagenham	13.07.26	Welter	1946–1953	50	25	19	6
Jack Hobbs	Shepherds Bush	01.12.29	Heavy	1950–1954	18	15	3	0
Len Hobbs	Battersea	01.05.35	Heavy	1963–1964	6	5	1	0
Reg Hoblyn	Fulham	03.10.18	Middle	1942–1949	38	22	14	2
Clive Hogben	Kettering	15.12.51	Feather	1972–1977	18	10	7	1
Alby Hollister	Islington	15.02.23	Middle	1946–1952	55	28	24	3
Steve Hopkin ø	Ely	11.08.57	L. Middle	1977–1981	20	14	4	2
Bert Hornby	Bolton	10.03.25	Light	1943–1954	59	39	17	3
Jackie Horseman	West Hartlepool	02.03.21	Feather	1938–1955	108	30	76	2
Ronnie Hough	Liverpool	23.08.46	Middle	1968–1973	43	22	17	4
Arthur Howard ø	Islington	05.06.30	L. Heavy	1951–1960	54	37	15	2
Johnny Howard	Holloway	21.10.34	Feather	1955–1964	35	13	14	8

Name	Domicile	Born	Weight	Career	Record C	W	L	D
Gareth Howells	Llanelli	27.05.48	Bantam	1968–1971	13	7	6	0
Charlie Howe	West Ham	29.06.29	Middle	1950–1957	26	19	5	2
Roger Howes	Norwich	13.01.44	Feather	1968–1972	25	14	10	1
Brian Huckfield	Warley	05.01.51	Heavy	1975–1979	23	15	6	2
Brian Hudson ø	Woodford	28.12.45	Light	1967–1971	22	18	4	0
Johnny Hudson	Covent Garden	27.07.30	Light	1946–1955	86	51	28	7
Tony Hudson	Peckham	18.10.54	L. Middle	1975–1977	16	13	3	0
Darkie Hughes ø	Cardiff	10.04.31	Light	1953–1964	45	33	10	2
Eddie Hughes	Walworth	06.02.34	Light	1957–1959	17	10	7	0
Harry Hughes ø	Wishaw	07.12.22	Light	1944–1952	79	51	25	3
Jackie Hughes	Pontypridd	13.12.23	Feather	1943–1950	42	20	19	3
Tony Humm	Tottenham	08.03.47	Bantam	1967–1971	21	15	4	2
Colin Humphreys	Pyle	06.09.42	Welter	1960–1963	16	13	3	0
Danny Hurley	Morden	08.04.30	Light	1951–1954	24	15	8	1
Brian Husband	Hull	03.08.39	Welter	1957–1963	45	24	19	2
Isaac Hussein	Streatham	09.12.56	Heavy	1975–1981	25	15	10	0
Mick Hussey	Peckham	02.06.39	Bantam	1961–1965	18	9	9	0
Tommy Icke	Birmingham	18.02.30	Bantam	1951–1955	27	17	10	0
Tom Imrie	Edinburgh	18.06.47	L. Middle	1971–1976	14	10	4	0
Brendan Ingle	Sheffield	19.06.41	Middle	1965–1973	33	19	14	0
Gene Innocent	Cardiff	04.01.45	Heavy	1967–1973	17	11	5	1
Mal Issaacs	Brynmawr	17.08.50	Heavy	1972–1973	9	6	3	0
Bert Jackson	Fleetwood	06.08.21	Feather	1937–1951	142	91	41	10
Fred Jackson	Custom House	14.01.29	L. Heavy	1951–1956	25	11	11	3
Ron Jackson	Newcastle	12.08.34	Welter	1952–1960	22	12	9	1
Nat Jacobs ø	Manchester	01.12.39	Middle	1967–1970	56	28	26	2
George James	Cwm	17.10.15	Heavy	1933–1949	53	31	18	4
Percy James	Southport	29.10.31	Feather	1950–1957	86	38	43	5
Brian Jelley	Bury	06.12.31	Light	1950–1955	50	25	21	4
Chris Jenkins	Stourbridge	20.10.23	Light	1946–1951	55	26	23	6
Ritchie Jenkins	Pontypool	28.12.23	Bantam	1953–1955	12	11	1	0
Jimmy Jennings	Clapton	24.06.25	Fly	1948–1953	50	29	18	3
Brian Jewitt	Newcastle	09.06.44	Heavy	1969–1973	28	12	14	2
Chris Jobson	East Ham	11.10.45	Welter	1964–1972	48	26	18	4
Roy John ø	Nelson	13.10.47	L. Heavy	1967–1978	43	25	17	1
Bobby Johnson	Plymouth	22.11.33	Welter	1950–1957	48	22	23	3
Les Johnson	Finsbury Park	26.12.11	Fly	1936–1950	88	39	37	12
Mias Johnson	Jacksdale	12.02.29	Welter	1947–1952	91	44	36	11
Owen Johnson	Jacksdale	02.10.27	Feather	1947–1950	79	46	22	11
Ron Johnson	Bethnal Green	12.04.26	Bantam	1949–1956	37	22	11	4
Tom Johnston	Belfast	05.11.29	Welter	1950–1953	25	19	5	1
Brian Jones	Nottingham	30.10.32	Light	1957–1963	57	36	17	4
Emrys Jones	Trefonen	01.11.31	Light	1949–1956	65	34	24	7
Gerald Jones	Merthyr	05.11.43	Fly	1962–1968	35	16	17	2
Haydn Jones	Tiryberth	01.02.27	Feather	1946–1953	20	11	8	1
Ken Jones	Gorseinon	03.09.51	L. Heavy	1978–1980	15	8	6	1
Morry Jones	Liverpool	25.10.22	Light	1947–1950	28	14	14	0
Phil Jones	Cardiff	20.04.38	Feather	1957–1962	33	25	8	0
Tommy Jones	Derby	1919	Middle	1937–1950	147	121	21	5
Tommy Joyce	Doncaster	08.08.47	Welter	1971–1980	52	26	23	3
George Judge	Glasgow	02.11.36	Feather	1959–1962	23	14	8	1
Jimmy Jury	Bournemouth		Light	1936–1949	116	46	50	20
Jim Keery	Lisburn	04.02.21	Light	1932–1953	137	86	37	14
John Kellie ø	Livingstone	15.01.45	Bantam	1968–1975	30	17	11	2
Chris Kelly	Liverpool	24.11.27	Feather	1944–1953	75	34	33	8
Frankie Kelly	Birkenhead	25.09.24	Feather	1942–1950	58	40	15	3
Paddy Kelly	Derry	15.03.39	Feather	1957–1962	37	24	12	1
Warren Kendall	Tonyrefail		Light	1936–1949	103	57	35	11
John Kennedy	Draycott	30.04.57	Welter	1979–1981	11	9	2	0

LEADING BRITISH BASED BOXERS, 1946–1982: CAREER SUMMARY

Name	Domicile	Born	Weight	Career	Record C	W	L	D
Emmett Kenny	St. Helens	09.11.25	Light	1946–1954	48	29	14	5
Frank Kenny	Glasgow	28.11.19	Feather	1936–1949	79	49	24	6
Jim Kenny ø	Polmont	27.03.28	Feather	1947–1953	53	39	12	2
Ron Kensington	Tooting	01.08.31	Welter	1951–1955	38	15	17	6
Johnny Kent	Covent Garden	06.12.22	Bantam	1946–1950	30	18	8	4
Jackie Keough	Chester-le-Street	24.06.30	Welter	1949–1955	36	25	11	0
Charlie Kerr	Glasgow	28.11.21	Bantam	1944–1949	29	18	10	1
Tony Kerr	Aberdeen	19.05.53	Bantam	1974–1979	17	8	8	1
Basil Kew	Putney	28.11.28	L. Heavy	1954–1958	25	13	10	2
Johnny Kidd	Aberdeen	30.05.36	Light	1957–1963	40	24	15	1
Tommy Kiely	Brighton	25.09.55	Heavy	1976–1982	30	19	11	0
Freddie King ø	Wandsworth	06.01.31	Feather	1950–1955	54	35	14	5
Paul King	Torquay	07.08.31	Welter	1951–1958	60	33	20	7
Peter King	Manchester	10.08.33	Welter	1952–1958	45	28	15	2
Rocco King	Askern	24.05.33	Middle	1950–1958	48	23	24	1
Paul Kinsella	Liverpool	29.12.55	Heavy	1975–1978	12	5	6	1
Gordon Kirk	Kirkby	17.12.48	L. Welter	1974–1980	24	12	10	2
Billy Knight ø	Walworth	26.07.61	L. Heavy	1974–1978	24	18	5	1
Johnny Kramer	Canning Town	28.10.40	Middle	1959–1970	68	39	26	3
John Laine	Grimsby	01.12.54	L. Middle	1973–1976	17	10	3	4
Colin Lake ø	Islington	24.11.41	Light	1963–1969	30	20	9	1
George Lamont	Glasgow	12.12.28	Feather	1949–1954	26	12	12	2
Kenny Langford	Slough	25.03.33	Bantam	1955–1957	11	6	5	0
Dick Langley	Peckham	29.08.27	Middle	1946–1952	60	44	14	2
Mick Laud	St. Ives	29.07.43	Welter	1962–1973	62	28	28	6
Monty Laud	St. Ives	17.10.44	Bantam	1964–1967	20	14	2	4
Winston Laud	St. Ives	16.06.43	Light	1964–1968	27	16	11	0
George Lavery	Belfast	25.05.30	Middle	1954–1959	27	19	5	3
Peter Lavery	Belfast	28.02.37	Feather	1959–1967	33	8	22	3
Danny Lawford	Manchester	17.10.56	L. Heavy	1979–1982	24	15	6	3
Ken Lawrence	Southampton	20.01.32	Feather	1951–1957	36	20	15	1
Harry Lazar	Aldgate	06.09.22	Welter	1938–1950	115	84	25	6
Lew Lazar ø	Aldgate	03.02.31	Middle	1951–1958	60	48	8	4
Danny Lee	Port Glasgow	05.01.40	Fly	1961–1965	20	12	7	1
Jackie Lee	Hoxton	11.05.47	Light	1967–1971	16	10	6	0
Lloyd Lee	Harlesden	16.03.58	Welter	1977–1979	13	10	3	0
Teddy Lee	Clerkenwell	27.09.24	Welter	1946–1951	36	24	12	0
Harry Legge	Bournemouth	06.09.21	Light	1943–1954	166	84	54	28
Ron Lendrum	Pontypridd	02.07.38	Feather	1963–1965	11	8	3	0
Des Lennon	Banbridge	19.01.28	Light	1951–1954	34	24	8	2
Dick Levers	Chesterfield		Light	1937–1952	117	59	54	4
Bryn Lewis	Porthcawl	22.12.43	Light	1967–1971	23	11	11	1
Norman Lewis ø	Nantymoel	13.11.23	Bantam	1939–1950	113	83	25	5
Teddy Lewis	Dagenham	24.08.30	Light	1947–1951	38	29	8	1
Tony Lewis	Camden Town	30.03.42	Welter	1961–1964	19	14	4	1
Derek Liversidge	Retford	14.01.36	Welter	1956–1960	36	21	14	1
Tony Llanelly	Doncaster	22.06.28	Feather	1948–1953	34	22	6	6
Derek Lloyd ø	Chingford	31.01.36	Fly	1958–1961	24	18	4	2
Jim Lloyd	Liverpool	05.07.39	Welter	1962–1966	20	10	7	3
Willie Lloyd	Brecon	12.05.33	Light	1953–1957	47	25	19	3
Sammy Lockhart	Belfast	20.07.46	Light	1967–1973	19	11	7	1
Jack London	Blackpool	08.05.33	L. Heavy	1954–1966	45	29	13	3
Peter Longo	Covent Garden	15.08.30	Middle	1952–1957	32	20	10	2
Tony Lord	Liverpool	01.11.26	L. Heavy	1948–1956	44	24	19	1
Len Lowther	Doncaster	23.03.33	Middle	1954–1956	17	14	3	0
Frankie Lucas ø	Croydon	15.08.53	Middle	1974–1980	17	10	7	0
Jackie Lucraft	Islington	07.11.22	Feather	1945–1952	47	28	15	4
Eric Ludlam	Sheffield	11.02.32	L. Heavy	1953–1960	29	17	11	1

Name	Domicile	Born	Weight	Career	Record			
					C	W	L	D
Phil Lundgren	Bermondsey	02.01.40	Feather	1961–1967	34	19	13	2
Jim Lynas	Coventry	28.03.34	Middle	1952–1959	54	26	21	7
Carlton Lyons	Manchester	23.03.52	L. Middle	1976–1977	11	6	5	0
Dan McAllister	Belfast	1918	Light	1937–1947	48	35	10	3
Gordon McAteer	Liverpool	24.02.42	Light	1963–1967	31	22	7	2
Jim McAuley	Belfast	26.08.46	Feather	1967–1970	15	9	6	0
Gerry McBride	Manchester	20.10.46	Feather	1966–1976	54	19	31	4
Danny McCafferty	Glasgow	27.06.50	Middle	1972–1977	15	10	4	1
Sean McCafferty	Belfast	17.12.44	Feather	1965–1970	18	12	6	0
Brian McCaffrey ø	Liverpool	04.04.38	Welter	1963–1967	27	19	4	4
Jim McCann	Belfast	1919	Feather	1935–1952	139	73	57	9
Jim McCann	Belfast	01.03.44	Bantam	1965–1967	12	10	2	0
Pat McCann	Harrow	09.12.51	L. Heavy	1971–1981	29	23	6	0
Pat McCarthy	Birkenhead	21.01.33	Feather	1952–1956	36	19	14	3
Mike McCluskie	Croeserw	24.01.50	Middle	1971–1973	27	14	12	1
Spike McCormack	Belfast	29.12.36	Light	1956–1968	96	44	40	12
Frank McCoy	Portadown	15.05.28	Fly	1947–1952	32	14	16	2
Rickie McCulloch	Belfast	12.07.26	Light	1947–1953	65	27	32	6
George McDade	Glasgow	17.01.33	Fly	1957–1961	23	12	9	2
John McDermott	Cambuslang	24.03.39	Feather	1963–1967	8	5	2	1
Stan McDermott	East Ham	03.01.53	Heavy	1977–1982	20	13	6	1
Billy McDonald	Liverpool		Light	1947–1950	27	17	7	3
Terry McDonald	Cudworth	11.08.31	Heavy	1950–1955	35	27	7	1
Garfield McEwan	Birmingham	03.12.53	Heavy	1975–1978	14	7	7	0
Jackie McGill	Glasgow	07.01.56	Feather	1976–1978	12	7	5	0
Jim McGinness	Wishaw	25.11.35	Welter	1955–1960	22	17	5	0
Johnny McGowan	Leeds	10.07.25	Light	1946–1952	47	31	15	1
Jimmy McGrail	Liverpool	10.12.36	Welter	1959–1964	37	31	6	0
Roy McGregor	Glasgow	24.04.49	Welter	1947–1955	45	26	17	2
Tommy McGuinness	Edinburgh	10.11.34	Light	1957–1960	19	10	8	1
George McGurk	Jarrow	27.05.50	L. Welter	1970–1980	63	33	27	3
Noel McIvor	Luton	06.01.47	Light	1970–1976	47	25	18	4
Danny MacKay	Edinburgh	23.06.22	Welter	1939–1951	67	29	30	8
George McKay	Edinburgh	25.02.53	Feather	1972–1974	17	6	8	3
John McKenna	Southend	22.01.42	Light	1961–1967	35	18	15	2
Sean McKenna	Downpatrick	30.01.54	Heavy	1975–1978	6	1	5	0
Errol McKenzie	Cardiff	07.01.54	Middle	1974–1980	24	13	11	0
Ian McKenzie	Ayr	22.07.41	Middle	1961–1967	25	14	10	1
John McLaren	Glasgow	06.02.35	Light	1954–1962	23	9	12	2
Peter McLaren	Brixton	24.02.40	Welter	1961–1967	39	31	8	0
Neil McLaughlin ø	Derry	10.05.48	Fly	1976–1982	28	5	20	3
Herbie McLean	Edinburgh	28.02.48	L. Welter	1970–1980	33	16	14	3
Tim McLeary	Wrexham	02.04.32	Welter	1949–1955	50	34	16	0
Johnny McLeavy	Dagenham		Heavy	1949–1955	23	12	9	2
Tom McMenemy	Belfast	18.04.27	Welter	1946–1954	49	28	17	4
Angus McMillan	Glasgow	30.06.46	L. Welter	1970–1975	32	21	8	3
Don McMillan ø	Glasgow	12.09.38	Middle	1963–1974	53	30	18	5
Harry McMurdie	Edgware	24.12.25	Light	1947–1951	42	24	14	4
Gerry McNally	Liverpool	02.09.32	L. Heavy	1953–1963	44	25	15	4
John McNally	Belfast	03.11.32	Light	1954–1957	22	13	7	2
Eric McQuade	Downham	21.07.26	Middle	1949–1953	34	23	11	0
Sammy McSpadden ø	Fulham	16.05.41	Light	1960–1966	38	27	10	1
Don McTaggart	Dundee	14.04.31	Light	1949–1956	56	39	13	4
Brian McTigue	Wigan	08.08.30	L. Heavy	1947–1951	30	14	15	1
Terry McTigue	Belfast	09.11.42	Middle	1965–1970	15	8	6	1
Tommy Madine	Belfast	25.04.20	Bantam	1939–1950	76	38	32	6
Jan Magdziarz	Eastleigh	26.01.48	Middle	1972–1979	27	15	10	2
Eddie Magee	Belfast	22.05.24	Feather	1946–1954	80	50	23	7

LEADING BRITISH BASED BOXERS, 1946–1982: CAREER SUMMARY

Name	Domicile	Born	Weight	Career	Record C	W	L	D
Tim Mahoney	Downham	22.09.23	Bantam	1944–1952	24	17	6	1
Danny Malloy	Bonnybridge	09.02.29	Welter	1951–1954	20	12	8	0
Leo Maloney	Hillingdon	10.01.32	Welter	1953–1960	63	32	23	8
Maurice Mancini	Leamington	06.01.27	Light	1947–1953	67	37	27	3
Tony Mancini ø	Hammersmith	30.11.32	Welter	1950–1962	38	30	4	4
Vic Manini	Lambeth		Light	1946–1949	30	16	14	0
Johnny Mann	Birmingham	11.04.32	Light	1948–1958	92	53	25	14
Johnny Mantle	Battersea	15.06.42	Feather	1961–1967	37	27	9	1
Billy Marlow	Cardiff	21.11.42	Light	1965–1968	11	10	1	0
Eric Marsden ø	St. Helens	20.08.30	Fly	1949–1955	32	27	4	1
Bernard Marshall	Manchester	20.08.30	Fly	1950–1951	15	12	3	0
Jackie Marshall	Glasgow	10.07.28	Welter	1946–1951	48	37	9	2
Vince Marshall	Manchester	11.07.28	Light	1949–1955	39	25	12	2
Al Marson	Stepney	13.04.13	L. Heavy	1938–1950	82	56	20	6
George Martin	Bermondsey	05.09.34	Light	1956–1959	16	8	8	0
Phil Martin ø	Manchester	05.04.50	L. Heavy	1974–1978	20	14	6	0
Bobby Mason	Liverpool	12.06.31	Feather	1949–1955	25	16	7	2
Ted Mason	Bournemouth	01.06.29	L. Heavy	1949–1953	33	20	12	1
Alf Matthews	Liverpool	07.10.38	Middle	1963–1965	13	10	3	0
Jimmy Matthews	Belfast	04.07.32	Fly	1954–1955	7	5	2	0
Phil Matthews ø	Rossendale	24.04.48	Middle	1970–1976	22	16	6	0
Billy May	Newport	16.05.48	Middle	1971–1972	12	11	1	0
Wally Mays	Hull	31.03.32	Welter	1951–1955	21	18	2	1
Tom Meli	Belfast	28.03.30	Middle	1948–1955	47	28	15	4
Jim Melrose	Glasgow	03.03.51	L. Welter	1971–1975	14	10	3	1
George Metcalf	Leeds	21.05.55	Light	1978–1982	20	12	8	0
Colin Miles	Tonyrefail	28.10.49	Feather	1969–1978	38	22	14	2
Johnny Miller	North Shields	09.08.30	Light	1947–1957	48	35	7	6
Tommy Miller	West Lothian	01.05.29	Bantam	1950–1959	34	23	8	3
Howard Mills ø	Huddersfield	09.12.53	Middle	1976–1981	18	10	7	1
Ken Millsom	Doncaster	01.09.29	L. Heavy	1950–1954	24	17	4	3
Mick Minter	Crawley	25.05.56	L. Middle	1976–1979	27	12	13	2
Achille Mitchell	Coventry	12.05.54	L. Middle	1975–1981	38	15	19	4
Ivor Mitchell	Chatham	29.11.25	Middle	1948–1951	36	19	14	3
Jimmy Mitchell	Wandsworth	05.02.41	Light	1962–1966	28	15	11	2
Jimmy Molloy	Liverpool		Welter	1939–1952	75	47	27	1
Johnny Molloy ø	St. Helens	26.03.26	Feather	1943–1953	67	40	24	3
Tony Monaghan	Derry	21.07.43	Heavy	1967–1979	20	8	11	1
Jim Montague ø	Antrim	11.04.50	L. Welter	1974–1978	40	15	23	2
Dave Mooney	Wishaw	02.04.32	L. Heavy	1956–1958	16	12	4	0
Colin Moore	Derby	21.02.38	Welter	1957–1961	25	20	4	1
Jimmy Moore	Birkenhead		Welter	1936–1950	83	52	30	1
Rees Moore	Mardy	23.12.23	Welter	1948–1957	80	43	31	6
Tony Moore	Hendon	28.02.53	Heavy	1974–1982	54	22	25	7
Tony Moore	Stepney	27.04.44	L. Heavy	1965–1969	24	21	2	1
Eddie Moran	Leeds	29.03.29	Feather	1949–1956	41	23	14	4
Jim Moran	Leeds	07.02.29	Heavy	1948–1956	32	22	8	2
Les Morgan	Acton	24.02.33	Welter	1954–1961	23	18	5	0
Ted Morgan	Worcester	22.12.30	L. Heavy	1948–1955	37	22	15	0
Cliff Morris	Pontypridd	08.03.20	Feather	1942–1949	36	18	17	1
Peter Morris	Bridgnorth	10.05.54	Middle	1975–1980	21	10	9	2
Peter Morrison	Hull	21.06.29	Feather	1949–1953	37	16	18	3
John Morrissey ø	Newarthill	17.08.37	Feather	1957–1964	32	24	6	2
Laurie Morrow	West Hartlepool	06.06.29	Bantam	1946–1952	41	26	14	1
Len Mullen	Glasgow	17.09.34	Middle	1956–1958	13	7	6	0
Alex Murphy	Glasgow	08.08.22	Fly	1943–1946	19	11	5	3
Arthur Murphy	Camden Town	24.08.36	Light	1955–1959	39	29	10	0
Joe Murphy	Glasgow	07.07.27	Fly	1947–1956	22	12	10	0

Name	Domicile	Born	Weight	Career	Record C	W	L	D
Terence Murphy	Canning Town	19.08.34	L. Heavy	1953–1957	28	20	7	1
Duggie Myers	Rotherham	30.05.23	Middle	1946–1951	55	30	23	2
Willie Myles	Dundee	14.05.21	Feather	1947–1951	31	16	13	2
Rocky Nelson	Brixton	07.05.40	L. Heavy	1961–1964	8	7	1	0
Bernie Newcombe	Dagenham	24.11.30	Welter	1950–1954	43	31	9	3
Jimmy Newman ø	Walthamstow	12.08.34	Welter	1953–1960	25	18	6	1
Irvin Newton	Thorne	09.12.33	Feather	1951–1955	30	23	5	2
Bob Nicolson ø	Farnborough	19.07.40	L. Heavy	1960–1968	29	19	7	3
Gerry Nolan	Liverpool	05.02.29	L Heavy	1949–1952	18	8	7	3
Rugger North	South Elmsall	08.01.26	Welter	1944–1948	55	43	8	4
Salvo Nuciforo	Falmouth	18.05.54	L. Middle	1977–1980	21	12	9	0
George Nuttall	Stockport	17.03.27	Heavy	1947–1957	46	25	19	2
Danny O'Brien	Kilburn	10.07.39	Feather	1960–1963	24	17	7	0
Jimmy O'Connell	Bootle	18.06.31	Welter	1949–1958	37	26	10	1
Pat O'Grady	Bermondsey	22.06.38	Middle	1960–1964	24	12	10	2
Alex O'Neill	Belfast	30.09.40	Fly	1960–1965	16	7	8	1
George O'Neill ø	Belfast	26.04.32	Bantam	1952–1963	47	20	25	2
George O'Neill	Wolverhampton	17.12.44	Feather	1965–1978	37	22	13	2
Gerry O'Neill	Glasgow	09.02.58	Feather	1977–1980	18	7	9	2
Mickey O'Neill	Belfast	06.12.26	Welter	1947–1955	67	38	28	1
Teddy O'Neill	Dumbarton		Bantam	1934–1948	74	39	28	7
Tommy O'Neill	Salford	16.12.32	Welter	1949–1955	37	21	11	5
Freddie Orr	Belfast	06.12.29	Fly	1949–1953	28	14	11	3
Jeff Oscroft	Sutton-in-Ashfield	18.02.29	Fly	1946–1952	29	22	5	2
Dickie O'Sullivan ø	Finsbury Park	24.05.25	Fly	1945–1951	38	20	14	4
Mickey O'Sullivan	Finsbury Park	05.09.28	Bantam	1949–1955	39	25	9	5
Dave Ould	Bermondsey	19.05.40	Heavy	1960–1968	33	22	11	0
John Ould	Bermondsey	19.05.40	L. Heavy	1961–1967	24	10	11	3
Austin Owens	Reading	14.07.56	Feather	1978–1982	14	11	2	1
Dave Owens	Castleford	11.12.54	Middle	1976–1980	20	12	7	1
Dickie Owens	Reading	30.08.48	L. Heavy	1967–1971	29	18	11	0
Brian Packer	Dartford	02.03.44	Bantam	1965–1968	15	14	1	0
Kevin Paddock	Southampton	28.02.56	Middle	1974–1978	23	11	10	2
Charlie Page	Stepney	07.01.33	Welter	1953–1954	16	11	3	2
George Palin	Crewe	13.02.36	Welter	1960–1964	37	22	14	1
Gerry Parker	Nottingham	24.07.38	Fly	1956–1960	47	23	22	2
Frank Parkes	Beeston	06.06.20	Light	1934–1956	102	79	18	5
Larry Parkes	Stoke	17.08.30	Middle	1952–1954	21	17	4	0
Sid Parkinson	Wakefield	06.05.38	Middle	1961–1963	20	17	3	0
Dave Parsons	Northolt	23.03.40	Light	1960–1964	26	15	8	3
Joey Parsons	Ilford	03.04.31	L. Heavy	1951–1957	25	14	9	2
Charlie Parvin	Wishaw	15.01.51	Bantam	1972–1980	20	9	10	1
Alan Peacock	Hull	29.03.36	L. Heavy	1958–1963	15	7	7	1
George Peacock	Greenock	23.04.56	L. Welter	1976–1982	28	19	8	1
Jimmy Pearce	Middlesbrough	13.02.28	Fly	1948–1953	45	33	11	1
Les Pearson	Pontefract	08.09.46	Welter	1968–1977	39	20	14	5
Bobby Peart	South Elmsall	27.02.30	Welter	1947–1951	26	21	4	1
Teddy Peckham	Bournemouth	16.12.28	Feather	1944–1959	160	94	52	14
Joe Perks	Liskeard		Welter	1935–1950	36	30	4	2
Vic Phayer	Woolwich	21.04.31	L. Heavy	1948–1954	45	26	14	5
Eddie Phillips	Edinburgh	23.05.30	Welter	1950–1957	54	24	22	8
Neilly Phillips	Motherwell	27.08.29	Light	1950–1952	26	16	7	3
Terry Phillips	Cardiff	13.06.39	Welter	1959–1966	48	12	33	3
Harry Pickard	Battersea	20.09.43	Feather	1962–1966	24	22	1	1
Les Pickett ø	Merthyr	04.04.49	Feather	1971–1979	25	15	8	2
Johnny Pincham	Crawley	09.05.56	Welter	1976–1981	30	13	15	2
Mick Piner	Camberley	27.05.50	Feather	1972–1973	10	5	5	0
Denny Pleace	Cardiff	14.03.45	Middle	1962–1970	36	27	8	1

LEADING BRITISH BASED BOXERS, 1946–1982: CAREER SUMMARY

Name	Domicile	Born	Weight	Career	Record C	W	L	D
Mick Piner	Camberley	27.05.50	Feather	1972–1973	10	5	5	0
Denny Pleace	Cardiff	14.03.45	Middle	1962–1970	36	27	8	1
Robin Polak	Nottingham	18.01.48	Welter	1968–1972	24	12	9	3
George Pook	Torquay		Feather	1928–1950	99	59	32	8
Tony Poole ø	Northampton	05.10.53	L. Middle	1972–1978	35	24	10	1
Ricky Porter	Swindon	27.04.43	Welter	1962–1973	76	26	44	6
Ken Potter	Battersea	10.06.41	Heavy	1961–1963	16	13	2	1
Eric Powell	Ashton-under-Lyne	1915	Feather	1936–1949	35	19	15	1
Fred Powell	Walworth	25.08.28	Heavy	1949–1960	52	34	16	2
Fred Powney	Doncaster	05.06.40	Middle	1962–1971	78	33	36	9
Johnny Prescott ø	Birmingham	20.08.38	Heavy	1961–1970	49	34	11	4
Ron Price	Bilston	19.08.22	Light	1944–1953	67	38	21	8
Jeff Pritchard	Merthyr	27.11.54	Light	1974–1980	46	22	22	2
Tommy Proffitt	Manchester	13.07.27	Bantam	1948–1953	47	34	12	1
Dave Proud ø	Penge	20.08.49	Welter	1968–1979	33	29	4	0
Ron Pudney	Croydon	12.12.23	Middle	1947–1954	65	43	16	6
Bernard Pugh	Liverpool	12.08.25	Feather	1945–1952	100	61	35	4
Reg Quinlan	Ammanford	02.05.25	Light	1944–1951	40	27	10	3
Jimmy Quinn	Kirkintilloch	04.05.28	Fly	1951–1956	31	18	12	1
Joe Quinn	Belfast	13.02.26	Feather	1949–1958	46	33	11	2
Peter Quinn	Swindon	30.08.48	Welter	1967–1971	16	12	4	0
Billy Rafferty ø	Glasgow	14.08.33	Bantam	1956–1962	31	24	6	1
Harry Ramsden	Brixton	20.12.31	Feather	1951–1955	28	20	5	3
Bob Ramsey	Stepney	26.02.22	Light	1938–1947	89	44	35	10
Jackie Rankin	Southall		Feather	1935–1947	95	51	36	8
Terry Ratcliffe	Bristol	19.08.30	Welter	1950–1954	51	33	16	2
Bill Rattray	Dundee	06.04.29	Welter	1948–1952	41	31	7	3
Johnny Rawlings	Billingsgate	04.04.26	Feather	1942–1951	49	37	7	5
Willie Rea	Belfast	15.08.39	Welter	1966–1970	11	6	5	0
Dennis Read	Chelsea	09.05.33	Middle	1953–1965	38	21	10	7
Johnny Read	Norwood	08.02.32	Middle	1953–1959	30	22	7	1
Freddie Reardon	Downham	19.04.31	Light	1953–1956	15	10	4	1
Tom Reddington	Salford	30.04.18	Heavy	1934–1948	81	60	18	3
Ron Redrup	West Ham	30.05.35	L. Heavy	1957–1968	52	22	25	5
Len Luggy Reece ø	Cardiff	05.04.32	Fly	1956–1961	28	18	9	1
Terry Rees	Catford	12.06.37	Feather	1957–1961	26	11	15	0
Ken Regan	Blackpool	25.01.32	Welter	1949–1955	62	42	17	3
Owen Reilly	Glasgow	21.01.37	Feather	1957–1961	16	10	5	1
Les Rendle	Hull	21.07.24	Welter	1948–1951	40	24	9	7
Sammy Reynolds	Wolverhampton	25.07.22	Bantam	1936–1949	104	63	36	5
Derek Richards ø	Merthyr	14.03.41	L. Heavy	1962–1969	25	16	7	2
Doug Richards	Gorseinon	20.03.20	L. Heavy	1946–1950	30	16	14	0
Ron Richardson	Canning Town	26.07.34	Welter	1953–1963	71	39	29	3
Hugh Riley	Edinburgh	11.08.29	Fly	1950–1961	20	10	9	1
Ronnie Riley	Preston	13.12.30	Middle	1946–1961	43	35	6	2
Terry Riley	Liverpool	29.12.25	Feather	1947–1952	49	24	21	4
Tony Riley ø	Coventry	30.09.43	Light	1963–1971	26	18	7	1
Ginger Roberts	Whitley Bay	23.04.17	Welter	1932–1951	129	90	29	10
Jimmy Roberts	Newbridge	09.11.26	Middle	1951–1952	14	9	3	2
Dave Robins	Camberwell	29.11.33	Bantam	1954–1955	8	5	3	0
Al Robinson	Leeds	1920	Heavy	1937–1948	61	36	23	2
Dave Roden	Birmingham	30.01.50	Heavy	1971–1974	19	11	8	0
George Roe	Wolverhampton	29.03.30	Middle	1950–1957	76	44	31	1
Frank Ronan	Fulham	18.05.26	Heavy	1943–1950	33	21	11	1
Joe Rood	Aldgate	11.11.28	Middle	1946–1953	39	21	15	3
Ken Rowlands	Luton	03.07.27	L. Heavy	1948–1958	69	41	23	5
Denton Ruddock	Camberwell	08.11.51	Heavy	1975–1981	18	9	8	1
Johnny Russell	Covent Garden	07.10.22	Light	1942–1950	58	31	21	6

Name	Domicile	Born	Weight	Career	Record			
					C	W	L	D
Ken Ryan	Islington	23.01.29	Feather	1950–1952	18	15	3	0
Ginger Sadd ø	Norwich	27.03.14	Middle	1932–1951	224	164	44	16
Dennis Sale	Northwich		Fly	1946–1952	52	24	23	5
Alan Salter ø	Peckham	23.10.50	L. Welter	1969–1976	32	13	18	1
Bert Sanders	Kilburn	04.10.23	Middle	1942–1954	114	49	55	10
Ric Sanders	Leicester	24.11.25	Welter	1945–1950	108	69	31	8
Redvers Sangoe	Cardiff	06.07.36	L. Heavy	1956–1960	28	17	11	0
Paul Schutt	Leicester	13.01.56	Middle	1976–1979	19	11	7	1
Don Scott	Derby	23.07.28	L. Heavy	1950–1953	20	15	5	0
George Scott	Newcastle	02.12.55	Heavy	1977–1982	22	11	8	3
Harry Scott	Bootle	27.10.37	Middle	1960–1973	79	39	34	6
Vernon Scott	Willesden	23.10.50	L. Heavy	1974–1981	30	14	14	2
Wally Scott	West Ham	04.02.32	Middle	1956–1958	22	11	7	4
Billy Seasman	Liverpool	30.09.45	Welter	1962–1972	34	21	12	1
Ray Seward	Lincoln	05.01.37	L. Heavy	1961–1965	22	10	11	1
Al Sharpe	Belfast	29.01.34	Light	1952–1968	119	71	45	3
Howard Sharpe	Harlesden	17.02.48	Middle	1969–1972	25	18	6	1
Roy Sharples	Burnley	30.10.24	Light	1947–1951	49	34	13	2
Billy Shaw	Manchester	19.06.27	Light	1949–1953	40	18	19	3
Jeff Shaw	Manchester	15.12.45	L. Heavy	1968–1973	26	15	10	1
Ken Shaw	Dundee	10.06.20	Heavy	1942–1951	39	23	12	4
Ray Shiel	St. Helens	23.12.38	Heavy	1960–1965	44	22	20	2
Young Silky	Leeds	19.12.48	Light	1968–1975	32	9	21	2
Alan Sillett	Acton	19.02.33	Bantam	1954–1956	15	10	3	2
Harry Silver	Clapton		Feather	1936–1946	89	64	16	9
Charlie Simpkins	Bridlington	31.07.28	Feather	1948–1954	37	17	18	2
Derek Simpson	Kilmarnock	25.04.48	Welter	1969–1975	55	26	25	4
Ivor Simpson	Basingstoke	12.10.24	Feather	1942–1951	66	42	18	6
Graham Sines	Wandsworth	13.11.50	Heavy	1971–1977	18	12	6	0
Eric Skidmore	Wednesbury	11.05.28	Welter	1943–1955	41	19	18	4
Stan Skinkiss	Manchester	17.10.31	Light	1951–1957	50	24	22	4
Paddy Slavin	Belfast	09.01.27	Heavy	1947–1960	49	23	24	2
Billy Smart	Corby	02.03.55	Feather	1974–1976	17	8	6	3
John Smillie ø	Fauldhouse	12.11.33	Feather	1955–1962	44	30	13	1
Algar Smith	Stoke Newington	31.05.31	Light	1949–1954	20	17	3	0
Billy Smith	Croydon	29.07.32	L. Heavy	1956–1960	24	13	9	2
Brian Smith	Porthcawl	07.05.38	Light	1960–1963	24	17	6	1
Dave Smith ø	Eltham	13.08.53	Bantam	1976–1981	23	16	6	1
Dusty Smith	Cricklewood	23.10.46	Middle	1968–1976	30	15	13	2
Freddie Smith	Sheffield		Light	1947–1951	37	20	15	2
Hugh Smith	Chapelhall	19.11.50	Welter	1974–1981	40	27	12	1
Hughie Smith	Sunderland	05.10.23	Light	1940–1951	79	37	36	6
Jack Smith	Worcester	1919	Heavy	1936–1948	42	32	7	3
John Smith	Glasgow	19.10.50	L. Middle	1970–1980	72	24	44	4
John Smith	Portsmouth	19.08.29	L. Heavy	1953–1959	28	16	12	0
Johnny Smith	Clydebank	01.03.23	Light	1940–1951	112	82	27	3
Kris Smith	Sutton	05.10.51	Heavy	1975–1978	15	10	5	0
Maxie Smith ø	Stockton	03.11.42	L. Heavy	1968–1975	26	20	6	0
Maxie Smith	Wolverhampton	05.08.36	Middle	1959–1963	25	16	8	1
Peter Smith	Huddersfield	28.02.32	Welter	1951–1958	68	36	27	5
Tom Smith ø	Sunderland	26.09.18	Feather	1932–1947	124	107	14	3
Tony Smith ø	Bootle	22.08.36	Welter	1958–1965	48	32	14	2
Tony Smith	Wolverhampton	08.11.37	Heavy	1958–1965	23	13	10	0
Gerry Smyth	Belfast	07.07.23	Light	1946–1956	70	40	28	2
Trevor Snell	Cardiff	18.02.33	L. Heavy	1955–1957	14	8	6	0
Tommy Sobles	Leeds	17.11.48	Light	1970–1973	31	22	7	2
Jackie Sommerville	Greenwich	19.04.28	Feather	1949–1953	28	15	8	5

Name	Domicile	Born	Weight	Career	Record			
					C	W	L	D
Carl Speare	Liverpool	17.12.52	Middle	1974–1978	17	8	8	1
Reg Spring	Southall	20.03.24	L. Heavy	1946–1952	78	45	25	8
Charlie Squire	Coventry	18.10.20	Fly	1946–1949	24	17	7	0
Michael Stack	Leamington	27.07.28	Middle	1949–1954	46	23	20	3
Mario Stango	Bedford	23.10.53	Feather	1973–1976	22	11	9	2
Lacey Stannard	Kings Lynn	18.06.36	L. Heavy	1958–1963	25	16	9	0
George Stern	Glasgow	27.02.27	Heavy	1948–1954	28	18	10	0
Billy Stevens	Tillycoutry		Middle	1937–1950	174	100	63	11
Les Stevens	Reading	07.03.51	Heavy	1971–1979	28	23	5	0
George Stewart	Hamilton	23.05.26	Feather	1948–1952	44	28	13	3
Ginger Stewart	Hamilton		Welter	1936–1950	76	60	12	4
Dave Stone	Battersea	21.04.35	Light	1958–1961	38	24	12	2
Billy Straub	Motherwell	06.03.54	Bantam	1979–1981	10	7	3	0
Pat Stribling	Croydon	08.01.27	L. Heavy.	1946–1951	46	26	16	4
Jimmy Stubbs	Runcorn		Feather	1936–1947	77	52	21	4
Bernie Sutton	Willesden	06.05.44	L. Heavy	1963–1967	16	15	1	0
George Sutton	Cardiff	15.09.22	Fly	1944–1952	20	3	15	2
Jackie Sutton	Cardiff	28.03.23	Fly	1947–1951	26	12	11	3
Jim Swords	Manchester	05.02.42	Middle	1961–1969	30	15	14	1
Paul Sykes ø	Wakefield	23.05.46	Heavy	1978–1980	10	6	3	1
Amos Talbot	Manchester	09.10.47	Welter	1967–1973	36	19	16	1
Billy Tansey	Middleton		Fly	1926–1949	136	68	55	13
Billy Tarrant	Bermondsey	20.06.39	Welter	1960–1964	34	18	14	2
Keith Tate	Leeds	30.01.45	Bantam	1964–1966	16	11	3	2
Alf Taylor	Warrington	30.03.22	Welter	1938–1949	60	38	22	0
Billy Taylor	Stirling	03.05.26	Bantam	1950–1954	30	18	11	1
Carl Taylor	Richmond	27.09.40	Bantam	1960–1968	36	20	12	4
Frankie Taylor	Lancaster	02.09.42	Feather	1962–1966	31	27	3	1
Jock Taylor	Sidcup	02.08.25	L. Heavy	1946–1951	43	21	18	4
Kenny Taylor	Norwich	16.03.30	Light	1950–1957	30	23	7	0
Ronnie Taylor	Horwich	23.10.26	Feather	1946–1952	41	25	15	1
Norman Tennant	Dundee	26.04.23	Fly	1946–1952	47	31	11	5
Bernie Terrell ø	Edmonton	17.11.44	Welter	1968–1972	28	23	4	1
Neville Tetlow	Manchester	09.05.31	Bantam	1950–1956	50	33	14	3
Billy Thomas	Cardiff	28.03.44	Feather	1962–1967	30	18	9	3
Carl Thomas	Cardiff	23.01.47	Middle	1966–1977	24	15	8	1
Hughie Thomas	Merthyr	26.11.28	Bantam	1950–1955	16	13	3	0
Johnny Thomas	Cardiff	12.01.38	Bantam	1958–1960	16	15	1	0
Maurice Thomas	Bradford	23.09.45	Middle	1967–1973	37	15	18	4
Nat Thomas	Colsterworth	06.04.28	Welter	1949–1951	25	23	2	0
Ernie Thompson	Bedworth	08.08.24	Light	1946–1951	33	16	13	4
Mickey Thompson	Lowestoft	00.00.00	Welter	1932–1948	73	59	8	6
Pat Thompson	Liverpool	21.03.48	L. Heavy	1972–1976	60	30	25	5
Jimmy Thomson	Glasgow	19.12.27	Fly	1950–1955	36	21	14	1
Jack Thornbury	Covent Garden	12.06.27	Welter	1952–1955	30	18	10	2
George Thresher	Edmonton	25.02.22	Light	1947–1954	39	23	14	2
Jimmy Tibbs	West Ham	09.09.46	Middle	1966–1970	20	17	2	1
Roger Tighe	Hull	23.07.44	Heavy	1966–1976	37	21	13	3
Jimmy Tippett	Greenwich	28.03.31	Light	1949–1958	38	27	10	1
Jeff Tite	Spratton	29.10.26	Welter	1947–1952	84	64	19	1
Terry Toole	Hackney	01.06.34	Feather	1956–1960	27	13	11	3
Alan Tottoh	Manchester	21.10.44	Welter	1969–1974	21	10	8	3
Owen Trainor	Manchester	29.09.29	Welter	1950–1952	33	19	13	1
Steve Trainor	Manchester	14.11.31	Feather	1952–1954	20	16	2	2
Jim Travers	Airdrie	03.09.29	Feather	1951–1954	17	9	5	3
Derry Treanor ø	Glasgow	17.07.37	Feather	1956–1962	23	17	6	0
Noel Trigg	Newport	28.11.34	L. Heavy	1952–1959	25	16	9	0
Charlie Tucker	Camberwell	01.10.28	Feather	1950–1957	47	32	13	2

Name	Domicile	Born	Weight	Career	Record			
					C	W	L	D
George Turpin	Liverpool	10.01.52	Feather	1973–1977	16	11	3	2
Jackie Turpin	Leamington	04.05.49	Welter	1967–1975	32	24	7	1
Jackie Turpin	Leamington	06.06.25	Feather	1946–1954	130	87	35	8
Dave Underwood	Plymouth	22.12.33	Welter	1953–1955	37	20	15	2
Eddie Vann	Shoeburyness	17.11.28	Heavy	1947–1951	20	12	5	3
Sammy Vernon	Belfast	11.10.48	Bantam	1967–1972	22	11	9	2
Ernie Vickers	Middlesbrough	30.07.24	Welter	1949–1956	58	39	19	0
Billy Vivian	Tredegar	24.11.55	L. Welter	1976–1981	28	11	16	1
Johnny Waddingham	Islington	28.12.51	Light	1969–1971	13	8	3	2
Billy Wadham	Tottenham	09.04.34	Welter	1957–1961	17	9	7	1
Jackie Wakelam	Normanton	17.07.25	Light	1945–1952	51	28	20	3
Johnny Waldron	Poplar	12.01.54	L. Heavy	1976–1979	12	9	1	2
Lloyd Walford	Bradford	22.02.42	L. Heavy	1964–1976	64	26	34	4
Billy Walker	Kings Cross	25.02.38	Fly	1959–1961	16	11	5	0
Billy Walker ø	West Ham	03.03.39	Heavy	1962–1969	31	21	8	2
Chris Walker ø	Retford	23.04.51	L. Welter	1976–1979	27	15	11	1
George Walker ø	Stepney	14.04.29	L. Heavy	1951–1954	16	10	6	0
Steve Walker	Birmingham	28.04.50	L. Heavy	1973–1978	25	4	20	1
John Wall	Shoreditch	23.05.51	L. Heavy	1971–1979	24	16	7	1
Steve Walsh	Liverpool	23.11.27	Feather	1949–1953	19	13	6	0
Jeff Walters	Scarborough	05.07.31	Light	1950–1956	51	23	24	4
Ron Warnes	Erith	31.12.36	Welter	1958–1960	17	14	3	0
Jimmy Warnock	Belfast	1913	Fly	1931–1948	100	74	20	6
Phil Watford	Forest Gate	16.06.44	L. Heavy	1966–1972	21	16	4	1
Carl Watson	Camberwell	08.02.56	L. Heavy	1974–1977	12	6	6	0
Harry Watson	Aldgate		Middle	1940–1946	40	33	6	1
Norman Watts	Kennington	25.07.23	Fly	1951–1952	14	11	3	0
Freddie Webb	Belfast	25.09.25	Middle	1944–1952	45	25	20	0
Kelvin Webber	Porth	16.01.53	Light	1977–1978	13	7	5	1
Kenny Webber	Manchester	08.11.52	L. Middle	1972–1981	30	18	8	4
Jimmy Webster	Canning Town	16.09.24	Bantam	1945–1952	55	28	24	3
Jim Wellard	Northampton	27.03.22	Welter	1937–1951	96	57	34	5
Don Weller	Battersea	11.11.36	Bantam	1959–1969	41	23	15	3
George Whelan	Acton	20.05.34	Light	1955–1957	23	15	8	0
Al White	Forest Hill	18.09.45	Light	1965–1969	28	20	7	1
Harry White	Northampton	11.06.51	L. Heavy	1974–1981	24	13	11	0
Kevin White ø	Wells	19.06.49	Welter	1972–1977	35	15	16	4
Ivan Whiter	Tooting	04.01.40	Welter	1962–1969	40	23	4	13
Dave Whittaker	Battersea	05.12.39	Bantam	1959–1962	27	17	8	2
Jack Whittaker	Warwick	19.12.34	L. Heavy	1955–1965	44	25	16	3
Willie Whyte	Glasgow	20.06.17	Welter	1939–1953	86	53	28	5
Al Wilburn	Hickleton Main	16.04.26	Light	1947–1953	36	19	13	4
Ray Wilding	Northwich	06.09.29	Heavy	1947–1956	50	42	4	4
Alan Wilkins	Ystradgynlais	15.07.26	Welter	1946–1953	41	28	10	3
Billy Williams	Barking	19.03.52	L. Heavy	1973–1974	16	15	1	0
Dave Williams	Barry	18.08.26	L. Heavy	1949–1954	35	20	14	1
Dave Williams	Borehamwood	27.04.57	Light	1978–1981	21	20	0	1
Frankie Williams ø	Birkenhead	12.02.25	Bantam	1944–1953	41	29	12	0
Freddie Williams	Nuneaton	25.09.49	Light	1969–1972	29	19	9	1
Gwyn Williams ø	Pontycymmer	08.01.22	Welter	1938–1951	72	55	15	2
Lance Williams	Manchester	19.07.60	Light	1978–1982	27	19	5	3
Lennie Williams ø	Maesteg	02.02.44	Feather	1961–1966	37	33	3	1
Ollie Williams	West Ham	05.01.24	Middle	1947–1952	30	20	7	3
Ted Williams	Huddersfield	13.04.38	L. Heavy	1954–1960	57	30	23	4
Barney Wilson	Belfast	08.08.42	L. Heavy	1964–1967	10	6	4	0
Charlie Wisdom	Peckham	01.06.26	Light	1948–1952	21	17	4	0
Billy Wooding	Birmingham	19.07.32	Welter	1953–1958	33	22	8	3
Ernie Woodman	Battersea	28.02.16	L. Heavy	1937–1948	78	41	29	8
Alex Woods	Randalstown	24.12.19	L. Heavy	1937–1948	57	38	16	3

Name	Domicile	Born	Weight	Career	Record C	W	L	D
Danny Woods	Clydebank	25.09.16	Light	1936–1950	53	37	14	2
Syd Worgan	Llanharan		Feather	1935–1948	109	56	38	15
Norman Wormall	Birmingham	28.06.32	Light	1952–1954	19	13	5	1
Ronnie Wormall	Birmingham	21.07.30	Light	1948–1954	30	16	10	4
Malcolm Worthington	Crewe	29.09.39	L. Heavy	1959–1978	52	25	25	2
Eddie Wright	Mile End	28.10.32	L. Heavy	1953–1959	23	13	8	2
Johnny Wright	Potters Bar	19.05.29	Middle	1951–1953	13	10	2	1
Ken Wyatt	Minehead	29.05.23	Heavy	1949–1956	28	19	9	0
Andy Wyper	Newmilns	25.03.40	Welter	1963–1967	20	14	5	1
Gary Yean	Liverpool	16.04.50	Light	1968–1972	20	13	7	0
Frank Young	Belfast	06.10.46	Middle	1968–1974	39	19	17	3
Mo Younis	Walsall	04.05.57	Bantam	1977–1981	22	8	11	3

21.10.52 *Eric Marsden (left) ducks under a left hook thrown by Terry Allen during their bout for the vacant British Flyweight title. Marsden was unfortunate to receive an accidental punch on the sciatic nerve in the sixth round and was unable to continue.*

British Area Title Bouts, 1946 – 1984

The results of Area Title bouts since the Second World War shown by individual Area Councils and weight class. Bouts for vacant Titles that resulted in draws or no contests are not included. Champions are stated first throughout.

Central Area Title Bouts

Flyweight
12.02.51 Jimmy Pearce **W** PTS 12 Jeff Oscroft
25.09.53 Eric Marsden **W** RSC 8 Colin Clitheroe

Bantamweight
12.11.50 Gus Foran **W** RTD 7 Jimmy Gill
10.10.66 Tony Barlow **W** CO 7 Billy Hardacre
10.03.74 George Turpin **W** RSC 8 Frank Taberner
09.05.74 George Turpin **W** RSC 3 Frank Taberner
24.03.80 Steve Enright **W** PTS 10 Jimmy Bott
08.04.83 John Farrell **W** RSC 7 George Bailey
09.12.83 John Farrell DREW 10 Ray Gilbody

Featherweight
24.05.51 Tommy Bailey **W** CO 8 Bert Jackson
08.05.53 Denny Dawson **W** PTS 12 Johnny Molloy
15.03.60 Billy Calvert **W** PTS 12 Eddie Burns
25.05.64 Mick Carney **W** CO 7 Freddie Dobson
01.04.68 Gerry McBride **W** PTS 10 Terry Halpin
21.01.69 Gerry McBride L PTS 10 Billy Hardacre
19.02.73 Billy Hardacre **W** PTS 10 Alan Richardson
09.05.73 Billy Hardacre L PTS 10 Alan Richardson
10.12.73 Alan Richardson **W** RSC 3 Barry Harris
23.11.81 Steve Farnsworth **W** PTS 10 Ian Murray
29.03.83 Steve Farnsworth L RSC 2 Steve Pollard
Steve Pollard *yet to defend Title*

Lightweight
19.10.50 Peter Fallon **W** PTS 12 Frank Parkes
12.11.53 Johnny Butterworth **W** RSC 10 Tom Bailey
10.06.54 Johnny Butterworth **W** RSC 6 Colin Harrison
10.12.54 Johnny Butterworth L PTS 12 Frank Johnson
Frank Johnson *did not defend Title*
02.12.59 Ken Hignett **W** CO 6 Alf Cottam
30.01.62 Johnny Cooke **W** PTS 12 Dave Coventry
02.11.70 Young Silky **W** PTS 10 Gerry McBride
24.05.71 Young Silky L PTS 10 Gary Yean
Gary Yean *did not defend Title*
27.11.73 Billy Hardacre **W** RSC 5 Billy Hall
18.06.79 Najib Daho **W** PTS 10 Brian Snagg
19.11.81 George Metcalf **W** CO 5 George Schofield
22.11.82 Glyn Rhodes **W** CO 5 Kevin Pritchard
14.03.83 Glyn Rhodes L PTS 10 Jimmy Bunclark
23.05.83 Jimmy Bunclark **W** RSC 1 Vince Vahey

L. Welterweight
20.09.73 Joey Singleton **W** PTS 10 Jess Harper
09.04.75 Jess Harper **W** RSC 7 Gordon Kirk
02.12.75 Jess Harper L PTS 10 Terry Petersen
27.09.76 Terry Petersen L PTS 12 Gordon Kirk
17.01.77 Gordon Kirk L PTS 10 Chris Walker
Chris Walker *did not defend Title*
23.04.79 Martin Bridge **W** PTS 10 Dave Taylor
30.04.81 Alan Lamb **W** PTS 10 Tony Carroll
03.06.82 Alan Lamb **W** PTS 10 Dave Taylor
14.03.83 Tony Brown **W** PTS 10 Walter Clayton

Welterweight

26.10.50 Wally Thom **W** PTS 12 Jimmy Molloy
29.02.52 Jackie Braddock **W** PTS 12 Peter Fallon
29.03.62 Tony Smith **W** PTS 12 Jimmy McGrail
28.01.65 Tony Smith L PTS 10 Johnny Cooke
Johnny Cooke *did not defend Title*
18.11.65 Shaun Doyle **W** PTS 10 Gordon McAteer
26.02.68 Fred Powney **W** RTD 8 Billy Seasman
11.11.68 Fred Powney L RSC 8 Amos Talbot
21.03.69 Amos Talbot L PTS 10 Billy Seasman
04.05.70 Barry Calderwood **W** PTS 10 Alan Tottoh
05.10.70 Barry Calderwood L PTS 10 Les Pearson
Les Pearson *did not defend Title*
10.04.72 Mickey Flynn **W** RSC 6 Amos Talbot
07.05.73 Mickey Flynn **W** RSC 2 Tommy Joyce
11.10.73 Mickey Flynn DREW 10 Alan Tottoh
11.11.75 Mickey Flynn L DIS 5 Jeff Gale
30.11.76 Jeff Gale L PTS 12 Terry Petersen
06.12.77 Terry Petersen **W** PTS 12 Chris Glover
19.02.79 Terry Petersen **W** RSC 6 Chris Glover
04.02.80 Terry Petersen L PTS 10 Joey Singleton
26.10.81 Joey Singleton **W** PTS 10 Lee Hartshorn
25.11.82 Joey Frost **W** RSC 4 Peter Bennett
24.02.83 Joey Frost **W** RSC 5 Lee Hartshorn

L. Middleweight

31.03.76 Carlton Lyons **W** RSC 6 Brian Gregory
03.10.77 Kenny Webber **W** PTS 10 Jim Devanney
24.10.78 Prince Rodney **W** DIS 5 Joe Lally
16.05.79 Prince Rodney **W** RSC 4 Mick Mills
06.04.82 Prince Rodney **W** RSC 4 Mick Mills
14.03.83 Prince Rodney **W** RSC 5 Brian Anderson
18.04.84 Paul Mitchell **W** RSC 5 Wayne Crolla

Middleweight

19.09.60 Ronnie Riley **W** PTS 12 Johnny Cunningham
10.09.62 Harry Scott **W** RSC 1 Sid Parkinson
10.06.63 Harry Scott **W** RSC 9 Jim Swords
28.01.65 Harry Scott **W** PTS 10 Alf Matthews
10.05.65 Nat Jacobs **W** CO 2 Jim Swords
07.03.67 Les McAteer **W** PTS 10 Jackie Harwood
04.05.70 Ronnie Hough **W** RSC 10 Nat Jacobs
01.03.71 Ronnie Hough L RSC 10 Pat Dwyer
21.10.73 Pat Dwyer **W** PTS 10 Brendan Ingle
06.03.75 Carl Speare **W** PTS 10 Tim McHugh
10.07.77 Dave Owens **W** RSC 9 Pat Brogan
17.10.79 Dave Owens **W** RSC 4 Jimmy Pickard
23.05.83 Brian Anderson **W** RSC 9 Jimmy Ellis
21.05.84 Brian Anderson **W** RTD 1 Sammy Brennan

L. Heavyweight

01.06.51 Johnny McGowan **W** RTD 7 Jimmy Carroll
05.04.60 Ted Williams **W** RSC 4 Alan Peacock
17.09.68 Ray Ako **W** CO 3 Sean Dolan
21.11.72 Lloyd Walford **W** PTS 10 Geoff Shaw
29.04.75 Phil Martin **W** PTS 10 Pat Thompson
01.04.76 Pat Thompson **W** PTS 10 Terry Armstrong
05.03.77 Pat Thompson L PTS 10 Alek Penarski
24.10.78 Alek Penarski L PTS 10 Francis Hands
Francis Hands *did not defend Title*
25.02.80 Tom Collins **W** RSC 1 Greg Evans
20.02.84 Ian Lazarus **W** PTS 10 Bernie Kavanagh

Heavyweight

01.09.50 Ray Wilding **W** RSC 10 Frank Bell
20.05.52 Ray Wilding **W** RTD 8 Frank Bell
07.09.70 Billy Aird **W** RSC 6 Richard Dunn
14.01.76 Peter Freeman **W** CO 6 Roger Tighe
20.02.78 Peter Freeman L CO 2 Neil Malpass
20.03.78 Neil Malpass **W** DIS 7 Paul Sykes
18.07.78 Neil Malpass DREW 10 Paul Sykes
28.11.79 Neil Malpass L DIS 5 Terry Mintus
20.10.81 Terry Mintus L RSC 3 Neil Malpass
Neil Malpass *yet to defend Title*

Central Area North Title Bouts

Flyweight

15.04.48 Eddie Douglas **W** DIS 11 Tommy Farricker
20.03.50 Billy Ashton **W** PTS 12 Tommy Farricker

Bantamweight

24.06.48 Gus Foran **W** CO 1 Billy Tansey

Featherweight

21.07.49 Bert Jackson **W** CO 5 Frankie Kelly

Lightweight
25.08.49 Peter Fallon W PTS 12 Bert Hornby

Middleweight
15.12.47 Jimmy Bray W DIS 3 George Dilkes
26.04.48 Jimmy Bray L CO 4 George Dilkes
21.10.49 George Dilkes W PTS 12 Tommy Whelan

Note: Area disbanded 19 May 1950

Eastern Area Title Bouts

Bantamweight
23.11.48 Gus Harris W PTS 12 Charlie Waters

Featherweight
04.11.47 Len Dunthorpe W PTS 12 Billy Barnard

Lightweight
02.07.49 John Newman W CO 2 Colin Wilson

Welterweight
28.06.47 Mickey Thompson W RSC 7 Keith Weston
23.09.48 Mickey Thompson W RSC 11 Eric Hall
02.07.49 Bert Buxton W CO 6 Keith Weston

Middleweight
07.06.48 Ginger Sadd W RTD 8 Joe Beckett
29.09.49 Ginger Sadd L PTS 12 Joe Beckett
Joe Beckett *did not defend Title*

Note: Area Disbanded 19th May, 1950

Midlands Area Title Bouts

Flyweight
27.04.83 Gary Roberts W CO 1 Cliff Storey

Bantamweight
19.01.53 Johnny Haywood W RTD 8 Tommy Icke
16.01.63 Brian Cartwright W PTS 10 Billy Williams
12.03.63 Brian Cartwright W CO 9 Billy Williams

Featherweight
19.01.53 Jackie Turpin W PTS 12 Tommy Higgins
10.08.53 Jackie Turpin L PTS 12 Harry Ramsden
Harry Ramsden *did not defend Title*
13.02.66 George O'Neill W RSC 2 Brian Cartwright
01.10.68 George O'Neill L PTS 10 Kenny Cooper
12.11.68 Kenny Cooper L PTS 10 Brian Cartwright
12.09.79 Doug Hill W PTS 10 Alec Irvine
24.09.80 Doug Hill W PTS 10 Don Aagesen
11.03.81 Jarvis Greenidge W CO 3 Steve Topliss
19.03.82 Jarvis Greenidge L PTS 10 Alec Irvine
28.02.83 Alec Irvine L PTS 10 Steve Topliss
10.02.84 Steve Topliss W PTS 10 Alec Irvine

Lightweight
02.03.53 Frank Parkes W DIS 2 Stan Parkes
26.10.53 Frank Parkes W PTS 12 Norman Wormall
09.11.54 Frank Parkes W RTD 7 Johnny Mann
30.01.56 Frank Parkes W PTS 12 Ray Corbett
17.04.56 Frank Parkes L RTD 3 Johnny Mann
Johnny Mann *did not defend Title*
25.09.61 Terry Edwards W PTS 12 Tony Icke
02.04.62 Terry Edwards L PTS 12 Chris Elliott
01.07.62 Chris Elliott W RTD 7 Terry Edwards
20.05.64 Chris Elliott L PTS 12 Harry Edwards
Harry Edwards *did not defend Title*
18.03.69 George O'Neill W PTS 10 Tony Riley
27.05.69 George O'Neill L DIS 4 Tony Riley
20.09.71 Tony Riley W RSC 10 Paul Bromley
25.09.74 Billy Belnavis W PTS 10 Ray Holdcroft
01.07.75 Billy Belnavis W RSC 7 Kevin Evans
29.10.75 Billy Belnavis W PTS 10 Ray Holdcroft
22.02.77 Geoff Butler W RSC 6 Von Reid
27.04.77 Geoff Butler L PTS 10 Kevin Davies
Kevin Davies *did not defend Title*
31.10.78 Des Gwilliam W PTS 10 Bingo Crooks
29.10.79 Des Gwilliam L PTS 10 Paul Chance
25.09.80 Paul Chance L CO 9 Bingo Crooks
Bingo Crooks *did not defend Title*
25.01.82 Paul Chance W PTS 10 Mickey Baker
01.12.82 Stuart Shaw W RSC 6 Lee Halford
16.04.84 Gerry Beard W CO 8 Lee Halford

L. Welterweight
18.04.78 Roy Varden W PTS 10 Des Gwilliam
19.11.79 Roger Guest W CO 1 Steve Early
19.10.80 Roger Guest L PTS 10 Adey Allen
09.07.81 Adey Allen W RSC 7 Mickey Baker
05.10.83 Adey Allen L PTS 10 Steve Early
Steve Early *yet to defend Title*

Welterweight
02.02.53 Eric Skidmore W RTD 3 Maurice Mancini

26.10.53 Eric Skidmore L PTS 12 Billy Wooding
03.09.56 Billy Wooding W PTS 12 Leo Maloney
17.09.59 Wally Swift W RTD 6 Ray Corbett
09.10.72 Robin Polak W PTS 10 Dave Moore
22.10.76 Larry Paul W RTD 2 Peter Morris
02.05.79 Joey Mack W CO 4 Achille Mitchell
18.10.80 Joey Mack W PTS 10 Roy Varden
01.12.81 Joey Mack W PTS 10 John F. Kennedy
07.06.82 Joey Mack W RTD 6 Martin McGough
17.11.82 Joey Mack L PTS 10 Cliff Gilpin
Cliff Gilpin *did not defend Title*
13.06.83 Kostas Petrou W RSC 5 Joey Mack
10.05.84 Kostas Petrou W PTS 12 Lloyd Christie

L. Middleweight
02.12.74 John Laine W PTS 10 Keith Nugent
24.05.82 Cliff Gilpin W RSC 6 Lloyd Hibbert
26.01.83 Dennis Sheehan W RSC 5 Bert Myrie

Middleweight
28.10.52 George Roe W PTS 12 Les Allen
08.09.53 George Roe L CO 7 Les Allen
17.04.56 Les Allen W PTS 12 George Roe
06.05.57 Les Allen W PTS 12 George Roe
03.02.58 Les Allen L PTS 12 George Aldridge
29.09.59 George Aldridge W PTS 12 Derek Liversidge
04.02.60 George Aldridge W RTD 6 Teddy Haynes
13.02.62 Maxie Smith W DIS 9 Ron Vale
23.10.62 Maxie Smith L PTS 10 Wally Swift
01.05.63 Wally Swift L RSC 5 Teddy Haynes
Teddy Haynes *did not defend Title*
21.02.79 Romal Ambrose W CO 7 Paul Shutt
05.02.80 Romal Ambrose W PTS 10 Martin McEwan
19.03.80 Romal Ambrose L CO 10 Glen McEwan
20.10.80 Glen McEwan W CO 6 Romal Ambrose

L. Heavyweight
16.02.53 Don Scott W RSC 3 Ted Morgan
07.06.62 Jack Bodell W RSC 5 Roy Seward
10.12.62 Jack Bodel W RSC 3 Roy Seward
02.12.63 Jack Grant W RSC 3 Roy Seward
13.02.76 Steve Walker W RSC 9 Billy Baggott
21.02.79 Tony Allen W RSC 9 Steve Fenton
02.05.79 Tony Allen L DIS 7 Eddie Fenton
27.11.79 Eddie Fenton L PTS 10 Harry White
19.03.80 Harry White L PTS 10 Eddie Fenton
08.07.80 Eddie Fenton L RSC 6 Roy Skeldon
10.03.82 Roy Skeldon L PTS 10 Antonio Harris
Antonio Harris *yet to defend Title*

Heavyweight
24.10.60 Tony Smith W CO 3 Ken Brady
09.01.62 Tony Smith L RTD 9 Johnny Prescott
27.02.62 Johnny Prescott W CO 2 Jack Whittaker
20.01.65 Jack Bodell W PTS 10 Ron Gray
06.02.68 Jack Bodell W PTS 10 Johnny Prescott
16.09.74 Rocky Campbell W PTS 10 Dave Roden
09.04.76 Garfield McEwan W PTS 10 Eddie Fenton
06.11.78 Brian Huckfield W PTS 10 Terry O'Connor
29.09.80 Terry O'Connor W RSC 6 Rocky Burton
25.09.81 Terry O'Connor L PTS 10 Ricky James
10.11.81 Ricky James W CO 6 Rocky Burton
17.02.83 Ricky James W CO 3 Rocky Burton

Midlands Area North Title Bouts

Flyweight
20.03.50 Jeff Oscroft W CO 9 Sid Hiom

Bantamweight
21.11.49 Jimmy Gill W PTS 12 Sammy Reynolds

Featherweight
30.01.50 Owen Johnson W PTS 12 Tommy Cummings

Lightweight
11.04.49 Frank Parkes W PTS 12 Chris Jenkins
24.04.50 Frank Parkes W RSC 6 Johnny Carrington

Welterweight
07.03.49 Ric Sanders W PTS 12 Ken Page

Middleweight
03.03.50 Albert Southall W PTS 12 Sam Burgoyne

L. Heavyweight
14.03.49 Dave Goodwin W RTD 4 Allan Cooke
07.03.50 Allan Cooke W RTD 7 Derek Alexander

Note: Area disbanded 19 May 1950

Midlands Area West Title Bouts

Lightweight
27.01.48 Chris Jenkins W PTS 12 Ron Smith

Note: Area Disbanded 19 May 1950

Northern Area Title Bouts

Featherweight
20.06.46 *Ronnie Clayton **W** PTS 15 Bert Jackson
22.08.46 *Ronnie Clayton **W** PTS 15 Ben Duffy
08.08.49 Tommy Burns **W** PTS 12 Ben Duffy
07.05.51 Jackie Horseman **W** PTS 12 Don Scott

Lightweight
12.09.46 Stan Hawthorne **W** PTS 12 Billy Thompson
17.08.49 Hughie Smith **W** PTS 12 Jimmy Trotter

Welterweight
30.01.50 Ginger Roberts **W** PTS 12 Billy Exley
17.12.51 Ginger Roberts L PTS 12 Ernie Vickers
Ernie Vickers *did not defend Title*
30.05.77 Colin Deans **W** PTS 10 Terry Schofield

Middleweight
20.02.50 George Casson **W** PTS 12 Bert Ingram

L. Heavyweight
20.07.49 Dave Davis **W** CO 8 Charel Baert
28.03.51 Dave Davis **W** CO 12 Charel Baert
08.11.77 Reg Long **W** PTS 10 Ralph Green
09.11.81 Reg Long L PTS 10 P. T. Grant
P. T. Grant *did not defend Title*

Heavyweight
12.11.79 George Scott **W** PTS 10 Reg Long
26.11.81 George Scott L PTS 10 Stewart Lithgo
Stewart Lithgo *yet to defend Title*

* Denotes original Northern Area Title Fights

Northern Ireland Area Title Bouts

Flyweight
26.11.48 Jackie Briers **W** RTD 6 Frank McCoy
06.10.51 Frank McCoy **W** RSC 2 Mickey McLaughlin
02.02.57 Dave Moore **W** PTS 12 Jim Loughrey

Bantamweight
24.03.47 Tommy Madine **W** PTS 15 Max Brady
05.05.47 Tommy Madine L CO 4 Bunty Doran
26.12.51 Bunty Doran **W** PTS 15 Jackie Briers
27.06.53 Bunty Doran L RTD 11 John Kelly
John Kelly *did not defend Title*
04.10.58 Billy Skelly **W** PTS 12 George O'Neill
12.10.65 Jim McCann **W** RSC 9 Alex O'Neill
13.12.66 Jim McCann **W** PTS 12 Sean McCafferty
10.02.70 Sammy Lockhart **W** DIS 4 Sean McCafferty
26.07.77 Neil McLaughlin **W** RSC 5 Terry Hanna
27.10.78 Neil McLaughlin L PTS 10 Davy Larmour
05.10.82 Davy Larmour L PTS 12 Hugh Russell
02.03.83 Hugh Russell L PTS 12 Davy Larmour
Davy Larmour *yet to defend Title*

Featherweight
28.12.49 Jim McCann **W** PTS 15 Dave Watson
22.02.50 Jim McCann **W** PTS 15 Eddie Magee
13.06.53 John Griffen **W** RSC 4 Pat Kelly
29.07.53 John Griffen L PTS 12 Billy Kelly
Billy Kelly *did not defend Title*
18.12.54 Joe Quinn **W** RTD 7 Billy Smith
26.03.55 Joe Quinn **W** PTS 12 John McNally
23.02.65 Peter Lavery **W** PTS 10 Brian Smyth
04.03.69 Jim McAuley **W** PTS 10 Jim Henry
26.04.77 Jim McAuley L RTD 4 Damien McDermott
Damien McDermott *did not defend Title*

Lightweight
30.11.49 Mickey O'Neill **W** RTD 9 Gerry Smyth
16.06.50 Mickey O'Neill **W** RTD 12 Jim Keery
23.02.52 Mickey O'Neill L PTS 12 Gerry Smyth
27.06.53 Gerry Smyth L PTS 12 Ricky McCulloch
25.09.53 Ricky McCulloch L PTS 12 Gerry Smyth
26.03.55 Gerry Smyth **W** PTS 12 Paddy Graham
23.11.57 Al Sharpe **W** RTD 8 John McNally
02.08.58 Al Sharpe L CO 6 Jimmy Brown
04.10.58 Jimmy Brown L PTS 12 Spike McCormack
Spike McCormack *did not defend Title*
02.10.75 Charlie Nash **W** PTS 10 Ray Ross
Charlie Nash *did not defend Title*

L. Welterweight
25.02.80 Davy Campbell **W** RTD 7 Ray Heaney

Welterweight
30.11.49 Tommy Armour **W** PTS 12 Jackie King
28.04.51 Tommy Armour **W** RTD 10 Billy O'Neill

11.10.52 Bunty Adamson **W** PTS 12 Mickey O'Neill
25.12.54 Roy Baird **W** RTD 5 Mickey O'Neill
30.06.56 Roy Baird **W** RTD 9 Gerry Smyth
18.04.59 Al Sharpe **W** PTS 12 Paddy Graham
03.03.62 Al Sharpe L PTS 10 Paddy Graham
Paddy Graham *did not defend Title*
29.09.65 Des Rea **W** PTS 10 Bob Sempey

Middleweight
28.10.47 Jackie Wilson **W** PTS 15 Frank Boylan
19.08.49 Jackie Wilson L PTS 12 Freddie Webb
27.01.51 Freddie Webb L PTS 12 Jackie Wilson
01.12.51 Jackie Wilson L RTD 4 Tom Meli
22.01.55 Tom Meli L PTS 12 George Lavery
21.04.56 George Lavery **W** PTS 12 Sammy Hamilton
12.10.65 Al Sharpe **W** RSC 9 Henry Turkington
21.02.67 Al Sharpe **W** PTS 12 Terry McTigue

L. Heavyweight
22.10.47 Alex Woods **W** CO 8 Matt Locke
11.10.52 Tom Meli **W** PTS 12 Garnett Denny
01.04.69 Terry McTigue **W** CO 5 Gerry Hassett
04.03.76 Ian Glenn **W** CO 2 Roy Baillie
28.10.76 Ian Glenn L RTD 2 Tony Monaghan
Tony Monaghan *did not defend Title*
17.02.81 Liam Coleman **W** PTS 10 Trevor Kerr
30.11.81 Liam Coleman **W** RTD 6 Trevor Kerr

Heavyweight
25.12.48 Paddy Slavin **W** RSC 2 Alec Woods
22.11.66 Barney Wilson **W** RSC 5 Jim Monaghan
21.05.75 Sean McKenna **W** CO 3 Des Reynolds
26.07.77 Sean McKenna L RSC 2 Danny McAlinden
Danny McAlinden *did not defend Title*

Scottish Area Title Bouts

Flyweight
12.12.46 Jackie Bryce **W** PTS 15 Johnny Summers
26.02.47 Jackie Bryce **W** PTS 15 Johnny Summers
10.12.47 Jackie Bryce **W** RSC 7 Hugh Cameron
08.12.48 Jackie Bryce L CO 2 Norman Tennant
23.08.49 Norman Tennant **W** PTS 12 Eddie Carson
17.01.51 Norman Tennant L PTS 12 Vic Herman
20.08.52 Vic Herman L PTS 12 Joe Cairney
28.01.53 Joe Cairney L PTS 12 Jimmy Quinn
17.06.53 Jimmy Quinn **W** CO 12 Jimmy Thomson
24.02.54 Jimmy Quinn **W** RTD 4 Jimmy Thomson
07.12.54 Jimmy Quinn **W** RTD 4 Joe Cairney
13.01.56 Jimmy Quinn L PTS 12 Dick Currie
19.09.56 Dick Currie L PTS 12 Frankie Jones
Frankie Jones *did not defend Title*
13.11.57 George McDade **W** PTS 12 Pat Glancy
02.07.58 George McDade L PTS 12 Alex Ambrose
25.02.59 Alex Ambrose DREW 12 George McDade
10.09.59 Alex Ambrose L RTD 10 Jackie Brown
Jackie Brown *did not defend Title*
08.11.62 Danny Lee **W** PTS 10 John Mallon

Bantamweight
17.04.47 Teddy O'Neil **W** CO 4 Jackie Bryce
21.04.48 Teddy O'Neil L PTS 15 Charlie Kerr
03.03.49 Charlie Kerr L CO 11 Eddie Carson
14.10.49 Eddie Carson **W** RSC 6 Jimmy Stewart
21.03.51 Eddie Carson **W** PTS 2 Jim Dwyer
26.02.52 Eddie Carson **W** RSC 2 Billy Taylor
20.08.52 Eddie Carson **W** CO 10 Billy Taylor
13.10.53 Eddie Carson **W** PTS 12 Hugh Riley
24.02.54 Eddie Carson L PTS 12 Peter Keenan
Peter Keenan *did not defend Title*
20.06.56 Malcolm Grant **W** PTS 12 Chic Brogan
19.09.56 Malcolm Grant L PTS 12 Chic Brogan
Chic Brogan *did not defend Title*
10.09.59 John Morrissey **W** RTD 5 Tommy Miller
14.11.62 Tommy Burgoyne **W** RSC 8 Lewie Mackay
24.02.64 Tommy Burgoyne L PTS 10 Jackie Brown
19.09.66 Jackie Brown L CO 4 Evan Armstrong
Evan Armstrong *did not defend Title*
27.04.70 John Kellie **W** PTS 10 John Mitchell
18.10.76 John Kellie **W** PTS 10 Charlie Parvin
23.10.78 Charlie Parvin **W** PTS 10 Tony Kerr

10.10.83 Danny Flynn **W** RSC 5 Robert Dickie

06.04.84 Danny Flynn **W** CO 2 Jim Harvey

Featherweight

15.12.47 Frank Kenny **W** CO 6 Jimmy Dunn

20.04.49 Jim Kenny **W** RTD 3 Jackie Robertson

28.02.51 Jim Kenny L PTS 12 George Stewart

20.08.52 George Stewart L PTS 12 Tommy Miller

Tommy Miller *did not defend Title*

07.12.54 Charlie Hill **W** PTS 12 Chic Brogan

19.09.56 Bobby Neil **W** RTD 8 Matt Fulton

19.02.58 Chic Brogan **W** PTS 12 Owen Reilly

11.09.59 Chic Brogan L CO 2 Dave Croll

Dave Croll *did not defend Title*

28.04.69 Jimmy Bell **W** PTS 10 Hugh Baxter

21.09.70 Evan Armstrong **W** RSC 9 Jimmy Bell

25.11.74 Alan Buchanan **W** PTS 10 George McKay

26.05.75 Alan Buchanan **W** RTD 8 John Mitchell

11.03.76 Gerry Duffy **W** RSC 6 John Mitchell

14.03.80 Gerry O'Neill **W** PTS 10 Terry McKeown

Lightweight

29.10.47 Harry Hughes **W** CO 6 Danny Woods

30.06.48 Harry Hughes **W** PTS 15 Johnny Smith

18.10.49 Harry Hughes **W** RTD 6 Don Cameron

01.09.50 Harry Hughes **W** PTS 12 Jim Findlay

22.06.51 Harry Hughes L PTS 12 Johnny Flannigan

Johnny Flannigan *did not defend Title*

05.03.52 Jim Findlay **W** RSC 8 Neilly Phillips

28.01.53 Jim Findlay L PTS 12 Don McTaggart

Don McTaggart *did not defend Title*

02.04.58 John McLaren **W** RSC 12 Tommy McGuinness

25.07.58 John McLaren L CO 9 Johnny Kidd

Johnny Kidd *did not defend Title*

02.11.60 Jimmy Gibson **W** PTS 12 Alex McMillan

26.06.61 Jimmy Gibson **W** RTD 9 Dave Higgins

27.11.61 Jimmy Gibson L PTS 12 Johnny Kidd

Johnny Kidd *did not defend Title*

23.01.67 Ken Buchanan **W** PTS 10 John McMillan

25.02.74 Alan Buchanan **W** CO 3 Johnny Cheshire

04.03.76 Tommy Glencross **W** PTS 10 Tommy Wright

26.04.76 Tommy Glencross **W** PTS 10 John Gillan

14.11.77 Tommy Glencross L PTS 10 Willie Booth

07.06.80 Willie Booth **W** PTS 10 Duncan Hamilton

23.02.81 Willie Booth L PTS 10 Peter Harrison

Peter Harrison *did not defend Title*

31.05.82 Willie Booth **W** PTS 10 Ian McLeod

L. Welterweight

27.11.78 Willie Booth **W** RSC 8 Mick Bell

18.06.79 Willie Booth L PTS 10 George Peacock

24.03.80 George Peacock **W** RSC 7 John Smith

09.11.81 George Peacock **W** RSC 8 Steve McLeod

Welterweight

22.05.46 Ginger Stewart **W** PTS 15 Billy Stevens

29.10.47 Ginger Stewart L PTS 15 Willie Whyte

21.09.50 Willie Whyte L PTS 12 Bill Rattray

Bill Rattray *did not defend Title*

12.08.52 Willie Whyte **W** PTS 12 Danny Malloy

03.10.53 Willie Whyte L RSC 5 Dann Malloy

Danny Malloy *did not defend Title*

07.12.54 Roy McGregor **W** PTS 12 Danny Harvey

20.12.55 Roy McGregor L PTS 12 Jimmy Croll

Jimmy Croll *did not defend Title*

10.03.60 Jim McGinness **W** PTS 12 Tommy McGuinness

21.01.64 Andy Wyper **W** RSC 7 Don McMillan

26.02.73 Alan Reid **W** PTS 10 Derek Simpson

02.06.80 Dave Douglas **W** RSC 9 Liam Linnen

09.11.81 Dave Douglas **W** PTS 10 Hugh Smith

30.01.84 Dave Douglas L CO 6 Jim Kelly

Jim Kelly *yet to defend Title*

L. Middleweight

24.03.75 John Smith **W** PTS 10 Derek Simpson

22.03.76 John Smith **W** PTS 10 Derek Simpson

23.04.79 John Smith L PTS 12 Charlie Malarkey

Charlie Malarkey *yet to defend Title*

Middleweight

11.09.46 Jake Kilrain **W** RTD 4 Eddie Starrs

18.05.49 Jake Kilrain **W** PTS 12 Willie Whyte

03.08.51 Willie Armstrong **W** RSC 10 Dave Finnie
02.07.58 John Cowboy McCormack **W** PTS 12 Len Mullen
30.05.63 Ian McKenzie **W** PTS 10 Willie Hart
24.05.71 Don McMillan **W** PTS 10 Andy Peace

L. Heavyweight
09.02.49 Bert Gilroy **W** RSC 8 Jock Todd
29.10.58 Chic Calderwood **W** RSC 5 Dave Mooney

Heavyweight
09.03.49 Ken Shaw **W** PTS 12 Bert Gilroy
22.06.51 George Stern **W** DIS 7 Hugh McDonald

South Central Area Title Bouts

Bantamweight
10.10.49 Ronnie Draper **W** PTS 12 Peter Fay

Featherweight
28.10.47 Albert Bessell **W** PTS 15 Ronnie Draper
12.04.48 Albert Bessell **W** PTS 15 Jackie Turpin
21.03.49 Albert Bessell **W** PTS 12 Ivor Simpson
01.05.50 Albert Bessell **L** RTD 7 Ivor Simpson
Ivor Simpson *did not defend Title*

Lightweight
22.12.47 Hal Bagwell **W** PTS 15 Harry Legge
07.09.48 Hal Bagwell **W** RTD 3 Billy Davies
05.12.49 Hal Bagwell **L** PTS 12 Maurice Mancini
Maurice Mancini *did not defend Title*

Welterweight
14.04.49 Frank McAvoy **W** RSC 10 Ron Jones
01.05.50 Frank McAvoy **W** PTS 12 Ron Jones

Note: Area disbanded 19th May, 1950

South East Area Title Bouts

Flyweight
16.03.48 Terry Allen **W** DIS 2 Dickie O'Sullivan

Bantamweight
29.10.46 Jimmy Webster **W** RSC 10 Sammy Reynolds
08.04.48 Jimmy Webster **L** PTS 12 Danny O'Sullivan
Danny O'Sullivan *did not defend Title*

Lightweight
17.06.48 Claude Dennington **W** PTS 15 Tommy Barnham
12.07.49 Tommy McGovern **W** RSC 6 George Daly

Welterweight
19.12.49 Alf Danahar **W** PTS 12 Jeff Tite

Middleweight
16.04.47 Mark Hart **W** PTS 12 Albert Finch
11.10.48 Mark Hart **L** PTS 12 Albert Finch
Albert Finch *did not defend Title*

L. Heavyweight
01.03.48 Al Marson **W** PTS 12 Jock Taylor
15.02.49 Al Marson **L** RTD 7 Reg Spring
13.12.49 Reg Spring **L** PTS 12 Mark Hart
Mark Hart *did not defend Title*

Heavyweight
18.02.47 Alf Brown **W** CO 8 Reg Andrews

Note: Area Disbanded 19 May 1950

South West Area Title Bouts

Featherweight
25.03.50 George Pook **W** PTS 15 Billy Parsons

Lightweight
25.09.48 Roy Coote **W** PTS 15 Harry Legge
19.11.49 Roy Coote **W** PTS 15 Harry Legge

Note: Area Disbanded 19 May 1950

Southern Area Title Bouts

Bantamweight
28.03.55 Jimmy Cardew **W** PTS 12 Ron Johnson
28.11.60 Don Weller **W** PTS 12 Dennis East
09.01.62 Don Weller **W** DIS 7 Danny Wells
19.11.62 Don Weller **W** RSC 7 Mick Hussey
25.03.63 Don Weller **W** PTS 10 Brian Bissmire
23.11.64 Don Weller **W** PTS 10 Mick Hussey
15.08.65 Don Weller **L** PTS 10 Monty Laud
18.04.66 Monty Laud **W** RSC 11 Carl Taylor
21.11.66 Carl Taylor **W** PTS 10 Don Weller
13.11.67 Carl Taylor **L** DIS 10 Brian Packer
Brian Packer *did not defend Title*
23.06.70 Tony Humm **W** PTS 10 Ron Elliott
14.09.71 Tony Humm **W** PTS 10 Eric Elderfield
25.10.71 Tony Humm **W** PTS 10 Eric Elderfield
04.04.78 Gary Davidson **W** PTS 10 Dave Smith
21.11.78 Gary Davidson **L** RTD 6 Dave Smith
Dave Smith *did not defend Title*
22.03.83 Johnny Dorey **W** PTS 10 Ivor Jones

Featherweight
02.03.55 Teddy Peckham **W** CO 1 Charlie Tucker
09.04.56 Teddy Peckham L PTS 12 Ken Lawrence
Ken Lawrence *did not defend Title*
28.04.58 George Carroll **W** PTS 12 Arthur Devlin
10.02.59 George Carroll L RSC 6 Johnny Howard
19.03.63 Johnny Howard **W** PTS 10 Bobby Davies
08.10.63 Johnny Howard L DIS 6 Phil Lundgren
22.08.64 Phil Lunderen **W** RSC 10 Johnny Howard
31.10.66 Jimmy Anderson **W** RSC 7 Johnny Mantle
14.11.67 Monty Laud **W** PTS 10 Johnny Mantle
09.05.73 Mickey Piner **W** PTS 10 Clive Hogben
06.05.74 Mario Stango **W** RSC 2 Jimmy Revie
14.10.74 Mario Stango L RTD 4 Jimmy Revie
Jimmy Revie *did not defend Title*
12.11.75 Mark Bliss **W** PTS 10 Clive Hogben
23.03.76 Mark Bliss **W** PTS 12 Billy Smart
31.05.77 Mark Bliss L RSC 4 Jimmy Flint
Jimmy Flint *did not defend Title*
21.02.83 Paul Huggins **W** PTS 10 Clyde Ruan
25.04.83 Paul Huggins **W** RSC 7 Rory Burke
07.12.83 Paul Huggins L PTS 10 Clyde Ruan
05.06.84 Clyde Ruan **W** PTS 12 Pat Doherty

Lightweight
05.12.50 Tommy McGovern **W** PTS 12 Tommy Barnham
26.02.52 Tommy Barnham **W** PTS 12 Joe Lucy
20.01.53 Joe Lucy **W** PTS 12 Tommy McGovern
28.03.55 Freddie King **W** CO 9 Jimmy Tippett
19.09.55 Freddie King L CO 5 Gordon Goodman
Gordon Goodman *did not defend Title*
18.02.58 Ron Hinson **W** RSC 11 Ernie Fossey
07.07.59 Ron Hinson L RSC 12 Dave Stone
Dave Stone *did not defend Title*
21.01.63 Dave Parsons **W** CO 6 Danny O'Brien
05.04.65 Brian Brazier **W** DIS 6 Mick Laud
15.02.66 Brian Brazier L CO 2 Jimmy Mitchell
15.05.66 Jimmy Mitchell L RSC 9 Phil Lundgren
14.07.66 Phil Lundgren L PTS 10 Vic Andreetti
Vic Andreetti *did not defend Title*
18.10.66 Ivan Whiter **W** PTS 10 Phil Lundgren
22.10.67 Ronnie Davies **W** RSC 9 Winston Laud
25.02.68 Ronnie Davies L PTS 10 Winston Laud
Winston Laud *did not defend Title*
12.05.69 Brian Hudson **W** CO 3 Jackie Lee
24.11.70 Brian Hudson **W** CO 4 Jackie Lee
26.04.71 Brian Hudson L RTD 8 Willie Reilly
Willie Reilly *did not defend Title*
12.06.72 Noel McIvor **W** RSC 2 Alan Salter
11.12.74 Noel McIvor L PTS 10 Tommy Dunn
14.07.75 Tommy Dunn **W** RSC 7 Noel McIvor
26.01.76 Tommy Dunn DREW 10 Jimmy Revie
21.09.76 Tommy Dunn DREW 12 Johnny Claydon
28.10.76 Tommy Dunn L PTS 12 Johnny Claydon
13.02.79 Johnny Claydon L RSC 10 Ray Cattouse
Ray Cattouse *did not defend Title*
01.02.82 Winston Spencer **W** RSC 6 Billy O'Grady

L. Welterweight
22.09.76 Des Morrison **W** RSC 5 Colin Power
30.11.81 Chris Sanigar **W** CO 4 Sid Smith
20.04.82 Chris Sanigar L RSC 9 Sylvester Mittee
Sylvester Mittee *did not defend Title*
26.04.83 Terry Marsh **W** PTS 10 Vernon Entertainer Vanriel

Welterweight
30.05.50 Alf Danahar **W** PTS 12 Eric McQuade
28.11.50 Alf Danahar **W** PTS 12 Bob Frost
12.03.51 Alf Danahar **W** PTS 12 Jeff Tite
04.02.52 Alf Danahar **W** PTS 12 Bob Frost
03.02.58 Terry Gill **W** RSC 8 Ron Richardson
22.04.58 Terry Gill **W** PTS 12 Ron Richardson
13.10.58 Terry Gill **W** PTS 12 Albert Carroll
11.06.59 Terry Gill L PTS 12 Albert Carroll
05.07.60 Albert Carroll **W** PTS 12 Tony Mancini
07.03.61 Albert Carroll L RSC 6 Tony Mancini
Tony Mancini *did not defend Title*
25.09.62 Johnny Kramer **W** RSC 7 Billy Tarrant
10.06.63 Johnny Kramer L PTS 10 Peter McLaren

07.10.63 Peter McLaren L PTS 10 Johnny Kramer
08.02.64 Johnny Kramer L RSC 10 Tony Lewis
25.11.64 Tony Lewis L CO 3 Peter McLaren
07.02.66 Peter McLaren **W** PTS 10 Ricky Porter
06.04.66 Peter McLaren L RSC 8 Ralph Charles
Ralph Charles *did not defend Title*
12.12.67 Ivan Whiter **W** PTS 10 Chris Jobson
26.05.68 Ivan Whiter L PTS 10 Chris Jobson
30.09.68 Chris Jobson L RSC 1 Peter Cragg
04.11.69 Peter Cragg L RSC 1 Bernie Terrell
20.04.71 Bernie Terrell **W** PTS 10 Ricky Porter
27.06.71 Bernie Terrell **W** RSC 8 Chris Jobson
11.09.72 Ricky Porter **W** PTS 12 Des Morrison
02.07.73 Ricky Porter L PTS 12 Des Morrison
02.09.74 Des Morrison **W** RSC 8 Steve Angell
24.03.75 Des Morrison L PTS 12 Tony Poole
Tony Poole *did not defend Title*
25.10.76 Henry Rhiney **W** RSC 8 Mickey Ryce
02.05.77 Johnny Pincham **W** PTS 10 Mickey Ryce
10.10.77 Johnny Pincham L PTS 7 Dave Proud
Dave Proud *did not defend Title*
12.12.77 Peter Neal **W** PTS 12 Johnny Pincham
22.03.78 Peter Neal **W** PTS 10 Steve Angell
03.10.79 Peter Neal **W** PTS 12 Henry Rhiney
18.10.82 Peter Neal L RSC 6 Sid Smith
01.03.83 Sid Smith L CO 4 Lloyd Honeyghan
Lloyd Honeyghan *did not defend Title*
22.02.84 Rocky Kelly **W** PTS 10 Chris Sanigar

L. Middleweight
14.06.76 Albert Hillman **W** PTS 10 Mickey Ryce
22.11.76 Albert Hillman **W** RTD 7 Tony Poole
02.05.77 Albert Hillman L PTS 10 Tony Hudson
17.10.77 Tony Hudson L CO 8 Tony Poole
24.01.78 Tony Poole **W** RSC 11 Dave Proud
22.01.79 Steve Hopkin **W** RTD 7 Mick Minter
19.10.81 Steve Hopkin L RTD 7 Chris Christian
21.06.82 Chris Christian L PTS 10 Jimmy Cable
Jimmy Cable *did not defend Title*

Middleweight
12.02.51 Ron Pudney **W** PTS 12 Alex Buxton
20.08.51 Ron Pudney **W** CO 12 Les Allen
27.07.53 Ron Pudney L PTS 12 Wally Beckett
Wally Beckett *did not defend Title*
22.09.55 Lew Lazar **W** PTS 12 Terence Murphy
23.07.62 George Aldridge **W** PTS 10 Pat O'Grady
25.02.63 Dennis Read **W** PTS 10 Dave George
08.07.63 Dennis Read **W** PTS 10 Dave Wakefield
08.06.64 Dennis Read **W** PTS 10 Billy Tarrant
01.03.66 Johnny Kramer **W** RSC 6 Len Gibbs
16.01.67 Johnny Kramer **W** RSC 8 Len Gibbs
06.05.68 Johnny Kramer **W** PTS 10 Bunny Sterling
11.11.68 Johnny Kramer L RSC 8 Bunny Sterling
Bunny Sterling *did not defend Title*
26.10.70 Howard Sharpe **W** PTS 10 Mick Cain
10.12.70 Howard Sharpe L RSC 2 Eric Blake
16.04.71 Eric Blake **W** CO 2 Howard Sharpe
10.04.72 Eric Blake L PTS 10 Kevin Finnegan
Kevin Finnegan *did not defend Title*
27.10.75 Frankie Lucas **W** RSC 7 Jan Magdziarz
29.03.76 Frankie Lucas L RSC 6 Jan Magdziarz
17.07.76 Jan Magdziarz L RSC 9 Peter Cain
22.02.77 Peter Cain L CO 1 Alex Tompkins
18.07.77 Alex Tompkins L RSC 5 Jan Magdziarz
06.10.77 Jan Magdziarz **W** RSC 4 Oscar Angus
19.02.79 Jan Magdziarz L RSC 7 Roy Gumbs
18.02.80 Roy Gumbs **W** PTS 10 Frankie Lucas
03.03.81 Earl Edwards **W** RSC 2 Dave Armstrong
23.03.82 Earl Edwards L RSC 6 Dave Armstrong
18.05.83 Dave Armstrong L RSC 1 Gary Hobbs
Gary Hobbs *did not defend Title*
05.06.84 James Cook **W** RSC 9 T. P. Jenkins

L. Heavyweight
02.12.52 George Walker **W** DIS 5 Albert Finch
16.02.54 George Walker L RSC 9 Brian Anders
Brian Anders *did not defend Title*
26.03.57 Albert Finch **W** PTS 12 Terence Murphy

13.05.58 Eddie Wright **W** DIS 10 Ron Redrup
26.08.59 Eddie Wright L RTD 7 Arthur Howard
Arthur Howard *did not defend Title*
12.05.60 Johnny Cole **W** RSC 8 Billy Smith
11.05.61 Johnny Cole L RSC 11 Stan Cullis
19.06.62 Stan Cullis **W** CO 9 Johnny Ould
23.01.64 Stan Cullis L RSC 10 Bob Nicolson
21.02.66 Bob Nicolson DREW 10 Johnny Ould
25.11.68 Bob Nicolson L PTS 10 Phil Watford
26.06.69 Phil Watford L RSC 4 Dickie Owens
15.09.69 Dickie Owens L PTS 10 Ray Brittle
16.02.70 Ray Brittle L RSC · Chris Finnegan
Chris Finnegan *did not defend Title*
25.05.71 Johnny Frankham **W** PTS 12 Dave Hawkes
22.05.73 Johnny Frankham L PTS 10 Pat McCann
12.02.74 Pat McCann **W** PTS 12 Johnny Frankham
17.11.75 John Wall **W** PTS 10 Sid Falconer
16.02.76 John Wall L RSC 7 Tim Wood
Tim Wood *did not defend Title*
15.09.77 Johnny Waldron **W** CO 5 Bob Pollard
21.11.78 Johnny Waldron **W** DIS 3 Vernon Scott
19.09.79 Johnny Waldron L RTD 10 Dennis Andries
Dennis Andries *did not defend Title*
22.09.80 Shaun Chalcroft **W** PTS 10 Carlton Benoit
23.03.81 Shaun Chalcroft L PTS 10 Dennis Andries
13.08.82 Dennis Andries **W** PTS 10 Keith Bristol
28.02.83 Dennis Andries **W** CO 4 Carl Canwell
22.09.83 Dennis Andries **W** CO 4 Keith Bristol

Heavyweight
09.11.64 Dave Ould **W** PTS 10 Len Hobbs
02.05.67 Roy Enifer **W** PTS 10 Dave Ould
04.01.74 Les Stevens **W** PTS 10 Tim Wood
16.02.76 Denton Ruddock **W** PTS 10 Tony Moore
10.05.76 Denton Ruddock **W** RSC 2 Sid Falconer
05.04.77 Denton Ruddock **W** PTS 10 Ishaq Hussein
06.12.77 Denton Ruddock L RSC 8 John L. Gardner
John L. Gardner *did not defend Title*
12.02.79 Tommy Kiely **W** PTS 10 Les Stevens
06.03.80 Tommy Kiely **W** PTS 10 Tony Moore
19.01.81 Tommy Kiely **W** PTS 10 Denton Ruddock
13.05.84 Funso Banjo **W** PTS 10 Hughroy Currie

Welsh Area Title Bouts

Flyweight
21.04.47 Billy Davies **W** RSC 11 Gilbert Hughes
14.06.48 Billy Davies L PTS 15 George Sutton
28.03.49 George Sutton L RTD 12 Norman Lewis
Norman Lewis *did not defend Title*
23.08.50 Glyn David **W** PTS 12 George Sutton
04.10.51 Glyn David L PTS 12 George Sutton
George Sutton *did not defend Title*

Bantamweight
28.11.49 Jackie Sutton **W** PTS 12 Norman Lewis
23.08.50 Jackie Sutton NC 5 Roy Ball
21.03.51 Jackie Sutton **W** RSC 12 Roy Ball
26.05.52 Hughie Thomas **W** RTD 8 Roy Ball
28.06.65 Terry Gale **W** PTS 10 Gerald Jones
23.09.65 Terry Gale DREW 10 Gerald Jones
12.07.66 Terry Gale L RTD 8 Gerald Jones
Gerald Jones *did not defend Title*
02.07.69 Steve Curtis **W** PTS 10 Glyn Davies
22.06.70 Colin Miles **W** RTD 7 Gareth Howells
19.10.70 Colin Miles **W** PTS 10 Glyn Davies
22.02.71 Colin Miles **W** PTS 10 Gareth Howells
12.09.73 Tony Davies **W** RSC 10 Joey Deriu
06.05.74 Tony Davies **W** RSC 6 Tony Williams
29.03.77 Johnny Owen **W** PTS 10 George Sutton
04.10.79 Glyn Davies **W** RSC 7 Pip Coleman
01.10.80 Glyn Davies L PTS 10 Pip Coleman
Pip Coleman *did not defend Title*

Featherweight
28.02.49 Jackie Hughes **W** PTS 15 Len Davies
06.03.50 Jackie Hughes **W** RSC 5 Dai Davies
23.08.50 Jackie Hughes **W** RTD 10 Len Davies
24.09.51 Dai Davies **W** RSC 5 Jackie Sutton
16.02.53 Haydn Jones **W** PTS 12 Dave Lloyd
04.05.53 Haydn Jones **W** PTS 12 Dave Lloyd
26.10.53 Haydn Jones **W** PTS 12 Hughie Thomas
01.09.59 Terry Rees **W** DIS 6 Gordon Blakey
30.06.64 Lennie Williams **W** RSC 3 Billy Thomas
12.09.65 Lennie Williams **W** CO 2 Billy Thomas
26.03.74 Colin Miles **W** RSC 5 Martyn Galleozzie
10.11.75 Les Pickett **W** PTS 10 Alun Trembath

17.11.76 Les Pickett **W** RTD 9 Jeff Pritchard
19.11.81 Don George **W** PTS 10 Mervyn Bennett

Lightweight
23.02.48 Warren Kendall **W** PTS 15 Vernon Ball
16.11.49 Warren Kendall **L** RSC 1 Reg Quinlan
04.12.50 Reg Quinlan **W** RSC 10 Ron Bruzas
22.08.51 Selwyn Evans **W** RSC 8 Dennis Sewell
03.03.52 Selwyn Evans **W** PTS 12 Len Davies
21.11.52 Selwyn Evans DREW Dai Davies
01.06.53 Selwyn Evans **L** CO 10 Dai Davies
Dai Davies *did not defend Title*
24.05.54 Willie Lloyd **W** DIS 8 Parry Dando
26.09.55 Willie Lloyd **L** PTS 12 Emrys Jones
Emrys Jones *did not defend Title*
16.07.56 Willie Lloyd **W** PTS 12 Darkie Hughes
21.08.57 Teddy Best **W** RTD 9 Bryn Phillips
10.08.63 Teddy Best DREW 10 Gordon Davies
22.05.68 Bryn Lewis **W** RSC 5 George Evans
13.12.76 Martyn Galleozzie **W** PTS 10 Dil Collins
15.02.77 Martyn Galleozzie **L** PTS 10 Johnny Wall
16.06.77 Johnny Wall **W** PTS 10 Billy Vivian
21.11.77 Johnny Wall **W** PTS 10 Dil Collins
20.03.78 Johnny Wall **L** PTS 10 Kelvin Webber
10.07.78 Kelvin Webber **L** PTS 10 Martyn Galleozzie
21.09.78 Martyn Galleozzie **W** PTS 10 Jeff Pritchard
04.03.83 Ray Hood **W** PTS 10 Andy Thomas

L. Welterweight
10.07.78 Billy Vivian **W** PTS 10 Dil Collins
22.03.82 Ray Price **W** PTS 10 Geoff Pegler
19.12.83 Ray Price **L** RTD 8 Geoff Pegler
Geoff Pegler *did not defend Title*
13.06.84 Michael Harris **W** PTS 10 Ray Price

Welterweight
21.09.48 Eddie Thomas **W** PTS 15 Gwyn Williams
21.06.50 Alan Wilkins **W** DIS 6 Ken Curvis
26.10.53 Rees Moore **W** PTS 12 Dennis Rowley
10.01.55 Rees Moore **W** RSC 11 Eric Davies
27.08.56 Rees Moore **W** PTS 12 Eddie Williams
18.02.57 Rees Moore **L** RSC 9 Les Morgan
Les Morgan *did not defend Title*
29.06.65 Terry Phillips **W** RSC 4 Geoff Rees
10.07.78 Horace McKenzie **W** PTS 10 Mike Copp
11.03.80 Horace McKenzie **W** PTS 10 Gary Pearce
07.06.82 Billy Waith **W** PTS 10 Frank McCord
10.12.83 Billy Waith **W** PTS 10 Frank McCord

L. Middleweight
26.03.74 Dave Davies **W** RSC 8 Colin Davies
05.03.77 Dave Davies **L** RSC 8 Pat Thomas
Pat Thomas *did not defend Title*
07.11.81 Gary Pearce **W** RSC 9 Terry Matthews
17.02.84 Rocky Feliciello **W** RSC 8 John McGlynn

Middleweight
11.04.46 Tommy Davies **W** RSC 4 Taffy Williams
12.01.48 Tommy Davies **W** PTS 15 Johnny Houlston
19.07.48 Tommy Davies **W** RSC 14 Ron Cooper
23.05.49 Tommy Davies **W** PTS 15 Des Jones
11.06.52 Ron Cooper **W** PTS 12 Bob Burniston
20.08.52 Ron Cooper **L** PTS 12 Jimmy Roberts
01.12.52 Jimmy Roberts **L** CO 12 Roy Agland
Roy Agland *did not defend Title*
16.01.57 Freddie Cross **W** RSC 11 Teddy Barrow
21.08.57 Freddie Cross **L** PTS 12 Phil Edwards
23.04.58 Phil Edwards **W** PTS 12 Freddie Cross
27.11.68 Carl Thomas **W** PTS 10 Roy John
12.07.69 Carl Thomas **W** DIS 3 Denny Pleace
27.06.73 Mike McCluskie **W** CO 8 Jeff Burns
28.01.83 Doug James **W** RSC 9 Horace McKenzie

L. Heavyweight
28.04.48 Jack Farr **W** PTS 15 Elfryn Morris
09.07.49 Jack Farr **L** CO 1 Dennis Powell
06.11.49 Dennis Powell **W** CO 5 Doug Richards
27.04.53 Ken Rowlands **W** RTD 7 Nick Fisher
26.08.53 Ken Rowlands **L** RSC 5 Dave Williams
10.10.55 Ken Rowlands **W** RTD 6 Terry Gooding
07.05.56 Ken Rowlands **L** PTS 12 Noel Trigg
18.03.57 Noel Trigg **W** PTS 12 Don Sainsbury
23.04.58 Noel Trigg **L** PTS 12 Redvers Sangoe
01.09.59 Redvers Sangoe **W** RTD 9 Don Sainsbury
21.03.60 Redvers Sangoe **W** RTD 9 Don Sainsbury
28.07.64 Derek Richards **W** RTD 7 Stuart Price
12.07.65 Derek Richards **W** PTS 10 Eddie Avoth

29.11.78 Chris Lawson **W** PTS 10 Bonny McKenzie
19.03.79 Chris Lawson **W** PTS 10 Ken Jones
12.08.80 Chris Lawson L PTS 10 Ken Jones
Ken Jones *did not defend Title*
21.09.81 Bonny McKenzie **W** PTS 10 Chris Lawson
27.10.83 Nye Williams **W** PTS 10 Chris Lawson

Heavyweight
06.08.49 Dennis Powell **W** CO 2 George James
07.07.51 Dennis Powell L RSC 6 Tommy Farr
Tommy Farr *did not defend Title*
28.06.65 Carl Gizzi **W** RSC 5 Rocky James
11.10.71 Carl Gizzi L PTS 10 Dennis Avoth
24.04.72 Dennis Avoth **W** PTS 10 Del Phillips
27.06.73 Dennis Avoth **W** PTS 10 Gene Innocent
29.03.76 Neville Meade **W** RSC 4 Tony Blackburn
22.01.80 Neville Meade **W** RSC 2 David Pearce
01.10.80 Neville Meade **W** RSC 2 Winston Allen
22.09.83 Neville Meade L RSC 9 David Pearce
David Pearce *did not defend Title*

Western Area Title Bouts

Lightweight
17.12.51 Harry Legge **W** RSC 4 Roy Coote
10.05.52 Harry Legge L PTS 12 Roy Coote
Roy Coote *did not defend Title*

Welterweight
22.02.54 Terry Ratcliffe **W** PTS 12 Paul King

06.04.84 *Scottish Bantamweight Champion Danny Flynn standing over his challenger Jim Harvey who is counted out in the second round.* SCOTSMAN/EVENING NEWS

The Commonwealth Boxing Championships Committee

Simon Block, Honorary Secretary, Commonwealth Boxing Championships Committee

Possibly there were boxers at the end of the last century who fought for and claimed Empire Championships, but it was not until 1908, when Jim Driscoll defeated Charlie Griffin on points in London to take the Featherweight Title, that records were started and universal recognition accorded.

'Peerless' Jim is acknowledged as one of the 'greats' of his division and he set the standard for the many fine Empire and later Commonwealth Champions at all weights who were to follow him. In 1910 Tommy Burns became the first Heavyweight Champion by defeating Bill Lang in Sydney, Australia, and to this day the Canadian holds the distinction of being the only Commonwealth Champion ever to claim sport's richest prize – the World Heavyweight Championship. From other weight divisions, Freddie Mills, Randolph Turpin, Ted Kid Lewis, Freddie Welsh, Vic Toweel, Rinty Monaghan, Jackie Paterson and Jimmy Carruthers all went on from the Empire Championship to win World Titles over the next four and a half decades.

In 1954 the idea of setting up a governing authority to regulate and control the Championships was advanced. On 12 October of that year an inaugural meeting was held in London, resulting in the formation of the British Commonwealth and Empire Boxing Championships Committee under the Chairmanship of J. Onslow Fane, Chairman of the British Boxing Board of Control and future co-founder of the World Boxing Council. The Committee was made up of nominated delegates each representing a National Commission within the Empire and Commonwealth, with additional elected members acting in an advisory capacity. A Constitution and set of Objects and Regulations were drawn up, these being by design simple and minimal. It was never intended that the Committee should develop into a structured licensing, judicial and administrative organization, but merely to serve as the means to ensure regular Championship defences in all weight divisions against contenders of approved status, and to assist the representation of Empire and Commonwealth boxers at World level. The General Secretary of the British Board, Teddy Waltham, was appointed Honorary Secretary and the Board's offices were to serve as headquarters.

These clear and concise aims were achieved quite successfully over the next 18 years. The tendency for some weight divisions to fall into disuse was halted, with regular Championship matches producing many a thrilling contest and worthy Champion. Well-known names like Henry Cooper, Chris Finnigan, Yvon Durelle, Brian Curvis, Dave Charnley, Floyd Robertson and Bunny Grant all won Empire Championships during this time. Again there were those who went on to win World Titles: Nigeria's Dick Tiger, World Champion at two weights, Hogan Kid Bassey, Lionel Rose of Australia, Scotland's Walter McGowan and Johnny Caldwell of Northern Ireland.

The 1950s and 1960s, however, saw major changes in the World and in the old established order of things. New nations were emerging divorced from their colonial past, and with their own voice in International affairs. The British Empire of the days of Jim Driscoll and Tommy Burns, which had once extended across the globe, had dwindled to a handful of colonies. By the end of the 1960s the old Committee, which had achieved so much, had, like the Empire, all but ceased to exist. Between 1969 and 1972 no meeting took place, even though Championship matches were still being fought. Fortunately, at a time when it might have petered out altogether, a meeting was held in London on 22 November 1972 with a view to reviving the aims of 1954 and making them work in the modern boxing world. A new Committee was formed which approved an amended set of

Regulations. The structure of the Committee would remain the same, but as boxing developed in Commonwealth countries and new Commissions were formed, they in time would be affiliated. J. Onslow Fane remained as the Chairman and the new Board General Secretary, Ray Clarke, replaced the by now retired Teddy Waltham. New weight divisions which were now recognized elsewhere in the World were adopted at Light Middleweight and Light Welterweight. Junior Lightweight being added two years later in 1974 and Cruiserweight in 1983.

The Committee was renamed The British Commonwealth Boxing Championships Committee, although the qualifying 'British' was later dropped in accordance with current terminology. 'Pop' Fane remained in the Chair until 1976, when after years of distinguished service to British, Commonwealth and World boxing he decided to retire. He was succeeded by Alexander Elliot, then Chairman of the British Board.

Ray Clarke resigned as Secretary in 1980 to concentrate on his ever-increasing workload as General Secretary of the BBBC and WBC representative, but in order that his wide experience in Commonwealth matters should not be lost he was elected to serve as a member in his own right. His assistant at the BBBC, Simon Block, is now the current Secretary.

From 1972 to the present day the Championships have continued to produce great names in the sport. David 'Poison' Kotey, John Conteh, Ayub Kalule, Maurice Hope and Claude Noel were all World Champions. Others came close: Colin Jones (twice against Milton McCrory for the Welterweight Title), Pat Ford and Azumah Nelson (both against Salvador Sanchez for the Featherweight Title). In addition, boxers like Clyde Gray of Canada, Paul Ferreri of Australia and Lotte Mwale of Zambia have become permanent national sporting heroes in their own countries, as has Henry Cooper in Britain, through their achievements as Commonwealth Champions.

The winning of a Commonwealth Title, whilst carrying no automatic guarantee of a World ranking, will almost certainly result in a WBC top 20 ranking. Apart from Britain, where the winning of a European Title brings the greater prestige and financial reward, it is to the Commonwealth Crown that many promising eligible boxers set their sights, prior to an advance on the World Championship. Most member Commissions are affiliated to the WBC via their own continental Federations, such as the African Boxing Union or Orient and Pacific Boxing Federation, each with its own prestigious International Title. One of the prime aims of the Committee in the coming years will be to ensure that these high standards are maintained.

Meetings are held twice yearly in London and although the odd heated exchange is not unknown, decisions are usually arrived at in a spirit of co-operation and good sense. The goodwill that has carried the Committee through the 30 years of its existence at a time when the World, as well as the sport of professional boxing, has undergone so much change, is still very much in evidence and looks certain to keep the Commonwealth Championships in the forum of International boxing for many years to come.

Commonwealth Champions (Excluding British Titleholders), 1908 – 1984: Championship Records

Includes complete Championship records of all Commonwealth Champions who did not hold the British Championship (the records of British and Commonwealth Champions appear under the British Champions sections). Prior to 1970 the Championship was contested as the British Empire Title.
*Current Champions

Title Holder	Country	Date	Opponent	Result	Venue	Weight
Johnny Aba	Papua N.G.	01.12.77	Billy Moeller	W PTS 15	Boroko	J. Light
		05.05.78	Brian Roberts	W CO 12	Port Morseby	J. Light
		11.08.78	Billy Moeller	W RSC 2	Rabaul	J. Light
		20.10.79	Willie Tarika	W PTS 15	Suva	J. Light
		21.03.80	Willie Tarika	W PTS 15	Port Moresby	J. Light
		28.10.81	Billy Moeller	DREW 15	Orange	J. Light
		17.09.82	Gary Williams	W PTS 15	Port Moresby	J. Light
Steve Aczel	Australia	19.02.75	Maxie Smith	W RSC 3	Manchester	L. Heavy
		30.10.75	Tony Mundine	L CO 12	Blacktown	L. Heavy
		14.05.84	Stewart Lithgo	L CO 11	Brisbane	Cruiser
Dennis Adams	S Africa	23.10.57	Frankie Jones	W CO 3	Glasgow	Fly
		24.01.58	Warner Batchelor	W CO 2	Durban	Fly
		16.07.60	Les Smith	W CO 1	Durban	Fly
		13.05.61	John Mtimkulu	NC 9	Luanshya	Fly
Love Allotey	Ghana	04.08.62	Floyd Robertson	L PTS 15	Accra	Feather
		07.10.67	Bunny Grant	W PTS 15	Accra	Light
		27.07.68	Percy Hayles	L PTS 15	Kingston	Light
Ray Amoo	Nigeria	08.02.80	Neil McLaughlin	W PTS 15	Lagos	Fly
		17.10.80	Steve Muchoki	L RSC 12	Copenhagen	Fly
Roy Ankrah	Ghana	30.04.51	Ronnie Clayton	W PTS 15	London	Feather
		25.02.52	Ronnie Clayton	W RTD 13	Nottingham	Feather
		02.10.54	Billy Spider Kelly	L PTS 15	Belfast	Feather
Baby Cassius Austin	Australia	28.04.77	Hector Thompson	W RSC 15	Perth	L. Welter
		16.06.77	Hector Thompson	L PTS 15	Perth	L. Welter
		15.09.77	Hector Thompson	W PTS 15	Perth	L. Welter
		21.04.78	Tony Aba	W CO 4	Boroko	L. Welter
		24.09.78	Jeff Malcolm	L PTS 15	Melbourne	L. Welter
		15.12.78	Jeff Malcolm	L PTS 15	Griffith	L. Welter
George Barnes	Australia	24.11.54	Barry Brown	W CO 11	Sydney	Welter
		28.11.55	Attu Clottey	W PTS 15	Sydney	Welter
		14.04.56	Benny Nieuwenhuizen	W RSC 13	Johannesburg	Welter
		06.08.56	Darby Brown	L PTS 15	Sydney	Welter
		12.11.56	Darby Brown	W PTS 15	Sydney	Welter
		12.08.57	Attu Clottey	W PTS 15	Sydney	Welter
		17.05.58	Johnny Van Rensburg	L PTS 15	Salisbury	Welter
		18.08.58	Johnny Van Rensburg	W RSC 13	Sydney	Welter
		07.08.59	Billy Todd	W PTS 15	Brisbane	Welter
		07.12.59	Billy Todd	W RSC 6	Sydney	Welter
		09.05.60	Brian Curvis	L PTS 15	Swansea	Welter

Title Holder	Country	Date	Opponent	Result	Venue	Weight
Hogan Bassey	Nigeria	19.11.55	Billy Kelly	W CO 8	Belfast	Feather
		01.04.57	Percy Lewis	W PTS 15	Nottingham	Feather
Trevor Berbick*	Canada	21.07.81	Conroy Nelson	W RSC 2	Halifax, NS	Heavy
		09.09.83	Ken Lakusa	W CO 10	Alberta	Heavy
Monty Betham	N Zealand	24.07.75	Carlos Marks	W PTS 15	Wellington	Middle
		19.01.76	Semi Bula	W RSC 9	Port Kembia	Middle
		11.03.76	Al Korovou	W PTS 15	Wellington	Middle
		05.06.76	Jone Mataitini	W CO 7	Suva	Middle
		30.07.76	Carlos Marks	W PTS 15	Port of Spain	Middle
		23.09.76	Wally Carr	W CO 11	Wellington	Middle
		17.03.78	Al Korovou	W CO 12	Suva	Middle
Lennox Blackmore	Guyana	30.09.77	Jonathan Dele	W PTS 15	Lagos	Light
		25.10.78	Hogan Jimoh	L CO 5	Lagos	Light
Gomeo Brennan	Bahamas	22.10.63	Mick Leahy	W PTS 15	London	Middle
		14.03.64	Tuna Scanlon	L PTS 15	Auckland	Middle
		12.11.64	Earl Nikora	W PTS 15	Auckland	Middle
		15.06.65	Earl Nikora	W PTS 15	Auckland	Middle
		25.09.65	Blair Richardson	W CO 11	Glace Bay	Middle
		25.03.66	Blair Richardson	L PTS 15	Glace Bay	Middle
Kenny Bristol	Guyana	29.07.79	Pat Thomas	W PTS 15	Georgetown	L. Middle
		24.02.80	Eddie Marcelle	W PTS 15	Georgetown	L. Middle
		25.11.81	Herol Graham	L PTS 15	Sheffield	L. Middle
Barry Brown	N Zealand	15.01.54	Gerald Dreyer	W RSC 7	Wellington	Welter
		24.11.54	George Barnes	L CO 11	Sydney	Welter
Darby Brown	Australia	06.08.56	George Barnes	W PTS 15	Sydney	Welter
		12.11.56	George Barnes	L PTS 15	Sydney	Welter
Tommy Burns	Canada	07.04.10	Bill Lang	W PTS 20	Sydney	Heavy
		17.07.20	Joe Beckett	L RTD 7	London	Heavy
Joe Bygraves	Jamaica	26.06.56	Kitione Lave	W PTS 15	London	Heavy
		19.02.57	Henry Cooper	W CO 9	London	Heavy
		27.05.57	Dick Richardson	DREW 15	Cardiff	Heavy
		25.11.57	Joe Erskine	L PTS 15	Leicester	Heavy
Milo Calhoun	Jamaica	28.07.67	Johnny Meilleur	W PTS 12	Glace Bay	Middle
		09.10.67	Johnny Pritchett	L RTD 8	Manchester	Middle
Jimmy Carruthers	Australia	15.11.52	Vic Toweel	W CO 1	Johannesburg	Bantam
		21.03.53	Vic Toweel	W CO 10	Johannesburg	Bantam
Chris Clarke	Canada	28.08.79	Clyde Gray	W RSC 10	Halifax, NS	Welter
		13.11.79	Clyde Gray	L RSC 10	Halifax, NS	Welter
Jonathan Dele	Nigeria	03.05.75	Jim Watt	W PTS 15	Lagos	Light
		16.07.76	Percy Hayles	W PTS 15	Lagos	Light
		04.03.77	Hogan Jimoh	W PTS 15	Lagos	Light
		30.09.77	Lennox Blackmore	L PTS 15	Lagos	Light
Gerald Dreyer	S Africa	08.12.52	Cliff Curvis	W PTS 15	Johannesburg	Welter
		15.01.54	Barry Brown	L RSC 7	Wellington	Welter
Bob Dunlop	Australia	12.02.68	Young John McCormack	W RSC 7	Sydney	L. Heavy
		01.01.69	Al Sparks	W PTS 15	Melbourne	L. Heavy
Bobby Dunne	Australia	03.11.72	Toro George	W PTS 15	Melbourne	Feather
		05.04.74	Evan Armstrong	L RSC 8	Brisbane	Feather
Yvon Durelle	Canada	30.05.57	Gordon Wallace	W CO 2	Moncton	L. Heavy
		16.07.58	Mike Holt	W RTD 8	Montreal	L. Heavy
Johnny Famechon	Australia	24.11.67	John O'Brien	W RSC 11	Melbourne	Feather
		13.09.68	Billy McGrandle	W RSC 12	Melbourne	Feather
Billy Famous*	Nigeria	28.05.83	Obisia Nwankpa	W PTS 12	Lagos	L. Welter
		17.03.84	Obisia Nwankpa	W CO 5	Lagos	L. Welter
Paul Ferreri*	Australia	16.09.72	John Kellie	W PTS 15	Melbourne	Bantam
		26.04.73	Fred Burns	W PTS 15	Carlton	Bantam
		07.03.75	Paddy Maguire	W RSC 8	Melbourne	Bantam

CONTINUED OVERLEAF

Title Holder	Country	Date	Opponent	Result	Venue	Weight
		25.03.76	Brian Roberts	W PTS 15	Blacktown	Bantam
		29.01.77	Sulley Shittu	L PTS 15	Accra	Bantam
		02.11.78	Johnny Owen	L PTS 15	Ebbw Vale	Bantam
		21.05.81	Mike Irungu	W PTS 15	Copenhagen	Bantam
		16.12.81	Stix Macloud	W RSC 12	Sydney	Bantam
		02.04.82	John Feeney	W RSC 13	Sydney	Bantam
		24.09.82	Francis Musankabala	W RSC 12	Melbourne	Bantam
		07.05.83	Stix Macloud	W CO 9	Harare	Bantam
Pat Ford	Australia	28.08.53	Frank Johnson	W PTS 15	Melbourne	Light
		09.10.53	Frank Johnson	W CO 13	Melbourne	Light
		09.04.54	Ivor Germain	L PTS 15	Melbourne	Light
		02.07.54	Ivor Germain	W PTS 15	Melbourne	Light
Pat Ford	Guyana	01.08.80	Eddie Ndukwu	W RTD 9	Lagos	Feather
Larry Gains	Canada	13.06.31	Phil Scott	W CO 2	Leicester	Heavy
		28.01.32	Don McCorkindale	DREW 15	London	Heavy
		03.03.32	Don McCorkindale	W PTS 15	London	Heavy
		18.05.33	George Cook	W PTS 15	London	Heavy
		08.02.34	Len Harvey	L PTS 15	London	Heavy
		10.09.34	Jack Petersen	L RTD 13	London	Heavy
		10.03.39	Len Harvey	L RTD 13	London	Heavy
Toro George	N Zealand	12.12.70	Ken Bradley	W RSC 6	Canberra	Feather
		06.09.71	Evan Armstrong	W PTS 15	Melbourne	Feather
		03.11.72	Bobby Dunne	L PTS 15	Melbourne	Feather
Ivor Germain	Barbados	09.04.54	Pat Ford	W PTS 15	Melbourne	Light
		02.07.54	Pat Ford	L PTS 15	Melbourne	Light
Bunny Grant	Jamaica	04.08.62	Dave Charnley	W PTS 15	Kingston	Light
		13.02.65	Percy Hayles	W PTS 15	Kingston	Light
		15.03.67	Manny Santos	L PTS 15	Wellington	Light
		07.10.67	Love Allotey	L PTS 15	Accra	Light
		18.02.74	Clyde Gray	L RTD 8	Toronto	Welter
Clyde Gray	Canada	12.02.73	Eddie Blay	W PTS 15	Toronto	Welter
		18.02.74	Bunny Grant	W RTD 8	Toronto	Weltr
		03.03.75	Marc Gervais	W CO 5	Calgary	Welter
		01.12.75	Lawrence Hafey	W RSC 8	Halifax, NS	Welter
		23.11.76	Kevin Odus	W RSC 5	Halifax, NS	Welter
		09.12.77	Vernon Lewis	W PTS 15	Port of Spain	Welter
		19.08.78	Sakaria Ve	W RSC 8	Suva	Welter
		15.12.78	Sakaria Ve	W CO 9	Lautoka	Welter
		28.08.79	Chris Clarke	L RSC 10	Halifax, NS	Welter
		13.11.79	Chris Clarke	W RSC 10	Halifax, NS	Welter
Wilf Greaves	Canada	22.06.60	Dick Tiger	W PTS 15	Edmonton	Middle
		30.11.60	Dick Tiger	L RSC 9	Edmonton	Middle
Percy Hayles	Jamaica	13.02.65	Bunny Grant	L PTS 15	Kingston	Light
		27.07.68	Love Allotey	W PTS 15	Kingston	Light
		14.08.70	Jeff White	W PTS 15	Brisbane	Light
		10.07.71	Al Ford	W PTS 15	Kingston	Light
		22.01.73	Al Ford	W RSC 12	Kingston	Light
		22.07.74	Manny Santos	W PTS 15	Kingston	Light
		16.07.76	Jonathan Dele	L PTS 15	Lagos	Light
Hogan Jimoh	Nigeria	04.03.77	Jonathan Dele	L PTS 15	Lagos	Light
		25.10.78	Lennox Blackmore	W CO 5	Lagos	Light
		30.11.79	Johnny Claydon	W RSC 8	Lagos	Light
		07.12.80	Langton Tinago	L RSC 7	Lagos	Light
Ayub Kalule	Uganda	25.05.78	Al Korovou	W RSC 14	Copenhagen	Middle
		14.09.78	Reg Ford	W CO 5	Randers	Middle
Jimmy Kelso	Australia	24.04.33	Al Foreman	W PTS 15	Sydney	Light
		22.05.33	Al Foreman	L DIS 3	Sydney	Light

Title Holder	Country	Date	Opponent	Result	Venue	Weight
Arthur King	Canada	01.10.48	Billy Thompson	W RTD 7	Manchester	Light
Al Korovou	Australia	11.03.76	Monty Betham	L PTS 15	Wellington	Middle
		17.03.78	Monty Betham	W CO 12	Suva	Middle
		25.05.78	Ayub Kalule	L RSC 14	Copenhagen	Middle
David Kotey	Ghana	07.12.74	Evan Armstrong	W RTD 10	Accra	Feather
		03.10.78	Eddie Ndukwu	L PTS 15	Lagos	Feather
Percy Lewis	Trinidad	01.04.57	Hogan Bassey	L PTS 15	Nottingham	Feather
		09.12.57	Charlie Hill	W RSC 10	Nottingham	Feather
		07.12.59	John O'Brien	W CO 2	Nottingham	Feather
		26.11.60	Floyd Robertson	L PTS 15	Belfast	Feather
Jeff Malcolm	Australia	24.09.78	Baby Cassius Austin	W PTS 15	Melbourne	L. Welter
		15.12.78	Baby Cassius Austin	W PTS 15	Griffith	L. Welter
		03.03.79	Obisia Nwankpa	L PTS 15	Lagos	L. Welter
Patrick Mambwe	Zambia	03.07.76	Gwyn Jones	W RSC 9	Lusaka	Fly
Barry Michael	Australia	22.12.76	Billy Moeller	L PTS 15	Orange	J. Light
		06.05.81	Langton Tinago	W PTS 15	Melbourne	Light
		20.07.81	Dave McCabe	W RSC 7	Melbourne	Light
		11.12.81	Willie Tarika	W RSC 10	Melbourne	Light
		22.07.82	Claude Noel	L PTS 15	Melbourne	Light
Billy Moeller	Australia	13.05.15	Jimmy Bell	W PTS 15	Sydney	J. Light
		25.05.76	Mama Clay	W PTS 15	Lagos	J. Light
		22.12.76	Barry Michael	W PTS 15	Orange	J. Light
		01.12.77	Johnny Aba	L PTS 15	Boroko	J. Light
		11.08.78	Johnny Aba	L RSC 2	Rabaul	J. Light
		28.10.81	Johnny Aba	DREW 15	Orange	J. Light
Steve Muchoki	Kenya	17.10.80	Ray Amoo	W RSC 12	Copenhagen	Fly
		03.02.83	Keith Wallace	L RSC 10	London	Fly
Tony Mundine	Australia	21.01.71	Bunny Sterling	DREW 15	Sydney	Middle
		14.04.72	Bunny Sterling	W RSC 15	Brisbane	Middle
		07.02.73	Matt Donovan	W RSC 3	Sydney	Middle
		20.08.73	Fred Etuati	W CO 1	Auckland	Middle
		28.09.73	Carlos Marks	W PTS 15	Brisbane	Middle
		30.10.75	Steve Aczel	W CO 12	Blacktown	L. Heavy
		04.12.75	Victor Attivor	W RSC 2	Blacktown	L. Heavy
		26.03.76	Baby Boy Rolle	W CO 3	Brisbane	L. Heavy
		04.09.76	Victor Attivor	W RSC 9	Accra	L. Heavy
		08.07.77	Ernie Barr	W PTS 15	Brisbane	L. Heavy
		27.02.78	Gary Summerhays	L CO 11	Melbourne	L. Heavy
Bos Murphy	N Zealand	26.01.48	Vince Hawkins	W PTS 15	London	Middle
		18.05.48	Dick Turpin	L CO 1	Coventry	Middle
Lottie Mwale*	Zambia	31.03.79	Gary Summerhays	W RSC 5	Lusaka	L. Heavy
		04.06.82	Chisanda Mutti	W RSC 13	Lusaka	L. Heavy
		05.12.82	Kid Power	W CO 13	Lusaka	L. Heavy
		30.01.83	Billy Savage	W RSC 2	Lusaka	L. Heavy
		12.03.83	Mustafa Wasajja	W RSC 3	Lusaka	L. Heavy
		08.10.83	Chisanda Mutti	W PTS 12	Lusaka	L. Heavy
Eddie Ndukwu	Nigeria	17.06.77	Evan Armstrong	W RSC 12	Lagos	Feather
		09.12.77	Alan Richardson	W RTD 8	Lagos	Feather
		03.10.78	David Kotey	W PTS 15	Lagos	Feather
		28.09.79	Henry Saddler	W RTD 8	Lagos	Feather
		01.08.80	Pat Ford	L RTD 9	Lagos	Feather
Azumah Nelson*	Ghana	26.09.81	Brian Roberts	W CO 5	Accra	Feather
		28.02.82	Charm Chiteule	W RSC 10	Lusaka	Feather
		02.12.83	Kabiru Akindele	W CO 9	Lagos	Feather

Title Holder	Country	Date	Opponent	Result	Venue	Weight
Henry Nissen	Australia	06.08.71	John McCluskey	W RTD 8	Melbourne	Fly
		14.03.74	Big Jim West	L RTD 4	Melbourne	Fly
Claude Noel*	Trinidad	22.07.82	Barry Michael	W PTS 15	Melbourne	Light
		02.12.83	Steve Assoon	W PTS 12	Port of Spain	Light
		16.03.84	Davidson Andeh	W CO 7	Port of Spain	Light
Obisia Nwankpa	Nigeria	03.03.79	Jeff Malcolm	W PTS 15	Lagos	L. Welter
		04.07.80	Clinton McKenzie	W PTS 15	Lagos	L. Welter
		07.11.80	Derrick McKenzie	W RSC 2	Lagos	L. Welter
		13.06.82	Des Morrison	W RTD 10	Aba	L. Welter
		28.05.83	Billy Famous	L PTS 12	Lagos	L. Welter
		17.03.84	Billy Famous	L CO 5	Lagos	L. Welter
Charkey Ramon	Australia	30.10.72	Pat Dwyer	W RSC 8	Melbourne	L. Middle
		07.06.73	Donato Paduano	W RSC 11	Sydney	L. Middle
Ron Richards	Australia	26.02.40	Fred Henneberry	W DIS 11	Sydney	Middle
		16.12.40	Fred Henneberry	W DIS 12	Sydney	Middle
		27.11.41	Fred Henneberry	W DIS 13	Sydney	Middle
Blair Richardson	Canada	25.09.65	Gomeo Brennan	L CO 11	Glace Bay	Middle
		25.03.66	Gomeo Brennan	W PTS 15	Glace Bay	Middle
Floyd Robertson	Ghana	26.11.60	Percy Lewis	W PTS 15	Belfast	Feather
		04.08.62	Love Allotey	W PTS 15	Accra	Feather
		05.10.63	Joe Tetteh	W RSC 11	Accra	Feather
		03.02.67	John O'Brien	L RTD 12	Accra	Feather
Lionel Rose	Australia	08.03.69	Alan Rudkin	W PTS 15	Melbourne	Bantam
Dave Sands	Australia	06.09.49	Dick Turpin	W CO 1	London	Middle
		09.05.52	Al Bourke	W CO 5	Melbourne	Middle
Manny Santos	N Zealand	15.03.67	Bunny Grant	W PTS 15	Wellington	Light
		22.07.74	Percy Hayles	L PTS 15	Kingston	Light
Tuna Scanlon	N Zealand	14.03.64	Gomeo Brennan	W PTS 15	Auckland	Middle
Sulley Shittu	Ghana	29.01.77	Paul Ferreri	W PTS 15	Accra	Bantam
John Sichula	Zambia	04.02.84	Langton Tinago	W CO 5	Harare	Light
Laurie Stevens	S Africa	11.01.36	Jackie Kid Berg	W PTS 12	Johannesburg	Light
Gary Summerhays	Canada	27.02.78	Tony Mundine	W CO 11	Melbourne	L. Heavy
		31.03.79	Lottie Mwale	L RSC 5	Lusaka	L. Heavy
Joe Tetteh	Ghana	05.10.63	Floyd Robertson	L RSC 11	Accra	Feather
		21.09.72	Joey Santos	W RSC 10	Wellington	L. Welter
		26.03.73	Hector Thompson	L PTS 15	Brisbane	L. Welter
		16.07.73	Hector Thompson	L PTS 15	Brisbane	L. Welter
Hector Thompson	Australia	26.03.73	Joe Tetteh	W PTS 15	Brisbane	L. Welter
		16.07.73	Joe Tetteh	W PTS 15	Brisbane	L. Welter
		19.05.75	Ali Afakasi	W RSC 10	Brisbane	L. Welter
		16.08.76	Andy Broome	W CO 6	Tweed Heads	L. Welter
		03.12.76	Ross Eadie	W RSC 15	Wollongong	L. Welter
		16.12.76	Martin Beni	W RSC 10	Broad Meadow	L. Welter
		28.04.77	Baby Cassius Austin	L RSC 15	Perth	L. Welter
		16.06.77	Baby Cassius Austin	W PTS 15	Perth	L. Welter
		15.09.77	Baby Cassius Austin	W PTS 15	Perth	L. Welter

Title Holder	Country	Date	Opponent	Result	Venue	Weight
Dick Tiger	Nigeria	27.03.58	Pat McAteer	W CO 9	Liverpool	Middle
		22.06.60	Wilf Greaves	L PTS 15	Edmonton	Middle
		30.11.60	Wilf Greaves	W RSC 9	Edmonton	Middle
Langton Tinago	Zimbabwe	07.12.80	Hogan Jimoh	W RSC 7	Lagos	Light
		06.05.81	Barry Michael	L PTS 15	Melbourne	Light
		07.05.83	Safiu Okebadan	W PTS 12	Harare	J. Light
		04.02.84	John Sichula	L CO 5	Harare	J. Light
Vic Toweel	S Africa	12.11.49	Stan Rowan	W PTS 15	Johannesburg	Bantam
		08.04.50	Fernando Gagnon	W PTS 15	Johannesburg	Bantam
		02.12.50	Danny O'Sullivan	W RTD 10	Johannesburg	Bantam
		26.01.52	Peter Keenan	W PTS 15	Johannesburg	Bantam
		15.11.52	Jimmy Carruthers	L CO 1	Johannesburg	Bantam
		21.03.53	Jimmy Carruthers	L CO 10	Johannesburg	Bantam
Willie Toweel	S Africa	10.12.55	Johnny Van Rensburg	L RTD 9	Johannesburg	Light
		16.06.56	Johnny Van Rensburg	W PTS 15	Johannesburg	Light
		11.08.56	Johnny Van Rensburg	DREW 15	Johannesburg	Light
		10.11.56	Richie Howard	W PTS 15	Johannesburg	Light
		14.02.57	Johnny Van Rensburg	W RTD 4	Johannesburg	Light
		09.07.57	Dave Charnley	W PTS 15	London	Light
		12.05.59	Dave Charnley	L CO 10	London	Light
Jake Tuli	S Africa	08.09.52	Teddy Gardner	W RSC 12	Newcastle	Fly
		19.10.54	Dai Dower	L PTS 15	London	Fly
		14.09.55	Peter Keenan	L CO 14	Glasgow	Bantam
		06.12.55	Dai Dower	L PTS 15	London	Fly
Johnny Van Rensburg	S Africa	12.02.55	Joe Lucy	W PTS 15	Johannesburg	Light
		11.06.55	Louis Klopper	W PTS 12	Johannesburg	Light
		20.08.55	Roy Louw	W RSC 8	Cape Town	Light
		10.12.55	Willie Toweel	W RTD 9	Johannesburg	Light
		16.06.56	Willie Toweel	L PTS 15	Johannesburg	Light
		11.08.56	Willie Toweel	DREW 15	Johannesburg	Light
		14.02.57	Willie Toweel	L RTD 4	Johannesburg	Light
		17.05.58	George Barnes	W PTS 15	Salisbury	Welter
		18.08.58	George Barnes	L RSC 13	Sydney	Welter
Gordon Wallace	Canada	19.06.56	Ron Barton	W PTS 15	London	L. Heavy
		30.05.57	Yvon Durelle	L CO 2	Moncton	L. Heavy
Big Jim West	Australia	14.03.74	Henry Nissen	W RTD 4	Melbourne	Fly

Undefeated Champions

Johnny Aba, J. Lightweight, 1977 – 1982; *Dennis Adams*, Flyweight, 1957 – 1962; *Hogan Bassey*, Featherweight, 1955 – 1957; *Tommy Burns*, Heavyweight, 1910; *Jimmy Carruthers*, Bantamweight, 1952 – 1954; *Bob Dunlop*, L. Heavyweight, 1968 – 1970; *Yvon Durelle*, L. Heavyweight, 1957 – 1959; *Johnny Famechon*, Featherweight, 1967 – 1969; *Pat Ford*, Lightweight, 1954 – 1955; *Pat Ford*, Featherweight, 1980 – 1981; *Clyde Gray*, Welterweight, 1979 – 1981; *Percy Hayles*, Lightweight, 1968 – 1975; *Ayub Kalule*, Middleweight, 1978 – 1980; *Arthur King*, Lightweight, 1948 – 1951; *David Kotey*, Featherweight, 1974 – 1975; *Patrick Mambwe*, Flyweight, 1976 – 1979; *Tony Mundine*, Middleweight, 1972 – 1975; *Charkey Ramon*, L. Middleweight, 1972 – 1975; *Ron Richards*, Middleweight, 1940 – 1941; *Blair Richardson*, Middleweight, 1966 – 1967; *Lionel Rose*, Bantamweight, 1969; *Dave Sands*, Middleweight, 1949 – 1952; *Manny Santos*, Lightweight, 1967; *Tuna Scanlon*, Middleweight, 1964; *Sulley Shittu*, Bantamweight, 1977 – 1978; *Laurie Stevens*, Lightweight, 1936; *Dick Tiger*, Middleweight, 1960 – 1962; *Big Jim West*, Flyweight, 1974 – 1975.

European Champions, 1906 – 1984

Shows the tenure of each European Champion at each weight.

EUROPEAN COUNTRY CODE
AU = Austria; BEL = Belgium; DEN = Denmark; FIN = Finland; FR = France; GB = Great Britain; GER = Germany; GRE = Greece; HOL = Holland; HUN = Hungary; ITA = Italy; POR = Portugal; RUM = Rumania; SP = Spain; SWE = Sweden; SWI = Switzerland; TU = Turkey; YUG = Yugoslavia.

* Undefeated Champions.

Flyweight

Sid Smith	GB	1913
Bill Ladbury	GB	1913 – 1914
Percy Jones	GB	1914
Tancy Lee	GB	1914 – 1916
Jimmy Wilde *	GB	1916 – 1917
Michel Montreuil	BEL	1923 – 1925
Elky Clark *	GB	1925 – 1927
Victor Ferrand *	SP	1927
Emile Pladner	FR	1928
Johnny Hill	GB	1928 – 1929
Emile Pladner	FR	1929
Eugene Huat *	FR	1929
Kid Oliva	FR	1930
Lucien Popescu	RUM	1930 – 1931
Jackie Brown *	GB	1931 – 1932
Praxille Gyde	FR	1932 – 1935
Kid David *	BEL	1935
Ernst Weiss	AU	1936
Valentin Angelmann *	FR	1936 – 1938
Enrico Urbinati *	ITA	1938 – 1943
Raoul Degryse	BEL	1946 – 1947
Maurice Sandeyron	FR	1947 – 1949
Rinty Monaghan *	GB	1949 – 1950
Terry Allen	GB	1950
Jean Sneyers *	BEL	1950 – 1951
Teddy Gardner *	GB	1952
Louis Skena *	FR	1953 – 1954
Nazzareno Giannelli	ITA	1954 – 1955
Dai Dower	GB	1955
Young Martin	SP	1955 – 1959
Risto Luukkonen	FIN	1959 – 1961
Salvatore Burruni *	ITA	1961 – 1964
Rene Libeer *	FR	1965 – 1966
Fernando Atzori	ITA	1967 – 1972
Fritz Chervet *	SWI	1972
Fernando Atzori	ITA	1973
Fritz Chervet *	SWI	1973 – 1974
Franco Udella	ITA	1974 – 1979
Charlie Magri *	GB	1979 – 1983
Antoine Montero *	FR	1983 – 1984

Bantamweight

Joe Bowker	GB	1910
Digger Stanley	GB	1910 – 1912
Charles Ledoux	FR	1912 – 1921
Tommy Harrison	GB	1921 – 1922
Charles Ledoux	FR	1922 – 1923
Bugler Lake	GB	1923
Johnny Brown *	GB	1923 – 1924
Henri Scillie *	BEL	1925 – 1927
Domenico Bernasconi*	ITA	1927 – 1929
Carlos Flix	SP	1929 – 1931
Lucien Popescu	RUM	1931 – 1932
Domenico Bernasconi*	ITA	1932
Nicholas Biquet	BEL	1932 – 1935
Maurice Dubois	SWI	1935 – 1936
Joseph Decico	FR	1936
Aurel Toma *	RUM	1936 – 1937
Nicholas Biquet *	BEL	1937 – 1938
Aurel Toma	RUM	1938 – 1939
Ernst Weiss	AU	1939
Gino Cattaneo	ITA	1939 – 1941
Gino Bondavilli *	ITA	1941 – 1943
Jackie Paterson	GB	1946
Theo Medina	FR	1946 – 1947
Peter Kane	GB	1947 – 1948
Guido Ferracin	ITA	1948 – 1949
Luis Romero	SP	1949 – 1951
Peter Keenan	GB	1951 – 1952
Jean Sneyers *	BEL	1952
Peter Keenan	GB	1953
John Kelly	GB	1953 – 1954
Robert Cohen *	FR	1954
Mario D'Agata	ITA	1955 – 1958
Piero Rollo	ITA	1958 – 1959
Freddie Gilroy *	GB	1959 – 1960
Pierre Cossemyns	BEL	1961 – 1962
Piero Rollo	ITA	1962
Alphonse Halimi	FR	1962
Piero Rollo	ITA	1962 – 1963
Mimoun Ben Ali	SP	1963
Risto Luukkonen *	FIN	1963 – 1964
Mimoun Ben Ali	SP	1965
Tommaso Galli	ITA	1965 – 1966
Mimoun Ben Ali	SP	1966 – 1968

Salvatore Burruni *	ITA	1968 – 1969
Franco Zurlo	ITA	1969 – 1971
Alan Rudkin	GB	1971
Agustin Senin *	SP	1971 – 1972
Johnny Clark *	GB	1973 – 1974
Bob Allotey	SP	1974 – 1975
Daniel Trioulaire	FR	1975 – 1976
Salvatore Fabrizio	ITA	1976 – 1977
Franco Zurlo	ITA	1977 – 1978
Juan Francisco Rodriguez	SP	1978 – 1980
Johnny Owen *	GB	1980
Valerio Nati	ITA	1980 – 1982
Giuseppe Fossati	ITA	1982 – 1983
Walter Giorgetti	ITA	1983 –

Featherweight

Jim Driscoll *	GB	1912 – 1913
Ted Kid Lewis *	GB	1913 – 1914
Louis De Ponthieu *	FR	1919 – 1920
Arthur Wyns	BEL	1920 – 1922
Eugene Criqui *	FR	1922
Edouard Mascart	FR	1923 – 1924
Charles Ledoux	FR	1924
Henri Hebrans	BEL	1924 – 1925
Antonio Ruiz	SP	1925 – 1928
Luigi Quadrini	ITA	1928 – 1929
Knud Larsen	DEN	1929
Jose Girones *	SP	1929 – 1934
Maurice Holtzer *	FR	1935 – 1938
Phil Dolhem	BEL	1938 – 1939
Lucien Popescu	RUM	1939 – 1941
Ernst Weiss	AU	1941
Gino Bondavilli	ITA	1941 – 1945
Ermanno Bonetti *	ITA	1945 – 1946
Tiger Al Phillips	GB	1947
Ronnie Clayton	GB	1947 – 1948
Ray Famechon	FR	1948 – 1953
Jean Sneyers	BEL	1953 – 1954
Ray Famechon	FR	1954 – 1955
Fred Galiana *	SP	1955 – 1956
Cherif Hamia *	FR	1957 – 1958
Sergio Caprari	ITA	1958 – 1959
Gracieux Lamperti	FR	1959 – 1962
Alberto Serti	ITA	1962 – 1963
Howard Winstone *	GB	1963 – 1967
Jose Legra *	SP	1967 – 1968
Manuel Calvo	SP	1968 – 1969
Tommaso Galli	ITA	1969 – 1970
Jose Legra *	SP	1970 – 1972
Gitano Jiminez	SP	1973 – 1975
Elio Cotena	ITA	1975 – 1976
Nino Jiminez	SP	1976 – 1977
Manuel Masso	SP	1977
Roberto Castanon *	SP	1977 – 1981
Salvatore Melluzzo	ITA	1981 – 1982
Pat Cowdell *	GB	1982 – 1983
Loris Stecca *	ITA	1983
Barry McGuigan	GB	1983 –

J. Lightweight

Tommaso Galli *	ITA	1971 – 1972
Lothar Abend	GER	1972 – 1974
Sven-Erik Paulsen *	NOR	1974 – 1975
Roland Cazeaux	FR	1976
Natale Vezzoli	ITA	1976 – 1979
Carlos Hernandez	SP	1979
Rodolfo Sanchez	SP	1979
Carlos Hernandez	SP	1979 – 1982
Cornelius Boza-Edwards *	GB	1982
Roberto Castanon	SP	1982 – 1983
Alfredo Raininger	ITA	1983 – 1984
Jean-Marc Renard	BEL	1984 –

Lightweight

Freddie Welsh	GB	1909 – 1911
Matt Wells	GB	1911 – 1912
Freddie Welsh *	GB	1912 – 1914
Bob Marriott	GB	1919 – 1920
Georges Papin	FR	1920 – 1921
Ernie Rice	GB	1921 – 1922
Seaman Hall	GB	1922 – 1923
Harry Mason *	GB	1923
Fred Bretonnel	FR	1924
Lucien Vinez	FR	1924 – 1927
Luis Rayo *	SP	1927 – 1928
Alme Raphael	FR	1928 – 1929
Francois Sybille	BEL	1929 – 1930
Alf Howard	GB	1930
Francois Sybille	BEL	1930 – 1931
Bep Van Klaveren	HOL	1931 – 1932
Cleto Locatelli	ITA	1932
Francois Sybille	BEL	1932 – 1933
Cleto Locatelli *	ITA	1933
Francois Sybille	BEL	1934
Carlo Orlandi *	ITA	1934 – 1935
Enrico Venturi *	ITA	1935 – 1936
Vittorio Tamagnini	ITA	1936 – 1937
Maurice Arnault	FR	1937
Gustave Humery *	FR	1937 – 1938
Aldo Spoldi *	ITA	1938 – 1939
Karl Blaho	AU	1940 – 1941
Bruno Bisterzo	ITA	1941
Ascenzo Botta	ITA	1941
Bruno Bisterzo	ITA	1941 – 1942
Ascenzo Botta	ITA	1942
Roberto Proietti	ITA	1942 – 1943
Bruno Bisterzo	ITA	1943 – 1946
Roberto Proietti *	ITA	1946
Emile Dicristo	FR	1946 – 1947
Kid Dussart	BEL	1947
Roberto Proietti	ITA	1947 – 1948
Billy Thompson	GB	1948 – 1949
Kid Dussart	BEL	1949
Roberto Proietti *	ITA	1949 – 1950
Pierre Montane	FR	1951
Elis Ask	FIN	1951 – 1952
Jorgen Johansen	DEN	1952 – 1954
Duilio Loi *	ITA	1954 – 1959

Mario Vecchiatto	ITA	1959 – 1960
Dave Charnley *	GB	1960 – 1961
Conny Rudhof *	GER	1963 – 1964
Willi Quatuor *	GER	1964
Franco Brondi	ITA	1965
Maurice Tavant	FR	1965 – 1966
Borge Krogh	DEN	1966 – 1967
Pedro Carrasco *	SP	1967 – 1969
Miguel Velazquez	SP	1970 – 1971
Antonio Puddu	ITA	1971 – 1974
Ken Buchanan *	GB	1974 – 1975
Fernand Roelandts	BEL	1976
Perico Fernandez *	SP	1976
Jim Watt *	GB	1977 – 1979
Charlie Nash *	GB	1979 – 1980
Francisco Leon	SP	1980
Charlie Nash	GB	1980 – 1981
Joey Gibilisco	ITA	1981 – 1983
Licio Cusma	ITA	1983 – 1984
Rene Weller	GER	1984 –

L. Welterweight

Olli Maki *	FIN	1964 – 1965
Juan Sombrita Albornoz	SP	1965
Willi Quatuor *	GER	1965 – 1966
Conny Rudhof	GER	1967
Johann Orsolics	AU	1967 – 1968
Bruno Arcari *	ITA	1968 – 1970
Rene Roque	FR	1970 – 1971
Pedro Carrasco *	SP	1971
Roger Zami	FR	1972
Cemal Kamaci	TU	1972 – 1973
Toni Ortiz	SP	1973 – 1974
Perico Fernandez *	SP	1974
Jose Ramon Gomez-Fouz	SP	1975
Cemal Kamaci *	TU	1975 – 1976
Dave Boy Green *	GB	1976
Primo Bandini	ITA	1977
Jean-Baptiste Piedvache	FR	1977 – 1978
Colin Power	GB	1978
Fernando Sanchez	SP	1978 – 1979
Jose Luis Heredia	SP	1979
Jo Kimpuani *	FR	1979 – 1980
Giuseppe Martinese	ITA	1980
Antonio Guinaldo	SP	1980 – 1981
Clinton McKenzie	GB	1981 – 1982
Robert Gambini	FR	1982 – 1983
Patrizio Oliva	ITA	1983 –

Welterweight

Young Joseph	GB	1910 – 1911
Georges Carpentier *	FR	1911 – 1912
Albert Badoud *	SWI	1915 – 1919
Johnny Basham	GB	1919 – 1920
Ted Kid Lewis *	GB	1920
Piet Hobin	BEL	1921 – 1925
Mario Bosisio *	ITA	1925 – 1928
Alf Genon	BEL	1928 – 1929
Gustave Roth	BEL	1929 – 1932
Adrien Aneet	BEL	1932 – 1933
Jack Hood *	GB	1933
Gustave Eder *	GER	1934 – 1936
Felix Wouters	BEL	1936 – 1938
Saverio Turiello	ITA	1938 – 1939
Marcel Cerdan *	FR	1939 – 1942
Ernie Roderick	GB	1946 – 1947
Robert Villemain *	FR	1947 – 1948
Livio Minelli	ITA	1949 – 1950
Michele Palermo	ITA	1950 – 1951
Eddie Thomas	GB	1951
Charles Humez *	FR	1951 – 1952
Gilbert Lavoine	FR	1953 – 1954
Wally Thom	GB	1954 – 1955
Idrissa Dione	FR	1955 – 1956
Emilio Marconi	ITA	1956 – 1958
Peter Waterman *	GB	1958
Emilio Marconi	ITA	1958 – 1959
Duilio Loi *	ITA	1959 – 1963
Fortunata Manca *	ITA	1964 – 1965
Jean Josselin	FR	1966 – 1967
Carmelo Bossi	ITA	1967 – 1968
Fighting Mack	HOL	1968 – 1969
Silvano Bertini	ITA	1969
Jean Josselin	FR	1969
Johann Orsolics	AU	1969 – 1970
Ralph Charles	GB	1970 – 1971
Roger Menetrey	FR	1971 – 1974
John H. Stracey *	GB	1974 – 1975
Marco Scano	ITA	1976 – 1977
Jorgen Hansen	DEN	1977
Jorg Eipel	GER	1977
Alain Marion	FR	1977
Jorgen Hansen	DEN	1978
Josef Pachler	AU	1978
Henry Rhiney	GB	1978 – 1979
Dave Boy Green	GB	1979
Jorgen Hansen *	DEN	1979 – 1981
Hans-Henrik Palm	DEN	1982
Colin Jones *	GB	1982 – 1983
Gilles Elbilia *	FR	1983 – 1984

L. Middleweight

Bruno Visintin	ITA	1964 – 1966
Bo Hogberg	SWE	1966
Yolande Leveque	FR	1966
Sandro Mazzinghi *	ITA	1966 – 1968
Remo Golfarini	ITA	1968 – 1969
Gerhard Piaskowy	GER	1969 – 1970
Jose Hernandez	SP	1970 – 1972
Carlos Duran	ITA	1972 – 1973
Jacques Kechichian	FR	1973 – 1974
Jose Duran	SP	1974 – 1975
Eckhard Dagge	GER	1975 – 1976
Vito Antuofermo	ITA	1976
Maurice Hope *	GB	1976 – 1978
Gilbert Cohen	FR	1978 – 1979
Marijan Benes	YUG	1979 – 1981

Louis Acaries	FR	1981
Luigi Minchillo *	ITA	1981 – 1983
Herol Graham *	GB	1983 – 1984
Jimmy Cable	GB	1984 –

Middleweight

Georges Carpentier *	FR	1912 – 1928
Ercole Balzac	FR	1920 – 1921
Gus Platts	GB	1921
Johnny Basham	GB	1921
Ted Kid Lewis	GB	1921 – 1923
Roland Todd	GB	1923 – 1924
Bruno Frattini	ITA	1924 – 1925
Tommy Milligan *	GB	1925
Rene Devos *	BEL	1926 – 1927
Mario Bosisio	ITA	1928
Leone Jacovacci	ITA	1928 – 1929
Marcel Thil	FR	1929 – 1930
Mario Bosisio	ITA	1930 – 1931
Poldi Steinbach	AU	1931
Hein Domgorgen *	GER	1931
Ignacio Ara *	SP	1932 – 1933
Gustave Roth	BEL	1933 – 1934
Marcel Thil *	FR	1934 – 1938
Edouard Tenet	FR	1938
Bep Van Klaveren	HOL	1938
Anton Christoforidis	GRE	1938 – 1939
Edouard Tenet *	FR	1939
Josef Besselmann *	GER	1942 – 1943
Marcel Cerdan	FR	1947 – 1948
Cyrille Delannoit	BEL	1948
Marcel Cerdan *	FR	1948
Cyrille Delannoit	BEL	1948 – 1949
Tiberio Mitri *	ITA	1949 – 1950
Randy Turpin	GB	1951 – 1954
Tiberio Mitri	ITA	1954
Charles Humez	FR	1954 – 1958
Gustav Scholz *	GER	1958 – 1961
John Cowboy McCormack	GB	1961 – 1962
Chris Christensen	DEN	1962
Laszlo Papp *	HUN	1962 – 1964
Nino Benvenuti *	ITA	1965 – 1967
Juan Carlos Duran	ITA	1967 – 1969
Tom Bogs	DEN	1969 – 1970
Juan Carlos Duran	ITA	1970 – 1971
Jean-Claude Bouttier *	FR	1971 – 1972
Tom Bogs *	DEN	1973
Elio Calcabrini	ITA	1973 – 1974
Jean-Claude Bouttier	FR	1974
Kevin Finnegan	GB	1974 – 1975
Gratien Tonna *	FR	1975
Bunny Sterling	GB	1976
Angelo Jacopucci	ITA	1976
Germano Valsecchi	ITA	1976 – 1977
Alan Minter	GB	1977
Gratien Tonna *	FR	1977 – 1978
Alan Minter *	GB	1978 – 1979
Kevin Finnegan	GB	1980
Matteo Salvemini	ITA	1980
Tony Sibson *	GB	1980 – 1982
Louis Acaries	FR	1982 – 1984
Tony Sibson	GB	1984 –

L. Heavyweight

Georges Carpentier	FR	1913 – 1922
Battling Siki	FR	1922 – 1923
Emile Morelle	FR	1923
Raymond Bonnel	FR	1923 – 1924
Louis Clement	SWI	1924 – 1926
Herman Van T'Hof	HOL	1926
Fernand Delarge	BEL	1926 – 1927
Max Schmeling *	GER	1927 – 1928
Michele Bonaglia *	ITA	1929 – 1930
Ernst Pistulla *	GER	1931 – 1932
Adolf Heuser *	GER	1932
John Andersson *	SWE	1933
Martinez de Alfara	SP	1934
Marcel Thil *	FR	1934 – 1935
Merlo Preciso	ITA	1935
Hein Lazek	AU	1935 – 1936
Gustave Roth	BEL	1936 – 1938
Adolf Heuser *	GER	1938 – 1939
Luigi Musina *	ITA	1942 – 1946
Freddie Mills *	GB	1947 – 1950
Albert Yvel	FR	1950 – 1951
Don Cockell *	GB	1951 – 1952
Conny Rux *	GER	1952
Jacques Hairabedian	FR	1953 – 1954
Gerhard Hecht	GER	1954 – 1955
Willi Hoepner	GER	1955
Gerhard Hecht	GER	1955 – 1957
Artemio Calzavara	ITA	1957 – 1958
Willi Hoepner	GER	1958
Eric Schoepner *	GER	1958 – 1962
Giulio Rinaldi	ITA	1962 – 1964
Gustav Scholz *	GER	1964 – 1965
Giulio Rinaldi	ITA	1965 – 1966
Piero Del Papa	ITA	1966 – 1967
Lothar Stengel	GER	1967 – 1968
Tom Bogs *	DEN	1968 – 1969
Yvan Prebeg	YUG	1970 – 1971
Piero Del Papa	ITA	1970 – 1971
Conny Velensek	GER	1971 – 1972
Chris Finnegan	GB	1972
Rudiger Schmidtke	GER	1972 – 1973
John Conteh *	GB	1973 – 1974
Domenico Adinolfi	ITA	1974 – 1976
Mate Parlov *	YUG	1976 – 1977
Aldo Traversaro	ITA	1977 – 1979
Rudi Koopmans	HOL	1979 – 1984
Richard Caramonolis	FR	1984
Alex Blanchard	HOL	1984 –

Heavyweight

Gunner Moir	GB	1906 – 1909
Iron Hague	GB	1909 – 1911
Bomb. Billy Wells	GB	1911 – 1913
Georges Carpentier	FR	1913 – 1922

EUROPEAN CHAMPIONS, 1906–1984

Battling Siki *	FR	1922 – 1923
Erminio Spalla	ITA	1923 – 1926
Paolino Uzcudun *	SP	1926 – 1928
Pierre Charles	BEL	1929 – 1931
Hein Muller	GER	1931 – 1932
Pierre Charles	BEL	1932 – 1933
Paolino Uzcudun	SP	1933
Primo Carnera *	ITA	1933 – 1935
Pierre Charles	BEL	1935 – 1937
Arno Kolblin	GER	1937 – 1938
Hein Lazek	AU	1938 – 1939
Adolf Heuser	GER	1939
Max Schmeling *	GER	1939 – 1941
Olle Tandberg	SWE	1943
Karel Sys *	BEL	1943 – 1946
Bruce Woodcock *	GB	1946 – 1949
Jo Weidin	AU	1950 – 1951
Jack Gardner	GB	1951
Hein Ten Hoff	GER	1951 – 1952
Karel Sys	BEL	1952
Heinz Neuhaus	GER	1952 – 1955
Franco Cavicchi	ITA	1955 – 1956
Ingemar Johansson *	SWE	1956 – 1959
Dick Richardson	GB	1960 – 1962
Ingemar Johansson *	SWE	1962 – 1963
Henry Cooper *	GB	1964
Karl Mildenberger	GER	1964 – 1968
Henry Cooper *	GB	1968 – 1969
Peter Weiland	GER	1969 – 1970
Jose Urtain	SP	1970
Henry Cooper	GB	1970 – 1971
Joe Bugner	GB	1971
Jack Bodell	GB	1971
Jose Urtain	SP	1971 – 1972
Jurgen Blin	GER	1972
Joe Bugner *	GB	1972 – 1975
Richard Dunn	GB	1976
Joe Bugner *	GB	1976 – 1977
Jean-Pierre Coopman	BEL	1977
Lucien Rodriguez	SP	1977
Alfredo Evangelista	SP	1977 – 1979
Lorenzo Zanon *	SP	1979 – 1980
John L. Gardner *	GB	1980 – 1981
Lucien Rodriguez	SP	1981 –

17.01.49 *Billy Thompson (left) shown successfully defending his European Lightweight title against the Belgian Joseph Pieys.*

World Champions, 1891 – 1984

Shows the tenure of every World Champion at each weight. Under the heading of Status, recognition is defined for WBA/WBC Champions or Champions not generally recognised and Champions from weight divisions that were not generally recognised at the time. Note that Champions **in bold** are recognised in general as having the strongest claim to the Title. The Champions representing the WBA/WBC are viewed as undisputed.

CHAMPIONSHIP STATUS CODE:
AUSTR = Australia; CALIF = California; CAN = Canada; CLEVE = Cleveland; EBU = European Boxing Union; GB = Great Britain; IBU = International Boxing Union; LOUIS = Louisiana; MASS = Massachusets; MEX = Mexico; MICH = Michegan; NBA = National Boxing Association; NY = New York; USA = United States; WBA = World Boxing Association; WBC = World Boxing Council; † = Claimants.

*Undefeated champions

Title Holder	Birthplace	Tenure	Status
L. Flyweight			
Franco Udella *	Italy	1975	WBC
Jaime Rios	Panama	1975 – 1976	WBA
Luis Estaba	Venezuela	1975 – 1978	WBC
Juan Jose Guzman	Dom. Republic	1976	WBA
Yoko Gushiken	Japan	1976 – 1981	WBA
Freddie Castillo	Mexico	1978	WBC
Sor Vorasingh	Thailand	1978	WBC
Sung-Jun Kim	Korea	1978 – 1980	WBC
Shigeo Nakajima	Japan	1980	WBC
Hilario Zapata	Panama	1980 – 1982	WBC
Pedro Flores	Mexico	1981	WBA
Hwan-Jin Kim	Korea	1981 – 1982	WBA
Katsuo Tokashika	Japan	1981 – 1983	WBA
Amado Ursua	Mexico	1982	WBC
Tadashi Tomori	Japan	1982	WBC
Hilario Zapata	Panama	1982 – 1983	WBC
Jung-Koo Chang	Korea	1983 –	WBC
Lupe Madera	Mexico	1983 – 1984	WBA
Francisco Quiroz	Dom. Republic	1984 –	WBA
Flyweight			
Sid Smith	England	1913	GB
Bill Ladbury	England	1913 – 1914	GB
Percy Jones	Wales	1914	GB
Joe Symonds	England	1914 – 1916	GB
Jimmy Wilde	Wales	1916 – 1923	
Pancho Villa *	Philippines	1923 – 1925	
Fidel La Barba *	USA	1925 – 1927	
Frenchy Belanger	Canada	1927 – 1928	
Izzy Schwartz	USA	1927 – 1929	NY
Johnny McCoy	USA	1927 – 1928	CALIF
Newsboy Brown	Russia	1928	CALIF
Frankie Genaro	USA	1928 – 1929	
Johnny Hill	Scotland	1928 – 1929	GB/CALIF

Title Holder	Birthplace	Tenure	Status
Emile Pladner	France	1929	
Frankie Genaro	USA	1929 – 1931	
Willie La Morte	USA	1929 – 1930	NY
Midget Wolgast	USA	1930 – 1935	NY
Young Perez	Tunisia	1931 – 1932	
Jackie Brown	England	1932 – 1935	
Benny Lynch*	Scotland	1935 – 1938	
Small Montana	Philippines	1935 – 1937	NY
Valentin Angelmann	France	1936 – 1937	IBU
Peter Kane	England	1938 – 1943	
Jackie Paterson	Scotland	1943 – 1948	
Rinty Monaghan	Ireland	1947 – 1948	NBA
Rinty Monaghan *	Ireland	1948 – 1950	
Terry Allen	England	1950	
Dado Marino	Hawaii	1950 – 1952	
Yoshio Shirai	Japan	1952 – 1954	
Pascuel Perez	Argentina	1954 – 1960	
Pone Kingpetch	Thailand	1960 – 1962	
Fighting Harada	Japan	1962 – 1963	
Pone Kingpetch	Thailand	1963	
Hiroyuki Ebihara	Japan	1963 – 1964	
Pone Kingpetch	Thailand	1964 – 1965	
Salvatore Burruni	Italy	1965 – 1966	
Horacio Accavallo *	Argentina	1966 – 1968	WBA
Walter McGowan	Scotland	1966	WBC
Chartchai Chionoi	Thailand	1966 – 1969	WBC
Efren Torres	Mexico	1969 – 1970	WBC
Hiroyuki Ebihara	Japan	1969	WBA
Bernabe Villacampo	Philippines	1969 – 1970	WBA
Chartchai Chionoi	Thailand	1970	WBC
Berkrerk Chartvanchai	Thailand	1970	WBA
Masao Ohba *	Japan	1970 – 1973	WBA
Erbito Salavarria	Philippines	1970 – 1973	WBC
Betulio Gonzalez	Venezuela	1972	WBC
Venice Borkorsor *	Thailand	1972 – 1973	WBC
Chartchai Chionoi	Thailand	1973 – 1974	WBA
Betulio Gonzalez	Venezuela	1973 – 1974	WBC
Shoji Oguma	Japan	1974 –1975	WBC
Susumu Hanagata	Japan	1974 – 1975	WBA
Miguel Canto	Mexico	1975 – 1979	WBC
Erbito Salavarria	Philippines	1975 – 1976	WBA
Alfonso Lopez	Panama	1976	WBA
Guty Espadas	Mexico	1976 – 1978	WBA
Betulio Gonzalez	Venezuela	1978 – 1979	WBA
Chan-Hee Park	Korea	1979 – 1980	WBC
Luis Ibarra	Panama	1979 – 1980	WBA
Tae-Shik Kim	Korea	1980	WBA
Shoji Oguma	Japan	1980 – 1981	WBC
Peter Mathebula	S Africa	1980	WBA
Santos Laciar	Argentina	1981	WBA
Antonio Avelar	Mexico	1981 – 1982	WBC
Luis Ibarra	Panama	1981	WBA
Juan Herrera	Mexico	1981 – 1982	WBA
Prudencio Cardona	Colombia	1982	WBC
Santos Laciar	Argentina	1982 –	WBA
Freddie Castillo	Mexico	1982	WBC
Eleoncio Mercedes	Dom Republic	1982 – 1983	WBC
Charlic Magri	Tunisia	1983	WBC
Frank Cedeno	Philippines	1983 – 1984	WBC

Title Holder	Birthplace	Tenure	Status
Kojï Koboyashi	Japan	1984	WBC
Gabriel Bernal	Mexico	1984 –	WBC

S. Flyweight

Title Holder	Birthplace	Tenure	Status
Rafael Orono	Venezuela	1980 – 1981	WBC
Chulho Kim	Korea	1981 – 1982	WBC
Gustavo Ballas	Argentina	1981 – 1982	WBA
Jiro Watanabe	Japan	1982 –	WBA
Rafael Orono	Venezuela	1982 – 1983	WBC
Payo Pooltarat	Thailand	1983 –	WBC

Bantamweight

Title Holder	Birthplace	Tenure	Status
George Dixon	Canada	– 1891	
Tommy Kelly	USA	– 1892	†
Billy Plimmer	England	1892 – 1895	
Jimmy Barry	USA	1894 – 1899	USA
Pedlar Palmer	England	1895 – 1899	
Terry McGovern *	USA	1899 – 1900	
Harry Harris	USA	1901	
Harry Forbes	USA	1901 – 1903	
Frankie Neil	USA	1903 – 1904	
Joe Bowker *	England	1904 – 1905	
Jimmy Walsh *	USA	1905 – 1906	
Digger Stanley	England	1906 – 1910	
Kid Murphy	USA	1907 – 1908	USA
Johnny Coulon	Canada	1908 – 1914	
Digger Stanley	England	1910 – 1912	GB
Frankie Conley	Italy	1910 – 1911	CALIF
Charles Ledoux	France	1912 – 1913	GB
Kid Williams	Denmark	1913 – 1914	GB
Kid Williams	Denmark	1914 – 1917	
Pete Herman	USA	1917 – 1920	
Joe Lynch	USA	1920 – 1921	
Pete Herman	USA	1921	
Johnny Buff	USA	1921 – 1922	
Joe Lynch	USA	1922 – 1924	
Abe Goldstein	USA	1924	
Eddie Martin	USA	1924 – 1925	
Charlie Rosenberg *	USA	1925 – 1927	
Teddy Baldock	England	1927	GB
Bud Taylor	USA	1927 – 1928	
Willie Smith	S Africa	1927 – 1929	GB
Bushy Graham	Italy	1928 – 1929	
Al Brown	Panama	1929 – 1935	
Pete Sanstol	Norway	1931	CAN
Sixto Escobar	Spain	1934 – 1935	NBA
Baltazar Sangchilli	Spain	1935 – 1936	
Lou Salica	USA	1935	NBA
Sixto Escobar	Spain	1935 – 1936	NBA
Tony Marino	USA	1936	
Sixto Escobar	Spain	1936 – 1937	
Harry Jeffra	USA	1937 – 1938	
Sixto Escobar *	Spain	1938 – 1939	
Lou Salica	USA	1940 – 1942	
Manuel Ortiz	USA	1942 – 1947	
Harold Dade	USA	1947	

Title Holder	Birthplace	Tenure	Status
Manuel Ortiz	USA	1947 – 1950	
Vic Toweel	S Africa	1950 – 1952	
Jimmy Carruthers *	Australia	1952 – 1954	
Robert Cohen	Algeria	1954 – 1956	
Raton Macias	Mexico	1955 – 1957	NBA
Mario D'Agata	Italy	1956 – 1957	
Alphonse Halimi	Algeria	1957 – 1959	
Joe Becerra	Mexico	1959 – 1960	
Alphonse Halimi	Algeria	1960 – 1961	EBU
Eder Jofre	Brazil	1960 – 1965	
Johnny Caldwell	Ireland	1961 – 1962	EBU
Fighting Harada	Japan	1965 – 1968	
Lionel Rose	Australia	1968 – 1969	
Ruben Olivares	Mexico	1969 – 1970	
Chucho Castillo	Mexico	1970 – 1971	
Ruben Olivares	Mexico	1971 – 1972	
Rafael Herrera	Mexico	1972	
Enrique Pinder	Panama	1972 – 1973	
Romeo Anaya	Mexico	1973	WBA
Rafael Herrera	Mexico	1973 – 1974	WBC
Arnold Taylor	S Africa	1973 – 1974	WBA
Soo-Hwan Hong	Korea	1974 – 1975	WBA
Rodolfo Martinez	Mexico	1974 – 1976	WBC
Alfonso Zamora	Mexico	1975 – 1977	WBA
Carlos Zarate	Mexico	1976 – 1979	WBC
Jorge Lujan	Panama	1977 – 1980	WBA
Lupe Pintor *	Mexico	1979 – 1983	WBC
Julian Solis	Puerto Rico	1980	WBA
Jeff Chandler	USA	1980 – 1984	WBA
Alberto Davila	USA	1983 –	WBC
Richard Sandoval	USA	1984 –	WBA

J. Featherweight

Title Holder	Birthplace	Tenure	Status
Jack Kid Wolfe	USA	1922 – 1923	NY
Carl Duane	USA	1923 – 1924	NY
Rigoberto Riasca	Panama	1976	WBC
Royal Kobayashi	Japan	1976	WBC
Dong-Kyun Yum	Korea	1976 – 1977	WBC
Wilfredo Gomez *	Puerto Rico	1977 – 1983	WBC
Soo-Hwan Hong	Korea	1977 –1978	WBA
Ricardo Cardona	Colombia	1978 – 1980	WBA
Leo Randolph	USA	1980	WBA
Sergio Palma	Argentina	1980 – 1982	WBA
Leo Cruz	Dom Republic	1982 – 1984	WBA
Jaime Garza	USA	1983 –	WBC
Loris Stecca	Italy	1984	WBA
Victor Callejas	Puerto Rica	1984	WBA

Featherweight

Title Holder	Birthplace	Tenure	Status
Young Griffo *	Australia	– 1891	
George Dixon	Canada	1891 – 1897	
Solly Smith	USA	1897 – 1898	
Ben Jordan	England	1898 – 1899	GB

Title Holder	Birthplace	Tenure	Status
Dave Sullivan	Ireland	1898	
George Dixon	Canada	1898 – 1900	
Eddie Santry	USA	1899 – 1900	GB
Terry McGovern	USA	1900 – 1901	
Young Corbett II	USA	1901 – 1904	
Jimmy Britt *	USA	1904	
Abe Attell	USA	1904	
Brooklyn Tommy Sullivan *	USA	1904 – 1905	
Abe Attell	USA	1906 – 1912	
Jim Driscoll	Wales	1912 – 1913	GB
Johnny Kilbane	USA	1912 – 1923	
Johnny Dundee	Italy	1922 – 1923	NY
Eugene Criqui	France	1923	
Johnny Dundee *	Italy	1923 – 1924	
Kid Kaplan *	Russia	1925 – 1927	
Honeyboy Finnegan	USA	1926 – 1927	MASS
Benny Bass	Russia	1927 – 1928	
Tony Canzoneri	USA	1928	
Andre Routis	France	1928 – 1929	
Battling Battalino *	USA	1929 – 1932	
Tommy Paul	USA	1932 – 1933	NBA
Kid Chocolate	Cuba	1932 – 1933	
Freddie Miller	USA	1933 – 1936	
Baby Arizmendi	Mexico	1935 – 1936	MEX/CALIF
Mike Belloise	USA	1936	NY
Pete Sarron	USA	1936 – 1937	
Henry Armstrong *	USA	1936 – 1938	
Maurice Holtzer	France	1937 – 1938	IBU
Joey Archibald	USA	1938 – 1940	
Leo Rodak	USA	1938 – 1939	NBA
Pete Scalzo	USA	1940 – 1941	NBA
Jimmy Perrin	USA	1940	LOUIS
Harry Jeffra	USA	1940 – 1941	
Joey Archibald	USA	1941	
Richie Lemos	USA	1941	NBA
Chalkey Wright	Mexico	1941 – 1942	
Jackie Wilson	USA	1941 – 1943	NBA
Willie Pep	USA	1942 – 1946	
Jackie Callura	Canada	1943	NBA
Phil Terranova	USA	1943 – 1944	NBA
Sal Bartolo	USA	1944 – 1946	NBA
Willie Pep	USA	1946 – 1948	
Sandy Saddler	USA	1948 – 1949	
Willie Pep	USA	1949 – 1950	
Sandy Saddler *	USA	1950 – 1957	
Hogan Kid Bassey	Nigeria	1957 – 1959	
Davey Moore	USA	1959 – 1963	
Sugar Ramos	Cuba	1963 – 1964	
Vicente Saldivar *	Mexico	1964 – 1967	
Howard Winstone	Wales	1968	
Paul Rojas	USA	1968	WBA
Jose Legra	Cuba	1968 – 1969	WBC
Shozo Saijyo	Japan	1968 – 1971	WBA
Johnny Famechon	France	1969 – 1970	WBC
Vicente Saldivar	Mexico	1970	WBC
Kuniaki Shibata	Japan	1970 – 1972	WBC
Antonio Gomez	Venezuela	1971 – 1972	WBA
Clemente Sanchez	Mexico	1972	WBC
Ernesto Marcel *	Panama	1972 – 1974	WBA

Title Holder	Birthplace	Tenure	Status
Jose Legra	Cuba	1972 – 1973	WBC
Eder Jofre *	Brazil	1973 – 1974	WBC
Ruben Olivares	Mexico	1974	WBA
Bobby Chacon	USA	1974 – 1975	WBC
Alexis Arguello *	Nicaragua	1974 – 1977	WBA
Ruben Olivares	Mexico	1975	WBC
David Kotey	Ghana	1975 – 1976	WBC
Danny Lopez	USA	1976 – 1980	WBC
Rafael Ortega	Panama	1977	WBA
Cecilio Lastra	Spain	1977 – 1978	WBA
Eusebio Pedroza	Panama	1978 –	WBA
Salvador Sanchez *	Mexico	1980 – 1982	WBC
Juan Laporte	Puerto Rico	1982 – 1984	WBC
Wilfredo Gomez	Puerto Rico	1984 –	WBC

J. Lightweight

Title Holder	Birthplace	Tenure	Status
Johnny Dundee	Italy	1921 – 1923	NY
Jack Bernstein	USA	1923	NY
Johnny Dundee	Italy	1923 – 1924	NY
Kid Sullivan	USA	1924 – 1925	NY
Mike Ballerino	USA	1925	NY
Tod Morgan	USA	1925 – 1929	NY
Benny Bass	Russia	1929 – 1931	NY
Kid Chocolate	Cuba	1931 – 1933	NY
Frankie Klick	USA	1933 – 1934	NY
Sandy Saddler	USA	1949 – 1950	CLEVE
Harold Gomes	USA	1959 – 1960	
Flash Elorde	Philippines	1960 – 1967	
Yoshiaki Numata	Japan	1967	
Hiroshi Kobayashi	Japan	1967 – 1969	
Hiroshi Kobayashi	Japan	1969 – 1971	WBA
Rene Barrientos	Philippines	1969 – 1970	WBC
Yoshiaki Numata	Japan	1970 – 1971	WBC
Alfredo Marcano	Venezuela	1971 – 1972	WBA
Ricardo Arrendondo	Mexico	1971 – 1974	WBC
Ben Villaflor	Philippines	1972 – 1973	WBA
Kuniaki Shibata	Japan	1973	WBA
Ben Villaflor	Philippines	1973 – 1976	WBA
Kuniaki Shibata	Japan	1974 – 1975	WBC
Alfredo Escalera	Puerto Rico	1975 – 1978	WBC
Sam Serrano	Puerto Rico	1976 – 1980	WBA
Alexis Arguello *	Nicaragua	1978 – 1980	WBC
Yasutsune Uehara	Japan	1980 – 1981	WBA
Rafael Limon	Mexico	1980 – 1981	WBC
Cornelius Boza-Edwards	Uganda	1981	WBC
Sam Serrano	Puerto Rico	1981 – 1983	WBA
Rolando Navarrete	Philippines	1981 – 1982	WBC
Rafael Limon	Mexico	1982	WBC
Bobby Chacon *	USA	1982 – 1983	WBC
Roger Mayweather	USA	1983 – 1984	WBA
Hector Camacho	Puerto Rico	1983 –	WBC
Rocky Lockridge	USA	1984 –	WBA

Lightweight

Title Holder	Birthplace	Tenure	Status
George Lavigne	USA	1896 – 1899	
Frank Erne	Switzerland	1899 – 1902	

Title Holder	Birthplace	Tenure	Status
Joe Gans	USA	1902 – 1908	
Jimmy Britt	USA	1904 – 1905	CALIF
Battling Nelson	Denmark	1905 – 1906	CALIF
Battling Nelson	Denmark	1908 – 1910	
Ad Wolgast	USA	1910 – 1912	
Willie Ritchie	USA	1912 – 1914	
Freddie Welsh	Wales	1914 – 1917	
Benny Leonard *	USA	1917 – 1925	
Jimmy Goodrich	USA	1925	
Rocky Kansas	USA	1925 – 1926	
Sammy Mandell	USA	1926 – 1930	
Al Singer	USA	1930	
Tony Canzoneri	USA	1930 – 1933	
Barney Ross *	USA	1933 – 1935	
Tony Canzoneri	USA	1935 – 1936	
Lou Ambers	USA	1936 – 1938	
Henry Armstrong	USA	1938 – 1939	
Lou Ambers	USA	1939 – 1940	
Sammy Angott	USA	1940 – 1941	NBA
Lew Jenkins	USA	1940 – 1941	
Sammy Angott *	USA	1941 – 1942	
Beau Jack	USA	1942 – 1943	
Bob Montgomery	USA	1943	NY
Sammy Angott	USA	1943 – 1944	
Beau Jack	USA	1943 – 1944	NY
Bob Montgomery	USA	1944 – 1947	NY
Juan Zurita	Mexico	1944 – 1945	
Ike Williams	USA	1945 – 1951	
Jimmy Carter	USA	1951 – 1952	
Lauro Salas	Mexico	1952	
Jimmy Carter	USA	1952 – 1954	
Paddy De Marco	USA	1954	
Jimmy Carter	USA	1954 – 1955	
Wallace Bud Smith	USA	1955 – 1956	
Joe Brown	USA	1956 – 1962	
Carlos Ortiz	Puerto Rico	1962 – 1965	
Kenny Lane	USA	1963 – 1964	MICH
Ismael Laguna	Panama	1965	
Carlos Ortiz	Puerto Rico	1965 – 1968	
Carlos Teo Cruz	Dom Republic	1968 – 1969	
Mando Ramos	USA	1969 – 1970	
Ismael Laguna	Panama	1970	
Ken Buchanan	Scotland	1970 – 1971	
Ken Buchanan	Scotland	1971 – 1972	WBA
Pedro Carasco	Spain	1971 – 1972	WBC
Mando Ramos	USA	1972	WBC
Roberto Duran	Panama	1972 – 1979	WBA
Chango Carmona	Mexico	1972	WBC
Rodolfo Gonzalez	Mexico	1972 – 1974	WBC
Guts Ishimatsu	Japan	1974 – 1976	WBC
Esteban de Jesus *	Puerto Rico	1976 – 1978	WBC
Roberto Duran *	Panama	1978 – 1979	
Jim Watt	Scotland	1979 – 1981	WBC
Ernesto Espana	Venezuela	1979 – 1980	WBA
Hilmer Kenty	USA	1980 – 1981	WBA
Sean O'Grady *	USA	1981	WBA
Alexis Arguello *	Nicaragua	1981 – 1983	WBC
Claude Noel	Trinidad	1981	WBA
Arturo Frias	USA	1981 – 1982	WBA

Title Holder	Birthplace	Tenure	Status
Ray Mancini	USA	1982 – 1984	WBA
Edwin Rosario	Puerto Rico	1983 –	WBC
Livingstone Bramble	USA	1984 –	WBA

J. Welterweight

Pinky Mitchell	USA	1922 – 1926	NY
Mushy Callahan	USA	1926 – 1930	NY/NBA
Jack Kid Berg	England	1930 – 1931	NY/NBA
Tony Canzoneri	USA	1931 – 1932	NY/NBA
Johnny Jadick	USA	1932 – 1933	NY/NBA
Battling Shaw	Mexico	1933	NY/NBA
Tony Canzoneri	USA	1933	NY/NBA
Barney Ross	USA	1933 – 1935	NY/NBA
Tippy Larkin	USA	1946	NY/NBA
Carlos Ortiz	Puerto Rico	1959 – 1960	
Duilio Loi	Italy	1960 – 1962	
Eddie Perkins	USA	1962	
Duilio Loi *	Italy	1962 – 1963	
Roberto Cruz	Philippines	1963	
Eddie Perkins	USA	1963 – 1965	
Carlos Hernandez	Venezuela	1965 – 1966	
Sandro Lopopolo	Italy	1966 – 1967	
Paul Fujii	Hawaii	1967 – 1968	
Nicolino Loche	Argentina	1968 – 1972	WBA
Pedro Adigue	Philippines	1968 – 1970	WBC
Bruno Arcari	Italy	1970 – 1974	WBC
Alfonso Frazer	Panama	1972	WBA
Antonio Cervantes	Colombia	1972 – 1976	WBA
Perico Fernandez	Spain	1974 – 1975	WBC
Saensak Muangsurin	Thailand	1975 – 1976	WBC
Wilfred Benitez *	USA	1976 – 1977	WBA
Miguel Velasquez	Spain	1976	WBC
Saensak Muangsurin	Thailand	1976 – 1978	WBC
Antonio Cervantes	Colombia	1977 – 1980	WBA
Sang-Hyun Kim	Korea	1978 – 1980	WBC
Saoul Mamby	USA	1980 – 1982	WBC
Aaron Pryor *	USA	1980 – 1983	WBA
Leroy Haley	USA	1982 – 1983	WBC
Bruce Curry	USA	1983 – 1984	WBC
Johnny Bumphus	USA	1984	WBA
Bill Costello	USA	1984 –	WBC
Gene Hatcher	USA	1984 –	WBA

Welterweight

Billy Smith	USA	1892 – 1894
Tommy Ryan	USA	1894 – 1896
Kid McCoy *	USA	1896 – 1898
Billy Smith	USA	1898 – 1900
Rube Ferns	USA	1900
Matty Matthews	USA	1900 – 1901
Rube Ferns	USA	1901
Joe Walcott	Barbados	1901 – 1904
Dixie Kid *	USA	1904

Title Holder	Birthplace	Tenure	Status
Joe Walcott	USA	1904 – 1906	
Honey Mellody	USA	1906 – 1907	
Mike Twin Sullivan *	USA	1907 – 1908	
Harry Lewis	USA	1908 – 1913	
Jimmy Gardner	Ireland	1908	†
Jimmy Clabby	USA	1910 – 1911	†
Waldemar Holberg	Denmark	1914	
Tom McCormick	Ireland	1914	
Matt Wells	England	1914 – 1915	
Mike Glover	USA	1915	
Jack Britton	USA	1915	
Ted Kid Lewis	England	1915 – 1916	
Jack Britton	USA	1916 – 1917	
Ted Kid Lewis	England	1917 – 1919	
Jack Britton	USA	1919 – 1922	
Mickey Walker	USA	1922 – 1926	
Pete Latzo	USA	1926 – 1927	
Joe Dundee	Italy	1927 – 1928	
Young Jack Thompson	USA	1928 – 1929	
Jackie Fields	USA	1929 – 1930	
Young Jack Thompson	USA	1930	
Tommy Freeman	USA	1930 – 1931	
Young Jack Thompson	USA	1931	
Lou Brouillard	Canada	1931 – 1932	
Jackie Fields	USA	1932 – 1933	
Young Corbett III	Italy	1933	
Jimmy McClarnin	Ireland	1933 – 1934	
Barney Ross	USA	1934	
Jimmy McLarnin	Ireland	1934 – 1935	
Barney Ross	USA	1935 – 1938	
Henry Armstrong	USA	1938 – 1940	
Fritzie Zivic	USA	1940 – 1941	
Red Cochrane	USA	1941 – 1946	
Marty Servo *	USA	1946	
Sugar Ray Robinson *	USA	1946 – 1951	
Johnny Bratton	USA	1951	NBA
Kid Gavilan	Cuba	1951 – 1954	
Johnny Saxton	USA	1954 – 1955	
Tony de Marco	USA	1955	
Carmen Basilio	USA	1955 – 1956	
Johnny Saxton	USA	1956	
Carmen Basilio	USA	1956 – 1957	
Virgil Akins *	USA	1958	
Don Jordan	USA	1958 – 1960	
Benny Kid Paret	Cuba	1960 – 1961	
Emile Griffiths	Virgin Islands	1961	
Benny Kid Paret	Cuba	1961 – 1962	
Emile Griffith	Virgin Islands	1962 – 1963	
Louis Rodriguez	Cuba	1963	
Emile Griffith *	Virgin Islands	1963 – 1966	
Charley Shipes	USA	1966 – 1967	CALIF
Curtis Cokes	USA	1966 – 1969	
Jose Napoles	Cuba	1969 – 1970	
Billy Backus	USA	1970 – 1971	
Jose Napoles	Cuba	1971 – 1975	
Hedgemon Lewis	USA	1972 – 1974	NY
Angel Espada	Puerto Rico	1975 – 1976	WBA
John H. Stracey	England	1975 – 1976	WBC
Carlos Palomino	Mexico	1976 – 1979	WBC
Pipino Cuevas	Mexico	1976 – 1980	WBA

Title Holder	Birthplace	Tenure	Status
Wilfred Benitez	USA	1979	WBC
Sugar Ray Leonard	USA	1979 – 1980	WBC
Roberto Duran	Panama	1980	WBC
Thomas Hearns	USA	1980 – 1981	WBA
Sugar Ray Leonard	USA	1980 – 1981	WBC
Sugar Ray Leonard *	USA	1981 – 1982	
Don Curry	USA	1983 –	WBA
Milton McCrory	USA	1983 –	WBC

L. Middleweight

Title Holder	Birthplace	Tenure	Status
Denny Moyer	USA	1962 – 1963	
Ralph Dupas	USA	1963	
Sandro Mazzinghi	Italy	1963 – 1965	
Nino Benvenuti	Italy	1965 – 1966	
Ki-Soo Kim	Korea	1966 – 1968	
Sandro Mazzinghi *	Italy	1968	
Freddie Little	USA	1969 – 1970	
Carmelo Bossi	Italy	1970 – 1971	
Koichi Wajima	Japan	1971 – 1974	
Oscar Albarado	USA	1974 – 1975	
Koichi Wajima	Japan	1975	
Miguel De Oliveira	Brazil	1975 – 1976	WBC
Jae-Do Yuh	Korea	1975 – 1976	WBA
Elisha Obed	Bahamas	1975 – 1976	WBC
Koichi Wajima	Japan	1976	WBA
Jose Duran	Spain	1976	WBA
Eckhard Dagge	Germany	1976 – 1977	WBC
Angel Castellini	Argentina	1976 – 1977	WBA
Eddie Gazo	Nicaragua	1977 – 1978	WBA
Rocky Mattioli	Italy	1977 – 1979	WBC
Masashi Kudo	Japan	1978 – 1979	WBA
Maurice Hope	Antigua	1979 – 1981	WBC
Ayub Kalule	Uganda	1979 – 1981	WBA
Wilfred Benitez	USA	1981 – 1982	WBC
Sugar Ray Leonard *	USA	1981	WBA
Tadashi Mihara	Japan	1981 – 1982	WBA
Davey Moore	USA	1982 – 1983	WBA
Thomas Hearns	USA	1982 –	WBC
Roberto Duran *	Panama	1983 – 1984	WBA

Middleweight

Title Holder	Birthplace	Tenure	Status
Nonpareil Dempsey	Ireland	– 1891	
Bob Fitzsimmons *	England	1891 – 1896	
Kid McCoy *	USA	1896 – 1898	
Tommy Ryan *	USA	1898 – 1907	
Stanley Ketchel	USA	1907 – 1908	
Billy Papke	USA	1908	
Stanley Ketchell	USA	1908 – 1910	
Billy Papke	USA	1910 – 1913	
Cyclone Thompson	USA	1911	†
Frank Mantell	USA	1912	†
Frank Klaus	USA	1913	
George Chip	USA	1913 – 1914	
Eddie McGoorty	USA	1914	AUSTR

Title Holder	Birthplace	Tenure	Status
Al McCoy	USA	1914 – 1917	
Jeff Smith	USA	1914	AUSTR
Mick King	Australia	1914	AUSTR
Jeff Smith	USA	1914 – 1915	AUSTR
Les D'Arcy	Australia	1915 – 1917	AUSTR
Mike O'Dowd	USA	1917 – 1920	
Johnny Wilson	USA	1920 – 1923	
Bryan Downey	USA	1921	OHIO
Dave Rosenberg	USA	1922	NY
Jock Malone	USA	1922 – 1923	OHIO
Mike O'Dowd	USA	1922	NY
Harry Greb	USA	1923 – 1926	
Tiger Flowers	USA	1926	
Mickey Walker *	USA	1926 – 1931	
Gorilla Jones	USA	1931 – 1932	
Marcel Thil	France	1932 – 1937	
Ben Jeby	USA	1932	NY
Lou Brouillard	Canada	1933	NY/NBA
Vince Dundee	USA	1933 – 1934	NY/NBA
Teddy Yarosz	USA	1934 – 1935	NY/NBA
Babe Risko	USA	1935 – 1936	NY/NBA
Freddie Steele	USA	1936 – 1938	NY/NBA
Fred Apostoli	USA	1937 – 1939	
Al Hostak	USA	1938	NBA
Solly Krieger	USA	1938 – 1939	NBA
Al Hostak	USA	1939 – 1940	NBA
Ceferino Garcia	Philippines	1939 – 1940	
Ken Overlin	USA	1940 – 1941	
Tony Zale	USA	1940 – 1941	NBA
Billy Soose	USA	1941	
Tony Zale	USA	1941 – 1947	
Rocky Graziano	USA	1947 – 1948	
Tony Zale	USA	1948	
Marcel Cerdan	Algeria	1948 – 1949	
Jake La Motta	USA	1949 – 1951	
Sugar Ray Robinson	USA	1951	
Randy Turpin	England	1951	
Sugar Ray Robinson *	USA	1951 – 1952	
Carl Bobo Olson	Hawaii	1953 – 1955	
Sugar Ray Robinson	USA	1955 – 1957	
Gene Fullmer	USA	1957	
Sugar Ray Robinson	USA	1957	
Carmen Basilio	USA	1957 – 1958	
Sugar Ray Robinson	USA	1958 – 1960	
Gene Fullmer	USA	1959 – 1962	NBA
Paul Pender	USA	1960 – 1961	
Terry Downes	England	1961 – 1962	
Paul Pender *	USA	1962	
Dick Tiger	Nigeria	1962 – 1963	
Joey Giardello	USA	1963 – 1965	
Dick Tiger	Nigeria	1965 – 1966	
Emile Griffith	Virgin Islands	1966 – 1967	
Nino Benvenuti	Italy	1967	
Emile Griffith	Virgin Islands	1967 – 1968	
Nino Benvenuti	Italy	1968 – 1970	
Carlos Monzon	Argentina	1970 – 1974	
Carlos Monzon	Argentina	1974 – 1976	WBA
Rodrigo Valdez	Colombia	1974 – 1976	WBC
Carlos Monzon *	Argentina	1976 – 1977	

Title Holder	Birthplace	Tenure	Status
Rodrigo Valdez	Colombia	1977 – 1978	
Hugo Corro	Argentina	1978 – 1979	
Vito Antuofermo	Italy	1979 – 1980	
Alan Minter	England	1980	
Marvin Hagler	USA	1980 –	

L. Heavyweight

Jack Root	Austria	1903	
George Gardner	Ireland	1903	
Bob Fitzsimmons	England	1903 – 1905	
Jack O'Brien *	USA	1905 – 1912	
Jack Dillon	USA	1912 – 1916	
Battling Levinsky	USA	1916 – 1920	
Georges Carpentier	France	1920 – 1922	
Battling Siki	Senegal	1922 – 1923	
Mike McTigue	Ireland	1923 – 1925	
Paul Berlenbach	USA	1925 – 1926	
Jack Delaney *	Canada	1926 – 1927	
Jim Slattery	USA	1927	NBA
Tommy Loughran *	USA	1927 – 1929	
Jim Slattery	USA	1930	
Maxie Rosenbloom	USA	1930 – 1934	
George Nichols	USA	1932	NBA
Lou Scozza	USA	1932	NBA
Bob Godwin	USA	1933	NBA
Bob Olin	USA	1934 – 1935	
Heinz Lazek	Austria	1935 – 1936	IBU
John Henry Lewis *	USA	1935 – 1939	
Gustave Roth	Belgium	1936 – 1938	IBU
Adolf Heuser	Germany	1938	IBU
Tiger Jack Fox	USA	1938 – 1939	NY
Melio Bettina	USA	1939	
Len Harvey	England	1939 – 1942	GB
Billy Conn *	USA	1939 – 1940	
Anton Christoforidis	Greece	1941	NBA
Gus Lesnevich	USA	1941 – 1948	
Freddie Mills	England	1942 – 1946	GB
Freddie Mills	England	1948 – 1950	
Joey Maxim	USA	1950 – 1952	
Archie Moore	USA	1952 – 1962	
Harold Johnson	USA	1961 – 1962	NBA
Harold Johnson	USA	1962 – 1963	
Willie Pastrano	USA	1963 – 1965	
Eddie Cotton	USA	1963 – 1966	MICH
Jose Torres	Puerto Rico	1965 – 1966	
Dick Tiger	Nigeria	1966 – 1968	
Bob Foster	USA	1968 – 1970	
Bob Foster	USA	1970 – 1972	WBC
Vicente Rondon	Venezuela	1971 – 1972	WBA
Bob Foster *	USA	1972 – 1974	
John Conteh *	England	1974 – 1977	WBC
Victor Galindez	Argentina	1974 – 1978	WBA
Miguel Cuello	Argentina	1977 – 1978	WBC
Mate Parlov	Yugoslavia	1978	WBC
Mike Rossman	USA	1978 – 1979	WBA
Marvin Johnson	USA	1978 – 1979	WBC
Victor Galindez	Argentina	1979	WBA
Matthew Saad Muhammad	USA	1979 – 1981	WBC

Title Holder	Birthplace	Tenure	Status
Marvin Johnson	USA	1979 – 1981	WBA
Eddie Mustafa Muhammad	USA	1980 – 1981	WBA
Michael Spinks	USA	1981 –	WBA
Dwight Braxton	USA	1981 – 1983	WBC
Michael Spinks	USA	1983 –	

Cruiserweight

Marvin Camel	USA	1979 – 1980	WBC
Carlos De Leon	Puerto Rico	1980 – 1982	WBC
Ossie Ocasio	Puerto Rico	1982 –	WBA
S. T. Gordon	USA	1982 – 1983	WBC
Carlos De Leon	Puerto Rico	1983 –	WBC

Heavyweight

John L. Sullivan	USA	– 1892	
James J. Corbett	USA	1892 – 1897	
Bob Fitzsimmons	England	1897 – 1899	
James J. Jeffries *	USA	1899 – 1905	
Marvin Hart	USA	1905 – 1906	
Tommy Burns	Canada	1906 – 1908	
Jack Johnson	USA	1908 – 1915	
Jess Willard	USA	1915 – 1919	
Jack Dempsey	USA	1919 – 1926	
Gene Tunney *	USA	1926 – 1928	
Max Schmeling	Germany	1930 – 1932	
Jack Sharkey	USA	1932 – 1933	
Primo Carnera	Italy	1933 – 1934	
Max Baer	USA	1934 – 1935	
James J. Braddock	USA	1935 – 1937	
Joe Louis *	USA	1937 – 1949	
Ezzard Charles	USA	1949 – 1951	
Jersey Joe Walcott	USA	1951 – 1952	
Rocky Marciano *	USA	1952 – 1956	
Floyd Patterson	USA	1956 – 1959	
Ingemar Johansson	Sweden	1959 – 1960	
Floyd Patterson	USA	1960 – 1962	
Sonny Liston	USA	1962 – 1964	
Muhammad Ali *	USA	1964 – 1970	
Ernie Terrell	USA	1965 – 1967	WBA
Joe Frazier	USA	1968 – 1970	NY
Jimmy Ellis	USA	1968 – 1970	WBA
Joe Frazier	USA	1970 – 1973	
George Foreman	USA	1973 – 1974	
Muhammad Ali	USA	1974 – 1978	
Leon Spinks	USA	1978	
Larry Holmes *	USA	1978 – 1983	WBC
Muhammad Ali *	USA	1978 – 1979	WBA
John Tate	USA	1979 – 1980	WBA
Mike Weaver	USA	1980 – 1982	WBA
Mike Dokes	USA	1982 – 1983	WBA
Gerrie Coetzee	S Africa	1983 –	WBA
Tim Witherspoon	USA	1984 –	WBC

World Champions who boxed in British Rings 1929 – 1984

Includes all non-British disputed or undisputed World Champions who at any stage of their careers boxed in British rings following the inception of the BBBC (1929). World Championship contests are indicated by printing the opponent's name in **bold**. The complete records of both Dick Tiger and Hogan Kid Bassey are shown separately at the end of this section as a large part of their careers were spent in Britain.

Championship Status Code:
EBU = European Boxing Union; GB = Great Britain; IBU = International Boxing Union; NBA = National Boxing Association; WBA = World Boxing Association; WBC = World Boxing Council

Virgil Akins World Welterweight Champion (Undisputed), 06.06.58 – 05.12.58

08.03.60 Wally Swift **L** PTS 10 London

Muhammad Ali World Heavyweight Champion (WBC Version) 25.02.64 – 03.02.70; (Undisputed) 30.10.74 – 15.02.78; (WBA Version) 15.09.78 – 01.09.79

18.06.63 Henry Cooper **W** RSC 5 London
21.05.66 **Henry Cooper** **W** RSC 6 London
06.08.66 **Brian London** **W** CO 3 London

Vito Antuofermo World Middleweight Champion (Undisputed) 30.06.79 – 16.03.80

28.06.80 **Alan Minter** **L** RTD 8 London

Valentin Angelmann World Flyweight Champion (IBU Version) 06.01.36 – 03.09.37

10.11.30 Tommy Brown **L** PTS 10 Manchester
12.06.33 **Jackie Brown** **L** PTS 15 London
11.09.33 Jackie Brown **L** PTS 15 Manchester
30.10.33 Herbie Hill **W** RSC 5 London
18.12.33 Mickey Maguire **L** DIS 8 Newcastle
05.03.34 Mickey Maguire **W** PTS 12 Newcastle
16.04.34 Mickey Maguire **W** RTD 10 Manchester
18.06.34 **Jackie Brown** DREW 15 Manchester
26.09.34 Benny Lynch **L** PTS 12 Glasgow
12.11.36 Peter Kane **L** PTS 12 Liverpool
20.10.37 Jim McStravick **W** PTS 10 Belfast
30.03.38 Jimmy Warnock **W** RSC 5 Belfast
15.05.39 Jackie Paterson DREW 10 Glasgow

Alexis Arguello World Featherweight Champion (WBA Version) 23.11.74 – 20.06.77; World J. Lightweight Champion (WBC Version) 28.01.78 – 09.08.80; World Lightweight Champion (WBC Version) 20.06.81 – 26.02.83

20.06.81 **Jim Watt** **W** PTS 15 London

Henry Armstrong World Featherweight Champion (Californian/Mexico/New York Version) 04.08.36 – 29.10.37; (Undisputed) 29.10.37 – 17.08.38; World Lightweight Champion (Undisputed) 17.08.38 – 22.08.39; World Welterweight Champion (Undisputed) 31.05.38 – 04.10.40

25.05.39 **Ernie Roderick** **W** PTS 15 London

Max Baer World Heavyweight Champion (Undisputed) 14.06.34 – 13.06.35

15.04.37 Tommy Farr **L** PTS 12 London
27.05.37 Ben Foord **W** RSC 9 London

Al Brown World Bantamweight Champion (Undisputed) 18.06.29 – 26.06.34; (Disputed) 26.06.34 – 01.06.35

10.03.31 Willie Farrell **W** CO 3 Manchester
31.03.31 Doug Parker **W** RSC 11 Newcastle
13.04.31 Jack Garland **W** PTS 15 London
21.05.31 Teddy Baldock **W** RSC 12 London
15.06.31 Johnny Cuthbert **L** DIS 8 London
13.06.32 Nel Tarleton DREW 15 Liverpool
01.12.32 Dick Burke **W** PTS 12 Sheffield
04.03.33 Johnny Peters **W** PTS 15 London
30.04.33 Tommy Hyams **W** RSC 9 London
.06.33 Art Boddington **W** CO 4 London
12.06.33 Dave Crowley **W** PTS 10 London
03.07.33 **Johnny King** **W** PTS 15 London

Joe Brown World Lightweight Champion (Undisputed) 24.08.56 – 21.04.62

18.04.61 **Dave Charnley** **W** PTS 15 London
25.02.63 Dave Charnley **L** CO 6 Manchester
09.03.65 Vic Andreetti **L** RSC 5 London

Salvatore Burruni World Flyweight Champion (Undisputed) 23.04.65 – 14.06.66

14.06.66 **Walter McGowan** L PTS 15 London

Mushy Callahan World J. Welterweight Champion (Undisputed) 21.09.26 – 18.02.30

18.02.30 **Jackie Kid Berg** L RTD 10 London

Primo Carnera World Heavyweight Champion (Undisputed) 29.06.33 – 14.06.34

17.10.29 Jack Stanley **W** CO 1 London
18.11.29 Young Stribling **W** DIS 4 London
17.12.29 Franz Diener **W** RSC 6 London
18.12.30 Reg Meen **W** CO 2 London
23.03.32 George Cook **W** CO 4 London
07.04.32 Don McCorkindale **W** PTS 10 London
30.05.32 Larry Gains **L** PTS 10 London

Jimmy Carter World Lightweight Champion (Undisputed) 25.05.51 – 14.05.52, 15.10.52 – 05.03.54 and 17.11.54 – 29.06.55

08.10.57 Willie Toweel **L** PTS 10 London

Frank Cedeno World Flyweight Champion (WBC Version) 27.09.83 – 18.01.84

27.09.83 **Charlie Magri** **W** RSC 6 London

Marcel Cerdan World Middleweight Champion (Undisputed) 21.09.48 – 16.06.49

09.01.39 Harry Craster **L** DIS 5 London
11.02.47 Bert Gilroy **W** CO 4 London
29.03.49 Dick Turpin **W** CO 7 London

Ezzard Charles World Heavyweight Champion (Undisputed) 22.06.49 – 18.07.51

02.10.56 Dick Richardson **L** DIS 2 London

Chartchai Chionoi World Flyweight Champion (WBC Version) 30.12.66 – 23.02.69, 20.03.70 – 07.12.70 (WBA Version) 17.05.73 – 18.10.74

19.09.67 **Walter McGowan** **W** RSC 7 London

Robert Cohen World Bantamweight Champion (Undisputed) 19.09.54 – 09.03.55, (Disputed) 09.03.55 – 29.06.56

25.09.53 Teddy Peckham **W** CO 6 Manchester
14.12.53 Jake Tuli **W** PTS 10 Manchester
27.02.54 John Kelly **W** RSC 3 Belfast
07.04.54 Eddie Carson **W** PTS 10 Glasgow
30.04.54 Manny Francis **W** PTS 10 Manchester

Eddie Cotton World L. Heavyweight Champion (Michigan Version) 29.10.63 – 15.08.66

27.06.63 Chic Calderwood **W** PTS 10 Glasgow

Carlos Teo Cruz World Lightweight Champion (Undisputed) 29.06.68 – 18.02.69

06.07.65 Frankie Taylor **W** PTS 10 London

Mario D'Agata World Bantamweight Champion (Disputed) 29.06.56 – 01.04.57

15.09.59 Freddie Gilroy **L** PTS 10 London
09.06.60 Jackie Brown **L** PTS 10 Glasgow

Vince Dundee World Middleweight Champion (New York/NBA Version) 30.10.33 – 11.09.34

26.07.31 Jack Hood DREW 10 London

Ralph Dupas World L. Middleweight Champion (Undisputed) 29.04.63 – 07.09.63

11.09.62 Brian Curvis **L** DIS 6 London

Jimmy Ellis World Heavyweight Champion (WBA Version) 27.04.68 – 16.02.70

18.06.63 Johnny Halafihi **W** RSC 1 London
21.05.66 Leweni Waqa **W** RSC 1 London
12.11.74 Joe Bugner **L** PTS 10 London

Johnny Famechon World Featherweight Champion (WBC Version) 21.01.69 – 09.05.70

21.01.69 **Jose Legra** **W** PTS 15 London
21.03.69 Giovanni Gergenti **W** PTS 10 London
20.05.69 Jimmy Anderson **W** PTS 10 London
11.11.69 Miguel Herrera **W** PTS 10 London
09.12.69 Pete Gonzalez **W** RSC 3 London

Bob Foster World L. Heavyweight Champion (Undisputed) 24.05.68 – 09.12.70, (WBC Version) 09.12.70 – 07.04.72, (Undisputed) 07.04.72 – 16.09.74

26.09.72 **Chris Finnegan** **W** CO 14 London

Joe Frazier World Heavyweight Champion (New York Version) 04.03.68 – 16.02.70, (Undisputed) 16.02.70 – 22.01.73

02.07.73 Joe Bugner **W** PTS 12 London

Kid Gavilan World Welterweight Champion (Undisputed) 18.05.51 – 20.10.54

07.02.56 Peter Waterman **L** PTS 10 London
24.04.56 Peter Waterman **W** PTS 10 London

Frankie Genaro World Flyweight Champion (NBA Version) 06.02.28 – 02.03.29, (NBA/IBU Version) 18.04.29 – 27.10.31

17.10.29 **Ernie Jarvis** **W** PTS 15 London

Joey Giardello World Middleweight Champion (Undisputed) 07.12.63 – 21.10.65

11.10.60 Terry Downes L PTS 10 London

Harold Gomes World J. Lightweight Champion (Undisputed) 20.07.59 – 16.03.60

08.10.63 Frankie Taylor L RSC 9 London
29.10.63 Dave Coventry L CO 1 London

Emile Griffith World Welterweight Champion (Undisputed) 01.04.61 – 30.09.61, 24.03.62 – 21.03.63 and 08.06.63 – 25.04.66. World Middleweight Champion (Undisputed) 25.04.66 – 17.04.67 and 29.09.67 – 04.03.68

22.09.64 **Brian Curvis** **W** PTS 15 London
01.12.64 Dave Charnley **W** RSC 9 London
04.10.65 Harry Scott **W** RTD 7 London

Marvin Hagler World Middleweight Champion (Undisputed) 27.09.80 –

27.09.80 **Alan Minter** **W** RSC 3 London

Alphonse Halimi World Bantamweight Champion (Undisputed) 01.04.57 – 08.07.59, (EBU Version) 25.10.60 – 30.05.61

04.06.57 Jimmy Carson L RSC 9 London
25.10.60 **Freddie Gilroy** **W** PTS 15 London
30.05.61 **Johnny Caldwell** L PTS 15 London
31.10.61 **Johnny Caldwell** L PTS 15 London

Carlos Hernandez World J. Welterweight Champion (Undisputed) 18.01.65 – 29.04.66

11.05.71 Ken Buchanan L RSC 8 London

Maurice Holtzer World Featherweight Champion (IBU Version) 05.10.37 – 11.07.38

09.04.33 Tommy Hyams **W** RTD 14 London
08.02.34 Louis Botes **W** PTS 10 London
08.03.34 Phineas John **W** PTS 8 London
05.09.34 Jimmy Walsh L DIS 6 London
01.10.34 Jimmy Walsh L PTS 10 London
12.03.36 Dick Corbett L PTS 10 London
23.04.36 Benny Sharkey DREW 8 London
09.07.36 Ginger Foran **W** PTS 12 Liverpool
27.03.39 Dave Finn DREW 8 London
10.05.39 Ginger Stewart L PTS 10 Glasgow

Don Jordan World Welterweight Champion (Undisputed) 05.12.58 – 27.05.60

28.01.58 Dave Charnley L PTS 10 London

Ayub Kalule World L. Middleweight Champion (WBA Version) 24.10.79 – 25.06.81

25.04.84 Jimmy Price **W** RSC 1 London

Santos Laciar World Flyweight Champion (WBA Version) 28.03.81 – 06.06.81 and 01.05.82 –

08.12.80 Charlie Magri L PTS 10 London

Kenny Lane World Lightweight Champion (Michigan Version) 19.08.63 – 11.04.64

02.06.64 Dave Charnley L PTS 10 London

Hein Lazek World L. Heavyweight Champion (IBU Version) 17.09.35 – 01.09.36

21.11.37 Tommy Martin **W** CO 1 London
20.12.37 Frank Hough **W** PTS 10 London
31.01.38 Jim Wilde DREW 10 London

Jose Legra World Featherweight Champion (WBC Version) 24.07.68 – 21.01.69 and 16.12.72 – 05.05.73

22.06.65 Howard Winstone L PTS 10 Blackpool
24.07.68 **Howard Winstone** **W** RSC 5 Porthcawl
21.01.69 **Johnny Famechon** L PTS 15 London
25.01.71 Jimmy Revie **W** PTS 15 London
15.02.72 Evan Armstrong **W** PTS 15 London
17.05.72 Tommy Glencross **W** PTS 15 Birmingham

Gus Lesnevich World L. Heavyweight Champion (Disputed) 22.05.41 – 14.05.46, (Undisputed) 14.05.46 – 26.07.48

14.05.46 **Freddie Mills** **W** RSC 10 London
17.09.46 Bruce Woodcock L CO 8 London
26.07.48 **Freddie Mills** L PTS 15 London

Hedgemon Lewis World Welterweight Champion (New York Version) 16.06.72 – 03.08.74

20.03.76 **John H. Stracey** L RSC 10 London

John Henry Lewis World L. Heavyweight Champion (Disputed) 31.10.35 – 25.01.39

09.11.36 **Len Harvey** **W** PTS 15 London

Duilio Loi World J. Welterweight Champion (Undisputed) 01.09.60 – 14.09.62 and 15.12.62 – 23.01.63

12.12.51 Tommy Barnham **W** PTS 10 London

Alfonso Lopez World Flyweight Champion (WBA Version) 27.02.76 – 02.10.76

16.09.80 Charlie Magri L PTS 10 London

Tommy Loughran World L. Heavyweight Champion (Undisputed) 07.10.27 – 18.07.29

13.11.35 Maurice Strickland **W** PTS 10 London
15.01.36 Tommy Farr **L** PTS 10 London
10.02.36 Ben Foord **L** PTS 12 Leicester
14.03.36 Jack London **W** PTS 10 Bristol

Dado Marino World Flyweight Champion (Undisputed) 01.08.50 – 19.05.52

16.07.47 Rinty Monaghan **W** DIS 9 Glasgow
08.08.47 Peter Kane **L** PTS 10 Manchester
20.10.47 **Rinty Monaghan** **L** PTS 15 London

Rocky Mattioli World L. Middleweight Champion (WBC Version) 06.08.77 – 04.03.79

12.07.80 **Maurice Hope** **L** RSC 11 London

Joey Maxim World L. Heavyweight Champion (Undisputed) 24.01.50 – 17.12.52

24.01.50 **Freddie Mills** **W** CO 10 London

Eleoncio Mercedes World Flyweight Champion (WBC Version) 06.11.82 – 15.03.83

15.03.83 **Charlie Magri** **L** RSC 7 London

Freddie Miller World Featherweight Champion (NBA Version) 13.01.33 – 11.05.36

21.09.34 **Nel Tarleton** **W** PTS 15 Liverpool
24.09.34 Billy Hazelgrove **W** CO 5 Manchester
01.10.34 Dave Crowley **W** PTS 10 London
08.10.34 Benny Sharkey **W** CO 1 Newcastle
15.10.34 Billy Gannon **L** DIS 6 Manchester
18.10.34 Jimmy Walsh **W** PTS 12 Liverpool
25.10.34 Gilbert Johnstone **W** DIS 10 Glasgow
22.11.34 Johnny Cuthbert **W** CO 2 Liverpool
06.12.34 Cuthbert Taylor **W** PTS 12 Liverpool
06.01.35 Joe Connolly **W** PTS 10 London
14.01.35 Tommy Rogers **W** PTS 12 Birmingham
20.01.35 Benny Caplan DREW 10 London
24.02.35 Benny Caplan **W** PTS 10 London
26.02.35 Doug Kestrall **W** PTS 8 Belfast
28.02.35 Johnny Peters **W** RSC 4 Liverpool
02.03.35 Stan Jehu **W** PTS 10 London
23.03.35 Harry Brooks **W** CO 6 London
11.04.35 Jimmy Stewart **W** PTS 10 Liverpool
23.05.35 Jimmy Walsh **W** PTS 10 Liverpool
12.06.35 **Nel Tarleton** **W** PTS 15 Liverpool
27.06.35 Seaman Tommy Watson **W** PTS 10 Liverpool
25.07.35 Seaman Tommy Watson **W** CO 2 Liverpool
27.01.38 Billy Charlton **W** PTS 12 Liverpool
21.02.38 Len Wickwar **W** PTS 12 Leicester
10.03.38 Billy Charlton **W** PTS 12 Liverpool
28.03.38 Tommy Hyams **W** CO 9 Bristol
28.04.38 Johnny Cusick **W** CO 7 Liverpool
12.05.38 Len Beynon **W** PTS 12 Swansea
26.05.38 Frank McCudden **W** PTS 12 Edinburgh
13.06.38 Billy Charlton **W** PTS 12 Newcastle
27.06.38 Ronnie James **W** DIS 8 Swansea
21.07.38 Jack Carrick **W** PTS 10 Liverpool
01.09.38 Johnny King **W** PTS 10 Liverpool

Small Montana World Flyweight Champion (New York Version) 16.09.35 – 19.01.37

19.01.37 **Benny Lynch** **L** PTS 15 London
08.02.37 Tiny Bostock **L** PTS 12 Manchester
04.03.37 Pat Palmer **W** PTS 10 London
27.04.37 Pat Palmer **W** PTS 10 London

Archie Moore World L. Heavyweight Champion (Undisputed) 17.12.52 – 25.10.60, (Disputed) 25.10.60 – 10.02.62

05.06.56 **Yolande Pompey** **W** RSC 10 London

Davey Moore World Featherweight Champion (Undisputed) 18.03.59 – 21.03.63

20.10.59 Bobby Neill **W** RSC 1 London

Ossie Ocasio World Cruiserweight Champion (WBA Version) 13.02.82 –

17.03.81 John L. Gardner **L** CO 6 London

Sean O'Grady World Lightweight Champion (WBA Version) 12.04.81 – 12.09.81

01.11.80 **Jim Watt** **L** RSC 12 Glasgow

Bob Olin World L. Heavyweight Champion (Undisputed) 16.11.34 – 31.10.35

02.04.36 Tommy Farr **L** PTS 10 London

Carlos Ortiz World Lightweight Champion (Undisputed) 21.04.62 – 19.08.63, (Disputed) 19.08.63 – 11.04.64, (Undisputed) 11.04.64 – 10.04.65 and 13.11.65 – 29.06.68. World J. Welterweight Champion (Undisputed) 12.06.59 – 01.09.60

28.10.58 Dave Charnley **W** PTS 10 London
22.10.63 Maurice Cullen **W** PTS 10 London

Manuel Ortiz World Bantamweight Champion (Undisputed) 07.08.42 – 06.01.47 and 11.03.47 – 31.05.50

03.10.49 Ronnie Clayton L PTS 10 Manchester
26.10.49 Jackie Paterson **W** PTS 10 Glasgow

Carlos Palomino World Welterweight Champion (WBC Version) 22.06.76 – 14.01.79

22.06.76 **John H. Stracey W** RSC 12 London
14.06.77 **Dave Boy Green W** CO 11 London

Willie Pastrano World L. Heavyweight Champion (Undisputed) 01.06.63 – 30.03.65

22.10.57 Dick Richardson **W** PTS 10 London
25.02.58 Brian London **W** PTS 10 London
21.04.58 Joe Bygraves **W** PTS 10 Leicester
30.09.58 Brian London L RSC 5 London
24.02.59 Joe Erskine L PTS 10 London
16.09.60 Chic Calderwood L PTS 10 Glasgow
30.11.64 **Terry Downes W** RSC 11 Manchester

Floyd Patterson World Heavyweight Champion (Undisputed) 30.11.56 – 26.06.59 and 20.06.60 – 25.09.62

20.09.66 Henry Cooper **W** CO 4 London

Paul Pender World Middleweight Champion (Disputed) 22.01.60 – 11.07.61 and 07.04.62 – 09.11.62

11.07.61 **Terry Downes** L RTD 9 London

Young Perez World Flyweight Champion (IBU/NBA Version) 26.10.31 – 31.10.32

30.11.30 Johnny King DREW 15 Manchester
03.11.31 Johnny King DREW 15 Manchester
28.01.32 Len Beynon **W** PTS 10 London
12.09.32 Mickey Maguire L CO 2 Newcastle
31.10.32 **Jackie Brown** L RSC 13 Manchester
03.07.33 Jackie Brown L PTS 10 London

Eddie Perkins World J. Welterweight Champion (Undisputed) 14.09.62 – 15.12.62 and 15.06.63 – 18.01.65

14.02.67 Vic Andreetti **W** RSC 8 London

Emile Pladner World Flyweight Champion (IBU/NBA Version) 02.03.29 – 18.04.29

22.01.30 Teddy Baldock L DIS 6 London
18.02.30 Dick Corbett L PTS 12 London
22.04.31 Benny Sharkey L PTS 8 London
09.05.31 Tom Cowley **W** PTS 12 Sheffield
09.11.31 Johnny Peters DREW 8 London

Sugar Ramos World Featherweight Champion (Undisputed) 21.03.63 – 26.09.64

22.10.63 Sammy McSpadden **W** RSC 2 London

Sugar Ray Robinson World Welterweight Champion (Undisputed) 20.12.46 – 14.02.51. World Middleweight Champion (Undisputed) 14.02.51 – 10.07.51, 12.09.51 – 18.12.52, 09.12.55 – 02.01.57, 01.05.57 – 27.09.57 and 25.03.58 – 28.08.59. (Disputed) 28.08.59 – 22.01.60

10.07.51 **Randy Turpin** L PTS 15 London
25.09.62 Terry Downes L PTS 10 London
03.09.64 Mick Leahy L PTS 10 Paisley
12.10.64 Johnny Angel **W** RSC 6 London

Luis Rodriguez World Welterweight Champion (Undisputed) 21.03.63 – 08.06.63

25.05.71 Bunny Sterling L PTS 10 London

Vicente Rondon World L. Heavyweight Champion (WBA Version) 27.02.71 – 07.04.72

10.09.73 John Conteh L RSC 9 London

Gustave Roth World L. Heavyweight Champion (IBU Version) 01.09.36 – 25.03.38

26.02.31 Alf Howard **W** PTS 15 Liverpool
02.02.33 Eddie Maguire **W** PTS 15 Liverpool

Sandy Sadler World Featherweight Champion (Undisputed) 29.10.48 – 11.02.49 and 08.09.50 – 21.01.57. World J. Lightweight Champion (Cleveland Version) 06.12.49 – 08.09.50

02.06.49 Jim Keery **W** CO 4 London

Vicente Saldivar World Featherweight Champion (Undisputed) 26.09.64 – 14.10.67, (WBC Version) 09.05.70 – 11.12.70

07.09.65 **Howard Winstone W** PTS 15 London
15.06.67 **Howard Winstone W** PTS 15 Cardiff

Baltazar Sangchilli World Bantamweight Champion (Undisputed) 01.06.35 – 29.06.36

31.03.36 Ronnie James **W** PTS 10 London
10.04.36 Benny Sharkey L PTS 10 Newcastle
13.03.39 Jim Brady L PTS 12 Manchester
03.04.39 Peter Kane L PTS 10 London

Petey Sarron World Featherweight Champion (NBA Version) 11.05.36 – 29.10.37

15.04.37 Harry Mizler L DIS 1 London
07.05.37 Dave Crowley L DIS 9 London

Willie Smith World Bantamweight Champion (GB Version) 06.10.27 – 09.02.29

22.05.30 Dick Corbett **L** PTS 15 London

Leon Spinks World Heavyweight Champion (Undisputed) 15.02.78 – 15.09.78

08.03.77 Peter Freeman **W** CO 1 Liverpool

Arnold Taylor World Bantamweight Champion (WBA Version) 03.11.73 – 03.07.74

24.11.76 Vernon Sollas **L** RTD 8 London

Marcel Thil World Middleweight Champion (IBU Version) 11.06.32 – 23.09.37

05.11.29 Fred Shaw **L** PTS 15 Manchester
09.11.31 Jack Casey **W** PTS 10 London
04.07.32 **Len Harvey** **W** PTS 15 London

Franco Udella World L. Flyweight Champion (WBC Version) 04.04.75 – 31.05.75

01.05.79 Charlie Magri **L** PTS 12 London

Ike Williams World Lightweight Champion (NBA Version) 18.04.45 – 04.08.47 (Undisputed) 04.08.47 – 25.05.51

04.09.46 **Ronnie James** **W** CO 9 Cardiff

Jackie Wilson World Featherweight Champion (NBA Version) 18.11.41 – 18.01.43

10.01.35 Billy Gannon **W** PTS 10 Liverpool
24.10.35 Spike Robinson **W** PTS 12 Belfast
07.11.35 Cuthbert Taylor **W** PTS 10 Liverpool
12.12.35 Gilbert Johnstone **W** RTD 5 Liverpool
12.01.36 Ronnie James **L** PTS 10 London
21.02.36 Stan Jehu **W** PTS 10 Manchester
06.03.36 Doug Kestrall **W** PTS 10 Manchester
31.03.36 Johnny McGrory **W** RSC 10 Glasgow
08.05.36 Jack Middleton **W** CO 2 Plymouth
22.05.36 George Gee **W** CO 7 Plymouth
16.06.36 Tommy Rogers **W** RSC 4 Wolverhampton

Midget Wolgast World Flyweight Champion (New York Version) 21.03.30 – 16.09.35

30.10.33 Jackie Brown **W** PTS 12 London

Chalky Wright World Featherweight Champion (New York Version) 11.09.41 – 20.11.42

27.04.39 Dan McAllister **W** RSC 5 Liverpool
25.05.39 George Daly **W** PTS 8 London
06.06.39 Kid Tanner **W** CO 7 Liverpool

Hogan Kid Bassey

Undefeated Nigerian Flyweight Champion 1949 – 1950. Undefeated Nigerian Bantamweight Champion 1950 – 1952. Undefeated West African Bantamweight Champion 1951 – 1952. Undefeated British Empire Featherweight Champion 1955 – 1957. World Featherweight Champion 1957 – 1959.
Born 03.06.32 *from* Calabar, Nigeria (Birthname Okon Bassey Asuquo)
Pro. Career 1949 – 1959 (74 Contests, Won 59, Drew 2, Lost 13)

CHAMPIONSHIP CONTESTS (12)

Date	Opponent	Result	Venue		Title
1949	Dick Turpin	W PTS 12	Lagos	Nigerian	Flyweight Title
1949	Dick Turpin	L DIS 5	Lagos	Nigerian	Flyweight Title
31.05.50	Ogli Tettey	DREW 12	Lagos	W. African	Flyweight Title
10.11.50	Joe Bennetts	W RSC 10	Lagos	Nigerian	Bantamweight Title
29.08.51	Steve Jeffra	W PTS 12	Lagos	Nigerian	Bantamweight Title
28.09.51	Spider Neequayo	W PTS 12	Lagos	W. African	Bantamweight Title
19.11.55	Billy Kelly	W CO 8	Belfast	BE	Featherweight Title
01.04.57	Percy Lewis	W PTS 15	Nottingham	BE	Featherweight Title
24.06.57	Cherif Hamia	W RSC 10	Paris	W	Featherweight Title
01.04.58	Ricardo Moreno	W CO 3	Los Angeles	W	Featherweight Title
18.03.59	Davey Moore	L RTD 13	Los Angeles	W	Featherweight Title
19.08.59	Davey Moore	L RTD 10	Los Angeles	W	Featherweight Title

NON CHAMPIONSHIP CONTESTS (62)

Nigerian Record (7) — **1950** Steve Jeffra W; Eddie Phillips W; Bola Lawal L. **1951** Dick Turpin W PTS 6; Kid Chukudi W RSC 3; Jack Salami W PTS 8; Adjetey Sowah W PTS 10

WON PTS (29) — **1952** Peter Fay, Tommy Higgins(2), Len Shaw, Jimmy Cardew, Eddie McCormick, Eddie Carson, Tommy Proffitt. **1953** Jackie Briers,

	Tommy Higgins, Sammy McCarthy. **1954** Johnny Butterworth, Jean Sneyers, Enrico Macale, Jacques LeGendre, Louis Romero, Harry Ramsden, Aime Devisch. **1955** Percy Lewis, Andre Pierson, Juan Alvarez. **1956** Aldo Pravisani, Alby Tissong, Dos Santos. **1957** Miguel Berrios, Victor Pepeder. **1958** Pierre Cossemyns, Carmelo Costa, Ernesto Parra.
WON CO (6)	**1952** Bobby Boland, Ivor Davies, Johnny Barclay. **1953** Denny Dawson. **1955** Marcel Ranvial, Joe Quinn.
WON RSC/RTD (10)	**1952** Ray Hillyard, Stan Skinkiss, Tommy Proffitt, Bobby Boland. **1953** Ken Lawrence, Luis Romero. **1956** Jean Sneyers, Louis Cabo. **1958** Jules Touan, Willie Pep
DREW (1)	**1952** Glyn Evans
LOST PTS (6)	**1952** John Kelly, Frankie Williams, Pierre Cossemyns. **1953** Juan Alvarez, Billy Kelly. **1954** Joe Woussem
LOST RSC/RTD (2)	**1953** Emile Chemama. **1956** Jean Sneyers
LOST DIS (1)	**1953** Johnny Haywood

Dick Tiger

Undefeated Nigerian Middleweight Champion 1954 – 1955. British Empire Middleweight Champion, 1958 – 1960 and Undefeated British Empire Middleweight Champion 1960 – 1962. World Middleweight Champion 1962 – 1963 and 1965 – 1966. World L. Heavyweight Champion 1966 – 1968

Born 14.08.29 *From* Aba, Nigeria. (Birthname, Richard Ihetu) *Died* 1971.
Pro. Career 1952 – 1970 (81 Contests, Won 61, Drew 3, Lost 17)

CHAMPIONSHIP CONTESTS (15)

06.05.53	Tommy West	L RTD 7	Lagos	Nigerian	Middleweight Title
1954	Tommy West	**W** PTS 12	Lagos	Nigerian	Middleweight Title
27.03.58	Pat McAteer	**W** CO 9	Liverpool	BE	Middleweight Title
22.06.60	Wilf Greaves	L PTS 15	Edmonton	BE	Middleweight Title
30.11.60	Wilf Greaves	**W** RSC 9	Edmonton	BE	Middleweight Title
23.10.62	Gene Fullmer	**W** PTS 15	San Fransisco	W	Middleweight Title
23.02.63	Gene Fullmer	DREW 15	San Fransisco	W	Middleweight Title
10.08.63	Gene Fullmer	**W** RSC 7	Ibadan	W	Middleweight Title
07.12.63	Joey Giardello	L PTS 15	Atlantic City	W	Middleweight Title
22.10.65	Joey Giardello	**W** PTS 15	New York	W	Middleweight Title
25.04.66	Emile Griffith	L PTS 15	New York	W	Middleweight Title
16.12.66	Jose Torres	**W** PTS 15	New York	W	L. Heavyweight Title
16.05.67	Jose Torres	**W** PTS 15	New York	W	L. Heavyweight Title
17.11.67	Roger Rouse	**W** RSC 12	Las Vegas	W	L. Heavyweight Title
24.05.68	Bob Foster	L CO 4	New York	W	L. Heavyweight Title

NON CHAMPIONSHIP CONTESTS (66)

Nigerian Record (14)	Simon Eme W CO 2; Easy Dynamite W CO 1; Mighty Joe W PTS 8; Lion Ring W RTD 6; Simon Eme W PTS 8; Koko Kid W PTS 8; Black Power W PTS 8; Bolaji Johnson W PTS 8; Robert Nwanne W CO 2; Ray Fargbemy W PTS 8; Peter Okptra W CO 8; Koko Kid W RTD 6; Super Human Power W PTS 8; John Ama W CO 2
WON PTS (23)	**1956** Alan Dean(2), Jimmy Lynas. **1957** Alan Dean, Phil Edwards, Jean Poisson. **1958** Jean Ruellet, Yolande Pompey. **1959** Randy Sandy, Gene Armstrong, Joey Giardello, Holly Mims. **1960** Gene Armstrong, Victor Zalazar. **1961** Hank Casey, Billy Pickett. **1962** Henry Hank. **1964** Don Fullmer. **1965** Rubin Carter. **1967** Abraham Tomica. **1968** Frank De Paula. **1969** Nino Benvenuti, Andy Kendall.
WON CO (2)	**1956** Dennis Rowley. **1966** Peter Muller

WON RSC/RTD (13)	**1956** Wally Scott. **1957** Johnny Read, Terry Downes, Marius Dori, Paddy Delargy. **1958** Jimmy Lynas, Johnny Read, Billy Ellaway. **1961** Gene Armstrong, Spider Webb. **1962** Florentino Fernandez. **1964** Jose Gonzalez. **1965** Rocky Rivero
DREW (2)	**1957** Pat McAteer. **1959** Rory Calhoun
LOST PTS (12)	**1955** Alan Dean. **1956** Gerry McNally, Jimmy Lynas, George Roe, Alan Dean. **1957** Willie Armstrong. **1958** Spider Webb. **1959** Randy Sandy, Rory Calhoun, Joey Giardello. **1964** Joey Archer. **1970** Emile Griffith

25.05.39 *Former triple World Champion Henry Armstrong (right) at the weigh in for his Welterweight title defence against Ernie Roderick who was well beaten at Harringay Arena.*

Medical Aspects of Boxing

Dr Adrian Whiteson, Chairman, Medical Committee, British Boxing Board of Control

The Medical Committee of the British Boxing Board of Control was founded in the early 1950s by Colonel Graham, who remained its Chairman for some 20 years. It is now under the Chairmanship of Dr Adrian Whiteson. The eight Area Councils of Great Britain have their own Senior Medical Officer who is responsible for appointing firstly his own deputy and secondly a panel of Medical Practitioners to officiate at the various boxing venues. There is normally close liaison between the Area Medical Officers and Head Office and at least once a year there is a conference where medical matters relating to boxing are discussed and rules and regulations formulated.

Each doctor appointed to the Boxing Board must have a working knowledge of sports medicine, and must be able to recognise and treat any emergency that may arise in any contact sport. He must also be prepared to advise the boxer, trainer, second, manager or any other interested party on training methods, dietetic advice and other such factors.

The Medical Committee over the last few years has introduced many rules and regulations to improve the safety of the sport and many of these have been adopted by 'safe' sports with great benefit to competitors.

No boxer is granted a licence without first completing a very thorough medical examination, preferably by a member of the Boxing Board's Panel and the report must be countersigned by a Senior Medical Officer. The examination that the boxer has to undergo is a very vigorous and searching one and is divided into two parts. A questionnaire involves checking the boxer's past and present medical history, including his family background and past boxing performances. This is followed by a searching physical examination with special attention being paid to the nervous system and the eyes, plus the bones and joints. Should any untoward factors be revealed either in the history or examination, the boxer is referred for further specialist advice. Then, when all the reports are obtained, a decision will be made initially by the examining doctor and subsequently by the Board's Medical Panel to consider whether the boxer is fit enough to undertake a professional career. This examination occurs anually and at any other time that the Board may think fit. It is also carried out prior to a boxer competing abroad and when a boxer becomes 'World Rated'. The medical records are then filed at Head Office and are available at all times for reference.

All boxers must be examined at one o'clock PM on the day of a contest and should also be checked prior to and immediately after the bout. Should any untoward problems arise, the doctor's decision as to whether or not to allow the boxer to participate in a contest must be final. At the end of each tournament a report is sent to the Boxing Board to be filed for future reference.

In the past two years the Medical Panel has instituted the requirement of a skull x-ray at least once in the career of a boxer, but at present both EEGs and brain scans are only required should there be any medical indication for them. The lay public is unfortunately under a misapprehension that a normal brain scan will prevent a boxer from suffering any brain damage, which unfortunately is not the case. A scan is only used as a diagnostic procedure to confirm or refute the presence of any brain damage, and should only be used in conjunction with a thorough medical examination along with an observation of the boxer in previous contests.

Some 20 years ago the Medical Panel introduced the necessity for two doctors to attend each tournament, one of whom must remain ringside throughout the duration of each contest. This enables one doctor to be available to treat any emergency which may arise during a contest, whilst the other is available firstly as medical back up ringside and secondly to deal with any medical problems that may arise in the dressing room. Each venue must have a fully equipped medical room including an examination couch, which should be well lit. There should be hot and cold running water, with the various pieces of equipment available for treating lacerations and other such minor injuries that may arise during the boxing. There must also be a stretcher under the ring apron. It is the duty of the promoter to provide this, but it is always wise for the doctor to check on its position and also to delegate Stewards to carry it if required. The Medical Officers for each tournament have also been primed to liaise and advise the casualty departments of local hospitals and the ambulance service that the tournament is taking place. Should any emergency arise this ensures that there is a minimum delay in transporting the boxer to hospital, as there is no doubt that speed of recovery from any injury is directly proportionate to the speed at which emergency treatment is given.

During each tournament both doctors follow the performance of all contestants very carefully, and should any signs of lack of fitness or deterioration in performance level be noted, then they should immediately inform the officials in charge or subsequently write to the Chief Office. In that way, a dossier of a boxer's performance is gradually built up. Very often the boxer's performance level will deteriorate long before he shows any signs of the brain damage which was all too common in the boxing of yesteryear. By retiring a boxer when his performance level slips, the Board often prevents nowadays the kind of tragedy that used to occur.

The Board's Medical Panel has very strict control over the use of stimulants in boxing and in fact none whatsoever are allowed other than a cold sponge plus the harsh word of the trainer. The use of all types of drugs is banned, as is the use of any artificial covering over the eyes such as new skin or a substance to stop bleeding from a cut around the eye, other than 1:1000 aqueous solution of Adrenaline. These rules are very strictly applied by the Board's Inspectors in conjunction with the Medical Officers. No linaments are allowed prior to or during a contest, as should they rub off onto a glove and enter an opponent's eye, severe problems could arise.

Another medical regulation of value is the requirement to examine a boxer's career should he lose four consecutive contests. The Council at its discretion may interview the boxer, his seconds and manager with a view to deciding whether he has any future in boxing. At the same time, the Council can direct the way future contests are made on his behalf.

Among other safety factors constantly under review is the use of adequate floor covering to prevent any concussional damage that may occur as a result of a boxer striking his head. The Board is also examining the possibility of thumbless gloves, and has in fact already modified the original boxing glove. This modification protects the boxer's hand along with his opponent's face, his eyes in particular. The use of headguards is also under constant review, but at present the Medical Panel do not feel that their use will in fact prevent injuries from occurring.

The Medical Panel of the Board is only too aware of the dangers involved in boxing. It is thus only by constantly updating and examining their own medical procedures that the safety of both boxing and other contact sports can be improved upon. Unfortunately considering its nature, there is no way that boxing can be made 100 per cent safe, but we feel, on reviewing our sport with others, that we have a safety record second to none. However we are not complacent and will continue to work toward higher safety levels.

The aim of the Medical Panel has always been to ensure that a boxer is as fit when he leaves the ring and his profession as he was when he entered it. This will allow him to benefit from all the lessons learned concerning fitness and discipline, as well as from the financial rewards, which are many in boxing.

Open Letter to The British Medical Association

From Dr. Adrian Whiteson, Chief Medical Officer of the British Boxing Board of Control

FOLLOWING the outcome of the debate on the motion to ban boxing at the recent BMA Conference and the ensuing publicity on this matter, I would like to put on record the views of the British Boxing Board of Control regarding certain key points arising from the debate.

In the first instance I would emphasise that we are always looking for ways to increase safety in boxing and protect boxers. We are also very willing to participate in any independent study on boxing.

Much has been made of the British Boxing Board of Control declining to give evidence to the Working Party. The reason that the Board did not wish to submit evidence was because it felt the Working Party, as constituted, could not be accepted as an independent or objective body.

Furthermore, how could the Board be expected to participate in the study, when the motion tabled for the BMA conference assumed that the findings of the Working Party would sustain the motion?

The Board has always said that it would co-operate with independent organisations. In 1969 the British Boxing Board of Control worked closely with the Royal College of Physicians on the major study on boxing it carried out.

As a result of the Board's non-involvement, the final report of the Science and Education Working Party on boxing is a study in part of amateur boxing today; in part a study of boxing in Europe, America and elsewhere; and in part a study of professional boxing in the past.

Much of the debate that took place at the Conference relied on this evidence of the Report. We believe there are some serious errors of fact and misinterpretation in the Report.

The Board is particularly concerned about the survey on the incidence of eye injuries (page 18), which the BMA has quoted as one of the reasons for campaigning for the abolition of professional boxing.

The section relies on recall and supposition, and therefore the validity of its conclusions is highly questionable. The authors even acknowledge the problem of "over-reporting" and to refer to "proven ocular damage" on the basis of such unreliable evidence is irresponsible.

Moreover, the report misses the point about the Board's philosophy on the medical protection of boxers. As Chief Medical Officer my approach has always been that preventive controls are the key to making a physically hazardous sport as safe as possible.

It is little known that the Board is often accused of forcing boxers to retire too early in their careers.

I think it is also important to put the results of the voting on the motion into perspective. Over 600 delegates registered for the Conference, but only 254 participated in the debate on boxing, out of which 144 voted in favour and 110 against.

Those supporting the motion represented something less than 28% of the medical delegates at the conference.

In any event, in campaigning to ban boxing the BMA is setting a very questionable precedent by seeking to deprive individuals of the freedom to choose how they wish to conduct their lives, develop their careers and/or earn their livings.

If the BMA is primarily concerned with statistics of injuries and fatalities in sport, why not seek to ban mountaineering, horse riding, football and rugby where in each case the figures on deaths are much higher?

Furthermore, if you extend the logic of the BMA's case why not ban drinking and smoking, both of which, unlike boxing, have consequences which affect those who do not participate?

Yours sincerely, Dr. Adrian Whiteson.

The Boxing Writers' Club

The Boxing Writers' Club reflects the media coverage of the sport because virtually no regular boxing writers fail to become members. It was founded as a social club, and in many ways has remained just that with membership by invitation only.

Each year the Club members vote for the 'Best Young Boxer,' and the trophy is presented at the annual dinner, held traditionally on the third Wednesday in January each year. When Barry McGuigan was voted 'Best Young Boxer' of 1983 he became the 33rd in a line of succession dating back to the formation of the British Boxing Writers' Club in the early 1950s and including many great names of British boxing. The 'Best Young Boxer' award is named after the late Geoffrey Simpson of the *Daily Mail*, the Club's first Chairman, and since 1967 a second award 'For outstanding Services to Boxing' has been made commemorating another former Chairman, the late Joe Bromley of *Sporting Life*. The most recent recipient of this award was the former professional referee and three times ABA Heavyweight Champion, Pat Floyd.

The present Chairman of the Club is John Morris of the *Yorkshire Post*, who is also the boxing writer for the United Newspapers group. John has recently been appointed an Administrative Steward of the Board of Control. The Honorary Secretary is Frank Butler, OBE, the former sports editor of the *News of the World* and a famous sports columnist, with the Treasurer being Colin Hart of the *Sun*, and the Vice-Chairman, Alan Hoby of the *Sunday Express*. One of the great characters of the Club is Walter Bartleman of the London *Evening Standard*, a past Chairman and a man with more than 50 years experience in Fleet Street behind him.

On the television side of the sport, Harry Carpenter, formerly of the *Daily Mail*, is the BBC's man at the ringside, whilst for ITV the regular commentator is Reg Gutteridge, for many years the boxing correspondent of the London *Evening News*.

Bill Martin (Press Association) and Dave Field (Exchange Telegraph) cover for Britain's leading domestic agencies. A former Chairman, Alan Hubbard, is now a senior executive of the *Straits Times* in Singapore after service in Britain with *Now* magazine and the *Mail on Sunday*.

Other writers based in London include Neil Allen of the *New Standard*, Peter Batt of the *Daily Star*, Dave Brenner (LBC), Dan Garrett of *Sporting Life*, Ken Jones of the *Sunday Mirror* and Sydney Hulls of the *Daily Express*, son of a former leading promoter. John Rodda and Frank Keating write for *The Guardian*, Donald Saunders and Ken Mays for the *Daily Telegraph* and former Oxford boxing blue Srikumar Sen for *The Times*. Frank McGhee is the *Daily Mirror* man, with assistance from Ron Wills. Hugh McIlvanney of *The Observer* is a former 'Sportswriter of the Year.' Fred Burcombe writes for the *News of the World*, Peter Moss for the *Daily Mail*, Colin Malam for the *Sunday Telegraph* and Maurice Wolff for the *South East London Mercury*. Frankie Taylor, a former European amateur champion and later a leading professional featherweight, and himself a past winner of the Geoffrey Simpson award, writes for the *Sunday People*. Still on the London scene, Jon Robinson is active on East London papers plus several magazines, whilst that great South London character Dave Caldwell is also a valued member of the Club.

Harry Mullan edits *Boxing News* and former editor Gilbert Odd, now the doyen of the Club, remains an acknowledged historian of the sport. When it comes to world-wide boxers' records, Eric Armit, also an advisor on ratings to the Board and the World Boxing Council, is the king. Former *Boxing News* editor Tim Riley still contributes, and remains a leading freelance along with Ron Olver, who was the former assistant editor and now specialises in the excellent Old-Timers feature plus the Professionals for *Boxing News*.

In Scotland the Club is strong with men like Dick Currie, twice ABA Flyweight Champion and then Scottish professional Flyweight Champion, who now writes for the

Daily Record, Pat Garrow of *The Scotsman*, who is based in London, John Quinn of the *Glasgow Evening Times* and Jim Reynolds of the *Glasgow Herald*.

Over in Belfast, Jack McGowan carries the Club colours with distinction.

In the English provinces there is Sidney Dye of the *Liverpool Echo*, Pat Forrest from the *Evening Post* at Reading, Eddie Griffiths from the *Wolverhampton Express and Star* and Ian Johnson from the *Evening Mail* in Birmingham. Alan Parr covers the sport for the *Leicester Mercury*, John Wilkinson for the *Evening Telegraph* at Kettering, and Bob Walker, Len Whaley and Terry Poskitt for papers in Essex and East London.

There are many other distinguished former writers, now retired, and others who operate as back-up on a number of papers. Apologies are offered to any overlooked.

GEOFFREY SIMPSON AWARD (*Annual Award to the Best Young Boxer of the year, in memory of the Club's first Chairman*)

1951 Randy Turpin; 1952 Sammy McCarthy; 1953 John Kelly; 1954 Dai Dower; 1955 Joe Erskine; 1956 Bobby Neill; 1957 Terry Spinks; 1958 Terry Downes; 1959 Freddie Gilroy; 1960 Brian Curvis; 1961 Howard Winstone; 1962 Frankie Taylor; 1963 Walter McGowan; 1964 Alan Rudkin; 1965 Johnny Pritchett; 1966 Ken Buchanan; 1967 John McCluskey; 1968 Johnny Clark; 1969 Joe Bugner; 1970 Bunny Sterling; 1971 Jackie Turpin; 1972 John H. Stracey; 1973 John Conteh; 1974 Dave Needham; 1975 Vernon Sollas; 1976 Dave Boy Green; 1977 Charlie Magri; 1978 Johnny Owen; 1979 Tony Sibson; 1980 Colin Jones; 1981 Herol Graham; 1982 Keith Wallace; 1983 Barry McGuigan.

Note: Of the above 33 Award winners, 21 were already National or International Champions, whilst a further ten went on to achieve the same prominence. Only Jackie Turpin and Frankie Taylor, who both unfortunately had to retire prematurely, failed to attain Titles. Terry Downes, Howard Winstone, Walter McGowan, Ken Buchanan, John H. Stracey, John Conteh and Charlie Magri all went on to win World Titles after being tipped for stardom by the Club.

JOE BROMLEY RING AWARD (*For outstanding services to Boxing*)

1967 Len Harvey; 1968 Larry Gains; 1969 Chris Finnegan; 1970 Jack Petersen; 1971 Ken Buchanan, 1972 Teddy Waltham; 1974 Terry Waller; 1975 Henry Cooper; 1976 Harry Vines; 1977 Tommy Farr; 1978 George Biddles; 1979 J. Onslow Fane; 1980 Maurice Hope/Jim Watt; 1981 Terry Downes; 1982 Pat Cowdell; 1983 Pat Floyd.
Note: In 1973 no Award was made.

Licensed Referees

The following referees are licensed by the British Boxing Board of Control:

Class 'B'	**Ivor Bassett**	Welsh Area
	David Booth	Midlands Area
	Geoffrey Clarke	Midlands Area
	Richard Davies	Southern Area
	Brian Donald	Scottish Area
	Roddy Evans	Welsh Area
	Roy Francis	Southern Area
	Keith Garner	Central Area
	Brian Hogg	Central Area
	Douglas Jenkins	Southern Area
	Wynford Jones	Welsh Area
	John Keane	Midlands Area
	Danny McCafferty	Scottish Area
	Ricky Nicholson	Central Area
	Dave Parris	Southern Area
	James Pridding	Midlands Area
	Billy Rafferty	Scottish Area
	Jack Snipe	Southern Area
	Paddy Sower	Southern Area
	Anthony Walker	Southern Area
	Nicholas White	Southern Area
	Barney Wilson	Northern Ireland Area
Class 'A'	**Arnold Bryson**	Northern Area
	Bob Galloway	Southern Area
	Ron Hackett	Central Area
	Denzil Lewis	Western Area
	Adrian Morgan	Welsh Area
	Len Mullen	Scottish Area
	Larry O'Connell	Southern Area
	Frank Parkes	Midlands Area
	Fred Potter	Northern Area
	Paul Thomas	Midlands Area
	Mickey Vann	Central Area
	Harry Warner	Central Area
Class 'A' Star	**James Brimmell**	Welsh Area
	John Coyle	Midlands Area
	Roland Dakin	Southern Area
	Harry Gibbs OBE	Southern Area
	Michael Jacobs	Southern Area
	Sidney Nathan	Southern Area

Licensed Managers

The following managers are licensed by the British Boxing Board of Control:

Joe Aitchison
32 Ettrick Crescent
Burnside
Rutherglen
Glasgow

Derek Alexander
1 Conway Crescent
Short Heath
Willenhall
West Midlands W12 5TP

Les Anderson
49 Hales Crescent
Smethwick
Warley
West Midlands B67 6QR

Jarvis Astaire
21 Cavendish Place
London W1M 9DL

Michael Atkinson
9 Tudor Road
Ainsdale
Southport
Merseyside PR8 2RU

Wally Atkinson
25 Sewerby Heads
Bridlington
North Humberside

Don Austen
14 Whinchat Road
Broadwaters
Thamesmead
London SE28

Robert Avoth
8 Fairfield Avenue
Victoria Park
Cardiff
South Wales

Johnny Barclay
2 The Beeches
Beech Grove
Tring
Herts

Mike Barrett
National House
60–66 Wardour Street
London W1

Robert Barron
1 Templemore Park
Londonderry
Northern Ireland

Albert Barrow
236 Freshfield Road
Brighton
Sussex

Nat Basso
38 Windsor Road
Prestwich
Lancashire

Peter Bates
Red Lion Inn
Vicar Lane
Chesterfield
Derby

Teddy Best
76 Neville Street
Canton
Cardiff

Doug Bidwell
19 Squires Close
Crawley Down
Sussex RH10 1 BQ

Jack Bishop
76 Gordon Road
Fareham
Hants

Gerald Boustead
46 Coombe Lane
St Mary Church
Torquay
Devon

George Bowes
Fairfield Coast Road
Blackhall Rocks
Cleveland

Eric Bradshaw
Har Vista House
3 Druids Road
Illogan Highway
Redruth
Cornwall JK15 3EG

Tony Brazil
106 Maresfield Road
Manor Farm
Brighton
Sussex

Colin Breen
31 Penlan Road
Treboeth
Swansea
West Glamorgan

Jackie Briers
9 Benview Drive
Bailysillian
Belfast 14
Northern Ireland

Frederick Britton
71 Henrietta Street
Leigh
Lancashire WN7 1LH

Pat Brogan
42 Talke Road
Alsager
Stoke on Trent
Staffordshire

Arthur Brooks
20 Longford Gardens
Sutton
Surrey

Harry Burgess
25 Calthorpe Street
London WC1

Sam Burns
7 Denning Close
Hall Road
London NW8 9PJ

Alex Buxton
2 Romola Road
London SE24

Paddy Byrne
70 Benfield Way
Portslade-by-Sea
Sussex

Sid Cain
49 Westcourt Road
Worthing
Sussex BN14 7DJ

Trevor Callighan
The Stump Cross Inn
Halifax
Yorkshire

Ernie Cashmore
18 North Drive
Handsworth
Birmingham B20 B5Z

John Celebanski
The Lord Clyde
86 Thornton Road
Bradford 1
West Yorkshire

Nigel Christian
41 Station Road
Keyham
Plymouth
Devon PL2 1NG

William Clark
Darag
16 Mossfield Drive
Lochyside
Fort William
Highland
Scotland

Edward Coakley
6 Hillview Crescent
Bellshill
Glasgow

Roger Colson
63 Amwell Street
Roseberry Avenue
London EC1

Tommy Conroy
144 High Street
Sunderland
Tyne and Wear

George Cooper
40 Bannister Close
Greenford
Middlesex

Philip Coren
16 Highcliffe Gardens
Redbridge
Ilford
Essex

John Cox
5 Newby Court
Eastfield
Northampton

Tommy Cumiskey
28 Halstead Square
Hylton Lane
Sunderland
Tyne and Wear

Joseph Dakin
8 Earl Way
Thurmaston
Leicester

Gary Davidson
The Thomas A'Beckett
320 Old Kent Road
London SE1

David Davies
10 Bryingalli
Carmal
Llanelli
Dyfed

Glyn Davies
29 Glyncoed Terrace
Half Way
Llanelli
Dyfed

Gordon Davies
Bryn-View
15 Old Blaenavon Road
Brynmawr
Gwent

Ronnie Davies
3 Vallensdean Cottages
Hangleton Lane
Portslade
Sussex

David Davis
179 West Heath Road
Hampstead
London NW3

Denny Dawson
33 Badger Drive
Woodhouse
Sheffield S13 7TH

Fred Deakin
7 Meakin House
Newcastle Road
Stone
Staffordshire

Frank Deans
7 Stirling Avenue
Primrose
Jarrow
Tyne and Wear

George Donaghy
9 Denise Drive
Kingshurst
Birmingham B37 6NN

George Dougan
24 Cornhadock Street
Greenock
Renfrewshire
Scotland

Terry Downes
Milestone
Milespit Hill
London NW7

Mickey Duff
National House
60–66 Wardour Street
London W1

Pat Dwyer
128 Roxburgh Street
Walton
Liverpool 4
Merseyside

Bernard Eastwood
Eastwood House
Chapel Lane
Belfast
Northern Ireland

Jack Edwards
29 The Fold
Lionfold
Hill Lane
Blackley
Manchester M9 2PE

Ron Elvin
92 Woolaston Avenue
Lakeside
Cardiff

Billy Evans
33 Stewards Avenues
Widnes
Cheshire

George Evans
14 Donald Street
Abercanaid
Merthyr Tydfil
Glamorgan

Jack Evans
Morlee House
Hanbury Road
Pontypool
Monmouth

Peter Fay
44 Avenue Road
Christchurch
Dorset

Reg Fishlock
79 Kings Road
Farmcombe
Surrey

Vince Flynn
1 Ledger Lane
Lofthouse
Near Wakefield
Yorkshire

Ernie Fossey
26 Bell Lane
Hatfield
Herts

George Francis
11 Hill Way
Holly Lodge Estate
London N6

Dai Gardiner
13 Hengoed Hall Drive
Cefn Hengoed
Hengoed
Glamorgan

Teddy Gardner
293 Whitehorse Road
West Croydon
Surrey

John Gaynor
7 Westhorne Fold
Counthill Drive
Brooklands Road
Crumpsall
Manchester M8 6JN

Jimmy Gill
96 Portland Road
Toton
Nottingham

Tommy Gilmour
46 Tanzieknowe Road
West Greenlees
Cambuslang
Glasgow G72

Manny Goodall
190 Newton Drive
Blackpool
Lancashire FY3 8JE

Jack Goodyear
16 Flat
Wellington Close
Blockhouse
Worcester WR1 2BB

Ben Grant
16 Southgate Street
Neath
Glamorgan

Ron Gray
Ingrams Oak
19 Hatherton Road
Cannock
Staffordshire

Johnny Griffin
26 Christow Street
St Mathews Estate
Leicester LE1 2GN

Harry Griver
198 Redbridge Lane East
Redbridge
Essex

Gus Grubb
15 Herma Street
Glasgow

Dick Gunn
43 Moray Avenue
Hayes
Middlesex

Clive Hall
23 Linnet Drive
Barton Seagrave
Kettering
Northants

Terry Hardwick
100 Hampshire Court
Upper St James Street
Brighton
Sussex

David Harris
16 Battle Crescent
St Leonards on Sea
Sussex

Bernard Hart
17 Grosvenor Gardens
Oakwood
London N14 4TU

Gerry Hassett
29 Saul Street
Down Patrick
Belfast BT30 6NQ

Patrick Healy
1 Cranley Buildings
Brookes Market
Holborn
London EC1

Dennis Hill
38 Old Barn Way
Abergavenny
Wales

George Hill
52 Hathaway
Marton
Blackpool
Lancashire

Mick Hill
35 Shenstone House
Aldrington Road
Streatham
London SW16

John Hillier
9 Silkin Walk
Broadfield
Crawley
Sussex

Henry Hoey
5 Balquhidoer Court
Airdrie
Lanarks
Scotland

Harry Holland
178 Cranford Lane
Heston
Middlesex

Gordon Holmes
Wayland House
Shipdam Road
Scoulton
Norwich
Norfolk

Maurice Hope
582 Kingsland Road
London E8

Brendan Ingle
26 Newman Road
Wincobank
Sheffield 2

Mick Inskip
8 Pembroke Avenue
Syston
Leicester LE7 8BZ

Joe Jackson
8 Romford Road
Holbrooke
Coventry

Donald James
42 Aneurin Crescent
Twynyrodyn
Merthyr Tydfil
South Wales

Duncan Jowett
Cedarhouse
Caplethill Road
Paisley
Renfrewshire
Scotland

Archie Kasler
17 Claude Road
Leyton
London E10 6NE

Alan Kay
Beaverley
26 Park Street
Salford
Lancashire M7 0NH

John Kittle
Queensbury
1 The Mount
Cranleigh
Surrey

Johnny Kramer
115 Crofton Road
Plaistow
London E13

Colin Lake
4 Downham Court
Downham Road
London N1

Lennie Lake
3 Pool House
Penfold Street
London NW8

Tony Lavelle
23 Ruvigny Gardens
Putney
London SW15

Terry Lawless
4 Banyards
Off Nelmes Way
Emerson Park
Hornchurch
Essex

Philip Lee
13 Pembroke Avenue
Blackpool
Lancashire
FY2 9PS

Barney Lewis
18 Manor Farm Road
Alderton
Wembley
Middlesex

Benjamin Lloyd
27 High Street
Rhyl Clwyd
North Wales

Joe Lucy
The Ruskin Arms
386 High Street North
London E12

Pat Lynch
Gotherinton
68 Kelsey Lane
Balsall Common
Near Coventry
West Midlands

Gordon McAteer
36 Derby Road
Birkenhead
Merseyside

Burt McCarthy
Danecourt
Copt Hill
Danbury
Essex

Billy MacDonald
70 Longfellow Street
Liverpool 8

Sam McIlvenna
10 Pinewood Place
Lenzie
Glasgow

Tony McKenna
211 High Greave
Ecclesfield
Sheffield 5

Danny Mahoney
Villa Dandor
3 Merlewood Close
Bournemouth
Dorset BH2 6JQ

Frank Maloney
The Castle
44 Commercial Road
London E1

Dennie Mancini
10 Laurel View
Finchley
London N12 7DT

Tony Mancini
The Golden Gloves
80 Fulham Palace Road
Hammersmith
London W6

Kenrick March
17 Addy House
Rotherhithe New Road
London SE16

Teddy Mason
55 Hall Green Lane
Hutton
Brentwood
Essex

Billy May
25 Partridge Way
Duffryn Estate
Newport
Gwent

Tommy Miller
128 Clapton Mount
King Cross Road
Halifax
West Yorkshire

Jimmy Molloy
2 Kildonan Road,
Aigburth
Liverpool 17

Christopher Moorcroft
52 Rawcliffe Road
Walton
Liverpol 9

Alexander Morrison
9 Magnus Crescent
Simshill
Glasgow G44

James Murray
Top Flat
63 Barrington Drive
Glasgow G4 9ES

Bobby Neill
The Alexandra
163 Parish Lane
Penge
London SE20

Philip Oliphant
12 Jacobs Court
Spencer Road
Bromley
Kent

Danny Peacock
30 Queen Mary Avenue
Morden
Surrey SM4 4JR

Billy Pearce
36 Courtfield Gardens
South Kensington
London SW5

Tony Penpraze
83 Chaucer Way
Manadon
Plymouth

Allen Pompey
Flat 3
34 Oxford Gardens
London W10

John Pook
75 Stapley Road
Hove
Sussex

Ricky Porter
115 County Road
Swindon
Wiltshire

Ronald Price
18 Elphin Crescent
Townhill
Swansea SA1 6LW

Jimmy Quill
111–113 London Road
Plaistow
London E14

Dennis Read
65 Bridle Road
Shirley
Croydon
Surrey

Earnest Rea
27 Meldrum Mains
Glenmavis
Airdrie

Owen Reilly
10 Glenfinnan Drive
Glasgow G20

Ken Richardson
15 East Walk
North Road Estate
Retford
Notts DN22 7YF

Barry Ridge
79 Rowanberry Avenue
Leicester

Graham Riley
34 Charlemont Road
Walsall
Staffordshire

Fred Rix
14 Broom Road
Shirley
Croydon
Surrey CR0 8NE

Les Roberts
214 Stewarts Road
Wandsworth
London SW8

Brian Robinson
12 Rutland Road
Ellesmere Park
Eccles
Manchester

David Roden
The Lantern House
22 Beaks Hill Road
Kings Norton
Birmingham 38

Joe Rossi
51 Shirley Street
Leicester

John Rushton
20 Alverley Lane
Balby
Doncaster

Mike Sendell
The Poplars
23 Belvedere Road
Shrewsbury
Shropshire

Tommy Sharp
52 Arkle Green
Derby DE2 9NW

Billy Shinfield
43 Cedar Avenue
Alfreton
Derbyshire

Charles Shorey
48 Newlands Road
Norbury
London SW16

Johnnie Simmons
327 Malden Road
New Malden
Surrey

Joey Singleton
190 Peckham High Street
Peckham
London SE15

Len Slater
28 Sutcliffe Avenue
Nunsthorpe
Grimsby
Lincolnshire

Andy Smith
Valandra
St Audrey's Lane
St Ives
Cambridgeshire

Darkie Smith
21 Northumberland House
Gaisford Street
London NW5

John P. Smith
6 Kildare Road
Chorlton
Manchester 21

Maxie Smith
45 Carlton Drive
Bassleton Court
Thornaby on Tees
Cleveland

Richard Smith
36 Henlow Avenue
Southdene
Kirkby
Liverpool L32 9EW

John Spensley
36 Wilson Street (c/o Jas Video)
Conversation Street
Middlesbrough
Cleveland

Albert Spriggs
71 Renfrew Close
New Beckton
London E6

Walter Springett
Stonehaven
Troy Road
Morley
Leeds LS28

Ken Squires
27 University Close
Syston
Leicester

Greg Steene
Panton House
Panton Street
London W1

Danny Sullivan
77 Lanbydrock Road
St Judes
Plymouth

Johnny Sullivan
26 Great Meadow
Astley Village
Chorley
Lancashire

Norrie Sweeney
46 George Street
Paisley
Scotland PA1 2LD

Wally Swift
Grove House
54 Grove Road
Knowle
Solihull
West Midlands B93 0PJ

Heddwyn Taylor
Fairways
The Walk
Ystrad Mynach
Mid Glamorgan

Eddie Thomas
Runnington
Penydarren Park
Merthyr Tydfil
Glamorgan

Roger Tighe
8 West Park Avenue
Granville Street
Anlaby Road
Hull
Humberside

Terence Toole
Goring Arms
24 Broadway Market
London Fields
Hackney
London E8

Mick Toomey
153 Newlyn Close
Bransholme
Hull
Humberside HU7 4PJ

Alum Trembath
36 Arthur Street
Williamstown
Tonypandy
Rhondda
Mid Glamorgan
Wales

Noel Trigg
The Gladiator Inn
Pillmawr Road
Malpass
Newport
Gwent

Terry Tulley
149 Greenacres
Shoreham
West Sussex

Frankie Turner
7 Delancy Street
London NW1

Danny Urry
26 Nella Road
Hammersmith
London W6

David Veal
13 Southampton Road
Lymington
Hants

Bev Walker
Wallhurst House
Wallhurst Estate
Cowfold
Horsham
West Sussex

Frank Warren
Bloomsbury Crest Hotel
Coram Street
London WC1N 1HT

Robert Watt
32 Dowanhill Street
Glasgow G11

James Wellard
1 Franklin Street
St James End
Northampton

Ken Whitney
The George Inn
Glapthorn Road
Oundle
Peterborough
Northants

William Wigley
44 Fernwood Crescent
Wollaton
Nottingham

Mac Williams
Dolphin Inn
Dolphin Street
Newport
Gwent

Michael Williamson
34A St Mary's Grove
London N1

Jack Wilson
24 Althorp Road
St James
Northampton

Howard Winstone
30 Gilfach Cynon
Twyneodyn
Merthyr Tydfil
Mid Glamorgan

Walter Witts
7 Law Street
Pembroke Dock
Dyfed

Fred Wolfindale
20 Hamilton Road
Smethwick
Warley
West Midlands

Tex Woodward
Spaniorum Farm
Berwick Lane
Compton Greenfield
Bristol

Billy Wynter
26 Newick Road
Clapton
London E5

Matchmakers

The following matchmakers are licensed by the British Boxing Board of Control:

Nat Basso
38 Windsor Road
Prestwich
Lancashire

Jack Bishop
76 Gordon Road
Fareham
Hampshire

Harry Burgess
25 Calthorpe Street
London WC1

Paddy Byrne
70 Benfield Way
Portslade-by-Sea
Sussex

David Davis
179 West Heath Road
Hampstead
London NW3

Selwyn Demmy
58a Swan Street
Manchester 4

Mickey Duff
National House
60–66 Wardour Street
London W1

Pat Dwyer
128 Roxburgh Street
Walton
Liverpool 4

Ernie Fossey
26 Bell Lane
Hatfield
Herts

Tommy Gilmour
46 Tanzieknowe Road
West Greenlees
Cambuslang
Glasgow G72

Ron Gray
Ingrams Oak
19 Hatherton Road
Cannock
Staffordshire

Clive Hall
23 Linnet Drive
Barton Seagrave
Kettering
Northants

Pat Healey
1 Cranley Buildings
Brookes Market
Holborn
London EC1

George Ingram
The Lodge
Bants Lane
Northampton

Archie Kasler
17 Claude Road
Leyton
London E10 6NE

Terry Lawless
4 Banyards
Off Nelmes Way
Emerson Park
Hornchurch
Essex

Phil Lee
13 Pembroke Avenue
Blackpool
Lancs FY2 9PS

Danny Mahoney
Villa Dandor
3 Merlewood Close
Bournemouth
Dorset BH2 6JQ

Dennie Mancini
10 Laurel View
Finchley
London N12 7DT

Tommy Miller
128 Clapton Mount
King Cross Road
Halifax
West Yorkshire

Danny Peacock
30 Queen Mary Avenue
Morden
Surrey SM4 4JR

Al Phillips
30 Sunningdale Close
Stanmore
Middlesex HA7 3QL

Ricky Porter
115 County Road
Swindon
Wiltshire

Ken Richardson
15 East Walk
North Road Estate
Retford
Notts DN22 7YF

Les Roberts
214 Stewarts Road
Wandsworth
London SW8

Tommy Sharp
52 Arkle Green
Derby DE2 9NW

Charles Shorey
48 Newlands Road
Norbury
London SW16

Len Slater
78 Sutcliffe Avenue
Nunsthorpe
Grimsby
Lincs

Darkie Smith
21 Northumberland House
Gaisford Street
London NW5

Terry Toole
Goring Arms
24 Broadway Market
London Fields
Hackney
London E8

Licensed Promoters

The following promoters are licensed by the British Boxing Board of Control:

William Aird
Lilliput Hall
9 Old Jamaica Road
Bermondsey
London SE16
(01-237 5903)

Anglo-American Sporting Club
National House
60–66 Wardour Street
London W1
(01–437 5956)

Arden Sporting Club
National House
60–66 Wardour Street
London W1
(01–734 1041)

Michael Atkinson
9 Tudor Road
Ainsdale
Southport
Merseyside PR8 2RY
(Southport 77799)

William Ball
6 Copse Close
Marlow
Bucks SL7 2NY
(062 846179)

Mike Barrett
National House
60–66 Wardour Street
London W1
(01–437 5956)

Basso Duff Promotions
38 Windsor Road
Prestwich
Lancashire
(061–834 9945)

Peter Bates
The Red Lion Inn
Vicar Lane
Chesterfield
(0246 76968)

Bowes and Bewick Promotions
Bewick's Lodge
Ryhope Road
Sunderland
Tyne and Wear
(0783 59479)

Pat Brogan
42 Talke Road
Alsager
Stoke-on-Trent
Staffordshire
(Alsager 4825)

Harry Burgess
25 Calthorpe Street
London WC1
(01–837 8324)

Pat Button
20 Hook Close,
Chatham,
Kent.
(0634 666 881)

Paddy Byrne
70 Benfield Way
Portslade-by-Sea
Sussex
(0273 412498)

Ernest Cashmore
18 North Drive
Handsworth
Birmingham B20 3SZ
(021–554 2868)

Conroy & Deans Proms.
144 High Street East
Sunderland
Tyne & Wear

Crewe Police Athletic Club
County Police Office
Crewe
Cheshire
(Crewe 55111)

Alan Davies
1020 Carmarthen Road
Fforestfach
Swansea
(0792 587571)

Brian J. Davies
27 Cross Acre
West Cross
Swansea
(0792 403 850)

Dawn Promotions
The Stump Cross Inn
Halifax
West Yorkshire
(0422 66004)

Dawson Promotions
Jurby Hotel
Jurby
Isle of Man
(Andreas 492)

Thomas Donnelly
26 High Park
Southway
Derry City
Northern Ireland
(0504 62060)

Shaun Doyle
15 Jermyn Croft
Dodworth
Barnsley
South Yorkshire
(0226 298 492)

Mickey Duff Promotions
National House
60–66 Wardour Street
London W1
(01–734 1041)

Bernard & Stephen Eastwood
Eastwood House
2–4 Chapel Lane
Belfast 1
Northern Ireland
(0232 09491)

K Lindsay Eaton
Holiday Inn
St Nicholas Circle
Leicester
(0533 531161)

George Evans
14 Donald Street
Abercanaid
Merthyr Tydfil
(0685 690337)

Evesham Sporting Club
17 Worcester Road
Evesham
Worcester WR11 4JU
(Evesham 41539)

Firkin-Flood, Douglas
Nut Bank House
Blackley
Manchester 9

(061 643 0068)**Gill Promotions**
96 Portland Road
Toton
Nottingham
(06076 60964)

Gilligan Promotions
399 Burton Road
Derby DE3 6AN
(Derby 362105)

Thomas Gilmour
46 Tanzieknowe Road
Cambuslang
Glasgow G72
(041–641 7599)

Glasgow Sporting Club
6 Hillview Crescent
Bellshill
Lanarkshire
(041–474 9954)

Ruth & Emanuel Goodall
190 Newton Drive
Blackpool
Lancashire FY3 8JE
(0253 326888)

Ron Gray (Boxing) Promotions
Ingrams Oak
19 Hatherton Road
Cannock
Staffordshire
(05435 2279)

Great International Sporting Club
Commodore International
Nuthall Road
Nottingham NG8 5DR
(0602 781746)

Johnny Griffin
26 Christow Street
Leicester LE1 2GN
(Leicester 29287)

Harry Grossmith
1–2 Boleyn Road
Dalston Junction
London N16

Harry Holland
178 Cranford Lane
Heston
Middlesex
(01–574 1032)

Gordon Holmes
Wayland House
Shipdham Road
Scoulton
Norwich NR9 4PH
(0953 850561)

Alma Ingle
26 Newman Road
Wincobank
Sheffield S9 1LP
(0742 383392)

Ron Jackson
The Old Mill
Kirkley
Northumberland
(Ponteland 25018)

Alan Kay
Berkeley House
26 Pack Street
Salford
Lancashire
(Chatham Hill 3781)

Kennington and Kenningham
389–395 Anlaby Road
Hull
North Humberside
(0482 53146)

John Kidd
59 Monmouth Drive
Sutton Coldfield
West Midlands

Harry Levene
National House
60–66 Wardour Street
London W1
(01–437 5956)

Lawrence Lewis
166 St. Anne's Road East
St Anne's-on-Sea
Lancashire
(Blackpool 26948)

Liver International Sporting Club
Holiday Inn
Paradise Street
Liverpool L1 8JD
(051–709 0181)

Benjamin Lloyd
27 High Street
Rhyl Clywd
North Wales
(0745 2409)

McAteer Promotions
39 Derby Road
Tranmere
Birkenhead
Merseyside
(051–647 9608)

Burt McCarthy
Danecourt
Copt Hill
Danbury
Essex
(024541 5383)

M and M Promotions
142 Butterthwaite Lane
Ecclesfield
Sheffield S30 3WA
(07415 63977)

Peter Mason
4 Manor Road
South Woodham Ferrers
Chelmsford
Essex
(Chelmsford 320786)

Walter Mays
26 Woodland Drive
Anlaby
N. Humberside HU10 7HG
(0482 655575)

Mens Aid Jewish Blind Society
Glanly House
Middleton Road
Manchester

Midlands Sporting Club
Xanadu
Main Road
Meriden
Coventry CV7 7NH
(0676 22050)

Mid Staffs Sporting Club
c/o Evening Sentinel
24 Salter Street
Stafford
Staffs

Alan Minter International Sporting Club (1980)
19 Squires Close
Crawley Down
Sussex RH10 4JH
(0342 714 309)

John Gilmour Morrison
58 Ledi Drive
Bearsden
Strathclyde
(041–942 7969)

Moyle-Roberts Promotions
Selsdon Guest House
Barncoose
Redruth
Cornwall
(0209 215791)

National Sporting Club
National House
60–66 Wardour Street
London W1
(01–437 5956)

North Staffs Sporting Club
D W Eardley Esq
Mercury Sports Equipment Limited
Victoria Road
Fenton
Stoke on Trent
Staffordshire
(Stoke on Trent 23526)

North-West Promotions
128 Roxburgh Street
Walton
Liverpool 4
(051–523 4772)

Patara, and Sharp
28 Florence Road
Southall
Middlesex
(01–571 4377)

Ricky Porter
115 County Road
Swindon
Wiltshire
(0793 22093)

James Quill
74 Manor Road
Chigwell
Essex
(01–500 9501)

Raymond Randall
14 St. Stephen's Road
Newport
Gwent
(Newport 52389)

Regency Sporting Club
70 Benfield Way
Portslade-by-Sea
Sussex
(0273 412498)

Les Roberts
214 Stewarts Road
Wandsworth Road
London SW8
(01–622 3128)

Brian Robinson
12 Rutland Road
Ellesmere Park
Manchester M30 9FA
(061–789 8477)

Roden Lynch Promotions
144 Charles Henry Street
Highgate
Birmingham
(021–622 6162)

S. and F. Promotions
1 Ledger Lane
Lofthouse
Wakefield
Yorkshire
(Wakefield 823275)

St. Andrew's Sporting Club
12 Sherwood Street
London W1V 7RD
(01–734 6435)

Mike Sendell
23 Belvedere Road
Shrewsbury
Shropshire
(0745 69103)

Billy Shinfield
43 Cedar Avenue
Afreton
Derbyshire
(0773 832360)

Charles Shorey
48 Newlands Road
Norbury
London SW16
(01–764 7619)

Leonard Slater
78 Sutcliffe Avenue
Nunsthorpe
Grimsby

James Smith
49 Allington Street
Aigburth
Liverpool 17
(051 727 7536)

John Smith
33 Salisbury Road
St. Judes
Plymouth
Devon
(Plymouth 25251)

John H. Spensley
Jas Video
36 Wilson Street
Middlesbrough
Cleveland
(0642 240040)

Walter Springett
Stone Haven
Troy Road
Morley
Leeds
(0532 535286)

Greg Steene
Panton House
25 Haymarket
London SW1
(01–930 5600)

Stoke on Trent European Sporting Club
42 Talke Road
Alsager
Stoke-on-Trent
Staffordshire
(0782 614077)

Heddwyn Taylor
Fairways
The Walk
Ystrad Mynach
Hengoed
Mid Glamorgan
(0443 814604)

Edward Thomas
Runnington
Penydarren Park
Merthyr Tydfil
Mid Glamorgan
(0685 4176)

John Trickett
7 Cotswold Avenue
Hazel Grove
Stockport
Staffordshire
(061 428 2212)

Twentieth Century Sporting Club
38 St. Vincent's Road
Westcliffe-on-Sea
Essex
(0702 48782)

Frank Warren
Bloomsbury Crest Hotel
Coram Street
London WC1N 1HT
(01–837 1200)

James Watt
30 Northbank Road
Kirkintilloch
Glasgow

Welsh Executive Sporting Club
31 Commercial Road
Newport
Gwent
(Newport 65723)

John Williamson
Valley Hotel
Fivemiletown
Co Tyrone
Northern Ireland
(0365 52505)

Roy Witts
30 Water Street
Pembroke Dock
Dyfed
(0646 681089)

Wolverhampton Sporting Club
100 Dudley Road East
Oldbury
Warley
Wolverhampton
(021 552 2803)

Tex and Jeff Woodward
Spanorium Farm
Compton Greenfield
Bristol BS12 3RX
(Pilning 2448)

World Sporting Club
Eastgate House
16--19 Eastcote Street,
London, W.1.

Yorkshire Executive Sporting Club
190 Newton Drive
Blackpool
Lancashire
(0253 32688)

Diary of British Boxing Tournaments, 01.01.83 to 30.06.84

Tournaments are listed by date, town, venue, and promoter. (Code: SC = Sporting Club)

Date	Town	Venue	Promoters
07.01.83	Durham	Van Mildert College	Spensley
17.01.83	Manchester	Hotel Piccadilly	Anglo-American SC
18.01.83	Kensington	Albert Hall	Barrett/Duff
19.01.83	Birmingham	Metropole Hotel	Midland SC
19.01.83	Stoke	North Stafford Hotel	Stoke-on-Trent European SC
20.01.83	Birkenhead	Hamilton Club	North-West Promotions
24.01.83	Piccadilly	Cafe Royal	National SC
24.01.83	Bradford	Norfolk Gardens Hotel	Yorkshire Executive SC
24.01.83	Glasgow	Albany Hotel	St. Andrews SC
24.01.83	Mayfair	Hilton Hotel	Anglo American SC
25.01.83	Bethnal Green	York Hall	Barrett/Duff
25.01.83	Belfast	Ulster Hall	Eastwood
26.01.83	Stoke	Trentham Gardens	North Staffs SC
28.01.83	Swansea	Top Rank Suite	A. Davies
31.01.83	Southwark	Elephant & C Rec. Centre	Byrne
31.01.83	Birmingham	Albany Hotel	Arden SC
01.02.83	Southend	Garons Suite	Twentieth Century SC
03.02.83	Bloomsbury	Crest Hotel	Warren
07.02.83	Marylebone	Regents Crest Hotel	Warren
07.02.83	Piccadilly	Cafe Royal	National SC
07.02.83	Brighton	Metropole Hotel	Regency SC
07.02.83	Liverpool	Holiday Inn	Liver International SC
08.02.83	Kensington	Albert Hall	Barrett/Duff
10.02.83	Walthamstow	Assembly Hall	Quill
10.02.83	Sunderland	Greyhound Stadium	Conroy/Deans
14.02.83	Liverpool	Rotters Night Club	North-West Promotions
14.02.83	Manchester	Hotel Piccadilly	Anglo-American SC
14.02.83	Lewisham	Concert Hall	Burgess
15.02.83	Wolverhampton	Park Hall Hotel	Wolverhampton SC
16.02.83	Muswell Hill	Alexandra Pavilion	Warren
17.02.83	Coventry	Leisure Centre	McCarthy
17.02.83	Morley	Town Hall	Springett
21.02.83	Mayfair	Grosvenor House	World SC
21.02.83	Piccadilly	Cafe Royal	National SC
21.02.83	Glasgow	Albany Hotel	St. Andrews SC
21.02.83	Nottingham	Commodore Hotel	Great International SC
21.02.83	Edgbaston	Tower Ballroom	Roden/Lynch
21.02.83	Bradford	Norfolk Gardens Hotel	Yorkshire Executive SC
22.02.83	Bethnal Green	York Hall	Barrett/Duff
23.02.83	Chesterfield	Aquarius Nightclub	Bates
23.02.83	Mayfair	Europa Hotel	Alan Minter International SC
24.02.83	Liverpool	The Stadium	Goodall
25.02.83	Doncaster	Brodsworth M.W.	Shinfield
28.02.83	Strand	The Lyceum	Steene
28.02.83	Birmingham	Albany Hotel	Arden SC
01.03.83	Kensington	Albert Hall	Barrett/Duff
01.03.83	Southend	Garons Suite	Twentieth Century SC
02.03.83	Evesham	Marine Ballroom	Evesham SC
02.03.83	Belfast	Kings Hall	Eastwood

04.03.83	Queensferry	Deeside Leisure Centre	North-West Promotions
07.03.83	Piccadilly	Cafe Royal	National SC
07.03.83	Liverpool	Holiday Inn	Liver International SC
07.03.83	Glasgow	Morleys Nite Spot	Glasgow SC
09.03.83	Solihull	Civic Hall	Midland SC
09.03.83	Stoke	North Stafford Hotel	Stoke-on-Trent European SC
12.03.83	Swindon	County Ground	Porter
14.03.83	Manchester	Hotel Piccadilly	Anglo-American SC
14.03.83	Sheffield	City Hall	Ingle
15.03.83	Wembley	Empire Pool	Barrett/Duff/Levene
16.03.83	Stoke	Trentham Gardens	North Staffs SC
16.03.83	Cheltenham	Town Hall	Warren
17.03.83	Marylebone	Regent Crest Hotel	Barrett
21.03.83	Nottingham	Commodore Hotel	Great International SC
21.03.83	Bradford	Norfolk Gardens Hotel	Yorkshire Executive SC
21.03.83	Mayfair	Hilton Hotel	Anglo-American SC
21.03.83	Piccadilly	Cafe Royal	National SC
21.03.83	Glasgow	Albany Hotel	St. Andrews SC
22.03.83	Bethnal Green	York Hall	Barrett/Duff
22.03.83	Wolverhampton	Park Hall Hotel	Wolverhampton SC
25.03.83	Bloomsbury	Crest Hotel	Warren
28.03.83	Birmingham	Albany Hotel	Arden SC
28.03.83	Manchester	Belle Vue	Robinson
29.03.83	Hull	Tiffanys Night Club	Kennington and Kenningham
05.04.83	Kensington	Albert Hall	Barrett/Duff
06.04.83	Mayfair	Europa Hotel	Alan Minter International SC
07.04.83	Strand	The Lyceum	Steene
08.04.83	Liverpool	The Stadium	Burgess
11.04.83	Gosforth	Park Hotel	Spensley
11.04.83	Manchester	Hotel Piccadilly	Anglo-American SC
11.04.83	Glasgow	Morleys Nite Spot	Glasgow SC
12.04.83	Belfast	Ulster Hall	Eastwood
12.04.83	Southend	Garons Suite	Twentieth Century SC
13.04.83	Evesham	Marine Ballroom	Evesham SC
14.04.83	Basildon	Festival Hall	Mason
15.04.83	Piccadilly	Cafe Royal	National SC
16.04.83	Bristol	Redwood Lodge	Woodward
18.04.83	Glasgow	Albany Hotel	St. Andrews SC
18.04.83	Bradford	Norfolk Gardens Hotel	Yorkshire Executive SC
20.04.83	Muswell Hill	Alexandra Pavilion	Warren
20.04.83	South Shields	Prince Regent Club	Conroy/Deans
20.04.83	Solihull	Civic Hall	Midland SC
21.04.83	Piccadilly	Cafe Royal	National SC
21.04.83	Stevenage	Leisure Centre	McCarthy
25.04.83	Acton	Town Hall	Warren
25.04.83	Mayfair	Grosvenor House	Anglo-American SC
25.04.83	Aberdeen	Skean Dhu Hotel	Glasgow SC
25.04.83	Piccadilly	Cafe Royal	National SC
24.05.83	Southwark	Elephant & C. Rec. Centre	Byrne
25.04.83	Liverpool	Holiday Inn	Liver International SC
26.04.83	Bethnal Green	York Hall	Barrett/Duff
27.04.83	Stoke	Mayfair Ballroom	Stoke-on-Trent European SC
27.04.83	Rhyl	Dixieland	Lloyd
28.04.83	Leicester	Granby Halls	Griffin
29.04.83	Liverpool	Rotters Night Club	North-West Promotions
03.05.83	Wembley	Empire Pool	Barrett/Duff/Levene
09.05.83	Nottingham	Commodore Hotel	Great International SC
09.05.83	Piccadilly	Cafe Royal	National SC
10.05.83	Southend	Garons Suite	Twentieth Century SC
12.05.83	Morley	Town Hall	Springett

16.05.83	Bradford	Norfolk Gardens Hotel	Yorkshire Executive SC
16.05.83	Mayfair	Hilton Hotel	Anglo-American SC
16.05.83	Manchester	Belle Vue	Robinson
16.05.83	Birmingham	Albany Hotel	Arden SC
17.05.83	Bethnal Green	York Hall	Barrett/Duff
17.05.83	Piccadilly	Cafe Royal	National SC
18.05.83	Bloomsbury	Crest Hotel	Warren
19.05.83	Queensway	Porchester Hall	Steene
19.05.83	Sunderland	Greyhound Stadium	Conroy/Deans
23.05.83	Sheffield	City Hall	Barrett
23.05.83	Mayfair	Hilton Hotel	Anglo-American SC
23.05.83	Glasgow	Normandy Hotel	Glasgow SC
25.05.83	Rhyl	Dixieland	Lloyd
27.05.83	Swansea	Top Rank Suite	A. Davies
27.05.83	Wolverhampton	Civic Hall	Gray
31.05.83	Kensington	Albert Hall	Barrett/Duff
06.06.83	Piccadilly	Cafe Royal	National SC
07.06.83	Southend	Garons Suite	Twentieth Century SC
12.06.83	Middlesbrough	Gaskins Club	Spensley
13.06.83	Coventry	Leisure Centre	McCarthy
13.06.83	Doncaster	Adwick Leisure Centre	Shinfield
13.06.83	Nottingham	Commodore Hotel	Great International SC
13.06.83	Glasgow	Albany Hotel	St. Andrews SC
14.06.83	Newport	Tiffanys Night Club	Welsh Executive SC
17.06.83	Queensferry	Deeside Leisure Centre	North-West Promotions
20.06.83	Piccadilly	Cafe Royal	National SC
20.06.83	Manchester	Free Trade Hall	Men's Aid Jewish Blind Society
23.06.83	Bethnal Green	York Hall	Warren
23.06.83	Wolverhampton	Civic Hall	Gray
01.09.83	Bloomsbury	Crest Hotel	Warren
05.09.83	Mayfair	Europa Hotel	Alan Minter International SC
05.09.83	Liverpool	Holiday Inn	Liver International SC
05.09.83	Glasgow	Grosvenor Hotel	Gilmour
08.09.83	Queensway	Porchester Hall	Steene
12.09.83	Glasgow	Holiday Inn	Glasgow SC
12.09.83	Leicester	Holiday Inn	Lindsay Eaton
14.09.83	Muswell Hill	Alexandra Pavilion	Warren
15.09.83	Liverpool	The Stadium	Goodall
16.09.83	Swindon	Oasis Leisure Centre	Porter
16.09.83	Rhyl	Dixieland	Lloyd
19.09.83	Glasgow	Albany Hotel	St. Andrews SC
19.09.83	Nottingham	Commodore Hotel	Great International SC
19.09.83	Manchester	Hotel Piccadilly	Anglo-American SC
20.09.83	Piccadilly	Cafe Royal	National SC
20.09.83	Southend	Garons Suite	Twentieth Century SC
20.09.83	Dudley	Town Hall	Gray
22.09.83	Cardiff	St. Davids Hall	Barrett
22.09.83	Strand	The Lyceum	Steene
22.09.83	Stockport	Quaffers Club	Brogan
23.09.83	Longford	Crest Hotel	Holland
26.09.83	Manchester	Belle Vue	Robinson
26.09.83	Mayfair	Grosvenor House	National SC
27.09.83	Wembley	Empire Pool	Barrett/Duff/Levene
27.09.83	Stoke	Kings Hall	Stoke-on-Trent European SC
30.09.83	Leicester	Granby Halls	Griffin
03.10.83	Eltham	Yorkshire Grey	Aird
03.10.83	Bradford	Norfolk Gardens Hotel	Yorkshire Executive SC
03.10.83	Glasgow	Normandy Hotel	Glasgow SC
03.10.83	Liverpool	Holiday Inn	Liver International SC
04.10.83	Bethnal Green	York Hall	Barrett/Duff

05.10.83	Belfast	Ulster Hall	Eastwood
05.10.83	Solihull	Civic Hall	Midland SC
05.10.83	Stoke	Trentham Gardens	North Staffs SC
06.10.83	Basildon	Festival Hall	Mason
10.10.83	Glasgow	Albany Hotel	St Andrews SC
10.10.83	Birmingham	Albany Hotel	Arden SC
11.10.83	Kensington	Albert Hall	Barrett/Duff
12.10.83	Evesham	Marine Ballroom	Evesham SC
13.10.83	Bloomsbury	Crest Hotel	Warren
15.10.83	Coventry	Willenhall Soc. Club	McCarthy
17.10.83	Manchester	Hotel Piccadilly	Anglo-American SC
17.10.83	Southwark	Elephant & C. Rec. Centre	Byrne
18.10.83	Wolverhampton	Park Hall Hotel	Wolverhampton SC
19.10.83	Hull	Tiffanys Night Club	Kennington & Kenningham
24.10.83	Mayfair	Grosvenor House	National SC
24.10.83	Nottingham	Commodore Hotel	Great International SC
26.10.83	Stoke	Kings Hall	Stoke-on-Trent European SC
27.10.83	Ebbw Vale	Leisure Centre	Taylor
28.10.83	Queensferry	Deeside Leisure Centre	North-West Promotions
31.10.83	Mayfair	Europa Hotel	Alan Minter International SC
01.11.83	Dudley	Town Hall	Gray
02.11.83	Bloomsbury	Crest Hotel	Warren
07.11.83	Liverpool	Holiday Inn	Liver International SC
07.11.83	Birmingham	Albany Hotel	Arden SC
08.11.83	Bethnal Green	York Hall	Barrett/Duff
09.11.83	Sheffield	Cutlers Hall	Ingle
09.11.83	Evesham	Marine Ballroom	Evesham SC
09.11.83	Southend	Cliffs Pavilion	Twentieth Century SC
10.11.83	Stafford	Top of the World Club	Mid Staffs SC
14.11.83	Glasgow	Normandy Hotel	Glasgow SC
14.11.83	Nantwich	Civic Hall	Crewe Police Athletic Club
14.11.83	Manchester	Hotel Piccadilly	Anglo-American SC
16.11.83	Belfast	Kings Hall	Eastwood
17.11.83	Basildon	Festival Hall	Mason
18.11.83	Sheffield	Cutlers Hall	M & M Promotions
21.11.83	Eltham	Yorkshire Grey	Aird
21.11.83	Glasgow	Albany Hotel	St. Andrews SC
22.11.83	Wembley	Empire Pool	Barrett/Duff/Levene
22.11.83	Manchester	Belle Vue	Trickett
22.11.83	Wolverhampton	Park Hall Hotel	Wolverhampton SC
23.11.83	Solihull	Civic Hall	Midland SC
24.11.83	Kirkby	Sports Centre	Atkinson
28.11.83	Southwark	Elephant & C. Rec. Centre	Byrne
28.11.83	Bayswater	Royal Lancaster Hotel	Warren
28.11.83	Rhyl	Dixieland	Lloyd
29.11.83	Cardiff	St. Davids Hall	Barrett
30.11.83	Piccadilly	Cafe Royal	National SC
01.12.83	Basildon	Festival Hall	Mason
01.12.83	Dudley	Town Hall	Gray
05.12.83	Manchester	Hotel Piccadilly	Anglo-American SC
03.12.83	Marylebone	Regent Crest Hotel	Warren
05.12.83	Nottingham	Commodore Hotel	Great International SC
05.12.83	Manchester	Rotters Night Club	Robinson
06.12.83	Kensington	Albert Hall	Barrett/Duff
06.12.83	Southend	Garons Suite	Twentieth Century SC
07.12.83	Bloomsbury	Crest Hotel	Warren
07.12.83	Stoke	Trentham Gardens	North Staffs SC
09.12.83	Liverpool	The Stadium	Goodall
10.12.83	Swansea	Top Rank Suite	A. Davies
12.12.83	Bedworth	Civic Hall	McCarthy

12.12.83	Birmingham	Albany Hotel	Arden SC
14.12.83	Stoke	Kings Hall	Stoke-on-Trent European SC
19.12.83	Bradford	Norfolk Gardens Hotel	Yorkshire Executive SC
19.12.83	Swansea	Dolphin Hotel	B.J. Davies
16.01.84	Bradford	Norfolk Gardens Hotel	Yorkshire Executive SC
18.01.84	Stoke	Kings Hall	Stoke-on-Trent European SC
19.01.84	Digbeth	Civic Hall	Roden/Lynch
23.01.84	Mayfair	Grosvenor House	National SC
23.01.84	Glasgow	Albany Hotel	St. Andrews SC
25.01.84	Solihull	Civic Hall	Midland SC
25.01.84	Belfast	Kings Hall	Eastwood
25.01.84	Stoke	Trentham Gardens	North Staffs SC
26.01.84	Strand	The Lyceum	Steene
27.01.84	Longford	Crest Hotel	Holland
28.01.84	Hanley	Victoria Hall	Brogan
30.01.84	Birmingham	Albany Hotel	Arden SC
30.01.84	Glasgow	Normandy Hotel	Glasgow SC
30.01.84	Manchester	Belle Vue	Trickett
31.01.84	Kensington	Albert Hall	Barrett/Duff
01.02.84	Bloomsbury	Crest Hotel	Warren
03.02.84	Maidenhead	Magnet Leisure Centre	Ball
06.02.84	Bethnal Green	York Hall	Barrett/Duff
06.02.84	Liverpool	Holiday Inn	Liver International SC
06.02.84	Mayfair	Marriott Hotel	Alan Minter International SC
09.02.84	Manchester	New Century Hall	Brogan
10.02.84	Dudley	Town Hall	Gray
13.02.84	Eltham	Yorkshire Grey	Aird
13.02.84	Manchester	Hotel Piccadilly	Anglo-American SC
14.02.84	Wolverhampton	Park Hall Hotel	Wolverhampton SC
14.02.84	Southend	Garons Suite	Twentieth Century SC
16.02.84	Basildon	Festival Hall	Mason
17.02.84	Rhyl	Ford Glas Social Club	North-West Promotions
20.02.84	Mayfair	Grosvenor House	National SC
20.02.84	Bradford	Norfolk Gardens Hotel	Yorkshire Executive SC
22.02.84	Kensington	Albert Hall	Barrett/Duff
22.02.84	Evesham	Marine Ballroom	Evesham SC
23.02.84	Digbeth	Civic Hall	Roden/Lynch
27.02.84	Birmingham	Albany Hotel	Arden SC
27.02.84	Glasgow	Albany Hotel	St. Andrews SC
27.02.84	Nottingham	Commodore Hotel	Great International SC
29.02.84	Sheffield	Cutlers Hall	Ingle
01.03.84	Queensway	Porchester Hall	Steene
05.03.84	Glasgow	Normandy Hotel	Glasgow SC
05.03.84	Liverpool	Holiday Inn	Liver International SC
06.03.84	Stoke	Kings Hall	Stoke-on-Trent European SC
07.03.84	Brighton	Corn Exchange	Byrne
12.03.84	Liverpool	Holiday Inn	Liver International SC
12.03.84	Manchester	Hotel Piccadilly	Anglo-American SC
13.03.84	Hull	Tower Theatre	Mays
13.03.84	Wembley	Empire Pool	Barrett/Duff/Levene
14.03.84	Mayfair	Grosvenor House	National SC
14.03.84	Stoke	Trentham Gardens	North Staffs SC
15.03.84	Kirkby	Sports Centre	Atkinson
15.03.84	Leicester	Granby Halls	Griffin
19.03.84	Bradford	Norfolk Gardens Hotel	Yorkshire Executive SC
19.03.84	Manchester	Belle Vue	Trickett
21.03.84	Solihull	Civic Hall	Midland SC
21.03.84	Bloomsbury	Crest Hotel	Warren
21.03.84	Mayfair	Marriotts Hotel	Alan Minter International SC
22.03.84	Maidenhead	Magnet Leisure Centre	Ball

26.03.84	Leicester	Holiday Inn	Lindsay Eaton
26.03.84	Barnsley	Civic Hall	Doyle
26.03.84	Glasgow	Albany Hotel	St. Andrews SC
27.03.84	Bethnal Green	York Hall	Barrett/Duff
27.03.84	Battersea	Town Hall	Holland
27.03.84	Wolverhampton	Park Hall Hotel	Wolverhampton SC
27.03.84	Southend	Garons Suite	Twentieth Century SC
28.03.84	Aberavon	Afan Lido	Thomas/Warren
31.03.84	Derby	Sports Centre	Patara/Sharp
02.04.84	Mayfair	Grosvenor House	National SC
03.04.84	Lewisham	Concert Hall	Burgess
04.04.84	Belfast	Kings Hall	Eastwood
04.04.84	Evesham	Marine Ballroom	Evesham SC
06.04.84	Edinburgh	Playhouse Theatre	Gilmour
06.04 84	Watford	Town Hall	Steene
09.04.84	Glasgow	Normandy Hotel	Glasgow SC
09.04.84	Manchester	Hotel Piccadilly	Anglo-American SC
11.04.84	Kensington	Albert Hall	Barrett/Duff
12.04.84	Piccadilly	Cafe Royal	National SC
16.04.84	Birmingham	Albany Hotel	Arden SC
16.04.84	Glasgow	Albany Hotel	St. Andrews SC
16.04.84	Bradford	Norfolk Gardens Hotel	Yorkshire Executive SC
16.04.84	Nottingham	Commodore Hotel	Great International SC
17.04.84	Merton	Civic Hall	Shorey
17.04.84	Piccadilly	Cafe Royal	National SC
18.04.84	Stoke	Kings Hall	Stoke-on-Trent European SC
19.04.84	Basildon	Festival Hall	Mason
25.04.84	Muswell Hill	Alexandra Pavilion	Warren
27.04.84	Wolverhampton	Civic Hall	Gray
30.04.84	Rhyl	Dixieland	Lloyd
30.04.84	Liverpool	Holiday Inn	Liver International SC
30.04.84	Glasgow	Skean Dhu Hotel	Glasgow SC
30.04.84	Mayfair	Grosvenor House	National SC
01.05.84	Maidstone	Royal Star Hotel	Button
01.05.84	Bethnal Green	York Hall	Barrett/Duff
02.05.84	Solihull	Civic Hall	Midland SC
09.05.84	Leicester	Granby Halls	Griffin
09.05.84	Mayfair	Marriotts Hotel	Alan Minter International SC
10.05.84	Digbeth	Civic Hall	Roden/Lynch
12.05.84	Hanley	Victoria Hall	Brogan
13.05.84	Wembley	Empire Pool	Barrett/Duff/Levene
14.05.84	Manchester	Hotel Piccadilly	Anglo-American SC
14.05.84	Nottingham	Albany Hotel	Great International SC
14.05.84	Glasgow	Normandy Hotel	Glasgow SC
19.05.84	Bristol	Redwood Lodge	Woodward
21.05.84	Bradford	Norfolk Gardens Hotel	Yorkshire Executive SC
21.05.84	Aberdeen	Skean Dhu Hotel	Glasgow SC
23.05.84	Mayfair	Grosvenor House	National SC
31.05.84	Basildon	Festival Hall	Mason
04.06.84	Nottingham	Commodore Hotel	Great International SC
04.06.84	Manchester	Belle Vue	Trickett
04.06.84	Mayfair	Grosvenor House	National SC
04.06.84	Glasgow	Normandy Hotel	Glasgow SC
05.06.84	Kensington	Albert Hall	Barrett/Duff
06.06.84	Sheffield	Cutlers Hall	Ingle
07.06.84	Piccadilly	Cafe Royal	National SC
07.06.84	Dudley	Town Hall	Gray
11.06.84	Glasgow	Albany Hotel	St. Andrews SC
11.06.84	Manchester	Hotel Piccadilly	Anglo-American SC
12.06.84	Southend	Garons Suite	Twentieth Century SC

12.06.84	St. Helens	Cindys Night Spot	North-West Promotions
13.06.84	Aberavon	Afan Lido	Thomas/Warren
15.06.84	Liverpool	The Stadium	Aird/James Smith
18.06.84	Manchester	Free Trade Hall	Men's Aid Jewish Blind Society
30.06.84	Belfast	Kings Hall	Eastwood

10.02.84 *When topping the bill at Dudley Town Hall, George Feeney (right) the British Lightweight Champion successfully defended his title over 12 rounds against the tough local, Paul Chance*
Fred Cicharski

British Boxing Board of Control (1929): Boxing Rules

No. 1 Contests
All Contests to be decided in a three-roped ring with the ropes joined in the centre at each side, not less than 16 feet or more than 20 feet square and not less than 18 inches margin of ring floor outside the ropes. The floor to be covered with canvas over a safety mat approved by the Board. 'Each corner shall be padded from the top to the bottom rope with one whole length of padding not less than 2 inches thick and 6 inches in width'.

No. 2 Dress and Bandages
Boxers must shake hands before the commencement of the Contest and at the beginning of the final round and must defend themselves at all times.

Contestants must be stripped to the waist, box in Regulation boots without heels or spikes, with Regulation shorts.

The gloves to be of a weight of 6 ounces each for Flyweights to Light Middleweights and 8 ounces each for Middleweights to Heavyweights. (Breaking by twisting, removal of padding by fingering and thumbing from the potential part of the glove is prohibited.) Contestants to weigh on the day of the Contest.

Bandages are permitted for the protection of the hands. If used, they must not exceed 18 feet of 2 inch soft bandage (W.C.W.) for all weights, and/or 9 feet of 1 inch Zinc Oxide plaster tape for weights up to and including Middleweights and 11 feet of 1 inch Zinc Oxide plaster tape for Light-heavy and Heavyweights. In all cases these lengths are for each hand. The tape must **not** be applied over the knuckles.

No. 3 Officials
In all Contests a Referee who must officiate inside the Ring and a Timekeeper shall be appointed.

In all Contests no more than four persons acting as Second shall be allowed in each corner.

The Seconds shall leave the Ring when ordered to do so by the Timekeeper; the Referee to see this is carried out.

The Seconds shall give no advice or assistance to the contestants during the progress of any round.

No. 4 Medical Examination and Number of Rounds
'Contestants shall be medically examined after the weigh-in or immediately prior to the commencement of the tournament'.

In all Contests the number of rounds shall be specified. No Contest shall exceed 12 rounds nor be of less than 12 minutes' duration; except in the case of novice competitions which may be of eight minutes duration. Rounds shall be of three minutes' duration except in Contests of ten rounds and under when rounds may be of two minutes duration.

The interval between the rounds shall be one minute.

No. 5 Referee's Marking
The Referee shall award a maximum number of ten marks at the end of each round to the better man and a proportionate number to the other contestant or, when equal, the maximum number to each.

Marks shall be awarded for 'attack' – direct clean hits with the knuckle part of the glove of either hand on any part of the front or sides of the head, or body above the belt (the belt is an imaginary line drawn across the body from the top of the hip bones); 'defence' – guarding, slipping, ducking, or getting away. Where contestants are otherwise equal, the majority of marks shall be given to the one who does most part of the leading off or who displays the better style.

If a contestant is down he must get up unassisted within ten seconds; his opponent meanwhile shall retire to the farthest neutral corner and shall not resume Boxing until ordered to do so by the Referee. A man is to be considered down even when he is on one foot or both feet, if at the same time any other part of his body is touching the ground, or when he is in the act of rising. A contestant failing to continue the Contest at the expiration of ten seconds shall not be awarded any marks for that round, and the Contest shall then terminate.

In the event of the count being interrupted by the bell signifying the end of the round, the contest and count shall continue, either until the Boxer who is down rises, or until the 'out' is reached, in which case the Contest shall terminate.

The count shall not continue when the bell signifies the termination of the final round of the Contest.

If at the conclusion of any round during the Contest one of the contestants should attain such a lead on points as to render it an impossibility for his opponent to win, he must then be declared the winner.

The Referee shall decide each Contest in favour of the contestant who obtains the greater number of marks.

(*a*) When ordered by the Referee to 'break', both Boxers shall immediately take one step back before re-commencing to box. A Boxer shall not strike or attempt to strike his opponent on the 'break'.

At the end of each Contest which lasts the scheduled number of rounds, the M.C. shall announce the Referee's final score.

No. 6 Disqualification

The Referee shall have power to disqualify a contestant for any of the following acts: (a) hitting below the belt; (b) using the 'pivot blow'; (c) hitting on the back of the head or neck; (d) kidney punching; (e) hitting with the open glove, the inside or butt of the hand, or with the wrist or elbow; (f) holding, butting or careless use of the head, shouldering, wrestling, roughing; (g) not trying; (h) persistently ducking below the waist line; (i) intentional falling without receiving a blow; (j) failing to break when so ordered, or striking or attempting to strike an opponent on the break; (k) for deliberately striking an opponent when he is dropping to the floor or when he is down; (l) for ungentlemanly conduct; (m) for any other act or conduct which he may deem foul.

A contestant disqualified for any cause whatever shall not be entitled to any prize or remuneration, except in accordance with Regulation 20, Para. 15.

No. 7 Referee's Power

The Referee shall have power to stop the Contest if in his opinion a contestant is outclassed or accidentally disabled.

No. 8 Discretion

The Referee shall decide (1) any question not provided for in these Rules (2) the interpretation of any of these Rules on matters arising during the time the contestants are in the Ring.

No. 9 Referee's Decision

The Referee's decision shall be final.

Standard Weights

Flyweight	8st. and under	Welterweight	10 st. 7 lb. and under
Bantamweight	8st. 6lb. and under	Light-Middleweight	11 st. and under
Featherweight	9 st. and under	Middleweight	11 st. 6 lb. and under
Lightweight	9 st. 9 lb. and under	Light-Heavyweight	12 st. 7 lb. and under
Light-Welterweight	10 st. and under	Heavyweight	Any weight

First published 2021 by HarperCollins Children's Books
This edition published in Great Britain 2021 by Farshore
An imprint of HarperCollins*Publishers*
1 London Bridge Street, London SE1 9GF
www.farshore.co.uk

HarperCollins*Publishers*
1st Floor, Watermarque Building, Ringsend Road
Dublin 4, Ireland

Book design by Elaine Lopez-Levine

DUNGEONS & DRAGONS®

ISBN 978 0 7555 0382 7
Printed and bound by CPI Group (UK) Ltd, Croydon CR0 4YY
1

A CIP catalogue record for this title is available from the British Library.

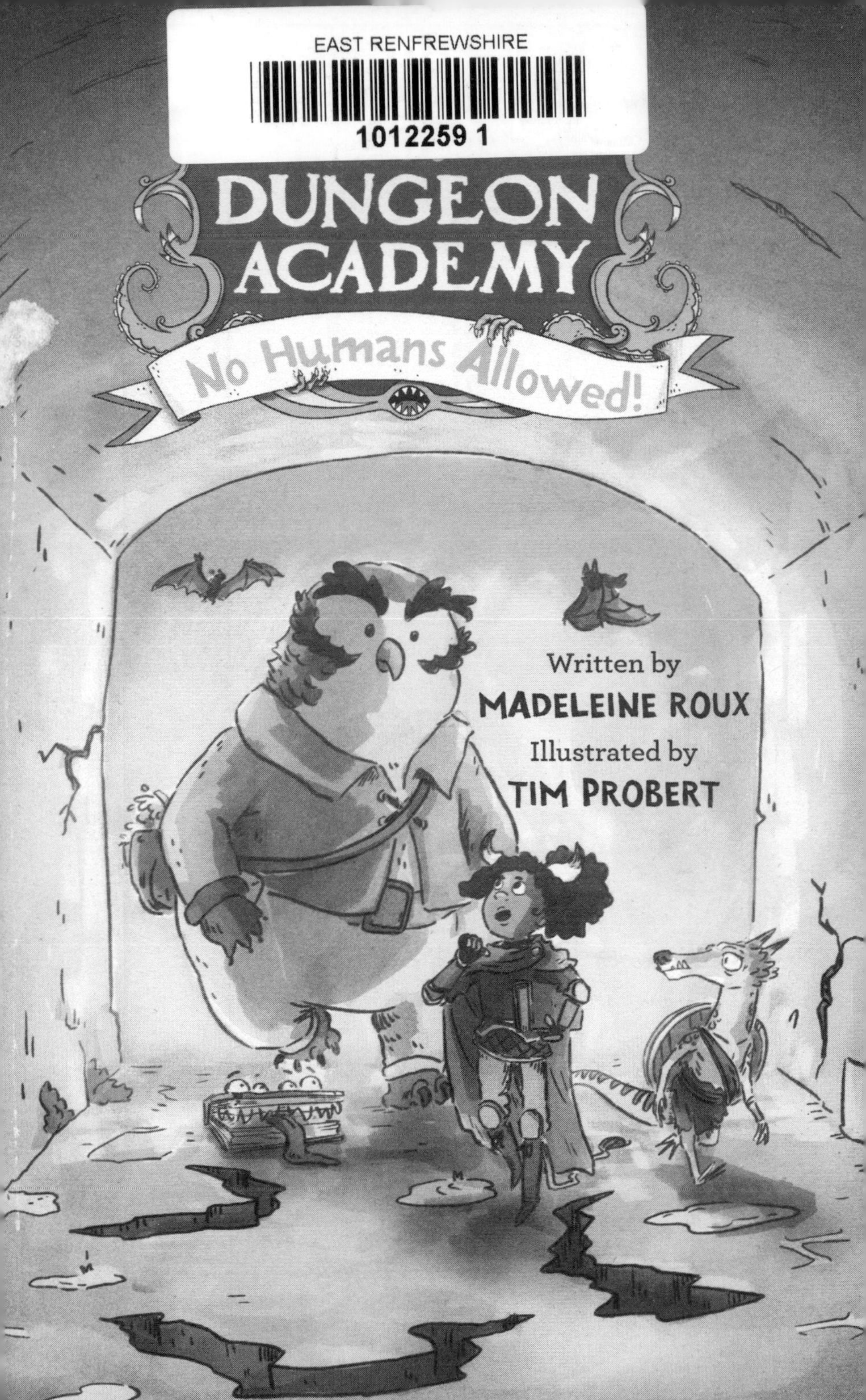

EAST RENFREWSHIRE
1012259 1
DUNGEON ACADEMY
No Humans Allowed!
Written by
MADELEINE ROUX
Illustrated by
TIM PROBERT